THE CHANGING WORLD

The Changing World

Studies in Political Geography

edited by

W. GORDON EAST M.A.

PROFESSOR OF GEOGRAPHY IN THE UNIVERSITY OF LONDON

and

A. E. MOODIE B.A. Ph.D.

READER IN GEOGRAPHY IN THE UNIVERSITY OF LONDON

All is in flux, nor stays, but changes on.
No sunrise hymns the self-same orison.

WALTER DE LA MARE, *Winged Chariot*

WORLD BOOK COMPANY
Yonkers-on-Hudson, New York

Preface

"A MAN needs rub up his geography in these days": so wrote *The Times* newspaper on March 10, 1848. To-day, no less than in 1848 or in 1921, when the first edition of Isaiah Bowman's *The New World* appeared, the time is appropriate for an appraisal of the geography of national and international affairs, subject as these are to continual change. Change, too, has always been the concern of students of geography, for the parts of the earth are always being revalued as ideas and technologies change. Certainly at no time has the tempo of change in the international scene—some of it revolutionary in kind—been greater than during the decade which followed the second world war: in more senses than one the world is on the move. Ironically enough, its component parts are now more closely associated than ever, despite the political ideologies which divide it. Scientific and technological advances could now, more than ever before, lead to improved standards of living, and we possess to-day a more accurate inventory of the "estate of man" than was ever available to our ancestors. No less important in our politically divided world are the invigorating new mental climates which find expression in the desires for further political, social, and economic changes. The nature and direction of these changes call for objective analysis, such as is attempted in the studies which are gathered together in this book.

A survey of these widespread developments, together with analyses of the geographical and historical conditions which lie behind them, is best achieved through an editorial plan executed by a team of contributors, each of whom has made special studies in his particular field. We are deeply indebted to our many collaborators, drawn as they are from various parts of the Anglo-American world. In particular, we are grateful to them for their ready acceptance of the limitations which the character and scope of this book necessarily impose. The least we could do was to give them freedom of expression in all but length: a balanced discussion of the world's major problem areas and problems calls for a judicious allocation of the limited space.

The fact that this work is the co-operative effort of no fewer than twenty experts drawn from five countries has involved only minor difficulties for the editors. For example, the language of the English-speaking world reveals some interesting variations in spellings which we have left as written by the authors. It is of greater importance in a book which is illustrated by numerous statistical tables to remind the more attentive reader that the English billion is one thousand times as large as the American.

We are indebted to our publishers for their assistance at every turn. The exposition of political geography requires many maps, no less than words and tables, and we appreciate their willingness to include so many maps, most of which have been specially drawn for this book. Contributors have been able to incorporate very recent changes at and after the galley-proof stage, and even, in some chapters, to include statistical data for 1955. Nevertheless, in a work of this kind which, while being topical and interpretative, does not attempt to be encyclopædic, it is impossible to be completely up to date. Such is the measure of the rapidity of change in an ever-changing world.

The map at p. 903 is reproduced from Prestan James's *Latin America* by kind permission of the Odyssey Press, Inc.

LONDON,   W.G.E.
June 1956   A.E.M.

The Contributors

EDWARD A. ACKERMAN, Ph.D.

Director, Resources for the Future, Inc., Washington, D.C.

The United States: Economic Aspects of Domestic Governmental Affairs

H. J. BRUMAN, Ph.D.

Professor of Geography, University of California at Los Angeles

The Caribbean and the Panama Canal

KEITH M. BUCHANAN, B.A.

Professor of Geography, University of New Zealand, Victoria University College, Wellington

The Union of South Africa

MISS EILA M. J. CAMPBELL, M.A.

Lecturer in Geography, University of London, Birkbeck College

New Zealand and its Dependencies

W. GORDON EAST, M.A.

Professor of Geography, University of London, Birkbeck College

Introduction: The World Background (*part author*)
The Mediterranean: Some Internal Problems
The Mediterranean Theatre of International Politics
The Soviet Union: its Geographical Setting and Historical Background
Land Frontiers and Frontier Problems of the Soviet Union
The Soviet Union and the 'Heartland'
Postscript (*part author*)

ERIC FISCHER, Ph.D.

Professorial Lecturer in Geography, George Washington University

The Passing of Mitteleuropa

CHARLES A. FISHER, M.A.

Lecturer in Geography, University College, Leicester

The Prospect for Japan
Communist China
Korea, Formosa, and Hong Kong
Mainland South-east Asia
The Malaysian Realm: Indonesia, British South-east Asia, and the Philippines

W. B. FISHER, B.A., D. de l'U.

Professor of Geography, University of Durham

South-west Asia: Internal Problems
South-west Asia: External Relations

R. J. HARRISON CHURCH, B.Sc. (Econ.), Ph.D.

Lecturer in Geography, University of London, The London School of
    Economics and Political Science

The Impact of the Outer World in Africa
African Boundaries
Policies and Problems in Africa

PRESTON E. JAMES, Ph.D.

Professor of Geography, Syracuse University

Latin America: State Patterns and Boundary Problems
Latin America: Economic and Demographic Problems
Latin American States: Four Case Studies

L. P. KIRWAN, M.A., B.Litt.

Director and Secretary of the Royal Geographical Society, London

The Partition of Antarctica

TREVOR LLOYD, Ph.D., D.Sc.

Professor of Geography, Dartmouth College

The Political Geography of the Arctic

W. R. MEAD, B.Sc. (Econ.), Ph.D.

Reader in Geography, University of London, University College

Problems of Scandinavia and Finland

A. E. MOODIE, B.A., Ph.D.

Reader in Geography, University of London, Birkbeck College

Introduction: The World Background (*part author*)
Fragmented Europe
Britain, France, and the Benelux Countries
The Eastern Marchlands of Europe
Intra-European Circulation
Maritime Boundaries
Postscript (*part author*)

N. L. NICHOLSON, B.A., M.Sc., Ph.D.

Acting Director, Geographical Branch, Department of Mines and
    Technical Surveys, Ottawa

The Confederation of Canada

THEODORE SHABAD, B.S.

Staff Member of the Foreign News Desk of the *New York Times*

The Administrative-territorial Patterns of the Soviet Union
The Soviet Union: Demographic and Economic Aspects

O. H. K. SPATE, M.A., Ph.D.

Professor of Geography in the Australian National University, Canberra

The Resurgence of Asia
India and Pakistan: Internal Political Geography
The Neighbours of India and Pakistan
The Pacific: Some Strategic Considerations
Australia and its Dependencies

L. DUDLEY STAMP, C.B.E., D.Lit., D.Sc., LL.D.

Professor of Social Geography, University of London, The London School of Economics and Political Science

Some Aspects of Applied Geography

G. TATHAM, M.A., Ph.D.

Associate Professor of Geography, University of Toronto

Canada: Economic Aspect

DERWENT WHITTLESEY, Ph.D., Sc.D.

Professor of Geography, Harvard University

The United States: the Origin of a Federal State
The United States: Expansion and Consolidation

A*

Contents

CHAPTER   PAGE

Maps and Diagrams

Chapter XI. The United States: Economic Aspects of Domestic Governmental Affairs

Chapter XII. The Confederation of Canada

Chapter XIII. Canada: Economic Aspect

Chapter XIV. The Soviet Union: its Geographical Setting and Historical Background

Chapter XV. The Administrative-territorial Patterns of the Soviet Union

Chapter XVI. The Soviet Union: Demographic and Economic Aspects

Chapter XVII. Land Frontiers and Frontier Problems of the Soviet Union

Chapter XXVII. The Malaysian Realm: Indonesia, British South-east Asia, and the Philippines

Chapter XXVIII. South-west Asia: Internal Problems

Chapter XXIX. South-west Asia: External Relations

Chapter XXX. The Impact of the Outer World on Africa

Chapter XXXI. African Boundaries

Chapter XXXII. The Union of South Africa

Chapter XXXIV. Australia and its Dependencies

Chapter XXXV. New Zealand and its Dependencies

Chapter XXXVI. The Caribbean and the Panama Canal

Chapter XXXVII. Latin America: State Patterns and Boundary Problems

Chapter XXXVIII. Latin America—Economic and Demographic Problems

Chapter XXXIX. Latin America—Four Case Studies

Chapter XL. Maritime Boundaries

The World Background

W. GORDON EAST
and
A. E. MOODIE

The Physical Setting

FEW parts of the earth's surface remain *terra incognita* to-day, for ease of movement and other technological developments have made possible an almost comprehensive knowledge of the terrain, much of which is now accurately mapped.[1] Not least in importance is the contribution made recently by aerial surveys, which, besides speeding mapping, frequently reveal previously unknown features and are often used in the detection of valuable mineral deposits.

All this vast range of knowledge serves, among other things, to emphasize the great physical diversity of the home of man. Long ago the Greeks introduced the concept of a threefold division of the world into torrid, temperate, and frigid zones. In broad outline the Greek division remains substantially correct, but modern knowledge has brought about many refinements of this concept and has fostered the growth of regional geography, which seeks to define distinct areas which are commonly identified with physical conditions. Hence geomorphology, oceanography, climatology, and biogeography are recognized as essential parts of geographical studies in so far as they explain the physical aspect of human environments, and various classifications of regions have been based on the findings of their exponents. Yet, despite the repetition of broadly similar characteristics in many parts of the world, each region remains unique: precisely homologous areas do not exist. This statement is not a denial of the validity of regional geography, but it serves to emphasize the great variety of the many habitats of man. Nevertheless, the study of the areal differentiation of

---

[1] For details of the current state of mapping in the various countries see *World Cartography* (United Nations, New York, published annually).

B

the earth's surface is thereby limited to the extent that selected features are used as criteria for the definition of the characters of regions. Hence all regional divisions carry elements of arbitrariness. They have their value as 'tools,' but they can be misleading if regarded as final and irrevocable. If, therefore, we seek to find patterns in the world physical setting we should do so with the reservation that generalizations are subject to modification on closer investigation. The so-called temperate lands, for example, include areas which are far from 'temperate' in their climatic regimes, and Professor Gourou has demonstrated recently[2] that, although the hot, wet lands reveal some common physical characteristics, they also exhibit great variety. Deviation from the mean is as common in geography as it is in mathematics.

Despite the repetition of similar climates and land forms, diversity is therefore characteristic of all the world's physical environments. Complete regional homogeneity being absent, classifications of environments call for subdivision. This heterogeneity of physical conditions helps to explain the occurrence of the numerous types of society to be found, the differences in their population densities and in their levels of social, economic, and political development, and the varying degrees of influence which they exert in world affairs. Every physical environment provides opportunities for its occupants; but decisions as to the manner and pace of their exploitation rest with their human inhabitants either through their own initiative or with the help, or sometimes compulsion, of others. Thus man-land relationships are made more complex by the combination of physical and social diversity. The understanding of these relationships requires careful attention to the time factor as expressed in the stage reached in the evolution of societies.

Physical conditions undoubtedly exert a strong 'control' over human activities at a low cultural level, but they grow less effective with the development and application of new techniques and forms of mechanical energy. This waning influence appears to coincide with the growth of organization both within States and on a larger scale, and nothing has been more inducive of organization than the ever-increasing rate of contact between the many and diverse parts of the earth. Not only have methods and ideas been copied and modified, but fear, on social, economic, and military grounds, has evoked strong associations. As man's powers of destruction increase so is he driven to greater efforts to produce more material goods. There may be no single yardstick for mea-

---

[2] P. Gourou, *The Tropical World* (Longmans, London, 1953).

suring the 'power' of nations, but what State can hope for 'a place in the sun' unless its economy is geared to increasing productivity? It is unlikely that complete freedom from the physical environment will ever be achieved, but it must be admitted that its 'control' has been greatly reduced. If the potentialities of a so-called 'chemistic age'[3] can be realized man may achieve 'freedom from the plant' and 'freedom from the mine.'

Of the world's physical setting the sea forms a conspicuous part. For many centuries the seas were effective barriers to human movement, so much so that the ancient empires were continental politico-territorial structures; even the Cretan and Greek thalassocracies were restricted to an inland sea. To-day human societies are still land-based, but many of them possess the great advantage of accessibility to the oceans, which have become links instead of barriers to circulation. The four greatest concentrations of population in the world, in Western Europe, Eastern North America, South-east Asia, and the Far East, all lie accessible to ocean waters; in common with many other areas, they are closely linked by ocean highways. So important are these connexions in world trade and so great is the strategic rôle of the seas in world affairs that it is permissible to use the term 'one ocean.' Facilitated by the construction of inter-oceanic canals and by the developments of marine engineering, economic interdependence of the shorelands has become possible.

Protracted and often bitter arguments on the regime of the High Seas and of the so-called Territorial Seas reflect the importance of the ocean to maritime Powers. Some of the participants in these disputes demand new seaward boundaries[4] not only for strategic reasons, but also to secure control of food supplies in their adjacent waters as well as exclusive rights over the mineral deposits of the appropriate parts of the subjacent floor. Confronted with dwindling resources on land, these Powers are therefore attempting to extend their sovereignty over large areas of sea, thus posing many fresh problems in international law. This new development may represent an attempt to share out the ocean. For centuries the exercise of sovereign powers over restricted coastal waters has been recognized, but the numerous unilateral claims made since 1945 to extension of these rights may lead to further demands which, in their turn, may make the politico-territorial pattern of the ocean more closely resemble that of the land.

[3] See J. Rosin and M. Eastman, *The Road to Abundance* (Rider, London, 1955).
[4] See Chapter XL below.

The Politico-economic World

The extreme diversity of physical environments is matched by an equally wide range of human activities, all of which are basically directed towards the production and distribution of the means of existence. Food, clothing, and shelter retain their importance as the primary material needs of mankind even in the most advanced communities. The unceasing struggle for survival is therefore closely associated with the production of these staple commodities, however much the methods of production have changed and vary regionally. Parallel with the introduction of new technological devices has been the development of closer relationships between these economic activities and political organization. Thus a characteristic feature of the twentieth century is the growth of State control in national economies. In effect, political and economic organization of human activities now proceed hand in hand on the territory of individual States. In the world as a whole, however, political and economic forces are commonly opposed to each other, and this conflict explains many of the stresses and strains which bedevil international relations in the twentieth-century world. Unilateral action in each of a hundred independent States can only increase this tension.

Economic Aspect. One result of the great diversity of physical environments mentioned above is the uneven spread of material resources over the surface of the earth. This is particularly true of mineral deposits, but applies no less to soil and plant resources. In the first place, the uneven distribution of land and sea masses gives the Northern Hemisphere greater actual and potential production of 'the sinews of peace and war' than the lands to the south of the equator. Secondly, varied combinations of geological and climatic conditions ensure that economic resources are unevenly spread on the continents and in the political entities of which they are composed. Before large-scale organized interchange of commodities was developed the great majority of communities were compelled to follow subsistence economies, which, however efficient within their limited capacities, were unable to provide high standards of living for most of their members. World-wide changes have resulted from the growth of international commerce during the last one hundred and fifty years. So widespread are the ramifications of world trade to-day that only remote and primitive peoples are relatively free from economic interdependence; and even they are being brought, directly or indirectly, into closer relations with more advanced societies.

Because of these changes, something approaching a world-wide specialization of labour, by which areas concentrate on the production of those commodities for which they are best equipped and obtain other goods from elsewhere, has already been achieved and, but for political and other restrictions, might have conferred greater benefits on mankind. At the same time, it must be admitted that economic interdependence has so far resulted from *ad hoc*, piecemeal measures. With all the advantages of greatly increased means of circulation and advanced technologies, the greater part of the world's population remains inadequately fed and unsatisfactorily housed. Such schemes as the Colombo Plan, the American Point Four Programme, the British Colonial Development scheme, and the various plans of the Communist States represent tacit admissions of the backwardness of many parts of the world, of the existence of 'have' and 'have not' peoples, and of the many other urgent economic problems which are disturbing the world's peace. As in the past, however, these schemes originate from different centres of political gravity. Lacking co-ordination, they can hardly be more than palliatives, although they may help in the attack on local and regional problems; while each is implemented independently of the others because of the different political and economic interests of certain major groups, the catalytic influence of expanding world trade is sadly restricted. Add to this the powerful effects of prejudices and fears, in part resulting from ignorance, and it is not difficult to appreciate the reasons for the absence of full international co-operation. The belief of the sceptics that such co-operation is unrealizable rests on the disruptive strength of nationalistic policies, yet the inter-war experiments in economic autarchy were disastrous failures, and in 1955 there were some signs of a change for the better in east-west relationships, at least in the economic field. Still, the hard core of this major problem remains. An eminent authority summarized the matter clearly when he wrote: "There is no doubt that it is physically possible to create absolute abundance but it would be politically difficult. All nations would need to co-operate in creating it."[5] Thus the mid-twentieth-century world is faced with a conflict between economic interdependence and political independence. Certain adjustments in national economies illustrate the

[5] Lord Boyd Orr, Introduction to *The Road to Abundance*, p. 16. See footnote 3 above.

effects of this conflict; outstanding are the changes in agriculture and industry.

Fifty years ago a reasonably clear-cut distinction could be drawn between countries with an almost completely agricultural economy and those in which industrial occupations provided the greater part of the national income. The latter group contained the United Kingdom, France, Belgium, and Germany; the United States was well on its way to warrant inclusion also. The rest of the world was concerned very largely with the production of such primary commodities as foodstuffs, fibres, and timber. Of course, domestic industries were widespread and provided the 'manufactured' goods for local consumption, but the character of the economy was dictated by the emphasis placed on agriculture.

TABLE 1

Population employed in Agriculture (millions)

DIVISION	TOTAL		EMPLOYED IN AGRICULTURE		AGRICULTURAL POPULATION AS PERCENTAGE OF TOTAL	
	1937	1950	1937	1950	1937	1950
World[1]	1954	2205	1211	1301	62	59
Europe[1]	371	394	134	130	36	33
N. and C. Americas	179	216	63	67	35	31
S. America	84	110	52	66	62	60
Asia[1]	1139	1273	832	891	73	70
Africa	169	198	129	146	76	74
Oceania	11	13	4	4	34	30

[1] Excluding present territory of the U.S.S.R.; European Turkey included in Asia.

Source: *Food and Agriculture Organization Yearbook, 1951* (Rome, 1952), p. 15.

The above table shows that over half the world's population was still engaged in agriculture in 1950, but two other points are worth noticing. First, that, although the total population increased during the period covered in Table 1, the percentage working on the land has decreased. Second, the percentages given in the fifth and sixth columns of this table do not represent fractions of the economically active population. If they had been computed on this basis they would have been considerably larger. It is almost certain, therefore, that two out of every three active people in the world are agricultural workers; yet they are unable, at present, to produce enough food to eliminate hunger from every land.

Furthermore, the highest densities of agricultural workers are found in areas where little or no expansion of the farmland can take place. This means agricultural overpopulation—*i.e.*, there are too many people working too little land—and provides one of the keys to many economic and social problems in such overcrowded territories. It is especially prominent in those areas where the land is cultivated by peasants, and was the root cause of collectivization in the U.S.S.R. and its satellite States.

Table 1 shows the variations in ratio between land-workers and total population by continental divisions, and therefore omits differences between smaller areas. It conceals striking changes, for example, in certain countries. Between 1880 and 1950 the percentages of total active males in agriculture fell from seventeen to six in the United Kingdom, from forty to sixteen in Germany, and from fifty-four to sixteen in the United States. The decrease in the numbers of males engaged in agriculture was striking also in the Soviet Union, where between 1920 and 1950 the percentage fell from seventy-eight to fifty-three.

The numbers of people working on the land are clearly decreasing, although at differential rates. In those countries where the decrease has been large, the absorption of surplus agricultural labour in other occupations has been possible, and capital has been available for investment in agriculture, farm production has become more efficient. Elsewhere there has been little change in agricultural methods and productivity.

That there is a close relationship between environmental conditions (including climate) and agriculture and industry is not open to doubt. Here, again, the maldistribution of the world's population in relation to available resources becomes evident by comparing total population, agricultural population, agricultural area, and industrial production, expressed as percentages of world totals for each of the major areas of the earth's surface (Table 2).

In North America 14 per cent. of the world's agricultural area is worked by 2 per cent. of the world's agricultural population, whereas the comparable figures for Asia, excluding the U.S.S.R., are 21 and 63. Quite apart from differences in farming methods and types of land use, North Americans have far greater opportunities for agricultural production than have Asians. Furthermore, North American farmers have the backing of highly organized industry in providing markets, and capital for investment; such support is almost entirely lacking at present in

TABLE 2

*The World: Population, Agricultural Area, and Industrial
Production by Major Areas about 1950*

(In percentages of world totals)

DIVISION	POPULATION		AGRICULTURAL AREA	INDUSTRIAL PRODUCTION[1]
	TOTAL	AGRICULTURAL		
Oceania	0·5	0·3	11	1
N. America	7	2	14	43
Africa	8	10	24	2
Latin America	7	8	10	3
U.S.S.R.	9	8	13	14
Europe[2]	17	9	7	33
Asia[2]	52	63	21	4
World	100	100	100	100

[1] Includes mining.   [2] Excluding the U.S.S.R.

Source: *European Agriculture* (F.A.O., Geneva, 1954).

Asia. These are extreme examples, but there are many cases where the lack of balance between branches of the economy is an adverse factor. It follows, therefore, that the demand for industrialization arises in all those countries where over-reliance on agriculture has retarded economic development. To the peoples of these under-developed lands industrialization has become the panacea for all their economic ills. Not least is this true of those Communist States where obsession with industrialization has led to the neglect of agriculture, which yet remains the basic sector of their economies.

The fourth column in Table 2 shows that 76 per cent. of the world's industrial production is still concentrated in two major areas, North America and Europe, excluding the Soviet Union. This is a further example of the uneven spread of human phenomena, but it should be regarded as representing a stage in global economic development. Here, too, changes are taking place; the Industrial Revolution began in Western Europe, was effective later but at a much more rapid rate in the United States, and is now in process of spreading to many other parts of the world. Whether we regard recent industrial developments as a continuation of processes which were initiated during the eighteenth century or as evidence of a new industrial age, there can be no doubt that they call for an attack on traditional industrial and economic practices, as did the introduction of the steam-engine and the factory system two hundred years ago. The use of synthetic materials to replace or supplement natural materials, the application of atomic energy and the by-products of nuclear fission, and the development of automatic machines and instruments all raise issues which demand the attention of modern industrialists.

Undoubtedly the two major wars of this century stimulated the production of manufactured goods in those lands which were deprived of their peacetime sources of supply. One result of the first world war, for example, was the initiation of a change from the production of primary goods, such as foodstuffs and other raw materials, to that of factory-made commodities in countries such as Australia, India, Brazil, and Argentina. The war of 1939–45 hastened this change, but did not lead to its completion. Nevertheless, the consequential loss of markets to the industrial countries of Western Europe and the entry of competitors, such as Japan, into world trade led to disruptions in world economy. The great economic depression of the nineteen-thirties was partly the result of inadequate adjustments to the changed conditions in the world.

Closely associated with these economic changes is the loss of prestige which has been suffered by western peoples. No longer are Asians, Africans, and South Americans content to be 'hewers of wood and drawers of water.' Their leaders have been quick to seize the opportunities created by war and to copy western industrial technologies. In effect, the world is passing through a second phase of readjustment in the distribution of industrial and commercial activities. For Europeans, especially those who live in the western part of this continent, the most serious result of this change is the relative decline in their share of an increasing world trade[6] despite their rapid and hard-won post-war recovery.

Political Aspect. The developments briefly outlined above are linked with equally important political changes which are also characteristic of the twentieth century. In this context the most important politico-geographical features are the spread of political independence and the increasing power wielded by central governmental organs in each of the individual States.

The most striking change in the world political map (see Figs. 1, 2, and 3) is the decrease in the number of dependent territories.[7] In Asia

[6] An excellent analysis of this change is available in I. Svennilson's *Growth and Stagnation in the European Economy* (United Nations, Geneva, 1954).
[7] Or "non-self-governing territories and dependencies," as they are now styled in the *Demographic Yearbook* (United Nations, New York, 1954).

B*

alone fifteen important areas[8] have acquired independent status since 1945; in Africa progress towards self-government is also making rapid strides. These two continents (excluding the U.S.S.R.) occupy 42 per cent. of the earth's habitable surface and have generally been regarded as politically backward areas. With certain minor exceptions, Asia is now made up of independent States, and Africa is following in its wake. Containing fully 60 per cent. of the world's population, they now, or will soon, exhibit politico-territorial patterns comparable in certain respects with those of Europe, the Americas, and Oceania. In short, the organization of human activities under the ægis of sovereign independent States has now become the norm throughout the greater part of the œcumene. This remarkable change, marking as it does the end of a long phase of imperialism, is largely the outcome of the diffusion of that intangible but powerful force which is known as nationalism.[9] Perhaps best defined as a feeling of belonging together and finding its origins in man's gregarious instincts, nationalism, in one form or another, has come to play a dominant rôle in international relations. Many of the older political entities and most of the new ones claim to be nation States, however much they lack national homogeneity. They vary greatly in area, numbers of people, economy, and political institutions, but they possess at least two common features—they all insist on the right to exercise sovereign powers, and their territorial limits are clearly defined and usually demarcated. In other words, the surface of the earth is divided into politically water-tight compartments at a time when, because of the inability of any one State to be completely self-supporting, there is an urgent need for closer international co-operation. In this conflict between the economic and political aspects of national interests lies the root cause of the failure of many international schemes for the improvement of the lot of mankind. It explains the failure of the League of Nations and lies behind the inadequacy of the United Nations in many spheres.

Solutions of the problems which arise from this conflict are made more difficult by the growth of centralized power in all modern States. State interference, as the exercise of this power is commonly called, dominates the internal affairs of most countries; even in the United States the Federal Government wields increased economic power, as has been well

---

[8] Burma, Cambodia, Ceylon, India, Indonesia, Iraq, Israel, Jordan, South Korea, Lebanon, Pakistan, Philippines, Saudi Arabia, Syria, and Viet Nam.

[9] For a useful study of this phenomenon see *Nationalism* (Royal Institute of International Affairs, London, 1939).

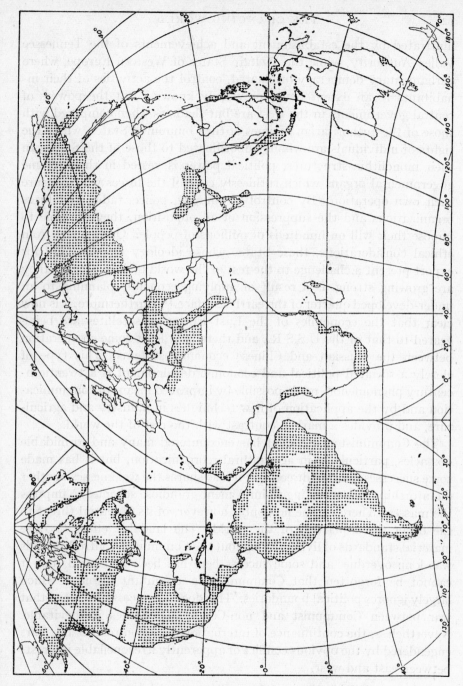

FIG. 1. EUROPEAN TERRITORIAL HOLDINGS IN THE OTHER CONTINENTS, 1815

Projection by courtesy of the Cartographical Department of the Clarendon Press

illustrated by the establishment and achievements of the Tennessee Valley Authority, while the Welfare States of Western Europe, where parliamentary democracy originated, control the activities of their inhabitants to an extent never previously known. But the powers of central governments in the west are but shadows when compared with those of the authoritarian regimes of the Communist States, where the rights of individuals are wholly subordinated to those of the State. In their monolithic structures, political power is vested in the supreme governmental organs which ruthlessly control the forces which ensure their own operation. By control of military, police, radio, and Press organizations and the suppression of all opposition, they are able to impose their will on hundreds of millions of people. Quite apart from ethical considerations, these States whose ideology is essentially for export present a challenge to the rest of the world mainly because they are growing strong as a result of applying economic planning to an under-developed quarter of the earth's surface.[10] Furthermore, it is now clear that the economies of the East European satellites are being geared to that of the U.S.S.R., and there is at least some co-operation between the Russian and Chinese economic systems. This type of closely associated political and economic development is a twentieth-century phenomenon, made possible by improved means of communication and by the application of new techniques in industry and agriculture, and provides a marked contrast with the rest of the world.

The Communist experiment has encountered many and formidable obstacles, particularly in agricultural reorganization, but it has made some successes in other directions; it also shares the weaknesses of other dictatorships in attempting to implement grandiose schemes to impress the masses. There can be no doubt, however, of its potential threat to the other three-quarters of the world. The laudable effort to raise material standards of living throughout the Communist-controlled lands was long overdue, and some success here has been registered; but it cannot be forgotten that Communism is a militant ideology which largely ignores political boundaries. This does not necessarily mean that war between Communist and non-Communist States is inevitable. Nevertheless, the continuance of international tension reflects the fears engendered by the obvious conflict of apparently irreconcilable interests between east and west.

[10] Thirty-three out of 135 million square kilometres.

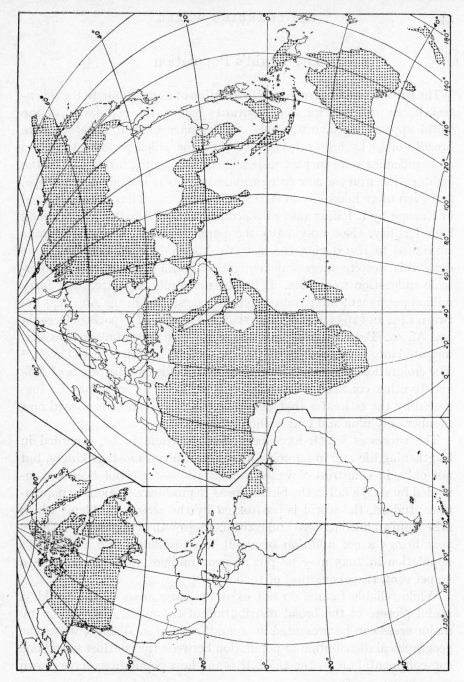

FIG. 2. EUROPEAN TERRITORIAL HOLDINGS IN THE OTHER CONTINENTS, 1914

Projection by courtesy of the Cartographical Department of the Clarendon Press

The World's Population

The Growth and Geographical Distribution of Population. In the seventeenth century, and for some centuries before, the population of the world appears to have remained stable, since natural increases were broadly offset by high rates of mortality, for which periodical famines and epidemics were in part responsible. During the latter half of the eighteenth century a new rising trend of numbers is evident in Europe, and even more markedly in Asia. This rising trend has been sustained in Europe by a falling rate of mortality and in Asia by a continuing high fertility. Not only have the populations of Asia and Europe continued to rise during the last two hundred years, but they have done this despite large-scale emigration from Europe and smaller-scale emigration from Asia. It has been roundly estimated that forty million permanent immigrants from Europe settled in the Americas between 1492 and 1935;[11] and about six millions moved to parts of Oceania and Africa. Between 1800 and 1914 more than seven million Russians migrated into what are now the Asiatic territories of the Soviet Union.[12] The emigration of Asiatics from their homelands to other areas of Asia and to other continents was relatively smaller. Its scale may be suggested by the estimates that Chinese and Indian nationals abroad now number only nine and four millions respectively.

The successes which have been, and continue to be, recorded in lengthening life and in reducing infant mortality—most strikingly, but not only, in countries of western civilization—have not been accompanied by such a fall in the birth-rate as to produce a stationary population. Indeed, the world is confronted by the serious problems which arise from an uncontrolled and continuous growth of population. Every year brings a net addition of about forty millions, and the world's population in 1955 may be put at 2700 millions, which represents a 50 per cent. rise above that of 1920.

While reliable figures do not exist for large areas of the world, a useful picture of the broad distribution of the world's population by major areas can be presented in 'round' estimates. Table 3 shows the geographical distribution of population between the continents and one sub-continental area—the U.S.S.R.—and how populations have grown

[11] R. R. Kuczynski, *Population Movements* (Oxford University Press, 1936), p. 22.
[12] W. F. Willcox, *International Migrations* (New York, 1931), vol. ii, p. 557.

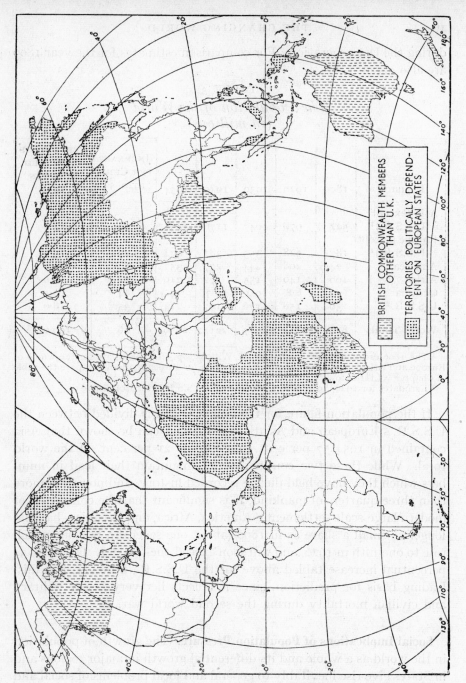

FIG. 3. EUROPEAN TERRITORIAL HOLDINGS IN THE OTHER CONTINENTS, 1955
Note that in 1956 Tunisia and Morocco became independent of France.
Projection by courtesy of the Cartographical Department of the Clarendon Press

during the last generation. For comparison estimates for the year 1800
are also given.

TABLE 3

The Population of the World
(in millions)

DIVISION	1800	1920	1930	1940	1954	INCREASE PER CENT. 1920–54	PERCENTAGE OF WORLD TOTAL IN 1954
Asia (except U.S.S.R.)[1]	522	970	1047	1176	1451	50	55·0
Europe (except U.S.S.R.)[1]	187	328	355	381	404	23	15·0
America	24·6	208	244	277	357	72	13·5
Africa	100	140	155	172	210	50	8·0
Oceania	2	8·8	10·4	11·3	14·4	64	0·5
U.S.S.R.[2]	36	158	176	197	214	35	8·0
World Totals	872	1813	1987	2214	2650	46	100·0

[1] The 1800 estimates, taken from W. F. Willcox, *op. cit.*, vol. ii, are for the whole of
Europe and Asia, but a separate estimate is given for Russia *c.* 1800. Compare the table
in Chapter XLIII below.
[2] Estimates for 1920, 1930, and 1950 relate to U.S.S.R.'s territory in 1955.

If the population figure for the Soviet Union is divided between the
U.S.S.R.'s European and Asiatic territories it can be shown that Asia
contained in 1954 57 per cent. and Europe 21 per cent. of the world
total. While these two continents thus maintain their lead in numbers which they have held during recorded history, and now hold more
than three-quarters of mankind, it is significant that the continents of
modern large-scale settlement—America, Africa, and Oceania—have no
longer so small a share as in 1800 (about one-seventh), but one which
rose to one-fifth in 1920, and will soon exceed one-quarter. The 1920–54
percentual increase tabled above for the U.S.S.R., however, is a misleading basis for prediction, since it reflects her very heavy military
and civilian mortality during the second world war.

Social Implications of Population Pressure. The growth of population
in the world as a whole and its differential growth in major regions and
in States give rise inevitably to general and local problems of social and
political importance. One variety of problem springs from the pressure
of population on natural resources. This may become so acute as to

create a condition of overpopulation in the strict sense, revealed in the downward trend of real income per head. In some of the crowded lands of monsoon Asia, notably in India, China, and Japan, as also in Egypt, this condition may well obtain. Unless expedients are found and applied—birth-control would appear the most relevant though not the easiest to apply—such dangers as famine, civil war, and political aggression cannot be ruled out. A substantial relief to overpopulated States of high fertility, in Europe at least, was formerly provided by emigration; but freedom of movement across State borders has become conspicuously limited in recent years. Some such movements are still possible—witness the resettlement of 800,000 refugees and displaced persons, chiefly from Europe, during the years between 1947 and 1951. Some limited scope for emigration exists to those lands still incompletely settled, especially to North and South America and to Australia and New Zealand; but there, as elsewhere, opportunities are rigidly controlled by governments.

Another kind of problem of politico-geographical interest arises from the differential trends of population which have been operating in the States of the world. Although no simple and direct relationship exists between population numbers and the economic and military strength of States, for there are striking qualitative differences to be reckoned with, population numbers, regarded as man-power numbers, clearly have an economic and political importance. The huge numbers of the Chinese and Indian republics do not, above all because of deficiencies in modern capitalized industry, command a commensurate political stature in the world. They represent, nevertheless, a formidable political fact, and may come to exert increasing economic and military force. It may be recalled that until about the year 1800 the population of France was the highest in Europe. From that time onward it became dwarfed by that of Russia; already by 1871 it had fallen also below that of the German Empire. The fact that the population of the Soviet Union is growing much faster than that of the countries of Western Europe, and, moreover, contains a higher proportion of the more active age-groups, is of evident political interest. As with specific States, so also with whole continents and sub-continents, demographic trends have political effects, even if they are slow to appear. The increasingly positive rôle assumed by the United States in world affairs in recent decades reflects the attitude and vigour of a rapidly growing population. In short, there are continued ups and downs in the relative status of nations and consequent changes in the strength and alignments of States which are grounded on the dynamism of population.

So, also, growing population numbers are one factor behind the new evaluations of dependent territories, making possible, where favourable conditions occur, political advancement, or at the least stimulating more effective development of natural resources. Clearly Africa has made a striking demographic advance. Since the winding up of the slave-trade this loss of population by emigration to the Americas and elsewhere has ended; it has now a population in excess of that of Latin America. It presents interesting 'case studies' in political evolution, while, under mainly European tutelage, it has many areas of expanding economy. In the main, however, the more acute problems of Africa's future, in certain areas at least, spring less from absolute numbers than from the presence of minorities of Whites living with a predominantly Black population.

One problem of world interest in particular claims attention as a result of population growth—that of food supply. The apparently insoluble problem that haunted Malthus a hundred and fifty years ago has reappeared to challenge the statesmen, scientists, and technologists of to-day. It is an encouraging fact that in this politically divided world there is international awareness of the seriousness of the food problem in many lands and, expressed in the Food and Agriculture Organization of the United Nations, a genuinely felt desire to raise nutritional levels for that half of the world's inhabitants who are clearly underfed. In contrast to the position three hundred years or less ago, when people depended on local supplies of basic foods which set limits to population growth, the world now includes a few areas which have foodstuffs surplus to their own needs and others which are in varying degrees deficient. These contrasting positions reflect the very unequal distribution of cultivated land in the world (Table 4).

TABLE 4

Cultivated Land per Head of Population
(in acres)

NORTH AMERICA	SOUTH AMERICA	WESTERN EUROPE	U.S.S.R.	EASTERN ASIA	SOUTHERN ASIA
4·0	1·5	0·7	2·0	0·5	0·8

Source: *World Food Survey* (F.A.O., Washington, 1946).

While these figures do not make allowance for a number of variables —the use of cultivated land for non-food crops, marked regional differences in diet, and varying yields per acre—high, for instance, in Western Europe and Japan, and low in North America and the U.S.S.R.—they suggest, nevertheless, that Asia in particular, but also Europe, produces insufficient agricultural foodstuffs, and that the American continent, potentially at least, has the largest surplus. Nor is the problem so simple that an efficient system of trade and transport between the 'haves' and the 'have nots' could solve it. If it were there would surely be no need for the United States to impose restrictions on its own production of food crops. The distribution of surplus foodstuffs encounters many political difficulties. The low standard of living in monsoon Asia, the provision of dollar currency by countries which can pay only in goods, the very serious practical difficulty of greatly enlarging transport capacity, and, not least, the limited scale of total supplies—all these are challenging hurdles to surmount. Food production has not even kept pace with increasing population: food supplies during the years 1948–50 averaged only 95 per cent. of the 1934–38 level, whereas potential consumers had increased by about 10 per cent.

While the easement of regional food shortages can be sought by various means—the raising of yields, a small expansion of the cultivated area, the diversification of farming, the breeding of new hybrid plants, the reduction of waste in store and by disease and pests in the field, and by the increase of fish catches—geographical study can help appreciably by turning attention to existing land use throughout the world and to the difficulties and possibilities which arise regionally.[13]

Urbanization. A further demographic aspect which is of interest to geographers and others is the spread of urbanization throughout the world. Since early times towns have been important as administrative or commercial centres, as ports or strategic points, or, indeed, for two or more of these functions; yet at no time has their growth been so great as during the last century and a half. There has been a well-marked 'drift to the towns' in every major State, with consequences which should not be ignored. Unfortunately, sufficient and reliable statistical data are not available for precise measurement of this important change in the proportions of rural and urban population. For

[13] See Chapter XLIII, below.

one thing, national classifications of urban population have not been standardized; for another, appropriate Census returns are sometimes restricted to the numbers of people living in urban administrative areas, whereas a more useful return would be the population of 'urban agglomerations'—*i.e.*, of peripheral areas together with those of the administrative unit. In spite of these and other shortcomings, however, it is possible to obtain a general view of the extent and rate of urbanization. Table 5, for example, illustrates changes in selected countries which reveal marked differences in their economic structures.

TABLE 5

Increases in the Urban Percentages of Population in Selected Countries

England and Wales	1901	77·0	France .	1921	46·4
	1951	80·7		1946	52·9
Germany . .	1900	56·1	Canada .	1901	37·5
	1939	69·9		1951	57·4
U.S.A. . .	1900	39·7	Egypt .	1937	25·1
	1950	59·0		1947	30·1
Japan . .	1920	18·1	New Zealand	1901	43·1
	1950	37·5		1951	61·3
U.S.S.R. . .	1926	17·9			
	1939	32·8			

Dates refer to Census years.
Source: *Demographic Yearbook, 1952* (United Nations, 1953).

A further expression of urbanization is seen in the increasing number of cities containing over a million inhabitants. These increased from thirty-four in 1940 to sixty-four in 1953, distributed as follows: Africa 1, North America 15, South America 4, Asia (including Istanbul) 20, Europe (including East and West Berlin as separate entities) 20, Oceania 2, the U.S.S.R. 2. Even this number will probably soon be exceeded, as there are many towns which are now rapidly approaching the million mark.

The causes of these migrations to the towns are many and complex. Excess of births over deaths is only a partial cause of the increases in numbers, since many town-dwellers are born outside the urban limits—

between the Censuses of 1926 and 1939 in the U.S.S.R., for example, thirteen million people moved into towns from the countryside. Undoubtedly the major cause of urbanization is to be found in industrialization. This was especially so during the nineteenth-century phase of the Industrial Revolution in Western Europe and seems to be characteristic of similar stages of economic development in other areas, although modern means of transport make it increasingly possible to site factories outside urban centres. Nevertheless, the greater range of employment, recreational, and other social facilities remain strong attractions, and easy accessibility to expanding markets, particularly for manufacturers of consumer goods, also exerts a strong pull to the larger towns.

Whatever the reasons for its existence, urbanization has far-reaching influences on the demographic structures of all but the least developed States. In effect, it leads to an ever-increasing concentration of population, which, in its turn, gives birth to social, economic, and political problems. In the first of these categories health and housing questions are paramount. The effects of 'urban sprawl' are seen not only in increasing difficulties in the journey to work, but also in a lack of a sense of community in many of the suburban areas. Before the advent of electric railways and the internal-combustion engine work-people necessarily lived within walking distance of their places of employment; now they may travel several miles each day and waste countless hours in so doing. Prolonged and detailed research would be necessary to ascertain the number of commuters in the world, but in the industrial countries it must run into many millions.

The divorce of place of work and place of residence, rarely if ever revealed in censuses, also has its economic repercussions. Vast capital investment is required for the provision of modern means of transport in towns, largely because of the high cost of land, and enormous sums must be spent annually on travelling costs. On the other hand, urbanization means a concentration of the labour force and should entail a greater mobility in the sense that it is easier to change jobs where a greater variety of employment is available within daily travelling distance. At the same time, the organization of workers in 'craft' and 'general' trade unions militates against the easy transfer of employees from one type of industrial employment to another. Economic planning would be greatly facilitated if direction of labour were feasible, but, outside authoritarian States, such a drastic measure is unlikely to be used except in wartime. This brings us to the political implications of urbanization.

Experience in the Communist-ruled States indicates that rural peoples, especially when they work on the land, are less amenable to political control than townspeople. Rural workers are more widely dispersed than those in towns and, accordingly, they are less easily organized in trade unions and for political purposes—concurrently they possess greater powers of resistance to political and economic pressures. In the last resort, they are less likely to starve than industrial, urban workers. Nowhere is this better illustrated than in the Communist States, where the existence of large numbers of peasants has hindered economic and political planning. The Soviet Union may have overcome the resistance of its agricultural workers by draconian measures; but the satellite States of Eastern Europe[14] have so far failed to collectivize their land, and Communist China is experiencing great difficulties among the peasants, who, numerically, are its chief supporters. In spite of their lack of organization when compared with industrial workers, and their high degree of illiteracy, peasants can be a powerful factor in the internal affairs of the States in which they live. Agriculture is less amenable than industry to large-scale changes. The tempo of development is slower, largely for reasons connected with climate and soils, but also because of the innate conservatism of land-workers. Rural people live more closely to Nature and have deeper roots in their particular environments; townsmen necessarily live in artificially created conditions and tend to be rootless. In this context it is significant that Marxism in its original form was largely based on its author's experience in industrial Western Europe, which was already highly urbanized. The 'dictatorship of the proletariat' is inappropriate to peasant communities even when coercion is practised. This explains the political background of collectivization in agriculture—it was an attempt to turn farms into factories, to convert peasants into 'proles,' and its success is by no means assured.

Finally urbanization presents serious strategic problems. In the past sieges of towns often played important parts in warfare, but the great decisive battles of history were fought at sea or in more or less open country where manœuvrability could be achieved. Bombing from the air has vastly increased the vulnerability of towns, as the second world war showed. The advent of new weapons, notably the atomic and

[14] See Chapter IV, below.

hydrogen bombs, makes towns wholly indefensible in total war. We witness the greatest military revolution of all time, if only because of the concentrated powers of destruction possessed by the new weapons and the high speed at which they can be transported. Hence the conflict of opinion on the efficacy of so-called 'civil defence'; the American slogan "Dig, die, or get out" predicates a grim future should total war break out again.

Geopolitical Problems

The term 'geopolitics,' although invented in Sweden,[15] fell into disrepute, since it was vigorously adopted in Nazi Germany as a pseudo-scientific cloak to cover the geographical discussion of Nazi territorial claims and an expansionist foreign policy. The term can, however, be used, and is used here, conveniently to refer to the external geographical relationships of States and, more specifically, the geographical aspect of those external relationships and problems of States which affect the whole world.

Bowman's 'New World' of the 1920's. A generation ago Dr Isaiah Bowman demonstrated in *The New World* the value and relevance of a geographical analysis of the problems which then faced the world. It is helpful before reviewing present problems to recall this outstanding book and the problems with which Bowman then grappled. *The New World*, which has as its sub-title *Problems in Political Geography*, first appeared in New York and London in 1921–22, soon after the first world war and the Treaty of Versailles had been concluded. It ran through four editions, the last of which, subsequently reprinted, was issued in 1928. Owing to the many political changes since then, it has become an historical text, a picture of a bygone time.

In the Preface to the first edition of his book Bowman insisted that it was necessary to grasp the world situation, because it posed problems which called for action by statesmen. He was very well aware how ill-informed about the outside world was the American electorate, which had been recently enlarged by women's suffrage, and he noted—what must strike us now as surprising—the complete lack in the United States of a "trained and permanent foreign-office staff." The questions discussed in his book had, he stated, "a geographical and historical setting and require scholarly consideration." Bowman was, however, in no doubt about the difficulty of presenting "a wholly balanced account" of the problems before him, but his method was to let the facts on both sides of a problem speak for themselves, except where grave dangers loomed ahead and there did not appear to him two sides to the question.[16] One further point may be recalled from Bowman's work—the large number, range, and nature of the maps, which were a striking and illuminating feature of his book. While the maps reached high standards in cartography and content and were assembled from many sources, it is noteworthy that the Mercator projection—for world maps and for the British Empire, for example—was much used. The fact that Mercator maps in a geopolitical context are no longer satisfying is one illustration of the changes of the last thirty years.

The first world war, which spread over a large part of the world, had shattered what had been economically a 'going concern'—this term goes back to Sir Halford Mackinder[17]—and produced territorial changes not only in Europe. The proportions of *The New World* which Bowman devoted to the several continents afford an interesting commentary on the problems of those times as he assessed them. In round figures 61 per cent. of his pages are given to Europe; 23 per cent. to Asia; 7·5 per cent. to Africa; 4 per cent. to America; and 2 per cent. to Australia, New Zealand, and the Pacific islands. Certainly Europe had been very much the main theatre of the war, and its political map was redrawn: not only were the boundaries of many existing States changed, but also many new States—Poland, Yugoslavia, Czechoslovakia, Albania, and the four Baltic States—emerged. While this may explain why so much attention was directed to Europe, the little space accorded to America is surprising.[18] Bowman's *New World* was emphatically concerned with the Old World, and the United States, for whose readers Bowman primarily wrote, was not itself brought under review, except incidentally: the United States stood like a stable rock while much of Europe was foundering. This omission must strike us now as strange, and could not be made to-day in any study of the political geography of the world. Russia got thirty-three pages in *The New World*, only five

---

[16] This avowal underlines the difficulty of wholly detached and objective discussion of current affairs, and signposts a danger which political geographers must face and try to overcome, if, unlike *Geopolitik*, their craft is to have academic value.

[17] *Democratic Ideals and Reality* (Constable, London, 1919), pp. 10–11.

[18] These proportions relate to the first edition of the *New World*, and they were changed substantially in the fourth edition, where the Americas were given about 14 per cent. of the space.

of which related to its Asiatic territory. India and the other British Dominions were discussed under the title "Problems of Imperial Britain." There was no reference to any Arctic or Antarctic problems—neither area was given in the index. Above all, the reader is left in no doubt as to the importance of European Powers in international affairs at a time when the United States, having become involved for the first time in a major European war, was seeking to withdraw within its own continent.

The Far East presented actual and potential problems of political interest both to the United States and to European Powers when Bowman wrote. He was careful to note the extraordinarily rapid growth of the trade and power of Japan, and what this might entail. The term 'Middle East' as a political concept had not been born, although there were live problems bound up with the British Mandate and the Jewish National Home in Palestine, Mesopotamian as well as Persian oil, and the status of Egypt. 'Imperialism'—implying the control by one country of the affairs of dependent peoples—was a recurrent theme, even though the first world war had brought to an end four imperial structures in Europe—the Russian, Turkish, German, and Austro-Hungarian. 'Imperialism' appeared then very much a speciality of Britain and, to a less extent, of France, Italy, the Netherlands, Belgium, Spain, and Portugal. Even so—and it is a tribute to Bowman's objectivity that he called attention to this—'imperialism' was not lacking in the policy of the United States in relation to Latin America. A new principle in dealing with dependent peoples was being applied in a modest degree and was summed up in the term 'Mandate,' of which there were three graded types. This marked a new and liberal experiment, as did the creation of the League of Nations, which the United States did not, however, join.

We should fail to recall the world of Bowman's book if we did not take account of one of the chief dangers which had already arisen. "There has been growing, chiefly in Russia," wrote Bowman, "an internationalist movement, and we have seen it in the form of Bolshevism carry devastation and fear into every corner of old Russia. It has sent its agents abroad to carry its revolutionary beliefs into peaceful communities and even into the democracies of the western world." While Bowman believed that the Bolshevik revolution of 1917, which gave rise to the U.S.S.R., was justifiable—after all, his own country had also been born of revolution—Bolshevism, he wrote in 1921, appeared to mean "a step backward toward the barbarism of earlier times."

And now, a generation after Bowman wrote, we confront a world politically changed again and still changing, in large measure as the direct or indirect result of war. Hardly a 'new' world as Bowman described that of the 1920's, for in the policies of States so much remains constant; yet a world presenting situations hardly then foreseen. The political changes produced during and after the second world war, although again prominent in Europe, extended markedly to Asia and in smaller measure to Africa and Oceania. In the studies which follow this Introduction space has had to be allocated differently from that of *The New World*. One-quarter of our pages is devoted to America, rather more than one-quarter to Europe, and nearly one-third to Asia. Both Africa and Asia call for a larger share than they were accorded in Bowman's work, while the Soviet Union is given twice as much. And it has seemed fitting, having regard to the present international scene, to include chapters on the Arctic, the Antarctic, the Seas, and the geographical aspect of the world's food problem.

Some Political Patterns in the Mid-century World. Let us try at least to glimpse how the present world differs from that of a generation ago. The earth's surface now appears to have contracted, spanned as it is by airways for which no barriers exist. A variety of new maps, based on suitable projections, must replace those, like Mercator's, which were specially adapted to a seaman's age. We have no longer the United States which recoiled from the League of Nations and the outer world it little knew. Rather, it seeks to lead the world through the United Nations Organization, to which most (but by no means all) of the independent States of the world now belong (see Postscript). No longer concerned solely with the local defence of the American continent, and aware from hard experience that its own defence must be organized also at long range near to the danger areas of international life, the United States now projects its influence and power throughout the world, except where the Soviet and Chinese realms extend. In short, the United States, conscious of its economic and technological strength, now assumes abroad the leading part which falls to, and cannot with impunity be shirked by, the greatest of the Great Powers. Its foreign policy outside the Americas is now interventionist where formerly isolationism tended to prevail. "Westward the course of Empire takes its way." The terms 'empire' and 'imperialism' take on new shades of meaning, and apply to new species of the same genus. For while the 'imperialism' of the United States involves neither the possession nor the administration of large overseas dependencies, it involves "economic and cultural penetration combined with a reluctance to assume political responsibilities for the results."[19]

In recent centuries 'imperialism' has been largely but not exclusively a function of European States in so far as it is reflected in the extent of overseas territories which are in varying degrees dependent politically. Figs. 1, 2, and 3 show that imperialism was flourishing a hundred and forty years ago, was still vigorous in 1914—although it had largely abandoned its hold on the Americas, it had extended widely in Africa— but by 1955 it had declined sharply.

'The British Empire' has proved a remarkably adaptable and lasting political structure. When the first world war began the 'Dominions' of Canada, Newfoundland,[20] Australia, New Zealand, and South Africa, although autonomous, were not wholly independent, since their defence and foreign relations were controlled by the United Kingdom. This limitation to their sovereignty no longer exists; they are now more correctly styled 'Kingdoms' than 'Dominions.' In association with the United Kingdom of Great Britain and Northern Ireland, whose Queen is also theirs, they are members of the British Commonwealth of Nations, of which their Queen is head. Britain's Indian Empire formally ended in 1947, to give rise to the two independent federations of India and Pakistan; both are Commonwealth members, but, as Republics, they acknowledge the British Queen only as head of the Common- wealth. Ceylon, formerly a British colony, is now a Dominion within the same Commonwealth, and in 1953 the newly organized Rhodesia and Nyasaland Federation became the ninth member State, but its sovereignty is limited in respect of foreign policy.

On the other hand, the Republic of Ireland and the Union of Burma have seceded from the Commonwealth. The British Mandate in Palestine ended in 1948; ended, too, is the British condominium with Egypt in the Sudan, which has achieved independence. Britain no longer retains a special position in Egypt, having carried out an agreement of 1954 to withdraw her armed forces from the Suez Canal Zone by June 1956. Britain's colonial empire, including 'Trust

[19] E. A. Walker, *Colonies* (Cambridge University Press, 1944), p. 18.
[20] Newfoundland became a province of the Canadian Confederation in 1949: see Chapter XII, below.

Territories,' still includes holdings large and small, at different levels of dependence, in all the continents: inter-tropical territories in Africa, Central America, and the East Indies, as well as numerous maritime bases, acquired to facilitate the commerce and defence of a world-wide empire and scattered between the Falkland Islands, Aden, Singapore, Hong Kong, and the South-west Pacific.

It is not easy to assess the effect of these and other external changes on the importance of Britain as a world Power. Clearly power and policy, once centred in Britain, have been diffused, and Britain has lost, except under specified conditions of emergency, her strategical position in the Suez Canal Zone. She has lost in India the major base of man-power and supplies which she held during the two world wars of this century, but her withdrawal from India has made possible friendly relations with the new States of India and Pakistan. Indeed, political changes within the Commonwealth, as also political advances and pro-gress in the colonial territories, would appear on balance to strengthen rather than weaken Britain, for they have widened the area of political freedom and free co-operation in policy-making. After all, the Com-monwealth members are linked on a basis of consent and are free to secede. Despite the great diversities of peoples and culture, and despite the fact that for certain members, notably India, there are no bonds of sentiment with Britain, membership carries a balance of advantage—some addition to the independence which each enjoys. The Common-wealth does not, however, assume in the world the predominant status which its population numbers—nearly one-quarter of mankind—might suggest. While the leaders of Commonwealth members confer con-tinually on matters of common interest, the Commonwealth does not act as a unit in international affairs. Nor is it free from weakening internal strains and stresses.[21] The effects of economic progress and of wars in this century by raising two dominant Powers—the United States and the Soviet Union—chiefly account for the reduction of Britain's relative stature in the world since its heyday in the nineteenth century. Clearly the more powerful United States, now the leading naval Power, undertakes many of the tasks in international affairs which once fell to Britain. But it would be easy to underestimate the importance of the Commonwealth in world politics: thanks to its wide measure of agree-ment on democratic principles and political ends, its material resources,

[21] Such, for example, as those caused by the Kashmir dispute between India and Pakistan (see below, Ch. XX), by the position of Indians in the Union of South Africa (see below, Ch. XXXII), and by the 'White Australia' policy (see below, Ch. XXXIV).

and the geographical range of its territories, it exerts considerable influence.

While the old-established British Empire has shown its capacity at the same time to change and to endure, the twentieth-century Empire of Japan, built up chiefly at the expense of China, reached its zenith in the second world war, only to pass rapidly away. Other empires have survived, some of them shrunken and under strain. The French Empire is now correctly described as the French Union; its administration is centred at Paris, to which representatives from member States are sent. While France preserves intact vast territories in Algeria, West and Equatorial Africa, as well as Madagascar, Somaliland, Guiana, and many other insular and coastal holdings, it has lost its Mandate in Syria and Lebanon and its holding in Indo-China. The Italian Empire lost Libya, now independent, the Dodecanese Islands, and Eritrea. Italians, however, administer the United Nations' Trust Territory of Somalia. Spain retains some scantily settled areas of West Africa and the Canary Islands. The Republic of Portugal still controls a vast colonial area five times that of California—in Guinea, Angola, and Moçambique in Africa, in the Azores, Madeira, and Cape Verde Islands, at Goa in India, Maçao in China, and Timor in the East Indies. The Kingdom of the Netherlands lost its most valuable colonial possessions with the creation of the Indonesian Republic, but retains the western half of New Guinea, Surinam (Dutch Guiana), and some West Indian islands. Belgium holds a vast colony in the Congo basin. Of the former Danish colonies, Iceland has become a republic, but Greenland and the Faeroes remain autonomous parts of Denmark.

Although the countries of Western Europe have been historically, and remain, the chief colonial Powers, others both in the Old World and the New have political control of under-developed areas and of peoples not yet culturally advanced and strong enough to stand alone. While the Philippines and Puerto Rico are now independent States and Alaska and the Hawaiian Islands have not yet been admitted as members to the federation, dependent territories of the United States include the Panama Canal Zone and island bases in the West Pacific. Many areas of Asiatic U.S.S.R. are inevitably Russian colonies in all but name and expressed intention. Australia has charge of the Mandated Territory of Papua in New Guinea; the Union of South Africa holds the Mandate of South-west Africa, which it has virtually annexed; and New Zealand has some island dependencies. Even in Antarctica the following States have territorial holdings or claims: Argentina, Australia, Chile, France, Norway, and the United Kingdom.

Fig. 3, which shows overseas territories still politically dependent on European States, emphasizes how Africa remains the most dependent of all the continents. The achievement of independence by Morocco and Tunisia early in 1956 marks, however, a significant trend.

The Principal Theatres of International Politics. It is a truism of geography that phenomena, human and physical alike, are unevenly distributed on the face of the earth. The jigsaw pattern of States sovereign and dependent covers the lands (and Territorial Seas) of the world everywhere, except for most of the Antarctic continent. If all sovereign States are equal in international law,[22] some are clearly more equal—or rather superior in man-power, the extent and position of their territory, natural resources, economy and technology, and the will to exert their strength. In geopolitics special interest attaches to the 'Great' and 'Middle' Powers, because in their hands lies the direction of international affairs. Special interest necessarily attaches also to certain regions which, owing to the facts of physical geography and the events of political history, have attracted the attention and interests of the Great Powers, for which reason they have become, and can again become, danger areas of international relations and theatres of major war.

A refined analysis might be made of the concepts 'Great' and 'Middle' Power, and existing States might with some difficulty be allocated to these categories. It is enough to suggest here that no single criterion—be it man-power, extent of territory, economic resources, or cultural level—underlies this classification, and that, as a result of social, economic, and political changes, particular States may, and do, alter their classification. That the Security Council of U.N.O. was allotted in 1945 five permanent members—the United States, the Soviet Union, the United Kingdom, France, and China—suggests that these five States were then thought to be the Great Powers. In contrast, only two Great Powers now survive—the U.S.A. and the U.S.S.R.— each conscious of the other's power. What is clear beyond doubt is that changes in the relative status of the leading Powers have occurred

[22] The principle 'one State, one vote' which is applied in the Assembly of UNO bears no relationship to the unequal responsibilities and power of its members. It provides however, a workable principle. The idea of 'weighted voting,' which has been mooted, would involve the classification of States and thus inevitable dissension. See A. de Rusett, "Large and Small States in International Organization—I," *International Affairs*, vol. xxx, No. 4 (October 1954).

in this century and that on the eve of the first world war no fewer that eight States were rated Great Powers—Germany, France, Italy, the British Empire, the United States, Austria-Hungary, Russia, and Japan. The classification of the British Commonwealth to-day is not beyond doubt: its Great Power status can only clearly appear if in specific circumstances it is acting as a unit. Into the category of 'Middle Powers' Canada, Brazil, and Argentina in the New World, and India, Italy, Turkey, and Yugoslavia in the Old, would appear (with others) to fall, despite their remarkable inequalities in area, population, and resources. These others now clearly include France, gravely weakened by the wars of this century and by political difficulties at home and abroad; China, whose status is rising rapidly as industrialization proceeds; and the United Kingdom, which no longer enjoys the power and prestige which went with her control of India and the Middle East.

Niceties of classification apart, the existence and operations of the more powerful and influential members of the hierarchy of States draw our attention to certain regions of especial interest and danger. Our concern here is with a few large-scale regions, each of which contains local areas of strategical importance—such as Korea, Indo-China, the isthmus of Suez, and the Malaccan, Moroccan, and Turkish straits. The Far East, the Middle East, South-east Asia, and Central Europe above all invite discussion.

Some explanation of these geographical divisions is called for. Fifty years or so ago geographers applied the term 'Far East' to that part of South Asia which lay north-east of the peninsula of Malaya.[23] Present usage narrows its content by lopping off Indo-China and Siam, which, together with Malaya, the East Indies, and the Philippine islands, make up South-east Asia, one of the six realms of Asia.[21] Thus the Far East (so far to the west of the United States, which is now the most interested extraneous Power) consists of China—including Manchuria, Hainan, and Formosa—Korea, Japan, and the mainland and insular Pacific territories of the Soviet Union. The term 'Middle East,' which gained currency and persists as a result of the military organization and operations of the second world war, includes the geographer's divisions of South-west Asia and the eastern basin of the Mediterranean Sea and

[23] *Cf.* A. Little, *The Far East* (Clarendon Press, Oxford, 1905), p. 1 and Fig. 3. See also Chapters XIX and XXV, below.
[24] See W. G. East and O. H. K. Spate, *The Changing Map of Asia* (Methuen, London, and Dutton, New York; third edition, 1956), pp. 6–8 and Fig. 1.

invites confusion with an earlier conception of 'Middle East,' of which the Indian sub-continent was the chief component. In its current sense Middle East denotes, therefore, an area of doubtful limits, and, although the term has not been ignored in this book, discussion has been related rather to South-west Asia and the Mediterranean basin than to the Middle East as such. Lastly, there is 'Central Europe,' which has an interior if dubiously central position within this continent. Its extent has been very variously delimited by geographers, not least by German writers of the inter-war period who were interested in the political concept of *Mitteleuropa*. Perhaps the key to the geographical content of Central Europe and a partial explanation of its indefiniteness are to be found in the changing area of contact of German and Slav peoples throughout their long history.

The Far East sprang to the forefront of the international stage in the first decade of this century as a result of the extension to Vladivostock of the Trans-Siberian Railway and of the rise of the Japanese Empire as a strong naval, military, and expansionist Power. Bowman foresaw in the 1920's the dangers to world peace consequent on the continued growth of the power of Japan, which had fought in, and profited by, association with the victorious western Powers in the first world war. That phase of history ended abruptly with the defeat of Japan in the second world war. The new phase opened with the unforeseen Communist control of China, certainly one of the most pregnant changes in the geopolitical situation of the last decade. The new Chinese Republic, now in alliance with its mighty neighbour, the U.S.S.R., and ruled from the old imperial capital of Peking, undergoes drastic social and economic reorganization, which must greatly develop its latent resources and strength. While it has control of China proper and Manchuria, it has extended its control to North Korea, Tibet, and Sinkiang, and only the island of Formosa, held by its defeated rivals of the Kuomintang, eludes its grasp.

Among the leading Powers the United States now takes the greatest interest in this theatre—an interest which began with her opening up of Japan in 1854, and her acquisition of the Philippine islands from Spain in 1898. American interests in the Far East, at once commercial, cultural, and political, developed vigorously during the inter-war period, only to be strengthened by the realization of the dangers (made evident by the Japanese assault on Pearl Harbour) to which she could be exposed from this quarter. The earlier interest of Tsarist Russia in the

Far East is clearly maintained by the U.S.S.R. in this Pacific borderland of its territories. The peninsula of Korea, a gateway to China's workshop in Manchuria and to the U.S.S.R.'s Far East, and zone of contact between long-range maritime and short-range continental power, became again during the years 1950–53 a battlefield in a war of world concern. And Japan, the imperialist and enemy of yesterday, together with Formosa, assumes a new rôle within the outer defence system of the United States.

The 'Middle East' is the old 'Near East' writ large. Dr Bowman's problems in the 1920's were concerned there with Turkey, Palestine, South Caucasus, as well as Persia and Egypt. During the first world war Britain successfully led national revolts of Arab peoples against the Turks, and, under treaties which followed, successor States were set up in the Arabian area torn from Turkey. The Turkish Empire was replaced by the Turkish Republic, the territory of which was reduced to Anatolia and Eastern Thrace. Britain abandoned her protectorate in Egypt, but retained rights to maintain armed forces there. France acquired Mandates over the new States of Syria and Lebanon; Britain took over Mandates in Iraq and Palestine, which included the newly created Jewish National Home. Britain already in the 1920's held the dominant financial, commercial, and strategic position in the Middle East. She had for some time been exploiting the petroleum resources of South Persia and, with France and the Netherlands, was extending activities to the oilfields of Iraq. The interest in petroleum persists and increases, as the scale of production rises rapidly, and outside industrial countries, including the United States, work their concessions.

Geopolitical interest in the Middle East also persists, as it is bound to do in a troubled world, because it springs from basic facts of geography. The Middle East is the 'waist' of Asia: through or across it pass the sea and air routes between Western Europe and the Indian sub-continent. Moreover, the Soviet Union borders the Middle East in the north, and is the only Great Power to do so. The advent of the Republic of Israel in the teeth of the hostility of the surrounding Moslem world intrudes a new disturbing element into the Middle East situation which is not without other serious problems, both internal and external.

Internally there are the major difficulties of fighting widespread poverty, disease, and illiteracy, and of increasing agricultural productivity. The countries of the Middle East react increasingly to Western intrusion—witness the ending of the Anglo-Iranian Company's

c

operations in Persia and Egypt's success in eliminating British forces
from the Suez Canal Zone. The formation of the Arab League in 1945,
to which we shall refer again, is another instance of the desire of Middle
East countries to assert their independence against foreign intervention. Many delicate problems thus arise in the Middle East, chief of
which is the need to reconcile local aspirations with external interests.

South-east Asia, like the Far East and Middle East, became a theatre
of war when Japanese forces overran it during the second world war,
and in recent years protracted fighting in Indo-China, Burma, and
Malaya has necessarily claimed world-wide attention. The old imperialism which characterized this area, which consists of peninsular and
insular territories between Burma and Indo-China and between Sumatra,
Borneo, and the Philippines, has largely disappeared with the creation
of independent national States in Burma, Indonesia, the Philippines, and
Indo-China. The Federation of Malaya will soon become independent
(and probably join the Commonwealth); Singapore enjoys a measure of
self-government. Problems of economic and strategical interest arise,
since South-east Asia is both valuable to the Western Powers as the
chief source of natural rubber and tin, and necessary to their defence
organization, based on control of the sea. Danger is seen in the expansionist tendencies of Communist China, which might threaten not only
the freedom of sea communications to South-east Asia, but also the
independence of countries accessible therefrom—India and Ceylon, the
Philippines, Australia, and New Zealand. Thus in South-east Asia new
national States, weak in material resources, are now charting their own
courses, but they lie within a borderland of international tension between continental and maritime Powers.

And lastly, among regions of outstanding geopolitical interest, stands
Europe, and especially Central Europe. Despite the ravages of war
Europe, west of the Soviet realm, remains, because of its population
numbers, its industrial skill and potential, its command of mechanical
energy, and its long-held oversea interests, one of the major areas of
political power. Sharp changes have occurred in Europe since the 1920's.
Bowman was largely concerned with discussions of the boundary changes
of existing States and with the boundaries of States set up afresh as
results of the collapse of the German, Austro-Hungarian, Russian, and
Turkish empires. The new Bolshevik Russia, although its revolutionary
dogma was already feared, had then neither political nor economic
strength. The boundaries of the Soviet Union were withdrawn east-

ward, and a tier of States from Finland, through the Baltic States and Poland to Hungary and Romania, was organized as a *cordon sanitaire* to shield the West from Bolshevism. The length of boundaries in Europe increased from 13,000 in 1914 to 17,000 by 1938,[25] when Europe contained no less than two-fifths of the independent States of the world. Beyond doubt the political map of Europe was redrawn after the first world war: "frontiers," quoted Bowman, "are snap-shots of the life of nations"—a dynamic element in historical geography. And in the Europe of those days France, despite its man-power losses through wars, still appeared to hold the leading rôle in the affairs of the continent.

"A man needs rub up his geography in these days": so wrote *The Times* newspaper in 1848. The need recurred a century later at the end of the second world war. The power area in Central Europe, built up by Hitler, was destroyed, and with it went German pretensions to control the continent from the English Channel to the Urals. Defeat involved Germany in both territorial loss and partition. It entailed, too, the advance territorially and in military strength of the Soviet Union. A new stage in the old conflict between German and Slav now presents itself: Germany is politically divided and militarily weak, while the Soviet Union, dominated by the Great Russian Slavs, exercises control from its own and satellite territories strung out between the Pacific in the Far East and the Danube and the Elbe rivers in Central Europe. And the strength of France has clearly weakened, a weakness intensified by her losses in the Indo-China war and unrest in North Africa.

Europe after the second world war witnessed not the marking out of new States, but the disappearance of some—the three Baltic States lost their independent status—and above all, the expansion of one—the U.S.S.R. Instead of a *cordon sanitaire*, designed by the Western Powers to defend themselves from Communism, the U.S.S.R. created a tier of satellite States to insulate herself from the West and to permit her political and economic organization of East-Central Europe.

FURTHER READING

C. B. FAWCETT, *The Bases of a World Commonwealth* (Watts, 1941).
W. G. EAST and O. H. K. SPATE, *The Changing Map of Asia* (Methuen, London, and Dutton, New York; third edition, 1956).

---

[25] S. Whittemore Boggs, *International Boundaries* (Columbia University Press and Oxford University Press, 1940), p. 13.

Y. M. Goblet, *Political Geography and the World Map* (Philip, London, 1955).

Sir Ivor Jennings, *The British Commonwealth of Nations* (Hutchinson's University Library; second edition, London, 1954); *The Commonwealth in Asia* (Clarendon Press, Oxford, 1951).

R. Linton, *Most of the World* (Columbia University Press, New York, 1949).

N. Mansergh, *The Commonwealth and the Nations* (Royal Institute of International Affairs, London, 1948); *The Name and Nature of the British Commonwealth* (Cambridge University Press, 1954).

M. Roberts, *The Estate of Man* (Faber, London, 1951).

E. Staley, *The Future of Underdeveloped Countries* (Harper Brothers, for the Council of Foreign Relations, New York, 1955).

World Planning and Resources (Political and Economic Planning, London, 1955).

World Population and Resources (Political and Economic Planning, London, 1955).

W. S. and E. S. Woytinsky, *World Population and Production* (Twentieth Century Fund, New York, 1953).

E. W. Zimmerman, *World Resources and Industry* (Harper Brothers; second edition, New York, 1951).

CHAPTER I

Fragmented Europe

A. E. MOODIE

EUROPE[1] leads the world in the degree of fragmentation of its territory into independent States. Of the six continental divisions shown in Table 1, Europe is easily the smallest, yet it contains twenty-six of the world's important political units; in the number of its States it is exceeded only by Asia, excluding the U.S.S.R., and that position would be reversed if the Sheikdoms of Kuwait, Qatar,

TABLE 1
The Continental Divisions of the World in 1952

DIVISION	TOTAL AREA (000's sq. km.)	NUMBER OF INDEPENDENT STATES	AGGREGATE AREA OF INDEPENDENT STATES (000's sq. km.)	AGGREGATE POPULATION OF INDEPENDENT STATES (000's)	AVERAGE AREA OF INDEPENDENT STATES (000's sq. km.)
Europe[1]	4,921	26[2]	4,851	393,268	187
Asia[1]	27,091	28[3]	27,048	1,276,376	966
Africa	30,313	6	5,279	43,238	880
Oceania	8,557	2	7,972	10,876	3,986
Americas	42,102	22	37,716	348,787	1,715
U.S.S.R.	22,271	1	22,271	193,467	22,271
World	135,255	85	105,137	2,266,012	1,237

[1] Excluding U.S.S.R.
[2] Excluding micro-States such as Liechtenstein, Andorra, etc.
[3] Including sheikdoms of Persian Gulf area.

Source: *Demographic Yearbook, United Nations, 1953* (New York, 1954).

Bahrain, and Oman were not included in the Asian total. Europe is thus made up of a mosaic of States, varying in size from half a million sq. km. (France) to 2586 (Luxembourg), with population totals ranging from fifty-one millions (United Kingdom) to 148,000 (Iceland). There

[1] The U.S.S.R. is excluded from this chapter, except for incidental references, mainly because it is treated in detail in Chapters XIV–XVIII below.

is clearly no uniformity among these European States in area, population totals, and density (see Table 2, below); the one common denomina-
tor which they all claim is their sovereign independence, but it will be
shown later that even this political quality is subject to modification.

This large number of States, unevenly distributed on a relatively
small area, means that in Europe they are never far from each other;
nor are peripheral ones separated by such wide national spaces as in
North America and Asia. In other words, territorial contiguity is a
characteristic feature of the States of Europe, Iceland alone excepted.
Within the British Isles there is one inter-State boundary, but Germany
has nine immediate neighbours, Austria has six, and peripheral Italy
has four. This geographical factor of contiguity, an essential concomitant of the conditions of space and numbers in Europe, results in an
excessive length of international boundaries. When these are expressed
in miles per 1000 square miles of territory, Europe has nearly three
times as many miles of boundary as South America, its nearest rival in
this category. Reference will be made later to the implications of this
fact, but, in the present context, the words of an eminent Cambridge
historian are relevant: "In regions where power exists without local
and immediate check, territorial contiguity gives it such enormous
leverage that it ought to be regarded as equivalent to a formidable
increase of strength."[2]

Two other general facts concerning the political fragmentation of
Europe may be mentioned at this stage. First, the evolution of the
European States has been characterized by instability. With few
exceptions, their areas and boundaries have been subject to change at
irregularly spaced intervals. Even in the United Kingdom, which is
generally regarded as one of the most stable political entities in the
world, a new international boundary (between Eire and United Kingdom territory in Northern Ireland) was drawn in 1921. The use of the
epithet 'dynamic' as applied to the politico-territorial history of
Europe is, therefore, fully justified, both in the past and the present,
and who would dare to forecast what may happen in the future?

Secondly, Europe's range of political units is matched by its diversity
in national economies. As E. de Martonne pointed out in 1931,[3] there
is a general economic and social gradient eastward and south-eastward,
between the highly industrialized and urbanized countries of Western

[2] H. Butterfield, "The Scientific versus the Moralistic Approach in International
Affairs," in *International Affairs*, vol. xxvii, No. 4 (London, 1951).
[3] E. de Martonne, "Europe Centrale," in *Géographie Universelle*, Tome IV (Paris, 1931).

TABLE 2

Areas and Populations of the Leading European States in 1952

(excluding U.S.S.R.)

COUNTRY	AREA (sq. km.)	POPULATION (000's)	DENSITY (per sq. km.)	PERCENTAGE OF URBAN POPULATION
Albania .	28,748	1,246	43	n.a.
Austria .	83,850	6,949	83	49·1
Belgium .	30,507	8,706	285	62·7
Bulgaria .	110,842	7,390	67	24·6
Czechoslovakia	127,827	12,340	97	48·8
Denmark (excl. Faeroes)	42,936	4,334	101	67·3
Finland .	337,009	4,140	12	32·3
France .	550,986	42,600	77	52·9
East Germany.	107,173	17,180	160	65·4
West Germany	245,289	49,005	198	71·1
Greece .	132,562	7,776	59	47·2
Hungary .	93,011	9,460	102	34·5
Iceland .	103,000	148	1	71·7
Ireland (Eire) .	70,282	2,942	42	40·5
Italy .	301,023	47,015	156	44·6
Luxembourg .	2,586	302	117	58·3
Netherlands .	32,388	10,377	320	54·6
Norway .	323,917	3,327	10	50·5
Poland .	311,730	24,977	80	35·8
Portugal .	92,150	8,621	93	31·1
Romania .	237,502	16,300	69	23·4
Spain .	503,061	28,528	56	60·5
Sweden .	440,122	7,125	16	56·3
Switzerland .	41,295	4,884	117	36·5
United Kingdom .	244,002	50,592	207	80·7
Yugoslavia .	256,880	17,004	65	16·2
TOTALS .	4,850,678	393,268	81	—

Sources: *Demographic Yearbook, United Nations, 1952 and 1953.*

Europe and the largely agrarian, predominantly rural communities of its eastern and south-eastern States. In spite of recent political and economic developments in Eastern Europe,[4] directed mainly towards achieving better balanced and differently oriented economies, there is evidence that these countries are still underdeveloped. In addition to these broad differences between the major areas of the continent, there

[4] See Chapter IV below.

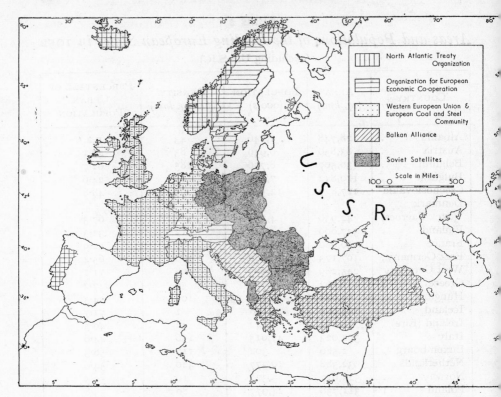

FIG. 1. THE STATES OF EUROPE AND THEIR MEMBERSHIP OF POLITICO-ECONOMIC
GROUPINGS IN JANUARY 1955

are other important differences between the States of which they are
composed, and these differences of policy, stage of economic development, and cultural level in Europe were emphasized during the inter-
war years by national efforts directed towards economic autarchy.

The pattern of States which is therefore represented on the present
political map of Europe is the result of a combination of geographical
conditions and historical forces. These, in themselves, exert pressures
which increase or decline at different times, thus evoking varying responses from the human occupants of this dynamic environment. In
consequence, the tempo of territorial change has fluctuated, but never
has it reached a greater rate than during the first half of the twentieth
century. Before the outbreak of the first world war there were twenty
independent States in Europe west of Russia. After that war the
number increased to twenty-eight, and since 1945 has decreased to

twenty-six,[5] if we accept the *de facto* division of Germany. These numbers represent the disappearance of some States, the division of others, and the emergence of new members of the European polity. The changes which they indicate are symptomatic of the ferment which has permeated Europe during the last fifty years.

The Physical Background

Eminent geographers of the recent past saw in the physical background of Europe, as well as of other areas, a measure of control of the development of States, and tended to exaggerate its importance. This determinist attitude to the relationships between human activities and physical conditions has now been modified, yet it is manifest that such relationships do exist. It is evident that every State must possess territory, the character and resources of which present opportunities to its occupants. The ways in which these resources are utilized, the level of efficiency attained and expressed in the standard of living of the people concerned, serve as useful criteria in differentiating between developed and under-developed States. On a highly diversified terrain, presenting a large number of habitats, the possibilities available to the inhabitants are therefore likely to be of a greater range than in more monotonous, less variegated areas. In this respect, Europe, in spite of its relatively small size, offers a physical make-up to which its equally diverse peoples have adapted their economic, social, and political activities. This peculiar physical background, moreover, is found in an unusual location which itself has been a contributory factor to the development of the European States.

Locational Factors

The well-worn truism that Europe is 'a peninsula of peninsulas' retains its value to the extent that it points to some of the outstanding geographical features of the continent. Itself a westward extension of the great land mass of Eurasia, and, for the greater part, lying between latitudes 40° and 60° N., Europe derives great benefits, both in commercial development and in climatic conditions, from the possession of

[5] Excluding the U.S.S.R. and the micro-States.

c*

a long, ice-free Atlantic frontage. At the same time, the major trend lines of European geological structure and the associated land forms run approximately west–east. This feature, in its turn, is reflected in the deep penetration of water bodies, especially the Baltic and Mediterranean Seas, a penetration which is enhanced by the presence of deep-water estuaries and their rivers, which are frequently navigable. As a result, Europe possesses a greater length of coastline in relation to its total area than any other continental division of the world. Its peninsularity has played a major part in facilitating the growth of that maritime supremacy which it has held until recently.

While it is true that straight lines joining North Cape (Norway) and Cape St Vincent (Portugal), and the latter with Cape Matapan (Greece), indicate the roughly triangular shape of Europe, the run of the coasts of the continental mainland shows two marked narrowings of its north–south extent—one between the head of the Adriatic and the southern part of the Baltic, the second between the English Channel and the Bay of Biscay on the one hand and the Gulf of Lions on the other. A straight line from Szczecin (Stettin) to Trieste is just over 500 miles long, while the air distance from Bordeaux to the Mediterranean is less than 250 miles. The former of these two isthmian regions coincides with the Eastern Marchlands of Europe,[6] and the latter is occupied by France. In each, locational factors have influenced the political geography of the States concerned.

The marked ease of access to the sea which most of the European States enjoy, combined with the unusual irregularity of the coasts, lends emphasis to the strategic value of the surrounding seas. This is not simply a matter of access to and from deep water, but includes control of the strategically important narrows within the adjacent seas. Such areas as those which command the entries to the Baltic, the straits of Dover and of Gibraltar, the Sicilian narrows, the Dardanelles, and the Bosporus have consistently and continually acted as sources of friction between interested States. It is not insignificant that the North Sea, Strait of Dover, and the English Channel are often called the Narrow Seas, and their strategic value needs no elaboration here.

Europe's forward position in the Atlantic made it a capital bridgehead from which to develop overseas trade and the associated building of maritime empires by the countries on its oceanic seaboard. The wealth derived from such overseas expansion brought increased power

---

[6] See Chapter IV below.

to the States of Western Europe, and gave them the means to maintain their influence in world affairs. The so-called Colonial Powers (the United Kingdom, France, Belgium, the Netherlands, Spain, and Portugal) of Western Europe are sometimes described as maritime nations, although until recent times it is unlikely that more than a minority of their inhabitants ever saw the sea. Nevertheless, they have preserved and still retain a distinguishing character derived from their association with the sea. By contrast, the States of Eastern Europe are essentially continental Powers which have played a negligible part in world maritime activities. This difference between east and west, generalized as it is here, is perhaps best illustrated by the duality of the former German Reich. Centrally located in Europe, and consequently facing at least two ways, modern Germany's expansionist efforts were divided between maritime and continental outlets. German strategy in both world wars exemplifies only too clearly and tragically how an energetic nation may strive to exploit locational possibilities with disastrous results.

Finally, and still of major importance, is that climatic diversity which arises from Europe's location in the Old World and in relation to the ocean. The continent exhibits examples of maritime and continental temperate climates; it contains the largest area of Mediterranean climate in the world, as well as considerable areas of sub-arctic conditions, the latter being closely comparable with the mountain climates of the higher parts of the Alps and Carpathians. For our present purpose it is enough to indicate that this climatic diversity is favourable to the production of a wide range of food and industrial crops. Taken into consideration with the unequal spread of mineral wealth, it helps to explain some of the economic differences between the varied European States.

Factors of Terrain

Europe's surface is even more diversified than its pattern of States. Only by reference to its geological structure and to the effects of erosional activities can this complex arrangement of land forms be understood. Caledonian, Hercynian, and Alpine earth movements have been responsible for the major lineaments of the continents, but ice action, running water, wind, and the waves of the sea have brought about widespread modifications of the original morphological units. The outcome of this long geological history differentiates Europe from all the other continents, so that it has probably a greater degree of physical diversity, and so of human environments, than any area of comparable size. Its lowlands include regions of exceptional value as cradlelands for the evolution of national groups, and became later the 'core areas' of States, but in no case does a modern European State coincide precisely with any one morphological or climatic unit. Small as they are when compared with many of the giant States of other parts of the world, they usually contain parts of more than one physical region. Only exceptionally, as in Finland and Denmark, do they fall completely within one physical province.

This great diversity of terrain has encouraged the evolution of a large number of human groups which were rarely isolated because of the possibilities of movement throughout the continent from prehistoric times onward. The coming of new means of communication increased this freedom until modern States introduced artificial barriers. In effect there are few severe physical barriers in Europe. Because of their dissection, the mountain regions are passable and rarely impeded the spread of peoples. Witness the distribution of the Basques astride the Western Pyrenees, the Slovenes in the South-eastern Alps, the German-speaking people in South Tyrol, and a dozen other examples. Again, on the plains and in basins circulation has been generally easier than in highlands, and intercourse between groups has not been prohibited. Perhaps the greatest demonstration of human use of all these facilities was given by the Romans in the way they linked the component parts of their Empire by paved roads. The desert stopped their expansion in Africa, and the Atlantic presented an insurmountable barrier westward, but on mainland Europe no physical hindrance barred their way except the Hercynian forests of Germania. Nearly two millennia later, Europe now possesses the densest network of railways and motorable roads in the world.[7] Before the results of the second world war imposed certain rigid political and economic barriers it was a most informative experience to spend an hour or so at one of the great continental railway stations such as Basel, where the indicator boards on trains showed destinations as far apart as Paris, Copenhagen, Bucharest, Rome, and Madrid. They were but the twentieth-century expression of the ease of circulation in Europe.

[7] See Chapter VIII below.

Certain States have exploited these physical facilities to better advantage than others. France has made the maximum use of the concentration of routeways on the Paris basin to weld its parts into one of the first highly unified modern States. At the same time, its isthmian location in Europe, between the Mediterranean and the Atlantic, between the sub-continent of Iberia and Central Europe, gave France unrivalled opportunities for exerting influences as well as receiving them. Switzerland provides an outstanding example of the importance of the control of mountain passages in economic and political affairs, while the dominance of London in the United Kingdom has been fostered by the convergence of lines of movement, past and present, on it. By contrast, the less fragmented lands of Eastern Europe are even more open than those of the Atlantic countries. The Carpathians are no more difficult to cross than the Alps; the Germano-Polish plains open out eastward and invite movements of people.

This difference between east and west may well be reflected in the greater stability of the West European States in recent times. What is more important, however, is that whereas the East European States lie open to the U.S.S.R., those of Western Europe face the open sea, with all the possibilities it presents for overseas expansion. Between them, pre-war Germany exploited its transitional character, neither fully western nor completely eastern in its outlook and resultant policies. In this geographical context, the Iron Curtain symbolizes a European dichotomy. The fact that it has no historical precedent as an international boundary in Germany serves to emphasize the *Zwischenraum* character of that country.

A further factor of terrain may be seen in the uneven distribution of mineral resources in Europe. This is a direct result of its complex geological structure. Such common minerals as sand, gravel, and building stone are widespread in their occurrence, and could play little or no significant part in the differential evolution of States, but the more valuable minerals, particularly coal and iron ore, are in a different class. Since the beginning of the Industrial Revolution, they have become increasingly important as two of the main bases of the economic power of certain European States. Rich and accessible deposits of coal and iron ore have contributed greatly to the wealth of the United Kingdom, France, Belgium, and Germany, and have therefore fostered their viability as political units. On the other hand, relative absence of such resources in Eastern and Southern Europe has hindered their industrial development. It is not surprising, therefore, to find that the desire to acquire or to augment mineral resources has led to inter-State political conflicts.

The aggregate of all these elements in the physical make-up of Europe may be regarded as the stage on which the drama of European politico-territorial evolution has unfolded itself. This unique physical endowment has been very differently exploited at different times. The natural resources have been available all the time, but the tempo of their human exploitation has varied greatly. Clearly the abilities, purposes, and energy of the various European nations are the decisive factor in the physico-human relationships, whether these are developed within the territorial framework of States or more widely. Hence, in analysing the political fragmentation of Europe it is necessary to examine the role of historical forces.

The Historical Forces

The present pattern of European States represents a stage in the evolution of relationships which has lasted well over two thousand years. This long history has passed through many phases and carries the marks of prolonged struggles by European peoples in their efforts to satisfy their gregarious instincts and their growing needs. What differentiates this continent from all others, however, is the way in which Europe has become the home of the nation State, a form of politico-territorial organization which has now spread to many other parts of the world. While this is mainly a modern phenomenon, its roots go back far into European history.

Under the *Pax Romana* a very large part of the continent was welded into one centralized Empire which must have assumed the appearance of permanence to its builders. With the collapse of that magnificent achievement Europe reverted to extreme disunity. For centuries lack of organization became so marked that the Dark Ages were characterized by anarchic tendencies. The feudal States which ultimately replaced the Roman Empire in the West, and, indeed, occupied virtually the whole of the continent as here defined, rested on a system of contractual relations. Furthermore, and unlike the Romans, the feudal overlords had poor means of communication for controlling their vassals, so that persistent fluctuations in area were common features of their domains, to which the term State was hardly applicable. This medieval attempt at territorial organization was replaced by the absolutist States, in which a combination of royal power and the financial resources of a newly evolved merchant class made possible a higher degree of organization in which rulers commonly identified themselves with the State: *L'État, c'est moi*. In this political development it is possible to see the growth of what have been called capitalist societies, but it is also possible to detect the seeds of their successors, the nation States.

The Nation State

The dynastic States of Europe died a slow death—some of them survived until the opening years of the twentieth century—and they have not yet been replaced by fully homogeneous nation States. Nevertheless, Europe's 400 million people live to-day in politico-territorial entities which have a strong national flavour. Among the many contributions which this continent has made to the world's cultural development the concept of the nation State ranks high. Hence, the nation and its concomitant, nationalism, are of paramount importance in the political geography of Europe. It is no exaggeration to say that we live in a nationalist age and that "The principle of nationalism is the strongest principle alive in the world to-day."[8]

The terrain of Western Europe was appropriate to the growth of nations. The favourably endowed lowlands such as the English plain, the Paris and Brussels basins, were particularly suitable as areas around which later States were to grow. Within them, circulation was relatively easy, so that gradually their inhabitants came to recognize common interests out of which grew a feeling of belonging together which is the essence of nationalism. No such emotion resulting from shared experiences was possible on the vast plains of the Old or the New Worlds until railways, the internal-combustion engine, and other means of communication came into being. Long before that time Western Europe was divided into a number of ill-defined but recognizable political units, in each of which the people became fused into a nation. Nowhere were they separated by insurmountable physical barriers. They not only inherited the dynastic quarrels of the preceding absolutist States, but also initiated their own expansionist policies.

[8] Sir Winston Churchill, in a speech in the House of Commons, 1933: quoted by G. Schwarzenberger, *Power Politics* (second edition; Stevens, London, 1951).

The absence of impassable physical obstacles meant that each embryonic nation State was subject to threats from its neighbours, and there is no greater incentive to group unity than such threats, be they real or imagined. Thus, while the United Kingdom was able to become a political unity behind the shelter of the Narrow Seas, Western and Central Europe were riven by wars which steadily assumed a national character. One of the most important results of these conflicts, whether they began as religious, imperialist, or dynastic quarrels, was a strengthening of nationalism. The surface of Western Europe in particular was an anvil on which the principle of nationalism was forged by constant hammerings.

While military and religious conflicts were decisive elements in the evolution of nationalism in Europe, other factors played an important part during the nineteenth and twentieth centuries. The steady growth of liberalism, with which is associated respect for the individual, the breakdown of the earlier local loyalties connected with feudalism, the rapidly increasing power of the third estate, especially in those countries which were becoming industrialized and therefore urbanized, all fostered the rise of new social and political traditions and new attitudes of mind. Then the railways and greatly improved road communications facilitated intercourse both within the individual States and internationally. But, in the final analysis, it may well be that the most cogent factor of all is to be found in the spread of educational facilities. As late as the end of the nineteenth century illiteracy was common throughout Europe, even elementary schooling was not available to the majority, and universal suffrage, by which the nation may express its wishes, was little more than an aspiration in most countries. By the middle of the twentieth century all these geographical, social, and economic forces had helped in cementing those bonds of relationship which are the life-blood of nationalism. The almost frenzied enthusiasm with which the European participants in the first world war entered that conflict and, even more striking, the success of the appeals made to national interests in the U.S.S.R. during the second world war are perhaps the most outstanding symptoms of national feelings in recent times. Their most tangible expression was seen in the collapse of the Habsburg Empire in 1918, when the principle of national self-determination was applied for the first time on a large scale, and led to the establishment of a number of nation States.[9]

[9] See Chapter IV below.

We have seen that the basis of nationalism is the emotion described as a feeling of belonging together. This intangible psychological phenomenon, as yet impossible to measure precisely, is usually assessed in relation to certain other factors. Of these, language stands out largely because human beings find it difficult, if not impossible, to share the experiences and emotions of their fellows unless they are able to speak their language. In many countries, therefore, national Censuses include data on "the language of common usage" or "the mother tongue." Comparison of the cartographic representation of this information with the political map reveals a lack of complete coincidence; in other words, linguistic minorities exist in all the States of Europe. France has its German-speaking people in Alsace, Belgium is a bilingual country, four languages are used in Switzerland, and in the United Kingdom there remain areas where English is not the language commonly used in the home. There is even more linguistic differentiation in the States of Eastern Europe. Thus the linguistic map of Europe not only reveals a highly diversified distributional pattern which is often assumed to coincide with the ethnic characteristics of the various groups, but still contains numerous islands of language.

So much emphasis has been placed on language as a criterion of both ethnic and national qualities that determined efforts have been made to impose the language of the ruling State on the inhabitants of disputed territories. Complete prohibition of a mother tongue is impracticable, but such measures as making the use of the official language obligatory in all State documents, in all legal proceedings, and in newspapers and other publications, and its utilization as the instrument of instruction in schools, undoubtedly inflicted hardships on the minorities. Hence the preservation of the mother tongue became one of the chief aims of linguistic minorities, so that great diversity of tongues in Europe has been kept alive and has contributed to the political fragmentation of the continent. It was largely through such cultural activities that Polish and Czech nationalism survived long periods of political subjugation. Preservation of language and literature was the chief weapon against assimilation, yet when some millions of Europeans migrated across the Atlantic the majority of them appear to have forgotten their opposition to assimilation. Their change of habitat was accompanied by a change in mental outlook; their country of adoption was indeed a "New World," where the strains and conflicts of a thousand years could disappear in one or two generations. In view of this it is a little difficult to deny that there is some *genius loci* in Europe, more especially in its eastern parts.

While accepting the powerful influence of language as a factor in differentiating national allegiance in Europe, it must be admitted that linguistic usage does not lend itself to the drawing of satisfactory boundary lines. Although the great majority of Europeans speak languages derived from the Indo-European or Aryan linguistic family (excluding Magyar, Finnish, Estonian, Turkish, and Basque), invasions, conquests, and migrations have brought about modifications to such an extent that the forty-odd languages of the continent act as real barriers to international co-operation. This separative force is augmented by the transitional linguistic character of the frontier zones which lie between the more compact masses of people each using a common language. When political boundaries are drawn through such zones of mixed languages it is inevitable that linguistic minorities should be left on the wrong side of the line. Short of compulsory transfers, there seems to be no solution to this particular problem. During the inter-war years several attempts were made to overcome this difficulty by plebiscites—for example, in Austrian Carinthia, Silesia, and the Saar—but nowhere were the results accepted finally by the contending parties.

So-called racial characteristics have sometimes been postulated as national determinants, the most striking case being the racial policy of National Socialist Germany. In Europe the identification of race and nation is patently absurd; the former is a biological, the latter a political, concept, and the two are not interchangeable. In any case, the peoples of Europe, whatever their racial origins may have been, have become so inextricably mixed by inter-marriage that it is impossible to group them effectively on racial grounds.

Common religious beliefs, modes of living, shared traditions, also make their contribution to unification of a nation, but of even greater importance is attachment to a specific territory, which becomes known as the motherland or homeland. Here, again, the relation between territory and nationalism does not lend itself to precise measurement. There is no way of knowing how many members of a nation act in accordance with the dogma "My country, first and last." At the same time, however, a nation State is inconceivable except in terms of politically organized people and territory.

The relationship between people and territory is a specifically geographical factor in the evolution of a nation. Before the advent of indus-

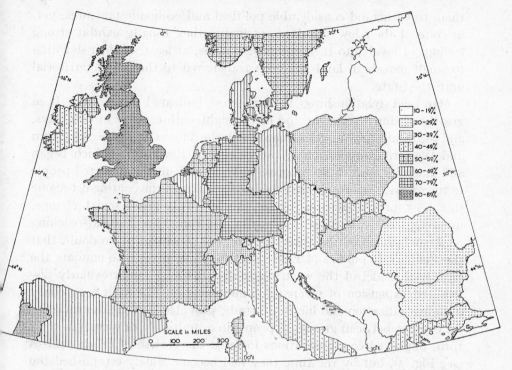

FIG. 2. DEGREES OF URBANIZATION IN WESTERN AND CENTRAL EUROPE

It should be noted that the percentages of urbanization for the various countries are not strictly comparable because of differences in the official interpretation of 'urbanization.'

Based on data from the United Nations "Demographic Yearbook, 1952"

trialization and the associated drift to towns the great majority of Europeans were intimately and directly tied to the land as their primary source of subsistence. Their social and economic roots were firmly embedded in the soil, which they regarded with something approaching reverence. Their desire to possess land was the overriding passion in their lives, and lay behind the many revolts against the feudal system. With the abolition of serfdom, achieved at different times in different parts of the continent, the European peasants retained their deep attachment to land as such, but this relationship gradually became enlarged and dualistic in character in those countries where agrarian economies survived. Thus the peoples of the States of Eastern Europe have remained predominantly rural (see Fig. 2); they are still largely peasant communities. Their techniques of subsistence farming enable them to withstand considerable political and economic pressures, yet, in spite of their low standards of living, they usually exhibit strong feelings of loyalty to their countries. Some, at least, of their devotion to small parcels of land has been transferred to the larger territorial unit, the State.

Man-land relationships, in the sense indicated here, have been greatly modified since the end of the eighteenth century in two ways, and the results are especially manifest in the differences between Eastern and Western Europe. First, the Industrial Revolution, which began and made its most rapid progress in Western Europe, attracted people to towns, with the result that the western part of the continent became the most urbanized area in the world. This great social change, involving the tearing up of centuries-old roots, has had far-reaching results which cannot be analysed here, but there can be no doubt that the People's Republics of Eastern Europe are anxious to emulate the industrial model of the west. Secondly, the vast but irregularly distributed expansion of means of communications, in itself a corollary of industrialization and increased trade, provided ever greater facilities for contact between groups of people in a multitude of ways. In their turn, improved communications fostered the growth of urban centres (see Fig. 3), but by the time they had become widely established the political pattern of Europe had begun to be fixed. Thus, for example, the railway systems grew into national networks. In some cases they were designed to serve national interests, economic and strategic. Perhaps it was only incidental that they increased national political solidarity, but they certainly made possible the concentration of political power and added to the administrative efficiency of the unitary States of Europe. Paradoxically enough, this high degree of national centralization, which is an outstanding feature of European life in the twentieth century, has developed into one of the strongest separative forces of all time in the way it has reinforced political independence. Just when facilities for human movement reached a stage previously unknown, political boundaries became equally unprecedented barriers. Passports were largely unnecessary before the end of the nineteenth century.

The interaction of all these geographical and historical influences has brought about the political fragmentation of Europe—a mosaic of sovereign nation States. On less than 5 per cent. of the aggregate area of the world's eighty-five States, the twenty-six major political

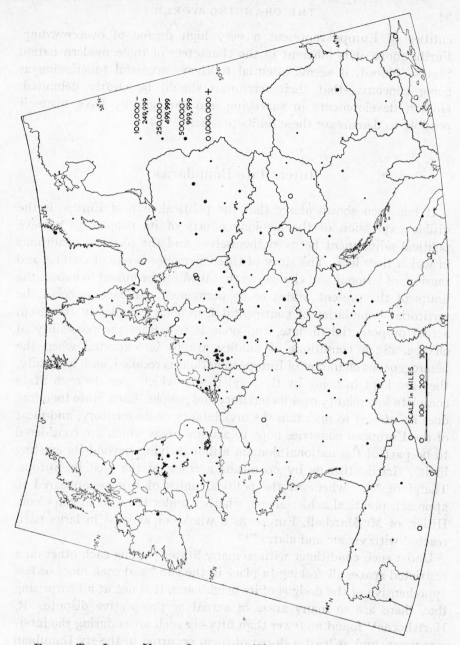

FIG. 3. THE LARGE URBAN CENTRES OF WESTERN AND CENTRAL EUROPE

Compared with Western Europe, and excluding Upper Silesia, there are no clusters of large towns in eastern Central Europe, thus indicating differences in industrial development.

entities of Europe represent a very high degree of overcrowding. Furthermore, it is inherent in the characters of these modern nation States—indeed, it seems essential to their successful functioning as going concerns—that their territories should be clearly delimited. Modern developments in surveying and cartography have made it possible to demarcate these limits precisely.

Inter-State Boundaries

It has been shown above that the political map of Europe is the visible expression of the age-long efforts of its peoples to achieve political adjustment between themselves and the physical conditions in which they live. The story of those struggles is one of conflict and tension, of ferment and change, so that it would be unreal to expect the limits of the present States to be permanent. In fact, none of the territorial boundaries of continental Europe is completely free from actual or potential dispute, and none is free from the possibility of change. Such conditions of fluidity are to be expected when the heterogeneous character of European nations is recalled, and, ironically, they are kept in being by the legal theory which gives to each State complete sovereignty over its territory and people. Each State therefore does its utmost to maintain the inviolability of its territory, and most of the European countries hope to acquire areas which are considered to be part of the national domain although lying beyond its existing limits. Irredentism is by no means a thing of the past in Europe. Therefore ". . . whenever the political unity of Europe appeared to approach practical achievement, whether under the ægis of Napoleon, Hitler, or Mr Marshall, Europe as a whole, or at least in large part, reacted with vigour and alarm."[10]

Under such conditions, with so many States jostling each other on a restricted space, all seeking 'a place in the sun,' and each more or less apprehensive of the designs of its neighbours, it is not at all surprising that there are so many areas of actual or prospective dispute. R. Hartshorne[11] found no fewer than fifty-six such areas during the inter-war years, and at least a dozen of them occurred in the six Danubian

[10] W. G. East, *The Political Division of Europe* (Birkbeck College, London, 1948).
[11] R. Hartshorne, "A Study of the Boundary Problems of Europe," in *Geographic Aspects of International Relations*, edited by C. C. Colby (Chicago University Press and Cambridge University Press, 1938).

countries.[12] All these areas of contention lay in those frontier zones within which European State boundaries are invariably drawn. They are commonly inhabited by mixed nationalities and are peripheral to the inner areas of States where national solidarity is most pronounced; it is no wonder that boundary problems receive much attention at peace and other international conferences.

The Function of the Inter-State Boundaries

In view of the difficulties associated with international boundaries it has been suggested that their abolition would contribute to the well-being of the European peoples. Two aspects of the character of these lines should be considered before this suggestion can be seen in a proper perspective. First, and in spite of numerous attempts to classify them, all political boundaries are artificial in the sense that they are defined and demarcated by man. Statesmen may use physical features such as mountain crest lines, water divides (rarely coincident with crest lines), and rivers as the sites of boundaries, or they may draw geometrical lines, but they do select the line which may be approved by the States concerned or imposed by a successful belligerent. Such boundaries, being established by man, are mutable. Secondly, the organization of the modern State demands linear boundaries. It is essential that its inhabitants should be aware of their obligations to the State, and in the case of contiguous countries the spheres of loyalties and duties must be clearly delimited. Even if the dividing lines ceased to be inter-State boundaries through some scheme of federation or even by absorption, they might well survive as internal boundaries with reduced functions and less separative force. Once a boundary is established it tends to acquire a politico-economic momentum. Where rivers, for example, have been used as dividing lines and have changed their courses, the earlier lines are normally retained as boundaries. In addition, therefore, to the other stresses and strains which are reflected in territorial disputes, there is an inherent tendency to conflict in the character of boundaries. Mutability and conservatism are uneasy bed-fellows. As the European States were the first to develop their national status and also the first to acquire demarcated boundaries, it should give no cause for surprise to find so many international disputes within the riven political structure of Europe.

[12] See Chapter IV below.

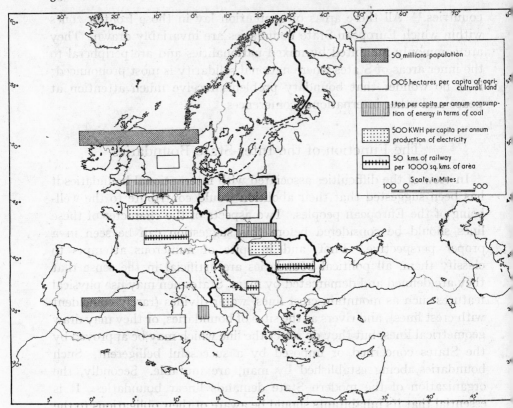

FIG. 4, CRITERIA OF ECONOMIC DEVELOPMENT IN EUROPE

The division into Western, Southern, and Central Europe is that of the Economic Commission for Europe.

Based on data in the "Economic Survey of Europe in 1953" (United Nations, Geneva, 1954)

The separative function of inter-State boundaries has been greatly reinforced during the last hundred years by the coincidental growth of nationalism and the increasing tightness of State organization. "Nationalism is no doubt a vivifying and inspiring force. It makes for national unity and—when it is genuine, and not merely a cloak for political ambitions—it acts as a curb upon the selfish instincts of individuals, and of classes and professions."[13] It is when national emotions are misused by political leaders that they become a menace. Such aggressive policies as those of Germany and Italy during the inter-war period provide adequate evidence of the tragedies in which misguided national-

[13] H. M. Chadwick, *The Nationalities of Europe and the Growth of National Ideologies* (Cambridge University Press, 1945).

ism can involve its members. It was impossible to unite national sentiments solidly in support of the leaders of a State in the days when 'public opinion' was incapable of being moulded by the agencies which are now available. Hence the modern importance of propaganda, in all its forms, whereby nationalism frequently becomes irrational if not hysterical. As means of fostering national consciousness, the Press, the radio, and the cinema have been used ruthlessly, and it is significant that among the first actions of those who aim at a *putsch* or *coup d'état* is the seizure of broadcasting stations.

As a result of the close interdependence of nationalism and the forces which encourage it ". . . the State apparatus has become incomparably stronger than it ever was before. Democratic and totalitarian States alike have today a crushing supremacy over dissident groups, let alone the individual citizen."[14] As long as the cohesive power of nationalism is confined to its own territory peaceful co-existence is possible, but, it may be suggested, wrongly directed nationalism is also explosive, especially when it exists alongside one or more equally powerful and similar developments. Then inter-State boundaries may be fortified and also used as instruments of economic warfare until their dividing functions are overthrown by military aggression. Europe has been, and remains, a prey to such politico-economic conditions, largely because it is a congeries of nation States, each closely knit internally and each striving to maintain its own sovereignty irrespective of size or power. Its 13,600 miles of inter-State boundaries[15] are the tangible evidence of its capacity for international strife, and are, therefore, an important aspect of its political geography. Added force is given to this view by the fact that, as the two world wars of the twentieth century showed beyond doubt, when European conflicts develop into war the consequences cannot be restricted to this small continent.

Conclusion

No other part of the earth's surface comparable with that of Europe is so politically divided—as a result of the long and peculiar history staged on its variegated surface. Sporadic attempts in the past to combine parts of this continent and its nations into Imperial States, some of which achieved a measure of unity, but at a price paid in

[14] G. Schwarzenberger, *op. cit.*, p. 63.   [15] Excluding those of the micro-States.

social discontent—succeeded only for a time, and failed when internal stresses and/or external forces overthrew the empires alike of the Habsburgs and the Hohenzollerns and of dictators like Napoleon and Hitler. The inequality of European States in area and population is now enhanced by the facilities available for integrating their political and economic activities and thus increasing and centralizing the power of their governments. Yet during at least part of the twenty inter-war years every country in Europe professed to practise one variant or another of the parliamentary system of government. It was not until the middle twenties and early thirties that dictatorships, with their distinctive ideologies, were established west of the U.S.S.R. The Italian and German dictatorships vanished at the end of the second world war, but in the Eastern Marchlands the parliamentary systems of Poland, Czechoslovakia, Hungary, Romania, Bulgaria, and Yugoslavia, however much these countries preserve a façade of elections and representative government, have fallen under the sway of the Communist ideology. Hence the Europe of the 1950's stands divided in an unprecedented manner. The Roman bifurcation of the continent reflected the difference between an organized and an unorganized Europe; to-day the Iron Curtain separates two great areas of completely different types of political organization and political philosophy. Modern history has never witnessed so separative a boundary, which, by analogy, may be said to mark a political fault zone. It is one of the realities of European life, and is all the more emphatic because it epitomizes the division of the world into two opposed camps.

The establishment of the Iron Curtain has certainly made possible a degree of simplification of some of the nationalist problems of Eastern Europe, so that its linguistic map is very different from that of 1938. The change has been brought about at the cost of much hardship for the displaced persons and has been achieved under the ægis of a State which professes to give autonomy to its national groups. It has been assumed that on the fragmented territory of Europe transfers of population are the only means of solving the problems associated with areas of mixed nationalities. Such draconian measures were not considered necessary in the past, if exception be made of the exchanges of population between Greece and Turkey after the first world war, and certainly nothing on the scale of the compulsory movements of Germans during the decade 1940–50 has ever been attempted before. On the other hand, the dominating power of nationalism reached its peak in the first half of this century, so that assimilation of non-nationals became virtually impossible in most European States. The dilemma still facing governments appears to lie in the choice between compulsory transfers and the tolerant acceptance of minorities. The post-war evidence goes to show that the desire for national self-determination is at least as strong as it was a century ago, even when allowance is made for the subordination of the satellite States of the U.S.S.R. This raises a further and pressing problem of fragmented Europe—the economic viability of its numerous smaller States—which will be considered in Chapter VIII.

CHAPTER II

The Passing of Mitteleuropa

ERIC FISCHER

THERE are geographic names which have only one meaning and are understood by everybody. *Mitteleuropa* does not belong to this group of names, but means different things to different people. It is a term fraught with political and economic connotations. The English form 'Central Europe' has fewer such connotations, and will be used in this chapter to designate a major but variously delimited physical division of this continent. Mitteleuropa is used here as a politico-geographical term,[1] which in the usage and mind of every author has a very definite meaning, but, unfortunately, for every author a different one.[2]

The Concept 'Mitteleuropa'

During the first world war, following the publication of *Mitteleuropa* by the German politician and writer Friedrich Naumann, the concept of Mitteleuropa[3] became the basis of a program of economic and political conquest. Though geographers and historians had previously tried to find a suitable definition of this term, after the publication of Naumann's book this quest turned toward finding some physical features suitable to delimit Mitteleuropa.[4] The emotionally and politically

[1] W. Gordon East, in the discussion following Mrs J. A. Steers's paper, "The Middle People," in *Geographical Journal*, vol. cxii (July–December 1948), p. 41.

[2] It is strange that non-German authors in many cases have adopted a delimitation of Central Europe, used only by the most expansionist German authors, though derived from a geographer, Partsch. See *Encyclopædia Britannica*, vol. viii (1944), p. 840; *Schweizer Lexicon*, vol. v (1947), p. 616.

[3] Friedrich Naumann, *Mitteleuropa* (G. Reimer, Berlin, 1915). For other literature on this concept of Naumann's see *Bibliographie zur Geschichte Österreich-Ungarns im Weltkrieg*, in *Bibliographische Vierteljahrshefte der Weltkriegsbücherei*, Doppelheft, 2/3 (Stuttgart, July–October 1934); this bibliography lists thirty-four items.

[4] For a discussion of the development of this term see Henry Cord Meyer, "Mitteleuropa in German Political Geography," in *Annals of the Association of American Geographers*, vol. xxxvi (September 1946), pp. 178–194.

tainted use of geographical names had been common in this part of the world for a long time. Metternich, a hundred years ago, said that the Balkans began at the eastern city gate of Vienna,[5] using the geographical term 'Balkans' to connote a semi-barbaric civilization on a level far below that of either Central or Western Europe. With this connotation the term Balkans has been saddled, used by some,[6] misunderstood by many, and frequently resented, whether the slight was intended or not. Hungarian and Romanian writers especially have tried to prove with pseudo-geographic arguments that their countries are wholly within Mitteleuropa, implying thereby that they had endured centuries of Turkish rule without forfeiting their cultural standing among the nations of the European center.

Modern text-books in the English language define the area of Central Europe in several different ways. It is correct to state that Central Europe is a zone of transition[7] or that it is the opposite to periphery;[8] to call it the tidal lands of Europe[9] is a picturesque, allegorical designation without accurate meaning. One author defines Mitteleuropa in terms of political units having a transitional climate,[10] others simply enumerate those political units which they want to include,[11] while others try to prove that it has nothing to do with the patterns of States.[12]

If we accept 'Central Europe' as a physical division and Mitteleuropa as a politico-geographical unit we can hardly speak of the passing of Central Europe, but can certainly discuss the passing of Mitteleuropa.

[5] "Der Balkan beginnt an der Marxer Linie."
[6] Among recent text-books in English Norman J. G. Pounds, *Europe and the Mediterranean* (McGraw-Hill, New York, 1953), p. 271, excludes Hungary and Romania from Central Europe, and has a separate chapter on "Danubian and Balkan Countries." His meaning is clear when he writes on p. 273: "The Danubian countries have a common heritage from the long period of Turkish domination and misrule—their poverty and backwardness," overlooking that this period ended for southern Yugoslavia and Bulgaria only forty years ago, for Hungary more than 225 years earlier.
[7] Samuel Van Valkenburg and Colbert C. Held, *Europe* (second edition; Wiley and Son, New York; Chapman and Hall, London, 1952), p. 526, and similarly Margaret Reid Shackleton, *Europe* (fourth edition; Longmans, Green and Co., London, 1950), p. 240. N. J. G. Pounds, *op. cit.*, p. 210, uses this characteristic to refer to the area "dominated by German political power and settlement . . . and speech."
[8] Jean Gottmann, *A Geography of Europe* (Holt and Co., New York, and Harrap, London, 1951), p. 332, and similarly Derwent Whittlesey, *The Earth and the State* (Holt and Co., New York, 1944), p. 90.
[9] Gottmann, *op. cit.*
[10] George D. Hubbard, *Geography of Europe* (second edition; Appleton Century-Crofts, New York, 1952), p. 605.
[11] George W. Hoffman (ed.), *A Geography of Europe* (Ronald Press Co., New York, and Methuen, London, 1953), p. 325.
[12] Joseph Aulneau, *Histoire de l'Europe Centrale* (Paris, 1926), p. 8, quoted by Meyer, *op. cit.*, p. 179, footnote.

This formerly very vital core of Europe has disappeared from the political scene. Instead of Mitteleuropa occupying the ill-defined middle of the continent, a line now divides Western Europe and the Soviet Realm. In other words, Mitteleuropa has contracted to a line. It is the purpose of this chapter to discuss the development and the implications of this political division and the geographical factors which make it more than a temporary accident.

The Historical Development of Mitteleuropa

Mitteleuropa, as here conceived, had its widest possibilities in the days when only the Old World was known—in the Europe of the Middle Ages, when America was unknown and the countries of Asia and Africa belonged to different civilizations and had only slender contacts with the rest of the world. In such a world the center of Europe could easily, though not necessarily, be a center of political gravity. In the modern world there is no longer one single center of the entire modern world; for the Old World alone the center lies farther east, in the Heartland, as formulated by Sir Halford Mackinder and believed by Haushofer. The latter drew the conclusion that Germany and the U.S.S.R., if closely associated, could dominate the world, and he, as a German, preferred, of course, that Germany should be the senior partner in this combination. Hitler, in his crude way of thinking, drew the conclusion that Germany had to conquer Russia. However, as early as 1919, at a time when neither Mackinder's nor Haushofer's ideas were widely known, a rumor circulated in Germany that Lenin did not support a Bolshevist revolution in Germany at that time because he was afraid that, given the undeveloped state of Russia, in a Bolshevized Russia and Germany the tail would wag the dog.

Central Europe no longer has centrality in the world. We have to go far back in history to find a somewhat comparable situation. During Classical times Central Europe stood on the very periphery of the known and civilized world; in the lengthy earlier period of Egyptian-Mesopotamian predominance its position was even more remote and marginal. This position could not change as long as civilization was centered on, and had not spread far beyond, the basin of the Mediterranean Sea. Later, when Islam conquered its eastern and southern shores, Mediterranean Europe became a frontier region. However, it

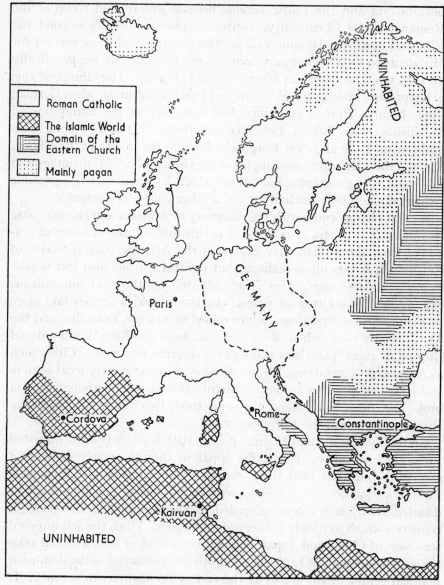

FIG. 1. SELF-CONTAINED CHRISTIAN EUROPE, APPROXIMATELY A.D. 1000

was slow to lose its importance as the central area of the European world; notably, it retained the Papal center at Rome.

In the later Middle Ages Europe, in the modern sense, emerged.

Scandinavia and the Baltic regions became known and received the Roman form of Christianity. Germans colonized widely beyond the Elbe and down the Danube valley. The geographical stage was set for Mitteleuropa to strive for supremacy over Christian Europe, practically all that was known of the Western world (Fig. 1). The climax of this attempt came during the eleventh and twelfth centuries, when German kings became Roman emperors, had their say in the foundation of archbishoprics in Poland, Bohemia, and Hungary, ruled over northern and central Italy and over Burgundy down to the mouth of the Rhône. Though this 'Holy Roman Empire of the German Nation' disintegrated gradually, the geographic conditions which had made its rise possible remained essentially unchanged for another couple of centuries.

A great change came with the discovery of America and the sea route to India. It is generally realized that this fostered the transfer of sea-power from the Italian City States to the Atlantic coastal States of Europe. It is less often realized that Central Europe also lost importance by this change. This is accentuated by the contemporaneous expansion of the Ottoman power. In 1529 Turkish armies laid siege to Vienna for the first time. Silver mined in Saxony, Bohemia, and the Tyrol lost its value when silver and gold from the New World entered Europe in great quantities through the Iberian peninsula. Cities such as Augsburg, Nuremberg, Vienna, Cracow, became merely local centers and lost their position as central distribution points. Although Russia broke the Tatar yoke about the same time, this did not yet signalize Russia's entry into the European world.

Gradually Europe and to some degree Mitteleuropa became adjusted to the new situation. It became apparent that the newly discovered countries could not hold their own as equal partners with European Powers. Most became colonies (even India, where the Moghul power disintegrated), and a few succeeded in keeping outside the circle of countries which mutually influenced each other. Thus, the self-imposed seclusion of China and Japan reduced the world of international relations for another three centuries. Europe later emerged as the dominant political center of the world at the end of the eighteenth century. It was also geographically the center, as the westward and southward expansion was balanced by Russia's expansion into Siberia. At the same time Russia was spreading its version of European Christian civilization to the borders of China and the Pacific, and under Catherine the Great it finally entered the 'Concert of Europe.'

Geographically, Central Europe was again at the center of the world. However, its geographical position had suffered since medieval times: it labored under a severe handicap, because it touched the sea only at a few peripheral points. The central position of Europe and European rule over the outer world was based on sea-power. At the critical period just before and after the discovery of America several Power combinations had emerged which tried to rule over a wider area from a base in Mitteleuropa. Hungary under the Anjous and the Hunyadis, and Poland at the period when Polish troops entered Moscow and Kiev, enjoyed only short periods of success. The Austrian Habsburgs were more fortunate, or perhaps more persistent, combining at times with Spain to rule over the Low Countries, Burgundy, and Italy, as well as Austria, Hungary, and Bohemia, and dominating Italy and the northern Balkans. A final attempt was made by the Prussian Hohenzollerns to use a part of Mitteleuropa as a power base. Unlike the Habsburgs, who allied with the Pope, they co-operated closely with the nascent German nationalism.

This Prussian-German attempt was doomed to failure from the very beginning, because it was undertaken at the very moment when a world-wide reorganization took place, comparable with that which occurred at the time of the Renaissance and the great geographical discoveries. The non-European continents entered the stage, leaving their colonial status behind.[13] The Spanish-American War in 1898 and the Russian-Japanese War in 1904–5 brought recognition as Great Powers to two non-European nations. During the first world war, when Germany made its bid to consolidate Mitteleuropa and make it the basis of world domination, failure became inevitable when the United States entered the war. Japan had previously joined the conflict.

The inter-war period saw a rapid shift away from the European center: the British Empire became the Commonwealth, in which strength increasingly derived from the overseas members; France based its power reluctantly on non-European sources, primarily by the use of non-European troops; and the Soviet Union, by developing the Urals and Siberia, shifted its center perceptibly eastward, even if the capital moved only from St Petersburg (Leningrad) to Moscow.

In the face of these changing, but unappreciated, conditions

[13] For a detailed description of this development see Eric Fischer, *The Passing of the European Age* (second edition; Harvard University Press, Cambridge, Mass., and Oxford University Press, 1948).

D

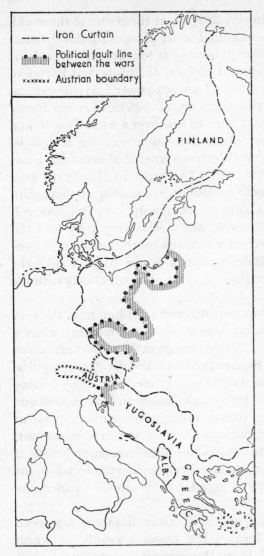

Iron Curtain
Political fault line between the wars
Austrian boundary

FINLAND

AUSTRIA

YUGOSLAVIA

ALB.

GREECE

FIG. 2. THE IRON CURTAIN AND ITS PRE-
DECESSOR BETWEEN THE WARS

Hitler and his Third Reich attempted the renewed conquest of the world from the Mitteleuropa base. However, the main power centers were out of Hitler's reach, and his violent outburst served only to precipitate a development that might have taken much longer to mature under peaceful conditions. Mitteleuropa was no longer so located that it could be a major power center. Under the tremendous stress it broke into halves. The fault line, called the Iron Curtain, follows approximately a line of cleavage which had become visible after the first world war (Fig. 2). At that time it separated the new, mostly Slavic-speaking national successor States from Germany, running, therefore, straight across the Mitteleuropa of German dreams. Whether Austria belonged east or west of this line remained undetermined. However, all the countries, like Poland, east of this line regarded themselves as Central European nations, and felt themselves more strongly separated from Eastern Europe than from Germany, the leader of western Mitteleuropa.

The two lines drawn after the first and second world wars show significant differences, though the shift is not very great in miles. The new line runs across Germany herself. The position of Austria, now neutralized, is no longer as ambiguous as it was between the wars. Adjacent to both the northern and the southern ends of the line are two more countries in somewhat dubious position, Finland and Yugoslavia. The main fact, however, is that Mitteleuropa ceased to exist even as a potential unit.

Factors of Disintegration

This historical summary gives, however, only one side of the picture. It shows the waxing and waning significance of the central position of Mitteleuropa in its dependence on world-wide developments. If we focus our view on a wide perspective, Mitteleuropa may easily appear as a unit. It never was. There were, indeed, forces striving for unity. They never accomplished their goal. Several times they came very close to it, the first time under the emperors of the Saxon dynasty in the early Middle Ages, later under the Emperor Charles V, who was also King of Spain, and finally during both world wars. Characteristic of this failure is that Mitteleuropa never had a capital city. Indeed, for most of the time Germany also lacked a capital city. Its individual components had capitals, ranging from petty residences such as Gotha or Brunswick to large centers such as Vienna or Prague. Otto III, one of the Saxon emperors, resided in Rome. Most of the early German kings and emperors migrated from castle to castle, from city to city. Perhaps Prague under the Luxembourg dynasty came closest to playing the role of a capital for most of Mitteleuropa. Berlin is a latecomer; but under Kaiser Wilhelm II and Hitler it came as close as any other city to the role of a capital of Mitteleuropa. To-day the dividing line runs through this city and its fate symbolizes that of Mitteleuropa. However, it is significant that Berlin's fall did not make room for another city. Vienna, the one-time rival, is hardly in a better position; Budapest, Warsaw, and Prague are seats of satellite governments. Bonn lacks tradition, lies near the border, and is regarded by most Germans as a temporary expedient.

Though world-wide conditions opened the road to domination for Mitteleuropa at certain times and condemned it to a backward position at other times, a Power strong enough to take advantage of favorable circumstances did not always arise, nor did Mitteleuropa always withdraw to a secondary position under favorable conditions.

When, in the course of its history, Mitteleuropa disintegrated into a hodge-podge of small, mutually hostile Powers, another aspect of its central position came to the fore. It became a power vacuum, into which adjacent Powers were tempted to intrude. Countries at the margin of the œcumene, such as Japan, Iceland, or Sweden, could sometimes pass through a period of internal disintegration without interference from outside. If some of the many neighbours of Mitteleuropa were either too weak or too involved in other pressing problems to take advantage of the weakness at the centre, there was always a strong one remaining to do so.

In the seventeenth century such a situation developed after the critical shift of the political and economic strength of Europe to its Atlantic coastlands had occurred, and when religious fanatics and representatives of new and old social forces were locked in deadly conflict. At this critical period Danish, Swedish, French, and Turkish armies on occasions, and sometimes simultaneously, roamed over most of Mitteleuropa. Previously, in the late fifteenth and early sixteenth centuries, when feudal conflicts and the disrupting forces of newly emergent social order weakened the Hungarian kingdom, it had fallen prey to the invading Turks. A similar tragic fate befell Poland in the two succeeding centuries. Devastated by Swedish and Russian armies, it was finally partitioned in such a way that the largest part was annexed by Russia, an East European country and civilization, and lost to Central Europe.

It is possible to interpret the happenings after the first world war as the irruption of neighboring Powers into a power vacuum; but such an interpretation is insufficient to explain what happened after the second world war. During World War I, even at its very end, either the Central Powers or even Germany alone held an area which might be designated as Mitteleuropa. The collapse of the Central Powers created the power vacuum into which foreign armies irrupted from west, south, and south-east. The armies coming from the west stopped soon, and at their own free will, at the Rhine. In the east, because there were hardly any armies left to invade, the local populations, supplemented by small groups of returning soldiers (Polish and Czech legionaries and remnants of the Serbian and Romanian armies), were able to create new States and to claim new boundaries, some of them rather haphazardly. Only in Hungary and Bavaria, and then only for periods of a few weeks, did Bolshevism enter the vacuum from the east.

The picture of the second world war is quite different: strong armies from the east and west had to fight their way into the innermost parts of Mitteleuropa until they met. The tenacity of Hitler prevented the development of a power vacuum for the time being. In its place a line of division between west and east developed, at first tentatively, but soon firmly. Czechoslovakia and, to some degree, Hungary and Poland, near the center of the Continent, tried for a while to operate on a policy completely dependent neither on the west nor on the east. After a few years of a losing struggle they were drawn into the eastern orbit and are firmly incorporated in the Soviet system for the foreseeable future. If the political and military ties of the West German Republic and Austria to the west are less tightly drawn there can be no doubt that these countries belong to the economic and ideological structure of the west. There is now no Mitteleuropa which is independent ideologically of either the west or the east.

The Northern Plain of Central Europe

In the final phase of the second world war the Allies invaded Central Europe by four main routes. The Russians moved across the Polish and North German Plain and also through the Pannonian Plain and the Vienna Gate; the western Allies came from the plains of Flanders and the Saverne Gate of Lorraine. All of these four routes are great historical corridors of movement in peace and war, used for ingress as well as for egress, exchange, invasion, and conquest. Such an arrangement of routes is closely connected with the geological structure of Central Europe and its east–west zonal arrangement.

Central Europe is bordered in the north by two minor water bodies, the North Sea and the Baltic Sea. Between them and the low mountains which trend in an east–west direction through much of Europe is a plain, narrow in the west, gradually widening toward the east. This east–west trend is accentuated in the broader eastern part by low morainic ridges and intervening wide sandy valleys. In the Great Ice Age the latter served as glacial spillways; now they are a favorable location for canals connecting the rivers which flow from the mountains in a generally northward direction to the sea.

The narrow westward continuation of this North German Plain contains the regions of Flanders and Brabant in present-day Belgium. It leads without break into the lowlands and plains of Northern France.

On these terminal lowlands, since the dawn of history, routes converged and merchants settled down. The fringing mountains to the south belong to the Hercynian system. The Belgian edge of these old mountains has coal and iron deposits, which also occur elsewhere along their northern edge. The coast, on the North Sea, lies near to the Strait of

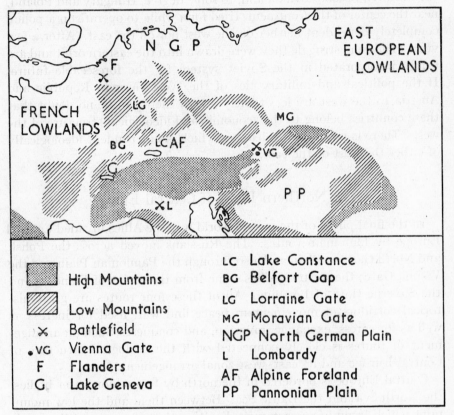

FIG. 3. THE MOUNTAIN ZONES OF CENTRAL EUROPE

Dover and the exit to the Atlantic Ocean. In this favored location one of the most densely populated and most intensively industrialized regions of the world has developed. However, it has also attracted armies from the east and west, and places such as Oudenaarde, Waterloo, and Ypres are best known as battlefields (Fig. 3).

In the east the North German Plain is too wide to permit the development of small, distinctive, individualized areas, such as Flanders in the west. There are inland mining and industrial areas, first of all that of

Upper Silesia, at the northern edge of the Hercynian belt in the east. There are maritime cities from Lübeck to Riga; but they are not necessarily at or near the path of west–east land communications. There are battlefields; they are widely dispersed. The German peasant colonists, moving east, occupied the plain in its full width as far as east of the middle Oder, but split up farther east into numerous unconnected groups.

It is remarkable that until recently there was only one period when enemy armies crossed the whole length of this plain. Napoleon marched his army there from France to Moscow, and the Russians followed it on his retreat. In the second world war armies invading east and west met in the center between the Elbe and the Oder. The only comparable event occurred in the seventeenth century, when Swedish armies and French armies crossed Germany and Poland by different routes, without, however, occupying them in the modern sense.

The great rivers of Central Europe, the Danube excepted, cross the plain from south to north (Fig. 4). They have been the main routes in past centuries, and still carry much traffic, while more follows their valleys. Most of these rivers connect important inland centers with the sea. The Vistula leads from the vicinity of the only low and wide gap in the eastern Hercynian belt, the Moravian Gate, past the old Polish capitals of Cracow and Warsaw to Danzig (Gdańsk); the Oder comes from the same area, and is the main water outlet of the Upper Silesian industrial region to Stettin (Szczecin). The Elbe rises farther inland and is the main artery of Bohemia. The rich Saxon coal, salt, and potash mines are within its drainage basin, as is Berlin. At its mouth Hamburg became one of the largest ports of the world; its rivals are Bremen at the mouth of the relatively insignificant Weser river, and Rotterdam at the mouth of the Rhine. This last river is unique in Europe, as it rises in the Alps, breaks through the whole width of the Hercynian mountain belt, and serves the largest and most diversified hinterland. In modern times it has received its largest impulse from its connexion with the industrial heart of Germany, the Ruhr region.

None of these rivers was ever a major obstacle to east–west traffic on the plain, though communication lines converged at a few bridge cities, especially toward Cologne on the Rhine and Magdeburg on the Elbe. These river systems have tended in modern times to facilitate trade and traffic within their basins, which were seldom, if ever, political units. The rivers served to unite and not to divide, though

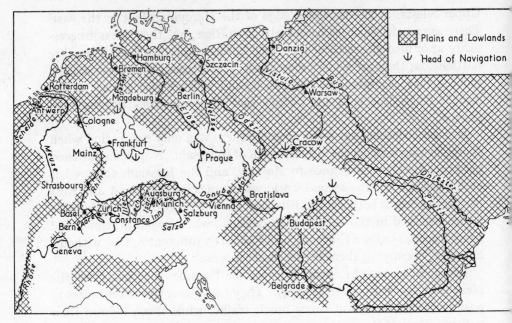

FIG. 4. LOWLANDS, RIVERS, AND BRIDGE-TOWNS IN CENTRAL EUROPE

political slogans may evoke a different impression. The Rhine boundary upstream to Basel has been a goal of French politics, but it became a reality, and then very briefly, only during the years 1801–13. The Elbe line played an important role in German social and political history, and it has been held to be a significant dividing line within Germany. It was regarded as the boundary between the area of the great feudal landowners and their serf-tenants, and the peasant owners in the west; between autocratic, militaristic Prussia and the more or less liberal small principalities; between the home of the reactionary 'east-Elbian Junkers' and the democratic and capitalistic, industrial western Germany. As useful as this distinction may be for the understanding of much in German life, nobody would regard the term 'Elbe line' as more than an approximate, rather symbolic designation, and not an exact boundary line.[14]

At present the Oder-Neisse line has become the best known of international river boundaries. The Poles try to justify the selection of this boundary line by referring to an historical precedent. It is more than

[14] E.g., Isaiah Bowman, *The New World* (fourth edition; World Book Co., Yonkers-on-Hudson, New York, and Chicago, and Harrap, London, 1928), p. 261.

900 years since these rivers served as a boundary between Germanic and Polish tribes for approximately half a century. Since then no part of these rivers has been an international boundary.

The Uplands of Central Europe

The upland belt south of these northern plains is not uniform. In its western part it is a mosaic of low mountains, hills, and basins. In the center is the diamond-shaped block of the Bohemian Massif. In the east the Carpathians are no longer a part of the Hercynian system, but belong to the Alpine fold mountains. From the Danube near Vienna they trend north-east, east, and finally curve south and west to reach the river again. These three sections of the Uplands of Central Europe have offered a varied environmental background to much of Mitteleuropa's history.

The western section is fairly well opened up by basins, broad valleys, and corridors. Two low gaps connect the upper Rhine valley and associated smaller basins with the lowlands of France—the Lorraine (Saverne) Gate and, between the Vosges and Jura, the Belfort Gap. Both are highroads of commerce and war. Several routes cross the Rhine, the most important where the Main joins the Rhine at Mainz (with the associated crossings over the Main at Frankfurt), near Strasbourg, and in Switzerland at Basel. Patton's 3rd Army entering through the Lorraine Gate and the French 1st Army through the Belfort Gap are only the last of a long series of armies passing through. Not all came from the west. The heights between the gaps are thinly populated, and have few, mostly secondary, transportation lines. Thus the German attack over the rough plateau of the Eifel took the Allies by surprise in the famous Battle of the Bulge in December 1944.

Throughout history the mountain rim of the Bohemian Massif exerted its influence in two directions. In the Middle Ages its wedge-like shape divided the eastward movement of the German colonists into two separate currents.[15] The country to the south and north became German-speaking; within the wedge in Bohemia the Slavic-speaking population consolidated itself into the Czech nation. On the other hand, the forested mountain rim of Bohemia surrounds a very rich agricultural basin, and the mountains themselves are rich in minerals.

[15] W. G. East, *loc. cit.*, p. 41.

D*

In the Middle Ages they were mined for silver, gold, and copper; to-day for coal and uranium. This natural endowment attracted German settlers, especially miners, into and across the mountains. Bohemia's history shows oscillations of the language boundary throughout the centuries, with that of Czech either retreating into the interior or barely able to regain the mountain rim. Only once, and then only for a few decades, did the Bohemian Massif become a mountain fortress from which Czech armies sallied forward into the surrounding lowlands. This was in the fifteenth century, when the Czechs embraced the heretic Hussite doctrine. Driven by fanaticism and desperation from persecution, they overran the surrounding countries at a time when almost complete anarchy reigned in Germany and Hungary. German nationalistic propagandists used this atypical movement to depict western Czechoslovakia as the dagger-point aimed at the very heart of Germany.[16] Thus this insidious propaganda tried to justify the fight against Czechoslovakia. This misuse of the facts of historical geography was possible only because of the widespread lack of historical knowledge in the west.

The western Carpathian mountains have few passes, most of them rather high; they include the highest part of the upland belt of Central Europe, with summits reaching to nearly 9000 feet. Despite minor changes, parts of the Western Carpathians have proved a fairly stable border between the Slovak and Polish national areas and between the kingdoms of Hungary and Poland politically.[17] Occasionally one of these kingdoms conquered the opposite slope of the mountains for short periods. It is perhaps characteristic that, although the Habsburgs acquired Galicia, the country on the northern slopes of the Carpathians and extending into their foreland, they administered it throughout as a part of their Austrian dominion and kept it from any political connexion with, or dependence on, Hungary. Militarily, they regarded Galicia as the outwork of the mountain-rimmed fortress of Hungary. Neither then nor in previous periods of conquest was any political connexion

---

[16] Haushofer published a map purporting to show how large parts of Germany could be covered by long-range artillery fire because of the unfavorable tracing of the German boundaries at Versailles. Bohemia plays a great role in this argument. Haushofer forgot conveniently that the whole of Bohemia could be covered by long-range artillery fire from inside Germany even if the guns were placed some distance from the boundary. Karl Haushofer, *Grenzen* (Vowinkel, Berlin-Grunewald, 1927), p. 244.

[17] S. Columb Gilfillan, "European Political Boundaries," in *Political Science Quarterly*, vol. xxxix (September 1924), pp. 458–484. Gilfillan's map was reprinted by S. Whittemore Boggs, *International Boundaries* (Columbia University Press, New York, and Oxford University Press, 1940), pp. 116–117.

followed by a migration of people, by economic integration, or by cultural assimilation. The western Carpathians shielded Hungary from the Russian danger and Poland from Turkish conquest to a large degree. The year 1944 is a landmark, as for the first time this part of the Carpathians is no longer a cultural divide, Russian Communism having become victorious north and south of them.[18]

Similarly, the role of the eastern Carpathians has changed. In the past Hungarian kings had dominated the Moldavian and Wallachian plains off and on by advancing over the mountains east and south. By such conquests the Romanian people came under the influence of cultural currents from Central Europe, despite their strong resistance to such foreign domination. However the discussion may range on the questions whether or how far Romania belonged culturally to Mitteleuropa, or to Eastern Europe, or to the Balkan region of Byzantium and Turkey, or to the Romance group of nations, there is no doubt that it is now submerged under the Soviet Russian flood.

The Southern Plains of Central Europe

South of the Hercynian-Carpathian upland belt is a zone of rather level areas. Different from the northern plains, it is in no way a uniform landscape. The western and central part is the Alpine Foreland; the eastern the Pannonian Plain.[19] The Alpine Foreland is in some places a plain, in others a hilly country, and generally slopes away from the Alps. It is built of material (*molasse*) brought down from the Alps in the Tertiary era and partly covered by products of later erosion, especially during the Great Ice Age. Moraines, terraces, outwash plains, and lakes surrounded by morainic amphitheaters show that the contributions of the glacial period belong to a geologically recent past.

Politically the Foreland is shared by three countries—Switzerland in the west, the West German Republic in the center, and Austria in the east. Switzerland and Austria join their parts of the Foreland with the Alps south of it into two political units. For many centuries Bavaria tried to accomplish a similar combination, but succeeded only in holding the outer rim of the mountains, while the Austrian

---

[18] See below, p. 420.
[19] The expression 'Hungarian' Plain is now unsatisfactory because the plain extends on all sides beyond the present boundaries of Hungary.

Habsburgs joined the Tyrol, south of Bavaria, to their more eastern Alpine dominions.

This Foreland, though relatively level, is much inferior to the North German Plain in many respects. Much of it is infertile, and it lacks mineral resources.[20] Industrial development came late and has remained sporadic. In addition, there are many obstacles which limit its use as a passageway between east and west. In the south-west the Foreland tapers where the Alps and Jura mountains come close together. Between them the Lake of Geneva intervenes. Another lake, Constance, interrupts the Foreland farther to the north-east, and its median line has been the boundary between Switzerland and Germany since the sixteenth century. The Foreland thus has connexions with the west only over passes or through narrow valleys, usable enough for trade routes, less usable for armies, least usable for migrations. They have fostered the spread of cultural influences, but have been used in the delimitation of political boundaries. The rivers which cross the Foreland are quite different from those which cross the North German and Polish Plains. They are unsuitable for navigation, but have sufficient volume and are rapid enough to be serious obstacles. All the larger cities of the Foreland, from Geneva, Bern, and Zurich in Switzerland to the German cities Augsburg and Munich, and to the Austrian Salzburg and Vienna, grew out of bridgeheads. In the east as in the west, the Foreland narrows. But there also the Alps end, only to continue after a short break across the Danube as the Carpathians. Vienna is located in this critical gap. Here a level avenue opens into the Pannonian Plain. Another passageway leads from there north-eastward between the Bohemian Massif and the Carpathians through the Moravian Gate into the North German Plain. Here, again, is one of the chief battlefields of European history, rivalled only by the plains of Flanders and Lombardy. Here the Habsburgs found a favorable location for a capital from which they could keep in easy touch with their diversified possessions.

The Pannonian Plain is a wide basin, surrounded by moderately high, but inhospitable, mountains. The greater part of the Plain lies in the domain of the Hungarian State. From there Hungarian influence reached out, frequently to the rim of the mountains, even crossing them occasionally, most persistently in the south-west across the karstic limestone plateaux which separate the Pannonian Plain from the

[20] Oil exists on its very margin in the east.

Adriatic Sea. Time and again enemies invaded the interior of the Plain, most frequently through the two natural gateways, the Vienna Gate and the Serbian Morava valley, an easy route from Istanbul via Sofia or from Salonica to Belgrade. This is the route which the armies of the Crusaders took from Central Europe into Asia; the invading Turks came in the opposite direction. Cultural influences followed generally the same route, supplemented by others from Italy coming from the south-west. Thus culturally and in its physiographic structure the Pannonian Plain is less closely bound to the other potential areas of Mitteleuropa than any other area discussed; historical accident, especially German colonization and Habsburg dynastic policies, did much to link the Pannonian Plain to the rest of Mitteleuropa for long periods.

Mitteleuropa has a definite border in the south. The Alps provide a bold frontier zone between the central parts of Europe and the Mediterranean countries. From the high plains of the Foreland most valleys can be easily entered, while only a few good routes lead from the North Italian Plain far into the mountains and to the passes. Only in Roman times did a Power, based on Italy, rule over the Alps. However, from the fifteenth to the nineteenth century Italian cultural influence was strong in Switzerland, southern Germany, Austria, Bohemia, Hungary, and as far as Poland, especially in architecture and music. In the past, political boundaries in the Alps have been more stable than in the western and eastern boundary regions of Mitteleuropa. The present changed political, cultural, and ideological alignments, which have redrawn the political map of Europe, have not appreciably affected this Alpine border zone.

Germans and Mitteleuropa

It is doubtless clear to the reader that the Mitteleuropa concept has a weak geographical base. German writers in gathering their arguments often fell back on the fact that throughout this area German was the only language generally understood. It was the *lingua franca* for all the smaller nations. In the east and south-east many Germans lived in small or large isolated areas, so-called language islands. More radical German writers and map-makers claimed large areas either as originally German 'settlement areas' or as German 'national soil' or at least as German 'cultural soil.' German language and civilization, rather than the German State, were alleged to be the unassailable basis of the concept of Mitteleuropa.[21]

This thesis can no longer be maintained. German minorities were withdrawn or expelled from all the countries which now lie east of the Iron Curtain. The use of German in the schools of the People's Republics has been largely supplanted by that of Russian. West of the Iron Curtain, although German is the sole language of scores of millions of people, there is no longer the feeling that this native language is enough for success in the present world. French and English are taught more widely here than ever. Editors of German scientific journals feel that they have to provide a summary in a foreign language; these and other signs all point in one direction: German is becoming only one of many national languages, one of the most widely spoken, but no longer the sole medium of culture. Germany, the apparently irreducible core of Mitteleuropa, is now politically divided, and the two parts are torn asunder, one drawn into the orbit of the United States, the other into that of the Soviet Union. Mitteleuropa, the German Mitteleuropa, seat of great political and military power since Bismarck created the German Empire in 1871, is in eclipse, and contains within it a zone of contention between two seemingly irreconcilable worlds.

FURTHER READING

CAHNMANN, WERNER, JR., "Frontiers between East and West in Europe," in *Geographical Review*, vol. xxxix (October 1949).

DICKINSON, ROBERT E., *The German Lebensraum* (Penguin Special, London, 1943).

EAST, W. GORDON, *An Historical Geography of Europe* (fifth edition; Methuen, London, and Dutton, New York, 1956).

FISCHER, ERIC, *The Passing of the European Age* (second edition; Harvard University Press, Cambridge, Mass., and Oxford University Press, 1948).

HASSINGER, HUGO, "Geographische Grundlagen der Geschichte," in Heinrich Finke, Hermann Junker, and Gustav Schnürer, *Geschichte der führenden Völker*, vol. ii (Herder and Co., Freiburg i.B., 1930; second edition, 1953).

[21] See, *e.g.*, Putzger's, *Historischer Schulatlas* (fifty-sixth edition; Vienna and Leipzig, 1939), p. 123, apparently derived from a map in *Zeitschrift für Geopolitik*, vol. xi (1934). But even a conservative Catholic writer stated: "The German cultural influence is so strong in some parts of the western Slavic region that it is possible to speak directly of German cultural soil, in which Czechs, Slovenes, Wends, and parts of the Poles are living" (Hugo Hassinger, p. 291). An English writer, N. J. G. Pounds, has adopted the German thesis most completely. He wrote: "This ancient German settlement has encouraged in recent years the assertion of German political control over this area. . . . But Poland and Czechoslovakia nevertheless bear deeply the imprint of German civilization . . . they cannot wholly remove their debt to Germany. In this sense the region . . . may be called the German realm" (*op. cit.*, p. 210).

NALKOWSKI, WACLAW, *Poland as a Geographical Entity* (Allen and Unwin, London, 1917).

NETTL, PETER, "Economic Checks on German Unity," in *Foreign Affairs*, vol. xxx (July 1952).

ORMSBY, H., "The Definition of Mitteleuropa and its Relation to the Conception of Deutschland in the Writings of Modern German Geographers," in *Scottish Geographical Magazine*, vol. li (1945).

POUNDS, N. J. G., *An Historical and Political Geography of Europe* (Harrap, London, 1947).

SETON-WATSON, HUGH, *Eastern Europe between the Wars, 1918–1940* (Cambridge University Press, London, 1945).

VAN VALKENBURG, SAMUEL, "The Rise and Decline of German 'Lebensraum,'" in Hans Weigert and others, *New Compass of the World* (Macmillan, New York, and Harrap, London, 1949).

WANKLYN, H. G. (MRS J. A. STEERS), *Czechoslovakia: A Geographical and Historical Study* (Philip, London, 1954).

CHAPTER III

Britain, France, and the Benelux Countries

A. E. MOODIE

Atlantic Europe

DESPITE differences in area, population, and economy, the six countries of Britain, France, Belgium, Luxembourg, the Netherlands, and Ireland have much in common, and, together, may be described as Atlantic Europe because their geographical location has played a dominant role in their separate histories and continues to influence their present relationships. Luxembourg, although a small inland State, enjoys close economic association with Belgium, and thus shares in the advantages of location on those coasts of Europe which front the world's most important maritime trade area—*i.e.*, what Mackinder called "the British Seas." The combined area of these territories is 931,419 square kilometres, representing 18·8 per cent. of Europe (excluding the U.S.S.R.), but its population is 117 millions, or 29 per cent.

TABLE 1

Area, Population, and Densities of Atlantic Europe

Country	Area (sq. km.)	Estimated Population in 1953 (thousands)	Density per sq. km.
United Kingdom .	244,022	50,592	208
France[1] . . .	551,694	43,836	78[2]
Belgium-Luxembourg	33,093	9,082	288[3]
Netherlands . .	32,328	10,493	324
Ireland . . .	70,282	2,942	42
Total .	931,419	116,945	126
Europe[4] . . .	4,930,000	402,000	82

[1] Including the Saar.   [2] Excluding the Saar (292 per square kilometre).
[3] Belgium only.   [4] Excluding U.S.S.R.
Source: *Demographic Yearbook, United Nations,* 1954 (New York, 1955).

of all Europeans west of the Soviet boundary. Densities per square kilometre vary from forty-two in Ireland to 324 in the Netherlands (see
Table 1), but this is to be expected because of the diversity of terrain and
the uneven spread of material resources and industrial developments in
Atlantic Europe.

The chief reason for discussing these countries together here lies, then,
in their maritime character. Norway, Denmark, Spain, and Portugal
enjoy similar advantages of location, but their trade by sea is much
smaller. Germany also has a North Sea coastline which she has exploited fully since the establishment of the first Reich, but her energies are divided between maritime and continental interests, largely
because of her interior position in Europe. In contrast, Britain, France,
the Netherlands, and Belgium have used their bridgehead situations at
the western end of the Eurasian land mass to become not only great
world trading countries but also four of the leading Colonial Powers.

Table 2 shows that Britain and France are largely dependent on over-

TABLE 2

Trade Relationships of the Countries of Atlantic Europe in 1953

(millions of current dollars)

AREA	UNITED KINGDOM		FRANCE		NETHERLANDS		BELGIUM-LUXEMBOURG	
	Imports	Exports	Imports	Exports	Imports	Exports	Imports	Exports
World . .	9,300·9	7,175·5	3,937·9	3,764·9	2,372·7	2,103·3	2,422·2	2,245·2
West European Countries[1] .	721·9	679·2	336·8	455·7	534·3	481·2	661·2	643·9
Total Europe[2]	2,699·9	2,299·5	1,187·8	1,494·0	1,416·8	1,411·1	1,433·8	1,502·3
Total Overseas Countries .	6,601·0	4,876·0	2,750·1	2,270·9	955·9	692·2	988·4	742·9
Overseas Sterling Area[3] . .	3,844·0	3,156·8	767·3	140·5	213·2	178·2	236·3	120·0
Dollar Area[4] .	1,770·8	1,051·4	481·0	393·4	336·2	237·3	377·9	324·4
Affiliated Overseas Areas[5] . .	251·0	141·2	1,088·9	1,509·1	92·0	82·4	214·1	167·1

[1] France, Netherlands, Belgium-Luxembourg, Switzerland.
[2] Including U.S.S.R.   [3] Including British colonies.
[4] U.S.A., Canada, Latin America (Venezuela, Colombia, Ecuador, Bolivia), Philippines, and
Central American countries.
[5] Affiliated overseas areas excluding sterling area.

Source: Table XXX, *Economic Survey of Europe in 1954* (Economic Commission for Europe
(E.C.E.), Geneva, 1955).

seas trade. (See also Fig. 1.) Sixty-eight per cent. of Britain's exports
went overseas and she received 71 per cent. of her imports from overseas
sources in 1953; comparable figures for France were 63 and 69 per cent.
respectively. The Netherlands and Belgium-Luxembourg had a proportionately smaller share in overseas trade (Netherlands 33 and 40 per
cent., Belgium-Luxembourg 32 and 42 per cent.), largely because of their
participation in the foreign trade of Germany. A notable feature of these
commercial relationships has been the maintenance of the relative importance of these four countries in total European trade[1] during the
twentieth century. Together they have been responsible for one-half of
the exports and imports of Europe for over fifty years.

Maritime location alone does not, of course, account for these achievements: Atlantic Europe's foreign trade could not have reached and held
its twentieth-century level without the backing of industrialization and
skill of its peoples. Britain led the world in the Industrial Revolution;

TABLE 3

Industrial Production in Atlantic Europe in 1953

COUNTRY	HARD COAL (*million tons*)	ELECTRIC POWER[1] (*billion kWh*)	FINISHED STEEL (*thousand tons*)	CRUDE STEEL (*million long tons*)	NUMBERS IN INDUSTRY[2] (*millions*)	IRON ORE[3] (*million tons*)
United Kingdom	227·8	66·0 (1·8)	14,106	17·61	10·0	4·5
France[4] . .	69·0	43·0 (21·0)	9,484	12·48	4·6	11·7
Belgium-						
Luxembourg	30·1	10·7 (0·1)	5,716	7·05	1·1[5]	1·7[6]
Netherlands .	12·3	9·1 (0·0)	710	0·86	1·1	—
Total .	339·2	128·8 (22·9)	30,016	38·0	16·8	17·9
E.C.S.C. . . .	237·0	—	30,114	—	—	—

[1] Hydro-electricity production in brackets.
[2] Numbers in industry—*i.e.*, wage- and salary-earners in mining and quarrying, manufacturing,
gas-, water-, and electricity-production, but not in building and construction.
[3] Metal content.   [4] Including the Saar.   [5] Excluding Luxembourg.   [6] Luxembourg only.
Source: As for Table 2.

France and Belgium were quick to follow. This was made possible
by the availability of the essential raw materials of industry, at least in
the early stages, and Table 3 shows that they continue to hold a strong
position in the production of the basic elements of modern industry.

Among the results of rapid industrialization, common to all the

[1] Excluding the U.S.S.R.'s.

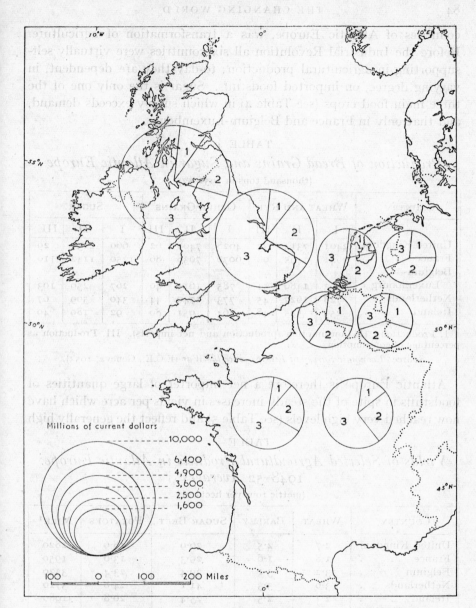

FIG. 1. TRADE RELATIONSHIPS OF BRITAIN, FRANCE, AND THE BENELUX COUNTRIES

Left-hand circles represent imports, right-hand circles exports, by value, of each country (Belgium and Luxembourg as one economic unit). Segments represent: 1. Trade with Western European industrial countries (France, Netherlands, Belgium-Luxembourg, and Switzerland); 1 + 2. Trade with Europe including the U.S.S.R.; 3. Trade with overseas countries.

countries of Atlantic Europe, was a transformation of agriculture. Before the Industrial Revolution all six countries were virtually self-supporting in agricultural production; to-day they are dependent, in varying degree, on imported foodstuffs. Sugar is the only one of the three main food crops (see Table 4) in which supply exceeds demand, and that only in France and Belgium-Luxembourg.

TABLE 4

Production of Bread Grains and Sugar in Atlantic Europe

(thousand tons in 1951–52)

COUNTRY	WHEAT AND RYE			OTHER GRAINS			SUGAR		
	I	II	III	I	II	III	I	II	III
United Kingdom	2401	7313	33	4628	7408	62	660	2251	29
France . ..	7641	7495	96	6076	7038	86	1250	1142	110
Belgium-									
Luxembourg	763	1489	51	785	1615	49	267	259	103
Netherlands .	728	1627	45	773	1740	44	340	509	67
Ireland . .	255	535	48	764	951	80	92	189	49

I. Production. II. Consumption (production and net imports). III. Production as percentage of consumption.

Source: *Economic Survey of Europe since the War* (E.C.E., Geneva, 1953).

Atlantic Europe is therefore a net importer of large quantities of foodstuffs in spite of the steady increases in yields per acre which have now reached very high levels (see Table 5) and reflect the generally high

TABLE 5

Yields of Selected Agricultural Products in Atlantic Europe: 1948–52 Averages

(metric tons per hectare)

COUNTRY	WHEAT	BARLEY	SUGAR BEET	POTATOES	MILK[1]
United Kingdom	2·7	2·5	26·9	18·9	2820
France . .	1·8	1·6	29·3	13·0	1950
Belgium . .	3·2	3·1	39·4	23·4	3530
Netherlands .	3·6	3·3	41·1	24·8	3710
Ireland . .	2·4	2·5	25·4	20·8	1980

[1] In kilogrammes per cow per annum.

Source: As for Table 4.

efficiency of farming in these lands. The average number of active workers per 100 hectares of agricultural land is only fourteen (ranging from twenty-two in the Netherlands to eight in the United Kingdom),

TABLE 6

Urban Centres of 50,000 or More Inhabitants in Atlantic Europe

COUNTRY	50,000–99,999		100,000–999,999		MORE THAN 1 MILLION IN URBAN AGGLOMERATIONS		CENSUS YEAR
	Number	Population	Number	Population	Number	Population	
England and Wales	91	6,216,522	66	16,812,461	5	16,078,305	1951
Northern Ireland	1	50,099	1	443,670			1951
Scotland	3	238,140	4	1,916,372	1	1,758,193	1951
France	32	1,194,592	22	6,592,957	1	4,775,711	1946
Belgium	10	629,403	5	894,046			1947
Luxembourg	1	26,851	1	61,996			1947
Netherlands	12	825,426	11	3,145,183			1947
Ireland	1	75,595	1	506,051			1946
	151	9,256,628	111	30,372,736	7	22,612,209	

Source: *Demographic Yearbook, United Nations, 1952* (New York, 1953).

compared with thirty in the Danubian countries (Romania, Yugoslavia, and Bulgaria), while the average number of tractors per thousand hectares of agricultural land in Atlantic Europe is fourteen, against 1·6 in the Danubian countries. The rate of mechanization of agriculture, not exceeded anywhere else in the world, is all the more impressive in view of the relatively small size of farms. Only in the United Kingdom and Ireland are more than half the farms above ten hectares in size, while in France and the Netherlands two-thirds are between one and ten hectares; in Belgium about five-sixths of the farms are less than ten hectares. Much of the agricultural land of all but the British Isles is worked by peasants, and their production rates are very high for this type of farming.

TABLE

Land Use in Atlantic Europe

(Areas of agricultural land in thousands of hectares;

COUNTRY	TOTAL AREA (sq. km.)	AGRICULTURAL AREA[1]	ARABLE AREA	PERMANENT GRASS
United Kingdom[2]	244,769	19,520 (100)	7,425 (140)	12,096 (85)
France .	551,694	39,286 (97)	21,174 (91)	18,113 (106)
Belgium-				
Luxembourg .	33,093	1,929 (97)	1,112 (92)	817 (104)
Netherlands .	32,328	2,344 (101)	1,060 (108)	1,284 (97)
Ireland . .	70,282	5,488 (99)	2,476 (110)	3,012 (92)

[1] Excluding rough pasture.

Source: *Economic Survey of Europe*

Table 7 gives the areas of land devoted to various types of crops in each of the five countries for the year 1951–52, and also indicates changes in these areas since before the second world war. The total agricultural area has remained stationary, but there have been large changes in the individual crop areas. These represent efforts to combat wartime and post-war domestic demands, and reflect a degree of flexibility in farming methods which, in its turn, reflects the skill and adaptability of the peoples of the whole region.

Closely associated with industrialization and the consequential decline of rural population is the 'drift to the towns,' which again is a characteristic feature of Atlantic Europe. More than half of its total population (sixty-two out of 117 millions) lives in towns of 50,000 or more inhabitants, and more than twenty-two millions live in cities of over one million (see Table 6). Although the rate of increase of population slowed down towards the end of the nineteenth century, urbanization has steadily increased since *c.* 1900, with the result that only Ireland of the countries listed in Table 8 has less than half of its population urbanized. The percentages of urban and rural population given in Table 8 are not strictly comparable, because the several countries use different methods of classification, but it is valid to deduce from them that Atlantic Europe is one of the most highly urbanized areas in the world. The tradition of living in towns in this part of Europe is by no means modern—it dates back to Roman times—but the rapid acceleration of urbanization in the twentieth century is remarkable, and has caused problems with which the various governments have to contend.

7

in 1951–52 *and Pre-war*

figures in brackets give the percentages of pre-war areas.)

Wheat and Rye	Other Grains	Sugar Beet	Potatoes	Vineyards	Temporary Grass
921 (121)	2,360 (168)	170 (118)	520 (176)	—	2,296 (136)
4,769 (81)	3,736 (84)	353 (111)	1,098 (72)	1,564 (97)	5,101 (118)
268 (73)	284 (91)	58 (116)	100 (57)	—	161 (n.a.)
267 (74)	215 (118)	62 (144)	182 (135)	—	70 (n.a.)
157 (199)	341 (118)	25 (119)	141 (104)	—	1,698 (105)

[2] Includes Channel Islands and Isle of Man.

since the War (E.C.E., Geneva, 1953).

A further factor common to Atlantic Europe is a high standard of living. Although the index numbers of the cost of living[2] have risen steadily since 1945 and the incidence of taxation remains high, the peoples of Atlantic Europe are better fed and housed than those of the rest of the Continent. In daily food consumption per capita measured in calories, they compare reasonably well with the inhabitants of the United States and Canada, although their diets are probably less well-balanced.[3] Nevertheless, the average daily consumption of animal protein is well above "the 25–30 grammes held by most experts to be the desirable minimum level."[4]

[2] See *Economic Survey of Europe in 1953* (Economic Commission for Europe, Geneva, 1954), Table XIV.
[3] See *European Agriculture* (Food and Agriculture Organization, Geneva, 1954), Table 13.   [4] *Ibid.,* p. 27.

TABLE 8

Urbanization in Atlantic Europe in the Twentieth Century

COUNTRY	CENSUS YEAR	POPULATION (millions)	URBAN (percentage)	RURAL (percentage)
England and Wales	1901	32·5	77·0	23·0
	1951	43·7	80·7	19·3
Northern Ireland .	1926	1·3	50·9	49·1
	1951	1·4	53·1	46·9
Scotland . .	1901	4·5	69·8	30·2
	1951	5·1	82·9	17·1
France . . .	1901[1]	38·96	41·0	59·0
	1946	39·8	52·9	47·1
Saar . . .	1946	0·9	77·9	22·1
Belgium . .	1900	6·7	52·3	47·7
	1947	8·5	62·7	37·3
Luxembourg . .	1935	0·3	56·9	43·1
	1947	0·3	58·3	41·7
Netherlands . .	1909	5·9	40·5	59·5
	1947	9·6	54·6	45·4
Ireland . .	1926	2·97	31·7	68·3
	1951	2·96	40·5	59·5

[1] Excluding Alsace-Lorraine.

Source: *Demographic Yearbook, United Nations, 1952* (New York, 1953).

Here, then, is a group of European countries which enjoy many economic advantages and which have achieved a high level of social and cultural progress. Not less important is the relative stability of government which they enjoy. France and Ireland are republics, the United Kingdom, Belgium, and the Netherlands are constitutional monarchies, and Luxembourg is a Grand Duchy, but each is a unitary State with full parliamentary representation based on universal suffrage and the secret ballot at elections. In Atlantic Europe the nation State saw its first full development, and set an example which has been copied widely, perhaps too widely. This political form has led to the evolution of the Welfare State with its highly centralized administration which, in itself, fails to overcome regional differences but does emphasize the increasing interdependence of political, economic, and social affairs in each of the countries. These States have much in common in their methods of economic development, in foreign trade, in parliamentary institutions and governmental methods, in well-developed circulation,[5] and, possibly most vital, they recognize their common interests, strategic, commercial, and

[5] See Chapter VIII.

cultural. The States of Atlantic Europe are fully mature; no major territorial changes have taken place during the twentieth century except the detachment of the Irish Republic from the United Kingdom and the restoration of Alsace-Lorraine to France in 1919 (see Table 9). With the exception of Luxembourg, they share colonial responsibilities and pursue colonial policies which, despite their individual differences, have something in common.

TABLE 9

Territorial Changes in Atlantic Europe during the Twentieth Century

COUNTRY	DATE	AREA (sq. km.)	CHANGES (sq. km.)
United Kingdom .	Pre-1921	314,304	
	Post-1921	244,022	− 70,282
France . .	1871–1921	536,464	
	1921–1947	550,986	+ 14,522
	1947—	551,694	+ 708
Saar . .	1920	1,924	
	1949	2,567	+ 643
Belgium . .	Pre-1925	29,452	
	Post-1925	30,507	+ 1,055
Luxembourg .	Unchanged	2,586	Nil
Netherlands .	Pre-1949	32,328	
	1949—	32,388	+ 60

Britain, France, the Netherlands, and Belgium have world-wide relationships as Colonial Powers. The first three were pioneers in 'empire-building,' an occupation which frequently resulted in conflicting interests. These activities were shared at first by the Dutch Republic and continued by the United Kingdom of Belgium and the Netherlands (1815–39), but after 1839 the independent States of Belgium and the Netherlands followed separate courses. The two world wars combined with movements for independence have brought about considerable decreases in the non-self-governing territories, but their aggregate area remains large, as Table 10 shows.

Area by itself is never a safe criterion of importance. The greater part of these dependent territories has relatively little economic value as yet. Much of France's possessions in Africa, for example, lies in the Sahara Desert, and the Netherlands' remaining territories in Asia (New Guinea) are of little present value to the home country. Furthermore,

TABLE 10

Atlantic Europe's Non-self-governing Territories in 1954

(in square kilometres)

Country	Africa	N. America	S. America	Asia	Europe	Oceania	Totals
United Kingdom	5,917,929	58,389	226,922	662,262	1,089	132	6,866,723
France .	10,607,105	3,122	91,000	501	Nil	23,651	10,725,379
Belgium	2,343,930	Nil	Nil	Nil	Nil	Nil	2,343,930
Nether- lands .	Nil	947	142,822	412,781	Nil	Nil	556,550
Totals	18,868,964	62,458	460,744	1,075,544	1,089	23,783	20,492,582

and with certain exceptions, these colonial lands are economically under-developed. Yet they have a high potential value, and it would be un-wise to predict that the future development of their resources has no significance for Atlantic Europe; 90 per cent. of these territories lie in Africa, which has been dubbed 'the continent of the future.' On the other hand, the possession of such vast areas (in the aggregate nearly twenty-four times the size of the metropolitan countries) gives grounds for criticism by the non-colonial Powers as well as by the inhabitants of the dependent territories. Whatever advantages may have been derived from 'imperialism' in the past, the possession of large colonial areas to-day is not an unmixed blessing. The United Kingdom, France, and the Netherlands cannot but be aware of the drain on their resources, in wealth and man-power, which has resulted from their efforts to retain their status as Colonial Powers.

Finally in this assemblage of common features which characterize Atlantic Europe may be placed the emphasis which is laid on the rights of the individual. "The differentiation of the individual from the mass, the liberation of the human personality not only from the grosser servi-tudes of the environment—getting food, keeping warm, and so on—but also from inner bondage to ancestral fears and resentments, these great marks of progress depend upon a non-materialist framework of thought."[6] It cannot be claimed that such 'marks of progress' are restricted to the countries under discussion, nor that they have fully extended such privileges to the inhabitants of their overseas posses-

[6] F. L. Woodward, "The Heritage of Western Civilization," in *International Affairs*, vol. xxv (London, 1949), p. 146.

sions. Nevertheless, the importance attached to the rights of the individual and the methods of maintaining them through parliamentary democracy and the administration of justice were first evolved in Atlantic Europe and remain fundamental to its culture.

Britain

The study of the peculiar politico-territorial organization of the archipelago which lies off the shores of Western Europe is properly a branch of political science, but, for the sake of clarity in what follows, certain of its features should be indicated. The two major islands, Great Britain (England, Scotland, and Wales) and Ireland, together with a large number of off-shore islands, constitute the British Isles. This geographical area is not a political unit; it is divided into the United Kingdom of Great Britain and Northern Ireland, and the Republic of Ireland. The former is by no means a completely unitary State. Northern Ireland (the six counties) has its own Parliament, with a Senate and a House of Commons, and a Governor appointed by the Crown. This local parliament is responsible for all aspects of government except those affecting foreign relations, defence, and postal services. At the same time, Northern Ireland sends twelve representatives to the House of Commons in London. Scotland and Wales are more fully integrated with England politically. Each is represented by an appropriate number of Members of Parliament, but, whereas some aspects of Scottish affairs have spokesmen at Westminster, Welsh 'nationalists' are chagrined at the refusal of their request for a Minister of Welsh Affairs; they are dissatisfied with the parliamentary arrangement whereby the Home Secretary speaks for Wales, although in the present parliament[7] he is a Welshman. Two other political anomalies exist in the Isle of Man and in the Channel Islands; in the former, Manxmen claim that their Tynwald is the oldest parliament in the world, while the Channel Islands, last territorial remnant of the Anglo-Norman union of nine hundred years ago, exercise considerable autonomy.

The Republic of Ireland stands in a category by itself. Under the Anglo-Irish Treaty of 1921 the twenty-six counties became the Irish Free State with the status of a Dominion. In 1937 the Free State Parliament passed the External Relations Act, which established a new Irish

[7] June 1956.

Constitution, rechristened the country Eire (*i.e.*, Ireland), forswore allegiance to the Crown, but remained associated with the Commonwealth, such 'association' being symbolized in the acceptance of the monarch's signature to the letters of appointment of Irish representatives to foreign countries. In 1948, after being neutral throughout the second world war, Ireland formally seceded from the Commonwealth, without becoming a foreign State, and adopted the title of the Republic of Ireland. Her citizens retain a non-foreign status in relation to the United Kingdom, and Irish trade enjoys preferential treatment in the British market.

These differences in status and terminology raise difficulties in discussing the political geography of the British Isles. For our present purposes, Britain is used as a synonym for United Kingdom, and the adjective British is applied to the four countries. Similarly, the words Ireland and Irish are used only in relation to the Republic, although this may be resented in Northern Ireland.

External Problems. Britain's position in the world is unique. Only the United States has a greater share of world trade [8] and larger merchant and naval fleets; only France has a larger colonial empire (see Table 10). More people speak English than any other European language, and British methods in legal, administrative, commercial, and industrial affairs have been widely adopted. No other country has shown greater recuperative powers after major world wars and other crises, yet in few countries has the struggle for economic survival called for greater efforts. With the emergence of the United States and the Soviet Union as the two leading world Powers, Britain has lost the rank which she held throughout the nineteenth century; yet who would deny that her spokesmen still command respect in world affairs? Lacking the resources in materials and man-power on her island territory to justify full-scale competition with the United States and the U.S.S.R., seriously weakened by the loss of overseas capital investments and with an economy undermined by the other effects of two world wars, Britain has been compelled to re-adjust her outlook and foreign policy to changing world conditions. Writing in 1948, a Canadian geographer considered that "Britain faces a bleak future." [9] Yet, in 1955, although many serious

---

[8] U.S.A. imports 10,779 and exports 11,476 million dollars, against 9301 and 7176 million dollars for the United Kingdom, in 1953.

[9] G. Tatham, "Great Britain and the Dependent Empire," in *World Political Geography*, edited by G. E. Pearcy and R. H. Fifield (New York, 1948), p. 109.

and difficult problems still confront the British people, confidence has been restored, the standard of living of the great majority has been raised, industrial production has grown at an annual rate of 8 per cent. since 1946, and Britain is now producing nearly half of her foodstuffs at home. These are no mean achievements even when allowances are made for the generous assistance received from the United States during the post-war years.

Commonwealth and Colonial Relations. Recent changes in relations within the Commonwealth have been remarkable not only in the numbers of people and areas of territory involved but also in the relative ease with which they have come about. Since 1945 India, Pakistan, and Ceylon have acquired Dominion status and several other territories are moving towards this goal. Britain has recognized the force of nationalist aspirations in lands which were formerly dependent, and also her own inability to hold them against the wishes of their people. Each Dominion is fully independent politically; each sends her own representatives to foreign Powers as well as to the other Dominions. Britain has no powers of compulsion in their affairs—witness the existence of Canada as a member-State of the Dollar Area, the association of Australia and New Zealand with the United States in the ANZUS pact, and the independent role of India in international affairs. Apart from the Commonwealth Relations Office in London and the irregularly held conferences of Prime Ministers, there is no machinery for regulating Commonwealth affairs; yet, despite great economic and social differences between the Dominions, this arrangement works smoothly; at least it bears no resemblance to nineteenth-century imperialism. It may well be that this example of association of independent States could be followed with advantage elsewhere.

The first British Empire—*i.e.*, before the secession of the United States —and its successor of the late eighteenth and nineteenth centuries were maritime structures, created through the use of the world ocean and maintained by the effective control of its waters by the Royal Navy. For the successful survival of such an imperial system and of its commercial connexions, strategic bases together with naval organization in a number of separate fleets were necessary. The temporary closure of the Mediterranean and the fall of Singapore during the second world war demonstrated conclusively that full reliance on naval power was at an end; Britannia could no longer "rule the waves." Air power, reinforced

by the post-war development of immensely powerful new weapons, has
largely superseded the earlier dominance of warships alone. Nevertheless, the important economic relations between the members of the
Commonwealth, which persist in spite of political differences, remain
dependent on ocean highways.

In the British Commonwealth of to-day it is probably true to say that
economic co-operation is the most effective single link. A detailed
analysis of these relationships would "reveal a close contexture of commercial and financial links, held together by long-standing friendly
agreements between merchants, tradesmen, bankers, organized in the
same way, maintaining the same standards of conduct, and thoroughly
understanding one another."[10] Their maintenance is of vital importance
to Britain, as the creation of the Sterling Area in 1940 and its continuing
existence demonstrate.

The Sterling Area[11] is neither coincident with nor confined to the
Commonwealth. Canada is not a member, but provides an effective
'bridge' between it and the Dollar Area. The remaining Dominions and
the British colonies are all members, as are Burma, Ireland, Iraq, and
Iceland. Each country of the Area, although it may have its own currency, uses the pound sterling in settling its accounts with other members and in carrying out most of its foreign business. In the aggregate,
the Sterling Area constitutes the largest area in the world where a common currency is used for international purposes. Reference to Table 2
shows that it is also the largest major world trade area with which
Britain is concerned. Within it the Dominions play a leading part,
being responsible for 53 per cent. of the trade turnover of the Area with
Britain in 1953.

The Sterling Area is not economically self-sufficient, although it
stretches through most of the climatic regions of the earth. Although it
produces practically all the world supply of jute and mica, it is short of
newsprint and wood pulp; it mines 75 per cent. of the world's diamonds
and grows 60 per cent. of its natural rubber and tea, yet it has to import
petroleum, cotton, and tobacco in large quantities; it is not self-sufficient
in grain or meat or vegetable oils, yet it supplies the world with half its
gold, half of its wool and cocoa. In 1953 40 per cent. of Britain's imports
came from the Area, which took four-ninths of Britain's exports. The

[10] C. E. Carrington, "A New Theory of the Commonwealth," in *International Affairs*,
vol. xxxi (London, 1955), p. 144.
[11] For a detailed study of this organization see *The Sterling Area—An American
Analysis* (Economic Co-operative Administration Special Mission to the United Kingdom, London, 1951).

remainder of its trade is with non-sterling areas, and enables its members to acquire credit facilities without which the Area could scarcely survive as a going concern.

The economic cohesion of these politically independent and dependent countries which together contain one quarter of the world's population and handle a fourth of the world's international trade has been achieved in the face of serious difficulties. In the first place, the Dominions are anxious to grow out of their earlier status as primary producers; each is striving to become industrialized, with the result that their demands for Britain's consumer goods will decrease. Such economic developments require capital investment, and Britain no longer exercises her earlier function as the world's financial centre. The so-called 'colonial system' of economic relations within the Commonwealth is dying rapidly, if it is not already dead. The Dominions will continue to require capital goods, especially machinery for their secondary industries, but they are under no obligation to buy them from Britain. Secondly, large areas of the associated countries may be legitimately described as under-developed and again require large-scale capital investment. This is particularly the case in the dependent territories, where the existence of the problem is frankly recognized by Her Majesty's Government in London in its colonial development policy. Three Colonial Development and Welfare Acts (1929, 1940, and 1945) have been passed in the last twenty-seven years. The last of them provided for the expenditure of £120,000,000 over the ten years ending in March 1956, including not more than one million pounds a year for research. These are not great sums when seen against the needs of the colonies, but they loom large against Britain's post-war economic situation. Their value should also be considered in the light of Britain's declared policy that the colonies should be helped along the road to self-government.

Emphasis has been laid here on the economic aspects of Britain's relationships with the Dominions and colonies, but let us not forget other aspects. In the administration of justice and local affairs in the colonies, long and devoted service by colonial civil servants and others has borne fruit. In spite of the expression of strong anti-British feelings—in India, for example—the work of British administrators is admired and copied. Perhaps the most striking case of vision in social matters, however, is shown in the establishment of institutions of university rank in British Tropical Africa. There are now (summer of 1956) university colleges at Achimota, Ibadan, and Makerere, working in close association with the

University of London; University College, Khartoum, has acquired
independent status, and a new multi-racial university is being established at Salisbury in Rhodesia. These centres of learning, largely
financed by the British taxpayer, will become the sources of inspiration
and drive for the development of education in areas where it is essential
to social progress.

Britain and Europe. Since the dawn of the Columban Age British
foreign policy has been progressively dominated by maritime considerations. Once the discovery of America demonstrated that the earlier
barrier function of the ocean could be overcome the way was open to
overseas expansion, territorially and commercially; the seal was set on
this development when the Industrial Revolution created new supplies
of goods and demanded new markets as well as new sources of raw
materials. Thus, from the late fifteenth century onward, Britain turned
her attention overseas, using her geographical location as an admirable
base for this purpose, and steadily sought to free herself from European
entanglements. Nevertheless, the effects of propinquity were not to be
denied. Insularity was often confused with isolation between 1500 and
1900. Naval control of the Narrow Seas was of decisive importance in
precluding military invasion after 1066, but Britain could not avoid
commitments on the Continent; instead she strove to bring about a kind
of 'containment' of Europe through the Balance of Power, while she
devoted most of her energies to overseas affairs. This policy, implemented by a long series of continental alliances, called for changes of
political alignment which help to explain the description of Britain as
"perfidious Albion." For long, France was the 'enemy,' but Spain,
Austria, and imperialist Russia shared in this dubious distinction until
finally Germany, then the most powerful continental State and with
strong expansionist tendencies, took the centre of the European stage.
Hence the Entente Cordiale of 1904. As the two world wars proved,
Britain was to be involved in European affairs almost to her destruction. No longer was diplomacy able to maintain the balance; it was
replaced by military action at a frightful cost. The well-worn descrip-
tive cliché 'Of Europe but not in Europe' is still applicable to Britain.
Her people do not regard themselves as Europeans, not unexpectedly,
perhaps, after the events of the last five centuries, and the results are
displayed in a certain unwillingness to enter into direct commitments
with Europe.

Twice in the last fifty years Britain has fought successfully on the Continent and maintained armies of occupation there. Her statesmen have participated fully in the political settlements which have followed the wars, but have shown a reluctance to enter whole-heartedly into the economic plans which have been put forward at various times. Since 1945 Britain has become an active member of the North Atlantic Treaty Organization (N.A.T.O.), and in 1954 Her Majesty's Government "indicated their desire for the closest political and military association"[12] with the European Defence Community. When the French Parliament refused to ratify the E.D.C. Treaty in August 1954, the Brussels Treaty of 1948 was revised and put into operation, largely at the instigation of the British Foreign Secretary, but Britain's military and political commitments in Western European Union were made subject to an interesting reservation in the Treaty. "This undertaking shall not, however, bind Her Majesty in the event of an acute overseas emergency."[13] The Paris and London Agreements of 1954, which have been ratified by the Governments of the States concerned, form the basis of a potentially successful defence system for Western Europe, but it should be noted that they and the N.A.T.O. Treaty are the only cases where Britain has been willing to concede some part of its national sovereign rights to supra-national bodies.

No such willingness has been shown in economic affairs. "Britain's present Continental role in economic affairs arises simply from her membership of a number of European institutions of which the most important is the Organization for European Economic Co-operation to which the European Payments Union is attached."[14] In particular Britain refuses to become a full member of the European Coal and Steel Community, although in December 1954 she signed a Treaty of Association with E.C.S.C. To many people Britain's attitude towards Europe seems half-hearted and hesitant, if not vacillating; she goes forward with political and military safeguards, but hangs back in economic matters. These criticisms ignore the dilemma in which Britain finds herself. Somewhere between the Scylla of overseas commitments and the Charybdis of continental dangers she must steer a middle course. The then Minister of Defence claimed that, in Western European Union, "a way

[12] *Memorandum regarding United Kingdom Association with the European Defence Community*, Cmd. 9126 (London, 1954), p. 5.

[13] *Documents agreed on by the Conference of Ministers held in Paris, October 20–23, 1954*, Cmd. 9304 (London, 1954), p. 38.

[14] "Britain and the European Continent," in *The World To-day*, vol. xi (London, 1955), p. 25.

E

has now been found which enables Britain to play her full part, both as a great Imperial and as a great European Power."[15] That, briefly, is the expression of the conflict of interests which every British Government must attempt to reconcile, a conflict which is the inevitable outcome of Britain's geographical location, history, and economy.

France

Unlike Britain, France does not enjoy the advantages of insularity. The key to her location lies in her occupation of one of the most important isthmuses in Europe. This gives her three marine frontages, on the Narrow Seas, the Atlantic, and the Mediterranean, but also two land limits, one with the Iberian Peninsula and the other with Belgium-Luxembourg, Germany, Italy, and Switzerland. Thus the French people have been subject to both continental and maritime influences, but concurrently their country has been a valuable base for expansion, territorially and culturally.[16] The French knew how to exploit this geographical situation with success as long as their domestic economy was organized more efficiently than that of their neighbours. But in recent years that organization has shown a strong tendency to run down; at least it has not kept pace with that of either Britain or Germany. This is no denial of France's right to be considered an important part of Atlantic Europe, but it does mean that, although the country has important overseas commitments, her people are fully alive to the results of contiguity with their continental neighbours. France has been invaded no less than three times during the lives of some of her oldest inhabitants.

As long as agriculture and commerce remained the chief means of employment in Western Europe France's position as a leading Power was secure, especially as it was the first State to become highly unified. Owing to marked diversity of terrain and climate, the French reached a higher level of self-sufficiency than any other people of Atlantic Europe. Good internal means of circulation, even before the railway age, made possible the exchange of commodities of regions as different as the Midi and the Paris Basin, as Flanders and Aquitaine. Furthermore, three stretches of coast, often well-endowed with good natural harbours, en-

---

[15] Mr H. Macmillan, House of Commons, November 1954.
[16] "France, this crossroads where nations meet, this crucible of ideas, is the country where the unreconcilable can be reconciled": Monsieur A. Pinay, "France's Political and Economic Problems," in *International Affairs*, vol. xxx (London, 1954).

couraged the export of surplus commodities to foreign markets as well as imperialist aspirations overseas. Add to these geographical advantages the might and prestige of French armies, and it is not surprising to find France possessed of great authority in international affairs right down to the inter-war years of the twentieth century. Long before this time, however, changes had begun to take place in the French economy, changes which have gradually become apparent, although "The decline in the economic importance of France, compared with other European countries, does, however, often escape attention."[17] This relative decline is the result of a combination of a number of processes, among which demographic and industrial developments are of outstanding importance.

Reference to Table 1 shows that France occupies more than half of the total area of Atlantic Europe, and is more than twice the size of the United Kingdom; indeed, it is the largest State in Europe west of the Soviet Union. Yet France supports fewer people than Great Britain and only just over one-third of the total population of Atlantic Europe; this demographic fact is well illustrated in the average density of population, which is well below that of all her immediate neighbours except Spain (see Table 1). Decrease in number of people has proceeded steadily—a century ago France accounted for one-seventh of the population of Europe, including Russia west of the Urals, while her share to-day is only one-fourteenth—but it was not until the nineteen-thirties that serious official attention was given to this problem. The pre-war population policy has been reinforced since 1945, and the system of family allowances and the fiscal advantages accorded to large families are now the most favourable in Europe. This policy helps to explain the post-war population increase from 39·8 millions in 1946 to 42 millions in 1953 (excluding the Saar), which is in marked contrast with the pre-war decrease, but it is not yet effective in the occupational structure of the country, because children born since the war have not yet entered employment. Thus France, despite substantial immigration of European workers (Italians and Poles), and also of Africans, has a smaller share of her people in the important age group of 15–59 years than either the United Kingdom or Western Germany, and that proportion has fallen since 1860, whereas Britain's share has risen. In effect, the number in this age group has stagnated in France (60·7 per cent. in

[17] *Economic Survey of Europe in 1954* (E.C.E., Geneva, 1955), p. 173. Chapter 7 in this volume is a useful study of "Basic Problems of the Occupational Structure and Regional Balance" in the French economy.

1860 and 60·6 per cent. in 1950). Furthermore, the numbers employed
in industry and agriculture have not increased in the last twenty-five
years. Decline in numbers of agricultural workers is characteristic of
Atlantic Europe, but all the other countries have added to the totals
of their industrial workers. Thus, although the decrease in the French
labour force has not been catastrophic, it has been effective in restricting economic expansion. Table 11 exposes the relative lack of change
in the occupational structure of France between 1896 and 1936.

TABLE 11

Structure of Active Population in France,[1] *1896–1936*

PERCENTAGES

Agriculture		Industry		Other	
1896	1936	1896	1936	1896	1936
46	37	30	31	24	32

[1] Excluding Alsace-Lorraine and armed forces.
Source: *Economic Survey of Europe in 1954*, Table 84.

In addition to its labour problems, the French industrial structure
suffers from other deep-seated weaknesses which are closely associated
with the geography of the country. France was in the van in the early
days of the Industrial Revolution, and, indeed, "As recently as a century
ago it was still—almost certainly—the most highly industrialized country
on the Continent."[18] Yet now she lags behind the other countries of
Atlantic Europe as well as Germany. This is largely the result of insufficient resources in the basic raw materials of modern industry, and also
because of their peculiar distribution within the country. Nearly all the
coal and the majority of the iron ore are mined in the north-eastern part
of the country—*i.e.*, near the critical boundary with Germany. Hence
the extractive and metallurgical industries are highly concentrated.
Furthermore, Paris, like all the capital cities of industrial and unitary
States, has attracted a large proportion of the manufacturing industries.
With a few exceptions, such as the Grenoble, Rouen, and Marseilles districts, the rest of France plays little part in industrial production. It
has, therefore, been almost impossible to achieve a balance between
agricultural and industrial activities in a very large part of the country.
Over-centralization has been a very real weakness in the French industrial economy; 24 per cent. of the output of all manufacturing industries
were concentrated in the Paris Region (Seine and Seine et Oise) in 1946.

Once the German occupation of France ended, serious efforts were

[18] *Economic Survey of Europe in 1954*, p. 173.

made to overcome this weakness. In general, two lines have been followed—internal reorganization, primarily through the Monnet Plan, and
closer integration with the west European economy by means of various
international schemes. In the former case, progress has been considerable. According to Monsieur Pinay,[19] the production of electrical
energy has been doubled, petroleum refining capacity has been trebled,
output of coal has increased by ten million tons a year, steel production
has increased by 75 per cent., and reconstruction has cost more than
£2000 million. All this has been done in seven years and, very largely,
under Government control, so that France stands out among the non-
Communist countries as a land where the influence of the State in the
development of basic industries has been most systematic. Outstanding
has been the attempt to meet industrial energy requirements by expanding hydro-electric generation. Nearly a half of France's electric power
is now generated by running water (see Table 3), and is produced in areas
far from the Franco-German boundary.

These are commendable results of State planning within a private
enterprise economy, but a further weakness of the French system is
revealed in her foreign trade. Like the other countries of Atlantic
Europe, France has an adverse balance in foreign trade, but her industrial shortcomings are apparent in the relatively small share of manufactured goods in her exports (see Table 12).

TABLE 12

Exports from France, the United Kingdom, and Western Germany in 1953

(Exports are shown as percentages of total exports by value.)

	FRANCE	W. GERMANY	UNITED KINGDOM
Manufactures . .	65	81	79
Food . . .	12	2	6
Fuel and Raw Materials .	19	17	12
Miscellaneous . .	4	—	3
Total .	100	100	100

Steel (13 per cent.) is the major item listed under the manufactures
exported from France, and, since it is usually exported in 'semi-
finished' form, it does not earn as much foreign credit as it would if it
were turned into consumer goods. Thus over one-third of French

[19] *Op. cit.*

exports are commodities which do not require a large proportion of skill in their preparation, and this in part explains the big difference in the value of the export trade of France and the United Kingdom (see Table 2).

France and Europe. In her relationships with the rest of Europe, France has developed along new lines since the end of the second world war and has shown herself willing to make considerable sacrifices of national sovereignty. Two directive elements are detectable in what amounts to a revolutionary change. First and foremost is the necessity to avoid those mistakes of the past which derived from reliance on alliances and bilateral commercial agreements. Humiliating experiences during the second world war combined with post-war increases in the cost of armaments have convinced the French realists that States of forty to fifty million inhabitants cannot adequately defend themselves in the world of to-day. New means of obtaining security must be found, and the French Government seeks them in and through supra-national organizations. Secondly, by integrating her economy with those of her nearest neighbours, France hopes not only to prevent the organization of German industries towards war preparations but also to participate in the large European common market which full integration alone makes possible. This has proved possible in the coal and steel industries, through the E.C.S.C., because they are organized on a large scale, but it is unlikely to achieve success while France retains a rigid small-town economic structure. A report[20] submitted to the Committee of Public Accounts in 1953 revealed that out of a total of just under a million industrial establishments almost half employ no wage-earners, and of just over a million commercial undertakings 700,000 are in the same category. A third of French farms are so small or so inefficient as to be uneconomic, while the agricultural community, which pays only some 13 milliard francs in taxation, receives 16 milliards in subsidies and the equivalent of about 100 milliards in the form of legal fiscal privileges of different kinds.

The European policy of France is therefore directed towards security, largely through the elimination of German militarism, and economic integration with her neighbours. Both objectives are obstructed by territorial problems connected with the French eastern boundaries. The

[20] Quoted in "France's Economic Outlook," in *The World To-day*, vol. ix (London, 1953).

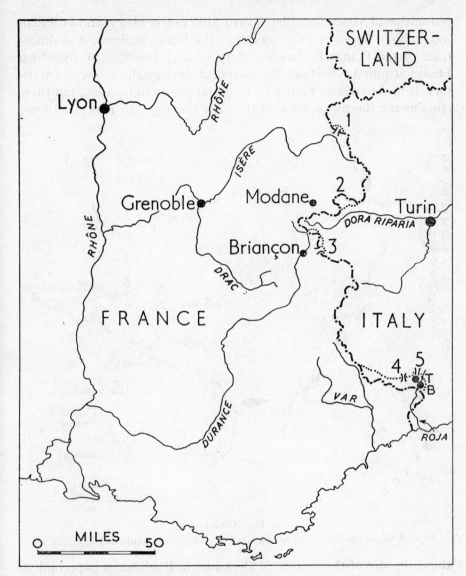

FIG. 2. CHANGES IN THE FRANCO-ITALIAN BOUNDARY IN 1947

1. Little St Bernard Col. 2. Mont Cenis Plateau. 3. Mont Genèvre Col.
4. Col del Agnei. 5. Col di Tenda. T. Tenda. B. Briga. The dotted lines indicate
the 1947 changes, which, together, added 708 square kilometres to the previous
area of France.

restoration of Alsace-Lorraine in 1919, after nearly fifty years of German 'occupation,' brought France back to the Rhine, and minor modifications of the Franco-Italian boundary in 1947 (see Fig. 2), by which France acquired 708 square kilometres of strategically important territory, helped to relieve French fears of 'dangers from the east,' but there remains the thorny problem of the Saar (see Fig. 3). This small area,

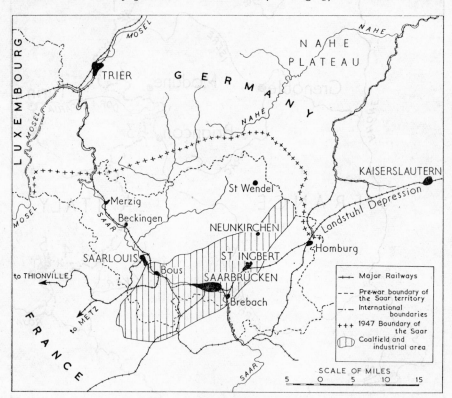

FIG. 3. THE SAAR IN 1954

A slight modification of the 1947 boundary was made in 1949.

about the size of the County of Berkshire in England, is important to both France and Germany, partly because of its valuable coal resources (sixteen million tons production in 1953), but also because of its strategic situation between the two countries which rests on its control of the important Landstuhl depression (see Fig. 3).

The Saar problem[21] is a comparatively recent one. During the period

[21] See C. C. Held, "The New Saarland," in *Geographical Review*, vol. xli (New York, 1951).

of the French Revolution the territory was occupied by France, but it was ceded to Prussia by the Congress of Vienna in 1815. Until about 1880 it had little economic significance, but thereafter its coal deposits were intensively developed in close association with Lorraine iron ore. Saar coal was sent to Lorraine, and ore from that region was smelted at the Rochling works at Volklingen and at those of Stum at Dillingen and Neunkirchen. German capital and labour were largely responsible for the industrial development of an area which was, and still is, predominantly German-speaking. After the first world war the treaty makers attempted a compromise settlement; they established the Saar Territory to be ruled by a commission of the League of Nations from January 1920 for fifteen years, gave the Saar coal mines to France for that period as part of German reparations, and arranged for a plebiscite to decide the future of the Territory at the end of the period. In 1935 the Saarlanders voted overwhelmingly for return to Germany, but this political arrangement did not solve their economic problems. The Saar was still dependent on neighbouring French territory for food and labour supplies, and, because of its distance from the important industrial regions of Germany, it did not fit as conveniently into the economy of that country as it had done into that of France.

Immediately after the second world war the Saar formed a part of the French Zone of Germany. A plan for economic union with France and political autonomy was put forward by the French Government. When the western zones of Germany were fused together in 1947, a Franco-Saar customs and currency union was established, and the Saarlanders retained their political autonomy on a territory which had been enlarged in 1946 by 942 square kilometres and the population of which was 20 per cent. greater than that of the former Saar Territory. As a result of Anglo-American protests this area was reduced to 2559 square kilometres in 1947 (see Fig. 3), and a further slight adjustment was made in 1949, thus giving the Saar its present area of 2567 square kilometres. In the meantime British and American spokesmen had made it abundantly clear that a permanent settlement of the Saar problem must await the conclusion of a peace treaty with Germany—*i.e.*, the same policy should be applied as to the Oder-Neisse line between Poland and Eastern Germany.

In October 1954 a new agreement was reached between France and Germany which "shows that a new territorial conception has been introduced, establishing something that is neither a State, nor a protectorate,

E*

nor a condominium."[22] This agreement provided for the 'Europeaniza-
tion' of the Saar—*i.e.*, it would have been given a European statute
within the framework of Western European Union, and a European
commission appointed by W.E.U. would have undertaken representation of Saar interests in foreign affairs and defence; internal affairs
would have been the responsibility of an elected parliament, and the
coal mines and iron and steel works would have been in the hands of Saarlanders. These ingenious arrangements marked a new stage in Franco-
German relationships connected with the Saar, but they were subject
to approval, or otherwise, by a referendum among the Saarlanders
which was held in October 1955; if the Statute had been approved it
would not have been brought into question until the conclusion of a
peace treaty with Germany.

The clearly stated objectives of the French and West German Governments in this matter were "to develop the economy of the Saar to the
broadest extent, and to do away with any occasion of conflict in their
mutual relations." These commendable policies might have made it
possible for the Saarland to function as a bridge between the two States,
instead of as a bone of contention. The Saarlanders, however, rejected
the Statute, and, with it, a possible 'middle way' of solving one of
Europe's most difficult politico-territorial problems.

The French Union. France emerged from the second world war with
a disrupted economy and a serious loss of prestige; burdened with the
weight of European problems and apparently unable to find a stable
government, she was compelled to face a series of crises at home and
overseas. This is not unusual in the restless times which have followed
the war, but France, because of the colonial policy which she had
adopted, found herself called upon to deal with colonial problems which
called for a new approach.

From its inception in the seventeenth century French 'imperialism'
has been dominated by the policies of administrative centralization,
mercantilism, and assimilation. Under the Republic the colonies were
ruled by Presidential decrees, which were implemented by a body of
civil servants; in the protectorates the sovereigns retained the right to
make laws, but it was the French Resident who prepared and enforced
legislation. It has been no part of the French programme to guide the

[22] *The Times*, October 26, 1954. This issue gave the text of the Franco-German Agreement, and its first leader contains an analysis of the political and economic problems
involved.

colonies towards self-government. As late as 1944 the rapporteur of an Imperial Conference at Brazzaville said, "We visualize the Empire in the Roman sense of the word, not in the Anglo-Saxon sense."[23]

The war and its effects, including the growth of nationalism in Asia and Africa, as well as the sheer inability of France to maintain adequate civil and military forces overseas, brought about a change of attitude towards colonial territories which received special consideration in the new Constitution of 1946. Under this Constitution the French Empire became the French Union, which now consists of the French Republic, comprising Metropolitan France and the departments and territories overseas, and associated States and territories. The overseas departments include the old colonies of Martinique, Guadeloupe, Guiana, and Réunion, together with Algeria, where the three northern departments hold a special status. The overseas territories, formerly colonies and now an integral part of the Republic, are Madagascar, Comoro Islands, Somaliland, New Caledonia, Pacific islands, St Pierre and Miquelon, and West and Equatorial Africa; they are administered by officials from the mother country, but they have elected assemblies for local affairs. The associated States are Viet-Nam, Laos, and Cambodia, but Tunisia and Morocco were in a peculiar category before their attainment of political independence in 1956. While they do not now form part of the French Union, it appears likely that they will stand in special treaty relations with France.[24]

The organization of the French Union is basically different from that of the British Commonwealth or of the Colonial Empire. The French conception is clearly far more rigid than that of the British. Not only is it expressed in a written Constitution, but also in the provisions for three central organs—the office of President, the Higher Council, and the Assembly. There is nothing comparable with the Dominions in the French Union.

The Benelux Countries

The three members of the Benelux economic union—Belgium, Luxembourg, and the Netherlands—together occupy only 7 per cent. of the area of Atlantic Europe, but contain one-sixth of its total population. With an average density of 300 per square kilometre, they are the most

[23] Quoted by C. A. Julian, "From the French Empire to the French Union," in *International Affairs*, vol. xxvi (London, 1953), p. 493.
[24] See below, pp. 179–183.

thickly peopled part of Europe. All three are now highly industrialized and have developed their agriculture along progressive lines; each has over half her population living in towns, and each is largely dependent on international trade. The very factor of location, which has played such a large part in making their growth possible, has also been a serious cause of trouble in the past and present conditions of Belgium and the Netherlands. Their coastal situation, precisely where the vast European plain, narrowed here by a north-western extension of the Hercynian Uplands of Central Europe, meets the North Sea, also coincides generally with the estuaries of the Rhine and Meuse. For centuries, therefore, the important Powers of Europe have been interested in the politico-territorial status of these lands. Britain has striven to prevent their domination by a rival State; Spain, Austria, and France have incorporated parts of them at various times; and the evolution of modern Germany has further emphasized the strategic importance of these Low Countries. Strategic considerations have therefore overshadowed the fortunes of Belgium and the Netherlands, which occupy such a vulnerable situation; no wonder the Dutch have long wished to be neutral and that, when Belgium was separated from the former United Kingdom of the Netherlands in 1839, her neutral status was guaranteed by the European Powers.

Again, their maritime location, combined with motives similar to those of Britain and France, has enabled the Netherlands and Belgium to build up overseas empires. Together they control three million square kilometres of colonial territory, but, whereas that of Belgium is restricted to one unit, the Belgian Congo, the Dutch colonies are located in Asia and the Americas (see Table 10), although the Netherlands suffered a severe blow in the loss of Indonesia. Thus the two most important members of Benelux are caught up in the conflict between continental and maritime interests, but their case differs from those of Britain and France. For Belgium and the Netherlands, trade with Europe as a whole occupies a far more important position in their total trade than it does in the rest of Atlantic Europe, and trade with affiliated overseas territories is relatively and absolutely much smaller (see Table 2). This, again, is largely an expression of location, for the two countries are not only contiguous with Germany but are also intimately connected with German foreign trade by way of the Rhine Waterway. Thus much of their trade is composed of transit traffic. In 1953 Antwerp handled 90 per cent. of Belgian international seaborne trade, and over a quarter was in transit; in the Netherlands there was an even greater share of such transit traffic, 43 per cent., of which 83 per cent. was handled at Rotterdam. Both countries have a strong interest in maintaining and increasing this type of trade, as it brings employment in the docks, in the shipyards, and on the waterways. The handling of 30·7 million tons of goods in Belgium and 51·9 million tons in the Netherlands per annum is a large item in the economy of two small countries, even if much of the traffic is in transit. The well-being of the Low Countries is, therefore, closely linked with economic stability in the world, but particularly in Europe, and it should not occasion surprise that their Governments have tried to overcome the difficulties inherent in their mutual interests by creating an economic union.

Belgium and Luxembourg have been economically united in a customs union since 1922. Fifteen years later the three countries set up a permanent economic commission to explore the possibilities of co-operation, but the war delayed progress, although it compelled both the Dutch and the Belgians to appreciate their economic interdependence and to realize that neutrality was a thing of the past for them. As soon as the German occupation ended six commissions of administrators fully explored the problems of economic union; in 1948 customs duties were abolished and a common tariff against third countries was adopted, while a year later the Pre-Union was created. Full working of the Union has not yet been achieved, although it was expected to be in operation by 1950. Looked at superficially, Benelux should have succeeded much more rapidly, but consideration must be paid to important differences, in particular, between the two larger members.

One Dutch author stated recently that "the economic and financial circumstances in the three countries still differ so greatly that the union cannot be realized. It is not intended, however, to abandon the plan on which continuous work is being done."[25] Manufactured goods are moving freely among the Benelux countries, and their participation in the European Coal and Steel Community overrides any necessity to integrate their mining and heavy metallurgical industries. The major hindrance to the implementation of further economic association stems from differences in their agricultural economies and in their monetary policies. Belgian agriculture has been organized to feed the urban population of this highly industrialized country, while the Netherlands

[25] B. H. M. Vlekke, "A Dutch View of the World Situation," in *International Affairs*, vol. xxvii (London, 1952), p. 418.

directed their farming towards the export of foodstuffs, especially to Germany and Britain. Hence Dutch foodstuffs tend to be cheaper than Belgian, so that the export of the former to Belgium is restricted to limited quantities, and only against payment of a tax which raises the price to the Belgian level. Furthermore, agriculture and farm prices are among the most inhibited subjects for all European governments. As long ago as 1951 it was asserted that this problem "is the rock on which the Benelux union is foundering."[26] On the other hand, a recent publication of the Economic Commission for Europe stated: "The Benelux unification has proceeded slowly. . . . The Benelux is undoubtedly a relative success when considered against the background of so many vain attempts in other regions, but it also serves to stress the difficulties inherent in any attempt at close economic union between countries which for a long time have developed as independent units."[27] This last statement provides a key to the problem of Benelux and similar schemes. Judging by results, European economic unions are unlikely to be successful unless accompanied by close political co-ordination; in practice they are inseparable, as the Russians have found in Eastern Europe. Participation in E.C.S.C., N.A.T.O., in the revised Brussels Treaty and in the new scheme for the future of the Saar, involves a degree of sacrifice of national sovereign rights. Benelux is a purely economic scheme—no political union is contemplated—and although the assiduity of the officials and other experts is beyond doubt, it seems that some political co-ordination, leading to currency standardization and integration of financial policies, is required.

[26] S. Strange, "A European Agricultural Authority," in *World Affairs*, vol. v (London, 1951), p. 463.
[27] *Economic Survey of Europe since the War* (E.C.E., Geneva, 1953), p. 226.

CHAPTER IV

The Eastern Marchlands of Europe

A. E. MOODIE

The Geographical Character of the Eastern Marchlands

THERE is little or no agreement on the extent of the several geographical divisions of Europe, and a degree of arbitrariness therefore enters into the definition of any one of them. To avoid confusion, the subject of this chapter is called the Eastern Marchlands of Europe—a title borrowed from H. G. Wanklyn[1]— although the area discussed here is restricted to the six States of Poland, Czechoslovakia, Hungary, Romania, Yugoslavia, and Bulgaria. Justification for this grouping may be found in the common features of their histories, in the Communist character of their present governments, and in the westward spread of Soviet influence into their territories.

The Eastern Marchlands have no physical unity save in one connexion—their location. In Chapter I above, attention was drawn to the reduction of the north–south extent of Europe between the Baltic and the Adriatic. Eastward of this isthmus stretch the vast territories of the Soviet Union, so that land movements of peoples, goods, and ideas between the Russian realm, on the one hand, and Central and Western Europe, on the other, have inevitably utilized the 500-mile-wide corridor which the peculiar configuration of Europe places between them. In the upshot, and even before States were organized in their present form, the Eastern Marchlands were a transitional zone between, not two countries, but two different worlds. This geographical character provides the key to understanding the strategic, economic, and social conditions which have developed there, and goes far to explain their present politico-territorial structure.

Physiographically the Eastern Marchlands are highly diversified.

[1] *The Eastern Marchlands of Europe*, by H. G. Wanklyn (Philip, London, 1941). Miss Wanklyn (Mrs J. A. Steers) was the first to give prominence to her title in English geographical literature.

Land forms range from the drift-covered plains of Poland to the lofty alpine chains of the Carpathian arc, from the karstlands of western Yugoslavia to the flat lowlands of the Alföld and Wallachia. Geological structures are equally diverse, since the area lies athwart the major geological trend lines of Europe. In brief, the Eastern Marchlands reveal many of the physical characteristics of continental Europe, but, whereas the western part of the continent faces the Atlantic, Poland and Romania in particular lie wide open to the Soviet Union. Furthermore, the Carpathian arc is no more a barrier than the Alps. Especially in its central sector, between Slovakia and northern Romania, it is breached by relatively low passes, four of which are used by railways. Thus, although the deeply incised section of the valley of the Danube which separates the Transylvanian Alps and the Balkan Mountains (Stara Planina) is a serious hindrance to both land transport and river navigation, east–west movement through the Marchlands as a whole has never been seriously impeded naturally. The early medieval Barbarian invaders of Europe were able to select lines of movement westward; the Slavs reached the Elbe, to be succeeded by a compensatory later movement of Germanic peoples in the opposite direction; after the Ottoman Turks had been compelled to retreat south-eastward through the Morava-Vardar corridor, by which they had previously .penetrated to the Middle Danube plains, the Habsburgs were able to extend their imperial sway to the western slopes of the Carpathians and to Galicia beyond the Tatra and Beskide mountains. During the present century German economic and military penetration of the Marchlands was facilitated by the network of railways, as all the main lines have a generally east–west orientation and Russian strategy towards the end of the second world war exploited the lines of movement which had assisted the earlier invaders.

For nearly two millennia, therefore, this part of Eastern Europe has witnessed the ebb and flow of peoples; armies, merchants, and migrants have traversed its surface, but predominantly in a latitudinal direction. It is no matter for surprise that many of them found their journey's end in the Marchlands, which became thereby a territory occupied by peoples of extremely mixed ethnic origins. Nowhere did the area settled by any one ethnic group coincide exactly with a physical region. The original homeland of the Poles was the Vistula basin, but they spread as far west as the Oder and beyond; Czechs concentrated in the Bohemian Massif, but Germans penetrated to the inner slopes of the mountain rim of this block; the majority of the Magyars, distinct ethnically and linguistically from the Slav peoples of Eastern Europe, settled on the Great Alföld, but many of them found homes in the southern valleys of the mountains of Slovakia, and more passed round or through the Bihor mountains into the high basin of Transylvania. While the lower Danube, with its broad flood plain dotted with numerous lagoons, effectively separated Romanians and Bulgars, the Yugoslavs were able to survive in two such contrasting regions as their northern plains (Voivodina) and the mountains of Bosnia, Hercegovina, and Montenegro. Little did all these peoples with their different languages anticipate the problems which their distribution would create for twentieth-century statesmen. Even less here than elsewhere was there any possibility of 'natural frontiers' for the States which were to be established after the first world war. In the heyday of self-determination, no part of the earth's surface comparable in area with the Eastern Marchlands had a greater number of minorities.[2]

Against such a background of historical and geographical conditions, instability in the politico-territorial structure may be expected, but the Eastern Marchlands are not a 'shatter belt' merely because of their surface and ethnic qualities. Lying open to east and west, their fortunes are largely dependent on the power and policies of the larger States which they separate.

Twentieth-century Territorial Changes in the Eastern Marchlands

The Situation in 1914. Before the outbreak of the first world war the three great Empires of continental Europe—German, Russian, and Habsburg—met in the Eastern Marchlands (Fig. 1) and effectively suppressed numerous nationalist aspirations. Poland had been partitioned towards the end of the eighteenth century, and so gave contiguity to the three empires in Upper Silesia, although the mineral wealth of this area was not developed until the second half of the nineteenth century. The former Kingdom of Bohemia had long disappeared, but the Habsburg domain was flanked on the south-east by a series of independent States. Romania had acquired completely independent

[2] For an excellent account of the minorities problems see P. de Azcárate, *The League of Nations and National Minorities: An Experiment* (Carnegie Endowment for International Peace, Washington, 1945).

FIG. I. TWENTIETH-CENTURY BOUNDARY CHANGES IN THE EASTERN
MARCHLANDS (EXCLUDING CHANGES DURING THE SECOND WORLD WAR)

1. Boundaries in 1914.   2. Boundaries resulting from the first world war.
3. Boundaries resulting from the second world war. 4. Russian territory in 1914.
5. The Habsburg Empire in 1914. Boundary-lines are thinned where coincident.
The Free Territory of Trieste ceased to exist as a separate entity in 1954.

status in 1878, and Bulgaria in 1908. Serbia had gained a degree of
freedom from Turkish rule in 1817 and full independence by the Treaty
of Berlin in 1878, while Montenegro, which had escaped complete
Turkish occupation, was also recognized by the Powers as an independent State in 1878.

This territorial arrangement in the Eastern Marchlands made them
the locus of three types of conflict. Firstly, as the meeting place of

three great empires during a period of expansionism, there was at least the possibility of conflict between imperialist ambitions. Secondly, and within the imperial domains, the desires of national groups for freedom from their overlords could not be resisted permanently. Thirdly, the small independent States of the south-east were not only in conflict among themselves, but were also subject to external pressures from Russia, Austria-Hungary, and other Powers, so that the "Balkan Question" was a constantly recurring theme in pre-war European affairs. In this context it is hardly surprising that the first world war was initiated by the Austrian declaration of war on Serbia as a result of the assassination of Archduke Francis Ferdinand and his wife at Sarajevo in June 1914.

The Situation after the First World War. For the Eastern Marchlands the decisive results of the first world war were the defeat of Germany and Austria-Hungary and the replacement of the Russian Empire by the Soviet Union. The collapse of the Habsburg Empire and the complete absorption of the newly created Soviet Union with internal disruption left a temporary vacuum in Eastern Europe, which the statesmen of the victorious Allied Powers sought to fill by the political and territorial provisions of the Peace Treaties.[3] Fig. 1 shows that their work led to the division of the Eastern Marchlands into six small States. Poland was re-created;[4] Austria and Hungary became 'residual' States on a greatly reduced scale. Czechoslovakia was the only true 'successor' State, in that its post-war territory consisted entirely of land which had previously been within one of the pre-war empires. Romania expanded to nearly double its pre-war size by the acquisition of Bessarabia and Transylvania. Yugoslavia represented an amalgamation of formerly independent Serbia and Montenegro and most of the territory occupied by Croats and Slovenes under previous Habsburg rule. Bulgaria alone emerged from the first world war with but minor territorial changes.

Thus the political map of the Eastern Marchlands immediately after the first world war revealed major boundary changes. In one sense the new territorial arrangement may be described as 'idealistic,' because it

[3] Treaties of Versailles, Trianon, Saint-Germain-en-Laye, and Neuilly, and the Pact of Rome. For details see H. W. V. Temperley (ed.), *A History of the Peace Conference of Paris*, vols. iii–iv, Hodder and Stoughton, London, 1924).
[4] For a useful series of maps of Poland since 1660 see Map 7, Y. M. Goblet, *Political Geography and the World Map* (Philip, London, 1955).

was based on the principle of self-determination; but the nature of the shatter belt did not lend itself to the application of this principle—it is not composed of a series of homogeneous physical units, nor did it contain clearly definable linguistic or ethnic groups. In such conditions it was very unlikely that the territorial changes, on the scale attempted in the Peace Treaties, could succeed permanently. Little or no consideration was given to the viability of the six States in their new form. In fact, the dangers of conflict were increased—witness the boundary disputes and the 'revisionist' efforts which marred their inter-war relationships. Furthermore, external political and economic influences were not removed by the Peace Treaties. For a time French, British, and American interests were dominant, but, with the renewal of isolationism in the United States and the failure of such political groupings as the Little Entente and the Balkan Entente, Germany was soon able to extend its economic activities into the Marchlands, and thus paved the way for later political infiltration, for which the numerous groups of Auslanddeutsche provided good spearheads.

Looking back over the inter-war period, it seems that the Western policy of attempting to create a tier of small independent States on the western flank of the Soviet Union, designed to act as a *cordon sanitaire* for the isolation of that new political phenomenon, failed for two main reasons. Firstly, the six States were left to work out their own economic salvation with little or no external assistance. The treaty makers appear to have been satisfied that economic, social, and nationalist problems could be solved by drawing new political boundaries. They failed to realize that the Eastern Marchlands were under-developed areas—as, indeed, they remain thirty-five years later. Overwhelmingly agrarian in their economies, they had completely inadequate industrial provision for consumer goods, and, what is more, lacked capital for the building of factories and means of communication. The manufacturing industries of the Czech lands were primarily concerned with markets outside Eastern Europe, while such foreign capital as was available found its way into extractive industries and the like that were organized to provide raw materials or semi-finished goods for external use. In spite of various land-reform schemes, none of which was completed, agricultural conditions were marred by the continued existence of many large private estates, and there seemed to be no hope of appeasing the land hunger of the peasants. Discontent was therefore prevalent throughout the Eastern Marchlands. The long overdue concessions to nationalist aspirations, as reflected in the new politico-territorial organization, were not in themselves sufficient to ensure the redress of social grievances that rapid economic development alone could satisfy.

Secondly, neither the Allied Powers nor the six new States could have foreseen the emergence of the U.S.S.R. as one of the most powerful elements in world affairs. Within twenty years of the Bolshevik Revolution in 1917 Soviet economic reconstruction and military strength had reached such a stage that the disunited Marchland States could no longer be expected to function as a *cordon sanitaire* if and when the Russians decided to expand westward. Within the same period German economic control had grown powerful, particularly in the southern sections of the Marchlands, so that a new alignment of external forces came into existence, although political boundaries remained unchanged. This explains the Soviet-German agreement of September 1939, which was a recognition of Russian and German interests in Eastern Europe, albeit a temporary recognition until the fortunes of war were to remove one of the competitors.

The Second World War and its Aftermath. While Western Europe was settling down to the 'phoney' war the Eastern Marchlands were being carved up in a way unknown even in their eventful history. Before fighting began Austria was annexed by Germany and the Munich Agreement had compelled the Czechs to cede the Sudetenland. The new *Drang nach Osten* achieved two victories without striking a military blow. Then followed the invasion of Poland and the rapid advances eastward and south-eastward, until in 1941 Germany had subdued, directly or indirectly, practically the whole of the Marchlands. In the meantime the U.S.S.R. had incorporated the Baltic Republics, occupied Eastern Poland, and regained Bessarabia from Romania. Hungary, Romania, and Bulgaria became German satellites and sought to settle some of their territorial problems by accepting the provisions of the two Vienna Awards. The duality of conflict in this part of Europe was clearly reflected in the territorial readjustments which took place between 1938 and 1941. The external aspect was seen in the renewed contiguity of Soviet and German territories, and internal disunity was represented by intra-Marchland land grabbing. A further indication of the interests of external Powers in Eastern Europe was provided by the somewhat meagre rewards Italy received for its support of German aims.

Fig. 2 summarizes the state of territorial mutilation in the March-lands at the time of the German invasion of the U.S.S.R. in June 1941. Already considerable shifts of population had taken place either as refugees or under German organization, but the invasion of the U.S.S.R. entailed human movements on an unprecedented scale even if armies are excluded. The 'scorched earth' policy of the retreating Red Army necessitated the compulsory migration of many more German civilians, and millions of East Europeans were compelled to leave their homes. When the German advance was halted at Stalingrad and the tide of war turned, a further series of flights and expulsions came about, and the numbers of displaced persons reached enormous proportions. "More than 30,000,000 Europeans were transported, deported, or dispersed between the outbreak of war and the beginning of 1943."[5] Not all of these were inhabitants of the Marchlands, but by the end of the war the total number of displaced persons in the shatter belt probably reached between twenty and thirty millions. Many have since returned to their homelands, but the most striking result of wartime and post-war human movements was the virtual elimination of Germans from the Marchlands. Included among the agreements reached at the Potsdam Conference was a decision that Germans remaining in Poland, Czechoslovakia, and Hungary should be transferred to Germany. This set the seal on the collapse of German economic and political domination in the Marchlands and smoothed the way for the westward advance of Communism. The stage was set for the fall of the Iron Curtain.

The post-war territorial settlement in the Marchlands presented many difficult problems to the Allied statesmen.[6] Hungary, Bulgaria, and Romania had been enemy States, but Poland, Czechoslovakia, and Yugoslavia had been closely associated with the Allied Powers, all three having been represented by governments-in-exile in London. But more important than the question of status was the fact that all the six States had been 'liberated' by the Red Army, which strengthened the hands of the Soviet representatives at Potsdam in 1945. Furthermore, many Poles, Czechs, and Slovaks remembered the inability of the Western Powers to help them in the years immediately

---

[5] E. M. Kulischer, *Europe on the Move* (Columbia University Press, New York, and Oxford University Press, 1948), p. 264.

[6] The new boundaries are shown on Fig. 1. Those of Poland are *de facto*, but those of the other five States have been agreed by treaty. For details see *Treaties of Peace with Italy, Bulgaria, Hungary, and Romania* (Treaty Series, London, 1948). Also A. Leiss (ed.), *European Peace Treaties* (World Peace Foundation, Boston, 1954), which contains a valuable commentary.

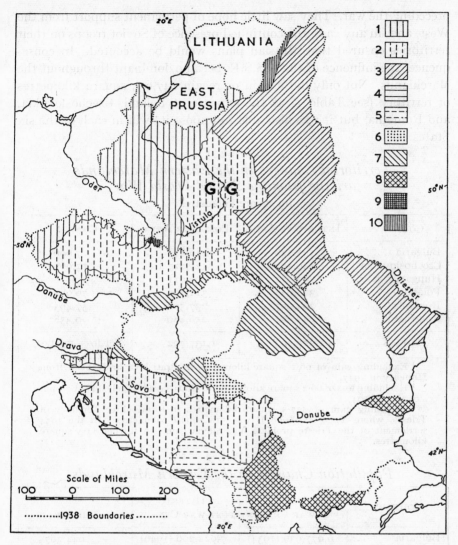

FIG. 2. TERRITORIAL CHANGES IN THE EASTERN MARCHLANDS, 1938–41

The greater part of the Eastern Marchlands was either annexed or occupied by Germany, the U.S.S.R., and Italy. Hungary, Romania, and Bulgaria were German satellites during most of the second world war. The symbols indicate the following territorial changes: 1. Annexed by Germany, 1938–41. 2. Occupied by Germany, 1938–41. 3. Annexed by the U.S.S.R., 1939–40. 4. Annexed by Italy, 1941. 5. Occupied by Italy, 1941. 6. Annexed by Romania, 1941. 7. Annexed by Hungary, 1941. 8. Annexed by Bulgaria, 1941. 9. Annexed by Poland, 1939. 10. Annexed by Lithuania, 1939. GG="Government General" of Poland.

preceding the war. They saw little hope of permanent support from the
West, and, in any case, the continued presence of Soviet troops on their
territories ensured that Russian plans would be accepted. In consequence, the influence of the U.S.S.R. became dominant throughout the
Marchlands. Not only did it gain or regain 147,035 square kilometres
of territory (see Table 1) at the expense of Poland, Czechoslovakia,
and Romania, but it was also able to impose its will in each of the six
States.

TABLE 1

Territorial Changes in the Eastern Marchlands arising from the Second World War

(in square kilometres)

COUNTRY	INTER-WAR AREA	POST-WAR AREA	CHANGE
Bulgaria .	103,146	110,842	+ 7,696
Czechoslovakia	140,493	127,827	− 12,666[1]
Hungary .	93,011	93,011	— [2]
Poland .	388,634	311,730	− 76,904
Romania .	294,967	237,502	− 57,465
Yugoslavia .	247,542	256,880	+ 9,338[3]
TOTALS .	1,267,793	1,137,792	Net loss 130,001

[1] Excluding gain of 66·2 square kilometres in Bratislava bridgehead from
Hungary in 1947.
[2] Excluding loss of 66·2 square kilometres in Bratislava bridgehead to Czechoslovakia in 1947.
[3] Excluding gain of 527·5 square kilometres in former Free Territory of
Trieste, where Yugoslav Zone B was 516 square kilometres. In the 1954
settlement of the Trieste problem Yugoslavia gained a further 11·5 square
kilometres.

TABLE 2

Population Changes in the Eastern Marchlands

COUNTRY	LAST PRE-WAR CENSUS	LATEST POST-WAR CENSUS	CHANGE
Bulgaria .	6,077,939 (1934)	7,022,206 (1946)	+ 944,267
Czechoslovakia	14,729,536 (1930)	12,339,674 (1950)	− 2,389,862[1]
Hungary .	8,685,109 (1930)	9,204,799 (1949)	+ 519,690[2]
Poland .	32,107,252 (1931)	24,976,926 (1950)	− 7,130,326
Romania .	14,282,172 (1930)	15,872,624 (1948)	+ 1,590,452
Yugoslavia .	13,934,038 (1931)	16,927,275 (1953)	+ 2,993,237[3]
TOTALS .	89,816,046	86,343,504	Net loss 3,472,542

[1] Excluding gain of population in Bratislava bridgehead.
[2] Excluding loss of population in Bratislava bridgehead.
[3] Excluding gain of population in Yugoslav Zone of F.T. Trieste.

With the single exception of Poland, the principle behind the territorial settlement was the restoration of the *status quo ante bellum*. In practice, each of the other five States experienced certain boundary changes. Czechoslovakia gained a small bridgehead opposite its chief Danubian port, Bratislava, but ceded Ruthenia to the Soviet Union by a bilateral agreement. Hungary suffered a minor loss of pre-war territory by the cession of this bridgehead to Czechoslovakia, but Romania lost 57,465 square kilometres by returning Bessarabia and Northern Bukowina to the U.S.S.R. and by confirming the Treaty of Craiova (1941), whereby Southern Dobruja became a part of Bulgaria. Yugoslavia, which had staged the most successful resistance movement during the war years, gained the greater part of the Julian March,[7] but was unsuccessful in its claims to the port of Trieste, where the Free Territory of Trieste came under international administration for over nine years. The Statute of the Free Territory was never put into practice; Yugoslavia remained in occupation of the southern part, Zone B (516 sq. km.), while the northern part, Zone A (222 sq. km.), came under Anglo-American military government. This unsatisfactory arrangement was dissolved in October 1954, when the Yugoslavs consented to the transfer of Zone A (including the port of Trieste) to Italy, subject to a minor modification of the inter-zonal boundary whereby Yugoslavia acquired a small strip of land (11·5 sq. km.) immediately to the south of Milje.

Poland presented different problems, which are not yet legally settled; the limits of post-war Poland still await confirmation in a treaty of peace with Germany. The *de facto* settlement was in effect a westward shift of the country's eastern and western boundaries. Eastern Poland was incorporated in the Soviet Union, and East Prussia was shared unevenly by the U.S.S.R. and Poland. Danzig and its corridor became Polish, and the western boundary of inter-war Poland was moved to the Oder-Neisse line. On balance, and in spite of its losses of territory and population (see Tables 1 and 2), Poland emerged from the second world war with better chances of economic survival than any other of the Marchland States. Its acquisitions from Germany gave it better agricultural land than that it had ceded to Russia, while the control of the whole of Upper Silesia ensured the basis of a reasonable industrial development. On the other hand, the Soviet

[7] A. E. Moodie, *The Italo-Yugoslav Boundary* (Philip, London, 1945), and "Some New Boundary Problems in the Julian March," in *Transactions of the Institute of British Geographers* (London, 1950).

Union in addition to control of the new States made enormous gains, not so much in territory as in strategic considerations. Annexation of Estonia, Latvia, and Lithuania greatly strengthened the Russian position in the Baltic, while the shift of the Soviet-Romanian boundary from the Dniester to the Prut and lower Danube has brought back Russian power to a dominant position on the Danube. Although the full extent of pre-1914 Russian territory has not been regained (see Fig. 1), the U.S.S.R. has acquired contiguity with four of her western neighbours—Poland, Czechoslovakia, Hungary and Romania—while Bulgaria is easily accessible by the Black Sea. This geographical factor is of decisive importance in Soviet policy in Eastern Europe. Yugoslavia alone of the Eastern Marchlands is separated from the U.S.S.R. by land, and this may have been a significant element in their strange relationships since 1945.

In spite of all these changes, however, the territorial pattern of the Eastern Marchlands shows a similarity with that of the inter-war years. The six States are nominally independent, but their economic difficulties remained as intractable in 1945 as they had been previously—indeed, the disruptions of war exacerbated them. Furthermore, it would be unwise to assume that the final settlement of boundary disputes has been reached. As long as Soviet authority retains its present ascendancy there is unlikely to be open conflict over the areas shown in Fig. 3, but the history of Eastern Europe suggests that neither military nor economic pressures have been able to subdue permanently the internal conflicts which have bedevilled relationships in the Marchlands. Any serious relaxation in Russian policy may lead to the resuscitation of boundary disputes in an active form. The close political, military, and economic integration of the U.S.S.R. and the satellite States[8] is a present safeguard against such a revival, but the Soviet authorities cannot but be aware of the existence, however dormant, of these territorial problems.

The Eastern Marchlands since 1945

In the decade since the second world war ended the Marchlands have passed through revolutionary changes in economic, social, and political conditions. Complete statistical evidence of these changes is not

---

[8] Since the Yugoslav deviation of 1948 it is convenient to refer to Poland, Czechoslovakia, Hungary, Romania, and Bulgaria as the satellite States.

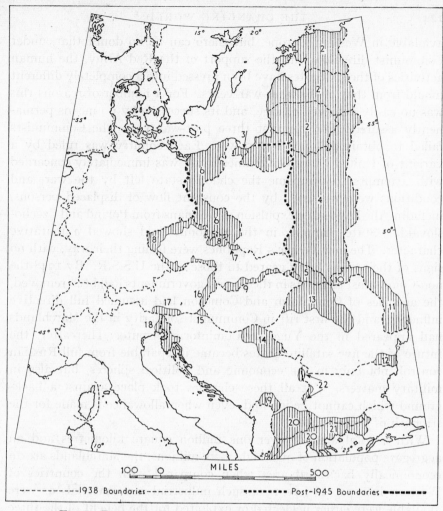

FIG. 3. DISPUTED TERRITORIES IN THE EASTERN MARCHLANDS

In spite of treaty settlements, these areas may still cause conflicts between the countries named in brackets: 1. East Prussia (Poland, Germany, U.S.S.R.). 2. The former Baltic Republics (Poland, U.S.S.R.). 3. Danzig (Poland, Germany). 4. Former Eastern Poland (Poland, U.S.S.R.). 5. Ruthenia (Hungary, Czechoslovakia, U.S.S.R.). 6. The "Western Territories" of Poland (Poland, Germany). 7. The Teschen Area (Poland, Czechoslovakia). 8. The "Border Districts" of Czechoslovakia-Sudetenland (Germany, Czechoslovakia). 9. Southern Slovakia (Czechoslovakia, Hungary). 10. Northern Bukovina (Romania, U.S.S.R.). 11. Bessarabia (Romania, U.S.S.R.). 12. Southern Dobruja (Bulgaria, Romania). 13. Transylvania (Romania, Hungary). 14. The Banat (Romania, Hungary, Yugoslovia). 15. Medjmurje (Hungary, Yugoslavia). 16. Burgenland (Austria, Yugoslavia). 17. Slovene Carinthia (Austria, Yugoslavia). 18. The Julian March (Italy, Yugoslavia). 19. "Northern Albania" (Albania, Yugoslavia). 20. Macedonia (Greece, Bulgaria, Yugoslavia). 21. Eastern Thrace (Greece, Bulgaria). 22. The Frontier Districts (Bulgaria, Yugoslavia).

available in Western Europe, but there can be no doubt that, under Communist direction with the support of the Red Army, the human activities of the six States have been pressed into a completely different mould from that of the inter-war years. For a number of reasons this was no easily achieved change, and its success is by no means permanently assured. For the first three post-war years the Communists failed to obtain full political power. Each country was ruled by a variant of United Front Government, and was immediately concerned with attempts to overcome the chaotic state left by the war, and conditions were worsened by the constant flow of displaced persons, including the large-scale expulsion of Germans from Poland and Czechoslovakia. State planning in the economic field showed a tentative character. The new People's Republics were feeling their way, with no signs of their plans being geared to those of the U.S.S.R. By 1948 the non-Communist elements in the several governments had been removed, the agencies of Cominform and Comecon had assumed full directive influence, and the first rift in Communist solidarity in the Marchlands had appeared in the Yugoslav-Cominform dispute. Thereafter, the future of the five satellite States became inseparable from full Russian control, not only in the economic and political spheres, but also in military matters. Yet all these changes took place against a background which cannot be ignored, even when allowance is made for the strength of Soviet power.

With a total area of over one million square kilometres and an aggregate population of over eighty-six millions, the Marchlands are an economically backward area when compared with the countries of Western Europe. Before 1914 such industrial raw materials as were available were either neglected or exploited for the benefit of the three empires. It was not until the end of the nineteenth century that Prussia made serious efforts to develop Upper Silesia, [9] while the mineral resources of Bohemia and Galicia were used for the benefit of Austria. Furthermore, such means of communication as were available at the outbreak of the first world war had been designed to suit the needs of either Prussia or the Habsburgs, so that the highly centralized States which were created at the end of that war were in a poor position to organize their industrial affairs even where raw materials were available, and the economic situation was worsened by the lack of capital. Indus-

[9] W. J. Rose, *The Drama of Upper Silesia* (Battleboro, U.S.A., 1935; Williams and Norgate, London, 1936).

trial backwardness was accompanied by low-level agricultural organization. For centuries the characteristic land holding of the Marchlands had been the large private estate, frequently owned by absentee

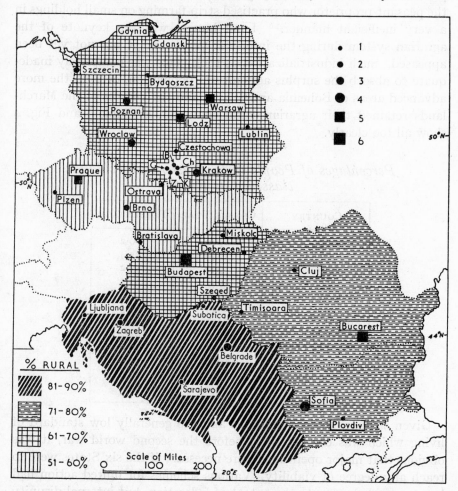

FIG. 4. RURAL POPULATION IN THE EASTERN MARCHLANDS

Based on definitions of 'rural' by the Governments concerned. Key to size of towns: 1. 100,000. 2. 200,000–300,000. 3. 300,000–400,000. 4. 400,000–500,000. 5. 500,000–1,000,000. 6. Over 1,000,000. B=Bytom. G=Gliwice. Ch=Chorzow. Z=Zabrze. K=Katowice (Stalinograd).

landlords and generally inefficiently utilized. This *latifundia* system and its associated serfdom had been a constant source of friction between owners and agricultural workers. From the early nineteenth century onward it gradually passed through a process of disintegration, although it was not finally abandoned in some areas until 1945. By 1939 the predominant element in the populations of the Marchland States was the peasant-proprietor who practised strip-farming on small holdings in a very inefficient manner.[10] Land hunger was the keynote of the agrarian system during the inter-war years, and it has not yet been appeased. Such industrialization as took place was completely inadequate to absorb the surplus agricultural population, even in the more advanced areas of Bohemia and Silesia, and the peoples of the Marchlands retained their agrarian, rural character, as Table 3 and Fig. 4 show all too clearly.

TABLE 3

Percentages of People in the Eastern Marchlands classified as Rural

COUNTRY	CENSUS YEAR	PERCENTAGE
Bulgaria .	1900	80·2
	1946	75·4
Czechoslovakia .	1930	53·2
	1947	51·1
Hungary .	1900	69·4
	1949	65·5
Poland .	1931	63·2
	1949	64·2
Romania .	1930	79·8
	1948	76·8
Yugoslavia .	1931	81·0
	1948	83·8

Given such economic conditions and the generally low standard of living which was characteristic before the second world war, it was obvious that major operations were necessary if the six States were to reach any degree of viability. Various schemes for united action had been suggested, even to the extent of federation, but internal disunity had prevented their implementation. Because of their 'liberation' of Eastern Europe and the power of the Red Army and once they had obtained full political control, the Communists had practically a free hand in reorganizing the economic life of the lands which fell under their sway, although, on the surface, the planned economies were put into effect separately in the individual countries. Whatever success or

[10] D. Warriner, *Economics of Peasant Farming* (Oxford University Press, 1939).

failure they have achieved must be measured against the background of the conditions which existed before the war and which gave them their opportunity.

Industrial Changes. Before 1939 Czechoslovakia was the only Marchland State able to meet most of its needs in industrial production. The others were largely dependent on external sources, predominantly German, so that the disappearance of German supplies after the war created widespread shortages, even allowing for the low purchasing capacity of the peasants. Among the first steps taken in the post-war economic plans, therefore, were efforts to reorganize the industrial economies of the People's Republics. First place was given in the several investment policies to the development of heavy industries, and the people were expected, indeed encouraged, to suffer continued shortages of consumer goods. In retrospect it can be seen that too much emphasis was given to the production of capital goods—many of the schemes were too ambitious—although there was some logic in putting their production before that of consumer goods. Had more capital and raw materials been available, and had the Soviet Union been in a position to supply the goods which the six States were unable to make, industrial development might have been much more successful. The Marchlands were not allowed to accept Marshall Aid or any other form of Western assistance. Thus, in spite of the existence of trade agreements, both between the satellite States and with the U.S.S.R., they were unable to meet each other's needs—at least, not sufficiently to overcome the loss of West European supplies. Hence the cessation of east–west trade in Europe meant further deprivations for the peoples of the Marchlands.

Industrial changes were preceded by the nationalization of all credit and production, as is to be expected under Communist rule. The assumption of complete financial control by the State helped to overcome one of the greatest difficulties in Marchland economics—the lack of capital for investment purposes. Nevertheless, and in spite of the confiscation of properties of ex-enemy nationals and of other foreign-owned resources, there was still insufficient capital for industrial development at the desired rate. The U.S.S.R. was either unable or unwilling to do for the Marchlands what American financial assistance did for Western Europe and other parts of the world. In fact, the chief weakness of the industrial reforms is to be seen in the sometimes reckless speed with which plans were prepared and executed. Local targets were often set too high, the privileged workers in heavy industry often failed to reach their planned output, and inadequate attention to agricultural production led to shortages in food supplies. To make matters worse, the means of communication which are vital to any industrial development were inadequate in the Marchlands. The length of railway lines in proportion to the population is about equal to that of Western Europe; the ratio of railways to area is considerably lower.[11] Furthermore, the tracks are poorly laid, and the rolling stock, seriously depleted during the war, is of lower efficiency than that of Western Europe. For short-haul traffic the road systems of all but parts of Poland and Czechoslovakia are incapable of acting as effective feeders to the railways.

Yet, despite these formidable difficulties, the overall targets in heavy industry were fulfilled. Particular attention was paid to fuel and power production, as Table 4 indicates.

TABLE 4

Industrial Production in the Eastern Marchlands in 1954

COUNTRY	HARD COAL (million tons)	LIGNITE (million tons)	ELECTRIC POWER (million MWh)	FINISHED STEEL (million tons)
Bulgaria .	—	8·6	1·8 (0·2)	—
Czecho- slovakia	20·3 (16·8)	32·8	13·5 (4·1)	3·0
Hungary .	2·1 (1·0)	19·2	4·6 (1·4)	1·1
Poland .	91·3 (69·4)	6·9	15·4 (7·0)	2·5
Romania .	0·5 (0·3)	4·4	3·4 (1·1)	0·5
Yugoslavia	1·0 (0·5)	—	3·0 (1·1)	0·4
TOTALS .	115·2 (88·0)	71·9	41·7 (14·9)	7·5

Figures in brackets are 1938 productions adjusted for post-war territories.

Clearly the energy base of the economies has been greatly strengthened since 1938. Coal output has risen by over a quarter, and the generation of electric power[12] has nearly trebled; but the output of light industry shows relatively less progress, largely because of the deliberate policy of fostering the production of heavy industry at the expense of all other branches.

[11] Eastern Europe, 0·8 km. of railway per 1000 persons; Western Europe, 0·8 km. Eastern Europe, 73 km. of railways per 1000 sq. km.; Western Europe, 85 km. (*Economic Survey of Europe in 1953* (United Nations, Geneva, 1954), Table 31, p. 76.)
[12] See Fig. 5.

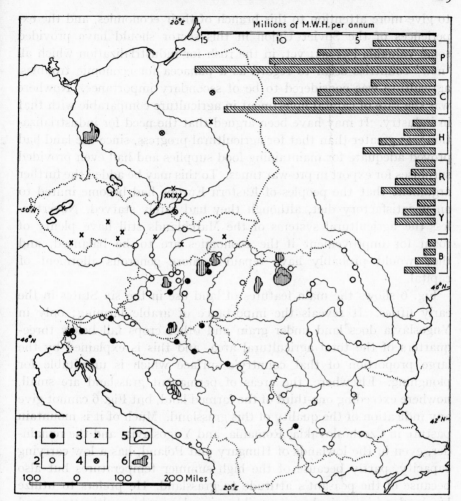

FIG. 5. PRODUCTION OF ELECTRICITY IN THE EASTERN MARCHLANDS

The horizontal blocks represent production for the years 1939, 1948, 1951, and 1954, except for Yugoslavia, where data are not available for 1954. 1. Existing hydro-electric plants. 2. Projected or partly completed hydro-electric plants. 3. Completed (post-war) thermal electric plants. 4. Partly completed new thermal stations. 5. Hard-coal deposits. 6. Lignite deposits.

Agrarian Reform and Collectivization. The new regimes in the Marchlands have probably made their greatest mistakes in dealing with agriculture.[13] At first glance, and in view of the peasant character of the great majority of their populations, they might have been expected

[13] In this connexion it is worth recalling that agricultural reorganization has not been completely successful in the U.S.S.R.

F

to give more attention to this branch of their economies, and the experiences of the Soviet Union in this sector should have provided
some valuable lessons; yet, in the rush for industrialization which all
'new' countries seem to regard as a panacea for economic troubles,
agriculture was considered to be of secondary importance. Nowhere
was the rate of capital investment in agriculture comparable with that
in industry. It may have been argued that the need for industrialization was greater than that for agricultural progress, since the land had
proved adequate for maintaining food supplies and had even provided
surpluses for export in pre-war times. To this may be added the further
argument that the peoples of Eastern Europe had become inured to
an unsatisfactory diet, although they had rarely starved. Nevertheless the agricultural systems of the Marchlands still have plenty of
room for improvement if the economies are to be balanced, and
they would probably have repaid a more generous allotment of
capital.

Fig. 6 shows the main features of land use in the six States in the
early fifties. It reveals the importance of arable farming; only in
Yugoslavia does land under grain and other crops fall below three-
quarters of the total agricultural area, and this is explained by the
large proportion of that country's surface which is unsuitable for
ploughing. Elsewhere, the areas of permanent grassland are small,
nowhere exceeding one-third of the farmed land, but Fig. 6 cannot give
any indication of the quality of this grassland. Much of it is mountain
pasture in Czechoslovakia, Romania, and Yugoslavia, and the remainder, even in the lowlands of Hungary and Poland, has a low carrying
capacity, partly because of the high summer temperatures but also
because of the peasant's attitude to grassland. He prefers to utilize
his land as intensively as possible—i.e., by arable cultivation—and
so produces fodder crops for stall-fed cattle. Only the poorest soils
and steep slopes are left in grass, and well-tended meadows are
rare.

The emphasis on grain-crop production which is demonstrated in
Fig. 6 remains a serious weakness in the agrarian economy of the Marchlands. Most of each peasant's holding is under grains—wheat or rye in
Poland and Czechoslovakia, wheat or maize in the other countries—
so that proper rotations are impossible and, in consequence, soil
impoverishment is widespread. Adequate supplies of fertilizers are not
maintained, and little attention is paid to improved farming tech-

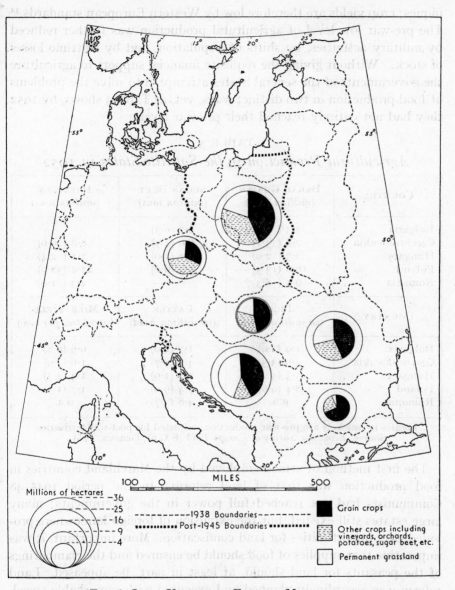

MILES

100   0   500

Millions of hectares
—36
—25
—16
—9
—4

- - - - 1938 Boundaries - - - - -
▪▪▪▪▪ Post-1945 Boundaries ▪▪▪▪▪

■ Grain crops

▨ Other crops including
vineyards, orchards,
potatoes, sugar beet, etc.

□ Permanent grassland

FIG. 6. LAND USE IN THE EASTERN MARCHLANDS

Over-emphasis on grain cultivation remains the chief weakness in the agrarian economy. Outer circles represent total areas of the States; inner circles represent total agricultural areas. Average areas 1948/49 to 1951/52 for Poland, Hungary, and Yugoslavia. 1954 areas for Bulgaria and Romania.

niques; crop yields are therefore low by Western European standards.[14] The pre-war low level of agricultural production was further reduced by military activities, by shifts of population, and by wartime losses of stock.   Without giving the requisite financial support to agriculture the governments of the several States attempted to solve the problems of food production in two distinct ways, yet, as Table 5 shows, by 1952 they had not entirely reached their pre-war levels.

TABLE 5

Agricultural Production in the Satellite States in 1952

COUNTRY	BREAD GRAINS (*million tons*)	SUGAR BEET (*million tons*)	POTATOES (*million tons*)
Bulgaria .	2·3 (2·2)	0·7 (0·3)	— —
Czechoslovakia .	2·8 (3·1)	6·0 (4·7)	8·8 (9·6)
Hungary .	2·3 (2·9)	1·2 (1·0)	1·1 (2·4)
Poland .	10·9 (13·3)	7·7 (6·0)	28·2 (38·0)
Romania .	6·5 (8·3)	— —	2·3 (1·0)

COUNTRY	PIGS (*in million head*)	CATTLE (*in million head*)	MILK YIELD (*000 litres per cow*)
Bulgaria .	1·9 (1·0)	1·7 (2·0)	0·6 (0·8)
Czechoslovakia .	4·6 (3·5)	4·3 (4·7)	1·6 (1·9)
Hungary .	5·3 (5·2)	2·1 (1·9)	1·4 (2·3)
Poland .	8·4 (9·6)	7·4 (9·9)	1·7 (1·5)
Romania .	n.a.	4·8 (3·7)	n.a.

Figures in brackets are pre-war productions adjusted for post-war territories.
Source: *Economic Survey of Europe 1953* (E.C.E., Geneva, 1954).

The first method of attack employed by the Marchland countries in food production was that of land reform.   In the period 1945–48 Communists had not reached full power in the governments; many large estates still existed, but the expulsion of foreign landowners provided easy opportunities for land confiscation.   More important, it was imperative that supplies of food should be ensured and the clamourings of the peasants for land should, at least in part, be appeased.   Land reform was accordingly planned and executed with remarkable speed, in marked contrast with the delays and non-fulfilment of similar plans after the first world war.   In three years forty-eight million acres of

[14] Average annual yields of wheat for 1948–52 in 100 kilogrammes per hectare were: Bulgaria, 12·5; Czechoslovakia, 18·6; Hungary, 13·1; Poland, 12·2; Romania, 10·3; Yugoslavia, 12·0; United Kingdom (for comparison), 27·0.

land (including forests) were confiscated, and over thirty million acres of agricultural land were distributed among nearly three million peasants or landless agricultural workers. Fig. 7 shows that the area of expropriated land varied greatly from country to country. In Hungary,

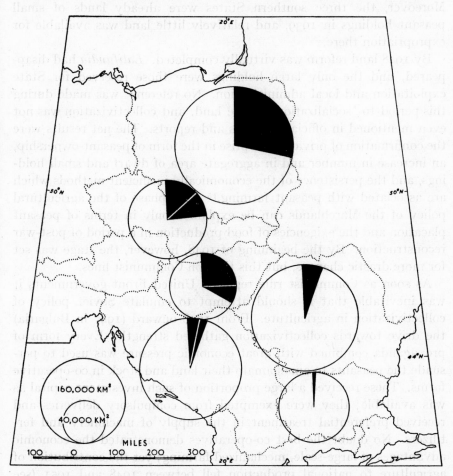

FIG. 7. LAND EXPROPRIATION, 1945–47, DURING THE AGRARIAN REFORM IN THE EASTERN MARCHLANDS

Circles represent the total areas of the States; segments represent the areas expropriated, which are divided into agricultural land (left-hand side) and forests (right-hand side) where data are available.

Poland, and Czechoslovakia the percentages of total State area confiscated were 34, 28·6, and 24 respectively, while in Yugoslavia, Romania, and Bulgaria they were only 6, 6, and 4·5. This general difference between the northern and southern parts of the Marchlands was largely the result of the survival of greater numbers of large estates, particularly in Poland and Hungary, combined with the expulsion of German landowners from Czechoslovakia and Poland. Moreover, the three southern States were already lands of small peasant holdings in 1939, and relatively little land was available for expropriation there.

By 1948 land reform was virtually completed. *Latifundia* had disappeared, and the only large holdings were those reserved for State exploitation and local administration. No reference was made during this period to 'socialization' of the land, and collectivization was not even mentioned in official speeches and reports. The net results were the confirmation of private enterprise in the form of peasant-ownership, an increase in number and in aggregate area of dwarf and small holdings, and the persistence of the economically inefficient methods which are associated with peasant farming.[15] This phase of the agricultural policy of the Marchlands can be explained only in terms of peasant placation and the exigencies of food production in a period of post-war reconstruction. By the beginning of 1948, however, the stage was set for more drastic changes, but this time on Communist lines.

As soon as Communist rule replaced United Front governments it was inevitable that it should attempt to emulate Soviet policy of collectivization in agriculture. From 1948 onward (1947 in Bulgaria) the drive towards collectivization gathered strength. Every form of propaganda combined with great economic pressure was used to persuade the peasants to amalgamate their land and stock in co-operative farms. These received a large proportion of such investment capital as was available; they were exempted from compulsory deliveries and received preferential treatment in the supply of machinery and fertilizers. No doubt the best co-operatives demonstrated the economic advantages of large-scale, mechanized farming; yet the contribution of agriculture to national production fell between 1948 and 1951 (see Table 6). Even after allowances are made for serious droughts during this period, and for the increase in the contribution of industry, the actual decline in agricultural production was a serious matter.

In spite of this decline, collectivization proceeded, until in 1953, following an exceptionally bad harvest, food shortages became acute

[15] For the results in detail of the land reform see A. E. Moodie, "Agrarian Reform in East-Central Europe," in *Yearbook of World Affairs* (London, 1954).

TABLE 6

Percentage Contribution of Agriculture to National Production by Value in Four Satellite States

COUNTRY	1948	1951
Czechoslovakia	17·6	15·1
Hungary .	26·7	20·1
Poland .	24·0	19·6
Romania .	50·0	33·0

Source: *Economic Survey of Europe since the War* (E.C.E., Geneva, 1953).

and a new line was adopted in dealing with the peasants. In Hungary, Czechoslovakia, and Yugoslavia pressure to join the co-operatives was eased, compulsory deliveries by peasant-proprietors were abandoned, and, most striking of all, farmers who had pooled their land were allowed to withdraw from the co-operatives. In the Voivodina of Yugoslavia, by far the best farming land in the country, where collective farming should have been an economic success, the aggregate area of co-operative farms fell from 53·6 per cent. to 14·6 per cent. of the total agricultural land. Bulgaria alone retained its high level of collectivization. There can be little doubt that everywhere else in the Marchlands the peasants have won a victory in their resistance to Communist rulers. On a long term-view this may well be a serious misfortune both for the governments and for the peoples. The greatest single economic problem of Eastern Europe is still agricultural overpopulation—too many people living on too little land as long as it is worked by peasant methods. While it must be admitted that much of the terrain is completely unsuitable for collectivization, mechanized, large-scale farming on the plains might have led to higher productivity and would certainly have released labour for industrial occupations as the need grew. Forecasting developments is as dangerous in Eastern Europe as anywhere else in the world, but it does seem that the decline in collectivization is a temporary matter. Just how long the peasants will be allowed to hold their Communist masters at bay is an open question.

Conclusion

In spite of Yugoslavia's deviation in 1948, which was followed by an unexpected *rapprochement* in May 1955, the U.S.S.R. is in full control

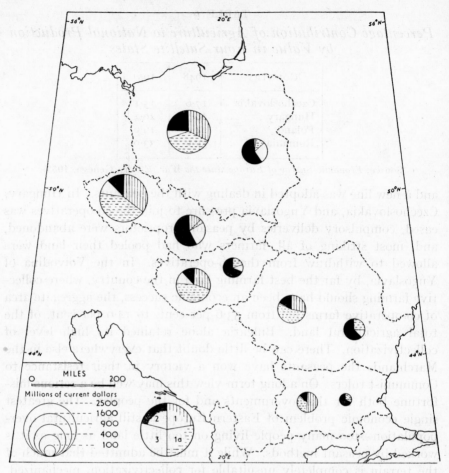

FIG. 8. DISTRIBUTION OF TRADE TURNOVER (EXPORTS PLUS IMPORTS)
OF THE SOVIET SATELLITE STATES IN 1953 (LEFT-HAND SIDE) AND 1937
(RIGHT-HAND SIDE)

Circles represent total foreign trade in millions of current dollars. 1. Trade with
U.S.S.R. 1a. Trade with other Satellite States. 2. Trade with Western European
countries, including Yugoslavia. 3. Trade with overseas countries. Poland's
trade with U.S.S.R. in 1937 was so small that the appropriate symbol could not
be used in this diagram.

of all aspects of life in the satellite States, and there appears to be little
hope of any serious relaxation of Russian power in the near future.
The five States are firmly tied by treaties of friendship and trade agreements, and the long-term plans of each are geared to Soviet requirements. The creation of a unified high command under the leadership

of a Soviet-trained general may be interpreted as putting their armed forces at the disposal of the U.S.S.R. if and when they are needed. In effect, the satellite States, as the name implies, have lost their independence of action, however much they have been able to preserve a façade of separate government. With the signing of a State Treaty with Austria, they stand, together with Eastern Germany, as a great economic, political, and military bastion between the Soviet Union and the West. This may avail the U.S.S.R. little in the event of an atomic war, but the reorientation of the satellite States eastward, nowhere better exemplified than in commercial relationships as shown in Fig. 8, must be regarded as a triumph of Communist policy.

FURTHER READING

BASCH, A., *The Danube Basin and the German Economic Sphere* (Kegan Paul, London, 1944).

Demographic Yearbook (United Nations, New York, annually).

Economic Development in S.E. Europe (Political and Economic Planning, London, 1945).

Economic Survey of Europe (United Nations, Geneva, annually).

GEORGE, P., and TRICART, J., *L'Europe Centrale* (two vols.; Presses Universitaire de France, Paris, 1954).

LEPRETTE, J., *Le Statut International de Trieste* (Editions A. Pedone, Paris, 1949).

MOUSSET, A., *The World of the Slavs* (Stevens, London, 1950).

SCHECHTMAN, J. B., *European Population Transfers, 1939–1945* (Oxford University Press, New York and London, 1946).

SCHLESINGER, R., *Federalism in Central and Eastern Europe* (Kegan Paul, London, 1945).

WARRINER, D., *Revolution in Eastern Europe* (Turnstile Press, London, 1950).

The World To-day (Royal Institute of International Affairs, London, monthly).

F*

CHAPTER V

Problems of Scandinavia and Finland

W. R. MEAD

Land and People

SCANDINAVIA is a fact geographically: a marriage culturally: a chimera politically," a North European historian once wrote. As an omnibus term, Scandinavia, which strictly includes Norway, Sweden, Denmark, and Iceland, is loosely applied to include also Finland; but these countries prefer the collective expression *Norden*—in English, "The Northern Countries." Common to all five are certain characteristics—high-latitude location and climate, a peripheral position in Europe, a maritime orientation, relatively sparse population, economic and political dependence. As a group they have experienced reduction in international status in the eighteenth century and a compensating transformation in the last century from economic obscurity to significance. They possess a high degree of cultural unity: but, though of all countries they are the group most near to federation, political combination remains a chimera.

The catalogue of common features, despite differences in detail, is extended in the common division of Scandinavia by its human geographers into a developed southern half and an under-developed northern half. In Finland, J. G. Granö has contrasted *Kultur Finnland* and *Natur Finnland*; in Sweden, Åke Campbell describes a similar dichotomy. The northern territories of Norway, Sweden, and Finland —the better part of a thousand kilometres from their metropolitan centres and traditionally neglected by them—command intermittent attention. A domestic objective of the last two generations has been to integrate by rail, road, and air the 'colonial' north with the metropolitan south and to reduce the lag in development which prevails from Norwegian Troms and Finnmark through to Finnish Lappi and Oulu. State enterprise has naturally taken precedence over private schemes:

witness the hydro-electric plants at Røsåga, Mo-i-Rana, and the Luleå iron works in North Sweden.[1] The division also has meaning equally for Denmark through Greenland (and formerly Iceland).

The division of the land cannot be appreciated without reference to the people. There was a time when the land was not sufficient to support the people, and the great emigration saga of fifty years ago, ending in a demand for a *National Union against Emigration*, was in part a sequel to this fact.[2] To-day the seventeen million people concentrating steadily in urban areas are not sufficient for the land. Table 1 summarizes the situation.

TABLE 1

COUNTRY	SURFACE AREA (*square miles*)	CULTIVATED AREA (*thousand acres*)	POPULATION (*thousands*)	DENSITY PER SQUARE MILE	CRUDE BIRTH RATE PER 1000
Denmark	17,000	6,739	4,281	250	17·9
Finland	130,000	6,833	4,032	30	23·0
Iceland	36,000	125[1]	144	3	27·0
Norway	121,000	2,005	3,277	27	18·5
Sweden	170,000	9,208	7,044	41	15·6
Fenno-Scandi-navia	474,000	24,910	18,778	39	20·4

[1] No cultivated area is returned by the Icelandic Ministry of Agriculture. This figure consists of 122,500 acres of "manured grassland" and 2500 acres of garden.

Denmark apart, the Scandinavian countries present some of the most thinly peopled areas in Europe (though the extent of their wasteland must be remembered). Under-population is essentially a relative term; but both Sweden and Norway could probably support more people. Some economists argue that the intensified settlement occasioned by the loss of a tenth of its area to the U.S.S.R. may have a positive long-term effect for Finland.[3] Birth rates also differ in the Northern Coun-

[1] Cf. *Norrlandskommittens betänkande* (1949) and North Norway Committee for Reconstruction. Among geographers who have sought to place the north in its true perspective are W. William-Olsen, *Norrland* (Stockholm, 1933), and I. Hustich in his work on Finnish Lapland. *Ymer*, 3, 4, 1942, is devoted to papers on Norrland.

[2] *Cf.* H. Nelson, *The Swedes and Swedish Settlement in North America* (Lund, 1943); Ingrid Semmingsen, *Veien mot vest* (Oslo, 1950); T. Blegen, *Norwegian Migrations* (Northfield, 1931–40); G. Sundbärg, *Emigrations utredningen betänkande* (Stockholm, 1913); and J. H. Kolehmainen, *Haven in the Woods* (Madison, 1951).

[3] Directly relevant are *Migration from Europe* (Geneva, 1951), S. S. Nilson, "Immigrants for Norway," in *The Norseman*, vol. xi, 5 (1953), and also the interesting contribution by J. E. Rosberg, "Tankar om huru många invånare Finland kunde nära," in *Terra* (1923), pp. 102–124.

tries. Finland has a steadily increasing population; while recommendations for arresting population decline were the central theme of Sweden's

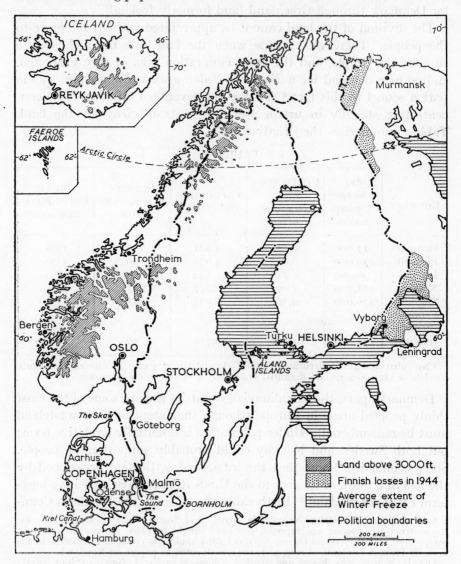

FIG. 1. THE FENNO-SCANDINAVIAN SETTING

Population Commission which reported in 1935. Indeed, some of the most informative demographic literature has come from Sweden— Gunnar and Alva Myrdal, for example, continue a tradition which began with the first modern census of *Tabellverket* over two centuries ago. The Scandinavian countries have ethnographic identity; while Finland's long association with Sweden has reduced the difference of a distinctive racial origin. Thirty-one thousand Lapps, two-thirds in Norway, maintain their identity and are among the world's protected minorities.[4] Fig. 1 presents the Scandinavian setting.

Theme and Implications

While Scandinavia and Finland have had many able geographers, political geographers have been rare. These cannot, however, be dismissed. One theme may be found in the works of the most exceptional of them—Rudolf Kjellén (1864–1922),[5] professor of political science, instructor and examiner in geography at the University of Göteborg. His lectures from 1899, printed the following year as *Inledning till Sveriges geografi*, belonged to the borderlands of geography and international affairs and had a strongly determinist flavour. Marrying geography and politics, Kjellén invented the term *Geopolitik*—an unconsidered trifle in Sweden rapidly seized upon elsewhere. His books, which began with *Stormakterna* (Stockholm, 1911–13),[6] analysed the great continental and maritime powers which ringed the Scandinavian world. Atlantic Scandinavia (Denmark and Norway, with their outlands) was most responsive to maritime power; Baltic Scandinavia (Sweden and Finland) reacted most strongly to continental power. Maritime power tended to assert itself commercially; continental power, militarily. The pressure of Britain, Germany, and Russia tended to neutralize themselves across Scandinavia: their "planetary struggles" produced an equilibrium in which Scandinavia contrived to exist. Kjellén was concerned with location, other aspects of which must be recalled. First, the area has lain aside from the main stream of European movement. Next, the winter freeze obstructs nearly a third of the Swedish coast and two-thirds of the Finnish coast for several months,[7] while even

[4] The best general study is B. Collinder, *The Lapps* (Princeton University Press, 1949; Oxford University Press, 1950); *cf.* also on Finnish Lapps, K. Nikula, *Fennia*, 36, 3 (Helsinki, 1953) (in English); on Norwegian Lapps, G. Sjessing, *Changing Lapps* (Royal Anthropological Institute, London, 1954).

[5] There is a useful account of his work by E. Thermanius, "Geopolitics and Political Geography," in *Baltic and Scandinavian Countries*, iv, 2 (Torun, 1938), pp. 165–173.

[6] Translated, in more senses than one, and published by K. Haushofer as *Die Grossmächte vor und nach dem Weltkriege* (Leipzig, 1930), with eighty diagrams.

[7] Cf. *Ice Atlas of the Northern Hemisphere* (U.S. Navy Department, Washington, 1946), which incorporates the evidence of expert Swedish and Finnish studies and includes a full bibliography.

during open water the uncharted skerries offer only a dangerous passage. Third, the area has been traditional famine country [8]— unattractive to the outsider. Nor has physical geography eased communication.

While, to-day, it is the balance between continental and maritime power which matters for Scandinavia, in the past it was the fate of continental and maritime countries which was held in the balance by the north. The great northern Powers, as seen in Anders Bure's seventeenth-century baroque maps, are best described as twin States— Denmark-Norway and Sweden-Finland. Yet, although 300 years ago Sweden's population was a full quarter that of Great Britain, deficiencies were foreshadowed. Mercenaries were required to conduct the Vasan and Adolphan campaigns—the names of descendants of Scottish soldiery and merchants fill pages in the telephone directories of modern Sweden. Sweden may have had a supply base adequate for the needs of empire; but it lacked men to maintain such an extensive territory.

Atlantic Norway retains the vestiges of its imperial North Sea "outlands." The adjustment of political boundaries within Scandinavia by the Treaty of Kiel (January 14, 1814) broke the association of Denmark and Norway formed in 1490. Denmark retained (by Art. 4) Greenland, Iceland, and the Faeroes, [9] while independent Norway sought and gained a decision from the International Court at The Hague over the east coast of Greenland (1931–32). Norway's right to the Spitsbergen archipelago (renamed collectively Svalbard)[10] was accorded by twelve Powers in 1920 and by the U.S.S.R. in 1924. Jan Mayen Island, which has a weather station, was acquired in 1929. In the Antarctic, Bouvet Island (1927), Peter I Island (1931), and a sector of the mainland (Queen Maud Land) are legacies from whaling.

During the Renaissance, Denmark (with Norway) aspired to a tropical empire and thereafter clung to its fragments tenaciously. The five fortresses on the Guinea coast were ceded to Britain by the London Convention of August 17, 1850; Tranquebar on the Coromandel coast and Serampore in Bengal were sold (February 22, 1845) to "the Honorable East India Company." The Virgin Islands, outermost of the

[8] W. R. Mead, "The Conquest of Finland," in *The Norseman*, 9, i and ii (1951).

[9] The best study in English is K. Williamson, *The Atlantic Islands* (Collins, London, 1948). The affairs of Greenland are most fully treated in *Grønlandskommissionens Betaenkning* (six vols.; Copenhagen, 1950).

[10] Scientific publications concerning the area are published regularly in *Skrifter om Svalbard og Ishavet* (Oslo), and *Meddelelser om Grønland* (Copenhagen). *Cf.* also *Polar Record*, 6, 44 (1952).

Caribbean archipelagos, were sold after nearly 300 years to the U.S.A. (August 4, 1916). A recent superb publication (*Vore gamle Tropekolonier* (Copenhagen, 1952)) bespeaks a nostalgia for tropical possessions. Swedish feeling for the past is differently oriented: expansion has been mostly trans-Baltic. This lure of the opposite coast preceded Swedish political expansion. Dark Age finds from the Baltic States attest it, while the Novgorod Chronicles (1014–1417)[11] attribute the foundations of proto-Russia to Swedish *Varangians*. There was no stronger latter-day *Varangian* than Sven Hedin (1865–1952), who published more than a score of volumes on his Eurasian wanderings. Attraction is coupled with fear: *Faran från östen* (the danger from the east) is a phrase encountered in many of the recent historico-political texts of Sweden.[12] Concern over the continental front has reduced Sweden's interest in overseas possession. The colony on the Delaware was absorbed by Dutch and British, while diminutive St Barthelmey lingered in the West Indies until 1877. As "compensation" for the attachment of the Grand Duchy of Finland to Russia in 1809, Norway was united to Sweden in a dual monarchy in 1814. The three younger members of the northern countries have all acquired independence in the present century—Norway (October 20, 1905), Finland (December 6, 1917), Iceland (June 17, 1944).

Matters of Strategy

The Scandinavian countries have locational importance for continental power in relation to maritime power as also for maritime power in its dealings with continental. With this in mind, three points may be considered. First, each country, possessing a different geographical character, has a different capacity to resist interference. Second, characteristics of location must not obscure those of resources. Third, some locations within the frame will be more significant than others, and four are isolated for detailed treatment under the heading—"the problem of the narrows."

Assessment by Country. Of the five northern countries, *Denmark* is the most continental. It is territorially the smallest, and the most

[11] Camden series, vol. xxv (London, 1914).
[12] A useful general review of Swedo-Russian relations is Ture Nerman, *Svensk och Ryss* (Stockholm, 1946), and an interesting historical publication is L. Maury, *Le Nationalisme suédois et la guerre 1914–18* (Paris, 1918).

discontinuous, has 4600 miles of open coastline and few natural topographical lines of defence. Its historical boundary—the Danevirke—is
an artificial earthwork which now lies deep in German territory. The
essential communications which bind together its parts, like the Little
Belt Bridge and Laaland Bridge (second longest in the world) are
vulnerable lines. The most isolated territory is Bornholm, seven hours
by packet-boat from the capital. In 1944 it was surrendered by a
German garrison to Soviet forces and eventually returned to Denmark.
The population shows a disproportionate concentration in Copenhagen
(one quarter).

In war and peace, *Norway* is beset by the difficulty of communication.
By sea, express coastal steamers take a week to go from South Norway
to Varanger Fiord. Though the journey has been speeded by diesel
train to Lönsdal and bus thereafter, it is still four days' journey by the
quickest land route from Oslo to the Russian border. Given good
weather, hydroplanes cover the distance in twenty-four hours. The
deeply dissected cul-de-sacs of Norway's western fiords and eastern
valleys prohibit communication between many of the lowland areas.
Waterways can be negotiated only by slow-moving ferry: bridging is
frequently impossible. Bridges and wharves were the first structures to
be rebuilt in north Norway after the war. Where there are fell highways
snow frequently closes them seasonally or intermittently. To defend
Norway against a well-planned sea-borne assault is therefore almost
impossible, though to subject a country with such a complex littoral
and such uncontrollable fells is equally difficult.[13] Norway's urban
centres are also exposed, as their effective subjugation by Germany in
1940 showed. The detachment of Troms and Finnmark and their
adjacency to the Murmansk coast have long caused speculation about
Soviet aims.

Finland, the least insular of the group, has, however, a land frontier
which has been effectively described as "geographically demilitarized"
—with rock, swamp, and lake opposing any large-scale modern military
campaign. Finland is most exposed in winter, when frozen coastal and
interior waterways open routes of swift movement. Olaus Magnus, first
great geographer of the north, has pertinent sixteenth-century remarks
on winter warfare; while the experience of the Finnish Winter War

---

[13] *Cf.* David Howarth, *The Shetland Bus* (Nelson, London, 1951). The difficulty of
communications, for invader and defender alike, comes out clearly in T. W. Derry, *The
Campaign in Norway* (H.M.S.O., 1952).

(November 1939–March 1940) provides more recent evidence.[14] Unlike the Scandinavian countries, Finland has suffered the greatest fluidity of boundaries.

Iceland, a third as big as Great Britain, lies 500 miles from the nearest part of the Norwegian coast and nearly 950 miles from Copenhagen. The island has a number of bus services (mostly operated seasonally), but lacks railways. Its position in relation to North Atlantic air and sea routes gives it significance. Nineteenth-century stagnation has been succeeded by twentieth-century renaissance.[15] It should not be overlooked that the current phase of domestic prosperity is attributed in geographical quarters at least as much to physical as to strategic change. Profuse and reliable evidence on the positive effects of long-term climatic improvement has been put forward.[16]

Sweden has the best communications of the Scandinavian States. North–south axial rail routes bind together a country which from Malmö to the Three States cairn is as far as from Malmö to Rome. The electrified coastal route, which brings Stockholm to within a day's journey of Lapland, contrasts with the slow *Inlandsbanan* (1904) of the piedmont. *Inlandsbanan*[17] not only gives access to the backwoods; it duplicates the coastal route. Sweden has, of course, for nearly 150 years sought to detach itself from Baltic entanglements and Atlantic commitments; but it cannot ignore the re-adjustment of Soviet boundaries in the Baltic or the twelve-mile extension of Soviet territorial waters, which eliminates old fishing grounds.

Assessment by Resources. Matters of strategy are inseparable from economics. The Northern Countries' reservoir of resources does not make for self-sufficiency, but it does provide a rich pool from which a surplus is available for exchange. This reservoir must attract extra-Scandinavian attention. In 1745 Jonas Ahlströmer pointed out that Great Britain had such an interest in Sweden's mineral resources that unless the Swedes were careful they would find themselves with nothing

---

[14] *Compendious History of the Goths, Visigoths, and other Northern Nations* (London, 1656), and *cf.* the strategic summary translated by B. Collinder, *Försvaret om Finland* (Stockholm, 1940).

[15] V. Stefansson, *Iceland* (New York, 1939). The most up-to-date statement is Th. Krabbe, *Island og dets tekniske Udvikling* (Copenhagen, 1946). A range of historical and contemporary maps are bound in the single volume *Islands Kortlaegning* (Copenhagen, 1944).

[16] S. Thorarinsson, in papers to *Museum of Natural History Publications* (Reykjavik) and *Ymer* (Stockholm).

[17] *Statens järnvägar, 1856–1906*, v, IV (Stockholm).

left but the "black hands of smiths." In the meantime the form and centre of gravity of the iron industry have changed. Two hundred years ago, with superior charcoal-smelted steels and the oldest chartered copper company in the world, Central Sweden was a primary centre of European supply. To-day the use of phosphoric ores, together with rail construction (culminating in the Ofoten line), have enabled exploita- tion of the iron mountains of Kiruna and its neighbourhood.[18] Five- sixths of Sweden's high-quality iron ore (*i.e.*, 60 per cent. ore content) derives from Norrland. About eleven million tons move annually by way of the open, tidal water of Narvik port or the seasonally closed, non-tidal port of Luleå. Two-thirds (8,600,000 tons, 1952) of the exports use the Narvik funnel to Great Britain, Belgium, Germany, and the U.S.A.; one third (4,500,000 tons, 1952), by the Luleå funnel, principally to Germany. At the current rate of extraction estimated reserves are adequate for three hundred years.

Norway, too, has invested heavily in its mines. During the Danish era it was a source of military supply (*e.g.*, iron foundries at Moss, copper at Röros). To-day mining is less rewarding than in Sweden. Of greater ultimate significance than iron development in Dunderland and Kirkenes are the electro-chemical plants (*e.g.*, at Rjukan, Notodden Herøya) and the electro-metallurgical (*e.g.*, aluminium reducers at Årdal, Tyssedal, Høyanger in Sogn, and Sunndalsøra). Finland's metalliferous wealth is latent, although Outokumpu is the principal copper mine in Europe. An astute Finnish 'John Gabriel Borkman' once commented that "Finland's future lies not in farming or forestry but in mining." Kolosjoki, Petsamo's large nickel mine opened by Canadian Nickel Mond, was, however, lost to the U.S.S.R. by purchase, when it acquired the corridor in 1944.

Scandinavia lacks mineral fuels. There is no oil—save in the meagre shales of central Sweden. Skåne's annual production of 500,000 tons has disillusioned the coal hopes of Sweden's mid-nineteenth-century forecasters, while Svalbard's output from Norwegian mines of 400,000 tons per year partly meets the needs of the treeless coasts of Finnmark and Troms. Water-power resources compensate in part for these deficiencies, except in Finland and Denmark, where the former in time

---

[18] Output figures are summarized annually (in English) in *Bergshantering*, Sweden's Official Statistics. A useful map is P. Geijer, "Geological Map of the Iron-bearing Region" (Kiruna, etc.), in *Mineral Resources of the World* (New York, 1952), p. 52. Prob- ably the best and most accessible article is Lucile Carlson, "The Mining District of Kiruna Stad," in *Scientific Monthly*, 1952, lxxiv, 2, pp. 76–83.

of duress falls back on forest fuel and the latter on low-quality brown coal and peat.

Scandinavia's economic strength has more recently been supplemented by its forest products. At the time of the Crimean War British strategic interests in the Baltic hinged upon the uninterrupted provision of naval supplies. Single London companies were importing as much as 10,000 barrels of tar a year from Bothnian ports. To-day Finland and Sweden meet the needs of what a German economist called "wood- and paper-hungry Europe," so that the forester offers international exchange. In an ideal trading world Finland and much of Sweden and Norway would turn their attention more to silvicultural than agricultural matters; but in Sweden social policy and in Finland national security have forbidden this. It is asserted that Finland could not have escaped the second world war, since it was vital to get food from outside sources. To-day the domestic deficiency of roughly 300,000 tons of grain per year is met principally from the U.S.S.R.

While Baltic Scandinavia supplements farming with forestry, Atlantic Scandinavia complements farming with fishing. Denmark's fisheries are insignificant beside its highly developed and export-oriented agriculture; but Norway is the world's third greatest fishing country and is excessively jealous of its European rights. The litigious business of coastal fisheries has vexed Anglo-Norse and Anglo-Danish (now Icelandic) relations through the centuries. A recent British Ambassador to Norway once declared, complimentarily to Norway, that his position would be unnecessary but for fish; while the Ministry of Agriculture and Fisheries maintains an attaché in Atlantic Scandinavia. Since 1874 Norway and Sweden have claimed a four-mile (7·24 km.) fishery limit.[19] Largely on the score of its fisher-farmers,[20] a further extension of territorial sovereignty was internationally conceded to Norway by the High Court of Justice at The Hague in 1952. This award settled an Anglo-Norwegian dispute about fishing rights in the broad embayments between Norway's headlands.[21] Its practical effects can be clearly seen on topographical sheet 1 : 100,000 for coastal Tromsö and Nordland. Beyond this, a precedent is established for Iceland to practise a similar exclusion—especially in the great bight of Faxa Floi. Indeed,

[19] The evolution of Swedish territorial waters is told in detail (but without maps) in *Gränsen för Sveriges territorialvatten* (Utrikesdepartementet, Stockholm, 1930).
[20] The significance of this community is clearly evidenced cartographically in A. Somme, *Jordbrukets geografi i Norge* (Bergen, 1954), pp. 14–15.
[21] Summarized succinctly in Helge Givenholdt, *Den norsk-britiske Fiskerigrensetvisten* (Bergen, 1953).

a delicate problem is raised, because Britain, principal among nearly a dozen transgressors, is also a principal market for Icelandic fish exports.

Contrasting surpluses and deficiencies in the Scandinavian economies favour active trading, which, because of geographical configuration, is conducted mostly over sea routes. Each of the countries has accordingly built up a mercantile marine. In Norway, which with more than six million gross registered tons has the world's third merchant fleet, specialization has accompanied expansion. During the eighteenth-century wars Britain turned to Norway for supplementary commercial shipping; in the mid-nineteenth century it relaxed its Navigation Acts; and in this century the pattern of two hundred years ago has been repeated.

The flow of trade shows remarkable similarities in the five northern countries. All are dominantly European traders; all buy and sell in much the same markets (especially the British); for each the market of purchase largely coincides with the market of sale. Common commercial action *vis-à-vis* their international markets has in many ways been more important than attempts to promote inter-Scandinavian exchange. In this century uncertainties have encouraged movements towards self-sufficiency; but, with the possible exception of Sweden, which also distinguishes itself in the Northern Countries on industrial grounds, none of the Scandinavian States can aspire to follow the advice of Peer Gynt's troll: "Be sufficient unto thyself." Economic renaissance for Scandinavia has brought with it the problem of international dependence.

The Political Geography of the Narrows

Within the 'northern' setting two sea and two land narrows continually engage political attention. The sea narrows are the Danish Sound and the Aland Sea; the land narrows are the Jutish isthmus and the Karelian isthmus. The latter are not only of strategic consequence in themselves; they are also territories of ethnographic transition, and it is almost impossible to separate the two facts.

The Sea Narrows

The Sound. Denmark commands the Baltic entrances, of which the chief is the Øresund. For more than 500 years it capitalized this three-mile-wide, deep-water strait between Elsinore and Helsingborg—continuing even after the loss of the Skånian shore to Sweden in 1656. Toll was collected at "Hamlet's Castle," from which gunshot could intercept men-of-war and merchantmen who preferred not to risk the shifting channels and beaconless waters of the Great and Little Belts. Returns went to the personal exchequer of the Danish king.[22] Denmark's naval power, destroyed by British action during the Napoleonic Wars, never fully recovered. Baltic naval activity during the Crimean War made it clear that Danish control was of a token nature. By international agreement of all parties with a Baltic interest, the dues were rescinded and amortized on March 14, 1857.[23] The Baltic entrance, however, continued to be of interest. Sweden had sought in some measure to by-pass the Sound by its modest Göta Canal (1832), though this picturesque historical folly never achieved commercial significance.[24] Germany created a new entrance to the Baltic in the Kiel Canal (1896). This was in part a manœuvre to give German naval craft independent access to the North Sea, but it also made a certain contribution to maritime security. Shipping losses and strandings were unbelievably great on the Skaw route even seventy years ago.[25] Insurance rates favoured the Kiel route independently of sea-mile economies. In the White Sea Canal (1933) the U.S.S.R. also possesses a private entrance, though it is of use for only half of the year.

Åland and its Sea. The Åland islands, a "kingdom of 6554 islands," was accepted as an autonomous unit within the republic of Finland in 1921.[26] Its population (1951) totals 22,500; its area, 730 sq. m. This rocky, low-lying, tree-covered, and most maritime part of Finland has been contrastingly described by North Bothnians as a "Garden of the Hesperides" and by Mediterranean travellers (unwise enough to travel in winter) as "An Arctic Hades." On physical grounds, a case can be

[22] And the records of these dues, telling of tonnage moved and cargoes carried, are among the most enlightening documents on North European economic strategy. *Cf.* N. Bang, *Tabeller over Skibsfart og Varetransport gennem Øresund, 1661–1783*, etc. (Copenhagen, 1930–45).
[23] C. M. Hill, *The Danish Sound Dues and the Command of the Baltic* (Durham, North Carolina, 1925).
[24] *Cf.* S. E. Bring, *Göta Kanals historia* (Uppsala, 1922–30).
[25] Demonstrated in the striking map accompanying G. Beseke, *Der Nord-Ostsee Kanal* (Kiel, 1893).
[26] Probably the most concise and rounded treatment is A. J. Grüssner, "Die Åland Inseln im Ostseeraum," in *Deutsche Geographische Blätter* (Bremen, 1937). R. Hausen, *Bibliografi öfver Åland* (Helsingfors, 1923), is an index to the author's collection in Åbo Academy Library: supplementary to it is A. L. Lindstedt, *Forteckning över literatur rörande Åland* (Stockholm, 1940).

made for its adherence to either Sweden or Finland. Save for Skiftet, a submarine rut as nicely defined on eighteenth-century maps as on current naval charts, there is skerry continuity for fifty miles across a shallow sea with peninsular Finland. Navigation routes are, however, tortuous and in winter kept open only with the aid of ice-breakers. To the west is the contrasting island-free Åland Sea, dropping to depths of 1500 ft. and detaching the archipelago from the coast of Uppland. The twenty-five-mile strait, however, is navigationally plain-sailing and freezes only one winter in ten. Mariehamn, chief port and administrative centre of the *län* (population 3500), lies equidistantly between Turku and Stockholm. Åland Mainland—the principal island —has enough level land for an airport, which is in daily communication with Sweden and Finland.

The Åland archipelago controls the Bothnian sea. Already, by the late eighteenth century, this sea was becoming important for Western Europe's naval supplies. Though the character of supply has changed, Bothnian shores still supply significant raw materials and the Åland narrows retain their importance. Swedish and Finnish documents, representing the extreme points of view, have mobilized other arguments. Thus, for Finland, Åland threatens the local approaches to Turku and Hangö (the essential winter ports), Rauma and Pori, which in turn give access to the south Finnish rail junctions of Toijala and Hyvinkää. For Sweden, Åland ownership carries with it a threat to the Stockholm area.

Swedish control of the Åland Islands ended on September 17, 1809, when after six months resistance to the Russians the Ålanders became a part of the Grand Duchy of Finland. Although it established strong points in Reval (Tallinn) and Suomenlinna, Imperial Russia was clearly anxious to push them westward towards Dagö, Ösel, and Åland.[27] It was argued that Russia had no excuse for the construction of Bomarsund fortress in the 1830's, having no mercantile marine to defend. The British and French fleets effectively destroyed its fortifications in August 1854, and the islands were subsequently demilitarized and neutralized by the Treaty of Paris, 1856.[28] After lengthy deliberations in the League of Nations the islands were accorded regional autonomy within Finland on Midsummer Day, 1921;[29] while the London Conven-

[27] J. O. Soderhjelm, *Démilitarisation et neutralisation des Iles d'Åland, 1856 et 1921* (Helsingfors, 1928).
[28] See *The Norseman, op. cit.*, IX, 1, 2, 1951.
[29] A. Tollet and J. Uggla, *Lagskiftningen angående självstyrelse för Åland* (Helsingfors, 1930).

tion of October 20, 1921, provided for renewed demilitarization and
neutralization (including freedom from Finnish military service).

In times of territorial dispute, stones have tongues and the ghosts of
geographers past live in the briefs of international lawyers. To detach
Åland from Finland would be "Une partage arbitraire de terres reliées
par la nature elle-même," declared the Finns. Eighteenth-century
geographers like Djurberg and Tuneld were summoned to testify on
either side, and the old jingle of Johannes Messenius:

> Ålanders with Sweden's land
> Have always most preferred to stand,

was brought in to underline the "unanimity, constancy, and spon-
taniety" of the Åland wish for Swedish union. It is curious that the
League of Nations, pledged to national self-determination, should give
a decision diametrically opposed to the 95 per cent. pro-Swedish vote
in the Åland plebiscite.[30] It did not solve the problem, and the second
world war has heightened Åland dissatisfaction with the division.[31] An
imposing maritime museum dominates Mariehamn's western harbour
to symbolize Åland's marriage with the sea. War meant losses of
shipping as well as of trade (save, perhaps, smuggling, "the hereditary
sin of the coast" as Zachris Topelius put it). The reduction of the
celebrated Ericsson sailing fleet illustrates this. Ålanders have not
given up hope of aspiring like the Faroese to independence in a pigmy
State or, alternatively, of associating with a richer Sweden. But to
pare Finland's south-western fringes, following the amputation of its
south-eastern marchlands, would mean a serious loss in prestige even if
territory and population were reduced but little.

The Isthmian Narrows

Slesvig-Holstein. Scandinavia has nowhere experienced the pressure
of continental power more incisively than in the Jutish isthmus. Two
issues have been involved: three phases are detectable. The two issues

---

[30] The principal documents appertaining to the Swedish case are given in *Ålands
frågan inför Nationernas Förbund* (Utrikesdepartementet, Stockholm, I–III, 1920–21).
See also H. Tingsten, *The Debate on the Foreign Policy of Sweden* (Oxford University
Press, 1950), pp. 82–137, 242–277. Finnish documents are reproduced in *La Question
des Iles d'Åland: Documents diplomatiques publiées par le ministère des affaires étrangères
de Finlande* (Helsingfors, 1920).

[31] *Cf.* Finnish-Swedish negotiations in 1938–39, C. G. Mannerheim, *Minnen*, II, 75
et seq. (Stockholm, 1952).

are ethnographic and strategic. Ethnographically, Dane and German meet in the root of the peninsula (Frisian, too, on the western margins); strategically, the isthmus between Baltic and North Sea looks to Germany's second river (the Elbe) and first seaport (Hamburg). Historically, the territory has been Danish: in its early history Denmark's boundary lay along the line of the Eider river. Racially and linguistically, the zone of transition has been a broad one, with the distribution of German settlement established well within the historical Danish boundary. For a politically fragmented Germany such a distribution was of little consequence; Pan-Germanism saw in it an irredentism.[32]

This marked the first phase of the problem. After a generation of friction a six-week war acquired for Prussia the duchies of Slesvig and Holstein with Lauenburg by the Treaty of Vienna (October 30, 1864). The boundary was shifted northward to a line "from Herteminde to midway between Manoe and Roemoe," thus reversing the position and creating a substantial Danish minority in the annexed German territory. There was but little migration as a result; though, within Denmark, domestic policy urged land reclamation in order "to make good the loss without." The annexation was regardless of popular wishes, though the ethnographic map as a document for political consideration was ready at hand. The claims of Denmark (by Mr Allen) and of Prussia (by Mr Geertz) are juxtaposed in a publication dated 1862, "showing the distribution of the popular idioms compared with the official arrangement for the public use of Danish and High German."[33] Such means of expression became of increasing significance as a policy of germanization was imposed (cf. the language decree of 1888). From this era dates Jessen's *Carte linguistique de Slesvig*,[34] which shows on a commune basis the number of Danish-speaking, bilingual, and German-speaking farmers.

The second phase reached a peak during the Versailles settlement, when revision in favour of the Danish minority was proposed. The debate centred on Slesvig only; Holstein's status was not questioned. The crux of the issue lay in the zone of mixed population between Viding and Bokings *herred* in the west and Flensburg fiord in the east. It is an interesting reflection on the ethnographical knowledge of the day that the *British Foreign Office Handbook* (H.M.S.O., London, 1920)

[32] The most comprehensive publications covering the issue are those of F. C. von Jessen, *Manuel historique de la question de Slesvig* (Copenhagen, 1906 and 1938).
[33] C. A. Gosch, *Denmark and Germany since 1815* (London, 1862).
[34] Jessen, *op. cit.*, p. 346.

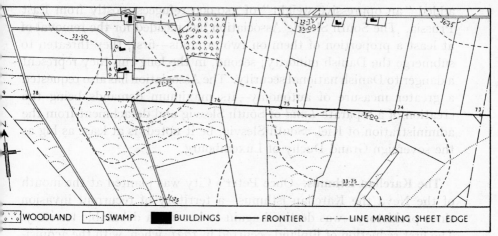

WOODLAND   SWAMP   **BUILDINGS**   ⸺ FRONTIER   ⸺ LINE MARKING SHEET EDGE

FIG. 2. A PORTION OF THE DANO-GERMAN BOUNDARY TO SHOW THE EFFECTS OF BOUNDARY-DRAWING ON THE FARMS OF SLESVIG

From *Carte de la frontière entre l'Allemagne et le Danemark établie par la Commission de Délimitation, juillet 1920–mai 1921.* 1:5000

and the Versailles *Travaux du Comité d'Études* (Paris, 1918–19), edited by Vidal de la Blache, both employed the linguistic outlines drawn up by F. H. I. Geertz in 1838. Ruling out the proposals of extremists, the solution clearly lay in a compromise line running through those towns (or most of them) which requested a plebiscite. The result for a sample tract is embodied in Fig. 2. The wisdom of Solomon could not have prevented a residual Danish element to the south or German element to the north of the forty-two-mile boundary. Systematic purchase of Danish-owned property exerted a pressure in the 1930's which was difficult to resist.

The third phase of the Slesvig question has a substantially different character. German defeat in 1945 aroused Danish minority aspirations in South Slesvig. The full aims of the resulting South Slesvig movement were partly subscribed to by Denmark and partly proscribed by the British military government. Denmark has not pressed for either a population or a boundary adjustment. The Danish-speaking population of Slesvig, totalling a little over 70,000, is mostly a rural population, whereas the German population in Denmark has been essentially an urban population.[35] To the 370,000 natives of South Slesvig has been

[35] A situation the consequences of which were summarized in R. Andersen, "Le Danemark et la minorité allemande de Slesvig du Nord," in *Le Nord* (1938), pp. 59–74. The contemporary issue is dealt with officially in *Aktstykker vedrørende det sydslesvigske Spørgsmal* (Copenhagen, 1950). The publication includes all of the British reports and documents.

added "an oppressive weight" of 350,000 refugees mostly from East Prussia. The South Slesvig Association has pleaded for the removal of at least a proportion of them on two grounds—first, they threaten to submerge the Danish minority; second, in the long run they represent a danger to Danish national security. The Association has also requested a greater measure of autonomy—its maximum demands being the creation of a separate *Land* of South Slesvig and detachment from the administration of Kiel. South Slesvig, be it noted, is at least as big as the sovereign Grand Duchy of Luxembourg.

The Karelian Isthmus. Once Peter's City was planted at the mouth of the Neva the Karelian isthmus—a territory of recurrent invasion since prehistory—was destined again to become a debatable territory. The first reduction of Finland occurred in 1721, when, with the acquisition of the isthmus, including its medieval fortress and bishopric of Viborg, Russian opinion proclaimed: "St Petersburg now has a pillow on which it can sleep soundly." But bolsters were needed too. By two subsequent steps—in 1743 and 1809—Russia advanced across the eastern wing of Sweden's empire to the Tornio-Muonio river line.

The contemporary dispute over Karelia dates from 1811, when "Gamla Finland" was reunited with the new Russian Grand Duchy and bounded in the south-west by a boundary between Terijoki and Metsäpirtti. Revisionist claims were pressed by such as N. N. Kovero in 1910 in "A lecture to the united nobility of the Russian Empire at St Petersburg." The following resolutions were put forward:

(a) the province of Viborg, if left in its present condition, with a frontier not more than twenty miles distant from the capital and not subjected to the supervision of the Russian authorities, is a menace to the political and strategic interests of the Empire,

(b) that the long-continued opposition to Russian imperial measures centres precisely in Viborg,

(c) the State can no longer tolerate at the gates of the capital an independently governed territory.

Such claims were repeated to the echo in the 1930's, culminating in the ultimatum presented by the U.S.S.R. to Finland in October 1939.[36]

Formerly, boundaries passed to and fro above the heads of people who accepted a change of sovereignty. In Eastern Finland this gave a

---

[36] The general outline of this situation is given by J. H. Wuorinen, *Finland and World War II* (New York, 1948). Proposal and counter-proposal for a peaceful solution are given with geographical precision in V. Tanner, *Finlands väg, 1939-40* (Helsingfors, 1950). *Cf.* also W. Kolarz, *Russia and her Colonies* (Philip, London, 1952), pp. 88–104.

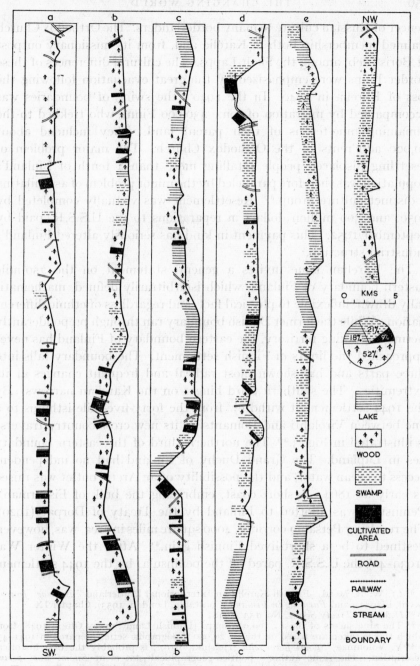

FIG. 3. THE CROSS-COUNTRY TRAVERSE OF THE NEW FINNISH BOUNDARY
THROUGH KARELIA FROM VIROLAHTI TO ILOMANTSI

veneer of Russian culture to many borderlanders. The Orthodox Church claimed membership both in Karelia and, from its missionary outpost at Boris Gleb, among the Skolt Lapps. The cultural differences of these border Finns were emphasized by the great evacuation following the loss of Karelia in 1940. In the 1940's the swing of boundaries was accompanied by migration of some 430,000 Finns, who trekked to the remaining nine-tenths of their parent land. They included about 70,000 adherents of the Orthodox Church. The major problem of resettling displaced people totalling more than a tenth of Finland's population was therefore paralleled by the minor problem of assimilating a distinct culture group.[37] Resettlement was virtually completed by 1950, and 300 million dollars in reparations to the U.S.S.R. paid by September 1952. This payment in kind has seriously altered Finland's industrial structure.

The Karelian issue invites a general statement on the 750-mile eastern boundary of Finland, which is arbitrarily defined, mathematically drawn, inflexible to physical fact, and regardless of ethnic differentiation. While the former Danish boundary ran through preponderantly German-speaking territory, the eastern boundary of Finland has never approached the limits of Finnish settlement. The boundary falls into three parts and has shown most radical and frequent changes at its extremities. The southern third hinges on the Karelian narrows. By the 1944 settlement it withdrew from the forty-five-mile isthmus to a line between Virolahti and Ilomantsi:[38] its new cross-country traverse is illustrated in Fig. 3.[39] The northern third of the eastern boundary lies in Lapland. The Grand Duchy of Finland had no independent access to ocean water, and the possibility of an Arctic outlet was raised as early as 1864. A short coast, embracing the bulk of Fisherman's Peninsula, was allotted to Finland by the Treaty of Dorpat (1920). The resulting Petsamo corridor, 4000 square miles in area, was, however, destined to be a short-lived Finnish gain.[40] After the Winter War (1939–40) the U.S.S.R. pared off the peninsula; by the 1944 settlement

[37] *Cf.* W. R. Mead "Finnish Karelia an International Borderland," in *Geog. Journ.*, cxviii, i (1952), and *Farming in Finland* (Constable, London, 1953), Chapter IX.
[38] *H.M.S.O. Treaty Series*, No. 153 (1948).
[39] The nine sheets of the 1 : 100,000 maps (Finnish Land Survey Office, 1948) from which this is taken are based on the 1 : 20,000 topographic series prepared in 1941–43.
[40] V. Voionmaa, *Suomi jäämereltä* (Helsinki, 1919), is probably the best historical description. The same author's politico-geographical statement *Suomi uusi asema* (Porvoo, 1919) contains one of the earliest maps projecting a Petsamo railway (p. 152). *Valtakunnan rajankäynti Petsamossa, v. 1921* (Helsinki, 1927) (English summary), discusses the field work involved in drawing the boundary.

it acquired the corridor. The northern boundary of Finland (with minor adjustments like the Jääniskoski and Niskakoski appendectomy of sixty-six square miles) has therefore resumed its nineteenth-century outline. The central third of the boundary has shown greatest stability; but the 1941 and 1944 revisions narrowed the waist of Finland between the head of the Gulf of Bothnia and the Gulf of Kandalaksha by the eastern halves of Salla and Kuusamo parishes (3000 square miles). In demanding Finnish construction of a railway line from the railhead of Kemijärvi to the boundary village of Kelloselkä, the U.S.S.R. has acquired virtual continuity of communication to Tornio.

Intra-Scandinavian Differences

Ethnographic Matters. Within the confines of 'Norden' there is only ethnographic friction between Finnish- and Scandinavian-speaking peoples, and this has manifested itself with different degrees of intensity in different areas. In the High North there is Finnish settlement in both Swedish and Norwegian territory. Most of Sweden's 30,000 Finns are in Norrbotten *län*, where they are old-established; recruitment by immigration remains substantial.[41] Finnish migration to Finnmark and Troms is a river-valley movement. Typical of its legacy are Finnish-speaking fisher-farmers, commonly called Kvens, found in the dales from Lyngen to Pasvik.[42] Historically, the migration has been encouraged by famine conditions in the home country. Formerly a Finnish newspaper, *Ruijan suomenkiellinenölehti*, was published in Vadsö (in Finnish, Vesisaari) and a Finnish service held monthly in its Lutheran Church. Finnish atlases have their own name for North Norway (Ruija), and chauvinists regarded it as a territory to be won—*e.g.*, map in *Aito-soumalainen* (Helsinki, June 24, 1933). Planned sixteenth- and seventeenth-century emigration to Central Sweden produced an area of Finnish ethnic differentiation in Värmland. Place-names and family names are all that remain to-day;[43] though certain atlases give erroneous

---

[41] *Cf.* Swedish Central Statistical Bureau, *Ut-och Invandring*, annual tables, and V. Voionmaa, *op. cit.*, sketch map, p. 203. The struggle is also outlined in E. Jutikkala, *Atlas of Finnish History*, Map 14.

[42] J. E. Rosberg, "Finnerna i Tromsö amt," in *Terra* (1915), pp. 219–236, and S. Pauluharju, *Ruijan suomalaisia* (Helsinki, 1928). The most definitive document, though dated, is probably "Official Statistics of Norway," in *Population*, vol. vii, Nr. 76.

[43] T. Wennerström, *Svenskarna i Finland och Estland* (Göteborg, 1931). . Finnskoga, in Norwegian Hedemark, also recalls a Finnish colony; *cf.* L. Ostberg, "A Norwegian Minority Problem in the 1820's," in *Norsk Geografisk Tidskrift* (1939 and earlier vols.).

emphasis to it (probably basing their evidence on the century-old maps of C. A. Gottlund).

Much more significant is the historical field of Swedish settlement in Finland—to-day found chiefly in Ostrobothnia, south-west Finland, and coastal Uusimaa. Finnish-Swedes, more correctly defined as Swedish-speaking Finns, for many Finnish-speaking families are of Swedish stock, account for 9 per cent. of the Finnish population. During the period of the Swedish Grand Duchy the language issue was not of consequence. Daniel Juslenius's first Finnish-Swedish dictionary dates from 1745; Jaako Juteini's first Finnish grammar from 1819. The association of Finnish language and national feeling was such that intellectual leaders like J. V. Snellman declared, "The Swedish language and nationality belong to a foreign nation." Finnish became an official language in the 1880's—complicating topographical maps and country signposts with dual place-names. Swedish-speaking Finns were split over such issues as the pressure of Russia grew. In 1906 alone, 16,000 Swedish-speaking families changed their names to Finnish forms as a patriotic demonstration against russification.[44] Such changes were calculated to disturb ethnographic tables in the Census returns. By the language law of June 1, 1922 (based on the Swiss Compromise Law of 1874), Finnish and Swedish have common rights.

The Swedish-speaking minority of Finland to-day, including that of Åland, totals 370,000. The position of the minority is weakened because of steady loss through inter-marriage with Finnish-speaking people and by a lower birth rate. Protective clauses in the constitution have aided its resistance to invasion by the army of displaced people. It is concentrated to-day in twenty-two parishes. The three main Swedish-speaking blocks are now detached from each other, and the process of contraction is seen by comparing the successive editions of the *Atlas of Finland* (1899, 1910, 1925).[45] The dichotomy makes for many social problems. An indirect effect has been to encourage emigration of Swedish-speaking people—for example, from Ostrobothnia to Vestrobothnia and the New World. The Swedish-speaking Ostrobothnian, his land already intensely sub-divided, is loath to migrate to the workshops

[44] J. H. Wuorinen, *Nationalism in Modern Finland* (New York, 1931).
[45] The topic offers great opportunities for ethnological field work. The South Finland student society in the University of Helsinki undertook farm-by-farm studies half a century ago—e.g., F. W. Klingstedt, *Statistiska undersökningar av språk förhållandena i Nylands län åren 1895-1905* (Helsingfors, 1909); cf. also G. Modeen, "Språk forhållanderna i det svenska Finland år 1920," in *Fennia*, 47, 1. A contemporary investigator is M. Kloverkorn, University of Bonn.

of south-west Finland among people who speak a different tongue. " Yksi mieli, kaksi kieli" (One mind, two tongues) is more trite than true as a summary of Finland's domestic position.

Boundary Settlements. There was a time when Sweden and Denmark warred over their boundaries. But since Sweden achieved its objective of "peninsular completeness" with the acquisition of Jämtland and Härjedalen (1645), Bohuslän and Halland, Skåne and Blekinge (1653), its national boundaries have been peaceably accepted. Russia dictated the last intra-Scandinavian boundary along river lines in the High North in 1810. In 1825–26 a Swedish-Norwegian boundary commission set about delimiting the 1661 boundary of Bohuslän and the boldly limned 1751 fell boundary found in the manuscript maps of Riksarkivet, Oslo. A nominal twenty-five to forty-five foot boundary zone in the north was to be complemented by a three-mile neutral zone in the south (since widened and extended to 61° N.).[46] The Russo-Norwegian boundary, paced and surveyed in 1829, was later accepted by the Republic of Finland. Since Finland's loss of the Petsamo area Russia again marches for seventy-five miles beside Norway along the Pasvik river. By the boundary agreement of 1947 the 1829 line was reaffirmed with slight adjustments in its southern reaches.[47]

Boundaries in the High North have not been drawn regardless of human geography. The Lapps have paid scant regard to international boundaries: their movements, responsive to reindeer migration, cut across political boundaries. On February 5, 1919, Norway and Sweden defined their especial status in a series of international agreements. Since the adherence of Finland, a common Lapp border document has been issued. This Arctic condominium has never been joined by the U.S.S.R.: a reindeer seeking pasturage east of the Scandinavian boundary is a lost reindeer.

[46] The succession of treaties are reprinted in the official series *Sveriges traktater*, published intermittently in Stockholm. R. Kjellén, "Studier ofver Sveriges politiska gränser," in *Ymer* (1899), pp. 283–331, lists where many relevant manuscripts may be found.
[47] On the actual field problems *cf.* K. Gleditsch, "Rivers as international boundaries," in *Nordisk Tidsskrift for International Ret*, 22, 1 (1952) (Copenhagen). A useful statement with sketch maps of the area is T. Lloyd, *The Norwegian-Soviet Boundary* (Hanover, N.H., 1954).

The Idea of Fenno-Scandinavian Unity

Differing locations and disparate resources give to the Scandinavian countries distinct characters. Where historical associations have existed (Denmark–Iceland, Norway–Sweden, even Sweden–Finland) the particularism of the parts has been pleaded as basis for separation. Since separation, the group has periodically paid lip-service to federation. The differences between the separate countries are represented as being no greater than the differences within them. The federal solution has always been a chimera in the North. At the higher level (conclave of kings or council of foreign ministers) there is seen a pendulum swing of policy between two poles. In time of adversity, be it physical such as famine or strategic such as war, the States draw together: in times of stability the search for political union relaxes. *In extremis* the group splits geographically—Denmark, Norway, and Iceland falling into the Atlantic camp, Sweden and Finland into the Middle European.

Proposals for the geographical identification of a Scandinavian federal unit vary widely. When continental power relaxed in the Baltic arena in the 1920's Sten de Geer drew lines of distinction between "das geologische Fennoskandia" and "das geographische Baltoskandia."[48] The circle of the Baltic States, which reflected the maximum extent of Scandinavian influence to the east, was balanced against the ethnological core of Scandinavia proper. In the post-war period a noticeable contraction of the area of discussion has occurred. 'Danosve,' proposed as a northern equivalent to Benelux, omits Finland. Yet, if restraint and frustration characterize high-level schemes, at lower levels a web of integration has been woven which is unparalleled among any other group of sovereign States. It is seen in the functional unity of industrialists and trade unionists, farmers and foresters, academic and professional people. The integration ignores political boundaries. Perhaps, in the end, it is co-operation and not federation which will dominate the Scandinavian world. Group co-operation is the sustaining force which persists when greater propelling forces lose their impulse.

[48] *Geografiska Annaler*, 1928. *Cf.* also T. Jorgenson, *Norway's Relation to Scandinavian Unionism* (Minneapolis, 1935), and J. Henning-Friis, *Scandinavia between East and West* (Ithaca, 1950).

FURTHER READING

Additional to those mentioned in footnotes, the following publications are recommended:

ROYAL INSTITUTE OF INTERNATIONAL AFFAIRS, *Scandinavian States and Finland* (London, 1951).
FINNISH GEOGRAPHICAL SOCIETY, *Handbook of Finnish Geography* (Helsinki, 1952).
FEDERATION OF SWEDISH INDUSTRIES, *Industry in Sweden* (Stockholm, 1953).
ADAMSON, O. J., *Industries of Norway* (Oslo, 1952).
Suomen teollidustus (Finnish Industry) (Helsinki, 1951).
JUTIKKALA, E., *Atlas of Finnish History* (Helsinki, 1949).
SWEDISH GEOGRAPHICAL SOCIETY, *Atlas of Sweden* (1953–   ).
DANISH GEOGRAPHICAL SOCIETY, *Atlas of Denmark* (Copenhagen, 1950–   ).
Agricultural Atlas of Sweden (Stockholm, 1952).
SØMME, A., *Atlas of Norwegian Agriculture* (Bergen, 1950).

The geographical societies of all the northern countries publish a substantial amount of their material in English. A lively German interest in Scandinavian and Finnish geography was shown at the University of Greifswald between the wars when, under the stimulus of Professor G. Braun, many monographs and pamphlets were published.

G

CHAPTER VI

The Mediterranean:
Some Internal Problems

W. GORDON EAST

IN Chapter VII the Mediterranean region will be looked at from outside and its place in world politics and strategy broadly assessed. In this chapter the region is looked at from within, and attention is turned to some of its parts and to the geographical aspect of the special political problems which they present. Many of these local problems—demographic pressure in Italy, nationalist aspirations in French North Africa, the prospects for Israel and for 'Enosis' in Cyprus, to cite some outstanding examples—have more than local implications: success or failure in dealing with them must inevitably react on the outer world.

The Mediterranean region long held the lead in the cultural and political life of the Western world, but after losing this much of its area fell into political dependence on States of Western Europe. It lost, too, the progressiveness which once characterized its economy, and it retains many traditional cultural features slow to change. Yet it has changed much during the last hundred years. And the second world war, of which it was an important theatre, clearly brought changes of various kinds and stimulated currents of change.

The Mediterranean Environment

The Mediterranean 'region' can be variously delimited by geographers, yet there can be little doubt of its actuality. Many factors of physical and biogeography combine to mark off a Mediterranean environment different and somewhat detached from those of surrounding lands in Europe, Asia, and Africa. The Mediterranean Sea itself,

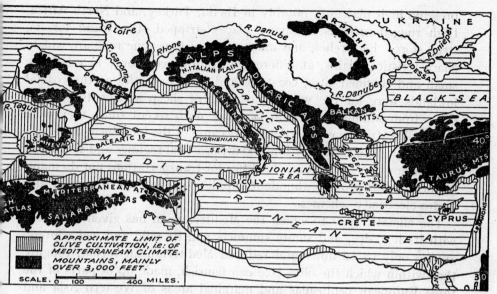

FIG. 1. THE MEDITERRANEAN SEA WITH ITS MOUNTAINOUS GIRDLE

From "Mediterranean Problems," by W. G. East. By courtesy of Messrs Thomas Nelson and Sons, Ltd

which provides means of intercourse, contributes most to the individuality of the Mediterranean environment. Although this sea dips southward in its eastern basin, the fact that it is elongated for some 2100 miles within a latitudinal zone makes for a wide measure of uniformity in the climate of its coastlands. The sea itself is unequally divided into an eastern and western basin, which merge in the Sicilian strait. These two basins in turn are made up of a number of semi-enclosed seas: in the western lie the Tyrrhenian and Ligurian seas, in the eastern the Adriatic, Ionian, Ægean, and Marmora, the last of which is part of the confined waters which link the Mediterranean with the Black Sea. Many island groups, especially in the eastern basin, emphasize the lake-like character of the Mediterranean, as they epitomize much of its geological and human history.

The lands around the sea show marked similarities and contrasts (Fig. 1). Those on its northern flank—Iberia, Italy, the Balkans, Greece, and Asia Minor—contrast in their peninsular form with the Levant coastlands of Syria, Lebanon, and Israel, and with those of Egypt and North Africa, where only Cyrenaica and Tunisia project northward on either side of the broad Great Syrtis Bay. Much the greater part of the Mediterranean landscape is truly mountainous or presents high plateaux, notably in Iberia, Turkey, and North Africa. High rugged surfaces, in many places stripped of soil and forests, steep slopes, high relief, and much exposed limestone rock are widely characteristic. Plains, at different altitudes, occur only in relatively small and confined sites, coastally and inland. Useful as the coastal lowlands were for the winter pasturing of sheep and goats brought down from summer mountain pastures, until recent times they were not wholly attractive to settlement because of the incidence of malaria and piracy. The rivers, with markedly seasonal regimes and flowing in immature valleys, afford few facilities for transportation; nor do many of their basins provide abundant supplies of water for irrigation and hydro-electricity schemes.

The climatic type to which the Mediterranean has given its name, with its hot, dry, and sunny summers and its mild and wet winters, applies only to an inner and reduced Mediterranean region, roughly that within which the olive-tree can flourish, made up of parts of the three European peninsulas and marginal areas of Western Asia and Northern Africa. The Mediterranean region thus narrowly defined presents many common features of vegetation, soils, agricultural and pastoral husbandry, maritime activity, and even the ethnic type of its peoples. But no less significant is the larger Mediterranean region conceived broadly on grounds of physical and biogeography. As such, the bounds of the Mediterranean region are extended to the outer ranges of the Atlas mountain system of North Africa, to the Pyrenees, Alps, Dinaric Alps, and Balkan mountains in Europe, and to the Anatolian plateau of Asia Minor, the Lebanon mountains, and the highlands of Jordan in South-west Asia. This region, oriented towards the sea, along which passes much the greater part of its trade, is enclosed by lands with contrasting climates and vegetations: the hot deserts of Africa and Arabia, the deciduous forests of Western and Central Europe, and the steppe grasslands of the lower Danubian basin, South Russia, and Anatolia. And while the mountains, steppes, and deserts which girdle this Mediterranean region continue to lose their former character as obstacles to passage, especially since the advent of aeroplanes and motor vehicles, they still serve to mark off a peculiar inter-continental Mediterranean world.

The Mediterranean lands suffer many natural disadvantages for agriculture, yet this is in fact the main basis of their economy, providing employment for at least half of the male workers (Table 1). The climate,

TABLE 1

COUNTRY	AREA (square miles)	POPULATION (millions) 1952	ACTIVE MALES IN AGRICULTURE (per cent.) 1950	ARABLE AREA[1] (square miles)	POPULATION PER SQUARE MILE OF ARABLE LAND
Italy	119,764	47·1	48	62,800	750
South Italy	48,000	17·6	50	24,200	730
Greece	50,147	7·8	48	11,190	700
Portugal	35,490	8·5	54	12,100	700
Spain	196,607	28·3	53	61,300	470
Turkey	296,432	22·0	67	68,750	320

[1] Since these figures include arable land in fallow, they are substantially in excess of the area which is cropped annually. These figures do not include areas devoted to arboriculture.

while congenial to live in, presents many difficulties. The summers are very sunny, but very dry; the rainfall is often inadequate, very unequal from one year to another, and capricious seasonally. Deep-rooted trees, like the olive, vine, and fig, are well adapted; 'dry farming' has to be resorted to in many areas; high yields are won, and citrous fruits are grown, only where irrigation can be employed. The scarcity of flat land and the qualities of the soil (mostly poor) set further limits to farming. In many parts of the region the arduous task of terracing of hill slopes has to be undertaken. And generally peasant agriculture is remarkably intensive—so much depends on unremitting human toil. Except in a few areas where conditions have made possible the introduction of capitalized farming—as in Greek Macedonia and eastern Tunisia —Mediterranean agriculture is mainly horticulture, gardening rather than farming as it is understood in the great grain-lands of North America and the U.S.S.R. Simple farm implements—light ploughs, sickles, and hoes—are still widely used. While the crops are grown primarily for subsistence, and grain supplies fall short of requirements, many crops—notably olive oil, citrous and dried fruits, vines, tobacco, 'early' fruits and vegetables—provide exports. The rearing of sheep, goats, mules, and asses is widespread and well suited to the rough, hilly ground and to the seasonal pastures at different altitudes, but the virtual lack of perennial pastures largely excludes cattle- and horse-rearing within the area of Mediterranean climate.

Physical conditions, hard though they are, do not, however, account for the unproductiveness and inefficiency of Mediterranean agriculture, which are illustrated by the fact that wheat yields are only half those of Western Europe. Wasteful practices survive, such as that of fallowing in alternate years and the one-crop system on the *latifundia* of central and southern Spain. Little use is made of fertilizers, and of the considerable scientific and technical knowledge now available. It is possible, for example, to eliminate fallows in many areas by introducing suitable rotations, with crops like lucerne and unirrigated sugar beet. Much could be done—and the work has at least begun—to increase the productivity of Mediterranean agriculture, but numerous difficulties prevent rapid and spectacular improvement: the shortage of capital; widespread rural poverty; the lack of private enterprise; and the ignorance and often illiteracy of the peasants—these are only some of the obstacles to overcome.

The Mediterranean region has not been very generously endowed with the sources of fuel and power and with those natural resources—minerals, timber, and fish—which condition extractive industries. The Mediterranean is mostly too deep to be rich in supplies of fish. The forest cover has long been removed from the hilly lands—with much consequent loss of soil, although some good sources of timber remain in northern Turkey and north and north-west Spain. While petroleum has been struck in Egypt, Albania, Turkey, Sicily, Tunisia, and Morocco, as yet its production is very small. Similarly, while some coal or lignite is mined, for example, in Morocco, Turkey, and Yugoslavia, and France and Spain have fair supplies in their extra-Mediterranean areas, the outputs are generally small. Water power offers a more promising source of energy, and is developed in some scale in North Italy (from Alpine waters) and in north-east Spain (from Pyrenean waters), and is being developed in French North Africa (especially in Morocco), but the potentialities are not great.

The mineral wealth of the Mediterranean lands is not yet known: both geological mapping and, still more, geological prospecting are far from complete, and in respect of metallic ores and other minerals, as also of agriculture, these lands remain under-developed. In the earlier decades of this century mineral exploitation was started by foreign interests in search of new sources of supply. As more minerals become available in the Mediterranean lands they might fittingly be now used in domestic industries. Meanwhile production is mainly for export. North Africa produces phosphates on a very large scale, and also an increasing supply of iron ore, manganese ore, and lead. Southern

Spain produces mercury, copper, lead, and zinc; Cyprus has copper and chrome ores; Italy, France, and Yugoslavia produce an exportable surplus of bauxite, Turkey of chrome ore, and Italy of mercury and sulphur. These various and valuable supplies are, however, widely distributed, and the deficiencies as yet of iron ore and sources of power, together with the lack of both capital and enterprise, have militated against any substantial industrialization in the Mediterranean lands.

Brief reference should be made to the demographic geography of the Mediterranean lands. Within and around the Mediterranean basin towns appeared early—in prehistory and, more signally, in ancient Græco-Roman times. The economic life and culture of the region are largely concentrated in the towns to-day, and the outsize city—one with a million or more inhabitants—is well represented: there are two in Spain (Madrid and Barcelona), three in Italy (Rome, Milan, and Naples), one in European Turkey (Istanbul), and one in Egypt (Cairo). In the countryside the nucleated village is widely characteristic, and in many areas its great size, by withdrawing peasants from their fields, means waste of the time and energy of rural workers. In their population numbers the Mediterranean countries show steady growth and have long provided a stream of emigrants to the New World. This steady increase in numbers has been accompanied by widespread poverty, for the ever-increasing supply of labour has not been fully used to raise the living standards of the mainly peasant masses. Under-employment occurs widely, hand in hand with under-development. Neither has to continue inevitably once greater use is made of modern science and technology and enlightened leadership and supplies of capital are applied.

Some Problems of Italy

As a single State, replacing a patchwork of kingdoms and duchies, Italy appeared only in 1871, thanks to the successful statecraft of the Kingdom of Sardinia, which, with the support of French arms and with British encouragement, overthrew Austria, whose military power and territories in North Italy had prevented Italian political unity (Fig. 2). That Italy is less than a century old and that it arose under the leadership of a dynasty whose base lay in Piedmont in the extreme north-west are background facts which help to explain Italian foreign policy and internal problems. On the one hand, the new Italy was concerned to improve its frontiers so as to increase its security: this led to an opportunist foreign policy, both before and during the Fascist phase, which aimed at territorial aggrandizement. On the other, the specially difficult demographic and economic problem of South Italy (including Sicily) is not a little due to past neglect by a government whose primary interests were focused on its northern territory.

Italy entered the Mediterranean scene when the Suez Canal had just been opened and that new phase of imperialism known as "the scramble for Africa" was about to begin. Despite her relative weakness, Italy did not fail to claim her share of African lands. For Italy, her Foreign Minister Mancini declared, the keys of the Mediterranean were in the Red Sea. Although the first attempt to hold Abyssinia as a protectorate failed by Italy's defeat at Adowa in 1896, she annexed Eritrea bordering the Red Sea and won Libya and the Dodecanese Islands from Turkey during a war in 1911–12. The African dependencies, though extensive, had little economic value, their population in 1914 amounting to only about one and a half millions.

The geographical content of Italy, made up of a more populous and richer northern area, linked to Western and Central Europe by the Alpine railways and passways, and a southern peninsular and insular area, which is essentially Mediterranean alike in position, climate, and landscapes, has made it possible for her during the major wars of this century to choose whether she should throw in her lot with the Powers whose military forces dominated Central Europe or with the Western Powers whose naval forces tended to dominate the Mediterranean. During the first world war, lured by promises of large territorial gains, Italy joined Britain and France. While she gained much less than she had hoped, and thus professed herself an 'unsatisfied Power,' her gains were in fact substantial, greater indeed than her efforts in the war might seem to have earned. She secured a strategical frontier on the Brenner Pass by the incorporation of South Tyrol, which included 230,000 Germans, the peninsula of Istria (which contained a large Slav majority), the port of Trieste, Zara on the Dalmatian coast, a number of islands in the Adriatic sea, and the port of Fiume, which she occupied in defiance of the Allied Powers.[1] Her right to the Dodecanese Islands was recognized formally, and there were minor gains in Africa. She had, however, failed in her wider imperialistic ambitions to acquire

[1] See A. E. Moodie, *The Italo-Yugoslav Boundary* (Philip, London, 1945).

northern Dalmatia, a protectorate over Albania, and sovereignty over parts of Turkish Asia Minor.

Under Fascist rule Italy built up air and naval forces and asserted

FIG. 2. ITALY IN A.D. 1859

From "Mediterranean Problems," by W. G. East. By courtesy of Messrs Thomas Nelson and Sons, Ltd

herself as a Mediterranean Power. She has 5300 miles of sea frontiers, compared with only 1200 miles by land. Unlike France and Spain, her shores are wholly Mediterranean, and her position in this sea, supplemented by bases on the Libyan coast and in the Dodecanese, suggested

G*

strategical possibilities which Mussolini sought to exploit. Although he succeeded by the campaigns of 1935 and 1936 in conquering Abyssinia and joined the winning side in the Spanish Civil War, his association with Germany and Japan in the second world war brought the collapse of his regime and of the monarchy and the end of the Italian Empire. After the treaties of peace in 1947, Libya and Ethiopia (Abyssinia) became independent, Eritrea was federated with Ethiopia, and the Dodecanese Islands, whose population is Greek, passed to Greece. Since then, as a Republic, Italy has readjusted her foreign policy by aligning herself with the Western Powers in the North Atlantic Treaty Organization. Moreover, a long and dangerous disagreement with Yugoslavia, centred on their Istrian borderland, has been settled by the Agreement of London in 1954, to which the United States and the United Kingdom are parties.

The role cast for Italy by Mussolini was beyond her capacity: she has not as yet the economic resources, nor indeed does she appear to possess the requisite natural resources of a Great Power. Certainly she commands a large and growing labour force—and one that is not fully employed in either the industrial or the agricultural sector of the economy. Relatively and absolutely Italy is the most populous of the Mediterranean countries. Her population at forty-eight millions exceeds that of France, while its density approaches that of Western Germany. The lowlands of North Italy, enclosed between the Alps and the Apennines, form the hub of the State, for there lie the chief food-producing lands, some of the leading seaports, notably Genoa, manufacturing cities, of which Milan and Turin are the greatest, and near by the main hydro-electric plants, worked by the rapid and continual flow of water from the Alps. Peninsular Italy, together with the islands of Sicily and Sardinia, have so far contributed less to the national economy, largely because of neglect, although geographical conditions are rather unfavourable. Much the greater part of this area is mountain or rough highland, useful only for sheep and goats; forests—and soil too—have been removed from some of the many slopes; climate forbids cattle-raising and dairying, unless irrigation is employed; much of the flatter land, especially in the south-east, suffers from aridity, and there is not enough water either from rain or from melted snow to facilitate irrigation and the generation of electricity on the North Italian scale. The primary industry is agriculture and arboriculture, which produce wheat, vines, and olives, as well as citrous fruits by irrigation.

While labour (mostly unskilled) is abundant, the major deficiencies for large-scale industrialization so far are metals and, above all, sources of fuel and power. There are good coal reserves in Sardinia as well as some iron; Apulia has bauxite deposits; oil has been struck in Sicily, and iron resources await prospecting in Calabria. But as yet Italy has only very small outputs of coal, petroleum, and iron ore, and virtually all metals except mercury, lead, zinc, and aluminium have to be imported. Other major deficiencies are potash fertilizer, cotton, and rubber. Exportable goods include machines, textiles, sulphur, wine, olive oil, and foodstuffs. There are good domestic supplies of flax, hemp, and silk, to supply the textile industry. In foodstuffs, however, the country is not self-sufficient, and although reclamation works, such as the drainage of the Pontine marshes, add to supplies, much wheat and meat are needed from overseas.

Italy thus depends on seaborne trade for the efficient functioning of her economy. Over 80 per cent. of her imports are seaborne: Italy is virtually an island, like Britain. As Lord Balfour remarked, as long ago as 1921, "I doubt whether she [Italy] could feed herself or supply herself, or continue as an efficient fighting unit, if she were blockaded and her sea commerce were cut off." The experience of the second world war affords a commentary on this text, and N.A.T.O.'s naval forces in the Mediterranean clearly include among their main functions the safeguarding of the shipping lanes to Italy.

Perhaps the most serious internal problem of Italy concerns the arrested economic development of the South, where, in contrast to the North, a high natural increase persists and population pressure and poverty are acute and an 'under-developed' region challenges national effort.[2] Marked regional differences between North and South Italy (Sicily included) run deep and can be discerned throughout Italian history and even prehistory, and before the unification of Italy in 1871 the South constituted a separate kingdom with its capital at Naples.[3] In this century emigration from Italy as a whole, and especially from the South, afforded some relief to the pressure of population on the means of subsistence, and even in recent years (1949–52) more than 150,000 permanent migrants have been leaving Italy annually, chiefly

[2] For a revealing analysis of the backward social and economic conditions in South Italy and the problem of its development, see United Nations, *Economic Survey of Europe in 1953* (Geneva, 1954), especially Chapter 9.

[3] Significantly the referendum of June 1946 revealed the preference of the cities of the South for a monarchy, but this was outweighed by the preference of the northern cities for a republic.

for Latin America and for other European countries, above all for France. Whereas experts before the second world war discovered 'over-population' in South Italy—and, indeed, Mussolini argued that, owing to the pressure of population, Italy had either "to expand or explode"—it is now suggested that emigration, by drawing off a high proportion of adult workers, weakens the economy of the country of origin, and, further, that South Italy suffers not so much from over-population as under-development. Mineral resources await exploitation and even exploration, while expert surveys indicate large possible improvements in agricultural technique and the range of crops. Legislation is now being specially directed to the problem of raising the productive level of agriculture in the South, in which at least half the active population is engaged, the development of suitable industries, and the exploitation of its water resources for power and irrigation; these and other long-term projects, calling for much enterprise and capital investment, promise a rise in the living standards and an end to economic stagnation. The continuance of migration from South to North Italy, too, when northern industry is working to capacity, should also help the national economy by providing for export manufactures needed in other less industrialized Mediterranean countries.

The Iberian States

The Iberian Peninsula, which includes the kingdom of Spain, the republic of Portugal, and the Pyrenean statelet of Andorra, has almost twice the area but only about three-quarters of the population of Italy (Table 1). In its location at one extremity of the Mediterranean basin, as in the extent, elevation, and land forms of its surface and the length of its coastline, the Iberian Peninsula is comparable with Asia Minor, the main territorial base of modern Turkey. Both are lands which have fallen behind in the recent centuries of industrialization elsewhere and may fittingly be classed as 'under-developed'; both were centres of ancient civilizations and extensive empires. Spain and Portugal, lying somewhat aloof from Europe beyond the Pyrenees, yet close to North Africa and between the Mediterranean and the North Atlantic, retain their remarkable strategical position, although they have lost the political power and status which they formerly achieved, above all, in the sixteenth century. Even so, the chances of history have preserved for Portugal vast overseas territories twenty-four times the area of the home plot.

Franco's Spain. The great days of Spanish civilization and power lie far behind: only fragments survive of an empire which once stretched from north-west Europe and the Mediterranean to the Americas and the Far East, and her economy, which was still flourishing in the early seventeenth century on the bases of the fine fleeces of her merino sheep and the precious metals of Latin America, is now replaced by one which is probably the most arrested and unproductive in the whole of Europe. The American-Spanish war of 1898–99 marked the last stage in the dismemberment of the old Spanish Empire, bringing with it the loss of the Philippines and Cuba. Spain now retains outside the peninsula only the Balearic and Canary Islands, which are administratively part of Spain, her three coastal cities in Morocco, and Rio de Oro and Spanish Guinea in West Africa.[4]

Spain faces many serious internal problems, which can be in part explained and illuminated by reference to their geographical background. The country is much divided and diversified as a result of both geological and human history. Spain is essentially a highland area, made up of extensive plateaux within and around which rise mountain ranges. Although Spain has so long a coastline and necessarily makes most of its trade and other external contacts by sea, the coastal plains, where indeed they occur, are confined landward by mountains which obstruct circulation and serve everywhere to compart the country. There are sharp contrasts of climate and vegetation forms, notably between the wet north-west and the arid south-east, and contrasting landscapes range from the irrigated orange-groves and vineyards of Valencia and Murcia, to the interior sheep-walks and grain fields of Castile, and to the wet woodlands, pastures, and maize fields of Galicia, in the north-west. Apart from Madrid, which was built in the sixteenth century to provide a capital for a united Spain, the chief cities and most populous areas lie peripherally, in or towards the coastlands. Thus the less densely settled interior, although it contains the capital and focuses the slender railway system, at the same time separates the main regions of settlement and economic activity. In contrast to the position in prehistoric and Roman times, it is now the north, not the south, which supports the highest densities of population: Catalonia, with its textile,

[4] See below, pp. 750–751.

chemical, metallurgical, and paper industries, its water-power, its commercial interests, and its agriculture and arboriculture; Bilbao in Vizcaya, with its iron mines and ferrous metallurgy; Oviedo and Aviles in Asturias, with their steel plants and near-by coalfields; and Galicia, where the densest provincial population of Spain is engaged mainly in mixed farming and fishing.

In common with other parts of Europe where the worn-down but uplifted rocks of Hercynian folding are exposed, Spain possesses a wide range of mineral wealth. Iron ore reserves are considerable, but the annual yield is only three million tons and mostly exported; coal resources are smaller, and the production—about thirteen million tons —is not enough for domestic needs. Non-ferrous metals include copper, zinc, lead, silver, mercury, and wolfram, while in Navarre very large reserves of potash provide a valuable product for industry, agriculture, and export.

The present economy of Spain, despite the variety of its agriculture, pastoral husbandry, and mineral resources, is clearly maladjusted and arrested. While there is no shortage of labour—for the population is increasing by over 200,000 a year—it is by no means fully used in agriculture, which under-employs half the male workers. Agricultural production stagnates, and the real wages of rural workers have actually fallen since 1935. It has become necessary in recent years to import one tenth, and at times even a quarter, of the domestic wheat requirement. Even the numbers of livestock have fallen since the 1930's. Industry shows no marked progress, and the agricultural staples of Spanish trade meet damaging competition in outside markets. The symptoms of an ailing economy are many, and they cannot be explained merely as the result of difficult physical conditions, despite the fluctuating and unreliable rainfall in 'dry' Spain and the extent of mountains and steppes.

Undoubtedly, since changes come very slowly in Spain and although farm efficiency varies regionally, shortcomings of the economy result from the survival of old systems of land tenure and traditional farm practices—for agriculture is the principal branch of activity. In parts of the country, especially the north, holdings are too small to be economically worked; in Andalusia and the interior, in contrast, enormous estates, owned by absentee landlords and worked by hired labour, are farmed without regard to their full productive potentialities. Bad crop rotations, involving fallows, are still adopted, and wheat yields are low.

The use of nitrogenous fertilizers and of machinery is much neglected; capital and enterprise are largely lacking; hydraulic works to provide more water for irrigation await construction; and the low living standards of the agricultural workers, nearly half of whom are casual labourers, continue to fall.

The destruction inflicted by the civil war of 1936–39 certainly added to Spain's difficulties and helped to worsen already inadequate transport facilities. Industrial development suffers seriously from this deficiency as well as from lack of capital and enterprise. The supply of mechanical energy is not enough for existing industries; hydro-electricity has to be supplemented by the use of thermal plants, and the output of coal falls short. The production of steel is only about one million tons per year.

Nor does the political system of Spain make for any liberalization and expansion of the economy. The country was long ruled by an absolute monarchy, supported by the nobility and Roman Catholic Church—that is, by the great landowners. The creation of a republic in 1931 brought the promise of long-needed and drastic internal reforms, but these hopes were dashed by the success of the reactionary forces led by General Franco in the civil war.[5] Thus, under a dictatorship, which is to eventually succeeded by a constitutional monarchy, Spain presents many archaic, indeed fossil, features of political organization. She has yet successfully to reconcile strong centrifugal forces—notably those exerted by the Catalan and Basque industrial regions and that exerted from Madrid and Castile—regional forces which are reflected in some measure by survival of languages other than Spanish: a Portuguese dialect in Galicia, Catalan in Catalonia and Valencia, and Basque in Vizcaya. Meanwhile Spain occupies an anomalous position in international affairs: staunchly anti-Communist in attitude, although undemocratic in her own form of government, she remains outside the North Atlantic Treaty Organization, and was admitted to the United Nations Organization only in December 1955. Recent United States interest in Spain, born of the recognition of her strategical importance and reflected in the American-Spanish agreement of 1953, is stimulating some new developments in Spain, notably an improvement in the transport system. So far, however, capital expenditure has been devoted mainly to the expansion of airfields near Saragossa, Madrid, and Seville, and the provision of naval facilities at Cartagena and near Cadiz.

[1] General Franco received the active support of the Axis Powers.

Salazar's Portugal. The home territory of Portugal, together with Madeira and the Azores, which are administratively part of Portugal, and her dependency the Cape Verde Islands, are wholly extra-Mediterranean, but they have obvious strategical importance in covering the oceanic approach to the Mediterranean (Fig. 3). Divided from Spain by the gorge of the Minho river in the north and by wide areas of little-settled steppe to the east, Portugal turns her back on Spain as she faces the ocean with its fish resources and routes of commerce and empire. The centuries-old independence of the Portuguese State illustrates the strong regional pulls and divisions within the Iberian Peninsula, and the incorporation of Portugal into Spain in 1581 lasted only sixty years.

Portugal enjoys a better physical endowment than Spain, for it contains proportionately more lowland and less mountains and arid steppe: thus, with only 15 per cent. of the peninsula, she supports 23 per cent.

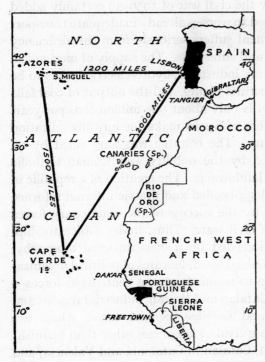

FIG. 3. THE PORTUGUESE STRATEGIC TRIANGLE
From "Mediterranean Problems," by W. G. East. By courtesy of Messrs Thomas Nelson and Sons, Ltd

of its population, mainly by agriculture. Portugal enjoys, too, the advantages of enormous colonial possessions,[6] which, though at an early stage of their development, nevertheless provide many valuable minerals and tropical commodities and a quarter of her trade. Portugal's under-developed economy, however, conforms closely with that of so much of the Mediterranean world. Agriculture is backward, industry is arrested, and poverty abounds. Yet many opportunities are offered. There is an abundance of labour, although much is illiterate and un-

---

[6] On the African territories, see below, Chapter XXXIII. See also Jose Shercliff, "Portugal's Strategic Territories," in *Foreign Affairs*, vol. 31, No. 2 (January 1953).

skilled; hydro-electricity and irrigation can be greatly expanded; iron ore (at Moncorvo), wolfram, copper, and other non-ferrous metals are known to be available, although the necessary geological mapping has only begun. Under an authoritarian regime Portugal has followed the narrow path of 'orthodox' economics, although she held the foreign assets which would have permitted a bolder policy of profitable, large-scale investments at home.

Since she has long ruled an extensive overseas empire and depends much on the oceanic routes, Portugal has long pursued a foreign policy which associates her with the leading sea Powers. The Anglo-Portuguese treaty of mutual defence, which was first made in 1386, remains in force: it was invoked during the second world war to secure bases for the Allies in the Azores. Like Spain, Portugal was not admitted to U.N.O. until December 1955, but, unlike Spain, she is a member of N.A.T.O. By an alliance in 1952, Portugal granted the United States full use of bases in the Azores, both in peace and in war. Britain enjoys the same facilities in wartime.

The States of North Africa

The term 'North Africa' has come to be applied by geographers—a little selectively—to the countries of northern Africa other than Egypt. Together with Egypt, these fall within that area of military organization known during and since the second world war as 'The Middle East.'[7] North Africa thus consists of Libya, Tunisia, Algeria, and Morocco. They were historically parts of the Roman Empire (as also was Egypt) and areas of either Greek or Latin speech, but the Arab conquests of medieval times replaced these languages by Arabic speech as they introduced the Moslem religion. The four countries of North Africa occupy one-sixth of the continent, but, with a total population of about twenty-four millions, contain only one-eighth of its population. Except for minorities of Europeans and even smaller numbers of Jews, this population is Moslem in religion. Europeans average only about 7 per cent. of the whole population. The African peoples belong to the Mediterranean ethnic type, being Arabs, Berbers, Moors, and Senussi in nationality, and show a high rate of natural increase; about one-third of the Libyans are negroid, a result of the old overland slave-trade route which reached the Tripolitanian coast from West Africa.

[7] See below Chapters XXVIII and XXIX, and W. B. Fisher, "Unity and Diversity in the Middle East," in *Geog. Review*, vol. xxxvii (1947), pp. 414–435.

Table 2 below summarizes some basic statistical data for 1954:

TABLE 2

COUNTRY	AREA in square miles (estimated)	POPULATION in millions (1954) (estimated)	EUROPEANS (as percentage of total population)	CULTIVATED LAND[1] (square) miles)	POPULATION PER SQUARE MILE OF CULTIVATED LAND
MOROCCO	172,104	9·7	5	—	—
French Zone	153,870	8·3	5	17,000	465
Spanish Zone	18,009	1·2	7	—	—
Tangier	225	0·2	16	—	—
ALGERIA	847,552	9·5	12	24,400	390
Northern Algeria	80,117	8·7	—	—	—
Southern Territories	767,435	0·8	—	—	—
TUNISIA	48,300	3·7	7	16,250	228
LIBYA	700,000	1·2	—	975	—
Tripolitania	—	0·8	6	780[2]	1,000
Cyrenaica	—	0·3	—	195[2]	1,500
Fezzan	—	0·05	—	—	—
NORTH AFRICA	1,767,956	24·1	7		

[1] These figures exclude arable land in fallow.
[2] These figures refer only to areas of sedentary agriculture.

Much the greater part of North Africa consists of the Saharan and Libyan deserts, where some widely scattered springs and wells permit only scanty settlement. Thus less than one-tenth of the population of Algeria lives in the desert nine-tenths of its area. All but a trivial proportion of the North Africans are concentrated on the coastlands or in a zone behind the coasts of the Mediterranean and Atlantic Ocean where the rainfall or irrigation permits agriculture, arboriculture, and pastoral farming. Even in these areas population is by no means evenly spread. West of Tunis and Sousse confined coastal or interior plains are separated by, or enclosed within, the mountains of the Atlas system, which dominate most of the coast and support only a low density of population engaged in pastoral farming. Morocco, however, has a large populous area in the well-watered parts of its Atlantic coastal plain. To the east of Tunisia, in contrast, much of the coastal belt of Libya, with less than eight inches of annual rainfall, is semi-desert and thus settled only where water is available from wells and springs.

North Africa came to assume a dependent status politically as the result of the intervention of European Powers—France, Italy, and Spain. Only Libya, which was subject in turn to Turkey and to Italy, had achieved before 1955 the formal status of a sovereign State. Algeria assumes a special political position, for it is juridically part of France.

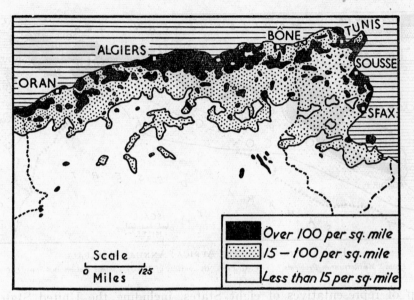

FIG. 4. POPULATION DENSITIES IN ALGERIA AND TUNISIA

From "Mediterranean Problems," by W. G. East. By courtesy of Messrs Thomas Nelson and Sons, Ltd

Algeria, Tunisia, and Morocco. These countries, the former Barbary States, from whose coasts pirates infested the western basin of the Mediterranean, occupy a natural region long known to Moslem geographers as "Maghreb" (= "the West"). This is broadly an 'island' made up of mountains, high plateaux, and flanking or interior plains, between the sea and the desert. Algeria was the first to be occupied by a European Power, and the French conquest was a costly and arduous venture which involved intermittent fighting for over fifty years (1830–84). Tunisia (Fig. 6) was occupied by France, very much more easily in 1881, and became a French 'protectorate' two years later by a Convention with the ruling Bey. Lastly, Morocco, which was an old-established Moslem State, became a protectorate of France, with the concurrence of Britain, by treaty with the Sultan in 1912, although the country was not pacified until 1934. The northern part, which largely fronts the Mediterranean opposite Spain, passed to that country as a 'sphere of influence' by a Franco-Spanish treaty, also in 1912; the coastal cities of Ceuta and Melilla, however, had already been in Spanish hands for several centuries. Finally, the city and seaport of Tangier is administered as an international zone by a Committee of Control made

FIG. 5. FRENCH NORTH AFRICA: ANNUAL RAINFALL

From " Mediterranean Problems," by W. G. East. By courtesy of Messrs Thomas Nelson and Sons, Ltd

up of representatives of eight States, including the United States. The three zones of Morocco formed separate political units with little inter-communication. The Sultan's authority, however, was exercised in all three zones. That this was not purely nominal and ceremonial became clear when France expelled the Sultan in 1953. The Spanish Zone, however, continued to recognize the representative of the exiled Sultan, who returned to Morocco from Madagascar in November 1955.

By her treaty with the Sultan of Morocco, France virtually committed Spain to relinquish her protectorate over the Spanish Zone, although there is no question of her surrendering her coastal cities. General Franco, who has carefully cultivated the Arab World, was quick to fall into line by surrendering his zone to the Sultan. Reconsideration of the status of Tangier must follow soon.

A 'protectorate' is a clear-cut conception in international law which implies that the 'protecting' Power reserves to itself specified duties on behalf of the 'protected' State, such as defence, foreign affairs, currency, and finance. Thus in international law Morocco and Tunisia, which were granted full independence by France early in 1956, were not

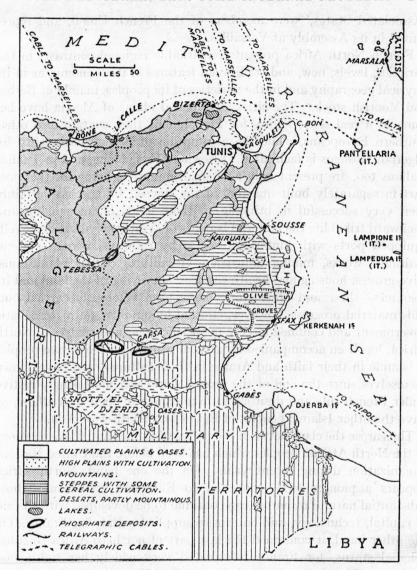

FIG. 6. TUNISIA: ITS GEOGRAPHICAL BACKGROUND

From "Mediterranean Problems," by W. G. East. By courtesy of Messrs Thomas Nelson and Sons, Ltd

dependencies of France, and relations with them fell to the Ministry of Foreign Affairs at Paris. (In contrast, because of its special status, Algerian affairs fall to the French Ministry of the Interior.) In accordance with the French Constitution of 1946, Morocco and Tunisia, as

'Associated States,' were members of the French Union, and represented in its Assembly at Versailles.

French North Africa presents remarkable regional contrasts in the
varieties, levels, new, and traditional features of its economy, as in its
physical geography and in the varieties of its peoples, mainly of Berber
and Moorish stock.[8] The cities and coastal plains of Algeria have become in a real sense homes for Frenchmen; they contain also other
southern Europeans, while the assumption of French nationality by
Algerian Moslems is facilitated. Elsewhere Frenchmen, and in Tunisia
Italians too, are present only as a small minority, living for the most
part in separately built quarters of the towns. France has certainly
been very successful in bringing to these lands of unchanging and
backward tribal life the material benefits of Western civilization. Well-
equipped ports with hinterland access by railways, a road system,
hydraulic works, mining industries, viticulture, citrous plantations,
olive-groves, housing and health services, surveying of the land and its
resources—these and other works have been vigorously carried out.
This material progress, however, effected by an alien and paternalistic
government and confined largely to specific areas and centres of North
Africa, has been accompanied by a vocal reaction of the native peoples
—Islamic in their faith and Arabic in their culture—who have shown
themselves since the end of the second world war increasingly restive
under French rule and desirous to take charge of their own affairs, as
have the other Islamic peoples of Egypt and South-west Asia.

Thus arose the clash between the policy of France and the aspirations
of the North African peoples which has been before the United Nations
Organization during recent years. On the one hand, North Africa
appears a pioneer land, congenial to European settlement, whose
substantial natural resources can continue to be developed with the aid
of capital, technology, and enterprise supplied mainly by France. On
the other hand, it contained the last part of northern Africa to suffer
colonial status, for France interpreted very widely her rights and
duties as a protectorate Power in Tunisia and Morocco. It might appear
that the development of North African resources of minerals, soil, and
water power serves the common interest of the native populations (who
exceed 90 per cent. of the whole) and of France and the other commercially interested Western Powers. Prolonged economic effort is

_____

[8] See *Atlas des Colonies Françaises* (published under the direction of G. Grandidier,
Paris, 1934).

required to raise the low living standards of a mainly peasant population, and the export products of North Africa are now of some scale and value.

For France herself, North Africa means much, not least in prestige, the more so since she has lost some of her overseas possessions. The proximity of North Africa to France increases its political and strategical value as a source of man-power and supplies. France hoped to meet the nationalist aspirations in Tunisia and Morocco by the grant of autonomy, but was compelled in February and March 1956 to concede by treaty full independence. She intends, however, to keep them if possible within her political orbit and linked by special treaty relationships. The French formula for this special, if loose, relationship is 'independence with inter-dependence.' In Algeria, which France holds by right of hard-earned conquest, and where she has settled a million Frenchmen, it appears likely, given the strength and violence of the internal nationalist movement, that she will have to concede domestic self-government—*i.e.*, reach a political rather than a military, decision. The destiny of North Africa, which played an important role in the strategy of the second world war, is a matter of much importance to the United States, as indeed to the security of the Western world (see below, p. 199). The attitude of the United States towards the Moroccan and Tunisian problems before the United Nations clearly reflected their difficulty, for, while the United States disapproves of colonialism, it is mindful of the fact that a tranquil North Africa is essential as a life-line to N.A.T.O. in the Mediterranean theatre.

The Kingdom of Libya. Most of the vast territory of Libya, with a negligible rainfall, is sheer desert except for some oases of which the Fezzan group is the chief. Libya's long sea coast facing the central Mediterranean, however, gives this country strategical interest, and it is in parts of the coastland—around Tripoli and between Benghazi and Derna in Cyrenaica—where the annual rainfall averages about twenty inches, that sedentary agriculture as well as arboriculture and pastoral farming are practicable and support the bulk of the population.

The coastlands were in turn part of the ancient Græco-Roman world and of the Arab Caliphate. Later they were held as an outpost of the Ottoman Empire, until conquered by Italy between 1912 and 1929. Fascist Italy built a coastal road and at some cost established colonies of Italian peasants. At the end of the second world war, during which

northern Libya became a battlefield in the defence of Egypt, Britain
remained in military occupation of Tripolitania and Cyrenaica, while
France occupied the Fezzan. Military administration ended in 1951,
when Libya was set up as an independent kingdom with a representative form of government under the Amir of Cyrenaica, Mohammed
Idris el Senussi.

Libya is organized as a federal State: recognition is thus given to the
fact that its three autonomous territories—Tripolitania, Cyrenaica, and
the Fezzan—lie remote from each other and have their distinctive
interests and problems. Before the second world war Italian colonists,
either as townsmen or as farmers, made up 10 per cent. of the population. Now that their number has decreased to less than half, the survival of Italian farms, which are valuable agriculturally, but involve a
financial charge on Libyan funds, presents a delicate problem.[9] Libya
joined the Arab League in 1954, and a year later was granted membership of the United Nations Organization. Her viability as a sovereign
State rests on a somewhat precarious economic basis. Less than 1 per
cent. of the area is potentially productive, and then mainly for grazing.
The economy depends on the products of pastoral husbandry, chiefly
of sheep, goats, and camels, and of arboriculture, which yields olives,
figs, almonds, oranges, dates, and grapes. Shifting cultivation adds little
to the yields of barley, wheat, and millet grown on settled farms. Libya
receives a subsidy from Britain, in accordance with the Anglo-Libyan
treaty of friendship and alliance of 1953, and receives similar aid from
the United States; to each she grants in return facilities for troops and
air forces on Libyan soil. Libya has no fewer than six neighbours and
a great length of boundaries: these are mainly demarcated, being
geometric in type and drawn for the most part across desert wastes.
A motor road near the coast links the chief towns of northern Libya
with Tunisia and Egypt, and motorable roads connect Tripoli with the
Fezzan oasis and El Agheila with Wadi Halfa on the Nile where it
leaves the Sudan to enter Egypt.

British Territories in the Mediterranean

Gibraltar, the Maltese Islands, and Cyprus are the surviving British
holdings in the Mediterranean. They were acquired at different times,

[9] See W. B. Fisher, "Problems of Modern Libya," in *Geographical Journal*, vol. cxix
(June 1953).

chiefly for strategical and commercial purposes, which they still serve. The importance of the first two in British and international history has been out of all proportion to their size. All three were Crown Colonies, although enjoying different degrees of self-government, and two so remain. Malta, however, since 1948 has been autonomous. The table below summarizes some contrasting facts about them.

TABLE 3

Country	Area (square miles)	Population (estimated 1952)	Population (per square mile)	Crop Area (square miles)	Population per Square Mile of Crop Area
Gibraltar	2·25	24,084	10,700	—	—
Maltese Islands	121	316,619	2,620	60	4,370
Cyprus	3,572	497,970	139	900	553

Gibraltar. This small rocky peninsula commands a large sheltered bay and was ideally situated for a naval base, thanks to its location at the entry to the Mediterranean from the Atlantic and to its easy defence from landward attack. It was captured in 1704 by an English admiral Sir George Rooke, who suffered dismissal on his return home,[10] and passed from Spain to Britain at the Peace of Utrecht of 1713–14. It has remained continuously in British hands, notwithstanding some conditional offers to return it to Spain in the first part of the eighteenth century and the Spanish siege during the years 1779–83. It has played a signal part in war and peace as a well-defended base and port of call on a well-frequented sea route from the days of sail to those of oil-fuelled ships. Its deep harbour is marked off by moles, while the Bay of Algeciras affords anchorage facilities. Its water supply is collected from the rain which falls on its rocky spine, and elaborate underground storage places have been provided by tunnelling.

Gibraltar is administered by a Governor, who is also Commander-in-Chief, with the help of a nominated Executive Council and a Legislative Council, one half of which is elected. The population, mostly of Spanish or Italian descent, is virtually all crowded into a single town; immigration is forbidden, while much of the labour force of the colony is drawn from La Linea, the Spanish town just beyond the narrow 'neutral

[10] G. Callender, *The Naval Side of British History* (Christophers, London, 1924), p. 139. On Gibraltar, see W. C. Abbott, *An Introduction to the Documents relating to the International Status of Gibraltar*, 1704–1934 (New York, 1934; Macmillan, London, 1935).

ground' which separates Gibraltar from Spain. All supplies have to be imported to maintain the garrison, the needs of the shipyards, the local population, and calling ships.

Although the usefulness of Gibraltar during the second world war was very considerable—it is *inter alia* an outpost in the naval defence of Britain itself—it has long been recognized that Gibraltar is too confined a site for the aero-naval base which modern conditions require. Suggestions have from time to time been made that Gibraltar should be exchanged for an ampler site (*e.g.*, Ceuta) on the opposite side of the Strait in Spanish Morocco. In recent years demonstrations in Spain have urged that Gibraltar should be returned. While this issue for Spaniards is clearly one of national psychology, Gibraltar has also a symbolic interest to the British. Its strategical importance, however, is certainly less to-day now that the United States has acquired bases in Spain and in Morocco (see below, p. 201).

The Maltese Islands. Malta, the largest island of a group of three, is a hilly limestone area of about ninety square miles situated at the eastern approach to the Sicilian Channel which joins the eastern and western basins of the sea. There are other smaller islands in or near the Sicilian Channel—*e.g.*, Pantelleria, which is held by Italy—but they lack good harbours, whereas Malta contains the Grand Harbour of Valetta, reached through a narrow entry. The islands were formerly ruled by the Knights of St John, from whom Napoleon seized them in 1798 when en route for Egypt, but the French were ejected with British help in the following year. Nelson shrewdly described them as "a most important outwork to India," and, agreeably to the local inhabitants, they passed formally to Britain in 1814. They have long served as a naval base and port of call—half-way between Gibraltar and Port Said—and they now offer their facilities to the navies of N.A.T.O. The value of this base was largely but never wholly lost during the second world war, despite the hostility of Italy, near at hand.

The population of the Maltese Islands has more than tripled during the last hundred years; 90 per cent. of the total live in Malta itself. Thus with an average density of 2600 per square mile—and more than this in Malta proper—the islands are among the densest settled parts of the world, and a steady emigration has taken place during most of this century. Although nearly 60 per cent. of the islands' area is cultivated, virtually all supplies, including some food, have to be imported.

Abundant labour is available for the needs of the port and shipyards. While the Maltese are Roman Catholics, they are not Italian either in language or sentiment. Their language is mainly Semitic—a survival from the Arab conquest in the ninth century—and English, not Italian, is the second official language. The Maltese, indeed, have shown marked loyalty to Britain. The use of Valetta as a naval headquarters brings both employment and business to the islands and provides a material basis to this loyalty. But goodwill towards Britain has not prevented minor difficulties centring on the political status of the islands. Malta has its own elected legislative assembly and self-chosen ministers responsible to it; certain matters—*e.g.*, of defence and foreign relations—however, are reserved to the Governor (as representative of the Queen), who is also Commander-in-Chief. The Maltese Government has suggested that Malta should become part of the United Kingdom and send its representatives to the Parliament at Westminster. This would give give Malta a status broadly comparable to that of Northern Ireland. The United Kingdom has expressed its willingness to implement this proposal, if Malta shows beyond doubt that it is desired.

Cyprus. One of the larger islands of the Mediterranean, situated in its eastern basin forty miles from the southern coast of Turkey and sixty miles from Syria, Cyprus covers the seaward approach to an area of increasing strategical interest—the Turkish port of Alexandretta and the Gulf of Iskanderun, behind which run the railway and a historic highway linking Turkish Anatolia and Syria. The United Kingdom assumed the administration of Cyprus in 1878 by agreement with the Sultan of the Ottoman Empire, so that it might be used as "the key to Western Asia"—a forward base from which to check Russian encroachment against Turkey. Although it was not in fact needed for this purpose, Britain annexed it in 1914 on the outbreak of war with Turkey, which recognized this annexation in 1924. Not much was done until the second world war to equip Cyprus as a base or to exploit its substantial natural resources, although ordered government was established, a railway and roads were built, copper—the word derives from 'Cyprus'—was mined, and efforts were made to reafforest, conserve soil, and to develop irrigation and water supplies. Even if, as is alleged, Britain treated the island with some neglect, it revitalized its economy, wasted during three centuries of Turkish rule, and its population has grown between two and three times during the last seventy years.

Cyprus acquired an enhanced value during and since the second world war and is becoming relatively very prosperous. With Britain's abandonment of its mandate over Palestine and withdrawal from the Suez Canal Zone, Cyprus is officially regarded as essential, as an advanced British base, to the fulfilment of British responsibilities in the Middle East. Its size and relatively low population density, coupled with its varied resources, afford much scope for development. The extensive, treeless plain of Mesaoria (the best agricultural area) provides ample sites for airfields, and Lake Akrotiri affords a landing-place for seaplanes in rough weather. In recent years the airport of Nicosia, the capital, has become a highly frequented junction for air traffic to and from the Middle East. Cyprus lies close not only to Turkey and Syria, but also to Lebanon, Israel, and the Suez Canal. The nearest Soviet territory—in South Caucasus—is over 600 miles away.

Cyprus produces a wide range of crops—grain, olives, grapes, almonds, and tobacco, and, by irrigation, potatoes, cotton, and citrus fruits; sheep, goats, donkeys, and mules are reared. On balance more foodstuffs are imported than exported, although thanks to the 1946-56 Development Programme and to the stimulus of increasing local military requirements Cyprus should become almost self-sufficient in food. It has a variety of light industries, a growing tourist trade, and a considerable mining industry: copper concentrates, copper and iron pyrites, chrome ore, and asbestos make up (with some other minerals) 60 per cent. of the exports and pay for imports such as wheat, meat, and dairy products, iron and steel, machinery, timber, cement, fertilizers, and textiles.

Malaria, which gravely afflicted the island as recently as the 1930's, has now been wiped out, and the death rate in Cyprus is almost the lowest in the world. The population, except for a Moslem–Turkish minority of 18 per cent., is Greek, alike in language, national sentiment, and allegiance to the Greek Orthodox Church. British rule, despite the material benefits which it has brought, has never evoked enthusiasm. Indeed, the movement for political union with Greece—*Enosis*—led by the Church and now supported by a vigorous Communist party, unites all Greek Cypriots and is welcomed by the Greek State, to which Cyprus has never belonged. Already in 1931 this movement caused widespread disturbances, and the elective Legislative Council was abolished. A proposal to reintroduce representative government, made by the United Kingdom in 1948, was not accepted, so that a provisional central government, without elected representatives, was set up. Greece sponsored the Cypriot claim for *Enosis* at the United Nations, but the question was temporarily shelved in December 1954.

This issue, which clearly invites Communist interest, is not under present conditions easy to resolve. The United Kingdom, while desirous to establish self-government by stages and in co-operation with Cypriots, is unwilling to give up its sovereignty, because Cyprus is held to be necessary for Middle East security—a matter of more than British interest.[11] Turkey, which held the island for three centuries yet prefers that it remains under British rule, is wholly opposed to its cession to Greece. Since Greece and Turkey are members of N.A.T.O., as also of a Balkan Pact with Yugoslavia, differences over Cyprus clearly weaken an important sector of Western defence. While Cyprus now prospers as a result of its new value to the defence organization of the Western Powers, its usefulness as a base is reduced, unless the co-operation of its Greek population (80 per cent. of the whole) can be won.

[11] For an official exposition of the Cyprus problem, see *Cyprus* (Central Office of Information, London, April 8, 1954).

CHAPTER VII

The Mediterranean Theatre of International Politics[*]

W. GORDON EAST

Post-war Changes in the Mediterranean Area

THE Mediterranean has always played a conspicuous part in history. Alike in prehistoric, ancient, and medieval times—in peace and in war—high civilizations and great political activity characterized it. It is not one of those regions, like pre-war Germany and the present Soviet Union, whose concentration of population and economic resources is great enough to make it a political base for a bid for world mastery. It engages the interest of the Great Powers, notably the great naval Powers, because of its political disunity and weakness, and its geographical location and character. Only once in history—in the heyday of the Roman Empire—did all the Mediterranean lands form one political unit.

In modern times, with the decline of Turkish and Spanish power, and in a world which had become 'oceanic' in its relationships, Britain intruded her sea power into the Mediterranean to suppress piracy, to protect her commercial interests, to help to maintain the balance of power in Europe, and to defend her territories east of Suez. Certainly Britain made good use of the geographical opportunity presented by the Mediterranean–Red Sea short route, which flanked or pierced great desert obstacles and linked the two most populous regions of the Old World—Europe and Monsoon Asia. It was possible for her to exploit this opportunity, among other reasons, because the entries from the Atlantic Ocean and the Arabian Sea were restricted and thus easily controllable, because island groups in the Mediterranean provided necessary ports of call and bases, and, not least, because the African

* Thanks are due to the Editor of *Foreign Affairs* (New York) for permission to use in this chapter material published under the title "The Mediterranean: Pivot of Peace and War."

flank of the Mediterranean and the desert coastlands of the Red Sea offered few political or naval dangers.

But to-day, when so much has changed politically both inside and outside the Mediterranean basin, it does not follow automatically that the part which this sea played for Britain in the past is the one it should now play for the American-led Western world. The place of the Mediterranean and the Middle East in British defence policy was seriously questioned before the second world war, and although their role in the defence policy of the West has been much discussed, it has never been clarified. It should be remembered that this continuous waterway is made up of two unequal and distinct parts, which until 1869 perforce functioned separately—the Mediterranean proper and the Red Sea—the two tenuously linked at the Suez isthmus. And while the present defence policy of the West, expressed above all in the formation and activities of N.A.T.O., assigns unmistakable functions to the Mediterranean area, policy in respect of the Red Sea-Middle East area encounters serious difficulties.

The scale and nature of the political changes wrought since 1939 must be recalled, because they help to define the practical problems. Nazi Germany and Fascist Italy together only narrowly failed to dominate the Mediterranean, and the former won control of the inner Black Sea basin. When they were destroyed the Soviet Union emerged as the danger to world peace and the catalyst of Western defence planning; and the Soviet Union, beyond the Turkish Straits, is the chief Black Sea Power. Alongside Britain, driven by the stream of events, the United States found itself in 1945 in control of the whole Mediterranean and Middle East areas. France, which had occupied a powerful position in the Mediterranean in 1939, was greatly weakened by 1945 and had been deprived of her emplacements in Syria and Lebanon, which became independent States in 1944. She has been further weakened by her loss of control over Morocco and Tunisia, two strategic territories of North Africa,[1] while even Algeria has become (mid-1956) a heavy military liability.

Britain's relationships with her overseas territories have also changed greatly. Although most of these are still within the British Commonwealth of Nations, so many have ceased to be controlled from London that it is necessary to reassess Britain's defence responsibilities and her

---

[1] See General de Monsabert, "North Africa in Atlantic Strategy," in *Foreign Affairs*, vol. xxxi (April 1953).

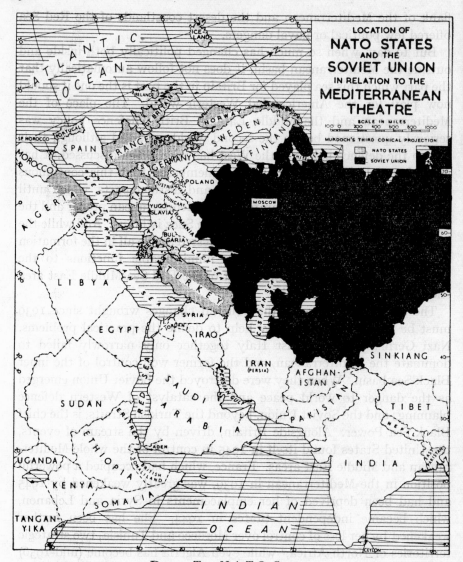

FIG. I. THE N.A.T.O. STATES

facilities for carrying them out. India, Pakistan, and Ceylon have
assumed Dominion status and thus taken full control of their foreign
policies; and Burma opted for complete independence of the Commonwealth. Thus Britain lost not only the principal (though restive) base
which made her a formidable Power in the Indian Ocean, but also a
strong support to her position in the neighbouring Middle East. The

termination of Britain's Palestine mandate and her withdrawal from the condominium with Egypt in the Sudan and from the Suez Canal Zone are also basic facts which must affect plans of defence both for the British Commonwealth and for the whole world.

And there are other well-known changes around the shores of the Mediterranean, notably the revolutionary advent of Israel and the creation of an independent Libya in place of Italian North Africa. Many, but not all, of the Mediterranean countries share a new political and military allegiance under the North Atlantic Treaty Organization (Fig. 1). Yugoslavia and Spain occupy politically interesting yet anomalous positions, the latter clearly oriented to the West. Albania, whose coast controls the Strait of Otranto, is the sole Mediterranean outpost of the Soviet World.

The Role of the Mediterranean in Recent Times

Given a world of changing political attitudes and forces, in which air mastery invites new geographical evaluations, it is clearly necessary to re-examine the political interests which focus on this sea and the assumptions on which they rest. Britain's interest in the Mediterranean began as early as the sixteenth century, with the Levant trade, which helped to establish good relations with the Turkish Empire, the principal territorial Power in the eastern basin. For three centuries the sea was a useful field of political and military operations for her. In the western basin naval pressure could be exerted against France and Spain. In the eastern basin sea-power, supplemented at times by military forces, was effectively applied at two points and for two distinct purposes. On the one hand, by supporting Turkey, especially in the area of the Turkish Straits, Britain sought consistently in the nineteenth century to thwart Russian expansion and thus to preserve the balance of power in Europe and Asia. On the other, as the failure of Napoleon's attack on Egypt in 1798 showed, Britain could defend India at long range, in Egypt, mainly by naval superiority. The maintenance of naval forces in, or available for, the Mediterranean and Red Seas contributed to Britain's political independence, commercial progress, imperial unity and security, and stature as a World Power. Nor was this policy merely national and self-interested. Greek independence, the unification of Italy, the liberation of Arab peoples from Turkey,

H

the creation of the Jewish National Home in Palestine and of the present Libyan State, were all in some sense by-products of British naval power and political initiative in the Mediterranean area. It can also at least be claimed that—as Captain Mahan argued—the application of naval power there, as in other waters, contributed to peaceful international relations.

It should not be thought that naval control of the Mediterranean by Britain was either easily or continuously held. Physically it depended on the possession of a few well-selected bases, of which some remain: Gibraltar, since 1704; the Maltese Islands, which voluntarily joined Britain in 1814; Aden, originally leased to the East India Company in 1839; and Cyprus, leased to Britain by Turkey in 1878. But these small footholds would scarcely have proved adequate but for two powerful supports: political control of Egypt from 1882 until 1936, of which the military base in the Suez Canal Zone marked until recently the last vestige; and a skilful diplomacy which produced allies and neutrals within the Mediterranean basin. Indeed, Britain's delicately poised position there seemed at times untenable: in 1893–94, when war with France and Russia appeared imminent; in 1935–37, when Mussolini was waging war in Abyssinia and talking of *mare nostrum*; and in 1940, when, with the fall of France, Italy joined Germany during the second world war.

These dangers were met successfully, but raised a broad strategical problem. Is the Mediterranean a vital link in British Commonwealth defence, to be preserved at all costs? Have developments in the art of war, notably aircraft and rocket projectiles, undermined the efficacy of naval warfare in such confined waters? Can this sea be virtually closed to merchant shipping by the air forces of peripheral land Powers aided by submarines? Is the Suez Canal now defensible from all likely forms of attack? Is the Mediterranean–Red Sea only a 'short cut,' and, if so, should it in a major war be abandoned in favour of the longer, oceanic (Cape) route, where fewer hazards are to be expected? Do air routes across Africa dispense with this waterway as a direct route to the Middle East? In short, is the Mediterranean–Red Sea route a major factor in world politics or only a local convenience?

The experience of the second world war provides provisional answers. While France stood firm and Italy remained non-belligerent—*i.e.*, until June 1940—use of the Mediterranean raised no difficulties. With the fall of France and Italy's entry into the war the situation was worse

than could have been envisaged: apart from her controlling position in
Egypt and her local bases, the sole factors favourable to the operations
of Britain were the neutrality of Portugal, Spain, and Turkey and the
temporary availability of Crete and the Cyrenaica coast. Only shortcomings in the technical equipment of the Italian naval and air forces—
notably their lack of radar, aircraft carriers, and dive bombers armed
with torpedoes, as well as their shortage of oil—made it possible to
continue war there; and as a route for through traffic the sea was
useless for some time. The epic struggle waged in the Mediterranean,
costly on both sides, was virtually won, however, late in 1942, when
Malta was not only relieved but again became a base for offensive
operations.

Various factors were essential for the success of this effort. Thanks
to both military and naval action, control of the Red Sea approach to
Egypt was never lost. Malta was supplied with fighter aircraft flown
from carriers. The Takoradi air route was organized across Africa;
and, above all, a powerful base was created in Egypt, from which
Libya was finally conquered before the end of 1942. While Hitler's
employment of submarines and torpedo-bombers had added greatly
to the hazards of Mediterranean warfare, his strategical failures were
probably the greatest cause of Allied success, for had he succeeded in
carrying out his plan for the capture of Gibraltar in the winter of
1940–41 the gate to the Mediterranean nearest to the United States
and Britain would have been closed. Had either Malta or Egypt been
occupied, or had the Suez Canal been more than temporarily closed by
enemy action, the sea would have lost much of its strategical value.
Actually, the enemy was successful in only one of the critical sectors of
the sea—the approach to the Turkish Straits, which he controlled
largely by air-power based on Greek territory and the Italian Dodecanese Islands. In short, the Mediterranean seaway was preserved only
with great difficulty to facilitate the first Anglo-American invasion of
Europe.

Allied sea-power, taking advantage of the peninsular form of Europe,
thus made practicable the invasion of Italy; and Sir Winston Churchill
argued that further advantage of this might have been taken by an
invasion of the Balkan Peninsula. The 'Mediterranean' school of
strategists had justified its views, and the grandiose strategy of the
enemy, which would have outflanked the Allied position in the Mediterranean by a gigantic pincer movement directed towards the Middle

East from the Caucasus and from Libya, came to nothing. This success contrasts with the failure of the Mediterranean strategists—"Easterners" they were called—in the first world war. While the "Westerners" had then argued that only an all-out effort against the Germans in the West could win the war, the "Easterners," led by Churchill, urged an attack on Turkey (then allied with the Central Powers) in the area of the Straits. This was attempted, but just failed to force the Dardanelles in the Gallipoli campaign of 1915.

These experiences offer some help in our present problems. In the defence of Europe, at least, the Mediterranean has a clear role, although a powerful and resolute enemy who had gained territorial bases on the sea could intervene with powerful effect against shipping. Some of the questions raised remain unanswered, however, and to pursue them we must turn to the history of Russian political and military operations during the nineteenth century.

The U.S.S.R.'s Interests in the Mediterranean Basin

If only because her territories front the Black Sea, from the Danube delta to the coast of Georgia S.S.R., the Soviet Union necessarily has political interests in the Mediterranean, and above all in the Straits which link these two seas. Yet they developed late, when Britain and France had become well-established Mediterranean Powers. It was only in the latter part of the eighteenth century that Russia expanded southward to the Sea of Azov and the Black Sea and set about building a Black Sea fleet. By the Treaty of Kutchuk-Kainardji in 1774 the Turkish Black Sea outpost of the Crimea was ceded to Russia, and it was then also that the Straits were forced open to her commercial navigation. Thereafter Russia's relations with the Ottoman Empire, whose European and Asiatic territories flanked the Straits, were the prime factor in the so-called Eastern Question which engaged the continual attention of the European Powers. Either control of the Ottoman Empire by Russia, or its disruption, would have upset the whole balance of power in Europe; and now that the U.S.S.R. and the Turkish Republic replace the former Tsarist and Ottoman Empires, the problem in some measure persists, especially as concerns the Straits.

Certain basic geographical facts lie behind these problems. The Straits consist of the narrow and winding Dardanelles channel, which leads from the Ægean Sea to the Sea of Marmara, and the yet narrower but shorter Bosporus, which in turn links this sea to the Black Sea. The work of Nature here has defined a critical inter-continental area where land and seaways cross. Within the Straits stands the historic city of Istanbul—the Constantinople and Byzantium of earlier days. Situated on a hill by a natural harbour where the Bosporus enters the Sea of Marmara, Istanbul controls access between the Black and Mediterranean Seas. The capital in turn of two remarkably long-lived empires—the Byzantine (or East Roman) and the Ottoman Turkish —it was in itself so tempting a prize to imperialist ambitions that no great Power could afford to let it fall to another.[2] Further, the neighbouring lands of the Balkan Peninsula and Asia Minor are the meeting-places of political pressures generated respectively by land-based military power and of long-range sea-power, and as the Ottoman Empire weakened they were bound to become areas of high international tension. In his well-known analysis of the political significance of the Heartland, Sir Halford Mackinder showed[3] how the strategic prize of Constantinople and the Straits was in contest throughout history between Continental and Mediterranean Powers. Moreover, Istanbul is a key point on the land route from Central Europe via Iraq to the Persian Gulf, a potential path of imperialism which outflanks the Mediterranean Sea—as Kaiser Wilhelm II, for example, was well aware.

For the Soviet Union, as formerly for Russia, the mere geographical fact of the Straits inevitably affected its foreign policy. For legitimate reasons of defence Russia had perforce to keep a steady eye on these confined waters: they were and remain "keys to her house."[4] This did not, however, exclude territorial aspirations at the expense of Turkey. While the dissolution of the Ottoman Empire might have best served Russia, provided certain Balkan areas, the Straits included, fell safely

---

[2] Napoleon I is reported to have countered the Tsar Alexander's hope of obtaining this city by exclaiming: "Constantinople, Constantinople, never! That is the empire of the world." Cited by V. J. Puryear, *Napoleon and the Dardanelles* (University of California Press, 1951), p. 191.

[3] *Democratic Ideals and Reality* (Pelican Books, London, 1944), p. 85 and Fig. 25.

[4] As Count Nesselrode, the Russian Chancellor, explained in 1833: "No ships can want to enter the Black Sea except with intentions hostile to Russia, and she did not demand an exit for her own ships which might have given umbrage to other Powers, but her object was purely defensive." Cited by Sir Charles K. Webster, *The Foreign Policy of Palmerston, 1830–41* (G. Bell and Sons, Ltd, London, 1951), vol. i, p. 317. Milyutin, War Minister to Tsar Alexander II, believed that the acquisition of the Straits was not vital to Russia, so long as they did not fall into the hands of a great Power. Russia "could not let England hold these keys to her house"; B. H. Sumner, *Russia and the Balkans, 1870–1880* (Oxford University Press, 1937), pp. 574–575.

into her hands, other watchful Powers—Britain, Austria, and France—
had every reason to prevent this. Britain especially saw in a Russian control of the Straits a danger to her own Mediterranean position and to
India.

The Straits' question engaged international attention continually
during the nineteenth century. While Turkey had accorded the right
of passage to merchant ships of the chief maritime nations, it held firm
to its ancient rule which closed them to foreign warships, a rule essential
to its survival as an independent State. At one time—in 1833—when
British sea-power was at a low ebb, Russian influence dominated at
Constantinople. At another—in 1841—a workmanlike compromise,
upholding the Turkish view, was written into the public law of Europe,
thanks mainly to Lord Palmerston's diplomacy, backed by a newly
built fleet. The Crimean War of 1854–56 showed the danger to Russia
of the intrusion into the Black Sea of the sea-power of Britain and
France, in alliance with Turkey. In 1856 and 1878 settlements of the
question of the Straits (which always eluded Russia's grasp) veered in
favour of Britain; but the Straits tended to remain, under international
law, a zone of insulation between the Black Sea forces of Russia and the
Mediterranean forces of the Western Powers. And this facet of the
political geography of the nineteenth century suggests a conclusion still
valid. The area of Istanbul and the Straits (like Korea, a meeting
point of maritime and continental power) is one of the pivots on which
the wheel of peace and war turns.

During the first world war, when Turkey was at war with Russia,
Britain, and France (but not with the United States), use of the Straits,
which were then fortified with German help, was denied to its enemies,
so that the western Allies could not send help to Russia by this convenient route. With the disruption of Turkey at the end of that war,
it was hoped to neutralize the Straits under the authority of the League
of Nations, but the success of Mustafa Kemal, as leader of the Turkish
Republic, necessitated a different solution. By the Treaty of Lausanne
in 1923 the Straits were demilitarized and left in Turkish hands. When,
however, new dangers arose in the Mediterranean, especially from
Fascist Italy, the Lausanne treaty was replaced (in 1936) by the Convention of Montreux, to which ten States, including the U.S.S.R. and
Australia, were signatories.[5] By implication Turkey was left free to

---

[5] The signatories were Bulgaria, France, Great Britain, Australia, Japan, Greece,
Romania, Turkey, the U.S.S.R., and Yugoslavia. Italy signed the Convention in 1938.

fortify the Straits, full freedom was accorded to merchant shipping, and it was provided that in time of war, if Turkey was not a belligerent—the position which obtained during World War II—belligerent warships could not pass through the Straits; if, however, Turkey was a belligerent, or if she were "threatened with imminent danger of war," the passage of foreign warships through the Straits would be left "entirely to the discretion of the Turkish Government." It is this provision of the Convention of Montreux which greatly disturbs Soviet sensibilities, and its importance needs no emphasis.

By a direct approach to Turkey in 1946 the Soviet Union sought to revise this convention in a way which would transfer control of the Straits to her own hands. Her proposal—that defence, control, and use of the Straits by warships should be the concern solely of the "Black Sea Powers"—was tantamount to reasserting the position temporarily won in 1833 by the Treaty of Unkiar-Skelessi. But this Soviet démarche failed (as did the Soviet claim to trusteeship over Tripolitania in 1947). The Montreux Convention, however, expires in 1956, unless renewed; prior notice of two years, required for its "denunciation," has not been given by any of the signatories.

The United States and N.A.T.O. in the Mediterranean

The interest of the United States in the Mediterranean area, which finds powerful expression politically in its moral, financial, and technical support of Italy, Greece, Turkey, and Yugoslavia and strategically in the maintenance there of its Sixth Fleet, is clearly a legacy of the second world war. Before that war the Mediterranean had no particular importance to the United States, although the scene of occasional American activity. A United States squadron was kept there during the first half of the nineteenth century and took its part in the suppression of piracy based on the North African coast. The foundation of the American University at Beirut was an interesting cultural enterprise in the Levant. At the end of the century, during the Spanish-American War, the United States came to appreciate the strategical importance of the Suez Canal.[6] American warships operated in the Mediterranean

[6] In order to impede the passage of a Spanish fleet at Port Said into the Suez Canal *en route* for the Far East, the American deputy consul at Cairo, acting on instructions from the Secretary of State, bought up all the local supplies of coal. See P. Crabitès, *The Spoliation of Suez* (George Routledge and Sons, Ltd, London, 1940), chapter xxii.

during World War I, and an American Naval Mission was stationed in the Adriatic from 1918 until 1921. Rather later—from 1928 onward—American oil companies, and, indeed, the State Department, intervened in the Middle East to secure oil interests or concessions—in Iraq, Kuweit, Bahrain, and Saudi Arabia. Americans found themselves there in commercial rivalry with Britain, which had aided national movements against Turkey and then assumed administrative control of many areas. But none of these earlier considerations accounts for the present large-scale American commitments in the Mediterranean theatre which are clearly one aspect of the revolution in American foreign policy which has taken place since the second world war began in Europe. The challenges of German and Japanese armed might, developments in the art of war, and the consequent weakening of the defensive value of the flanking oceans, no longer dominated as in the nineteenth century by British sea-power, and the awareness of its economic strength, overseas interests, and the responsibilities which attach themselves to political power, help to explain the present American policy which seeks defence by economic and military co-operation, beyond the oceans, with States near to areas of likely conflict.

It seems clear that American foreign policy in the Mediterranean area was at first determined by the logic of events rather than applied as part of a preconceived plan. American intervention in North Africa in 1942 (Operation Torch) brought American armed forces into the Mediterranean when the assault which they would have then preferred —an invasion of France—was too hazardous a venture. By 1944 there were nearly a million American troops, as well as the Sixth Fleet, in the Mediterranean theatre, and, jointly with Britain, the United States found itself in 1945 in a controlling position from the western Mediterranean to the Middle East. As French influence and power in this area had declined and as Britain reduced its commitments in Greece, withdrew from Palestine, India, Burma, and Ceylon, the United States projected its material aid, influence, and power into the Mediterranean area under the symbols—beneficent to Europe, but disquieting to the U.S.S.R.—of Marshall Aid, the Truman Doctrine, and N.A.T.O.

This policy has given practical effect to the realization that Mediterranean Europe, linked by the sea, is N.A.T.O.'s right flank in the military defence of Europe. It has achieved notable success, marked by the inclusion of Greece and Turkey in N.A.T.O., the support of Tito, the recent military agreement between Greece, Turkey, and Yugoslavia, and the American military and economic agreement with Spain. But it is on the abrupt edges of regional pacts that attention should be focused.[7] Until the settlement of the Trieste dispute in October 1954 one such edge lay in the Yugoslav-Italian frontier of tension in Istria, where a militarily exposed gap made vulnerable not only Trieste but the whole of North Italy. Another edge flanks the Middle East from Syria to Egypt, a politically unstable and militarily vulnerable region, where Western defence policy is faced with difficult and far-reaching decisions. For it should be clearly recognized that the geopolitical value of the Mediterranean Sea has hitherto rested on the British position in Egypt, junction of the sea routes from the outer oceans and passageway between them. This position has been lost, although the military base in the Canal Zone is being maintained by civilian experts and can be reoccupied under certain specified conditions. The British Middle East base is being built up in Cyprus, and Britain still retains a special position in Jordan (under a treaty of 1947). Britain's withdrawal from Egypt and the Sudan, taken together with her withdrawal from Palestine and India and the loss of French emplacements in Syria and Lebanon, raises urgently the role in Western defence of that large region which we oddly call the " Middle East."

Before grappling with this question, however, let us review the main functions of the Mediterranean area proper in Western defence and note the territorial bases available for performing them. The fleets of N.A.T.O., which rule their waters, have at their disposal the many mainland and insular harbours and bases of Britain, France, Italy, Greece, and Turkey—all member States. Since Spain, like Egypt, occupies so outstandingly important a position in relation to the Mediterranean—her territories border both ocean and inland sea and command both sides of the Strait of Gibraltar—it is not surprising that the United States has been at pains to seek an agreement with her. With the development of naval bases near Cadiz and at Cartagena, air bases in Spain, and the other American establishments at Port Lyautey, Rabat, Casablanca, and elsewhere in French Morocco, defence in depth will become available at the Mediterranean's Atlantic entry. The United States is thus quietly writing a new page of history by replacing Britain as the guardian of the western gateway to the Mediterranean. As the use of this narrow seaway must depend increasingly on

[7] See Hamilton Fish Armstrong, "Eisenhower's Right Flank," in *Foreign Affairs*, vol. xxix (July 1951).

H*

air support from the land, it is advantageous that Libya, fronting the centre of the basin, stands in friendly relations with the West and permits the maintenance of British and American airfields on its territory. Only Albania, which is another delicate area in Italo-Yugoslav relations, constitutes an outlier of the Soviet world on the shores of the Mediterranean. But in wartime, peacetime maps sometimes need rapid revision; there are weak spots, such as Macedonia and Thrace, at which —despite the Balkan Defence Pact of August 1954[8]—a powerful continental enemy might quickly strike.

The functions which are, or can be, carried out by N.A.T.O. naval power in the Mediterranean may be briefly listed. This long, ready, and mobile arm helps to defend vital objectives, such as the Strait of Gibraltar, and to apply the policy of containment to potential aggressors. Together with land-based strategic air forces, it provides a strong southern flank to the N.A.T.O. forces in western Europe which occupy defensive positions determined by political necessity, not by military choice. Control of the Mediterranean seaway is indispensable to the efficient co-operation of the member States of N.A.T.O., and to France as a link with Africa, an important source of its manpower and supplies. The possibilities in war both of flank attack from this sea and of support to land operations, by means of inter-service co-operation, clearly exist so long as aero-naval supremacy is held: such operations have been a recurrent feature of Mediterranean warfare and owe their success in part to deficiencies in surface transport in many areas around the basin. The seaport of Trieste, from which Anglo-American occupation forces were withdrawn in 1954, has a striking strategical position where the Mediterranean projects farthest north into Europe and, by way of Alpine passes, leads to the middle Danube basin and Vienna, for which it was originally created.

Moreover, naval control of the Mediterranean can, in some areas at least, gain prestige—no mean consideration. It provides, for example, the opportunity of winning friends and of diverting neutrals from hostile action. It guards the Turkish Straits, one of the water gates to the Soviet Union, which leads not only to its industrialized South but also to the Caucasus regions. Then, again, the Mediterranean provides the shortest route to the Middle East for both the United States and

---

[8] This agreement between Greece, Turkey, and Yugoslavia does not provide for automatic action by the signatories if one of them is a victim of aggression. The military value of this pact is seriously weakened by the conflicting attitudes of Turkey and Greece to the problem of Cyprus.

Britain. To the holders of this sea, in time of war, falls the trade in the many valuable commodities which its ports provide: oil (piped to the Levant coastlands), iron, copper and chrome, fertilizers and foodstuffs; control of these waters makes possible economic warfare generally, and maritime blockade in particular. And, lastly, since Africa is virtually an island and contains large areas dependent politically on west European countries, its defence, and all that this implies economically and strategically for its defenders, rests primarily on aero-naval supremacy in the Mediterranean-Red Sea area.

The Middle East and the Defence of the West

But if Western defence in the Mediterranean area appears firmly grounded, it is still weak in the Middle East—"the land of the five seas." Although during the inter-war period Britain and France were strongly established in this area, their tenure of power in the face of nationalistic pressures has either ended or is waning. Britain's position there in 1939 was still strong enough to enable her to create in Egypt a powerful, elaborate, and highly organized base for the defence not only of Egypt but of the whole Middle East. In retrospect, the British positions in Egypt, Jordan, Palestine, and Iraq would appear to have served more than a narrowly British Commonwealth interest in the war against the Axis Powers. It is now open to discussion whether this costly defence commitment in the Middle East—even if it is still practicable to continue it—is strategically justified in the best interests of the British Commonwealth. No other base in the Middle East can possibly be as efficient as Egypt,[9] where the Suez Canal Zone, accessible to shipping from both the Atlantic and Indian Oceans, commands the single invasion route into Egypt from the Levant coastlands. The loss of this linchpin of the British Middle East defence position has inevitably weakened the remaining defence foothold in Jordan. The practical possibility of preserving the Canal from all likely forms of attack also appears more than doubtful, and though the loss of its use would not be disastrous to the base it would be serious.

In short, although it may take time to adjust thought to such fundamental reorganization of the British defence system—if time is allowed —it would seem sound British policy to build up defence in depth, as

[9] It is Egypt, not merely the Canal, which makes the base so important. During the second world war it provided a large labour force and repair centre as well as airfields, railroads, headquarters, and ports.

some military experts have long argued, in and around the Indian Ocean, on the shores of which lie three-fifths of the area of the British Commonwealth. There the Gulf of Aden and the Red Sea entry could be held from near-by British territories; Kenya, linked with West Africa by air routes and roads might be made a base for supplies, while the Persian and Ormuz Gulfs might be held with the aid of outlying defence positions in Iraq. For this the co-operation of Pakistan, India, and Ceylon would be most desirable. Such a deployment of forces would impose on an aggressor from the north the weakness of lengthened lines of communication through difficult country, shield the oilfields of Iraq and the Persian Gulf, and utilize the facilities provided by command of the sea for the movement of men and *matériel* to required points.

Such a change in the geography of British defence organization, which might in any case be enforced by events, has its clear implications for the United States. Americans must necessarily have pondered the questions whether, and to what extent, their own foreign and defence policies were at times underwriting the waning imperialism of Britain. A delicate and careful analysis would be necessary to explore these questions, and the concept 'imperialism' in its more decent modern dress would need due evaluation. But the power vacuum created by the British withdrawal from Egypt cannot easily be filled. Defences, now barely strong enough for their possible tasks, become inadequate. While Turkey may appear a substantial obstacle set between the Black Sea and the Mediterranean, both Persia on her eastern flank and the Arab States to the south remain areas of political and military weakness exposed to the Soviet Union's sharpest weapon, ideological infiltration. The co-operation and bases which are necessary if the Middle East defence gap is to be filled are not to be easily obtained, in some at least of the States of the Arab League. Recollection of American support for the new Israel, with which, in their view, a state of war still exists, distrust of alliances with Great Powers, the aspiration for full independence in countries whose faith and culture are alien to those of the West, unwillingness to incur Soviet hostility by defence arrangements that will be deemed provocative in Moscow, predilection for that scarcely rejoicing third 'neutralist' bloc which cries "A plague o' both your houses!"—all present a stern challenge to Western diplomacy.[10]

[10] For a critical analysis of Middle East problems, see Albert Hourani, "The Decline of the West in the Middle East—I," in *International Affairs*, London, vol. xxix (January 1953).

If the age of miracles has not passed, and if Stalin's successors were actually thinking of peace and not merely talking about it, the Middle East, east of Egypt, might be made the test case in an attempt at settlement between the U.S.S.R. and the West. Here Nature has provided a spacious and largely desert frontier of separation between the Soviet Union on the one hand and Africa and the Indian sub-continent and ocean on the other—an area of ancient cultures and historic interest, as also of poverty and ill-health despite its oases of Western industrialism. Here, in a dream world of sanity, the rich petroleum resources could be exploited not only for consumers within the dollar and sterling areas. Westerners and Russians would agree to leave these Middle Eastern peoples free to develop in their own ways, with such financial and technical aid as they were willing to accept and able to absorb.

But, pending the miracle, the broad strategical problem persists, and it is primarily an Anglo-American problem. Complete withdrawal from British positions in the Middle East would leave the eastern flank of N.A.T.O.'s Mediterranean position exposed to land attack and threaten the loss of the Suez Canal passway; available forward defences would exist only in Turkey, Cyprus, Crete, and Libya. To hold the area in strength for adequate defence clearly requires the collaboration of the Arab States and Israel—and the enmity between these introduces at once a factor of political weakness. The League of the Arab States, although it rests on a basis of common cultural ideas and ensures inter-Arab co-operation in economic, financial, and other matters, is in no sense an effective military organization for defence. Its leader, Egypt, has sought above all so to integrate it that in its dealings with the Great Powers it should act as one. Iraq, however, mindful of external dangers and of the need to defend its rich petroleum resources, has challenged this Egyptian policy by following an independent line. She noted with interest Pakistan's acceptance of military aid from the United States and the conclusion of the Turco-Pakistan Pact of 1954. Unlike Egypt, Iraq has accepted American military aid and signed a mutual defence treaty with Turkey which Arab States and others able to help in the defence of this area may join. Britain quickly seized the opportunity of relinquishing her outworn treaty of 1930—which gave the Royal Air Force the use of two airfields in Iraq—by herself joining this system of regional defence. Persia too joined this pact in 1955.

Thus the Western Powers have made some progress towards strengthening the defences of the Middle East. Moreover, Britain's relations

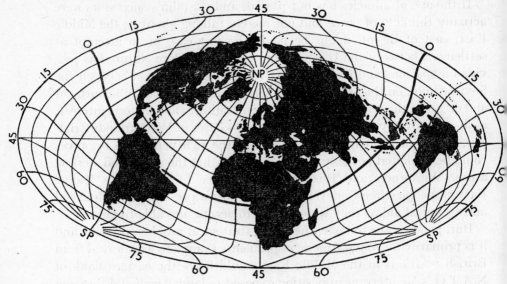

FIG. 2. THE WORLD CENTRED ON THE MEDITERRANEAN SEA

From the world map "Nordic Projection." By courtesy of Messrs John Bartholomew and Son, Ltd

with Egypt have improved, and under her recent treaty the base in the Suez Canal zone can be reactivated in certain eventualities, one of which is aggression against Turkey. The direct actions of Pakistan and Iraq have, through their reactions, caused fresh international difficulties. India, still at loggerheads with Pakistan over Kashmir, resents Pakistan's acceptance of American military aid and consequent increase of military strength. The Arab League has become a riven structure: Egypt, backed by Saudi Arabia and Syria, strongly objects to Iraq's defiance of the League and of her direct association with one of the Great Powers and also with Turkey, which has maintained normal relations with the Arabs' enemy Israel. And the last named, beset by the unsolved problems of her frontiers, the Jordan waters and Arab refugees, notes with some concern the departure of British forces from the Canal Zone, the increasing strength of Iraq, and the growth in Egypt's military strength as a result of armaments imported from Czechoslovakia. Certainly Israel's difficulties abound, although the tripartite declaration of the United States, the United Kingdom, and France, does at least promise her support against an aggressor.

It has been said that "Who holds the Mediterranean holds the World"

(Fig. 2). There is no need to apply this simplification to the present international complexities and dangers. It will be clear, however, that aero-naval control of the Mediterranean-Red Sea interior line of movement, where three continents adjoin, is for the Western Powers of first-class importance to the strategy of peace, as it proved in war.

FURTHER READING

BELOT, R. DE, *The Struggle for the Mediterranean, 1939–45,* translated by D. A. Field, Jr. (Princeton University Press, 1951; Oxford University Press, 1952).

BIROT, PIERRE, and DRESCH, JEAN, *La Méditerranée et le Moyen-Orient:* vol. i, *La Méditerranée occidentale: Géographie physique et humaine, Péninsule ibérique, Italie, Afrique du Nord.* 'Orbis': Introduction aux études de géographie (Presses Universitaires de France, Paris, 1953).

CHURCHILL, SIR WINSTON S., *The Second World War* (six vols.; Cassell, London, 1948–54). (Vols. 3, 4, and 5 discuss the Mediterranean war.)

CORBETT, JULIAN S., *England in the Mediterranean, 1603–1713* (two vols.; Longmans, Green, London, 1904).

CRABITÈS, PIERRE, *The Spoliation of Suez* (Routledge, London, 1940).

DESPOIR, J., *La Colonisation italienne en Libye* (Paris, 1953).

EAST, W. GORDON, *Mediterranean Problems* (Nelson, London; revised edition, 1943). (A short introduction.)

FANNING, L. M., *American Oil Operations Abroad* (McGraw-Hill, New York, 1947).

HERTSLET, SIR E. (editor), *The Map of Europe by Treaty* (four vols.; Butterworth, London, 1875–91).

HOSKINS, H. L., *The Middle East: Problem Area in World Politics* (Macmillan, New York, 1954); *British Routes to India* (Longmans, Green, New York and London, 1928).

ISSAWI, CHARLES, *Egypt at Mid-Century: An Economic Survey* (revised edition; Oxford University Press, London and New York, 1954).

LEDVE, G. (editor), *Les Industries de l'Afrique du Nord* (Paris, 1952).

MONROE, ELIZABETH, *The Mediterranean in Politics* (Oxford University Press, London, 1938).

PURYEAR, V. J., *Napoleon and the Dardanelles* (University of California Press, Berkeley and Los Angeles, and Cambridge University Press, 1951).

REITZEL, WILLIAM, *The Mediterranean: Its Role in America's Foreign Policy* (Harcourt Brace, New York, 1948).

RENNELL OF RODD, LORD, *British Military Administration of Occupied Territories in Africa during the Years 1941–47* (H.M.S.O., London, 1948).

SIEGFRIED, ANDRÉ, *Suez and Panama* (translation; Cape, London and Toronto, 1940).

SPEISER, E. A., *The United States and the Near East* (Harvard University Press, Cambridge, Mass., and Oxford University Press, 1947).

UNITED NATIONS, *Economic Survey of Europe in 1953* (Geneva, 1954).

UNITED NATIONS, *Non-Self-governing Territories* (New York, 1954).

CHAPTER VIII

Intra-European Circulation

A. E. MOODIE

THE title of this chapter calls for a short explanation. The term 'circulation' is used here to include all those movements of goods, passengers, news, ideas, and capital which are essential to both national and international well-being. There is no one synonym for this word in the English terminologies of geography and economics. 'Trade' refers to the exchange of goods, 'communications' usually means rail, road, and water transport systems, while 'telecommunications' includes telegraph, wireless, and cable services; 'transport' is commonly used to describe the movements of both goods and passengers, but 'transport facilities' is restricted to the services and vehicles (including ships, barges, and aircraft, as well as trains and road vehicles) which carry them. 'Circulation' covers all these activities and is all the more valuable to geographers in that it is a comprehensive term. It was first widely used by French geographers, notably and recently by Capot-Rey;[1] its adoption in English obviates a number of ambiguities and misuses.

Circulation, in this sense, is basic to the economic and political organization of every State, but its development varies within wide limits. No period in history is comparable with the first half of the twentieth century in its growth of facilities for all kinds of movement both within countries and internationally. So highly valued are they that internal networks are subject to some degree of governmental control in all countries. Almost all the railway systems of Europe are 'nationalized,' postal services are usually State monopolies, and national air lines are normally in receipt of subsidies in some form. This appreciation of the importance of circulation in national affairs, so clearly exemplified in such different realms as those of the private enterprise

[1] P. Capot-Rey, *Géographie de la Circulation sur les Continents* (Paris, 1946).

economies of Western Europe[2] and the centrally planned economies of the Communist States, indicates that it is a vital factor in internal political organization. In international relations, too, it is equally if not more important, since intercourse between States rests on circulation. The commonly used phrase 'the shrinking world' is merely geographical shorthand for saying that the facilities for world circulation have greatly expanded so that speed, volume, and ease of movement have reached a level never before achieved. Yet there remains an important contrast between internal and external circulation. Within national boundaries, and making allowance for physical and economic limitations, everything possible is done to increase circulation. On the other hand, politico-economic barriers are a common feature of the relationships between States, so that international circulation is artificially restricted. Undoubtedly, the outstanding example of this restriction is to be seen in the sealing off of the Communist world by the continued existence of the Iron Curtain, which has become so effective that a recent United Nations publication has introduced the terms 'Eastern World Market' and 'Western World Market.'[3] At the same time, however, all is not 'free' in international relations in the western world, where the wealthiest and most highly productive State is unwilling to open its markets freely to European or other exporters. This contrast between the freedom of internal circulation and the relative lack of freedom in international movements reaches a climax in regions where territorial fragmentation is excessive. The United States, nearly eight million square kilometres in area, constitutes one vast common market for its producers, and, within it, movement is completely free to all its citizens. Similarly, the twenty-two million square kilometres of the U.S.S.R. have no internal trade barriers. By contrast, Europe has an area of nearly five million square kilometres, which is unevenly shared among twenty-six States, and the interruptive functions of its international boundaries are made even worse by that of the Iron Curtain. Attempts have been made since 1945 to create limited common markets in Europe, but at the present time it must be admitted that hindrances to circulation are of greater force in this continent than in any other area of comparable scale. This is one of the penalties which Europe pays for its development of the idea of the small nation State.

[2] Unless otherwise stated, Western Europe in this chapter comprises the United Kingdom, Ireland, Finland, Norway, Sweden, Denmark, the Netherlands, Belgium-Luxembourg, Western Germany, France, Portugal, Italy, Switzerland, Greece, Turkey, and Yugoslavia. The last of these is a Communist country, but not a satellite of the U.S.S.R.

[3] *Economic Survey of Europe in 1954* (E.C.E., Geneva, 1955).

Politics and Circulation in Europe

During the forty years preceding the second world war Europe "moved . . . towards an almost complete disintegration. Movements of capital and labour were, in the inter-war period, progressively restricted, the result being that, on the European level, labour, capital, new technology and natural resources were far from being harmonized in optimal combinations."[4] While changes in the terms of trade throughout the world and, not least important, the effects of two world wars have added greatly to the difficulties of European economic development, the continued existence of a large number of unco-ordinated national policies remains the chief barrier to a fuller growth of trade and other branches of circulation. The intractable character of this problem is well illustrated by the numerous attempts which have been made, with varying but limited success, to overcome difficulties of movement.[5] Since the end of the second world war even greater activities have been directed towards finding solutions to Europe's economic difficulties. Some of these are non-governmental, several are sponsored by the United Nations Organization through its appropriate specialized agencies, and others are organized at governmental level.[6] The formidable array of institutions through which these efforts are conducted has made valuable studies of various aspects of European life, in particular the individual institutions have compiled statistical data which are prerequisites to further development, yet with one or two exceptions, circulation within Europe remains hindered by the policies of its component States.

The severity of this hindrance is worsened by the fact that, for most of the continental countries, intra-European trade is more important than trade with the rest of the world. In 1938 the United Kingdom and France were the only two of the twenty-two countries listed in Table 1 which sent more than half of their exports to and received more than half of their imports from non-European States. In that year 61·3 per cent. of European exports circulated within the continent, as did 50·4

[4] I. Svennilson, *Growth and Stagnation in the European Economy* (E.C.E., Geneva, 1954), p. 42. This penetrating analysis is indispensable to the student of European economic problems, including those of circulation.

[5] Most of these inter-war attempts are described in a valuable series of studies, compiled under the direction of Sir Osborne Mance for the Royal Institute of International Affairs and published by the Oxford University Press. In particular, see O. Mance, *Frontiers, Peace Treaties and International Organization* (Oxford University Press, 1946).

[6] See Lord Layton, "Introductory Report on International Economic Institutions," in *The Economic Future of Europe*, by René Boël and others, (Deutsch, London, 1954, and Praeger, New York).

per cent. of its total imports. The trade figures for 1950 show a marked decrease (53·4 per cent. and 46·1 per cent. respectively), but this is largely the result of the reorientation of the trade of the East European satellite States towards the U.S.S.R.[7] In effect, therefore, the European

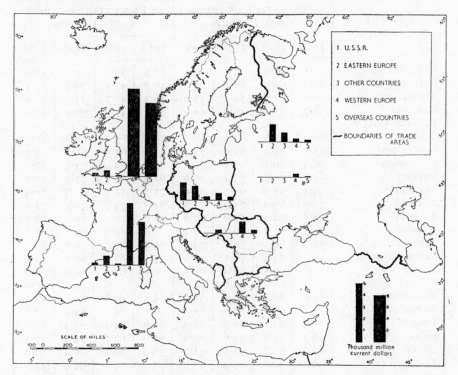

FIG. 1. EUROPEAN TRADE BY MAJOR AREAS IN 1937 AND 1953

The upper diagram represents 1953 trade and the lower 1937 trade for Western Europe (O.E.E.C. Europe), Eastern Europe (Eastern Germany, Poland, Czechoslovakia, Hungary, Romania, and Bulgaria), and the U.S.S.R. The reorientation of Eastern Europe's trade since 1937 is clearly shown. 'Other countries' are Mainland China, Mongolia, North Korea, and Albania.

Based on data in *Economic Survey of Europe in 1954* (E.C.E., Geneva, 1955).

economy, viewed as a whole, is largely a 'subsistence' economy, even if allowance is made for the large quantities of goods imported from and exported to overseas areas. Since none of the European countries is self-supporting, neither in raw materials nor in manufactured goods, the free flow of goods between them is necessary to maintain their economic well-being and is even more essential if stagnation is to be overcome.

[7] See Fig. 8, Chapter IV above.

TABLE 1

European Trade in the Twentieth Century[1]

COUNTRY	EXPORTS FROM INDIVIDUAL COUNTRIES TO EUROPE AS PERCENTAGE OF THEIR TOTAL EXPORTS				IMPORTS OF INDIVIDUAL COUNTRIES FROM EUROPE AS PERCENTAGE OF THEIR TOTAL IMPORTS			
	1913	1928	1938	1950	1913	1928	1938	1950
United Kingdom	30·1	31·6	32·1	29·8	37·5	38·9	31·0	27·9
Germany . .	66·3	69·9	65·1	71·6	40·7	47·1	50·3	53·4
France . .	66·6	62·5	54·2	43·6	46·5	42·7	33·7	29·9
Italy . .	58·7	57·4	48·7	56·0	58·2	47·0	60·0	38·2
Belgium-Luxembourg .	79·2	69·9	69·1	66·5	58·6	65·2	54·8	51·7
Netherlands .	65·2	74·3	69·0	72·3	47·0	61·4	58·7	58·2
Switzerland .	69·3	69·2	69·4	58·9	79·1	72·5	73·3	57·8
Sweden .	83·6	74·9	77·4	70·9	81·5	74·0	75·2	76·7
Denmark .	95·4	93·9	93·1	88·8	73·5	71·3	83·3	81·5
Norway .	73·9	69·2	81·9	71·0	84·5	74·7	77·1	67·3
Finland .	68·8	82·3	84·0	67·8	71·6	78·2	82·5	69·8
Ireland .	—	98·2	99·2	96·4	—	86·3	66·8	68·1
Austria .	80·3	86·5	83·7	74·4	65·8	83·6	74·7	82·3
Czechoslovakia .	—	84·4	70·1	48·9	—	82·9	66·1	53·3
Hungary .	—	96·5	88·4	66·1	—	93·4	89·3	66·9
Poland .	—	92·2	85·0	74·7	—	75·6	62·8	46·0
Romania .	87·0	89·4	86·4	35·6	89·5	90·8	89·1	42·1
Yugoslavia .	—	95·6	88·9	71·5	—	88·4	84·2	63·8
Bulgaria .	83·3	91·1	92·6	42·3	80·6	94·1	93·3	35·8
Greece .	78·3	78·2	75·6	67·0	71·0	62·7	73·3	46·1
Spain .	69·4	69·7	73·5	41·3	58·9	49·5	66·4	33·9
Portugal .	59·4	69·8	69·4	45·9	75·0	74·2	64·4	47·6
Total Europe .	59·6	63·0	61·3	53·4	49·4	53·6	50·4	46·1

[1] Imports and exports by value.

Source: I. Svennilson, *Growth and Stagnation in the European Economy* (Economic Commission for Europe, Geneva, 1954).

The maintenance of the separative functions of Europe's 21,788 kilometres of land boundaries, given existing policies, is the greatest single obstacle to this freedom of circulation on the continent.

National policies thus play the most prominent part in the pattern and machinery of circulation in all its aspects, but particularly in the movement of goods. Nothing short of full federation of all the countries west of the Soviet boundary will allow the establishment of a European common market and its desirable concomitants in the free movement of people, ideas, and capital, comparable with that of the United States, but, in the presence of Communism in Eastern Europe and the forces which lie behind national sovereignty in Western Europe, this is not a short-term expectation. The idea of a 'United States of Europe' has much to commend it, but its implementation calls for circumstances which simply do not exist at present.

Disintegration in Intra-European Trade

Trade between any two areas reflects a combination of physical, economic, social, and political factors, and it is rarely possible to give a correct weighting to each of them. In an ideal world, solutions of many economic problems could be found through national specialization of production accompanied by free exchanges of surpluses; in the existing world, emphasis has been laid on attempts to achieve economic autarky —*i.e.*, many countries have sought to be self-supporting in all those commodities which they could produce even to the extent of incurring higher costs than those obtaining elsewhere. Particularly during the inter-war period in Europe, economic independence was given priority over interdependence with a resultant reduction in intra-European trade as well as exchanges with other parts of the world. War disruption and the generally unstable terms of trade throughout the world during the middle years of that period were factors conducive to such policies, but their effects were not evenly important on the Continent. Their most striking manifestation was seen in the trade between the three large industrial countries—the United Kingdom, Germany, and France —as Table 2 shows.

Not only did the decline in trade within this group proceed almost continuously from 1913 to 1938, but it has shown little indication of recovery since the second world war. Furthermore, disintegration was also exemplified in the expansion of trade between the smaller countries. In effect, intra-European trade is more and more being carried on outside the group of the three big countries. "The trade in which the latter had no share rose from one-fifth of the total of intra-European trade in 1913, to one-quarter in 1938 and to one-third in 1950."[8]

The 'Big Three' were also differentiated from the rest of Europe by the high proportion of total European trade for which they were responsible. But, whereas their share of exports fell from 64·4 per cent. in 1913

[8] Svennilson, *op. cit.*, p. 197.

TABLE 2
Trade between the United Kingdom, Germany, and France
(1913, 1928, 1938, 1950)

Per 1000 of total intra-European trade (excluding U.S.S.R.)

EXPORTING COUNTRIES	IMPORTING COUNTRIES			TOTAL
	U.K.	Germany	France	
United Kingdom—				
1913 . .	—	33	24	57
1928 . .	—	22	14	36
1938 . .	—	16	12	28
1950 . .	—	11	10	21
Germany—				
1913 . .	57	—	31	88
1928 . .	31	—	21	52
1938 . .	22	—	14	36
1950[1] . .	9	—	16	25
France—				
1913 . .	31	23	—	54
1928 . .	34	24	—	58
1938 . .	16	9	—	25
1950 . .	24	20	—	44
Total—				
1913 . .	88	56	55	199
1928 . .	65	46	35	146
1938 . .	38	25	26	89
1950 . .	33	31	26	90

[1] W. Germany only.

Source: I. Svennilson, op. cit., Table 58, p. 198. The figures given in this table represent a combination of value and approximate volume of trade for four selected years.

to 50·5 per cent. in 1950 and their share of imports from 61·4 to 49·1 per cent., that of the rest of Europe rose from 45·6 to 49·5 per cent. (exports) and from 38·6 to 50·9 per cent. (imports) during the same thirty-seven years. Clearly the dominance of the United Kingdom, Germany, and France in European trade, both overseas and within the continent, has declined since c. 1900. This is partly explained, since the second world war, by the defection of the Communist States of Eastern Europe (excepting Yugoslavia), but of greater significance have been the protectionist policies and bilateral trade agreements of the countries which lie west of the Iron Curtain. This disintegration has continued in spite of increased production and overall trade. "The task which Western Europe now faces is to build a better economy than that existing before the war. For member countries have completed—indeed, exceeded—the economic recovery which, when the Marshall Plan began, was no more than a hope. Their recent achievements have paved the way for further progress."[9] Such a "better economy" calls at least for a discontinuance of disintegration, but, preferably, for closer politico-economic integration. Attempts in this direction will be discussed later in this chapter, but some of the problems associated with the means of intra-European circulation should be noticed here.

The Means of Circulation in Europe

Economic development in the modern world is closely dependent on the ability to move industrial raw materials and finished products, food-stuffs and people, together with the availability of those other branches of circulation which convey knowledge and ideas—e.g., telecommunications and postal services. In this respect Europe is very well equipped with a dense network of railways, roads, and inland waterways and good postal, telegraph, and radio communications, but mere length of transport arteries is an inadequate criterion of their effective use, nor, indeed, is accessibility to them in terms of distance always of decisive importance. Differential tariff rates and other restrictive factors frequently reduce the movement of traffic, and the more a given area is divided into independent political units, the more commonly are political considerations likely to interfere with the flow of goods and passengers. "In almost every country of the world inland transport has become a political issue for fiscal or other reasons; . . . transport is too much at the whim of domestic politics," recently stated the chairman of a manufacturing organization with world-wide connexions.[10] Because Europe is excessively fragmented politically, its internal circulation is particularly subject to "the whim of domestic politics." The establishment of special tariffs, import quotas, and other discriminatory measures is usually 'justified' on commercial and national grounds, but their existence, and particularly their liability to rapid change, are drawbacks to the full utilization of the means of circulation. During the inter-war years political interference with the use of both domestic and

---

[9] *From Recovery towards Economic Strength*, Sixth Report of the Organization for European Economic Co-operation (O.E.E.C.) (Paris, 1955), p. 15.
[10] Sir G. Heyworth, *Transport* (Unilever, Ltd, London, 1955), p. 15.

international means of transport reached a maximum,[11] and there remains a strong carry-over of these policies into the post-war period. There can be little doubt that it is the most powerful factor militating against integration of the European economy.

The political fragmentation of Europe has modified its circulation in another way. In each of its countries all forms of transport facilities were originally created to serve either local or regional needs.[12] Gradually they became welded into national systems which were certainly not designed for international movement, which had to be adapted to existing conditions as the need arose. In contrast with the United States and Canada, where railway construction commonly preceded the opening up of parts of the State territory, the primary purpose of railways in most parts of Europe was to link already existing towns and/or industrial areas. Once the regional lines became parts of national systems the latter showed a strong tendency to focus on State capitals. A similar trend, but with less clear-cut results, is observable in the network of main roads in most European countries, provided that conditions of terrain make this possible. By the beginning of the twentieth century, after which relatively little new railway construction has been undertaken, the major arteries of movements and goods showed a pattern which clearly reflected national interests.

Differences in economic development in the several parts of Europe were, and still are, revealed in the density of their national networks. The advanced industrial countries of Western Europe, particularly the United Kingdom, Germany, and France, developed their transport facilities far more rapidly than the rest of the continent in length of track, roads, and inland waterways, and certainly in the numbers of passengers and the tonnages of goods carried. In this, as in other ways, Southern Europe remained a region of arrested development and Eastern Europe stayed under-developed (see Table 3). A similar degree of differentiation is revealed if we use the criterion of ton/kilometres to measure the intensity of traffic of each of the countries (see Fig. 2), and also, as Table 4 shows, by the relationships between length of railways and area and population respectively (see Fig. 3). Judged by the availa-

[11] "In 1936 the Reichsbahn [German State Railways] had 550 exceptional tariffs, of which 133 were export and 49 import tariffs."—R. L. Wedgwood, *International Rail Transport* (Oxford University Press, 1946), p. 58. The reader is referred to Chapter IV of this work for further examples of political control of railway and inland waterway transport.

[12] The only important European exception to this rule was the network of roads of the Roman Empire.

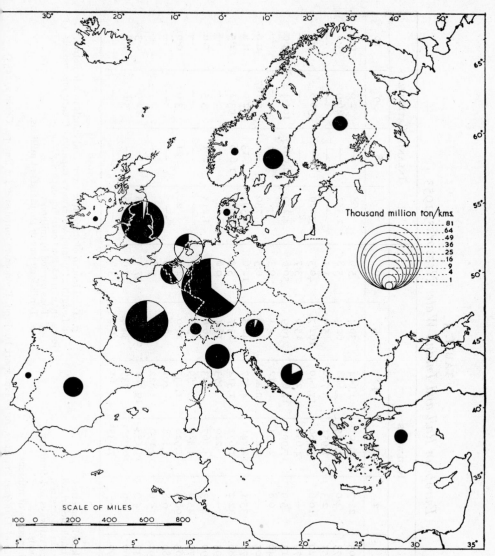

Fig. 2. The Rail and Inland Waterways Goods Traffic of Western Europe (O.E.E.C. Europe) in Ton/Kms. in 1953

The areas of the circles represent total traffic by rail and inland waterways; the black segments represent total rail traffic. Inland waterways goods traffic data are not available for Sweden and Italy; that for Switzerland is too small to be shown on this scale.

Based on data in *Annual Statistical Bulletin, 1953* (Transport Division, E.C.E., Geneva, 1955).

TABLE 3

European Rail and Inland Water Networks, 1953

	RAILWAYS						INLAND WATERWAYS			
	1	2	3	4	5	6	7	8	9	10
Austria	6,005	22·7	4,401	1,604	36·4	5·9	368	—	2·6	0·4
Belgium	4,973	4·0	2,285	2,688	62·4	5·8	1,552	—	46·9	3·8
Denmark	2,651	2·3	1,951	700	5·9	1·1	—	—	—	—
France	41,420	10·6	23,780	17,640	162·7	40·5	13,229	—	50·8	7·8
Finland	4,879	—	4,659	220	15·6	3·7	—	—	—	—
W. Germany	30,513	5·9	17,903	12,610	219·9	50·6	4,259	2,091	101·4	23·0
Greece[1]	2,546	0·8	2,534	12	2·1	0·3	—	—	—	n.a.
Ireland	4,105	—	n.a.	n.a.	3·8	0·5	730	—	0·167	n.a.
Italy	16,478	35·1	12,241	4,237	48·5	12·6	2,397	13	2·0	n.a.
Netherlands	3,186	42·2	1,672	1,514	23·7	3·3	6,918	1,616	93·4	12·5
Luxembourg	393	—	220	173	16·1	0·6	—	—	—	—
Sweden	15,090	40·3	14,267	823	36·6	8·3	1,213	261	3·5	n.a.
Norway	4,379	25·6	4,320	59	5·0	1·0	—	—	—	—
Switzerland	3,165	96·5	1,928	1,237	22·0	2·6	21	21	3·9	0·01
Portugal	3,589	0·8	3,188	401	3·5	0·6	—	—	—	—
Spain	12,992	5·6	11,170	1,822	27·7	7·8	—	—	—	—
U.K.	30,935	4·9	11,153	19,782	293·1	37·1	3,833	—	12·9	0·345
Yugoslavia	11,660	0·9	10,921	739	34·4	7·9	2,035[2]	—	5·6	1·8
Turkey	7,696	—	7,635	61	10·2	3·6	—	—	—	—

[1] 1952.   [2] 1950.

1. Total length of track in kilometres.
2. Percentage of total track electrified.
3. Single-track railways in kilometres.
4. Double or more track railways in kilometres.
5. Tons carried in millions.
6. Ton/kilometres in thousands of millions.
7. Total length of navigable rivers and canals in kilometres.
8. Length of inland waterways capable of carrying vessels of more than 1000 tons carrying capacity.
9. Tons carried in millions.
10. Ton/kilometres in thousands of millions.

Source: *Annual Bulletin of Transport Statistics, 1953* (Transport Division, Economic Commission for Europe, Geneva, 1955).

bility of transport facilities, and the annual rate of ton/kilometres, as well as by almost any other criteria, the Big Three together with the Benelux countries and Switzerland constitute the centre of economic

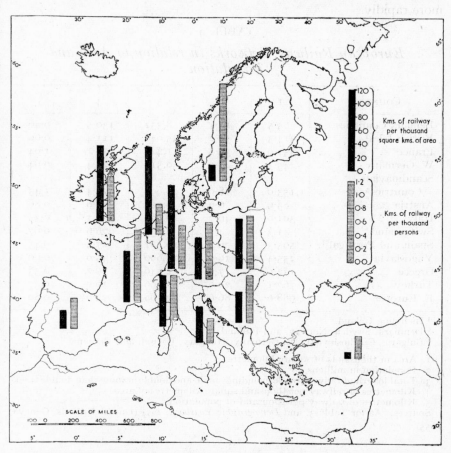

FIG. 3. EUROPEAN RAIL NETWORKS IN RELATION TO AREA AND POPULATION

The following countries are grouped: Denmark, Norway, Sweden and Finland, Netherlands and Belgium-Luxembourg, Spain and Portugal, Eastern Germany, Poland, Czechoslovakia, Hungary, Romania and Bulgaria. The base-lines of the blocks rest on the area of each country or group, except for Switzerland, where the blocks are inverted.

Based on data in *Annual Statistical Bulletin, 1953* (Transport Division, E.C.E., Geneva, 1955).

gravity in Western Europe. The peripheral countries are less well served and have a generally less well-developed economy. Here it is difficult to separate cause and effect, but it seems likely that if the transport systems of these areas had been more fully developed, and if they had been more closely and effectively linked with those of the Big Three, then their production and international trade would have grown more rapidly.

TABLE 4

European Railway Networks in relation to Area and Population

COUNTRY	1	2	3	4	5
Benelux Countries .	65·5	18·4	8,552	130·5	0·46
British Isles[1] . .	314·3	53·2	35,040	111·4	0·66
France . . .	551·0	39·8	41,420	75·1	1·04
W. Germany . .	245·3	47·7	30,513	124·4	0·64
Scandinavian					
Countries[2] . .	1,153·0	18·6	26,999	23·4	1·43
Austria . . .	83·9	6·9	6,005	71·6	0·86
Italy . . .	301·0	46·7	16,478	54·7	0·35
Switzerland . .	41·3	4·7	3,165	76·6	0·67
Spain and Portugal .	595·3	36·4	16,581	27·9	0·45
Yugoslavia . .	255·4	16·9	11,660	45·6	0·69
Greece . . .	132·6	7·6	2,546	19·2	0·33
Turkey . . .	767·1	20·9	7,696	10·0	0·37
E. Europe[3] . .	988·6	86·6	72,168	73·0	0·80

[1] Including Ireland.
[2] Denmark, Sweden, Norway, and Finland.
[3] Bulgaria, Czechoslovakia, E. Germany, Hungary, Poland, and Romania.

1. Area in thousands of square kilometres.
2. Population in millions.
3. Total length of railway track including single and double or more than double track.
4. Kilometres of railway per thousand square kilometres of area.
5. Kilometres of railway per thousand of population.
Sources: As for Table 3, and *Demographic Yearbook, 1954* (United Nations, Geneva, 1955).

Rail Transport. Compared with most other parts of the world, Europe possesses good facilities for rail transport, both for goods and passengers, yet rail traffic has lost its position of relative importance in European circulation. Prior to the first world war the railway systems had reached a high level of performance and showed marked stability both in services rendered and in tariff rates. Employment by the railway companies was considered a 'safe job' and investment in railway shares was comparable with that in 'gilt-edged.' New lines were still being constructed, although most of Western Europe was approaching saturation, and the future of the railway industry seemed secure. Nevertheless, the war of

1914–18 and its effects brought about a transformation on the European railways which could hardly have been foreseen. The causes of this change fall into two groups—economic and political.

Among the economic causes, rising costs of railway operation, increased by the cost of post-war reconstruction, led to increased passenger fares and freight rates, and thus reduced the competitive capacity of the railways. Far more important, however, was the advent of road transport both as a substitute for and a complement to rail traffic. "The negative side of this development was a slowing-down in the growth of transport by rail, a loss of income by the railways as a result of this new competition from the roads, and a financial weakness which tended to make the railways a depressed industry with a slow rate of modernization."[13] This new development took some years to make its effects felt and was certainly unevenly spread throughout the Continent, mainly for financial reasons. In Eastern and Southern Europe capital for investment in roads and vehicles was not adequately available, so that the railways remained the prime movers of goods and passengers in those areas, as they still do. In contrast, the change-over to road transport in the industrialized countries of Western Europe has been remarkable. No longer do the railways hold a dominant position in the transport of goods within these countries, as Table 5 shows.

TABLE 5

Percentages of Total Traffic carried by Rail, Road, and Inland Waterways

COUNTRY	YEAR	RAIL	ROAD	INLAND WATERWAYS
France	1952	21	73	6
W. Germany	1952	26	63	11
Netherlands	1952	9	57	34
Switzerland	1951	43	48	9
United Kingdom	1952	24	75	1

Source: *Annual Bulletin of Transport Statistics, 1953* (Geneva, 1955).

A further factor which affected transport conditions during the inter-war years was the change from pre-war stability to post-war instability in the European economy. No longer was it possible for the operating concerns to rely on a steady flow of traffic, nor could they fix permanent freight rates. Increased operating costs, including the investments con-

[13] Svennilson, *op. cit.*, p. 144.

cerned with the growth of electrification of track,[14] combined with the uneasy state of European trade generally, undermined the international efficiency and the financial position of the railways in spite of the efforts of such organizations as the League of Nations Committee on Rail Transport, the International Chamber of Commerce, and the International Railway Union. Under these economic conditions the railways became subject to increasing State control, partly because they found it necessary to bolster up their new policy of speculation by governmental financial assistance, but also because nationalism became rampant between the wars. This brings us to the second group of causes of the changes in railway affairs in Europe.

The outstanding characteristic of political interference with rail transport during the inter-war years was the use of special rail tariffs as a means to further national aims—e.g., the stimulation of depressed industries, the encouragement of a national port policy, or the implementation of some international trade bargain. Germany, in virtue of her interior location in Europe and her consequently powerful strategic position in intra-European trade, together with her highly nationalist policy after the Nazis came into power, led the way. Under the Versailles Treaty Germany undertook not to discriminate against goods coming from the Allied and Associated Powers, but once the five-year period of this agreement expired she began an intensive national policy, so that by 1938 nearly 75 per cent. of all traffic on the Reichsbahn was being carried at special rates. In international trade the two most interesting aspects of this policy were the well-known Adriatic Tariffs and the competition for the foreign trade of Poland between the German railways and the Polish ports. By the former, Germany sought to favour the trade of Hamburg and Bremen with Austria and Czechoslovakia by reducing the railway rates to those ports to the level of those between these two countries and Trieste and Fiume (Rijeka), in spite of their shorter distances from the Adriatic ports.[15] Thus was the severance of Trieste and Fiume from their former hinterlands expedited. Similarly, Germany did all in its power to attract traffic from the hinterland of Danzig to its own North Sea ports, a political move which was strongly resisted by the newly revived Polish State. After Danzig and

[14] In Austria, Germany, France, Italy, the Netherlands, Sweden, and Switzerland the aggregate of electrified track increased from 8502 kilometres to 16,333 kilometres between 1930 and 1937.
[15] Hamburg–Vienna, 987 kilometres; Trieste–Vienna, 555 kilometres (railway distances). For further details on this point, see A. E. Moodie, *The Italo-Yugoslav Boundary* (Philip, London, 1945), particularly Chapter VIII.

its immediate surroundings were erected into a Free Territory Poland developed the new port of Gdynia and granted favourable rail and port tariffs to Hungary, Austria, and Czechoslovakia. The situation of the German ports, the shorter distances, and the river transport on the Elbe were all in favour of Hamburg, but the German-Polish 'tariff war' resulted in the rapid expansion of the trade of Gdynia and a large decrease in the German share of Polish international trade from over 50 per cent. in 1922 to 19 per cent. in 1937.

The case of nationalist German policy has been stressed here because of that country's important situation in European circulation, but every other country in Europe experimented with special tariffs on its railway system for national purposes. Such moves were facilitated by State ownership of practically all the rail networks so that they could be used freely as instruments of governmental policy and, often, at the expense of domestic taxpayers. The juggling with tariffs led to such chaotic conditions that numerous tariff unions were set up during the thirties in efforts to re-establish more satisfactory freight rates for international movement.

The politico-territorial consequences of the first world war also affected the pattern and utilization of the European rail networks. When large areas of territory change hands their transport systems come under the control of the acquiring State and their use and organization are adjusted accordingly. Since the largest transfers of territory followed on the collapse of the Austro-Hungarian Empire, that area provides the best illustration of the effects of such changes on railway transport. Before 1914 the Imperial Railway System had been designed with two major objectives—to link the industrial districts of the north (Bohemia, Moravia, Silesia, and Galicia) with the agrarian districts of the south (the Alfold and Slavonia) as well as with the newly developed ports of Trieste and Fiume, and to make Vienna and Budapest the twin nuclei of the imperial network. Although the Austro-Hungarian railways were neither as well-constructed nor as efficiently organized as those of Western Europe, their lay-out was logical and appropriate to the economic needs of the Empire. North–south traffic was much greater than east–west—the latter tracks were of secondary importance, largely because such heavy freights as were available could be transported on the Danube. The Treaties of Trianon, St Germain, and Rapallo completely disrupted this system, since one administration was replaced by six (those of Poland, Czechoslovakia, Austria, Hungary, Yugoslavia, and

Italy). To give but two examples of the effects on individual lines, the main route from Silesia to Vienna was split into three sections, Polish, Czech, and Austrian, while the important route for overseas trade, Vienna–Trieste, was divided among Austria, Yugoslavia, and Italy. This latter line, the former Austrian Southern Railway (Sudbahn), was the subject of prolonged discussions which were finally settled by two agreements signed at Rome in 1923. They contained fifty-two articles and two annexes and seventy-one articles respectively, the two together requiring fifty-seven pages of close print in the English translation;[16] few of the agreed provisions were ever put into practice. It is not surprising, therefore, that Trieste's total trade, which had reached a peak of 6·15 million tons in 1913, fell to 5·38 million tons in 1938, and that its mean annual traffic over the period was still lower at 3·96 million tons.

In addition to such disruption of traffic, there was another problem for some of the so-called Successor States inasmuch as the Austro-Hungarian lines had not been planned to serve their needs as independent countries. Thus Bohemia-Moravia found itself quite inadequately linked with Slovakia, a factor which contributed to the lack of unity in the new republic; furthermore, Ruthenia was almost inaccessible from the Czech lands. The newly formed Kingdom of the Serbs, Croats, and Slovenes, later to become Yugoslavia, was in an even worse plight, since that part of its territory which had formerly been under Habsburg rule had been largely neglected, except for parts of Slovenia, Slavonia, and the ports of Trieste and Fiume. As late as 1918 the rest of the country south of the Sava had to be content with one main line.[17] In spite of extensive new construction and improvement of existing tracks, the present Yugoslav network still shows the effects of changes in the political regime of the Danubian Lands and South-eastern Europe, and the failure of the inter-war Government to weld its territory into a unitary State may, in part, be attributed to the difficulties of, indeed for some areas the absence of, railway facilities.

Inland Water Transport. For many centuries the numerous navigable rivers of Europe have been utilized for the circulation of goods and passengers. Long before wheeled transport, on road or railway, came into its own, the rivers were carrying short- and long-distance traffic and

---

[16] *Documents No. 593 and No. 594*, Treaty Series, No. 23, 1924.
[17] For an interesting series of maps showing development of Yugoslav railways see A. Melik, "The Development of the Railway Network on Yugoslav Territory," in *Geografskega* (Ljubljana), vol. xiv (1938).

played a considerable part in the economies of the several countries, but
the growth of trade, national and international, the great increases in
production, and above all the demand for greater speed in movement
called for new transport facilities, with the result that railways and
metalled roads largely superseded rivers as traffic arteries for many commodities during the nineteenth century. Nevertheless, competition between rail and inland waterways gave rise to many improvements in the
latter.[18] Of particular importance was the regularization of navigable
stretches of rivers with the installation of lighted buoys and quayage
facilities, but even more important was the construction of navigation
canals, which, in continental Europe, were primarily designed and constructed as links between the major rivers. Thus a well-adapted pattern
of inland waterways has grown up, although the continental coverage of
such routes is less complete than that of railways, largely because of the
insuperable physical difficulties of building canals in mountainous
country.[19]

Water-borne traffic enjoys a great advantage over rail freights in that
it is normally much cheaper,[20] but it is much slower. Furthermore, river
traffic is subject to the vagaries of the regime of the streams, fluctuations
in volume and consequently in depths of the navigable channels, shifting
sandbanks, and, in Eastern Europe, the possibilities of blockage by ice
in winter. As a result of a combination of these two factors, inland water
transport tends to specialize in its cargoes. Except in the British Isles,
where inland navigation is largely moribund for special reasons, rivers
and canals carry heavy, bulky commodities in the movement of which
speed is less important than the regularity of flow. Coal, coke, mineral
oil, timber, building stone, and, in some cases, cereals constitute the
main cargoes. For example, solid fuel, minerals, building materials,
and petroleum together accounted for 75 per cent. of the tonnage carried
on the inland waterways of France in 1953.

Political considerations played almost as important a part in the
utilization of inland waterways during the inter-war years as they did in

---

[18] The British experience is not typical in this context.

[19] See Fig. 4. For more detailed maps see *Annual Bulletin of Transport Statistics, 1953*,
Appendix 3, and also *Chisholm's Handbook of Commercial Geography* (fourteenth edition,
London), p. 408.

[20] For example, Belgian freight rates per ton/kilometre are 0·38 francs by barge, 0·90
francs by rail, and 2·2 francs by a ten-ton motor vehicle. At the same time, a 150 h.p.
tug can pull a 2000-ton barge, but a 1000 h.p. locomotive is needed for a 1000-ton train.
It is not surprising, therefore, that Belgian inland water traffic increased from 30·5
million tons in 1949 to 51 million tons in 1954. See "Modernization of Rivers and Canals
in Belgium," in *The Times*, August 10, 1955.

I

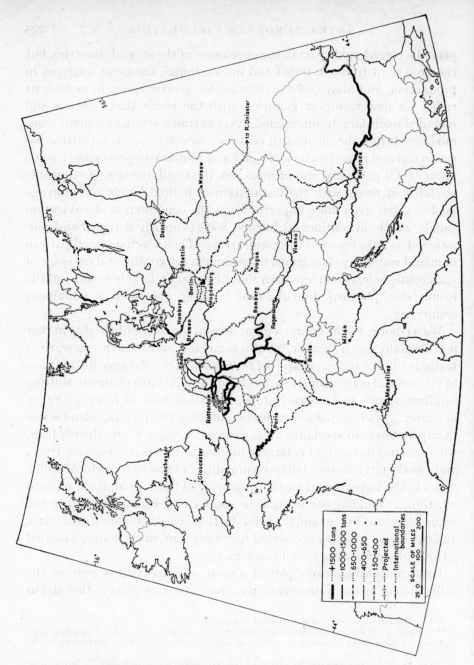

FIG. 4. THE MAJOR INLAND WATERWAYS OF EUROPE

The waterways are classified according to the maximum carrying capacity of the vessels which they can carry. The absence of standardization of carrying capacity is apparent.

Based on data in *Annual Statistical Bulletin, 1953* (Transport Division, E.C.E., Geneva, 1955).

that of the railways; in fact, the two systems were often equally affected by the application of the same tariffs. Germany again led the way in attempts to use its waterways in competition with those of neighbouring countries, even going as far as to build the Dortmund–Ems canal to drain Rhine–Ruhr traffic from Rotterdam and Antwerp to Emden and Bremen. National policies also affected the rivers and canals in another way. With the exceptions of those of the U.S.S.R. and Iberia, all the European railways are standard gauge, so that, provided suitable arrangements are made, goods wagons and passenger coaches may be moved from one country to another; train ferries make this movement possible between Great Britain and the Continent and between Sweden and Denmark. Similarly, the great majority of road vehicles find no physical obstacle in the way of international movement. The case of inland waterways is a very different one. The uses of steamships, barges (self-propelled or otherwise), and other river craft are determined by the depth of the navigable channel. Hence a map of waterways which gives no indication of their carrying capacity is of little geographical value. Fig. 4 has been drawn with this point in mind to show the capacity of the major European waterways as reflected in the maximum capacity of the vessels for which they were built, with the reservation that the data given are 'normal'—*i.e.*, they are only applicable to traffic carried when rivers have a normal volume.

Most of the waterways of Europe are State-controlled, yet few of them have a 'standard gauge' over long distances. The Rhine can carry barges of over 1500 tons capacity from the North Sea to Rheinfelden in Switzerland (twenty-one kilometres above Basel), and the Danube is capable of carrying vessels of 1000–1500 tons capacity from Regensburg to the Black Sea. Apart from these two major waterways, there is no standardization of 'gauge' on the European water systems, so that circulation is hindered by frequent and necessary breaks of bulk. It would greatly ease the movement of bulky, heavy goods if international co-operation, such as that which is responsible for the construction of the St Lawrence Seaway in North America, could standardize depth of channel, carrying capacity of vessels, and customs formalities in Europe. That this is still desirable is suggested by the steady increase of water-borne traffic since the end of the second world war shown in Table 6.

That such co-operation might be achieved is indicated by the pre-war development of international control of rivers and their traffic. "Freedom of navigation on international rivers was first proclaimed by the

TABLE 6

Traffic Density on Inland Waterways

(in ton/kilometres per kilometre of waterway per annum)

COUNTRY	1949	1950	1951	1952	1953
Austria . . .	205	461	712	928	1,031
Belgium . .	1,483	1,691	2,239	2,184	2,458
France . .	473	509	571	581	593
W. Germany .	2,898	3,755	4,719	5,257	5,410
Netherlands .	1,162	1,445	1,668	1,684	1,805
United Kingdom	81	82	85	87	90
Yugoslavia .	694	642	809	948	863
R. Rhine . .	—	19,637	24,068	25,082	26,050

Source: Table 34, *Annual Bulletin of Transport Statistics, 1953.*

Executive Council of the French Republic in 1792. It was codified by the Congress of Vienna and ranks as one of the outstanding achievements of that body."[21] This Congress was primarily concerned with the international control of the Danube, but it must be admitted that its admirable recommendations were frustrated by the nationalist policy of Austria-Hungary. The regime[22] laid down at Vienna in 1815 was incorporated in the Treaty of Paris of 1856 whereby the maritime Danube (*i.e.*, below Braila) came under a fully independent international body, the European Commission of the Danube, including non-riparians, with extra-territorial powers to carry out works of improvement on the river and to safeguard the rights of all comers. The same treaty led to the Mannheim Convention, which governed the international regime of the Rhine and which also established a Central Commission for that river, although this had no executive powers comparable with those of the E.C.D. After the first world war the Treaty of Versailles added three more commissions—for the Elbe, the Oder, and the fluvial Danube (*i.e.*, above Braila)—and in spite of certain national efforts to undermine the effectiveness of these bodies, on the whole the rivers and their users gained in the increased volume of trade which was carried.

Since the end of the second world war navigation on the Rhine has increased considerably without, as yet, reaching its pre-war level.

[21] O. Mance and J. E. Wheeler, *International River and Canal Transport* (Oxford University Press, 1944), p. 1.

[22] It is necessary to distinguish between the *physical* regime of rivers, which includes fluctuations in volume, rates of flow, etc., and the *legal* regime—i.e., the sum of the regulations controlling the use of the river for all purposes. The term 'commercial regime' is sometimes used to describe the volume of trade carried, the types of goods carried, and the freight rates charged.

TABLE 7

Traffic on the Rhine (in millions of tons)

	1949	1950	1951	1952	1953
Rheinfelden[1] .					
to Lobith[2] .	43	56	68	71	77
Lobith to the sea	47	60	68	69	67
Total .	70	88	102	104	112
Traffic passing Lobith—					
Downstream	12·8	16·9	15·6	14·3	17·0
Upstream .	8·2	11·4	19·5	22·3	20·2
Total .	21·0	28·3	35·1	36·6	37·2

[1] Head of navigation in Switzerland for barges with carrying capacity of more than 1500 tons.
[2] Dutch-German frontier.

Source: Table 12, *Annual Bulletin of Transport Statistics, 1953.*

The Elbe and Oder Commissions have disappeared and the reappearance of the Soviet Union as a Danubian riparian has completely changed the composition of the two Danube Commissions with temporarily disastrous results for traffic on the river. For several years after the war the bulk of the river fleet was immobilized above Vienna and traffic was brought to a standstill. No figures are available for trade on the river as a whole, but data for the Yugoslav section show that the transit traffic (*i.e.*, through Yugoslavia) in 1953 (2·44 million tons) exceeded that of 1937 (2·06 million tons). As this is the most important section of the waterway, the Danube may have recovered its pre-war commercial value, although the abandonment of the construction of the Danube–Black Sea Canal, which was intended to avoid the detour round Dobrudja, is hardly a happy augury.

Road Transport. The transformation brought about in European circulation by the rapid expansion of road transport during the twentieth century has already been mentioned in the section on Rail Transport, where Table 5 reveals the commanding position of road haulage in the internal circulation of the States of Western Europe during the early fifties. "International goods traffic by road, however, remains relatively small; even in the Netherlands, where the tonnage of goods entering and leaving by road was higher than in other countries, it was equivalent to 6 per cent. of inter-urban road traffic and to 2 per cent. of all tonnage carried by road in that country."[23] The main effects of the turnover to the roads has therefore been an internal matter, although there has been a considerable increase in the number of international tourists travelling by road as well as by air.

Other Means of Circulation. Railways, roads, and inland waterways are the primary agents for the movement of goods and passengers in Europe, but other means of circulation play their part, more particularly in the exchange of knowledge and ideas. Postal services are regulated by the provisions of the Universal Postal Union, to which all European countries subscribe, but liability to censorship is a restrictive factor in some countries. Telecommunications, of special value to commercial interests, are theoretically controlled through the International Telecommunications Union, but there is no way of compelling member-countries to implement agreed regulations. This is very noticeable in the wireless branch of telecommunications. During the second world war the device of 'jamming' broadcasts was fully exploited by the two sets of combatants. Since 1945 there have been many complaints against the continuance of this practice by the Communist States. An interesting example of the completely successful international use of telecommunications is that achieved through the Organization for Meteorological Information, which is universal in its exchange of weather information.

The latest and most rapidly developed form of transport is that by aeroplanes, and the growth of this new means of circulation has raised important issues. Quite apart from technical problems, such as suitable location of airports and approach lanes to them, safety regulations, and time-tables, international air transport bristles with difficulties arising from political factors. Every State is jealous of its sovereign rights in its national air space and will normally grant 'right of way' to members of other States only on a reciprocal basis if at all. It is obviously difficult for an airman, in these days of high-level flying, to know precisely when he is crossing an international boundary or to be sure that he is following the prescribed 'lanes' across foreign territory, a difficulty well illustrated by a number of unfortunate 'incidents' in recent years. Another political factor in this branch of circulation, however, is that all the important European countries and many overseas States compete with each other for a limited traffic through the agency of their own national air corpora-

[23] *Annual Bulletin of Transport Statistics, 1953*, p. 27.

tions, which are frequently subsidized. The desire for prestige in the air and, in some cases, to foster the aircraft manufacturing industry both for civil and military purposes, has resulted in the evolution of numerous overlapping and competitive services which are commonly uneconomic. Only recently, for example, has British European Airways shown a profit, while Air France continues to run at a loss.

One last means of circulation may be briefly mentioned—*i.e.*, the international transmission of electrical energy.

The growing need for power in connexion with the industrial development of many countries; the pressure to utilize water power where coal is not readily available; the improvement in the technique of the long-distance transmission of electric power and latterly its value as an export, have all tended to expand the distribution of electric power from the national to the international field despite the nationalistic tendencies of the inter-war period.[24]

This succinct summary of pre-war development is equally applicable to the international transmission of electricity since the second world war if we remember that expanding production in Europe calls for ever greater supplies of current and that the war had not only destroyed many power plants but had also delayed replacement of obsolescent generating plant. In 1938 total exchanges of current in Western Europe had reached the equivalent of over 2000 million kWh, and by 1949 this had increased to 2569 million kWh. The chief countries participating in this traffic are shown in Table 8.

The balancing of hydro- and thermal-electricity supplies to meet fluctuating, albeit expanding, requirements in Western Europe offers opportunities of wide scope for international co-operation. Swedish export to Denmark has been made possible by the laying of the world's largest submarine power cable between Hälsingborg in Sweden and Elsinore in Denmark.[25] In 1955 experiments were initiated to find the most suitable methods of transmitting electricity between France and Britain, where peak load demands are not coincident. Projects for connecting both Poland and Czechoslovakia are temporarily in abeyance, while the Russian satellites in Eastern Europe have a scheme in hand for supplying power derived from Silesian coal to Czechoslovakia and Hungary. Perhaps the most striking new development is the 'Emalp' project

[24] O. Mance and J. E. Wheeler, *op. cit.*, p. 128.
[25] The Earl of Verulamium, J. Houston Angus, and S. Chapman, "The Geography of Power: its Sources and Transmission," in *Geographical Journal*, vol. cxviii (September 1952).

TABLE 8

West European Electricity Exchanges in 1949 (*in Millions of kWh*)

COUNTRY	GERMANY	AUSTRIA	BELGIUM	LUXEMBOURG	NETHERLANDS	DENMARK	FRANCE	ITALY	SWITZERLAND	MISCELLANEOUS	TOTAL IMPORTED
Germany	—	565	40	0	14·7	0·06	2·5	0	66	19	707·26
Austria	141	—	0	0	0	0	0	0	0	0	141[2]
Belgium	40	0	—	0	21	0	22·8	0	0	0	83·8
Luxembourg	0	0	0	—	0	0	10	0	0	0	10
Netherlands	0·8	0	1	0	—	0	0	0	0	0	1·8
Denmark	0	0	0	0	0	—	0	0	0	0	—
France	520	0	13·6	4·9	0	0	—	8·1	241·5	235·5[3]	1,023·6
Italy	0	0	0	0	0	0	80·4	—	102	0	182·4
Switzerland	35	0	0	0	0	0	91·3	45	—	0	171·3
Miscellaneous	40[1]	45	0	0	0	150[4]	13	0	0	—	248
Total Exported	776·8	610	54·6	4·9	35·7	150·06	220	53·1	409·5	254·5	2,569·16

[1] Power going to Switzerland in transit through Germany.
[2] Excluding the output of border power stations.
[3] Saar.   [4] Sweden.

Horizontal lines give the imports; vertical lines give the exports.

Source: *Interconnected Power Systems in the U.S.A. and Western Europe* (O.E.E.C., Paris, 1950).

in the western Alps, which is in course of construction with the help of Swiss, Italian, and French capital. When it is completed it will greatly increase the amount of power available to the three countries concerned, and possibly to others.[26] In the fairly near future, current generated by atomic power plants should become available. If this, and electricity from other sources, could be fed into a European grid, it would be possible to overcome the shortages of power available to agriculture and industry.

The Integration of European Circulation

Europe has shown extraordinary recuperative powers since the end of the second world war. Even when allowances are made for the contributions of U.N.R.R.A. and Marshall Aid, recovery in production has been outstanding. By 1947 industrial output had reached its pre-war level, and between that year and 1954 it increased by 20 per cent. in Western Germany and in the rest of Western Europe by 50 per cent. above the level of 1938. Agriculture responded less readily to post-war conditions; Austria, Greece, and Ireland have not yet reached their pre-war levels, and serious difficulties in food production have been experienced in Eastern Europe. During the first post-war decade transport facilities have been rehabilitated and international trade generally has increased; most European countries now enjoy full employment or a near approach to it; in fact, in some countries there are shortages of certain types of labour. This relatively satisfactory state of economic affairs cannot be maintained if the strong pre-war trend towards disintegration is allowed to redevelop. This explains the strenuous and carefully planned efforts to achieve integration in recent years, but it cannot be too strongly emphasized that, although the effects of war and the great depression of the thirties accelerated the trend towards economic disintegration, the increasing interference of the State in economic affairs was the basic factor involved. In the sober words of a publication of the Economic Commission for Europe, "The natural concomitant of a growing significance of national Governments in economic matters was the enhanced significance of political frontiers."[27] European integration cannot be achieved without harmonizing the interests of its several States, and

[26] See A. F. A. Mutton, "Hydro-electric Power in Western Europe," in *Geographical Journal*, vol. cxvii (September 1951).
[27] *Economic Survey of Europe since the War* (E.C.E., Geneva, 1953), p. 215. Chapter 12 of this volume, entitled "Problems of Economic Integration," is an illuminating study.

I*

this depends on finding ways of combining the purposeful direction of governments with a more intricate international division of labour. A first and essential step in this direction is the release of the means of circulation from the restrictive measures indicated earlier in this chapter, so that goods, passengers, knowledge, and labour may move more easily. This calls for some sacrifice of national sovereign rights and therefore will not be brought about easily; even in matters of defence the States of Europe show a tardiness to suffer any infringement of this authority, as the collapse of the plans for the European Defence Community indicates. Only those who are ignorant of European history, traditions, and methods of organization will expect a sudden conversion of its national governments and its peoples to federation or even to an international customs union, although the latter has been advocated for over thirty years. Hence the importance of the policy of 'integration by sector,' which has gradually been adopted since 1950. A few examples of what has been achieved under this policy in the integration of European circulation are noted in the following sections.

TABLE 9

Intra-Benelux Trade: Percentages of Total Imports and Exports

	1936–38	1947	1948	1949	1950	1951
Belgium-Luxembourg—						
Imports from Netherlands	8·7	5·9	8·2	9·4	10·0	10·9
Exports to Netherlands .	11·6	12·7	15·5	14·7	12·4	17·9
Netherlands—						
Exports to Belgium-Luxembourg . .	10·8	15·7	15·8	13·4	13·7	14·6
Imports from Belgium-Luxembourg . .	11·6	12·3	14·8	14·3	18·4	18·3

Source: *Economic Survey of Europe since the War* (E.C.E., Geneva, 1953).

Benelux.[28] The decision of the Netherlands, Belgium, and Luxembourg to come together in a close economic union, without trade barriers and with free movement of labour and capital, dates back to 1943, but five years passed before customs duties were abolished and a common tariff against third countries was established, and it was not until 1949 that quantitative trade restrictions, with some important exceptions, were removed. The main obstacles to full economic union were found in basic

[28] See also Chapter III above.

differences in the economies of Belgium-Luxembourg, on the one hand, and of the Netherlands on the other, which have led to problems such as differences in price and wage levels and in currency questions.[29] Nevertheless, trade steadily improved within the union (see Table 9) in spite of these difficulties, which also included the strong competition between Antwerp and Rotterdam for German traffic.

The European Coal and Steel Community (E.C.S.C.). This supranational organization, including representatives of France, Western Germany, Italy, Belgium, the Netherlands, and Luxembourg, is primarily concerned with establishing and maintaining a free market for its commodities in the six countries involved. For our present purpose, the most significant developments are connected with finance, labour, and transport. Under Article 49 of the Treaty[30] which established the Community, it is empowered to procure the funds necessary to the accomplishment of its mission by imposing levies on the production of coal and steel, by borrowing or by receiving grants. This represents a very real attempt to facilitate the circulation of capital for investment. Under Article 69 the member-States bind themselves to renounce any restriction, based on nationality, on the employment in the coal and steel industries of workers of recognized qualifications from any of the six countries, and Article 70 expressly forbids discrimination in transport rates and conditions among the member-States. As by far the largest share of European coal and steel production is now the responsibility of E.C.S.C., and, as these industries are the twin pillars of industrial economy, such progress towards integration is of inestimable value and may well go far to eliminate those Franco-German rivalries which have bedevilled European relations for many years.

Liberalization of Trade in Western Europe. In July 1951 the Council of the Organization for European Economic Co-operation (O.E.E.C.) approved a Code of Liberalization which was designed to eliminate quantitative restrictions (import and export quotas, etc.) in trade between the seventeen European States which are members.[31] The Code

[29] For further details, see "Benelux in Operation," in *The World To-day* (Royal Institute of International Affairs, London, December 1948).

[30] *Treaty establishing the European Coal and Steel Community* (British Iron and Steel Federation, London, 1954).

[31] Austria, Belgium, Denmark, France, Western Germany, Greece, Iceland, Ireland, Italy, Luxembourg, the Netherlands, Norway, Portugal, Sweden, Switzerland, Turkey, and the United Kingdom. Yugoslavia began to send 'observers' to meetings early in 1955.

is applicable only to trade on private account, but, as the volume of European imports subject to State trading has decreased considerably since 1952, the increase in liberalization is all the more commendable. By the end of 1954 the average amount of trade freed from quantitative restrictions in this way reached 83·3 per cent. for O.E.E.C. Europe, Italy, Portugal, the Netherlands, Switzerland, Sweden, Western Germany, and Greece leading the way with over 90 per cent. of their trade liberalized.

The Code is not directly concerned with the vexed problems of tariffs, which remain the most serious difficulty in the circulation of goods in Europe. During the inter-war years international attempts to control the imposition of tariffs, including those of the first World Economic Conference in 1927, were unsuccessful. Similar post-war efforts have resulted in the General Agreement on Tariffs and Trade (G.A.T.T.), which is not restricted to Europe. In accordance with international agreements, any tariff concession by one member-State must automatically be extended to all countries participating in G.A.T.T. As many of these countries lie outside Europe, including Japan since August 1955, and have important trade relationships with Western Europe, it is extremely difficult for intra-European tariff reductions to take place.

"The Green Pool." The European Conference on Organization of Agricultural Markets, more often called the Green Pool, was established in 1951 and has attempted to break down the autarkic character of European agriculture. Intra-European trade in agricultural commodities has steadily declined since the first world war, and all countries in Europe made determined efforts to be self-supporting in food production, efforts which have been stimulated by the great risks in being exposed to wide changes in supply and demand on the world market since the great depression and also by the disruption of world trade engendered by the second world war. In the upshot, "The protective devices employed are sometimes so intricate as to make it impossible even for Governments to ascertain which products are really competitive and which are only 'feather-bedded' by unnecessarily high support."[32] Green Pool plans envisage the erection of an international body rather like the Coal and Steel Community which would gradually remove the barriers to trade in agricultural products, but little has so far been achieved.

[32] *European Agriculture: A Statement of Problems* (Food and Agriculture Organization, Geneva, 1954).

East-West Trade. Of all the examples of political interference with intra-European circulation, that represented by the Iron Curtain is the most outstanding and intractable. Between 1918 and 1939 Eastern and Western Europe were far from being closely integrated. Trade with the Soviet Union was small, irregular, and hindered by political factors, while West European exchanges with what are now Russian satellite States were hampered by a combination of economic stagnation and extreme protectionist policies. Since 1945 the domination of the economies of the satellites by the U.S.S.R. and the ban on the export of 'strategic' commodities from Western Europe inevitably caused an almost complete severance of trade relationships between the two areas which was accompanied by a very pronounced weakening of cultural and other links. In 1953 a change in Communist policy regarding foreign trade became noticeable. By that year satellite reparation payments to the Soviet Union had ceased, and in 1954 the Soviet shares in joint trading companies were sold to Bulgaria, Hungary, Romania, and Eastern Germany. At the same time efforts were being made to expand trade with Western Europe, with the result that east–west trade increased by 22 per cent. during the first nine months of 1954 compared with the similar period in 1953. For the same periods Western European imports from Eastern Europe (including the U.S.S.R.) rose from 629 to 714 million dollars and exports from 526 to 700 million dollars. A highly significant development in this improvement of relations was the conclusion of a trade agreement between the Soviet Union and Yugoslavia in January 1955 which provided for an annual turnover of twenty million dollars, for this follows a complete break in trade since the Cominform split of 1948.

Further and rather surprising developments have taken place during the summer of 1955. Both the Soviet Union and its satellites have run into serious economic difficulties, particularly in agriculture, and they may consider that the time is ripe for a different approach to the West. This is borne out by their participation in the 'Summit' Conference at Geneva and the more recently held scientific conference in the same city at which Russian scientists seem to have been willing to release some of their secrets. Even more striking is a report that the Red Army is to be reduced by 1,500,000 men, who are probably needed to strengthen the agricultural and industrial sectors of the Soviet economy. Caution is necessary in assessing the influence of these and similar developments. The one thing certain about Communist policy, in the economic as well as the political and military spheres, is its unpredictability.

Conclusion

This chapter has been concerned with the means of circulation within Europe, the problems of intra-European movement of all kinds, and the efforts which have been made to bring about that greater international co-operation which is essential to closer integration. The close relationships between governmental policies and economic development at the national level is indisputable, especially since the evolution of the Welfare State in Western Europe and the centrally planned economies of Eastern Europe. The analyses attempted here cannot be exhaustive, if only because of the limitations of space, but the interruptive functions of national policies have been shown to be of major importance.

CHAPTER IX

The United States: The Origin of a Federal State

DERWENT WHITTLESEY

THE United States of America is a political framework of contrasting but complementary regions held together in tension and reciprocation. The regional diversity itself sets up the primary stresses, of which some are centripetal, others centrifugal. They change in force and incidence with every modification in the natural or the cultural aspect of any of the constituent regions.

Secondary stresses are exerted in the wake of changeful regional tension. Always present are conflicting views as to the use of regional resources, both natural and human. They often find political expression in a clash between conservative and radical opinion. Another stress, perennial until lately, has resulted from the antithesis between territorial expansion and territorial limitation of the country.

Chapters IX–XI deal with the geography of a Federal State which came to possess a generous share of every major environment within middle latitudes. The origins of the American nation, in contrast, lay in environments of much narrower range.

The Setting

The part of North America to which European pioneers turned was the seaboard on the opposite side of the North Atlantic Ocean, a many-harbored coast extending from sub-polar to sub-tropical climates. Inland stretched a vast forest. The continent's natural resources had been little altered by the Amerind tribes that made up its small aboriginal population.

Lacking domestic animals except the dog, and restricted to tools and weapons of stone, they lived mainly by hunting and fishing, with pauses in their roving life to burn off clearings in the forest for planting maize, squash, and beans—husbandry auxiliary to the pursuit of game and fish. This shifting cultivation yielded uncertain harvests, but in the aggregate the clearings, including abandoned 'old fields,' presented considerable farmland to the European settlers at little cost of labor for preparation.

The long and broken coastline (Fig. 1) furnished separate points of contact for nationals of several Atlantic States of Europe. At the extreme south of what became the United States of America, Spain planted a few forts as a protective screen for the convoyed ships that carried precious metals to the European homeland from its far western American colonies. The broadly spreading, generally navigable members of the Mississippi river system funnelled into this Spanish gulf. Toward the northern margin of the habitable and wooded Atlantic coast, in what became Canada, France occupied the approaches to the St Lawrence river—the outlet of the Great Lakes—and established a ribbon of close settlement in the valley of the broad lower stream. This was intended as a base for the fur trade, which flung its gossamer net of canoe routes and fur trappers' lines over the vast interior lowland of both the St Lawrence and Mississippi basins.

Between the Spanish and the French settlements groups of English colonists, and a few Dutch and Swedes, disembarked in harbors that

---

FIG. 1. MAJOR PHYSICAL CONDITIONS AND EARLY COLONIAL GROUPINGS IN EASTERN NORTH AMERICA

Physiographic divisions (after N. M. Fenneman, *Annals of the Association of American Geographers*):

    I.   Gentle coastal lowland (Low Country and Middle Country).
    II. Somewhat hilly piedmont (Upper Country). (The boundary between I and II is the fall line.)
  III. Appalachian ridges and valleys.
  IV. Dissected Appalachian plateaux. (The boundary between III and IV is the Allegheny Front.)
    V. Rugged New England highlands.
  VI. Rugged interior highlands.
 VII. Limestone basins.
VIII. Interior plains (glacial deposition north of the Ohio river).
  IX. Ice-scoured Laurentian upland.

Broken lines show limits of holdings of European Colonial Powers about 1750. Dotted lines show groupings of British Colonies:

    A.   Southern.
    B.   Middle.
    C.   North-eastern or New England.

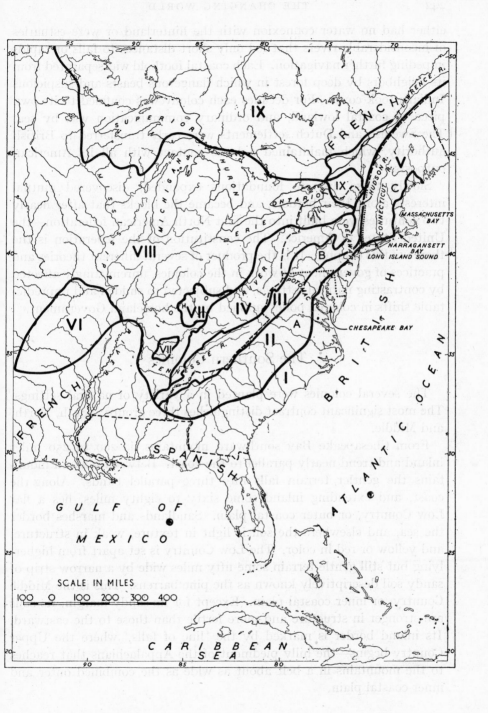

either had no water connexion with the hinterland or were estuaries of inconsiderable rivers that led only short distances to falls or rapids impeding further navigation. Each coastal foothold was separated from its neighbors by deep forest in which dangerous beasts and suspicious Indians took cover. For decades each colony was confined to its own piece of coastal lowland, and ordinary communication was by sea. The Swedish and Dutch settlements were early transferred to British authority, which maintained a loose contact with all its American outposts.

Slowly these discrete foundations expanded, discovered mutual interests along their borders, and became the blocks that after nearly two centuries were built into the first North American federation—the United States of America. The constitution of the federation is the theme of this chapter. It is the product of several different theories and practices of government at work in the colonies, unremittingly affected by contrasting natural settings, and subjected to sudden and unpredictable shifts in colonial policy applied by the homeland Government.

The Southern Colonies

The several colonies were planted in a variety of natural settings. The most significant contrast distinguishes three groups: South, North, and Middle.

From Chesapeake Bay southward mountains lie 200 to 250 miles inland and trend nearly parallel to the coast. Between sea and mountains the gentler terrain falls into three parallel bands. Along the coast, and extending inland some sixty to eighty miles, lies a flat Low Country, or outer coastal plain. Sandlands and marshes border the sea, and elsewhere the soil is light in texture, weak in structure, and yellow or red in color. The Low Country is set apart from higher-lying but still gentle terrain some fifty miles wide by a narrow strip of sandy soil descriptively known as the pine barrens. This is the Middle Country, or inner coastal plain. Except for its sandy margin, its soils are stronger in structure and more fertile than those to the eastward. Its inland border is marked by the 'line of falls,' where the Upper Country begins—the hilly piedmont of the Appalachians that reaches to the mountains in a belt about as wide as the combined outer and inner coastal plain.

All three belts are crossed nearly at right angles by a succession of rivers that reach the sea in tidal estuaries. In their course across the lightly consolidated sediments of both outer and inner coastal plain they have carved shallow valleys surfaced with swampy alluvial deposits, through which they flow quietly in broad, navigable channels. The head of navigation is abruptly marked by falls or rapids where the rivers are slowly cutting into the hard crystalline rocks of the piedmont. Above the Fall Line they are generally unnavigable.

The whole southern seaboard has a climate very different from that of the British Isles. It is warm most of the year, and the summers are hot, but in winter visitations of cold air-masses from the continental interior occasionally bring freezing weather. Rain is copious, and much of it falls in heavy downpours. Crops that were familiar to the immigrants from England thrive only in favored localities, mainly in the piedmont. Malaria (fever and ague) was rife, especially near the swamps, until the twentieth century.

In spite of its strangeness, the coastal plain was largely settled soon after a colony was started. The soils were easily worked and the climate proved suited to crops that readily found a market abroad. In the northern part the streams draining into Chesapeake Bay penetrated the whole of Low Country Virginia and Maryland and part of North Carolina (Figs. 1 and 2). There tobacco became the sovereign crop. Each plantation had its own wharf and exported directly via ocean-going ships. The river-banks were dotted with houses of the planters. For several decades holdings were not large, and were worked in large part by white indentured servants. As Negro slaves increased in number larger acreages were cultivated. Tobacco was hard on the weak soil, and new land had to be cleared every three or four years. For a time old fields could be used for subsistence crops, needed to feed the Negro slave labor, which was prodigally expended in the miasmic climate. But after a few years of use the land had to be abandoned. For several decades large fortunes were made by the tidewater planters, who formed an aristocracy that adapted English country life to their novel environment and maintained close social as well as economic relations with the mother country. Within a century of its beginnings, however, each neighborhood was deteriorating, and the old aristocracy was losing not only its wealth but also its hold on the colonial governments. Only the innermost coastal plain had soils that could continue to bear successive crops, mainly tobacco and upland cotton. By the eighteenth century those lands, together with the adjoining piedmont, came to support a group of planters born in the New World. They were farther removed in time and place from England than the immigrants who had farmed the Low Country, but, as planters of crops for export, they also were dependent upon trade within the British Empire. When their prosperity began to suffer from restraints on that trade, these new men became leading supporters of revolt against Britain.

Far to the south of the Chesapeake outlet lay Charleston amid fresh-water swamps and alongshore "Sea Islands" (Fig. 2). There the swamps could be diked, and rice became the dominant export crop, produced by a landholding society essentially like that on tidewater farther north, but with a larger proportion of Negro slaves used in the arduous paddy cultivation. All the trade moved through Charleston, which became the first real urban center in the southern colonies.

During the eighteenth century long-staple cotton proved suited to the near-by "sea islands," while upland cotton, and, for a time, indigo, were grown up-river on the coastal plain of Georgia as well as South Carolina. During the same decades farmers from up north settled along the piedmont and in the easternmost mountain valleys of all the southern colonies. Masts, pitch, and tar were perennial products of the extensive pine forests of both coastal plain and piedmont.

Whether above or below the Fall Line, life continued to revolve around the plantation houses where the needs of owners, white dependents, and Negro slaves were supplied by household crafts, and where social life was centered. The political organization of the southern colonies required county towns, but these might consist of nothing more than the court house, some hostelries, and a general store. Com-

---

FIG. 2. SETTLEMENTS AND ROUTES IN THE EARLY UNITED STATES OF AMERICA
A. Landward boundary of the new United States of America, 1783.
B. Frontier of settlement, 1760 (after H. R. Friis, *Geographical Review*).
C. Proclaimed boundary between British settlements and Indian country, 1763.
D. Frontier of settlement, 1790 (after H. R. Friis, *ibid.*).
E. The National Road.
F. Inland canals and their connexions:

1. Boston and Lowell (Merrimac River-Boston Harbor).
2. Erie (Hudson River-Lake Erie).
3. Chesapeake and Ohio (Potomac River-Allegheny Front).
4. Ohio and Erie (Lake Erie-Ohio River via Cleveland and Columbus).
5. Miami and Erie (Lake Erie-Ohio River via Toledo and Cincinnati).
6. Wabash-Erie (Lake Erie-Ohio River via Toledo and Fort Wayne).
7. Illinois and Michigan (Lake Michigan-Mississippi River via Chicago and the Illinois River).

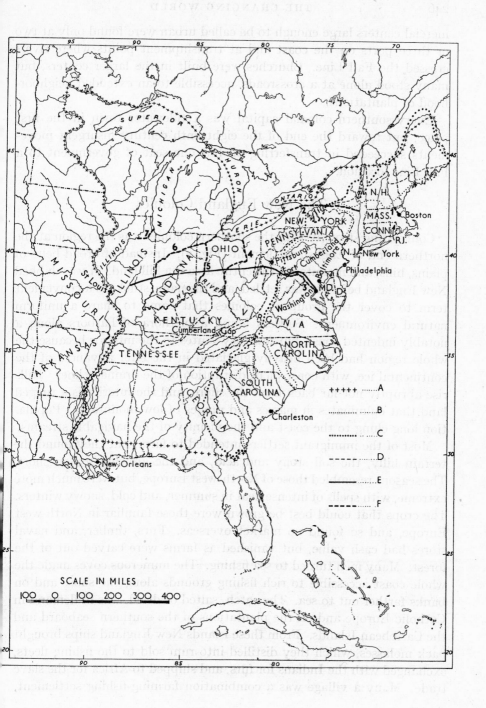

mercial centers large enough to be called urban were found only at two or three ports on the coast and at transhipment points where rivers crossed the Fall Line. Churches were built in the larger centers, but many stood alone at a crossroads, accessible to·an extended neighborhood of plantations.

Every southern colonial capital was a tidewater town in the first place, but toward the end of the eighteenth century insurgent movements succeeded in transferring all but one seat of government to a Fall Line location.

The New England Colonies

Contrasting strongly with the southern colonies was the region at the northern end of English settlement (Fig. 2). Instead of broad belts of plains, hills, and mountains, the entire area is a hill land. It was dubbed New England before it was settled, and the name stuck, as a convenient term to cover the group of colonies that came to share a uniform natural environment. Settlers found a plethora of harbors along a notably indented coast, but few easy routes to the interior because the whole region had been heavily glaciated in the later advances of the continental ice, with consequent disruption of the drainage lines. Hills rise abruptly not far back from the shore, and the interior is a rugged land that culminates in masses and ranges of low mountains. Population long clung to the coast and the vicinity of the navigable streams.

Most of the immigrant settlers intended to farm, but they found the terrain hilly, the soil stony and acid, and the growing season short. The seasons resembled those of North-west Europe, but were much more extreme, with spells of intense heat in summer, and cold, snowy winters. The crops that could best be grown were those familiar in North-west Europe, and so found no market overseas. Furs, timber, and naval stores had cash value, but vanished as farms were carved out of the forest. Many men turned to sea fishing. The numerous coves made the whole coast accessible to rich fishing grounds along the shore and on banks farther out to sea. The catch, salted or dried, was in demand in Catholic Europe and on the plantations of the southern seaboard and the Caribbean Islands. From these islands New England ships brought back molasses, which they distilled into rum sold to the fishing fleets, exchanged with the Indians for furs, and shipped to Africa for the slave trade. Many a village was a combination farming-fishing settlement, located at the head of a cove surrounded by a crescent of level, arable land and patches of salt marsh where coarse hay grew, and provided with a small waterpower for grist and saw mills by a stream tumbling from its glaciated channel into tidewater. Fishermen naturally lived in tight clusters close to their boats. But most New England farmers, whether on the sea or inland, also lived in villages in the manner of most European farmers of that time.

Communities that grew into cities were located on those coastal and river harbors best suited to overseas shipping which at the same time had the easiest access to the hinterland. Trade was their business, including the building of ships in which to carry it. Centers that functioned as seats of colonial government had a marked initial advantage. The pattern of settlement during a century was oriented to the coastline. New England faced the sea. Boston early became and long remained the leading port and largest city in the English colonies.

Whether small or large, the New England settlement was centered on a 'meeting house,' which served the residents as a church and also as a gathering-place for political activities. Every colony was founded as a theocracy, in which religious and political affairs were two facets of a single endeavor. When a settlement became overpopulated a group banded together to found a new village on the frontier. Before setting out, the emigrants generally made a formal compact to act in concert under the leadership of their pastor. The same formula was adopted by groups that migrated beyond the bounds of the mother colony to form new political units. The concepts of voluntary compact and of formal deliberations by the men of property were deep roots, both philosophical and practical, of constitutional government by representative assembly in the later United States.

The two earliest New England settlements were colonized direct from England, but Massachusetts, the second in point of time (Fig. 2), assumed leadership (never relinquished) when several members of the sponsoring company emigrated to the New World with their charter and governed the colony without recourse to backers in England. As time passed its capital proved to be the most favorable harbor in New England.

Almost at once groups broke away from this thriving colony to form new settlements in the wilderness. Some retained friendly relations with the mother colony, others were hostile, but all except those clearly within Massachusetts jurisdiction strove to obtain charters from

England that would give them legal standing. All were on waterways that served for communication with the outside world: Massachusetts Bay, the coast north of the Merrimac river, Narragansett Bay, and the Connecticut river and adjacent coasts of Long Island Sound.

Before the end of the seventeenth century all these settlements were consolidated into four colonies, each operating under its own charter. The constituent communities were organized into 'towns,' as befitted a society living in clustered settlements. County government was unknown until imposed by imitation, and remained secondary. Only the colonial capitals possessed a special political quality. Several of the early coastal seats of government long retained their political functions, and two are still state capitals. The main sources of wealth remained at and near the coast, and the political center did not gravitate beyond navigable waters, except in New Hampshire, which possessed very little coastline.

The New England colonies lay closer together than the southern foundations, and soon found they had interests to bring them together, but also rivalries to hold them apart. Four of them were the first English offshoots in North America to join in a voluntary association, "The United Colonies of New England," a federation intended to meet a threat of Indian war at a time when the oldest member of the confederation had been in existence only twenty-three years. Each colony chose representatives to act for it. The commissioners dealt with Indian affairs and undertook mutual defense against the Dutch colony to the west, but after a decade, when the danger of war diminished, the association ceased to function, because of divergence of interests.

Thirty years later a systematic attempt of the homeland to unify its American colonies was launched in New England, where close settlement and the earlier voluntary confederation made the scheme appear feasible. Intended as the first step in a larger consolidation, it was undertaken when the restored English kingship was eager to reduce the independence of colonies that exemplified non-conformist and republican institutions, as the New England foundations conspicuously did, even though they acknowledged the supremacy of the motherland. Their several charters were abrogated, and a royal governor was sent out to set up a single government for them all. This was resented by the inhabitants as a violation of their rights. Before the new regime was accepted the king lost his throne. Two of the smaller colonies promptly resumed government under their charters, which they had not surrendered. Massachusetts Bay had to accept a new charter that provided for a governor appointed by the Crown, but reaffirmed a number of privileges not usual in other royal colonies.

Expanding ocean traffic became the main dependence of New England, where pioneer privations gave way to the comforts of successful trading, at least in the ports. The United Kingdom continued to try to keep the traffic within the empire by laws prohibiting trade with territory not under the British flag. The Molasses Act of 1733 seriously hampered New England's lucrative traffic with French and Dutch sugar islands, and every subsequent law restricting trade increased the opposition to the homeland. The New England colonies took the lead in the revolt, when merchants and working men of the urban centers found common ground in resisting further encroachments on traditional practices. The issues were debated in town meetings and colonial assemblies.

The Middle Colonies

Lying between the South and New England, the Middle Colonies (Fig. 1) show resemblances to both, but differences more than offset similarities, and give the region a character of its own.

South-west of Long Island Sound the hills and low mountains recede from the coast, and both the piedmont and the coastal plain fan out until they merge into the well-marked belts beyond Chesapeake Bay. As in the South, the two lowland zones meet along the Fall Line, but both are diversified by basins standing at different levels, surfaced with different soils, and partially separated by ridges. The coastal plain is cut into peninsulas by the three broad estuaries of the principal streams, which flow almost due south. Several of the piedmont basins are the most fertile districts on the entire seaboard, and much of the coastal plain is moderately productive.

The arable land was taken up rapidly by waves of colonists who came from the continent of Europe as well as the British Isles. The small original communities of Dutch and Swedes were early followed by English immigrants, who settled along the estuaries and the outer piedmont. Germans came later, and moved westward to the frontier of settlement, where they took up land. They clustered in districts having high-grade soil, which they are reputed to have chosen because it bore trees similar to the best land in their native Germany. 'Scotch-Irish' arrived still later and settled mainly on the western piedmont, but also pushed into the northern end of the long trough that lies behind the front range of low mountains. Extensions of the trough far into the Southern Colonies directed farther migration of this element of the population.

Diversity of origin carried with it cultural variety, most sharply expressed in religious views not represented in the English colonies to the north and south. The early Dutch Reformed and Lutheran settlers were followed by Roman Catholics and Quakers, who welcomed Presbyterians from Scotland and Ireland and a variety of sectarians from Germany, as well as Anglicans and Puritans. All these elements found it possible to live under the same laws and in the same habitats, so long as they were allowed to think and believe as they wished.

Except for some large Dutch estates along the Hudson river, the farmland of the Middle Colonies was taken up in holdings small enough to be worked by family units. The soil and climate favored diversified agriculture not unlike that practiced in North-west Europe. Besides producing ample food for themselves, the people came to export wheat and flour, beef and pork, and beer to the other North American colonies of Britain. Exports that went chiefly to Europe were lumber and furs, the latter from the Indian country as far west as the Great Lakes via the Mohawk-Hudson gateway.

This ocean-going commerce was handled by four or five port cities located on the estuaries of the main rivers (Fig. 2). Philadelphia and New York grew to take rank a little behind Boston in both population and traffic. They were also early seats of government, but at the end of the eighteenth century all the Middle Colonies chose new political capitals closer to the centers of the expanding population. Ports and other towns also profited from small manufactures for local consumption, chiefly coarse woolens and linens, and crude iron wares. Rural and urban life were in balance in this region, as attested by the co-existence of county and municipal governments.

All the Middle Colonies were at one time or another chartered as grants to individual proprietors, some of whom retained control of their lands and headed their governments until the end of the colonial period—perhaps a further evidence of the tolerance exercised in these composite communities.

In this connexion Maryland may be thought of as one of the Middle Colonies. It also resembled its neighbors, Delaware and Pennsylvania, in producing varied foodstuffs, grown with the aid of a white servitor class rather than Negro slaves. Baltimore, on Chesapeake Bay, although a very small place, served as an outlet port much as did its large neighbors on the Delaware and Hudson estuaries. As tobacco planting on extensive holdings became the dominant business, Maryland grew more and more like Virginia and the number of slaves rose while indentured Europeans diminished. Manufacturing never developed, in sharp contrast to Pennsylvania. Before the end of colonial days the line between North and South was clearly drawn along the northern boundary of Maryland—a surveyed line that happened to coincide roughly with a major cleavage in natural environment and in character of occupance.

The Political Forces

The British colonies of the North American Atlantic seaboard were set up during the 125 years after 1607. Every one was launched as a commercial or trading organization, with profit as a prime objective. Each operated under charter, nearly always issued by the English Government to a group of merchants or settlers, or to an individual proprietor. The charters functioned also as frameworks for governing the colonies, but subsequently most of them were altered by Great Britain, generally to install a governor appointed by the Crown. Not only did the financial backers of the ventures hope for returns on their investments, but the individuals who emigrated to the New World also expected to improve their condition. Some sought adventure; a larger number, deprived of a living by radical changes in land use in Britain, looked for a livelihood; many took passage as indentured servants; some were convicts seeking to start life anew.

In the mercantile system then prevailing in European economic society colonies were supposed to send frontier products to the metropole in exchange for goods fabricated by the more advanced technology of the homeland. Laws to keep this trade in the desired channels were passed by the English Parliament from the mid-seventeenth century onward, and as the colonial share in ocean trade grew these Navigation Acts became an increasing cause of friction between the mother country and the colonies.

Economic betterment was not the only motive for colonization. In seventeenth-century England religious issues were ascendant, as attested in the charters obtained by Puritan groups and by Quakers and Roman Catholics. Freedom of worship outside the Anglican established communion was a major object of those grantees and of many emigrants —in some colonies all of them.

The century and more during which the colonies were founded was a period of turmoil in England. Religious controversy was an important manifestation of the strife, but mixed with it was a prolonged struggle between Crown and Parliament. This was the political expression of a fundamental clash in the philosophy of government between the divine right of kings to rule, and rule by representatives of the population. Crisis after crisis absorbed England's attention and left the newly founded colonies to manage their own affairs. For considerable periods they were forced to rely upon themselves to hold the land taken from resentful aborigines, to govern unruly and dissident individuals, and to improve their economic position.

In the course of handling such problems self-government, which had been slowly progressing in England under restraints of tradition, was given free rein in America. The charters were generally so drawn that property-owners were entitled to meet to discuss their affairs, and by the end of the seventeenth century every one of the colonies had a representative assembly that became well practiced in making laws. In nearly every colony such laws were subject to veto by the Crown, and many were disallowed. But the elected assemblies reserved the vital power to consent to all taxes used to defray costs of government, including the salary of those governors who were appointed by the Crown. Usually the treasurer, who handled expenditures of tax money, was chosen by the assembly, and in some colonies other administrative officers as well.

With changes in government in England, different colonial foundations came into favor or fell out of it, and a colony might find its charter altered or revoked. Noteworthy examples of these vicissitudes were the Puritan settlements of New England. All were granted a large degree of self-government at their inception, and they were well treated by the Puritan Commonwealth Government, but when the kingship was restored they were faced with abrogation of their charters and subordination to governors appointed by the Crown.

New England also furnishes practical examples of the "social compact," a philosophy of government widely held in the seventeenth and eighteenth centuries. It assumes that society, including government, rests on agreement among individuals. The most famous of these agreements, the Mayflower Compact, was a spontaneous solution of the problem faced by the emigrant company of Pilgrims when they made their landfall to the north of the territory of the chartered company from which they held a patent. Before landing, they formed themselves into a "civil body politic" and proceeded to choose a governor and pass ordinances.

Local autonomy turned out to be good policy in the transatlantic world, separated by many weeks from the homeland, and confronted with unfamiliar habitats where novel problems in economic and social life required political action on the spot.

The wide latitude permitted by most of the original charters functioned variously in the different sections of the seaboard. Not only did the charters provide for diverse political machinery, but in each principal habitat the particular economic and social procedures introduced by the colonists were modified, and thereby affected the political structure ultimately accepted. The Atlantic seaboard under English rule became a laboratory of political geography.

Steps toward a Federal Constitution

As the outpost footholds grew into substantial provinces, friction between the colonies and the motherland increased. The early days of liberal charters and intermittent attention came to a close with the end of constitutional strife in Britain, marked by the accession of the Hanoverian line to the throne in 1714. Thereafter Parliament was paramount at home, and the earlier sporadic efforts to consolidate the empire hardened into fixed policy.

Besides the general desirability of uniform government, more urgent specific matters arose. The western frontier of the mainland colonies (Fig. 2) was being subjected to increasing Indian warfare, partly as an incident in the struggle of Britain and France for the North American continent, and partly as tribal retaliation against encroaching white settlement on Indian hunting grounds. To wage war effectively it was important to have a unified military command, and it also seemed appropriate that the colonies should help defray the cost of their own protection. Money could most feasibly be raised by taxing the ocean trade between the several colonies and with Britain. This traffic had already been subject to regulation by Navigation Acts, although they had proved difficult to enforce except in the parts that suited colonial interests. The new regulations embodied taxes levied by Parliament, and a storm of protest arose in the colonies on the constitutional ground that there should be no taxation without representation.

This issue was an outgrowth of contrary governmental practice on the opposite sides of the Atlantic.

The franchise for the British Parliament was based on ancient rights which included plural votes for some, while many others had no vote at all, notably residents of recently founded cities. Moreover, individual Members of Parliament were not required to dwell in the district they represented. Collectively the membership was held to give virtual representation to the whole British body politic. In the eyes of the mother country Parliament represented the colonies no less than Britain, even though the ocean barred colonial participation in its election. The authority of Parliament was supreme, because after 1714 the Crown no longer exercised a veto upon its acts.

The colonies acknowledged this unique supremacy of the British legislature, but thought of their own provincial assemblies as minor parliaments, with like prerogatives inside their smaller orbits. By 1700 every province had established the right to a representative assembly, elected by those entitled to vote (usually adult males who possessed property above a small minimum). Electors voted by local political unit—*i.e.*, county or town—and each member elected had to be a resident of his district.

To people accustomed to so large a degree of local autonomy taxes imposed from across the Atlantic seemed to violate rights cherished on both sides of the ocean. The clash over taxes was a collision that showed both imperial control and colonial independence to have been growing in strength, side by side. The paradox could be resolved only by submission on the part of the colonies, capitulation by Parliament, or a compromise that would establish a new *modus vivendi*.

Imperial uniformity was fostered by officers of the Crown resident in the colonies. In 1624 a royal governor was sent to Virginia, and subsequently other colonial charters were revoked or modified to provide for governors appointed by the Crown, until only two colonies continued to elect their own governor, while in two others proprietors retained office. During the first third of the eighteenth century New Hampshire and Massachusetts shared a single governor, as did also

New York and New Jersey. But no comprehensive plan of provincial union was undertaken.

Each royal and proprietary governor was aided by a council of officials, appointees of the Crown, who acted as an upper legislative House and also had a hand in judicial matters. The Privy Council in England sent out collectors of customs, who served the commercial interests of imperial authority. All laws passed by the colonial legislatures were subject to review and veto by the Crown. This right was exercised freely while imperial control was being built up, but slackened as major policies were worked out. The veto was more frequent in some colonies than in others, but local matters were generally left to the individual governments.

Countering the trends toward imperial uniformity was the variety in natural environment, economic life, and social attitudes from colony to colony that found expression through the provincial assemblies. These bodies shared with the governors' councils the right to initiate legislation, and no tax law was valid without their consent. Being close to the electorate, they stood for local interests. As lesser parliaments, their existence was unassailable after the Parliament in London made itself the supreme arm of government. By keeping agents in London colonies were often able to forestall adverse laws and obtain their individual objectives.

Equally independent of both imperial and local aspirations was the unremitting growth of British America. The allocation of territory in the several colonial charters generally mentioned boundaries running from the coast inland. Because of imperfect knowledge of the country when the charters were drawn, several of them overlapped. Until after 1700 no attempt was made to demarcate the boundaries, because unoccupied wilderness separated even the closest neighbors. As the forest gave way to farms, questions arose about these early but still unmarked boundaries.

By the mid-eighteenth century land had generally been taken up as far inland as the mountains (Fig. 1), and projects were afoot for planting settlements in the Ohio Basin, beyond the Appalachians. The movement inland into Indian country involved making treaties with claimant tribes, and at times the frontier flamed into warfare, notably whenever Britain and France went to war. In making war and peace more than a single colony was likely to be engaged, on the battlefields and in the pacifications.

All the issues arising from expansion of the population engendered disputes between the colonies, but also led to co-operation in joint conferences of colonial officials to deal with specific mutual concerns—generally boundaries or Indians. The usefulness of these discussions gave rise to unofficial proposals looking toward a broader and more permanent federation of the colonies. In 1754 commissioners from seven of the colonies north of Virginia met in Albany, New York, to treat with the Iroquois tribes. Incidental to its objective, the convention adopted a Plan of Union for the British provinces, subject to confirmation by the provincial assemblies and by the home government. It was rejected by the assemblies as giving too much authority to the Crown, and by the Crown as being too democratic, but it served as a prototype for later constitutions. Mutual jealousy among the colonies doubtless contributed to their rejection of a super-government which would have required them to surrender some prerogatives.

A decade later all but four of the colonies sent delegates to meet in New York to protest against the Stamp Act passed by Parliament, a law opposed in the colonies because in their view it imposed taxation without representation. This issue was the climax of several grievances. Britain had been at war with France, and tax moneys were wanted to help maintain regular English troops in America. Quartering of soldiers on the citizenry in itself was looked upon as an instrument of tyranny. During the war regulations were enforced to prevent traffic with the enemy, after decades of laxity. To limit Indian warfare all migration to the country west of the Appalachians was forbidden (Fig. 2). As a result of protest by the congress of colonial delegates, and nullification throughout the colonies, the Stamp Act was repealed, but to pay colonial governors and judges a new law levied import duties to be collected at the custom houses. These duties were stoutly resisted and were later attenuated to a moderate tax on tea, retained as a symbol of the right of Parliament to levy taxes on the colonies. Drastic steps taken to prevent landing of the tea at several ports, including destruction of a cargo in Boston harbor, drew the issue clearly: should the British Empire be a unitary or a federal State? A century and a half of active but largely separate political life on opposite sides of the Atlantic Ocean, in natural habitats basically unlike and at different stages of land use, had brought Britain and British North America to the verge of war.

In Massachusetts towns committees of correspondence had been formed a little earlier to keep each other informed of developments in the struggle over taxation. Standing committees of the assemblies were shortly set up in several of the colonies to serve the same purpose at the higher political level. While leaders in the different colonies were getting to know each other and losing some of their mutual distrust Parliament passed measures that were considered intolerable in America and repressive in England. They closed the port of Boston until the destroyed tea should be paid for, occupied the town with British troops quartered on the townsfolk, and annulled the charter of Massachusetts. These measures alarmed the other colonies, and all were directly affronted by another law which extended the colony of Quebec to the Ohio River, thus extinguishing claims of several colonies to trans-Appalachian territory and putting a stop to westward migration.

At this juncture, about a decade after the Stamp Act Congress, twelve of the colonies responded to a call by Massachusetts for a congress to meet in Philadelphia. This became known as the First Continental Congress, and it worked out a scheme for union of Britain and the colonies intended to safeguard the rights of both, a plan that narrowly missed adoption. It announced a *Declaration of Rights and Grievances* setting forth the issues as seen from the American side of the Atlantic, and it sent to the colonial governments a proposed agreement to suspend trade with Great Britain and the Caribbean colonies. The trade agreement was ratified by eleven colonies. The discussion of mutual concerns by men drawn from widely different habitats marked a further step away from the particularism that had dominated life in the several colonies.

The Second Continental Congress, which followed close on the first, conducted the war that broke out even before it met in Philadelphia. The American Revolution was in large measure a civil war. In the colonies many people were loyal to the mother country and opposed to independence. In Britain many people believed that the colonies were fighting for the cause of freedom on both sides of the Atlantic. The prolonged war went far toward bringing the individualistic Americans together, although the task was formidable and not completed when hostilities were over. Britain possessed vastly greater forces than the colonies, but was compelled to fight at ocean's distance. Although the British Navy had the most powerful fleet extant, and with it the power to strangle the trade that supported colonial prosperity, the strategists chose to put down the rebellion by fighting mainly on land. By that

K

decision European armies, including mercenary troops, were compelled to wage war in environments to which they were unaccustomed, and to confront men habituated to firearms, who were defending their homes and often employed guerrilla tactics they had learned in Indian wars.

The close of war brought to the several colonies their independence, and a title to all British North American territory south of the Great Lakes (Fig. 2).

During the war each of the colonies had revised its charter into a constitution for a sovereign State. All had the same background in English institutions, and the autonomy of each was unchallenged. The representative congress by which the war had been conducted was a temporary expedient. It had acted in an emergency and with no sort of written constitution, although some of its actions became precedents for later written documents.

The necessity for a more permanent union was recognized, and a committee of the Second Continental Congress to draw up *Articles of Confederation* was appointed as an accompaniment to the *Declaration of Independence*. After nearly a year and a half the instrument was sent to the States for ratification, and more than three more years elapsed before the last of the States put it into operation by ratifying it. As a voluntary framework for federal government, it rested on the delegation of sovereign powers of a general nature to the central government, while reserving to the States the local powers.[1] Two vital general powers were witheld from the federal government—the power to raise money and the power to regulate commerce. These were two of the issues that had precipitated the revolt against Britain. A third long-standing source of conflict, the allocation of the trans-Appalachian lands, was settled when the States having western claims agreed that new States be carved out of the territory beyond the mountains. The Articles were thereupon ratified by the thirteenth State and became the organic law of the new federation. Jurisdiction over the western lands imposed common action and served as a tangible evidence of unity. The Ordinance of 1787, providing for the organization of the "North-

[1] The United States federation affords contrasts with that of Canada. Whereas the main powers in the U.S.A. were originally intended to rest with the individual States, in Canada (see Chapter XII, below) the provinces were assigned major responsibilities only in matters where local autonomy was thought desirable. However, the central government in the United States has been increasing its powers *vis-à-vis* the States, while in Canada the provinces have been increasing theirs at the expense of the federal government.—EDITORS' NOTE.

west Territory" (*i.e.*, west of existing States and north of the Ohio River), prepared the way for a growing federation in which local problems were to be solved in accord with regional needs.

The Articles showed weaknesses as soon as they were adopted, and the Congress that met according to their provisions found itself helpless because it had no power to raise money, and the States, freed from the threat of defeat in war, had reverted to their former individualism and pulled tight the purse-strings. The formula for a federal union that left vital general powers to the member States was inadequate.

After six years the Congress called a convention to meet in Philadelphia for the purpose of revising the Articles of Confederation. Twelve States appointed delegates. The deliberations created a novel form of government that was worked out by compromising issues inherent in the geography of the country.

The populous States immediately found themselves at variance with those whose numbers were small. The discrepancy was great. Unplanned occupance of an unknown environment had given some States large and undefined areas, while others were rigidly restricted to narrow confines. The population roughly accorded with area, although the natural resources also varied from State to State, and modified the ratio between population and area. Thus populous little Massachusetts ranged itself with the large States while big but undeveloped Georgia sometimes voted with the small States. The primary issue between the large and the small States was settled when a bicameral legislature was provided, with representation in proportion to population in the lower House and equal representation by States in the upper branch.

Other compromises grew out of the opposed views of the northern and the southern States over slaveholding. In the north slaves were unprofitable, and therefore few; in the plantation south they filled a need, and were numerous. It was agreed that three-fifths of the slaves should be counted in apportioning representatives to the lower legislative House. Importation of slaves was not to be prohibited for twenty years, but otherwise Congress should have power to pass navigation laws. Both the compromises on slavery bore witness to the hardening of a regional division of the States into northern and southern, separated by the Maryland-Pennsylvania boundary (Fig. 2), and replacing the earlier threefold division. The cleavage was already extending into the west, for the continuance of the slave trade was intended to permit new States in the national domain to stock up on labor. But the Ordinance of 1787, passed by Congress while the constitutional convention was sitting, forbade slavery in the territory north of the Ohio river, which thus became the extension of the boundary between slave States and free.

In framing the allocation of federal and state powers, the convention hit upon a happy solution. The general government was to rest, not upon the states, but directly upon the individuals inhabiting the federal union. Thus each citizen was subject to two governments, but he was not subjected to conflicting loyalties, because the federal constitution was declared to be the supreme law of the land, and the judges in the state courts as well as those in the federal courts were required to render decisions on this basis. This arrangement has permitted co-ordinated development of a vast and varied territory without sacrificing desirable local distinctions arising from regional differences.

CHAPTER X

The United States:
Expansion and Consolidation

DERWENT WHITTLESEY

THE new United States of America was a weak string of political units on the Atlantic seaboard of North America. Although they had gained their independence by standing precariously together in the emergency of war, they were absorbed by their divergent economic pursuits and dissonant social practices, both of which stemmed from wide contrasts in natural environment. Recognizing the need for a union more permanent and more effective, they set up a federal government based on a written constitution. Within that political framework they expanded across the continent, moved through the swiftest technological revolution in history, and at the same time consolidated the power derived from their evolving natural and human resources. Territorial and technological expansion coupled with political and legal consolidation are the subject of this chapter.

The West

The political geography of the century and a quarter between adoption of the Constitution and entry of the United States into the first world war was stamped with the impress of "the west." This was no fixed region, but a succession of frontiers of occupance. To the initial settlers on the seaboard the piedmont was the west. Beyond it lay the Appalachians, a dual barrier composed of a number of ridges and valleys, and a dissected plateau sharply defined by a steep, east-facing slope called the Allegheny Front. By the time the new United States were seeking a suitable frame of government the piedmont had demonstrated its partnership with the coastal plain in each colony-state that embraced both types of country, and the mountain barrier was already breached. In Pennsylvania, Maryland, and Virginia settlers had poured into and along a trough behind a single low ridge. South of Virginia the trough lies farther west, behind the highest ranges, and hardy individualists were moving into it by way of headwaters of the Tennessee river. Others penetrated the plateau front at Cumberland Gap and passed beyond the mountains into the exceptionally fertile limestone basins of Middle Tennessee and Kentucky, regions notable for expanses of nutritious native grass, blue when in blossom, interspersed with groves of deciduous trees. A little later the country north of the Ohio river received immigrants by way of that stream and its tributaries. Its unleached soils, deposits of the Ice Age, many of them ground from limestone beds, made excellent farmland.

The first of the newcomers into the west did not hesitate to band themselves into political units that disregarded both the parent seaboard states and the new federal government. Their reasons for such a show of independence arose from their location. Nothing they could produce from forest or farm could stand the costly haul back east across the mountains. An outside market for surplus goods could be profitably reached only by way of the Mississippi river, on whose tributaries their settlements lay. The mouth of the master stream and the port city of New Orleans had been settled by the French, but lately ceded to Spain, and the Spanish authorities undertook to close the river to traffic from United States territory. The frontier was also beset by Indian attacks, and the government east of the Appalachians was unable or unwilling to protect the isolated settlements.

A treaty with Spain finally opened the river outlet, Indian depredations were stopped, and the blocks of country south of the Ohio river, which had been organized as districts of Virginia and North Carolina, were admitted to the federal union as states equal in all respects to the original seaboard members.

The balance was soon upset by Spain's retrocession of New Orleans to France and the prospect of a French empire dominating the Mississippi Basin. At that juncture the federal government, in order to obtain the New Orleans outlet, purchased the entire river basin west of the master stream (Fig. 1). This was clearly beyond the powers specified in the Constitution. Nevertheless a President who stood for strict interpretation of that instrument negotiated the treaty of purchase, the Upper House of Congress ratified it, and the courts made no

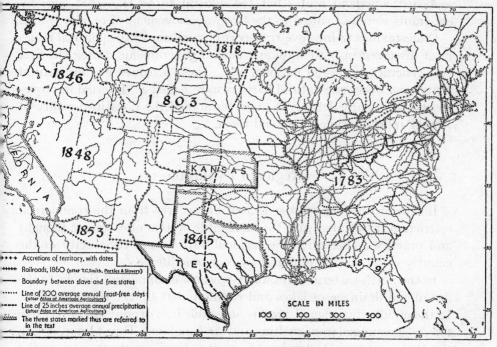

FIG. 1. TERRITORIAL EXPANSION AND SECTIONAL DIVISION

protest. In the same year the Supreme Court of the United States for the first time declared a law passed by Congress to be unconstitutional, and therefore might well have disallowed the treaty on constitutional grounds. All three branches of the federal government concurred in loose construction in order to facilitate an improvement in the geography of the transmontane west felt to be necessary. Not long afterward the remainder of south-eastern North America was obtained from Spain.

With the entire Mississippi Basin in the hands of a single government, the patterns of mountain ranges, river systems, soils, and natural vegetation could and did condition the expanding occupance. The navigable Mississippi and its tributaries gave the vast interior some cohesion by encouraging movement downstream and making New Orleans a clearing-house for the settlements on the 'western waters.' A dozen years after the Basin was politically united steamboats unified its commercial life by carrying traffic both down and upstream. For a longer term the mountains segregated the west from the Atlantic seaboard; overland routes not too difficult to be traversed once by emigrants were not suited to the two-way movement of regular traffic.

Undertakings to improve transport became one of the political issues most discussed in both state and federal governments during the first two generations of the national life. These schemes to link natural routes and overcome natural barriers were hailed as 'internal improvements,' and many debates in Congress argued the Constitutionality of federal appropriations to extend them.

Regional Evolution

Independence had set the United States free from the commercial restrictions associated with the mercantile system of economic thought and practice. Thereafter the regional variety and reciprocity of the country could make its impress on economic life.

In the north-eastern states water-power was abundant, thanks to the disordered drainage of lakes and cataracts left by the Great Ice Age. In the middle states small, readily accessible iron deposits and extensive forests encouraged iron-smelting and steel-making. Thus equipped with the basic instruments for manufacturing, textile and other industries sprang up, and the once distinct New England and middle regions came to have much in common, including designation as the North (Fig. 2). They took advantage of their numerous harbors to send fabricated goods by sea to the agricultural South and to foreign countries. The burgeoning port cities found that regulation of trade by the federal government was advantageous. Inland points urged that canals and roads to the west likewise be built under the constitutional authority over inter-state commerce.

Most of the seaboard South was as cut off from the west as was the North, but where the Appalachians give way to merging coastal plains that slope both to the Atlantic and to the Gulf of Mexico, east and west run together without physical impediment. Experiment soon proved that nearly all of the farther or 'deep' South had the right climate for growing cotton, a raw material in strong demand in the new textile mills of western European countries and New England. Just when the west was opened to settlement the cotton gin for removing seeds from fiber was invented. This eliminated the one high-cost item in cotton production, and opened to cotton plantations all the country on both sides of the Appalachians, south of the line of 200 frost-free days (Fig. 1). In less than forty years cotton became the dominant crop throughout that climatic region except in the sandy barrens. The northern west found a swiftly growing market for its foodstuffs in the booming South.

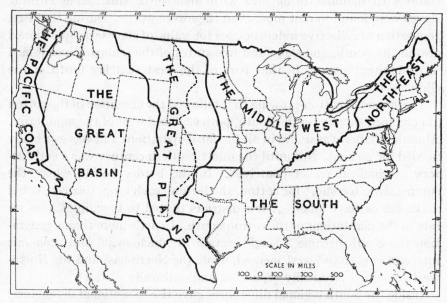

FIG. 2. GEOGRAPHIC REGIONS OF THE EARLY TWENTIETH CENTURY

Geographic regions. The regional limits on the north and the south are national boundaries; the limits of the three western regions are physiographic lines (after N. M. Fenneman, *Annals of the Association of American Geographers*); the other regional limits are anthropo-geographic.

Natural vegetation. Forest to the east, grass to the west (after A. W. Küchler, *Goode's World Atlas*).

Climate. Humid to the east, semi-arid to the west (after C. W. Thornthwaite, *Geographical Review*).

The nation was clearly separating into regions, usually called sections. Each reflected earth conditions and resources that distinguished its economic and social life from the others. Regional variety is inherent in the natural environment of any large segment of the earth's surface, and carries over into economic, social, and political life. It may result in reciprocity between regions, or in antagonism, depending upon the nature of their resources and upon group attitudes that help to shape the regional character.

An attitude that underlay and often overrode the political march of

K*

the time was the regional viewpoint on slavery. Slave-holding had once been legal in every British North American colony, but was abolished in all the northern states within a generation after their separation from Britain. In a climate with a long winter and an economy that combined trade with manufacturing and with diversified, small-scale farming slaves were found to cost more than they were worth. During that first generation of collective independence the value of slaves was questioned also in the South, and slave and free states of the seaboard had joined in prohibiting slavery in that part of the west that lay north of the Ohio river.

The spread of cotton-growing that followed the invention of the cotton gin clamped slavery on the South, both east and west of the mountains. Abundant labor was useful in all the farm operations and was especially needed for picking. Not until the mid-twentieth century was a satisfactory mechanical picker contrived. In the border South, where the summers are too short for cotton, the leading cash crop, tobacco, could make use of slave labor. A few districts turned to breeding slaves for sale to the plantations of the cotton South. In little more than a generation the South became a single section in which social and economic interests of east and west merged, while the North-east and the North-west remained physically separated and culturally distinct.

Inside the South regional differences gave rise to sectional dissonance. In the mountainous parts of Virginia, Tennessee, Kentucky, Missouri, and Arkansas cropland was confined to small fields, and slave-holding was by no means profitable. These less prosperous regions, however, were dominated politically by the richer plains, and the issues remained local. The larger regional divisions into which the United States fell absorbed more and more of the national attention. This was most obvious in matters having to do with the west, the frontier zone that began with the back country of the Atlantic seaboard settlements and continued until the Pacific Ocean was reached two centuries later.

In admitting new states to the Union after 1800 it became accepted practice to pair slave and free territories, in order to maintain equipoise in Congress on the burning sectional issue. Thus a provision of the Constitution inserted to give representation to both population (in the Lower House) and states (in the Upper House) became subordinated to the territorial extension of slavery. The conflict sharpened as the part of the Mississippi Basin west of the river grew in population and qualified for statehood, because the fan-shaped domain belonging to the United States before 1845 contains much more land in the north than in the south (Fig. 1). Toward the middle of the century the balance of territory between the sections was believed to be redressed by incorporating Texas and all the country farther west extending to the Pacific Ocean. Some time later it was discovered that the grass-lands, deserts, and rugged mountains that comprise most of the land west of the line of twenty-five inches of annual rainfall (roughly longitude 100° W.) were as little suited to a slave economy as were the cold-winter climates of the north.

The end of national domain which could be subdivided into pairs of states devoted to slavery and freedom was one of the conditions that brought North and South to civil war. A forerunner of that conflict was an armed clash in Kansas (Fig. 1). Lying immediately west of slave states, Kansas was early designated by Congress as free territory, but a generation later was opened to slave-holding if desired by the inhabitants. Thereupon, settlement took on the unfamiliar form of migration from both North and South, planned and organized to occupy and hold the territory. Two groups of communities were set up, and rival state constitutions were submitted to Congress. After con-siderable bloodshed the Kansas issue was swallowed up in the greater conflict between the North and South. After southern states had seceded from the Union Kansas was admitted as a free state. Nature all along favored this conclusion, because the new state lies north of the cotton requirement of 200 frost-free days, and its western half receives less than twenty-five inches of rainfall a year.

The slave and free states reached the point of civil war only after the three sections of the federation coalesced into two. So long as transport was confined to the natural waterways the inland North-west found its only market in the South. That market increased, and its center shifted westward with amalgamation of the entire South to and beyond the Mississippi river into a region based on one or the other of two cash crops grown with slave labor.

Meantime, the movement for improved transport was gaining momentum, and by the year 1800 beginnings had been made by indivi-dual states. Massachusetts constructed a canal from the great bend of the Merrimac river to Boston harbor as a means of tapping the expanding trade of northern New England; Pennsylvania began an elaborate system of canals. Where waterways were impracticable wagon roads were built inland from port cities. A good many were turnpikes, a name that came to denote a reliable degree of upkeep paid for by charging tolls. Some roads penetrated far into the frontier zone that separated the northern seaboard from the northern interior.

In a quarter-century some states achieved a considerable network of routes, and were ready to undertake ambitious projects. In 1825 New York State, utilizing a glacial drainway from the Great Lakes to the mouth of the Hudson river, opened the Erie Canal and so laid the foundation for New York City's becoming the nation's metropolis. That same year the State of Ohio began a series of canals connecting Lake Erie with the Ohio river, thus linking the two most-used waterway systems of the continent. Ohio's example was followed by Indiana and Illinois.

Completion of the Erie Canal stimulated Pennsylvania to connect its eastern and western lowlands by canals along its east- and west-flowing river systems, joined across thirty-six miles of intervening mountain (including the Allegheny Front) via inclined planes operated by station-ary engines. Construction went on for a decade before the seaport of Philadelphia was linked to Pittsburgh, at the confluence of streams that form the Ohio river.

Farther south the Potomac river likewise pointed toward Pittsburgh. The states of Virginia and Maryland, with the approval of Pennsylvania, projected a canal from tidewater at Washington, the federal capital, to the Monongahela tributary of the Ohio. It was constructed only as far as the Allegheny Front at Cumberland, Maryland. By a dramatic coincidence this canal was begun on the same day as the Baltimore and Ohio Railroad, which did reach its objective at Pittsburgh from its starting-point on Chesapeake Bay, passing through the very gap where the canal was stalled. It was the first fruits of the steam railroad age of overland transport, without which the United States might never have reached and held its present boundaries.

By 1800 a wagon road was being pushed from Washington to the upper Potomac, reaching the same pass through the Allegheny Front that later became an objective for canal and railroad. Extension of this road through the mountains was authorized by Congress in 1806, but another five years elapsed before work was begun. The project came to be called the "National Road," and it was planned to pass through three state capitals and to reach St Louis, starting-point of trans-Mississippi overland trade. Congress alternated in granting and refusing funds for its extension, but in forty years it figured in thirty-four federal laws, touched off fundamental debates on strict versus loose construction of the power conferred by the Constitution to provide for defense and to regulate inter-state commerce. Representatives of the West voted for federal aid, except for particular districts when a proposed line of transport threatened to compete with their own connexions already established. Federal support for the National Road ceased only when railroads superseded it. Before that day canals had already been given aid in the form of congressional grants of land to the states, which passed them on to the canal companies. The principle was extended to railroads being built by private capital in 1850 and later years.

Canals were the first means of linking the Atlantic seaboard and the trans-Appalachian West with effective two-way transport. Of them the only all-water route, via the Erie Canal, was incomparably the most useful. Railroads intensified the connexions across the grain of the country by providing several alternative routes, reducing the time of transit, and ramifying into areas far from waterways and hitherto not easily reached (Fig. 1). Machines for planting and harvesting grain from the large fields of the interior plains were invented before the middle of the century, and bumper crops were taken from the virgin soil. The North-west could now buy manufactures direct from the North-east in exchange for surplus foodstuffs, and the trade mounted swiftly. Along with freight, canals and railroads brought about a notable increase in westward emigration, particularly from rocky hill-farms abandoned in the mountainous North-east, to the deep, fine-textured soils typically deposited by the continental ice-sheets throughout the northern interior to and beyond the Missouri river (Fig. 3). By mid-century the American migration was joined by Europeans, who came from countries where slavery had been abolished or had never existed. Most immigrants brought with them an antipathy to slave-holding. Economic reciprocity and cultural ties shifted the balance of political power in the North-west, which soon after the middle of the century had a railroad density and continuity far greater than any part of the South (Fig. 1).

The outbreak of the Civil War signalized the amalgamation of North-east and North-west into a single section—the pro-Union North. It had been foreshadowed fifteen years before the clash of arms by cleavage into northern and southern units of nation-wide organizations, the most notable being several of the larger Church denominations. It was precipitated as a protest by the South against control of the federal government by a newly organized sectional party that drew its strength from the North and was dedicated to the elimination of slavery. This shift in hegemony from the South to the North arose largely from the coalescing interests of North-east and North-west, but it was made intolerable to the South by admission of free states which could not be matched by balancing slave states after 1850. In that year California was admitted with a constitution that did not mention slavery. Admission was forced upon the federal government by threats of the isolated Californian population to set up as an independent sovereignty unless granted statehood, and both North and South hoped to add it to their ranks. Most of it lay west of slave territory, but it was primarily a mining country, and its remote location and Mediterranean climate favored livestock ranching and extensive wheat farming. None of those pursuits could readily use slaves. Equal representation of slave and free states in the Upper House of Congress was overthrown, a fact that became inescapable with the admission of two unquestionably free states before another decade passed, and the prospect that most of the remaining federal domain would demand admission as free territory.

The Civil War took the form of secession by the eleven slave states farthest south and coercion by the federal government to preserve the union. In the South the struggle was called "The War between the States"; in the North "The War of the Rebellion." These names invite attention to the basic political philosophies underlying the American federal State. In the philosophy of the South the sovereign states voluntarily entered the federal union, and might voluntarily withdraw from it and reassert their sovereignty. In the philosophy of the North the States relinquished a part of their sovereignty on entering the union, and might regain it only by majority vote of all the members. In practice, this assumption means that no minority can ever withdraw from the union. Presumably no majority will ever wish to do so. It is significant that before the Civil War the country was referred to in the plural ("The United States are . . ."). Since then the singular verb has become universal usage in spite of its derogation of grammatical English ("The United States is . . ."). Slavery was abolished in the seceding states as a war measure, and the border states that did not secede emancipated their slaves shortly after the end of the conflict. The strategy and tactics of the war were based on the transport by rail of troops and supplies. As the first such use in history the Civil War is a milestone in military annals.

The Dry West

Railroads likewise figured critically in the territorial expansion of the United States to the Pacific Coast. The frontier of settlement at mid-century was approaching the western margin of humid climate, and emigrants were being attracted to fertile, adequately watered, lowland basins on and near the Pacific coast. In the intervening thousand miles, climate, land-forms, and vegetation combined to throw formidable barriers in the path of pioneers (Fig. 3). Two chains of lofty, forested mountains embraced deeply dissected plateaux and basins interrupted by lesser ranges. Inadequate water supplies and widespread desert shrub gave the intermont area the name "Great American Desert." East of the mountains lay a broad belt of semi-arid grassland. The first emigrants sought farmlands; then the discovery of rich gold deposits caused a rush to the hinterland of San Francisco. The booming mining settlement demanded statehood and rail connexion to the east as the price of remaining in the Union. California became a state in 1850, but the proposed railroad precipitated sharp debates in Congress. Northern interests favored Chicago or St Louis as the starting point for a transcontinental line; each city was already a rail center. But the South was in the political saddle and advanced claims for Memphis and New Orleans. No action had been taken when war intervened.

Before the end of the war and re-admission of the seceding states Congress subsidized construction of a railroad to extend lines then building from Chicago almost due west to Omaha on the Missouri river. The transcontinental line was advanced simultaneously from both ends (Omaha and the California port of San Francisco), and was completed in six years, only two years after Omaha was connected by rail with the east. Construction was made attractive to private capital by large land grants from the federal domain along the right-of-way. Similar land largesse was subsequently voted to encourage construction of other lines to the Pacific North-west and South-west.

The railroads were built primarily to link the populous east with the growing Pacific settlements on the opposite side of intervening harsh environments that constituted impediments to movement and drawbacks to settlement: lofty mountain ranges trending north–south, intervening arid basins, and a broad semi-arid steppe east of the mountains. The streams are unsuited to navigation, and the dry climate was unfamiliar to people whose backgrounds were Northern Europe and Eastern United States.

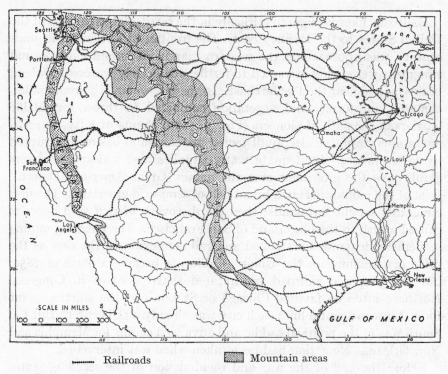

    ━━━━ Railroads   ▨ Mountain areas

FIG. 3. NATURAL FEATURES AND MAIN RAILROADS WEST OF THE GREAT LAKES AND THE MISSISSIPPI RIVER

All transcontinental railroads were built between the Civil War and the first world war. The mountain areas are after N. M. Fenneman, *Annals of the Association of American Geographers*. Most of the area between longitude 100° W. and the mountains was originally grassland; *cf.* Fig. 2. Between the mountain ranges shown lie broad plateaux, waste-filled basins (bolsons), and peaks and ranges. Higher lands are generally wooded; basins bear desert shrubs. Between the western major range and the Pacific Ocean lie lowland basins and low mountain ranges.

Once railroads were built the time and toil of crossing the country were greatly reduced. As a by-product the natural resources of the hitherto isolated interior could be exploited. Rich mineral deposits were promptly found and mined; sheep and meat cattle browsed on the open range until sent east for fattening and marketing; before long the grasslands on fertile black soil were being converted into wheat fields; and after refrigerator railroad cars were invented fresh fruits and vegetables grown by irrigation began to move to the markets of the eastern half of the country. In most places production was specialized. A single mineral, or a group of minerals derived from a single ore body, would be mined by a company organized to exploit each claim. Output fluctuated wildly with new strikes and unexpected failure of ore in mines already operating. Each farm or livestock ranch grew a single crop or grazed either cattle or sheep. Farm and range production varied widely, because the unreliable rainfall characteristic of dry climates resulted in frequent but unpredictable drouth. Only the small districts that grew irrigated crops could depend on a stable output.

The uncertainties of production were not the fault of the railroads, which made it possible for the dry half of the country to become settled and participate in the economic life of the nation. Nevertheless, the western pioneers and their descendants generally blamed railroad companies for their reverses, accusing them of charging exorbitant freight rates. This was a natural reaction in a region dependent on a cash economy that had no alternative means of reaching a market. When a drop in world price reduced the return from a year's toil to less than cost, while freight rates remained unchanged, the producers clamored for political regulation of the carriers. As the whole nation became enmeshed in a net of rails that supplanted canals and rivers, demands for federal control came also from the South, and indeed from all parts of the country except the North-east, where lived the capitalists who built and owned most of the lines.

Railroads had grown piecemeal, and charges for their services were more likely to be determined by competition of waterways or other rail lines than by distance, cost, or any other equitable principle. It was a railroad official of the time who is reported to have expressed the viewpoint of big business in the often-quoted phrase: "The public be damned."

Rapid extension altered the rail pattern from individually operated, isolated lines to an uninterrupted network, and many independent companies were merged into systems that combined trunk lines between convenient terminal cities and branches to tap tributary resources of farm, range, forest, and mine. The federal government favored this preliminary consolidation. Competition was sharpened and service was improved by unifying the gauge of the rails, expediting shipments, and reducing transfers from line to line. Well before the end of the century it was possible for freight to move anywhere in the same car. The great east–west extent of the principal lines and differences in travelling conditions between the humid, populous east and the dry, sparsely settled west were instrumental in fixing upon passengers a change of trains, and often stations, at Chicago, or alternatively at St Louis. After three-quarters of a century competition from through air services resulted in a few through trains between New York and Los Angeles, but the time consumed in routing over the maze of railyards in Chicago largely offsets the advantage.

The breadth of the country covers 58 degrees of longitude, equivalent to nearly four hours elapsed time. Railroads, as the first form of transport operating on precise schedules, adopted the local time of principal cities on their lines until seventy-five standards were in use. In 1883 they agreed upon four time zones, each centered upon a meridian of longitude of an even multiple of 15° west of Greenwich, England— namely, 75°, 90°, 105°, and 120° W. The borders of the zones do not follow meridians exactly, but conform to local convenience. These divisions are accepted by the general public; a few have been fixed by state laws, to which the railroads have conformed.

In spite of improvements in service, inequalities of charges remained. Several states undertook to regulate rail transport after 1870, but they had no power beyond their own boundaries.

In 1887 Congress finally set up an Interstate Commerce Commission as an executive agency having power to investigate railroad practices, including alleged discrimination. This was a pioneer federal agency for dealing with the economic revolution taking place in the utilization of the rich natural resources of the nation. The creation of a privately owned rail net, operated as a unit, and guided between specified limits by a federal agency, consolidated the sprawling Union to a degree impossible before the railroad age.

Not only the new transport system but also the mechanization of workshop and farm provided more goods with the available labor— never enough in a new and rapidly expanding country. Improved farm implements made it possible to break the tough prairie sod of the highly productive black soils between the Great Lakes and the Rocky Mountains (Fig. 1) and to harvest bonanza crops on fields too large to be worked by hand tools. On the land and in factories mechanical power supplemented human and animal energy. Wind and tide had long been used in a small way, but the rapid advances came in steps between the beginning and the end of the period covered by this chapter: falling water applied directly as motive force; coal burned to make steam; petroleum exploded in internal-combustion motors; water, coal, and petroleum applied to generate electric current. Richly endowed with all these sources of power and unhampered by tradition, the country moved swiftly into the mechanized age.

Immigration from overseas, which had been the basis of the new nation, did not cease with independence. On the contrary, it swelled to one of the largest migrations in history, reaching its peak about the end of the nineteenth century. Each succeeding wave brought in a different segment of European society. Motives were diverse. Some came to gain political asylum, particularly after the repression of Central European revolts in 1848; others left their homelands because of economic disaster, such as the failure of potato crops in Ireland at about the same time; many came as individuals or families in the hope of finding a better living. They brought with them ideas and ideals as varied as the lands from which they came, and thereby further diversi- fied the national life along lines foreshadowed by the several nationali- ties who had settled the middle colonies long before (Chapter IX).

Whatever their reasons for coming, they were accustomed to work hard, and generally they set as their goal the economic level of living current among 'old Americans,' as they understood it. They generally avoided the South, because they could not compete with Negro labor, whether enslaved or freed. Hordes stayed in the seaports, where they disembarked, and for a generation remained undigested economic, social, and political enclaves of Europe (and of Asia on the Pacific coast). Those who settled in the farming country were first to become identified with their longer-settled neighbors, but until after the first world war such class distinctions as existed were based, in most parts of the nation, on recency of national affiliation.

National Uniformity and Regional Variety

The objective of most immigrants was to be accepted as part of American society. As their children grew up, attending free public schools and speaking English without a foreign accent, the zeal to conform erased distinctions based on national origins. At the same time it helped to foster a growing unison in American society as a whole, facilitated by mass transport and mass education. The individuality that had been an outstanding characteristic of original immigrants from the earliest settlement, and of pioneers on successive and distinctive frontiers, gradually faded into a uniformity astonishing in a nation so vast and so diverse in natural environment. After the first world war immigration was narrowly restricted.

The United States, along with Canada, has the most mobile population on earth. It is customary for many young people to migrate to near-by cities, but this is also true of other countries. Nowhere else is it so much the custom for executives and professional people to shift from one part of the country to another as steps in their careers; nowhere else do larger numbers of laborers individually seek permanent or temporary jobs far from their homelands; nowhere else is there so heavy a seasonal flow to resorts and so considerable a permanent re-settlement of people retired from their lifetime occupations. The magnitude of these movements has increased greatly since the beginning of the century, but the trends were in operation long before—in the peopling of the country by pioneer immigrants, and in travel by canal and later by rail. The permanence of mobility as a feature of American life is closely related to the internal regional contrasts that provide at once an incentive and an opportunity to move.

The South

At the close of the Civil War the South was bankrupt and powerless, but in essentials was the same as before. It retained its character as the most distinctive region of the country, with its large colored population, its white people mainly of 'old American' stock, its stress on ownership of land as a mark of prestige, its intonation of the English language, and its consciousness of its own distinctiveness. These regional traits can be directly related to the humid sub-tropical climate that favored large-scale one-crop agriculture, discouraged livestock rearing and diversification of crops, and accelerated deterioration of the farmland. Few of the South's natural resources other than soil rose to first rank until late in the nineteenth century. Then its distinctive pine-trees, long the source of naval stores (tar and pitch), found wider markets for turpentine and gums in numerous manufacturing processes. The forests also became a principal source of the nation's lumber after the woodlands of New England and the Great Lakes region were depleted. Steel-making was begun in one center having an exceptional combination of coal, iron ore, and limestone, but outside the Appalachian Mountains the South is not well endowed with minerals of the sorts long familiar in industry. Instead it had to await the era of petroleum, bauxite, and the minerals basic to the chemical industry. Its abundant falling water could likewise be utilized effectively only after power came to be profitably transported as electric current. This age began only at the close of the period covered by this chapter.

The regional combination of North-east and Old North-west that fought and won the Civil War thereafter continued to expand along similar lines, but their differences again set them apart as two regions once the issues of the war had been settled. These and other regions discussed below are delineated in Fig. 2.

The North-east

The Atlantic seaboard from Chesapeake Bay northward remained the nation's main gateway to the outside world. The port cities attracted manufactures, as did also many inland places on water-power, near coalfields, or favorably located on through routes. As manufacturing came to depend more on the location of markets and less on other locative conditions the densely peopled, urban North-east maintained its economic headway. When local resources were depleted substitutes flowed in from outside. After canals and railroads were built it surpassed in population its seaboard neighbor, and its cities kept well ahead of those in other regions of the nation. The growing market encouraged farmers to abandon staples and to specialize on perishable foods. Rural production became geared to urban consumption, and few farm products ever left the region. Staple foods and raw materials of manufacture were drawn from the interior by rail or came by sea from coastal regions of the United States and from other countries. In every sense the North-east became the focal region of the nation in the decades following the Civil War.

The Middle West

On the interior side of the Appalachian Mountains a large and richly
endowed region came to be known as the Middle West during the years
that followed settlement of the regions still farther west. It extends,
between the Canadian border and the South, westward to the margin
of humid climate and associated 'mixed farming,' so called because
crops are raised and livestock reared on the same farm. During the
nineteenth century the Middle West became the nation's principal
producer of a long list of staple foodstuffs and the first region to use
successively improved, mechanical farm implements. Large-scale
mechanized agriculture was favored by hot summers with ample rainfall, by extensive flat and gently rolling land surfaces, and by soils of
durable structure derived in large part from limestone pulverized into
rock flour by the continental ice-sheets, and in the western half of the
region high in humus accrued from the dense mat of prairie grasses.
By the time it had proved itself the premier farm region of the country
parts of it developed manufacturing on a scale rivalling the North-east.
At scattered points convenient to the farmland factories engaged in
processing farm products, notably flour-mills and meat-packing plants,
stimulated the growth of cities favored by transport lines and, in some
places, by water-power or coal. Timber from the extensive forests of
the Upper Great Lakes was sawn into lumber for markets in the fast-
growing cities and on the treeless prairies. Iron ore from the vicinity of
Lake Superior was shipped by water to the southern shores of Lakes
Erie and Michigan (Fig. 2, Ch. IX). Thence it went by rail to steel-mills
on Appalachian coalfields, or met coal brought to lakeside blast furnaces.
Steel gave rise to varied manufactures using steel. Toward the end of
the period under discussion the Middle West became the chief center
of automobile manufacture; it put to use its considerable resource of
petroleum, and its largest cities (all on the Great Lakes or the Mississippi river system) took rank in population among the seaports of the
North-east.

The Great Plains

West of the South and the Middle West the regional orientation of
the country shifts from east–west to north–south. Temperature and

soil cease to be the environmental keys to regional variety and are replaced by rainfall and mountain ranges. Outlier settlements along the Pacific and in a few intermont basins were made at mid-century, but the rest of the vast area, amounting to half the entire United States, remained unoccupied for another quarter-century or more.

East of the Rocky Mountains lies a broad band of semi-arid country known (from its contrast with the lofty ranges) as the Great Plains. Its eastern border is indeterminate, because there is no observable break in land surface, and fluctuating rainfall has resulted in alternate encroachment and retraction of corn, wheat, and cotton about once in a human generation. The region is essentially rural, and two distinct systems of agriculture exist side by side and in places interpenetrate. Where effective moisture suffices (mainly in the east and north), a single crop, generally wheat, dominates the landscape; it may be grown by special 'dry-farming' methods, and crops fail at frequent but unpredictable intervals. Elsewhere the natural grassland or planted forage nurtures livestock, mainly cattle and sheep. Along some streams, especially near the mountains, are irrigated strips, several of them devoted to winter forage for the animals. The rest specialize on fruits and vegetables. The mesh of the rail net is coarser than farther east, but the sparse population has been from the first entirely dependent on overland transport to outside markets for practically all of its produce and most of its needs. Until long after the close of the century few minerals were known to exist, and in sources of power the region has ranked lowest in the nation.

The Great Basin

The Rocky Mountains form the conspicuous eastern flank of a broad region of ranges and basins that extends to include the equally prominent Cascade and Sierra Nevada ranges. The pioneer wagon routes and the later trunk railroads, all built between 1867 and 1912, are channelled by the mountain passes that lie between the Great Plains and the few outlets to the Pacific Ocean, and serve the intermont region only incidentally (Fig. 3). The surpluses requiring shipment to distant markets before rails penetrated the region were minerals, ranging from gold to borax, but predominantly metals. Mining has remained basic to the economy. The region was long mapped as "The

Great American Desert," and considerable parts of it have never been put to agricultural use. Most of the rest came to be grazed by cattle or sheep as soon as transport became available. The business is transhumant, animals being driven seasonally between desert shrub in the basins and open woodland in the mountains, with an annual round-up at the ranch house. Indians and Mormons practiced irrigation for subsistence long before rails crossed the desert. As waves of settlers moved into the dry country numerous small patches were co-operatively irrigated where water could be controlled without heavy outlay of capital. By 1890 such oases dotted the entire mountainous west. Subsequently large-scale projects financed by the federal government opened to irrigation tracts generally larger. Much irrigated cropland came to be planted to fruits and vegetables for rail shipment to the populous eastern half of the nation. In the extreme north a grassy, rolling plateau proved suited to wheat, and the heavy forests of the adjacent Rocky Mountains began to be cut when railroads provided an outlet for lumber (Figs. 2 and 3). The federal government and the states own much land in the dry country of mountain plateaux and basins. They lease much of it for grazing or lumbering under supervision intended to minimize soil erosion and insure permanence of the resource. Notably scenic districts are administered by the federal government as national parks and monuments. In this century scenery has drawn increasing numbers of tourists, especially in summer.

The (Pacific) Coast

Between the Cascade-Sierras and the Pacific Ocean lie lowland basins, most of which are cut off from the sea by a low Coast Range, except at a few points. The economy of this Pacific Region, often called "The Coast," is made up of the same elements as that of the Great Basin, and during the last half of the nineteenth century prefigured the development of its inland neighbor. As time has passed the two regions have become differentiated. In the Coast Region much land formerly planted to small grains has been irrigated. Lumbering has become a major industry. Gold, the predominant mineral resource of the early days, has been outranked by petroleum. Districts notably scenic, or merely wild if handy, have been set aside for recreation. These areas are much visited, both by outsiders and by local residents of the many cities and towns. The population is both larger and denser than in any other western region, and it is urban to a degree comparable only to the North-east Region. Like the North-east, the Pacific Region is a terminus of seaways, and all the largest cities are ports.

Climatic and other environmental differences between the northern and the southern parts of the Coast Region made themselves felt in the human geography from the beginnings of occupance. The divergence grew with every decade, although the tempo of change was slow until the end of the century. California's showery but sunny winters enticed seasonal tourists, its hot but dry summers did not deter visitors accustomed to take annual holidays at that time of year, and both seasons were favored by people retiring from lifework in the harsher continental climates farther east. Bright weather and varied scenery drew the moving-picture industry to the vicinity of Los Angeles. Petroleum and hydro-electric power laid the foundation for manufactures in step with the growing local market and labor supply. In contrast, the equally scenic northern half of the Coast came to be visited by tourists only during the summers—cool and less cloudy and rainy than the chilly winters. The extensive forests of huge trees could be cut for lumber all year round, and provided building material, first for the Coast, later for the entire nation. While the region is more bountifully supplied with water-power than any other part of the country, utilization had to await the second world war before it found accessible markets for manufactured products.

Regional Interrelations

Interaction among the six regions that made up the United States between the Civil War and the first world war calls to attention a rearrangement of the federal structure. The issue of slavery no longer vexed the nation; instead, the striking contrasts between the humid east and the dry west became the basis of a new alinement in Congress. Groups of adjacent states roughly corresponding to the several regions found they had economic and social interests in common that grew out of similarity in natural environment and set them apart from other groups. At the same time, regions widely separated might discover themselves in frequent agreement, because of the complementary nature of their natural resources and the goods they produced. The entire dry west has undeviatingly favored federal distribution of funds for local improvements. The Great Basin has generally worked with the North-east for stable currency and high tariffs, because one produces minerals and animal products needed in the factories of the other, and both fear foreign competition. In contrast, the Great Plains and the South have combined to demand regulation of railroads, cheap money, and low tariffs, because they are exporters of foodstuffs and raw materials. The Pacific Coast and the Middle West are reciprocal in many respects. Borderline zones may change sides, as when the western Middle West for a time stood beside its Great Plains neighbor in agitating for lower freight rates.

Toward the close of the century it was recognized that the frontier of settlement had ceased to exist with the end of government land available at a nominal price. Indeed, westward from the Rocky Mountains the frontier had never been an uninterrupted zone, but rather a spotting of settlements accessible to transportation lines or coterminous with favored terrain and climate. The last territories to become states were in the Great Plains (1908) and the Great Basin (1912).

Constitutional Evolution

The territorial growth of the United States engulfed half a continent in a century and a quarter and embraced natural environments of the widest variety to be found in middle latitudes. The federation func-tioned under a written constitution that was not amended, save for technical adjustments in the first years, for three-quarters of a century, and only ten times in the succeeding period of like length. All but three of the amendments that were added mark a trend to centralization of authority in the Federal Government at the expense of the states. They more than doubled the electorate, broadened the power to tax, and even imposed a sumptuary measure (prohibition of alcoholic liquors), although this was subsequently repealed.

The original Constitution was notably positive in statement, and action was forbidden to the states only in respect of powers delegated by them to the federation. It is therefore noteworthy that four of the eight later amendments still operative expressly prohibit the states from actions that have no reference to delegated powers. One of them declares that the states may not "deprive any person of life, liberty, or property, without due process of law." This clause has been made a platform for far-reaching judicial decisions, extending to the states a restriction on legislative and executive authority that was applied only to the Federal Government in the original document.

The capacity of the Constitution to meet the varied conditions of the expanding United States over a long period with so few amendments lies in the comprehensive nature of its provisions, coupled with the practice of construing its provisions loosely, to permit actions not specifically empowered, but desired by the people. As decades have passed revolutionary alterations in the economic and social life of the nation, based on areas and resources unknown or unused at the beginning, have been brought within the federal authority by this means. All three coordinate branches of the government have participated in making modifications. Congress has passed laws to deal with the novel conditions, the President has applied them, and the courts have felt free to disallow or interpret them.

The right of the federal courts to declare unconstitutional, and therefore inoperative, legislation by Congress and state legislatures was announced at the beginning of the nineteenth century, and at once became an accepted part of United States legal procedure. Up to 1954 the Supreme Court declared unconstitutional seventy-eight Acts or parts of Acts passed by Congress. This does not take into account state laws that have been disallowed. Neither does it measure the deterrent effect of the Judiciary on legislation that might have been passed if testing in the courts had not been in prospect. If the courts have been rather more conservative than the legislatures, their decisions have usually kept within hailing distance of trends in public opinion. The established practice of liberal construction of the Constitution, as formally amended, has fostered changes in the judicial viewpoint. Some earlier decisions have actually been reversed.

If this broadening of its literal terms had not occurred the document must long ago have been radically revised as the price of continuing to serve as the basic law in a country that has multiplied its settled area eleven times, its population forty times, and its productivity immeasurably.

A World Power

After a prolonged engrossment in internal affairs while settlement advanced across the continent the United States discovered toward the end of the last century that it had become a World Power. Early evidences were annexation of lands beyond the borders of the North American continent and inhabited by peoples with radically different traditions: the Hawaiian and Philippine archipelagoes in the Pacific Ocean, Puerto Rico and the Virgin Islands in the Caribbean Sea. A long lease to permit digging an inter-oceanic canal across the Isthmus of Panama manifested the conviction that the American navy must thenceforth be able to operate in both the Atlantic and the Pacific, to protect both coasts of the mainland, and also the newly possessed islands.

A further long stride into the political sphere beyond North America came when the United States entered the first world war and sent troops to fight on European soil. This put an end to the policy of 'no foreign entanglements' that had dominated the era of internal expansion. The oceans had all but ceased to function as defense in spatial depth. The two decades in which the nation moved from isolation to association saw the invention of the airplane and its first use in warfare. Movement by air has made unrealistic a return to isolation behind the wastes of the Atlantic and Pacific Oceans and the Arctic Icecap.

BIBLIOGRAPHICAL NOTE ON CHAPTERS IX AND X

Published contributions to the political geography of the United States are cited, with annotations, in *The Harvard Guide to American History* (Cambridge, Massachusetts, Harvard University Press, 1954; distributed in Britain by the Oxford University Press, London).

A large part of the guide is devoted to lists classified by topics under short periods. These lists are prefaced by a general section, two parts of which deal particularly with geographic matters:

Physiography and Geography, pp. 249–250;
Maps and Gazetteers, pp. 70–79.

CHAPTER XI

The United States: Economic Aspects of Domestic Governmental Affairs

EDWARD A. ACKERMAN[1]

THE important politico-economic characteristics of the present-day United States are illuminated by an understanding of four features of its geographical environment and its occupance. The United States occupies a living-room which is large and diverse even for this day of rapid and readily available inter-continental communication. The Federation is composed of economically unequal partner states, many of which have territorial jurisdictions ill-suited to the realities of their environment. A rapidly changing technology is being reflected in some fundamental changes in the pattern of occupance. And the people of the United States are still a vital group, continuing to grow in numbers.

The forces which have grown in response to the limits and pressure imposed by these four features have not been consistent influences on either governmental administration of economic affairs or upon economic activity itself. Instead they have often been contending forces. The present administrative structure of the United States, as it concerns economic affairs, in a sense may be considered in a condition of unstable equilibrium, responsive to any change in weight which these forces exert.

Effects of Size and Diversity and the Legend of Inexhaustibility

The effects of size and physical diversity of the territory on the development and characteristics of the United States have been well

[1] Prepared with the assistance of W. Brinton Whitall, Philadelphia, Pennsylvania.

outlined in the preceding chapters on the making of the Federation and its internal problems. Those effects are still manifest, and in some instances intensified. In general, the forces which have found territorial size and diversity a favorable environment have resulted in pressures against coherent federal participation in economic activity, and have strongly promoted sectionalism in the nation. This was the effect of the transportation system which was developed to cover the country, of the very high per capita resource endowment, and of the diversity of the physical environment among the several regions.

The effect of size has had great influence in present-day American life. The three million square miles available to a relatively sparse population from the mid-nineteenth century onward meant that the national psychology for a long time was predominantly oriented toward development for the immediate future, rather than planned long-term progress. It meant that enterprise was likely to cause a minimum of immediate infringement upon the rights of all citizens. Enterprise was to be encouraged, and regulation of economic activity to be minimized. Thus, lands could be given away to those willing to farm them, as under the Homestead Acts of 1862, 1891, 1909, and 1916, because it was more important to the development of the nation to have those lands in production than for the nation to realize upon the full investment value of its great holdings. Similarly, valuable mineral rights were given for the filing of a claim; and millions of acres of timber and grazing lands fell to the corporations willing to undertake the construction of transcontinental railways.[2]

Great size has contributed in other ways to psychological attitudes which have characterized the inhabitants of the United States from colonial days. Size in this instance has meant lands and other natural resources which seemed inexhaustible to several generations of pioneers. Where great forest resources were actual handicaps to the culture and economy of the frontier, as they were in eighteenth- and nineteenth-century United States, the legend of inexhaustibility is understandable. It was also understandable wherever new lands were being opened to farm operators who faced declining income from farms 'mined' of their fertility. Only in a land of great size could either of these situations have long prevailed. The legend has been further nurtured by the recurring discoveries of petroleum and natural gas in this century, by

---

[2] See V. W. Johnson and R. Barlowe, *Land Problems and Policies* (McGraw-Hill Book Company, Inc., New York, 1954), pp. 45–46.

the estimates of trillions of tons of coal reserves, by the discovery and exploitation of huge deposits of iron and copper ores, and many other lesser natural resources. Since the early 1900's, and particularly since the administration of President Theodore Roosevelt, efforts have been made to reorient public attitudes in the United States toward an appreciation of some resource problems of the longer-term future, and to attack the legend of inexhaustibility. These have been successful to the extent that there are general impressions which endorse 'conservation' activities and efficient resource development and management. However, the legend of inexhaustibility of resources has continued to have astonishing tenacity, fed most recently by faith in the capacity of science to produce in time every needed technological compensation for declining supplies of materials.[3]

Belief in the essential correctness of the legend may be considered a deep-rooted part of the folklore of the United States, even though many technical, political, and educational leaders view the future more cautiously. The effects of the legend are exhibited in many aspects of American economic life. They are shown particularly in the relatively high per capita consumption of all materials, from the paper for newsprint and commerce (381 pounds per person[4]) to the steel for tools, structures, implements, and automobiles (886 pounds per person[5]). While design for economy of operation is highly developed in American industrial establishments, most consumers' goods in the United States are not economically designed, because consumer preferences ignore such economy. The size and embellishment of the typical United States automobile is a very good example.

Whatever its origin, the legend is important in the future of the United States, and probably in the future of the world. It means that popular pressures will do little to abate trends toward rising demands for materials in the United States, short of a serious emergency. It may mean ever stronger competition by the United States in the world markets for materials, and difficulty on the part of Americans in

[3] For an example of this point of view see Eugene Holman, "Our Inexhaustible Resources," in *Atlantic Monthly* (June 1952), pp. 29-32.

[4] *Statistical Abstract of the United States*, 1952 (Government Printing Office, Washington, 1952), Appendix I, Table A, p. 962. Figure is for paper and paperboard consumption in 1950.

[5] Total civilian consumption of finished steel and steel castings, 1950—*Resources for Freedom*, Vol. II of the Report of President's Materials Policy Commission, 1952, p. 124. (Steel ingot production for the same year was 1278 pounds per capita—*Statistical Abstract of the United States*, 1952, pp. 80-91, and *Business Statistics*: a Supplement to *Survey of Current Business*, Department of Commerce, 1953 Biennial Edition, p. 156.)

understanding controls which may be needed for a fair sharing of eventually limited world supplies. At home it is likely to mean a tendency to assume the risks associated with a minimum public control over resource use and development and a heavy reliance on technical ingenuity to solve long-run resource-use and materials-supply problems. The legend will be a continued stimulus to American support of resource development abroad, and it is likely to continue as long as satisfactory solutions to some United States resource problems are found abroad.

Size, Transportation Problems, and Organization of Transportation

The great size of the United States also has meant transportation problems and a considerable influence of transport organization on national life. Thus a first problem in the development of resources and territory in the nineteenth and early twentieth centuries was the accumulation or attraction of the vast amounts of investment funds required for adequate railroad service. This was solved by making railroad service a clear field for private enterprise, by the attraction of foreign investment funds, and by connecting rail development with resource opportunities. Such a pattern for the development and later administration of the most important means of transportation inevitably led to a differential system of freight rates, because some regions were more lucrative sources of revenues than others. Freight rates and long hauls governed the course of development in different regions of the United States.

The United States is divided into five principal rate zones for the purposes of rail revenues: Southern, Western Trunk-Line, Southwestern, Mountain-Pacific, and Official (North-eastern) (Fig. 1). For the same service the Southern and three Western territories until 1947 were generally higher rate zones than the Official territory, which happened also to be the developing center of manufacturing. Thus the South and the West, until relatively recently, had an important handicap to their manufacturing development, because rates for the movement of goods within those areas were set in fashion which generally magnified, rather than minimized, the effects of distance by comparison with the North-eastern and Middle Western regions. This has been reflected in the generally lesser manufactural development of both regions. Only California, at the western extremity of the country and with better than average balance to its resource base, escaped the blight which freight rates brought upon the southern and western rail territories.

Distance has meant that new and cheaper forms of bulk-goods movement have been issues within the United States for many decades.

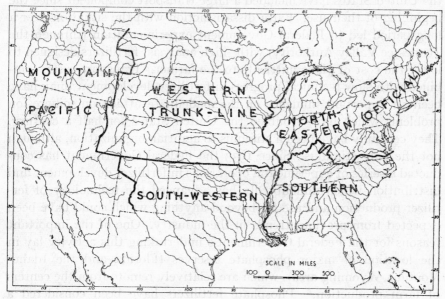

FIG. 1. RAILROAD FREIGHT-CLASS RATE TERRITORIES, 1942

Indeed, as noted in Chapter X, those issues date from the time of the Thirteen Colonies, when there were numerous efforts to improve rivers, construct canals, and open harbors. Provision of water transportation has been an issue down to the present day, particularly in those inland areas which have suffered from comparative rail-rate disadvantages. In general it has meant a tendency to encourage Federal Government participation in transportation development through the United States Army Corps of Engineers and other agencies.

Distance has also meant a readiness to capitalize quickly on technological innovations in transportation. Thus, as soon as technically feasible the United States developed a relatively complete network of air transport. The most recent development has been a system of pipe-line transportation, particularly for petroleum and natural gas. Pipeline mileage now exceeds railroad mileage in the country, although

L

the first long-distance pipelines came only during the second world war. These have been important influences in counteracting some sectional differences in natural-resource endowment.

The importance of transportation costs and distance is further illustrated in the stimulus to experiment with space- or weight-saving forms of bulk commodities. For example, the delivered costs of fertilizers in the United States have included a large transport component since the beginning of their use. Farm dissatisfaction with the situation over a long period led to Federal Government experimentation (through the Tennessee Valley Authority) with 'high analysis' fertilizers designed to lower the cost of plant nutrients to the farmer. Transport costs, combined with slow technical progress in fertilizer development, may have been an important influence on the inadequate attack on soil-erosion problems which have troubled the United States for half a century. They certainly have been a stimulus to agrarian organization, although not the only stimulus. Since 1933 the Federal Government has conducted a series of experimental operations in fertilizer development and distribution which undoubtedly has advanced the technology of fertilizer production and use far beyond anything which could have been expected from previous trends in the industry. One of the important reasons for the Federal Government's undertaking this activity lay in the location of major phosphate reserves (Florida and the Idaho-Montana-Wyoming area), which are relatively remote from the centers of farm production.[6] Phosphate fertilizers have been considered a major need of cultivated soils in eastern United States.

Thus size as it has affected the transportation system has acted to promote federal activity in economic development. Perhaps its major practical result, until recently, however, was a reinforcement of the naturally encouraged sectionalism.

Environmental Diversity and Sectionalism

The United States is not only huge but also diverse, and that diversity is reflected in sectionalism.

Sectionalism, which has been so notable a feature of United States

[6] K. D. Jacob, "Phosphate Resources and Processing Facilities," and J. H. Walthall, "Chemistry and Technology of New Phosphate Materials," in *Fertilizer Technology and Resources in the United States*, edited by K. D. Jacob (Academic Press Inc., New York, 1953).

history since the beginning of the Federation, is still a part of the country's political and economic life. While its manifestations are often less direct than 150 years ago, its effects are real, and in many ways a force to be reckoned with. The several very different physical environments are no less potent influences on the creation of sectional economic and political differences than in the eighteenth and nineteenth centuries.

Sectional interest in the United States still follows the same broad lines as it did from the time that all major regions contained appreciable settlement. There is still a major division of interest between the arid and semi-arid seventeen western states[7] and the more humid thirty-one eastern states. Within the humid area there are similar distinctions between South, Midwest, and Maritime North-east.

The seventeen western states, being dependent on large-scale irrigation and water development, having a relatively large percentage of their area in the public domain (owned by the Federal Government), having large areas and sparse populations, and being deficient in capital, have presented strong pressures for federal investment and grants-in-aid for resource and economic development of all kinds. They are the only large group of states in the Union represented in the Executive Branch of the Federal Government by a professedly regional agency, the competent, politically powerful Bureau of Reclamation.[8] The western states have consistently pressed for and obtained federally financed and constructed irrigation and electric power projects (Fig. 2). They have favored and obtained federal financial assistance through highway aid, in-lieu tax payments on federally owned lands, and special concessions in the taxation of the mining industry. The now famous depletion allowance, which has given several parts of the mining industry more favored treatment than all other industries in federal income taxes, has always been strongly supported from these states, because of their extensive mining interests. Concessions of this kind were under serious consideration as recently as 1954.[9] The western states also have been increasingly greater beneficiaries of federal water-resource development in such projects as those of the Central Valley of

[7] Arizona, California, Colorado, Idaho, Kansas, Montana, Nebraska, Nevada, New Mexico, North Dakota, Oklahoma, Oregon, South Dakota, Texas, Utah, Washington, Wyoming.

[8] The parts of the seven states making up the Tennessee Valley are also represented regionally in the Executive Branch of the Federal Government by the Tennessee Valley Authority.

[9] Two Bills (S. 3227 and H.R. 8300) were introduced "to encourage and assist the protection of strategic and critical metals and minerals in the United States by allowing increased percentage depletion therefor." (83rd Congress, 2nd Session.)

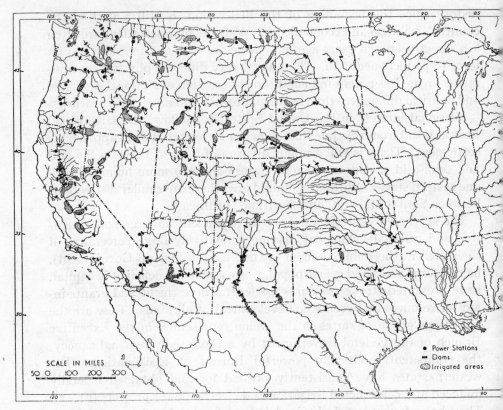

FIG. 2. FEDERAL IRRIGATION, FLOOD CONTROL, AND POWER PROJECTS OF THE
WESTERN STATES

California, the Columbia and Snake rivers, the Missouri Basin, and that
recently proposed for the Upper Colorado Basin.

The states of the humid East, on the other hand, have presented no
such consistent group pattern of pressure for special federal action. The
closest approach to group action probably comes in matters of general
agrarian interest, like the pressure for price supports under 'parity'
formulas[10] in the last two decades. Interest in federal experimentation
with and production of low-cost fertilizers is another example. However, some of the more important issues have also concerned the West
and therefore do not result in a sectional distinction. The humid East
cannot be considered a section; it is, instead, a set of sections.

[10] In simplest terms, parity prices are governmentally determined prices which would
give farm products the same purchasing power per unit, in terms of things farmers buy,
as prevailed during a base period.

North and South at the Present Day

The old distinction between North and South as definite sections of differing interest still may be found. The North, with a major share of the nation's iron and coal deposits, a favored position for maritime trade, a great internal waterway on the Great Lakes, and early capital accumulations, was favored for the nation's first large industrial developments. The South, on the other hand, centered its attention for too long on a technically obsolete agriculture, handicapped by the legacy of reconstruction after the Civil War, a difficult physical environment,[11] and a position opposite regions which were far less productive of trade than Europe until a relatively few years ago. These differences were better known as national issues in such matters as tariffs on manufactured goods (the South favored low tariffs and the low-tariff Democratic Party), and civil rights or segregation. The latter cultural issue proved an economic handicap to the South, because its maintenance forced not a few economic concessions which favored the northern part of the Union.

The differences between South and North were reflected most strikingly in statistics of per capita income as late as twenty years ago. In 1930 the income per capita of nineteen north-eastern states averaged 733 dollars; that of twelve south-eastern states was 312 dollars.[12]

However, the South is changing. Over the past several decades many fundamental changes have come about in the economy of the South-east which have altered its place in the nation as a whole. From 1929 to 1948 the South-east doubled its share of total national mineral output and increased by one-fourth its share of absorption of all goods sold in the United States at retail. From 1931 to 1953 it more than tripled its installed electric utility generating capacity—from 5 million kilowatts to 18·1 million kilowatts—and amassed capital at a rate well above the national average. Production workers in manufacturing increased by 49 per cent. from 1939 to 1950, and over the same period farm employment decreased by 31 per cent. Most significant of all, perhaps, has been

[11] Wide incidence of physical conditions favoring malaria; large land areas unsuited for extensive farming; high intensity rainfall, contributing to soil erosion and floods; soils easily exhausted of nutrient minerals; and high summertime temperatures.

[12] U.S. Department of Commerce, Bureau of the Census, 1950 *Census of Population, General Characteristics* (Government Printing Office, Washington, 1952), Vol. i, Table 6, and U.S. Department of Commerce, Office of Business Economics, *Survey of Current Business* (Government Printing Office, Washington, August 1952), Table 4, p. 12.

the increase in per capita income of about 160 per cent., a rate of 1·5 times that of the United States as a whole.[13]

New Sectional Alinements

The old distinctions between North and South are beginning to matter less. There is some evidence of a new set of sectional alinements arising, although the old differences are dying hard. One great change has come in the redistribution of the Negro population of the United States, which has moved relatively rapidly northward in the last fifteen years in response to opportunities for industrial and service employment in northern states (Table 1). This is probably more a rural-urban change than a sectional change, but it is nonetheless an event of great

TABLE 1

Negro Population as Percentage of Total Population for Selected States[14]

STATE	1930	1940	1950
Mississippi	50·2	49·2	45·2
Kentucky	8·6	7·5	6·8
Illinois	4·3	4·9	7·4
Michigan	3·5	3·9	6·9
New York	3·2	4·2	6·1

sectional significance. A reduction in numbers of Negroes in the South eventually must have an effect on local cultural attitudes to race relations,[15] including the fixation that the South-east has had on this issue.

Interesting differences between sections within the southern states also are beginning to show. These differences appear to have centered particularly on available regional energy resources. One of the more prominent domestic issues of the last twenty years in the United States has related to the manner of developing its electric energy resources.

[13] C. A. R. Wardwell, *Regional Trends in the United States Economy*, U.S. Department of Commerce (Government Printing Office, Washington, 1951), pp. 31–37, and *Statistical Abstract of the United States*, 1952, Table 309, p. 258.

[14] U.S. Department of Commerce, Bureau of the Census, *1950 Census of Population*, vol. ii (Government Printing Office, Washington, 1952), Table 14 (for states indicated).

[15] Large emigration of Negroes from the delta areas of western Mississippi to northern defense plants during the second world war brought about revaluation of the worth of Negro labor, and also tended to reduce racial conflict stemming from economic competition. Mr Arthur F. Raper, in *The Tragedy of Lynching* (University of North Carolina Press, 1933), discusses the direct relationship between inter-racial conflict and size of Negro population.

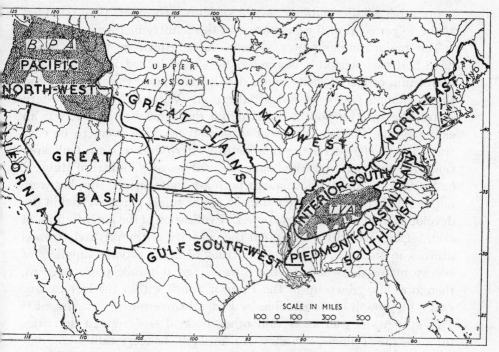

FIG. 3. GENERAL DIVISIONS OF SECTIONAL INTEREST

It is an issue which has crystallized along sectional lines, although it exists in one form or another in all regions. It is a good indicator among the evidences of new sectional alinements which are influenced by economic considerations. It also indicates that the dominantly agrarian motivations for sectional interest in the pre-1914 United States are being replaced by other forces.

The issue is that of public power development. Two methods of organizing, supporting, and managing electric power systems have grown side by side in the United States since electricity first became an important means of transmitting energy in the 1880's. Under one, privately managed companies undertake the development of resources and provision of service through a monopoly franchise. The second method is that of public investment from publicly derived funds, with appointive management directly responsible to elective governmental bodies. This is the "public power." The Bonneville Power Administration's system and that of the Tennessee Valley Authority are two outstanding examples in the United States (Fig. 3), although there are

296 THE CHANGING WORLD

many other smaller publicly owned systems. Together, they provided about 20 per cent. of the generation of the country in 1953.

The major public power systems have grown in regions which have had two economic characteristics; they lacked important coal, petroleum, or gas deposits under development, and they were only in the beginning stages of industrialization. Within the south-eastern states, the Interior South, centering on the Tennessee Valley, was an example; the Pacific Northwest was another. They were to be contrasted with the petroleum-rich south-western and western Gulf area centering on Texas and Oklahoma, the coal-bearing, industrial Midwest or North-east, and California. In both adequate energy supplies were not available before large amounts of public funds were invested in the development of hydro-electric power. Realization of the potentialities of each region seemed to be beyond the capacity of the privately owned utilities in the region, and beyond that of other private suppliers of energy materials, whatever the form. A great public power system, therefore, has grown up in the Interior South within the last twenty years, its growth made possible by Federal Government investment.[16] This system, as well as certain other Federal Government activities through the Tennessee Valley Authority,[17] has crystallized a new sectional unit, not only distinct within the South, but in the United States.[18] It is generally characterized by a 'liberal' approach in political economy, by a sensitivity to the need for common regional action on matters affecting its future economic development, well-organized state- and community-planning activities, and a generally mature understanding of the relation of Federal and State Government responsibilities. The Interior South is now distinctly both a political and economic force to be reckoned with in American national life.

A neighboring region of the Interior South may be used as a second brief illustration of the emergence of new sectional alinements in the United States. This is what might be called the Gulf South-west. One of the most highly mineralized regions on the continent, it is not only one of the major sources of energy supply for the nation, but a very nearly ideal environment for major chemical industries. Petroleum, natural gas, sulfur, salt, potash, and other materials not only have been

[16] This is the T.V.A. system, now one of the largest electric power systems in the world.
[17] *E.g.*, educational activities in fertilizer usage and other agricultural methods, in forestry, and in other resource developments.
[18] As suggested in Chapter X, this region has presented certain elements of 'dissonance' from the remainder of the South for over a hundred years. However, it lacked a focal interest until problems of energy supply became important in the 1930's.

increasingly important resources to the United States economy for the past three decades, but they also have been very well adapted to exploitation by private enterprise. Their major reserves are in this region, which centers on Texas, but extends into Louisiana, Oklahoma, and New Mexico. As one of the foremost areas of recent capital accumulation in the nation, this region generally has been able to support a vigorous development from its own financial resources, or readily attract outside private funds. The Gulf South-west therefore has found relatively little of common cause with the capital-poor Interior South in recent years. Even though it has some serious problem areas within it, like the Arkansas-Red and the middle and upper Rio Grande Valleys, the spokesmen for this region have taken a strongly independent attitude in federal-state relations. This was illustrated between 1951 and 1953 in the tidal oil lands issue before the United States Congress, in which the Gulf South-west took leadership in pressing for exclusive state control of the mineral rights on tidal lands and in offshore waters, rather than Federal Government control.[19] In this, as in other recent issues, the Gulf South-west has revealed itself to be a sectional entity in American political and economic life.

The Interior South and the Gulf South-west have been taken only as illustrations of the emergence of a different pattern in sectional interest and sectional pressure. Other parts of the pattern are regions which have long been recognized as distinctive, like California, the Pacific North-west, New England, the Piedmont–Coastal Plain South-east, the Great Basin, the Midwest, the Great Plains. One other area which shows some possibility of emerging as a distinct section is the upper Missouri Basin, particularly the Dakotas and Montana. Common interests have been discovered in the development of the Missouri river and the other resources which can be associated with river development. While the upper Missouri Basin area has shown its sectional cohesion mainly in conflicts of interest with the lower Missouri areas on activities related to river development, other signs also promise that this common interest will be continued.

[19] The tidal lands issue was decided by the 83rd Congress in favor of state control (May 1953). (See "Submerged Lands Act," H.R. 4198 and Public Law 31, 83rd Congress, 1st Session.) It was considered an important victory for state sovereignty in economic matters by those who favor a minimum of Federal Government activity in domestic economic affairs.

L*

The Division of Territory among the States

In addition to the great size and diversity of United States territory its federal system continues to be another reality of the twentieth-century nation. The forty-eight states of 1956 show great disparity in their population, wealth, size, resources, and economic capacity. Further, state boundaries in many instances show a singular disregard for the realities of the physical environment that each state must share with its neighbors. An extremely large percentage of their total length is surveyed straight lines. Both phenomena are related to issues which have developed a high emotional charge in United States politics in the last two decades—those related to the expanding economic activity of the Federal Government and its expanding power over all economic activity in the nation.

In general the disparities among the states may be assessed by their fiscal capacity, which varies greatly. Uniform governmental services thus cannot be provided, and in some cases not even minimal services for a modern economy. California and New York in 1950 operated on budgets in excess of 1,000,000,000 dollars, while states such as Nebraska and South Dakota were limited to budgets of less than one-tenth that amount. Connecticut and Arkansas have approximately equal numerical populations, yet the former received a 61 per cent. greater revenue in 1950.[20]

Thus, as the complexity of national economic life has grown, not a few activities have fallen to the Federal Government by default, because the weaker states obviously were unable to undertake a full range of developmental or regulatory activities. Services such as pure food and drug regulation or fair trade practice legislation became the province of the Federal Government from the beginning, and were given only infrequent attention by state authorities. The earliest example of all was the attention given by the Federal Government to the development of navigation facilities, which dates from the first decades of the nineteenth century. The Interstate Commerce Act of 1887 was in part another expression of the Federal Government's answer to a need arising out of the disparate capacities of the states. The apogee came during the administration of President Franklin Roosevelt, when in effect a majority of the states laid the many troubles of the Great

[20] *Statistical Abstract of the United States*, 1952, Table 420, p. 366.

Depression at the door of the Federal Government. The latter thereupon concerned itself directly with almost every aspect of the nation's economic life. Whether or not this would have happened if the several states had been better balanced economic units is not likely to be decided. However, the very specialized nature of the economies of a number of the states, and the relatively small populations of some certainly aggravated the conditions of the Depression for them.

Another result of the disparate economic strength of the states has been the inducement of compensating federal programs called "grants-in-aid." Early grants to the states were in the form of land grants to build schools, to expedite the construction of railroads, and to encourage education in agriculture. These early grants were unconditional. Starting in 1916, however, federal grants-in-aid became conditional,[21] and are now made in such diverse fields as agricultural education, extension and research, forest protection, highway and airport construction, and civil defense. The expanding impact of financial grants upon the states is suggested in terms of figures. In 1931 it was about 220 million dollars; in 1941 it was 615 million dollars; and by 1951 it had climbed to 2200 million dollars.[22]

The significance of this trend for federal-state governmental relations may be seen in the fact that approximately 18 per cent. of the average state budget depends on federal grants.[23] The fear that such a degree of fiscal dependence may erase the constitutional division of power has existed for many years. However, these figures should not be taken as support for the view, expressed by Harold Laski and others, that the epoch of federalism is past in the United States. The states themselves are far from "withering away." They now spend annually about 15,000 million dollars, whereas twenty years ago they spent about 2000 million dollars.[24]

The peculiar allotment of territory to the individual states also has had its effect on the need for Federal Government activity. This situation has been recognized particularly since the full development of regional water resources has come to be a necessity. State boundaries rarely make sense in terms of the drainage pattern of the United States.

[21] In most programs the state is required to match federal grants with an equal appropriation of its own funds.

[22] Leonard D. White, *The States and the Nation* (Baton Rouge: Louisiana State University Press, 1953), p. 18.

[23] Richard L. Neuberger, "The Decay of State Governments," in *Harper's Magazine*, October 1953, p. 40.

[24] White, *The States and the Nation*, p. 36.

Those internal boundaries which are not straight lines often follow river channels. The grand scale of most of the river basins also contributes to the confusion of state jurisdictions within them. Thus the development of the Tennessee and of the Colorado concerns seven states in each instance, that of the Ohio ten states, and of the Missouri ten. If the entire Mississippi river system is taken, thirty states are concerned. Among all the major basins only the Central Valley of California is within one state. A single state, like Colorado, may be drawn into the developmental problems of as many as four major river basins. The principal results over a long period were two. Where development of streams was not a matter of critical concern (generally east of the 100th meridian) very little positive action was taken by the states themselves on major development. Where water development was vital to any substantial progress, as in the states with territory west of the 100th meridian, there has been a history of inter-state conflict[25] and unnatural compartmentalizing of the basins. The compartmentalizing of the Colorado river, with water withdrawals of specified amounts for each of the seven states of the Basin, is illustrative of the barriers which state boundaries impose upon development where appropriative water law has become necessary.

About twenty years ago it became very clear that if the wealth of the nation's major streams were not to be allowed to waste indefinitely some federal action toward basin development would be necessary. For this reason, among others, the Tennessee Valley Authority experiment was started, and has been pursued successfully in the South-east. While other federal water development activities, through the United States Army Corps of Engineers and the Bureau of Reclamation, had taken place previous to the 1930's, they were usually of a localized character. Even the levee systems of the lower Mississippi were of this nature. From 1933 onward, however, not only the Tennessee Valley Authority but also the Department of the Interior[26] and the Corps of Engineers have been actively concerned with planning, construction, and management of the nation's streams in a manner which will yield as near full benefits as possible from the rivers' potential for power production, navigation, flood prevention, and water supply, and other

[25] *E.g.*, the Platte river controversy between Nebraska and Wyoming and Colorado. See "Ten Rivers in America's Future," Volume II of the President's Water Resources Policy Commission (Government Printing Office, Washington, 1950), p. 201.

[26] The Department of the Interior includes the Bureau of Reclamation as a subsidiary agency.

purposes. While the organization needed to manage such activities is still very much a matter of controversy in the United States,[27] few now raise questions as to the need for federal leadership and participation if such development is to be accomplished. The unsuitability of individual state jurisdictions to comprehensive basin development was too long demonstrated.

Technology, Changes in Settlement Pattern, and Administrative Responsibilities

Within the larger pattern of economic and governmental activity imposed by size, by environmental diversity, and by the peculiarities of the American federal system, some fundamental changes are taking place which are affecting every section of the country. They can be traced to a dynamic technology, buttressed by a huge national expenditure for scientific and engineering research (3800 million dollars in 1952). Development of new industrial processes, of new uses for erstwhile unknown or unusable natural resources, of highly mechanized farming techniques, and introduction of new methods of transport, energy distribution, and communication are having a profound influence upon American patterns of economic and political life.

The influence of technological innovation is widespread in American life, as indeed in that of any other advanced modern nation. Advances in the techniques of transmitting and generating electrical energy have encouraged decentralization of manufacturing industry, both to new regions and to new localities within the old regions. The growth of industry in both the South and the Pacific North-west, the early sites of all nuclear-energy work in the United States, and the sites of much of the country's large expansion of electro-metallurgical industries in the last decade, has been much aided by these advances. Technological advances in the use of petroleum and natural gas brought a major growth of chemical industries in the Gulf South-west. Advances in pipe-line transmission of natural gas are redressing the balance by bringing that new important fuel and material into the industrial north-eastern states.

But in addition to the regional changes, technical changes also have

[27] The controversy is nourished principally by the privately owned electric utility companies, who fear and vehemently oppose the growth of publicly owned utility systems. It also receives some support from irrigation areas where water rights are vital issues.

made possible decentralization of industry intra-regionally. With some corporations it is now a matter of fixed policy to locate manufacturing plants outside the larger industrial centers. Many hundreds of smaller towns throughout the Midwest and North-east now have manufacturing plants; and the same process is taking place in the South-east. In part this has become possible because of improvements in motor-truck transportation; but the development of the electric motor as a prime mover, petroleum and gas pipelines, and other phases of industrial change have helped.

In the wake of this industrialization of the countryside have come important social changes. The great increase of suburban and rural residence in the last twenty years[23] and the growth of labor unions into organizations with pervading influence throughout a region as well as in large industrial centers may be mentioned as examples. (See Table 2.)

With the spread of urban folkways and techniques into hitherto rural areas, tensions are created as the older, and frequently distinctive, rural values are displaced by more uniform urban methods. Industrialization of rural areas tends also to create inter-regional tensions, such as the series of political charges and bargains exchanged in the 1950's between New England and the South-east. Developing rural areas are beginning to bite into the business 'cake' which, until recently, the older industrial regions have had all to themselves.

[23] In 1950, 20·8 million people (30·1 per cent. of the population) lived in what the United States Bureau of the Census called the "urban fringe areas" surrounding or contiguous to urban centers. Evidence of the change which has taken place is provided in the following data on United States rural population:

TABLE 2

YEAR	RURAL NON-FARM		RURAL FARM		TOTAL RURAL POPULATION	
	Number	Percentage of United States Total	Number	Percentage of United States Total	Number	Percentage of United States Total
1930	23,662,710	19·3	30,157,513	24·6	53,820,223	43·8
1940	27,029,385	20·5	30,216,188	22·9	57,245,573	43·5
1950	38,693,358	25·7	23,076,539	15·3	61,769,897	41·0

Source: U.S. Department of Commerce Bureau of the Census, *1950 Census of Population*, Volume II, Part I, Tables 17 and 34.

Technology and the Farm

One of the most interesting and important changes which technology has made possible is that which has occurred on American farms. American farming practices have changed radically in the last three decades. Even since 1940 the change to greater mechanization has been striking. In 1954 there were 4·65 million tractors in use on American farms as against 1·5 million in 1940. With this assistance, and with better crop varieties, better pest control, and other improvements, 6·9 million farmers produced 31 per cent. more farm products in 1952 than did 9·5 million farm workers in 1940. Technical change has relieved one man in five on the farm in 1940.[29] It also has raised the level of cash investment required to enter agriculture on a competitive basis.

These production changes have been paralleled by changes in the farm population, which decreased from 32 million in 1910 to 22 million in 1954. In 1910 the farm population was 35 per cent. of the total; in 1954 it was 13·5 per cent. While farm population has been decreasing, land area in farms has increased, from 46 per cent. of the total United States land area in 1910 to 61 per cent. in 1950. The size of American farms therefore has been increasing steadily, from an average of 138 acres in 1910 to 215 acres in 1950. Average farm size in 1950 ranged from 74 acres in Rhode Island to 3834 acres in Arizona.[30]

Interesting social and political changes have followed the change in farm methods. For one thing, the family farm has become a less important factor in agricultural production than ever before. The number of corporation farms is rising, and the number of independent landowners is declining relatively. In 1950 full owners of farms comprised only 5·1 per cent. of the civilian gainfully employed.[31]

The declining farm population, instead of weakening the voice of agriculture in public affairs, has tended to centralize and strengthen it, a tendency enhanced by the American custom of isolating segments of public policy for decision by those most directly affected. The interests of the 'farm bloc' are watched over closely by the well-organized American Farm Bureau Federation, the National Grange, and the Farmers

---

[29] C. Wright Mills, *White Collar: the American Middle Classes* (Oxford University Press, New York, 1951), p. 19.
[30] *Statistical Abstract of the United States*, 1952, pp. 573–581. *Ibid.*, 1955, p. 13.
[31] *Statistical Abstract of the United States*, 1953 (Government Printing Office, Washington, 1953), Table 205, p. 185, and Table 717, p. 618.

Union. Together they have an estimated membership of about 2·8 million persons.[32] Additional farm political strength is derived from the fact that within the constitutional system the farmer is over-represented, because he was relatively more numerous previously. At both the state and national levels of government, rural populations exercise a voting strength which remains disproportionately large as the appointment of legislative representatives lags behind the shift of population to urban centers.

Farm production has improved so rapidly that it has outrun the capacity of the nation to absorb it, even though the average American diet is better than ever before, the population has been rising steadily, and the capacity of industry to absorb farm products has improved. American agriculture may not now be able to depend fully on a free competitive market and remain prosperous. Because of this, and because of the political strength of the farm groups, farm problems have continued to be important political issues in spite of the declining farm population. To help the farmer meet the problem of unpredictable markets the Government maintains a system of agricultural commodity price supports which, through supporting farm income, has succeeded in stabilizing an economically and politically troublesome situation. Thus in November 1953 government-purchased surplus products on hand included 6 million bales of cotton, 1109 million pounds of fats and oils, 1021 million pounds of dairy products, 854 million bushels of wheat, and many other commodities in equally large amounts.[33] The Federal Government, in 1953, was paying 168 million dollars a year just to store agricultural surpluses in addition to some 2500 million dollars 'loaned' to farmers for price supports.[34]

Mobility of the People

Changes on the farm have also contributed to a demographic characteristic of present-day United States: the relatively high mobility of its

[32] For a full and recent treatment of American farm trends and their political implications see Grant McConnell, *The Decline of Agrarian Democracy* (University of California Press, Berkeley, and Cambridge University Press, 1953). Also, Charles M. Hardin, *The Politics of Agriculture* (The Farm Press, Glencoe, Illinois, 1952).

[33] Figures released by Agricultural Marketing service of the United States Department of Agriculture, and quoted in the American Farm Bureau Federation *Newsletter* of February 1, 1954, p. 3.

[34] Friends Committee on National Legislation, *Washington Newsletters*, No. 124 (February 5, 1954), p. 2.

people. In recent years it has been particularly a movement of rural people to the cities. In 1900, 39·7 per cent. of the American population lived in cities or towns of 2500 or more; by 1950 this proportion had grown to 59 per cent. In 1950, 168 metropolitan areas accounted for more than half (56 per cent.) of the entire population of the country. In 1900, America had 78 cities of over 50,000 population; by 1940, there were 199; and in 1950, 230 such cities.[35] Whether it is to the city or elsewhere, ten million Americans make a major change in their place of residence each year, moving either to another part of one state or into another state.[36]

Population mobility continues to create several major problems and effect certain political and social changes. Movement from place to place breaks the continuity of social bonds, with the result that the migrant often becomes socially detached and indifferent to the problems of the local or regional community. Expanding urban populations have meant an ever-increasing demand for governmental services; services which in rural life were either unnecessary or else taken care of among family chores. Included are many of the expanding municipal responsibilities: sanitation, water-supply, waste removal, recreation and parks, and local transportation. In political activity urbanism counteracts tendencies toward agrarian sectionalism. The growing cities, with their mixtures of economic, racial, and social interests, interject new forces into the older patterns of political balance. Thus, in the South-east the city of Atlanta, Georgia, once known as a seat of conservatism, has responded to the needs of its industrial growth with many 'progressive' changes. Urbanization introduces class politics. It compels increased legislative action on issues such as housing, race relations, and social security, since these are matters of more real and pressing concern to urban voters than to rural.

Conclusion

The comments here made are only illustrative of the many intricate relationships among the natural environment, economic development, and governmental affairs in the United States. They serve to emphasize that the present-day United States is the product of contending, if not

[35] U.S. Department of Commerce, Bureau of the Census, *Historical Statistics of the United States*, 1798–1945 (Government Printing Office, Washington, 1949), Series B145–159, p. 29, and Bureau of the Census, *Census of Population*, 1945, Table 16, p. 24.
[36] *Statistical Abstract of the United States*, 1955, p. 42.

conflicting, forces working within it. Some of these forces derive from the past, when relatively few people were called upon to shape a culture, economy, and society within a vast and diverse living room. Habits of consumption and methods of economic organization, developed in relation to the room provided by great resources and large space, encourage acceptance of the idea of an ever-expanding economy. So also does an

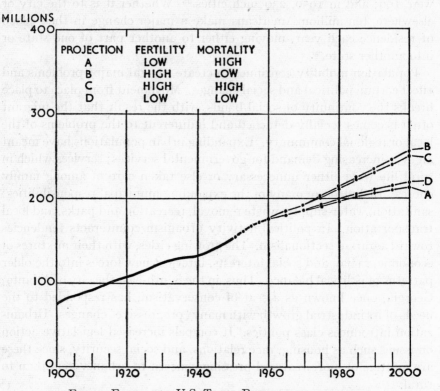

PROJECTION	FERTILITY	MORTALITY
A	LOW	HIGH
B	HIGH	LOW
C	HIGH	HIGH
D	LOW	LOW

FIG. 4. ESTIMATED U.S. TOTAL POPULATION, 1900–2000

expanding population, which has risen from 122·8 million in 1930 to an estimated 166 million in 1955,[37] and the enormous demands for production of a modern defense establishment. All of these influences give rise to an ever-greater need to exploit the resources of United States territory, and to improve the efficiency of the government and business organizations responsible for resource development. They will also assure continuing American interest in the economic development of other

[37] United States Bureau of the Census estimate for October 1955. See also Fig. 4 for estimate of future trends.

parts of the world, particularly those having low ratios of population to resources.

The United States in a sense is now in a transition from a period in which it supported its economy from 'funded' resources[38] to a time still in the future when it will depend most heavily upon managed production from renewable resources on a sustained-yield basis. American agriculture even now is making the turn. Instead of the traditional reliance on the stored fertility of the soil, the American farmer, like those of older, longer-cultivated lands, is now becoming expert in the use of farm and commercial fertilizers. Since 1930 the farm consumption of commercial fertilizers has risen about three and a half times.[39] American forestry is following the same pattern, with a distinct trend toward carefully managed forest plantations, whether publicly or privately owned. There is also a movement toward orderly development of water resources.

As per capita consumption continues to rise, and as population increases still more, the trend toward a more carefully managed use of resources may be expected to gain momentum. The need for more careful management is likely in turn to mean pressures for public attention to development and regulation of resource use. Both state and federal governments are certain to be increasingly concerned with activities related to economic development and resource management. This will be particularly true in eastern United States, within which the major opportunities for popular support seem to lie, and where we can expect the major land, water, and industrial developments of the future. An interesting future event in this connexion is likely to be the spread of irrigation into eastern, and particularly south-eastern, United States, with all of its potentiality for increasing the complexity of administering resources and local economic development.

There are thus some basic forces at work in the United States which press the nation in the direction of greater federal and state administrative concern for economic development and resource management. The pressure of these basic forces must be considered in the light of the pattern of territorial division among the states. Because of territorial characteristics, all but a few states lack capacity to deal effectively with

[38] Any resource being consumed at a rate higher than it is being replaced or restored is here considered to be used on a 'funded' basis. Mineral deposits are the most common example.

[39] Measured on basis of nitrogen, phosphorus pentoxide, and potassium chloride content.—United States Department of Agriculture, *Agricultural Statistics* (United States Government Printing Office, Washington, 1952 and 1953).

some of the more important problems of development and management. Because of this, the basic pressure in many cases will fall more heavily on the federal administrative structure than on that of the states.

The direction of these pressures toward the federal[40] establishment is reinforced by the changes in American social structure and geographical pattern which are being caused by technology. The growing specialization of the economy and the increasingly greater number of people resident in or dependent on urban communities with quasi-national service responsibilities create economic relations which can be dealt with successfully only on a national scale, particularly in emergency. Migration and growing urban or suburban residence furthermore favor psychological attitudes which tend to weaken local and regional ties, and leave dominant the identification of the individual with the nation.

The changes which technology has brought about in agriculture have also resulted in pressure for federal action and federal responsibility. The problem of stabilizing agriculture is of such great size that no state has yet shown itself capable of meeting it. The Eisenhower Administration, committed to a policy of lessening federal participation in economic affairs, has not been able to change federal responsibility for agricultural stabilization materially. Furthermore, the fact that the only logical outlet for United States agricultural surpluses lies in foreign aid and development programs will assist in keeping farm problems tied to national policy.

On the other hand, there are also strong contending forces which generally press in the opposite direction. Sectionalism, emphasizing differences and contrasts, encompasses many of these forces. A few sections, like the Interior South, undoubtedly will continue to favor a co-operative federal-state approach to many problems of economic development which permits both federal and state initiative. In general, however, sectional forces in the United States are anti-federal in their expressions. The spokesmen for the Gulf South-west and New England seem to want no federal interference with the pattern of resource development they have worked out on a state basis. Often their expressions appear to be stimulated and prompted by vested private economic interest, particularly privately owned utilities, which can better maintain positions of political power where federal activity is restricted.

The voices which interpret sectionalism are reinforced by the inheri-

40 'Federal' here and in succeeding paragraphs means 'federal government' as contrasted with individual state government administration.

tance of attitudes from past periods of sparse population and oversized territory. The tendency to emphasize immediate development problems and the tenacity of the inexhaustibility legend still strongly favor minimum participation by public agencies in economic affairs. These voices still are very strong.

Yet there appears to be an underlying understanding about many activities relating to economic development, even on the part of those who promote sectional positions most strongly, which admits state inadequacies. The pressure for federal investment funds for resource development is a good example. No section so strongly believes in its regional identity that it has not pressed for increasingly large federal investment in the last twenty years. Preferably it is a non-reimbursable federal investment which is sought. But federal management of any economic activity is consistently opposed in the same breath, even though it often is obvious that the individual states at present are no more prepared to handle some management problems than to meet investment needs. Consequently there have arisen new occasions to experiment with regional combinations of states to deal with inter-state problems like those attending river-basin development. Most are referred to in legal terms as 'inter-state compacts.'

Thus proposals and negotiations have arisen for inter-state compacts on the Missouri river and Columbia river developments and several others. There have been further experiments with 'interagency' committees which combine federal and state representation for resource–development planning purposes. While compact agreements are not new in the United States, their proposed use for broad purposes of economic development is. Their potentialities have assumed new importance since 1953, when a national policy discouraging the regionalization of federal agencies was adopted. For twenty years previously there had been a trend toward decentralization of administrative structure on a regional pattern among the important operational agencies of the Federal Government. This had been looked upon as undesirable strengthening of the federal administrative structure by many proponents of sectional views.

In 1954 the sectional influence was thus still powerful in determining the pattern of governmental participation in United States economic activity. While exercising this power, however, there was overt admission by sectional interests that their administrative outlet, the state, was inadequate to undertake the increasingly complex task of economic development, resource management, and economic regulation. It would seem that the basic forces at work in the United States combine unrelentingly to demand a certain degree of federal administrative participation in the future of these affairs. At the same time there are possibilities of more effective co-operation organization which transcends the limits imposed by state territorial jurisdictions, but permitting independent regional expression. In this respect also the United States may be considered to be in a period of experimentation and transition. An interesting aspect of present activities is that some of the best organized independent inter-state regional activities are being carried on in an area where federal activity has been most coherently organized, the Interior South, which centers in the Tennessee Valley. This would tend to prove that coherent, well-coordinated federal administrative organization which responds to the basic needs for economic development, resource management, and economic regulation is not incompatible with strong expressions of sectional identity. This pattern may well lie beyond the present period of transition, and even confusion, in administrative structure relating to economic affairs. When the change to smoother, more efficient co-operative relations between necessary federal organization and state activities is achieved consistency in foreign and domestic economic policy should be more easily obtained, and sectional interests should be recognized as more compatible with national interest.

FURTHER READING

BEHRMAN, JACK N., "Political Factors in U.S. International Financial Cooperation, 1945–1950," in *American Political Science Review*, vol. xlvii (June 1953).

FABRICANT, SOLOMON, *The Trend in Government Activity in the United States since 1900* (National Bureau of Economic Research, Inc., New York, 1952).

KEY, V. O. JR., *Politics, Parties, and Pressure Groups* (Thomas Y. Crowell Company, New York, 1948).

MILLS, C. WRIGHT, *White Collar: The American Middle Class* (Oxford University Press, New York, 1953).

ODUM, HOWARD W., and MOORE, HARRY E., *American Regionalism* (Holt, New York, 1938).

OSTROM, VINCENT, "State Administration of Natural Resources in the West," in *American Political Science Review*, vol. xlvii (June 1953).

REPORT OF THE PRESIDENT'S MATERIALS POLICY COMMISSION, *Resources for Freedom* (five vols.; United States Government Printing Office, Washington, 1952).

SYNDER, RICHARD C., and WILSON, H. HUBERT, *Roots of Political Behaviour* (American Book Company, New York, 1949).

UNITED STATES DEPARTMENT OF COMMERCE. *Statistical Abstract of the United States, 1953* (United States Government Printing Office, Washington, 1953).

UNITED STATES DEPARTMENT OF COMMERCE, *Historical Statistics of the United States, 1789–1945* (United States Government Printing Office, Washington, 1949).

UNITED STATES DEPARTMENT OF COMMERCE, *Regional Trends in the United States Economy* (United States Government Printing Office, Washington, 1951).

WHITAKER, J. RUSSELL, and ACKERMAN, EDWARD A., *American Resources* (Harcourt Brace, New York, 1951).

WHITE, GILBERT F., "New Stage in Resources History," in *Soil and Water Conservation Journal*, vol. viii, No. 5 (September 1953).

WHITE, LEONARD D., *The States and the Nation* (Louisiana State University Press, Baton Rouge, 1953).

ZIMMERMAN, ERICH W., *World Resources and Industries* (Harper, New York, revised edition, 1951).

CHAPTER XII

The Confederation of Canada

N. L. NICHOLSON

THE rise of the Canadian nation is an event of very recent times. It is usual to date it from 1867, when, by an Act of the British Parliament, the three former colonies of Canada, New Brunswick, and Nova Scotia became four provinces of a federal union collectively named Canada. In 1870 "Rupert's Land and the North-Western Territory" were placed under the new federal government when the Hudson's Bay Company surrendered exclusive control of those areas, and in 1871 and 1873 the colonies of British Columbia and Prince Edward Island became additional provinces of Canada. In 1880 Canada acquired the British title to the Arctic Archipelago, which, in 1925, was officially claimed to extend to the North Pole, and in 1949 she embraced the remaining portions of the north Atlantic coast when Newfoundland and its dependency (Labrador) joined the Confederation (Fig. 1).

As a result, Canada is now the second largest political unit in the world, a huge country, with an area of about 3,846,000 square miles and an extent of over 88 degrees of longitude and 48 degrees of latitude. At the same time it has a sea-coast of no less than 60,000 miles (more than twice the circumference of the earth), and faces three oceans—the Pacific, the Arctic, and the Atlantic.

These astronomical figures are questionable assets when it is realized that about 25 per cent. of the country experiences an arctic[1] climate and more than 50 per cent. is subarctic.[1] Of the remaining areas those which experience microthermal, mesothermal, and continental steppe climates cover less than 20 per cent. of the total area of the country, yet support most of the fifteen million Canadian people. This œcumene is a long, narrow tract stretching from east to west along the southern part of the country. It borders the United States of America, and this close

[1] These terms are used in Köppen's sense—*i.e.*, "arctic" includes the ET and EF areas and "subarctic" the Dfc.

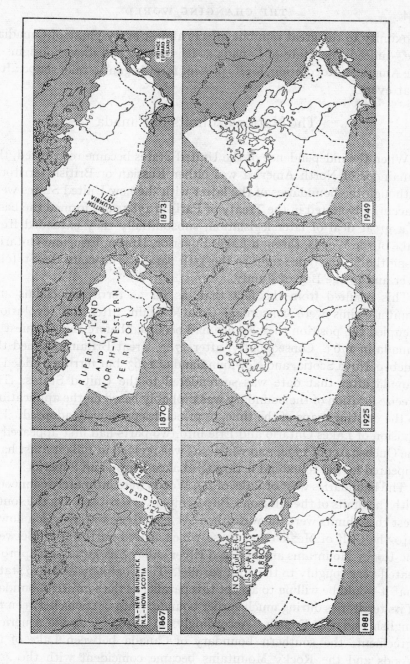

FIG. 1. THE TERRITORIAL DEVELOPMENT OF CANADA, 1867–1949
Note the gradual acquisition of a three-ocean coast. The **broken lines** indicate
the provincial and territorial boundaries at the date shown.

proximity to the great republic affects almost every phase of Canadian life. Indeed, the State of Canada as it is to-day had its very origins in the American Revolution, for its present form began to take shape after that event.

The National Limits of Canada

When the independence of the United States became recognized, the remainder of North America was either Russian or British territory. Although the boundaries of the latter with the new United States were inaccurately stated in the Treaty of Paris in 1783, and formed the basis of a great deal of later legislation, substantially they extended from Lake of the Woods, through Lakes Superior, Huron, Erie, and Ontario, along the St Lawrence river to the 45th parallel, thence to the St John river and to the Bay of Fundy.

This resulted from the fact that, as far as territorial claims and counter-claims were concerned, Great Britain, after the revolution, occupied the position that France had occupied before the conquest of Canada in 1763. Consequently, after 1783, Great Britain retained the Quebec, Nova Scotia, and Newfoundland of 1763, but territory added to Canada after that date was surrendered to the United States. The precise location of the boundary was probably based on the application, to the existing maps of the time, of principles previously adopted. The division of Lakes Ontario and Erie into two parts had first appeared in the Quebec Act of 1774, and when this was revived in 1783 it must have appeared logical to extend it through Lakes Huron and Superior.

The boundaries west of Lake of the Woods were intimately connected with the limits of the Hudson's Bay Company's territory. On the south-west these limits were the watershed between those waters which flowed into the Gulf of Mexico and those which flowed northward. Between the Rocky Mountains and the Red River valley this watershed approximated very roughly to the 49th parallel. The Company had also stated that it would be willing to accept this parallel as the southern boundary of its territories during much earlier boundary negotiations between the English and the French. Accordingly, in 1818, by Anglo-American agreement, the southern boundary of Canada between Lake of the Woods and the Rocky Mountains became coincident with the 49th parallel. It was extended farther westward to the Pacific Ocean in 1846, partly because it was convenient to do so and partly because it roughly bisected Columbia, an area which had legally been under joint American-British occupation since 1818.

That much of the 49th parallel is approximately a watershed and is in places marked by low hills[2] does not lessen the fact that it, and the international boundary east of it to the Atlantic Ocean, cut across every major physiographic unit of the North American continent and have little effect on the underlying unity of Canada and the United States. But the one physiographic province that is almost entirely included in the Canada of to-day is the Canadian Shield. The rivers and lakes which fringe it link up with the lower Great Lakes–St Lawrence waterways and the river systems of the northwest "in a manner that has given the northern portion of the continent a peculiar measure of east and west unity."[3] It was along these waterways that the earliest explorers, traders, missionaries, and settlers moved. Later the transcontinental railways followed them, and, in facilitating east–west migration, enormously strengthened the longitudinal rather than the latitudinal forces at work. To-day millions of Canadians live around the fringes of the Shield, deriving their livelihood from its rich forests and mineral resources, which are becoming even more productive as technology advances.

The boundary between Russian and British territory in North America, which is to-day the boundary between Canada and Alaska, was substantially settled in 1825. The two Governments were guided in their negotiations by the representations of two trading companies—the Russian-American on the one hand, whose chief interest was in exploiting the resources of the sea, and the Hudson's Bay on the other, which was primarily engaged in hunting the resources of the land. Therefore, the Russians were particularly anxious to retain control of the Pacific coast north of 55° N., the southern limit mentioned in their charter of 1799, as it included the trading settlements which they had established. On the other hand, the British wished to retain control of the Mackenzie river area. The ultimate selection of the 141st meridian as the northern part of the boundary was probably due to the fact that it ran north from Mount St Elias, one of the few outstanding and unmistakable features in a relatively unknown land, and supplied a point of reference for the

[2] Stephen B. Jones, "The Forty-ninth Parallel in the Great Plains," in *Jour. of Geog.*, vol. xxxi (1932), pp. 357–367. Another of the rather rare truly geographical studies of Canada's boundaries is by the same author: "The Cordilleran Section of the Canada-United States Borderland," in *Geog. Jour.*, vol. lxxxix (1937), pp. 439–450.
[3] R. G. Trotter, "The Canadian Back Fence in Anglo-American Relations," in *Queen's Quarterly*, vol. xl (1933), pp. 383–397.

northern part of the boundary as well as the southern "panhandle" part.

In the north, Canada's title to the Arctic islands was obtained from Britain in 1880, mainly on the ground that the British had carried out most of the exploration in that area. The Norwegian claim to certain islands as a result of Sverdrup's explorations of 1898–1901, was withdrawn in favour of Canada in 1930, and there now seems to be no doubt as to her sovereignty in the area. The claim to the sector between 141° W. and 60° W. was first made by Senator Poirier in 1907, although it was not officially supported by a member of the Canadian Cabinet until 1925.

The Growth of the Internal Political Structure

Canada's size alone would have made a unitary state almost unworkable, quite apart from its historical development. Thus it is to-day a federation of ten provinces and two territories. The provinces are all fundamentally south of 60° N., whereas the two territories extend south of 60° N. only in the Hudson Bay and James Bay areas, and include those water bodies and the islands within them.

Each of these major internal political units varies greatly in area, shape, and national significance. Of the present provinces, five have the same extent which they had as British colonies. In four of them— British Columbia, Prince Edward Island, New Brunswick, and Nova Scotia—their boundaries resulted from forces which were significant at the time of their creation in the eighteenth and nineteenth centuries, but which have long since lost that significance.

British Columbia evolved from the earlier colonies of Vancouver Island, British Columbia, and Stickeen Territory. Its present extent dates from 1863 and is largely due to the discoveries of placer gold along the mountain rivers and creeks after 1850. It was thought that the gold found along the lower courses of the rivers was but debris from larger deposits along the headwaters, and the colonial boundaries were therefore established in such a way as to include as many of these headwater areas as possible.[4]

The three smallest maritime provinces really originated in 1763,

[4] Willard E. Ireland, "The Evolution of the Boundaries of British Columbia," in *Brit. Col. Hist. Quart.*, vol. iii (1939), pp. 263–282.

when, as a result of the Treaty of Paris, France withdrew from North America except for the islands of St Pierre and Miquelon. In order to provide for the administration of this newly acquired territory, the British extended the government of Nova Scotia over the peninsula proper, Cape Breton Island, Prince Edward Island,[5] and the present New Brunswick. Prince Edward Island, which was practically deserted after the withdrawal of the French, was re-colonized by the British, but no sooner had this been accomplished than the landlords petitioned the Crown for complete political separation from the government of Nova Scotia. They stressed the inconvenience of having to refer all judicial and legal matters to Halifax, the capital of Nova Scotia. At the best of times the journey from the island to the mainland was tedious and expensive, and during the winter months it was impracticable because of the ice in Northumberland Strait. These and other reasons ultimately resulted in the separation of Prince Edward Island in 1769.

In 1784 New Brunswick was established as a separate colony. This clearly resulted from the American Revolution. During and immediately after its close thousands of people who adhered to the royal standard, now known as "United Empire Loyalists," moved into what remained of British North America. In Nova Scotia, these lands were mainly in the St John valley and along the north shore of the Bay of Fundy, and it was to these areas that most of the Americans went in Eastern Canada. This sudden advent of thousands of migrants, many of whom were destitute, created judicial and administrative problems with which the government in Halifax was unable to deal adequately, the more so as it was relatively inaccessible to the remoter parts of the province. Ultimately, the division was made across the fourteen-mile-wide Chignecto Isthmus, from Cumberland Arm to Baie Verte.

Thus the existence to-day of three small provinces on the Atlantic seaboard of Canada stems essentially from the state of the transportation system of the late eighteenth century.[6] Nevertheless, other factors were also involved. The decision to separate New Brunswick from peninsular Nova Scotia, for example, was in part due to the 'divide-and-rule' policy of the British Government. With the experience of the American Revolution fresh in their minds, they took the view that small, separate colonies would show less independence than large ones.

[5] It did not receive this name until 1798. Before that date it was referred to as either St John's Island or Ile St Jean, the old French name.
[6] N. L. Nicholson, "Boundary Evolution in the Gulf of St Lawrence Region," in The Newfoundland Quarterly, vol. liii (1954), pp. 13–17.

Indeed, the British colonial administration had even suggested the creation of another province between New Brunswick and Maine. A separate New Brunswick also served another useful purpose; for, being a 'Loyalist' province, it acted as a 'buffer' between the United States and Nova Scotia, which had during the Revolution shown signs of sympathizing with the rebels. This was, of course, hardly surprising, as on the eve of the Revolution more than half the population of Nova Scotia was American.

However, the core of the new Confederation in 1867 was the Colony of Canada. This had undergone a somewhat complicated political evolution since the time of the earliest settlements along the shores of the St Lawrence, but at the close of the American Revolution it was called Quebec and extended from the Atlantic coast westward to the shores of Lakes Huron and St Clair. Most of its unsettled lands lay south-west of the Ottawa river and along the north shores of Lakes Erie and Ontario, between the lands granted in seigniory during the French regime and the small settlement of French origin near the present city of Windsor. To these lands went large numbers of United Empire Loyalists, and after 1789 many other Americans migrated northward to take advantage of the offer of free land.[7] The French feudal system of land tenure was contrary to the ideas of these newcomers, who held their land in free and common socage. Furthermore, having become accustomed to popular government, they resented its absence in their new country. The factor of accessibility was also present. The distance from Windsor to Montreal, the colonial capital, was some six hundred miles, and no road connected them, while the journey on the Great Lakes–St Lawrence waterways was "exceedingly tedious, precarious, and during the winter season, absolutely impossible."[8] Consequently, the movement for political separation of the New Canadians from the Old Canadians grew, and, following the Constitutional Act of 1791, the Province of Quebec was divided into the two provinces of Upper and Lower Canada. The boundary ran northward from the St Lawrence river, following the westernmost limits of the seigniories to the Ottawa river, and thence up the river. Thus the "triangle" south of the Ottawa river and north of the St Lawrence was included in the Province of Lower Canada, but this area, from the point of view of regional geography, is properly part

[7] Many of these were doubtless Loyalists during the American Revolution, but are more correctly described as "late Loyalists."
[8] A. Shortt and Arthur G. Doughty, *Documents relating to the Constitutional History of Canada, 1759–1791* (King's Printer, Ottawa, 1918).

of the Montreal plain, and the boundary, therefore, approximated to a physiographic division as well as being a line dividing people of different origins.

The Canadians of French descent, having acquired their own government, were able to preserve their own laws and customs without conflict with the Canadians of American and British descent, who had established a different set of institutions. But the division came to an end in 1840, for a number of reasons. Among them was the fact that, as a result of the division, Upper Canada was compelled to import all seaborne articles through territory under the administration of another government, either through Lower Canada or the United States. Thus trade via the St Lawrence River was commanded by Lower Canada, and in order to collect customs revenue it was necessary for Upper Canada either to establish customs houses on her eastern boundary or to come to some arrangement whereby a certain proportion of the duties levied at Quebec, the port of entry for Lower Canada, would be given to the administration of Upper Canada. The latter course was taken, but it resulted in perpetual friction and temporary arrangements.

As separate parts of a federated country, however, such difficulties would not arise, and as the factors of human geography were as valid in 1867 as they had been in 1791, re-division occurred in 1867 along the 1791 boundary, when, by the British North America Act, the colony of Canada became the two provinces of Ontario and Quebec.

Ontario and Quebec, however, differed from the other provinces which became part of Canada in 1867, or shortly afterwards, in that their northern limits were not precisely known. This was one of the problems in internal political geography with which the Government of Canada was faced almost as soon as it was created. Its solution was complicated by the formation of a new province (Manitoba) in response to the demands of the people who had settled in the Canadian portion of the Red River Valley. Both Manitoba and Ontario claimed the area between Lake of the Woods and the present Port Arthur–Fort William, and the controversy was not settled until 1889. The northern limits of Quebec were not defined until 1898.

Meanwhile the former Hudson's Bay Company territory was being peopled. The first response, from the point of view of political geography, was to divide the area into provisional districts for administrative and postal purposes. These districts underwent several modifications in response to the geographical changes which resulted from in-

creased settlement and development, and by 1905 much of the area was
deemed ready for provincial responsibilities. The Government was of
the opinion that the area north of 60° N. and west of the District of
Keewatin was "absolutely unfit for agriculture," and that without agriculture there could be little hope of "thick and permanent settlement,"
and thus of stable provincial government. They also considered that the
area within these limits was too large for a single province when compared with the other members of the Confederation, and therefore it was
divided into two, of approximately equal size, named Alberta and
Saskatchewan. The boundary between them followed the 110th meridian W. and was admittedly an arbitrary one. But although at the time
there was some criticism, because it divided the cattle-raising area between Calgary and Swift Current, it does not appear to have caused any
permanent hardship.

The real effect of the creation of Alberta and Saskatchewan was felt
outside those provinces, for now three provinces extended as far north
as 60° N. Manitoba, Ontario, and Quebec, therefore, felt justified in
requesting northward extensions. The main difficulty seemed to concern
Manitoba and Ontario, as both laid claim to the area between the Albany
and Churchill rivers. This was ultimately divided more or less equally
between the two. The boundary was intended to follow the watershed
between the Hayes and Nelson rivers on the one hand, and the Severn
river on the other. However, when it was discovered that this boundary
did not extend in a reasonably straight line to Hudson Bay, because it
was met some distance from the shore by another watershed running
east and west, the boundary effecting the desired division was expressed
geometrically as two straight lines. [9] These extensions came into force
in 1912, at the same time as Quebec was extended northward to the
shores of Hudson Strait and Bay.

The only remaining major boundary to be settled was that between
Canada and Newfoundland. Labrador, east of Rivière St-Jean, Anticosti Island, and the Magdalen Islands first came under the jurisdiction of Newfoundland in 1763, but they were transferred to Quebec in
1774, as it was thought that this would be in the best interests of the
Quebec fishermen. By 1809, however, this had become inconvenient
from an administrative point of view, and Labrador and Anticosti
Island were returned to Newfoundland. This still led to difficulties,

[9] N. L. Nicholson, "Some Aspects of the Political Geography of Keewatin," in *The Canadian Geographer*, 3 (1953), pp. 73–84.

however, as the laws of Newfoundland were unfamiliar to the fishermen of French origin, so that in 1825 Anticosti Island and that part of the Labrador coast between Rivière St-Jean and Ance Sablon, now known as Blanc Sablon, became part of Quebec. The major part, however, remained under Newfoundland, but its boundaries on the landward side were never precisely delimited. This did not become a practical problem until 1902, when the Government of Newfoundland granted leases for the cutting of timber in a 297-square-mile area on the north and south sides of the Hamilton river, between Lake Melville and Grand Falls, and the Government of Quebec maintained that this was an area properly under their jurisdiction. Eventually, the matter was referred to the Imperial Privy Council, who decided that the boundary was essentially the watershed of those rivers flowing into the Atlantic Ocean. In 1949, when Newfoundland joined Canada as a province, the terms of union guaranteed these limits to it (Fig. 1).

The People of Canada

The people of Canada came originally from many different parts of the world. Although most of them were European in origin, the population as a whole generally lacks homogeneity, and the fact that the Canadian Citizenship Act of 1947 conferred upon them a legal status quite apart from British citizenship has hardly lessened their tendency to describe themselves variously as English, Scottish, Polish, etc.

The aboriginal inhabitants of the country were Indians and Eskimos. Together they now number about 166,000—a little more than one-hundredth of the total population. Regionally, however, their significance varies. Their relative concentration in the western provinces is mainly an expression of the fact that much of the land there is unsuited to colonization by other groups, and industrialization is lacking. More Indians live in Ontario than in any of these provinces, but conditions there are much more favourable for other groups, and immigration into Ontario has therefore reduced the relative numbers of Indians. A completely reversed situation exists in the Territories, and consequently almost half the population is of Indian and Eskimo origin, although their total numbers are less than those for Quebec, where, in turn, they form less than 1 per cent. of the total population of the province.

All the other inhabitants of Canada are relatively recent immigrants

M

or their descendants. The first colonies of settlement were established in the early seventeenth century, by the French, in the lower St Lawrence valley[10] and by the English, on the south-eastern part of the island of Newfoundland,[11] although proclamations of sovereignty had been made by both countries, as well as others, at much earlier dates. These colonies differed in character, for the French settlements were intended to establish a New France in North America, while the English settlements were merely intended to safeguard the property of the fishermen, and the island of Newfoundland was regarded rather as a ship moored near the fishing grounds than as a colony. However, these colonies progressed, particularly those in the St Lawrence valley, and to them were added similar settlements in the peninsula of Nova Scotia and Prince Edward Island, which were either British or French depending upon the fortunes of war and the tenacity of the original colonists.

The third great wave of settlement was the northward movement of people from the United States at the close of the American Revolution. They occupied the best agricultural portions of New Brunswick and were the founders of Ontario. They simply settled near the people of French origin without the two groups assimilating or making much impression on one another. Settlement in British Columbia began around the Hudson's Bay Company's posts at the present Victoria and Vancouver and was also principally British in origin.

The fourth influx of people into Canada occurred between 1901 and 1913, when the Prairies were opened for development and the great transcontinental railways were being built. It was as a result of this addition to the population that Canada began to lose its more purely French-British characteristics, for although the countries of North-west Europe were still the principal sources of immigrants, the newcomers contained significant numbers from Eastern Europe and the Eastern Mediterranean. Canadians of French and British origin, who in 1901 had constituted 88 per cent. of the total population, made up but 84 per cent. ten years later (Fig. 2).

There was a similar wave of migration after the second world war, when significant numbers of Germans, Italians, Poles, and Netherlanders came to Canada, in addition to those from the British Isles. These continental Europeans exceeded in number immigrants from the British Commonwealth.

[10] Quebec, the first settlement in Canada that has had an uninterrupted existence to the present day, was founded in 1608.
[11] Cupids was founded in 1610.

The distribution of the Canadian people to-day, according to origin,[12] shows the impress of early colonization and subsequent waves of migration. Thus in Quebec 82 per cent. of the people are of French origin,

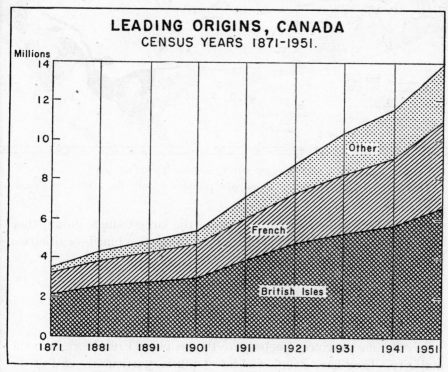

LEADING ORIGINS, CANADA
CENSUS YEARS 1871-1951.

FIG. 2. THE GROWTH OF THE CANADIAN POPULATION BY LEADING ORIGINS, 1871–1951

while in Newfoundland almost 94 per cent. of the people are of British Isles origin. These high percentages stem directly from the origin of the earliest settlers. Increases in the population of Canadians of French descent since 1745, and Newfoundlanders since 1830, have been primarily the result of natural increases, not immigration. The people of Nova Scotia and Prince Edward Island are more than 75 per cent. British in origin, and those of Ontario and British Columbia over 65 per cent. so (Fig. 3). In New Brunswick those of British Isles origin form 57 per cent. of the population, but in the other provinces, although

[12] For Canadian Census purposes a person's origin is traced through his father. For example, if a person's father is German and his mother Norwegian the origin is entered as "German."

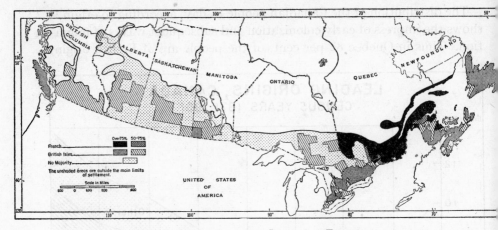

FIG. 3. ORIGINS OF THE CANADIAN PEOPLE, 1951

This is based on statistics which are published only by arbitrary Census divisions.

people of British Isles origin constitute the largest single group, they are exceeded in numbers by all the other groups combined—a situation which holds good for Canada as a whole.

Les Québeçios

In only one province, Quebec, are the people of French origin in the majority. They have overflowed into Ontario, particularly east of the Frontenac axis, where this outlier of the Canadian Shield extends across the St Lawrence into the United States and forms a relatively sparsely populated area because of its unsuitability for agriculture. The people of French origin are also to be found in considerable numbers in northern New Brunswick, where they have penetrated the valleys through the Appalachians and the coastal plains around them to join smaller concentrations in Nova Scotia, whose ancestors formed the other early French colony of Acadia.

Elsewhere in Canada the people of French origin are scattered, although they form locally important minorities. Their distinct survival in Quebec is not hard to explain, for the British North America Act guarantees French as an official language, on an equality with English, in Quebec, in the proceedings of the Parliament of Canada, and in Federal Courts throughout Canada. It also guarantees to Quebec the right to a Roman Catholic school system under the control of the Roman Catholic population of the province. Almost all the Canadians of French origin are Roman Catholic, and their branch of this Church differs in several respects from the English-speaking branch, in which the leadership is mainly provided by people of Irish origin. Les Québeçois have, therefore, developed a culture of their own, which is different in many respects from the culture of the rest of Canada, and, indeed, the rest of North America. "Comme, par instinct et par volonté, il entend se garder français et catholique, le but de la politique pour lui, ce n'est ni la prospérité, comme pour l'Américain, ni même la liberté, comme pour l'Anglais, mais sa survivance ethnique. C'est sous ce seul angle qu'il envisage tout le problème national."[13] The political consequences of this are important, for Les Québeçois, conscious of being a national minority, tend to act as a unit in national politics and support whichever party is paying attention to their claims.[14]

Political Regionalism

But, quite apart from the origins of the people, the great differences in area and population between the ten provinces have their effect upon the government of Canada, just as the presence of major and minor powers does in the United Nations.

On a population basis alone, the Provinces of Ontario and Quebec compare with independent States like Norway, Finland, and Venezuela, while the population of Prince Edward Island is barely one-quarter that of the Grand Duchy of Luxembourg.

Furthermore, it must be remembered that the boundaries of the larger provinces all cut across major geographical regions (Fig. 4).[15] Thus each of them includes a wide variety of regions and resources which, if found in an independent State, would enhance its international standing. The same result is found in the provinces, where there are tendencies to behave like quasi-independent countries, which tendencies are often accentuated by the factors of human geography, particularly in Quebec. The result is a problem in national unity—one

[13] Gustave Lanctot, "Le Québec et les Etats-Unis, 1867–1937," in Les Canadiens Français et leurs Voisins du Sud (Editions Bernard Valiquette, Montreal, 1941), p. 280.
[14] B. K. Sandwell, "The French Canadians," in The Annals of the American Academy of Political and Social Science, vol. ccliii (1947), pp. 169–175.
[15] The geographical regions shown in Fig. 4 are based on G. Helwecke, "Eleven Regions of Canada," in Canadian Geographical Journal, vol. xli (1950), pp. 84–89.

which really arises out of a failure to realize that the principles on which
the provincial boundaries were based at the time of their original
establishment have been almost completely invalidated by later events.
But the political map of to-day is so well known that the internal

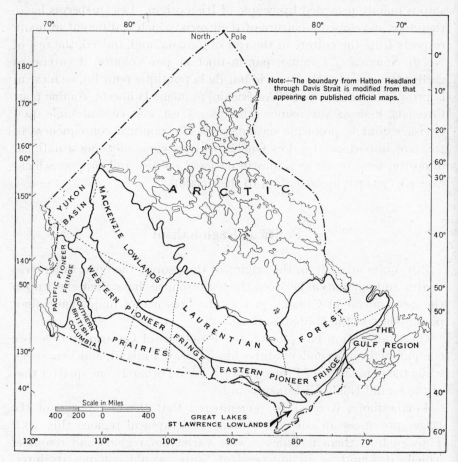

FIG. 4. GEOGRAPHICAL REGIONS AND POLITICAL AREAS OF CANADA

The boundaries of the major political divisions, where they do not coincide with
regional boundaries, are indicated by broken lines.

boundaries are looked upon as though they were created by the same
agencies which produced the Rocky Mountains or the St Lawrence
river.

From this point of view the provinces of Canada can be divided into
three groups. Ontario and Quebec can be regarded as major powers;

TABLE I

rea and Population Relationships of the Internal Political Divisions of Canada in 1951

POLITICAL AREA	AREA (square) miles)	PERCEN-TAGE OF TOTAL AREA	POPULA-TION	PERCEN-TAGE OF TOTAL POPULA-TION	DENSITY OF POPULATION PER SQUARE MILE OF LAND	NATURAL INCREASE PER 1000 PER ANNUM
ewfoundland	155,364	4·0	361,416	2·6	2·4	24·2
rince Edward Island .	2,184	0·1	98,429	0·7	45·1	17·9
ova Scotia .	21,068	0·6	642,584	4·6	31·0	17·6
ew Brunswick	27,985	0·7	515,697	3·7	18·8	21·8
uebec .	594,860	15·5	4,055,681	29·0	7·7	21·2
ntario .	412,582	10·7	4,597,542	32·8	13·2	15·4
anitoba .	246,512	6·4	776,541	5·5	3·5	17·0
askatchewan	251,700	6·6	831,728	5·9	3·8	18·4
lberta .	255,285	6·6	939,501	6·7	3·8	21·1
ritish Columbia .	366,255	9·5	1,165,210	8·3	3·2	14·1
ukon .	207,076	5·4	9,096	> 0·1	> 0·1	—
orthwest Territories .	1,304,903	33·9	16,004	0·1	> 0·1	—

British Columbia, Alberta, Saskatchewan, and Manitoba as middle powers; and Newfoundland, Prince Edward Island, Nova Scotia, and New Brunswick, as minor powers. To offset the influences of Ontario and Quebec, the other provinces often group themselves sectionally along these lines, so that within Canada it is common to speak of the East or Atlantic Provinces; Ontario; Quebec; and the West, or Western Provinces. Because its physical environment is in such great contrast to that of the other western provinces, British Columbia is sometimes considered separately from Alberta, Saskatchewan, and Manitoba, which are often referred to as "The Prairie Provinces" despite the fact that the prairie landscape occupies less than one fifth of their total area. In a somewhat similar way, Newfoundland is often considered as a separate 'section,' partly because it was outside Canada until recently, and partly because of its relative remoteness from Nova Scotia, Prince Edward Island, and New Brunswick, which are still collectively referred to as "The Maritime Provinces."

TABLE 2

Distribution of Seats in the Canadian House of Commons 1952[16]

POLITICAL UNIT	NUMBER OF SEATS IN FEDERAL PARLIAMENT		SECTION
Newfoundland . .	7		
Prince Edward Island .	4	33	Atlantic
New Brunswick . .	10		Provinces
Nova Scotia . .	12		
Quebec . . .	75	75	Quebec
Ontario . . .	85	85	Ontario
Manitoba . . .	14		
Saskatchewan . .	17	70	The
Alberta . . .	17		West
British Columbia .	22		
Yukon Territory .	1	2	The
Northwest Territories .	1		North
TOTAL .	265		

The North

Canada north of the provinces is divided into Yukon Territory and Northwest Territories. It does not enter directly into the internal political arena, because, with its widely scattered population of 25,000, it has but two members in the Federal Parliament of 265. In an indirect way, however, the Territories have representation in the Canadian Cabinet, just as the provinces do, as their administration is the responsibility of the Minister of Northern Affairs and National Resources, who is not, at the moment, one of the elected members from the Territories. But the significance of "Territorial" Canada in national life goes beyond these facts. Its importance lies as much in its "mystic appeal"[17] as in its economic value. Indeed, until relatively recently it had no economic value, but no Canadian would ever disown it. To-day, increasing wealth is being obtained from the Territories in the form of furs, fish, and

[16] Statutes of Canada, 1 Eliz. II, c. 48.
[17] André Siegfried, *Le Canada: Puissance Internationale* (Armand Colin, Paris, 1947), p. 15.

minerals, and there are indications of continued developments of this kind even in the Queen Elizabeth Islands, which are in the far northern sector to which the Prime Minister of Canada as recently as 1953 reiterated his country's claim and determination to develop. This attitude stems from the acquisition of the Hudson's Bay Company's territories, when, as Sir John A. Macdonald, Canada's first Prime Minister, said, the Government had one great country before them to do with as they liked. The challenge to "go north" remains as fresh as ever.

By no means the least of the increasingly important aspects of northern Canada has resulted from developments in aviation. The fact that the most direct air route between America and Europe and America and Asia lies over the area is an indication of the location of the possible future air routes. Canadian Pacific Air Lines have already established a scheduled 'polar' route from Vancouver to Amsterdam via Churchill (Manitoba) and Sondrestom (Greenland). In the meantime, the need for further meteorological information from all parts of the world has led to the establishment of five weather stations in the Queen Elizabeth Islands, three of which are almost on the shores of the Arctic Sea itself.

FURTHER READING

BÉRIAULT, YVON, Les Problèmes politiques du Nord Canadien (Université d'Ottawa, Ottawa, 1942).

BROWN, GEORGE W. (editor), Canada (University of Toronto Press, Toronto, 1950).

Canada Year Book, 1954 (Queen's Printer, Ottawa, 1954).

COATS, ROBERT HAMILTON (editor), "Features of Present Day Canada," in Annals of the American Academy of Political and Social Science (Philadelphia, 1947).

JONES, LL. RODWELL, and BRYAN, P. W., North America (tenth edition; Methuen, London, 1954).

LANCTOT, GUSTAVE (editor), Les Canadiens français et leurs Voisins du Sud (Editions Bernard Valiquette, Montreal, 1941).

NICHOLSON, N. L., The Boundaries of Canada, its Provinces and Territories (Queen's Printer, Ottawa, 1954).

SIEGFRIED, ANDRÉ, Le Canada: Puissance Internationale (fourth edition; Armand Colin, Paris, 1947).

M*

CHAPTER XIII

Canada: Economic Aspect

G. TATHAM

CANADA is the second largest country in the world. Its area, about 3¾ million square miles, equals that of Europe, yet there are only fifteen million inhabitants, and virtually all of these are found in scattered groups along the southern border. Less than half a million square miles are effectively settled; the rest of the country is an uninhabited wilderness of coniferous forest and tundra. Empty space is the dominant feature of Canadian geography. Nevertheless, this young, almost empty country ranks as a Middle Power, and is exerting increasing influence in international affairs. Such apparently disproportionate influence is rooted in two geographical factors—space relations and economic resources.

The aeroplane and the opening up of sub-arctic lands have transformed Canada from a northern outpost of civilization to a nerve centre of the world. To the south, sharing a common frontier 3000 miles long, is the United States, the strongest single Power in the world. Across the Arctic, barely 2500 miles from the Canadian coast, is the second strongest—the U.S.S.R. All the shortest air routes between these opponents either cross Canadian territory or skirt Canadian shores, and, though mutual suspicion and Soviet isolationism have retarded their development, their ultimate importance cannot be doubted; indeed, the control of these routes may be decisive in any future war. Across the Atlantic, Canada faces the old and still important industrial Powers of Europe; to the west, across the Pacific, China and Japan, two of the three major Powers of Asia.

In a shrinking world the centrality of Canada's position, surrounded by most of the powerful nations, ensures her an abiding, if uncomfortable, importance. On a world scale it recalls the position of the Low Countries in Europe sufficiently closely to make one wonder whether Canada too may not have thrust upon her the role of an international cockpit.

Quite apart from its space relations, Canada derives importance from its natural resources. Large areas of agricultural land producing a great surplus of food, mineral deposits so vast as to seem unlimited, extensive forests and abundant water-power, all combine to give Canada great productive capacity and one of the highest material standards of living in the world. In 1952 annual production was 1600 dollars per capita (U.S., 2200 dollars) and per capita income 1230 dollars (U.S., 1785 dollars). As world population grows and pressure on resources increases, the development and use of Canadian resources will be of deepening concern to her neighbours. Already foreign investment in Canada is greater than in any other self-governing country. Non-residents own 40 per cent. of the manufacturing industry, 45 per cent. of mining and smelting, 42 per cent. of the railroads, and 50 per cent. of the oil industry, a matter of great significance in the political life of Canada.

Wealth and world position will thus maintain the interest of foreign nations in Canada. Physical geography, on the other hand, causes Canada to have a reciprocal interest in foreign areas.

Most of Canada is covered by Taiga and Tundra, and the more favoured sections lie wholly within the cool temperate belt. There is relatively little climatic variety, and this, by limiting the list of agricultural products, makes it impossible for Canada to attain any degree of economic autonomy comparable with that of the United States. Canada is, and always will be, more dependent on foreign supplies than its neighbour.

In 1952, when, for example, Canada exported 24 per cent. of her national output and spent 24 per cent. of her national outlay on imported foods and services, the corresponding figures for the United States were only 5 per cent. and 4 per cent. respectively.

This dependence on foreign areas is not new. It began with the first settlers and has persisted ever since. At every stage Canadian development has been shaped more by demands made on her by other nations, particularly the industrial nations, than by internal forces. The basic importance of agriculture, forestry, and mining in Canadian life bears witness to this. These three primary industries owe their expansion to the persistent stimulus of foreign demand. Under this stimulus they have come to be the very foundation of Canadian economy and to exert considerable influence on her external relations.

Material Resources and their Uses

Only 16 per cent. of the total area of Canada is suited to agriculture. Less than half of this, only 174 million acres (7 per cent. of the total area of Canada), is cultivated. Nevertheless, in 1952 farm income amounted to 2750 million dollars and agriculture provided 20 per cent. of the net value of production.

All the cultivated land lies south of 55° N. latitude. East of the Great Lakes and in British Columbia farming is diversified and concerned primarily with animal and dairy produce. Local areas (Niagara Peninsula, the Annapolis and Okanagan valleys) produce special crops— fruits, vegetables, and tobacco—but the bulk of production is sold locally, and very little moves to outside markets.

Farming in the Prairies is quite different. There, in a grassland environment, on pedocal soils, are large 300- to 400-acre farms, highly mechanized and devoted to the monoculture of cereals. It is an American type of farming, but is closely tied to world markets. Annual production of wheat varies between 300 and 500 million bushels, of which 120 to 240 million bushels are exported. Until 1929 Prairie wheat made up about 30 per cent. by value of all Canadian exports, and in some years Canada supplied over 40 per cent. of international requirements (48·6 per cent. in 1925–26). Since then, though the volume has increased, its relative importance has declined. To-day wheat and wheat flour together make up only 15 to 20 per cent. of all exports.

Prairie grain production is particularly sensitive to world conditions. The depression of the thirties, backed by natural disasters (pests, disease, droughts, frost), cut output in 1937 to 180 million bushels. The average annual income in the Prairie Provinces between 1930 and 1938 was only half what it had been in the years 1926–29, and emigration reduced their population by 250,000.

War restored prosperity, but then the demand was for animal products as well as wheat. Under this stimulus the cultivated area expanded. Production was diversified, livestock increased everywhere, and the proportion of Prairie farmers' cash income provided by wheat fell from 63 per cent. (1935–39 average) to 30 per cent. (1942). Receipts from livestock were multiplied four and a half times. In Alberta cash from the sale of hogs actually exceeded cash from wheat in the year 1942–43. With the end of hostilities, as markets returned to something resembling pre-war conditions, the Prairies immediately turned from livestock and began to concentrate once more on wheat. Many experts considered this unwise and campaigned for a continuance of mixed farming, but in vain; since 1945 the numbers of hogs and milk cattle have dropped by half.

So vulnerable is the economy of the Prairies to fluctuations in world demand that the whole outlook of the farmers is dominated by their search for stability. This makes them willing to accept, even welcome, a considerable measure of State control and direction, and their political attitude is closer to that of the Australian and New Zealander than to that of their neighbours in Eastern Canada and the United States. At the level of provincial government it has led to the support of parties with programmes of social security and a willingness to throw the whole weight of government support behind the farmer in a depression. It was on such a programme that the Social Credit Government swept into office in Alberta (1936) and the Socialist (C.C.F.[1]) Government in Saskatchewan (1946). Relations between the Prairie Provinces and the Federal Government are also determined by the willingness of the latter to maintain wheat prices and defend and expand wheat markets by international agreement.

Forestry ranks second to agriculture in value of production. From the great forests that still cover one third of the country comes 10 per cent. of the value of the total annual production and about 20 per cent. of the total exports. These forests extend from the Atlantic to the Pacific in a broad girdle around the open Prairies. Of the total 80 per cent. is in the boreal forest of the north, part of the circumpolar Taiga belt, which crosses Canada from the Rockies to Labrador and extends south from the northern limit of tree growth to the Great Lakes. Conifers predominate (spruce, balsam, jackpine), with a sprinkling of aspen and birch. 10 per cent. is mixed deciduous and coniferous woodland characterized by a great variety of species in the milder and more humid south-east (Southern Ontario to the Maritimes). The remaining 10 per cent. is in the western mountains and varies greatly in type. The richest and most accessible is the coastal forest in the area of heavy winter rains. Western hemlock and western red cedar, with Douglas fir in the south and Sitka spruce in the north, are typical.

Almost half (590,000 square miles) of the total $1\frac{1}{3}$ million square miles of forest is non-productive—i.e., not capable of producing a crop of

[1] Co-operative Commonwealth Federation.

marketable timber. The remaining 700,000 square miles form 19 per cent. of the total productive forest of the world. But, of this, much is inaccessible at present, and important only as a future reserve. Lumbering, consequently, is confined to about half a million square miles. Between two and a half and three million cubic feet of timber are produced each year. Of this two-thirds comes from Ontario and Quebec, and the Maritimes, just less than one quarter from British Columbia, and the rest from Newfoundland and the Prairies.

Although Canadian forests seem inexhaustible, the rate of cutting (3000 million cubic feet in the last decade) is beginning to cause concern, and most of the provinces are initiating conservation programmes. The fact that during the last ten years one fifth of the annual depletion has been due to forest fires, pests, and disease indicates that such programmes are long overdue.

Minerals stand third among the basic resources of Canada. Mining accounts for 8 per cent. of the net value of production, and provides one-third of the freight carried by Canadian railways and about one quarter of the total exports. Industries based on minerals produce 39 per cent. of the gross value of manufactures.

The minerals are as varied as they are abundant. Sixty-six different ones are listed. They occur in every part of the country, though, as one would expect, the bulk are in the Pre-Cambrian Shield. From these old rocks come nickel, copper, silver, gold, iron, cobalt, platinum, and uranium; the Appalachian region supplies coal and asbestos; the younger undisturbed rocks of the Prairies oil, coal, and lignite; and the Cordillera metals and coal. Annual production has an average value of 1250 million dollars.

Canada leads in world production of nickel (about 90 per cent. of the world's supply), asbestos (70 per cent.), and platinum. She is second in aluminium (from imported ore), gold, zinc, and probably in radium and uranium, third in silver, fourth in lead, copper, and cobalt. Large as the present known reserves are, they are probably only part of the total. Many new deposits have come to light during the past few years[2] and there are still large areas unexplored. How significant the new discoveries may be can be illustrated by the reference to iron ore.

Twenty years ago it was generally agreed that Canadian industrial development would always be handicapped by her lack of iron. At that

---

[2] Asbestos (Ontario and British Columbia), titanium (Quebec, the largest single deposit in the world), silver and zinc (also in Quebec).

time the known reserves were insignificant and production nil. Then ore was found at Steep Rock, 135 miles west of Lake Superior, with a reserve now estimated to be between 500 and 1000 million tons. Production, started in 1939, has already reached a yearly total of one and a half million tons, but this, it is believed, will eventually reach ten million. Minor ore bodies were next discovered in Southern Ontario near Renfrew and near Peterborough. Half a million tons are expected to be raised from the Peterborough deposit in 1954. Attention then shifted to Northern Quebec. As far back as 1893 iron-ore deposits were known to exist in a zone extending for 350 miles from Lake Ashuanipi (53° N. 66° W.) to Hudson Strait, but they were too inaccessible to be mined. With the second world war interest revived. A company was formed to explore the area more carefully. Almost immediately a reserve of 500 million tons of high-grade hæmatite was located near Knob Lake on the Quebec-Labrador boundary. All this lies in only fifty square miles of the total iron ore region, and as each year new deposits are located, estimates of an ultimate reserve of 1000 million tons are being confidently made and do not seem unreasonable.

Development, costing 200 million dollars, is proceeding at a rapid rate. A 360-mile railway, completed in January 1954, links Knob Lake with Sept Iles on the St Lawrence, where loading docks are being constructed. Hydro-electric stations on the Menihek and Ste Marguerite rivers, with capacities of 12,000 and 17,000 h.p. respectively, were finished in 1954, when the first ore was moved out. An initial production of ten million tons a year is planned. This will be expanded to twenty million.

In 1939 Canada's iron reserves were estimated at about 250 million tons. No ore had been mined for seventeen years. Newfoundland, not then part of Canada, was producing between one and two million tons a year from the Wabana mines, where reserves were believed to be 3500 million tons. To-day annual production is close to five million tons, 2 per cent. of the world's total. Canada, now including Newfoundland, ranks eighth among world producers. Within the foreseeable future annual production will most likely exceed thirty million tons, which is equivalent to present Soviet production.

The whole of Canada's industrial prospects has been changed. And there are political implications, too. Canadian resources have expanded just when the Mesabi deposits are approaching exhaustion. American iron and steel manufacturers, looking for new sources of supply, are showing keen interest in Labrador. The Hanna Company, of Cleveland, has already acquired a minority interest in the Labrador field. The probability that the United States will soon need Labrador ore has swung many Middle Western voters to the support of the St Lawrence Seaway.[3]

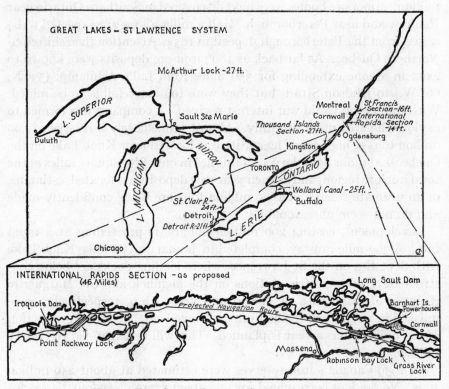

FIG. 1. THE GREAT LAKES—ST LAWRENCE SYSTEM

Canada's reserve of coal is roughly 1,400,000 million tons, seven times that of Great Britain and just a little below that of the U.S.S.R. Most of it is in western Alberta and is of inferior quality, sub-bituminous

[3] The St Lawrence Seaway project aims to provide a navigation channel with a minimum depth of twenty-seven feet from the Atlantic to the western end of Lake Superior. This requires relatively few changes. The ship canals linking Lakes Ontario, Erie, Huron, and Superior will have to be deepened, though their minimum depth is already twenty-five feet. The main task will be the cutting of a twenty-seven-foot channel through the Kingston axis between Montreal and Prescott, a distance of 114 miles. The existing canals in this section have a minimum depth of only fourteen feet. An agreement to construct this seaway was made by Canada and the United States in 1941, but so far it has not been ratified by the two Houses of the United States Congress. In 1951 Canada decided to undertake the task alone. Work has begun, but the door has not been closed against U.S. co-operation.

and lignite, though nearer the Rockies and extending into British Columbia good bituminous and anthracite occur. Other deposits are in Nova Scotia (Sydney) and Vancouver Island. Annual production varies around twenty million tons, Alberta producing 41 per cent., Nova Scotia 34 per cent., and British Columbia 10 per cent. This total, however, is only 40 per cent. of the annual consumption (average forty-five million tons). The other 60 per cent. is imported, 99 per cent. coming from eastern United States. This is the inevitable result of the excentric distribution of the Canadian deposits. The main market for coal is in the industrialized and densely settled southern section of Ontario and Quebec, 2000 miles from Aberta, 1000 from Nova Scotia, but only 250 from Pennsylvania and West Virginia. Ontario finds it cheaper to import American coal than to pay freight charges from Alberta, particularly since western coal moving eastward has to compete with wheat and iron ore for transport. Pennsylvanian coal, on the other hand, favoured by cheap rates in the returning empty ships and freight cars, can compete successfully with Alberta coal as far west as Winnipeg. Furthermore, Alberta coal does not ship well; it breaks easily and crumbles if exposed to the weather. Altogether, it seems that Alberta production will not expand rapidly and Canada must continue to rely on the U.S.A.

The outlook for Canadian oil is distinctly brighter. Just east of the Alberta coalfield a great sedimentary basin extends from the U.S. boundary for 1800 miles to the north between the Rockies and the Shield. Oil associated with Devonian limestone has been found in the southern section, but the structure makes it probable that the whole basin is a single oilfield comparable with the Mid-Continental Field of the United States. Minor strikes were made before 1947, but the present boom began with the discovery of oil at Leduc (1947) and Redwater (1948). Before this discovery Canada was producing (1946) only 20,000 barrels a day and had a meagre seventy-two million barrels reserve. By 1948 daily production had reached 34,000 barrels and reserves 500 million barrels (cf. U.S. reserves, 27,000 million; U.S.S.R., 40,000 half of Canadian requirements, potential output was 300,000 barrels, and estimated reserves 1679 million barrels. Prospecting is proceeding in both Alberta and Saskatchewan with considerable success. Estimates of Canada's potential reserve vary between 5000 million and 50,000 million barrels (cf. U.S. reserves, 300,000 million; U.S.S.R., 90,000 million).

To supplement this, there is a further reserve of 100 to 300 million barrels in the Athabaska tar sands. These lie in a broad belt thirty to fifty miles east and west of the river Athabaska below Fort McMurray, about 300 miles north-east of Edmonton.

No transport problem hampers the use of oil. A thirty-inch pipe-line from Edmonton to Lake Superior, a distance of 1150 miles, was completed in 1950. Its recent extension to Sarnia, at the southern end of Lake Huron, has eliminated the lake haul by tanker. This inter-provincial pipe-line will deliver 100,000 barrels a day to the Sarnia refineries. Another line carries refined oil to Toronto. Vancouver is also linked to Edmonton by a pipe-line with a daily capacity of 120,000 barrels, soon to be raised to 200,000 barrels. A branch from this line will cross the border to the new refineries at Bellingham in Washington.

By 1960 Canadian production will be sufficient to meet all her requirements.

Lastly in this survey of resources, there is the vast supply of water-power. Most of this is conveniently located near the main centres of population. In the west and east precipitation is heavy, reliable, and equally distributed throughout the year, and the terrain furnishes many admirable power sites. There are three main groups of sites: (1) along the numerous rivers re-developing on the glaciated surface of the Shield, (2) where the Appalachians fall precipitously to the sea, and (3) on the St Lawrence at Niagara and farther east where the river cuts through the Kingston axis, a neck of Pre-Cambrian shield rocks which links the Shield with the Adirondacks. British Columbia has many fine sites on the steep, well-watered slopes of the Coastal Mountains.

In potential power Canada ranks fourth among the nations (after U.S.A., India, and U.S.S.R.), but in installed capacity (13·3 million h.p.) is surpassed only by the United States. 80 per cent. of present capacity is in Ontario and Quebec, and 10 per cent. in British Columbia. Many projects destined to expand production are under way. Ontario will gain an additional $\frac{3}{4}$ million h.p. when the new Niagara plant is completed and another one million h.p. from sites built in connexion with the St Lawrence Seaway.

For a young country, apparently so fitted by its abundance of food and raw materials for a colonial type of economy, the rapid rise of Canadian manufacturing during the last fifty years is remarkable. It seems even more so when the obstacles to such a development are recognized. The home market is small and widely dispersed. Natural resources are also scattered, so that costs of assembling raw materials and distributing finished goods are high. Close by is a great industrial Power, whose well-protected home market, ten times as great as that of Canada, enables her to exploit mass-production methods more success-fully, and whose desire to penetrate the Canadian market is matched by her ability to do so. Contact with the United States affects wage rates. Canadian unions are affiliated with American, and though wages in the two countries are not equal, rates in Canada tend to approach the United States level, and to be far higher than those of Europe. This weakens Canada in competitive export markets. Nevertheless, despite these handicaps, industries have developed behind a high tariff wall. To-day they produce 14,000 million dollars a year, 53 per cent. of the total national income.

Their development too has been shaped by external influences. Three main periods of rapid growth can be recognized. Firstly, during the first world war, when war needs led to the start of the refining of non-ferrous metals and to the expansion of the steel industry. Secondly, in the boom years of the late twenties. This was due to heavy investments of American capital in the manufacture of pulp and paper, motor-cars, chemicals, and non-metallic minerals.[4] Thirdly, during the second world war, Canada then, as a major arsenal for the west, expanded her equip-ment for producing tools, precision instruments, chemicals, synthetic rubber, aluminium, aircraft, electrical apparatus, and ships.

To-day industries may be divided into three groups:

1. Those based on Canadian raw material and cheap power—pulp and paper, saw-mills, smelting and refining of non-ferrous metals, iron and steel, canning and processing of foodstuffs.

2. Offshoots of American firms producing in Canada to avoid Cana-dian tariff payments. The automobile industry is the main one. The plants are concentrated in south-western Ontario close to their parent industries, at Windsor (Ford, Chrysler), Hamilton (Studebaker), Oshawa (General Motors), Toronto (Ford, Nash, Reo, Kaiser-Frazer).

3. Consumer industries that under tariff protection have sprung up to supply the home market. Textiles (Eastern Townships, Montreal, and the Grand River Valley) are the chief. In contrast to the first two, foreign capital is not important in this third group.

Four-fifths of all Canadian manufacturing is in the triangular low-

---

[4] By 1929 American capital investment in Canada had reached 3500 million dollars, three and a half times what it had been in 1914.

land between the Great Lakes, the St Lawrence, and the southern edge of the Shield. Ontario (49 per cent. of the total) has almost all the motor-cars, machine tools, agricultural machinery, heavy electrical machinery; Quebec (30 per cent.) has tobacco, textiles, clothing, paper. Four cities—Toronto, Windsor, Hamilton, and Montreal—produce half of the Ontario and Quebec total. British Columbia (8 per cent.) has saw-mill products, pulp and paper, fish-processing, meat-packing, and raw-metal refining.

The heavy concentration of industry in central Canada creates there a social and political outlook very different from that of the Prairies. The difference between the two resembles that which in the mid-nineteenth century divided industrial New England, primarily interested in the home market, from the agricultural South, producing a cash crop for export. To reconcile these regional points of view is a perennial task of Canadian statesmanship.

Canada in International Trade

Canada is one of the leading trading nations of the world. In 1951 her total trade had a value of 8250 million dollars. This placed her fourth among the countries outside of the iron curtain, after U.S.A. (27,500 million), U.K. (18,500 million), France (8600 million dollars), all of which she surpassed in the amount of trade per capita (Canada 588 dollars; U.S. 175 dollars; U.K. 366 dollars; France 206 dollars).

The nature of this trade is simple. Canada exports a relatively few raw or processed natural products (newsprint, wheat, wheat flour, wood-pulp, lumber, base metals) and imports a large variety of manufactured goods (machinery, iron and steel goods, textiles, electrical apparatus, etc.). External rather than internal forces are responsible for this pattern. The two most important have been the economic demands of Western Europe and competition with the United States.

At first the demands of Europe were paramount. Fishing on the Grand Banks supplied salted cod for the Paris market, then sun-dried cod for the Roman Catholic populations of the Mediterranean and Caribbean. Later, as the French pushed west along the St Lawrence and Great Lakes and the British opened up the river routes from Hudson Bay, furs began to supplement fish. In the early nineteenth century white and red pine, potash, and, after 1840, wheat from the St Lawrence

and Southern Ontario were exported along with furs from the Prairie
and fish from the coast. Then, in the nineties, Prairie wheat began
to move out in increasing quantities until it became the major
export.

All this development proceeded on an east–west political axis, following the minor geographical features, but cutting across the dominant
north–south grain of the country which makes political and economic
links with the U.S. more natural and easier to forge. In the east the
great waterway facilitated the latitudinal movement of goods, but west
of Lake Superior communications had to be provided. Political as well
as economic necessities caused trunk railways to be pushed through to
the Pacific as quickly as possible. To keep within Canadian territory
these lines had to cross a great section of the Shield and the rugged
western mountains, areas which at first produced little revenue. Private
enterprise could not cope with such expensive undertakings, and government support had to be given.

Any hope of compensation for such an outlay through the development of Montreal as the chief outlet for the continent was frustrated
when the Erie Canal provided an all-water route to the superior harbour
of New York (1825), which, in addition to being deeper, was never
blocked by ice. New York's supremacy was confirmed after 1866 by
the tariff policy of the victorious North. The tariff wall tied Canada
more securely to the economy of Western Europe, and the eastward
movement of wheat was now balanced by the westward movement of
manufactures. In the nineties American industries turned to Canada for
raw materials. Their demand for gold, base metals, pulp, and paper
fostered a more diversified economy, especially in Ontario, Quebec, and
British Columbia, and caused a certain re-orientation of trade. Goods
now moved from north to south across the established current of trade,
and though this new trend did not change the nature of Canadian trade,
it had important political results. At home it complicated provincial-
federal relations by encouraging provincial independence. In foreign
relations the economic link with the United States gave Canada a
counterpoise to the politico-economic link with Britain, enabling her to
adopt a more independent attitude than would otherwise have been
possible. At the same time trade with Britain, the Commonwealth, and
Europe preserved Canada from American domination.

The United States and Britain still dominate Canadian trade relations.
In the inter-war years (1918–39) Canadian trade reached an unprece-

dented aggregate total of 38,000 million dollars. Of this, half was with the U.S.; 10,000 million dollars, or 27 per cent., with Britain.[5] Trade with the States has always been unbalanced. Of the total 19,000 million dollars, 11,500 million dollars were imports from the U.S. and 7500 million dollars exports. Proximity and the nature of her production make the United States the natural source for Canadian imports. The list of these is long and varied. Many are basic to Canadian manufacturing—sources of energy (coal, oil), raw materials (cotton, iron ore, hides, steel, chemicals) capital goods (mining equpiment, tanks, boilers, electrical goods). Consumer goods, foods (citrus and other fruits, vegetables), domestic machinery (refrigerators, washing machines, etc.), cars, and textiles are also imported, and have a strong competitive position in the Canadian market, owing to the popularity of American papers and journals in which they are advertised.

But though supplying two-thirds of the imports, the United States took only one-third (35 per cent.) of Canadian exports. These were mostly raw materials and partly processed goods: in 1939, wood and paper, non-ferrous metals, and minerals made up 30 per cent. Very few Canadian manufactures entered the United States. Canada consequently had a deficit in her trade with the U.S., and had to find a market outside the States for 65 per cent. of her products.

Of this 65 per cent. going overseas, 37 per cent. went to Britain (food, 17 per cent., lumber, and non-ferrous metals) 10 per cent. to the rest of the Commonwealth, 9 per cent. to Europe (food and metals), and 3·2 per cent. to Asia (lumber). From 1932 onward the credit balance in Canada's trade account with these overseas countries more than covered the deficit with the United States, and the practice of earning dollars in Europe to pay the United States was known as the Atlantic Triangle. This term, however, suggests greater simplicity than actually existed. Europe earned American dollars to pay Canada, not by trade with the United States, but by exporting to countries of south-east Asia which had an annual credit balance with the States. Canada's economic and political stability consequently rested on a freely moving, multilateral trade. The war wrecked all this. When hostilities ended, the former European customers of Canada, exhausted and burdened with debts, were forced to cut imports. At the same time, imports from the States to Canada shot up as American industry turned to peacetime produc-

---

[5] 1937: total trade, 1800 million dollars (U.S. 47 per cent.; U.K. 30 per cent.; Commonwealth, 11 per cent.; all others, 12 per cent.).

tion and Canadian savings were spent on consumer goods.[6] Canada was compelled to seek a new economic basis. There were two possibilities:

1. Canada could reorient her trade to the United States. It was, however, difficult to see how the latter could absorb all Canadian exports, particularly wheat and livestock products. Politically, too, reorientation would mean that, as an economic satellite of the United States, Canadian independence would be jeopardized.

2. Canada could help her former customers to rebuild their economies to the point where the pre-war trade pattern could be restored. In favour of this policy was a strong humanitarian desire to help those hurt by the war, as well as the realization that it would secure Canadian political independence.

It was this second policy which Canada adopted. Trade credits exceeding 1500 million dollars were extended to Europe, the bulk (1000 million dollars) going to Britain. The outcome is still uncertain. European nations, in their reconstruction, are making themselves somewhat more independent economically, even at the cost of a lower standard of living, and this will restrict the market for Canadian goods. At present they can still buy from Canada because of American loans to, and expenditure in, Europe, but it is impossible to foresee what will happen when American financial assistance ceases.

Canada seems destined, therefore, to a closer economic dependence on the United States. Already American investment in Canada has increased from 4500 million dollars in 1932 to 6500 million dollars in 1950. Indeed, only by this heavy import of capital (1500 million dollars in 1950 and 1951) has the large post-war trade deficit been covered. British investment in Canada in the same period dropped from 2700 million dollars (1933) to 1700 million dollars (1950). This dependence on the U.S.A. can be lessened only by reducing the trade deficit. Alberta oil and Labrador iron will help to do this, particularly after the St Lawrence Seaway is cut and ore moves cheaply into the Pittsburgh area. But, in addition, Canada must diversify her industries. A start was made during the war, and this diversification must be continued. It will not be easy. The small and dispersed home market is one handicap, but the greatest is the height and complexity of the United States tariff which so successfully keeps out Canadian goods. Canada can do little about this, though she might manage to make Americans buy processed

[6] The Canadian deficit on the U.S. trade was 430 million dollars in 1946, 890 million dollars in 1947. Later American stock-piling caused a heavy import of base metals which almost wiped out the deficit in 1950. Future trends are still not clear.

instead of raw materials, just as she has already got them to take news-print instead of wood-pulp.

These are all as much political as economic problems. American imports originate largely in the Shield, those to Europe and Britain in the Prairies, those to the Commonwealth countries in the industrial areas of Central Canada. So any reorientation of trade will affect not only the prosperity of one or other region, but also the relative political strength of the provinces. The more the solution of these problems is sought at the international level, the more it will require federal action, and thereby strengthen the federal at the expense of the provincial governments.

Canada's Empty Space and her Population Capacity

There remains to be considered the influence of empty space in Canadian life. The disparity between the size of Canada and its popula-tion has already been mentioned. The average density is 3½ people per square mile, fifth lowest in the world. In sharp contrast are conditions in overcrowded countries facing Canada across the Pacific and Atlantic.

World population is increasing at a rate that will double it in seventy years. Two-thirds of the present 2600 million are already living in a state of acute hunger as indicated by identifiable nutritional disease. Whether there are too many people on the earth to-day or not, there is no question that they are badly distributed. Any remedial action will require a high degree of international co-operation, and Canada will inevitably be involved.

It is surprising how conservative Canadians are about the absorptive capacity of their land. The U.S.S.R., with a territory twice the size of Canada, but lying in roughly the same latitudes and with comparable resources, has 215 million and is doing everything possible to increase this to 380 million. Some Canadians, on the other hand, believe their country, with only fifteen million, is already uncomfortably full. Griffith Taylor, having endured much criticism from Australians for telling them their country could not support more than thirty million, received almost as much abuse from Canadians for assuring them their population could reach 100 million. Australians, of course, living in an isolated outpost of white settlement facing the teeming lands of Asia, need a large population for defence. Canadians know America will have to defend them for the sake of her own security.

Most geographers are more cautious than Taylor.[7] After all, one million square miles of Canadian territory lie north of the tree line, where coasts are ice-bound nine to eleven months every year and no summer month has an average temperature above 50° F. Canadian known resources, too, are not inexhaustible. If worked at the rate planned they will be used up in a century. Modern estimates put the potential arable area at about 132 million acres, of which only 100 million could be cultivated every year. This would provide food for forty to fifty million people eating much as we do to-day. Such considerations make a figure of forty to fifty million more acceptable as the optimum population with present techniques of production.

Although this seems to err on the side of caution, it nevertheless means that there can be a threefold increase of population in the next fifty years without any threat to the standard of living. The present natural rate of increase is high—17·1 per cent. for the decade 1941–51 (1·82 and 1·88 in 1951 and 1952[8])—but even this will not raise the population to forty-five million by the end of the century. Immigration is therefore possible and perhaps desirable. It has long been the policy of the Federal Government to encourage immigration, and five million immigrants have entered since 1900. After 1945 the rate of entry rose sharply—over 700,000 entered in the last seven years.

Immigration necessarily imposes the problem of selection. Preference so far has been given to those who would appear to fit most easily into Canadian life, rather than to men and women from the areas of greatest overcrowding. Citizens of Great Britain, France, and the United States are thus given priority. All other would-be immigrants must satisfy the authorities that they are suitable. Asiatics, other than wives and children (under eighteen) of Canadian citizens, were excluded till 1951. Then restrictions were relaxed to allow 150 citizens from India, 100 from Pakistan, and fifty from Ceylon to enter each year. The result of this policy has been that in the decade 1941–51, 39 per cent. of all immigrants were from the British Isles, 59 per cent. from continental Europe, and only 1·3 per cent. from Asia.

Such discrimination is defended by the authorities as being in the interest of national unity. Inter-cultural friction already exists between

---

[7] G. Taylor, *Environment, Race, Migration* (University of Chicago Press, second edition, 1945), p. 370. See also G. Taylor, *Canada* (Methuen, London, second edition, 1947), p. 516.
[8] India, 1·3; U.S.A., 1·5.

the English and the French, and there has been a strong tendency for immigrant groups to form exclusive national associations, which add further complications, especially since these groups tend to perpetuate the political animosities of their homeland. Canada has not succeeded in developing a sense of Canadianism as strong as Americanism in the United States. Provincial loyalties and cultural separatism are everywhere strong. Moreover, education is a provincial concern and one most jealously guarded, so the Federal Government, in charge of immigration, has to rely on the provinces to provide educational programmes that will help immigrants to become assimilated. Much, it is true, has been done in this regard, but almost nothing has been done to curb prejudice against newcomers among those Canadians who have forgotten that they too are of immigrant stock. Alberta, in fact, has a government openly anti-semitic and actively hostile to inter-cultural education. The same tangle of governmental authority has also delayed the preparation of an adequate housing scheme. To-day over 700,000 homes are needed, and though 90,000 are being built each year, the annual natural increase in the number of families is 70,000. Lack of housing and high rents do much to create prejudice against newcomers. Empty space is thus a geographical factor affecting politics at every level. In external affairs there is the possibility of protests from the crowded nations of Asia against discriminatory practices which flout the basic principles of the United Nations;[9] at home there is the possibility of federal, provincial, and even municipal friction.

FURTHER READING

BROWN, G. W. (editor), *Canada* (United Nations Series, California University Press and Cambridge University Press, 1950). (Good bibliography.)

Canada on the March (Clarke, Irwin, Toronto, 1953). (Symposium; twenty authors.)

COATS, R. H. (editor), "Features of Present Day Canada," in *Annals of American Academy of Political and Social Science* (September 1947).

GIBSON, J. D. (editor), *Canada's Economy in a Changing World* (Macmillan, Toronto, 1948).

LAUGHARNE, O. K. S. (editor), *Springs of Canadian Power* (Royal Institute of International Affairs, London, Oxford, and Toronto, 1953).

PUTNAM, D. F. (editor), *Canadian Regions* (Dent, London, 1952).

SIEGFRIED, ANDRÉ, *Canada* (Duell, Sloan, and Pearce, New York, 1947).

TAYLOR, G., *Canada, an Advanced Geography* (Methuen, London, 1947).

[9] Friction might even develop between Canada and Britain, as Canada seeks to attract the highly skilled technicians whom Britain herself needs for her industrial reorganization. In 1926–31, 30·4 per cent. of all Canadian immigrants were agricultural workers and 10·3 per cent. manufacturing and mechanical workers. In 1946–51 the figures were 11·2 per cent. agricultural, 24·5 per cent. industrial.

CHAPTER XIV

The Soviet Union: its Geographical Setting and Historical Background

W. GORDON EAST

LITTLE more than a generation has elapsed since the Soviet Union first appeared as heir to the Russian Empire, yet in its vigorous and articulate youth, as a protagonist in world affairs, it compels widespread attention. Its ideology and its foreign policy supply a continual leaven to international politics, while its geographical position, its numbers, its economic and military strength, and its tenacity in diplomacy entitle it to the high place it now occupies in the hierarchy of states. The U.S.S.R. is the old Russia writ large—in territorial extent as in politico-economic potential. The federal union of republican states and nations of which the U.S.S.R. consists is dominated, as was Russia, by the Great Russian nation, and the area which this Union controls directly is that vast Euro-Asian territory which was settled, conquered, developed, and administered by Russian peoples during centuries of rule by the tsars. In the four succeeding chapters discussion turns on the internal political structure of the Soviet Union, its demographic and economic progress, its frontiers and frontier problems, and its place in contemporary world politics. A brief review of the history of the Russian land and the Russian peoples should help in the understanding of the Soviet Union and the problems which it begets. For, as the Soviet geographer Mikhaylov wrote,[1] "the lines on the map are the handwriting of history"—and not merely Soviet history, as he would have us believe. Nor can the words of Vidal de la Blache[2] be disputed: "the history of a people cannot be separated from the country which it inhabits."

[1] N. Mikhaylov, *Soviet Geography* (Methuen, London; second edition, 1937), p. xv.
[2] P. Vidal de la Blache, *Tableau de la Géographie de la France* (1911), p. 3.

The Great Russian Plain

A major physical unit of Europe, named after the Slav nation which
came to dominate it, the Great Russian Plain was the stage on which
Russian history began as it remains to-day the most important, though
only a fourth part, of the Soviet Union. Covering some two million
square miles, this plain occupies more than half of Europe and its broadest, eastern area. Inland waters—the Baltic Gulf of Finland, Lakes
Ladoga and Onega, and the White and Barents Seas—delimit it to the
north; the Azov, Black, and Caspian Seas to the south. Eastward it is
bounded by the Ural Mountains, worn remnants of Palæozoic folds,
which appear more striking features on the map than on the ground and
command approaches to the broad and lower plain of Western Siberia.
In the south-east the Great Russian Plain ends at the foothills of the
Caucasus Mountains, which recall—if not in their scale, at least in their
altitude, land forms, and scenery—mountain systems of like age, such
as the Rockies and the Alps. Westward, except where it abuts on the
Carpathian Mountains, the Great Russian Plain lies open to, as it forms
part of, the North European Lowland.

It is in the west, therefore, that the plain is inevitably joined to the
rest of Europe, from which it long stood aloof, and to which it did not
appear wholly to belong. Only the broad expanse of the Pripet marshes,
which are believed to have been the original homeland of the Slavs,
inject an obstacle (except when frozen over in winter) between this
plain and Peninsular Europe beyond. By European standards the
Great Russian Plain is an outsize unit: in places over 1500 miles broad
and over 2000 long from north to south. Indeed, it accords in scale and
uniformity with component parts of Asia, as it accords too with Asia
in the continentality of its climate. From the days of ancient Greece
onward into the Middle Ages the limit of Europe in the east bisected the
southern part of the plain along the line of the Azov Sea and the river
Don. How far Russia, in its varying extent throughout history, has
been part of Europe, part of Asia, or a world apart, has always been,
and remains, a theme for discussion. For if this plain appears physically
an integral part of Europe, it is linked closely too with Asia. The wide
Caspian Gate between the southern end of the Urals and the northern
shore of the Caspian Sea joins the steppes of Siberia and Central Asia
with those of South Russia, while narrow and difficult routes flanking

the Caucasus Mountains link Russia with the highlands of South-west Asia, the chief part of what is now called the Middle East.

The Great Russian Plain is by no means uniform either in its relief and soils or in its climate and vegetation cover. Deposits of glacial clays and sands in its northern half and thick deposits of interglacial loess in the southern, mantled in part by rich black-earth soils, introduce one important differential, while Palæozoic rocks of the underlying Russian Platform emerge at the surface in a few areas—as in Kola in the far north and in South-west Russia—to provide opportunities for the exploitation of economic minerals. Climate—with its winter severity and its limitation of the growing period for plants, most reduced in the northeast and longest in the south-west—has reacted on vegetation to produce the most fundamental division of the Great Russian Plain between a southern part formerly covered by steppe grasses, with few trees except in the valleys, and a larger part in Central and North Russia made up of either mixed or wholly coniferous forests, interspersed with marshes. Forest, grass steppe, and between them the transition zone of wooded steppe thus provided sharply contrasted habitats, each adapted historically to its own forms of society and economy, yet linked together potentially by a remarkably well-developed system of navigable rivers. These rivers, too, permitted transport between the interior lands and the neighbouring seas, as also between northern and southern ports. While to the south of Moscow the area of transition between the mixed forests and the wooded steppe marked a recognizable and significant geographical frontier, and while the inland seas set ultimately attainable limits to territorial expansion, the Great Russian Plain lacked the many small-scale regional compartments, congenial to national and political growth, which abounded in Peninsular Europe. Thus few physical limits were offered to Russia as it developed, and, as to-day, expansion and defence were inextricably bound.

The Origins of Kievan Russia

While archæologists by their studies of the *kurgans* (burial mounds) of South Russia have revealed a long prehistory of settled and civilized life, based on arable and pastoral husbandry, in the South Russian steppe, it is only with the immigration and settlement of the Eastern Slavs, largely within the zone of mixed forests, that Russian history begins, and the Principality of Kiev, created in the mid-ninth century, was the first Russian State. The Slavs, who make up to-day one of the distinct language groups of Europe, first appear in the lower Danube region of the Roman Empire, whence some of them, defeated in battle by the Emperor Trajan early in the second century A.D., moved off north-eastward. In the sixth century the Slavs, then known as the *Venedi*, were a populous race, tribally organized, dwelling not in towns but in forests and marshlands in the Carpathian Mountains, the Galician plateau, along the Vistula river, and eastward to the Dniester. The attacks of Slavonic tribes on the East Roman (Byzantine) Empire up to *c*. A.D. 650 testify to their military organization, and some of them appear soon after to have begun their eastward migration from the Carpathian region to the Dnieper. By the ninth century these so-called 'Eastern' Slavs had widely colonized the western half of the Great Russian Plain by setting up scattered, fortified homesteads along the rivers within an extensive area of mixed forests, wooded steppe, and swamps, in parts of which some Finnish and Germanic peoples had earlier penetrated.

The economy of the Slavs reflected the nature of their habitat and their own cultural limitations: there was at first little agriculture, but the trapping of animals for their furs and hides and the collection of wax and honey produced goods for trading. Already before *c*. A.D. 850 trading centres for the collection and exchange of these goods had grown up at points along the Dnieper and its tributaries, which clearly furnished the principal means of communication and transport. As early as the eighth century, it would seem, the Eastern Slavs had reopened the old river trade routes across the plain from the Baltic to the Black, Azov, and Caspian Seas—routes used in the days of ancient Greece—to carry on a lively trade with the Khazars of the Volga-Don steppes and with the Byzantine Empire.

The Russian land and the Russian State owe their name to the "men of Rus," Scandinavian intruders, chiefly from Denmark, who gradually and peacefully infiltrated the Slavonic population of Russia from the second half of the ninth century onward, as merchants, warriors, and later rulers of the Eastern Slavs. Already before their advent towns were growing up, especially along the lines of the Dnieper and Volkhov rivers, which provided from the Gulf of Finland water access to the Scandinavians or "Varangian" immigrants. Already, too, towns on the river trade routes had made themselves capitals of provincial areas which cut across tribal patterns. The arrival of the Varangians coincided broadly with the decline of thepower of the Khazars of the south-eastern steppe, to whom the Slavs had been subjected, and with the occupation of the steppe north of the Azov-Black Seas, by the Pechenegs, mounted nomads who threatened the safety of the Slavs and of their trade routes. It was the achievement of certain Varangian leaders to organize and apply armed force in the common interest of the Slavs by associating them into the Principality of Kiev, which replaced a number of small and weak principalities. A successful attack in A.D. 860 on Constantinople, capital of the Byzantine Empire and the most important market for Russian trade, showed the strength of this new State and the likelihood of its survival despite the recurrent enmity of the mobile horsemen of the steppe.

Kievan Russia between the tenth and the twelfth centuries consisted of the lands of the following rivers: the upper and middle Dnieper, the upper Dniester and southern Bug, the upper basins of the western Bug, the Niemen and Western Dvina, the upper Volga and the Volkhov. For the most part it thus comprised a watershed area and controlled easy portages between navigable rivers which diverged in all directions towards the neighbouring Baltic, Black, and Caspian Seas. In the north, overlapping the watershed area, it reached to Lake Ladoga, and although confined by lands of Finnish and Lithuanian settlement, it commanded access to the Baltic by one narrow gateway at the head of the Gulf of Finland, to which it had water access by way of the river Lovat, Lake Ilmen, Lake Ladoga, and the river Neva. In the north, where trade with the Baltic developed and where Russian colonists were pressing into the forests in search of new homes and of furs, the republic of Great Novgorod, despite its remoteness from Kiev, had acknowledged Kiev's political authority, for it depended on the wooded steppelands of the south for trade facilities and for grain which it could not sufficiently produce itself. In the south the settlements and fortifications of Kievan Russia extended to the limits of the wooded steppe, but at best only maintained effective passage along the Dnieper for its armed trading convoys across the hazardous grass steppe en route for the markets of the Greek and Arab worlds beyond. In the west the territories of the Principality impinged on those of the Prussians, the Poles (another Slavic people), and the Hungarians, the last two of which became Christian kingdoms which adopted their Christianity from Rome and became oriented to Western Europe.

In short, Kievan Russia, although not wholly land-locked—indeed, it was largely the political outcome of the overland routes between inland seas—had an interior location and was girt around by alien peoples. Doubtless external dangers helped towards the assimilation of the ruling Varangians with the subject Slavs, and in the eleventh and twelfth centuries the term "Rus" (whence "Russia"), formerly applied to the Varangian minority, was being applied to the whole Principality and also to its fusing Varangian and Slavic population.

Kievan Russia thus revolved around the north–south axis aligned along the Volkhov and Dnieper rivers, and it is not surprising, therefore, that the highly developed civilization which flourished in its metropolitan city Kiev was largely derived from that of the Byzantine Empire. But although it was already by European standards large in area and also populous (the population of Kievan Russia has been estimated at between seven and eight millions), it had no territories on the shores of the Black, Azov, and Caspian Seas, and suffered, to a greater degree than did the Byzantine Empire and the Hungarian kingdom, from "the historical scourge of Russia"—the continual assaults of warring, nomadic horsemen who moved along the broad grass steppe between the Ural-Caspian Gate and the lower Danube.

Kievan Russia, although essentially a mercantile State, turned increasingly from shifting to settled agriculture, especially within the wooded steppe, which provided its most productive lands, and introduced the variety of crops then grown in Western Europe. Princely, boyar, and monastic estates, worked by a peasantry of serfs, and, indeed, also by slaves, became characteristic. Kiev, the most southerly of the Dnieper towns and capital of the Principality, was at once an advanced stronghold for defence against enemies from the steppe and the chief collecting-point for the commodities traded with Constantinople and the Arab world.

The Principality of Moscow

If Kievan Russia is rightly regarded as the cradle of Russian nationality, the Principality of Moscow, which succeeded it, is clearly the Russian State which grew into the Russia of modern history. It owed its rise to the disruption and decline of Kievan Russia and to the stream of emigrants who left it to settle within the forests and marshes of Central

Russia in the second half of the twelfth century. Kievan Russia suffered from internal disruption related to the feuds of its ruling aristocracy and to social cleavages, while it failed to defend its lands and its trade route from successive attacks of the Polovtsi, who ruled the southern steppe. Some of the emigrants from Kievan Russia moved north-westward to resettle Galicia and Volhynia, lands from which their ancestors had originally come into Russia. Another stream moved north-eastward along the valley of the Desna river, a left-bank tributary of the Dnieper, and opened up (after c. A.D. 1150) a direct route from Kiev to Murom, on the lower Oka—through hitherto trackless forests. This emigration led to the colonization of the land of Suzdal, between the upper Volga and its tributary the Oka, which was to become the nucleus of the new Russian State ruled from Moscow.

Suzdal was a land of forests and marsh and intricately patterned streams. It differed sharply from the more congenial country around Kiev. The soils were heavier and less well drained; the forest and undergrowth more dense; the winters were longer and the growing period was shorter. Lying nearly 500 miles north-east of Kiev, Suzdal stood aside at first from the main water highways, although this loss was balanced by its relative security, since it lay remote from the steppe and was shielded by its oakwood forests. It did not lack means of communication with North Russia: indeed, a few agricultural townships already existed along or between the Oka and the upper Volga, such as Suzdal, Rostov,[3] Vladimir, and Murom, for some Slavs had early reached this region from the north-west. The later Russian immigrants were seeking new homes to settle in and new lands to cultivate, rather than trade opportunities. Actually the geographical position of Suzdal was potentially very good: situated at the geometric centre of the Great Russian Plain, it commanded water access to the Baltic, the White Sea, the Dnieper, the Azov Sea (by the Don river), and the Caspian (by the Volga). Moreover, Suzdal enjoyed a certain security, the lack of which had proved Kiev's downfall.

Out of the colonization of Russian peasants in Suzdal, and their peaceful association and then fusion with the less numerous native Finns, developed the 'Great Russian' nation, which to-day accounts for more than a half of the U.S.S.R.'s people and forms the dominant national group in the Soviet Union. Russian immigrants brought with them a material civilization superior to that of the Finns. They introduced and

[3] This should not be confused with the later Rostov-on-Don.

N

established the organization of the Orthodox (Greek) Church. Further, although much interested in the search for furs, they brought the vigour of true pioneers in colonization. Moving along the river valleys, they cleared and burnt strips of woodland, settled down in dispersed hamlets, cultivated their cleared land for several years, then moved on to make more clearings, ever north and north-eastward towards the White Sea and the Ural Mountains. Thus was slowly created the social and territorial fabric of Muscovy, the political leadership of which, in a vigorously assertive form, was won by the princes of Moscow in the mid-thirteenth century.

Moscow, a newcomer among the towns of central Russia and situated on the frontier of Suzdal, did not become its capital until 1263, yet less than a century later it had clearly become the political centre of gravity of Russia. Its success in achieving, first, primacy over the many other Russian principalities, and then in organizing and expanding its territory, owed much to Moscow's fine geographical position. Standing in an area of relatively dense colonization, protected by its marshes and forests, yet at the meeting-place of land and water routes across Russia, Moscow grew rich, and wealth fostered political power. Thanks to the rule of primogeniture, which was applied to the Principality of Moscow, its princes were able to follow a consistent and remunerative policy in their dealings with other princes within and outside Russia. By paying court to the Great Khan, whose Tatar hordes desolated most of Russia in the thirteenth century, the prince of Moscow obtained recognition from him (in 1328) as suzerain prince of Russia and as collector of the Russian tribute due to the Khan. The prestige of the prince of Moscow was further raised, at about the same time, when Moscow became the ecclesiastical capital of Russia, for the Metropolitan, head of the Russian Church, transferred his residence there from Vladimir, to which he had fled from Kiev owing to the Tatar danger. The prince of Moscow, too, had proved himself a successful military leader against Russia's enemies, the Lithuanians and the Tatars. Thus, although Russia seemed to be threatened with extinction between the converging pressures of the Golden Horde to the south-east and of the Lithuanians to the south-west, who (in the fourteenth century) conquered the Russian lands of Podolia, Volhynia, Galicia, and Kiev, the princes of Moscow consolidated the small nuclear State of Muscovy, which was to grow into the Russian Empire.

The Expansion of Russia in Europe and Asia

Russia moves East. The principality of Moscow, as it stood in 1462 at the accession of Ivan III, was merely part of Russia—that is, of the area originally colonized by the Eastern Slavs, or subsequently colonized by Russians (Fig. 1). To the west, in the basins of the upper Dnieper and upper Desna, were Russian principalities, while to the north, stretching from Lake Peipus to the White Sea, stood the vast forested area loosely administered by the landed and trading aristocracy of the Commonwealth of Great Novgorod, which fell to Moscow, by conquest, in 1478. A great part of the Russian land, in the middle Dnieper basin, as well as steppelands farther south as far as the Black Sea coast, had been conquered by the Grand Duchy of Lithuania, which in 1386 was united dynastically with Poland. This advance of Lithuania into Russian lands wasted by the Tatars led later on to their recolonization, largely by the descendants of Russians who had fled westward (to Galicia, Volhynia, and Polotsk), before the assaults of the Polovtsi in the twelfth century. And there, in the heartlands of the old Kievan Russia astride the middle Dnieper, developed by the sixteenth century the Little Russian, or Ukrainian, nation with its variant form of Slav speech. So also in the basin of the upper Dnieper west of Moscow, in a similar way, emerged the Byelorussians, or White Russians, with their language and nationality—distinct alike from those of the Great Russians and the Ukrainians.

South and east of Muscovy the much feared Tatars held the Don and Volga steppes and the middle Volga forests as the outposts of their vast Asiatic empire. The Great Khan, master from China and Korea to the Black Sea, held Russia tributary to him and ruled from his local capital at Serai, on the eastern side of the Volga bend, not far from the present Stalingrad. In short, the Russian States were tightly hemmed in virtually on all sides: the ring was broken to provide an outlet for their further expansion only in the north-east, into the basins of the North Dvina and Pechora, a vast expanse of coniferous forest and marsh with the longest and coldest winters of European Russia.

By 1584, when Ivan IV ("The Terrible") died, the territorial pattern of Russia had substantially changed, although not wholly to its advantage. Lithuania-Poland, controlling nearly the whole length of the Dnieper, still held Kiev "the mother of Russia" and approached closely to Smolensk, which, indeed, they later seized. In the north-west Ivan failed, despite a long struggle (1558–81), to broaden or even maintain his narrow outlet to the Baltic on the Gulf of Finland, for the Swedes succeeded in shutting Russia off from the Baltic by securing Ingria and Karelia on the two sides of this gulf. In the north, Russia had only the White Sea outlet, then closed by ice for half the year, but, thanks to the voyage of Chancellor in 1553, made accessible to maritime trade with Western Europe. In the east and south, in contrast, Russia's position was greatly improved. Ivan III had refused to pay tribute to the Khan, and Ivan IV, having fought the Tatars successfully, annexed extensive, scantily peopled, and mainly steppe areas. The basins of the Don and Volga, Astrakhan, and part of the northern shore of the Caspian Sea all fell into Russian hands. The capture of Kazan (in 1552) opened the way to the central Urals, which Russians had reached and crossed by 1581. Although Russia held almost the whole basin of the Don, it was denied the outlet which this gave to the Azov Sea, for the Crimean Tatars commanded it on one flank as subjects of the Ottoman Turks, who had extinguished and replaced the Byzantine Empire, controlled the Don outlet by its fortress at Azov, and, too, dominated the Black Sea.

Thus, shut off from the Baltic and the Black Seas and deprived of the Dnieper below Smolensk—the river which was the original artery of the Russian land—Russia was projected eastward, away from Europe. As a result, it absorbed more non-Russian peoples (Finno-Ugrian and Turkic-Tatar), and diverted much of its national energy to expansion into Siberia beyond the Urals. Indeed, during the century which followed the death of Ivan IV Russia appeared increasingly an Asiatic State. Sweden, Lithuania-Poland, and Turkey held it back firmly from Europe. The Poles even farther invaded Russian-settled lands—around Smolensk, and in Ukraine east of the Dnieper. And Russian pioneers made their way across Siberia to the Pacific.

Siberia (Turkic *Su beri*, meaning 'a watery wilderness') extended north from the Mongol Empire to the Arctic Ocean and from the Urals to the Pacific. Vast, mainly coniferous forests, interspersed with marshes especially west of the Yenisei, dominated its continental landscape, with winters longer and harder than in Russia. In the far north, tundra, and in the south, especially west of the Yenisei, steppe, bordered this world of forests. West of the Yenisei the West Siberian basin is mantled by glacial deposits and lies low with only a gentle slope towards the

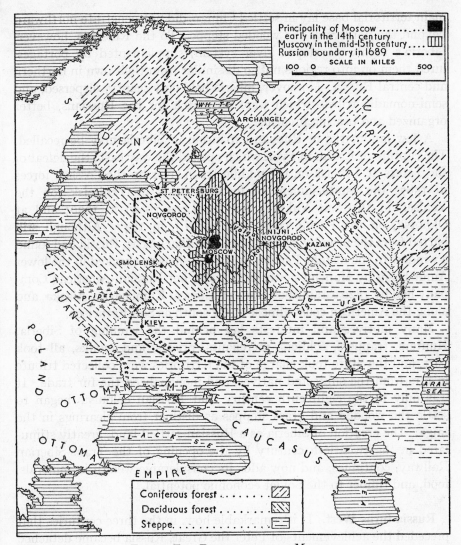

FIG. I. THE PRINCIPALITY OF MOSCOW

Arctic. East of the Yenisei, in contrast, plateau levels and mountain ranges diversify the landscape. The Arctic seas, with open water for only about two months a year, defied the efforts of the early Western explorers: there was no Hudson's Bay to permit their entry into this world with its wealth of timber, furs, and mammoth ivory. Thus, unlike Canada, Siberia was occupied and conquered only from the continental side. The Tatars—essentially a people of the steppe, although their main territorial base lay in settled China—did not penetrate northward beyond the borders of the wooded steppe. To the Russians, however, Siberia's highly developed river system, supplemented by portages, lured them on into regions not so dissimilar from their own in northern and central Russia. Moreover, Siberia held only scanty, dispersed, and semi-nomadic tribes, which were no match for the Russians, better organized and bearing firearms.

A few landmarks in Russian expansion in Siberia may be recalled. The capture of Kazan in 1552, which opened the way east; the defeat of the Tatars at Tobolsk on the middle Irtish river by the Cossack forces in 1587; the establishment of fortified posts at Yeniseisk (on the Yenisei) in 1618; at Yakutsk (on the Lena river) in 1630; and at Okhotsk, on the Pacific coast (lat. 59° N.), in 1647. Although still barred from the near-by Baltic, Azov, and Black Seas, Russia had found a window to the distant Pacific. Although she was checked in the lower Amur basin by Manchu power until 1860, her Russian-American Company had by 1820 established trade stations in Kamchatka, Alaska, and along the American coast almost as far south as San Francisco.

Many motives and interests lay behind the winning of Siberia. Hunters, trappers, soldiers, merchants, priests, and monks, all took part, and the State took charge of the territories won, collected tribute in furs from the subjected natives, and monopolized the fur trade. It was only in the eighteenth century that Russian colonists began to settle the wooded and grass steppes as distinct from clearings in the taïga. The creation of Siberia as a Russian-settled land, greatly stimulated in the twentieth century by the opening of the Trans-Siberian Railway, continues, and now adds its considerable wealth in minerals, food, and timber to the Soviet economic potential.

Russia turns West. It is remarkable how, in the three centuries that preceded the achievements of Peter the Great, Russia became detached from Europe and displaced into Asia. While sharpening its national consciousness, based on its dominantly Slav heritage and its attachment to the Orthodox Church, and reacting to dangers from outside, Russia stood aloof from the main cultural movements of Western Europe—the Renaissance, the Reformation, the Great Discoveries, and the growth of Science. The destruction of the Byzantine Empire by the Moslem Turks deprived it of this former source of its culture, and although its rulers proudly assumed, as tsars, the imperial title, they appeared destined merely to rule a vast, loosely organized, weak, and backward State.

The reign of Peter the Great (1689–1725) marks both a turning point and landmark in the history of Russia, as, indeed, in that of Europe and the world, since, as a result of his unremitting and statesmanlike efforts, Russia emerged (by 1721) as a State of the first rank and a European State at that. Tireless in his attempts to learn from the more advanced

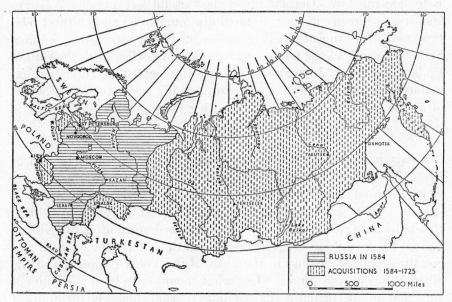

FIG. 2. RUSSIA, 1584–1725

material culture of the West, he brought foreign technicians to Russia, created a modernized standing army, built the first Russian navy, centralized government at his new capital at St Petersburg under his autocratic control, created a bureaucracy, reorganized the finances, consolidated serfdom, started many new industries (including the iron and copper industries of the Urals), and pursued relentlessly a foreign policy designed to increase the strength and status of Russia.

Peter's father, Alexis, had won back Smolensk, Kiev, and left-bank Ukraine from the Poles, but Russia was still cut off from the Baltic and Azov-Black Seas. In the south, despite initial successes, Peter failed to break through the outer defences of the Ottoman Empire and establish Russia as a Black Sea Power, but at least he prevented the Turks from reaching the Caspian Sea by overrunning a strip of Persian territory, which included Baku, along its western and southern sides. It was in the north, after a protracted war with Sweden (1700–21), that Peter was most successful. By the Treaty of Nystad in 1721 Sweden lost its pre-eminence in the Baltic, and Russia acquired Karelia, Ingria, Estonia, and Livonia—a secure frontage on the Baltic, protected by a fleet, and a direct seaway to the West (Fig. 2). These territories brought more non-Russians and non-Orthodox Christians into Russia: Letts and Estonians ruled by a German upper class, useful servants of a Western-izing tsar. Already in 1703, to facilitate commercial and cultural rela-tions with Western Europe, Peter had begun the gigantic task of building St Petersburg, and the fortress of Kronstadt to defend it in the Gulf of Finland near by. Although so ex-centrically located, St Petersburg re-mained the capital of Russia until 1918, and in and around it grew one of its major industrial regions. No other metropolitan city of its size occupies so northerly a location.

Russia moves West, North, and South. If, before the accession of Peter the Great, Russia was a world apart from Europe, in the centuries which followed down to the first world war it intervened in Europe (and in Asia too) as a Great Power. Hitherto the geographical extent of Russia had always fluctuated; it had decreased much after the Kievan period, but in the 220 years before the death of Peter the Great it had greatly expanded, mainly in the areas of the Volga steppe and of the Siberian forests and tundra. Just what should have been the limits of Russia at any particular period, or, indeed, what should be the limits of the Soviet Union to-day, is a scientifically unanswerable question. Actually in 1725 Russia by no means included in Europe all of "the Russian land"—that is, the area of settlement by Russian stock. No less evidently, in the east it had won for itself vast areas of scanty but alien populations, areas which, in this century especially, it has effec-tively colonized with Russians. After Peter the Great the problem of Russia's security and independence necessarily involved that of its territorial extent and frontiers, and for a strong and vigorous nation security has usually been sought by expansion. On all its European borders—west, north, and south—Russia markedly expanded during the two centuries after Peter the Great; in Asia, too, it colonized southward of the Siberian forests. Indeed, the successors of Peter the Great in large measure systematically pursued policies towards Russia's neigh-bours—Sweden, Poland, and Turkey—which he had himself initiated.

With their neighbours the Poles the Russians were continually at war between the fifteenth and the seventeenth centuries: their common Slav speech in no sense endeared them one to the other. Poland had merged dynastically with the Grand Duchy of Lithuania, whose territories, strung out across the European isthmus between the Black and Baltic Seas, included Russian-settled lands, formerly part of Kievan Russia: these lands lay mainly west but even east of the Dnieper and Dvina. Poland-Lithuania, which Poland came increasingly to dominate, was thus a multi-national State, made up of Lithuanians, Russians, and Poles, the last concentrated mainly within the basin of the Vistula. Into Poland's "eastern lands" (Russia's "western lands") Poles intruded to form the landed upper class, but the serf population there, little affected by Polish culture, remained either White Russian or Ukrainian in language and either Orthodox or Uniat[4] Christians. In its struggles with Poland Muscovy was at times worsted: between 1610 and 1612 a Polish tsar was actually imposed on Moscow, which was unable to win back Kiev and Smolensk from Poland until 1667. Pole and Russian were scarcely reconciled by Poland's claim to be the defender of European culture and Catholicism from barbarians to the east, while Russia coveted Courland, Poland's Baltic territory. Under Peter the Great the relative strengths of Poland and Russia changed decisively, and he devised the policy, followed by his successors, of keeping Poland internally weak and under Russian influence. He started, too, the practice of marching Russian troops across Poland en route for action in Germany. Russian pressure on Poland, on behalf of Poland's Orthodox subjects, made it clear also that Muscovy hoped to recover the lost lands of Kievan Russia.

In the late eighteenth century Russia won back its "western lands" —and more besides—but this success, achieved in partnership with Prussia and Austria, involved the complete effacement of Poland by the three partitions of 1772, 1793, and 1795 (Fig. 3). Russia's territorial gains were considerable, and she advanced more than 300 miles westward into Europe—to the Niemen, the headwaters of the Pripet, and the Dniester. To the lands, mainly Polish and Lithuanian in population, which she annexed in the third partition, Russia had, however, no title. Nor, indeed, had Austria and Prussia any justification for their annexation of truly Polish (so-called 'ethnographic') Poland. The Polish

[4] The Uniat Church, created in 1596, comprised those Orthodox Christians who, while retaining their rites and liturgy, accepted the Papacy.

N*

partitions extinguished Poland, but not the Polish nation. In 1809
Napoleon I created the short-lived Grand Duchy of Warsaw, and in 1815
a small Polish kingdom, "Congress Poland," was set up by the Congress
of Vienna, but under the tsar as king. This arrangement naturally failed

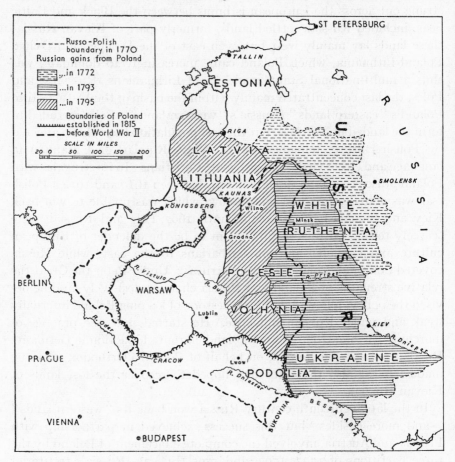

FIG. 3. THE TERRITORIAL EXPANSION OF RUSSIA

to satisfy the national aspirations of Polish leaders. It lasted a century,
however, until the collapse of Russia and the defeat of Germany in the
first world war made possible the creation of an independent Polish
republic. This Poland expanded eastward by winning back Russia's
"western lands"; during the second world war this situation was
drastically changed in favour of the Soviet Union.[5]

[5] See below, p. 418.

Not only in the west did Russia make felt its strength. In the north it completed its long struggle with Sweden—and consolidated its own position in the Baltic—by the conquest in 1809 of Finland, which was set up as a Grand Duchy within the Russian Empire, but allowed its own constitution, laws, and tariffs.

In the south, before the end of the eighteenth century, Russia had won control of the grass steppe to the shores of the Azov and Black Seas and of the Crimean peninsula, which facilitated Russian sea power in these waters. In 1812 its boundaries in the south-west were pushed beyond the Dniester to the Pruth river and the Danube delta by the absorption of Bessarabia from Turkey. Russian expansion in the south involved winning control of Cossack groups and peasant colonization, and also wars with the Ottoman Empire. Despite many successful campaigns spread over a century and a half, and despite its championship of the Slav and Orthodox subjects of the Turkish Empire, Russia never succeeded in reaching its main objective, Constantinople and the Straits, which controlled access to the Mediterranean Sea.[6]

By the 1860's Russia had expanded in Asia with remarkable vigour on three sectors—in the Caucasus region, in Turkestan, and in the Amur region of the Far East, where Vladivostok was founded in 1860. Railway building began to give some cohesion to the territorial hugeness of Russia. The end of the nineteenth century saw Russia controlling railways across Chinese Manchuria and established (by leasehold tenure) at Port Arthur. But defeat by the Japanese in 1904–5 and by the Central Powers in the first world war (1914–17), coupled with fatal internal weaknesses, brought the tsarist empire to its end. That it contained enormous, if latent, material strength has been shown by its successor, the Union of Soviet Socialist Republics.

FURTHER READING

BERG, L., *The Natural Regions of the U.S.S.R.* (trans.; Macmillan, New York, 1950).

ECK, A., *Le moyen age russe* (Maison du Livre étranger, Paris, 1938).

FISHER, R. H., *The Russian Fur Trade, 1500–1700* (University of California Press, 1943).

GROUSSET, R., *L'Empire des Steppes* (Luzac, Paris, 1939).

[6] See above, p. 196. Nevertheless the important part played by the Emperor Alexander I in the defeat of Napoleon and in the peace settlement made by the Congress of Vienna (1814–15) marked the political stature which Russia had come to assume among the Great Powers of Europe.

KERNER, R. J., *The Urge to the Sea* (University of California Press and Cambridge University Press, 1942).

KLUCHEVSKY, V. O., *A History of Russia*, translated by C. J. Hogarth (five vols.; Dent, London, and Dutton, New York, 1911–31).

KONOVALOV, S., *Russo-Polish Relations: an Historical Survey* (Cresset Press, London, 1945).

KRAUSSE, A. S., *Russia in Asia, 1558–1899* (New York, 1899; Richards, London, 1899).

LEROY-BEAULIEU, A., *L'Empire des Tsars et les Russes* (three vols.; Paris, 1881–89).

MOSELEY, P. E., *Russian Diplomacy and the Opening of the Eastern Question in 1833 and 1839* (Harvard University Press, Cambridge, Mass., 1934).

SETON-WATSON, G. H. N., *The Decline of Imperial Russia* (Methuen, London, 1952).

SKRINE, F. H., *The Expansion of Russia, 1815–1900* (new edition; Cambridge University Press, 1915).

SKRINE, F. H., and ROSS, E. D., *The Heart of Asia* (Methuen, London, 1899).

SUMNER, B. H., *Peter the Great and the Emergence of Russia* (The English Universities Press, London, 1950).

SUMNER, B. H., *Russia and the Balkans, 1870–80* (Clarendon Press, Oxford, 1937).

SUMNER, B. H., *Survey of Russian History* (Duckworth, London, 1944).

THOMSEN, V., *The Relations between Ancient Russia and Scandinavia and the Origin of the Russian State* (Parker, London, 1877).

WILLIAMS, HAROLD, *Russia of the Russians* (Pitman, London, 1914).

YAKHONTOFF, V. A., *Russia and the Soviet Union in the Far East* (Allen and Unwin, London, 1932).

CHAPTER XV

The Administrative-territorial Patterns of the Soviet Union

THEODORE SHABAD

A MORE than cursory examination of some of the administrative-territorial problems of the Soviet Union would appear to be justified by its unusually complex federal structure and the geographic importance of its political divisions.

In the Western world we are apt to regard the civil divisions of States as being of incidental significance geographically because such units generally owe their delineation to historical accident or administrative convenience and seldom reflect the realities of either physical or human geography. Internal political divisions in the West usually antedate the Industrial Revolution and the profound geographic changes that ensued. It is not unusual to find new integrated, homogeneous economic regions dissected by old administrative boundaries or even newly established cities situated astride a rigid political divide. In exceptional cases, the opposite sides of well-traveled urban thoroughfares may find themselves under different administrative jurisdiction.

Not so in the Soviet Union. There, as an integral part of the Soviet conception of political administration and economic planning, the territorial divisions of the country have come to reflect the dynamic character that typifies much of Soviet geography. No longer are we dealing with immutable historical lines that cut across the fabric of present-day activities; instead we find an extremely unstable structure of political-administrative units that keeps pace with, and sometimes even anticipates, changes wrought by man on the land.

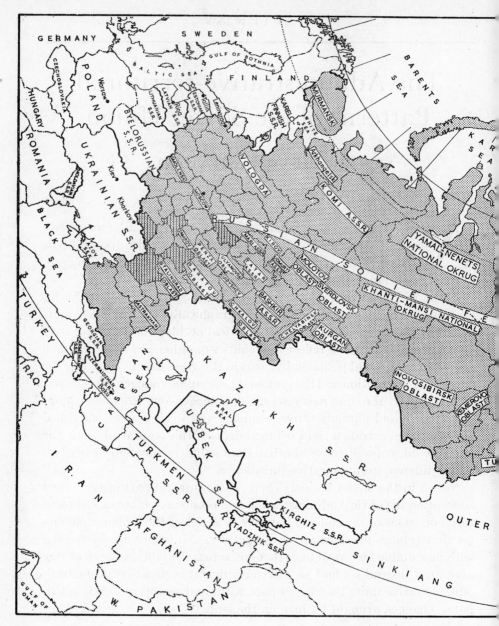

FIG. 1. THE ADMINISTRATIVE-TERRITORI.

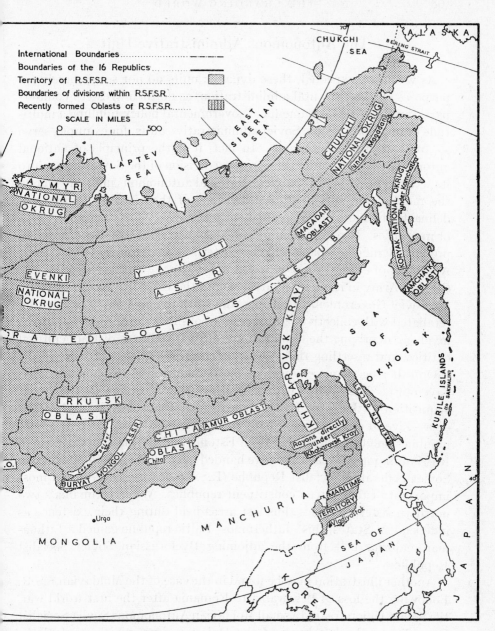

International Boundaries ....
Boundaries of the 16 Republics ....
Territory of R.S.F.S.R. .... ▦
Boundaries of divisions within R.S.F.S.R. ....
Recently formed Oblasts of R.S.F.S.R. .... ▦

SCALE IN MILES
0   500

CHUKCHI
SEA

ALASKA

BERING STRAIT

70

EAST
SIBERIAN
SEA

LAPTEV
SEA

TAYMYR
NATIONAL
OKRUG

CHUKCHI
NATIONAL OKRUG
(under Magadan)

KORYAK NATIONAL OKRUG
(under Kamchatka)

EVENKI
NATIONAL
OKRUG

Y A K U T

A . S . S . R .

MAGADAN
OBLAST

KAMCHATKA
OBLAST

─RATED   SOCIALIST   REPUBLIC

SEA
OF
OKHOTSK

KHABAROVSK   KRAY

KURILE   ISLANDS
(to SAKHALIN)

SAKHALIN

IRKUTSK
OBLAST

CHITA   AMUR OBLAST

.O.

OBLAST
•Chita

BURYAT MONGOL ASSR

Rayons directly
under
Khabarovsk Kray

•Urga

MANCHURIA

MARITIME
TERRITORY
•Vladivostok

SEA
OF
JAPAN

J A P A N

40

MONGOLIA

KOREA

TTERNS OF THE SOVIET UNION

The Autonomous Administrative Unit

As would be expected, these dynamic units do not serve merely for purposes of governmental administration, as do their Western counterparts, but are true instruments of governmental policy fulfilling a multitude of functions. Some Soviet administrative units, for example, serve as areas of ethnic autonomy. In fact, it is the principle of national autonomy that determines the primary division of the Soviet Union into its sixteen constituent republics. National autonomous units are among the most stable administrative divisions of the U.S.S.R., since they delineate the more or less permanently settled regions of ethnic groups or minorities. It required an upheaval such as the second world war to produce significant changes in the pattern of Soviet autonomous units. A number of ethnic groups situated in or near the area occupied by the German Army in its deepest advance into the U.S.S.R. were accused by the Soviet Government of collaboration with the invader. The Kremlin retaliated with collective punishment, abolishing the autonomous areas involved, depriving the ethnic groups of their rights as distinct cultural entities, and resettling the population elsewhere in the U.S.S.R.

On other occasions changes in the boundaries of autonomous units have not been associated with such arbitrariness. Following the Soviet acquisition of the three Baltic countries—Estonia, Latvia, and Lithuania—several changes were made in the boundaries of the new Soviet republics on ethnic grounds. Both Estonia and Latvia contained small Russian-majority areas that were handed over to the adjoining Russian Soviet Federated Socialist Republic (R.S.F.S.R.), the largest and most important of the sixteen constituent republics. While Lithuania's two northern sister republics thus lost areas held during their existence as independent States, this southernmost Baltic republic gained a Lithuanian-majority belt from the adjoining Byelorussian Soviet Socialist Republic.

Another illustration may be found in the case of the Moldavian S.S.R. Following the loss of Bessarabia to Romania after the first world war, the Soviet Union created a small Moldavian Autonomous Soviet Socialist Republic on the left bank of the Dniester river, which marked the boundary with Romania. Inasmuch as the Soviet Union never relinquished its claim to Bessarabia with its large Moldavian population, the area of the Moldavian A.S.S.R. was slightly inflated for propaganda reasons through the addition of some Ukrainian-majority areas along its border with the Ukraine. However, in 1940, when Romania was forced to return Bessarabia to the U.S.S.R., a new Moldavian S.S.R. was formed out of the greater part of Bessarabia and the old Soviet left-bank districts. In the ensuing shuffle of boundaries the Ukrainian-majority districts on the left bank were returned to the Ukraine, as the Moldavian S.S.R. had come to assume a sufficient stature.

These and similar changes were justified on ethnic grounds and generally reflected the areal distribution of a particular minority. It is more unusual to find boundary changes in national autonomous areas that are based on economic considerations. However, one such instance may be cited. In the late 1930's the U.S.S.R. began the development of the Vorkuta coalfield in north European Russia, within the Arctic Circle. The site of the future city of Vorkuta was situated just north of the Komi Autonomous Soviet Socialist Republic, which contained the greater part of the coal basin about to be exploited and the access railroad to be built. Because of its economic integration with the Komi A.S.S.R., Vorkuta was therefore included in that republic by a minor shift of the northern border.

The Soviet Union distinguishes various categories of national autonomous units in its administrative hierarchy. The category held by any given ethnic group depends on a number of factors, including size of population, location, and the degree of political and economic development. The hierarchy ranges from the sixteen constituent republics (Soviet Socialist Republics, or S.S.R.) through the autonomous republics (Autonomous Soviet Socialist Republics, or A.S.S.R.) and the autonomous oblasts (provinces) to the national okrugs (districts). There are also the very minor national rayons (counties) and national village areas.

Generally speaking, an ethnic group with a population of about a million constitutes one of the sixteen constituent or union republics, subject to the overriding factor of location. The present Soviet Constitution, promulgated in 1936, states that the constituent republics form a voluntary union of nations with the right of free secession. Of course, it is highly unlikely that any of the republics will ever raise the question of secession in such a rigid, monolithic system as exists in the U.S.S.R. But a literal interpretation of the right of secession requires that every constituent republic be located along the periphery of the country, with at least a section of its territory bordering on a foreign State. According to such a literal interpretation of the Constitution, no constituent republic could be formed, say, in the heart of the U.S.S.R., where enclosing Soviet territory would preclude possible secession in the physical sense. So it happens that a number of ethnic groups numbering far more than 1,000,000 in population and with a high degree of political and economic development are not likely to achieve the highest rung of the nationalities' ladder because they lie far from the Soviet border. Such groups, which are perforce relegated to the status of A.S.S.R., are the Tatars and Bashkirs situated in the country between the Volga and the Urals.

National autonomous areas send delegates to the Soviet of Nationalities, one of the chambers of the bicameral Supreme Soviet of the U.S.S.R., the country's highest, though entirely nominal, legislative body. The relative importance and standing of the autonomous units is clearly illustrated by the representation assigned to each: union republics send twenty-five delegates, autonomous republics eleven, autonomous oblasts five, and national okrugs one each. The second chamber, the Soviet of the Union, contains representatives elected on a population basis, one delegate per 300,000 persons.

We have seen how the principle of national autonomy determines the initial basis for a political division of the Soviet Union by assigning units of varying degrees of administrative standing to major and minor ethnic groups. Needless to say, the concept of autonomy discussed here must be viewed against the background of the specific Soviet situation. Soviet autonomy clearly does not imply self-rule or rights of self-determination in the Western sense. The concept is restricted largely to the cultural sphere, in which the ethnic groups are entitled to the use and development of their native languages, literature, and customs through the medium of the schools and the Press. But even such a cultural development is rigidly confined by the precepts of Soviet ideology. We are dealing here with cultures that are "national in form and Socialist in content," according to a Soviet slogan. The influence of Communist party doctrine and of the predominating culture of the Russian ethnic body thus directs the different peoples of the U.S.S.R., welding them at the same time into a solid entity.

The Economic Administrative Unit

The function of Soviet administrative-territorial units is not limited to comparting the country's ethnic groups and minorities. That is a rather static purpose, of interest geographically only in so far as it reveals changes in the distribution and settlement of nationalities. Of greater significance is the dynamic function fulfilled by Soviet administrative divisions in their capacity as economic regions.

In the late 1920's the Soviet Union embarked upon a program of economic planning and forced industrialization that is still continuing, though evidently at a reduced rate. The five-year plans, of which the sixth is currently in progress, served as the framework of this program. As part of this program, there was need for functional territorial units to be used in planning the economic development of the country. These units were visualized by the Soviet planners as the areal framework of their program, a framework that would be flexible enough to be adapted to the rapidly changing situation in the industrialization drive. And thus, as a result of the close integration of government and economy in the Soviet planning system, territorial divisions assumed a dual role as administrative-economic regions. This role must be viewed as being supplementary to the national autonomy function. Every territorial division in the U.S.S.R., whether autonomous or not, is designed to handle the customary problems of governmental administration, as well as the additional economic functions of economic planning and statistical reporting.

We have referred to Soviet political divisions as economic regions. The author has discussed elsewhere[1] in some detail the Soviet concept of economic regions. For the purpose of this discussion a few summary remarks will suffice. The common Western concept of an economic region implies uniformity or homogeneity. Homogeneity with respect to certain economic conditions has been the principal criterion in the classification and delineation of such regions. We speak of the Ruhr as an economic region, because of its homogeneous coal-mining and metallurgical characteristics, and we speak of the Corn Belt of the United States as an economic region, because of its broadly uniform crop aspect.

In the Soviet Union economic regions are regarded as heterogeneous or complementary areas, consisting of one or several industrial focal points, or perhaps an industrial area, with an associated agricultural hinterland. Soviet regional policy requires that any such economic region be developed to the utmost in all branches of production within the limits of available resources with the aim of ultimately achieving

[1] Theodore Shabad, "The Soviet Concept of Economic Regionalization," in *The Geographical Review*, vol. xliii (1953), pp. 214–222.

regional self-sufficiency. This many-sided or 'complex' development of the economy of Soviet regions is explained by considerations of national defense. The aim is twofold—to further the security of the country through regional autarky and to strengthen the economy by industrializing under-developed areas and by reducing the long-distance haul of commodities that can be produced locally.

We thus find that the Soviet administrative units are truly multi-purpose territorial divisions. They serve as national autonomy areas wherever a specific ethnic group is concerned; they constitute economic regions for planning and statistical reporting and for the ultimate achievement of autarky; and finally they fulfil administrative functions customarily associated with such divisions.

It has already been stressed that units of the autonomous type determine the initial division of the country. Now, within these autonomous divisions, smaller administrative-economic units are found. The largest division of this type is the oblast, which is found in most of the large union republics of the U.S.S.R. The oblast is apt to vary greatly in size, ranging from about 2000 square miles in densely populated oases of Central Asia to vast expanses of 500,000 square miles in sparsely settled Siberia. The administrative capital of an oblast is generally an industrial center. Soviet policy stresses the industrialization of the regional center, because industrial workers constitute historically the main source of support for the Soviet regime. When local conditions permit, the oblasts are so delineated as to provide the maximum prerequisites for the development of a heterogeneous economy.

Let us assume, for instance, that a Soviet area containing well-defined industrial and agricultural areas is to be divided into two oblasts for administrative purposes. The Western administrator, schooled in the principle of the homogeneous economic region, might well be inclined to divide this hypothetical area into an industrial oblast and into an agricultural oblast. The Soviet authorities, always concerned with the many-sided development of an area and the achievement of autarky, delineate the two oblasts so as to include in each an industrial and an agricultural section. This example finds illustrations in many parts of the Soviet Union. Whether in a densely populated coastal belt backed by sparsely settled mountains or an agricultural zone adjoining a forested area Soviet oblasts will always be found enclosing the greatest variety of natural conditions.

A unit similar to the oblast, known as the kray, is found only in the

Russian S.F.S.R.'s administrative structure. The kray differs from the oblast only in that it usually contains an autonomous oblast. An unusual situation existed in Khabarovsk kray and the Maritime kray of the Far East. These two areas once contained a special type of intra-kray oblast. These internal oblasts have gradually been abolished. The Maritime kray has had no international oblasts since 1943 and Khabarovsk kray lost its last such unit in January 1956 (see p. 383, note 6).

The administrative-economic division of second order in the hierarchy is the rayon. The rayon serves not only as a subdivision of the oblasts and krays, but also of autonomous units, such as small union republics, the autonomous republics, the autonomous oblasts, and the national okrugs. The rayon is actually a miniature oblast. Its center is usually the largest populated community, industrialized in so far as local conditions permit. Rayons are delineated so as to produce heterogeneous economic regions on a small scale. Like oblasts, rayons vary greatly in size, ranging from less than 100 square miles in densely populated areas to nearly 150,000 square miles in Siberia. Rayons, in turn, contain urban areas and rural areas. The rural areas, generally known as village councils (Russian *sel'sovet*), each contain a number of collective farms and constitute the lowest rural level of local government.

Urban Administrative Geography

Urban areas receive much attention in the Soviet administrative structure, because urbanization is so intimately linked with the industrialization process. Four types of urban areas of increasing importance are distinguished. The lowest type of urban center is the so-called workers' settlement, which may arise in the vicinity of a new mine, a new industrial plant, or any similar economic production unit, and is identified with the initial stage of industrialization. A workers' settlement is expected to have a minimum adult population of 400 persons, 65 per cent. of whom are employed in industry.

As the workers' settlement develops, population increases, and a greater proportion of the labor force enters into industry, the urban area reaches the status of 'city.' A city is expected to have an adult population of at least 1000 persons, 75 per cent. of whom are employed in industry. Both the workers' settlement and the city in its initial stage come under the jurisdiction of the rayon. Larger cities, of the order of

25,000 to 50,000 population, or cities of unusual economic importance are removed from the jurisdiction of the rayon and placed under the administration of the next highest administrative unit, which may be an oblast or kray, an autonomous republic, an autonomous oblast, or a national okrug. Finally, the largest cities in the Russian S.F.S.R., with a population of about 300,000 or more, are removed even from oblast jurisdiction and placed directly under the republic government. Such cities are Moscow, Leningrad, Sverdlovsk, Novosibirsk, and others.

Since this urban administrative structure reflects economic and demographic conditions in urban areas, any changes in existing conditions are reflected in the administrative pattern. Inversely, changes in the administrative structure provide valuable clues to Soviet economic development, which is so often veiled for security reasons. The relationship has its obvious applications in military intelligence, and is useful to the foreign geographer interested in keeping abreast of developments in the U.S.S.R.

Changes in administrative structure are published systematically by the Soviet authorities. Administrative-territorial guides listing all political divisions, including urban areas, in great detail are published annually or at longer intervals. Administrative changes are, moreover, announced periodically in the *Vedomosti Verkhovnogo Soveta* (Herald of the Supreme Soviet), which is the Soviet journal of laws and decrees.

How do these urban changes provide clues to economic development? The interested observer is first alerted by the announcement of the creation of a new workers' settlement. This means that at the stated locality an industrial enterprise is in the initial stage of its development. In perhaps the majority of cases the enterprise will not grow, and its modest size will continue to be associated with a workers' settlement. Such industries, which may range from saw-milling to mining, are not of unusual significance.

Assume, however, as frequently happens, that after a certain time interval the workers' settlement is raised one notch to the status of city under rayon jurisdiction. Such a change, based generally on the growth in population and industry, may mean either that the original industry has grown and attracted a larger labor force or that a second industry has been added to form a larger urban area. Although the city under rayon jurisdiction may be established by law with an adult population of 1000 persons, in practice the average city of such status has a population of 10,000 to 25,000. Most cities remain under rayon jurisdiction after their initial demographic and economic growth has leveled off to a more or less stable condition.

Occasionally such a city rises one more rung on the administrative ladder and becomes independent of the rayon in which it is situated, falling directly under the jurisdiction of an oblast, an autonomous republic, or similar unit. Such a rise may be caused by mere population growth, or the expansion of existing industry, or the addition of a new outstanding economic activity. Whatever the basis, the city has now reached a point where it may well be regarded as one of the leading industrial centers of the country. There are about 500 such cities in the Soviet Union. Although such centers are expected to have a population of about 50,000, other factors, such as special economic importance, frequently put a city in that category before the 50,000 limit has been reached.

A workers' settlement is sometimes raised directly to the status of city under oblast jurisdiction without passing through the intermediate stage of the rayon city category. Such an advance is invariably a clue to rapid economic growth and forced development. Industrial booms of this type marked the development of Almetyevsk, a new petroleum center of the Second Baku in the Tatar A.S.S.R.; Novokuibyshevsk, an oil town near Kuibyshev on the Volga; and Angarsk, a city with a synthetic fuels industry on the Angara river near Irkutsk, to cite only a few recent examples.

It has already been stressed that administrative changes in urban areas provide merely clues to economic development. No specific description of the nature of the economic development is normally associated with the administrative announcement. It remains for the observer to canvas all available literature, Soviet and non-Soviet, to obtain additional data about the rising industrial center. It is only through the meticulous assemblage of scattered bits of information that the full picture emerges. The importance of the administrative information lies in the fact that it places the industrial development in its proper perspective: in any investigation of this type less attention would normally be devoted to a workers' settlement than, say, to a city that is directly under oblast jurisdiction.

Frequently, even the most assiduous combing of overt sources fails to uncover the nature of an indicated economic boom or other industrial development. In many such cases it is safe to assume that the city in question harbors an industry of more or less direct military application.

Some such centers can be identified. For example, the cities of Kotovsk, a southern satellite of Tambov in central European Russia, and Chapayevsk, south-west of Kuibyshev near the Volga, appear to be concerned entirely with the production of munitions and similar military items, according to a German military intelligence source[2] that became available after the second world war.

In other cases, the name of the city provides a clue. In Dagestan, just south-east of the capital of Makhachkala on the Caspian shore, lies the city of Kaspisk. No economic information has been published about this center, which became a city under republic jurisdiction in 1947. Before its rise in status it had been a workers' settlement named Dvigatelstroi (engine construction). The name, its maritime location, and economic secrecy all indicate some kind of industry producing military marine engines, torpedoes, or similar items. About twenty miles south-east of Moscow, on a main rail line, lies the city of Zhukovskiy. This city has undergone steady administrative growth since pre-war days. In 1938 a workers' settlement of Stakhanovo was built on the site of the railroad station of Otdykh (meaning 'rest,' 'recreation' presumably a summer excursion stop). In 1947 this urban area was raised to the status of city under rayon jurisdiction and was renamed Zhukovskiy. Finally, in 1952, the city was raised one more notch and placed directly under the administration of Moscow oblast. Throughout the rise of this new urban center no economic data came forth to throw light on the nature of this development. The name of Zhukovskiy, however, provided a clue. He was a noted Russian aerodynamicist. The award of his name to the city indicates the existence of an aircraft center, probably engaged in experimental work.

History of Soviet Administrative Geography

It has been deemed of interest to go in some detail into these case studies to show how administrative urban changes closely reflect various types of economic developments. In the absence of explicit information much can thus be deduced from bare administrative announcements. While the meaning of urban growth has been unequivocal throughout the Soviet period, the significance of changes in larger administrative

[2] Generalstab des Heeres, Abteilung für Kriegskarten und Vermessungswesen, *Militärgeographische Angaben über das europäische und das asiatische Russland* (Berlin, 1941–42).

areas has not always been so clear. In fact, several stages can be distinguished in the development of the present administrative-economic divisions (oblasts, krays, rayons).

At the time of the Bolshevik Revolution in 1917 the Soviet regime inherited the Tsarist administrative structure, which served strictly administrative functions along the lines of its Western counterparts. The structure consisted essentially of a three-level hierarchy: guberniya, uyezd, volost. It was stressed soon after the revolution that the guberniya division was antiquated and no longer corresponded to the distribution of economic activities, that many small and unimportant towns were administrative seats, while major industrial and commercial centers lacked administrative functions, and that under the new regime administrative centers were expected to shift to the more important 'Soviet' (*i.e.*, proletarian) cities engaged in economic activity of one type or another.

The first two years of the Soviet regime were marked by haphazard administrative changes left largely to the local authorities without centralized guidance. The general trend was toward a splitting up of areas into smaller divisions to facilitate the introduction of Soviet control. While many new guberniyas, uyezds, and volosts were thus formed to bring the new government closer to the people, administrative functions were transferred to economic centers where the regime had proletarian support.

While these indiscriminate changes proceeded—they were slowed after 1919—a government commission formulated rules for the creation of new administrative-economic regions. The new policy was ratified in March 1921 by the All-Russian Central Executive Committee. It noted the pressing need for a new type of region in view of the lack of correspondence between the existing administrative structure and the new political and economic requirements of the Soviet State. The new rules provided for a transition period in which the existing guberniya structure was to be replaced by the new economic regions.

In 1922 the newly established State Planning Commission (Gosplan) proposed that the country be divided into twenty-one large economic regions. The Gosplan proposal was not adopted in its entirety, because it clashed with the division of the U.S.S.R. along national autonomous lines. But where no conflict existed Gosplan regions were in fact introduced. In the following discussion the complex Russian S.F.S.R. and its simpler sister republics will be treated separately.

In the course of the 1920's, the guberniya system was gradually replaced in the Russian S.F.S.R. by the Soviet system of administrative
divisions.[3] The transition involved the following adjustments: (1) Consolidated volosts and reduced uyezds were converted into the new small
economic region known as the rayon; (2) guberniyas were replaced by
okrugs, a larger type of economic region consisting of a number of
rayons; (3) the giant type of Gosplan region was introduced through the
merger of a number of okrugs. The Gosplan region was known as oblast
if it contained no autonomous units and as kray if it included autonomous republics or oblasts. (After 1936 only autonomous oblasts remained in the krays.) By 1929 the last guberniya had been abolished,
and the guberniya-uyezd-volost structure had been replaced entirely by
the new oblast (or kray)-okrug-rayon system.

For about five years, from 1929 to 1934, the Russian S.F.S.R., the
most complex of Soviet republics, was divided into the smallest number
of oblasts and krays in its history. Based in part on the Gosplan project,
this vast republic was divided during this period into fourteen major
economic divisions in addition to its autonomous republics. But whereas
consolidation of administrative units had preceded this simplified structure, a period of further subdivision was to follow.

In 1930 the okrug echelon was eliminated in the new administrative
structure. The okrug had been regarded as a transitory unit to be preserved during the change-over period of the 1920's. Now, with the new
system well established, its usefulness was no longer apparent. A more
important factor in its elimination was the start of the collectivization
of agriculture. The tremendous upheaval in the countryside that was
associated with the agricultural revolution at this time required more
direct Soviet control in the rural areas. "Bring government closer to the
rayons" was the slogan in 1930, and the okrug, as an intermediate division between the oblast and the rayon, was clearly superfluous.

The elimination of the okrug administration and the increased collectivization of the countryside soon drew attention to the excessively
large size of the rayons. The number of collective farms and state-
owned machine-tractor stations (M.T.S.) multiplied rapidly in the
rayons, and administration at the lower levels became unwieldy and
difficult. Many of the rayons contained two or three M.T.S. and twenty
to thirty collective farms, while the optimal rayon size was held to be

---

[3] Soviet administrative policy during the first two decades has been excellently treated
by John A. Morrison, "The Evolution of the Territorial-administrative System of the
U.S.S.R.," in *American Quarterly on the Soviet Union*, vol. i, No. 3 (1938), pp. 25-46.

that of an area served by a single M.T.S. The M.T.S., which controlled the agricultural machinery required by the farms, was envisaged as an arm of the government at the collective-farm level. Large rayons began to be broken down accordingly during the early 1930's. Soon the number of these units increased to such a point within the oblasts that oblast administration in turn became inefficient. That was the signal for the splitting up of the large oblasts of the Russian S.F.S.R., a trend that has continued to the present day. About thirty new oblasts were carved out of the large Gosplan units during the late 1930's, with about half formed during 1937. After a war-induced lull in administrative shifts, fifteen more oblasts were established in 1943 and 1944.

The reasons for these subdivisions of large oblasts were closely associated with the general economic growth of the country. The progress of collectivization continued to be an element in the 1930's, but the general industrial development of the country under the five-year plans and associated population increases and redistribution must also be taken into account. In his analysis of this period, Morrison attached special importance to the factor of administrative efficiency and discounted the Soviet policy of economic regionalization in this splitting-up process. Administrative efficiency in the sense of easier handling of smaller governmental areas undoubtedly played a role in this period, but it must be emphasized that the Soviet planners never lost sight of the principle of administrative-economic regionalization. Every new oblast was created with a strong industrial (proletarian) center at its nucleus and with a varied economy to ensure a degree of self-sufficiency. The number of economic regions thus kept increasing far beyond the relatively few originally envisaged by the Gosplan project, but the principle of economic regionalization was maintained.

In the union republics outside of the Russian S.F.S.R., the administrative reorganization was much less complex. Like their great sister republic, these smaller peripheral units were converted in the course of the 1920's from the old guberniya-uyezd-volost structure to the okrug-rayon system. The smaller union republics did not include any oblasts at that time, for they themselves were treated as economic oblasts in the Gosplan sense. With the abolition of the okrugs in 1930, the republics were divided directly into rayons. The immediate subdivision into a hundred or more rayons proved to be as unwieldy as were the large Gosplan oblasts of the Russian S.F.S.R. Accordingly, starting in 1932 with the Ukraine and Kazakhstan, the larger republics were divided into oblasts as an intermediate division above the rayon level. The smaller republics, such as Armenia, Azerbaidzhan, and Georgia in Transcaucasia, because of their size, retained the direct rayon subdivision.

The major role played by the Soviet administrative structure as an arm of Government policy was illustrated once again in 1940–41 and immediately after the second world war in the new union republics annexed by the U.S.S.R. along its western frontiers, in particular the three Baltic republics of Estonia, Latvia, and Lithuania, and the Moldavian S.S.R., carved out of Bessarabia. In these areas the Soviet rayon system was not introduced at once. Instead, the Soviet authorities preserved the existing structure of these areas as a transitory measure. For many years the countryside was not collectivized, and the former administrative system appeared suited to the continuing private farming. It was only with the completion of collectivization in 1950 that the Soviet system of rayon administration was introduced into the Baltic area, Moldavia having been converted as early as 1947.

Recent Administrative Developments

The oblast scene had been quiescent since the second world war, except for the creation of Sakhalin (1947) and Amur (1948) oblasts in the Soviet Far East, when a flood of changes suddenly occurred in 1952 in the last year of Stalin's regime. Not only was the oblast system introduced in all the small union republics that had been divided directly into rayons, but oblasts were even formed in three major autonomous republics of the Russian S.F.S.R.—the Tatar, Bashkir, and Dagestan republics. A new period of instability appeared in prospect. The new oblasts were short-lived, however. In April, May, and June 1953, after Stalin's death, the new Malenkov regime abolished all the oblasts created in 1952, stating that an oblast system had proved to be unnecessary in the small republics.

Subsequent oblast changes by the post-Stalin Government continued to reflect new administrative policies. In December 1953, for example, the formation of Magadan oblast in the Soviet Far East was announced. This oblast was organized in the Kolyma gold-mining area, which had been under the special supervision of the labor-camp administration of Beria's Ministry of Internal Affairs. After the fall of Beria the ministry apparently lost much of its power, including its complete control over forced-labor reserves, and the integration of Kolyma into the normal Soviet administrative structure appears to reflect this shift.

More recently, in January 1954, five new oblasts were established in the black-earth zone of European Russia, with their seats at Arzamas, Lipetsk, Belgorod, Balashov, and Kamensk.[4] A sixth oblast—Cherkassy —was added in the Ukraine.[5] As so often, reasons for this shift can only be inferred. The creation of new divisions in a predominantly agricultural zone suggests a connexion with the ambitious agricultural program announced by the post-Stalin regime in the fall of 1953. The creation of new oblasts may be regarded as an attempt to form more efficient units to carry out this program and to strengthen control at the rayon level. But it must be stressed once again that, while administrative efficiency may have been the deciding criterion in the establishment of these new oblasts, the new units conformed well to the Soviet standard of complex industrial-agricultural economic regions. For the new oblast centers are at the very least important for agricultural processing, with Lipetsk, moreover, the site of metallurgical and tractor plants and Kamensk the center of the easternmost wing of the industrial Donets Basin.

Other administrative consolidations are less easily explained, and must be attributed to efficiency and economy motives. Thus, in January 1954, the twelve oblasts of the Byelorussian S.S.R. were merged into seven oblasts. In August 1955 the Garm and Kulyab oblasts of the Tadzhik S.S.R. were abolished, and their rayons placed directly under the Tadzhik republic administration.

Late in February 1954 the Soviet Government transferred the Crimea from the Russian S.F.S.R., in which it had been included since the advent of the Bolshevik regime, to the Ukrainian S.S.R. Before the second world war the Crimea had been one of the autonomous republics of the Russian S.F.S.R., established in 1921 on the basis of its Tatar population. The Crimean Tatar khanate had been one of the remnants of the Golden Horde until it was absorbed by the Russian Empire in 1783. By the time of the Bolshevik revolution the Tatar element had been greatly reduced and was only 25 per cent. of the total population, the rest including Russians, Ukrainians, Germans, Greeks, and Jews. However, in spite of the minority of the Tatars, the autonomy of the Crimea was presumably based on the historical status of that population

---

[4] In August 1955 the capital of Kamensk oblast was moved to Shakhty, a coal-mining center.

[5] At the same time Izmail oblast of the Ukraine was incorporated into Odessa oblast.

group. At first the Tatar language and culture were stressed, in the early 1920's, but soon the Soviet Government had to face the realities of the Crimean population situation, and during the 1930's the predominant role played by the Tatars earlier gradually faded away. The Tatars of the Crimea surely resented their loss of prestige in the republic, and during the second world war, when the Crimea was occupied for three years by German troops, collaboration was widespread. In retaliation, the Soviet Government dissolved the Crimean autonomous republic in 1945, resettled the remaining Tatar elements elsewhere in the U.S.S.R., and brought in new settlers, predominantly Russians and Ukrainians. The Crimea became a simple administrative oblast within the Russian S.F.S.R.

Its recent transfer to the Ukraine can be explained in terms of political and economic factors. Politically, the cession may be regarded as a symbolic act, strengthening the ties between the Ukraine and Russia, which celebrated in 1954 the three-hundredth anniversary of their union. The Ukraine has been playing an increasingly important part since the death of Stalin, and the annexation of the Crimea may reflect this gain in stature. Economically, the Crimea is closely tied to the Ukraine, of which it always has been a southern appendage. Much Kerch iron ore, though phosphatic, is used in the ferrous metallurgy of the Ukraine, while Donets Basin coal and coke are shipped across the Sea of Azov to the Kerch iron and steel plant. Agriculturally most of the Crimea is largely a continuation of the south Ukrainian steppe, growing hard-grained spring wheat and some cotton.

The cession of the Crimea to the Ukraine, a logical step, was the first territorial change affecting boundaries of Soviet constituent republics since the agitated period of 1939–40, except for minor adjustments in the Caucasus in 1944. Although a transfer of the Crimea to the Ukraine would have been justified economically and politically immediately upon the abrogation of the area's autonomous status in 1945, the more rigid policies of the Stalin era prevented the cession at that time.

The minor adjustments in the Caucasus involved the boundary between the Russian S.F.S.R. and the Georgian S.S.R. In the Caucasus several ethnic minorities had been accused of wartime collaboration with the German occupying forces. Their autonomous areas, like the Tatar republic in the Crimea, were abolished in 1944, and at least part of the minority population was exiled to other regions of the U.S.S.R.

Some of the former minority territory passed from the Russian to the Georgian republic.

In this connexion, interesting developments occurred in 1955. One of the exiled Caucasian minority groups, the Chechen-Ingush nationality, was officially disclosed to be residing in Kazakhstan and Kirghizia. The announcement of the publication of Chechen-language newspapers was an indication of the cultural rehabilitation of the exiled minority under the more relaxed policies of the post-Stalin regime.

In the Caucasus itself some of the boundary adjustments made in 1944 were canceled. The territory formerly inhabited by the Karachay and Balkar peoples had been transferred to Georgia following the charges of wartime collaboration. In 1955, about the same time as the news of Chechen-Ingush rehabilitation in Kazakhstan, the former Karachay-Balkar areas were returned from Georgia to the Russian S.F.S.R. One year later, in June 1956, it was announced that Karachay and Balkar peoples had been banished to Khirgizia and were regaining their minority rights under the Soviet liberalization policy.

In summary, the complex Soviet administrative hierachy can be tabulated in three groups: the Russian Soviet Federated Socialist Republic, in a class by itself; the larger union republics; and the smaller union republics.

The Russian S.F.S.R. has undoubtedly the most complicated administrative system of any of the republics that make up the Soviet Union. Its special position is clearly expressed in the nomenclature that designates it as a 'federated' republic. In contrast to the other union republics, which are far more homogeneous ethnically, the Russian S.F.S.R. contains a large number of major nationalities in addition to the predominant Russian element, and thus forms a 'federation' of peoples. The purpose of the following table is to illustrate as clearly as possible the successive levels of administration in the Russian S.F.S.R.

Level A:
Russian S.F.S.R.

Level B (subordinated directly to the Russian S.F.S.R. administration):
Autonomous Republics—Oblasts—Krays[6]—Large Cities (with more than 300,000 inhabitants)

[6] Khabarovsk Kray contained two special 'intra-kray' oblasts—Lower Amur and Kamchatka until January 1956. Kamchatka was then separated from the Kray, and Lower Amur was abolished.

Level C:
Autonomous Oblasts (subordinated to Krays[7]) and National Okrugs (subordinated to Krays or Oblasts)
Level D (subordinated directly to any unit in Levels B or C, except the Large Cities):
Medium Cities[8] and Rayons
Level E (subordinated to the Rayons and occasionally to some Medium Cities in Level D):
Small Cities—Workers' Settlements—Village Councils

The larger union republics, other than the Russian S.F.S.R., that are divided into oblasts are: Byelorussian, Ukrainian, Kazakh, Turkmen, Uzbek, Kirghiz, and Tadzhik republics. Their administrative structure can be generalized as follows:

Level A:
Union Republic
Level B (subordinated to Level A):
Autonomous Republics or Oblasts—Oblasts—Largest Cities (generally the capitals of the republics)
Level C (subordinated to Level B):
Rayons and Medium Cities
Level D (subordinated to Level C):
Small Cities—Workers' Settlements—Village Councils

The smaller union republics that have no oblast division are: Karelo-Finnish S.S.R., the three Baltic republics (Estonia, Latvia, Lithuania), Moldavian S.S.R., and the three Transcaucasian republics (Georgia, Armenia, Azerbaidzhan). Their administrative structure can be generalized as follows:

Level A:
Union Republic
Level B (subordinated to Level A):
Autonomous Republic or Autonomous Oblast
Level C (subordinated to Levels A or B):
Rayons—Large Cities
Level D (subordinated to Level C):
Small Cities—Workers' Settlements—Village Councils

---

[7] An exception is Tuva Autonomous Oblast, the only one in this category that is subordinated directly to the Russian S.F.S.R. and is therefore equivalent to one of the units in Level B.

[8] Large Cities and the larger of the Medium Cities are divided into City Rayons (boroughs).

CHAPTER XVI

The Soviet Union:
Demographic and Economic Aspects

THEODORE SHABAD

THE preceding discussion of the administrative-territorial geography of the U.S.S.R. will have made clear the unusually close
relationship between the demographic and economic evolution
of the country, on the one hand, and the resulting political-territorial
pattern, on the other. It has been stressed throughout this discussion
that the dynamic nature of the administrative pattern is merely a reflection of equally rapid change in the human geography of the country. In
this chapter it is proposed to examine the nature and extent of demographic and economic changes in the Soviet Union, particularly during
the second world war and the post-war period, when published information was less plentiful than theretofore.

Both in the demographic and the economic fields, geographic change
generally proceeded along two directions: increases in total numbers for
the country as a whole and a territorial redistribution of the components,
usually associated with an eastward displacement.

The factors behind this development cannot easily be generalized and
will be treated separately for each element discussed. In general, however, the specific character of human geographic change in the Soviet
Union in the last fifteen to twenty years can be described as the product
of rigid, State-directed industrialization effort, under a planned economy
spurred and modified by the exigencies of the second world war.

Demographic Geography

It has been indicated in the discussion of the administrative geography of the U.S.S.R. that one of the key features of the Soviet population is its multi-national character. Other aspects that distinguish the

o

demographic evolution of the Soviet Union are (*a*) its relatively high rate
of natural increase—1·6 to 1·7 per cent. annually since the second world
war; (*b*) the spectacular urbanization that proceeds hand in hand with
the continuing industrialization drive; (*c*) the State-directed internal
migration of relatively large segments of the population.

Demographic evaluation of the Soviet population is necessarily based
to a large extent on available Census data. The Soviet Government carried out two Censuses, in 1926 and 1939. The 1926 Census was published in considerable detail and in many volumes. The 1939 Census, on
the other hand, was published in very rudimentary form in a few Press
releases. Since 1939 official information on demographic developments
has been extremely spasmodic, usually in the form of scattered references in speeches by Soviet leaders. In the absence of explicit data
students of Soviet affairs began to resort after the second world war to
a study of election district lists from which population changes could be
inferred.

On the occasion of any Soviet election the Government delimits election districts on the basis of the current state of the population. Under
the Soviet electoral system a single candidate is nominated (and subsequently elected) in each district. The election district lists are widely
published in the Press for the information of the electorate. Since the
population norm for an election district in any given election is set by
law and the number of districts in any given area is published, simple
multiplication yields a rather close approximation of the total population
of the given area.[1] Let us assume that an election in a given area provides for the setting up of eighty districts and that the population basis
per district is set by law at 50,000. The population that can be inferred
from this information is eighty times 50,000 equals 4,000,000. Let us
assume further that in a subsequent election in the area under consideration—say, after four years—eighty-five election districts are delimited.
It can be inferred that the population has risen to 4,250,000 in the intervening four-year period. Such inferred data are by no means to be taken
as precise demographic information. For one thing, the exact date of
the basic population data is unknown. It must be assumed that the
delimitation of election districts is based on a population register taken
some time before the election. Furthermore, such inferred figures are
subject to a considerable margin of error. In our example, although the

[1] The methodology used in inferring population estimates from election district lists
is discussed at some length in Theodore Shabad, *Geography of the U.S.S.R., a Regional
Survey* (Columbia University Press, New York, 1951), pp. xiii–xiv.

population norm is set at 50,000, not every district can be expected to be delimited in such a fashion as to include precisely 50,000 persons. Some districts may range as low as 35,000 or 40,000, others as high as 60,000 or 65,000. For working purposes in using this material it is assumed that the margin of error is plus or minus half the basic population norm. Thus, if a district is declared to have a legal population norm of 50,000, the population in various districts can conceivably range from 25,000 to 75,000. If the population of a prospective district were to fall below 25,000 it is assumed that no separate district would be formed and that the area would be attached to an adjoining district. If, on the other hand, the population of a prospective district were to be in excess of 75,000, it is assumed that two districts would then be created or that the excess would be attached to an adjoining district.

These comments have been presented because many estimates of the demographic situation in the U.S.S.R. after the second world war were based on precisely such election district data. Students of Soviet affairs were aware of the defects and the approximate nature of the source material, but, in the absence of official data, the election material was the only consistent source on Soviet population. In June 1956 the Russians published the first statistical yearbook since 1939, including population data. It showed that the population figures derived from the election data had in effect been inflated. The following discussion takes account of the newly released Soviet findings on population.

The Census taken in January 1939 yielded a total population figure of about 170,000,000. During 1939 and 1940 the U.S.S.R. annexed large sections of Eastern Europe, including the Baltic States, Eastern Poland, Northern Bukovina, and Bessarabia, with an estimated total population of 23,000,000 as of early 1939. The annexations brought the total Soviet population to 193,000,000. On the basis of the pre-war rate of increase of 1·5 per cent. the population of the U.S.S.R. at the time of the German invasion in June 1941 can be estimated at 200,000,000.

During the ensuing conflict the Germans swept through territory inhabited by 85,000,000 persons, or about 43 per cent. of the total Soviet population. Tremendous losses in manpower included not only military deaths, but also civilian deaths, a deficit in births, and emigration, forced or voluntary, to the western countries of Europe. If no war had occurred the population of the Soviet Union probably would have risen to about 212,000,000 by the summer of 1945. Actually, the total population of the U.S.S.R. was about 165,000,000 when the war came to a close in that summer. The Soviet population was thus set back by more than 45,000,000 as a consequence of the war.

During the post-war years the population of the U.S.S.R. continued to rise at a rate exceeding 3,000,000 annually. Late in 1949 and early in 1950 Soviet publications hinted that the nation's population had hit the 200,000,000 mark. This seemed supported by data released in connexion with the national elections in 1950. The elections provided for the delimitation of 671 electoral districts, each with a population norm of 300,000, thus indicating a population of 201,300,000. According to data published in the Soviet statistical handbook in June 1956, the population of the Soviet Union in early 1950 was 180,000,000. This would indicate that many election districts in 1950 had a population far below 300,000.

On the occasion of the 1951 anniversary of the Bolshevik Revolution, Lavrenty P. Beria, then one of the Soviet leaders, disclosed that the population of the Soviet Union had been increasing at a rate of more than 3,000,000 for a number of years, thus confirming earlier speculation to that effect.

In the 1954 national elections, the electoral districts numbered 700, which suggested, on the basis of the standard 300,000 norm, a total population of 210,000,000. The seemingly arbitrary roundness of this number and the circumstance that it was not in conformity with an annual increase of more than 3,000,000 suggested that the figure inferred from the election did not represent the true population. In effect, according to the statistical yearbook, the population in early 1954 was 192,200,000. According to the same source, the population in April 1956 was 200,200,000.

In addition to the electoral districts, outside students of the U.S.S.R. attempted to use the published numbers of registered voters for their post-war population estimates. Voting registration for all persons of 18 and over is compulsory in the Soviet Union, so that the number of registered voters represents with reasonable accuracy the number of persons of 18 and over with the exception of those who are disfranchised because of insanity or prison sentences. Before the second world war the proportion of the number of registered voters to the total population of the U.S.S.R. had been given as 55·4 per cent. in 1937. Post-war population estimates were frequently based on the same percentage. The new Soviet statistical yearbook shows, however, that the extremely low birth rate of the war period produced a major change in the age distribution of the post-war Soviet population. In early 1954 there were 120,750,000 registered voters, or 62·8 per cent. of the total population of 192,200,000, indicating a major decrease in the proportion of young people. The vital statistics for 1955 showed a crude birth rate of 25·6 per 1000, a crude death rate of 8·4 per 1000, and a natural increase of 17·2 per 1000.

The spectacular drive for industrialization, initiated with the first five-year plan, resulted in an equally striking rise in the urban population of the country. Urban population rose from 26,300,000, or 17·9 per cent. of the total population, in 1926, to 55,900,000, or 32·8 per cent. of the total, in 1939. Rural-urban migration to fill the increasing need for industrial manpower was undoubtedly a major factor in the doubling of the urban population. However, changes in the definition of 'urban' resulted in the reclassification of former 'rural' communities that were involved in any industrial activities. (The new Soviet concept of 'urban,' based on entirely economic criteria, was discussed in the preceding chapter.)

Urbanization continued at a rapid rate after 1939, particularly in the eastern regions of the U.S.S.R., which were not occupied during the second world war. The urban population of the unoccupied areas rose from 15,600,000 in 1939 to 20,300,000 in 1943. In his speech of April 1954 Mikoyan declared that the urban population of the Soviet Union was about 80,000,000. Later that year the Soviet Press said that the urban population in 1953 had been three times that of 1926. In February 1955 Nikita S. Khrushchev, Soviet Communist party secretary, said that the nation's urban population had increased by

TABLE 1

Urban and Rural Population Growth

YEAR (as of Jan. 1)	TOTAL (in millions)	URBAN (in millions)	RURAL (in millions)	PERCENTAGE URBAN
1926	147·0	26·3	120·7	17·9
1939 (in pre-1939 area)	170·5	55·9	114·6	32·8
1939 (in post-1939 area)	193	61	132	32
1945	165	50	115	30
1950	180	68	112	38
1956	200	87	113	43

17,000,000 since early 1950. These scattered figures make it possible, in conjunction with previous Census data, to trace the growth of the Soviet Union's population during the last three decades (Table 1).

The foregoing table shows that the urban percentage was set back somewhat as a result of Soviet annexations in Eastern Europe in 1939–40 of areas predominantly rural in character. In the country as a whole the urban percentage decreased as a result of the war. The peacetime trend returned after 1945. From 1950 to 1955 the natural urban increase was 8,000,000 and an additional 9,000,000 migrated from the rural areas to the cities.

Just as the most spectacular phase of Soviet urbanization was associated with the initial five-year plans, the greatest individual city growth occurred in the 1930's. The prototypes of Soviet boom cities are the two great eastern steel centers, Magnitogorsk in the Urals and Stalinsk in the Kuznetsk Basin of Western Siberia, and Karaganda, the new coal-mining city of Kazakhstan. The following table shows the growth of a number of new Soviet cities:

TABLE 2

Some Boom Cities of the U.S.S.R.

CITY	1926	1939	1956 *(estimates)*
Karaganda . .	—	166,000	350,000
Stalinsk . .	4,000	170,000	347,000
Magnitogorsk .	—	146,000	284,000
Stalinabad (Tadzhik S.S.R.) . .	6,000	83,000	191,000
Murmansk . .	9,000	117,000	168,000
Dzerzhinsk (Gorki Oblast) . .	9,000	103,000	—

As this table shows, by far the greatest population rise in these new cities, with the possible exception of Karaganda, took place before the second world war. There was no repetition in the post-war period of spectacular city growth similar to that of the great steel centers of Magnitogorsk and Stalinsk before the war. Nevertheless, urban population rose, though at a more modest and less spectacular rate. New urban centers established during the war and the post-war period no longer rocketed from village to city of 100,000-population rank. Instead, whatever urban rise did occur is reflected in the growth of existing centers or in the appearance of new medium-size cities reaching a population of, say, 50,000 at most. As would have been expected, new city growth during the war and after the war was most evident in eastern U.S.S.R., where industrialization proceeded unimpeded by the military operations in the west.

The foregoing comments apply to the largest metropolitan centers of the U.S.S.R. as well as to new cities that emerged in the 1930's. In the post-war period growth of the largest Soviet cities continued, although at a lesser rate than during the 1930's, when the rural-urban migration was at its peak. It should be noted, however, that cities unaffected by German occupation, such as Gorki, Kazan, Kuibyshev, and Saratov in the Volga valley, Sverdlovsk in the Urals, and Novosibirsk and Omsk in Siberia, grew more rapidly than such cities as Kiev, Kharkov, and Dnepropetrovsk, which had suffered a setback during the war.

The following table lists the cities of the Soviet Union with a population exceeding 500,000. The figures for 1897, 1926, and 1939 are based upon Censuses in those years; the 1956 estimate upon the new statistical yearbook.

TABLE 3
Population of Soviet Cities exceeding 500,000
(in thousands)

CITY	1897	1926	1939	1956
Moscow	1,039	2,029	4,137	4,839
Leningrad	1,265	1,690	3,191	3,176
Kiev	248	514	846	991
Baku	112	453	809	901
Kharkov	174	417	833	877
Gorki	90	222	644	876
Tashkent	156	324	585	778
Kuibyshev	92	176	390	760
Novosibirsk	8	120	406	731
Sverdlovsk	43	140	426	707
Tbilisi	161	294	519	635
Stalino	32	174	462	625
Chelyabinsk	—	59	273	612
Odessa	405	421	604	607
Dnepropetrovsk	121	237	501	576
Kazan	136	179	402	565
Riga	—	—	—	565
Rostov-on-Don	120	308	510	552
Molotov	45	120	255	538
Stalingrad	56	151	445	525
Saratov	137	220	376	518
Omsk	37	162	281	505

The industrial development of the Soviet Union under the five-year plans brought about not only a great increase in the urban population of the country, but also a regional redistribution of the population. While urbanization is related directly to the growth of new industrial centers and the expansion of older cities, the general redistribution of the population resulted from the new regional allocation of industry and a systematic settlement of sparsely populated regions. Before the start of the industrialization drive most of the Soviet population lived within the steppe and mixed-forest area roughly denoted by a triangle with apexes at Leningrad, Odessa, and Sverdlovsk. Most of the Soviet population still lives within this triangle, where natural and historical factors have been most favorable to settlement. However, as a result of the concerted Soviet effort to industrialize under-developed parts of the country, a significant part of the population has been shifted to formerly sparsely inhabited regions. The principal direction of this population shift has been eastward, both into the Asiatic regions of the Russian S.F.S.R. and into the Central Asian republics. To a lesser extent population has moved northward in European Russia.

Emigration did not occur uniformly throughout the 'population triangle' of European Russia. In fact, major industrial areas within the triangle, including the Moscow, Leningrad, and Donets Basin districts, increased in population at a rate about equal to that in the eastern regions. It was the overpopulated agricultural regions of central European Russia, Byelorussia, and the Ukraine that served as the

TABLE 4

Regional Shifts in the Population of the Soviet Union
(in millions)

	1926 CENSUS	1939 CENSUS	1956 ESTIMATE
U.S.S.R. in Europe . .	109·1	123·8	153·0
including			
Northern European Russia	2·7	3·9	4·8
U.S.S.R. in Asia . . .	37·9	46·7	47·0
including			
Urals	11·0	12·5	14·4
Siberia and Far East .	13·1	17·5	24·0
Central Asia and Kazakhstan	13·8	16·7	18·6
U.S.S.R.	147·0	170·5	200·0

principal areas of emigration eastward, northward, and to the cities.

Table 4 shows the distribution of Soviet population, with special reference to the northern and eastern regions, according to Census and election district data.

Economic Progress of the Soviet Union

Before the Bolshevik Revolution of 1917 Russia was primarily an agrarian nation. To-day it is an industrial Power second only to the United States. Before examining the dominant economic position that the Soviet Union occupies in the world to-day, it is well to recall the main stages of economic development that followed the political up-heaval of the first world war.

The Russian economy emerged from the years of revolution and civil war in a chaotic state. The period of so-called War Communism (1917–21), during which the State assumed rigid control of all phases of the economy, but was unable to maintain it, was followed by Lenin's New Economic Policy (N.E.P.). Under this program, which was to effect a temporary concession to free enterprise, domestic trade and small and medium industry were partly returned to private hands, while the State retained control over all key industries and transportation. Under this type of mixed economy the nation gradually raised its output, and by 1928 had regained or even exceeded its pre-war levels.

In that year began the vigorous industrialization movement designed to raise the Soviet Union to the forefront of the world's industrial Powers. This drive was implemented by means of the five-year plans, the sixth of which ends in 1960. The main effort was concentrated on the development of heavy industry, meaning metallurgy, fuels, power, machine building, and chemicals. This was essential, according to Soviet thinking, for economic and military reasons. In the Soviet view only the development of heavy industry made possible the subsequent rise of industry as a whole, of agriculture, and of transportation, thus ulti-mately insuring a rise in the standard of living of the people. The emphasis on heavy industry was necessitated, moreover, according to this view, by an international situation in which the Soviet Union stood alone in a generally hostile world.

As a result of this economic and strategic motivation the consumer in

o*

the U.S.S.R. has had to take a back seat, for while heavy industry rose steadily at an impressive rate, consumer industries and agriculture were either relegated to far lesser rates of growth or stagnated at or near pre-industrialization levels, as did animal husbandry. It was evidently in an effort to placate the long-neglected Soviet consumer that the post-Stalin Government in the autumn of 1953 inaugurated an intensified program of consumer goods and agricultural output. The results of this program were not very successful, and there can be little doubt, that, as before, it is heavy industry that continues to grow most rapidly.

Industry. Our survey of current Soviet industrial developments might well begin with the nation's power resources, the basis of any industrial system. They are, in their order of importance, coal, water power, fire-wood (used mainly for domestic heating), petroleum and natural gas, peat, and oil shale. We shall mainly consider the situation in coal, petroleum, and water-power, which play the leading role among the power sources for the Soviet economy.

The coal industry is typical of Soviet heavy industry on two counts: the extraordinary rapid rate of increase of output and the development of new fields that have brought about an eastward shift in the centers of production.

TABLE 5

Coal Production (in millions of metric tons)

MAJOR FIELDS	1913	1928	1940	1945	1950	1955
Donets Basin .	25·3	27·3	94·4	40	96	135
Kuznetsk Basin ..	·8	2·6	22·6	31·0	36·4	56
Karaganda . .	—	—	6·3	11·3	16·5	27
Others . .	3·0	5·6	42·7	66·7	112·1	173
U.S.S.R. . .	29·1	35·5	166	149	261	391

This table clearly shows that the Donets Basin, while still the uncontested leader among Soviet coal fields, produces a far lesser share of total coal than in 1913. Its contribution to the nation's production dropped from 87 per cent. in 1913 to 35 per cent. in 1955. In contrast, the new eastern fields of the Kuznetsk Basin and Karaganda have risen both in absolute terms and as a percentage of Soviet total output. The great increase in the output of 'other fields' demonstrates the increasing decentralization of Soviet coal production as additional fields, mainly of low-grade local coals, are being opened up.

While total Soviet petroleum output increased at a lower rate than coal after 1913, the recent shift in the geographical distribution of production centers has perhaps been even more spectacular.

TABLE 6

Petroleum Production (in millions of metric tons)

MAJOR FIELDS	1913	1928	1940	1945	1950	1955
Baku . . .	7·7	7·7	22·1	11·5	14·8	15·3
"Second Baku" .	—	—	1·9	3·0	11·1	40·4
Others . .	1·5	4·0	7·0	5·0	12·0	15·1
U.S.S.R. .	9·2	11·7	31·0	19·5	37·9	70·8

Until the second world war Baku's position in the petroleum industry was comparable to that of the Donets Basin in the coal industry. Although Baku's share in total output dropped from 84 per cent. in 1913 to 71 per cent. in 1940, actual output almost tripled within that period. However, the war ended the unchallenged dominance of Baku. A number of factors, such as the wartime shortage of pipe steel, German interdiction of shipping routes, the exhaustion of wells, and the lack of new drilling, combined to force a decline of output from 23·8 million tons in 1941 to about 11 million tons in 1944. After the war, in spite of the exploitation of new offshore wells in the Caspian Sea, the Baku production falls short of its pre-war level.

In the meantime attention had shifted to the so-called Second Baku, a vast petroliferous province between the Volga river and the Urals discovered in the early 1930's. Its great potentialities, of which the nickname was a hopeful expression, failed to materialize at first, and at the outbreak of the second world war the production of the Second Baku was only one-tenth of that of Baku. However, in 1944, just when Baku reached its lowest point, deeper drilling in the Second Baku disclosed rich Devonian oil-bearing strata that sent the area's output soaring. By 1952 the Second Baku had caught up with its limping predecessor and has now become the leading oil-producing region of the Soviet Union.

In the field of electric power production the most noteworthy development in the post-war period has been the marked shift to sources of hydro-electric energy.

TABLE 7

Electric Power Production (output in 1000 million
kilowatt-hours; capacity in million kilowatts)

	1913	1928	1940	1945	1950 (Plan)	1950	1953	1955 (Plan)	1955
Total Output .	1·9	5·0	48·3	43·3	82·0	91·2	134·4	162	170
Hydro-electric .	—	0·4	5·1	4·8	12	12·7	19·2	35	23
Total Capacity .	1·1	1·9	11·3	10·7	22·4	22	31	45	—
Hydro-electric	—	—	1·2	—	3	3	5	9	—

Soviet economic development is clearly reflected in the figures of electric power production, which is the backbone of any modern industrial economy. The stress placed by Soviet planners on this branch of the economy is evident from wartime developments. Although German occupation of the western part of European Russia resulted in the loss of five million kilowatts of power station capacity, or 44 per cent. of the Soviet total, new construction in the east virtually compensated for this loss, and by the end of the war both power output and capacity were nearly at pre-war levels.

Since 1945 the Soviet Union, both by rebuilding destroyed stations and constructing new ones, has been raising power-generating capacity at the rate of 2·5 to 3 million kilowatts a year. Within this rapid growth, hydro-electric power has been assuming an increasingly important share. According to the fifth five-year plan (1951–55), total electric power generating capacity doubled, while hydro-electric generating capacity tripled. Work has been proceeding in recent years on giant power plants on the Volga river, including the stations of Gorki, Kuibyshev, and Stalingrad on the Volga itself and the station of Molotov on the Kama, a major affluent. Construction is also to be started on the Cheboksary plant, the final link in the Volga power-station system, and on the Votkinsk plant, on the Kama river.

But of almost greater interest than these European projects are the large undertakings in Soviet Asia. Foremost among these is the long-planned Angara power system at the outlet of Lake Baikal. This project, which had been on Soviet books ever since the start of the five-year planning period, is finally beginning to be realized. In February 1954 the Soviet Press announced that construction of the first Angara station at Irkutsk with a planned capacity of more than 1,000,000

kilowatts was under way. Other major Asiatic power projects are at
Novosibirsk on the Ob river and at Ust-Kamenogorsk and Bukhtarma
on the Irtish river. In November 1955 the Soviet Press disclosed
that a second Angara project of 3,000,000 kilowatts would be built at
Bratsk.

Probably foremost among the consumers of these sources of fuel and
power has been the Soviet iron and steel industry. Here, again, the development under the Soviet industrialization drive has been marked
both by a rise in total output and an eastward redistribution of production.

TABLE 8

Iron and Steel Production (in millions of metric tons)

AREA		1913	1928	1940	1945	1950	1955
Ukraine—							
Pig Iron	. .	2·9	2·1	9·2	1·7	9·2	16
Steel	. .	2·5	2·3	8·6	1·4	8·3	17
Urals—							
Pig Iron	. .	·9	·7	2·8	5·5	7·3	13
Steel	. .	·9	1·0	4·4	7·2	11·9	18
Siberia—							
Pig Iron	. .	—	—	1·5	1·3	1·8	2
Steel	. .	—	—	1·8	2·5	3·1	4
Others—							
Pig Iron	. .	·4	·5	1·4	·4	1·0	2
Steel	. .	·8	1·0	3·5	1·2	4·0	6
Totals—							
Pig Iron	. .	4·2	3·3	14·9	8·9	19·3	33
Steel	. .	4·2	4·3	18·3	12·3	27·3	45

Table 8 illustrates the steady rise of ferrous metallurgy in the Urals,
particularly at the Magnitogorsk plant, and in Siberia, where most of the
output stems from Stalinsk in the Kuznetsk Basin. During the second
world war, when the Germans occupied the Ukraine, it was the eastern
plants that supported the Soviet war effort. It is noteworthy that,
while the Ukraine now produces little more than one-third of Soviet
steel, it still accounts for one-half of the nation's pig iron. This continuing importance in blast-furnace production is evidently the result
of favorable conditions, particularly the proximity of coal and iron-ore
sources.

In contrast to heavy industry's rapid rise of output and geographical decentralization, the development of consumer goods industries, such as clothing and food, has been marked by a very slight rate of increase if not stagnancy under the five-year plans.

TABLE 9

Production of Selected Soviet Consumer Goods

PRODUCT AND UNIT	1932	1940	1945	1950	1953	1955	1960 (Plan)
Cotton Cloth (million meters) . . .	2,694	3,954	1,700	3,899	5,300	5,904	7,270
Woolen Cloth (million meters) . . .	89	120	54	155	209	251	363
Linen Cloth (million meters) . . .	134	286	62	282	280	305	556
Leather Shoes (million pairs) . . .	87	211	63	203	239	275	455
Meat (thousand tons) .	596	1,501	530	1,556	2,150	2,522	3,950
Butter (thousand tons) .	72	226	110	336	369	459	—
Sugar (thousand tons) .	828	2,151	470	2,523	3,437	3,419	6,530
Canned Food (million cans) . . .	692	1,113	—	1,535	2,180	3,223	5,580

The trend shown in Table 9 is a slow rate of increase during the pre-war planning period, when emphasis was clearly placed on the development of heavy industry; a major drop during the second world war, frequently to the original 1932 levels or less; a return during the first post-war five-year plan to pre-war levels, and continued slow rise or stagnancy until 1953. Following the death of Stalin, the new Soviet regime introduced a policy of consumer goods expansion that set high goals for 1956 far exceeding levels previously achieved. Some of the consumer goods output figures become more meaningful when calculated on a per capita basis; for example, total Soviet output of leather shoes in 1940 and 1950 provided about one pair for each Soviet citizen. The output of food items must be related to the urban population (60 millions in 1940 and 80 millions in 1954), since only products of State industry or State-owned sales channels appear in food statistics. The considerable quantities sold directly by the farmers to city dwellers or consumed by the farmers themselves are excluded.

Major geographical shifts, such as those observed in heavy industry, have not been evident in the consumer-goods field. Soviet literature often points to the exploiting character of Tsarist policy in having concentrated industry in the heart of European Russia and having relegated peripheral areas to the role of raw-material suppliers. Soviet policy, by contrast, has been represented as one that brings industry to the sources of raw materials, thus raising the economic level of under-developed areas. In fact, however, relatively little such movement has taken place. The Moscow-Ivanovo textile region, which accounted for more than 90 per cent. of all Soviet cotton cloth output before the Revolution, still accounts for about 75 per cent. of the production. And Uzbekistan, which supplies three-fourths of the raw cotton, produces only about 4 per cent. of the nation's cotton cloth.

Agriculture. The Soviet Union is, as it was before the Revolution, one of the world's leading agricultural producers. But, unlike heavy industry, agriculture has not received much attention during the five-year plans, and together with the consumer industries has made little if any progress under the Soviet regime. The U.S.S.R. is nevertheless by virtue of its size the world's greatest producer of wheat, rye, barley, oats, flax, and sugar beets, with potatoes, sunflowers, and cotton other leading crops. In contrast to the United States, corn plays a minor role in the Soviet Union. However, a major corn-growing program was begun in the Soviet Union in 1955.

Although only about 7 per cent. of the total area is under cultivation, the total Soviet arable area is about 160 million hectares, or about 10 per cent. more than the arable area in the United States. The greatest part of the Soviet cultivated area lies in the black-earth steppe belt, extending east and west through the western half of the country, and in the adjoining sections of the podzol forest zone to the north and the drier steppes with chestnut-brown soils to the south. Essentially the Soviet sown area coincides with the area of greatest population concentration, forming a triangle with the base along the Leningrad–Odessa line and the apex in Western Siberia.

At the start of the first five-year plan, the dominant Soviet farming unit was the private farm with an average sown area of 4·5 hectares. There were about twenty million such farms. As the industrialization drive gathered speed and the urban population increased by leaps and bounds, the Soviet Government was faced with the problem of insuring an adequate food supply for the industrial workers and proceeded to collectivize agriculture. The emergent organizational pattern included about 250,000 collective farms with an average area of 500 hectares under cultivation and 5000 State-operated farms with an average sown area of 2500 hectares.

In 1950 the Soviet Government amalgamated many small collective farms into larger units, with a corresponding increase in the average farm area. After consolidation there were about 100,000 farms with an average sown area of 1300 hectares. An initial plan to associate the farm amalgamation with resettlement of the peasants in a central farm-city settlement, the so-called *agrogorod*, was opposed by the farmers and abandoned.

Throughout the five-year plans the major concern in Soviet agriculture has been to increase output either by raising yields per hectare or

TABLE 10

Sown Area and Output of Major Crops (in thousand hectares; output in thousand tons)

CROP	PRE-WAR AREA		PRESENT AREA			
	1913	1928	1940	1945	1950	1955
Grain—						
Area	94,360	92,170	111,100	85,200	102,900	126,400
Output	80,100	73,300	120,100[1]	66,500[1]	125,700[1]	
Cotton—						
Area	688	971	2,076	1,200	2,320	2,200
Output	740	820	2,700	1,290	3,750	4,090
Sugar Beets—						
Area	649	770	1,200	800	1,310	1,760
Output	10,900	10,100	20,900	8,900	23,500	30,600
Flax—						
Area	1,000	1,400	2,100	1,000	1,900	1,480
Output	330	320	570			
Sunflower Seed—						
Area	969	3,900	3,500	2,900	3,590	4,240
Output	740	2,100	3,300	1,800	3,100	6,400
Total Sown Areas	105,000	113,000	151,000	113,300	146,300	185,800

[1] These are gross official figures. Barn yields are estimated to be ± 20 per cent. below these totals.

expanding the sown area. In order to raise yields the Government has stressed the use of mineral fertilizer and the application of improved agricultural methods, such as moisture conservation and crop rotation. Quick-ripening and drought-resistant types of grains, for example, have been developed to enable the extension of the crop area into marginal lands with less favorable growing conditions. In spite of these measures, agricultural production has lagged and remains one of the problems in the Soviet economy.

Table 10 illustrates the trend in the sown area and gross output of some major crops during the Soviet five-year plans.

In 1953 the total Soviet grain area was 3·8 million hectares less than in 1940, partly through the abandoning of land and partly through the diversion of the land to other crops. In view of this reduction in area and since grain output over the years had barely been able to keep up with the rate of natural increase of the population of the Soviet Union, the Government launched a major grain area expansion program in 1954. The program called for the plowing and planting in grain of thirteen million hectares of abandoned and virgin lands during 1954 and 1955. The expansion is taking place chiefly in the steppes of Western Siberia and Northern Kazakhstan. A great share of the expanded area is being organized as State farms, staffed to a large extent by workers from the European part of the Soviet Union. In the spring of 1954, 124 new State farms with 2,532,000 million hectares of arable land were thus added to Soviet agriculture. In view of the apparent success of the expansion program the goals were raised late in 1954 to fifteen million hectares of new land by the end of 1955 and twenty-eight to thirty million hectares by the end of 1956. As this program has been achieved, the expected output at the rate of one ton of grain per hectare will be a welcome addition to the Soviet food supply.

The share of wheat has been steadily rising in total Soviet grain output. While it accounted for 43 per cent. of all grain in 1940, its share in 1952 was 61 per cent., with the rest made up of rye, barley, oats, and other cereals. The main wheat-producing areas of the Soviet Union, nearly all situated in the black-earth belt, are the Ukraine and the Kuban, which grow winter wheat, and the trans-Volga, West Siberian, and North Kazakhstan areas, which produce hard-grained spring wheat.

Cotton is the most important vegetable fiber of the Soviet Union. Its main producing areas are the irrigated regions of Central Asia (chiefly Uzbekistan) and Transcaucasia, where yields per hectare reached an average of two tons in 1953. Under the Soviet regime, cotton was expanded into the non-irrigated areas of the Southern Ukraine and the Northern Caucasus. But, while these areas occupy about 20–25 per cent. of the total cotton area of the Soviet Union, their low yield under non-irrigated conditions contributes only about 10 per cent. of the total cotton output.

While cotton has been expanded into non-irrigated areas, the reverse shift in production has taken place in the case of sugar beets. The basic beet-growing region includes the Ukraine and Kursk and Voronezh Oblasts of the Russian S.F.S.R. However, new sugar-beet areas in southern Kazakhstan and in Central Asia (particularly Kirghizia) are providing an increasing share of total Soviet output under irrigated conditions. While the Ukrainian yield is about eighteen to nineteen tons of beets per hectare, the irrigated yield in Kirghizia under normal conditions is as high as forty tons per hectare. In view of its far larger area, however, the Ukraine continues to account for about 65–70 per cent. of all Soviet sugar beets.

The U.S.S.R. has long been the world's leading producer of flax, the raw material of the linen industry. But flax has been in recent years one of the problem crops in the U.S.S.R. A plant that requires a high input in labor, flax suffered greatly during the second world war, when its main producing area—the north-west of European Russia—was overrun by the German Army. Flax area and output approached pre-war levels by 1950, but since that time decreased at an alarming rate. In March 1954 the Soviet Press announced that the sown area in flax had dropped by one-third since 1950. A flax-expansion program was promulgated, calling for a gradual return of the sown area to two million hectares by 1957, or approximately the level of 1940 and 1950. The 50-per-cent. increase in area is to be achieved by expanding flax holdings in the Urals and Siberia, outside of the main producing regions of the Baltic republics and Byelorussia.

Sunflowers, whose seed is the most important source of Soviet vegetable oil, are generally associated with the grain-growing areas of the dry and sunny south-eastern part of European Russia. The major areas are the Northern Caucasus, the Lower Volga, the south-eastern part of the Ukraine and Voronezh Oblast of the Russian S.F.S.R.

One of the most stagnant sectors of agriculture has been animal husbandry. Initially high numbers of livestock were greatly reduced in the early 1930's during the collectivization period, when farmers preferred to slaughter the stock rather than surrender it to common ownership. On the eve of the second world war, Soviet livestock numbers were still below pre-collectivization levels. The war further reduced livestock holdings, but during the post-war period 1941 levels were generally reached by 1951. In view of the continuing slow increase or even some decline during the early 1950's, the post-Stalin regime introduced a number of measures in 1953 designed to speed the rate of livestock increase. The Government expected to raise livestock levels by encouraging the increase of private holdings (theretofore discouraged), reducing forced livestock deliveries to the State, expanding veterinary aid, and so forth.

TABLE 11

Livestock Numbers in the Soviet Union (in million head at beginning of the year)

LIVESTOCK	1916	1928	1941	1945	1951	1955[1]
Cattle . . .	58·4	66·8	54·5	45·3	57·2	67·1
Hogs . . .	23·0	27·7	27·5	3·4	24·1	52·2
Sheep and Goats .	96·3	114·6	91·6	56·0	99·0	142·6
Horses .	38·2	36·1	21·0	9·1	13·7	—

[1] October.

Most of the Soviet livestock, as of the sown area, is found in the European part of the country. Hogs are reared chiefly in the potato-growing areas of central European Russia and Byelorussia, as well as on the basis of by-products of the food-processing industry in the Ukraine and the Northern Caucasus. Dairy cattle are raised in the moist meadows of the central and northern parts of European Russia, as well as in Western Siberia. In the vicinity of large urban markets dairying is oriented toward milk production, while in more remote areas butter and cheese are marketed. The steppe belt is the chief meat-cattle zone, with the animals reared on fodder crops in the west and on natural pastures in the east. Sheep-raising and wool production increase in importance toward the drier areas of Kazakhstan and Central Asia.

In its efforts to increase agricultural output, the Soviet Government is placing its hope in the major shelter-belt program initiated in 1949. This program is designed to provide a series of windbreaks in the southeastern part of European Russia against scorching winds from the deserts of Central Asia. In addition to the great State-sponsored windbreaks, totaling 3500 miles in length, the program envisages the planting of trees on individual farms in the drought-ridden area to act as local windbreaks and to prevent soil erosion. The completion of this grandiose program is scheduled for 1965, but the Soviet Press has been silent in recent years on progress, if any, of the shelter-belt program. Indications are that parts may have been abandoned.

Another factor to be taken into account in any future evaluation of the Soviet agricultural potential is a series of irrigation projects being carried forward at the present time. These projects, though greatly reduced in scope from the initial Stalinist plans, still call for the irrigation of the southern Ukrainian and Crimean steppes with water from the Dnieper river and of the Lower Volga and Caspian steppes with water from the Volga. Among the projects begun under Stalin's rule but abandoned after his death are the Turkmen Canal from the Aral Sea to the Caspian through the Kara Kum desert and the major canal linking the Volga and Ural rivers in the Caspian steppe. Instead, work has been resumed on the Kara Kum Canal in the southern part of the Turkmen Republic.

Transportation. The U.S.S.R. is one of the world's leading railroad Powers. A number of physical factors have favored railroad transportation over other means. The predominantly low relief has offered little obstacle to the building of railroad lines. The freezing of the rivers from three to nine months a year decreases the value of waterways as a major transportation factor. Moreover, most of the large rivers, such as those of Siberia, flow through economically undeveloped areas into hostile seas of the Arctic Ocean that are frozen the greater part of the year. Highway transportation is negligible, because of the lack of good roads and the small number of motor vehicles. And, finally, the continental nature of the Soviet Union and the lack of an indented coastline in temperate seas largely reduces the importance of coastwise shipping.

It is not surprising, in view of these factors, that railroads in the Soviet Union account for 80–85 per cent. of all freight carried and that the five-year plans should have placed great emphasis on the expansion of the rail network.

The Soviet regime inherited about 44,000 miles of railroad from Tsarist Russia. This network covered almost entirely only the European part of the country, with the Trans-Siberian and the Trans-Caspian railroads the only links with the outlying regions of Siberia and Central Asia. As a result of new construction during the five-year plans the Soviet rail mileage had risen to about 75,000 by 1955. The new construction occurred mainly in the peripheral regions of the U.S.S.R., where large-scale industrial development was undertaken.

One of the significant aspects of Soviet railroad geography has been the gradual decline of new construction during the five-year plans. The

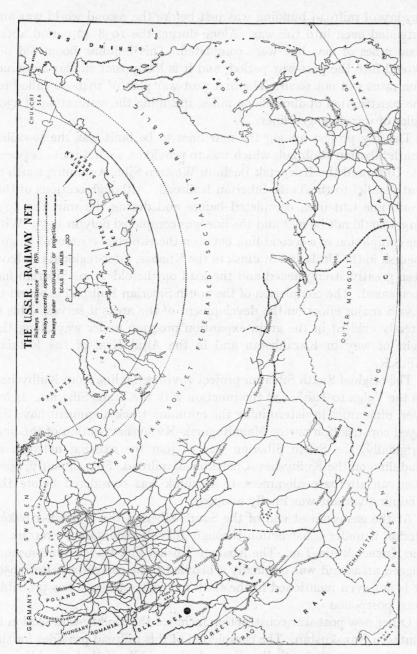

THE U.S.S.R.: RAILWAY NET

Railways in existence in 1939.
Railways recently opened.
Railways under construction or projection.

SCALE IN MILES

Fig. 1. The Railways of the Soviet Union

heyday of railroad building was just before the second world war and
extended even into the war. Alone during the 1938–42 period about
6000 miles of new line were completed. This building boom did not
extend into the post-war period, and it is likely that similar construction rates will not recur. The first post-war plan of 1946–50 called for
the construction of about 6000 miles, including the restoration of 2300
miles of war-damaged lines.

The key project among the new lines to be built was the so-called
South Siberian Railroad, which was to provide a second route between
the Urals and the Kuznetsk Basin in Western Siberia running south of
and parallel to the Trans-Siberian Railroad. Although sections of this
trunk line had been completed before and during the war, the 1950
target could not be met and the line was completed only in 1953. With
the completion of a second link between the two steel centers of Magnitogorsk in the Urals and Stalinsk in the Kuzbas, inter-regional ties have
been greatly strengthened and the load on the old Trans-Siberian has
been eased. The completion of the South Siberian Railroad is bound to
have a major effect on the development of the areas it serves. This is
already evident in the grain expansion program under way along the
right of way in Kazakhstan and in the Altai Krai of the Russian
S.F.S.R.

The original South Siberian project envisaged a line from Kuibyshev
on the Volga to Taishet at the junction with the Trans-Siberian. However, difficulties in determining the optimum track alignment have delayed construction on the Magnitogorsk–Kuibyshev section of the line.
Originally, the South Siberian was to join the existing network at
Abdulino on the Kuibyshev–Chelyabinsk railroad. Subsequently, however, an alternate alignment to Buzuluk was considered before the
Abdulino variant was finally adopted.

At the easternmost end of the South Siberian the Stalinsk–Abakan
section is under construction through difficult mountainous terrain of
the Kuznetsk Ala-Tau. The Abakan–Taishet link traverses even more
rugged areas and was originally scheduled to be completed after 1950.
It is not even mentioned in the sixth five-year plan and has probably
been postponed.

Other new post-war construction included the Mointy-Chu section in
southern Kazakhstan. The completion of this railroad provides for the
first time a north–south line through the middle of that republic and
greatly speeds the shipment of coal from Karaganda to the southern

part of Kazakhstan. Parallel to the Amu Darya, the Chardzhou-Kungrad project was undertaken after the war both to provide a rail line to the major irrigated farmlands of the lower Amu Darya and to supply the Turkmen Canal construction project. Work on an extension of this line north-westward to Makat, near Guryev on the north-east shore of the Caspian Sea, has been postponed.

The sixth five-year plan (1956–60) calls for the construction of the Astrakhan–Guryev railroad, which had been originally scheduled for the fifth five-year plan, but was not built. This line will fill a major transportation gap along the north shore of the Caspian Sea. Another current railroad project is the Achinsk–Abalakovo line in Siberia, which replaces the Krasnoyarsk–Yeniseisk railroad, another project that was scheduled under the fifth five-year plan and was not built. A total of 1900 miles of railroads was built in the course of the fifth five-year plan ending in 1955. About 4000 more miles are to be completed by 1960.

TABLE 12

Railroad Freight Traffic

	1913	1928	1940	1950	1955
Metric tons originated (*millions*)	132	156	593	828	1,267
Average length of haul (*kilometers*)	496	598	700	722	766
Metric ton-kilometers (*thousand millions*)	66	93	415	598	971
Average daily car-loadings (*2-axle units*)	27,400	32,333	97,852	118,850	—

The rise in Soviet freight traffic reflects the tremendous industrialization effort under the five-year plans. The increase in the physical output of the major transported commodities accounts for a seven-fold rise in the amount of freight carried by the railroads, the so-called tons originated. Foremost among these commodities is coal, which in 1955 accounted for 33 per cent. of all freight carried by the railroads. Other major commodities are ores and metals, petroleum, lumber, and grain.

The rise in the average length of haul of all these commodities is a reflection of the development of outlying regions and the increasing distances separating producers and consumers. The average figure conceals major differences in the lengths of haul of individual commodities. For example, cotton is carried regularly over a distance of about 2000 kilometers from the major producing areas in Central Asia to the textile mills of the Central Industrial Region of European Russia. A rise in the average length of haul of cotton from 1814 kilometers in 1940 to 2375 kilometers in 1953 demonstrates that by far the greatest share of Soviet cotton still travels huge distances from the fields to the mills. Other long hauls of about 1000 kilometers are typical of the transportation of lumber, metals, and coal. Building materials, on the other hand, being generally available locally, are carried an average of 275–300 kilometers.

Because of the limiting physical factors stated above, Soviet waterways account for only 6·3 per cent. of all freight carried. Moreover, about 70 per cent. of all waterways freight is carried in the Volga river system. Although the Volga empties into a closed inland sea, the Caspian, its canal links with other rivers systems have made it the main artery of the Soviet river transportation system. Among the most important of these canals are the old Mariinsk system connecting the Volga and Leningrad on the Baltic, the Baltic–White Sea Canal, the Moscow–Volga Canal, and the Volga–Don Canal, the last of which was completed in the summer of 1952. The leading types of freight on the rivers, in particular on the Volga, are petroleum, grain, and salt (moving upstream) and lumber (downstream). These four commodities, which make up less than 60 per cent. of the railroad freight, account for more than 90 per cent. of the goods carried on the waterways.

Other forms of transportation are maritime shipping, trucking, and air freight, as well as pipe-lines. The Soviet Union is not an important maritime nation, and by far the greatest part of the maritime freight moves in inland seas, particularly the Caspian. Here the shipping of crude oil from Baku to Astrakhan for trans-shipment up the Volga constitutes the most important item in Soviet maritime transportation. Trucking is restricted to short hauls to railheads and river ports, but is used also for longer distances in some peripheral areas that lack railroads. Airlines play a key role in supplying distant parts of Siberia, especially outposts in the Far North, where frequently no other means of transport are to be found.

FURTHER READING

BALZAK, S. S., VASYUTIN, V. F., and FEIGIN, YA. G., *Economic Geography of the U.S.S.R.* (American edition edited by Chauncy D. Harris; Macmillan, New York, 1950).

CRESSEY, GEORGE B., *How Strong is Russia?* (Syracuse University Press, Syracuse, N.Y., 1954).

GEORGE, PIERRE, *U.R.S.S., Haute Asie, Iran* (Presses Universitaires de France, Paris, 1947).

GRAY, G. D. B., *Soviet Land: the Country, its People, and their Work* (Black, London, 1947).

JORRÉ, GEORGES, *The Soviet Union, the Land and its People* (Longmans, Green, New York and London, 1950).

LEIMBACH, WERNER, *Die Sowjetunion: Natur, Volk, Wirtschaft* (Franck'sche Verlag, Stuttgart, 1950).

LORIMER, F., *The Population of the Soviet Union: History and Prospects* (League of Nations, Geneva, 1946).

SCHWARTZ, HARRY, *Russia's Soviet Economy* (second edition; Prentice-Hall, New York, 1954).

SHABAD, THEODORE, *Geography of the U.S.S.R., a Regional Survey* (Columbia University Press, New York, and Oxford University Press, 1951).

SHIMKIN, DEMITRI B., *Minerals, a Key to Soviet Power* (Harvard University Press, Cambridge, Mass., and Oxford University Press, 1953).

Note on Statistics. The figures tabled in this chapter have been assembled by the author from official and other sources, including the Soviet statistical handbook *Narodnoye Khozyaistvo S.S.S.R.* (National Economy of the U.S.S.R.), published in Moscow in June 1956.

CHAPTER XVII

Land Frontiers and Frontier Problems of the Soviet Union*

W. GORDON EAST

The Territorial Expansion of the U.S.S.R.

THE Soviet Union emerged from victory in the second world war with enlarged territories both in Europe and Asia. The effect of ideological factors on Soviet policy receives so much attention to-day that one often forgets how strong an influence territorial changes themselves exert upon subsequent policy. New boundaries may settle quarrels—or may exacerbate them. They may mark the limits of the expansion of a Power—or the jumping-off places for further advances. A careful scrutiny of the territorial acquisitions of the U.S.S.R. and of the strategical significance of the new frontiers which they have traced on the map of Europe and Asia may offer clues to the direction of future Soviet moves.

A British Foreign Secretary, Lord Curzon, himself an eminent geographer, wrote:[1] "Frontiers are indeed the razor's edge on which hang suspended the modern issues of war and peace, of life and death to nations." And although it is probably now true to say that frontier incidents alone are unlikely to be the cause—they can, of course, always be the pretext—of a major war, it is only too evident that certain frontiers, and not least those of the Soviet Union, give local expression to international tension. Of the danger spots of the years following the second world war—Greece, Berlin, Yugoslavia, Tibet, Indo-China, Formosa, Turkey, and Korea—only the last two lie strictly adjacent to the frontiers of the U.S.S.R., but it is not easily forgotten that the power of the U.S.S.R., thanks to its occupation forces in Germany, its permitted

---

* Thanks are due to the Editor of *Foreign Affairs* (New York) for permission to use in this chapter material published under the title "Frontiers and Frontier Problems of the Soviet Union."
[1] Lord Curzon, *Frontiers* (Cambridge University Press, 1907).

defence of its lines of communication through Romania, Hungary, and Poland, its creation of satellite neighbours, and its privileged position in Manchuria, extends territorially far beyond its own frontiers both in Europe and in Asia.

A State of such territorial extent and continuity as the Soviet Union has necessarily a great length of international boundaries, and, although these are only about half as long as its coastline, they stretch for 10,000 miles and delimit eleven bordering States, six in Europe and five in Asia. The sheer length of international boundaries and the physical geography of the frontier regions in which they lie—which may be such as either to facilitate or to minimize contact between the contiguous States—afford, of course, no criteria of frontier tension. Witness, for example, the war which Bolivia waged against Paraguay in 1932–35[2] in the Chaco, a tropical frontier zone which should have provided, so forbidding was its geographical character, natural and effective insulation between the settled and developed areas of the two States. Witness, too, in contrast, the peaceful stability of the long open frontier of contact between the United States and Canada, where such problems as do arise do not endanger friendly relations. But in the light of what is known both of traditional Russian territorial ambitions, which now appear to be subsumed in Soviet foreign policy, and also of the international character of Soviet Socialism (misnamed Communism), the great length and wide distribution of the frontiers of the U.S.S.R. acquire significance, since they provide a tempting choice of theatres for diverse action designed towards a common end: action in the form of propaganda, ideological infiltration, sabotage, allegedly 'civil' war (here, again, is a phrase that takes on new shades of meaning), and direct warfare undisguised.

"The old Europe has gone. The map is being rolled up and a new map is unrolling before us." So spoke Field-Marshal Smuts in 1943. The territorial expansion of the U.S.S.R. since 1938 has taken place mostly in Europe but also in Asia (Fig. 1), and in both there were other considerable gains which assumed less obvious forms. Along its frontier, 1000 miles long, between the Barents Sea and the Gulf of Finland its gains were secured first by the Treaty of Moscow with Finland in March 1940, only to be increased later, after the second Soviet-Finnish war, by the peace treaty of February 1947.[3] Those made

[2] Compare the short analysis made by Y. M. Goblet, *The Twilight of Treaties* (Bell, London, 1936), pp. 178–195.

[3] Cmd. 7484. H.M.S.O. Treaty Series, No. 53 (London, 1948).

in the area of similar length between the Baltic and Black Seas were
first effected under cover of the Nazi-Soviet non-aggression pact of
August 1939; they were subsequently lost, but recovered during the
Soviet-German war of 1941–45. There are peace treaties made in 1947
with Romania and Hungary governing some of these territorial changes;

FIG. I. U.S.S.R. TERRITORIAL GAINS SINCE 1938

for the rest they are mainly based on the Three-Power decisions made
at Yalta and Potsdam in 1945.

By its expansion in Europe the Soviet Union projected itself westward into the politically unstable 'shatter zone' of East-Central Europe,
but less far west than Tsarist Russia did in 1914. It was effected by the

incorporation of the three Baltic States, brought into the Union as constituent soviet socialist republics, and by accessions of territory from no fewer than five states—Finland, Germany, Poland, Czechoslovakia, and Romania. In area these additions amount to about 190,000 square miles: if they enlarge the U.S.S.R. by little more than 2 per cent., nevertheless they add an area larger than California, made up of lands strung out through 25 degrees of latitude—from the latitude of northern Alaska to that of Portland, Oregon. Moreover, the population of the Union is increased by some twenty-four millions—about half of whom are either Ukrainian or White Russian—which represent an increase of nearly 15 per cent. in Soviet man-power. U.S.S.R.'s maritime position is substantially improved; its boundary between the Baltic and the Black Sea is shortened, and in the extreme south overlaps the watershed of the Carpathian Mountains. At the same time Soviet territories conveniently flank Poland on its north-eastern side. Not the least important result of the Soviet gains in Europe is the establishment of direct contact with three states—Norway, Czechoslovakia, and Hungary—which were formerly separated from the U.S.S.R., the first by Finnish and the last two by Polish and Romanian territory.

Soviet Territorial Gains in the North

The U.S.S.R. advanced its boundaries at the expense of Finland in three sectors (Fig. 2), although 400,000 Finns migrated from the ceded areas to be resettled in Finland.[4] The most important adjustment was in the Karelian isthmus—the neck of land, narrowing to less than fifty miles in width between Lake Ladoga and the Gulf of Finland, at the head of which lie Leningrad and the insular base of Kronstadt. When, after the first world war, the Grand Duchy of Finland, attached to the Russian Empire since 1809, was replaced by an independent Finnish republic, the boundary was drawn across the isthmus favourably for the Finns, advantage then being taken there, as elsewhere, of the weakness of the new Bolshevik Russia. Behind this boundary, making full use of the constriction of the isthmus, Finland built its main defence works, known as the Mannerheim Line, which lay only about thirty miles from Leningrad. The vulnerability of Leningrad from this landward side,

[4] W. R. Mead, "The Finnish Outlook, East and West," in *The Geographical Journal* (London), vol. cix (October 1947).

should Finland become an enemy base, was doubtless the prime reason for the Soviet attack on Finland in November 1939. Leningrad, with its suburbs, was a city of over three million inhabitants—indeed, the largest city in the world in such high latitudes (60° N.)—and it actually accounted for fully one-tenth of the whole of Soviet industrial production, while it contained important ship-building yards and commanded the only Soviet outlet to the Baltic.

The area annexed from Finland in the Karelian isthmus extends from the head of the Gulf to and beyond the northern and eastern shores of Lake Ladoga: the southern part of it has been added to the Leningrad oblast of R.S.F.S.R., and the rest to the Karelian-Finnish S.S.R., which, as a result, obtains an outlet to the Baltic through the port of Viborg, formerly Viipuri. The U.S.S.R. therefore now holds not only the whole of the isthmus—possession of which alone made the military defence of Finland possible—but also the thriving seaport and water and rail focus of Viborg. Soviet control of the Gulf of Finland was confirmed by the acquisition, by the 1947 treaty, of a lease for fifty years of the Porkkala area and its peninsula, which commands marine access to Helsinki, for the U.S.S.R. already controlled the southern shore of the Gulf from the Estonian coast, notably from the port of Tallin, which is linked by rail to Leningrad. Porkkala was, however, returned to Finland in 1955.

The second area detached from Finland lies astride the Arctic Circle at the waist of Finland between the White Sea and the Gulf of Bothnia. This area is part of a great wilderness of lakes and forests, scantily peopled by Finns, Karelians—themselves a Finnish people—and Russians, which forms, in contrast to the well-populated Karelian isthmus, a frontier of separation between Finland and the U.S.S.R. The Soviet territory abutting this frontier consists of the Murmansk oblast of R.S.F.S.R. in the Kola peninsula, which was created in 1938, and southward of this, between the White Sea and Lake Ladoga, the Karelian-Finnish S.S.R., which, after the first Russo-Finnish war, replaced the Karelian-Finnish A.S.S.R.,[5] set up in 1923. These two areas cover 113,000 square miles, but only 760,000 inhabitants were recorded there in 1939, despite substantial mining, hydro-electric, transport, and urban development during the Soviet period. The Finns and Karelians of Karelian-Finnish A.S.S.R. were becoming mixed with immigrant Russians, whose speech was becoming dominant. These territories were

[5] An autonomous soviet socialist republic (A.S.S.R.) is administratively part of a soviet socialist republic (S.S.R.); the latter is a constituent republic of the federated Soviet Union (U.S.S.R.). See above, Chapter XV.

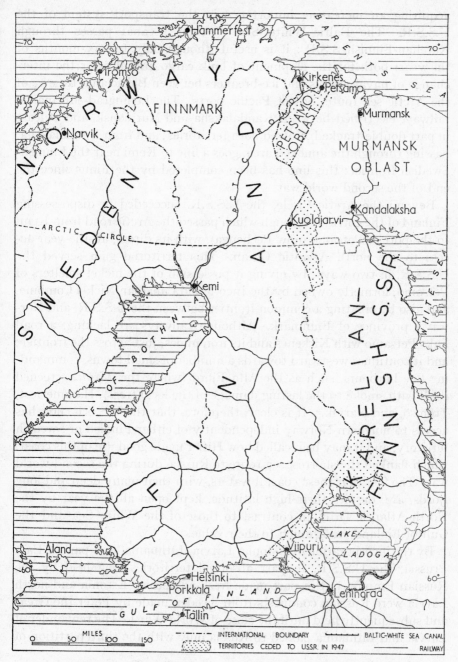

FIG. 2. U.S.S.R. TERRITORIAL GAINS FROM FINLAND

acquiring an increasing importance in the transport system of the U.S.S.R. The Baltic–White Sea ("Stalin") canal passes through Karelian-Finnish S.S.R.: it is useful (though only for six months of the year) both for the shipment of bulk cargo and also for the interchange of naval vessels and ice-breakers between Baltic and, by way of the Arctic sea route, Soviet Pacific ports. The Leningrad–Murmansk railway, electrified between Kandalaksha and Murmansk, and at least in part double-tracked, crossed both territories; and from Kandalaksha, passing through the annexed area, goes a line to Kemi near the Finnish-Swedish frontier: this line has been completed by the Finns since the end of the second world war.

Beyond the Arctic Circle, the U.S.S.R. succeeded in dispossessing Finland of the corridor through which passed the Arctic road from Kemi to the port of Petsamo (now Pechenga), with its direct, all-the-year access to the north Atlantic Ocean. This territorial gain served the U.S.S.R. in two ways: by giving it possession of the nickel smelters of Petsamo, formerly owned by the Inco-Mond Canadian Nickel Combine, and also by creating a common frontier between the U.S.S.R. and Norway's province of Finnmark. Although railways are lacking, a road links Petsamo with Kirkenes and its iron mines, just across the frontier; and it continues westward towards a number of small towns, commanding fine harbours, such as the Alta Fjord (where the *Tirpitz* screened itself with smoke to the lasting damage of the local trees), Hammerfest, Tromsö, and Narvik.[6] It is clear, therefore, that the U.S.S.R. now has access to northern Norway independently of either Finnish or Swedish territory, and it may be recalled how Hitler made good use of this coast, which flanked the shortest sea route to Russia, during the second world war. The fact that these coastal waters, with their many deep and long fjords, are, despite their high latitude, kept open all the year by the North Atlantic Drift, in contrast to those of the White Sea and the Gulf of Finland, adds much to their value.

By the incorporation of Estonia, Latvia, Lithuania, and part of East Prussia, the U.S.S.R. in part absorbed territories long held by the Russian Empire, but in part made fresh advances. Estonia and north Latvia were Russian conquests from Sweden made by Peter the Great and subsequently held until the close of World War I. The remainder of Latvia and Lithuania passed to Russia only with the third partition of

---

[6] D. H. Lund, "The Revival of Northern Norway," in *The Geographical Journal* (London), vol. cix (October 1947).

Poland in 1795. The division of German East Prussia—whereby the northern part, including Königsberg (renamed Kaliningrad) and the rail junction of Insterburg, are added to Lithuanian S.S.R. and thus to the U.S.S.R.—is a bold and novel change, for it was as long ago as the thirteenth century that the Teutonic Knights, as they wiped out the Balts of East Prussia, were colonizing and mastering this area.

The plebiscites of 1940, by which the peoples of Estonia, Latvia, and Lithuania expressed their desire to join the federal structure of the Soviet Union as constituent republics, need not be taken very seriously. It is true that the natural hinterlands of these countries lie in the Great Russian Plain, with which railways connect their ports, and that, on purely economic ground and national sentiment apart, their union with the U.S.S.R. might appear sensible and profitable. In any case certain positive advantages accrue to the U.S.S.R. Except for the important limitation that the gateways to the Baltic—the Danish Straits and the Kiel Canal—lie outside its control, its position in the Baltic, commercially and strategically, is now very strong. German pre-eminence has ended, Finland is deprived of its maritime defences, the demilitarization of the Åland Islands continues, the Soviet coastlands and insular emplacements front south-eastern Sweden, while friendly Polish ports lie westward of Kaliningrad. Protection for Leningrad, too, is secured on the side from which the Nazi attack was launched in 1941. The Soviet boundary is shortened, and Soviet East Prussia adjoins northern Poland. Apart from their useful seaports and their railroad connexions, these Baltic lands, being chiefly wooded and agricultural, add little of special value to the U.S.S.R.'s resources, except for the oil shales of Estonia, which provide a convenient supply of fuel oil for Leningrad and for Baltic shipping.

Soviet Territorial Gains in the West

The Soviet-Polish boundary now lies about 100–200 miles farther west than that of the inter-war years, although it no longer projects as far west as did that of Tsarist Russia in 1914, when so-called "Congress Poland"—all that survived of a Polish State—was ruled by the tsar as king. The new boundary (Fig. 3) helps to define yet another of the many territorial shapes which Poland has assumed in the course of a thousand years of history in this troubled borderland of Central Europe. It runs west–east in the north, where it delimits also Lithuanian S.S.R., and

P

then strikes south, leaving Grodno in Soviet hands. Farther south the boundary is aligned along the upper Bug river, so that the whole of the Pripet marshes fall to Byelorussian (White Russian) S.S.R., and then diverges south-westward across the Galician plateau to reach the Carpathian Mountains. The old fortress of Przemyśl lies just within Poland, but the large city of Lwow, originally founded by a Russian prince but held by Poland for several centuries, now passes to the U.S.S.R. as part of Ukraine S.S.R. The Soviet-Polish boundary, as defined by the Potsdam Agreement, except for some small adjustments in the south which roughly balance, agrees closely with the ethnographic boundary drawn up by Lord Curzon in 1920—the "Curzon Line." The proportion of Poles in the population of the area taken by the U.S.S.R. has been much debated, but seems unlikely to have much exceeded 20 per cent.;[7] indeed, White Russians and Ukrainians made up at least two-thirds of the total population of about thirteen millions, which included pre-war over a million Jews. In the Soviet view, these accessions marked the recovery of Russia's so-called "Western Lands," for which, on ethnographic ground and in contrast to other gains of territory, a sound case could be made.

The Western Lands lopped off from Poland consist of good farm lands in the old southern provinces of Podolia and Volhynia, but for the greater part of lowlands and marshlands in which transport facilities are poor and farming efficiency is low. Indeed, the Russian occupation since the late-eighteenth-century partitions,[8] did nothing to advance the economy of these lands which visibly contrast with the lands which Austria, and especially Prussia, annexed from Poland[9] and developed with some effect. Potentially, and above all when Soviet large-scale drainage works have improved the Pripet marshes, these lands, under the 'collectivized' system which has been introduced, should yield higher dividends from mixed farming; in other respects their economy has little to add to that of the U.S.S.R., for although the latter gets the larger part of the Galician oilfield, this has long been a trivial and dwindling asset. Control of the few railroads of the area has value for the U.S.S.R.: it now holds the junction of Brest-Litovsk on the main, double-tracked Moscow–Warsaw line, and, more important, perhaps, the

[7] These figures are reached from the 1931 Polish Census. See S. Konovalov, editor, *Russo-Polish Relations* (The Cresset Press, London, 1945).

[8] See Fig. 3 in Chapter XIV above.

[9] Compare O. S. Morgan, editor, *Agricultural Systems of Middle Europe* (Macmillan, New York, 1933).

FIG. 3. U.S.S.R. TERRITORIAL GAINS IN EUROPE

junction of Lwow on the main, double-tracked railway from Odessa to Cracow, Breslau, and Berlin; from Lwow, too, there are single-track lines north to Lublin and Warsaw and south across the Carpathians into Hungary. The now Ukrainian city of Lwow has for centuries served as a fortress and place of trade on a European thoroughfare: it lies on that diagonal route-way from the Black Sea to Belgium (where passage is confined between the Carpathians and the Pripet marshes) which has facilitated the movements of peoples and armies from prehistoric times.

Ruthenia, as the Hungarians call it, Sub-Carpathian Russia or Carpatho-Ukraine as Russians know it, is geographically and strategically more important than would appear from a glance at an atlas map. Part of the Carpathian mountain zone, it is sharply distinguished from the higher and more rugged Slovakian and Romanian Carpathians which lie respectively to the west and to the south-east, because it is so worn down and cut by river valleys and by passes as to form a natural passage-way between the Galician plateau and the Hungarian basin. Through its passes came the Magyars (Hungarians) who occupied Hungary at the end of the ninth century, the tsar's armies which overthrew so-called 'revolution' in Hungary in 1849 and attacked the Austro-Hungarian Empire in 1915, and the Red Army in 1945. Ruthenia is best known as the 'appendix' area in the extreme east of the Czechoslovak republic. Historically part of the Hungarian kingdom, it passed to Czechoslovakia on the settlement after World War I, and was returned to Hungary by Czechoslovakia, under Nazi pressure, in March 1939. Its small population of shepherds and peasants—about three-quarters of a million—are largely of Ukrainian descent, so that the U.S.S.R. was able to present its annexation as the liberation of brothers from alien rule. But to this ethnographic interest must clearly be added a strategical interest, for roads from Ruthenia lead into Slovakia and two single-track railways pass through it into Hungary, with which the Ukraine S.S.R., and thus the U.S.S.R., have now a common frontier.

As with the Poles, so also with the Romanians, the U.S.S.R. had old scores to settle when the chance arose in 1940, thanks to the Nazi-Soviet Pact of 1939. From Romania the U.S.S.R. seized and has retained the territories of northern Bukovina and Bessarabia, and thus advanced its boundaries to the Pruth river and the Danube delta. Historically Bukovina was part of the Principality of Moldavia, the union of which with that of Wallachia in 1859 led to the overthrow of Turkish suzerainty and the creation of the independent Romanian State. The drainage of its rivers—Pruth and Sereth—to the Black Sea also appears to attach it to Moldavia, but only in the south of Bukovina are the inhabitants mainly Romanian. In 1775 it was taken by Austria from the Ottoman Empire, to which the Romanian principalities then formally belonged, and incorporated in the Hungarian kingdom. It was returned to the Romanian kingdom as it emerged, much enlarged, after World War I. Soviet interest in this forested Carpathian area is partly ethnographic, since, in the northern part, which it has taken, Ukrainian people formed a large minority. Possession of northern Bukovina fits neatly the new Soviet frontier pattern, however, for it connects by single-track railways Bessarabia, Sub-Carpathian Russia, and Ukrainian Galicia. The chief city, Chernovtsy (Cernauti), passes to the U.S.S.R., and since 1940 north Bukovina has been merged in the Ukraine S.S.R.

Bessarabia has long been a contested frontier region. This area of steppe, of high productivity as farm land, lies between the Dniester and Pruth rivers and fronts both the Danube delta and the Black Sea. Its population of about three millions was very mixed, at least in the towns. Romanians—or, as the Russians preferred to call them, Moldavians— made up, however, about 56 per cent. of the total, Ukrainians and Russians made up 23 per cent., and Jews 12 per cent. Historically, like Bukovina, Bessarabia was part of Moldavia, but in 1812 the Tsar Alexander I, after a short and successful campaign against the Turks, acquired it by treaty. In 1856, after the Crimean War, although Russia retained Bessarabia, its southern boundary was withdrawn more than twenty miles north of the Danube delta. Only in 1919, after World War I, did Bessarabia become part of the Romanian kingdom.

Clearly the U.S.S.R. had no intention of permanently accepting the loss of this territory. Only 260,000 Romanians, enumerated under the heading "Moldavians," are recorded in the Soviet Census of 1939, and most of them dwelt in western Ukraine between the rivers Bug and Dniester. The organization in 1933 of the Moldavian A.S.S.R., although Moldavians constituted only about one-third of its population, gave them administrative recognition, and when Bessarabia was occupied in 1940 it was easy to create the Moldavian S.S.R. This small constituent republic of the Union—it is only 13,000 square miles in area, with a population (in 1940) of 2·4 millions—was formed by adding the greater part of Bessarabia to most of the much smaller Moldavian A.S.S.R. What remained of Bessarabia, including its coastland and the approach to the Danube, was assigned to Ukraine S.S.R.

The U.S.S.R. has derived some further advantages from the annexation of north Bukovina and Bessarabia. Its boundary along the Kilia branch of the Danube delta gives it the right to be regarded as a Danubian State. Given ascendancy over the satellite States of Romania, Bulgaria, and Hungary and its presence, until 1955, on the upper Danube in occupied Austria, the U.S.S.R. was able to prevent operation of the Danube Convention of 1922, by which the Danube, as an 'international river,' was declared open, under the safeguard of two international commissions, to the commerce of all nations.[10] This Convention, to which the U.S.S.R. was not a party, represented a 'seaman's solution' which is now replaced by a 'landsman's control,' and it is now clear that free navigation of the Danube, other than by the shipping of riparian States, is conceived as incompatible with Soviet ideas of secrecy and security; control of Danube navigation also provides a useful bargaining counter in any international discussions about the Turkish Straits.[11] In addition, Romania's 'maritime' ports on the Danube—Galatz and Braila—lie just beyond the Soviet boundary, while only the steppe corridor of Romanian Dobruja, carrying a railway which is, however, broken by the Danube delta between Ismail and Tulcea, separates the U.S.S.R. from Bulgaria, for which, less on ground of avowed Slav sentiment than for reasons of geography—since Bulgaria commands access to the Turkish Straits—it has always affected marked regard. Further, the U.S.S.R. now borders Romania all the way from the Danube, via Bessarabia and Bukovina, to Ruthenia. Lastly, Bessarabia's supplies of grain and animal products are not a negligible asset, for, unlike Ukraine, it has no large urban proletariat to consume the surplus produce of its farms.

The U.S.S.R.'s Frontier in the Middle East

The international frontiers of the U.S.S.R. in Asia extend for some 8000 miles, fall within three of its major components—South-west Asia,

[10] Compare L. F. L. Oppenheim, *International Law* (sixth edition, revised by H. Lauterpacht; Longmans, London, 1947, vol. 1, pp. 424–425. Desirable schemes for irrigation and water-power from the Danube, such as those discussed by G. Kiss, "T.V.A. on the Danube," in *The Geographical Review* (New York), vol. xxxvii (1947), are for the time being mere dreams.

[11] Denial of use of the Danube to non-riparian States would seem contrary to clauses of the peace treaties made between the Allied and Associated Powers and Hungary, Romania, and Bulgaria in 1947 which stipulated free and equal use of the Danube by commercial shipping of all states. Yugoslavia's control of the Iron Gate section of the Danube limits the U.S.S.R.'s domination of the waterway.

High (or Central) Asia, and the Far East—and they closely approach a fourth, the Indian sub-continent. Soviet acquisitions in Asia since 1938—Tannu-Tuva, south Sakhalin (Karafuto), the Aleutian Islands, and Port Arthur—total some 80,000 square miles. Even so, its Asiatic, as compared with its European, boundaries have been relatively stable. But although the frontiers of Asiatic U.S.S.R. might appear to be frontiers of separation—they mostly lie in country remarkable for its scanty settlement, lofty mountain chains, and high arid plateaux—international disquiet at many points has been considerable; nor should it be assumed that, because the Soviet boundaries in Asia have little changed, the Soviet position on its Asiatic marches has not been strengthened by other means. Indeed, the pattern of satellite states beyond the frontier in European U.S.S.R. is largely repeated in Asiatic U.S.S.R., and Soviet foreign policy has been, and remains, evidently active there. Its success has depended particularly on two facts: first the multi-national character of the Soviet Union, and second the application to Soviet Middle Asia and southern Siberia of Western technology.

Asiatic U.S.S.R. borders on Turkey, Persia, and Afghanistan in the South-west Asian (or "Middle East") theatre. The U.S.S.R.'s proximity to Turkey, both along its South Caucasian frontier and in Europe, where its satellite Bulgaria adjoins Turkey in Eastern Thrace, has clearly been useful to the U.S.S.R. in the pursuit since 1945 of a changed and forceful policy towards Turkey. It may be recalled that, following the Soviet-Turkish treaty of 1921, the relations between the two new political creations—the Soviet Union and the Republic of Turkey—long remained friendly. Turkey's secret treaty of neutrality with Nazi Germany in 1941, signed just before the German attack on the U.S.S.R., heralded, however, a worsening of Soviet-Turkish relations, which culminated in the Soviet denunciation in 1945 of the Soviet-Turkish treaty of non-aggression made in 1925. In essence this phase of Soviet policy, heir to that of the tsars, springs from two facts of strategic geography: Turkey controls the Straits between the Black Sea and the Mediterranean, which strategically and economically are very important to the U.S.S.R. Moreover, Turkey stands close, as air distances are measured, to major industrial areas of the Soviet Union, notably the Baku oilfield and the mining and heavy metallurgical industries of the Ukraine. During the years 1945–46 the U.S.S.R. tried, but failed, by a direct approach to Turkey, to secure the control and defence of the Straits jointly with Turkey and thus to replace the ruling Convention of

Montreux, to which it was a party in 1936. In 1945, too, the U.S.S.R. claimed from Turkey the areas around Ardahan and Kars which adjoin the Georgian and Armenian S.S.R.'s and contain a small minority of Armenians. These areas were in Russian hands between 1878 and 1917, but their cession to Turkey was confirmed by the Soviet-Turkish treaty of 1921.

Whereas Turkey is regarded by the U.S.S.R. as a barrier in its path to the Mediterranean and as a possible enemy base, so might Persia appear, since it is interposed between the U.S.S.R. and the Indian Ocean by way of the Persian Gulf and the Arabian Sea. The U.S.S.R. borders Persia both in South Caucasus and in Central Asia, and shares with it the navigation of the Caspian Sea. Weakly organized and incapable of defence against a powerful aggressor, Persia has survived, as a Buffer State, because this has suited equally Russian and British interests. Russia clearly had to guard against possible attack from this quarter, while Britain was at pains to prevent any great Power from establishing a foothold on the Persian Gulf, since this would outflank the north-west frontier defences of India. Accordingly, what are known technically in international law as "spheres of influence" were established by Britain and Russia in south and north Persia respectively, and when Nazi intervention in Persia threatened in 1941 British and Soviet troops temporarily occupied their respective zones. With American aid it was then possible, chiefly by road construction and by the provision of trucks, to make Persia, poorly equipped as it is for modern transport, a supply route of the U.S.S.R.

The U.S.S.R. showed marked reluctance to withdraw its troops from north Persia by the agreed date—March 2, 1946—since it wished, before the Red Army left, to obtain an oil concession in north Persia, the oil resources of which still appear somewhat problematical. The Soviet-occupied area of Persia included the province of Azerbaidzhan, which adjoins the Azerbaidzhan S.S.R., both being peopled mainly by Azerbaidzhan Turks. Tabriz, capital of Persian Azerbaidzhan, is an important strategical centre commanding roads into Turkey and Iraq, and linked to the Soviet broad-gauge railway system by a line to Julfa. In order to bring pressure to bear on the government at Tehran to grant the desired oil concession, the U.S.S.R. arranged, while its troops were still in Persia, that the Tudeh Party should set up a separatist regime in Azerbaidzhan. These manœuvres, and other similar attempts to separate the Kurds of Persia, failed: Soviet troops were withdrawn, the puppet regime was overthrown, and the Tudeh Party proscribed. But after a sufficient pause, and by changed tactics, the U.S.S.R. made a trade pact with Persia in November 1950 which might well have served as an instrument of Soviet political infiltration. However, despite the nationalization of the Persian oil industry, formerly controlled by the Anglo-Iranian Oil Company, relations between Persia and the Western Powers rather than with the U.S.S.R. have strengthened in recent years.

Three of the Soviet Central Asian republics—Turkmen S.S.R., Uzbek S.S.R., and Tadzhik S.S.R.—adjoin Afghanistan, which, as a semi-independent State, acquired international prominence only with the steady advance and railway-building of Russia in Central Asia during the later decades of the nineteenth century. This inland country of rugged mountains and semi-desert plains, the population of which comprises many ethnic elements, might well have passed under Russian rule but for the fact of its geographical position commanding the chief landward approach to India. Although railways reach the frontiers of Afghanistan—at Kushka and Termez on the Soviet side, and at the Khyber and Chaman Passes on the Pakistan side—Afghanistan still lacks railways but possesses a few historic highways leading, via Herat, Kabul, and Kandahar, to the gateways of India. British policy sought to create a friendly and viable Afghan State as a buffer to further Russian expansion, and to this end secured the delimitation (and partial demarcation) of its boundaries during the 1880's and 1890's. Russia formally avowed in a Convention of 1907 that Afghanistan lay outside its sphere of influence, while Britain conducted the foreign affairs of Afghanistan until 1919. The defence of the Indian sub-continent on its north-western marches now devolves primarily on Pakistan. Soviet interest in this borderland, remote from the major bases of the Union, appears restrained but not lacking. Afghanistan contains more Tadzhiks than does Tadzhik S.S.R., and also a smaller number of Uzbeks. The industrialization and westernization of which there are evident signs in the U.S.S.R.'s Middle Asian republics contrast sharply with the relatively unprogressive Afghan way of life. The Soviet-Afghan frontier thus could always provide possibilities for Soviet action on an ethnographic pretext.

In eastern Afghanistan, the Soviet-Afghan frontier, here undemarcated, lies in the Wakhan area between the forbidding Pamir and Hindu Kush Mountains, so that, although the U.S.S.R. and Pakistan

*P

are separated by only about twenty miles, their proximity has no strategical significance. Farther to the east the Soviet Tadzhik, Kirghiz, and Kazakhstan republics border Chinese Sinkiang, through which pass a few historic highways, some now motorable, linking Middle Asia to Szechwan and the Far East. Sinkiang is a vast and arid country with a population of only four millions, but its northern areas adjacent to the Soviet frontier are the most populous and potentially rich, since, apart from grain and wool, they are reported to contain wolfram, oil, and gold, as well as coal, iron, and copper. China's hold on Sinkiang since 1882, when it became a province of China, was always weak and locally resisted, for this remote province is not ethnically Chinese. Turki-speaking Moslems make up 77 per cent. of Sinkiang's population, 10 per cent. are Kazakhs, and only 8 per cent. Chinese. And although in the Sino-Soviet treaty of 1945 the U.S.S.R. avowed that it had no intention of interfering with China's internal affairs, it is as clear that Sinkiang was becoming an open field for Soviet politico-economic penetration as that it was also geographically (and by air services) oriented on the U.S.S.R. rather than on China. In 1944, not without help from across the border, the three northern districts of Sinkiang, whose population is half Kazakh, had set up the "Republic of East Sinkiang," in defiance of the Nationalist Government of China. The U.S.S.R.'s policy in respect of Sinkiang has necessarily undergone some change now that cordial relations exist between Moscow and Peking. Communist China clearly asserted its authority there. In accordance with the Sino-Soviet treaty of friendship, alliance, and mutual assistance of February 1950, joint Russo-Chinese companies were set up to exploit Sinkiang's mineral resources. And now a railway is being built jointly across Sinkiang to connect Peking, via Kanchow and Tihwa, with Alma Ata, the capital of Kazakhstan, which stands on the Turkestan-Siberian railroad.

The U.S.S.R.'s Gains from China and Japan

In South-west Asia, where the continental interests of the U.S.S.R. have been balanced by those of the Western maritime Powers, the Soviet boundaries at least have remained unchanged. In Central Asia, in contrast, where, remote from the oceans, the U.S.S.R. and China meet along a mountainous borderland, the former, at the expense of the latter's disorganization and weakness, was able to profit more clearly,

and even territorially. The absorption of the Tannu-Tuvan republic
into the U.S.S.R. in 1945, as an autonomous oblast of the R.S.F.S.R.,
is the logical culmination of a policy long pursued, in turn by Russia
and the U.S.S.R. (Fig. 4). In 1921 the latter was pleased to recognize
the new Tannu-Tuvan republic and thus to abandon the former Russian

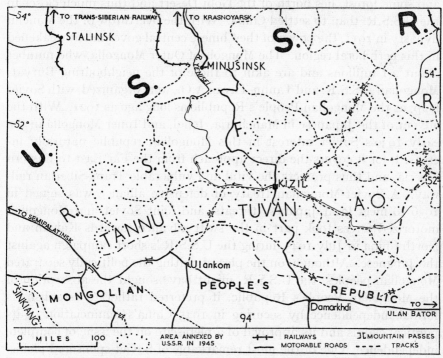

FIG. 4. U.S.S.R. TERRITORIAL GAINS FROM TANNU-TUVAN A.O.

protectorate over this area, titularly part of China. By the Sino-Soviet
treaty of 1945 China abandoned her tenuous claim to Tannu-Tuva, and,
for reasons not wholly clear, the U.S.S.R. preferred to end its nominal
independence. Tannu-Tuva is a mountainous area of about 65,000
square miles, with a Mongol population of only 70,000. It contains the
headwaters of the Yenisei river of Siberia, and is known to hold promise
for gold, other minerals, and hydro-electricity. A road crosses it, thus
linking Western Siberia to Outer Mongolia, so that it is not without
strategical as well as economic significance. Certainly it is geographically
understandable that Tannu-Tuva should have become part of the
U.S.S.R., to which it lies close, for it lies remote from the well-settled
parts of China.

For some 1800 miles from the Altai kray of Western Siberia to the Chita oblast of Eastern Siberia the R.S.F.S.R., the giant member state of the Soviet Union, borders Outer Mongolia. Here, as in Sinkiang and Tannu–Tuva, geography and politics have favoured the U.S.S.R.'s policy (Fig. 5). The better half of Outer Mongolia, made up of grassland and some forest, lies north of the Gobi Desert and thus much closer to the U.S.S.R. than to settled China. With the overthrow of the Manchu dynasty in 1911, the power of the Chinese central government weakened in this peripheral region. The Mongols of Outer Mongolia, who number about 2·1 millions and are akin to those of the neighbouring Buryat-Mongolian A.S.S.R. and Tannu-Tuvan A.O., were organized, with Soviet help, as the Mongolian People's Republic as long ago as 1921. With the advent of the Japanese in Manchuria, Jehol, and Inner Mongolia in the early 1930's Soviet interest in this Mongolian republic naturally increased, for it covers the direct approach from the Far East to Eastern Siberia, and thus protects the vital and vulnerable Trans-Siberian railway. A Soviet-Mongolian treaty of defensive alliance was signed in 1936 to meet local Japanese threats, and joint Soviet and Mongolian motorized forces took part in the swift advance towards Kalgan and North China in July 1945 during the U.S.S.R.'s short campaign against the Japanese. Although, on the plea of uniting the politically separated Mongolian peoples, the U.S.S.R. might have sought the absorption of the Mongolian People's Republic, it preferred rather to establish its formal independence by securing in 1945 China's renunciation of its political claims and its approval of a plebiscite on the issue of complete independence. One of the most remarkable of Soviet-sponsored plebiscites followed in October 1945;[12] it confirmed at one and the same time the nominal independence of the Mongolian People's Republic and its less nominal subjection to the U.S.S.R. The territory and resources of this republic are valuable to the U.S.S.R. economically as well as strategically. It yields wool and hides—Soviet deficiencies; like other parts of High Central Asia, it has mineral wealth. Soviet prospectors have already located deposits of coal, iron, copper, lead, gold, and silver, and coal is being mined in that part of the republic adjacent to Manchuria. The U.S.S.R. has brought into this vast region the capital,

[12] *Cf.* E. D. Carman, *Soviet Imperialism* (Public Affairs Press, Washington, D.C., 1950), p. 94: "Out of the total population of approximately 840,000 some 483,291 of these semi-nomadic people voted and signed their names to the ballots. The final result showed 483,291 votes in favor of independence from China with no invalid ballots and not one voter in favor of continuing even outward allegiance to the Chinese."

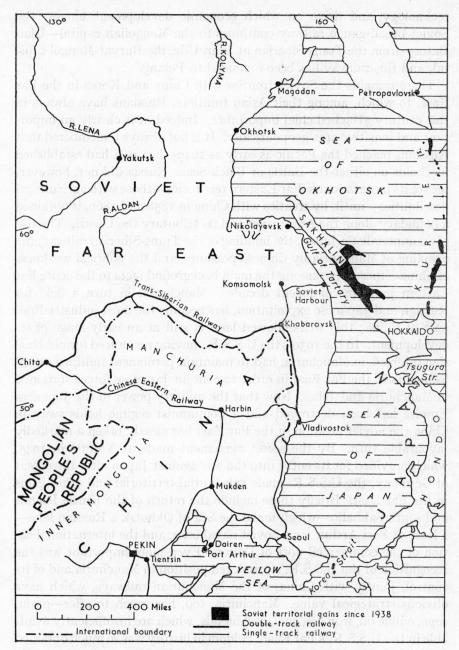

FIG. 5. U.S.S.R. TERRITORIAL GAINS IN THE FAR EAST

technology, and drive on which economic development hinges; the Soviet broad-gauge railway continues to the Mongolian capital—Ulan Bator—from the Trans-Siberian at Ulan Ude, the Buryat-Mongol capital, and this railway has been extended to Peking.

There remains the Soviet frontier with China and Korea in the Far East, to which, among their Asian frontiers, Russians have always in this century attached chief importance. Indeed, it is clearly an important and sensitive area geopolitically. It is not always remembered that Russians reached the Pacific as early as 1649—before it had established footholds on either the Baltic or Black Seas. Russia did not, however, secure its most valuable Far Eastern territories—those with agricultural possibilities—until, by treaties with China in 1858 and 1860, it obtained a boundary along the Amur river and its tributary the Ussuri. The rise of an imperialistic Japan, the building of the Trans-Siberian railway, the peopling of Manchuria by Chinese peasants, and the political weakness of China—these were among the main background facts to the acute Far Eastern problems of recent decades. Manchuria, in turn a field for Russian and Japanese exploitation, has become the most industrialized part of China; this well-endowed land is still at an early stage of its development. In the 1930's the U.S.S.R., having renounced former Russian interests in Manchuria, had to maintain permanent military establishments in the Far East in order to contain Japanese forces stationed in Manchuria and Jehol. Now that the military power of the Japanese Empire has been destroyed and a Communist regime holds sway in China the Soviet position in the Far East has clearly taken a markedly favourable turn. By the secret agreement made at Yalta[13] in 1945, which provided for its entry into the war against Japan after the defeat of Germany, the U.S.S.R. made substantial territorial and other gains in the Far East. Briefly these include the return of the Kurile Islands and south Sakhalin—which make the Sea of Okhotsk a Russian lake— a lease of Port Arthur for a Soviet naval base, and the internationalization of the commercial port of Dairen. Even more important was the recognition of the U.S.S.R.'s privileged position in Manchuria and of its control, jointly with China, of the Manchurian railways, which have obvious strategical value. Manchuria, too, has much to offer—grain, soya, edible oil, iron ore, coal, and metals, which are insufficiently available in the U.S.S.R.'s Far East. Seldom in history was so much obtained for such a little effort—the U.S.S.R.'s six-days' campaign against Japan.

[13] Cmd. 6735 (H.M.S.O., London, 1946).

The alliance of the U.S.S.R. with Communist China in recent years has created a delicate situation with respect to this rich and strategically placed borderland. The U.S.S.R. has deemed it expedient to return some of the industrial plant which it removed from Manchuria as "war booty," and also some of its gains from the Yalta agreement. The Changchun railway was restored to Chinese administration in 1952, and Port Arthur was returned to China in 1955.

'Lebensraum' for Defence?

The Soviet Union in its weakness during the inter-war period did not lack space; now in its strength it enjoys a spacious *Lebensraum* such as Hitler only dreamed of. The aggrandizement of the U.S.S.R., achieved by diplomacy and by war, can in some areas seek justification in terms of history and ethnography, although in others it appears merely the arbitrary decision of the victor. It must be allowed that no State can afford not to establish secure frontiers, and that the best frontiers, which strong States have always desired, have nearly always involved expansion, and never contraction, of their territory. It must be admitted, too, that in High Central Asia, and even in East-Central Europe to a lesser extent, the U.S.S.R. has been able to bring to backward countries those elements of Western material civilization on which the fuller development of their natural resources depends. In its first twenty years of revolutionary life the Soviet Union was a territorially curtailed Russia, confined by the *cordon sanitaire* of a suspicious and hostile world. Suspicion and anxiety still persist now that it has recovered its "Western Lands" and gained much else both in Europe and in Asia. And although it is not territorial expansion alone which justifies the suspicion and anxiety of the outer world, careful note should be taken of it, for the new frontier zones of the U.S.S.R., characterized by their great breadth, provide the thresholds to further Soviet adventure.

CHAPTER XVIII

The Soviet Union and the 'Heartland'*

W. GORDON EAST

The Prognostications of Sir Halford Mackinder

IT is virtually a generation since Sir Halford Mackinder first averred that "Who rules the Heartland commands the World-Island," yet, despite the apparent mutability of international affairs, this proposition raises the most momentous question of our times. Since the Soviet Union now controls almost all of the Heartland of Mackinder's conception, his proposition, translated into contemporary terms, invites, as a matter of no mere academic importance, the inquiry: how strong is the Soviet Union? The successive or concurrent phases of the now ironically named "cold war"—in Greece, Berlin, Malaya, Indo-China, Korea, and in the islands between Formosa and the Chinese mainland—are significantly located, in Mackinder's terminology, beyond the Heartland, and beyond its transitional zones, in the outer coastlands themselves. But it is both necessary and fitting, as Isaiah Bowman emphasized,[1] that in a world of rapid technological progress the geography of territory, since it is ever changing, should be continually revalued. It is important, too, to be ready to discard old geopolitical concepts if, with the passage of time, they can be shown to have lost their validity. While it must be admitted that Mackinder's geopolitical philosophy has not become irrelevant to the international world of to-day, it is nevertheless clear that it contains generalizations and assumptions which scarcely withstand close analysis. And if, as must be assumed, one of the possibilities of the near future is the renewal of war on a grand scale, it is well to re-examine his sweeping prognostications to determine their present worth.

* Thanks are due to the Editor of *Foreign Affairs* (New York) for permission to use in this chapter material published under the title "How Strong is the Heartland?"

[1] Isaiah Bowman, "The Strategy of Territorial Decisions," in *Foreign Affairs*, January 1946.

Prediction, a normal function of the experimental sciences, is inevitably more difficult as it is more unusual in the social sciences. A prediction of a political geographer,[2] originally foreshadowed in 1904, developed in a book in 1919, restated with some modifications in 1943, and republished in 1945, has attracted and must continue to attract wide and serious attention. This is due not merely to the rarity of such oracular utterances, but also to Mackinder's position as elder statesman among British geographers and to the world-wide importance of his prophecy. This he expressed in his *Democratic Ideals and Reality* in 1919 and repeated during the second world war in the following dramatic propositions:[3]

> *Who rules East Europe commands the Heartland.*
> *Who rules the Heartland commands the World-Island.*
> *Who rules the World-Island commands the World.*

What is so remarkable about these affirmations is the extent to which they have been accepted—the geopoliticians of Nazi Germany and Japan certainly tried to apply them—and the fact that they appear largely to have escaped critical examination. This daring and unnerving pronouncement of a single mind, albeit one maturely philosophic, steeped in the study of history and geography and sharpened in the world of affairs, still appears challengingly to define the ultimate and inescapable destiny of that deeply riven political structure of the world to the repair of which so much effort in thought and action is now being applied. The Delphic Oracle, it may be recalled, was often successful in its prophecies, for it had behind it what we should now call a good 'intelligence' organization. Sir Halford Mackinder had a sound knowledge of the world in its spatial and historical aspects upon which to base his prediction. But this was essentially a long-term one, and although it was subjected under his eyes to the partial test of at least a generation, which included two world wars, it belonged, of course, to that kind of prediction not easy to gainsay, since the chance of its being literally and exactly tested was small.

The world which Mackinder studied, as he was quick to see, was, and so it remains, a single 'going concern,' a delicate interlocking mechanism, susceptible to jarring by actions at any point. But this world,

[2] Sir H. J. Mackinder, *Democratic Ideals and Reality* (London, 1919; Pelican edition, 1944); "The Round World and the Winning of the Peace," in *Foreign Affairs*, July 1943, reprinted in *Compass of the World*, edited by H. W. Weigert and V. Stefansson (the Macmillan Co., New York, and Harrap, London, 1946).

[3] Pelican edition, p. 113.

finite though it is in its areal contours of land and sea, is for its human occupants rapidly and ever changing. Indeed, "geography changes as rapidly as ideas and technologies change"; we have continually to make new maps and newly evaluate the geography of land and sea areas. Notably our whole conception of mobility and accessibility, considerations to which Mackinder attached prime importance, have been revolutionized by the internal-combustion engine and the aeroplane. No less, too, have science and technology in their applications to industry and to the art of war wrought changes to which no end can be seen. The advent of new offensive weapons, notably the atom and hydrogen bombs, in themselves make it ever more necessary to re-examine time-honoured assumptions of geopolitical thinking. In the world of international relations, rooted although these are to a physically unchanging planet and conditioned as they are by a rich and perhaps too-well-remembered history, it is surely both unwise and dangerous to accept, as a predetermined end, the prediction that world hegemony must, on certain assumptions, inevitably pass to the rulers of one specified portion of the Earth. It is unwise, because neither History nor Geography, either singly or in combination, given the indeterminate character of social behaviour, warrants predictions of this precise kind. Dangerous, because, as the lawyers might say, even if Mackinder is right, to accept his prophecy as valid would be to stultify all our efforts towards the creation of a freely organized international society.

Let us look more closely at Mackinder's theses and the assumptions upon which they rest before considering their relation to the Soviet Union and their validity in the world of to-day.

The World-Island, East Europe, and the Heartland

The "World-Island" of Mackinder raises no problems: by this effective shorthand he embraced the land-linked continents of Europe, Asia, and Africa and emphasized their relation to the oceans. "East Europe," which he distinguished from "West Europe," also raises little difficulty: it was that broadening zone of Europe, dominated numerically by Slav-speaking peoples and continually a zone of political instability, which extended eastward of the peninsulas of Jutland and Istria as far as the Azov Sea, the Don, and the Volga above Stalingrad. Northward it included Sweden and south-eastward Asia Minor. Berlin and Vienna lay within its western confines. The Heartland is a somewhat more complicated geographical concept, although a remarkable achievement in generalization.

Mackinder conceived the Heartland in two ways—in terms of the area of internal drainage in Eurasia and also in terms of that area of Eurasia which was (under the ruling conditions of the time) inaccessible to sea-power. He regarded the Arctic Ocean east of the White Sea as virtually a physical barrier to human movement and as comparable with the Caspian Sea and Lakes Aral and Baikal, as basins of internal drainage affording no outlets to the routeways of the world oceans. On either basis the Heartland amounted territorially to much the same area. A colossal sub-continental entity, it was separated and almost barred off by transitional zones from the peripheral seaward lands of Europe and Monsoon Asia (see Fig. 2, p. 1021). The seclusion and natural security of the Heartland, it will be recalled, were attributed to facts of physical geography: the Arctic Ocean, frozen almost everywhere the whole year through, to the north, and mountain chains and vast desert plateaux to the south and east. In contrast, on its western flank the Heartland had easy contact with the well-settled lands of European Russia—with 'Russia' in the strict sense. The components of the Heartland, itemized in terms of regional geography, were the Volga Basin, Kazakhstan, Siberia, Central Asia, the Iranian and Tibetan plateaux. Politically the Heartland was largely Russian or Chinese, together with the semi-independent buffer states of Afghanistan and Persia, and Baluchistan.

Now, it might well seem paradoxical, in view of its remoteness, its climatic rigours, its vastness, and its relative emptiness of humanity, that the Heartland should possess marked geopolitical significance. Vast it certainly is—the equivalent of no less than five-ninths of Asia's area or of nearly one-fifth of the whole habitable earth. Virtually empty it was, and, to a lesser extent, still is. Its total population may be estimated to-day at 100 millions—about one-twenty-fifth of the world's population, although probably three times what it was when Mackinder first, and so emphatically, directed attention to it. Clearly his appreciation of the Heartland did not spring from demographic considerations, although he was the first to publicize the concept of 'man-power'[4] as an index of productivity and military power. The Heartland derived

[4] "Man Power as a Measure of National and Imperial Strength," in *The National Review*, 1905.

importance from its sheer extent. What mattered no less was its natural security and its median position in Eurasia. Nature, he argued, had endowed it not only with remarkable defensive strength, but also command of interior lines of overland communication. So, curiously to us, with memories fresh of the fundamental role of economic potential in modern war, Mackinder was little concerned here with either man-power or wealth, actual and potential. Geographical position, physical remoteness from the world oceans, natural security from attack afforded by the frozen Arctic seas and by the mountain-desert-steppe expanses of Central Asia, and space—so much space as virtually to defy the logistics of an enemy approaching from without: all these considerations seem to have entered into Mackinder's evaluation of the Heartland as a citadel for defence and as a secure base for offensive warfare.

That certain important and inescapable geographical realities entered into Mackinder's conception of the geopolitical role of the Heartland is abundantly clear. Whether so much can be deduced from the inert facts of physical geography is no less clearly a matter for discussion. It is true that in history Mackinder found in the recurrent theme of the movements of nomad horsemen from the steppes of Asia into the adjoining lands of Europe, Asia Minor, India, Manchuria, and China evidence of the pressure extended outward from the Heartland into the settled agricultural periphery. Within the southern areas of the Heartland the horse caravan did indeed provide much mobility along the almost endless road of the steppe. So far as it went, the historical record served to support Mackinder's theses in that the Heartland played a largely active and positive part *vis-à-vis* the settled peninsular lands of Asia and Europe. Yet the theme of nomadic migrations from Central Asia has been perhaps overemphasized: there were forceful movements into the Heartland which show at least its penetrability. Witness the penetration of the Russian boatmen, seeking furs, which started the Russification of Siberia. Some of the native peoples of north-west Siberia may have reached there from northern Russia or Finland rather than the Ural-Altai region; and in more recent times Japanese expansion into Manchuria and Inner Mongolia marked a successful approach at least to the threshold of the Heartland.

Let us return to the three assertions which summarize Mackinder's views. With the third, alleging that "Who rules the World-Island commands the World," there might appear little ground for critical comment. Given this hypothetical situation, the Americans and Australasia, even if assumed to be wholly united in an all-out military effort, might well hesitate before continuing so unequal a struggle, seeing their only chances of success in their margin of scientific, technological, and air and naval superiority, in the possible retention of bordering islands of the Old World, and in the inevitably large chinks in the armour of the World-Island empire at those points where the writ of its rulers failed to run. But at the most this surviving eighth of the world's population could hardly hope to stage more than a defensive war.

Similarly, Mackinder's first assertion—"Who rules East Europe commands the Heartland"—appears valid. The events of this century indeed have increasingly confirmed it, although there have been times when its challenge seemed likely—when (in 1918–20) Allied forces, supporting 'White' Russians, invested Russia in Asia and in Europe, but failed to wipe out Bolshevism soon after its seizure of power; and again with the expansion of the Japanese Empire into Korea, Manchuria, and China. For this assertion Mackinder had good geographical and historical warrant. Had the coastlands of the Siberian Arctic been accessible to the seamen of the Great Age of Geographical Discovery, as were those of the White Sea and Hudson Bay, the British or other west Europeans might well have sailed up the Ob or Yenisei rivers, sought Siberian sables direct, set up trading companies there, and made good political claims to Siberian territory. But navigation of the Arctic is a delicate and highly seasonal art, which only the technological achievements of this century have made possible. Control over the Heartland could practically be sought and established only from its marginal lands. It might conceivably have come, as partially it did come at certain periods of history, from South-west Asia—witness the conquests of Alexander the Great and of the Arab Empire. It was much more likely to be achieved from the populous bases of either Eastern Europe or China proper. The main base of the Mongol Empire, which was created in the thirteenth century, was China proper, although its original nucleus of power was the Mongolian steppes: this is an interesting historical instance of a Heartland power, based not on East Europe, but on part of Monsoon Asia, which penetrated but failed to hold much of East Europe, still less the European Coastlands or the World-Island Fig. 2, p. 1021).

The control of the Heartland by the principal State of East Europe, Russia, had at the time of Mackinder's book been long established.

With the emergence of medieval Muscovy in north and central Russia, the eclipse of Mongol ascendancy, and the organization of the Russian State in the sixteenth century, Russians began to penetrate Siberia in search of furs and to make good their control of this vast northern land. The Russian boatmen, using the river-ways and equipped with firearms which the scattered semi-nomadic population could not withstand, made their way through the coniferous forests and later pressed southward to control the wooded and treeless steppes of Siberia and the steppes and semi-deserts of Kazakhstan, which they called, with ethnographical inexactitude, the Kirghiz steppe. In this way Russia won a new pioneer land for colonization, so successfully that to-day Russians make up all but a tiny fraction of the population of Siberia and fully half of that of Kazakhstan. In the Caucasus and in those deserts and oases east of the Caspian and south of Kazakhstan, now known as the U.S.S.R.'s Middle Asia, Russia intervened in search of not so much new lands for colonization as new fields of economic opportunity. This intervention took place in the second half of the nineteenth century by means of military expeditions, difficult to execute because of great stretches of arid country. In Siberia the building of the Trans-Siberian railway (1891–1903) bound Siberia and its Pacific coast in no uncertain way to the Russian homeland in Europe; at the same time it permitted immigration into, and settlement of, Siberia at a new and faster pace, and projected Russia into the theatre of Far Eastern politics.

In Middle Asia, too, as necessary instruments of conquest and consolidation, railways were built, notably the Central Asian line from Orenburg (now Chkalov) to Tashkent and the Trans-Caspian line from Krasnovodsk (on the Caspian) to Merv, Bukhara, and Tashkent with a branch line to Kushka on the Afghan frontier. Quite apart from their internal value for government and trade, these railways had their international aspect. British 'merviness' at the possible threat to India, a threat not so much of direct invasion as of internal disorders such as the Indian Mutiny of 1857, was attributable to the new railways and their possible strategical implications. There can be no doubt that at the time Mackinder was developing his geopolitical ideas, staunch British imperialist as he was and sharer of the current suspicion of Russian designs, the Heartland had become very much a field of Russian control. Not quite completely, because China still held, though loosely, Mongolia, Sinkiang, and Tibet. But China's power was declining, and her hold on these borderlands, beyond the limits of a slender railway system, was weakening, the more so as her attention, too, was engaged on her maritime margins by the rising sun of Japanese imperialism.

East Europe in Control of the Heartland

At the present time the political control of East Europe and the political control of the Heartland by the rulers of East Europe, have been more exactly established than at any other time (see Fig. 2, p. 1021). In the first place, the Soviet Union, whose western boundaries were withdrawn eastward by the Treaty of Brest-Litovsk (1917), has expanded westward in Europe as a result of the Russo-German war of 1941–45, by the incorporation of the Baltic Republics, part of East Prussia, eastern Poland, Ruthenia, Bessarabia and even parts of eastern and southern Finland. Not only that, but its power and influence range farther west over a tier of states—namely, Finland, Poland, Czechoslovakia, Hungary, Romania, Bulgaria, and Albania—beyond which it holds its zone of military occupation in Germany (Fig. 2, p. 1021). With only a few exceptions—Sweden, Asia Minor, and Yugoslavia, with its independent Communism of Marshal Tito—East Europe in Mackinder's sense falls effectively under one rule. Moreover, if we turn to the Heartland as it now appears politically, it is evident that Soviet control has overflowed the U.S.S.R.'s borderlands into the greater part of what remains of the Heartland. The once Chinese-controlled territory of Tannu-Tuva was quietly incorporated into the Soviet Union in 1945. China's titular rights in Outer Mongolia were renounced in 1945, and the nominally independent Mongolian People's Republic is now, less nominally, a Soviet preserve. In Sinkiang, too, Russian influence was preponderant, although it has now to be shared with China's. The Turkestan-Siberian railway, built in the 1930's, opens up a new approach to the historic road through the 'dry strait' of Dzungaria to central China. Further, Russian prestige stands high among the medley of backward peoples of Central Asia, largely as a result of what the U.S.S.R. has achieved in its own Middle Asian republics by irrigation works, hydro-electric undertakings, mining operations, factory-building, and the operation of air services. All that remains of the Heartland which is not clearly under U.S.S.R. control are Tibet, Persia, and Afghanistan.

The first statement of Mackinder's triplet thus describes a situation which at the present time very nearly obtains. The U.S.S.R., as ruler of East Europe, commands nearly all of the Heartland. The word "commands" has, of course, its shades of meaning. If it is interpreted as "controls," it might well be argued that the Soviet "command" falls short in some important areas of the Heartland, markedly in Persia, and also in Afghanistan and Tibet. If "commands" means only "has at disposal" or "has within reach," the Soviet command does not appear so limited, for, as Mackinder foresaw in 1943, the destruction of German and Japanese armed forces leaves the U.S.S.R. the greatest military power in the world. Two of the Heartland areas outside the U.S.S.R., although within its field of special political interest, are, and have long been, geopolitically significant. British foreign policy has always sought the maintenance of the independence of Afghanistan and Persia as buffers essential to the defence of the Indian sub-continent, for the one provides the difficult but main highways towards the Indo-Gangetic plain, while the other conveniently holds the U.S.S.R. back from the Indian Ocean and guards one of the thresholds of South-west Asia. But it might well be argued that the weakening of the U.S.S.R.'s command of the Heartland due to the survival of the states of Persia and Afghanistan is more than counterbalanced by other extraneous sources of strength. For the Soviet Union obtained by the Yalta agreement a specially privileged position in Manchuria, and cannot fail to find satisfaction in the emergence of Communist China, now its ally.

The Economic Stature of the Heartland

The crux of Mackinder's prediction—that part of it which is of greatest immediate moment in international affairs and is most susceptible to criticism—is his proposition that "Who rules the Heartland commands the World-Island."

Now, it must be clearly realized that the events of the last twenty-five years have greatly increased the internal strength of the Heartland as a citadel of power. No less than an economic and social revolution has been effected in that part of the Heartland which falls strictly within the Soviet Union—namely, the Volga-Ural region and Asiatic U.S.S.R. beyond it, which together the Russians conveniently refer to as "The Eastern Regions." In pursuit of an objective set by Lenin, the U.S.S.R. has sought, by means of successive five-year plans, not only to achieve economic self-sufficiency but also to effect a geographical redistribution of the Union's resources by developing its Heartland area. Alike in agriculture, mineral exploitation, industry, and railway and airfield construction, substantial progress had already been effected there before the Germans fell upon Russia in 1941. One effect of enemy occupation of wide areas of European Russia was only to hasten the pace of economic development in the Urals and beyond. And, although the main purpose of the first post-war plan for the years 1946–50 was the restoration of the economy of war-devastated areas, there was no suggestion that the development of the Ural and Asiatic regions was to be discontinued; nor was there in the fifth five-year plan for 1951–55. In short, these areas, as they have received settlers from Russia, extended food production, fostered urban development, exploited coal deposits, and built up heavy metallurgical and armament industries, have acquired manpower and economic potential at a rate and to an extent unforeseen when Mackinder wrote his book. The industrial region of the Southern Urals is the outstandingly major component; Kuzbas, on the basis of its great coal resources, forms another, but smaller, industrial base; while others in Kazakhstan, Central Asia, and Eastern Siberia—notably that west of Irkutsk, which will use coal from the Cheremkhovo field and hydro-electricity from the Angara river—will continue to be developed. The Trans-Siberian Railway has been double-tracked, and duplicated in Western Siberia by the South Siberian Trunk line. The Soviet block of the Heartland is no longer an inert appendage of European Russia: although it is directed from Moscow, it now contains surplus food resources (in Western Siberia and Kazakhstan), sources of power (oil, coal, and hydro-electricity), steel, aluminium, and nitrate plants, and factories for motor and aircraft assembly and for locomotives and wagons. The mining of uranium among other rare metals, mainly in Kirghiz S.S.R., provides a basis for atomic energy applicable on a large scale to irrigation and mining undertakings. Indeed, the vast field for economic development in Siberia, Kazakhstan, and Central Asia could well occupy the major energies of the Soviet Union for at least a generation. Given, however, the ideological content and political posture of Soviet Communism, such a diversion of energy to solely internal projects can hardly be assumed.

It is important to grasp the fact that the geographical distribution of the Soviet economic potential has strikingly changed. Before the Russo-German war began in mid-1941 it would still have been true to emphasize that the main sources of Soviet power, whether measured in terms of man-power or of industrial output, lay preponderantly in European Russia west of the Volga, which accounted for about two-thirds of each. With the destruction and removal of much of the economic capital of western and southern Russia owing to war, the Heartland sprang into a position of pre-eminence, the more so when 1300 large industrial plants, evacuated from the west, were re-established there while the war still raged. The U.S.S.R. has claimed that the Eastern Regions became then "a powerful base of supply of ammunition, weapons, tanks, and aircraft for the Red Army"; that between mid-1941 and mid-1945 their industrial output doubled, while that of war industries increased five- to six-fold. The nature, tempo, and scale of industrial growth in the Heartland are clear enough: without its mounting production the Red Army's successful advance from the winter of 1942–43 onward could not have been achieved, even when full allowance is made for the substantial and well-selected supplies shipped from the United States and the United Kingdom. But whereas in 1940 the Eastern Regions (*i.e.*, virtually the Heartland) had only 34 per cent. of the U.S.S.R.'s industrial production, this proportion was to rise to 51 per cent. in 1950—and the 1946–50 Plan for industry as a whole was overfulfilled. It should not, however, be inferred that the economies of the Heartland and of Russia west of the Volga are not still in many ways interdependent: witness the interregional shipments of Baku oil, of Central Asian cotton, of West Siberian wheat, of East Siberian tin concentrates, and of nickel from Pechenga (Petsamo) and the Taimyr Peninsula. Nor should it be inferred that the population east of the Volga has so increased as to account for as much as half of the Union's total.

The fourth five-year plan (1946–50), for the "rehabilitation and development of the national economy of the U.S.S.R.," aimed not only at repairing the great damage inflicted on the railway system, the mines, and power and industrial installations of European U.S.S.R., but also at effecting by 1950 an increase of 48 per cent. in industrial output above the pre-war 1940 level. Actually an increase of 73 per cent. was achieved —one favourable factor being the increase of man-power by about 15 per cent. as a result of territorial gains. Thus, not only was industrial damage made good, but considerable advances were recorded. One striking aspect of this progress was the contribution made by the Heartland areas to the output of heavy industry. The Volga-Ural oilfield then began (as it continues) to justify much vaunted earlier claims;[5] the

[5] It produced eighteen million tons, 40 per cent. of total output in 1952.

application of modern equipment to the coalfields of Kuzbas (Western Siberia) and Karaganda (Kazakhstan) where the coal is easily accessible near the surface, yielded high dividends; and new iron and steel plants came into production. The following figures (in million metric tons) show that by 1950 the Heartland areas produced nearly half of four major items of energy and metal.

TABLE 1

PRODUCT	EASTERN REGION		WESTERN REGION		TOTALS	
	Pre-war	1950	Pre-war	1950	Pre-war	1950
Coal and lignite .	34	123	94	137	128	260
Crude petroleum .	2	16·7	27	21·3	29	38
Pig iron . .	4·4	8·5	10·6	10·9	15	19·4
Crude steel .	6·2	13·3	12·1	14	18·3	27·3

Source: *United Nations Economic Survey of Europe*, 1950 (Geneva, 1951), p. 41. Note that the pre-war figures for iron and steel are for 1940 and for coal and petroleum for 1937.

The fifth five-year plan (1951–55) set high targets for producer goods, some of which were exceeded, and the greater part of the increase since 1950 might appear to derive from the Eastern Regions. The following table lists the production of some major items for the U.S.S.R. as a whole, including planned figures for 1960.

TABLE 2

The U.S.S.R.'s Production (*million metric tons*)

PRODUCT	1940	1950	1955	1960 (PLAN)	PERCENTAGE INCREASE 1960 PLAN ON 1955 OUTPUT
Coal and lignite .	166	260	390·1	593	50·2
Crude petroleum .	31	37.8	70·7	135	91
Electric power (ooo million kwh) .	48.3	90.3	170·2	320	88
Crude steel .	18.3	27.3	45·2	68·3	51
Copper (ooo tons) .	161	255	—	—	—
Aluminium (ooo tons)	74.4	214 (Plan)	—	—	—

Sources: *United Nations Economic Survey of Europe since the War* (Geneva, 1953), Table 17, pp. 42–43, and *The Times*, January 16, 1956.

These are impressive figures, marking a rate of progress unequalled in any other industrial country. The sixth five-year plan (1956–60) sets out with the objective of overtaking and surpassing the major industrial

nations, not merely in absolute terms but in output per head of population. Fulfilment or overfulfilment of plans for industry as a whole does
not, of course, imply that there are not failures to record (or rather
conceal), and such weak spots are the more serious in a planned economy
which seeks a high degree of self-sufficiency and war preparedness.
Failures had to be admitted in both the fourth and fifth five-year plans
in respect of consumer goods. Failure, too, had to be admitted in
agriculture, despite vigorous improvised efforts to raise production.[6]

Does the Heartland command the World?

Emphasis has been put on the changing scale and distribution of the
U.S.S.R.'s economy, for it is clear, in retrospect, that owing to prejudice
and ignorance its strength was underestimated before the outbreak of
the second world war. Yet it would be equally wrong to exaggerate the
U.S.S.R.'s present might and wrong to conclude that, should another
major war ensue, the dice are as heavily weighted in favour of a combined East Europe and Heartland, as Mackinder asserted. The U.S.S.R.'s
industrial output, viewed comparatively or expressed in terms of output
per head of population, appears less striking. And, economic potential
apart, there are a number of considerations which challenge Mackinder's
belief in the great offensive and defensive strength of the vast area
which now falls under the U.S.S.R.'s control.

The conquest of Polar air by modern long-range aircraft introduces a
factor new since Mackinder first made his ominous pronouncements.
During the honeymoon period of American-Soviet relations late in the
second world war, as Henry A. Wallace has told,[7] useful air routes were
established in high latitudes between Alaska and Asiatic U.S.S.R.
Indeed, the ferrying of American aircraft by this route stimulated the
development of ground facilities on both sides of the Bering Strait, while
the activities of *Dalstroi*, seeking gold, tin, and other metals in the
Kolyma Basin, also focused Soviet attention on north-east Siberia where
it draws close to Alaska, which the Soviet Press described[8] a few years

[6] On the difficulties of the U.S.S.R.'s agricultural situation and the efforts to overcome
them, see V. P. Timoshenko, "Agriculture in the Soviet Spotlight," and C. D. Harris,
"Growing Grain by Decree in Soviet Russia," in *Foreign Affairs*, respectively January
1954 and January 1955. See also N. Jasny, "Soviet Grain Crops and their Distribution,"
in *International Affairs*, October 1952.
[7] *Soviet Asia Mission* (Reynal, New York, 1946).
[8] Cited by the Washington Correspondent of the London *Times*, July 7, 1950.

ago as "Soviet territory in the hands of an alien Power"! Just what are the possibilities of the Arctic regions as a theatre of war—cold desert, in contrast to the hot deserts in which valuable experience has already been gained—is not yet clear. Trans-Polar flights to worthwhile objectives in Eurasia and North America, since the return flight must normally be assumed, might strain the present range of non-stop flight and involve serious navigation difficulties. Aerial strikes and airborne and seaborne landings, using the shorter distances across the Bering Strait, certainly appear practicable—for example, in operations designed to achieve limited objectives or to divert and divide the military energies of adversaries. In any case, the U.S.S.R. can no longer militarily ignore its extended northern seaboard, leaving it safely secured by nature as Mackinder originally assumed; nor, given the vast distances and deficient means of surface transport, could it hope easily to protect all its scattered airfields, populated centres, and ports. Indeed, the general point emerges that, whatever value may attach to vast spaces in military strategy, in air defence they raise very serious difficulties. The task of defending from hostile aircraft the great length of the land and sea frontiers of the U.S.S.R. appears truly formidable, even if the U.S.S.R.'s spaciousness gives much scope for intercepting invading aircraft.

Further, there arises the problem to what extent the use, in a major war, of the newest weapons—notably the atomic and hydrogen bombs —injects a wholly revolutionary factor into geopolitical assessments. It is abundantly clear that dictatorship regimes and aggressor States enjoy the great military advantages of swift action and surprise: they are on the spot because they alone know beyond doubt where it lies. Yet it must be assumed that the Western Powers are well aware that in certain vitally important areas—Western Europe, the Mediterranean, the Middle East, and the Far East—military force must be ready to resist sudden aggression. It is in this context that the existence of the new bombs challenges Mackinder's views, for he assumed that expansion outward from the Heartland and East Europe would leave the victor able to enjoy the fruits of victory and thus to increase his war potential. The possession of atom and hydrogen bombs and long-range aircraft provide a means of depriving an enemy of economic and military assets on a greatly enlarged scale. There are objectives in and around the Heartland, accessible from peripheral bases in Britain, the Middle East, and the Far East, which it would appear necessary, on strictly military ground, to deny to a Heartland enemy. To enumerate some of the most

obvious of such objectives, there are the Baku oilfield, which accounts
for a third of the U.S.S.R.'s oil production, on which depend not only
its military and civil motor transport but also its industries and the food
supplies derived from a highly mechanized agriculture; the Ruhr industrial region, untroubled development of which would add greatly to the
military strength of its possessor; the Romanian oilfield; the heavy
industry of Ukraine and of upper Silesia; and so on in descending order
of importance. Nor, where it is practicable, should the high military
value of a thorough 'scorched earth' policy, as adopted with marked
success by Russians and Chinese, be underrated as a means of neutrali-
zing the economic advantages of enemy invasion.

There are other considerations, too, which the Mackinder thesis does
not take fully into account. The industrial potential of the Soviet Union
and of its East European satellites, despite its growth in recent decades,
does not much exceed that of European N.A.T.O. States, behind which
lies the towering industrial strength of the United States. The possibilities of direct invasion of coastlands under aero-naval cover, in the light
of the second world war, are now more seriously to be reckoned with by
a continental enemy. Is it also to be believed that the advantages of the
U.S.S.R.'s territorial extent and geographical location—now somewhat
impaired by the new skyways and by the increasing range of aircraft—
can more than offset the primacy of the United States in technology and
industrial capacity? And in a geopolitical power equation surely some
increase in military effectiveness must be allowed to the West European
States for the measures which they have already taken towards the
integration of their military and economic resources—measures very
difficult to effect yet practicable thanks to the external danger which
underlines their community of interest.

Expansion from an East European and Heartland base would involve
a war not on one but on many fronts and create a situation for the
U.S.S.R. unlike that which obtained in the second world war, when it
turned against Japan only after the war in Europe had ended. Such
widespread belligerency, despite the U.S.S.R.'s much-vaunted advantage of 'interior lines' of transportation, would impose a severe strain
on its railway system, on which the movement of men and material so
largely depends. Although the mileage of the Soviet railways is about
double that of 1913 and although official policy has sought to reduce
interregional transport by creating well-distributed regional bases of
population and industry as self-sufficient as possible, the fact remains

that the railroads are heavily burdened even in peacetime and would become in wartime, if subjected to hostile air attacks, a highly vulnerable part of the war machine. The railway system would appear most vulnerable at Moscow itself, since it is at once the chief node and the mainspring of a highly centralized economy. In the U.S.S.R. beyond the Urals, where motorable roads are under-developed and often useless during the spring thaw, great importance attaches to the skeletal railway system—there is no real network—in particular to the double-tracked Trans-Siberian and to the remaining single-track lines. It is true that the Red Army is distributed regionally and organized from bases towards the frontiers—from Tbilisi for South Caucasus, Alma Ata for Middle Asia, Irkutsk and Chita for Eastern Siberia, and Khabarovsk for the Far East[9]—but the supply of these widely spaced theatres in wartime would involve long hauls of men and equipment from the major sources of supply. The Soviet Union's interest in the aggression of North Korea, whatever else it included, could not have been unrelated to the vulnerability from air attack of the Trans-Siberian life-lines which diverged from Manchouli towards its Pacific ports of Vladivostok and Port Arthur.

There are other quite different considerations to which Mackinder paid no attention. What is the strength of Soviet *morale*? In a defensive war, it would seem, this can be relied on, for Russian nationalism is a powerful auxiliary to Soviet sentiment: that at least is the lesson of the Russo-German war of 1941–45. But in a war of world conquest, far from the Soviet borders? It is perhaps significant that the start of the U.S.S.R.'s short war against Japan—a war of offence—evoked little popular support in Russia. An aggressive war might at least strain the ideological solidarity of the numerous peoples of the Union, by revealing (what they are seldom told) the actual conditions of life in other countries. The solidarity, too, of Moscow's East European satellites might not prove too reliable: after all, the task of insulating the Soviet Union might prove very unenviable in time of war. Further, Mackinder did not envisage what is practically involved in an attempt to command or control that diversified half of humanity which occupies 'Asiatic' or Monsoon Asia.[10] Surely this is a formidable task from which even ardent

----

[9] John Scott, *Duel for Europe* (Houghton, Boston, 1942), p. 120.

[10] Mackinder's concept of these lands as merely a transitional zone between the Heartland and the Ocean becomes increasingly inadequate, as Indian experts have clearly shown. He saw the monsoon lands of Asia in European perspective and in terms of "a mariner's geography." To regard them primarily as hinterlands to seaports, and thus susceptible to sea-power, is a gross simplification in view of their age-long civilization

political planners might shy—unless, by methods of ideological propaganda and long-range infiltration, they had already imposed their will on these peoples by first conquering their minds. And, lastly, did Mackinder sufficiently appreciate that Africa, though part of the World-Island, since it is insular and almost wholly dependent politically on western Europe, might well prove defensible even against continental power in Europe and South-west Asia?

German authorities on the art of war have continually emphasized the "invulnerable hugeness of Russia" in the belief that space strengthens defensive as it weakens offensive warfare. But this is a traditional belief that does not reckon with the mobility of modern mechanized warfare. It has already been suggested that space can be a major difficulty in air defence, and in military campaigns long lines of communication with bases of supply can prove embarrassments. Certainly the interior lines of the East Europe Heartland area would be greatly stretched in a war of expansion and expose themselves to possible flank attack by air, land, or sea forces deployed from the periphery. Such vantage points are easily seen on a globe: the Baltic and Black Sea entries; the head of the Adriatic—hence Soviet interest in Albania, which commands the seaward approach; Greece; Turkey; Iraq; Persia; Afghanistan; Pakistan; and Japan.

Even though Mackinder's second assertion, that "Who rules the Heartland commands the World-Island," can no longer be sustained, it is scarcely necessary to insist that his geopolitical thinking is still relevant to the task of winning the peace. A strong believer in the British Empire and distrustful of Russian designs in Asia, he called attention to the danger of overweening continental power, noting in particular the defensive strength and strategical possibilities of a linked East Europe and Heartland. It is refreshing and perhaps even surprising to recall that the weight of Russian power has been thrown with effect against attempts at world domination in the three major wars of the last hundred and forty years: against Napoleon, against the German Empire, and against Nazi Germany and Japan. In the last-named struggle the contribution of the Heartland—its foodstuffs, oil, coal, steel, and armaments—were indispensable to victory. Should another world war break out, Sir Halford Mackinder's predictions will be more literally tested than ever before. What have been called here his 'predictions,' he

---

and reborn national consciousness. The "monsoon coastlands," the most populous segment of the world, clearly now assume an independent status in geopolitics. See K. M. Panikkar, *Geographical Factors in Indian History* (Bharatiya Vidya Bhavan, Bombay, 1955).

would have urged rather as 'warnings.' That the Western Powers have heeded these warnings seems clear enough when the geographical aspect of recent foreign policies is studied. There remain areas—great and small—outside and even within the Heartland, the retention of which permitted the containment of the U.S.S.R. during the sultry spell of 'cold war,' and loss of which might well upset the existing uneasy

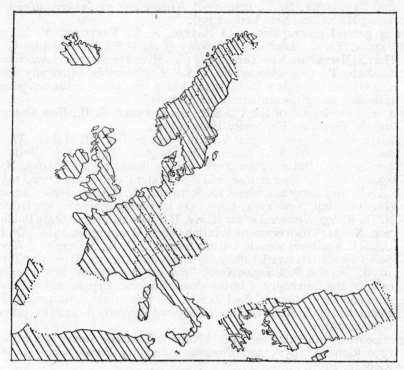

FIG. 1. SIXTEEN STATES WHICH RECEIVED MARSHALL AID

balance. These areas, accessible to sea power, are largely subsumed under three heads: the Marshall Aid States on the western and southern flanks of Europe (Fig. 1); the Middle East, with its rich oilfields and world crossways; and Japan, its role now recast as an advanced base from which to resist aggression. Consideration of the Heartland concept in relation to the Soviet Union and to the geopolitical realities of the present time, while it takes note of certain geographical advantages of the U.S.S.R. in warfare, does not justify Mackinder's implied prediction about the future mastery of the world.

Q

FURTHER READING

On the physical and vegetation geography, see BERG, L. S., *The Natural Regions of the U.S.S.R.* (translation; Macmillan, New York, 1950).

On the historical background, see SUMNER, B. H., *Survey of Russian History* (Duckworth, London, 1944); KERNER, R. J., *Russia's Urge to the Sea* (University of California Press and Cambridge University Press, 1942); and FLORINSKY, M. T., *Russia—A History and an Interpretation* (two vols.; Macmillan, New York, 1953).

Among general geographies, note BALZAC, S. S., VASYUTIN, V. F., and FEIGIN, YA. G., *Economic Geography of the U.S.S.R.*, edited by C. D. Harris (Macmillan, New York, 1949) (this gives a pre-war Soviet account); SHABAD, T., *Geography of the U.S.S.R.* (Columbia University Press and Oxford University Press, 1951), which treats each of the component republics and gives statistical information.

For a brief assessment of the U.S.S.R., see CRESSEY, G. B., *How Strong is Russia?* (Syracuse University Press, 1954).

On Asiatic U.S.S.R., see Chapter V (with select reading list) of EAST, W. G., and SPATE, O. H. K. (editors), *The Changing Map of Asia* (Methuen, London, and Dutton, New York; third edition, 1956); BELOFF, MAX, *Soviet Policy in the Far East, 1944–51* (Oxford University Press, 1953).

On U.S.S.R.'s economy as a whole, see SCHWARZ, H., *Russia's Soviet Economy* (Prentice-Hall, New York, 1950). On its energy resources, see GUYOL, N. B., *Energy Resources of the World*, U.S. Department of State Publication, No. 3428 (Government Printing Office, Washington, 1949). On the U.S.S.R.'s mineral wealth, consult SHIMKIN, D. B., *Minerals: A Key to Soviet Power* (Harvard University Press and Oxford University Press, 1953). See also *Bulletins on Soviet Economic Development*, issued periodically by the University of Birmingham, England, Department of Economics and Institutions of the U.S.S.R. On population, LORIMER, F., *The Population of the Soviet Union: History and Prospects* (League of Nations, Geneva, 1946).

For some recent statistics, see United Nations *Economic Survey of Europe in 1950* (Geneva, 1951), and *Economic Survey of Europe since the War* (Geneva, 1953).

On the Northern Sea Route, see T. Armstrong, *The Northern Sea Route* (Cambridge University Press, 1952).

Mention should be made of the valuable *Great Soviet World Atlas* (two vols.; Moscow, 1937–39), which is now somewhat out of date, and *Atlas of the World* (Moscow, 1954). A small Russian atlas is *Geographical Atlas of the U.S.S.R. for the Seventh and Eighth Classes of Middle Schools* (Moscow, 1951), 75 pages. In English a useful small atlas is *Soviet Union in Maps*, edited by G. Goodall (Philip, London; second edition, 1954).

CHAPTER XIX

The Resurgence of Asia

O. H. K. SPATE

"T HE struggle between Europe and Asia is the binding thread of
history; the trade between Europe and Asia is the foundation
of commerce; the thought of Asia is the basis of all European
religions."[1] These words were written over fifty years ago, when European power in Asia was near its height—four years before the Russo-
Japanese War heralded the resurgence of Asia. Even then, when the
Occident was virtually untouched by doubts of its own all-competence,
an observer of insight (but by no means a romantic orientalizer) could
ascribe so great a role to the greatest of continents. If for "Europe" we
read "the West" (whether in its older cultural sense or, in that now current politically, as antithetic to the Soviet world), and so take in
America, his words have to-day a force even more compelling. For we
are in the presence of one of the major revolutions of political geography:
the rise of Asian nationalism.

The resurgence of Asia, proclaimed in 1904–5, had, indeed, to await a
greater war—the Pacific War of 1941–45—before European domination
was seriously shaken; but within five years of its close the two greatest
of the classical imperialisms, those of the British and the Dutch,
existed, if at all, as shadows of their old selves.[2] As a consequence of this
struggle one Asian empire also had been overthrown, that of Japan; but
not before it had undermined the imposing structure of European rule.
It is, indeed, arguable that the West has begun its *revanche* with American intervention in the Far East; nevertheless, the attainment of independence in most of Southern Asia, and the new value to be attached,
since the Korean War, to Chinese military power, constitute a change in
political geography comparable with such world-events as the expansion
of Hellenism under Alexander the Great, the success of the wars of

[1] Meredith Townsend, *Asia and Europe* (Constable, London, 1901), p. ix.
[2] See the series of maps of the expansion and regression of European power in Asia
on pp. 22–23 of W. G. East and O. H. K. Spate (eds.): *The Changing Map of Asia*
(third edition; Methuen, London, and Dutton, New York, 1956).

independence in most of British and all of Latin America, or the victory
of the Bolsheviks in 1917.

The Continent of Asia

The vastness of Asia is a commonplace: its 18,000,000 square miles
comprise one-third of the land surface of the earth. No other continent
extends from within the Arctic Circle to the equator (or, with Indo-

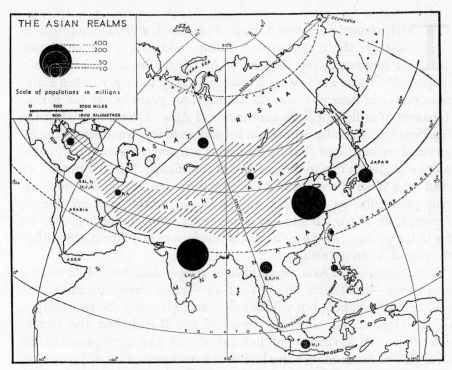

FIG. 1. THE ASIAN REALMS

Shading indicates plateau core; initials indicate States grouped together.

nesia, to 10 degrees beyond it). In longitude it extends for 165 degrees,
not far short of half-way round the globe. Bering Strait to Bab-el-
Mandeb is 6500 miles, the shorter diagonal from the Kara Sea to Singapore 5250; the heart of the continent is at least 2000 miles from the sea
in any direction (Fig. 1). The whole of continental North America could
lie comfortably on the main mass of Asia, barely trespassing on the three

southern peninsulas, which together are as large as Europe (including Russia) or Australia.

It is small wonder, then, that Mackinder seized on this fact of overwhelming bulk, with its corollaries of defence in depth and relative invulnerability, as the cornerstone of his concept of the World-Island and its Heartland.[3] Yet the immense range of latitude and longitude, which gives to Asia some representative of almost every physical environment found on the globe, imposes its own limitations. A very large proportion of the continent is humanly speaking negative, because of aridity or altitude (or both) in the interior, of low temperatures in the north, or (less decisively) of excessive humidity in the south-eastern archipelagos.

Environmental and Cultural Realms

About 7000 miles of the Asian coastline, nearly a fifth of the whole, fronts the Arctic: the northern seas are penetrated only by specially organized Soviet fleets, and that for but a few weeks of the short summer. Along these Arctic shores stretch immense and dreary tundras, backed by a greater immensity of coniferous forest, the taïga. South again a wedge of parkland and fairly well-watered steppe reaches out from European Russia across the great swampy plain of the Ob to about 85° E., around Barnaul; eastward hilly or mountainous forest country, yet not on the whole so unfavourable to man as the boreal taïga to the north, extends to the Manchurian steppes. This corridor, followed by the Trans-Siberian Railway, is the spinal cord of the U.S.S.R. in Asia; at its base in the west are the great metallurgical centres of the Urals, on the indeterminate marches of Europe and Asia, linked with the rapidly rising industrial centres of the Kuzbas on the Ob headwaters and of Karaganda in Kazakhstan.[4] Here, in the not distant future, will probably be the heart of the Heartland.

The southern borders of Asiatic U.S.S.R. (the term Soviet Asia must now have a less restricted use) overlap into the core of the continent, where the aridity and the extreme temperature ranges normally associated with such massive continentality are accentuated by the layout and the massive scale of the relief. From Turkey through Persia and High Asia to the borders of Manchuria, the dominant land-form character is basin-and-range topography on an enormous scale, culminating in the

[3] See Chapter XVIII.   [4] Cf. pp. 394–397 and 440–442.

lofty plateau of Tibet—nearly 500,000 square miles and mostly at over 14,000 feet above sea-level. Altogether this great belt of plateaux, flanked by the loftiest mountains of the world, is about 5000 miles long, and at its widest 2000 miles across (Fig. 1). Although seven of the twelve rivers of the world which exceed 2500 miles in length are in Asia, nowhere is there a watershed between Arctic and Indian Ocean streams; instead there are something like 5,000,000 square miles of inland drainage basins, lying at all altitudes from 16,000 feet above sea-level to 1000 feet below it.

This core of Asia, savage as it is in its ruggedness and aridity, is not without its oases. But in essence it forms a gigantic barrier alike to air-masses and to airways. East and south of it lies Monsoon Asia, "Asiatic Asia," where live over ten-elevenths of the people of the continent.

Two of the most fundamental environmental factors in the life of Monsoon Asia are the concentration of over 80 per cent. of the rainfall in the four or five warmer months, and the existence of great rivers which have built up large deltas and interior alluvial lowlands. The validity of the rainfall generalization is hardly offset by the anomalous regimes of such areas as the eastern littoral of Madras or the western shorelands of Japan. A more important exception is the definitely equatorial regime of Indonesia, but since the point of the tropical monsoon rhythm, humanly considered, is simply the coincidence of the warm season with the wet, the continuance throughout the year of both warmth and wetness rather accentuates than attenuates the agronomic characteristics associated with the monsoon lands proper.

The alluvial lowlands are, of course, a mere fraction of the total area, even in India and China. But in them lives the bulk of the people, in them were developed the characteristic techniques of irrigation and the traditions of society both rural and urban, and in them were the seats of empire, whether the rulers were indigenous or alien. In short, they set the tone, as it were, for the whole area: to give a simple example, although the Archæan portion of the Deccan is in general better suited to millets than to rice, and although such millets as jowar and ragi are more nutritious than rice and are grown over a larger area, yet their use is left to the poor and to the inmates of the gaols: the rich and the respectable eat rice, the staple crop of the deltas. This cultural disregard of dietetic values is, indeed, a very general phenomenon—the rice-barley relation in Japan is another case in point; but its significance in our context is as an illustration of the cultural dominance of the alluvial areas.

Though there are thus certain common patterns of environment and economy through most of Monsoon Asia, the range of diversity between West Pakistan and Manchuria is obviously great. There is first of all the distinction between tropical, sub-tropical, and temperate monsoon lands—between the rice and coconut of the Indian deltas and South-east Asia, the rice and silk of the Yangtse Basin, the wheat and millet and cotton of the North China Plain. Then, given the large areas and the hilly or mountainous relief of much of the monsoon lands, there are very large differences in the amount of rain: from under twenty-five inches a year in the Indo-Gangetic divide, in the lee of the Western Ghats, and in the North China Plain, to over 400 on the slopes of the Assam Plateau, fronting the moist air-masses sweeping up from the Bay of Bengal. Differences in the length of the dry season and the number of frost-free nights affect the possibilities of double-cropping and the choice of crops. The scope for irrigation and the techniques available or necessary for it differ widely; and so also with the amount and nature of forest cover, with soils, and with the availability and use of natural fibres.

To these variations (over-simplified in these few lines) we must add variations in the historical backgrounds and cultural affiliations of the populations of Monsoon Asia, in the distribution of industrial resources, in maritime contacts, in the nature, degree, and duration of contacts with Western Europe, Russia, and America. It is clear that Monsoon Asia is a world (or two or three worlds) in itself. Yet the similarities of seasonal work-rhythms, of techniques in the use of water and soil, of the peasant ethos and of agrarian poverty, provide an ever-persistent ground bass, whatever the variations on the theme.

This, then, is "Asiatic Asia": our stock associational response to the word "Asia" is most commonly a conflation of India and the Far East. In comparison, Asiatic U.S.S.R. is essentially "Eurasia"; not only is it "technologically a European extrusion into Asia," but it is the only area in the continent where European farmers have effectively occupied the soil, and European traditions and techniques (in their Russian variants) have here a history about as long as that of British and Dutch establishments on the coasts of southern Asia.[5]

[5] *Cf.* the dates on Fig. 2. Figs. 2–4 may profitably be compared with the map of "Civilisations en Asie" in P. Gourou, *L'Asie* (Hachette, Paris, 1953) Carte 2, and that of "Les grands foyers de civilisation de l'Asie" in M. Sorre, *Les Fondements de la Géographie humaine*, T. III (Colin, Paris, 1952), Fig. 32.

There remain two areas of the highest geopolitical significance. As we have seen, the major realms of Asiatic U.S.S.R. and of Monsoon Asia are essentially walled off from each other by the mighty ramparts of the plateau core. High Asia does, it is true, descend to the Siberian plains by a series of steps, in contrast to the single and stupendously abrupt fall on the Indian face; but, despite considerable encroachments on the northern glacis, this historic no man's land was only firmly gained for the Soviet world by the flank approach from China into Tibet. But both in the east and the west the barrier is to some extent broken into, by the lower plateaux of Mongolia and by the geocols of South-west Asia—the saddle between Turkestan and the Punjab, and the portages linking the Mediterranean with the Red Sea and the Persian Gulf. It is in these areas, Mongolia-Manchuria and "the Land of the Five Seas," that Asiatic U.S.S.R. has its most direct contact with the Western bloc. Of these two areas, South-west Asia has been of incomparably more direct importance in Euro-Asiatic relations.

The south-western extremities of Asia are not exempted from continentality by the fact that they are extremities; for south-west again lies the massive bulk of Africa. It is true that, north of Suez, South-west Asia lies in Mediterranean latitudes, accessible in the winter to westerly cyclonic influences; but it is 2000 miles from the open Atlantic to the Levant, and both here and in the Anatolian plateau to the north the highest relief is close to the coast, so that effective penetration by humid air-masses is rather limited, except across the low Syrian saddle. In the extreme south-west the mountains of Yemen are exposed to monsoonal influences from the Indian Ocean, but the area involved is small and isolated. The mass of the Arabian platform and the mountain-ringed basins of the Anatolian and Iranian plateaux are thus desert or semi-desert environments, and agriculture on any scale clings to the coasts, a few oases, and an arc ("the Fertile Crescent") from Jordan through Syria to the Euphrates, beyond which the alluvial plain of Iraq may be considered a huge oasis largely dependent on elaborate irrigation.

South-west Asia is the classic land of pastoral nomadism and caravan trading, the home of the purest and most intense Islamic culture. Lying as it does across the ancient highways between the foyers of civilization and commerce in the Mediterranean and India (and beyond to China), the region has been at once a bridge and a barrier, the marchland between Europe and Asia, swept by ever-recurrent waves of conquest both military and cultural. It is perhaps not surprising that here, where the universalist empires of the past most often clashed, where nomadic culture reached perhaps its highest pitch, and where urban traditions are most ancient, there arose three great faiths—Judaism, Christianity, Islam. All three are still of major importance in the tangled political geography of the Levant.

The fabric of a peasant society is tough enough to survive (even if on a low level of vitality) the shifts of political fortunes ruinous to many once-great empires and trading cities of this region; and so pronounced are the locational values of such sites as Damascus, Beirut, Baghdad, Istanbul, that they have retained urban identity for longer spans than any other cities in the world. Nevertheless, beyond merely local disaster and decadence, the area as a whole suffered at least one long-term eclipse, after it had been physically bypassed by the Portuguese opening of the Cape route in 1498. The caravan cities did not die —the local needs of the Orient kept them in being—but South-west Asia did not recover the world-importance then lost until the revival of interest in the Levantine portages around 1840. This revival was largely due to the need for more rapid communication between Britain and India and to the possibility of meeting this need by steam navigation combined with railways from the Mediterranean to the Red Sea and the Persian Gulf. The opening of the Suez Canal (ironically opposed by the major beneficiary, Britain) in 1869 provided a more radical solution of this problem. But there was still ample scope for the manœuvres of Britain, obsessed with the security of her 'life-line'; of France, anxious to assert her ancient cultural and political influence in the Levant; of Russia, perennially concerned with the problems of outlets either by the Turkish Straits or across Persia; of imperial Germany, ardent in the search for markets and allies. To-day the ancient highways are still followed, in their essential alignments, by airways; and the final, and most inflammable, ingredient in this witches' cauldron is oil. . . .

The upshot of this long and agitated history has been an extreme disunity, not only nationally and ideologically, but socially. Not only is South-west Asia riddled by the sectarian strife of its three great religions (and their numerous schismatics), but the gulf between urban élites and peasant masses is nowhere deeper, the contrast between degrading luxury and degrading poverty is nowhere more blatant, and nowhere are the forms of modern democracy more perverted to the purposes of corrupt oligarchies. To its weak and technologically retarded States its unrivalled strategic position and the treasures of its oilfields are at best

Q*

the raw material for bargain and blackmail. Strategy—the desire to contain the U.S.S.R.—and oil concession have led the United States to join the traditional rivals, so that South-west Asia is now once more an area of contention between East and West, in the revised political significance of the term. And the Arab States must cope with the intrusion of an entirely new and potentially revolutionary polity in Israel.[6]

In contrast to South-west Asia, the north-eastern flank of the central barrier (the Mongolian-Manchurian region), though always important in Asian history, is young as an area of direct critical significance in world affairs. To some extent, indeed, this is an expression of unfamiliarity and remoteness from European-centred history rather than of the facts; for the success or failure of Chinese dynasties in holding the steppe gateway, so grandly symbolized by the Great Wall, had an important influence on the movements of the steppe peoples, and so ultimately on the fortunes of civilization and barbarism on the Euro-Asiatic march-lands north of the Black Sea: a Chinese disaster might mean that the kings and bishops of medieval Central Europe could sleep better o' nights. But this was indirect; the rise of the region to an important geopolitical role had to wait until the opening of the Pacific as a theatre of geostrategy.

The curtain-raisers were two naval battles, the Japanese defeat of the Chinese at the Yalu river (1894), and the opening action of the Spanish-American War, the destruction of the Spanish fleet in Manila Bay (1898). These dramatically signalized the advent of the two most purely Pacific[7] world Powers. The decay of the Manchu dynasty in China left Manchuria open to the conflict between the old expansionism of Russia and the active new imperialism of Japan; the upshot of the Pacific phase of the second world war was to instal the United States on the ground in place of Japan, and so, in conjunction with the triumph of Communism in China itself, to bring the Soviet and the capitalist worlds into direct and explosive contact along the 38th Parallel.

---

[6] Turkey may fairly be exempted from the more damnatory implications of this paragraph.

[7] Japan, of course, was the only Power strictly confined to the Pacific, but strictly Pacific interests have been more vital to the United States than to any of the European Powers.

The Peoples of Asia: Numbers and Distribution

Within the borders of Asia live over 1,450,000,000 people, well over half the population of the world. In earlier times the proportion was probably still greater; for centuries India and China nourished highly organized societies, dominantly agrarian but with large urban elements, which maintained over large areas a density of population probably much greater than that of medieval Europe, apart from such few favoured pockets as Flanders and northern Italy. With the great increase of population which accompanied the Industrial Revolution in Europe, and the transplanting of its techniques to North America, the Asian preponderance was markedly lessened. (*Cf.* Table 3, p. 16.)

But in the last six or seven decades complex social causes have led to a very pronounced slackening of the rate of increase in North America and most European countries; on the other hand, some of the most densely populated countries of Asia, such as India, Java, and Japan, had enjoyed until 1941 nearly a century of unwonted internal peace, together with considerable economic development and the beginnings at least of modern preventive medicine; this last factor has applied more widely since the end of the second world war. Hence, while Asian death-rates (especially those of infants) remain very high, they have fallen more decidedly than have birth-rates, where, indeed, the latter have declined at all (*cf.* Table 1). The Asian fraction of the world's population is thus increasing, and on present trends would exceed 60 per cent. by the last decade of our century.

Internally there are of course great inequalities in the distribution of this vast population, inequalities probably more striking than those of any other continent. Java and fairly large areas in the great deltas of India and China have densities, preponderantly *rural*, around 1000 to the square mile, and some purely agricultural tracts reach 2000 or even 3000. Japan, with an average density of over 500, has nearly 3600 people to each square mile of cultivated ground. On the other hand, immense areas are barely inhabited: the vast stretches of tundra and taïga, the wind-swept wastes of Tibet, the burning deserts of the Tarim Basin. And in Arabia the 300,000 square miles of the Rub-'al Khali form emphatically "the Empty Quarter."

No fewer than a thousand million people live in five monsoon countries: India, Pakistan, China, Japan, and Java. These have a total area

TABLE 1

Some Comparative Vital Statistics

B = crude birth rates o/oo; D = crude death rates o/oo; I.M. = infant mortality (live births under 1 year) o/oo.
Averages for years given, but note that Indian figures are for 1921–24 (B, D, I.M.), 1930–34, and 1946–50 (B and D) or 1945–49 (I.M.).

COUNTRY	1920–24			1930–34			1947–51			PERCENTAGE CHANGE 1920–24 TO 1947–51		
	B	D	I.M.	B	D	I.M.	B	D	I.M.	B	D	I.M.
U.S.A.	22·8	12·0	76·7	17·6	11·0	60·4	24·4	9·8	30·7	+ 7·0	− 18·3	− 60·0
U.K.	21·7	12·5	79·2	15·8	12·2	65·5	17·6	11·9	35·2	− 19·0	− 4·8	− 55·5
France	19·9	17·3	97·1	17·2	13·6	80·1	20·6	13·0	57·0	+ 3·4	− 24·9	− 41·3
Netherlands	26·7	11·0	74·4	21·7	9·0	46·7	24·4	7·7	28·3	− 8·6	− 30·0	− 62·0
Australia	24·4	9·8	61·0	17·6	8·8	42·9	23·3	9·7	26·3	+ 4·5	− 1·0	− 56·9
India	33·0	26·8	184·2	34·0	23·7	176·2	26·5	17·5	137·2	− 22·7	− 34·7	− 25·5
Japan	35·0	23·0	164·7	31·8	18·1	124·2	30·9	11·8	63·6	− 12·7	− 48·7	− 61·4
Ceylon	38·5	28·9	192·3	37·8	22·4	165·1	39·5	12·9	90·0	+ 2·6	− 55·3	− 53·2

Source: *United Nations Demographic Yearbook*, 1952, Tables 10, 16, 19.

(excluding Mongolia, Sinkiang, and Tibet) of 3,200,000 square miles; all of them, except perhaps Java, contain large proportions of mountain or desert. Java has a very high proportion of intensively cultivated land, from much of which two crops of rice can be raised in one year; Japan's arable land is limited to about 16 per cent. of its area, but this is highly productive, and Japanese industrial development, unique in Asia, supports half of the 88,000,000 people. Apart from these, the great concentrations are in the larger alluvial plains and deltas: some 165,000,000 souls in the North China Plain, the loess lands, and Manchuria; 120,000,000 or more in the Yangtse Basins; 65,000,000 in the Bengal Delta, and some 140,000,000 more in the Indo-Gangetic plains.

Against such figures, the 1,200,000 square miles of Arabia support at most 14,000,000 people, about seventeen to the square mile; Tibet and Sinkiang have perhaps 8,000,000 on a similar area to Arabia; the 50,000,000 of Asiatic Russia are thin-spread over about 6,350,000 square miles: indeed, the Russian Far East is very comparable to Australia, with perhaps three persons to each of more than a million square miles. In the more arid lands of Soviet Central Asia and South-west Asia population concentrates in discontinuous lines and pockets of oasis irrigation, with notable thickenings in the greater oasis-lands of Turkestan (say, 10,000,000 people) and of the Tigris-Euphrates valley, which holds the bulk of Iraq's 5,000,000. At the other climatic extreme the equatorial rain forest is also relatively empty: while the 50,000 square miles of Java carry 50,000,000 people, the rest of Indonesia has less than half Java's population on an area fourteen times as large.

These great differences in density pose acute problems of *Lebensraum*. Already in Burma and Thailand, which for monsoon lands are thinly peopled (seventy to ninety to the square mile), Indian and Chinese immigrants form substantial minorities, holding a disproportionate share of commercial activity, and thus presenting very difficult social, economic, and political problems. There is also the very striking contrast between Monsoon Asia, with not far off half the world's people on one-fourteenth of its land, and tropical Australia, where the Northern Territory has over 500,000 square miles (one-third of which area receives over twenty inches annual rainfall), but only about 16,000 white inhabitants and about the same number of aborigines. Yet, as the increment for India and Pakistan alone has averaged about 5,000,000 a year for at least twenty years, it does not seem that migration on the most generous scale imaginable could offer real relief: it is simply not possible to pour the ocean of Asian increases into the pint-pot of Australian capacity.[8]

To most of Monsoon Asia it seems fair to apply the much-abused term over-population, if not absolute (and absolute it may be in some areas), at least relative to current techniques. The solution must be sought in internal development, agrarian as much as industrial; and also in limitation of births, to break the vicious cycle by which, hitherto, increases in food-production have been matched or out-matched by increases in the number of mouths to feed.

The Resources of Asia : Distribution and Development

Rich and varied as the resources of a continent so vast and so diverse must be, it may be questioned whether even their totality is adequate for industrial development on a scale commensurate with Asian populations and ambitions; and they are distributed with extreme inequality.[9]

Since the great majority of the people of Asia are agriculturists, and, moreover, largely subsistence agriculturists, this inequality is less marked in the cardinal article of food. Less marked internally, that is, since the nutritional intakes of nearly all the Asian peoples are probably no more than a quarter to a third of those of the peoples of North-western Europe, Anglo-America, or Australia. In most Asian countries the daily average calorie intake per person is probably not more than 2000 (for many millions it is less) against a desirable 2600 or more.

Even this low figure, however, is only attained by the adoption of badly unbalanced diets, in which fats and proteins are grossly deficient and carbohydrates excessively dominant: in Monsoon Asia poverty, if not religion, confines whole peoples to a diet not only vegetarian but in effect almost exclusively cereal. Since acre for acre the calorific output of rice-growing is about four times that of dairying and twenty times that of grazing for meat, Monsoon Asia can support populations which may be called inflated, their vast numbers being offset by the devaluation of the individual considered as a unit of energy.[10] Moreover, the

---

[8] *Cf.* Chapter XLIII.

[9] An excellent short survey, conveniently arranged by major regions, is given by H. A. Meyerhoff, in R. Linton (ed.), *Most of the World* (Columbia University Press, New York, and Oxford University Press, 1949), pp. 21–70.

[10] *Cf.* P. Gourou, *op. cit.*, chapter V ("Alimentation et géographie humaine"); H. H. Bennett: "International Contrasts in Food Consumption," in *Geogr. Rev.*, vol. xxxi (1941), pp. 365–376; W. S. and E. S. Woytinsky: *World Population and Production* (Twentieth-century Fund, New York, 1953), pp. 297–306.

toll of disease is immensely intensified by malnutrition. It is clear that for all of south and east Asia agrarian reconstruction is the primary problem.

In such reconstruction a great part must certainly be played by industrialization. It is very unlikely, however, that industrialization in itself will be able greatly to ease the pressure of population on the land by direct employment of labour surplus to rural needs: the absolute numbers involved are too great, and perhaps would only be made greater by agricultural mechanization. The greatest value of industrialization will probably lie in its contributions to increased agricultural productivity—by providing constructional material for irrigation and other 'developmental' works, some types of agricultural machinery (e.g., for new clearance, where that is possible), and (probably most important) artificial fertilizers. But the scope for industrialization is probably more limited than most Asian publicists would like to admit.

Coal and iron ore are badly localized. In Asiatic U.S.S.R. there has been much large-scale development—for instance, the Ural-Kuzbas-Karaganda linkage and the production of steel at Stalinsk, in the Kuzbas. This has involved accepting costs (especially in transport) which would probably be considered uneconomic in the capitalist world; but there is a strategic pay-off to be put on the credit side, in the form of the dispersal of industry into the innermost Heartland. China has vast reserves of coal, but with relatively small and badly scattered deposits of iron and base metal ores. Japanese industry, even when it had access to Manchurian coal, iron, and oil-shales, had to rely heavily on stockpiling and scraping together raw materials from all over the Far East. Reserves of first-class iron ores in India are immense, and the country is well-found in refractories and alloy metals (especially manganese); but coal reserves and output (especially of coking coal) are very strongly localized on the Bihar-Bengal border—fortunately a highly mineralized area—and local supplies of most non-ferrous metals are rather deficient.

All these countries, except Asiatic U.S.S.R., have but very small outputs of oil, and very little prospect of more; nor is the production of Sumatra and Burma really very large. On the other hand, the countries of South-west Asia collectively have now dislodged Venezuela from second place among the world's oil-producing regions, and their reserves are enormous; but they are completely lacking not only in the technology with which to exploit this wealth, but in the basic materials with which to construct this technology—at least, with the limited exception of Turkey. Capital, equipment, and technicians must all come from outside, whence arise political problems of the first order, exemplified by the Anglo-Persian oil dispute.

A further factor of disbalance, of far more than local import, is found in the quasi-monopolistic position of Malaya, Indonesia, and Ceylon in natural rubber, and the heavy concentration of tin in the first two countries. India also has a quasi-monopolistic share of world mica production, and apart from the considerable uranium resources of Russian Central Asia, the major known source of atomic minerals in the continent is in the thorium-loaded beachsands of Southern India.

In other raw materials the inequalities are not so marked, or at least they could be to some extent overcome. Most of the more important countries either grow or could grow appreciable quantities of cotton; nor need jute be for ever confined to Bengal, quite apart from the possibilities of developing substitutes. Wool of a sort is produced from South-west Asia to Manchuria and, except in China and Japan, hides and skins are available in quantity. All the major countries, apart from those of the dry south-west, have large areas under timber, though both in the boreal and the tropical forest exploitation is difficult, and in large areas, especially of India and China, conservation is urgently necessary; in China, indeed, much reafforestation is needed. The raw materials for cement and for heavy chemical industry also show a fairly wide scatter.

But on the whole it does not seem that any one country, or even any one 'sub-continental' area, of the continent is likely in the foreseeable future to rival in industrial weight of metal eastern Anglo-America, north-western Europe, or Russia from the Ukraine to the Urals. India and Asiatic U.S.S.R. certainly, China probably, have, however, at least the resources of good second-rank industrial Powers.[11] The Far East regarded as one block, despite disadvantages of distance for assembly, or even (as for the tin and tungsten of south-west China) inaccessibility, could make a similar unit if under some central direction. For such leadership Japan has obvious advantages of location and of prior tooling-up, and, indeed, the wartime "Greater East Asian Co-Prosperity Sphere" was an attempt to build such a structure; but to-day a similar effort is ruled out politically.

---

[11] Although India is often reckoned fifth among the industrial countries of the world, that is a function of size rather than of actual development, and her development is rather in textiles than in heavy industry: coal and steel outputs are small relative to area and population.

With all this, the scope for industrialization is great if limitations are heeded and (as hinted above) if concentration is on industry as ancillary to agriculture (both as supplier and market), rather than on an over-strained effort after basic heavy industry on a great scale. With the same rider, the need is urgent. And there is one factor of prime importance not yet mentioned: hydro-electricity.

Potential hydro-electric sites are well distributed; practically all the countries of Monsoon Asia, as well as Asiatic U.S.S.R., have a greater potential than they are likely to be able to harness in the near future; and the region with least water-power—South-west Asia—is that with most oil. Only in Japan and (oddly enough, until we recall former Japanese control) Korea is there anything like full exploitation of this resource: less than 10 per cent. of Asian capacity is yet utilized, and until recently 85 per cent. of developed power was generated in these two countries. In India potential is undoubtedly of the order of twenty-five to forty million kW, of which under one million are at present generated; the potential of China is of a similar order, the development still less.

Undoubtedly high initial cost is a limiting factor insufficiently appreciated by those numerous publicists to whom 'hydel' is a magic word; in some regions the added costs of long-distance transmission would be necessary, and progress on the more spectacular schemes is and will be slow. But, all allowance made, hydro-electric development remains one of the main keys to economic advance in Asia, the more so as it lends itself to a wide spread of light industry, and might thus play a big part in the rehabilitation of rural life, which in much of Monsoon Asia suffers severely from seasonal under-employment.

European Domination and the Asian Reaction

So much for the Asian setting: it remains to trace, in barest outline, some of the leading features in the evolution of the Asia of our day.

European expansion in Asia must always be considered under two heads: the land-based Russian expansion in the north, the domination of the maritime and mercantilist Powers in the south. In 1750 (a full 250 years after the Portuguese arrival) the latter group still held only scattered trading factories on the coasts, or at best dominated a few petty client-states; these posts, however, though scattered, were not

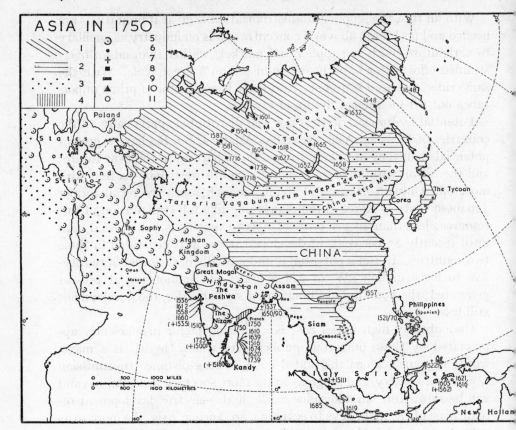

FIG. 2. ASIA IN 1750

1, Russia; 2, lands of Sinic civilization; 3, pastoral nomads; 4, territorial holdings of European maritime Powers; 5. Islamic States; 6–11, chief European posts, with dates of establishment: 6, Russian; 7, Portuguese; 8, British; 9, Danish; 10, French; 11, Dutch.

isolated, but rather links in chains which secured the bulk of overseas commerce. On the other hand the Russians, who started a century after the Portuguese (and only a few years before the Dutch and English East India Companies), had reached the Pacific by the mid-seventeenth century. Yet Asia was still fairly solidly under Asian control (Fig. 2).

The Industrial Revolution, however, with its insatiable demand for raw materials and markets, greatly accelerated the development of the maritime empires, so that by 1900 (Fig. 3) Southern Asia was all but completely under European control, while America had just supplanted Spain in the Philippines. The Turkish Empire, Persia, and Afghanistan were nominally free from this domination (though not from 'peaceful penetration'), but this was more by reason of the jealousies between the Great Powers than by their own strength. The same was very obviously true of Siam, and might even be said with some plausibility of China. In 1907 Persia was virtually partitioned economically between Britain and Russia, and after the first world war the core of South-west Asia, from Palestine to Iraq, was parcelled out into French and British Mandates. In the east China was powerless to prevent her Manchurian territory from being the theatre of the full-scale Russo-Japanese War, in which she herself was neutral.

By 1950 there had been, in Southern Asia, a great reversal (Fig. 4). In this Russia and Japan, in very different ways, had been catalysts. The Japanese, aided by a strongly cohesive ideology (lacking almost everywhere else in Asia), had succeeded in turning Western techniques against the West itself, both in war and peace; their victory in 1904–5 gave a powerful impetus to the nationalist reaction against the maritime empires.

More important still, the rapidity with which Japanese arms in 1942 overran all the lands and seas from Burma to the Solomons—a land area of 1,500,000 square miles, a population of 150 millions, subjugated in six months—shattered the belief in European invincibility, a belief only accepted, after all, with much kicking against the pricks. It also destroyed one of the major moral claims of European imperialism, the claim that it had secured peace to its subjects. And, while it obviously and grievously injured European morale, it gave new confidence to the peoples of South-east Asia, compelled to carry on somehow in the complete collapse of the pre-war economic structure in which the metropolitan countries took their cash crops and supplied many of their material needs. Nothing is more striking, for example, than the rapidity with which the Burmese matured in a country which was bombed from end to end, disrupted economically, yet politically compelled at once to aid the Japanese and to struggle against a new imperialism harsher than the old.

As for the cataclysmic effect of the Bolshevik Revolution, that is written in letters of fire: "who runs may read." The trouble is that the readings differ.[12]

[12] See, for example, the wide diversity of Asian reactions displayed in the short but brilliant section on Bolshevik Russia in Guy Wint, *The British in Asia* (Faber, London; second edition, 1954); not to mention the divergence of British and American approaches to Communist China.

One most important geopolitical change consequent on recent Communist successes must be noted. Russian expansion by land and that of the maritime Powers (whether Western European, American, or Japanese) had long been in contact and conflict on the wings: in South-

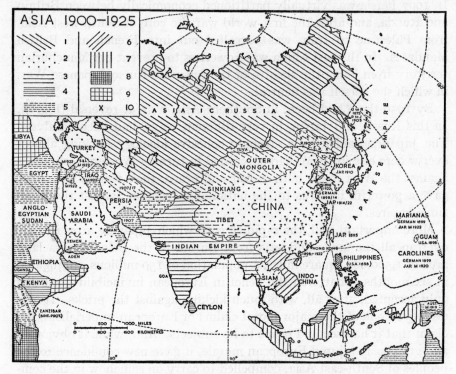

FIG. 3. ASIA, 1900–1925

1, Russia; 2, States not under European control; 3, Indian Empire; 4, other units of British Empire; 5, British Mandates (=M) or spheres of influence; 6, French; 7, Dutch; 8, Portuguese; 9, Italian; 10, areas reverting to Asian control during period. Broken lines indicate influence of adjacent power. T = Treaty Ports.

west Asia at least since the Russo-Turkish War of 1827–29, in the Far East since the jockeying for position which followed the Sino-Japanese War of 1894–95. But, in between, High Asia and interior China formed a wide no man's land, with no more than skirmishing between Britain and Russia around the listening-posts of Sinkiang. But the triumph of Communism in China and the assertion of Chinese authority in Tibet bring the Soviet and the Western worlds face to face on a front of thousands of miles: the entire Chinese coast, and even on the Himalayas, since India, though following her own international line, is in polity Western. The agreement for American bases in Pakistan highlights this change, and the struggle in Indo-China does so still more luridly.

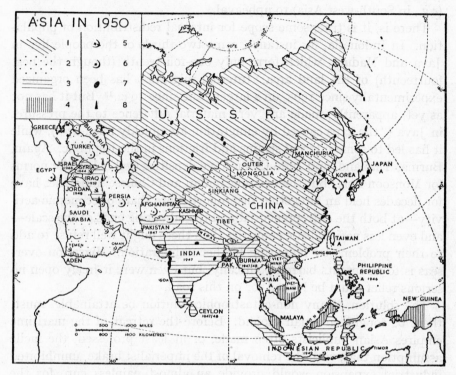

FIG. 4. ASIA IN 1950

1, Communist States; 2, independent Asian States other than: (3), successor States of maritime empires, with date of independence; 4, remaining European holdings; 5, States of Arab League; 6, other Islamic States; 7, chief industrial areas; 8, chief oil deposits. A=American influence; T.C. =Trucial Coast.

The Current Situation: Economic Aspects

It is clear enough, and, indeed, a commonplace, that the primary problem of Asiatic Asia is that of securing some relief from the mounting pressure of population against the resources of the land. This is hardly possible, in most of the area, within the framework of existing social and technological structures. Communists and liberals might assume, for example, that no further political revolution is needed in China and

India respectively; even so, great technological changes are necessary if rural populations of several hundreds to the square mile are to survive on any passable level of decency. And such changes are scarcely conceivable without great social changes, amounting in some countries (*e.g.*, in South-west Asia) to upheaval.

There is, it is true, some scope for internal redistribution of population. In Indonesia, for instance, some two-thirds of the people live in Java and Madura, which form only one-fourteenth (though the best fourteenth) of the land area. Internal migration has been organized experimentally since 1905, on a larger scale since 1932.[13] But it has not as yet, apparently, made any very material difference to the pressures in Java ("the gaps caused by emigration are quickly filled up"), while it has led to some internal strains and frictions in the Republic. Again, Burma, Thailand, and Indo-China have densities well below the norms for Monsoon Asia; but the existing Indian and Chinese minorities have for decades held an altogether disproportionate share of economic activity—at both the entrepreneurial and the labouring ends of the scale—and even less nationalistic countries than these might well refuse to add to their problems by favouring further immigration. Migration overseas is to all intents barred politically, but even were it freely open no serious relief could be looked for on this road.

The solution, if any non-catastrophic solution be attainable, must, then, be sought on Asian ground. Before the retreat of the maritime empires Asian publicists often made, or at least professed, the facile assumption that, with the removal of the imperialist brake, uninhibited industrial expansion would provide an almost painless cure for the chronic agrarian disease of Monsoon Asia. But the mobilizing of the undoubted non-agricultural resources needs outside capital and technical assistance, and even so a rate of industrialization capable of doing more than absorbing population increments (thus merely keeping a bad situation from getting worse) seems inconceivable; and, indeed, only the rash would assert that even this limited "containment" is sure to be attained. Some hopes are placed on industrialization and urbanization producing a fall in the birth-rate, and on the basis of Western experience this would probably come about in due course; it has at least begun in Japan. But, though the 'multiplier' value of industrialization in breeding consequential tertiary employment is not to be despised, the demo-

[13] *Cf.* K. Pelzer, *Pioneer Settlement in the Asiatic Tropics* (American Geographical Society, New York, 1945), pp. 191–231.

graphic crisis seems too urgent for reliance on such a long-term trend. Meanwhile the fall in death-rates is much more rapid (Table I).

Directly, then, industrialization is not a panacea. The extension of agriculture by irrigation works, its intensification by the provision of fertilizers, the diversification of rural economic opportunity and amenities by hydro-electricity—these are the real contributions of industrialization, and they are likely to be much more effective than any direct effect in absorbing surplus population. Now that the heyday of optimistic planning, which naturally followed on the attainment of independence in Southern Asia, is subsiding, the paramount importance of agrarian rehabilitation, and the role of industry as one of the main agents thereto, may be more fully recognized.

This recognition is one of the most refreshing features in the Indian First Five Year Plan, probably the most soundly based development programme yet put forward. Yet it is significant that the Plan's emphasis on agriculture has been widely criticized among the more articulate urban classes. Significant also is the almost desperate insistence of the Second Plan on the need for rehabilitating cottage industries to offset rural under-employment, limiting new factory investment largely to basic heavy and export industry. More hopefully, it is also of the highest significance that the Plan firmly advocates birth control, the third partner in the trinity of reconstruction: agricultural development, industrialization, family limitation. The causes of Asian poverty are deep-rooted and many-sided; its cure must be by measures not only radical, but also versatile in approach.

It is against this context of demographic urgency that programmes such as Point Four and the Colombo Plan must be assessed. It must be stressed that current plans, even if their targets are achieved, will simply support a larger population at the pre-war level of per capita consumption, or perhaps a little below it; but with the important rider that a sounder basis for real advance should have been secured by the acquisition of needed capital equipment.

The Current Situation: Political Aspects

Political scientists warn us that phrases imputing personality to a collective group are strictly speaking abstract symbols, a shorthand device to bypass the limitations of knowledge and language. When we

speak of "India's stand" we really mean the decisions of certain important Indian individuals; and *a fortiori* "Asia" is only a geographical
expression. This is a salutary warning against loose and emotive
generalization. Yet, on analysis, the decisions of individuals represent
calculations of common interests and opinions in the wider groups to
which these individuals belong. In this sense such abstractions have
meaning and even a real existence; and there is thus an "Asian" quality
which must be reckoned with, a feeling in much of the continent of an
identity over against the rest of the world.

Among the factors fostering such a feeling may be counted a felt
antithesis between "coloured races" and "whites," and the postulate of
"Eastern spirituality" versus "Western materialism." The inverted
commas are intended to suggest the large elements of fallacy or over-
simplification in these antitheses; nevertheless in all parts of the world
it takes a long time for objective facts to change such stereotypes, and it
is folly to ignore their potency.

Probably of more objective importance is the fact that practically all
of Southern Asia, from Syria to Indonesia and the Philippines, is occupied by States but recently freed from at least a large measure of alien
control; and for India, Pakistan, Burma, Ceylon, Indonesia, probably
the Philippines, and potentially Viet Nam, the timing of freedom is part
of one great historic act. Independence would probably have come about
in any case, but with varying time-lags, and in the actual event it is
impossible to divorce the practical simultaneity of its attainment from
the shattering upheaval of the Japanese conquest. On the other hand,
all these countries inherit (in greater or less degree) Western norms of
administration and representative institutions; and though it may often
seem that bureaucracy rather than democracy is the larger element in
this heritage, still the extent to which the spirit as well as the form of
democracy has been assimilated should not be underestimated.

Against the translation of pan-Asian sentiment into any sort of
political structure, however, are very powerful forces: the particularist
forces of local patriotisms and sectarian ideologies; the fears, well- or
ill-founded, of new imperialisms, Indian or Chinese; the enormous pull
of the universalist ideologies of the U.S.A. and the U.S.S.R.[14]

Even in the regional groupings of Asia, often even within one single
State, divisive forces are very strong: it suffices to mention the Arab-
Israeli conflict, the intrigues within the Arab League itself, the uneasi-

---

[14] *Cf.* East and Spate, *op. cit.*, pp. 391–407 ("The Unity of Asia?").

ness of the peace between India and Pakistan, the problems of plural society in Ceylon, Burma, Malaya, and Thailand, fissiparous tendencies within the Republic of Indonesia. And all these are apart from the clash of the world-ideologies which has left one Chinese government in possession of China and the other of a seat on the Security Council, and has brought disastrous civil war to Korea and Indo-China. Unity without leadership is impossible. The claimants to-day are four: the U.S.A., the U.S.S.R., and—in a different way—India and China.

Meredith Townsend, in the essay cited at the beginning of this chapter, shrewdly remarked that "the American has no interest in conquering Asia . . . it will be easier to acquire interest in Asia by protecting her from conquest than to begin conquering." And this, indeed, has seemed the role of America in Asia, in keeping with the great and generous tradition of the leaders of democratic action from Jefferson to F. D. Roosevelt. Undoubtedly the tradition often led to a naïve acceptance of the claims and charges of Asian nationalists and to an infuriating disregard of positive achievements in the British, Dutch, and French empires. But it did acquire a great deal of goodwill for America, in the eyes of the articulate middle-class leaders of nationalism, as the great anti-colonial power.

Townsend goes on to say that "the attitude of America will, I imagine, be one of rather contemptuous guardianship." Such an attitude on the part of the older colonialists was a serious factor in the revoking of Asian allegiance to them; it would be still more provocative to nations newly independent, and hence jealous to excess of their rights and dignities.

Virtually there is only one large and important buffer State in the divided world of to-day. That State is India, and although there is sentimentality in Indian "Neutralism," there is also calculation. At the least there is an assertion that Asians have a right to be called into equal judgment on Asian issues. The Indian stand is not without appeal to weaker states: Burma certainly (for whom "Chinese aggression" so far means Kuo Min Tang troops on her soil), Ceylon and Indonesia very probably.[15]

Although the world is not yet polarized around Moscow and Washington, it must be admitted that, in Asia as in Europe, the moral basis of

[15] Among the best-reasoned statements of the Indian case is a remarkable article by "P," clearly an observer on the highest level, "Middle Ground between America and Russia: An Indian View," in *Foreign Affairs* (New York), vol. xxxii (1954), pp. 259–269; and *cf.* the editorial pages of *The Eastern Economist* (New Delhi), *passim.*

Third Force ideas is weakened, perhaps fatally, by the necessity of accepting technical and fiscal assistance from one side or the other, and in practice from the U.S.A. Apart from this, it seems most unlikely that any solution can be enforced outside the great dichotomy. Yet States still retaining some freedom of action naturally wish to retain it as long as possible; they must therefore be "managed," and to this extent they do conversely limit the freedom of action of the great antagonists and do diminish the likelihood of precipitous and catastrophic action; and a year gained may be worth more than a general postponement of war for twelve months. In this view, the world may yet have reason to be grateful for the Indian refusal to take sides.

Be that as it may, it is clear that Asiatic Asia can no longer be regarded (as it was in effect by Mackinder) as simply the passive stage for the drama of Heartlanders versus Seamen, its peoples mere supers with no influence on the plot. But any positive influence is as yet inhibited by lack of a common objective.

In the unavowed rivalry between India and China for leadership of the Afro-Asian world, very much obviously depends on Indian success in the effort to carry through a radical planned reconstruction of her economy without sacrificing her inheritance of liberalism. But even success would not automatically ensure success in the wider aim. For effective leadership would imply an objective with sufficient common appeal to marshal behind it the conflicting nationalisms of the ex-colonial countries, and it is difficult to see where this is to be found. Attempts to form comprehensive blocks must reckon with very sharp antipathies: how shall Egypt and Israel be bedfellows, or the two Chinas? Egypt occupies, and seems determined to exploit a strategic position for leadership of the Islamic world; and in Burma and Ceylon also a revival of the traditional religious polity sorts ill both with Communism and the secularism of the new India.

As the 1955 Bandung Conference showed, then, it will be very difficult indeed to secure more than tactical rapprochements: a wider and independent strategy of the Afro-Asian world is far to seek. Only, it would seem, in anti-colonialism can any considerable measure of common outlook be found, and this is surely too sterile and negative to be the basis of a fruitful common policy.

FURTHER READING

Clear and well-organized factual introductions to the geography of Asia will be found in: STAMP, L. D., *Asia* (eighth edition; Methuen, London, and Dutton, New York, 1950); CRESSEY, G. B., *Asia's Lands and Peoples* (second edition; McGraw-Hill, New York, 1951). Two recent and stimulating works are GOUROU, P., *L'Asie* (Hachette, Paris, 1953) and SPENCER, J. E., *Asia East by South* (Wiley, New York, and Chapman and Hall, London, 1954).

A collective work on the political geography of the continent is EAST, W. G., and SPATE, O. H. K. (editors), *The Changing Map of Asia* (third edition; Methuen, London, and Dutton, New York, 1956). On the economic side, the United Nations (E.C.A.F.E.) annual *Economic Survey of Asia and the Far East* is invaluable.

Of the numerous Voices, Crises, Cross-roads, Minds, etc., of Asia, most are ephemeral or grossly tendentious. Perhaps the best of them is PAYNE, R., *The Revolt of Asia* (Gollancz, London, 1948); but the more valuable works are usually those dealing with particular regions, and so listed in the succeeding chapters. A very thoughtful and thought-provoking book is WINT, GUY, *The British in Asia* (second edition; Faber, London, 1954); PANIKKAR, K. M., *Asia and Western Dominance* (Allen and Unwin, London, 1953) is a provocative survey of European dominance in Asia (apparently accepting Soviet Russia as native to Asian soil); its sub-title—"A Survey of the Vasco da Gama Epoch of Asian History, 1498–1945"—gives an indication of its scope.

CHAPTER XX

India and Pakistan : Internal Political Geography

O. H. K. SPATE

THE complexity of life in the Indian sub-continent has been often stressed, and rightly so. There are, indeed, vast areas of monotonous terrain—the alluvium of the Indo-Gangetic plains, the lavas and gneisses of the Peninsular tablelands—and over areas as large as a major European State the aspect of the countryside, its towns and its villages, may appear remarkably uniform. Yet in human terms fragmentation, *morcellement*, seems the keynote. It is expressed in diverse ways: culturally in a host of castes and sects and tongues; economically in the patchwork of tiny holdings and tinier fields in the villages, or in the diffusion of industry into petty workshops and the persistent delegation of entrepreneurial responsibility to agents and sub-agents recruiting finance, labour, or know-how; legally in the myriad subtleties of land tenure and personal law; politically in the grotesque chaos of states and statelets which made or marred the map of India before 1948, and now in a proliferation of splinter parties. But, despite the division of the (British) Indian Empire into the Republics of *India*[1] and Pakistan, much of the intense interest of the contemporary scene (and perhaps especially to political geographers) lies precisely in the effort to transcend these particularisms, subsuming them into no more than two truly national States.

Some Factors of the Physical Setting

To attempt even a synopsis of the regional geography of India is obviously impossible in the space available, even were it appropriate to do so. A few leading features, however, demand remark.

[1] Italic for *India(n)* means specific reference to the present Republic, as against the old Empire or a geographical expression for the sub-continent as a whole.

The broad outlines of structure and relief are simple enough: on the landward side the lofty ramparts of the Himalaya-Karakoram ranges with their appendant mountain arcs in Baluchistan and Assam; within

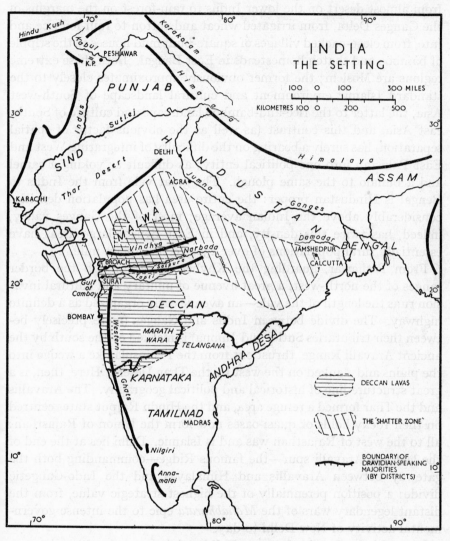

FIG. I. INDIA: THE SETTING

these the sweep of the Indo-Gangetic plains, like a vast silted moat around the base of the third element, the eastward-tilted block of the Peninsula.

The Indo-Gangetic plains, in terrain a vast monotony, are culturally a belt of almost imperceptible gradations between widely different extremes. The rationale of this transition is essentially climatic; it ranges from almost desert on the lower Indus to rain-forest on the margins of the Ganges Delta, from irrigated wheat and cotton to rain-fed rice and jute, from close-packed villages of square-built mud houses to the stipple of bamboo and thatch homesteads in East Bengal. Both these extreme regions are Moslem; the former obviously approximates closely to the standard Islamic environment and cultural landscape of South-west Asia, the latter to the rice-and-bamboo landscape and culture of South-east Asia, and this contrast (as well as the obvious factor of spatial separation) has surely a bearing on the difficulty of integrating West and East Pakistan into one political entity; as difficult as yoking a camel and a buffalo to the same plough. The great vale from the Indus to Bengal is Hindustan proper: the entire area has population densities considerably above the Indian average; most of the Ganges valley, indeed, has twice this density, and in East Bengal large areas have essentially rural populations of over 1300 to the square mile.

From Peshawar, guarding the Khyber entry through the border ranges of the north-west, a great avenue of military and cultural invasion runs the length of the vale—an avenue early organized as a definite highway. The divide between Indus and Ganges (more precisely between their tributaries Sutlej and Jumna) is marked on the south by the ancient Aravalli Range, thrust out from the Peninsula like a wedge into the plains and flanked on the west by the Thar Desert. Here, then, is a great structure-line of historical and political geography. The Aravallis and the Thar formed a refuge area, and the Hindu Rajput states centred on their rocky holds or quasi-oases now form the Union of Rajasthan: all to the west of Rajasthan was and is Islamic. Delhi lies at the end of the last low Aravalli spur—the famous Ridge—commanding both the gateway between Aravallis and Himalayas and the Indo-Gangetic divide: a position perennially of the highest strategic value, from the distant legendary wars of the *Mahabharata* epic to the intense governmental activity of New Delhi to-day.

From this focal region between Delhi and Agra another historic route —that of Malwa—strikes south into the Peninsula across the second great structure-line. This lies in the warped belt of scarped forested hills (Vindhya, Satpura, etc.) and rifts (Narbada and Tapti valleys) which lie across the Peninsula from the Gulf of Cambay to West Bengal. A refuge for the more important "aboriginal" tribes, this belt was politically a shatter-zone and is still rather backward, especially in the jungly Orissa hinterland in the east. Both the structure-lines converge in the Gulf of Cambay area, historically a major entry: its ports (Ptolemaic Barygaza, Renaissance Broach and Surat) were the terminals of the Malwa routeway. Malwa lies largely on Deccan Lava country, more open than most of the warped belt, and it is significant that it largely coincides with Madhyabharat, perhaps the most progressive of the Unions formed from the scores of princely states which occupied the shatter-belt. Conversely, the Union of Vindhya Pradesh, adjacent on the east of Madhyabharat, proved so backward that its administration was taken over by the central government.

Beyond the Narbada lies the Deccan, *Dakshinapatha*, "the South-land." In the north-west it is occupied by the open Deccan Lava country, and this was the threshold by which conqueror after conqueror, Hindustan once consolidated, advanced into the Peninsula. Here is also the seat of the very distinctive Maratha people, rivals with the East India Company for the virtual succession to the Mogul Empire. The boundary of their Aryan speech coincides remarkably with that of the Deccan Lavas, Hyderabad being split between basaltic Marathwara and gneissic Telangana, the land of the Dravidian-speaking Telugus, who also occupy the coast between Madras and Orissa. Finally the south-east quadrant of the Peninsula is solidly occupied by the Tamils, exponents of Dravidian culture in its highest form.

Very broadly, then, we have a repeated pattern: waves of cultural penetration entering from the north-west and constricted again in the Delhi and Malwa gateways, to spread out over the intervening plains or plateaux on broad fronts. These perennial routeways, frontier-zones, and nuclei of power have persisted at least from the Aryan invasions of the first millennium B.C., and they remain of great significance for the political geography of to-day. They have their part in the partition of the Punjab and Bengal, in the difficulty of yoking East and West Pakistan, in the layout of the new Unions of old princely states, in the problem of linguistic provinces, in the survival of large areas economically and politically backward, which set a problem of integration for such states as Orissa—a densely peopled coastland burdened with an immense hinterland of jungle.

Climate and the Agricultural Base

In the mountains and the hills the topographic texture is closely articulated; there are a multitude of *pays*. In the plains and on the tablelands it is, by and large, coarse: here climate provides the macro- and soil the micro-regional differentials. Temperature variations are not striking on the whole (apart from altitude effects, of course), though significant enough when we compare the almost equatorial regime of Travancore in the extreme south with the definite approach to continentality in the Punjab.

Although most of the sub-continent has a strictly monsoonal rhythm, annual rainfall varies from over 400 inches in Assam to under ten on the lower Indus. A factor of great agricultural significance is the contrast between the Himalayan rivers, which begin to fill with melt-water as early as mid-March (the height of the hot weather), and those of the Peninsula, which are practically dry from November or December to June. The advantages for irrigation and hydro-electricity generation of a high-flow season lasting a full three months longer than the Peninsular streams are obvious, although sometimes overlooked in optimistic visions of development; the best options are in the north, and for irrigation were taken up long ago, if not for 'hydel.'

Regional differences, then, are mainly matters of rainfall amount and distribution and of soil, with concomitant variations in the water-table. Putting things very simply, the wet Peninsular coasts and the Ganges Valley as far as a line N.N.E. from the Jumna–Ganges confluence are the domain of rice, though it is grown elsewhere (*e.g.*, in Sind) by irrigation; the upper Ganges and the Indus basins of wheat, in the latter for the most part dependent on great irrigation works; between these zones, and especially in the hillier or drier parts, or both, of the Peninsula (*e.g.*, in the rain-shadow of the Western Ghats), millets play a most important part in diet. Sugar-cane is most extensively grown in the middle and upper Ganges plains.

Nearly 80 per cent. of the total cropped area is in food-grains. Of commercial crops fibres are the most important: jute especially in East Pakistan, but increasingly extending in the lower Ganges plains and suitable coastal areas as *India* strives to make up for the loss of the main jute area; cotton in West Pakistan (where longer-stapled varieties are important), on the Deccan Lava *regur* or 'black cotton' soil behind

Bombay, and in the southern Peninsula: on a quarter or less of the total cotton area, Pakistan has a third of the output. Oil-seeds are widely grown, the most important concentrations being probably the ground-nuts areas of interior Andhra and the coastal plain south of Madras city. Tea is the most important plantation crop, and Assam (with East Bengal) the most important area; but it is also grown, with some coffee and a little rubber, on the hills in the extreme south of the Peninsula.

The cattle population is enormous—over 210,000,000 head, including buffaloes; they are primarily draft animals, and excessive numbers for the available feed, with very poor breeding, make many of them utterly uneconomic. Contrary to general belief, a considerable proportion of their dung—perhaps 40 per cent.—is in fact used as manure; but in the great plains where both men and cattle are most crowded and where there is next to no forest—or space to plant it—there is little alternative to its use as fuel.

Most of the sub-continent would naturally have had a forest cover, but over vast areas it has been replaced, either by almost continuous cultivation or, especially in the Peninsula, by cultivation mixed with scrub or short-grass savannah. Forest resources, however, remain important: teak along the Western Ghats, deciduous monsoon hardwoods in the jungly north-east of the Peninsula and along the lower Himalayan flanks, conifers on their higher levels. There are vast supplies of various grasses and bamboos for paper-making. The forest resources of West Pakistan are poor—on the plains negligible—and those of East Pakistan limited, although a bamboo-based paper industry is being developed.

The Peoples

For millennia India was a vast cul-de-sac, the end of countless migrations; in consequence culture has been imposed upon culture to produce perhaps the most complex social mosaic in the world. "Race," however, is of negligible significance; creed and speech are the fundamental divisive forces which find expression in terms of political geography—most patently, of course, in the primary partition, on the basis of religious ideology, into *India* and Pakistan. Hinduism and Islam are, of course, strong dominants in *India* and Pakistan respectively, but they are themselves much cross-divided.

R

It is easy to overstress the multiplicity of Indian tongues: six languages account for two-thirds of the people, which compares very favourably with Europe. But the deeply rooted culture of the Dravidian languages of the south (especially Tamil and Telugu) does inhibit the easy acceptance of Aryan Hindi as the national language of *India*, while the attachment of East Pakistan to Bengali (shared with *Indian* West Bengal, and heavily Sanskritized) has forced postponement of the official adoption as an all-Pakistan language of Urdu, which has a strongly Persianized higher vocabulary and is much more Islamic in its associations. The supersession of the old British Provinces, often arbitrarily delimited, by linguistic units has long been canvassed in *India*, and, indeed, Andhra has been carved out of Madras for the Telugus. It may be doubted whether this is sound as a general policy: there are too many outliers and debatable lands, too much risk of inter-state friction and of the disruption of viable economic regionalisms. Thus Andhra cannot be complete without Telangana in Hyderabad; the Marathi-speaking rump of that state would presumably be allotted to Bombay, and this weighting of the Maratha element might well touch off the incipient sectionalism of the Kanarese-speaking areas in the south of Bombay. The exorcizing of some cultural discontents might be too costly if purchased at the price of more particularism or even separatism, and this moral was forcibly pointed by the reception given to the definite proposals of the States Reorganization Commission in 1955. Differences in culture and tradition had struck so deep as to result in virtual sub-nationalisms, and when nationalism comes in at the door rationalism flies out of the window. The claims of West Bengal and Orissa against Bihar led to serious troubles, overshadowed by those in Bombay: the apprehensions of the Gujeratis, economically dominant in Bombay City, where Marathas were the largest single community, led to the proposal that Greater Bombay should be detached from Maharashtra and placed under Central control. The disturbances of January 1956 were a shock to national prestige and morale, perhaps salutary as pointing the danger to unity involved in a too literal acceptance of the linguistic principle.

Such divisions as these can be put on a map or even translated into territorial entities; others which have a distinct bearing on political geography are less easy to isolate geographically. Of these caste is the most difficult: an incredibly complex and intensely hierarchical organization of society, it undoubtedly still produces social, political, and economic frictions in a community which can ill afford them. Legislation enforcing the right of access to schools and wells by Untouchables (officially "Scheduled Castes"), and in some *milieux* at least public opinion, are curbing its extremist manifestations, and the institution is subject to erosion by the general modernization of life; but it remains a brake on the urgently needed mobilization of national energy. Conversely, while the never complete equation of caste with occupation is in general progressively weakening (except for definitely impure trades such as tanning, scavenging, and laundering), economic class is becoming more important every day, with the rise of an industrial proletariat on the one hand and the decay of the peasantry on the other. Already it affects significantly the geographical distribution of political allegiance—as, for example, where agrarian communism (or at least radicalism) has some hold, in Travancore-Cochin and Andhra especially.

Yet caste proper plays some part in these cases, and so also, in Travancore-Cochin, does religion. The Indian National Congress was in essence a Popular Front, and the prestige gained in the struggle for independence has so far kept it from splitting into parties on Western lines: only a few groups, mainly on the Left, have been shed. But in Travancore-Cochin Congress is merely one among the other parties, and not always a majority party; and this is at least in part associated with the fact that here nearly a third of the people are Christians. At the other extremity of *India*, the concentration of 90 per cent. of the 6,219,000 Sikhs in East Punjab and Pepsu—the frontier over against Pakistan—scarcely assists in the keeping of the peace, given their militant attitude to the Moslems.

Other minorities provide social rather than political problems. The most important are the 19,119,000 people still living as jungle tribesmen; they are found mainly in the forested hills in the north of the Peninsula and in the mountains of Assam. Their assimilation into modern *Indian* society will be difficult to achieve without exploitation: indeed, in Assam this finds formal recognition in the retention of definite "Autonomous Districts" and "Tribal Areas," though the difficulties of administration on forested mountain frontiers is perhaps also a factor. The Anglo-Indians (who would be more accurately styled Eurasians) are a sad but diminishing legacy of alien rule. A word is due to the altogether disproportionate share in economic activity held by the Parsees: they number only 112,000, but they have contributed very markedly to the civic life of Bombay and to modern industrial development, notably through the great house of Tata, whose interests range from the quasi-monopolistic iron and steel industry of Jamshedpur to chemicals, airways, textiles, hydro-electricity, and soap.

Population and Food

However diverse in other respects, all the peoples of India have in common the human facts that they eat, generally too little, and procreate, generally too much. This is by far the most fundamental problem of the sub-continent.

The over-all density of population is 276 to the square mile, over five times the world average, but not in itself excessive were resources fully utilized. Nor is the increase of population, though rapid, really extraordinary: if decennial increments of about 50,000,000 appear startling it must be remembered that they spring from high absolute numbers. The total increase 1891–1951 was 57 per cent., and this is quite comparable with increases in Western Europe over a similar period. The alarming aspects are that agricultural productivity is extremely low and cannot as yet be said to increase at anything like the rate of population increase,[2] and that industrial expansion, remarkable as it has been in some branches, has certainly not been on the scale which accompanied similar rates of increase in Europe.

India has all the classic features of *la misère*. Holdings are tiny; there is well under one acre of cultivated land for each member of a population of which over two-thirds depend *directly* on farming; half an acre and three-quarters of the people would probably be closer figures. The peasant, loaded with debt, can rarely hold his crop for a rise, and so is usually at the mercy of the local grain-broker, who may well be also the local moneylender and shopkeeper. The burden of landlordism is being eased, by legislation or voluntarily through the quasi-religious *Bhoodan Yagna* (Land-gift) movement, but it may well be that too little is being done too late, and even if all the land were in the hands of the actual cultivators the major problem remains: there is far too little cultivated,

---

[2] Much play has been made in *India* with the fact that in 1953–54 the index of food production was 119 (1936–39 = 100); this is much the same as the population index, if anything a little below it, and the sequence for the preceding years (1939–40 to 1952–53) is not reassuring: 99, 95, 93, 103, 107, 104, 95, 96, 102, 96, 99, 89, 100. Some of the nineteen points represent permanent net gain from development and agricultural improvement, but how much is from these sources and how much from a lucky monsoon is quite unclear. The increase in irrigated area by 1953 was only 1,400,000 acres, less than 3 per cent. on the 1948 figure. Perhaps half the increase is real gain.

or cultivable, land to ensure an adequate food supply with current farming techniques, and the peasant has rarely the skills, still less the capital, to apply better ones. Nevertheless great advances in productivity have been attained by the "Community Development Projects," which seek to extend, on a nation-wide scale and with more continuity, the experience of previous rural-uplift schemes. There are dangers of bureaucratic friction, and difficulties in securing adequate cadres of trained workers, but the peasant response is so far good.

More grandiose are the "Development Projects," such as Pakistan's Thal and Lower Sind schemes on the Indus, to produce over 1,000,000 tons of food-grains from 3,500,000 acres of new irrigation, or the multi-purpose T.V.A.-type schemes in *India*, of which the most outstanding are Bhakra-Nangal on the Sutlej, with ultimate objectives of some 1,200,000 kW of hydro-electric power and 3,500,000 acres of irrigation, and the complex Damodar Valley project.

It is true that in the sub-continent there are some 120,000,000 acres which used to be classified as "Culturable Waste," a vulgar error authoritatively denounced as long ago as 1928,[3] but still current both within and without. The maximum possible increase of cultivation in *India* would seem to be about 10 or 12 per cent. on the 1950 total sown area—say, 25-30,000,000 acres; but, once more, it seems impossible that expansion can keep pace with the expansion of population. West Pakistan could add about a quarter to the present cultivated area, but there is very little scope for expansion in East Pakistan.

It seems probable that a more rapid increase of food output could be obtained by a bolder artificial fertilizer policy. Against this must be set hydro-electric and other benefits from the multi-purpose schemes; and it may be held that it is necessary to increase not only unit yield but actual cultivated area, since consolidation of holdings—in many areas essential to real advance—implies that some cultivators must be displaced, and the problem of the landless labourer is already acute.

The undoubted increase in surplus rural population accounts in large part for the marked increase in urban population, and particularly in that of the larger cities. From 1921 to 1941 the urban population increased at over twice the general rate; there were two "million" cities in

[3] Report of Royal Commission on Agriculture in India, 1928, p. 605. The figure is for the area reporting agricultural statistics, about two-thirds of the total; but the non-reporting areas were so predominantly mountain, desert, or jungle that they may be disregarded in the argument.

1941, six in 1951. There is some hope that urbanization and industrialization may tend to slacken the rate of population increase, as in Western
Europe; but again it seems unlikely that this result will appear in time
to obviate what seems an impending food and population crisis.

It was one of the merits of the *Indian* First Five Year Plan that it
recognized the need for family limitation as well as for increased food
output: the two policies are complementary. While there seems to be
no definite sanction in Hinduism against birth control (though there is
a positive sanction in favour of male posterity), results have been disappointing, apparently less from hostility than from lack of interest and
understanding. It is perhaps difficult to whip up real enthusiasm for
what is after all a negative, if necessary, attitude to life.

Industrial Development: *India*

Although, as in other countries, the last years of the second world war
saw in India a turmoil of grandiose and incoherent schemes of reconstruction, little could be definitely initiated until the primary political
problem of independence and partition was resolved in 1947. Not un-
naturally, independence was succeeded by an even more tumultuous
mælstrom of plans and projects. But in 1951 a positive and realistic—
fiscally even orthodox—programme was set forth in the First Five
Year Plan. This was essentially devoted to the rehabilitation of agriculture (it was, indeed, criticized in *India* for undue agrarian bias) and the
tooling up of a transport system and an industrial apparatus unevenly
developed and badly overstrained during the war.

India's resources are not small, though they must always be considered against the great population. In fibres—jute, cotton, and wool
—she is not, indeed, self-sufficient, but has at least a firm base; there is
a great variety of oilseeds, both edible and industrial; timber and paper
materials are at least adequate; the huge cattle population provides for
a large, if primitive, leather industry and a big export of hides.

On the mineral side, oil production in Assam is only a fraction of
demand, and there is a deficiency of non-ferrous metals, especially tin,
lead, and zinc. Glass sands and cement materials are adequate, there
are large reserves of bauxite, and a quasi-monopoly of mica; the beaches
of Travancore carry heavy concentrations of the strategic minerals
monazite (a source of thorium) and ilmenite. But most notable are the

magnificent resources for iron and steel manufacture: perhaps 8000 to 10,000 million tons of iron ore, in large part first-class hæmatite; manganese to meet any foreseeable need and leave a large export surplus; fair supplies of chromite, vanadium, and other alloys; ample refractories and fluxes.

As for power, coal reserves are adequate (with some doubts as to the long-term supply of good coking coal), but too much concentrated in the Damodar Valley: there are many small scattered fields, but 80 to 85 per cent. of the annual output of around 35,000,000 tons comes from the Damodar. However, the north-eastern corner of the Peninsula, in which the Damodar lies, is by far the most heavily mineralized portion of the sub-continent. Few sites can have the locational advantages for heavy industry enjoyed by Jamshedpur, between Damodar coal and mountains of hæmatite on the Orissa border, seventy miles or less from all essential materials, and only 150 miles from the largest single market, Hooghlyside. This concentration is to some extent offset by the wider spread of hydro-electric potential: along the wildly dissected, rainswept flanks of the Himalayas, the Western Ghats, and the Nilgiri-Annamalai blocks in the far south, and in the zone where the major Peninsula rivers traverse, with a marked break of grade, the misnamed Eastern Ghats. The total potential must amount to at least thirty or forty million kW, of which under one million are developed.

Manufacturing industry in *India* is just a century old; since the attainment of tariff autonomy in 1922 its advance has been spectacular in some fields, though uneven. Textiles still account for nearly a third of factory employment, and though there is now a very wide range of consumption industries, entrepreneurial methods are still sometimes picturesque rather than sound. Since 1947 there have been very encouraging increases in basic output (Table 5), and on the whole the targets of the First Plan have been attained—a tribute to its modest realism. The great demand from the Development Projects can be met for cement, but steel at around 1,250,000 tons a year lags behind needs, and, of course, machine tools, high-grade electrical and electronic equipment, and so on must to a large extent still be imported.

It is clear that *India* has the makings of (at least) a good second-class industrial Power; but, encouraging as progress under the First Plan was, it is becoming apparent that it cannot be maintained at a rate commensurate with the needs of an ever-increasing population without a rather more dynamic fiscal policy than has been adopted so far. This, of course, carries with it the risk of inflation, or alternatively of controls of a range and rigidity difficult to accept in a country of 600,000 villages with a population still in great majority illiterate. Financial aid under the Colombo Plan is limited, and neither *India* nor the United States seems anxious for really large-scale American investment, unless with "strings" unacceptable to one party or the other.

The Second Five Year Plan is designed to meet some of these difficulties. It represents a shift from the agrarian bias of the First Plan towards more basic heavy industry: steel production, for instance, is to be quadrupled, two million-ton plants being already in hand with Russian and British technical aid. On the other hand, factory consumption industry is being as it were reined in and the labour-intensive but capital-light cottage industries fostered: thus production of mill cloth is to increase by 10 per cent., handloom cloth by 100 per cent. In view of the marked reserve displayed by capital, the experiment has a definitely socialist bias.

Beyond this is the major problem that, while a modest vision is at least more likely of attainment than the delightful dreams of the first fine careless rapture of independence, it may well be questioned whether it is really adequate to *India's* need. Food and clothing outputs *may* keep level with population, so that the pre-war standard is maintained for a larger population; but on any reasonable view pre-war India was grossly ill-clad and ill-fed. Once more we see the key importance of the food-man ratio: more fertility in the fields may not be enough unless there is less fertility in the home. Otherwise it seems very doubtful whether the most radical programme of agrarian and agricultural reform can do more than check the formation of rural population surplus (if, indeed, it can do that), and it is almost certain that no conceivable expansion of industry can cope with this problem. There are bright patches, but the further outlook remains unsettled.

Problems of Development: Pakistan

Pakistan's problem is essentially different from *India's*: it is not so much poverty of resources relative to population as simple poverty. So bald a statement obviously needs qualification, but it is nearer the truth than the optimism of official hand-outs. Yet West Pakistan, at least, has the makings of a well-found State provided that limitations are recognized. The main limitation is that Pakistan must remain essentially a primary producer and that the scope for industry, while not negligible, is essentially for industry based upon or ancillary to agriculture: processing and assembly, not basic production industry.

East Pakistan seems a precarious economic proposition. The density of population is over 775 to the square mile, and there is very little land still available for reclamation: over most of the unit the net cropped area is over 70 per cent. of the surface, over much of it over 80 per cent. The export standby is jute (which, indeed, normally accounts for half or more of all Pakistan's export values) and, apart from jute's notorious irregularity in output and market values, increasing competition with rice for the available land seems inevitable with increasing population pressure. Industrial resources to offset this are slight: except for lignite, mineral resources are about nil. The Karnaphuli river behind Chittagong will eventually generate about 160,000 kW and provide power for existing paper-mills and the big expansion of jute manufacture in progress at the capital, Dacca; this will certainly provide some relief, but hardly enough.

West Pakistan seems much more reasonable as an economic unit. Irrigation is practically essential to agriculture, and here good progress is being made in a programme to extend the 19,000,000 acres irrigated in 1947 to about 25,000,000 by 1957–58; despite a recent crisis, West Pakistan is normally at least self-sufficient in food. It has some oil at Attock in West Punjab, and great hopes are centred on the recent large strike of natural gas at Sui in Baluchistan. But even planned increases in the current output of around 500,000 tons of poor-quality coal would scarcely meet the needs of a serious industrial development, and the target for hydro-electric power is under 400,000 kW.

The mineral base is weak. There are scattered indications of various minor minerals in the hills, but the only important production so far is of chromite, salt, glass sand, and limestone, while the only assured unexploited reserve of much significance is of fair-quality iron ore in West Punjab.

Actual industrial production of significance is mainly in cotton, sugar, and cement, while woollens are being started. On these lines, and with the addition of light consumption goods such as cigarettes, matches, footwear, light electrical gear, and so on, prospects are fair. But such a development does not seem to measure up to Pakistani aspirations, and there seems real danger of squandering scarce resources of capital and

R*

trained personnel in pursuit of a visionary development of heavy industry. In any case Pakistan must remain a far weaker State than *India*,
and it might be further weakened by diffusing energy into blind alleys.

Political Evolution since 1947: *India*

India became a fully autonomous Dominion of the British Commonwealth on August 15, 1947, and proclaimed herself a Republic—retaining membership of the Commonwealth—on January 26, 1950. Independence was attended by the partition of the old Indian Empire into *India*
and Pakistan, essentially on a basis of religious allegiance.

India is a federal State, with a lower House of the People elected
by universal adult suffrage and an upper Council of States elected
indirectly through the legislatures of the various states. These fall into
three groups: Class A states are the old major British provinces, with
the addition of the new state of Andhra; Class B consists of old princely
states adhering either as single units (Hyderabad, Mysore) or as Unions
of a number of states. Class C states are smaller units, either old Chief
Commissioner's Provinces (Ajmer, Coorg, Delhi) or minor princely states
directly controlled from New Delhi, generally for strategic reasons.
Class D—Territories—has only one member, the Andaman and Nicobar
Islands. Residual powers rest with the Central Government seated at
New Delhi, but the states have a large sphere of operations.

With three exceptions—Kashmir (see below, p. 495), Junagadh, and
Hyderabad—the adhesion of the states was virtually automatic. The
small state of Junagadh, overwhelmingly Hindu but with a Moslem
ruler, acceded by plebiscite after *Indian* military occupation; it is now
included in the Union of Saurashtra, but still claimed by Pakistan.
Hyderabad also is in great majority Hindu, but again had a Moslem
ruler, descendant of the Mogul Viceroys of the Deccan, and its adhesion
was only secured by military action in September 1948.

The course of political development has in general been smooth
enough: indeed, the only internal changes of a geographical nature have
been the formation of Andhra in 1954 and the integration or suppression
of the 584 old princely states. These ranged from Hyderabad with
82,313 square miles and over 16,000,000 people to tiny estates of a
square mile or two and a hundred people; the smaller (and some of the
larger) states were fantastically intermingled with each other and with
old provincial territory, a scatter of ex- and en-claves, for the most part

much too small and poor to be anything but an administrative nuisance. Mediatization was carried through, in 1948, with a fine amalgam of adroitness, boldness, and tact. Seven Unions were formed (of which two, Himachal Pradesh and Vindhya Pradesh, became merely C states), while two fairly important states, Baroda and Kolhapur, were merged with Bombay, and a host of petty units of the shatter-zone (above, p. 479) were merged with Bombay, Madhya, Pradesh, and Orissa: the last state increased its area by 85 per cent. and its population by nearly 60 per cent. Figs. 2 and 3 give some idea of the territorial simplification thus achieved; the incredible fragmentation of the old regime can be grasped by the fact that Saurashtra unites 449 old 'states' (split into 860 bits of territory) into one block of 21,000 square miles and 3,500,000 people.[4] However, as we have seen, the demand for linguistic States raises serious and rather disturbing questions.

A different problem was presented by the relics of other Empires than the British. France held five towns with a total area of 200 square miles; the principle of adhesion to *India* should the local populations so desire was admitted at an early stage, but except for isolated Chandernagore (north of Calcutta) the actual handing-over was procrastinated until 1954. Portuguese possessions present a more serious issue: they consist of Diu and Damão in the Cambay area and the larger holding of Goa, which has a good and well-equipped port (the outlet for much of southern Bombay), and resources in salt and manganese. Over 40 per cent. of the population of Goa is Roman Catholic, and among these Portuguese culture has struck deep roots. There is thus some metropolitan sentiment; on the other hand, the natural *Indian* desire to round out the territory finds support from within. Goa would be far more of a loss to Portugal than a gain to *India*, and Portugal has so far taken up a completely *non possumus* attitude: the "Estado da India" is an integral part of Portugal. One might regret the disappearance of the last European flag, which was also the first: but it flies only on sufferance.

Political Evolution since 1947: Pakistan

"Evolution" is not perhaps the right word: in fact, it is probably not too much to say that, except South Africa, no major component of the

[4] For a fuller discussion of the geographical aspects of partition and integration, see W. G. East and O. H. K. Spate (eds.), *The Changing Map of Asia* (third edition, Methuen, London, 1956), pp. 130–31, 148–54, and especially Figure 15, p. 149. A further territorial simplification is envisaged.

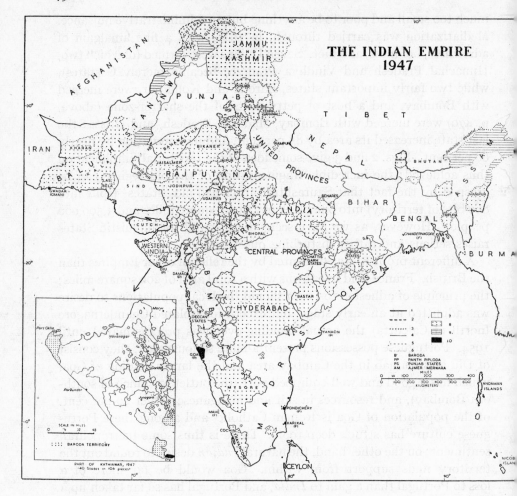

FIG. 2. THE INDIAN EMPIRE, 1947

1–6 boundaries: 1, international, demarcated; 2, international, undemarcated; 3, international, undelimited or undefined; 4, Provinces and Agencies; 5, internal states; 6, tribal areas; 7, British Provinces; 8, Princely states; 9, unadministered tribal areas; 10, foreign possessions.

British Commonwealth has so troubled a prospect. Indeed, it may be that Pakistan will be assimilated to South-west Asia not only by its Islamic policy but by its governmental tradition, and that is not an exhilarating view.

Fundamental is the division of the territory into two blocks, separated

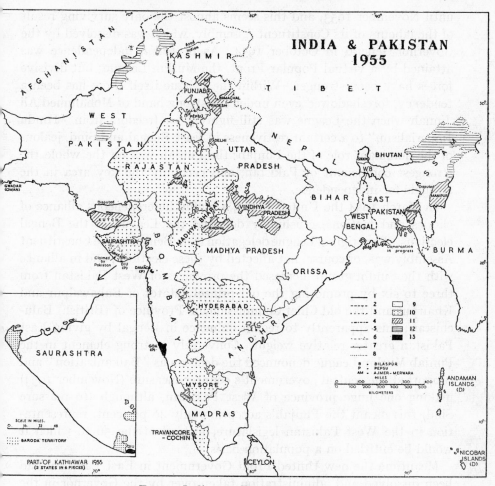

FIG. 3. *India* AND *Pakistan*, 1955

1–8 boundaries: 1, international, demarcated; 2, international, undemarcated; 3, international, undelimited or undefined; 4, Kashmir with India and Pakistan; 5, Provinces and Agencies; 6, internal States; 7, cease-fire line in Kashmir; 8, tribal areas; 9, Class A Indian states; 10, Class B Indian states; 11, Class C Indian states; 12, Class D states and Tribal areas; 13, foreign possessions. Sikkim is in effect an Indian protectorate.

by nearly 1000 miles of *India*. The western has six-sevenths of the area but only three-sevenths of the population, and although it is better found than East Pakistan, the hour-glass shape of its irrigated core, aligned along the single railway up the Indus Valley, would pose almost insuperable strategic problems in the event of any conflict with *India*.

Pakistan did not declare itself a Republic within the Commonwealth until November 1953, and this seems almost the only surviving result of the labours of its Constituent Assembly, which was dissolved by the Governor-General in October 1954. As in *India*, independence was attained by a virtual Popular Front, the Muslim League; but divisive forces have been stronger. Within the League itself there has been a tendency, foreshadowed even under the strong hand of Mohammed Ali Jinnah when the League was still fighting for freedom from "Hindu Imperialism," to a certain restiveness in East Bengal and Sind, jealous of the dominant role of the Punjab; the Punjab was on the whole the strongest component of Pakistan, and certainly the key area in the struggle for independence.

In March 1954 the United Front, a highly heterogeneous alliance of cliques and factions, crushingly defeated the League in the Bengal elections. The original League delegation from Bengal to the Constituent Assembly was, of course, not affected by these elections, and in alliance with the Sindhi group increased the provinces of West Pakistan from three to six by promoting the old princely states of Bahawalpur and Khairpur and the old Chief Commissioners' Province of (British) Baluchistan; this apparently to regain influence in Bengal by giving East Pakistan greater relative weight. Conversely a strong element in the Punjab Muslim League denounced the decision as "Balkanization" and supported the central government's counter-measure (November 1954) making one huge province of West Pakistan, although (to reassure Sind) this meant the Punjab's accepting only 40 per cent. representation in the West Pakistan legislature, instead of the 56 to which it would be entitled on a population basis.

Meantime the new United Front Government in East Pakistan had been dissolved and administration taken over by the Governor in the most approved manner of the British Raj: this on ground of corruption, but the more readily as there were some signs that East Pakistan might find her account in closer economic relations with *India*; and, indeed, the situation of East Pakistan is such that her interests might well diverge seriously from the general Pakistani line. The formation of two units is avowedly a *pis aller* necessitated by the impossibility of running two widely separated and geographically very different territories as a unitary State. It represents the very minimum of federation possible; its adoption, nearly nine years after Independence, should mean more stability and more concentration on the problems of development, which have not indeed been neglected.

With the disbalance between the eastern and western blocks, with an economy resting on a none too secure basis of resources, with the active interest of Afghanistan in Pathan separatism (below, p. 509), and with the ideological conflict between modernists and those who would build a backward-looking, purely Islamic polity, the weakness of Pakistan *vis-à-vis* her sister Republic is patent enough to discourage adventurism.

Although, then, some solid economic progress has been achieved, and although the socio-economic problems facing Pakistan are scarcely so vast or complex as those of *India*, it is perhaps not surprising that she should have sought to strengthen her position by securing economic assistance from the United States against the grant of facilities for the use of air-bases in Pakistan. To *India* this seemed to threaten the delicate structure of neutralism which she was endeavouring to build, and her reaction was the immediate ending of negotiations to implement the previous agreed policy for a plebiscite to resolve the problem of Kashmir.

Kashmir

This state—correctly "Jammu and Kashmir"—was the converse of Hyderabad: a Hindu ruler in a country three-quarters Moslem, but with a Hindu majority in the south-east, adjoining the *Indian* Punjab. Kashmir is of greater economic value to Pakistan than to *India*; much of the irrigation of West Punjab depends on the Indus and Jhelum; the Pir Panjal foothills supplied much timber to West Punjab, and here too are resources—hydro-electric potential, anthracite, bauxite, iron ore— marginal to *India's* needs but perhaps sufficient to make all the difference to Pakistan's industrial future. The natural economic links of Kashmir are decidedly with Pakistan.

The upheaval of August 1947 touched off a crisis always latent in this feudally exploited country. The accession of the ruler to *India* was legally indefeasible, but morally its acceptance (even subject to an ever-receding plebiscite) squared very oddly with the oft-proclaimed Congress attitude to the princes and their prerogatives; on the other hand, Pakistan weakened her moral case by complicity in the invasion of Moslem tribesmen from the hills and by accepting the adhesion of the Moslem ruler of Hindu Junagadh, which was not even contiguous to Pakistan. After much fighting an armistice (January 1, 1949) left *India* in possession of the greater part of the state, including the fertile Vale of Kashmir where the majority of the people live. Efforts by U.N.O. to produce an agreed solution failed; in the meantime the ruler was gradually pushed into the background by the agrarian reform government of Shaikh Abdullah, until he appeared to be playing his own hand and standing out for too much independence. Pakistan, bitterly hostile to this Moslem Quisling, yet saw in his supersession the threat of a coup; but *India* also had to face the warning that the Kashmiris might be far from acquiescent. Hence in August 1953 an agreement was reached to hold a plebiscite within twelve months; an agreement repudiated by *India* after the agreement on air-bases between Pakistan and America. Only in May 1954 were negotiations resumed.

Both sides are, indeed, so much committed that it is difficult to see any solution, other than the maintenance of an unsatisfactory status quo. Partition would seem logical, but the cease-fire line would be unacceptable to Pakistan, and after eight years of possession *Indian* opinion could scarcely be fobbed off with the Hindu corner. A solution of this Indo-Pakistani cold war by setting up an independent State under U.N.O. auspices might well end in transferring it into a greater cold war: Kashmir marches with Sinkiang and Tibet, and the extreme east is Tibetan by race and culture.

FURTHER READING

A comprehensive geographical analysis is given in SPATE, O. H. K., *India and Pakistan* (Methuen, London, 1954); this book contains many facts, most of them probably authentic, and some opinions. Two German surveys may be mentioned: KREBS, N., *Vorder Indien und Ceylon* (Koehler, Stuttgart, 1939); STECHE, H., *Indien und Pakistan* (Sofari, Berlin, 1952) (undocumented).

A book of great value, and wider scope than is implied by its title, is DAVIS, K., *The Population of India and Pakistan* (Princeton University Press, 1950).

Of other demographic works, perhaps the most useful geographically is GHOSH, D., *Pressure of Population and Economic Efficiency in India* (Indian Institute of International Affairs, New Delhi, 1950).

The standard works on the economy remain: JATHAR, G. B., and BERI, S. G., *Indian Economics* (eighth edition; Oxford University Press, Bombay, 1947–49); ANSTEY, V., *The Economic Development of India* (fourth edition; Longmans, London, 1948); but they should be supplemented by VAKIL, C. N., *Economic Consequences of Divided India* (Vora, Bombay, 1950).

There is, of course, a very large 'official' literature—reports and statistics of Ministries and the like—of which perhaps the most important are the

publications of the Ministry of Economic Planning, New Delhi, especially
those dealing with the Five Year Plans. Perhaps the most essential aid
in keeping abreast of the constantly changing economic and political
scene is *The Eastern Economist*, published weekly at the Hindustan
Times Press, New Delhi.

The volume of literature on the cultural background is vast; very useful
works are: O'MALLEY, L. S. S. (editor), *Modern India and the West*
(Oxford University Press, for Royal Institute of International Affairs,
London, 1941); GARRATT, G. T. (editor), *The Legacy of India* (Oxford
University Press, 1937); SMITH, W. C., *Modern Islam in India* (revised
edition; Gollancz, London, 1947).

On the more specifically political side the following may be noted: LUMBY,
E. W. R., *The Transfer of Power in India and Pakistan* (Allen and
Unwin, London, 1954); SYMONDS, R., *The Making of Pakistan* (Faber,
London, 1950).

The Kashmir problem is the subject of two monographs: BRECHER, M., *The
Struggle for Kashmir* (Canadian Institute of International Affairs and
Institute for Pacific Relations, by Ryerson Press, Toronto, 1953);
KORBEL, J., *Danger in Kashmir* (Princeton University Press and Oxford
University Press, 1954). The latter is perhaps the less objective, being
devoted to the thesis that Kashmir is a potential Korea: a view not
without some justification, but supported to some extent by extraneous
considerations.

TABLE 1

India and Adjacent Countries: Area and Population

	AREA (square miles)	POPULATION 1941	POPULATION 1951	PERCENTAGE OF INCREASE
India[1] . .	1,269,836	315,089,675	357,147,485	12·5
Pakistan . .	364,737	70,103,000	75,842,165	8·0
Kashmir . .	84,471	4,021,616	4,410,000E	9·65
Goa, Damão, Diu[2]	1,537	624,177	637,846	2·2
Afghanistan .	250,000 E	11,000,000–12,000,000 E		
Nepal . . .	54,000 E		8,946,000E	
Bhutan . .	18,000 E		300,000E	
Ceylon . .	25,332	6,693,945 (1946)	8,103,648 (1953)	21·7

[1] Including French India—196 square miles, population 323,295 (1941), 318,000
(1951, after loss of Chandernagore).

[2] Portuguese territory; Censuses 1940, 1950.

E = estimate.

TABLE 2

India: "Livelihood Categories"
(in thousands)

STATE	TOTAL POPULATION	AGRICULTURE	PER CENT.	OTHER PRODUCTION	PER CENT.
North					
Uttar Pradesh . .	63,216	46,897	74·2	5,301	8·4
East					
Bihar . . .	40,226	34,611	86·0	1,585	3·9
Orissa . . .	14,646	11,612	79·3	927	6·3
W. Bengal . .	24,810	14,195	57·2	3,811	15·4
Assam . . .	9,044	6,633	73·3	1,327	14·7
Manipur . . .	578	482	83·4	40	6·9
Tripura . . .	639	481	75·3	38	5·9
Sikkim . . .	138	126	91·3	1	0·6
South					
Madras[1] . .	57,016	37,022	64·9	7,043	12·4
Mysore . . .	9,075	6,343	69·9	930	10·2
Travancore-Cochin .	9,280	5,090	54·8	1,966	21·2
Coorg . . .	229	132	57·6	54	23·6
West					
Bombay . . .	35,956	22,098	61·5	4,949	13·8
Saurashtra . .	4,137	1,929	46·6	744	18·0
Kutch . . .	568	239	42·1	109	19·1
Central					
Madhya Pradesh .	21,248	16,149	76·0	2,252	10·6
Madhya Bharat .	7,954	5,744	72·2	793	10·0
Hyderabad . .	18,655	12,715	68·2	2,526	13·5
Bhopal . . .	836	548	65·6	88	10·5
Vindhya Pradesh .	3,575	3,114	87·1	164	4·6
Northwest					
Rajasthan . .	15,291	10,837	70·9	1,358	8·9
E. Punjab . .	12,506	8,069	64·5	915	7·3
Pepsu . . .	3,494	2,535	72·6	255	7·3
Ajmer . . .	693	315	45·5	134	19·3
Delhi . . .	1,744	172	9·9	302	17·3
Bilaspur . .	126	114	90·5	6	4·8
Himachal Pradesh .	983	914	93·0	23	2·3
INDIA .	356,663	249,118	69·8	37,641	10·6

[1] Including Andhra.
"Other production" includes factory and craft industry, mining, fishing, forestry, etc.; with totals in Census volumes due to rounding off.

and Urbanism, 1951

COMMERCE	PER CENT.	TRANSPORT	PER CENT.	OTHER	PER CENT.	URBAN POPULATION	PER CENT.
3,180	5·0	860	1·4	6,978	11·0	8,626	13·6
1,368	3·4	291	0·7	2,371	6·0	2,705	6·7
426	2·9	78	0·5	1,604	11·0	594	4·0
2,311	9·3	756	3·0	3,736	15·1	6,153	24·8
353	3·9	116	1·3	615	6·8	414	4·6
24	4·2	3	0·5	28	5·0	3	0·5
41	6·4	3	0·5	76	11·9	43	6·7
2	1·5	2	1·5	7	5·1	—	—
3,811	6·7	959	1·7	8,181	14·3	11,184	19·6
505	5·6	105	1·2	1,192	13·1	2,179	24·0
631	6·8	316	3·4	1,276	13·8	1,488	16·0
8	3·5	2	0·9	33	14·4	16	7·0
2,736	7·6	802	2·2	5,370	14·9	11,170	31·1
444	10·7	107	2·6	913	22·1	1,393	33·7
64	11·3	14	2·5	142	25·0	114	20·1
933	4·4	312	1·5	1,602	7·5	2,877	13·5
447	5·6	85	1·1	886	11·1	1,441	18·1
955	5·1	243	1·3	2,217	11·9	3,476	18·6
52	6·2	13	1·6	135	16·1	136	16·3
100	2·8	15	0·4	180	5·1	306	8·6
1,006	6·6	143	0·9	1,947	12·7	2,649	17·3
1,143	9·1	131	1·0	2,247	18·1	2,401	19·2
267	7·6	139	4·0	297	8·5	666	19·1
86	12·4	23	3·3	135	19·5	298	43·0
396	22·7	95	5·4	778	44·7	1,437	82·3
2	1·6	0	—	4	3·1	4	3·1
16	1·6	4	0·4	26	2·7	41	4·2
21,307	6·0	5,617	1·6	42,976	12·0	61,814	17·3

"other" professions, administration, domestic service, rentiers, etc. Minor discrepancies

TABLE 3
India: Population by States

Class A	AREA (square miles)	POPULATION (thousands)		DENSITY 1951	PERCENTAGE INCREASE
		1941	1951		
Andhra . .	67,025	18,783	20,283	303	8·0
Assam . .	85,012	7,593	9,044[1]	106	17·4
Bengal (W) .	30,775	21,837	24,810	806	12·7
Bihar . . .	70,330	36,528	40,226	572	9·6
Bombay . .	111,434	29,181	35,956	323	20·8
Madhya Pradesh .	130,272	19,632	21,248	163	7·9
Madras[2] .	60,765	31,048	36,733	605	18·3
Orissa . .	60,136	13,768	14,646	244	6·2
Punjab (E) .	37,378	12,699	12,641	338	− 0·5
Uttar Pradesh .	113,409	56,532	63,216	557	11·2
Class B	766,536	247,601	278,803	364	12·6
Hyderabad . .	82,168	16,327	18,655	227	13·3
Madhya Bharat .	46,478	7,170	7,954	171	10·4
Mysore . .	29,489	7,338	9,075	308	21·2
Pepsu[3] .	10,078	3,403	3,494	347	2·6
Rajasthan .	130,207	13,306	15,291	117	13·9
Saurashtra .	21,451	3,561	4,137	193	15·0
Travancore-Cochin .	9,144	7,500	9,280	1,015	21·2
Class C	329,015	58,605	67,886	206	15·8
Ajmer . . .	2,417	584	693	287	17·2
Bhopal . .	6,878	779	836	122	7·2
Bilaspur . .	453	110	126	278	13·3
Coorg . . .	1,586	169	229	144	30·5
Delhi . . .	578	918	1,774	3,017	93·2
Himachal Pradesh .	10,451	947	983	94	3·7
Kutch . . .	16,724	508	568	34	11·1
Manipur . .	8,628	512	578	67	12·0
Sikkim . .	2,744	122	138	50	12·5
Tripura . .	4,032	513	639	158	21·9
Vindhya Pradesh .	23,603	3,367	3,575	151	6·0
Class D	78,094	8,529	10,109	129	18·5
Andamans and Nicobars . .	3,215	34	31	10	− 8·6
TOTAL .	1,176,860	314,769	356,829	303	13·3

[1] Excluding an unreliable estimate of 560,000 for certain Tribal Areas.
[2] Excluding the 196 square miles with 318,000 people in French establishments, taken over in 1954.
[3] Patiala and East Punjab States' Union.

TABLE 4

India: Growth of Large Cities, 1941–51 (figures in thousands. Only states with cities of over 100,000 included)

| | CITIES OVER 100,000 | | | | | | | | PERCENTAGE OF INCREASE (1941–51) | | FEMALES TO 1,000 MALES | | |
	Number		Population		Percentage of State Population		Percentage of Urban Population[1]		State Population	Cities[2] Population	State	Cities	Cities
	1941	1951	1941	1951	1941	1951	1941	1951			1951	1941	1951
A States													
Bihar	3	5	467	857	1·3	2·1	22·4	31·7	9·6	37·6	989	755	824
Bombay	6	8	2,866	5,076	9·9	14·1	43·1	45·4	20·8	54·6	932	674	697
Madhya Pradesh	2	2	480	706	2·4	3·3	n.c.	24·5	7·9	47·1	993	881	887
Madras[3]	6	12	1,563	3,379	3·1	5·9	19·6	30·2	13·4	56·3	1,006	936	949
Orissa	0	1	0	102	0·0	0·7	n.c.	17·2	6·2	37·8	1,022	786	755
Punjab (E)	3	3	638	648	5·0	5·1	n.c.	27·0	− 0·5	1·6	863	724	802
Uttar Pradesh	12	16	2,510	3,908	4·4	6·2	35·9	45·3	11·2	31·7	910	767	786
West Bengal	3	7	2,605	3,610	11·9	14·6	n.c.	58·7	12·7	24·5	859	461	600
B States													
Hyderabad	1	2	739	1,219	4·5	6·5	33·7	35·1	13·3	46·5	921	919	985
Madhya Bharat	2	3	386	682	5·4	8·6	n.c.	47·3	10·4	46·0	925	801	876
Mysore	3	3	691	1,182	9·4	14·9	51·3	54·2	21·2	71·1	949	901	912
Rajasthan	3	3	430	589	3·2	3·9	21·1	22·2	13·9	40·0	921	853	896
Saurashtra	1	3	103	374	2·9	9·0	n.c.	26·8	15·0	64·8	975	891	943
T'core-Cochin	1	2	128	303	1·7	3·3	13·3	20·4	21·2	63·7	1,008	955	953
C States													
Ajmer	1	1	147	197	25·2	28·4	68·7	66·1	17·2	34·0	925	843	900
Bhopal[4]	0	1	0	102	0·0	12·2	n.c.	75·0	7·2	36·0	911	859	894
Delhi[4]	1	2	522	1,191	56·9	68·3	75·0	82·3	62·1	93·3	768	723	769
TOTAL (*all states*)	48	74	14,275	24,125	4·5	6·8	n.c.	39·0	13·3	44·2	947	716	785

[1] Urban population in 1941 not available for some states owing to boundary changes; indicated by n.c. = not comparable. For the same reason some of the figures given are somewhat in error, but not on a significant scale; the effect in all cases would be to lower the 1941 city proportion, so that the disproportionate growth of the large cities is in fact slightly understated.

[2] Increase in all cities over 100,000 in 1951, including those not ranking as such in 1941.

[3] Including Andhra.

[4] Details for Delhi, 1941 and 1951 respectively: 917,939/1,744,072; urban 695,686/1,437,134; Delhi city 521,849/914,790 New Delhi 93,733/276,314.

TABLE 5

India: Index of Industrial

Year	Cotton		Jute	Sugar	Paper
	Yarn	Cloth			
1946	100·0	100·0	100·0	100·0	100·0
1947	94·8	96·2	96·6	97·6	87·8
1948	105·9	110·5	100·2	116·5	92·4
1949	99·4	99·9	84·8	108·5	97·4
1950	85·9	93·8	76·8	105·8	102·7
1951	95·4	104·3	80·4	120·8	124·4
1952	106·0	117·7	87·4	161·9	129·7
1953	110·1	124·8	79·8	139·9	131·8

TABLE 6

Pakistan: Area and Population, 1951

State	Area (square miles)	Population (thousands)	Density to Square Mile	Percentage Increase 1941–51	Percentages 1951	
					Area	Popn.
Bahawalpur .	15,918	1,820	114	35·0	4·4	2·4
Baluchistan and Baluchi states	134,002	1,178	9	37·3	36·7	1·6
Khairpur . .	6,050	320	53	4·6	1·7	0·4
N.W. Frontier .	13,815	3,239	234	6·6	3·8	4·3
N.W. Tribal areas[1]	26,209	2,671	102	12·3	7·2	3·5
Punjab (W) .	62,987	18,814	299	19·7	17·3	24·8
Sind . .	50,443	4,619	92	26·5	13·8	6·1
Karachi Federal District .	812	1,118	1,377	?	0·2	1·5
West Pakistan .	310,236	33,779	109	19·4	85·1	44·5
East Pakistan .	54,501	42,063	772	0·5	14·9	55·5
Pakistan .	364,737	75,842	208	8·2	100·0	100·0

[1] Estimates.

Production, 1946–53

Coal	Cement	Sulphuric Acid	Steel Ingots and Metal for Castings	General Index
100·0	100·0	100·0	100·0	100·0
103·9	93·9	100·0	97·1	97·2
103·2	100·7	133·3	97·1	108·4
108·9	136·3	165·8	104·6	105·7
110·8	169·5	170·8	111·2	105·0
118·8	207·2	178·2	116·0	117·2
125·4	229·3	160·1	122·0	128·9
124·1	245·1	181·8	116·5	135·3

TABLE 7

India: Distribution of Religions, 1951

(A) Total Numbers (in thousands) and Percentages

	HINDUS	S.C.[1]	MOSLEMS	CHRISTIANS	SIKHS	TRIBAL[2]	JAINS	BUDDHISTS	PARSEES	OTHERS
	303,187		35,400	8,158	6,219	1,662	1,618	181	112	342
%	85·0	16·9	9·9	2·3	1·7	0·5	0·5			0·1%

[1] Scheduled Castes ("untouchables") as percentage of all Hindus.   [2] Tribal religions, not tribes as such, returned as 19,116,498.

(B) Major Concentrations of Minorities

(a) Percentage of total for religion in state which has 10 per cent. or more of Indian total; (b) Percentage of religion to total population of the state

STATE	MOSLEM (a)	(b)	CHRISTIAN (a)	(b)	SIKH (a)	(b)	TRIBAL (a)	(b)	JAIN (a)	(b)	BUDDHIST (a)	(b)	PARSEE (a)	(b)
Uttar Pradesh	25·5	14·3												
Bihar	12·9	13·3												
West Bengal	13·9	19·8					52·4	2·5			45·3	0·3		
Assam, Manipur and Tripura							39·2	6·4			21·0	0·4		
Sikkim											21·5	28·3		
Madras and Andhra	13·2	8·0	29·8	4·3										
Travancore-Cochin			36·4	32·0										
Bombay									35·4	1·6			87·5	0·3
Saurashtra and Kutch									11·6	4·0				
Rajasthan and Ajmer									22·2	2·3				
Punjab (E)					61·6	30·3								
Pepsu					27·7	49·3								
TOTAL	65·5		66·2		89·3		91·6		69·2		87·8		87·5	

CHAPTER XXI

The Neighbours of India and Pakistan

O. H. K. SPATE

The Landward Marches

THE "isolation of India" by sea and by land, save for the north-western entry, is a commonplace which has a good deal of truth in it; but it cannot be accepted without some refinement. The landward barrier, so clearly marked on the relief map, is in historical fact a blurred frontier zone. That Hinduism and Buddhism were once the dominants of society as far as the Hindu Kush is attested by the colossal rock-hewn Buddhas of Bamian, in the heart of Afghanistan, and many of the great empires of Hindustan were in fact saddle-states slung across the relatively low ranges around the Kabul river and the Khyber Pass; it is true that they were eventually faced with an enforced choice between a centre of power on the Afghan plateaux or in the Indo-Gangetic plains. Not only did "three empires meet" on the Pamirs, nearly making an actual trijunction of India, China, and Russia, but culturally Kashmir is divided between Islam, Hinduism, and Buddhism. Eastward, though Hinduism mingles with Buddhism on the Himalayan slope, the political boundary of India lies mainly in the malarial *terai* jungles—that is, below the outermost edge of the mountain mass. In the extreme east the wild country between Assam and Yunnan, deeply trenched and heavily forested, minimized direct contacts between India and China. But Assam itself was never subject to an Indian central power, not even that of the Moguls, until the British wrested it from Burmese invaders in 1824; its medieval rulers were in fact Shans, an offshoot of the Thai or Siamese peoples dominant east of the Irrawaddy.

In much of this frontier zone definite boundaries waited on the con-solidation of modern Powers, the British and the Russian Empires. Nor did this consolidation completely parcel out the mountainous no-man's-land between the three empires. States like Manipur and Kashmir, built around a core of paddy land in exceptionally large intermont basins, were brought within the bounds of India; but Afghanistan remained a buffer (with the Wakhan panhandle between Russian and Indian territory); Nepal and Bhutan were in the Indian orbit but not in the Indian Empire; much of the boundary with Tibet was never defined, let alone demarcated; and on both the north-west and the north-east frontiers of India a belt of unadministered tribal territory lay within the defined boundaries.

Nevertheless the most massive mountains of the globe, 1800 miles long and with ninety-two peaks over 24,000 feet, are obviously a military obstacle of the first class. The importance of the north-western entry, where the mountain core of Asia narrows to but 250 miles between Oxus and Indus and the main range (the Hindu Kush) has many practicable passes, has perhaps been too exclusively stressed: soldiers as well as monks have threaded through the complex ramparts and fosses of northern Kashmir, and the first Moslem incursion into India came not by the Khyber but through Makran, then perhaps more humid, when the Arabs took Sind in the seventh century A.D. But it is difficult to envisage more than the pettiest surface warfare around the Pamirs and the Karakoram, while rugged terrain and the rarefied atmosphere at ground level, with heavy summer cloud on the southern flanks of the mountain mass, render aviation exceedingly hazardous. Although in our day Communist domination of Tibet has revitalized a long-dormant frontier, the major strategic interest remains on the old North-west Frontier, and our survey may therefore begin here.[1]

The North-west Frontier and Afghanistan (Fig. 1). "The Frontier" of the old Indian Empire was simply that on the north-west, and more especially that with Afghanistan: all of it has been inherited by Pakistan. The boundary with Iran does not at present raise any special problems, although, of course, an extension of Russian influence into the old British sphere of southern Iran would do so at once. Along its northern border Baluchistan marches with Afghanistan, but here the border districts were under direct British rule. But in the North-west Frontier Province the administered areas lie back from the Afghan

[1] On the Himalayan barrier in general, see K. Mason, "The Himalayas as a Barrier to Modern Communications," in *Geogr. Journal*, vol. lxxxvii (1936), pp. 1–16; R. R. Rawson: "High Asia," in W. G. East and O. H. K. Spate (eds.): *The Changing Map of Asia* (third edition; Methuen, London, 1956), pp. 371–390.

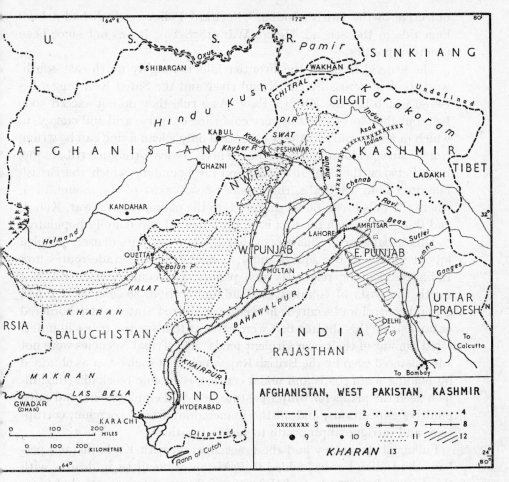

FIG. I. AFGHANISTAN, WEST PAKISTAN, AND KASHMIR

I, international boundaries, demarcated; 2, international boundaries, undemarcated; 3, boundary of Kashmir with India and Pakistan; 4, provincial
boundaries in Pakistan; 5, cease-fire line in Kashmir; 6–8, main railways of
strategic interest: 6, BG DT; 7, BG ST; 8, 2′ 6″ or 2′ ST; 9, capitals of countries;
10, other towns; 11, Administered Districts in N.W.F.P. and Baluchistan;
12, PEPSU (Patiala East Punjab States', Union, mainly Sikh); 13, princely states
adhering to Pakistan. N = Nepal. (BG, Broad Gauge; D(S)T, Double (Single)
Track.)

boundary (the Durand Line, in part undemarcated), and tribal movement, raiding or refugee, across the border is little impeded. This
frontier is thus very much alive; probably completely effective policing
could be obtained only by a single political control of both sides of
the quadrilateral Quetta-Peshawar-Kabul-Kandahar. This was the

objective of the British Indian "Forward Policy," which had a brief high tide in the Second Afghan War (1878–80); it has not since been practical politics.

The general trend of the Frontier hills is roughly north-east–south-west, broken across by the Kabul river and the Safed Koh range, between which lies the Khyber Pass. As a rule they do not exceed 5000 feet, but they form a belt of very confusing country, arid and craggy, in which (a few favoured valleys excepted) only a lean living can be wrung from scanty fields and poor grazing. This is the ever-troubled tribal zone, lying between the Afghan border and the boundary which the British inherited from the Sikhs, the *daman-i-koh* ("skirt of the mountain"), where the hills break down sharply into the plains of Peshawar, Kohat, and Bannu, of which the first is highly irrigated and densely populated.

This tribal zone is thus a poor, harsh land, yet quite densely peopled (about ninety to the square mile), lying astride the trade-routes into India, overlooking relatively rich plains. The country itself was not worth the costs of conquest and administration, so long as a rough general control was secured; hence the organized States which bordered or lay astride this shatter-belt were content to leave the tribes in unfettered pursuit of their own virulent feuds. The Tribal Agencies were not administered even by the British Raj, which kept such order as obtained by holding main roads and nodal centres, economic blockade (the hillmen need the plains for winter pasture, seasonal employment, and salt), punitive expeditions, and all the immemorial arts of coercion, corruption, and intrigue appropriate to such a frontier.

Financial stringency and the preoccupation with Kashmir (and perhaps the Indian border) added to Pakistan's difficulties in dealing with this thorny legacy; some of the major military outposts in tribal territory were abandoned, and defence relegated to local levies from subsidized tribes. For the same reason little can be done to settle the tribes by economic development, such as expansion of the rudimentary irrigation and orcharding which already exist; although, indeed, millennia of anarchic turbulence have set up an ethos likely to be very resistant to such peaceful penetration. But above all the problem is complicated by the issue of "Pathanistan" or, to use the current linguistic term, "Pakhtunistan."

Despite the often savage particularism of the tribes, all are generically Pathans and broadly of one culture; Sunni Moslem in religion, Pushtu or "Pakhtoon" in speech. But the Pathans are politically divided into the settled tribesmen of the Administered Districts (about one million), those of the Tribal Agencies (about two and a half million), and those of Afghanistan (anything from three to seven million). In recent years some sentiment of solidarity has grown up, culminating in the claim for Pakhtunistan; and behind Pakhtunistan stands the Afghan kingdom. Without Afghanistan, it is not very likely that the world would ever have heard of Pakhtunistan.

Afghanistan is generally a country of rugged hills and high, wind-swept plains, but includes a lowland strip along the Oxus and a number of reasonably fertile intermont valleys. The population, probably about ten or twelve million, is mainly tribal, some still nomadic. Mineral deposits include gold, iron, coal, and salt, of which the last two are to some extent worked; and there are significant oil reserves, notably at Shibargan, in the north-west and only forty-five miles from the Soviet border. Production includes cotton (with a small export to the U.S.S.R.), beet-sugar, and fruit; but the chief exports are wool and fine lamb-skins, the latter subject to a very fluctuant market.

Under able rulers considerable progress has been made over the last two decades in road-building, irrigation, a modest agriculturally based industrialization (powered by hydro-electricity), and a general moderni-zation of the country, especially round the capital, Kabul, which has over 200,000 inhabitants. Obviously this progress must depend largely on outside capital and technicians; and these in turn on political stability, internal and external.

Internally there are cleavages—tribal, occasionally dynastic, and even religious (Sunni versus Shiah); but the calculated preservation of the country as a buffer, and doubtless the reaction to a century of pressure between Britain and Russia, have greatly strengthened an older feeling of nationhood. The replacement of the British Raj by the relatively weak State of Pakistan, perennially embroiled with its great neighbour to the east, has seemed to offer an opening to Afghan aspirations, under cover of a solicitude for oppressed fellow-Pathans across the border: the old story of Piedmont and Serbia.

In its widest definition Pakhtunistan goes far beyond Pathan territory to include Baluchistan: the desire for a sea outlet is obvious. Since 1947 relations with Pakistan have often been strained, and to Pakistanis Kabul's links with New Delhi are disquieting. Discounting allegations of airborne arms traffic from India to Afghanistan, some remarks of Indian and Afghan leaders are at best ambiguous; only one country could be "squeezed in a fraternal embrace" between Kabul and Delhi.

The need for United Nations and American aid may discourage a forward policy on Pakhtunistan, especially since the Pakistan-U.S.A. agreement on arms and bases. On the other hand, the U.S.S.R. looks with most unfriendly eyes on American, or even U.N.O., technical missions around the Hindu Kush: Afghanistan remains a buffer State and, the case arising, may again become no more than a guarded pawn in the clash between the Powers of the Heartland and the Sea.

The Northern Frontiers of India (Fig. 2). India's long northern frontier—some 2000 miles—has taken on altogether novel significance with the far higher integration of Tibet with China, following on Communist control.

Kashmir is a joint Indo-Pakistani problem rather than one of external relations (see pp. 495–496); but we may note here a potential field for Tibetan irredentism in the solidly Buddhist population (some 40,000) in Ladakh, or Little Tibet. The cultural ties of the region are wholly with Lhasa; it is feudally dominated by the great monasteries, which fear, perhaps equally and with equal justice, Moslem rule should Kashmir go to Pakistan, the land expropriations of the new Indian regime, and the dominance of Chinese Communism in Tibet.

India is in direct contact with Tibet at the western and eastern ends of the frontier; the centre is occupied by three buffer States—Nepal, Sikkim, Bhutan. The short frontier athwart the Sutlej, north-west of Nepal, is perhaps too remote to raise serious difficulties; it is otherwise in Assam, where the McMahon line, along the Himalayan crest, was laid down as the boundary by the Anglo-Sino-Tibetan Convention of Simla in 1914: but this seems never to have been really accepted by the Chinese, and even before the Communist acquisition of Tibet there were petty violations of the border until the Himalayan glacis was organized into the Balipara and Sadiya Frontier Tracts during the second world war. The position is complicated by the fact that the real cultural and economic boundary lies at the foot of the mountain mass and not on its crest; since British maps often neglected to show the latter boundary, it is not surprising that Chinese maps habitually displayed the former. This geographical fact is recognized in the buffer States, which extend from the eternal snows to the hot marshy jungle of the *terai*. Bhutan may be briefly dismissed: 18,000 square miles of the wildest mountain and forest, its 300,000 Buddhists live an essentially feudal life, from

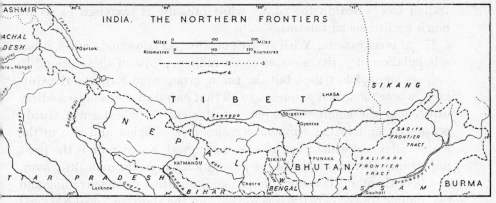

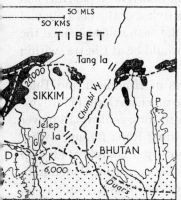

FIG. 2. INDIA: THE NORTHERN FRONTIERS

1–3, boundaries: 1, international demarcated; 2, international undemarcated, usually ill-defined; 3, internal; 4, main Himalayan watershed (not necessarily the crest) where not coincident with boundaries. *Map at left:* D = Darjeeling. G = Gangtok, K = Kalimpong, P = Punakha.

which foreigners are still excluded. Negotiations in 1948–49 led to a revision of the 1865 treaty by which the British Raj was responsible for such external relations as might exist; India took over this responsibility, increasing the annual subsidy to Bhutan and making a trifling retrocession (thirty-three square miles) from Assam.

Sikkim, though much the smallest of the three (2745 square miles, 136,000 people), is strategically the most significant: from it several easy passes cross into the Tibetan salient in the Chumbi Valley, at the head of which the wide Tang La, at only 15,200 feet with gently graded approaches, leads directly to the core-region of Tibet around Lhasa. This route carries as much trade as all other Indo-Tibetan trade-routes put together. Independence in India was followed by disorders in Sikkim, directed against the archaic autocratic government, and it is not surprising that Indian control has been stiffened; to the old British control of external relations has been added the right to maintain

Indian troops within the State, while pressure is exercised to secure much-needed social reforms.

Nepal is *sui generis*. With an area of about 54,000 square miles, it has a population of perhaps six or seven million. Most of these belong to various Mongoloid tribes, but the ruling group were Rajput—the Gurkhas, whose name was extended to all that excellent mercenary soldiery which was the country's major export. The Nepalis form a sturdy peasantry, cultivating temperate grains in the higher and rice in the lower valleys, of which that around the capital, Katmandu, is the most important. But two-fifths of the population live in the unhealthy *terai*, and here there was considerable Indian infiltration in little trading and rice-milling towns; here too was the base for the abortive Nepal National Congress *putsch* of 1949, which first shook the dykes of the old policy of seclusion. India has a particular interest in the eastern *terai*, since the great dam of the Kosi multi-purpose project would be at Chatra, within Nepal.

The culture of Nepal is a fascinating cross of Hinduism and Buddhism; its polity until 1950 was like nothing so much as that of Merovingian Gaul or the Tokugawa Shogunate in Japan: for a century all power was in the hands of the able, if backward-looking, Rana family, with a figurehead king. This regime was overthrown by a complicated *coup d'état*, from which King Tribhuvan emerged as a constitutional monarch, receiving economic aid and political guidance from India. Since 1952, however, the political life of Nepal has been a confused mêlée of factionalism in the capital and of peasant risings, in part Communist, in the countryside.

Some anxiety exists regarding the northern borders: difficult as the mountain country is, infiltration and petty warfare are always possible, and the social structure of Nepal is not secure enough for its rulers to face such strains with much confidence. Meanwhile Nepal is a camp-follower of India, and to retain even a qualified independence must probably remain so. But this policy is attacked, by both the reactionary Rana party and Communist or allied groups, as subservient to India or America, or both. It is significant that New Delhi advised the refusal of an American request for an embassy at Katmandu, since acceptance would make it difficult to refuse similar facilities for China, and this would bring the cold war right into the sub-continent.

The Tibetan frontier has thus come to life in a way not foreseeable by the British who forced the door to Lhasa in 1905. In an effort to secure stability on this newly agitated border, India signed an agreement with China (April 1954) by which the rest-houses and post and telegraph installations on the Lhasa road, secured as a result of the 1905 expedition, have been handed over to China, and the military escorts at Yatung and Gyantse withdrawn. It is arguable that Communist rule can at least prevent the irregular banditry responsible for the original insistence on these rights. In return India received little more than a pledge of non-interference with traders and pilgrims, and some small satisfaction in the timing of this purely intra-Asian agreement to coincide with an apparent disposition of the West to arrange Asian affairs without much reference to Asians.[2]

The Indian Ocean

If, as seems probable, the trade which undoubtedly took place between Sumeria and the Indus civilization was in part by sea, the Indian Ocean (or more precisely the Arabian Sea) was very likely the scene of the earliest long-distance navigation. Fascinating as its subsequent history is, for the purposes of political geography it is sufficient to begin our consideration with the virtual transformation of the Indian Ocean into a British lake.

Initiated by the successful outcome of the Anglo-French wars of the eighteenth century, this process was in essence completed by the British acquisition from the Dutch, as an incident of the Napoleonic Wars, of the Cape of Good Hope and Ceylon. As a sequel to the post-Napoleonic settlement British and Dutch spheres in the East Indies were also regularized, leaving Britain in undisputed possession of Penang, Malacca, and Singapore, and so with a firm grip on the passages into the eastern seas. On the other flank, Aden was secured in 1839 and control over the petty Sheikdoms of the Persian Gulf (the Trucial and Pirate Coasts) established by 1820. In 1869 the opening of the Suez Canal revolutionized the strategic pattern by providing an entirely new seaway to India and the Far East. Henceforth control of the Suez area became an overriding preoccupation of British foreign policy: Disraeli's purchase of a seven-sixteenths interest in the Canal Company in 1875

[2] See in general M. C. Feer, "India's Himalayan Frontier," in *Far Eastern Survey* (American Institute of Pacific Relations, New York), XXII/11 (October 1953); on Nepal, three articles in the same journal by W. Levi, XXI/12 (December 1952), XXII/1 (January 1953), XXIII/7 (July 1954); and, for the general background, O. H. K. Spate, *India and Pakistan* (Methuen, London, and Dutton, New York, 1954), pp. 405–421.

S

was soon followed by the occupation of Cyprus (1878) and Egypt (1882–83).

Territorially the British hold on Indian Ocean shores was not complete. Apart from the Dutch holdings in the East Indies and the short Siamese frontage in the Kra Isthmus, France retained Réunion, one of her old way-stations on the Cape route, and in the scramble for Africa added Madagascar with its dependencies and a small sector of Somaliland; Italy held Eritrea and much of the Somali coast, Germany Tanganyika, and Portugal Moçambique. But with both approaches from Europe, by Suez and the Cape, in British hands, these outliers were hostages to fortune: the argument is brought home by the rapid seizure of Madagascar by the British (May 5 to 7, 1942) and is not negatived by Italy's brief occupation of British Somaliland, so swiftly followed by the complete overthrow of her Ethiopian Empire. Apart from commerce-raiding such as that of the *Emden* in the 1914–18 war, naval operations in the Indian Ocean could take place only by British sufferance; most strangely, the only such operation on a large scale was the voyage, logistically a remarkable if crazy feat, of the Russian Baltic Fleet to its grave at Tsushima in 1905. As the antechamber to the Pacific and the Far East, the Indian Ocean was commercially an international highway of great importance; militarily it was virtually *mare clausum*.

This structure crumbled with astonishing suddenness in 1942. Mainland Malaya fell in seven weeks; the "island fortress" of Singapore, in the popular mind of Britain an image of impregnability, in two. The Japanese tide reached and lapped round the Andamans; but one strongpoint remained, admirably placed to rally British air and naval strength: Ceylon.

Ceylon. The locational significance of Ceylon surely needs no exposition: to the corner-site at the extremity of the Indian Peninsula it adds centrality in the Indian Ocean. Once the commercial meeting-place of the Græco-Roman and the Chinese worlds, it suffered little if any diminution of its importance in the age when the maritime entry by the Cape supplanted the old Levantine portages. Nowhere was the struggle between Portugal and Holland more bitter than in Ceylon, a warfare complicated by intrigue with the Sinhalese, who continued to hold their hill-kingdom of Kandy until it was annexed by the British in 1815.

In Dutch hands Ceylon was intrinsically valuable for the cinnamon trade; its role as a shipping node was probably to some extent diminished by the development of the new Dutch route to the Indies, making a long easting after leaving the Cape and then running north for Batavia. But the discovery of Australia sprang directly from this new course, and with the settlement of that continent and the opening of the Suez Canal Ceylon's nodal value was greatly enhanced; first Galle and later Colombo became an essential refuelling station on the long diagonal across the Indian Ocean.

While in global political geography this strategic nodality is the most significant fact about Ceylon, internal geographical factors are very important both economically and politically, and in both aspects ties with India are intimate.

The island has an area of over 25,000 square miles and a population around 8,250,000. Since the war a frontal attack on malaria has been remarkably successful, contributing very largely to a sharp fall in the death-rate (now over 55 per cent. lower than thirty years ago), while the birth-rate remains steady. But the cultivated area is barely one-fifth of the total, and plantations, mainly tea and rubber, account for well over one-third of the cultivated area. The bulk of the remainder is divided fairly equally between paddy and coconut, which latter can count both as a food and a cash crop.[3]

The "nutritional density" of population per square mile of food crops is thus very high indeed, probably ten times the average density of 320 in 1953. Energetic efforts are being made to increase home food production, notably by the remodelling of ancient tanks and irrigation channels (and adding new ones) in the Dry Zone, which in medieval times was one of the most flourishing regions of Ceylon, but for centuries has been little more than a sparsely populated waste of scrub: but progress, though not discouraging, is inevitably gradual, and large sums must be expended before any material improvement in the food-population position can be obtained by these means. Colonization in the Dry Zone has a marked psychological appeal, but so far only some 8000 families have been settled, and perhaps more immediate gains could be achieved by

[3] According to the 1946 Census of Agriculture, of a total acreage of 16,023,229, "cultivable" land amounted to 26·63 per cent.; of this figure 75·22 per cent. (= 20·03 per cent. of total area) was in fact cultivated. But "cultivable" land was that "opened out for cultivation," and a considerable area still remains for new settlement. Crop figures for 1953, in thousand acres: tea, 574; rubber, 650; (together 1224); paddy, 1047; coconut (1945), 1911 (*Statl. Abstract of Ceylon*, 1954). See B. H. Farmer, "Agriculture in Ceylon," in *Geogr. Rev.*, vol. xl (1950), pp. 42–66; *ibid.*, in O. H. K. Spate, *op. cit.*, pp. 743–784.

intensive agricultural improvement in already settled areas. Meanwhile Ceylon must still import 25–33 per cent. of her rice needs, and difficulties of procurement have led her to conclude a five-year agreement with China, exchanging rubber against rice. The increasing demographic pressure will obviously also affect relations with India, homeland of Ceylon's 984,000 "Indian Tamils."

Since tea, rubber, and coconut products normally account for over 90 per cent. of exports, diversification of this very unbalanced economy is clearly an urgent need. Resources for this task are none too good. The only minerals at present exploited to any extent are graphite and limestone for cement; deposits of thorianite and other rare earths, monazite and ilmenite sands, glass sands and kaolin, may be developed in the future. There is some fairly high-grade iron ore, but it is doubtful if any large-scale development is possible. The major resource is in the hydro-electric potential of the wet and deeply dissected highlands, and the large installation near Hatton (25,000 developed, 150,000 ultimate) may lead to a considerable expansion of consumption in industries such as textiles and rubber goods.

The socio-political problems are summed up by Farmer[4] with elegant conciseness: dual economy of peasant and plantation; plural society of Sinhalese peasantry, Tamils old and new, and a large number of "Moors" and Eurasians. This mixed population professes four creeds—Buddhism, Hinduism, Roman Catholicism, and Islam.

Both the major communities are themselves divided—the Sinhalese into those of the Low Country and those of the old Kandyan kingdom, the Indians (more importantly) between Ceylon and Indian Tamils.[5] The former are descendants of medieval invaders who conquered the north, and form a deeply rooted integrated community of all classes, with a disproportionate share of the island's entrepreneurial activity and professional and administrative cadres. The Indian Tamils are in the vast majority labourers on the plantations and their dependants, very poor and illiterate coolies. They present a considerable social, economic, and political problem: for example, from the Sinhalese viewpoint they

---

[4] *Loc. cit.*

[5] Numbers in thousands (1953 Census):

Low Country Sinhalese	. 3464	Ceylon Tamils .	909
Kandyan Sinhalese .	. 2157	Indian Tamils .	984
	5621 (69·4 per cent.)		1893 (23·4 per cent.)

The most important group of the remaining 585,000 are the "Moors" (Moslems), numbering 474,000.

are mostly sojourners who, if freely given the franchise, would be so much voting-fodder for the upper ranks of the Ceylon Tamils. Yet they are at present essential to the working of the export industries. There is thus always a latent possibility of friction with India over their status.

The small European community (6000) poses a different problem. The majority of the larger (and better-run) tea estates, and many of the rubber, are still European-owned or managed, or both, and this is a rock of offence to nationalists; conversely planters allege victimization through the administration of controls and welfare legislation, especially since the attainment of Dominion status in 1948. Sinhalese nationalism has not yet run its full course, as is shown by the recent increase of friction over the use of the Tamil language; while continued British use of the air and naval base at Trincomalee, in the undeveloped north-east, may be considered rather doubtful.

India and the Indian Ocean

Out of rather under 3,500,000 Indians overseas, about 2,855,000 are in Indian Ocean countries.[6] The large emigrations of labourers to Malaya, Ceylon, and Mauritius have also their professional and commercial cadres; in pre-war Burma an Indian sub-imperialism left but a small share of entrepreneurial activity to the Chinese, and still less to the Burmese; in East Africa Indians form a most important trading group between Africans and Europeans; the Indian problem in South Africa remains acute. Indians obviously occupy a key position in Africa, in a sense dependent on the framework of European rule, yet feeling themselves in a position of inferiority which leads to tactical alliances with the African majority, to whom they may teach the arts of politics. Pakistan's Indian Ocean interests are less direct and tangible: although she has important trading links with South-west Asia, Islamic ideology rather than economics is the real bond.

There is very little likelihood of any material increase in Indian emigration: indeed, since the depression of the 1930's the trend has been the other way, a trend accentuated in Burma (formerly the most important "colony") by the mass return of Indians before the Japanese inva-

[6] Main groups in thousands (estimates for various dates between 1946 and 1950): South Africa, 282; East Africa, 184; Ceylon, 732; Burma, 400–700; Malaya, 604; Mauritius, 285. The only other large concentrations are in Fiji (134) and the British West Indies (434). *Cf.* Fig. 16 in East and Spate, *op. cit.*, p. 167.

sion and the post-war determination of the Burmese to keep their Indian problem within the proportions thus reduced and made more manageable. In most of the countries concerned there is resentment against the Indians as exploiters or as cheap labour, the more so as Hinduism is socially very resistant to assimilation. Yet precisely because of this reaction the Government of India, itself not immune to nationalist pressures, is not likely to diminish its active solicitude on behalf of these colonies, which indeed provide extremely useful *points d'appui* for the expansion of the trade of an industrializing country.

Hence there are at least latent fears of "Indian imperialism" in Burma and Ceylon, and conversely some Indian groups might aspire to a *mare nostrum* in the Indian Ocean. But for the overriding menace of the Russo-American conflict, with its concomitant for southern Asians of a desire for neutralist solidarity, the situation would be more serious. In the context of the world to-day, rife with far more explosive tensions, the issue is not immediate: but there are definite potentialities of friction.

FURTHER READING

On the Northwest Frontier: DAVIES, C. C., *The Problem of the Northwest Frontier, 1890–1908* (Cambridge University Press, 1932; wider than title suggests); BARTON, W., *India's North-West Frontier* (Murray, London, 1939; official-popular in tone, but a clear survey).
Developments on the Himalayan frontiers must be followed in periodicals.
The literature of the Indian Ocean is mainly historical: see, *e.g.*, BALLARD, C. A. *Rulers of the Indian Ocean* (Duckworth, London, 1927); PANIKKAR, K. M., *India and the Indian Ocean* (Allen and Unwin, London, 1945; the most important book from a political geographer's point of view); POUJADE, J., *Le Route des Indes et ses Navires* (Payot, Paris, 1946); GONÇALVES, J., *Os Portugueses e o Mar das Índias* (Libraria Luso-Espanhola, Lisbon, 1947). ANSTEY, V., *The Trade of the Indian Ocean* (Longmans, London, 1929), has still some useful points.
More important than the elementary geographies of Ceylon by COOK, E. K., second edition, revised by KULARATNAM, K. (Macmillan, Madras, 1951), and DE SILVA, S. F. (second edition; Colombo Apothecaries Co., Colombo, 1945), are: JENNINGS, I., *The Economy of Ceylon* (Oxford University Press, Madras, etc., 1951); *The Economic Development of Ceylon* (Report of International Bank Mission, Colombo, 1952).
FARMER, B. H., has in preparation a book on Ceylon for the R.I.I.A., London, which will undoubtedly be most useful.
On Indian emigration: GANGULEE, N., *Indians in the Overseas Empire* (Hind Kitabs, Bombay, 1947); KONDAPI, K., *Indians Overseas, 1838–1949* (Indian Council for World Affairs, New Delhi; Oxford University Press, Bombay, etc., 1951).

CHAPTER XXII

The Pacific : Some Strategic Considerations[1]

O. H. K. SPATE

THIS chapter attempts no more than a general survey of some of the main geopolitical factors indicated by its title. So far as may be, it seeks to be objective in the most limiting sense of that word. To discuss the strategic situation in the Pacific without reference to the ideological cleavage of the world to-day would indeed produce vacancy in a vacuum; but that cleavage is regarded simply as a given fact. The ideological and material conquests of Communism, the social factors which have made these conquests possible, the desirability of containing it, the political tactics necessary to this end, the question of responsibility for wars past or future, the ethics of preventive war—with all these this survey has nothing to do.

This is a large self-limitation, but it is not self-stultification: there is virtue, now and then, in a rigid refusal to contemplate anything but the brute material facts of logistics and power. For once we go beyond this, we run serious risks of being caught up in our propaganda, as has, indeed, happened more than once to both the major antagonists in our divided world. These risks must, of course, be taken in any political action; nevertheless there is value in the attempt at a detached assessment, since the choice and use of political weapons largely depend, for their effect, on a realistic appraisal of geopolitical facts: the geography is in an important sense neutral.

To begin with, the ideological cleavage does give us our primary human fact. We must beware, however, of accepting this for more than it is worth. Even should both the centres of political magnetism,

[1] Originally prepared for the Australian Delegation to the Commonwealth Relations Conference, Lahore, April 1954. Thanks are due to Professor Gordon Greenwood, of the University of Queensland, and the Australian Institute of International Affairs for permission to reprint.

Washington and Moscow, adopt the view that "he who is not with us is against us," the fact remains that in a power sense, even if not psychologically, the division in the Pacific area is tripartite rather than dual.

On the one hand we have a great land-and-air Power which in the recent past has shown itself to be still expansive; on the other a great Power determined on at least containing the land Power and itself in this sphere based primarily on sea-and-air. Both have their outworks, round which a lively action of sorties takes place. But between them are a number of units of unequal value, some (as India) consciously neutralist, some (as Australia) consciously committed, but in neither case really strong enough to develop an independent strategy which would have any chance of enforcing a solution outside the major dichotomy. And yet the existence of these units as nations in their own right does impose some limits on the freedom of action of the major antagonists; for instance, minor but sovereign States can only be used on one side or the other by negotiation (which usually means publicity), and in some respects they cannot be used at all unless and until hostility culminates in open war.

The Proto-history of Pacific Strategy

In a rather recondite sense the strategic history of the Pacific might be said to begin with the first European intrusion into its waters, that of Magellan in 1519–21. To Spain at least the great ocean was of imperial significance as the link between the Philippines and Mexico, and although Anson's capture of the Manila galleon (1743), like Drake's foray, was a mere audacity, it is salutary to reflect that "global warfare" is not entirely a concept of our own age: the Ministry of All the Talents in Britain seriously considered in 1806 a double descent on Mexico, from the West Indies and from India via Manila;[2] a "pincer movement" grandiose enough for King Picrochole.

Nevertheless, by the end of the eighteenth century the Pacific was beginning to be definitely drawn within the ambit of Western power-politics. Penetration along its western flank had indeed begun much earlier (the Portuguese reached Japan in 1642), but was not of great importance until the opening-up of China by the Treaty Ports system

[2] See Sir John Fortescue, *History of the British Army* (Macmillan, London, 1901–30), vol. v, pp. 378–379; and for comment F. Rabelais, *The Heroic History of Gargantua and Pantagruel* (numerous editions), Book I, chapter xxiii.

after the Opium War (1839–41); though in the rather half-hearted jockeying for position on the approaches Raffles had already seized upon the key position of Singapore (1819), over against Dutch Batavia (Djakarta), which for just two centuries had guarded the Sunda Strait. In the southern Pacific the foundation of New South Wales (1788) was the first step in the creation of an altogether different type of base, formally complete by 1840, by which year the British claim to the whole continent of Australia had been asserted by settlement in every State, including what is now the Northern Territory; here, in 1824–29, abortive settlements were planted at Melville Island and Port Essington, designed in part to attract the Malay trade. In 1840 New Zealand also fell definitely under British control.

On the Pacific coast of North America there was a most extraordinary overlap of competing claims—Spanish, Russian, British, American. The great Russian drive to the East had spilled over from Siberia and Kamchatka into Alaska—and, indeed, the Russian-American Company, founded in 1799, actually extended its operations to Hawaii. Spanish claims, of course, were of longer standing, and hardly to be disposed of by Drake's proclamation of "New Albion" or by Dr Johnson's pamphlets; but there was no effective settlement north of San Francisco. In 1819 Spanish claims were limited to south of 42° N., and in 1824 Russia agreed to remain north of 54° 40'. The gap was open to Canadians and Americans, and was duly filled, not without friction ("Fifty-four forty or fight").

By 1840, then, all the margins of the Pacific (China, Indo-China, and Japan excepted) were firmly under European or American control—including Latin America, though the Pacific coast of South America was virtually *res nullius*, geopolitically speaking. So also, in effect, were the Dutch East Indies so long as Britain and the Netherlands remained on a friendly footing. But the oceanic Pacific, though well enough known as a field for whaling, trading, and evangelizing, was politically negligible. The antechamber to the Pacific—the Indian Ocean—was far more significant strategically, and its significance was enhanced by the opening of the Suez Canal (1869), after which it became in effect a British lake. It remained for the Americans to make the Pacific proper truly significant in the pattern of world power.

s*

The American Intrusion and the Rise of Japan

From the infancy of the Republic American interests had been wide-cast over the Pacific; it is sufficient to recall that the first private vessel to enter Sydney Harbour from overseas was a Yankee trader, and American merchants were also very early to the fore at Canton. But with the Oregon Treaty (1846), which settled the conflict with Britain over the Washington-Oregon-British Columbia area, and the seizure of California in the Mexican War (1846–47), the United States became a Pacific Power in the fullest sense of the word. Only seven years later it was an American commodore who definitively forced the Japanese to open their ports to Western trade. After the 1840's, then, the oceanic Pacific begins to have a political as well as a cultural and economic history. Despite the acrimony with which its islands were parcelled out between Americans, British, French, and Germans, however, too much importance need not be attached—in this phase—to these mostly minuscule territorial holdings; however useful as coaling and cable stations, or as trading *points d'appui*, the Pacific islands were after all only the small change of imperialism. Only to Australia and New Zealand were they of prime importance, and that was perhaps somewhat unreal: the amount of German "resistance" at Rabaul in 1914 justified Lord Salisbury's nonchalance rather than the Australian agitation of 1883–84.

In the next phase this estimate needs qualification. The modern history of the Pacific, in which it becomes an area of strategic importance in the strictest military sense, can be said to begin with two naval battles: the Japanese victory over China at the Yalu river (1894) and Dewey's destruction of the Spanish fleet in Manila Bay (1898). However, this was not yet oceanic war, since Dewey's fleet was not based on either trans- or even intra-Pacific bases, but sailed from Hong Kong. American control of the Philippines, and the rise of Japan as a first-class naval Power, immediately brought into importance the chain of islands north of the equator, staging-posts on the American line of communications: Hawaii, Midway, Wake, Guam. The point was emphasized after the first world war, when Japan took over the ex-German Marianas and Carolines, with at least two potentially important bases, Yap and Truk. The American northern flank was guarded, however, by the acquisition in 1867 of Alaska and the Aleutians from Russia. A very important by-product of the American extrusion right across the Pacific was the renewed urgency of the American need for the Panama Canal: five years after Manila Bay the United States recognized, in record time, the independence of the Republic of Panama, previously a part of recalcitrant Colombia.

For Britain and the British Commonwealth the oceanic Pacific was less vital: the approach from the United Kingdom to the Far East and to the South-west Pacific remained by the Indian Ocean, and Singapore was held to be a sufficient key to its defence from any Pacific threat. The Japanese acquisition of the Carolines, however, gave a new value to the screen of islands north of Australia and New Zealand, from New Guinea to the Cook group. The Japanese home base was only 1500 miles from the advanced base at Truk, and this was obviously a very different situation from that when they were in German hands. Once more the point was driven home by the lapse in 1921 of the Anglo-Japanese alliance and the construction of the Singapore naval base.

The Geopolitical Pattern: Bases and Potentials

By 1941 the strategic values of the Pacific were being transformed by air power; how revolutionary the transformation was to be could hardly be judged even by Pearl Harbor and the sinking of *Prince of Wales* and *Repulse*, but only by the succeeding four years of the first oceanic war. Put shortly, the effect is simply that the *offensive* power of island bases has been greatly enhanced for the Power with command over the air; but once this command is lost their garrisons can be written off, and hardly retain even a containing power of much significance. The further development of atomic power has reduced the defensive value of small island-bases, which of their nature offer very little scope—in extreme cases none at all—for dispersal, concealment, or going underground. Nevertheless air and atomic power do not alter the fundamentals of logistics, but, as it were, only the scale of their application and its tempo. Further, in what we may with some cynicism call "normal" cases, atomic onslaught will presumably still be followed by the occupation of hostile territory, not to mention the seizure of precariously neutral areas, and for this bases of assembly and supply are still needed. It is true, of course, that the uninhibited use of atomic power might well "make a desert and call it peace"; but, however likely this might be, in the long run it is not so likely (initially at least) to be the intention. Distances, land masses, populations, resources, are still of prime importance.

It is logical to consider circum-Pacific land areas before examining the logistic values of Pacific distances; for in the land masses are the primary bases. Indeed, it would be helpful if there were some word other than "base" for the islands, although the military usage of "base" for them has a pre-emptive right. The quantitative discrepancy between even a medium-sized continental country and the largest and most populous of the oceanic Pacific islands is so great as to be qualitative; there is no true base, able to set up and maintain independent force of more than negligible size, within the Pacific; the real bases are all marginal. This may be a truism, but the distinction is none the less a vitally important one.

As to man-power, the simplest and perhaps least adequate measure of war potential, the first and most striking fact is, of course, the dominance of the Asian sector. Following are rough approximations of population, in millions:

> *Pacific Asia*: 721, of which Pacific U.S.S.R. + China = 460; disputed Korea and Indo-China = 56; American bloc (Japan, Formosa, Malaya, Philippines) = 119; and Thailand and Indonesia, which may be regarded as doubtful and/or precarious = 93.
>
> *Pacific America*: 52·6, of which Latin America = 35·5.
>
> *Australia, New Zealand, and Pacific Islands*: 14.

Very roughly the Communist countries would amount to about 460 millions, excluding North Korea and Viet-Minh; those definitely following the American lead to about 194 millions; those doubtful, neutralist, precarious, or (as in the smaller Latin American States) of merely marginal significance to about 134 millions.

One point to which some consideration is probably due is the overwhelming preponderance of China's man-power in the Soviet Pacific bloc. To a large extent this is offset by dependence on the U.S.S.R. for major armaments; but in a general war the U.S.S.R. would, of course, have heavy commitments on other fronts, and, whatever the influence or control of Moscow over Peking in the "limited liability" Korean war, these factors taken together suggest that in the Pacific sphere of a general war the Soviet Union would have to rely heavily on

Chinese man-power, so heavily that it could hardly have a free strategic hand.

The situation is, of course, very different when we turn from man-power to consider war industrial potential. Space does not permit of any detailed survey, but a few significant figures may be noted under topical (as opposed to regional) heads. Atomic power is omitted: on the one hand the writer's competence does not extend to assessing such authentic technical data as pass through security screens; on the other the general picture and its changes are constantly before our eyes in the Press of the world.[3]

Oil. In 1950 crude-oil production in the U.S.S.R. was 270 million barrels. Very little of this can be credited to Sakhalin and the Soviet Far East generally; but a large area in western and central Siberia is possibly oil-bearing. China has oil-shales in Manchuria and a field which might be exploitable under the spur of necessity in Kansu; these do not amount to much, and the value of the Sinkiang fields (to be exploited under the 1954 Sino-Soviet economic pact) is unknown. Against these resources it is sufficient to cite some 1950 figures (in million barrels):

California	.	355
Venezuela	.	545 ('Pacific' by virtue of proximity to Panama)
Colombia	.	34
Peru	.	15
Canada	.	29
Indonesia	.	50
		1028

Coal. Pre-war estimates, rough as they are, suggest that the total coal reserves of China are very substantial—of the order of at least 250,000 million metric tons. Before 1948, however, actual raisings varied between *c.* 20 and 41 million tons a year; Manchurian output was of a similar order. Siberian output—the great bulk of it between the Urals and Kazakhstan—was 123 million tons in 1950. On the other side we have a total output in the Pacific area of about 45 to 65 million tons a

---

[3] Statistics in the rest of this section are based mainly on: E. W. Zimmerman, *World Resources and Industries* (Harpers, New York, 1951); W. G. East and O. H. K. Spate (eds.), *The Changing Map of Asia* (Methuen, London, and Dutton, New York; 3rd ed., 1956); T. Shabad, *Geography of the U.S.S.R.* (Columbia U.P., N.Y., 1951); W. S. and E. S. Woytinsky, *World Population and Production* (Twentieth-century Fund, New York, 1953).

year—30 to 50 million in Japan, 15 million in Australia (excluding lignite), small quantities in the Philippines, "Indo-China," and Chile.

Iron and Steel. In 1950 the U.S.S.R.'s output of crude steel was 27·3 million tons, of which about half came from the Urals and Asian centres, which include Komsomolsk on the Amur. Total iron-ore reserves in the U.S.S.R. are estimated at about 2000 million long tons—a fifth of those of the U.S.A. As for China, iron ores are widely scattered but except in Manchuria badly placed in relation to coal; in 1943, under the Japanese, Manchuria produced: iron ore, 5·3; pig iron, 1·7; steel, 0·8 million metric tons—figures of the same order as those of India. Against these figures may be set 1950 outputs of (a) iron ore, (b) pig iron, (c) crude steel (all in million metric tons) for:

	(a) ore	(b) pig	(c) steel
Japan	0·6	0·9	2·0
U.S.A.	113·3	61·0	88·4
Australia	c. 2·2	1·3	1·4
Chile	3·7	n.d.	c. 0·2
	119·8	63·2	92·0

Of the U.S.A. steel output, 5 million tons or so come from California and other western states.

Other war materials present a rather mixed picture. China has certainly large reserves of *bauxite*, estimated in 1952 at 10 per cent. of the world total; but bauxite figures are notoriously rough, and it is likely that this is an overestimate, less by exaggeration of China's reserves than by understatement of those in other countries. But these are merely reserves; the essential fact of the present is that, despite deficiencies in raw material, the U.S.A. produces about half of the world's aluminium, and one-third of the U.S.A. figure comes from Washington and California. Of *tin* and *tungsten* south-west China has important reserves; despite difficulties of access and primitive methods, China has at times been among the four or five leading producers. But her 1950 production of tin ore has been estimated at about 4,000,000 metric tons, against Malaya 58,000,000, Indonesia 33,000,000, and Bolivia 32,000,000. The U.S.S.R. has about 8 per cent. of world *copper* reserves, but output is not known; the U.S.A. produces 600,000 to 900,000 million metric tons of raw copper a year (about a third of world production), Chile about half as much. As for reserves, the U.S.A. controls half the world total (26 per cent. of world total in the U.S.A. itself, 21 per cent.

in Chile) and the British Commonwealth another quarter, mainly in Canada and south-central Africa. The Pacific proper has one important producer of one important metal: New Caledonia is the world's third producer of *nickel*, with Cuba second and both overshadowed by eastern Canada. But the U.S.S.R. reserves are the second largest in the world; and she has about a third of *manganese* reserves, and is self-sufficient in manganese production, unlike any other large steel producer. Finally, it is hardly necessary to stress the monopolistic position of Malaya and Indonesia in natural *rubber*, nor on the other hand the importance of synthetics in the U.S.A. and the U.S.S.R.

We may sum up this discussion, rather crudely, by tabulating the mineral position of the U.S.A. and the U.S.S.R. under four heads: A, available for export; B, adequate for domestic needs; C, some import necessary; D, dependent almost entirely on imports.

	U.S.A.	U.S.S.R.			U.S.A.	U.S.S.R.
antimony	C	C		mercury	C	B
asbestos	D	A		mica	D	B
bauxite	C	C		nickel	D	B
chromite	C	A		nitrate	D	B
coal	A	B		petroleum	A	A
copper	A	B		platinum	D	A
graphite	C	B		sulphur	A	B
iron ore	A	B		tin	D	C
lead	B	B		tungsten	C	C
manganese	D	A		zinc	B	B[4]

The Geopolitical Pattern: the Arsenals

Resources in men and raw materials, basic as they are to war potential, are in themselves merely latent factors. Although in the stress of revolutionary or ideological war the possibility of remarkable success in forming and organizing mass armies must be reckoned with, the decisive factor in a modern war is pre-existence of a technologically advanced base, capable of rapidly re-tooling itself for military ends. There are but three really first-class bases in the world, and none of them is in the Pacific. They are north-east Anglo-America, north-west Europe, and the Soviet industrial zones from the Ukraine to the Urals. North-west

[4] For details, see Zimmermann, *op. cit.*, p. 452; Woytinsky and Woytinsky, *op. cit.*, pp. 331-334; and D. B. Shimkin, *Minerals—a Key to Soviet Power* (Harvard University Press, 1953).

Europe is probably not as yet sufficiently integrated to count as a unit; the Soviet base hardly carries the weight of metal of the American, though its more interior situation and its greater dispersal—with out-liers as far as Kuznetsk and Karaganda, in the heart of Siberia—may to some extent offset this. The Pacific itself has in effect four arsenals. Two of these, Japan and the American west coast, rank at the top of the second class; south-east Australia is definitely below them; and there is an unknown quantity in the Sino-Soviet Far East. All other Pacific countries, whether in South-east Asia or South America, are virtually negligible quantities; which means in effect that they may readily be-come minus quantities for the side which they are nominally on. Yet their loss or retention might be of great importance psychologically (as affecting morale), economically (by virtue of special resources), or logis-tically (as sea- or air-bases); but again this might mean a diversion of forces to the detriment of strategically more vital areas. Weak bases may become traps; in a sense it was the over-extension of the 1890's which led to the loss of the British empire in South-east Asia in 1942, and the Japanese over-extension of that year which led to disaster by 1944.

The character and the geopolitical situation of the Pacific arsenals warrant some discussion. The *American west coast* is of relatively recent development industrially. It lacks the really heavy backing of coal and iron of the American east, relying rather on oil and hydro-electricity. This means, however, that its industries are completely modern in struc-ture: significant in this connexion is the fact that over one-third of the U.S.A.'s capacity in aluminium production is in the three Pacific states, which have about 9·5 per cent. of the country's population. A very large sector of industrial development is devoted to aircraft and to electronic equipment, all of which has a very obvious strategic impor-tance. On the other hand, the proximity of atomic plants and testing-grounds in Nevada and Arizona is perhaps of little significance owing to the easy portability of atomic munitions. As to vulnerability, this area is fronted by the wide moat of the eastern Pacific, empty of islands and defended on the farther side by American outworks in the Pacific. But some regard must be paid to the possibilities of approach by Great Circle routes across the Arctic (*cf.* pp. 444–445). Tokyo and Irkutsk are roughly equidistant from San Francisco, a fact not readily apparent from most atlases.

The *Japanese* arsenal suffers from the lack of a really sound raw-material basis; the pre-war development was a forced one, and indeed overstrained, made possible only by intensive stockpiling and the scraping together of raw materials from all over eastern Asia. The Manchurian resources in coal, iron ore, and oil-shales, while not absolutely large, were of great relative significance to the Japanese industrial structure, and these are now denied her. Furthermore, the extreme vulnerability of the Japanese islands to air attack from the adjacent mainland hardly needs stressing. Nor, perhaps, can the ideological adherence of Japan to the American bloc be regarded as secure beyond question. Hence, while Japan positionally appears a first-class base for operations against the Asian mainland, she might in practice be a liability quite as much as an asset.

Australian resources, or at least the developments so far based upon them, are secondary in scale, though capable of fairly rapid expansion to make a substantial contribution to war potential. Their situation in the south-east, turned away from Asia, makes them relatively little vulnerable, but the defence of the empty north-west against a power with advanced bases in Indonesia would be a serious liability.

The *Sino-Russian Far East* is industrially a little-known quantity, at least to the writer. The Soviet Far East is thinly populated even in the more settled districts: with about 3,500,000 people on an area of about 1,200,000 square miles it is indeed comparable to Australia. It is still essentially a primary producing area (gold, furs, fish, timber), but mineral resources are fairly substantial, including both coal and iron ore. There are steel mills at Komsomolsk on the Amur, and that town, Khabarovsk, and Vladivostok have a considerable variety of engineering industries, including aircraft and automobile assembly and shipbuilding. The total population of these three towns is probably around three-quarters of a million, and on the face of it the industrial and war potential of the area is at least comparable to that of Australia's only major extra-metropolitan industrial region, the lower Hunter Valley. But against this must be set the fact that the area is far from self-sufficient in food. A factor which might be of considerable logistic significance is the often-reported concentration of numerically large submarine flotillas in the ports of the Far East. As for China, it is not likely that the *heavy* war potential of her industries, even including Manchuria, will be very significant for some considerable time; in this respect she must continue to depend largely upon the U.S.S.R. But in the small change of modern war, expendable light armaments, she is probably even now by no means negligible. The Sino-Soviet Far East is, of course, vulnerable to attack both from offshore bases from the Philippines to the Aleutians, and by Arctic Great Circle routes.

The Geopolitical Pattern: Distance

The Pacific War of 1941–45 naturally enforced a striking change in the emphasis of logistic thinking. In Derwent Whittlesey's interesting section on the Pacific in *The Earth and the State* (1939) airways rate six lines out of seven pages: the emphasis is on surface naval activity. But by 1945 nearly 90 of the 460 pages of *Compass of the World*[5] are devoted specifically to the logistics of the air, besides numerous shorter references. Undoubtedly the distortions of Mercator's projection, so popular both in the U.S.S.R. and the British Commonwealth because of its poleward exaggeration, were reflected in the older view on strategy, and it was time that a "global" view should become more current. It is salutary to be forced to admit that "To men of my generation Greenland is farther east than New York City and therefore farther from New York than Tokyo. To the airmen, New York to Tokyo is 7000 miles; Greenland to Tokyo over the pole 5000," or again that "bombers based on North Cape, Norway, or Murmansk are as close to Vancouver and Chicago as to Washington."[6]

This revolution in thinking is in accordance with the nature of things; nevertheless some qualifications must be borne in mind:

(i) aircraft, like ships, are limited in their efficient action by the size and facilities of their ports; and (even allowing for non-economic military expenditure) maintenance and repair facilities will be best developed on major commercial routes—and there is not much of a payload in the Arctic;

(ii) as we have already noted, unless outright annihilation of the opponent is aimed at from the start, war will still include the occupation of territory, which on a large scale will call for surface supply lines; not to mention the supply or garrisoning of areas held for reasons of morale and economics;

(iii) winds and weather pay no attention to Great Circles.

[5] Ed. H. Weigert and V. Stefansson (Macmillan, New York, and Harrap, London, 1945).
[6] A. MacLeish and C. Hurd in *Compass of the World*, pp. 6, 110.

The limitations of the 'Great Circle' argument may be illustrated by a concrete case.

At the end of May, 1942, the Japanese, as Mercator-minded as many in this country [the U.S.A.], sent a major attack force to the Hawaiian Islands and a diversionary force to Alaska. Surprised by a handful of planes at Dutch Harbor [Alaska] they beat a hasty withdrawal and contented themselves with a comparatively harmless occupation of Kiska and Attu. Had they been globally-minded, these forces of course would have been reversed. We were still unprepared to stop a major force in Alaska, and it is highly probable that they could have been in British Columbia by fall. This would have revealed the true position of Pearl Harbor as a naval supply base for the eastern Pacific and a steppingstone to the south-west Pacific, relatively useless as a defense of our continent.

In short, "our only defense of the continent (at Pearl Harbor) was in reality only a flank defense."[7]

There are a number of fallacies in this argument. It is, of course, entirely true that a completely unprepared U.S.A. might have been knocked off balance by a serious Alaskan thrust; but this is beside the point. The concrete case is intended to illustrate a *general* principle; the argument purports to establish a new strategy superior to the "age-old flat-map strategy." But to do so we must construct a logistic "model" (in the economist's sense), and reduce our variables by assuming, on both sides, forces proportionate to the objective; but we must include other logistic variables than mere distance—factors of terrain and the possibilities of maintaining appropriate forces. To consider nothing but distance is a gross over-simplification; and to assume, as this argument does, that the other fellow sits still is naïve. It needs no very extensive acquaintance with the history of war to see that (given competent force and leadership) a flank defence is usually less costly to the defender, and more decisive in his favour, than the simple defence-to-the-front implicitly advocated here. For it is obvious that a diversion of main Japanese forces along the Alaskan route would leave the west-central Pacific "front" and the flank of their other major thrust—towards Australia—wide open to counter-attack; an attempt to execute the "Cannæ manœuvre," the envelopment of the enemy from the wings, cannot succeed if the wings are too widely extended and the enemy is solidly based for a counter-attack; all it does in such a case is to present the enemy with the advantage of interior lines. It is amusing to see the proponents of a dynamic strategy, fitted for the air age, completely

[7] R. E. Harrison and H. W. Weigert in *Compass of the World*, pp. 84–85.

ignoring the idea of the offensive defence and returning (in their theory rather than in actuality) to the direct approach. And, finally, the rather *opéra bouffe* character of some later operations in the Aleutians suggests that our authors neglect not only the "fog of war," but the physical fog of an area noted for its high average of low cloud.

The position is perhaps clearer if we envisage two types of hostilities, which might indeed represent two phases in a general war:

> (i) an atomic attack by large and "expendable" air forces, with the objective of striking a completely crippling blow at the war potential and the morale of the opponent;
>
> (ii) follow-up operations of a more conventional kind, as envisaged above.

In the first case, if the blow were devastating enough to be decisive no more need be said; air-distances would be almost the only logistic factor to count, and the Pacific might indeed be devalued in favour of the Arctic. It cannot be assumed, however, that such a blow would in fact be decisive in view of counter-measures both passive and offensive; and in the succeeding phases of a general war the Pacific would probably come into its own again. In that case the strategic advantages are indeed mixed. On the one hand the American mainland (which has itself strong "heartland" characteristics) is moated by the empty eastern Pacific, and holds valuable offensive bases on the farther side. But the fact must be reckoned with that many of these bases are probably hostages to fortune. In particular Japan, crowded, close to Asian mainland bases, with internal resources in food and raw material precariously (if at all) sufficient to carry on in a crisis, might well have to be written off in very short order. Perhaps the only outwork of the Western Hemisphere in the Pacific which is really significant quantitatively and qualitatively, and at the same time reliable, is Australia.

FURTHER READING

The standard modern book on the Pacific regionally considered is FREEMAN, O. W. (editor), *Geography of the Pacific* (Wiley, New York, 1951); but the essays in this book are of very unequal value. Other recent books such as KEESING, F. W., *The South Seas in the Modern World* (revised edition; John Day, New York, 1945), or STANNER, W. E. H., *The South Seas in Transition* (Australasian Publishing Co., Sydney, 1953), are mainly concerned with the changing economic and social order in the islands; but OLIVER, D. L., *The Pacific Islands* (Harvard University Press, Cambridge,

Mass., 1951), has an interesting short section on island bases. All these books contain good bibliographies. Books dealing strictly with geostrategics are for the most part now out of date; perhaps the best of them is BIENSTOCK, G., *The Struggle for the Pacific* (Allen and Unwin, London, 1937); it is interesting to compare his forecast with what actually happened in 1941–45.

CHAPTER XXIII

The Prospect for Japan

CHARLES A. FISHER

The Unsolved Problem of Population Pressure

THE overwhelming defeat of Japan in August 1945 marked the first major setback in that country's meteoric rise since the Meiji Restoration of 1868. Until 1853, when Commodore Perry, commanding a squadron of United States naval vessels, forced the Japanese to abandon the seclusionist policy introduced by the Tokugawa during the seventeenth century, their country had remained virtually unknown to the outside world. But within a few years of the Americans' arrival, the situation was dramatically reversed. Realizing the precarious position which their economically retarded land occupied in the nineteenth-century world, the Japanese decided upon a policy of intensive westernization as the only possible means of guaranteeing national survival. Accordingly, by sending able young men to study abroad, and by importing instructors and technicians of every kind, they sought to acquire the secrets of the West's supremacy and to lay the foundations of a modern industrial State.

Almost before the rest of the world had realized what was afoot, the new techniques were put to the test, and in two short but brilliantly executed wars Japan attacked and defeated first China (1894–95) and later Russia (1904–5). As a result it obtained substantial overseas dependencies, including Formosa (1895), Korea (1895–1910),[1] and Southern Sakhalin (1905), besides compelling the Russians to relinquish in its favour their newly acquired lease over the Liaotung peninsula and the railway zone of Southern Manchuria.

Even before the signing of the Anglo-Japanese Alliance in 1902 it seems that the Japanese had set themselves the task of turning their country into the Britain of the East. And, superficially at least, the

---

[1] See Chapter XXV for details of Japanese acquisition of Korea.

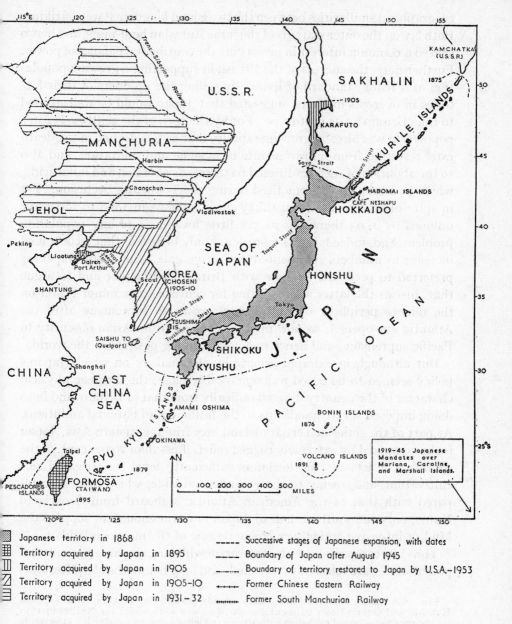

▨ Japanese territory in 1868	----- Successive stages of Japanese expansion, with dates
▦ Territory acquired by Japan in 1895	——— Boundary of Japan after August 1945
▥ Territory acquired by Japan in 1905	········· Boundary of territory restored to Japan by U.S.A.–1953
▧ Territory acquired by Japan in 1905–10	+++++ Former Chinese Eastern Railway
▤ Territory acquired by Japan in 1931–32	········· Former South Manchurian Railway

FIG. 1. THE RISE AND FALL OF THE JAPANESE EMPIRE, 1868–1954

geographical similarities between the two island kingdoms[2] were striking. Both lay on the outer margins of the same Eurasian land-mass, and hence shared a common interest in preserving the continental balance of power. Furthermore, the success of the British in supporting a growing population at a rising standard of living, by selling the products of their factories in overseas markets, suggested that Japan would be well advised to take Britain as its prototype. For by the turn of the century Japan's population was already growing rapidly, thanks to a decline in the death rate, resulting from improvements in hygiene and sanitation, and also to the abolition of such traditional restraints as abortion and infanticide, which had been widely practised during the Tokugawa Seclusion. Yet in spite of an increase from thirty-three millions in 1868 to forty-five millions by 1903 there was as yet little awareness of any population problem, and, indeed, it was more commonly believed[3] that a continued increase in numbers represented a positive gain. For many Japanese preferred to press the analogy with Britain still farther and to argue that, just as the latter after existing for centuries as a minor Power on the remote periphery of Europe had grown to supremacy after the Atlantic era opened, so now might Japan rise from Asian obscurity to Pacific supremacy, and hence to a commanding position in the world.

But although in external geography the analogy on which Japan's policy seemed to be based was remarkably close, the intrinsic physical character of the country differed radically from that of Britain, and in so doing imposed severe handicaps to the fulfilment of national ambitions. As part of the series of Tertiary island arcs fringing eastern Asia, Japan is characterized by extremely rugged relief. Less than 20 per cent. of the country consists of true lowlands sufficiently level for irrigated rice cultivation, and, owing to the extent in latitude, which may be compared with that of the American Atlantic seaboard from Georgia to Maine, only the southern half of Japan is warm enough to support the kind of intensive agriculture characteristic of the monsoon lands.[4]

Thus, in comparison with its near neighbours, Japan's agricultural potentialities are relatively restricted, and long before the Meiji Restora-

---

[2] In 1868 Japan comprised four main islands (Hokkaido, Honshu, Shikoku, and Kyushu) and certain lesser adjacent groups. To these were added the Kuriles in 1875 (as the result of a forced exchange with Russia, which obtained a valid title to the whole of Sakhalin), the Bonins in 1876, the Ryukus in 1876–79, and the Volcanoes in 1891.

[3] See Ryoichi Ishii, *Population Pressure and Economic Life in Japan* (King, London, 1937), p. 39.

[4] Two harvests a year are possible in most lowland areas of Japan south of latitude 37 degrees, but except in the extreme south only one of these is of rice.

tion nearly all the best land was already in use. Indeed, it was precisely because the limits of cultivation seemed to have been reached by the seventeenth century that families had been limited in the way already described.

Although in early Meiji times it was believed that western agricultural improvements, and in particular a greater use of fertilizer, would enable Japan to feed its growing population, the increase of foodstuffs did not keep pace with the demand, and by 1897 the country had become a regular importer of rice. Again, while in subsequent years various marginal tracts were gradually reclaimed for cultivation, the gains tended to be offset by the voracious swallowing up of better land by rapidly spreading cities, the great majority of which occupied lowland sites in southern Japan. Admittedly, with the substantial assistance of its overseas dependencies,[5] and by dint of intensively exploiting its own meagre agricultural resources and over-fishing the surrounding seas, Japan continued to avoid serious dependence on foreign purchases of foodstuffs until the end of the second world war. But in the meantime such industrial crops as cotton had been squeezed out, and animal husbandry, which could have provided further food and raw materials, had never been able to develop at all, partly because capital was not available either to purchase livestock or to replant the hillsides with suitable fodder grasses.[6]

Because of its inherent suitability to the congested conditions of rural Japan, sericulture formed an important exception to this general rule. But silk was a luxury, and, in view of American tariffs, it proved more economical for Japan to export most of its product raw to the United States, thereby paying for imports of cotton, than to concentrate on manufacturing silk textiles for which the market offered less scope.

Japan's shortage of industrial raw materials, however, was in no sense limited to those of agricultural origin. Indeed, the same geological youthfulness which accounts for the country's rugged surface and its proneness to earthquakes is also responsible for a pronounced shortage of nearly all the more important minerals. In this respect the parallel with Britain breaks down completely, and a much closer comparison

[5] During the 1930's Korea and Formosa respectively supplied 8 per cent. and 4 per cent. of Japan's total rice consumption, Japan itself producing 85 per cent. The dependencies also supplied sugar, fruit, etc., and, thanks to the export of appreciable quantities of canned crab, etc., Japan's exports of food (by value) slightly exceeded her imports in this category.

[6] The predominant types of grass on the Japanese hillsides are too coarse for consumption by most kinds of domesticated livestock.

would be with Italy, whose poverty in industrial raw materials is a byword.

Admittedly, reserves of the poorer grades of coal are fairly plentiful, but, owing to the highly contorted and severely faulted geological structure of the islands, mining is expensive and in any case coking coal is almost totally lacking. [7] Likewise iron ore, [8] bauxite, and petroleum occur on a quite inadequate scale to meet the needs of a major industrial Power, and it is only in copper and sulphur, the latter of considerable importance to the chemical industries, that Japan can be regarded as self-sufficient. From the industrialist's point of view, the greatest single natural asset which Japan possessed was its relatively large reserves of water-power, and in 1937 the country displaced Italy as the world's third producer of hydro-electricity. But again, although theoretically there was scope for still greater development, in practice it often happened that schemes for extending the use of hydro-electric power in industry clashed with plans for increasing the amount of irrigated land for rice. Thus a further complication was added to the persistent problem of both manufacturing and food production competing for the same restricted natural resources.

In view of these manifold difficulties, therefore, the measure of success which the Japanese attained in transforming their country into one of the world's greatest trading and military Powers within little more than half a century is truly remarkable. Fundamentally, the achievement was made possible because, notwithstanding grave deficiencies in both land and capital, Japan had human resources at its disposal which, in important respects, were virtually without parallel.

Thus, although Western technology had been avidly absorbed after 1868, the young Samurai statesmen who directed the Meiji Restoration were largely successful in their attempts to preserve Japan's traditional ethos, with its supreme emphasis on corporate rather than individual values. Moreover, a new mystique, centring on the person of the Emperor "reigning as deity incarnate," [9] was deliberately fostered as a means of ensuring national cohesion in an era of intense change. Not-

[7] Per capita reserves of coal are estimated at 220 metric tons, compared with 4200 metric tons in Great Britain. Annual output in 1937 was 37·8 million metric tons; in 1952 the figure was 43 millions.

[8] Reserves of high-grade iron ore (*i.e.*, magnetite averaging 60 per cent. iron) amount to only 35 million metric tons, and annual output of iron ore has been consistently below 20 per cent. of the country's needs. In 1951 steel production was 6·5 million tons, while local iron ore output was only approximately 1 million tons.

[9] *Kokutai no Hongi*, edited by Robert King Hall (Harvard University Press and Oxford University Press, 1949), p. 165.

withstanding the nominal abolition of feudalism in 1871[10] the countryside was insulated as far as possible from the revolutionary ideas surging in from abroad, and even the organization of industry, under the ægis of the handful of great family trusts, collectively known as the zaibatsu, faithfully repeated the closely knit pattern of Japan's traditional social structure.

As a result of these distinctive characteristics, Japan enjoyed competitive advantages of a unique kind. For to a people which thought in terms not of the value of every individual life but rather of the continuity of the family and the transcending glory of the national tradition, the call to sacrifice the material well-being of one or even more generations for the sake of the ultimate good did not meet with the sullen resentment or active resistance which it would have encountered in the West. Widespread rural poverty, combined with the restricted rights of women within the Japanese family system, also help to explain why a vast fund of female labour was always available to work at much lower wages than in any Western country. Naturally, scope for employment of this kind was greatest in the lighter grades of industry, and largely for this reason it was these which constituted the main strength of the export trade.[11]

The monolithic structure of the Japanese industrial economy also contributed greatly to its strength. Instead of many hundreds of rival firms competing with each other to produce distinctive individual articles, the concentration of industrial control into the hands of a few giant combines made it possible to specialize on the mass production of a few standardized lines. Whereas Lancashire turned out an immense range of textile patterns, Japan limited itself to a handful, but to the unsophisticated purchasers in backward lands this mattered little, while the consequent cheapness was an undoubted asset. Similarly tremendous savings were possible as a result of bulk purchase of raw materials, and it has been estimated that in 1936 Japanese manufacturers bought American cotton at least 10 per cent. more cheaply than did any of their European rivals.

It is, therefore, an over-simplification to argue that Japan's great

[10] To a considerable extent the abolition of feudalism merely meant a change in landlord so far as the peasant was concerned. By 1892 nearly 40 per cent. of the agricultural land was operated by tenants, and this proportion slowly increased. Rents amounting to 50 per cent. of the rice crop remained normal, and this, combined with the small average size of holdings—2½ acres—was the cause of widespread rural poverty. See p. 550.

[11] Even as late as 1939 raw silk (14·2 per cent.) and cotton tissues (11·3 per cent. were by far the largest items on Japan's export list.

successes in the manufacture and sale overseas of textiles and light goods (*e.g.*, bicycles, electrical fittings, rubber goods, toys, etc.) was due simply to sweated labour, for clearly industrial organization also played a major part. But this distinction is perhaps more academic than the facts warrant. The fundamental basis of Japan's successful competition with Western manufacturing States was her ability to control and regiment her population. Individuality and the satisfaction of personal desires were crushed as much by rigid organization as by excessive working hours and low wages. The whole nation worked in an atmosphere of ruthless austerity, and its almost blind obedience to those who spoke in the name of the Emperor constituted a potential threat of the utmost magnitude.

Yet even this combination of energy, docility, and austerity was not enough, for although in the inter-war years Japan had already become the world's first exporter of cotton textiles, as well as a major producer of many other consumer goods, the principal outlets for these—namely, the neighbouring lands of Monsoon Asia—were becoming increasingly precarious. For not only were the established imperial Powers able to discriminate against Japanese manufactures in the interests of their own products throughout most of South-east Asia, but the inexorable trend towards local industrialization threatened before long to reduce the market even more drastically.

In short, Japan was sailing against the current of the times, and, in attempting to play the part of nineteenth-century Britain in the twentieth-century world, with material resources no greater than those of Italy, the country seemed to be heading for disaster. Accordingly when, beginning in 1929, the world economic crisis led first to a catastrophic slump in the American demand for silk, and then to further difficulties in almost every other branch of Japan's export trade, support for a more ruthless policy speedily gained ground, and little effective opposition could be mustered.

Thus was Co-prosperity born. The attack on Manchuria in 1931, on the rest of China in 1937, and on South-east Asia in 1941 all formed part of the militarists' plan, which was carefully outlined in the Tanaka Memorial of 1927.[12] By seizing Manchuria and northern China Japan's own fatal stategic weakness in war materials, particularly coking coal and iron, would be made good, and once this new mainland arsenal and supply base had been effectively organized it would be safe to thrust

[12] See Charles A. Fisher, "The Expansion of Japan: a Study in Oriental Geopolitics," in *Geog. Journ.*, vol. cxv (1950), pp. 1–19 and 179–193, especially p. 13.

south to the rich colonies of the European Powers, with their great abundance of food and tropical produce. Thereafter the whole of Greater East Asia could be organized into a vast self-contained empire, providing unlimited opportunity for Japanese enterprise of every kind.

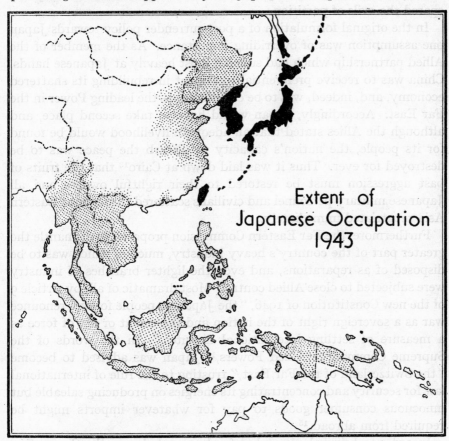

Extent of
Japanese Occupation
1943

FIG. 2. EXTENT OF JAPANESE OCCUPATION, 1943
Royal Geographical Society

Allied Occupation and Post-surrender Policy

In spite of an intensive effort to build up heavy industry both at home and in Manchuria after 1931, the Japanese were far from adequately prepared to wage a major war, and once their European allies had been eliminated their own defeat was a foregone conclusion. Thereafter, partly as a result of Russia's late entry into the Far Eastern war and of the evident intention of the British to reduce their commitments in the Pacific, the United States, which had played the preponderant role in the campaign against Japan, assumed virtually complete control over the Allied Occupation, with the result that the country was spared the evils of partition.

In the original formulation of a post-surrender policy towards Japan one assumption was of overriding importance. As the member of the Allied partnership which had suffered most heavily at Japanese hands, China was to receive preferential treatment in rebuilding its shattered economy, and, indeed, was to be established as the leading Power in the Far East. Accordingly, Japan would have to take second place, and although the Allies stated that an adequate livelihood would be found for its people, the nation's capacity to disturb the peace was to be destroyed for ever. Thus it was laid down at Cairo[13] that the fruits of past aggression must be restored to their rightful owners and all Japanese military personnel and civilians scattered throughout Eastern Asia repatriated immediately.

Furthermore, the Far Eastern Commission proposed to dismantle the greater part of the country's heavy industry, much of which was to be disposed of as reparations, and even the lighter branches of industry were subjected to close Allied control. Most dramatic of all, by Article 9 of the new Constitution of 1946, "the Japanese people forever renounce war as a sovereign right of the nation and the threat or use of force as a measure of settling international disputes." In the words of the Supreme Commander Allied Powers,[14] Japan was advised to become "the Switzerland of the Far East," trusting to the rule of international law for security and concentrating its energies on producing saleable but innocuous consumer goods to pay for whatever imports might be required from abroad.[15]

In order to bring about such a fundamental change the Occupation authorities proceeded by systematic legislation drastically to remodel the national life. The Meiji reforms, it was felt, had not gone deep enough, and, in failing to introduce liberal democracy as a necessary concomitant of Western technology, the builders of modern Japan had prepared the way for militarism and totalitarian rule. True

---

[13] See below, p. 545.
[14] *I.e.*, General of the (U.S.) Army Douglas MacArthur.
[15] The analogy with Switzerland was extremely superficial. For, while making neutrality the basis of its foreign policy, Switzerland has never renounced war nor dispensed with its armed forces.

democracy must therefore be inculcated forthwith. The new constitution, which represented an ingenious blend of American and British usage, dispensed at one stroke with the more stultifying restraints of its Prussian-style predecessor, and although the throne was retained as a stabilizing and unifying factor, the Emperor was divested of his divinity and reduced to the rank of a constitutional monarch.

Moreover, through the Land Reform Law of October 21, 1946, the Occupation authorities strove to replace the traditional forms of land tenure by a system of individual peasant proprietorship. In this way they hoped to strike at the roots of agrarian unrest and hence to remove one of the most potent inducements to an expansionist policy.[16] Finally, a mass of new legislation was directed towards loosening, and in some cases removing altogether, the traditional shackles on Japanese economy and society. By these means women were emancipated, new labour standards set up, and the employment of young children forbidden. Similarly, trade unionism was encouraged, the zaibatsu were ordered to disband, and a new commercial code, patterned on the American instead of the German model, was introduced.[17] Thus, by shifting the emphasis from loyalty and obedience to individual freedom of action and personal responsibility in every walk of life the authorities sought to re-educate the Japanese to a new and peaceful role in world society.

Whether this remarkable experiment could, without drastic modification, have provided a solution to the Japanese problem it is impossible to say. For within two years of its inauguration the basic assumption on which it rested had ceased to apply, and, in face of deepening chaos in China and the steady deterioration in relations with the Soviet Union, the United States was driven to revise its whole Far Eastern policy.

Thus, if the new doctrine of containment were to be applied in this critical region, Japan, rather than China, seemed by 1947 to be the obvious basis on which to build. For, while in the opinion of General Marshall there remained little that the United States could do to arrest the disintegration on the mainland, the island fringe from Japan to the

[16] Many of the younger officers who played a leading part in promoting aggressive policies were from the countryside and were keenly aware of the distress which prevailed there. See G. T. Trewartha, "Land Reform and Land Reclamation in Japan," in *Geog. Rev.*, July 1950, pp. 376–396, vol. xl, No. 3.

[17] As a result of these changes, "the working conditions of the majority of Japanese artisan classes are infinitely improved in comparison with the past. Hours of work have been reduced, and the eight-hour day, forty-eight-hour week has become an accepted principle in many establishments."—*Japan, Overseas Economic Surveys* (H.M.S.O., London, 1953), p. 38.

Philippines, and perhaps also the rest of South-east Asia, seemed politically more stable and might well be buttressed by economic aid, and where appropriate by American sea and air power, into forming a reliable dam against the spreading Communist tide.

Such a policy could hope to succeed, however, only if two important conditions were fulfilled. First, Japan would need to be given greater opportunities to earn a reasonable livelihood than seemed possible under the existing restrictions on the scale of its activity. And, secondly, living standards in the newly independent lands of South-east Asia would need to be underpinned, in particular by large outlays on rehabilitation works and the building up of local industries, lest these areas also should succumb to subversion.

It was in response to this combination of circumstances that, in March 1948, following the Draper Mission to Japan, the United States announced its intention of rebuilding that country as "the workshop of the Far East," with an authorized steel output by 1952 of approximately 140 per cent. of the 1930–34 level, and a comparable expansion in other branches of industry. But although the United States, which thereafter pressed for the speedy conclusion of a peace treaty, repeatedly disclaimed any intention of promoting Japanese re-armament, the Philippines, Australia, and New Zealand refused to sign the proposed treaty without supplementary guarantees of American aid in the event of a future attack by Japan. This point having been conceded,[18] the Peace Treaty with Japan was signed at San Francisco by the representatives of forty-nine countries on September 8, 1951,[19] and finally came into effect on April 29 of the following year. In order to provide for the defence of Japan after the Occupation ceased a bilateral U.S.–Japanese security pact, under which American forces were to be stationed in Japan "for the time being," was concluded on September 5, 1951. Finally, in November 1953, in an attempt to close the ring around the Soviet bloc while at the same time shedding some of its own vast burden

[18] The United States concluded a mutual defence treaty with the Philippines on August 29, 1951, and another with Australia and New Zealand on September 1, 1951.

[19] Several important nations did not sign the treaty. Both the U.S.S.R. and India were invited to do so, but refused; on June 9, 1952, India signed a separate treaty of "perpetual peace and amity with Japan." Owing to Anglo-American differences of opinion, the question which Government should sign on behalf of China was left unsettled and no Chinese representatives were invited to attend the San Francisco ceremony. But on August 6, 1952, a bilateral peace treaty was signed between Japan and Nationalist China (Formosa). Both Indonesia and Burma were reluctant to sign the Peace Treaty, since it contained no stipulation regarding the payment of reparations. In the event Burma did not participate, and though Indonesia signed the treaty, it has not yet ratified it.

of commitments, the United States called upon Japan to re-arm, and officially admitted that the decision to include Article 9 in the Constitution of 1946 had been mistaken.

Territorial Losses and Increasing Population

The coming into force of the Japanese Peace Treaty marks the beginning of a new era in the Far East, for, with full freedom of action regained, Japan must once again chart its own course in a world which has changed almost out of recognition since pre-war days. In most respects the "treaty of reconciliation," as it has been called, is far more generous than would have seemed possible in 1945, and though the great Powers expressed the hope that Japan would voluntarily pay reparations to her smaller neighbours, they renounced any such claims for themselves.[20] Indeed, it is only in respect of territorial readjustments, to which the Allies were bound by prior commitments, that the Treaty imposes any serious disability on Japan.

According to the Cairo Declaration of 1943, Manchuria and Formosa were to be restored to China once the war ended, Korea would "in due course" become independent, and Japan would cease to administer the Pacific Mandates.[21] At Yalta these arrangements underwent certain modifications as the price of Soviet participation in the war against Japan. Thus Russia was promised restoration of the rights it had lost in Manchuria in 1905 and also possession of the Kurile Islands. Finally, at Potsdam it was agreed that Japanese sovereignty should be restricted to "Honshu, Hokkaido, Kyushu, and Shikoku and such minor outlying islands as may be determined."

Following the surrender, both the U.S.S.R. and China claimed their appointed shares, the two zones of Korea came under Allied Occupation,[22] and the Pacific Mandates, together with the Ryukyus, Bonins, and Volcanoes, were occupied by the United States. By the time the Peace Treaty was drafted, therefore, all the more extensive of Japan's former dependencies were in the hands of either the U.S.S.R., Com-

---

[20] Japan accpteed the obligation to negotiate reparations settlements with the Asian countries it had invaded, and some progress was made in this respect during 1955–56.

[21] These consisted of various island groups—*e.g.*, the Carolines—formerly under German rule, which were occupied by Japan during the first world war and thereafter became C Class Mandates under Japanese administration. Long before 1941 many of the islands had been illegally fortified.

[22] See below, p. 604.

T

munist China, or the Nationalist Government of Formosa. And although, since none of these has signed the Peace Treaty, their tenure lacks legal validity, possession is clearly in all cases the decisive factor.[23]

Meanwhile, Japan has surrendered all claims to the former Mandated islands which have become United Nations Trust Territory under United States administration (July 18, 1947).[24] The position of the Ryukyus and Bonins, however, is less certain. According to the Peace Treaty, Japan will "concur in any proposal of the United States to the United Nations to place the islands under its trusteeship system, with the United States as the sole administering authority." But on Christmas Day 1953 the United States restored the northern—*i.e.*, Amami-Oshima—group of the Ryukus to Japan, and although at the same time it was stated that control would be retained over the remaining islands, particularly Okinawa, on which major American bases have been established, it seems possible that they may ultimately be returned to Japan.

Strategy and sentiment apart, however, none of these lesser islands has any great value, and their restoration to Japan would be of negligible economic importance. The loss of the larger dependencies, on the other hand, represents a tremendous setback, for immediately before the war nearly three-fifths of Japan's export and three-sevenths of its import trade took place with Manchukuo, Korea, and Formosa. Admittedly many of the exports, consisting of capital equipment required for the building up of Manchuria as the arsenal of the Co-prosperity Sphere, were of strategic rather than commercial significance. But the loss of political control over these lands, and of the large Japanese assets invested therein, undoubtedly means that Japan will no longer be able to obtain primary produce from them on anything like such favourable terms as in pre-war days. Particularly important among the commodities involved were the soya beans, iron, coking coal, grain, and timber from Manchuria, rice from Korea, rice, sugar, and camphor from Formosa, as well as valuable supplies of petroleum, coking coal, and wood pulp from Southern Sakhalin and important supplies of fish from the surrounding seas.

Besides the economic difficulties which the amputation of its former dependencies entails, Japan's military capacity has been even more

[23] As noted above, Nationalist China has since signed a bilateral treaty with Japan. This may entail complications whenever the matter of negotiating a peace settlement between Japan and Communist China is discussed.

[24] On January 1, 1953, control of Saipan and Tinian was transferred to the U.S. Navy.

strikingly reduced both by the cutting off of assured supplies of war materials and food and the loss of such vital strategic assets as the foot-hold on the mainland in Korea and the fortified island screen to the north and south.

Indeed, not only has Japan's ability to attack been drastically cur-tailed, but the question arises as to whether its own security has not been irreparably jeopardized by the post-war acquisitions of the U.S.S.R. in the Far East. With the occupation of Southern Sakhalin and the Kuriles, the Sea of Okhotsk became in effect a Soviet lake. Moreover, since this occupation extended even to the Habomai Islands, which had never previously been considered part of the Kuriles, Russian power now reaches to within two miles of the Japanese coast at Cape Neshapu. Already innumerable Japanese fishing vessels have disap-peared, presumably into Soviet hands, during the frequent fogs which descend upon these waters, and in such circumstances the Japanese fear of a surprise attack against Hokkaido[25] from the Kuriles and Sakhalin is understandable.

Even more valuable from the Soviet standpoint would be control of the Sea of Japan to which the three straits—Soya, Tsugaru, and Tsushima—provide the keys. By regaining possession of Southern Sakhalin the U.S.S.R. acquired a commanding hold over the Soya Strait so long as Japan remained disarmed, and the desire to win similar control over Tsushima was probably a major factor in bringing about the Korean War.[26] Similar in intention was the unsuccessful Soviet proposal, announced at San Francisco in September 1951, to include the following new article in the Japanese Peace Treaty:

> The Straits of La Perusa (Soya) and Nemuro all along the Japanese coast, as well as Sangara (Tsugaru) and Tsushima shall be demilitarized. . . . These straits shall be open for the passage of only those naval ships which belong to the powers adjacent to the Sea of Japan.

Although, as in 1861, Russia's attempt to close the Sea of Japan has been at least partially frustrated, the strategic relationship of Japan to its northern continental neighbour is now more unfavourable than at any time since 1875. For, while Japan has ceased to be "an island empire

[25] In 1869 the Japanese Government sponsored a project for the colonization of Hokkaido lest its sparse population should encourage Russian infiltration and later annexation. Even to-day, however, the northern part of the island, whose carrying capacity is very limited, is necessarily only sparsely populated, and hence strategically vulnerable.

[26] The Russians attempted to seize the Tsushima Islands in 1861, and were only pre-vented from doing so by the pressure of the British Navy.

with continental marches,"[27] the U.S.S.R. has extended its outer bulwarks from Kamchatka virtually to the shores of Hokkaido. And though this development may represent nothing more than an attempt to surround the U.S.S.R. with a protective series of satellite seas,[28] easier and more economical to defend than long stretches of sparsely populated coastline, the continued growth of the Soviet Navy may well suggest more sinister implications. Certainly the possibility of the U.S.S.R.'s basing a large fleet of submarines within these seas, from which it could menace the vital approaches to Japan, is as alarming to the latter as is the vulnerability of its major cities to air attack by shore-based planes from Vladivostok. Thus it has even been argued[29] that, in the last analysis, Japan may be driven to align itself with the Soviet Union rather than the Western bloc as the only possible means of ensuring national survival in the event of a third world war.

As a result of the territorial losses which Japan has sustained since 1945, its area to-day amounts to only 142,270 square miles. In the meantime, despite war mortalities of about $1\frac{1}{2}$ million, total population has risen from $72\frac{1}{2}$ millions in August 1945 to over 87 millions by December 1953. A considerable part of this increase is due to the repatriation of 6,241,548 Japanese, both military and civilian, from the surrounding lands between 1945 and 1949, though against these must be set the 1,192,157 foreigners, mostly Koreans and Chinese, who left the country during the same period. But a more lasting factor in the situation is the large excess of births over deaths since 1945 (Table 5).

Thanks to American improvements in public health, the Japanese death rate has recently shown a steep and continued decline to levels little above those in the West. The birth rate, however, has behaved less consistently. After rising in 1947 to one of the highest peaks ever recorded (34.3 per 1000) it also began to fall. But the gap between the two rates remains wider than before the war, and though total annual increase has fallen from $1\frac{3}{4}$ million during 1948 and 1949, it was still over a million in 1953.

As yet it is too early to appraise the full significance of these trends. During the 1930's Shimojo and other demographers argued that Japanese vital statistics were repeating the Western European pattern, with

---

[27] Y. M. Goblet, *The Twilight of Treaties* (Bell, London, 1936), p. 103.

[28] See "Soviet Satellite Seas," in *The Economist*, vol. clxviii, No. 5727 (May 30, 1953), p. 581.

[29] W. Macmahon Ball, *Nationalism and Communism in East Asia* (Melbourne University Press and Cambridge University Press, 1952), pp. 29–30.

a time-lag of between thirty and fifty years.[30] A slight decline in the birth rate, mainly the result of later marriage in the towns, was already apparent, and Shimojo calculated that by 1970 the rate of increase would be reduced to zero, by which time population would have reached a maximum of 85,542,100.

While this prophecy has clearly been falsified by events, it was not necessarily as unsound as it might appear. Undoubtedly the strong opposition of pre-war militarist governments to family limitation played a part in arresting the fall in the birth rate during the 1930's, and it also seems likely that the 1947–49 peak was merely a temporary feature associated with the return of military personnel to civil life. Thus, as more recent figures suggest, some levelling off may at last be in sight.

Nevertheless such a development is not inevitable. It is true that many influential Japanese have advocated the use of contraceptives, and the emancipation of women has doubtless contributed to the present decline in the size of families. But that decline, which has been brought about largely by the legalization of abortion under the Eugenics Protection Law of September 1948, did not set in until after Japan had been repeatedly rebuffed for continuing to suggest (1947–48) that new outlets should be found for its surplus population, preferably in eastern Indonesia or New Guinea. Moreover, many Japanese appear to suspect that Western propaganda in favour of birth control is merely a plot to reduce Japan's potential strength. Accordingly, while for a time expediency may dictate that population be kept in check, the possibility of a renewed rise in the birth rate cannot be entirely ruled out.

In short, it remains to be seen whether present trends are primarily a reflection of a real change in outlook, or whether they represent merely an interim adjustment to the constraints of the present economic situation. In either event, however, a considerable increase of population within the immediate future seems certain, and it is officially estimated that growth will continue until a maximum of 107 million is reached around the year 1990.[31]

[30] Ishii, *op. cit.*, p. 128 *et seq.*
[31] This estimate is by the Population Problem Research Institute of the Ministry of Welfare. See Chitoshi Yanaga, "Japan: Asiatic Co-operation," in *Current History*, vol. xxv, No. 147 (1953), p. 270. On October 1, 1954, the population was estimated to be 88,290,000.

The Contemporary Economic Problem

If therefore, as its propaganda claimed, Japan was already conscious before the war of having too many people on too little land, the position to-day is materially worse, and, with a density of 583 per square mile and 3575 per square mile cultivated, Japan is by far the most intensively populated of any of the major world Powers. Since emigration appears to offer no prospect of reducing the congestion, it is necessary to consider how these large and growing numbers can be supported within the Japanese Islands.

In agriculture, the scope for further expansion is severely limited. It must be stressed that the Land Reform Law of 1946 aimed solely at ameloriating the intolerable lot of Japan's tenant farmers, and in this it has had notable success. Whereas before 1946 approximately half of the cultivated land was owned by 7·5 per cent. of the farm households, to-day only 13·3 per cent. is worked by tenants and 95·5 per cent. of the agricultural population own some land. Thus, although the majority of holdings are still too small to provide a good livelihood, rural poverty has been greatly reduced. But this has had no significant effect on agricultural yields, and meanwhile the early post-surrender plans for reclaiming some 3¾ million acres by 1950 have not been realized. Indeed, little more than one quarter of that area has been added to the fourteen million or so acres under cultivation in 1946, and in view of the poor quality of most of the remainder the prospects are doubtful, though some experts still regard those in Hokkaido as relatively hopeful. Although only about 16 per cent. of Japan is at present cultivated, this includes virtually all the land which it is economically worthwhile to use, and most of this is already producing to capacity, thanks to an extremely intensive application of both labour and fertilizer. In these circumstances mechanization, even if it could be afforded, has little to contribute, and Japanese rice yields are far higher than those of any other major producer. Probably the best hope[32] for further increases in output lies in better drainage of the 46 per cent.

[32] For a discussion of the possibilities of livestock rearing, see Trewartha, *op. cit.*, and Yanaga, *op. cit.* The major difficulty in this respect is the continuing shortage of capital. Fishing has received a setback since the wars in that Japan has lost the valuable fishing grounds off Kamchatka and the Kuriles, which supplied the bulk of its exports of canned crab and salmon. Under the Occupation, moreover, Japanese fishermen were confined to the limited area of the Pacific within the so-called MacArthur line. Although Japan's total catch has almost regained the pre-war level and is once again the largest in the world, the danger of exhaustion must impose limits to further increases.

of the paddy fields in southern Japan which do not yet produce a second crop, and in improved pest control, which it is claimed could save more than the $2\frac{3}{4}$ million tons of grain which have been imported annually since 1950. But the disastrous crop failure of 1953 shows how near to the margin cultivation has been pressed, and it would be unwise to assume that Japan's present dependence on foreign sources for 20 per cent. of its food, representing some 30 per cent. of its total imports, can be substantially reduced in any foreseeable future.

The industrial outlook is hardly less bleak, for in almost every respect Japan's former disadvantages have been aggravated and its meagre assets still further whittled away. To begin with, war damage and dismantling reduced the total industrial capacity by some 30 per cent., and, while much of what survived was superfluous munitions plant, only one-quarter of the pre-war cotton spindles remained in working order in 1945. Since then United States loans have made a great contribution to industrial rehabilitation, but, except in the textiles, much of Japan's existing plant is seriously out of date and hence unduly expensive to operate.

Meanwhile raw-material costs have risen steeply, and in this respect the most important single factor has been the loss of cheap colonial produce. Hardly less serious, however, has been the stoppage of supplies from Communist China as the result of the trade ban imposed at United Nations' behest against that country, following its entry into the Korean War. Thus, with imports from China (including Manchuria) reduced to a mere 14 million dollars in 1952, Japan has had to turn to more distant sources, particularly for coking coal and iron, thereby practically doubling its expenditure on both these items.[33] At the same time dependence on imported raw materials for the textile industries is in no way diminished, and local timber supplies have fallen off sharply owing to continuous over-felling since 1933.

In the past, as has already been pointed out, Japan was able to compensate for many of its gravest handicaps by means of low wage bills and ruthless organization. But here, again, great changes have taken place, and many of the reforms introduced during the Occupation in the

[33] In the last six months of 1951 Japan's total coal imports were 1·2 million tons, of which 755,000 came from U.S.A. and 327,000 from India. During the same period iron ore imports amounted to *c.* 2 million tons, of which 594,000 came from the Philippines, 574,000 from the U.S.A., and 472,000 from Malaya. U.S. iron ore cost 14·5 dollars per ton as against 7 dollars for Chinese ore in 1949–50. See Jerome B. Cohen, *Economic Problems of Free Japan* (Center of International Studies, Princeton, 1952).

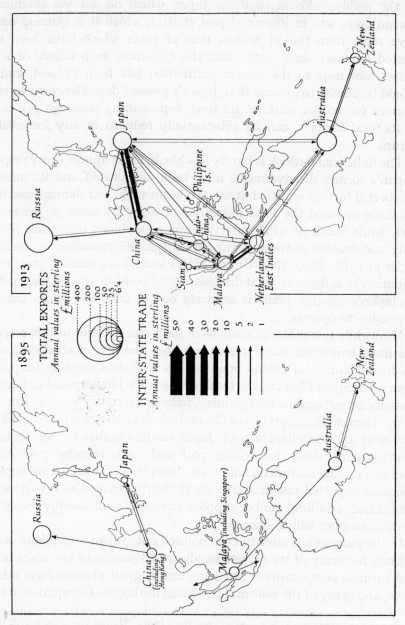

FIG. 3. EASTERN ASIA: EXPORTS, 1895–1913

Royal Geographical Society

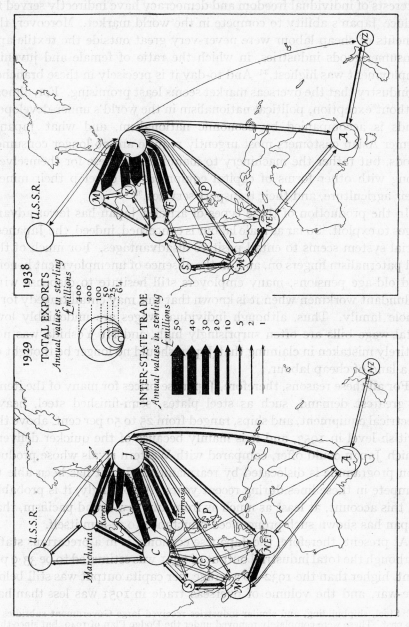

FIG. 4. EASTERN ASIA: EXPORTS, 1929–38

Royal Geographical Society

T*

interests of individual freedom and democracy have indirectly served to reduce Japan's ability to compete in the world market. Moreover, the benefits of cheap labour were never very great outside the textile and consumer-goods industries, in which the ratio of female and juvenile employment was highest.[34] And to-day it is precisely in these branches of industry that the overseas market seems least promising. For, almost without exception, political nationalism in the world's under-developed lands is accompanied by economic nationalism, and what Japan's former Asian customers most urgently require are no longer consumer goods, but rather the machinery to manufacture these for themselves, along with other forms of capital equipment to develop their mines, their agriculture, and their transport services.[35]

In the production of these types of articles Japan has fewer advantages to exploit. So far as male labour is concerned, indeed, the Japanese social system seems to entail positive disadvantages. For much of the old paternalism lingers on, and, in the absence of unemployment benefit and old-age pensions, many employers still hesitate to dispense with redundant workmen when it is known that this may entail tragedy for a whole family. Thus, although individual wages are undeniably low, total wage bills are often surprisingly high, and Mr Yoshida was not entirely mistaken in claiming that Japan should no longer be thought of as a land of cheap labour.

For all these reasons, therefore, Japanese prices for many of the items in greatest demand, such as steel plates, semi-finished steel, heavy electrical equipment, and ships, ranged from 25 to 50 per cent. above the British level in 1953, and it is mainly because of the quicker delivery which Japan could offer, compared with Western rivals whose production programme is dislocated by rearmament, that it has been able to compete in these lines during recent years. Accordingly, it is probably on this account, at least as much as from any new-found pacifism, that Japan has shown such pronounced reluctance to re-arm itself.

At present, therefore, the Japanese economy is in a precarious state. Although the total industrial output of 1951 was estimated to be 33·9 per cent. higher than the 1932–36 average, per capita output was still below pre-war, and the volume of overseas trade in 1951 was less than half

[34] Steel, shipbuilding, and similar industries received large Government subsidies in the past. These were completely removed under the Dodge Plan of 1949, but since then some have been reintroduced under various guises.
[35] The most spectacular example of this change is India, which was once a major importer of Japanese cotton, but in 1950 was the world's largest exporter of such manufactures.

that of 1934–36.[36] Moreover, textiles continued to form much the largest component in the exports, but despite the fact that in 1951 Japan had again become the world's first exporter of cottons, the amount involved was only about half the normal pre-war volume, and since early 1952 output has declined seriously owing to the world-wide textile recession.

Hitherto Japan's post-war economic survival has been possible only as a result of liberal American assistance in various forms. Altogether loans totalling some 2000 million dollars have been made available, and by June 1951 such funds had paid for 45 per cent. of the country's total imports since the surrender. Furthermore, this artificial situation has been extended beyond the expected period in that special procurement orders for United Nations forces in Korea led to a renewed flow of dollars, again totalling approximately 2000 million,[37] at precisely the time when direct aid was beginning to be turned off. But with the cessation of hostilities in Korea the period of ready money has come to an end. Thus, although further help is promised on condition that Japan rearms, and the rehabilitation of Southern Korea may afford other opportunities of earning dollars,[38] it is clear that Japan will no longer be able to pay its way without a great increase in exports of goods and services. In fact, thanks to the growth of population and the way in which the terms of trade have turned against manufacturing countries like Japan, it will be necessary to raise the flow of exports by about 60 per cent. over 1952 figures to maintain solvency at all, while to regain pre-war standards of living an increase of at least double that amount would be necessary. And in the meantime Japan has lost not only a considerable measure of its former competitive advantage, but also the greater part of its merchant fleet[39] and nearly the whole of its ready available capital, while in place of widespread goodwill it now has to face deep-seated hostility in many parts of East and South-east Asia.

Moreover, Japan's trade problem is not merely one of volume, but also

[36] Considerable advances in many branches of production were made during 1955–56, but the fundamental economic problems remained unsolved.

[37] In 1952 Japan received c. 800 million dollars special procurement and expenditures by U.S. personnel in the country. In 1953 the corresponding figure was estimated at 900 million dollars, which was equivalent to about three-quarters of the value of all Japanese exports in the same year.

[38] South Korean hostility may prevent this, however. President Syngman Rhee has declared that his country will refuse to accept materials manufactured in Japan under the proposed rehabilitation scheme. In 1955 U.S. Army expenditures provided Japan with some 300 million dollars.

[39] The Japanese merchant fleet amounted (December 1953) to 2,250,000 tons, compared with 6,300,000 in 1941 and 750,000 in 1945.

one of direction, and in particular of the acute lack of balance now prevailing between its transactions with the dollar and the sterling areas,
to neither of which the country belongs. In pre-war times the United
States was normally the largest single source of Japan's imports, mainly
of raw cotton, and these were paid for partly by a return flow of raw silk
and partly by means of a triangular trade in which Japan exported
manufactures to South-east Asia and the latter supplied primary produce to the United States. Since 1945, however, Japan under the Occupation came to rely more than ever on imports from North America,
and, in addition to cotton, these now include large quantities of other
raw materials and foodstuffs. But while imports from the United States
have risen to form nearly half of the total, the American demand for
Japanese silk has fallen to one-tenth of its pre-war volume, thanks to
the competition of nylon, and the old triangular trade has been blocked
because of the lack of convertibility between the major currencies.

Meanwhile many sterling area countries, notably India, Pakistan, and
Malaya, greatly expanded their imports of Japanese goods after 1951,[40]
but, on account of the higher prices of most of their commodities and
serious shortages in the supply of others, Japan has preferred instead to
buy from the United States, in spite of the latter's unwillingness to lower
its high tariffs against such Japanese goods as canned tuna and semi-
luxury manufactures. Thus, in 1952, when Japan's sterling balances
had risen to £130 million, the sterling area imposed new restrictions on
imports from Japan, which accordingly fell sharply. Though there has
since been a gradual easing in this respect the problem is far from solved,
and in the meantime the annual deficit in trade with the dollar area had
risen to over 700 million dollars by 1953.

The Prospect for National Survival

In the face of this formidable array of problems, Japan would appear
to possess singularly few assets of major significance. Among those that
remain the quality of the people is obviously a critical factor. Notwithstanding years of suffering and an almost unparalleled intensity of effort
during the war, the Japanese seem to have retained much of their tradi-

---

[40] In September 1951, when a new payments agreement was signed between the
United Kingdom and Japan, the dollar clause (whereby Japan's holdings of sterling in
excess of £17 million were convertible into dollars) was terminated.

tional energy, frugality, and resilience. Accordingly they may respond effectively to the call for further sacrifices which will undoubtedly be necessary if the country's export industries are to be put on a fully competitive footing. For only by reducing consumption to an even lower level can capital be made available to rebuild the merchant fleet,[41] to change over still further from consumer- to producer-goods industries, to re-equip existing factories with up-to-date machinery, and to increase the output of electrical power[42] so as to meet the needs of a much heavier industrial structure. Similarly, re-deployment of labour would be a painful process, and great hardships would result from drastic pruning of the present labour force in many industries. It remains, therefore, to be seen how far new social ideals may have reduced the Japanese capacity to submit to the austere discipline of the ant-heap. Certainly in the struggle to survive which now lies ahead it is to be feared that many more of the reforms introduced during the Occupation will be discarded as luxuries which the country cannot afford. Already the zaibatsu are regrouping and steadily regaining their hold on the economy, and a general return to a more highly integrated social and economic structure seems probable as the nation is driven back on to the reserves of its own experience.

If, therefore, one assumes that the Japanese will try to secure their own survival by continuing, in Lafcadio Hearn's poignant phrase, "to underlive the West," it is still necessary to consider which parts of the world offer the most rewarding prospects for their enterprise. To some extent it may be possible to find new outlets in Africa for the many types of consumer goods in which Japan excels, while the Latin American market for both these and capital equipment will probably repay the cultivation that has already begun with the sending out of trade missions in 1952. Again, if tariffs were not insurmountably high, the better grades of Japanese consumer goods, especially toys, cameras, optical equipment, and textiles, would sell at increasingly competitive prices in both Western Europe and North America. But since there seems to be little likelihood that such trade with the United States will expand sufficiently to close the dollar gap, Japan will clearly have to reorient its commerce so as to buy more of its primary produce from the countries which can be persuaded to take its manufactures, even though such

[41] It was planned to rebuild to a total of four million tons by 1955.

[42] It is proposed to utilize the greater part of the hydro-electric power reserves at present untapped, but this will be costly, as most of the remaining sites are relatively small and widely dispersed.

a change may involve purchasing in more expensive markets than at present.

In thus seeking to establish a more self-contained pattern of trade, Japan has no real alternative but to turn once again to the lands which comprised the former Greater East Asia Co-prosperity Sphere. Alike on historic, economic, and geographical grounds, these fall into two main groups—namely, the mainland territories of Korea, Manchuria, and China, which together formed both the continental arsenal and the main reserve granary, and the lands lying southward from Formosa, which were destined to become the tropical complement to the temperate nucleus centring in Japan itself. To-day, however, this division has taken on still deeper significance in that it coincides almost exactly with the post-war partition of Eastern Asia between the Communist bloc and the Western world.

Almost certainly the great majority of Japanese commercial leaders to-day wish to promote extensive trade with both of these regions, and, indeed, many claim that only by so doing is there any hope of solving their country's problem. That, however, is not the United States' view, nor, indeed, is it the British view, though both of these countries see the problem from markedly different standpoints. In American eyes, Japanese trade with Communist China, even after the signing of a Korean armistice, is likely, if effective, to be detrimental to the Western cause, since it will serve to build up a potential enemy and may also tend to draw Japan closer to the Communist bloc. Hence the United States administration favours greater Japanese concentration on the South and South-east Asian trade. Given internal stability, it is argued, Burma, Thailand, and Indo-China could produce rice surpluses more than adequate to meet Japan's needs, and, if better mining apparatus and transport facilities were installed, India, Pakistan, Malaya, and the Philippines could together make good its deficiencies in both coal and iron.[43] Conversely, these former dependent territories, which are still only on the threshold of modernization, could provide outlets for Japanese equipment of all kinds, and later, as their living standards begin in consequence to rise, they should be able to offer new markets for higher grade consumer goods as well. Already in 1951 this area absorbed 31 per cent. of Japan's iron and steel exports, and India alone took 90 per cent. of its diesel engines sold abroad, besides supplying

---

[43] This argument is sound so far as iron is concerned, but none of the areas in question has large reserves of coking coal. India is the best placed in this respect, but its resources are barely adequate to supply the likely increases in home demand.

Japan with nearly 500,000 tons of coal and substantial quantities of other commodities.[44] Moreover, owing to the inherent similarities in geographical environment and material culture, Japan, with its greater experience of westernization, is peculiarly fitted to supply technical advisers, both agricultural and industrial, to the lands of South and South-east Asia.[45] Though fully alive to these opportunities, however, the Japanese still suffer severe handicaps there. Thus, in many cases their prices are too high, and throughout the former Co-prosperity Sphere unhappy memories have been exacerbated by Japan's failure as yet to pay reparations. But these are not insuperable obstacles, and in the long run prospects for a considerable expansion of Japanese enterprise in this area seem encouraging.

Such a prospect, however, causes considerable concern to the British, who, despite their virtual withdrawal from the Far East, still retain very great interest in South and South-east Asia. For India, Pakistan, and Ceylon, despite their independence, still remain within the Commonwealth, along with Australia, which is seeking to expand its exports to the "Near North," and Malaya, whose tin and rubber provide an indispensable source of dollars for the sterling area. Accordingly, since the Commonwealth, largely under Australian inspiration, evolved in the Colombo Plan its own scheme for preserving both the economic and political stability of the Indian Ocean region, most of its members are apt to be critical of American attempts to encourage rival Japanese activity within this same area.

For this reason, therefore, the British Government has repeatedly stated its belief that the natural market for Japanese goods is mainland China, and that restrictions on trade between the two areas should be removed as quickly as possible. Nevertheless, although in the past China undoubtedly did provide the greatest single field of Japanese overseas enterprise, it is inconceivable that commercial relationships between the two countries will ever again be resumed on their former basis. For, whatever its regime, China is bent on industrialization, and though at present its Communist Government may be prepared to export foodstuffs and raw materials, it is China rather than Japan which now dictates the terms of trade, and demand is likely to be limited mainly to heavy capital goods. In short, trade with China appears to offer less remunerative prospects than does that with the lands to the

[44] See Cohen, *op. cit.*, p. 76.
[45] Japanese experts of various kinds were sought by India, Pakistan, Ceylon, Thailand, and Indonesia during 1952, though the numbers involved were small.

south, and so long as world tension remains acute it is difficult to refute the American argument that the latter area must play a major part in any solution of the Japanese problem.

It was on these grounds that in 1954 Japan was at last admitted as a donor member of the Colombo Plan, a development which was indicative of the growing realization that if Japan is to be kept within the Western fold many sacrifices, both economic and political, will have to be made.[46] And while the Commonwealth will clearly be called upon to play a leading part, notably by admitting more Japanese goods into many of its markets, the United States could also make a substantial contribution by reducing some of its more oppressive tariffs.

Paradoxical though it may seem, therefore, it is in Japan's geographical position relative to the two major power blocs of to-day that its greatest asset now lies. For, while in contemporary American strategy Japan has an indispensable role to play within the defensive girdle stretching from the Aleutians to Australia, there is no reason to dispute Stalin's pronouncement that possession of this, the most highly industrialized country in East Asia, would make international Communism invincible.

Thus, in a very real sense, as the Japanese are well aware, their country "holds the key to the balance of power between the two rivals."[47] Moreover, in view of their conspicuous lack of advantages of other kinds, it would be unrealistic to expect them not to exploit this situation for their own ends. Hence their seeming unwillingness to face unpleasant economic facts to-day rests on the belief that the United States dare not allow disaster to overtake the country and will accordingly make whatever further disbursements are necessary.

Whether the Japanese are wise to risk such a provocative policy remains to be seen. But it seems clear that, strategic considerations apart,[48] the prospect of absorption within the Communist bloc holds little attraction for Japan, since it would almost inevitably entail its assuming a subordinate role to that of China in the Far East.

For the time being, therefore, and unless economic catastrophe super-

[46] In spite of long-standing British (and other) opposition, Japan became a member of G.A.T.T. in September 1955, but fourteen of the member countries immediately announced their intention of withholding G.A.T.T. privileges from Japan under Article 35 of the agreement.

[47] See *Japan: her Security and Mission* (Japanese Government, Tokyo, April 28, 1952), Foreword.

[48] See above, footnote 29. Both the U.S.S.R. and the U.S.A. retain certain bargaining counters in the former Japanese territories which they now control and could offer to retrocede at an appropriate time.

venes, Japan's alignment with the West is likely to continue. Nevertheless in the light of past experience it would be unwise to assume that this
has any other basis than straightforward self-interest. That is not to
deny that many beneficial changes introduced during the Occupation
may have lasting significance, or in any way to decry the sincerity of
the democratic beliefs professed by important elements of the Japanese
population to-day. But democracy is a tender growth, and the particular variety of it that in recent years has been transplanted to Japan from
the opulent lands of the western hemisphere will not easily take root in
these impoverished and congested islands on the precarious fringe of a
hostile continent.

FURTHER READING

ACKERMAN, EDWARD A., *Japan's Natural Resources and their Relation to
Japan's Economic Future* (University of Chicago Press, 1953).

ALLEN, G. C., *A Short Economic History of Modern Japan, 1867–1937*
(Allen and Unwin, London, 1946).

BALL, W. MACMAHON, *Japan, Enemy or Ally?* (Melbourne University Press,
1948; Cassell, London, 1950).

BENEDICT, RUTH, *The Chrysanthemum and the Sword* (Secker and Warburg,
London, 1947).

BISSON, T. A., *Prospects for Democracy in Japan* (New York, 1949).

COHEN, JEROME B., *Japan's Economy in War and Reconstruction* (Minneapolis
University Press and Oxford University Press, 1949); *Economic Problems
of Free Japan* (Princeton, 1952).

CROCKER, W. R., *The Japanese Population Problem* (Allen and Unwin,
London, 1931).

FEAREY, R. A., *The Occupation of Japan—Second Phase: 1948–50* (New York,
1950; Allen and Unwin, London, 1951).

HAUSHOFER, KARL, *Dai Nihon* (Berlin, 1913); *Japan und die Japaner*
(Leipzig, 1933).

H.M.S.O., *Japan, Overseas Economic Surveys* (London, 1953).

ISHII, RYOICHI, *Population Pressure and Economic Life in Japan* (Chicago;
King, London, 1937).

JONES, F. C., *Japan's New Order in East Asia, 1937–45* (Oxford University
Press, 1954).

KASE, TOSHIKAZU, *The Eclipse of the Rising Sun* (U.S. title: *The Road to the
Missouri*) (Cape, London, 1951).

KUNO, YOSHIO S., *Japanese Expansion on the Asiatic Continent* (three vols.;
University of California Press and Cambridge University Press, 1937).

LATOURETTE, K. S., *The History of Japan* (Macmillan, New York, 1947).

NITOBE, INAZO, *Japan* (Benn, London, 1931); *Japanese Traits and Foreign
Influences* (Kegan Paul, London, 1927).

NORMAN, E. H., *Japan's Emergence as a Modern State* (New York; Allen and
Unwin, London, 1940).

ORCHARD, J. E., *Japan's Economic Position* (McGraw-Hill, New York, 1930).
SANSOM, G. B., *Japan: A Short Cultural History* (revised edition, New York, 1943); *Japan in World History* (New York, 1951; Allen and Unwin, London, 1952); *The Western World and Japan* (New York, 1950).
SMITH, G. H., and GOOD, D., *Japan: A Geographical View* (New York, 1943).
THOMPSON, WARREN S., *Population and Peace in the Pacific* (Chicago University Press and Cambridge University Press, 1946).
TREWARTHA, G. T., *Japan: A Physical, Cultural, and Regional Geography* (Wisconsin, 1945).
WAKEFIELD, HAROLD, *New Paths for Japan* (Royal Institute of International Affairs, Oxford, 1948).
WINT, GUY, *The Future of Japan* (Batchworth, London, 1952).
YANAGA, CHITOSHI, *Japan since Perry* (McGraw-Hill, New York, 1949).

TABLE 1

Changes in Direction of Japanese Trade

Figures are percentages, calculated on a value basis.

EXPORTS TO	1935–37 AVERAGE	1951	1951 AS PERCENTAGE OF 1935–37 AVERAGE
China . . .	18·17	0·4	1·0
Formosa . . .	6·64	3·6	23·7
Hong Kong . .	1·41	4·4	135·7
Rest of Asia . .	36·54	42·1	53·3
Europe . . .	9·21	10·4	49·0
Africa . . .	5·60	8·1	62·1
North America . .	17·43	15·4	40·8
South America . .	2·26	7·8	148·7
Australasia . .	2·69	7·8	124·9
Total Exports .	100·00	100·0	43·1
IMPORTS FROM			
China . . .	10·15	1·0	6·0
Formosa . . .	9·29	2·5	17·1
Hong Kong . .	0·98	0·3	194·7
Rest of Asia . .	30·08	24·7	50·1
Europe . . .	10·17	7·5	46·3
Africa . . .	3·29	4·1	78·4
North America . .	27·49	46·5	106·0
South America . .	2·72	5·6	129·9
Australasia . .	5·85	7·8	83·6
Total Imports .	100·00	100·0	62·8

Source: *Survey of Economic Conditions in Japan, Monthly Circular* (Mitsubishi Economic Research Institute, Tokyo, June 1952).

TABLE 2

Japanese Overseas Trade, by Commodities

Values 1951 in million yen (360 yen equal 1 U.S. dollar)

IMPORTS		
COMMODITY	VALUES	PERCENTAGES
Rice	3,573	5·8
Barley . . .	2,317	3·8
Wheat . . .	4,691	7·7
Sugar	2,575	4·2
Soya beans . . .	1,440	2·4
Hides and skins .	1,335	2·2
Crude rubber . .	2,354	3·8
Wool	6,316	11·3
Raw cotton . .	14,561	23·7
Iron ore . . .	1,737	2·8
Coal	3,050	5·0
Total (including others) .	61,324	100·0
EXPORTS		
Fish	1,012	2·5
Raw silk . . .	1,242	2·0
Cotton yarn . . .	1,020	2·5
Chemical fibre yarn .	824	2·0
Cotton fabrics . .	9,528	23·3
Silk tissues . . .	560	1·4
Chemical fibre fabrics .	2,629	6·4
Clothing . . .	996	2·4
Porcelain and earthen-ware . . .	1,033	2·5
Iron and steel manufac-tures . . .	6,192	15·1
Copper . . .	907	2·2
Ships	474	1·26
Total (including others) .	40,945	100·0

Source: As Table 1.

TABLE 3

Japanese Trade with South and South-east Asia, 1951

COUNTRY	IMPORTS TO JAPAN		EXPORTS FROM JAPAN	
	million yen	*million U.S. dollars*	*million yen*	*million U.S. dollars*
Burma	11,117	30·10	6,529	18·13
Malaya and Singapore .	22,820	63·38	24,551	68·20
Indonesia	22,128	61·46	46,220	128·38
India	20,024	55·62	18,622	51·72
Pakistan	46,992	130·53	42,128	117·02
Philippines . . .	18,708	51·96	13,813	38·37
Thailand	21,121	58·66	16,268	45·18
Other Asian countries, excluding Hong Kong, Korea, Formosa, China, and U.S.S.R. . . .	38,190	106·08	35,875	99·65

Source: Based on Jerome B. Cohen, *Economic Problems of Free Japan* (Princeton, 1952), Table 32, page 77.

TABLE 4

Japanese Indices of Industrial Activity and Production

Composite indices weighted by value added; 1934–36 average equals 100.

INDEX ITEMS	1934	1936	1940	1944	1946	1950	1951
Utilities . .	90·9	108·7	140·4	154·4	109·1	169·2	183·7
Mining . .	92·2	109·7	142·7	138·5	52·2	101·5	115·0
Food . .	96·8	103·6	119·3	60·8	36·3	771·2	107·2
Textiles . .	98·5	101·4	86·0	21·1	12·2	44·6	61·5
Lumber and wood	90·2	108·9	110·3	91·3	60·3	97·6	149·2
Chemicals . .	83·3	116·7	158·9	89·7	27·0	101·0	124·6
Ceramics . .	85·5	112·4	172·0	68·4	29·1	100·6	140·2
Metals . .	84·5	113·7	170·1	220·3	15·6	121·5	163·9
Machinery .	75·9	119·9	241·7	303·3	45·1	118·7	183·5
Electric machines	108·2	95·8	107·3	45·3	36·6	105·7	135·4
Transportation equipment .	76·4	126·8	259·4	960·9	68·3	113·8	180·7
Precision instruments . .	90·8	108·9	127·3	118·5	48·6	292·8	389·8
Total industrial activity . .	89·9	110·3	147·9	171·2	39·2	101·9	133·9

Source: Based on *Japan, Overseas Economic Surveys* (H.M.S.O., London, 1953), Appendix I, p. 96.

TABLE 5

Growth of Japanese Population, 1875–1951

YEAR	TOTAL POPULATION (*thousands*)	BIRTH RATE *per* 1000	DEATH RATE *per* 1000	NET INCREASE *per* 1000
1875	35,316	25·3	19·1	6·2
80	36,649	24·3	16·6	7·7
85	38,313	26·9	23·2	3·7
90	39,902	28·3	20·4	7·9
95	41,557	29·5	20·2	9·3
1900	43,847	31·7	20·3	11·4
05	46,620	30·4	21·1	9·3
10	49,184	33·9	21·1	12·8
15	52,752	33·1	20·1	13·0
20	55,963	36·2	25·4	10·8
25	59,737	34·9	20·3	14·6
30	64,450	32·4	18·2	14·2
35	69,254	31·6	16·8	14·8
40	71,540			
45	71,998			
46	73,114			
47	78,101	34·3	14·6	19·7
48	80,217	33·4	11·9	21·8
49	88,800	32·8	11·5	21·3
50	83,199	28·3	10·9	17·4
51	84,497	25·6	10·0	15·6

Source: *Outlook of the Japanese Economy Today* (Ministry of Finance, Tokyo, 1951).

CHAPTER XXIV

Communist China

CHARLES A. FISHER

The Geographical and Historical Setting

WITH the signing of the Sino-Soviet Treaty of February 1950, the Communist bloc added some three million square miles to its territories and more than trebled its population. To the Western world this new geopolitical alignment, which is without precedent save for the short-lived ascendancy of the Mongols during the thirteenth century, represents the outstanding and supremely disturbing consequence of the collapse of Nationalist power on the Chinese mainland in the years immediately following the second world war. But to many Asian observers these same events, coupled with the more recent developments in Korea and Indo-China, are above all significant in that they appear to portend the resumption by China of its traditional role as the dominant Power in eastern Asia.

This position of virtually undisputed supremacy[1] within the Orient[2] for at least 2000 years prior to the nineteenth century is indeed the cardinal fact in Chinese history, and, in comparison with this, Japan's bid for hegemony during the last fifty years may prove to be only a transitory phenomenon. For, in spite of the immense range of problems with which China is confronted to-day, it possesses many of the prerequisites for political power, and its new rulers seem determined ruthlessly to exploit all possible resources, both human and material, in pursuit of that goal.

Notwithstanding the isolating effect of its western mountain wall, reinforced by the Tibetan plateau and the inner Asian deserts, which delimit it to the west, China is in many respects well endowed by nature. Within the Orient as a whole its central position and the immense

---

[1] The only important challenge to this supremacy came from Japan's unsuccessful attempt, under Hideyoshi, to invade China in 1592.

[2] The term Orient is used here to cover the whole of the eastern and south-eastern fringe of Asia from Manchuria and Japan to Burma and Indonesia.

capacity of its great river basins and coastal plains for supporting population have done much to make possible its traditional supremacy. In large measure the great natural productivity of the country must be attributed to its climate. For, while the main rain-bearing onshore winds do not penetrate beyond the western mountain rim, which thus in a broad sense marks the divide between the Chinese agrarian way of life and that of the inner Asian steppe peoples, much the larger part of China proper comes under the direct influence of the monsoonal circulation, which has the great advantage of giving maximum precipitation at the season of highest temperature, and thus making possible a high intensity of cultivation. There is, it is true, considerable difference between the relatively drier and cooler north, and the warm and verdant countryside of the south, but the fact that the two halves are complementary is itself a further natural asset, and practically the whole of China lies within either the cool or the warm temperate zones.

Nevertheless during its long history even the immense agricultural resources of China have been strained to the limits by the slow but inexorable increase of population. Having originally entered via the Kansu gap in the north-west, the earliest Chinese peoples made their first major settlements in the Wei and Hwang Ho Valleys, from which they subsequently spread outward, and by the end of the Han Dynasty (206 B.C. to A.D. 214) Imperial China had already assumed something very like its modern proportions. (See Fig. 1.)

Although effective Chinese colonization of the mountainous country of the south-east, and more especially of the south-western border, was not accomplished until much later (and for this reason these areas still contain many and diverse minority groups), the rest of the country has ever since enjoyed a remarkable measure of cultural unity, which in most respects transcends the historic rivalries between north and south.

So far as can be ascertained it seems that the total population of China grew from around 70 million in 1650 to 140 million in 1740 and to some 300 million by the end of the eighteenth century. But while these enormous numbers were of themselves enough to ensure the final ascendancy over the inner Asian nomads who had intermittently attacked and ravaged China since the beginnings of recorded history, they were of little avail against the European Powers which, armed with all the new techniques of the Industrial Revolution, began in the early nineteenth century to break down the age-old isolation of the Middle Kingdom in order to find new markets for their manufactures.

Indeed, by this time population pressure was probably the basic cause of the agrarian discontent and multiplying corruption which undermined the effectiveness of the Manchu administration and, in so doing, played into the hands of the West. Long before the revolution of 1911, which finally expelled the Manchu Dynasty from Peking and

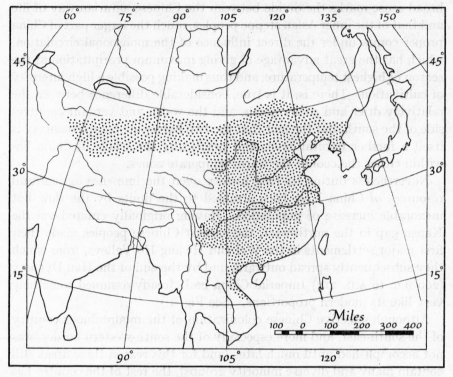

FIG. 1. THE EXTENT OF CHINA C. A.D. 100
(After Hermann.) *Royal Geographical Society*

established the first Chinese republic, the country had become in all but name an economic colony of the leading European Powers, which, from the 'treaty ports'[3] on the coast and the major rivers, dominated its overseas trade and controlled the greater part of its pitifully small array of modern industrial installations.

Notwithstanding the many achievements of Chiang Kai-shek's Nanking Government, which after October 1928 became the effective government of China, the immense problems still besetting the country

[3] *I.e.*, the series of ports which, under various agreements beginning with the Treaty of Nanking, 1843, the Chinese were compelled by the British (and later other Western Powers) to open to foreign trade.

were never satisfactorily solved. Virtually from the outset of his assumption of control the menace of Japan inevitably distracted attention from the economic front, and, furthermore, after 1931 the loss of Manchuria deprived China of its only major centre of heavy industry.[4] When in 1937 the Japanese attacked once again, both the Nationalist (Kuomintang) and the rival Communist armies (based on the north-western fastnesses of Shensi) formed a united front to resist. But after the Allied defeat of Japan in 1945 the disintegration of the wartime coalition quickly became complete, and in the civil war which ensued the Communists, after consolidating their hold in the north, succeeded in advancing rapidly southward. Thus by the end of 1949 they con-trolled virtually the whole of the country, apart from the island fortress of Formosa, in which Chiang Kai-shek and the remnants of his armies had finally taken refuge.

Territorial Organization of Communist China

Since the establishment of the Central People's Government at Peking in October 1949 it has become abundantly clear that the Com-munist revolution in China is at least as momentous an event as the Russian revolution of 1917. Moreover, while Mao Tse-Tung's "New Democracy" appears to depart in many respects from the tenets of Rus-sian Communism, the official view in both countries is that these new developments are merely 'adaptations' or 'enrichments' of the basic Marxist-Leninist doctrines to fit the special conditions of eastern Asia.

In fact, however, there are signs that the most fundamental of the supposed differences between Chinese and Russian Communism is al-ready beginning to disappear. Thus, although peasants, who formed the backbone of the armies which put the new regime into power, still accounted for 80 per cent. of the party's membership in 1951, the deci-sion had already been made as early as March 1949 to transfer the centre of activity to the urban districts.[5] More recently, the Five Year Plan and the new Constitution, dating respectively from 1953 and 1954, provide ample evidence that the primary aim is not to raise living standards or to advance the interests of the peasantry, but rather to

---

[4] See above, pp. 540–541.
[5] Richard L. Walker, "The 'Working Class' in Communist China," in *Problems of Communism*, vols. iii–iv, p. 3.

build up a politically united and industrially powerful State with the greatest possible speed.

Coupled with this drastic reorientation of the Chinese economy and polity are equally significant geographical changes. Whereas under the Kuomintang the national centre of gravity rested in the lower Yangtze Valley, since 1949 the focus has once again been shifted back to the north. For to the Communists the central position of Nanking is more than outweighed by its past associations with the West, while Peking, though peripheral to the country as a whole, occupies a remarkably focal position within the 'old liberated areas' of the north and north-east, which, on account of both natural resources and existing installations, offer the best potentialities for rapid industrialization.

Moreover, the imperial dignity and prestige of Peking, which on April 23, 1953, celebrated the eight-hundredth anniversary of its first adoption as the capital of China, are inestimable psychological assets, and, accordingly, are to be further emphasized by a spectacular fifteen-year development programme, during the execution of which the population (now 2,500,000) is expected to double. Thus, just as the Russian Communists turned their back on Peter the Great's "window on to Europe" and instead restored ancestral Moscow, "the Third Rome," to pre-eminence, so their Chinese counterparts have symbolized the reorientation of their outlook by abandoning Nanking in favour of Peking.[6]

The dominant role of the north was equally evident in the new administrative pattern introduced in 1949–50. Under this arrangement the traditional subdivisions—i.e., provinces, administrative regions, and counties (hsien) remained—though both the form of government and in many cases the details of their boundaries were changed. But, apparently in order to strengthen its hold over the country and to prevent any resurgence of the type of localism which flourished under the warlords, the central Government grouped the provinces together into a series of six new Greater Administrative Areas—namely, North, North-east, East, Central-south, North-west, and South-west (Fig. 2).

[6] Cf. the comment of H. A. L. Fisher (A History of Europe (Arnold, London, 1936), p. 722), referring to nineteenth-century Slavophiles and twentieth-century Communists: "To men of this type, Peter's city on the Neva appeared little better than a social centre for the Baltic barons and an outpost of Germany on Russian soil." The name Peking, which means 'northern capital,' is not admitted by the Nationalists, who call the city Peiping. Shanghai, the largest city in China, was even more Western in outlook than Nanking. In September 1955 it was officially stated that one million of its residents were to be moved to the countryside, and that ultimately the population would be reduced to half its present size.

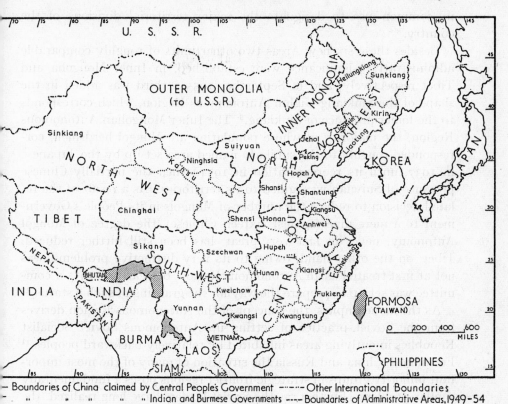

– Boundaries of China claimed by Central People's Government ––·–· Other International Boundaries
  "   "   "   "   " Indian and Burmese Governments ---- Boundaries of Administrative Areas,1949-54
· Provincial Boundaries   ▨ Territory claimed by both Central People's Government and other intererested
                             parties

FIG. 2. CHINA: ADMINISTRATIVE DIVISIONS, 1949–54

Of these six Areas the first two alone corresponded to any recognizable
geographical units, and in addition, as Ginsburg [7] has shown, enjoyed the
most privileged status. The remaining four Areas, however, had neither
geographical nor historical sanction, and, especially in the case of the
East and Central-south Areas, both of which extended from the winter-
wheat-growing lands of the north across the Yangtze to the subtropical
south coast, the main intention appears to have been to destroy the
latent regional consciousness and potential separatism of southern
China. Presumably this purpose has now been achieved, for in 1954 the
Area administrations were abolished, though the names still remain

[7] Norton S. Ginsburg, "China's Changing Political Geography," in *Geographical
Review*, vol. xlii (1952), pp. 102–117.

in common use to designate the major territorial divisions of the country. [8]

Besides these six new Areas two other units of roughly comparable administrative significance were established, in Inner Mongolia and Tibet respectively, and in September 1955 a third was added in the shape of the Sinkiang-Uighur Autonomous Region, which corresponds to the fomer province of Sinkiang.[9] The Inner Mongolian Autonomous Region, the majority of whose population are Mongol herdsmen, corresponded roughly to the similarly named area set up by the Japanese in 1937, until its reorganization in 1954, when the partially Chinese province of Suiyuan was added to its territories. As a result of the related decision to reduce the number of Mongols in its People's Government to a mere nine (against sixteen Chinese), the degree of Mongol Autonomy, never in fact very great, has been still further reduced. Tibet, on the other hand, owing to its very distinctive problems, was not at first treated as an Autonomous Region, but early in 1955 a committee was set up to prepare the way for the granting of such a status.[10]

As the name implies, the concept of the Autonomous Region derives from the Soviet practice of setting up Autonomous Soviet Socialist Republics in outlying areas inhabited by relatively backward peoples.[11] For in both China and Russia the situation of many of the most important minority groups in strategic frontier regions poses a fundamentally similar problem. Further, as the Soviet leaders have long realized, the winning over of such peoples to the new regime by granting them a measure of political and cultural autonomy was facilitated by their resentment against the forced assimilation to which they had traditionally been subjected, and could in turn provide a means of attracting the sympathies of related peoples in adjoining lands.

With this in mind, therefore, the Central People's Government, in addition to establishing Autonomous Regions for the large and relatively

[8] At the beginning of 1950 China contained thirty provinces, which were subdivided into 152 administrative regions, 2023 counties, 18930 chu, or districts, and over 200,000 hsiang, the last, composed of one or more villages, forming the lowest unit of administration in the rural areas (Shie I-yuan, "China's Administrative Divisions," in *People's China*, January 1, 1954, p. 14).

[9] These units still survive despite the abolition of the six Administrative Areas.

[10] On Mongolia, Tibet, and Sinkiang see below, pp. 588–591.

[11] These should not be confused with such advanced communities—*i.e.*, nations—as Ukraine, Byelorussia, etc., which form Soviet Socialist Republics (Union Republics) and alone enjoy, in theory, the right of secession. There is nothing corresponding to this category in the Chinese system. The Autonomous Soviet Socialist Republics are the level below this in the Soviet hierarchy, and include, for example, the Yakut A.S.S.R. Such republics, if they progress, may be upgraded, as were the Kazakh and Kirgiz, from A.S.S.R. status to that of Union Republics.

advanced population of Inner Mongolia, Sinkiang, and Tibet, has also copied Soviet practice in dealing with the smaller and often less coherent minorities in other parts of its territories. All told these are estimated at some forty million people, comprising over sixty different national groups. Already by 1953 it was claimed that forty-nine autonomous districts, corresponding to counties or to larger administrative units, had been established[12] (Fig. 3), and were being administered by suitably indoctrinated cadres drawn from the local population, and since then the number has been substantially increased.[13]

Towards certain religious groups also the Chinese Communists are following a conciliatory policy, and, like the Russians, have really tried to win the sympathies of their Moslem subjects. These include, besides some four million tribesmen in such outlying areas as Sinkiang, about six million 'Hui Tse,'[14] the descendants of former immigrants from Central Asia[15] who intermarried with Han Chinese. Moslems of this latter category form 26 per cent. of the population of Kansu and over 5 per cent. in Yunnan, and are also widely distributed as far east as Hopeh and Kiangsu. During land redistribution (see below, pp. 579–580), mosques have been allowed to retain their land, a privilege which has not been extended to the Christian churches. Nominally, it is true, the Christians, consisting of over four million Roman Catholics and three-quarters of a million Protestants, are also guaranteed religious liberty. But since Christianity has been associated in many cases with friendship towards the West and there are few large Christian communities in near-by countries to be wooed, the promised freedom is subject to severe qualifications.[16]

Buddhism, however, like Islam, can be more readily used as a vehicle for political propaganda in neighbouring lands, and although the number of genuine adherents in China proper probably does not exceed seven million, the opportunity was taken in June 1953 to hold a conference in Peking of the Chinese Buddhist Association, to which Government-sponsored delegates from Tibet, Mongolia, and the Thai territories of the South-west were invited, and "the unity of all Buddhists in China for the support of the motherland and of world peace" was duly proclaimed.

[12] Cf. the 'National Regions' of the U.S.S.R., which represent the lowest level in that hierarchy.
[13] Cadres are trained at the Central Nationalities Academy, Peking, founded in 1951.
[14] This, the traditional name, means 'rotten Moslem'; nowadays the Chinese are instructed to refer to them as Lao Piao—i.e., 'old cousin.'
[15] Largely mercenaries who came into China during T'ang and Manchu times.
[16] Christian missionaries have been expelled allegedly as subversive agents.

FIG. 3

COMMUNIST CHINA: MINORITY ADMINISTRATIVE UNITS

Titles of administrative units shown by numbers on the map. Minorities are indicated in brackets.

1. Orochon Autonomous Banner (Orochon)
2. Daghur Autonomous Area (Daghur)
3. Weng-niu-t'e (Ongniod) Autonomous Banner (Mongol)
4. Ao-han (Aokhan) Autonomous Banner (Mongol)
5. K'o-la-ch'in (Kharchin) Autonomous Banner (Mongol)
6. K'o-la-ch'in-tso (Kharchin East) Autonomous Banner (Mongol)
7. Ta-ch'ang Autonomous Area (Mongol)
8. Keui-sui Muslim Autonomous Area (Muslim)
9. Hui Autonomous Area (Muslim)
10. A-la-shan Autonomous Banner (Mongol)
11. O-chi-na Autonomous Banner (Mongol)
12. Su-pei Autonomous Area (Mongol)
13. T'ien-chu Tibetan Autonomous Area (Tibetan)
14. Hai-yen Tibetan Autonomous Area (Tibetan)
15. Kung-ho Kazak Autonomous Area (Kazak)
16. Tung-hsiang Autonomous Area (Muslim)
17. T'ung-te Autonomous Area (Tibetan)
18. P'ing-wu Tibetan Autonomous Area (Tibetan)
19. Lu-ting Democratic Coalition Area (Tibetan)
20. Hung-mao-ma-ku Yi Autonomous Area (Yi-chia)
21. Mu-li Tibetan Autonomous Area (Tibetan)
22. Kung-shan Li-su Autonomous Area (Li-su)
23. Pi-chiang Li-su Autonomous Area (Li-su)
24. Lu-ch'uan Democratic Coalition Area (Miao and Yi-chia)
25. Wu-ting Democratic Coalition Area (Yi-chia and Miao)
26. Mi-lo Yi Autonomous Area (Yi-chia)
27. O-shan Autonomous Area (Yi-chia)
28. Hsin-p'ing Democratic Coalition Area (Yi-chia and T'ai)
29. Yuan-yang Democratic Coalition Area (T'ai)
30. Lan-ts'ang La-hu Autonomous Area (La-hu)
31. Hui-shui Autonomous Area (T'ai)
32. Lu-shan Autonomous Area (Miao)
33. T'ai-chiang Miao Autonomous Area (Miao)
34. Tan-chai Miao Autonomous Area (Miao)
35. San-chiang T'ung Autonomous Area (T'ai)
36. Lung-sheng Democratic Coalition Area (Yao)
37. Tung-shan Yao Autonomous Area (Yao)
38. Lien-nan Yao Autonomous Area (Yao)
39. Ta-yao-shan Autonomous Area (Yao)
40. Shih-wan-shan Autonomous Area (Yao)
41. Ta Miao Autonomous Area (Miao)
42. Ling-lin Multinational Autonomous Area (Miao and T'ai)

Note. The terms 'league' and 'banner' apply to the Mongolian type of organization, leagues being the larger-scale units. Districts apply to the Chinese 'hsien' or 'county' units. The larger and more significant autonomous regions and districts are shaded.

Source: Herold J. Wiens, "China's March toward the Tropics" (The Shoe String Press, Hamden, Connecticut, 1954), pp. 263-266, by courtesy of the author and publishers.

Faithful copying of the Russian model is also evident in the new governmental structure set up under the Constitution of 1953–54, which provides for a system of "quasi-representative institutions similar to the

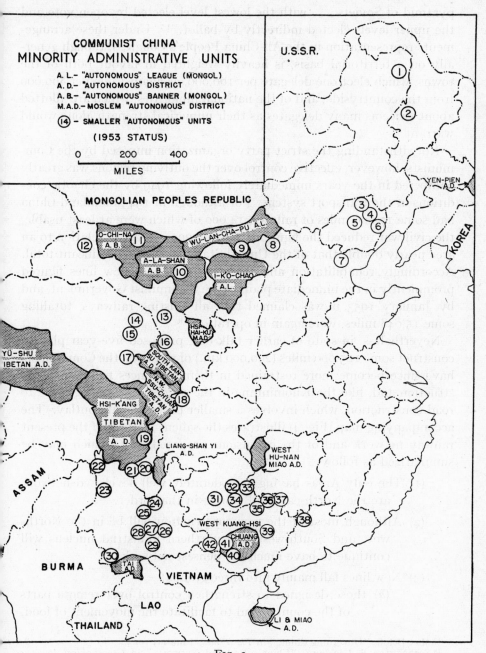

COMMUNIST CHINA
MINORITY ADMINISTRATIVE UNITS

A. L.– "AUTONOMOUS" LEAGUE (MONGOL)
A. D.– "AUTONOMOUS" DISTRICT
A. B.– "AUTONOMOUS" BANNER (MONGOL)
M. A.D.– MOSLEM "AUTONOMOUS" DISTRICT

(14) – SMALLER "AUTONOMOUS" UNITS

(1953 STATUS)

0   200   400
MILES

U.S.S.R.

YEN-PIEN A.D.

KOREA

MONGOLIAN PEOPLES REPUBLIC

O-CHI-NA A.B. (11)

WU-LAN-CHA-PU A.L.

(12)

A-LA-SHAN A.B. (10)

(9) (8)

I-K'O-CHAO A.L.

(3) (4)
(5) (6)
(7)

(14)
(15)

(13)

HSI HAI-KU M.A.D.

YÜ-SHU TIBETAN A.D.

(16)

(17)

SOUTH KAN SU TIBETAN A.D.

NW SSU-CHUAN TIBETAN A.D.

(18)

HSI-K'ANG TIBETAN A.D.

(19)

LIANG-SHAN YI A.D.

WEST HU-NAN MIAO A.D.

ASSAM

(22)
(23)

(21) (20)

(24)

(25)

(28) (27) (26)

(29)

(32) (33)

(31) (34)

(35)

(36) (37)

(38)

WEST KUANG-HSI

(42) (41)

(40)

(39)

WEST CHUANG A.D.

BURMA

(30)

TAI

VIETNAM

LAO

THAILAND

LI & MIAO A.D.

FIG. 3

pyramid of Soviets . . . with the lowest level elected by open vote and the upper levels elected indirectly by ballot."[17] Under these arrangements representation in the All-China People's Congress, though generally on a territorial basis, is heavily weighted in favour both of the towns, which elect one delegate per 100,000, as against one per 800,000 from the countryside, and of the national minorities, which are allotted about twice as many delegates as their numerical strength alone would warrant.

Notwithstanding the strict party organization imposed by the Communists, however, effective control over the outlying regions was greatly hampered in the years immediately following 1949 by the chaotic conditions of the transport system. For although in 1945 mainland China had some 17,000 miles of railway, 14,000 of which were at least usable, the civil war reduced the figure to a mere 5000, which, in relation to an area nearly double that of the United States, was an insignificant total. Accordingly rehabilitation and the construction of new lines figured prominently in the immediate plans of the Communist Government, and by January 1953 it was claimed that all existing railways, totalling some 15,048 miles, were again in operation.[18]

Nevertheless, in spite of earlier talk of a proposed five-year plan to construct some 125,000 miles (200,000 km.) of railways, the Communists have since become more restrained in their references to further construction and, like the Kuomintang in the 1930's, are turning more to road construction, which involves a smaller proportionate outlay. The accompanying map (Fig. 4) illustrates the salient features of the present railway network and of the extensions proposed to it, which may be summarized as follows:

(1) The only Areas having a moderately well-developed network are the North-east and North, in that order.

(2) Although most of the new construction will be in the North-west and South-west, the northern industrial nucleus will continue to have much the densest network.

(3) New lines fall mainly into three groups:
   (a) those designed to strengthen control over remote parts of the country and to facilitate the movement of food,

[17] Max Beloff, "Governing China," in *The Times*, June 11, 1953.
[18] See Norton S. Ginsburg, "China's Railroad Network," in *Geographical Review*, vol. xli (1951), pp. 470–474, and Li Chang, "Railway Construction in China," in *Far Eastern Survey*, March 1953, pp. 37–42.

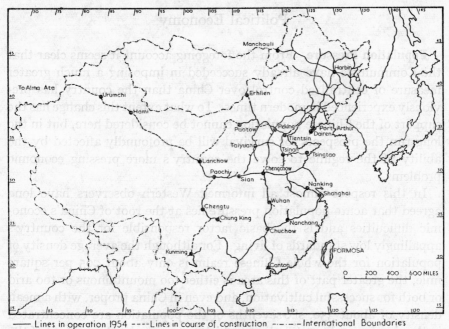

FIG. 4. CHINA: RAILWAYS

especially rice, from the rich but isolated province of Szechwan;

(b) those designed to open up key mining areas in the South-west and North-west;[19]

(c) two new through links with the U.S.S.R.:

    (i) Lanchow to Alma Ata, via Sinkiang, opening up *en route* the oil-bearing territories of Kansu and beyond;

    (ii) Kweisui to Ulan Ude, via Outer Mongolia (this was stated to have been completed in December 1954).

[19] E. Szczepanik suggests that the lines in the south-west are in part designed with a view to establishing overland communications with South Asia. E. Szczepanik: "On the Economic Theory of Maoism," in *Far Eastern Economic Review*, vol. xv, No. 25 (December 17, 1953).

U

Political Economy

Population Pressure. From the foregoing account it seems clear that the Communists have already succeeded in imposing a much greater measure of centralized control over China than the country has previously experienced in modern times. To what extent this change has the support of the Chinese population cannot be considered here, but in the long run the prospects for survival will be profoundly affected by the ability of the regime to solve the country's more pressing economic problems.

In this respect almost all informed Western observers have long agreed that acute population pressure lies at the root of China's economic difficulties and is the basic factor responsible for the country's appallingly low standards of living. For although the average density of population for the whole Chinese realm is only about 205 per square mile, the greater part of this area is either too mountainous or too arid or both for successful cultivation, and even in China proper, with a mean density of about 350, six-sevenths of the population are concentrated in the riverine and coastal plains, which comprise about one-third of the total area. It is thus in such lowland provinces as Kiangsu and Chekiang, which together contain some seventy million people in an area three-quarters the size of Great Britain and include large tracts supporting 3000 to 4000 persons per square mile almost solely by agriculture, that the problem appears in its true proportions. In fact, the economic history of China provides the outstanding illustration of the Malthusian doctrine, for had it not been for repeated famine, pestilence, civil war, and also, in many cases, infanticide, numbers would already have risen far above the present total of 582 million. Meanwhile the average size of agricultural holdings had fallen by the 1930's to around five acres in the wheat-growing regions of the north, to little over one acre in the more congested Yangtze rice-lands, and to even less in the southern coastal districts, which can produce two rice harvests within the year.

These regional variations in farming intensity are in the main a reflection of the different carrying capacity of north and south. In spite of the larger holdings in the north, living standards there have long been even lower than in the south, mainly as a result of less reliable rainfall and the tendency of the silt-laden Hwang Ho[20] to burst its banks

[20] This itself is an indirect consequence of overpopulation in that excessive depletion of the vegetation cover has fostered severe soil erosion.

and devastate wide expanses of cultivated land. But whatever the size of the holding and whether, as in three-quarters of the farm units in the north, the peasant in pre-Communist times owned his land, or whether, as in the south, some two-thirds of the farming population were tenants, most of the land was cropped virtually to capacity.[21] Moreover, thanks to the intensive application of labour per unit area and to highly skilled methods of hand cultivation, the yields of nearly all crops were above the world average, and of rice, much the most important single food crop raised, the output per acre was second only to Japan's among the major producers and approximately double that of India.

While the decline of handicraft industries and the often exorbitant rents, commonly amounting, as in many other parts of Asia, to over 60 per cent. of the crop, contributed to the general poverty, most Western observers have agreed that any programme for raising standards of living would be futile unless it tackled the basic problem of population increase. Such a policy, however, makes no appeal to the Central People's Government, which officially denies the existence of any population problem and, laying the blame for famine and poverty exclusively on the crimes of "the imperialists, feudalists, and bureaucrats in the old China," rejects the idea of birth control as being contrary to the interests of the State.[22] Moreover, in view of the rigorous and in themselves desirable measures now being taken to improve sanitation and public health, the death rate is falling sharply. Thus it is now estimated that population is increasing by ten to twelve million a year, and if these trends continue the total population will reach 800 million within the next fifteen to twenty years. But during 1955 there were unmistakable signs that the seriousness of the population problem had impressed itself on the Communist leadership, and a change in the official attitude towards birth control is now taking place.

Agricultural Policy. Foremost among the policies which the Communists have claimed were designed to cure the economic ills of China has been their much publicized 'land reform.' By the end of 1952 redistribution was complete except for some of the minority areas, and in all some 117 million acres have now changed hands. According to the Agrarian Reform Law of 1952, the agricultural population of China con-

[21] The lower incidence of tenancy in the north was mainly the result of an inadequate surplus of production there to support a landlord class.
[22] See Sun Ching-chih: "Eliminate Worship-America Ideology in the Field of Geography," in *Jen Min Jih Pao* (Peking, April 25, 1952). (Translation by Shannon McCune.)

sisted of five classes: landlords, rich peasants (cf. *kulaks*), middle peasants, poor peasants, and labourers. It was the aim of the new law to take land mainly from the first two groups, who allegedly owned some 60 to 70 per cent. of the total, and reallocate it to poor peasants and labourers. In theory both landlords and rich peasants were allowed to retain enough of their land to live on, unless they were 'enemies of the regime,' but in practice dispossession has been carried out with the utmost ruthlessness and brutality.[23]

As yet it is too early to assess the long-term effects of land redistribution, but it is clear that with a rural population of over 500 million and a total of less than 275 million acres of arable land, no programme of equalization of holdings can solve the basic problem of land hunger. Moreover, in spite of the Communist argument that "land reform would set free the rural productive forces, develop agricultural production, and thus pave the way for the New China's industrialization,"[24] it is doubtful whether the incentive to produce for oneself has offset the loss of efficiency entailed by breaking up the better-run units and penalizing the more successful cultivators. Certainly official statistics claiming percentage gains in output of up to 33 per cent. between 1949 and 1951–52 are valueless in view of the chaotic state of the country in the earlier year and the traditionally wide fluctuations in output between good harvests and bad.

Likewise the export of 66,000 tons of rice and 450,000 tons of grain sorghum to India in 1951, and the five-year trade agreement of 1952 with Ceylon, whereby China supplies 270,000 tons of rice annually in return for rubber, provide no more evidence of a real food surplus than did the Russian exports of wheat during the belt-tightening period of the First Five Year Plan.[25] In fact, such studiously vague statistics as are available suggest that total production of most agricultural commodities has no more than reached the pre-1937 level, and in some cases still remains below it, though it is reported that crops in 1955 were very

---

[23] The rates of land taxation, which in effect replaces the former rents, are graduated, poor peasants paying 10 per cent. of the summer yield, middle peasants 15 per cent., rich peasants 25 per cent., and landlords 50 to 80 per cent. (Szczepanik, *loc. cit.*) But in addition the cultivators are subjected to various other levies and have to make forced deliveries of produce to the authorities. It is impossible to obtain any accurate statistical data comparing the economic position of the peasantry to-day with that before land redistribution took place, but it is certain that the greater part of the cost of industrialization is being borne by the rural population, who form over 80 per cent. of the total.

[24] Agrarian Reform Law of 1952.

[25] However, centralized control of distribution under the new regime has played a large part in enabling China to export more agricultural produce than was normal in the past. But in 1954 China concluded a three-year agreement to buy rice, as well as timber and rubber, from Burma.

heavy. Accordingly, if the 1953 Five Year Plan is to succeed, the great increases in farm production which will be necessary to feed the industrial towns, to provide raw materials for the factories, and to pay for the import of capital goods will have to be obtained by other means than land redistribution,[26] as the Communists have been aware from the beginning.

The methods at present being pursued to bring about such an expansion fall into two categories—namely, those aimed at extending the area under cultivation and those directed towards increasing the yield per unit area. Within the former group the most publicized achievements have been in respect of drainage, flood control, and water conservancy, and in this kind of work many millions of political prisoners have been employed as unpaid coolie labour. Between 1949 and 1952 the flooded acreage is said to have been reduced from sixteen million to less than three million, and work has begun on some seventeen major water-conservancy schemes, nearly all of them in the drier northern half of the country. Of these the most notable is the Huai River Conservation scheme, which has reclaimed a vast area inundated after the Kuomintang armies breached the Hwang Ho dykes in order to hold up the Japanese advance in 1938. It has been variously estimated that between three and ten million forced labourers were employed on this task.[27]

Even more ambitious is the proposed Hwang Ho Basin Conservancy scheme, which aims at checking soil erosion by means of afforestation and the extension of grasslands (for animal husbandry) in the drier regions above the Wei confluence, as a first step towards better flood control in the lowlands. Complete success should bring another 6,800,000 acres under cultivation, though the main benefit would be in greater security from the extremes of water shortage and flooding to which much of the northern lowlands is at present liable. Similarly, plans are afoot for establishing four major protective forest belts, all of them in the north, in order to check wind erosion and the encroachment of deserts and coastal dunes. It is claimed that fifteen million acres were reforested during the first half of 1953.

In such ways as these Russian technicians have much specialized

---

[26] For details of Soviet loans to China see footnote 34. Under the 1953 ten-year trade and aid agreement between the two countries China is to repay the U.S.S.R. by exports of foodstuffs and other agricultural and mineral produce. It will also sell the U.S.S.R. 45 per cent. of the rubber it obtains from Ceylon.

[27] For sceptical comments on this scheme by an Indian observer see Raja Hutheesing, *Window on China* (Verschoyle, London, 1953), pp. 81–90.

knowledge to contribute to the solution of conservation problems in
northern China, which is geographically similar to many parts of the
U.S.S.R. In other respects, however, the applicability of Russian experience is altogether more questionable. Thus, although in the past
many Western experts have stressed the need for more careful use of the
extensive uplands of sub-tropical China,[28] its present rulers have shown
little interest in the possibilities of pastoralism, forestry, and fruit-
growing which these may afford. As regards the extension of the cultivated acreage, therefore, the gap between theory and practice remains
wide. Although according to the official view the arable area could be
trebled, the fact remains that virtually all the best land has long been
under intensive cultivation. Few areas at present uncultivated will ever
support the high densities of population already typical of most of the
riverine and coastal lowlands, and, even when this qualification is made,
it is still difficult to regard the prospective trebling of the cultivated
acreage as anything more than wishful thinking.

Even more significant, however, is the apparent belief that the key to
further intensification of output in the areas already cultivated is contained in the two magic words collectivization and mechanization. Thus,
speaking on Shanghai radio in late 1952, Hsu Pi-yu stated:

> New Democracy will be followed by nationalization of industry and col-
> lectivization of agriculture. . . . The participation of everyone in work
> necessitates large-scale production, whether in industry or agriculture, and
> there will be no small-scale production.[29]

Collectivization, it was explained, was necessary in order first to release
peasants for work in factories and mines and second to increase outputs
of food and raw materials for the towns.

For a time, however, the government moved cautiously in this
respect, for it had become clear by 1953 that the prospect of losing control over their newly acquired holdings was causing growing hostility
among the peasants. Thus, instead of an open drive for collectivization,
the authorities at first concentrated on promoting 'voluntary' mutual-
aid teams and producer co-operatives, by means of which they claimed
that it would be possible to recapture some of the efficiency of larger
units, to foster the development of a certain amount of handicraft
industry, and also to enable the peasants to purchase better tools and
to carry out local reclamation and irrigation work co-operatively.

[28] P. Gourou, "Notes on China's Unused Uplands," in *Pacific Affairs*, vol. xxi, No. 3
(1948), pp. 227–238.
[29] *Manchester Guardian*, November 4, 1952.

Already in 1953 it was reported that 43 per cent. of China's peasant households were organized in accordance with one or other of these schemes, and in the meantime the idea of collectivization and the supposed advantages of mechanization were advertised by demonstration farms. But in October 1955 Mao Tse-tung decided on a drastic speeding up of the programme, and it has since been stated that all of the 110 million peasant holdings are to be under collective management by the spring of 1958.

Although it seems likely that this acceleration springs from the desire to exert closer control over the traditionally individualistic peasantry, it is equally important to realize that the present policy begs the vital question of whether or not Russian methods are applicable to Chinese agrarian conditions. As Table 2 shows, practically all the demonstration farms are in the northern half of the country, and, indeed, a clear majority of them are in Manchuria alone, which in physique, climate, and population density is completely untypical of China as a whole.

Over the rest of China, as Table 2 illustrates, the basic agrarian problems are fundamentally different from those of Russia, and, with the solitary exception of cotton cultivation, which in the U.S.S.R. takes place under intensive oasis conditions in the Central Asian republics, no evidence whatever exists to suggest that the introduction of Russian methods will lead to any significant increase in yields. Indeed, the contrary is much more likely. For it cannot be too strongly emphasized that mechanization is efficient only in the sense of saving labour, and, so far as outputs per unit area are concerned, the extensive type of Russian cultivation falls far short of the intensive methods practised in the greater part of China.[30]

Far more relevant to China's problem is the experience of Japan, which between 1880 and 1930 increased its yields of rice per acre by some 60 to 65 per cent. above their previous level, which was somewhat lower than that of present-day China. This increased yield was made possible by maintaining the agricultural labour force at virtually the same level, introducing various improvements in cultivation methods, and greatly increasing the amount of chemical fertilizer used on the land. Even so, the increase in food production did not keep pace with the growth of population, and in China to-day the proportionate rate of

[30] It is probable that Russian instruction in such matters as seed selection could help, but the disclosures of agrarian shortcomings in 1953 confirm the impression that Russia has little to teach China in farming methods. See also F. H. King, *Farmers of Forty Centuries* (New York, 1926; Cape, London, 1927).

increase is at least as high as and probably higher than in Japan during the period under consideration. The apparent unconcern about how this vast and rapidly growing population was to be fed was in many respects the most baffling aspect of Chinese behaviour between 1949 and 1954. And although there are now signs that the authorities have realized the seriousness of the situation, it will obviously be many years before stability is reached, and during this time the problem of feeding the country will become increasingly difficult.

Industrialization. As formerly in the U.S.S.R., Communist China's first Five Year Plan (1953–57) is concerned above all with developing the basic heavy industries as rapidly as possible. Thus coal production is to be increased by 60 per cent. above the 1952 level, which Hsia[31] believes to have been approximately forty-seven million metric tons (as compared with over thirty-nine million in 1936 and over sixty-five million in 1942, when the Japanese were in control of the principal mines). Further, mainly as the result of constructing two large metallurgical plants, one at Paotow and the other in the Wuhan-Tayeh area,[32] and expanding the existing installations at Anshan, in Manchuria, the crude steel output is to be raised from 1·4 to 5·6 million metric tons (compared with 350,000 in 1936 and 2,079,000 in 1942). Meanwhile the production of electric power will be approximately doubled as new hydro-electric installations are built, notably at Fengman, on the Sungari river, and thermal electric plants set up at Fushun, Harbin, Fuhsin, and Dairen, in Manchuria, and also at Taiyuan, Sian, Lanchow, Paotow, and Tayeh. The principal advance in non-ferrous metal production will come from extending the present aluminium capacity at Fushun, and oil-refining capacity will be increased several-fold with the erection of a large refinery in Kansu to serve the newly discovered oilfields in the North-west.

With the sole exception of the Wuhan-Tayeh projects, all of these particular new developments will take place in the northern half of the country, and by far the greater part will be concentrated in Manchuria alone, where many of the larger towns are now growing at a rate comparable with that of the Siberian industrial cities twenty years ago.[33]

[31] Ronald Hsia, "The Chinese Economy under Communist Planning," in *Pacific Affairs*, vol. xxvii, No. 2 (June 1954), pp. 112–123. See also Table 5.
[32] These two centres, near the Outer Mongolian border and in the middle Yangtze Valley respectively, are already established producers of iron ore.
[33] Mukden, the focus of the industrial complex, has grown from less than one million in 1949 to over two million in 1952, and Anshan, some fifty miles to the south-west, from about 200,000 in 1949 to over 800,000 in 1952.

Moreover, the new industries will be exclusively State-controlled, as, indeed, is much the greater part of the heavy industry already in operation. This is notably true of Manchuria, where such Japanese-installed equipment as remained after the Russian depredations of 1945 became the property of the State. Since 1950 the U.S.S.R. claims to have replaced the equipment previously removed, though it has been suggested that the Russians may have taken this opportunity of ensuring the dependence of the Manchurian industrial complex on that of Far Eastern Russia by retaining certain key plant in the latter region.

Whether this be true or not, the agreement signed on September 15, 1953, whereby the U.S.S.R. promised increased long-term assistance[34] in order to sustain China's programme of industrial expansion, contains the significant proviso that China will seek Soviet advice in the location of ninety-one new enterprises which are now to be set up.[35] Although full details of the policy to be followed in this respect are not yet known, it seems that, while the main industrial concentration will remain in Manchuria and the North,[36] the North-west (along the route of the extended Lunghai railway) will be developed as a second great mining and metallurgical nucleus as a standby in the event of Manchuria's being devastated in a future war. In the still more distant future, according to E. Szczepanik,[37] a third major industrial base will be established in the South-west, and he draws an interesting parallel between this threefold sequence and that of Soviet industrial planning in the Leningrad-Moscow-Ukraine area, the Urals, and Western Siberia.

For the time being, however, industrial expansion no less than the more revolutionary developments in conservation will be largely restricted to northern China, and from many points of view this prior concentration on areas where Russian agricultural experience is applicable and where the foundations for a major industrial base were already in being, seems logical. According to this interpretation, the turn of the South as a whole would come in later Five Year Plans, when some margin for experiment had been acquired and a greater expansion could be

[34] The Sino-Soviet agreement of 1950 granted China a credit of 300 million dollars (U.S.). By the agreement of October 1954 the U.S.S.R. undertook to lend China a further 520 million roubles (*i.e.*, 130 million dollars (U.S.)).

[35] In addition to the sixty-five enterprises already established or under construction with Soviet assistance under the 1953 Five Year Plan. All told, the Plan envisages 694 industrial projects, of which the 156 enterprises planned, built, or largely equipped with Soviet aid are the crucial ones. 88 per cent. of total investment is in heavy industry.

[36] Including Paotow and also the pre-war complex at Tientsin.

[37] E. Szczepanik, *loc. cit.*

U*

afforded in the consumer-goods industries, for which the coastal cities, with their existing factory installations, and the South-west, with its large reserves of hydro-electric power, would be pre-eminently suited. But the present changes in the pattern of China's economic geography are also in part the result of a deliberate attempt to weaken the influence of the more Westernized and cosmopolitan southern cities in the national life. Like that of the U.S.S.R. under its Five Year Plans, the Chinese economy is becoming increasingly self-centred, and in its relations with the outside world China seems to be reverting to its traditional overland orientation, with the Jade Gate as the front door and the coastal ports as the back.

In the immediate future the prospects for the new plan's success will depend mainly on the supply of trained labour at home and of capital equipment from abroad. While at present Chinese trade unions claim to represent over ten million workers, most of these are unskilled and the training of technicians presents a major problem. Nevertheless, Russian experience can be of great help in overcoming this difficulty, and already many old and new colleges, again especially in the North and North-east, are mass-producing technicians. An important development in this connexion has been the recruitment of young and often well-educated Chinese from overseas for training and subsequent employment in China. Of the 7000 who were scheduled to arrive in 1953, 42 per cent. were to study engineering, 26 per cent. to become teachers, 10 per cent. to be trained as doctors, and another 10 per cent. to be taught various branches of applied science.[38]

If, therefore, the labour problem can be solved by these various means and sufficient capital equipment can be obtained from the U.S.S.R., whose own requirements in this respect, however, are prodigious, there would seem to be no reason why China should not experience a great industrial expansion. For, apart from the U.S.S.R., it is the best endowed of all Asian States with the most vital raw materials[39] and in Southern Manchuria it already controls the former 'continental arsenal,' without which Japan's spectacular conquests in recent years could not have been made. Undoubtedly the difficulties are many, and at the least

[38] Approximately 2800 Chinese are receiving technical training in the U.S.S.R. The number of Soviet experts of all kinds working in China is estimated at 30,000–50,000.

[39] China has by far the greatest coal reserves and the second largest iron reserves of any Asian country (apart from the U.S.S.R.). According to *Coal and Iron Ore Resources of Asia and the Far East* (U.N. Publications, ST/ECAFE/5, July 1952), China's coal reserves amount to 444,511 million metric tons (p. 18) and iron reserves to 4,167,820,000 metric tons (p. 20). In addition China is the world's leading producer of tungsten and antimony and a large producer of tin, copper, and salt.

it will take fifteen to twenty years for China to become a major industrial Power. But, given the time and the means to develop the resources already known to exist, and to regiment the vast reserves of man-power which it possesses, Communist China will become a formidable force to be reckoned with in international affairs. Moreover, if in the meantime the basic problem of land hunger remains unsolved, the temptation to use this growing strength as the foundation for an aggressive foreign policy will surely increase.

External Relations

In any attempt to evaluate the probable role of the new China in world affairs consideration of its relationship with the U.S.S.R. must clearly play a major part. In the economic sphere the drastic extent to which China has replaced its former links with the West by new ties with the Soviet bloc is shown in the latest trade statistics (Table 6) and in May 1952 British commercial firms, until then the most numerous foreign survivals, finally attempted to withdraw from the Chinese mainland.[40] From a political standpoint the situation is more difficult to assess, but it appears that China, as befits its size and potential strength, is being treated less as a satellite than as an ally, and that to a significant degree it has assumed the leadership of the Communist movement in eastern Asia. At present the mutual advantages of perpetuating this marriage of convenience between the two great Communist Powers seem overwhelming, and for the West to expect an early dissolution is merely to indulge in wishful thinking.

Nevertheless, sources of potential disagreement do exist, and the 5000-mile frontier between the two States has been the scene of repeated friction at numerous points during the past. In this context Manchuria clearly occupies a key position, but very little information is available about contemporary developments there. However, it is significant that in December 1952 the U.S.S.R., in fulfilment of the undertaking contained in the 1950 Treaty, restored the Changchun railway to

[40] The United Nations embargo on strategic trade with Communist China, following the latter's aggression in Korea, helped to accelerate this trend. But even before this the attitude to Western firms was far from encouraging. On May 19, 1952, the British Government informed the Central People's Government that British commercial firms intended to close their remaining establishments in China. During 1954 there were some indications of a Chinese desire for more trade with the West primarily in order to obtain more capital equipment than the U.S.S.R. alone is able to supply.

Chinese administration[41] and in May 1955 the Port Arthur naval base was handed back to China. It is none the less worth recalling that one reason for the original Russian occupation of Liaotung in 1898 lay in the potentialities which it offered for applying pressure on Peking, and the apparent insistence of the Russians that Chinese industry shall be concentrated primarily in Manchuria suggests that such considerations may not have been entirely forgotten.

The situation in the Inner Asian borderlands is, if anything, even more obscure. Yet there is no reason to assume that Chinese interest in this vital frontier region has undergone any diminution. Neither the first Republican Government (1912) nor the Nanking Government ever abandoned the claim that "the great Chinese family" comprised "five races"—i.e., Chinese, Mongols, Manchus, Tibetans, and Moslems—and the same five are symbolized to-day in the one large and four smaller stars on the flag of Communist China. Moreover, both of the former regimes sought to develop the agricultural, pastoral, and mineral resources of Inner Asia, and especially after the first world war this area received attention as a possible outlet for surplus population from other parts of the country.[42]

In the meantime, however, Russian influence has tended to increase at China's expense in several critical areas within this region. Although the Sino-Soviet Treaty of 1924 recognized Outer Mongolia as an integral part of China, the local inhabitants declared it to be an independent State, and by the 1930's it had become virtually a protectorate of the U.S.S.R. This alignment was reinforced by the building of the railway from the Trans-Siberian main line at Ulan Ude to Ulan Bator (Urga). Later, following the Yalta decision to maintain the political *status quo* in Outer Mongolia, a plebiscite was held in October 1945 among the 900,000 Mongols and Kalmycks who sparsely inhabit the territory, and this confirmed the creation of an 'independent' Mongolian People's Republic bound politically to the U.S.S.R. Thus the partition of the Mongol lands north and south of the Gobi desert has been regularized, though the arrangement cannot be said to satisfy the aspirations of the Mongol people as a whole, the greater part of whom—i.e., some four or five million—remain on the Chinese side of the boundary. Moreover, it is only the poorer lands of the desert and semi-desert borders which have

[41] *I.e.*, the old Chinese Eastern Railway from Manchuli to Sui-fen-ho, together with the spur extending from Harbin to Dairen and Port Arthur.
[42] See P. M. Roxby, "The Expansion of China," in *Scottish Geographical Magazine*, vol. xlvi (March 1930).

been formed into the Inner Mongolian Autonomous Region,[43] and the better grasslands farther to the south, formerly also a Mongol preserve, have during the present century been increasingly occupied by Chinese settlers and incorporated within the Chinese provincial system. For this reason Mongol nationalism in all these areas has tended to be more anti-Chinese than anti-Russian.

Nevertheless, Peking now seems determined to court the friendship of the Mongol peoples, and since the signature in October 1952 of a Treaty of Economic and Cultural Co-operation with Outer Mongolia has intensified its efforts to draw that area within the Chinese orbit. Whether this policy, which will take on a new significance with the linking of North China by rail with Ulan Bator, forms part of a wider defensive strategy aimed at surrounding China with a series of protective satellite States remains to be seen, but recent Chinese behaviour towards Korea and Vietnam[44] lends some support to this interpretation.

Sinkiang also presents many points of similarity with Mongolia, and, especially after the opening of the Turk-Sib Railway in 1930, its economic orientation towards the U.S.S.R. became more pronounced. In spite of the better relations between China and Russia when the Sinkiang road was developed as a supply route during the Sino-Japanese war, the Kuomintang Government was anxious to reassert its authority over the territory, which offers considerable possibilities for an extension of oasis cultivation and contains coal, copper, iron, and reputedly petroleum. It seems likely, therefore, that the incorporation of Sinkiang within the North-west Administrative Area of the Central People's Republic represented a continuation of this policy; but in September 1955 the territory, 77 per cent. of whose population of five million are Turki Uighurs, was constituted the Sinkiang-Uighur Autonomous Region.

By the terms of the 1950 Treaty, China and the U.S.S.R. agreed to set up joint companies to exploit the minerals of Sinkiang, and work on the new extension of the Lunghai railway, from Lanchow via Tihwa (Urumchi) to Alma Ata on the Turk-Sib Railway, has already begun.[45]

[43] See above, p. 572.
[44] See p. 592.
[45] This is essentially the same route as that followed by the motor road which carried supplies from Russia into China during the Sino-Japanese war after 1937. In January 1955 the U.S.S.R. handed over its shares in the joint companies to China, which will refund an equivalent value in exports over a period of years. It is claimed that the arable area of Sinkiang has been raised from 2·5 to 3·5 million acres between 1949 and 1955, and it is hoped ultimately to increase this figure to 10 million by means of irrigation.

Meanwhile many new roads have been built crossing the border into the Kirghiz and Tadzhik Soviet Republics, and in 1950 construction started, under Russian supervision, of a major highway which, passing through Kashgar and South-western Sinkiang, will extend into Tibet in an arc roughly parallel to the Kashmir frontier and ultimately afford a through route for mechanized vehicles from the U.S.S.R. to Lhasa. Another new road now under construction follows the line of the projected railway to Urumchi, and thence will run south-westward to Kashgar; considerable road-building is also in progress between South-western China and Eastern Tibet.

To many observers the reimposition of Chinese rule over Tibet in May 1951, following the capitulation of the Tibetan forces after some months of relatively small-scale fighting, seemed to substantiate the old dictum that a new and vigorous dynasty will automatically pursue an aggressive foreign policy. Admittedly, no Chinese Government ever recognized the independence of Tibet after 1912, and in this sense the Communists have merely succeeded where their predecessors failed in reasserting Chinese control over a former dependency. Nevertheless, although, according to the statement made by the Panchen Lama in Peking in April 1951, Tibet was "returning to the big family of China," the precise form of the 'autonomy' which was promised at that time remains to be demonstrated. Officially the administration is referred to simply as the Local Government of Tibet, but although the Chinese are attempting to govern through the native spiritual leaders, the trend towards political centralization in Peking is strong and has already provoked much local opposition.[46]

Since the greater part of Tibet consists of almost useless plateau averaging over 15,000 feet in altitude, and agriculture is out of the question except in the valleys of the south-east which support the bulk of its four million people, the value of the country to China is a matter of some speculation. Recent developments, however, provide certain clues. Although the food shortage, aggravated by the presence of Chinese forces, is acute and has helped to provoke riots against the new regime, there is evidence that the mineral wealth may repay exploitation. More significant, however, are the repeated references to road-building and the construction of air-strips, which suggest that strategic considerations may be uppermost in the Chinese mind. That does not mean that Tibet

[46] Werner Levi, "Tibet under Chinese Communist Rule," in *Far Eastern Survey*, vol. xxiii, No. 1 (January 1954), pp. 1–9. Preparations are now being made (1955) for granting Tibet the status of an Autonomous Region.

is likely to be used as the springboard for an attack on India in any foreseeable future, for to assemble a large army there would be impracticable, apart from the immense difficulties entailed in crossing the Himalayas.

However, China has continued to advance claims to substantial Indian territories both in Assam and Gharwal, and the construction of a military airfield in Tibet within 250 miles of Delhi has caused misgivings in that capital.[47] Accordingly, Indian policy towards Nepal, which also paid tribute to China before 1911, has aimed during recent years at counteracting the influence of those Nepalese who wish to associate themselves with Mongolian-Tibetan nationalism and, by linking their country's fortunes with those of the Chinese-controlled territories to the north, threaten India's defences along the southern slopes of the Himalayas. Finally, in June 1954, India and China ratified a non-aggression pact governing their relations with what was cryptically termed the "Tibet region of China."

From this brief consideration of Inner Asia only tentative conclusions can be drawn. In the absence of reliable surveys of resources it is unwise to take literally Communist reports of the great economic development now being undertaken in these remote regions. Nevertheless one thing is clear. Central Asia is ceasing to be a power vacuum, and although it will certainly be many years before its isolation is decisively broken down, the possibility of exploiting some of the strategic advantages implicit in its position as the pivot of Asia can no longer be discounted. Whether in these circumstances, and especially if important minerals are discovered there, Russian and Chinese interests will coincide, remains to be seen. But, in so far as past history is any guide, there would appear to be considerable room for divergence.

There is, however, one great field for possible Chinese activity in which no such complications arise. In the lands of South-east Asia, over much of which China claimed at least a vague suzerainty before the annexations of the Europeans in recent centuries, there is far greater opportunity for colonization than in the semi-arid interior of the continent. Moreover, not only is it possible to exploit the nationalist aspirations of such border peoples as the Thais and many lesser hill tribes who straddle the political boundaries between China and its neighbours to the south, but there is in addition an advance guard of some ten million Chinese scattered throughout the Nan Yang, many of whom occupy key

[47] See "China Liberates Tibet," in *The Economist*, June 14, 1952, pp. 756–757.

positions in industry and commerce. While for the time being China's principal interest in these overseas citizens may centre in the foreign exchange derived from the remittances which many contribute to relatives at home, their future use as a potential fifth column cannot be discounted.[48] And this, combined with the strategical advantage which China enjoys by virtue of her contiguity with the weak and divided States of the South-east Asian mainland, will become a cause of growing anxiety there as her industrial and military strength increases.

Clearly these are long-term considerations, but already the possibilities for slow piecemeal expansion along the southern landward border, wherever Western power is withdrawn, are great. Such is the threat facing Indo-China, which in many respects presents a close parallel to Korea. For northern Vietnam is not merely the one area in South-east Asia ever to have been an integral part of Imperial China, but in view of its geographical position and the lack of major natural barriers, the Chinese have argued that it provides a potential foothold from which an invasion could be launched by foreign Powers. However, as in the case of Korea, the rest of the world has more obvious reason to be concerned at the prospect of movement in the reverse direction.

If, as the events of 1953–54 suggest, Communist China has sought both to replace the U.S.S.R. as the controlling force in North Korea and to turn at least northern Vietnam into a Chinese satellite, a remarkable situation may arise. For, as reference to Fig. 1 makes clear, were China to succeed in these aims its territorial extent would become surprisingly similar to that which obtained during the later Han Dynasty. From another point of view, however, the policy of seeking to surround China with a series of buffer States, which can be manipulated for either defensive or offensive purposes, appears to derive directly from modern Soviet practice and, indeed, to take on its fullest significance only when considered in relation to a co-ordination of external policy on the part of these two allies.

In this respect, therefore, as in many others, the basic enigma presented by Communist China remains unsolved. For while it would be absurd to underestimate the determination of that country's contempor-

---

[48] China follows the *jus sanguinis* and accordingly regards all overseas Chinese, even though they may accept the nationality of their country of domicile, as being citizens of China. During conversations with Pandit Nehru during the summer of 1954 Mr Chou En-lai implied that this policy would be modified, and further statements were made to this effect at the Bandung Conference of April 1955. On April 22, 1955, a treaty was signed between China and Indonesia whereby Chinese in Indonesia were to have the option of choosing either Chinese or Indonesian nationality. China has also indicated its willingness to consider making similar agreements with other S.E. Asian countries.

ary leaders to break with the past and to refashion the national life on the Soviet model, it nevertheless appears that ingrained patterns of thought and behaviour may help to preserve a considerable element of continuity in the story.[49] Nevertheless, this much at least seems clear. If copying of the U.S.S.R. remains rigid and doctrinaire the probability of economic and political failure will be great. But if, over the years, the Chinese succeed in transforming what they are now learning from Russia into something truly relevant to the profoundly different problems of their own country, the future divergence of the two systems would appear to be no less inevitable.

FURTHER READING

BUCK, J. LOSSING, *Land Utilization in China* (three vols.; University of Chicago Press, 1937; Oxford University Press, 1938).

CHENG, F. T., *China Moulded by Confucius* (Stevens, London, 1946).

CHIANG KAI-SHEK, *China's Destiny* (with notes by Philip Jaffe) (Roy, New York; Dobson, London, 1947).

CRESSEY, G. B., *Land of the 500 Million* (McGraw-Hill, New York, 1955).

FEI, H. T., *Peasant Life in China* (Kegan Paul, London, 1943).

FEIS, H., *The China Tangle* (Princeton University Press and Oxford University Press, 1954).

FITZGERALD, C. P., *China: A Short Cultural History* (Cresset Press, London, 1935); *Revolution in China* (Cresset Press, London, 1952).

FONG, H. D., *The Post-war Industrialization of China* (National Planning Association, Washington, 1942).

GULL, E. M., *Facets of the Chinese Question* (Benn, London, 1931); *British Economic Interests in the Far East* (Oxford University Press, 1943).

HUDSON, G. F., *Europe and China* (Arnold, London, 1931); *The Far East in World Politics* (second edition, Oxford University Press, 1939).

HUTHEESING, RAJA, *Window on China* (U.S. title: *The Great Peace*) (Verschoyle, London, 1953).

JONES, F. C., *Manchuria since 1931* (Oxford University Press, 1949).

KING, F. H., *Farmers of Forty Centuries* (Harcourt, New York, 1926; Cape, London, 1927).

KIRBY, E. STUART, *Introduction to the Economic History of China* (Allen and Unwin, London, 1954).

LATOURETTE, K. S., *The Chinese: their History and Culture* (third edition, Macmillan, New York, 1946).

LATTIMORE, OWEN, *Inner Asian Frontiers of China* (American Geographical Society, New York, and Oxford University Press, 1940); *Manchuria: Cradle of Conflict* (Macmillan, New York, 1932).

MALLORY, W. H., *China: Land of Famine* (American Geographical Society, New York, 1926; Stevens and Brown, London, 1927).

MORAES, FRANK, *Report on Mao's China* (Macmillan, New York, 1953).

---

[49] A similar continuity with Tsarist policies is evident in many aspects of Russian affairs, both internal and external.

MURPHY, RHOADS, *Shanghai: Key to Modern China* (Harvard, 1953).

NEEDHAM, JOSPEH, *Science and Civilisation in China,* vol. i (Cambridge University Press, 1954).

ROSTOW, W. W., etc., *The Prospects for Communist China* (Chapman and Hall, London, 1955).

ROWE, DAVID N., *China among the Powers* (Harcourt, New York, 1945).

SCOTT, J. CAMERON, *Health and Agriculture in China* (Faber, London, 1952).

SHEN, T. H., *Agricultural Resources of China* (Cornell University Press and Oxford University Press, 1951).

TAWNEY, R. H., *Land and Labour in China* (Allen and Unwin, London, 1932).

SUN YAT-SEN, *The International Development of China* (Putnam, New York, 1929).

WU, A. K., *China and the Soviet Union* (Methuen, London, 1950).

WIENS, HEROLD J., *China's March toward the Tropics* (Hamden, Conn., 1954).

TABLE I

Comparative Densities of Population in pre-Revolutionary Russia and Contemporary China

(Figures are persons per square mile)

TYPES OF LAND	RUSSIA (1913)	CHINA (1949)
Most highly developed agriculture regions	Ukraine, and country-side in vicinity of Moscow—*c.* 130	Yangtze delta—*c.* 2000
Good farm-lands .	Black-earth belt—65–130	Yangtze valley—500–1000 North China plain—650
Poorer lands . .	Typical forest clearings in European Russia—30–65	Uplands of interior South and Central China—100–500
—	—	Manchuria—95

Note. It is not suggested that the intrinsic geographical character of the areas compared **is** identical. The purpose of the table is merely to emphasize the contrasts in density of rural population between the two countries before the introduction of Communist methods of tackling the agrarian problem.

Administrative Areas of China: Selected Statistical Data

ADMINISTRATIVE DIVISION	AREA (square miles)	POPULATION (estimated), 1952	CITIES OVER 1 MILLION (1950)	NATIONAL MINORITIES	CULTIVATED AREA (sq. miles)	NUMBER OF MECHANIZED FARMS	NUMBER OF STATE FARMS	HYDRO-ELECTRIC POTENTIAL kW
North ·	238,077	67,068,386	Peking 2,031,000 Tientsin 1,795,000		66,288	10	10	4,776,972
North-east ·	341,539	41,570,678	Mukden 1,551,000 Dairen 1,054,000		59,015	19	30	6,568,337
North-west ·	1,304,616	23,471,480		c. 6,300,000 (16 groups)	34,800	6	1	17,465,805
Central-south ·	242,692	136,775,290	Canton 1,496,000 Wuhan 1,200,000	c. 8,900,000 (16 groups)	82,746	1	1	18,510,768
East ·	443,077	140,928,712	Shanghai 5,407,000 Nanking 1,020,000		83,316	6	3	4,776,972
South-west ·	560,000	70,634,691	Chung-king 1,100,000	c. 20,000,000 (34 groups)	53,635	—	—	97,181,533
Inner Mongolian Autonomous Region ·	269,231	2,238,625		c. 2,200,000 (6 groups)	5,655	—	—	no data
Tibet ·	469,294	3,722,000		c. 3,700,000	no data	—	—	no data
Total ·	3,868,526	486,409,862[1]		c. 40,000,000	385,455 (excluding Tibet)	42	45	149,280,390 (excluding Inner Mongolia and Tibet)

Based on *Chung-hua Jen-min Kung-ho-ko-kuo Fen-sheng Ti-t'u* (Shanghai, 1952). (Translation by courtesy of Herold J. Wiens.)

[1] The Census of 1953 reported a total population of 601,938,035 which, however, included estimated totals of 7,591,295 in Formosa and 11,743,320 in foreign countries.

TABLE 3

Crop Yields in Selected Countries during the 1930's

PRODUCT	TOTAL OUTPUT, CHINA (*million bushels*)	YIELD PER ACRE (*bushels*)					
		China	Japan	India	U.S.S.R.	U.S.A.	World Average
Rice .	130,312	54	68	29	—	47	32
Wheat .	55,449	16	25	11	10	14	14
Sweet potatoes	35,745	139	—	—	—	—	95
Soya beans .	30,779	17	—	—	—	—	13·7
Barley .	17,093	28	—	—	—	—	20
Cotton .	3·1 million bales	203·2 lb.	—	102·2 lb.	284·1 lb.	212·4 lb.	178·9 lb.

Source: *International Yearbook of Agriculture.*

TABLE 4

China: Agricultural Outputs in 1949 *and* 1951

Expressed as percentage of "the highest annual production ever previously recorded."

PRODUCT	1949	1951
All types of food grain .	75	93
Rice	75	100
Wheat . . .	72	88
Soya beans . . .	34	72
Cotton . . .	52	133
Cured tobacco . .	27	130
Gunny-sack hemp .	13	304
Domestic animals .	84	90

Source: *Ta Kung Pao* (Shanghai, 1952).

Note: While these figures should be treated with reserve, they illustrate the great emphasis on raising the output of industrial raw materials.

TABLE 5

China: Industrial Outputs

ITEM	1952	1954	1957 (planned)
Steel . .	1·35 m. tons	2·25 m. tons	4·15 m. tons
Coal . .	63 m. tons	72 m. tons	110 m. tons
Oil . .	1·8 m. tons	2·2 m. tons	?
Electric power	7·2 m. kW	11 m. kW	15·5 m. kW

Source: *The Times*, September 7, 1955.

TABLE 6

Foreign Trade of Communist China (1952)

(Figures in million U.S. dollars)

AREAS OF ORIGIN AND DESTINATION	IMPORTS	EXPORTS
Russia and Eastern Europe . .	950	625
Japan	1	14
Other Far Eastern countries . .	4	2
Western Europe	31	44
Sterling area	195	221
(of which United Kingdom) .	12·8	?
Others	18	15
Total .	1211·8	921

Over 90 per cent. of China's imports from the Soviet bloc are industrial equipment. Exports include wood oil, bristles, soya beans, tungsten, and antimony.

Trade with non-Communist countries—*i.e.*, about 28 per cent. of the total—includes the following items (figures in million U.S. dollars):

IMPORTS		EXPORTS	
Raw cotton . .	87	Food . . .	130
Chemicals . . .	62	Vegetable oils . .	71
Raw rubber . . .	25	Bristles and feathers .	29
Machinery and vehicles .	12	Textiles and fibres .	26

Source: *New York Times*, December 20, 1953, Section 4, p. 4.

TABLE 7

Pre-war Foreign Trade of China: Figures for 1939

(Values in millions of standard dollars)

IMPORTS FROM	VALUE	PERCEN-TAGE	EXPORTS FROM	VALUE	PERCEN-TAGE
United States . .	214·1	15·9	United States .	225·9	21·9
Japan . . .	316·5	23·6	Japan . .	66·6	6·5
Germany .	87·2	6·5	Germany .	45·1	4·4
Hong Kong .	35·4	2·6	Hong Kong .	221·1	21·6
United Kingdom .	77·9	5·8	United Kingdom	90·9	8·8
N.E.I. . .	58·4	4·5	N.E.I. . .	17·7	1·7
India . . .	119·4	8·9	India . .	30·7	3·0
Total (including others) . .	1343·0	100·0	Total (including others) .	1030·4	100·0
Principal Commodities			*Principal Commodities*		
Raw silk . .	131·6	12·8	Raw cotton .	172·9	12·9
Eggs and egg products	87·4	8·5	Chemicals, etc. .	120·8	9·0
Bristles . . .	41·1	4·0	Wheat and flour	112·4	8·4
Wood oil . .	33·6	3·3	Metals and ores	73·1	5·4
Tin . . .	32·8	3·2	Machinery .	61·1	4·5
Cotton yarn .	31·8	3·1	Paper . .	55·9	4·2
Tea . . .	30·4	3·0	Rice and barley	55·1	4·1
Embroidery, etc. .	29·0	2·8	Sugar . .	52·6	3·9
Cereals . .	25·1	2·4	Tobacco . .	36·6	2·7
Hides and skins .	22·3	2·2	Motor vehicles .	35·6	2·7
Oil seeds . .	21·4	2·1	Timber . .	34·4	2·6

Based on K. R. C. Greene and J. D. Phillips, *Economic Survey of the Pacific Area* (I.P.R., New York, 1942), pp. 181–183.

CHAPTER XXV

Korea, Formosa, and Hong Kong*

CHARLES A. FISHER

THESE three territories have all in recent years assumed an international significance greater than either their size or economic importance warrants. Until well into the nineteenth century all three in various ways formed part of the great Chinese sphere of influence, but with the gradual dismemberment of that empire each in turn passed into foreign hands, Hong Kong being ceded to Britain in 1842 after the Opium War and Formosa and Korea coming under Japanese rule at the turn of the century. More recently, the change in the balance of power in Eastern Asia brought about by the defeat of Japan, the subsequent re-emergence of China as a Major Power, and the re-alignment of these two with the Western and the Soviet blocs respectively, has profoundly affected both the economic and the political prospects of all three areas. Indeed, in each, internal considerations are quite secondary to the external pressures to which each is subjected, and the future disposition of these intrinsically unimportant territories, which amount to little more than pawns on the Far Eastern chessboard, may well have profound effects upon the final outcome of the greater struggle which is now being played out in that area.

Korea

Korea before 1950. Korea has been developed in modern times almost entirely under the direction of the Japanese. For, in sharp contrast to the latter, the Korean people, who had also isolated themselves from the rest of the world since the seventeenth century, proved completely unresponsive to the Western challenge in the mid-nineteenth century.

---

* Thanks are due to the Royal Geographical Society for permission to use in this chapter some of the material published in the *Geographical Journal* of September 1954 (vol. cxx, No. 3) under the title of "The Role of Korea in the Far East."

This fact, combined with the equally ineffectual behaviour of their over-lords, the Manchu rulers of China, threatened during the years which followed to allow the peninsula, with its desirable ice-free harbours along the southern coast, to fall under Russian domination, and it was pri-marily in order to forestall such a move that the Japanese fought both the war against China (1894–95) and that against Russia a decade later.

As a result of the victory in the former, Japan was able, *inter alia*, to force China to abandon its claims to suzerainty over Korea, and by the Treaty of Portsmouth[1] it acquired a similarly privileged status in Korea to that which China had relinquished. This initial foothold was quickly consolidated, and in 1910 the peninsula was annexed outright. From then until 1919 the Japanese imposed on Korea a form of extremely brutal military rule, and this reached its culmination in the apparent annihilation of the independence movement, which had grown up under the stimulus of President Wilson's championship of the principle of self-determination. Thereafter, political exiles took refuge abroad—notably, according to taste, in either the United States or the U.S.S.R.[2] Even before 1917, however, agrarian distress and dislike of Japanese rule had led large numbers to migrate to Far Eastern Russia, where many received training later on as revolutionaries.[3]

After 1919 the extreme severity of Japanese rule was toned down, but the essential principle of completely subordinating Korea's interests to those of Japan remained unchanged whether, as until 1942, the country was administered as a colony under the Overseas Ministry or later, during the critical war years, as an integral part of Japan itself.

For Japan Korea had a twofold value, and both aspects were inti-mately bound up with its geography. Thus on the one hand its much older physical structure compared with that of Japan, together with a far lower density of population, meant that Korea could be developed to supply vital commodities in which the metropolitan country was seriously deficient. In particular, northern Korea contained valuable deposits of both iron and anthracite (as well as poorer grades of coal), and, notwithstanding the country's relatively large population of some thirteen millions in 1910, only about 10 per cent., or about half of the

---

[1] This marked the conclusion of the Russo-Japanese War in 1905.

[2] A self-appointed "Korean Government in Exile" also existed for a short time after 1919 in Shanghai.

[3] It was estimated that there were about 500,000 Koreans in the U.S.S.R. in 1945. Of these, some 185,000 were in Far Eastern Russia, but large numbers had been moved to Central Asia in 1937. Many served in the Red Army.

cultivable area, was then under the plough. Moreover, the proximity of Korea to the Japanese islands[4] made it a dependable source of these essential materials even in time of war.

This, in turn, is closely associated with the second advantage which Korea offered to Japan. Thanks to its general alignment and configuration, including the excellent series of natural harbours already noted, the peninsula provided a magnificent bridgehead on the mainland. As early as 1906 the Japanese had built a railway from Pusan, opposite Shimonoseki, via Seoul to Sinuijui near the mouth of the Yalu river, and after the latter was bridged in 1911 through running with the Manchurian rail system became possible.[5] Later, as Japanese plans for continental expansion came to be more elaborately formulated, the Korean harbours and rail facilities were rapidly extended, and, as its curious hourglass pattern might suggest, the overall network was designed primarily to facilitate the deployment of troops from Japan along the borders of Manchuria and Far Eastern Russia.

In this important sense, therefore, Korea under the Japanese ceased to be an entity in its own right. With the extension of Japanese rule over Manchuria in 1931 and over other parts of China after 1937, many Koreans were pressed into settlement schemes in these areas, and between 1931 and 1945 the number of Koreans there[6] rose from 800,000 to about 2,400,000. Others meanwhile emigrated to Japan to form the lowest-paid labouring class in the big cities, and in 1945 their numbers totalled about two million.

Again, between 1935 and 1945 the Japanese established some of the largest and most efficient hydro-electric power installations in the world along the Yalu river, which forms the divide between Korea and Manchuria, and, in supplying power both to the Manchurian industrial triangle and to manufacturing establishments in many parts of Korea, these served to integrate still further the areas on opposite sides of the frontier.[7]

For the most part, however, such industry as was established in Korea belonged to a few severely restricted categories and, indeed, consisted largely of fertilizer manufacturing plants, easily convertible to

---

[4] The shortest sea-crossing is approximately 120 miles.
[5] The Korean railways are standard gauge (4 ft. 8½ in.), in contrast with the 3 ft. 6 in. gauge in Japan.
[6] These were mostly in Eastern Manchuria.
[7] Korean manufactures in 1942 were valued at 2700 million won. They included: chemicals, 31 per cent. (by value); foodstuffs, 24 per cent.; textiles, 14 per cent.; metals and metal goods, 8 per cent.

produce explosives. Both for strategic reasons and also on account of the power supply these were located overwhelmingly in the north, while the only iron and steel plant, at Seoul, was somewhat more centrally situated, though equally dependent on northern sources for raw materials and fuel. But the promotion of consumer-goods industries outside the metropolitan islands ran counter to Japanese policy, and, apart from the setting up of some modern textile mills in Pusan and Seoul, little was done. Thus although there were numerous small factories in the main towns, industrial output was completely inadequate to supply even the extremely low consumption which the Korean people could afford. In the main, therefore, Korea under the Japanese was developed as a primary producer. During the thirty-five years following 1910, as a result of various reclamation schemes especially in the south, where more flat land is available and a warmer climate permits of intensive paddy cultivation and the raising of a second grain crop, the total culti-vated area was roughly doubled. In addition, reafforestation and other measures to counter soil erosion were undertaken, and by the use of much more fertilizer and improved rotation large agricultural surpluses were obtained. Of these rice[8] was by far the most important, and the quantity exported to Japan (over 40 per cent. of the normal crop of about 100 million bushels) had multiplied tenfold by the mid 1930's, by which time Korea, the largest single source of Japan's food imports, supplied 8 per cent. of its total consumption. Fishing also was revolu-tionized by the Japanese, and in the late 1930's Korea regularly ex-ported to Japan some 60 per cent. of its catch of nearly two million tons, which ranked as the sixth largest in the world. Likewise, soya beans, cotton, and silk, as well as appreciable quantities of the minerals already noted, figured prominently among the exports, 95·1 per cent. of which in 1931 were consigned to Japan.[9]

In general, however, this considerable economic development did not benefit the Koreans. So far from attempting to reduce the burdensome rents normally amounting to 50–60 per cent. of the annual crop, the Japanese sought to profit from this situation by acquiring control of much of the land themselves, and, indeed, during the period 1910–45 the percentage of land cultivated by tenants rose from forty to over seventy. As in China, and for the same reason—namely, that a more

---

[8] In the 1930's three-quarters of the cultivated area was under cereals, and approxi-mately one-third was double cropped. The main crops other than rice included barley, millet, soya beans, wheat, vegetables, fruit, cotton, and tobacco.

[9] In the same year 80·3 per cent. of Korean imports came from Japan.

productive climate leaves a greater margin to support a landlord class—tenancy was appreciably more common in the southern half of the country. Moreover, although large quantities of rice were exported to Japan at far lower cost than that of the home-grown commodity,[10] the average Korean consumption of rice per head fell by nearly a half between 1915 and 1938, and notwithstanding the import of large quantities of Manchurian millet and other poorer grains, this change undoubtedly represented a decline in the Korean standard of living. Again, while the population doubled its numbers from about thirteen millions in 1910 to about twenty-six millions in 1945, Koreans were consistently excluded from nearly all the more responsible and lucrative forms of employment. The senior posts in the civil service and in business were mostly reserved for Japanese, and even Korean landlords were compelled to have Japanese managers to supervise their estates. In short, the 750,000 Japanese who in 1945 formed only 3 per cent. of the total, but nearer 30 per cent. of the urban population,[11] of the country, constituted an alien upper class of the type characteristically associated with *colonies d'exploitation*, while the Koreans themselves were among the most poverty-stricken and depressed of any people in the whole of Asia.

Finally, not only was economic opportunity denied to the Koreans, but they were also subjected to a ruthless process of denationalization. In particular, the Japanese tried to exterminate the Korean language, but, as in many parallel cases elsewhere, this attempt produced an opposite effect to the one intended. Indeed, in spite of thirty-five years of Japanese rule, Korea retained a remarkably strong sense of national unity, and, notwithstanding the policies that had long been followed, it had at least the makings of a sound national economy in that its natural resources were relatively well-balanced, the transport network was among the best in Asia, and a beginning had already been made in industrialization.

Admittedly, as elsewhere in the Far East, the problem of a rising population loomed in the background,[12] but, with an average density of 285 per square mile and a lower intensity of agricultural production than

[10] Korean rice was cheaper than the Japanese product, both because of the lower living standards of the Korean cultivators and also because the amount of fertilizer used per acre was only about half that in Japan. This in turn largely explains why the Korean yield per acre was at most only two-thirds that in Japan.

[11] In 1933 10 per cent. of the total population of Korea lived in towns of over 45,000 people; the corresponding figure for Japanese in Korea was 70 per cent.

[12] During the period 1929 to 1938 growth had been very rapid, the birth rate averaging 32·4 and the death rate 19·9 per 1000.

in comparable parts of Japan, overcrowding had not yet reached an explosive stage, and the economy undoubtedly offered scope for further diversification.

Thus, as the defeat of Japan approached and the Cairo decision to establish Korean independence "in due course" was confirmed at Yalta, the future of the country appeared reasonably bright. With the expulsion of the Japanese and the freeing of the country from what amounted to a tributary relationship towards Japan the national spirit would at last find an outlet for constructive work, and the standard of the Korean people might be expected to rise significantly.

The Effect of Partition, 1945

These hopes, however, were speedily disappointed for, as on many previous occasions, external distractions again prevented the Koreans from tackling their country's internal problems. Owing to its geographical position in relation to the main Allied theatres in the Far Eastern War, Korea was bisected at the 38th Parallel for the immediate purposes of the Occupation, the Soviet Union being responsible for receiving the Japanese surrender in the north while the United States undertook the corresponding task in the south.

But, as relations between the two great power blocs swiftly deteriorated in the years which followed, this partition, which the West, at least, had never regarded as more than a temporary arrangement, acquired an unexpected air of permanence. Thus the plans for a Four Power Trusteeship[13] of a unified Korea, announced at Moscow in December 1945, were never put into effect. Instead, two new regimes were eventually set up—namely, in the south the Republic of Korea (formally proclaimed on August 15, 1948), which retained the old capital at Seoul, and the Korean People's Democratic Republic, inaugurated a month later in the north, with its capital at Pyong Yang. Each of these reflected in large measure the outlook of returning émigré politicians, from the United States and the Soviet Union respectively, and each, while hoping ultimately to unite the whole peninsula, set about introducing its own version of democracy within the territories it controlled.[14]

[13] I.e., U.S.A., U.S.S.R., Great Britain, and China. It was expected that such a phase would last five years.
[14] But it should be noted that the South Korean Government was established on the basis of elections observed by the United Nations Temporary Commission on Korea, which was denied access to the area north of the 38th Parallel.

Apart from the frustration of national aspirations and the international tension which partition entailed, its most serious consequence was to prevent the hoped-for improvement in the standard of living. In this respect, however, it should be noted that already by the end of 1945 other difficulties had become apparent. As a result of inadequate fertilizing during the war (when the relevant materials were mostly manufactured into explosives) the productivity of the land had fallen appreciably, and meanwhile intensive exploitation had seriously depleted many of the more accessible mineral reserves. Moreover, the exchange of population with Japan and near-by areas after the surrender meant that Korea was left with an extreme dearth of skilled labour of every kind, while at the same time its total numbers were augmented by over two millions,[15] in addition to those accruing as a result of the normally high rate of natural increase.

As can be seen from Table 2, these difficulties were seriously aggravated by partition, which had the effect of separating the principal centres of mineral, fertilizer and hydro-electric power production in the North from the predominantly agricultural South, which also contained virtually the whole of the textile industry. Furthermore, although in many respects the economy of the South seemed the more precariously based of the two, since, without fertilizer, its food surplus was rapidly turned into a deficit[16] and with greatly reduced power supplies its industries were threatened with breakdown, the political situation was such as to cause a net migration southward amounting to some two millions by June 1950. Meanwhile, owing to the superior medical facilities and sanitation introduced by the Americans, the death rate had fallen sharply, and in the absence of any decline in the birth rate the annual natural increase had risen to approximately twenty per 1000.

Nevertheless, thanks to the characteristic lavishness of American aid, the more pressing of these problems in the South were well on the way to being solved by 1950. Large imports of grain and fertilizer had staved off famine, and it was hoped to achieve agricultural self-sufficiency within a few years. In addition, new irrigation and power schemes were being planned, reserve thermal electric plant was brought into service and supplied with bituminous coal from Japan, and elaborate plans were under consideration for remodelling the economy of this decapitated land. Thus, despite the contention of the North that by

---

[15] See Table 2.
[16] Unlike the North, the South was cut off from the former imports of grain from Manchuria.

means of a 15 per cent. increase in agricultural productivity it had already attained self-sufficiency, the South appeared to be more than holding its own.

But in one respect the North had scored a notable propaganda success. By expropriating both the former Japanese and the Korean landlords and dividing their land among the local population the North Korean regime had undoubtedly won considerable initial popularity[17] among the peasantry, who there, as in the rest of the country, formed by far the most numerous section of the population. In the South, on the other hand, where tenancy had hitherto been more widespread, much less change had taken place, apart from the law reducing rents to one third of the annual crop, since the Government relied heavily on the support of the land-owning class. However, in 1948, largely as a result of American insistence, a start was made by selling the former Japanese lands, amounting to some 15·3 per cent. of the total farm area, to peasant cultivators, but the more extensive measures[18] outlined in the Land Reform Law of June 22, 1949, were only slowly coming into effect when the North Koreans attacked the South on June 25, 1950.

The Korean War and its Consequences

Behind this local aggression, which hoped to exploit the widespread desire for national unification, lay the more sinister plans of the U.S.S.R. The latter, apparently accepting at their face value earlier American statements about the expendability of Korea, assumed that the Communist perimeter might be further extended there by satellite aggression, without undue risk. But the speedy action of President Truman, followed by the U.N. Security Council decision of June 27, calling on all members to assist the Republic of Korea "to repel the armed attack and to restore international peace and security in the area," clearly dispelled such illusions.

Having thus been widened from a local incident to an ideological struggle between "the principle of collective security and the practice

[17] 'Initial' may prove to be the operative word. Though taxes, amounting to 27 per cent. of the crop on paddyland and 23 per cent. on dry land, are much less than the former rents, the peasants are periodically forced to make assessed contributions of various kinds and to render (unpaid) labour duty to the State.

[18] These were closely similar to those introduced in Japan (1946). All land owned by absentee landlords and all holdings in excess of c. 7½ acres were to be resold to cultivators on easy terms.

of aggression,"[19] the Korean war was further transformed into a contest between the two great power blocs when, in the following autumn, as the U.N. forces recrossed the 38th Parallel and approached the critical Yalu river boundary, the Chinese Communists sent large armies in support of the North Koreans.

Failure to distinguish between these three related but nevertheless distinct aspects of the Korean War has bedevilled the issue ever since. Thus, while President Syngman Rhee appears to regard it essentially as a war to unify Korea, the Western European nations, whose main preoccupations lie elsewhere, have concerned themselves almost solely with the ideological argument. Meanwhile the United States, though no less interested in this aspect, is nevertheless far more closely involved in the realities of power in the Pacific, has borne 95 per cent. of the Allied burden in Korea, and has paid correspondingly more attention to the broad strategic implications of the conflict.

Nevertheless, it remains to be proved that any greater sense of unity regarding the war exists on the Communist side. In this respect the fundamental question which still awaits an answer is whether the Chinese entered the war out of genuine fear, because of prior agreement with the U.S.S.R.,[20] or in order to displace the latter as the *de facto* suzerain Power in North Korea. Not impossibly more than one of these motives may have been involved, and doubtless the desire of the new Communist regime to strengthen its hold on Chinese public opinion, by the familiar device of rousing it against the West, played a part. On the other hand, in view of the military stalemate and the immense burden which the new Five Year Plan will impose on China,[21] it was not difficult to understand the latter's subsequent willingness to accept the Western terms for a truce in the summer of 1953.

What, then, are the prospects for Korea to-day? As a result of three years of war the peninsula has been drastically transformed. Extensive bombing has destroyed most of the cities and much of the industrial plant, over four million people have lost their lives and one in three of the survivors are homeless. Moreover, in spite of the great, though apparently only temporary, setback to the plans for agricultural self-sufficiency in the South, the latter has continued to be the more sought-

[19] W. MacMahon Ball, *Nationalism and Communism in East Asia* (Melbourne University Press and Cambridge University Press, 1953), p. 49.
[20] *E.g.*, that the U.S.S.R. should provide material equipment, while China supplied man power.
[21] See Chapter XXIV.

after of the two halves, and to-day its population stands at about twenty-one millions, compared with four millions in the North.[22] This situation, together with the existence of a superior army of 600,000 men in the South, may explain President Rhee's claim in 1954 that the time was ripe for a renewed attempt to unite the peninsula by force.

Yet to the impartial observer such a policy seems suicidal, for it is impossible to believe that the Communist bloc would remain passive if the South Korean army resumed the offensive. Equally, it is clear from the Mutual Defence Treaty signed between South Korea and the United States[23] that the latter is pursuing a policy of containment rather than liberation so far as Korea is concerned, though this treaty marks a significant departure in that it extends United States' commitments beyond the island fringe to the mainland of eastern Asia.

It may therefore be assumed that, in spite of undertakings to explore means of reuniting Korea, the existing division is likely to persist, and in the meantime the Western and the Communist blocs will seek to outbid each other in the rehabilitation of their respective halves of the country.

In this respect South Korea, which has been promised aid to the tune of 1000 million dollars by the United States in order to make it into the 'showcase of democracy,' would appear to be in a favoured position, despite its present dependence on approximately one million tons of imported food a year. But it remains to be seen whether the Government of President Rhee will carry out the more drastic land reform which needs to be introduced, and in the meantime his declared unwillingness to accept, even as much-needed aid for rehabilitation, any materials produced in Japan represents a setback to American plans for assisting both countries simultaneously. Indeed, the intense hostility which the South Korean Government continues to display towards Japan, as manifested, for example, in the seizure of Japanese fishing vessels which cross the unilaterally imposed " Rhee Line,"[24] is a major obstacle to the formulation of an overall American strategy in the Western Pacific in which Japan is clearly cast for a major role.

[22] These figures are at best rough estimates, and it has been stated by President Syngman Rhee that the population of North Korea in 1954 was only three millions. Some observers have suggested that the North is deliberately exporting some of its problems to the South by actively encouraging supposedly refugee migration thither.

[23] Signed at the U.S. State Department on October 1, 1953. The U.S. decision (December 26, 1953) to withdraw two divisions from Korea during 1954 bears out this interpretation.

[24] The " Rhee Line " runs some sixty miles from the shore of South Korea, and South Korea has claimed that no Japanese fishing may take place within the waters it encloses.

Hardly less complicated, however, is the corresponding situation in North Korea. For only two months after the U.S.S.R. in September 1953 promised a grant of 1000 million roubles (250 million dollars) for industrial reconstruction, the provision of technical and financial assistance, and the technical training of Koreans, this gift was overshadowed by a Chinese undertaking to grant 8,000,000,000,000 yuan (317,700,000 dollars) during the three years after 1954 for virtually identical purposes. While some Western observers have argued that the two schemes are complementary and that the Russians intend to supply heavy industrial plant, machine tools, and mining equipment, leaving the Chinese to provide textile and food-processing machinery and various consumer goods, it seems possible that at least some element of rivalry is involved. Such an interpretation would accord with both the strong historical sense of the Chinese and also with the contemporary utterances of some of their leaders,[25] though severe doubts are raised regarding China's capacity to fulfil its promises.

In any case, however, it is clear that in the coming years the economy of North Korea will once again, as under the Japanese, be closely integrated with that of southern Manchuria, both as regards industrial development and in the no less vital matter of food production. Thus, as in the more fundamental question of Russo-Chinese relationships, so also in the subsidiary problem of North Korea's relationship to both its northern neighbours, future developments in the Manchurian triangle may well provide the key. But it may be many years before the rest of the world is able to perceive with any assurance precisely what is happening in this vital but secluded region.

Formosa (Taiwan)[26]

Formosa under the Japanese. In many respects the role of Formosa has been remarkably similar to that of Korea. After an ancient if

[25] Thus Chou En-lai, announcing his Government's offer of assistance, stressed both the antiquity and the closeness of Korea's ties with China, and clearly implied that they should be altogether more intimate than those between Korea and the U.S.S.R. According to more recent reports, Chinese farmers, miners, and industrial workers are being settled in North Korea.

[26] With Formosa (area 13,808 square miles) it is customary to include some seventy-seven smaller islands in its vicinity, the most important of these being the Pescadores (total area forty-nine square miles, population c. 80,000). The series of small islands closer to the Chinese mainland, including Quemoy, Matsu, and the Tachens, traditionally formed parts of Fukien and Chekiang provinces, but were held after 1949 by the Kuomintang as outposts of Formosa. The Tachens were evacuated by the Kuomintang in February 1955.

X

tenuous relationship with mainland China the island for the first time became an integral part of the latter's territories under the Manchu dynasty. This followed an interregnum of over twenty years in the late seventeenth century when refugee supporters of the defeated Ming Dynasty held out in Formosa until 1683 against the new conquerors of the mainland, an incident which curiously foreshadowed contemporary events. In view of growing foreign interest in Formosa after it was opened to commerce in 1860, its administration underwent certain changes, and in 1887 it was constituted a province of the Chinese empire. But following the war of 1894–95 the island was ceded to Japan, whose interest in this, its first major overseas acquisition, showed the same blend of economic and strategic considerations as later became evident in its attitude towards Korea.

From the agricultural standpoint Formosa, which lies athwart the tropic of Cancer, was especially valuable as a source both of tropical commodities not easily grown in Japan and, even more, of rice and sugar, which could be intensively produced in the warm and generally well-watered lowlands forming the western third of this otherwise mountainous island. In mineral wealth, on the other hand, Formosa, which consists of a tilted block, uplifted along its eastern edge during the Tertiary folding of the Western Pacific island arcs, is as characteristically deficient as the metropolitan country itself. But the key position of the island, within the series of stepping-stones extending southward to Malaysia and at the same time less than 100 miles from the coast of southern China, gave it a high strategic value to Japan which even before the end of the last century was thinking in expansionist terms.[27]

As in Korea, a considerable local population (3,160,000 in 1905) accustomed to a lower standard of living than that in Japan virtually ruled out the possibility of Japanese agricultural settlement in Formosa. Nevertheless, given the altogether more productive climate and the fertility of much of the alluvial and volcanic soils, the agricultural carrying capacity of Formosa, area for area, is much higher than that of Korea. Thus although the population density in Formosa in 1905, about 261 per square mile, was higher than in Korea, such a comparison gives an entirely misleading impression, and a truer picture is obtained by comparing it with the 400–800 per square mile typical of essentially

[27] When Japan acquired Formosa in 1895 the Dutch, fearing that this move presaged an advance into the islands farther south, suggested that the Western Powers should compel Japan to renounce Formosa (as France, Germany, and Russia had meanwhile forced it to abandon Liaotung, which was originally acquired at the same time).

similar lands along the southern Chinese coast. Indeed, Formosa, the majority of whose population at that time were descendants of relatively recent immigrants from this part of China, was still by Oriental standards a relatively new country.

Accordingly, it was possible for the Japanese during the first years of the present century to more than double rice production and to increase sugar output to an even greater extent, by bringing more land under the plough, by improving irrigation, and by the use of imported fertilizer.[28] As a result, by 1939 virtually the whole of the 24 per cent. of the island suitable for cultivation was in use, more than half of it carrying two crops a year, and about 60 per cent. of it devoted to rice cultivation, which gave an average yield of 2·24 tons per hectare.

Since, in the meantime, the growth of population, though rapid, had not kept pace with the expansion of agriculture, Formosa was able in the late 1930's to export about half of the 1·4 million tons of rice grown each year, while still leaving enough to provide the local population with a rice diet, supplemented by adequate quantities of sweet potatoes, sugar, fruit, vegetables, pork, and fish. Moreover, holdings, which typically ranged between two and a half and four acres—*i.e.*, three or more times the normal size in the adjacent parts of China—were not unduly small, and, as a result, the living standards of the peasantry, even though most were tenants accustomed to paying rents equal to 60 per cent. of the crop, were distinctly above those in either China or Korea.

At the same time the Japanese benefited greatly from possession of the island, both through the large supplies of agricultural produce which they obtained at low rates, and by the high returns on invested capital. Thus, notwithstanding its small size and the lack of important mineral deposits,[29] Formosa was an extremely valuable component of the Japanese Empire, and appeared altogether more prosperous than most other parts of that country's overseas domains.

Indeed, the Japanese seem to have regarded Formosa as their most successful colonial venture, and this may well have played a decisive part in causing them to look increasingly to the south in their plans for further imperial expansion. In this connexion the establishment of the Taiwan Development Corporation in 1936,[30] for the purpose of pro-

[28] Fertilizer was not so intensively used as in Korea, only 600,000 tons being normally imported before the war and very little manufactured locally. Night soil and compost, however, were extensively used.

[29] The most important mineral was coal, of which 407,915 tons were exported in 1937.

[30] This was similar in character to the Manchurian Industrial Development Company, and the Oriental Development Company in Korea. See Norton S. Ginsburg, *Economic Resources and Development of Formosa* (I.P.R., New York, 1953), p. 28.

moting industry both in Formosa and elsewhere in South-east Asia, was significant, though little was achieved before the outbreak of war in 1941.

Formosa since the Second World War. In accordance with the Cairo Declaration, Japan was forced to relinquish possession of Formosa as soon as hostilities ceased. Shortly afterwards the repatriation of the 300,000 Japanese civilians, as well as members of the armed forces, began, and on October 25, 1945, Formosa, having reverted *de facto* to Chinese rule, was constituted the thirty-fifth province of the Republic. But partly because of severe war damage and dislocation, and partly because of the departure of nearly all the key personnel in agriculture, commerce, and government, the economy of the island was by this time in a state of chaos, which the incompetence and corruption of the new Chinese Governor, General Chen Yi, served only to aggravate.[31] In the meantime, following his defeat on the mainland, Chiang Kai-shek with 600,000 survivors from his former armies, as well as over a million other supporters, took refuge in the island, whose chief city, Taipei, became the temporary capital of (Nationalist) China on December 8, 1949.

How long this island fortress could have survived if left to its own devices it is impossible to say, but on June 27, 1950, the United States' Seventh Fleet was sent to neutralize Formosa for the duration of the Korean War. This action was a clear recognition of the threat that a Communist invasion of the island, such as could probably have been effected with Russian air support against the Nationalist forces alone, would present to the whole chain of defensive positions which the United States had begun to build up in the western Pacific. For, as events in the second world war showed, Formosa, lying almost at the centre of the triangle formed by Luzon, Kyushu, and Fukien, holds a commanding position between the East and South China Seas, and, in the event of future hostilities here, the United States would be loath to abandon this "unsinkable aircraft carrier off the China coast." (See Fig. 1.)

Largely for this reason, but also in the hope of preserving an alternative regime to that which now rules over the remainder of China, the United States has accordingly been granting economic aid of the order of some 100 million dollars a year to the Taipei Government, which, in

---

[31] The striking improvement in the administration of Formosa came with the appointment of K. C. Wu as Governor on December 21, 1949.

FIG. 1. FORMOSA AND MAINLAND CHINA

response to American suggestions, has carried out far-reaching reforms in the administration of Formosa. During recent years corruption and inflation have been greatly reduced and extensive land reforms put into effect. In this last respect the official policy is to realize the 'land-to-the-tillers' teaching bequeathed by the Republic of China's founding father, Dr Sun Yat-sen[32] and the measures adopted are therefore "equitable, peaceful, and gradual, not violent or radical." In fact, the programme which is now under way closely resembles that already introduced in Japan and more recently in South Korea. The first of its three phases (1949) involved the fixing of all rents at a maximum of 37·5 per cent. of the principal crop, and the second (beginning in 1951) consisted of Government sale of public land, mostly the former property of the Japanese, to peasant cultivators on easy credit terms. A further 35 per cent. of the farming population, numbering approximately 240,000 families, are to receive equitable shares on a similar basis of some 500,000 acres which are being compulsorily purchased by the Government from landowners holding more than the prescribed limit of three chia,[33] and it was claimed that by early 1954 land tenancy in Formosa would have been "reduced to a maximum of 20 per cent."

No doubt these reforms are more in line with the original proposals of Sun Yat-sen than are the measures introduced by the Communists on the mainland, and in several other respects also the claim of the present administration that Formosa has become a model province is substantially true. There is, however, little reason to assume that these developments will have any significant effect on the course of events in the rest of China, though, as the Overseas Chinese Conference held at Taipei in October 1952 suggested, it is not impossible that Formosa may provide a rival rallying point for Chinese communities in South-east Asia and elsewhere.

Nevertheless these peoples, and especially the commercial groups among them, are essentially realists, and, in spite of a widespread abhorrence of Communist aims, they will probably be more impressed by the power of the Communists than by the policies of the Nationalists. While, therefore, the heavy-handed behaviour of the former in southern China may cause some falling off of valuable remittances from the Nan Yang, few Chinese, at least outside of Formosa, have any illusions about

[32] This and the following quotations are from *Free China's Island Province of Taiwan* (Chinese News Service, New York, November 1953), p. 3.

[33] This figure varies somewhat according to the quality of the land, three chia being the limit in average land. One chia is approximately 2·4 acres.

the ability of the ageing armies[34] of the over-age Generalissimo to invade the mainland. Yet belief in such a possibility still appears to dominate Nationalist thinking, and, in doing so, threatens to prevent serious consideration from being given to the problem of creating a viable economy in Formosa itself.[35]

That this problem is both acute and urgent needs little demonstration. Already the population has increased by approximately 50 per cent. since 1943, and though this is partly due to the balance of refugee immigration over Japanese emigration, the most alarming aspect of the situation is revealed by current vital statistics. Thus with the death rate down to about 10 per 1000 (1951) and the birth rate still at the pre-war level of 44 per 1000, the annual natural rate of increase is 3·4 per cent., which implies a doubling of the present population (ten million in 1954) during the next twenty-one years.[36] Even before any further increase takes place, however, the present density of 724 per square mile is among the highest in the world, and, moreover, apart from current American aid, this population is almost solely dependent on agriculture.

For the time being, thanks to effective rehabilitation, an increasing use of fertilizer, and the conversion of much former sugar-growing land to paddy cultivation, food production is adequate for local needs, and, indeed, since 1951, when 103,000 tons of rice were exported, mainly to Japan, there has again been a small surplus. But virtually all available agricultural land is now in use, and, furthermore, without M.S.A. assistance, which in 1952 paid for 45 per cent. of the island's imports, the economy would be on the point of collapse. While to some extent industrialization,[37] making use of the considerable local hydro-electrical potentialities, would help, by freeing Formosa from dependence on imports against which it has little to offer apart from limited agricultural surpluses, the future prospect for supporting one of the world's most rapidly growing populations in this already congested island appears bleak in the extreme.

So long as the United States is prepared to bolster up the economy of

[34] The average age of the armed forces was twenty-eight in 1953. See "Formosa—the Island Fortress," in The Economist, August 29, 1953, pp. 578-579.

[35] The Four Year Plan of 1953 for putting the economy of the island on a self-sustaining basis is quite inadequate to meet the present situation, and, in the writer's opinion, is simply conceived as a stop-gap measure.

[36] Ginsburg, op. cit., p. 2.

[37] As part of the Four Year Plan the development of hydro-electric power installations and the manufacture of fertilizer, textiles, and petroleum products are being promoted. But in the absence of nearly all the more important raw materials there are clearly severe limits to such development.

this island outpost there need be no doubt as to the capacity of the present regime to survive, though its ability to serve as a focus for anti-Communist sentiment in Eastern Asia will be small if dependence on the West is too obvious. On the other hand, for the United States to abandon a cause which it has so long and so consistently upheld would raise even greater problems, both moral and political. Short of the operation of the Malthusian checks or a voluntary curtailment of numbers, the population problem appears insoluble. But so long as Nationalist China is obsessed with its military dreams of reconquering the mainland it is to be feared that this dilemma will be insufficiently heeded and the basic problem in consequence still further aggravated. Moreover, while strategic considerations remain uppermost, it seems inevitable that the interests of the locally born Formosans will continue to be subordinated to those of the 'mainlanders' (*i.e.*, those who have fled to the island since 1949), and this is a further source of potential trouble. For the moment, therefore, the situation remains precarious, and only time will show whether the present uneasy co-existence of the two rival Chinese Governments can continue without catastrophe.

Hong Kong

Hong Kong differs from the other two areas already discussed in this chapter first of all because it has been for over a century, with the exception of four years under Japanese rule, a British Colony. Furthermore, although there have subsequently been added to the original island, which was ceded in 1842, both the adjacent peninsula of Kowloon, obtained after the 1858–60 war, and the 'New Territories' leased by China in 1898, the total area still amounts to only 390 square miles and consists of little more than a single overcrowded city and barely enough near-by land to ensure a regular water supply. So far as food is concerned, the 20,500 acres under paddy and 4000 under vegetables are completely inadequate to provide for the present population of 2¼ millions,[38] and although the occupation of Kowloon may have been a sufficient guarantee against overland attack in the nineteenth century, such strategy was already outmoded before the second world war, and in 1941 Hong Kong was forced to capitulate to the Japanese after less than a month's resistance.

---

[38] Compared with 800,000 before the second world war.

Like Singapore, in company with which it was designed to control the South China Sea, Hong Kong is a monument to the nineteenth-century British belief in the supremacy of sea power and the efficacy of free trade. From this solitary fragment of British soil the whole southern

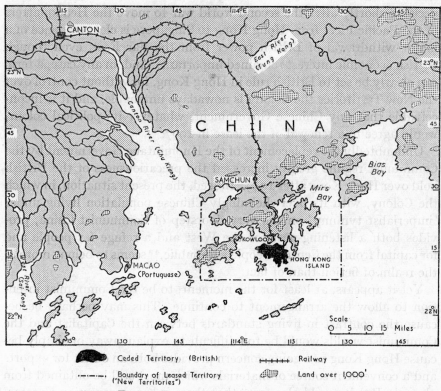

FIG. 2. THE POSITION OF HONG KONG

Chinese coastline could be kept under surveillance, and by developing its excellent anchorage as a free port where ocean shipping came in contact with smaller scale coastal vessels it was possible in large measure to control the whole trading pattern of southern China.[39] (See Fig. 2.)

To-day, a century later, when sea power is rapidly losing its former supremacy and Communist China is engaged in reorienting the geographical pattern of its economy to face inward instead of towards the great ocean highways, the very basis of Hong Kong's existence would seem to be called in question. Indeed, even before the second world war

[39] See above, p. 568.

x*

big changes were in progress, and although Chiang Kai-shek's plan to take over the territory from the Japanese in 1945 before the British could return was frustrated, such an arrangement would not have been entirely out of keeping with the spirit of the Cairo Declaration, which finally abolished extra-territoriality. Be that as it may, the British decision shortly after the second world war to move the Headquarters of the Pacific Fleet from Hong Kong to Singapore is clear evidence of a major withdrawal of British power from the Far East, even though British economic interest remained important. And, in any case, a term can clearly be set to British rule in Hong Kong, for without control over the New Territories the Colony is nowadays untenable, and it is inconceivable that any Chinese Government, whatever its political colour, would agree to a renewal of the lease in 1997.

Undoubtedly the replacement of the Kuomintang Government by the Communist regime greatly increased the precariousness of the British hold over Hong Kong after 1949. Indeed, the present situation, in which the Colony, with its overwhelmingly Chinese population living under 'imperialist tyranny' on the very doorstep of Communist China, provides both a listening-post for the West and a refuge for people and for capital from the Central People's Republic,[40] seems to belong more to the realm of fiction than of fact.

Yet it appears, at least for the moment, to be the Communist intention to allow the arrangement to continue. This may perhaps be because the contrast in living standards between the Capitalist and the Communist worlds would be too difficult to explain away or simply because Hong Kong as a going concern provides both an outlet for exports and a convenient source of materials which must still be obtained from abroad. But it would also seem that there is here a reversion to something closely akin to the Manchu policy of restricting Western trade to a single port, and that as remote from the imperial capital as possible. Under the Manchus this role was performed by Canton, but if to-day the foreign-administered city of Hong Kong can fulfil the task by proxy the Chinese may argue that the danger of contamination from Western ideas will be less than if a mainland port had to remain a centre of Western operations.

Nevertheless, since the imposition of the United Nations' embargo of May 17, 1951, on strategic trade with China during the Korean War, commerce with mainland China, which used to form the largest single

[40] Hong Kong provides a main escape route from mainland China to Formosa.

component in the entrepôt trade of Hong Kong, has sharply declined, and the considerable unemployment that this has occasioned may gravely impair the political stability of the Colony.[41] Yet, in spite of a much reduced volume of trade with China, there is no economic reason why Hong Kong should not be able to pay its way by commerce and manufacturing, for its hinterland also includes most of the lands bordering the South China Sea and in the north extends at least to the southern shores of Japan. Moreover, the channels of trade in these regions are well established, and manufacturing industry already supplies nearly half a million of the people with a livelihood.[42]

From the standpoint of power politics, however, it is clear that Hong Kong is now nothing more than an empty shell which the Communists, if they so desired, could seize at any time. Yet if the experience of near-by Macao, which has survived as a Portuguese possession for nearly 400 years, is any guide, such weakness may not prove fatal, and the Colony may yet continue for many years to fulfil its present role. And, in spite of occasional ill-founded statements to the contrary, this constitutes on balance a tremendous gain for the non-Communist world.

From the foregoing examination it is clear that Korea, Formosa, and Hong Kong are all actual or potential danger-points within the vast political fault zone which divides the two great power blocs in the Far East. But while from a geopolitical standpoint it is temptingly easy to oversimplify the problem in terms of continental versus oceanic strategy, the ideological issues involved belong to a different plane and are altogether more complex. Thus until it is possible to overcome such obstacles as contemporary Korean hostility to Japan, the difference between American and British attitudes towards trade with Communist China, and the widespread belief in the rest of Asia that the Formosan and South Korean Governments are nothing more than American puppets, the urgent task of knitting together these and other multifarious loose ends into a Pacific Pact Organization in some degree comparable with N.A.T.O. must remain unfulfilled.[43] It should, therefore, be a primary

[41] During 1953 Hong Kong's exports to mainland China were valued at 540·3 million (H.K.) dollars. None of this was material included in the U.N. list of strategic goods, and the largest items were wool tops, dyes, pharmaceuticals, watches, and fertilizers. During the same period Hong Kong imported from China 857·1 million (H.K.) dollars' worth of goods, mainly foodstuffs, silk, bristles, and tung oil.

[42] Hong Kong has shipyards, rolling mills, textile and other consumer-goods industries, which have been greatly expanded during recent years. Fishing is also an important occupation.

[43] S.E.A.T.O. does not include any of these territories within its terms of reference (see p. 646).

aim of Western statesmanship to seek by all available means to reach at least working agreement on the issues which at present impede collective action in this vital theatre.

FURTHER READING

BALLANTINE, J. W., *Formosa: A Problem for United States Foreign Policy* (Brookings, Washington, 1952; Faber, London, 1953).

COLLINS, SIR CHARLES, *Public Administration in Hong Kong* (Royal Institute of International Affairs, London, 1952).

DAVIS, S. G., *Hong Kong* (Hong Kong, 1949).

GINSBURG, NORTON S., *Economic Resources and Development of Formosa* (I.P.R., New York, 1953).

GRAJDANZEV, A. J., *Formosa Today* (I.P.R., New York, and Allen and Unwin, London, 1942); *Modern Korea* (I.P.R., New York, 1944).

INGRAMS, HAROLD, *Hong Kong* (H.M.S.O., London, 1952); *Korea: A Geographical Appreciation* (Foreign Geography Information Series, No. 4; Ottawa, 1951).

LAUTENSACH, HERMANN, *Korea: Land, Volk, Schicksal* (Stuttgart, 1950).

LEE, H. K., *Land Utilization and Rural Economy in Korea* (University of Chicago Press and Oxford University Press, 1936).

McCUNE, G., *Korea Today* (Harvard University Press and Allen and Unwin, London, 1950).

OLIVER, R. T., *Verdict in Korea* (Philadelphia, 1952).

PORTWAY, D., *Korea: Land of the Morning Calm* (Harrap, London, 1953).

RAND, CHRISTOPHER, *Hong Kong: The Island Between* (Knopf, New York, 1952).

RIGGS, FRED W., *Formosa under Chinese Nationalist Rule* (I.P.R., New York, and Allen and Unwin, London, 1952).

ZAICHIKOV, V. T., *Geography of Korea* (I.P.R., New York, 1952).

TABLE I

Occupations of Japanese in Korea, 1933–38

OCCUPATIONS	PERCENTAGES OF JAPANESE WORKING POPULATION SO EMPLOYED	PERCENTAGES OF TOTAL WORKING POPULATION SO EMPLOYED
Official and professional .	35·2	3·9
Commerce and transportation	29·4	8·0
Mining and manufacturing .	14·4	4·3
Agricultural and fishing .	10·9	75·1
Miscellaneous . . .	10·1	8·7

The Effects of Partition in Korea

ITEM	TOTAL	NORTH	PERCENTAGES OF TOTAL	SOUTH	PERCENTAGES OF TOTAL
Area, square miles	85,700	48,000	56	37,700	44
Population:					
1940	24,326,000	9,357,000	38	14,969,000	62
1949	29,570,000	9,170,000	31	20,400,000	69
1954 (estimate)	25,000,000	4,000,000	16	21,000,000	84
Density per square mile, 1949	345	191	—	541	—
Major cities, estimated populations, 1949		Pyong-Yang c. 500,000		Seoul 1,445,000; Pusan 474,000; Taegu 314,000; Inchon 266,000	
Rice production (koku[1]), 1944	16,051,879	5,791,952	36	10,259,927	64
Other grains (koku), 1944	20,020,989	7,318,554	37	12,702,435	63
Soya beans (koku), 1944	3,301,095	2,264,840	69	1,036,255	31
Fish catch (metric tons), 1944	690,000	428,350	62	261,650	38
Anthracite coal (metric tons), 1944	4,767,262	3,240,749	68	1,526,513	32
Iron ore (metric tons), 1944	3,331,814	3,221,057	97	110,757	3
Tungsten (metric tons), 1944	11,509	5,292	46	6,217	54
Chemical industries production (in ooo yen), 1940	699,442	615,509	88	83,933	12
Metal industries production (in ooo yen), 1940	129,669	110,219	85	19,450	15
Textiles (in ooo yen), 1940	232,178	32,504	14	199,674	86
Hydro-electric power capacity (installed kW), 1944	1,595,000	1,528,000	96	67,000	4
Thermal electric power capacity (installed kW), 1944	313,000	95,000	30	218,000	70

Based on (1) *Japan Year Book*; (2) G. M. McCune, *Korea Today* (Harvard, 1950), Chapter 3; (3) "Korean Backdrop," in *Focus*, vol. I, No. I (October 15, 1950); (4) Press reports.

[1] 1 koku = 5·12 bushels.

TABLE 3

Korea: Selected Population Statistics

KOREANS IN OTHER COUNTRIES	1944	1954
Japan	1,550,000*	450,000
China (mostly Manchuria)	1,500,000*	1,000,000
U.S.S.R. . . .	300,000	?
NON-KOREANS IN KOREA		
Japanese (civilians) .	708,449	(very few)
Chinese . . .	71,510	?

Note. The figures marked * are misleadingly low in that many Koreans normally resident in these areas were serving with the Japanese armies overseas.

TABLE 4

Korea: Overseas Trade, 1931 (*in million yen*)

IMPORTS FROM	VALUE	PERCEN-TAGES	EXPORTS FROM	VALUE	PERCEN-TAGES
Japan . .	217·8	80·3	Japan . .	249·0	95·1
China . .	39·5	14·5	China . .	12·0	4·5
U.S.A. . .	4·6	1·7	U.S.A. . .	·1	—
U.K. . .	1·3	·5	U.K. . .	·03	—
Total . . including:	270·5		Total . . including:	261·8	
Cotton tissues .	23·8	8·8	Rice . .	138·5	53·0
Iron . .	11·8	4·4	Beans . .	14·4	5·5
Machinery .	9·4	3·5	Raw silk .	12·0	4·6
Fertilizers .	8·6	3·2	Fish . .	9·8	3·8
Silk tissues .	8·5	3·2	Fertilizers .	8·5	3·2
Coal . .	8·5	3·2	Iron . .	3·2	1·2
Millet . .	7·9	2·9	Coal . .	3·0	1·1
Tussore silk .	7·1	2·6	Cotton . .	2·6	1·0
Sugar . .	5·6	2·1	Sugar . .	2·6	1·0

No post-war statistics are available for Korean trade as a whole. During the first five months of 1952 South Korean imports, valued at 19·2 million (U.S.) dollars, included food, clothing, and raw materials, while exports, valued at 7·6 million (U.S.) dollars, included tungsten and marine products.

TABLE 5

Formosa: Selected Economic Statistics

ITEM	1938	1952
Area cultivated (hectares) . . .	859,000	881,450
Farm families	424,500	c. 685,000
Rice hectarage (cropped) . . .	625,398	c. 790,000
Rice production (000 metric tons) . .	1,402	c. 1,570
Sweet potatoes production (000 metric tons)	1,726	2,090
Sugar production (000 metric tons) . .	967	520
Pineapple production (000 metric tons) .	116	c. 55
Swine (000 head)	1,827	c. 2,550
Mineral fertilizers consumed (000 metric tons) .	c. 466	c. 450
Mineral fertilizers produced (000 metric tons) .	c. 29	154
Power: installed capacity (kW) . .	190,000	331,000
Cotton cloth production (000 yards) . .	negligible	89,293
Coal production (000 metric tons) . .	2,199	2,286
Timber production (000 cubic metres) . .	327	451,000

Based on Norton S. Ginsburg, *The Economic Resources and Development of Formosa* (I.P.R., New York, 1953), pp. 53–56.

TABLE 6

Hong Kong Trade, 1951

All figures are in Hong Kong dollars. 1 Hong Kong dollar = ·175 U.S. $

IMPORTS		EXPORTS	
from:		to:	
China and Formosa	1,029,063,190	China and Formosa	1,971,527,809
Great Britain .	619,056,609	Malaya . . .	740,623,416
Malaya . . .	394,069,156	Great Britain .	214,598,413
Rest of British Com-		Rest of British Com-	
monwealth . .	617,964,406	monwealth . .	414,628,231
U.S.A. . . .	373,523,601	U.S.A. . . .	162,546,601
Total, including		Total (including	
others . .	4,870,314,536	others) . .	4,433,027,705
including:		including:	
Food, beverages, and		Textiles . .	810,515,272
tobacco . .	1,001,233,892	Chemicals and	
Textiles . .	873,662,809	pharmaceuticals .	675,597,540
Chemicals and		Food, beverages, and	
pharmaceuticals .	656,021,298	tobacco . .	556,682,936
Base metals and		Base metals and	
manufactures		manufactures	
thereof . .	378,805,401	thereof . .	162,546,601

In the twelve months ending June 1953 imports totalled 4,051,200,000 dollars and exports 3,133,300,000 dollars. Of these, imports from China totalled 684,320,000 dollars and exports to China 716,800,000 dollars.

CHAPTER XXVI

Mainland South-east Asia

CHARLES A. FISHER

The Duality of South-east Asia

IT is only since the second world war that the term South-east Asia has come into general use as a collective name for the lands lying to the east of the Indian sub-continent and to the south of China. Nor is it altogether surprising that Westerners should have been so slow to recognize the need for such a term, since the limited measure of unity which the region possesses is largely negative, deriving in the main from its transitional character between the two great demographic and cultural foci of India and China.

Moreover, because of the manner in which the land here is broken up by jungle-covered mountains and multitudinous arms of the sea into a series of relatively small units, and because also of its much lower average density of population[1] compared with that of these two great neighbours, it has always in the past been overshadowed by them and has tended to be divided into a series of separate States which were easily dominated by external Powers. In this sense, therefore, South-east Asia may fittingly be compared to the Balkans, and, as with the latter, though to a far greater extent, its diversities more than outweigh its still largely hypothetical unity.

Foremost among the geographical distinctions to be drawn is that between the mainland territories of Burma, Siam, and Indo-China, and the insular realm of Indonesia and the Philippines, with which Malaya should also be included. For whereas the Malaysian peoples of the archipelagos are mainly Moslem 'Malays'[2] and their traditional political units have evinced characteristically maritime patterns, the pre-

---

[1] The average density for all South-east Asia in 1949 was ninety-four to the square mile, which is approximately one-third of the corresponding figures for Indo-Pakistan and China proper.

[2] For a definition and description of the 'Malays' see Chapter XXVII, p. 659.

dominantly Buddhist[3] inhabitants of the mainland States, whose historic kingdoms have centred in the great river basins, are descended from more obviously Mongoloid stocks and show closer affinities with the Chinese.

Again, although no country in South-east Asia escaped the sudden intensification of economic activity which followed the opening of the Suez Canal in 1869, and was accompanied by the influx not merely of a Western managerial class but also of alien Asian middlemen and coolies, who were more responsive than the indigenes to the stimuli of money incentives, the pattern of this development on the mainland differed significantly from that in Malaysia. Thus, while the latter continued[4] to specialize in the production of plantation commodities destined for Western markets, the great deltas of the peninsula, thanks to their physique, their tropical monsoonal climate, and, except in Tonkin, their absence of serious population pressure, proved ideally suited for the commercialized production of rice, which has found its principal outlets in the more congested parts of Asia relatively close at hand.

On all these grounds, therefore, the division of South-east Asia into a continental and a maritime half appears well founded, and it will accordingly form the basis of the treatment to be followed in this and the ensuing chapter.

The Physical and Political Pattern of Mainland South-east Asia

Throughout the whole peninsula, which has a predominantly rugged surface, the main structural trend lines run roughly north–south. In the north the divides between the principal river valleys—the Irrawaddy, Salween, Mekong, and Songkoi—are narrow and serrated, though farther south, where the ranges simultaneously fan out and decrease in height, broad expanses of relatively level plateau occur, notably in the Shan country and Laos, which, in turn, nourish yet another major stream, the Menam. Notwithstanding the magnitude of these five great rivers, however, their valleys are in most cases unusually constricted and the total extent of good arable land is comparatively

---

[3] Except in the Annamite lands (see p. 636) the form of Buddhism practised in South-east Asia is that known as the Hinayana or Lesser Vehicle.

[4] Both the Philippines and the Netherlands Indies had been the scenes of continuous European influence since the sixteenth century. See Chapter XXVII, p. 654.

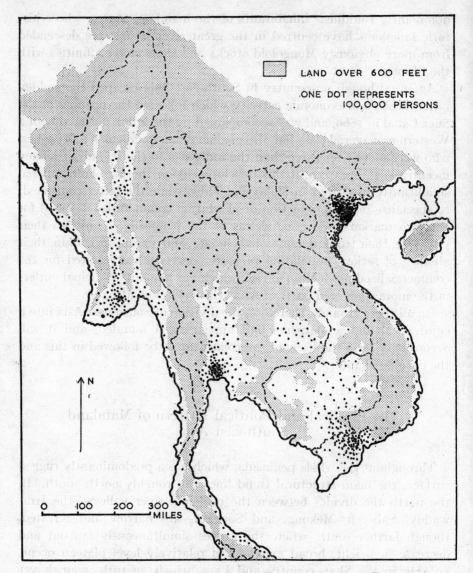

LAND OVER 600 FEET

ONE DOT REPRESENTS
100,000 PERSONS

Fig. 1. Peninsular South-east Asia: Distribution of Population

small. To-day some three-quarters of the region's population, which is
still almost exclusively agricultural, live in the deltas of the Irrawaddy,
the Menam, the Mekong, and the Songkoi.[5] (See Fig. 1.)

[5] The Salween Valley maintains its gorge-like character almost to the coast, and its
delta is much smaller than that of the other great rivers.

This extremely marked concentration on the immediate coastal fringe, however, is a relatively recent development, except in Tonkin and Annam, which, in a demographic sense, are a continuation of the Southern Chinese coastlands. But elsewhere, notwithstanding the critical role of sea-borne Indian colonization during the early centuries A.D., the historic nuclei of all the main States were some distance inland. Thus the heart of the Burmese kingdom lay in the relatively open lands of the dry belt in the vicinity of the Irrawaddy bend, the early capitals of Siam were all in the somewhat similar central part of the Menam Valley,[6] and the great Khmer empire, the predecessor of the modern Cambodia, focused on the inland basin of Tonlé Sap.[7]

Originally each of these kingdoms appears to have been peopled by relatively homogeneous ethnic groups corresponding to a distinct phase of southward migration from the Tibeto-Yunnan tableland, and furthermore their separate identities and linguistic individuality have in large measure been preserved to the present day, mainly because of the difficulty of lateral movement from one basin to the next. But, as time went on, each of the lowland peoples in question gradually extended its rule over portions of the hill and plateau country on its periphery, which in most cases was occupied by quite different ethnic groups at varying levels of cultural advancement.

Particularly important in this respect were the peoples known variously as Lao, Shan, and Thai, whose original homeland was the kingdom of Nan Chao in Yunnan. As a result of many centuries of Chinese pressure on this area, and the final sacking of its capital by Kublai Khan in 1253, the majority of the inhabitants were forced southward into the Menam valley, where they established their new State, Siam, and also into the plateau country which surrounds it on the landward sides.

During the course of history the allegiance of most of these various upland peoples underwent repeated changes as a result of the fluctuations in the relative strength of the lowland States. Moreover, because of their direct overland contact with China, many of the border territories were readily susceptible to its influence, and, indeed, even the major kingdoms themselves were all at times regarded by the Chinese emperors as tributaries. But only the Annamite lands ever formed part

[6] However, c. 1350 the capital was moved to Ayuthia on the edge of the delta, where it remained until 1767; thereafter it was moved to Bangkok.

[7] The ruins of Angkor, the capital of the former Khmer empire, lie slightly to the north of Siemreap.

of Imperial China, whose boundary in this vicinity extended virtually to the Annamite Cordillera for over a thousand years from III B.C. until A.D. 939. [8]

The possibility that the river valleys of peninsular South-east Asia might afford practicable routes to the interior of China was a principal cause of the growing Western, particularly French, interest in the region during the second half of the nineteenth century, though ever since the First Burmese War, of 1824–26, the main British preoccupation here had been to buttress the eastern frontier of the Indian Empire. But, in fact, apart from the Haiphong–Yunnan railway which was opened after great difficulty only in 1910, and the even more tenuous Burma road, completed under the stress of the Sino-Japanese war in 1939, the value of mainland South-east Asia in providing back-door entries into China has been negligible owing to the immensity of the physical obstacles. However, in the meantime the United Kingdom and France succeeded in carving out the two very valuable colonial dependencies of Burma and Indo-China before deciding, in a joint Convention of 1896, to preserve what remained of Siam as a buffer State between their respective spheres. [9]

After the opening of the Suez Canal the economic life of all the countries was rapidly transformed, and in this connexion the difference between the colonial status of Burma and Indo-China, and Siam's political independence, modified by extra-territoriality, was of small consequence. Thanks to a fundamental unity of geological structure and climate, the natural resources of the three were generally similar, though Burma's oilfields and the anthracite of Tonkin were each distinctive. Otherwise, with fairly widespread teak forests and more especially with opportunities for rice cultivation and rubber planting, all three were remarkably alike in potentialities.

Admittedly, there were significant differences in the way these resources were exploited. Thus, although the British policy of treating Burma, despite all cultural and historical realities, as a mere province of India, proved to be a major error, economically the country was much the most effectively developed of the three, and the bulk of its rice and

---

[8] During Ming times China reoccupied the Annamite lands from 1407 to 1428. Early in the nineteenth century the Annamite Emperor, Gia Long, attempted to strengthen his position against local rivals by obtaining investiture as a tributary ruler from the Manchu Empire of China.

[9] Nevertheless further annexations of Siamese territory did take place. In 1907 France seized Battambang and added it to Cambodia, and in 1909 Great Britain obtained the four northern states of Malaya—i.e., Kedah, Perlis, Kelantan, and Trengganu.

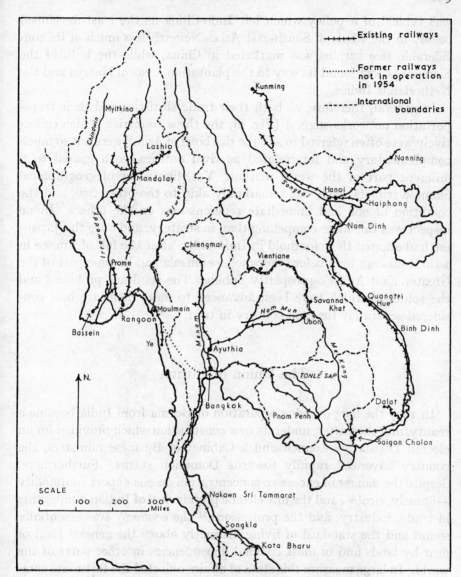

FIG. 2. PENINSULAR SOUTH-EAST ASIA: RAILWAYS

petroleum exports found a ready market in India and Ceylon. In Indo-China, on the other hand, the incongruities of the French assimilationist theory were displayed at their worst, and the doctrinaire attempt to divert the greater part of the rice exports, and even some of the coal, from their obvious markets close at hand in order to sell them in France was typical of a policy which left Indo-China as the least-developed colony in the whole of South-east Asia. Nevertheless much of its considerable rice surplus was marketed in China, while the bulk of the Siamese export found its way to the plantation areas of Malaya and the Netherlands Indies.

In general, therefore, as both their trade statistics and their transportation networks suggest (Fig. 2), the three countries, which collectively were often referred to as "the rice bowl of Asia," were not so much complementary and interrelated as rival entities, each geared to a different part of the world market. Yet, like a set of geographical Siamese triplets, each was remarkably akin to the other two, and the condition of one had immediate repercussions on the others. In no respect was this more compelling than in strategy, and once the Japanese had secured their foothold in Indo-China after the fall of France in 1940 it was not long before the whole peninsula had become part of the Greater East Asia Co-prosperity Sphere. The resultant problems and the solutions which have been advanced to meet them are best considered separately for each country in turn.

The Union of Burma

In 1937 the long overdue separation of Burma from India became a reality, and thereafter, under its new constitution which provided for an elected Legislative Council and a Cabinet of Burmese ministers, the country advanced rapidly towards Dominion status. Furthermore, despite the danger of excessive concentration on one export commodity —namely, rice[10]—and the unwelcome prominence of Indian immigrants in trade, industry, and the professions,[11] the economy was essentially sound and the standard of living distinctly above the general level of near-by lands and of most colonial dependencies in other parts of the world. In large measure this state of affairs reflected the fortunate combination of richly fertile soils in the riverine lowlands and a population

[10] In 1941 Burma exported 3,500,000 tons of rice—i.e., half its total production of rice and over 40 per cent. by value of its total exports. The Burmese rice export was the largest in the world and roughly equalled the amounts from Siam and Indo-China (its closest rivals) put together.

[11] Pre-war Indian investments in Burma were estimated at £56 million, a figure which slightly exceeded that of British investments (£53 million).—G. E. Harvey, *British Rule in Burma* (Faber, London, 1946), p. 7.

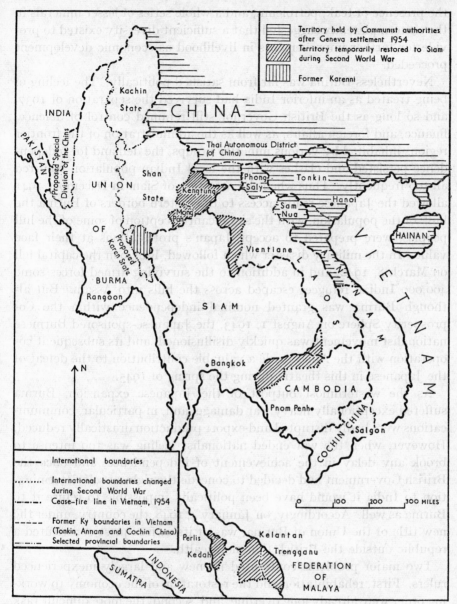

Territory held by Communist authorities after Geneva settlement 1954
Territory temporarily restored to Siam during Second World War
Former Karenni

International boundaries
International boundaries changed during Second World War
Cease-fire line in Vietnam, 1954
Former Ky boundaries in Vietnam (Tonkin, Annam and Cochin China)
Selected provincial boundaries

0   100   200   300 MILES

FIG. 3. PENINSULAR SOUTH-EAST ASIA: POLITICAL DIVISIONS

density lower than that of any other country in South-east Asia.[12] Moreover, at least a beginning had been made in industrialization, and

[12] The density in Burma was sixty-three per square mile in 1939 and seventy in 1949.

the presence of teak, petroleum, and a whole series of lesser minerals in the eastern plateaux suggested that a sufficient diversity existed to provide for further improvements in livelihood as economic development proceeded.

Nevertheless Burma was far from satisfied politically. The feeling of being treated as an inferior India had survived the separation of 1937, and so long as the British Governor still retained control of defence, finance, and foreign affairs, as well as the administration of the frontier regions inhabited by various minority groups, the demand for independence persisted and clashes with the local Indian population recurred all too frequently. Thus when the defection of Siam in December 1941 allowed the Japanese ready access to the eastern borders of Burma the bulk of the population, with the significant exception of some of the hill peoples, were prepared to accept Japan's protestations at their face value. In the military disaster which followed, Rangoon the capital fell on March 8, 1942, and in addition to the surviving armed forces some 400,000 Indian refugees escaped across the hills into Assam. But although Burma was granted nominal independence within the Co-prosperity Sphere on August 1, 1943, the Japanese-sponsored Burmese nationalist movement was quickly disillusioned, and its subsequent co-operation with the Allies made a valuable contribution to the defeat of the Japanese in this theatre during the spring of 1945.

As the westernmost outpost of the Japanese expansion, Burma suffered exceptionally heavy war damage, and, in particular, communications were badly disrupted and export production drastically reduced. However, when the war ended nationalist feeling was too intense to brook any delay in the achievement of independence, and once the British Government had decided to concede the right of self-determination to India it would have been politically impossible to refuse it to Burma as well. Accordingly, on January 4, 1948, the country, under the new title of the Union of Burma, was at its own request constituted a republic outside the British Commonwealth.

Two major problems confronted its new and largely inexperienced rulers. First, rehabilitation and the restoration of the economy to working order were already long overdue, and, second, the more difficult task of building a nation out of the country's diverse ethnic and cultural groups now had to be tackled. For a time these problems nearly proved too much for the new Socialist regime, which soon had to contend with three rival Communist or near Communist rebel factions, with the Karen insurgents, who demanded a larger area and a greater degree of autonomy than the Government would concede, and also, after 1949, with considerable remnants of the Chinese Nationalist forces which had been driven across the Yunnan frontier. But during 1951–52 the tide appeared to turn, and, barring interference from outside, the restoration of law and order should not now be long delayed.

The need to create a nation out of an ethnically diverse society is not in any sense unique to Burma, and, indeed, the problem is in many respects less acute there than in most other parts of South-east Asia. For a single linguistic group, the Burman, not only heavily outnumbers all the minorities put together[13] but also occupies the key central area, thus commanding the major routes and separating the several peripheral groups from each other.

Furthermore, in contrast to the rest of South-east Asia, the largest alien community in Burma is Indian and not Chinese, and, while the Indians, especially the small traders and money-lenders, have traditionally been extremely unpopular, their numbers have fallen from the pre-war total (1,018,000 in 1931) to some 700,000 to-day, and, since their mother country is not suspected of harbouring aggressive designs, they are not feared as a potential fifth column. However, the decline in both the size and relative importance of the Indian community has probably been more than offset by a growth in the Chinese population, from perhaps 200,000 before the war to over 300,000 to-day, and meanwhile many of the positions formerly held by Indians were taken over by Chinese after 1942. Moreover, although the concentration of the Chinese in Burma in three separate and fairly restricted localities—namely, Rangoon, the tin-mining districts of Tenasserim, and the north-eastern frontier—tends to reduce their prominence in the national life as a whole, the strategic importance of all these places is bound to deepen Burmese anxiety regarding the loyalties of this alien community.

Nevertheless the problem of national unity has in the main been that of satisfying the aspirations of the larger and more advanced indigenous minorities. Under the Constitution of 1948 it was hoped to solve the nationality problem both by making the country a federation of four units—namely, Burma proper, the Shan, Kachin, and Karen States— and also by establishing as an upper house a so-called Chamber of Nationalities. The latter, which was modelled on the Yugoslav pattern,

[13] The most recent Census data (1931) listed 9,627,196 Burmans out of a total population of 14,647,756. See Table 2.

has 125 members, of whom twenty-five represent the Shans, twenty-four the Karens, twelve the Kachins, eight the Chins, and the rest the inhabitants of Burma proper.

Although the measure of autonomy which the component states enjoy under the Constitution is not great, the arrangements seemed to have satisfied most of the minority groups, including the Shans, who are in many respects the most advanced of all.[14] As to the Karens, however, only a mere 70,000 out of a total population of $1\frac{1}{2}$ million live in the old feudatory Karenni (4506 square miles), and the remainder are dispersed over a wide area, mainly in the Irrawaddy delta and Tenasserim. But in much of this territory, which their leaders have optimistically claimed should all be constituted an autonomous State, the Karens do not form a majority, and the adherence of many of them to Christianity serves to estrange them still further from their Buddhist Burman neighbours. Thus, while the only satisfactory solution would appear to be a compromise giving the Karens a reasonable degree of autonomy in a somewhat more extensive area than was originally proposed,[15] together perhaps with some resettlement of population, the present psychological climate is hardly conducive to such an arrangement. Meanwhile the Mons, a smaller group, mostly inhabiting the vicinity of Moulmein, have shown signs of joining forces with the Karens,[16] and at the opposite extremity of the country the Kachins, who have always tended to be difficult to manage, have again become restive.

If the problems of national unification could finally be satisfactorily disposed of, however,[17] the economic difficulties facing the country, though serious, would not be by any means insuperable. Indeed, as recent export figures show (Table 3), substantial progress has already been made, though, mainly as a result of wartime demolitions in the oilfields and interruptions to communications with the eastern plateaux, mineral output is still far below the pre-war level.

Since the early days of independence the doctrinaire policy of wholesale nationalization has been toned down a good deal, and Burmese

[14] Unlike the great majority of the other hill peoples, who are either animists or recent converts to Christianity, the Shans are Buddhists. As a conciliatory gesture to the Shans, Sao Shwe Thaik, the Saophalong of Yawnghwe, was elected the first President of the Union of Burma.

[15] In 1947 it was proposed that the Karenni States, the Salween District, and certain other contiguous areas should be formed into a Karen State with limited autonomy, and that the interests of other Karens—e.g., those in the delta—should be given special protection.

[16] The Karens also joined forces for a time with both Burmese Communist and Chinese Nationalist troops.

[17] Considerable progress was made in this respect during 1953–54.

'Marxism' is in fact much modified by the all-pervasive influence of Buddhism in the national life. Thus to-day the emphasis is on *Pyidawtha*,[18] to be promoted by such means as industrialization, the modernization of rural handicrafts, the improvement of paddy and long-staple cotton cultivation, and a tempered programme of land redistribution, all of which has much more in common with present-day Indian practice than with the methods now being followed by Communist China. Similarly, the 1951 agreement between the Government and the three large British oil companies, whereby the former obtained a $33\frac{1}{3}$ per cent. share in the production and refining of the country's petroleum, was indicative of moderation, as was the decision of 1952 to participate in the Colombo Plan.

Nevertheless the unwillingness of Burma to accept any further aid from the United States after June 30, 1953, or to take part in S.E.A.T.O.[19] is symptomatic of an overriding determination to maintain a policy of strict neutrality in the cold war. Whether this policy is wise, in view of the long-standing, though legally and ethnically unjustifiable claims of China to substantial portions of northern and eastern Burma[20] and the recent creation of both Kachin and Thai autonomous states on the Chinese side of the disputed boundary, only time will show. But that Burma, with its relatively weak organization and obvious numerical inferiority, is acutely vulnerable to infiltration and attack via the traditional routes used by both the Mongols and the Chinese armies of the Manchu Dynasty is without doubt the dominant fact with which the framers of Burmese foreign policy to-day must contend.

The States of Indo-China: Vietnam, Laos, and Cambodia

The former French Indo-China was a much more complex dependency than Burma, but the familiar characterization of the country as "two bags of rice hanging from the two ends of a yoke" aptly summarizes the salient features of both its geography and its economy. Strictly speak-

---

[18] Which may be very loosely translated as 'national welfare.'

[19] See below, p. 646.

[20] Throughout the period of British rule in Upper Burma there were intermittent boundary disputes, and north of 26° 45' the boundary is not demarcated. Both before and since the Communist accession to power in China Chinese maps have shown large parts of northern and eastern Burma as Chinese territory.

ing, however, this image refers only to the Annamite lands[21]—*i.e.*, the two great deltas of the Song koi (Red River) and the Mekong, which form the "rice bags"—and the Annamite Cordillera which lies between. The latter, a rugged, jungle-covered, and fever-ridden upland, is sparsely inhabited, mainly by primitive hill tribes known collectively as Moi, though the small fertile pockets of lowland between the mountains and the coast support a much denser population of Annamites.

Both in physical appearance and in most aspects of their culture—notably, their language,[22] their traditional form of mandarin administration, and their religion, which contains elements of animism, Taoism, Confucianism, and Mahayana Buddhism—the Annamites show much the closest Chinese affinities of any South-east Asian people. Indeed, as has already been seen, the older Annamite lands—namely, the Tonkin delta and the northern coastal plain of Annam—were integral parts of Imperial China during the formative period of their civilization, and in many respects the Annamite Cordillera forms a more fundamental geographical divide than does the modern international boundary.

The force of this distinction may be seen by comparing the two deltas. In the north, the Red River delta, which has been continuously settled by Annamites for over 2000 years, is now extremely congested, its average density of population being well over 1250 to the square mile. Subdivision of holdings has reached an advanced stage, over three-fifths of the farms being less than one acre in size, and although all the rice grown is consumed locally, it has been necessary in recent decades to supplement this with imports from Cochin-China. However, the anthracite, tin, and zinc deposits of the hillier country to the north and north-east of the delta proper provided some compensating exports, as did the cement, glass, and textiles from the factories centred in Hanoi, Haiphong, and Nam Dinh.

The Mekong delta, on the other hand, has only been colonized by the Annamites during the last two hundred years, and, indeed, it was not until the later nineteenth century, when it was subjected to a process of European-controlled development comparable with that of the Irrawaddy delta, that its vast agricultural potentialities began to be system-

[21] Under French rule the Annamite lands had no official collective name but were subdivided into Tonkin, Annam, and Cochin-China. Since the second world war the old national name for the whole area, Vietnam, has been revived and is used by both the French Associated State (under Bao Dai) and the Communist "People's Democratic Republic of Vietnam" (under Ho Chi Minh). However, most Western writers refer to the latter by the name of its supporting movement, the Vietminh.

[22] The spoken language is basically similar to Chinese, though the traditional use of modified Chinese characters for writing it is dying out.

atically exploited. Even to-day, however, despite the relatively recent influx of Annamite cultivators and Chinese middlemen,[23] the average population density does not exceed 250 per square mile, and in pre-war days 80 per cent. of Indo-China's rice export of *c.* 1·5 million tons, which ranked next to Burma's and Siam's, came from this region.

As might be expected, individual holdings in Cochin-China are much larger than in Tonkin, but few of the cultivators own their plots and indebtedness is a serious problem. In addition to rice the French introduced the cultivation of rubber, for which the basaltic *terres rouges*, mostly in north-eastern Cochin-China, were particularly suitable, and many processing industries were established in Saigon and in Cholon, its Chinese twin.

But Indo-China included other components besides the Annamite lands. Immediately behind the Cochin-China delta lies the vast shallow basin of Cambodia, focusing in Tonlé Sap and endowed with a high degree of natural fertility. Since here, again, population density is generally low (about forty to eighty per square mile) a considerable food surplus, mainly of rice, maize, and fish,[24] is normally available, and the area is now known to possess also valuable reserves of iron ore, as yet little exploited. After the decline of the Indianized Khmer empire in the late twelfth century Cambodia was subjugated alternately by the Siamese and the Annamites. Of these two the former are culturally much the closer to the Cambodians and, in particular, practise the same (Hinayana) form of Buddhism.

Even more closely related to the Siamese, both physically and culturally, however, are the Lao[25] inhabitants of the plateau to the north of Cambodia. This area, mostly lying at an altitude of 3000 to 5000 feet, is essentially similar to the Shan country of Burma, and, though teak and other forests occur, its vegetation is generally more open and its climate far healthier than those of the Annamite Cordillera. Thus the Lao peoples, who tend to cluster in the many fertile valleys which break up the plateau, have been able to sustain a relatively advanced mode of existence, though primitive tribes, including Moi, Man, Miao, and Lolo, occupy the higher and more rugged parts of the Kingdom of Laos as well as the adjoining peripheries of Tonkin. But Laos has undoubtedly

[23] Some 80 per cent. of the half-million Chinese in Indo-China before the second world war lived in Cochin-China and Cambodia—*i.e.*, the areas in which commercial cultivation provided an opportunity for their talents as middlemen of all kinds.

[24] The annual fish catch of Tonlé Sap is about 120,000 tons.

[25] They also are Hinayana Buddhists.

suffered from the difficulty of communications both internally and with the outside world, and accordingly has tended to be by-passed by the advances which were taking place in adjacent areas.

Between 1887 and 1893 these varied and diverse lands were, for the first time in history, joined together by the French, in the allegedly federal Union of Indo-China. In fact, the federal character of the Union and the technical distinction between Cochin-China, which was a colony, and the remaining four protectorates were more imaginary than real. For although the traditional way of life was not greatly interfered with in Cambodia, Laos, or even Annam, all of which retained their native ruling houses, the two key economic areas—Cochin-China and Tonkin— were both closely controlled and in all but name directly administered by the French.

Nevertheless considerable rivalry existed between these two focal regions, and, despite the French decision at the turn of the century to move the capital from Saigon to Hanoi, the former city was unwilling to renounce entirely its claim to pre-eminence, and the Governor-General continued to reside there for a period every year.

This rivalry between the two principal cities, however, was by no means the most important of the tensions existing within the country, which was far from effectively integrated by physical communications and even less united in sentiment. Thus both the Cambodians and Laotians disliked the more hard-headed Annamites, who spread over to some extent into their territories, while the Annamites themselves proved almost from the outset exceedingly intractable to the French. For although the assimilationist doctrine might be expected to evoke a considerable response in isolated or backward parts of the world, the Annamites, possessed of cultural traditions which they felt to be in no sense inferior to those of France, were for the most part unsympathetic. Thus serious anti-French disturbances occurred repeatedly after 1905[26] and Annamite nationalism was among the most potent in all South-east Asia, though it differed significantly from related movements, notably in Burma and Indonesia, in taking its cue from China rather than from India.

In this respect, and in view of the acute agrarian problem in Tonkin, many Annamites showed great interest in both Sun Yat-sen's and later Communist proposals for land redistribution in China. Moreover, soon after its founding in 1927, the New Annam Revolutionary Association

[26] *I.e.*, following the Russo-Japanese war.

passed increasingly under the influence of its more left-wing members.[27] The same period also saw the rise, especially among the poorer peasants in Cochin-China, of a new reformist and semi-religious movement, Caodaism, which has been described as a "blend of Buddhism, Confucianism, Taoism, Roman Catholicism, and Free Masonry," but was strongly suspected by the French of being merely a cloak for subversive activity. Similar suspicions were even harboured against many of the two million or so Annamite converts to Roman Catholicism, who were largely concentrated in the coastal region around Phatdiem. But in fact, although nationalism in the sense of a desire for self-determination was undoubtedly strong among these groups, it was not incompatible with the maintenance of substantial ties with the French.[28] Among the Cambodians and Laotians, on the other hand, nationalism was much less widespread, and in general these peoples tended to look to the French for protection against their more aggressive neighbours.

From July 1941 until March 1945 Indo-China, whose capacity for resistance collapsed with the fall of France, was treated by the Japanese as "friendly occupied territory," and thus the gateway to the rest of peninsular South-east Asia was thrown open and the security of the Singapore base fatally undermined. But in March 1945 the Japanese, who had meanwhile withdrawn their regional headquarters from Singapore to Saigon, removed the French administration and set up three new and ostensibly independent national states—namely, Vietnam (*i.e.*, the Annamite lands of Tonkin, Annam, and Cochin-China), Cambodia, and Laos, respectively under the rule of the Emperor of Annam (Bao Dai) and the Kings of Cambodia and Luang Prabang.

This development marked the beginning of a process of political disintegration which was further aggravated a few months later by the Potsdam decision that Chinese (Nationalist) and British troops should occupy the areas respectively north and south of the sixteenth parallel. For in Cochin-China and southern Annam the French were quickly able to resume control and, owing to their command of the vital routes to the interior, could likewise exert their authority over Cambodia and Laos, whose rulers in due course reaffirmed their loyalty to France. But in Tonkin the long delay on the part of the Chinese in withdrawing pro-

---

[27] The movement was driven underground by the French.
[28] In the Indo-China war of 1946–54 (see below, p. 640) Roman Catholics and Caodaists (nearly two million in number) as well as the Hoa Hao sect (about one million adherents, in the areas south-west of Saigon) were strong opponents of the Communists. The same is true of the non-religious Binh Xuyen sect.

vided an opportunity for the new "Democratic Republic of Vietnam"[29] under the Presidency of the Communist Ho Chi Minh, to establish itself at Hanoi in place of the Japanese puppet regime which had collapsed with the defeat of Japan.

Beginning in December 1946, the French fought a long and dispiriting campaign in an endeavour to crush Vietminh resistance to their plans for refashioning Indo-China in accordance with the new post-war design for the overseas territories. To this end also, Vietnam, Cambodia, and Laos were each accorded the rank of *état associé*, and it was at first intended to group the three in a sub-federation of Indo-China within the wider federation of the *Union Française*. But although the latter undoubtedly affords a much greater degree of local autonomy, notably in economic affairs, to its component members than did the pre-war French colonial empire, it nevertheless retained considerable vestiges of assimilationism, and the independence which it offered was by no means complete.

For this reason the Government of Bao Dai in the Associated State of Vietnam failed to impress either a majority of the Vietnamese or the newly independent Asian Powers as being anything more than a French puppet regime. Furthermore, neither Laos nor Cambodia, both of which are now fully awake to the stirrings of nationalism, has been willing to lose its identity in an Indo-Chinese federation. But it was the Communist victory in China in 1949 and the consequent strengthening of the Vietminh from the rear which most drastically undermined the French position in Indo-China and, as in Korea, transformed a relatively localized issue into a problem of world-wide significance. Thus, in spite of the brilliant campaigns of Marshal de Lattre de Tassigny in 1951 and the land reform policy introduced by the Vietnam Government in 1952, the initiative passed increasingly into the hands of the Vietminh, and in the spring of 1954 the French[30] decided to seek a negotiated settlement.

By the terms of the Geneva cease-fire agreement of July 20, 1954,[31] Vietnam has temporarily been divided immediately south of the seventeenth parallel, ostensibly for the purpose of regrouping the Vietminh and French Union forces, respectively north and south of this line. Before July 1956, however, elections are to be held for a government

[29] See footnote 21.

[30] In spite of the fact that by this time the U.S.A. was paying more than three-quarters of the monetary cost of the war French losses in both men and material were causing increasing anxiety and there appeared to be little prospect of victory.

[31] Signed by France, the United Kingdom, the U.S.S.R., Communist China, the three Associated States, and Vietminh.

representing the whole of Vietnam, and in the meantime neither part is to place any military bases at the disposal of foreign Powers nor to participate in any military alliance.[32] In addition all Vietminh forces will be withdrawn from Laos, though the Laotian Communists retain control over the two northern provinces of Phong Saly and Sam Neua. Although permitted to maintain limited forces for self-defence, both Cambodia and Laos will, in effect, be neutralized, the apparent intention being to establish them as buffers between China and Siam. Immediately following the Geneva Conference the French announced that all three Associated States would be granted 'complete independence,' but it appears that this will not preclude their remaining within the French Union.

In so far as they concern Vietnam these terms afford an obvious parallel with Korea. Thus both countries have been bisected roughly according to the pattern of the 1945 occupation zones, an arrangement which clearly reflects the realities of external power rather than of local national aspirations. Moreover, in view of the landward contiguity of northern Vietnam with China, in comparison with the much more exposed position of the south, it would seem that the Communist Powers here, as in Korea, have gained a considerable strategic advantage.

In contrast to Korea, however, it is the northern half of Vietnam which has the larger population, and, in spite of provisions for moving refugees to the south, this distinction is not likely to disappear entirely. But though possessing important factory installations and considerable reserves of minerals, whose output can easily be increased now that hostilities have ended, the north will remain a food deficit area and, at least for the time being, the rice bowls as well as the rubber plantations of Cochin-China and Cambodia are not in Communist hands. Hitherto southern Vietnam has enjoyed a somewhat higher standard of living than the north, and if competent leadership were forthcoming to make wise use of the economic aid which the United States and France are willing to extend this advantage could probably be increased considerably. Meanwhile it remains to be seen whether the ties of the north with traditionally suspect China or the continued association of the south with France and the other predominantly non-Asian S.E.A.T.O. Powers[33] will prove to be the greater obstacle in winning popular support in the

---

[32] Early plans envisaged a southward movement of approximately one million people. By the summer of 1955 some 800,000 had been moved; no figures were available for any movement in the reverse direction.

[33] See below, p. 646.

country as a whole now that the war, with its confused national and ideological overtones, is at an end. In addition, the large concentrations of Chinese in the south are politically an unknown but by no means a negligible quantity in the equation.

Although from a tactical point of view the Geneva partition line is not favourable to the south, it has the important advantage of giving the latter complete control over the main route (the Quangtri–Savannakhet road) linking Laos with the outside world. But, as the recent Vietminh invasion implied, there is no fundamental reason why improved roads should not be developed between Laos and Tonkin, and in view of the continuing Communist control over Phong Saly and Sam Neua the stability of the new buffer may already be fatally undermined.

In both Cambodia and Laos the main obstacles to further Communist advances are the absence of acute agrarian discontent and the nationalist antipathies to the Vietnamese. But when the vigour and experience of the latter (to say nothing of the Chinese) are contrasted with the gentle insouciance of the Laotians and Cambodians, it is difficult to believe that these defences would be proof against open attack or even against covert subversion from the Communist lands near by.

Siam (Thailand)[34]

Alone among the States of South-east Asia Siam has never succumbed to Western imperial control, and this fact, together with its central position on the mainland, gives it a special importance at the present critical time. In its geographical layout the country presents a relatively simple pattern. From the nuclear region of the middle and lower Menam basin the Thais, as the result of intermittent warfare with their neighbours, have at various times since the fourteenth century extended their rule over most of Cambodia, Laos, the Tenasserim coast, and much of the Malay peninsula. But by the time that the British and French annexations ceased in 1909 nearly all of the remoter outlying territories had been lost, and the area which remained fell naturally into four main regions.

Of these, by far the most important is the central plain, an extremely

[34] The name Thailand came into general use under the regime of Pibul Songgram just before the outbreak of the second world war. Since then official usage has changed several times.

fertile alluvial lowland which, although the most densely populated part of the country, nevertheless appears capable of supporting much larger numbers than at present without undue congestion. Surrounding this area are, in turn, the northern hills, a territory closely resembling the Laos-Shan plateau and economically valuable mainly for its teak; the Nam Mun basin of the north-east, a semi-arid region of poor sandy soils and generally low productive capacity; and, in the south, the narrow strip of peninsular Siam, stretching down to the borders of Malaya and, like the latter, though on a much smaller scale, economically significant for its tin and rubber.

To a remarkable extent the riverine and coastal routes, still much the most important means of communication, focus upon Bangkok, which has also been made the hub of a fairly good railway network with lines radiating into all the main regions. Moreover, the direction of both political and economic affairs is overwhelmingly concentrated in this capital city, which, with a population of nearly one million, is several times larger than its nearest rival, Chiengmai.

Within much the greater part of Siam the rural population is almost exclusively Thai, though on the northern borders the distinction between lowland Thai and the essentially similar Shan and Lao uplanders is severely blurred, and in other mainly peripheral areas there are some 50,000 Cambodians and Vietnamese, a smaller number of Karens, and, in Patani, over 650,000 Malays who form a compact and resentful minority, differing sharply in both their language and their Islamic faith from the Thais themselves.

But without question the most serious minority problem is presented by the large Chinese community, estimated variously at from two to three million, and concentrated predominantly in Bangkok, the provincial towns, and the tin-mining districts of the south.[35] For although politically independent, Siam has nevertheless developed economically along similar lines to the former colonial lands near by. Thus to its indigenous subsistence economy has been added the production for export of vast quantities of rice, as well as lesser amounts of rubber, tin, and teak, and in all this activity both Western commercial houses and Chinese coolies, clerks, and business-men have played indispensable roles.

Nevertheless, in the absence of Western political control, nationalism

[35] There is also an Indian-Pakistani community of some 50,000, most of whom live in Bangkok, where they control the clothing industry.

in Siam assumed a form markedly different from that in other parts of South-east Asia. Thus the bloodless revolution of 1932 was primarily an attempt of the Western-educated minority to replace the old-fashioned absolute monarchy by a more nearly democratic form of government, and thereafter to negotiate, on a basis of equality with the Western Powers, a series of new treaties terminating such extra-territorial rights as had lingered on since the nineteenth century.[36] During the years which followed, successive enactments also restricted the rights of both the Malay and the Chinese communities, and much propaganda was made in favour of Pibul Songgram's Pan Thai movement, which aimed at bringing under Siamese rule all adjoining areas to which, on either historical or ethnic grounds, any claim, however tenuous, could be advanced.

During the second world war the Siamese showed considerable skill in maintaining good relations with whichever side was in the ascendant, and although the substantial portions of Cambodia, the Shan States, Laos, and Northern Malaya which were obtained under Japan's 'good offices' had to be returned after August 1945, Siam survived the conflict apparently without serious damage to its economic health or its internal political stability. Since then, moreover, it has been able to take advantage of the seller's market in rice and, as the world's leading exporter in recent years, has enjoyed considerable prosperity. Although, like all the states of peninsular South-east Asia, Siam has too small an internal market to justify any very extensive industrialization, there are reasonable prospects for developing the manufacture of the simpler types of consumer goods. And when, further, account is taken of the incidental benefits already accruing from Bangkok's new importance as the air focus of South-east Asia,[37] it would appear that the economic outlook for the country is by no means discouraging.

Against this, however, must be set the implicit threat posed by the stream of propaganda in favour of a 'free Thai' movement, nowadays emanating from Yunnan, and by the establishment of Communist control in two provinces of near-by Laos.[38] Moreover, although Siam, thanks to its history of complete freedom from Western political control

---

[36] The first of these was the Anglo-Siamese Treaty of 1937.

[37] While shipping has to make the detour via Singapore, the main air routes to Eastern Asia take the shorter route via Bangkok.

[38] The members of the Thai-Lao-Shan family to-day include c. 6 to 7 million in Yunnan, 1 million in Burma (Shans), 1½ million in Laos (Lao), and 17 million in Siam (Thai and Lao). In addition to the 'free Thai' movement with its headquarters at Cheli (Yungchinghung) in Yunnan, there is also a faction in Laos which aims at uniting the Lao subdivision of the family in Laos and northern Thailand.

and its present relatively high level of prosperity, lacks the two most potent inducements to the internal growth of Communism, it is a cause for anxiety that the one really depressed part of the country is the Nam Mun basin, which adjoins Laos and Cambodia, and the presence in the capital and elsewhere of the largest Chinese minority in the whole of South-east Asia does nothing to reduce the fear of subversion.

In view of this threat, and in the absence of any serious inhibiting factors, Siam, since the return to power of Pibul Songgram after the coup of 1947, has associated itself much more closely with the Western Powers than has any other South-east Asian country except the Philippines, and is now generally regarded by the West as the most stable State on the South-east Asian mainland. During January 1954, moreover, as Vietminh victories multiplied in Indo-China, the Siamese Government took the initiative in proposing the formation of a 'Buddhist bloc' to include, besides itself, both Laos and Cambodia, and possibly also Burma.[39]

From several points of view much can be said in favour of such a grouping, and at the very least the alignment of Laos and Cambodia with Siam would be far more reasonable than their past association with the Annamite lands. For not only is the Hinayana form of Buddhism a living force within all the countries concerned, but also, on a more mundane level, it would be a simple matter to extend the Siamese road and rail networks to provide new and much desired outlets for the other two land-locked States.[40] Nevertheless, resentment over former aggression by Siam is still a factor to be reckoned with in these lands, and many of their people, more especially in Cambodia, are inclined to regard such proposals as merely a revival of pre-war Pan Thai chauvinism. This argument is voiced even more strongly in Burma, whose sense of historic rivalry with Siam is strong, but it is noteworthy that in July 1954 a mission from Bangkok proposing to reopen the Burma–Siam railway[41] was received with interest in Rangoon.

[39] The formation of such a bloc has often been mooted before, but it is probable that any serious attempt to organize it would lead to disputes between Burma and Siam for the leadership. In 1954 the sixth great Buddhist Council (the second during the last 1900 years) was held under Government sponsorship near Rangoon and attended by representatives from the Hinayana Buddhist countries—*viz.*, Laos, Cambodia, Siam, Ceylon, and Burma itself.

[40] Cambodia has a short coastline but no modern ports. Resentment over Saigon's allegedly excessive 'squeeze' has led in recent years to proposals for the creation of a Cambodian port.

[41] As one of the 50,000 Allied prisoners of war who were employed in building this railway the writer may perhaps venture the opinion that it will never be of any use unless it is completely rebuilt. See Charles A. Fisher, "The Thailand–Burma Railway," in *Economic Geography*, vol. xxiii, No. 2 (October 1947), pp. 85–97.

For the present, however, only Siam among the peninsular Southeast Asian States has subscribed to the S.E.A.T.O. Defence Treaty signed at Manila on September 8, 1954, though the eight signatories[42] unanimously "designated" Cambodia and Laos, as well as "the free territory under the jurisdiction of the State of Vietnam," as areas against which an attack would be regarded as endangering their "own peace and safety."

If, as their propaganda claims, the objectives of the Chinese Communists are peaceful, and their sole desire is to prevent the establishment of Western bases close to their own borders, the Geneva agreement should assuage such fears and the terms of S.E.A.T.O. give no legitimate cause for alarm. If, however, the Communist aims are expansionist and aggressive, a very different situation arises. While, on account of the Chinese minority's role, the incentives of the Siamese to resist a Chinese advance are much stronger than those which operated against the Japanese invasion in 1941, it is impossible to say whether the existence of S.E.A.T.O. could prevent an internal coup of familiar pattern such as might restore to power the former Prime Minister, Pridi Panomyong, who is now openly supported by Communist China.

In respect of strategy, moreover, the lesson of the second world war is all too plain, and it remains to be proved that a hostile force in possession of Tonkin and supported in depth from the north could be prevented from extending its control over the whole of the South-east Asian peninsula.

FURTHER READING

Books on South-east Asia as a whole

BALL, W. MACMAHON, *Nationalism and Communism in East Asia* (Melbourne University Press and Cambridge University Press, 1953).

DOBBY, E. H. G., *Southeast Asia* (University of London Press, 1950).

DU BOIS, CORA, *Social Forces in Southeast Asia* (Minneapolis University Press and Oxford University Press, 1949).

ELDRIDGE, F. R., *The Background of Eastern Sea Power* (Phoenix House, London, 1948).

ELSBREE, WILLARD H., *Japan's Role in Southeast Asian Nationalist Movements, 1940–45* (Harvard University Press, 1953; Allen and Unwin, London, 1954).

EMERSON, R., MILLS, L. A., and THOMPSON, V., *Government and Nationalism in Southeast Asia* (I.P.R., New York, and Allen and Unwin, London, 1942).

---

[42] These were Australia, France, New Zealand, Pakistan, the Philippines, Siam, the United Kingdom, and the United States.

HARRISON, BRYAN, *Southeast Asia: A Short History* (Macmillan, London, 1954).

JACOBY, E. H., *Agrarian Unrest in Southeast Asia* (Columbia University Press and Oxford University Press, 1949).

KONDAPI, C., *Indians Overseas* (Bombay, 1951).

LASKER, BRUNO, *Peoples of South-east Asia* (Gollancz, London, 1944).

MILLS, L. A., and associates, *The New World of Southeast Asia* (University of Minnesota Press, 1949).

VAN MOOK, H. J., *The Stakes of Democracy in Southeast Asia* (Norton, New York, 1950).

PANIKKAR, K. M., *The Future of South-East Asia* (Allen and Unwin, London, 1943).

PURCELL, VICTOR, *The Chinese in Southeast Asia* (Oxford University Press, 1951).

QUARITCH WALES, H. G., *The Making of Greater India* (London, 1951).

THAYER, P. W. (editor), *Southeast Asia in the Coming World* (Johns Hopkins Press, Baltimore, and Oxford University Press, 1953).

Countries of Mainland South-east Asia

ANDRUS, J. RUSSELL, *Burmese Economic Life* (Stanford University Press and Oxford University Press, 1947).

CHRISTIAN, J. L., *Modern Burma* (California University Press and Cambridge University Press, 1942).

CROSBY, SIR J., *Siam: the Crossroads* (Hollis and Carter, London, 1945).

CREDNER, W., *Siam: das Land der Thai* (Stuttgart, 1935).

DONNISON, F. S. V., *Public Administration in Burma* (Oxford University Press, 1953).

FURNIVALL, J. S., *Colonial Policy and Practice* (Cambridge University Press, 1948).

GOUROU, P., *L'Indochine française* (Hanoi, 1929).

HAMMER, ELLEN J., *The Struggle for Indochina* (Stanford University Press and Oxford University Press, 1954).

HARVEY, G. E., *British Rule in Burma* (Faber, London, 1946).

Indo-China: A Geographical Appreciation (Foreign Geography Information Series, No. 6, Ottawa, 1953).

LANDON, K. P., *Siam in Transition* (Oxford University Press, 1940).

MUS, PAUL, *Viet-nam: Sociologie d'une guerre* (Paris, 1952).

NU, THAKIN, *Burma under the Japanese* (Macmillan, London, 1954).

REEVE, W. D., *Public Administration in Siam* (London, 1952).

ROBEQUAIN, C., *The Economic Development of French Indo-China* (Oxford University Press, 1945).

SASORITH, KATAY D., *Le Laos* (Paris, 1953).

THOMPSON, VIRGINIA, *Thailand: the new Siam* (I.P.R., New York, 1941); *French Indo-China* (Macmillan, New York; Allen and Unwin, London, 1937).

TABLE 1

Burma: Area and Population

Area: 261,789 square miles
Population (1931 Census): 14,647,756[1]
Population (1941 Census): 16,823,798
Population (1952 estimate; U.N.O.): 18,859,000
Population density (1952 estimate; U.N.O.): 72 per square mile
Population of Rangoon (1941 Census): 501,219

[1] 1931 figures do not include certain hill areas.

TABLE 2

Burma: Ethnic Groups and Religions[1]

Indigenous Groups		Non-indigenous Groups	
Burman	9,627,196	Indian	1,017,825[2]
Karen	1,367,673	Chinese	193,594[3]
Shan	1,037,406	Indo-Burman	182,166
Kachin (est.)	400,000	Eurasian	19,200
Chin	348,994	European	11,651
Mon	336,728		
Palaung-Wa	176,382		
Lolo-Muhso	93,224		
Naga (est.)	70,000		

Religions

Buddhist	12,348,037	Hindu	582,581
Animist	763,243	Christian	331,106
Moslem	584,839		

[1] 1931 Census in all cases (1941 Census data incomplete).
[2] 1954 estimate: Indian 600,000; Pakistani 100,000.
[3] 1947 estimate (Purcell) 300,000.

TABLE 3

Burma: Overseas Trade, 1951

IMPORTS

648 *million kyat* (136,080,000 *U.S. dollars;* £48,572,000)

COMMODITIES	PERCENTAGE	SOURCES	PERCENTAGE
Cotton yarn and fabric .	25	India . .	27
		U.K. . .	25
Machinery and transport equipment . . .	7	Japan . .	17
		Malaya .	7
		Hong Kong .	3
		U.S.A. . .	3
Metals and metal mfrs. .	6	China . .	2
		Indonesia .	1

EXPORTS

982 *million kyat* (206,640,000 *U.S. dollars;* £73,800,000)

COMMODITIES	PERCENTAGE	DESTINATIONS	PERCENTAGE
Rice and rice products .	73	India . .	24
		Ceylon .	22
Teak	5	Japan . .	14
		Indonesia .	12
Metals	4	Malaya . .	8
Rubber	3	U.K. . .	6
		Hong Kong .	1
		China . .	1
		Pakistan .	1

Y*

TABLE 4

Indo-China: Area and Population

DIVISION	AREA (*square miles*)	POPULATION (1949 *estimates*)	DENSITY PER SQUARE MILE	CAPITAL Name	CAPITAL Population
Vietnam . .	127,259	22,973,000	181	Saigon	1,179,000
Tonkin .	44,672	10,006,000	222	Hanoi	237,146
Annam . .	57,838	7,299,000	126	Hué	c. 50,000
Cochin-China	24,749	5,668,000	226	Saigon	—
Geneva Partition, 1954					
North Vietnam	c. 77,000	c. 12,750,000	c. 178	Hanoi	—
South Vietnam	c. 50,000	c. 10,250,000	c. 205	Saigon	—
Cambodia .	53,668	3,279,000	61	Pnompenh	110,639
Laos . .	91,428	1,208,000	13	Vientiane	c. 14,000

TABLE 5

Indo-China: Overseas Trade, 1951

(French-controlled territories only)

IMPORTS			
6276 *million piastres* (304,700,000 U.S. dollars; £108,821,000)			
COMMODITIES	PERCENTAGE	SOURCES	PERCENTAGE
Textiles . . .	32	France . .	77
Machinery and vehicles .	24	U.S.A. . .	5
		Indonesia .	2
Live animals and food .	16	China . .	2
		Siam . .	1
		India and Pakistan .	1
EXPORTS			
2784 *million piastres* (135,100,000 U.S. dollars; £48,250,000)			
COMMODITIES	PERCENTAGE	DESTINATIONS	PERCENTAGE
Rubber	44	France . .	38
Rice	32	U.S.A. .	11
Other foodstuffs . .	16	Malaya . .	11
Minerals	3	Hong Kong .	9
		Siam . .	2

TABLE 6

Siam: Area and Population

Area: 198,271 square miles
Population (1947 Census): 17,256,825
Population (1952 estimate; U.N.O.): 19,192,000
Population density per square mile (1952): 97
Population of Bangkok (city proper) (1947): 688,832

TABLE 7

Siam: Overseas Trade, 1951

IMPORTS			
3708 *million baht* (296,640,000 *U.S. dollars;* £105,940,000)			
COMMODITIES	PERCENTAGE	SOURCES	PERCENTAGE
No data		Malaya .	33
		Hong Kong .	25
		U.S.A. . .	9
		China . .	8
		U.K. . .	7
		Japan . .	3
		India . .	2
		Indo-China .	2
		Indonesia .	1
		Philippines .	1
EXPORTS			
4476 *million baht* (357,080,000 *U.S. dollars;* £127,500,000)			
COMMODITIES	PERCENTAGE	DESTINATIONS	PERCENTAGE
Rice	45	U.S.A. . .	31
Rubber	29	Malaya . .	14
Tin	5	Japan . .	9
Teak	3	India . .	6
		Indonesia .	5
		Hong Kong .	3
		Philippines .	3
		British Borneo	1

CHAPTER XXVII

The Malaysian Realm : Indonesia, British South-east Asia, and the Philippines*

CHARLES A. FISHER

The Geographical and Historical Setting

THE term Malaysia has long been used by anthropologists to denote the major cultural realm which comprises the Indonesian and Philippine archipelago and the Malay peninsula south of the Kra isthmus. Geographically, also, this area appears a distinctive region in that, notwithstanding its connexion with the continental mainland in southern Siam, Malaysia forms the maritime half of South-east Asia and as such exhibits significant differences, both physical and human, from the lands considered in Chapter XXVI. (See Fig. 1.)

Geologically, it is true, the Malaysian structures are essentially southward prolongations of those found on the mainland. But although the same two major components—namely, the older Indo-Malayan core and the more recent series of Tertiary folds—are likewise dominant here, their relative proportions are markedly different, and, except in Malaya and the Philippines, the characteristic north–south grain is absent. Thus, while the peninsula and the greater part of Borneo, together with such outlying islands as Banka and Billiton, form part of the stable massif of Sunda-land, the remainder, much of which is still volcanically active, is predominantly an area of island arc formation with the main trend lines running roughly east–west.

This broad geological contrast is fundamental to an understanding of economic potentialities. For while in peninsular Malaya and the related areas certain metallic minerals, notably tin, are abundant, but advanced

* Thanks are due to the Association of American Geographers for permission to use in this chapter some of the material published in the *Professional Geographer* of March 1955 under the title of "Changing Political Geography of British Malaysia."

laterization renders the soils for the most part infertile, the limited mineral wealth of the island arcs[1] is a much less important asset than the exceptional natural fertility of their volcanically enriched soils, particularly in Java and in scattered parts of Sumatra, the lesser Sundas, and the Philippines.

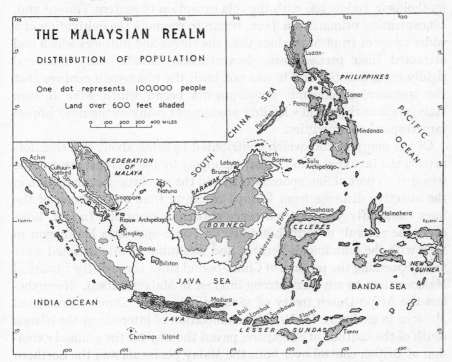

FIG. 1. THE MALAYSIAN REALM: DISTRIBUTION OF POPULATION

On this basis alone the carrying capacity of the islands in question would rank well above the average for the world's tropical and equatorial regions. But, in addition to its agricultural potentialities, the maritime character of Malaysia as a whole is a further major advantage, for it means that the greater part of the area's vast natural wealth is situated within easy reach of tide-water.

Indeed, it would be difficult to overestimate the role of the sea in Malaysian development. From the time of the earliest diffusion of peoples and cultures maritime patterns have prevailed, and this situa-

[1] The leading mineral of the archipelago is petroleum, which occurs in the gentler undulations between the main Tertiary ridges and the older core, notably in Sumatra, Java, and Borneo, and also, in parallel circumstances, in New Guinea.

tion was not fundamentally altered in the sixteenth century by the arrival—from opposite directions—of the Portuguese and Spaniards in search of the lucrative spice trade of the Moluccas. During the seventeenth century, while the Spaniards held their ground in the Philippines, the Dutch expelled the Portuguese from their dispersed and precarious footholds in Indonesia, with the sole exception of eastern Timor,[2] and, concentrating primarily on Java, began to promote the cultivation of a wider range of tropical produce than the cloves and nutmegs which had attracted their predecessors. Nevertheless, Dutch policy remained rigidly monopolistic, and it was not until the nineteenth century that the spectacular economic developments began which were to turn Malaysia into the world's leading producer of many of the most important tropical commodities.

Of the many factors which contributed to bring about this transformation the breaking of the Dutch monopoly by the establishment of the free British port of Singapore in 1819 and the revolutionary reduction in the effective distance from Europe resulting from the opening of the Suez Canal fifty years later deserve particular mention. In fact, however, the revival[3] of British activity in South-east Asia had begun in 1786 with the founding of Penang, and was subsequently directed more to safeguarding the passage of China-bound ships through the Straits of Malacca than to any very strong interest in Malaysia itself. Nevertheless the Anglo-Dutch treaty of 1824, by which the Dutch surrendered Malacca in exchange for British renunciation of interests in the islands south of the latitude of Singapore, paved the way for the gradual extension of British control over both the Malay peninsula and the northern third of Borneo.

Virtually from the outset Singapore, thanks to both its superb geographical position and the liberal policies introduced by its founder, Stamford Raffles, became a flourishing centre of entrepôt trade, much of which it obtained at the expense of Batavia. Moreover, the deliberate encouragement given by Raffles to Chinese and Indian immigrants was a principal factor in establishing in the Straits Settlements a multi-racial pattern of society which has since become almost equally characteristic of British Malaya as a whole.

In contrast to this, both Java and the Philippines, although they had

---

[2] Eastern Timor remains Portuguese to-day.
[3] English activity in Indonesia had languished after the "Massacre of Amboina" (1623), though in the eighteenth century factories were maintained at Benkoelen, Natal, and Tapanoeli on the western coast of Sumatra.

been the scenes of continuing Chinese settlement since the earliest days of European colonization, did not experience so great an influx during the nineteenth century. However, considerable Chinese immigration did accompany the extension of more effective Dutch control over many parts of the outer territories,[4] especially in the closing decades of the nineteenth century when the colonial forward movement was gaining momentum throughout South-east Asia. Particularly important was the decision to open up an entirely new area of estate cultivation in the more accessible coastlands of North-eastern Sumatra. For by 1870 little further land was available for new plantations in Java, and, though the latter long remained the primary centre of commercial cultivation, it had by the 1930's been outstripped by the Sumatran *Cultuurgebied*.

While rapid economic advances were thus under way on both sides of the Straits of Malacca, an equally momentous change took place at the opposite extremity of Malaysia when, in 1898, owing to the war with Spain, the Philippines passed under the control of the United States. Behind this radical innovation in American policy economic considerations were of minor importance compared with the desire to exclude other more aggressive nations from this crumbling but potentially significant outpost of Spanish power. For this reason, and in keeping with the anti-colonial tradition at home, the United States strove thereafter to promote efficient self-government within the shortest possible time.[5] On the other hand, however, the comparative lack of American interest in the economic exploitation of the Philippines was largely responsible for the islands' remaining a region of inefficient peasant production, whose low-value export crops, notably copra, sugar, and abaca, could never have competed with those from other parts of South-east Asia but for the inclusion of the territory within the United States' tariff wall after 1909.

As a result of this new political alignment the proportion of Philippine exports consigned to the United States rose from 26 per cent. in 1899 to 80 per cent. in 1941.[6] But although such a percentage greatly exceeded that of other parts of South-east Asia, a similar trend was discernible between the two world wars in the orientation of both British

[4] The term 'outer territories' has never had any strict political or administrative significance, but has been widely used to denote all the islands of Indonesia exclusive of Java and Madoera.

[5] There has nevertheless been considerable difference of opinion as to how short this should be, and Republican administrations in general have favoured a more cautious policy than that of the Democrats.

[6] Meanwhile the total annual value of external trade rose from 34 million dollars to 297 million dollars.

Malayan and Netherlands Indies' exports. For, notwithstanding their different imperial affiliations, both of these immensely productive dependencies found by far the largest single market for their principal exports in the United States. Thus there grew up a triangular pattern of trade which was extremely valuable to the metropolitan countries involved in helping to balance their trading accounts with the United States. Malaya, in short, became "the Empire's dollar arsenal" and the Indies the tail which wagged the Dutch dog with a truly transatlantic vigour.

Not surprisingly this situation exerted a compelling fascination on the Japanese, with their acute shortages of raw materials and their precarious dependence on silk exports to pay for vital purchases of American cotton. It is, therefore, at least in part against this background that both the Japanese trade offensive during the early 1930's and the subsequent invasion of the Nan Yo[7] should be seen. Moreover, although the Greater East Asia Co-prosperity Sphere did not survive the crushing defeat of Japan in August 1945, the effect of this remarkable interlude on the political and economic life of Malaysia has been profound. Some of the main outlines of the new patterns which are now gradually emerging from the chaos of recent years will be considered in the following pages.

The Republic of Indonesia

Of all the States in South-east Asia, Indonesia is by far the largest and the most diverse. Both in geographical extent and in the size of the population (c. eighty-two million) inhabiting over 2000 islands, Indonesia almost equals the whole of mainland South-east Asia. Moreover, in Java and Sumatra it contains the two major cultural foci of the Malaysian world of which to-day it forms the main component.

By comparison with Sumatra, the smaller and more compact island of Java, thanks mainly to its high fertility, its central position, and the absence of extensive coastal swamps, has in the long run proved to be the more favourably endowed as a base for controlling the archipelago. This function it fulfilled for the first time under Madjapahit (A.D. 1292–1500), a Hindu empire of great brilliance which, from its nucleus in east-central Java, succeeded in the fourteenth century in extending its sway

[7] Literally 'southern seas,' the traditional Japanese name for South-east Asia. Cf. Chinese Nan Yang, Chapter XXIV.

over an area remarkably similar to that of the Netherlands Indies in more recent times.[8] Thus, although under the impact of Islam and the coming of the Portuguese this pattern disappeared for a time, to be replaced by a mosaic of lesser succession states, the Dutch decision in 1619 to make Jakarta (renamed Batavia) their East Indian headquarters re-established the primacy of Java within the archipelago.

Indeed, because of the much longer connexion of the Dutch with Java than with all but a few scattered posts in the outer territories, this pre-eminence became still further emphasized. With the suppression of local warfare[9] and, later, the spread of sanitation and hygiene, the rapid increase of population in Java began nearly a century before comparable developments in other parts of the archipelago. Accordingly, from only three and a half million in 1795, Java's population rose to c. fifty-three million in 1954, and although the rate of growth in the outer islands as a whole now exceeds that in Java, their total population is still under thirty million. The resultant contrast in density between Java, with the phenomenal figure of 1039 to the square mile, and the remainder, whose average is only fifty-five, is the most striking fact in the complex human geography of Indonesia to-day.

Nevertheless, while, area for area, Java is undoubtedly the most productive of all the major Indonesian islands, the present distribution of population within the archipelago gives a far from accurate measure of the relative potentialities of its component parts. Thus, for example, although the cost of clearing the jungles and draining the swamps of the great peripheral lowlands of Borneo and eastern Sumatra would be enormous, many of these areas if suitably reclaimed could certainly support several times their present population.

So far as commercial cultivation is concerned, however, a relatively small proportion of the total arable area—namely, 2,604,000 acres of estate land in Java, and a further 3,476,000 in the outer islands— sufficed before the war to produce some 64 per cent. of the country's agricultural exports, the remainder coming from Indonesian small holdings, mostly in the outer territories. Yet, all-told, the Netherland Indies exported over 40 per cent. of the world's rubber and palm oil, 30 per cent. of its copra, and 90 per cent. of its cinchona, as well as

[8] There is, however, considerable doubt regarding the precise limits of Madjapahit's influence.

[9] It has been argued that the Culture System was also an important contributory factor in Java. See E. H. G. Dobby: "Some Aspects of the Human Ecology of Southeast Asia," in *Geographical Journal*, vol. cviii, Nos. 1–3 (July–September 1946), p. 44.

large quantities of coffee, sugar,[10] kapok, and spices. Second only to rubber in value, moreover, was the Indies export of petroleum (65 per cent. of it from Sumatra, 20 per cent. from Borneo, and 10 per cent from Java), and this in turn was followed by tin, which was worked in the three small islands of Banka, Billiton, and Singkep on the Sunda Shelf.

During the 350 years of their rule the Dutch made many changes in their colonial policy, though, in spite of the dissolution of the East India Company in 1798, the habit of viewing the Indies as a *bedrijf* (a business concern) never entirely disappeared. Thus, notwithstanding the attempt under the "Ethnical Policy" of 1902 to make amends for the excesses of past exploitation by means of a host of measures designed to promote native welfare, the economic dependence of the mother country on the profits drawn from the Indies proved a decisive obstacle to the adoption of policies aiming at eventual self-government.

On the contrary, the avowed basis of Dutch colonial rule in modern times was the promotion of a "synthesis between east and west." But, in striving to realize this somewhat grandiose ideal, the Dutch underestimated the strength of the antagonism it aroused among politically conscious Indonesians and, for the most part, neglected the more obvious task of promoting unity among the diverse peoples of the archipelago. Although, therefore, thanks to the high standards maintained by the Dutch civil administration and the excellent shipping services of the K.P.M. (Koninklijke Paketvaart Maatschappij), which linked the outlying islands to Java, the government of this vast region was unsurpassed in its efficiency by that of any other tropical dependency, the deeper problems still remained unsolved at the time of the Japanese invasion.

During the period of the occupation which followed, however, the Dutch Government in London seriously re-examined its colonial policy and elaborated plans for a drastic refashioning of the whole imperial structure. To provide full opportunities for local self-government a federal commonwealth was to be established, in which the Indies, as one of the constituent units, would, in turn, be reorganized on a federal basis. But before these plans could be put into effect the proclamation of the Indonesian Republic in Java on August 17, 1945, had unleashed forces which could not be arrested by such measures. Nevertheless it

[10] Before the slump in 1929 sugar was the country's leading export; this is unlikely to recur.

was not until December 27, 1949, by which time the Dutch had succeeded in setting up fifteen new states in the areas outside effective
Republican control, that the pressure of world opinion compelled them
to relinquish sovereignty over the whole of Indonesia with the exception
of western New Guinea.[11]

By the terms of the 1949 agreement a new federal republic, the United
States of Indonesia, was established, consisting of the sixteen states then
in being, and this was loosely linked to the metropolitan Power by
means of a Netherlands-Indonesian Union under the titular headship of
the Dutch monarch.[12] However, following the almost immediate outbreak of revolts in several parts of the archipelago, the new Government
announced on August 15, 1950, that the federal form of the State had
been abolished in favour of a new unitary structure, and that the name
had accordingly been changed to the Republic of Indonesia.[13] (See
Fig. 2.)

Thus, virtually from its inception, the new Indonesian State was
brought face to face with the decisive problem of how to maintain
national unity in this area of intense geographical fragmentation and
almost unparalleled ethnic diversity. While, so far as physical communications are concerned, recent developments in air transport have
already done much to offset the partial breakdown of inter-insular
traffic caused by wartime shipping losses, the more intangible human
problems still remain acute.

While some 90 per cent. of the indigenous population of Indonesia are
of the same basic Malay stock,[14] very considerable cultural differences
exist among them, which relate directly to the great distances and
natural barriers to movement between the several parts of the archipelago.[15] Thus over a dozen quite distinct—though related—languages
are current among the so-called Malay peoples alone, while in the deep

[11] Dutch insistence on retaining control over western New Guinea nearly wrecked the
Round Table Conference, and only the suggestion of the United Nations observers that
settlement of this question should be deferred for a year permitted agreement to be
reached on the other points. In 1955 the Dutch still held western New Guinea (Irian)
and the Indonesians continued to claim it.

[12] This arrangement was modelled on the formula adopted to preserve India's link
with the British Commonwealth; there were, therefore, no qualifications to Indonesia's
sovereignty.

[13] Owing to the widespread unrest both before and after the transfer of sovereignty
it was not until the autumn of 1955 that the first general elections were held. In the
meantime no formal constitution has been adopted.

[14] This very imprecise term is usually taken to include all descendants of either the
Proto- or Neo-Malays, who probably entered the archipelago between 1500 and 2000 B.C.

[15] In general the forested mountainous interiors of the islands proved the most serious
obstacles to movement. Indonesia is essentially an area in which "the land divides but
the sea unites."

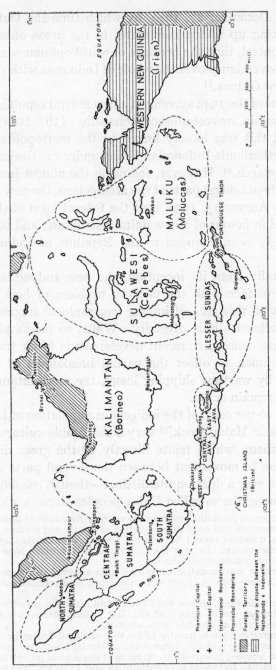

FIG. 2. INDONESIA: ADMINISTRATIVE DIVISIONS

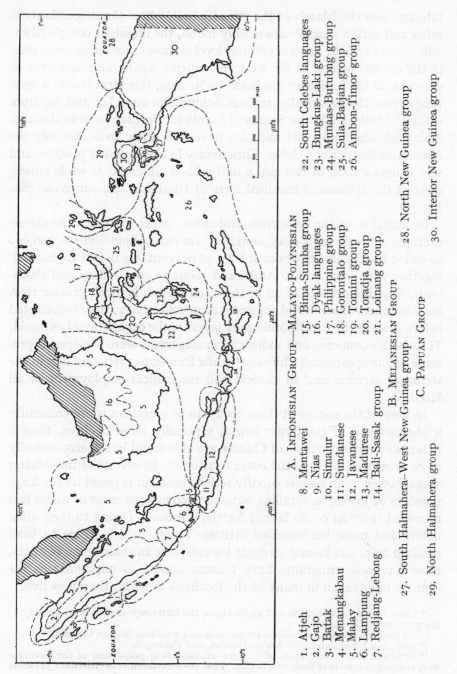

A. INDONESIAN GROUP—MALAYO-POLYNESIAN

1. Atjeh
2. Gajo
3. Batak
4. Menangkabau
5. Malay
6. Lampung
7. Redjang-Lebong
8. Mentawei
9. Nias
10. Simalur
11. Sundanese
12. Javanese
13. Madurese
14. Bali-Sasak group
15. Bima-Sumba group
16. Dyak languages
17. Philippine group
18. Gorontalo group
19. Tomini group
20. Toradja group
21. Loinang group
22. South Celebes languages
23. Bungkus-Laki group
24. Munaas-Butubng group
25. Sula-Batjan group
26. Ambon-Timor group

B. MELANESIAN GROUP

27. South Halmahera—West New Guinea group
28. North New Guinea group
29. North Halmahera group

C. PAPUAN GROUP

30. Interior New Guinea group

FIG. 3. INDONESIA: MAIN LANGUAGES

interiors and the islands of the remoter east, where the descendants of other and earlier stocks[16] are mainly found, the linguistic complexity is still greater and the general cultural level in most cases much lower than in the coastal regions of the west and centre. Again, although over 90 per cent. of the indigenes are listed as Moslem, this term covers a wide range from the fanatically zealous Achinese to such lax and far from orthodox believers as the Sasaks of Lombok. Further, both in the non-Malay islands of the east and also in several other areas, notably the Minahassa district of Celebes, Christianity has made great progress and now claims a total of two and a half million adherents,[17] while among most of the Balinese a modified form of Hinduism still survives. (See Fig. 3.)

In addition to the indigenes, Indonesia, which provides the classic example of the plural society, contains over two million Chinese, 250,000 so-called Europeans (of whom at least 70 per cent. are in fact Eurasians), together with some 70,000 Arabs and about 30,000 Indians and Pakistanis. The importance of all of these, moreover, is much greater than mere numbers alone would suggest, since, collectively, they constituted before the war the middle and upper layers of the occupational pyramid. Thus both commerce and industrial management were the special preserve of Europeans and Chinese,[18] while Eurasians predominated in the technical services and in clerical and mechanical employment of all kinds.

In view of the nature of these occupations pluralism is pre-eminently a phenomenon of the larger towns, especially those of Java, though important concentrations of Chinese are also found in the economically more developed parts of the outer territories. In several of these latter areas, however, an almost equally serious problem is posed by the large numbers of Javanese, totalling some 825,000 in 1930, most of whom had migrated there as coolie labour for the estates.[19] Owing to their alien habits and more hard-headed attitude to life, which seems to have resulted from the keener struggle for existence in their home districts, these Javanese emigrants have become almost as unpopular as the Chinese middlemen in many of the localities in which they now live.

[16] These include both negrito and negro types, the latter represented most notably by the present-day Papuans.

[17] All told, there are c. 1½ million Protestants and 1 million Roman Catholics.

[18] And, to a lesser extent, of Arabs, Indians, and Pakistanis.

[19] Although many were birds of passage, an increasing proportion of the Javanese were tending to remain in their new homes. Thus the total number of citizens of Javanese ancestry in the outer territories in 1930 was 1,150,000.

Clearly the task of forging a nation out of this extremely hetero-geneous material will not be easy, as, indeed, can already be seen from the lack of enthusiasm with which the Chinese and Eurasian com-munities have so far responded to the Government's offer of a common citizenship. Nevertheless, although their feelings are understandable, the Eurasians at least would be well advised to accept the prospect of assimilation, for while their skills should guarantee them a place in the new Indonesia, few opportunities are available elsewhere. The Chinese, on the other hand, present a more difficult problem, owing to their larger numbers and to their possible alternative loyalty,[20] though in Indonesia, unlike Siam and Malaya, they are only a small fraction of the total population (under 3 per cent.), which may appear reassuring.

As yet, however, the task of assimilating the non-Indonesian com-munities is proving less intractable than the problem of winning the allegiance of several of the 'national' minorities. In 1954 there were four main centres of active disaffection—namely, Achin, Pasundan (West Java), southern Celebes, and Ceram. Except for the last, where the largely Christian supporters of the "Republic of the South Moluc-cas," first proclaimed in April 1950, continue to resist the unitary policy of the Jakarta Government, all are centres of the fanatical and re-actionary Moslem movement, Darul Islam, which aims at establishing a theocratic State. But in all these areas resentment over excessive centralization in Jakarta and the employment of Javanese in preference to local officials further contributes to the present unrest, and the feeling is strong in many parts of the archipelago that the Central Government is bent on solving the problems of Java at the expense of the outlying territories.

This complaint is not unfounded. Indeed, when it is recalled that Java contains nearly two-thirds of the total population and that for several decades now, as a result of growing pressure on limited land, its standard of living has been declining, both absolutely and still more relatively to the outer territories, it would be naïve to assume that an Indonesian Government centred in Java could be wholly indifferent to such a solution.

The dangers inherent in the chronic unbalance between Java and the outer territories were foreseen many years ago by the Dutch, and before the war the problem was already being tackled in three main ways.

[20] Strictly speaking, there are now two such foci—*viz.*, Communist China and Formosa. See Chapter XXIV. By 1954 800,000 Chinese had adopted Indonesian nationality, but it was not until April 1955 that Communist China agreed to this procedure. See p. 592.

These included attempts at increasing food production in Java itself, an ambitious scheme of 'transmigration'—*i.e.*, resettling Javanese peasant cultivators in various pioneer tracts in Sumatra, Celebes, and Borneo—and, finally, extensive plans for developing factory and cottage industries in many parts of Java.

Notwithstanding certain minor changes of emphasis the same three approaches have in recent years been adopted by the Indonesians. So far as increased food production in Java is concerned, the main hope now lies in the use of more fertilizer and improved farming techniques, for, with virtually two-thirds of this mountainous island under cultivation and nearly half of it double-cropped, the limits in acreage appear to have been reached.[21]

Transmigration is now receiving much attention, and although under the Dutch the highest number of colonists moved in one year was 52,855 (in 1940), it was announced in 1953 that 500,000 persons from Java would be resettled, mainly in Sumatra, during the next five years, at a cost of 2000 million rupiah.[22] Whether, in fact, this goal can really be achieved remains to be seen, though a study of Pelzer's detailed analysis of the pre-war scheme is bound to raise doubts.[23] The number resettled in the first half of 1952 was 17,000, while the current population growth in Java is about 800,000 a year.

As outlined in the Sumitro Plan, the Indonesian Government's industrialization policy also does not differ radically from that of the Dutch, though a new motive is now present in the desire to remove the basis for the stigma which the term 'under-developed' is, rightly or wrongly, held to imply. While the Government proposes to establish several large factories for processing locally grown raw materials in various parts of the outer territories, notably in Sumatra and Borneo (rubber and petroleum), and Minahassa (copra), the major emphasis is still on Java, which is the obvious location for both large- and small-scale manufacture of consumer goods.[24]

This policy seems economically sound, for the most effective way of mopping up the concealed unemployment of the Javanese countryside is to develop the island still further as the manufacturing and managerial

[21] Some 23 per cent. of the total area of Java is State forest land. Any reduction of this would almost certainly lead to accelerated soil erosion.
[22] The current rate of exchange is 11·40 rupiah = 1 U.S. dollar.
[23] Karl J. Pelzer, *Pioneer Settlement in the Asiatic Tropics* (A.G.S., New York, 1945), pp. 185–231.
[24] The main factory industries so far developed are cotton textiles, tyres, soap and margarine, footwear, and glass bottles. Handicraft industries include *batik*, weaving, pottery, cigarettes, hats, and furniture.

nucleus of the archipelago. But to do this will nevertheless give rise to many difficulties. Already the urban population of Java is estimated to have more than doubled since the war, partly as the result of recent and continuing insecurity in many rural districts, but also owing to the proliferation of clerical and administrative jobs under the new regime.

Clearly this growth in the urban population must impose a new burden on the overstrained resources of the countryside, while at the same time to carry out the various projects already described will make heavy demands on the limited funds which the State has at its disposal. Meanwhile, although population has increased by at least 15 per cent., export production as a whole has barely regained the pre-war level. In this regard the Government's desire to avoid undue dependence on the vagaries of the export market for primary produce by establishing a more nearly self-contained economy, though understandable, is of doubtful wisdom at the present time. Similarly, the associated preference for peasant rather than estate production of such a highly competitive commodity as rubber may defeat its purpose unless greater care is taken to raise the quality of the output.

In any case, however, no serious prospect exists for maintaining, let alone raising, the living standards of Indonesia without considerable outside assistance of one kind or another. Yet to the Indonesians to-day foreign capital is almost pathologically suspect as the symbol of colonialism, and the anxieties caused by the preponderant share of the Dutch in the investments remaining in the country have been a major factor in bringing about the dissolution of the Netherlands-Indonesian Union in 1954–56.[25] Likewise, the mere suspicion of American interference with Indonesia's neutralist foreign policy led to the rejection of M.S.A. assistance in 1952, though an extension of aid under the Technical Assistance Program (Point Four) was subsequently accepted, and early in 1953 Indonesia agreed to participate as a full member of the Colombo Plan. Short of a major revolution in foreign policy, however, it will be most unlikely to align itself with the S.E.A.T.O. Powers.

In view of these many complexities in its attitude towards the outside world, the question is bound to arise as to what the aim of the present regime really is and on what foundations Indonesian nationhood is supposed to rest. For the moment, at least, religion has been officially

[25] In 1954 the Dutch controlled over 60 per cent. of production for export and ran practically all the shipping between the islands. In these circumstances many Indonesians have felt that colonialism was still not eliminated and the continued presence of the Dutch in western New Guinea has been a further irritant.

rejected as the primary integrating force, for, notwithstanding the attraction of becoming the largest Moslem State in the world,[26] the need to win the loyalties of key minority groups is clearly a more critical matter. Similarly, linguistic unity still remains a dream, though considerable success has already attended the efforts to promote *Bahasa Indonesia*, a modified form of Malay, as the national language. In the meantime, also, great play is made of historical and cultural arguments, and the garuda bird, the symbol of Madjapahit, has been adopted as the national emblem.

Nevertheless, if cultural unity be accepted as the criterion of Indonesian nationality the claim to western New Guinea and, indeed, to the dissident "Republic of the South Moluccas" can hardly be sustained. On the other hand, the cultural argument has been advanced by supporters of Indonesia Raya (Greater Indonesia) as the basis for seeking to incorporate British Malaysia, Portuguese Timor, and possibly even the Philippines within the Indonesian fold.

Obviously such a programme lies beyond the present bounds of practical politics, and the only official statements on Indonesia's territorial aspirations have been more restrained. Thus, for example, ". . . the territory which the Indonesian People claim its own is exactly the same territory not more and not less as the territory which formerly . . . was called the Netherland-Indies territory."[27] While the immediate purpose of this declaration was to substantiate Indonesia's claim to western New Guinea, a vast and almost completely undeveloped area, which ethnically and geographically belongs more to the South-west Pacific than to South-east Asia,[28] it nevertheless reveals only too clearly the great paradox inherent in contemporary Asian nationalism. Thus, despite all protests to the contrary, the real force which has hitherto united the Republic has been simply a common opposition to Dutch colonial rule. Yet in almost every outward respect the new State is cast in essentially the same mould as its predecessor. The territories which it claims are identical in extent, Batavia—renamed Jakarta—has been chosen as capital despite the sentimental appeal of Jogjakarta, and the major administrative divisions are no longer the sixteen federal states

---

[26] At present Pakistan claims that position, but Indonesia, though a secular State, has both a higher percentage and a greater total number of Moslems.

[27] *Report of the Committee on New Guinea (Irian), 1950* (The Hague, August, 1950), Part III (Indonesian Constituent Report), p. 30.

[28] For a fuller discussion of the New Guinea problem, see C. A. Fisher, "West New Guinea in its Regional Setting," in *The Year Book of World Affairs* (Stevens, London, 1952), pp. 189–210.

of 1950, but instead a series of ten provinces whose boundaries immediately recall those of the pre-war Dutch units and almost completely ignore all indigenous linguistic and historical units.

Admittedly these points in themselves do not necessarily constitute an indictment of the new regime, and in certain respects might even be cited as evidence of a sense of political realism. Nevertheless the fact remains that Indonesia has so far given little indication of ability to replace an outmoded anti-colonialism with any more positive philosophy.

Already the consequences of this weakness are becoming increasingly apparent in the internal affairs of the nation, and the threat of disintegration is unmistakable. Moreover, in view of the immense strategic importance of this vital portion of the island rim of Asia and of the temptations which the underpopulated portions of its outlying territories afford to more powerful but overcrowded neighbours, the problem is one of far more than local concern, as Australia in particular is keenly aware.

Yet, given vision and a willingness to accept help which friendly nations would readily extend, the problems are not insoluble. The fabulous wealth of the Indies, which lured the early explorers half-way round the globe, was not entirely a figment of the imagination, and, with the techniques of the twentieth century at its command, Indonesia could well provide a worthy livelihood for all its peoples.

British Malaysia

Although considerably smaller and more compact than the former Netherlands Indies, the British territories in Malaysia have never been administered as one unit, and, indeed, before the second world war their administrative pattern was almost ludicrously complex. (See Fig. 4.)

To begin with, the Crown Colony of the Straits Settlements included, besides the two great insular ports of Singapore and Penang, both Malacca and Province Wellesley on the Malayan mainland and the small island of Labuan off the coast of northern Borneo.[29] Both in its geographical layout and in the overriding importance of the entrepôt trade of its ports, the Straits Settlements constituted a perfect example of the type of sea-state which flourished under the ægis of the nineteenth-century *pax Britannica*, and its predominantly immigrant population

---

[29] For administrative convenience the Cocos-Keeling Islands and Christmas Island were also placed under the Straits Settlements.

(mainly Chinese, Malaysian, and Indian) had been drawn from all parts
of the vast trading region of which it formed the cross-roads. This latter
function was epitomized above all by Singapore, which, moreover, be-

FIG. 4. BRITISH MALAYA: POLITICAL DIVISIONS

tween the two world wars gained an enhanced significance from the
great naval base established there to protect both the Indian Ocean and
Australia against Japanese attack.[30]

[30] The defeat of Singapore during the second world war was made inevitable by the
collapse of French Indo-China and the priority that had to be given to supplying other

More recent in origin, but already of even greater economic importance, were the Federated Malay States, a union, dating from 1896, of
four British-protected sultanates—Perak, Selangor, Negri Sembilan, and
Pahang—with its capital at Kuala Lumpur. In contrast to the Colony,
whose life blood was commerce, the F.M.S., or, more precisely, its
western seaboard, was pre-eminently an area of primary production,
which had in turn led the world in the export of both tin and rubber.
But owing to the reluctance of the indigenes to work as wage labourers
the federation had attracted almost as mixed a population as the
Straits Settlements, and Chinese and Indians together far outnumbered
Malays.

During the early years of the twentieth century, when the phenomenal
boom in rubber suggested that the demand for further land for estates
would be insatiable, British protection was extended over the remaining
sultanates[31] in the peninsula. But, as subsequent experience revealed
that the western third of the country was capable of producing all the
rubber that the available markets could absorb, these unfederated
States, with the exception of Johore, were not seriously infiltrated by
commercialism and their population remained overwhelmingly Malay.

A comparable situation existed in northern Borneo. For although
British protection had been extended in 1888 over Sarawak (the territory ruled by the descendants of the first British Rajah, James Brooke),
over the extensive lands administered by the British North Borneo
Company, and also over what remained of the sultanate of Brunei, the
economic development of all these lagged far behind that of the highly
organized states of western Malaya,[32] and politically each remained a
separate entity.

After the second world war British policy towards the region changed
significantly, and, beginning in 1946, a series of measures was introduced with the twin aims of rationalizing the political structure and
preparing the way for the granting of self-government.

Nevertheless, there are many obstacles to the fulfilment of such
policies. Thus, for example, the disparate economic development of the
component regions is reflected in differences in both standards of living

---

more immediately critical theatres. Singapore, which is now the headquarters of the
British Far Eastern fleet, will remain of the utmost value so long as adequate forces
are available to defend the Malay peninsula.

[31] Kedah, Perlis, Kelantan, and Trengganu were acquired from Siam in 1909, and the
position of Johore, which had enjoyed a unique status since 1885, was regularized in 1914.

[32] The only economic development of any real importance was the oil industry of
Miri in Sarawak.

and political advancement. In particular, western Malaya has an exceedingly complex economy, based on the specialized production of tin and rubber, which have brought great profit to the country[33] and are responsible for its having a standard of living well above the average for South-east Asia. At the same time, however, the former British policy of guaranteeing the economic survival of the Malays by reserving most of the very limited paddy lands for their exclusive use has helped to bring about the present dependence of the peninsula on foreign sources for nearly two-thirds of its rice. For this reason, and in view of the wide fluctuations in the market price of its principal exports,[34] Malaya's comparative prosperity is precariously based. The Borneo territories, on the other hand, have witnessed no such economic development, apart from oil production, which has been relatively localized and is now mainly concentrated in Brunei, and accordingly their peoples remain much more closely attached to traditional and essentially self-sufficient ways of life.

Partly because of this retarded development of Borneo, and partly because its indigenous peoples, though related, are by no means identical with the peninsular Malays, the steps which the British Colonial Office has taken towards simplifying the political pattern of the area as a whole have hitherto stopped short of complete unification. So far as Borneo is concerned, both Sarawak and the Chartered Company's territory were constituted Crown Colonies in 1946, and at the same time Labuan was incorporated in North Borneo. These changes, together with the subsequent decision in May 1948 to make the Governor of Sarawak the *ex officio* High Commissioner for Brunei, were all symptomatic of the post-war trend towards closer regional association in the British dependent empire, and all were effected without serious difficulty.

The application of the same principle to Malaya, however, has been an altogether more formidable task. For there the degree of political sophistication and contact with the outside world is sufficient to create a demand for self-government, but at the same time, the stage has now been reached when, in the country as a whole, the Chinese have become the most numerous single ethnic group. Moreover, whereas before the war communal rivalries were never acute, latent animosities were exacerbated by the Japanese interregnum, with the result that in recent

---

[33] Great profits have also been taken out of the country, especially by British and Chinese, but even so enormous sums have been spent for the benefit of the country as a whole.

[34] In the case of rubber the competition of synthetics is particularly disturbing.

years communalism has emerged as a political issue of transcendental importance.

British post-war plans for Malayan unification have, therefore, at least for the time being, excluded Singapore from their terms of reference in the hope that, by subtracting some 730,000 Chinese from the total, the fears of the Malays of being politically swamped in their own country might be allayed. Nevertheless this anxiety survived the establishment of Singapore as a separate Crown Colony[35] and the amalgamation of the remaining territories in the Malayan Union of 1946, and, accordingly, in 1948 the British Government replaced the Union by the Federation of Malaya. The new arrangement, though retaining the territorial pattern of the Union, with nine component states, two settlements, and Kuala Lumpur as the capital, greatly increased the powers of the Malay sultanates and severely curtailed the numbers of Chinese and Indians eligible for citizenship.

Since then, however, the serious outbreak of terrorism by the predominantly Chinese Communists has served to emphasize the fact that any solution to Malaya's problems must take into account the interests of all communities and not merely those of the Malays alone. Thus the British have gradually prevailed upon the latter both to broaden the basis of citizenship[36] and to accept a much more extensive participation by non-Malays in subsistence farming than was ever contemplated in the past.[37] Finally, the declaration of the British Colonial Secretary, Mr Lyttelton, that self-government would be granted as soon as intercommunal co-operation had become a reality has led the United Malay Nationalist Organization, the Malayan Chinese Association, and the Malayan Indian Congress to form an alliance which won an overwhelming victory in the first elections (1955) for the new legislature.[38]

This fact, combined with the notable decline of terrorism since 1952,

[35] The declared reason for this special treatment was that Singapore "is a centre of entrepôt trade on a very large scale and has economic and social interests distinct from those of the mainland."—*Malayan Union and Singapore: Statement of Policy on Future Constitution* (Cmd. 6724, 1946), p. 3, para. 5. Since that time Singapore has remained apart.

[36] It was estimated by the High Commissioner in November 1952 that nearly 60 per cent. of the Chinese community, and about 35 per cent. of the Indians were eligible for citizenship. All Malays are automatically eligible.

[37] This has been largely the result of the Government's scheme for resettling some 500,000 squatters (mainly Chinese) many of whom were supplying the terrorists with food.

[38] The new Legislative Council contains fifty-two elected and forty-six nominated members.

suggests that the time is fast approaching when a complete transference of sovereignty should be made. For, as experience elsewhere has shown, it is only by anticipating the legitimate political aspirations of the colonial peoples that the metropolitan Powers can hope to preserve a basis for mutual co-operation in future. That such a relationship, preferably within the resilient framework of the Commonwealth, is desirable from the British standpoint is self-evident in view of the strategic significance of the country and the dollar-earning capacities of Malayan produce. Equally, so far as Malaya is concerned, the added security and opportunities which this arrangement should afford would seem to constitute sound arguments in its favour.

Before any final steps are taken and new patterns begin to solidify, however, it would surely be wise to develop a closer association between Malaya, Singapore, and the British Borneo territories. Northern Borneo, with its important reserves of petroleum and timber, and its not inconsiderable potentialities for food production, would add a welcome measure of diversity to the hitherto overspecialized economy of the peninsula. Further, the inclusion of the Borneo indigenes would help psychologically to assuage the Malays' fears of Chinese numerical predominance, while cosmopolitan Singapore would come into its own as a ready-made federal capital for the larger unit. And finally, so long as Indonesia persists in its neutralism, a closer knitting together of British Malaysia could contribute much towards closing the gap between the Pacific and Indian Ocean defence systems which at present appears so critical for the security of the free world.

The Republic of the Philippines

The political geography of the Philippines has undergone fewer and less spectacular changes in recent years than that of the other Malaysian lands considered in this chapter. With the coming into force of the Commonwealth Constitution in 1935 the country was already well on the way to independence and this fact goes far to explain its stubborn resistance to the Japanese attack in 1941–42. But although among the last to be defeated and the first to be reconquered of all the South-east Asian territories, the Philippines nevertheless suffered in proportion to their area the greatest material devastation of all. Particularly serious in this respect were the damage to mines and processing machinery and the almost complete loss of the excellent inter-island shipping fleet of some 160 vessels.[39]

Thanks to speedy and lavish United States' assistance, the work of rehabilitation is now far advanced, though per capita production as a whole in 1953 still fell short of the 1937 level. More important, however, has been the final fruition of United States' policy towards the Philippines marked by the proclamation of the Republic on July 4, 1946. By the terms of the Executive Arrangement then concluded, the United States retains access to certain key bases in the islands, and the shock to the latters' economy caused by exclusion from the American free-trade area is being cushioned by means of a graduated scale of tariffs, beginning in 1954 at only 5 per cent. of the comparable figure for imports from Cuba and rising to 100 per cent. in 1973.[40]

Nevertheless, although these arrangements should facilitate readjustment to a more nearly self-sufficient economy, the process is likely to be difficult. For, even apart from the destruction and dislocation caused by the war, the Philippine economy has long faced many acute problems. As in Indonesia (and many other parts of Monsoon Asia), the fundamental difficulty is that of maldistribution of population. Thus, although it is estimated that the islands could support three times their present population of c. 21 million, many agricultural areas—e.g., in Cebu and central Luzon—have densities of over 600 to the square mile, while others, not strikingly inferior, are altogether more sparsely peopled—e.g., Mindanao, 110.[41] But in contrast to other parts of Southeast Asia this basic problem is greatly complicated here by a pattern of land ownership derived from the Spanish colonial regime and resulting in an unusually high proportion of tenancy.[42]

These factors together have served to produce in the more congested parts of the country a combination of poverty, inefficiency, indebtedness, and despair which, as the Hukbalahap[43] movement has recently demonstrated, provides a fertile breeding ground for Communism. Moreover, although President Magsaysay has shown imagination in

[39] The importance of shipping can be judged from the fact that the Philippines number over 7000 islands, of which 740 are inhabited.

[40] An essentially similar reciprocal arrangement governs the admission of U.S. goods into the Philippines.

[41] Much lower densities occur in Palawan (average eighteen) and Mindoro (forty-one).

[42] Over 50 per cent. of all farms are tenant-operated in seven provinces, and in four the rate exceeds 60 per cent.

[43] This, like the terrorism in Malaya, is a legacy of the war-time anti-Japanese guerrilla movement. Unlike its Malayan counterpart, however, the Hukbalahap movement is not a predominantly Chinese affair.

Z

attacking the social roots of this political problem, a lasting solution will call for far more drastic agrarian reforms than have yet been introduced, and at the same time existing schemes for further transmigration[44] and industrialization will need to be implemented with the utmost vigour.

Notwithstanding the seriousness of their economic situation, the Philippines are far more favourably placed politically than most other parts of South-east Asia. Admittedly, real problems are posed by minority groups, notably the 650,000 Moslem Moros of Mindanao and Sulu, who have not always taken kindly to the assimilationist policies of Manila, and the 112,000 or so Chinese who, as elsewhere, control an utterly disproportionate share of the country's business and commerce. But, given the well-developed sense of national solidarity among the bulk of the 93 per cent. of the population who are described as "Christian Filipinos of Malay extraction," communalism is a far less serious issue than in most of the neighbouring lands.

Moreover, in comparison with nearly all other Asian peoples, the Filipinos have sustained only superficial spiritual wounds at the hands of the West. For, despite its many shortcomings, Spanish rule introduced a Christian culture without a colour bar, and the more recent phase under the Americans provided a thorough education—in English[45] —in the precepts of democracy. Thus the Filipinos as a nation are mentally much closer to the West than any other people in Monsoon Asia, and, almost alone in that realm, are capable of judging realistically the question of alignment versus neutralism in the cold war.

For this reason many observers, especially in the United States, look upon the Philippines to-day as the natural leader of South-east Asia. Such a role, moreover, is not without its appeal to certain Filipino politicians, as was shown a few years ago by General Romulo's scheme for a Pan-Malayan Union to embrace the Philippines, Indonesia, and Malaya.

Apart from the obvious objections to the latter proposal, however, it would seem that the measure of political leadership which the Philippines can exert in South-east Asia will remain relatively limited. For, as a result of its long-standing trans-Pacific affiliations, the country seems essentially alien to the rest of the region in which geographically

[44] See Karl J. Pelzer, *op. cit.*, pp. 81–159.
[45] In view of the multiplicity of dialects and the absence of any *lingua franca*, the United States from the outset made English the medium of instruction. To-day English is spoken by more Filipinos (4,428,709) than any other language, though Tagalog, the official national language, is a close second with 4,068,565.

it belongs, and so long as it remains culturally and politically an out-post of the Americas—whether English or Latin—it will never be accepted by its neighbours as truly Asian. But how long this alignment will prevail, in view of the impending relaxation of economic ties with the United States and the more obvious basis for mutual trade with Japan, remains to be seen.

Nevertheless, for the foreseeable future the sympathies of this vital component in the peripheral defensive bulwark of the western Pacific are not in doubt. And until the memory of past Japanese aggression and the possibility of further attack from the north have both disappeared there is every reason to assume that the Philippines will prefer the protection afforded by their treaty with the United States[46] to the precarious isolation which neutralism would entail. Such is the unmistakable import of the 1954 Manila Conference and of the participation of the Philippines as a founder member of S.E.A.T.O.

FURTHER READING

For books on South-east Asia as a whole, see list on pp. 646–647 above.

BOEKE, J. H., *Economics and Economic Policy of Dual Societies as exemplified by Indonesia* (New York, 1953).

BROEK, J. O. M., *The Economic Development of the Netherlands Indies* (I.P.R., New York, 1942).

EMERSON, RUPERT, *Malaysia: A Study in Direct and Indirect Rule* (Macmillan, New York, 1937).

FORBES, W. CAMERON, *The Philippine Islands* (Harvard University Press and Oxford University Press, 1945).

FURNIVALL, J. S., *Netherlands India* (Cambridge University Press, 1939); *Colonial Policy and Practice* (Cambridge University Press, 1948).

HAYDEN, J. R., *The Philippines* (Macmillan, New York, 1942).

JENKINS, SHIRLEY, *American Economic Policy towards the Philippines* (Stanford University Press and Oxford University Press, 1954).

JONES, S. W., *Public Administration in Malaya* (Royal Institute of International Affairs, London, 1953).

KAHIN, G. McT., *Nationalism and Revolution in Indonesia* (Ithaca, 1952).

KENNEDY, RAYMOND, *The Ageless Indies* (Day, New York, 1942).

KOLB, ALBERT, *Die Philippinen* (Leipzig, 1942).

MILLS, L. A., *British Rule in Eastern Asia* (Oxford University Press, 1942).

PELZER, K. J., *Pioneer Settlement in the Asiatic Tropics* (A.G.S., New York, 1945).

PURCELL, V., *Malaya: Outline of a Colony* (Nelson, London, 1946); *The Chinese in Malaya* (Oxford University Press, 1948); *Malaya: Communist or Free?* (Gollancz, London, 1954).

ROBEQUAIN, C., *Malaya, Indonesia, Borneo, and the Philippines* (Longmans, London, 1954).

[46] See above, p. 544.

SMITH, T. E., *Population Growth in Malaya* (Royal Institute of International Affairs, London, 1952).

SPENCER, JOSEPH E., *Land and People in the Philippines* (Berkeley, 1952).

VLEKKE, B. H. M., *Nusantara: A History of the East Indian Archipelago* (Harvard University Press, 1943).

WINSTEDT, R. O., *The Malays: A Short Cultural History* (Singapore, 1947); *Malaya and its History* (Hutchinson, London, 1948).

TABLE 1

Indonesia: Area and Population

DIVISIONS	AREA (*square miles*)	POPULATION (*millions*) (1954 *estimates*)	DENSITY PER SQUARE MILE
Java and Madura (three provinces—W., C., and E. Java) .	48,842	53	1,039
Sumatra (three provinces—N., C., and S.) . . .	187,600	13	69
Kalimantan (Borneo) . .	208,286	4	19
Sulawesi (Celebes) . . .	69,277	6	87
Maluku (Moluccas) . . .	32,307	1	31
Sunda Ketjil (Lesser Sundas) .	29,581	4	135
Total (without West New Guinea)	575,893	81	140
Irian (West New Guinea) .	159,375	1	6
Total (with West New Guinea) .	735,268	82	112

TABLE 2

Indonesia: Principal Towns

TOWN	ISLAND	POPULATION 1930 (*Census*)	POPULATION 1952 (*estimate*)
Jakarta (Batavia) .	Java	533,015	2,500,000
Surabaja . . .	,,	341,675	926,000
Bandung . . .	,,	166,815	724,000
Jogjakarta . . .	,,	136,649	500,000
Medan . . .	Sumatra	76,584	500,000
Malang . . .	Java	86,646	400,000
Surakarta . . .	,,	165,484	340,000
Semarang . . .	,,	217,796	335,000
Makassar . . .	Celebes	84,855	265,000
Palembang . . .	Sumatra	108,145	238,000
Banjermasin . .	Borneo	65,698	150,000

TABLE 3

Indonesia: Analysis of Overseas Trade, 1951

IMPORTS			
3060 million rupiah (805 million U.S. dollars; £287 million)			
COMMODITIES	PERCENTAGE	SOURCE	PERCENTAGE
Textiles . . .	27	U.S.A. . .	20
Food . . .	19	Japan . .	19
Base metals . . .	13	Netherlands .	12
Machinery . . .	13	U.K. . .	7
Transport equipment .	8	Hong Kong .	6
		Malaya . .	5
		India . .	3
		Burma . .	3
		Thailand .	3
		Australia .	1
EXPORTS			
4776 million rupiah (1257 million U.S. dollars; £449 million)			
COMMODITIES	PERCENTAGE	DESTINATION	PERCENTAGE
Rubber . . .	52	Malaya . .	33
Petroleum and products	13	Netherlands .	21
Copra . . .	10	U.S.A. . .	16
Tin and tin ore . .	6	U.K. . .	6
Tea . . .	3	Japan . .	3
		Australia .	2
		Philippines .	1

TABLE 4

Federation of Malaya and Singapore: Area and Population (1947 Census)

ETHNIC GROUP	FEDERATION	SINGAPORE	TOTAL
Malaysians . .	2,427,853	116,046	2,543,899
Chinese . . .	1,884,647	730,603	2,615,250
Indians . . .	535,092	73,496	608,588
Europeans . .	16,836	30,631	47,467
Eurasians . .	10,062	9,112	19,174
Others . . .	48,331	13,466	40,247
Total .	4,922,821	976,839	5,899,660
Area (square miles) .	50,690	224	50,914

TABLE 5

British Borneo: Area and Population (1947–51 Censuses)

ETHNIC GROUP	NORTH BORNEO (1951)	BRUNEI (1947)	SARAWAK (1947)	TOTAL (approximate)
Malaysians .	243,009	31,161	395,417	669,587
Chinese . .	74,374	8,300	145,158	227,832
Europeans .	1,213	394*	691	2,298
Others . .	15,545	802	5,119	21,466
Total .	334,141	40,657	546,385	921,183
Area (square miles) . .	29,387	2,226	47,071	78,684

TABLE 6

British Malaysia: Overseas Trade, 1951, in £ million

POLITICAL DIVISION	IMPORTS	EXPORTS
North Borneo . . .	8·2	14·3
Sarawak	44·8	59·3
Brunei	5·4	32·6
Malaya (including Singapore)	555·0	709·0
Total .	613·4	815·2

TABLE 7

Philippines: Cultural Diversity (data from 1939 Census)

RELIGION		LANGUAGE		DIALECT	
Roman Catholic	12,603,428	English	4,428,709	Visayan-Cebu	3,620,685
Aglipayan*	1,573,608	Tagalog	4,068,565	Iloko	2,263,297
Moslem	667,903	Spanish	415,888	Visayan-Panay	1,951,005
Pagan	626,008	Chinese	111,722	Bicol	1,287,197
Protestant	378,361	Japanese	27,450	Visayan-Samar	
Buddhist	47,852			Leyte	919,237
Shinto	13,861			Pampangan	639,571
Others	67,157			Pangasinan	574,609
				Visayan	388,634

Total population (1939) : 16,000,303 ; estimated total (1952): 21,120,000

* Independent Filipino Church

TABLE 8

Malaya (including Singapore): Analysis of Overseas Trade, 1951

IMPORTS £555 million (1554 million U.S. dollars)			
COMMODITIES	PERCENTAGE	SOURCE	PERCENTAGE
Raw materials . .	31	Indonesia .	30
Food	21	U.K. . .	16
Cotton manufactures .	8	Thailand .	8
Machinery . . .	6	Br. Borneo .	6
Metals . . .	4	Japan . .	5
Electrical goods . .	1	U.S.A. . .	5
		India . .	4
		China . .	3
		Australia .	3
		Hong Kong .	3

EXPORTS £709 million (1985 million U.S. dollars)			
COMMODITIES	PERCENTAGE	DESTINATION	PERCENTAGE
Rubber . . .	66	U.K. . .	20
Manufactured goods .	20	U.S.A. . .	20
Tin	9	Indonesia .	8
Food	5	Australia .	6
		Hong Kong .	4
		Japan . .	3
		Canada . .	3
		Br. Borneo .	2
		India . .	2
		China . .	2
		Thailand .	2

TABLE 9

Philippines: Principal Towns

TOWN	1939 CENSUS	1948 CENSUS
Manila . .	623,492	983,906
Cebu . .	146,817	167,503
Davao . .	95,564	111,263
Iloilo . .	90,480	110,122
Zamboanga .	131,455	103,317
Bacolod City .	57,474	101,432

TABLE 10
Philippines: Analysis of Overseas Trade, 1951

IMPORTS			
962·5 million pesos (481·25 million U.S. dollars; £171·8 million)			
COMMODITIES	PERCENTAGE	SOURCE	PERCENTAGE
Cottons . . .	15	U.S.A. . .	71
Grains, etc. . . .	9	Japan . .	7
Machinery and vehicles .	8	Thailand . .	3
Iron and steel manufac-		Indonesia .	2
tures . . .	8	Hong Kong .	2
Mineral oils . .	8	U.K. . .	1
Rayon, etc. . .	3	India . .	1
Electrical goods . .	2		
EXPORTS			
819·4 million pesos (409·7 million U.S. dollars; £146·3 million)			
COMMODITIES	PERCENTAGE	DESTINATION	PERCENTAGE
Coconut products . .	46	U.S.A. . .	61
Refined sugar . .	17	Japan . .	7
Abaca	16	U.K. . .	3

Sources of Tables 1–10: (a) Census reports of individual territories concerned; (b) *Economic Survey of Asia and the Far East*, 1952 (United Nations, Bangkok).

CHAPTER XXVIII

South-west Asia: Internal Problems

W. B. FISHER

HE influences of geographical environment in South-west Asia are strong and pervasive, but at the same time extremely complex, so that there occur widely differing and almost contradictory effects upon economic and political activity in the region. An excellent example of this situation can be seen in the mere attempt to define 'South-west Asia.' At the outset one may note certain overall tendencies making for geographical unity—a special regime of climate, a distinctive mode of life, and a characteristic culture-pattern—which justify the recognition of South-west Asia as a distinctive and separate region of the world. But we also have the disconcerting fact that national boundaries do not correspond even with the conventional limits of the major continents: most of Turkey lies in Asia, yet its largest and most important city is European; and Egypt extends from Asia into Africa. If, on the other hand, abandoning conventional physical criteria, we attempt a definition of South-west Asia purely in terms of human distributions further difficulties arise. Neither ethnic nor linguistic unity can be said to exist: instead, only a most bewildering alternation of physical types, ranging from Negroid through Caucasoid to Mongoloid, with a mosaic of languages, some ancient and others relatively recent in origin. Culturally, South-western Asia has been most affected by Islam, which is now the faith of over 90 per cent. of its inhabitants; but it is also the home of Judaism and Christianity, and important minorities of these sects still maintain a separate identity and outlook. Islam, moreover, has spread into other regions of the world; hence expressions such as 'Muhammadan Asia,' 'the Moslem World,' or even 'Arab Asia' cannot be applied with any exactitude to denote South-west Asia alone.[1]

---

[1] One step towards a solution of this problem of nomenclature in South-west Asia has been the extended use of the term 'Middle East' to denote South-west Asia and its immediate borderlands in European Turkey and North-east Africa. This proposal can in turn be criticized *inter alia* in that it ignores logic—where is, then, the 'Near East'?

z*

South-west Asia (or, interchangeably, the Middle East as defined in the footnote below) covers an area of some 2·1 million square miles, as compared with the 3·5 million square miles of Europe, and 3·7 million square miles of the United States. The population, which in some countries has not so far been accurately enumerated, totals approximately 60 million, giving an average overall density of twenty-nine persons per square mile. Owing, however, to extreme regional variation—as, for example, in Egypt, where 96 per cent. of the country has less than one inhabitant per square mile and the remaining 4 per cent. over 1000 persons per square mile—this figure has relatively little meaning.

Within South-west Asia occurs a surprising variety of geographical conditions (Fig. 1). Some 80 per cent. of Turkey and 65 to 70 per cent. of Persia lie at over 3000 feet above sea-level, and Asia Minor has over one hundred peaks of 10,000 feet and more; yet several millions of Egyptians and Iraqis pass their lives without seeing a hill of any kind. Climatically, there is a strongly marked single rhythm of hot dry summers and moist winters; but local incidence of temperature can vary in winter from an almost entire absence of frost close by the Mediterranean Sea, to the bitter winters of Eastern Asia Minor and Persia, where snow may lie for as many as 100 days annually, and night temperatures fall as low as those of the Canadian Arctic. Rainfall too is highly variable, not only in general distribution—from an annual total of 100 inches over the eastern Black Sea coastlands to the almost absolute aridity of the Rub' al Khali—but also in onset. Extremely heavy though capricious showers may occur for a short time over limited areas, watering one field and leaving its neighbour dry, or producing temporary floods in a region normally arid.

Despite this variety of physical environment within South-west Asia, there is one simple but outstanding environmental effect upon human life. Whether plainsmen or mountaineers, oppressed by summer heat or by winter cold, the large majority of Middle Eastern people have in general a low and precarious standard of living. This poverty arises from many factors, a number of which are directly or indirectly geographical in nature: a generally harsh physical environment; an unusual

---

—and also in that it merely puts the question of definition one stage further off. Nevertheless, usage of 'Middle East' to denote Asiatic lands lying south and west of the Caucasus Range and the Caspian Sea, together with European Turkey and Egypt, can be justified partly from the sanction gained during the second world war, and partly from the undeniable elements of geographical unity that occur, as outlined above in the text.

For fuller discussion of these points, see the writer's "Unity and Diversity in the Middle East," in *Geographical Review* (New York), vol. xxxvii, No. 3 (1947), pp. 414–435.

geographical position; and social organization the effect of which has been to retard initiative and inhibit the full and efficient use of existing resources.

A high proportion of South-western Asia is either too mountainous for cultivation, too arid, or covered by saline swamp. Climate is an

FIG. I. SOUTH-WEST ASIA
Land over 10,000 ft. in black. N = Neutral territory.

important obstacle, directly because of the scantiness and unreliability of rainfall, and of the sudden extremes of temperature; indirectly because conditions favour the existence of insect pests and the micro-organisms of plant, animal, and human disease, and, further, because of a remarkable effect of a regime of hot dry summers upon soil fertility. Humus and other organic matter are 'burnt out' of the soil, and the transfer of chemical compounds is towards the surface rather than downward into the lower soil. Thus there exists a considerable problem of maintaining soil fertility. Deep ploughing is both injurious, since it dries out the soil, and also ineffective, because fertilizers mixed in at depth ultimately return to the top layer. Western agriculturists, accustomed to moister cooler conditions, were at first inclined to suggest that the problem of maintaining soil fertility in the Middle East

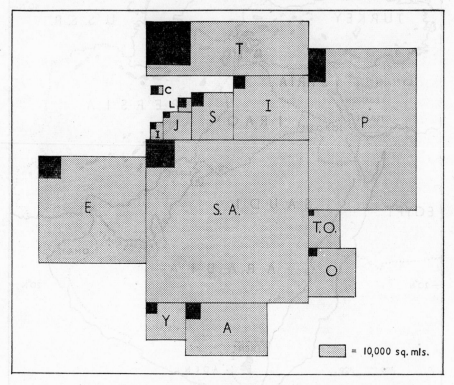

= 10,000 sq. mls.

FIG. 2. DIAGRAM SHOWING THE RELATIVE AREAS OF MIDDLE EASTERN
COUNTRIES

In black, the proportion of total surface actually under cultivation (approximative).

could be solved merely by adopting Western techniques of conservation, or by developing irrigation. After several costly failures—in south-west Persia, in the Konya region of southern Anatolia, and in the northern delta region of Egypt—there is now a realization that other approaches, more closely adapted to prevailing environmental conditions, are called for.

General geographical position may be considered to be a contributory factor to agricultural backwardness in that contiguity to other regions of the world—Africa, Central and Southern Asia, and Europe—brings pests and diseases from several endemic sources affecting plants, animals, and human beings. Most serious is perhaps the liability to plagues of locusts, which often originate in the deserts of Somaliland, Libya, or Arabia, and ultimately descend upon the agricultural lands of Egypt,

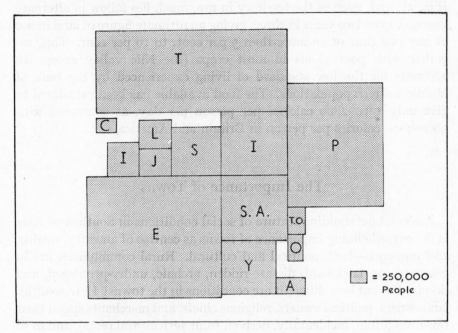

FIG. 3. DIAGRAM SHOWING THE RELATIVE SIZE OF POPULATIONS
IN THE COUNTRIES OF THE MIDDLE EAST

the Levant, Iraq, Turkey, and Persia. Human disease, especially malaria, is also a major factor in poverty, owing mainly to its debilitating effect, which reduces the intelligence and capacity for work of the peasant.[2]

The third group of factors contributing to low productivity is primarily social. Inordinately high rents and taxes, amounting to 50 per

[2] The incidence of disease among the populations of the Middle East is still extremely high, despite the efforts of local governments and of the World Health Organization. Between 70 per cent. and 80 per cent. of the entire population of Egypt suffers from serious disease, and this figure reaches 100 per cent. in certain parts of Persia and Iraq. It is an unfortunate feature that extension of irrigation has in some districts tended to spread malaria and parasitic diseases: this is particularly true of Iraq.

cent. or even 75 per cent. of the total yield of a holding; absenteeism among landlords, with resulting disinterest in improvements; religious influences, which can at times preclude change; and the perpetuance of tribal, communal, or group ownership of land, are all further elements in retarding initiative and development.

As a result, although over 80 per cent. of the inhabitants live as agriculturists, less than 15 per cent. of the land is actually cultivated (Fig. 2); and, even of the territory in use, much lies fallow in alternate years, or even two years in three, giving an ultimate figure of land in use at any one time of no more than 5 per cent. to 10 per cent. This, together with poor yields in most crops (the Nile valley excepted), accounts for the low standard of living experienced by the bulk of Middle Eastern populations. The food available has been calculated to give only 2300–2800 calories per person per day, as compared with 3000–4000 calories per person in Britain and America.

The Importance of Towns

A second outstanding feature of social conditions in South-west Asia is the overwhelming importance of towns as centres of amenity, wealth, and influence—both political and cultural. Rural communities are in general poor, backward, disease-ridden, archaic, under-privileged, and despised[3]—but how different are conditions in the towns! Here wealthy landowners, political leaders, religious chiefs, and merchants spend their revenues (often, incidentally, derived from agricultural rents), and in so doing provide a market for industry, commerce, and personal services. The cities, as outlets for trade and commerce, sometimes of world-wide connexion, possess wealth and historical tradition, and have at the same time the opportunity of acquiring new ideas and techniques from outside. Moreover, it would seem that religious feeling finds its highest expression in towns: some ritual observances even cannot easily be performed elsewhere.[4] Hence political power has also come to be concen-

---

[3] For example, very few doctors practise in rural areas. Of the total of 569 registered medical practitioners in Iraq (1945), some 308 alone resided within Baghdad city. In 1951 the present writer was informed by the Head of a Turkish Teachers' Training College that it was inadvisable for single women teachers to attempt to work in any but a few big towns.

[4] *Cf.* the celebration of Christian Eucharist, and the ritual ablutions carried out by Moslems.

It is significant that Jewish ritual includes the words "Next year *in Jerusalem*"; that

trated in towns to a degree that is not fully appreciated by outsiders, and this process has perceptibly extended rather than declined within the last fifteen years, with correspondingly significant effects upon political and social development.

Environment and Human Thought

It is possible to consider that the complex of geographical influences within the region would seem to have exerted a sustained influence upon human ideas. Broadly speaking, the Middle East may best be regarded as an isthmus—a tenuous, irregular land-mass deeply penetrated by seas and gulfs which are further prolonged by extensive river lowlands or fault-troughs. Yet the land-mass itself has remained sufficiently imposing to have given rise to conditions of a markedly continental kind, in sharp contrast to the maritime influences that prevail near the long coastline. This contrast between coast and interior is heightened by the presence of mountain chains that run parallel to the coast.[5] Here is a most important feature: duality of geographical environment, to which can be related significant human responses. In the valleys and basins of the interior there have grown up many indigenous cultures of an extremely high order; but along the coast an intimate juxtaposition of land and sea, and general geographical position as a link between three major continents, have together provided an invitation to movement and contact with the outside world. From this in turn has resulted much intercommunication and the diffusion of ideas, both native and from outside. Consequently the historic function of South-western Asia (or, in other words, the sustained human response to environment) has been on the one hand that of a zone of invention and development, where some of the outstanding steps in human progress were made, and, on the other, that of a region of intercourse and diffusion in which ideas and techniques originating in various other parts of the Old World could be transmitted elsewhere. Sometimes these latter were passed on with

the Lord's Supper and Descent of the Holy Ghost occurred within a city room; that men first called themselves Christians in Antioch, the metropolis of the time; and that Islam should have designated so many 'Holy Cities.'

[5] *Cf.* the contrast in outlook between the Phœnicians of the Levant coastlands, who penetrated as far as Britain and the Cape of Good Hope, and whose alphabet influenced Greece; and that of the Hebrews of Judea, living within sight of the Mediterranean but inveterate landsmen, whose millennium, as described by St John, would be ushered in when "there was no more sea."

little alteration, sometimes they became enriched by further local contributions.[6] The idea of duality in geographical environment, and hence
in human responses, can usefully be carried further. A remarkable feature of the Middle East is the rapid alternation of local conditions:
within a remarkably short distance one can pass from sea or plain to
mountain, from field to desert, or into a contrasting climatic regime;
and one also becomes conscious of the sharp distinction between the
bleakness and harshness of mountain and desert and the opulence of the
riverine plains, or the austerity of nomadic life contrasted with the
lavishness and complication of urban living. So one might suggest that
there can exist a similarly abrupt transition in mental climate: ease and
sensuality characteristic of the plains stand out against the simplicity
and sanctity of the Wilderness and high mountain. The fundamental
premise in Islam—acceptance of hardship in this life, with the expectation of voluptuous pleasure in the world to come—may derive from the
same concept.[7]

Moreover, this antithesis may colour political and ethical thinking.
Ways of life and outlook within South-western Asia are, generally
speaking, highly traditional and conservative, so that, "bowed by the
weight of centuries," habits change only slowly. But from time to time
there have appeared a number of outstandingly revolutionary figures,
both religious and political. Sir James Frazer spoke with horror of the
flood of Oriental ideas which, spread by mystics from South-west Asia,
"gradually undermined the whole fabric of ancient civilization in
Europe"[8]; and in our own time we have seen how leaders like Kemal
Atatürk, Ibn Saud, and Riza Shah could in a few years alter life and
thought within their respective countries.[9] Thus there would appear to

[6] As examples of developments that have originated within South-west Asia there may
be cited the development of settled civilization based on cereal cultivation, the invention
of the alphabet, and the remarkable flowering of ethical, monotheistic, and evangelical
religious systems on the borders of the Arabian and Persian deserts—Zoroastrianism,
Judaism, Christianity, Mithraism, and Islam. The function of transmission may be
illustrated by mention of the products and techniques introduced into Europe from the
Far East: garden irrigation, sugar, rice, citrus fruit, silk, silk-weaving, paper-making, and
navigation by magnetic compass; and in the remarkable synthesis of Greek and Hindu
science, enriched by the Arab inventions of numerals, that was passed on by Arab com-
mentators to Renaissance scholars in Western Europe.

[7] It may also be relevant to recall that while the Middle East gave to the world the
ideal and practice of austerity in the monasteries of the Thebaid and Palestine, the same
region held the courts of the Pharaohs, Solomon, the Byzantines, and of Haroun al
Rashid—all synonyms of luxury and splendour.

[8] J. Frazer, *The Golden Bough* (abridged edition, 1939), p. 357.

[9] *Cf.* Matt. x, 35 and 36, "For I am come to set a man at variance against his own
father. . . . And a man's foes shall be they of his own household."

It may also be pertinent to recall that, had he been born fifty years earlier, J. V. Stalin
would have been a Persian subject. His early training, moreover, was in a theological
seminary.

exist within the rooted conservatism of South-west Asia a complementary germ of subversion and revolutionary dissent. As T. E. Lawrence observed, "the thoughts of the Arabs are at ease only in extremes"—and in modern political events the outside observer must be ready to allow for a sudden swing from the normal traditionalism to a climate of impulsive, almost anarchic, experiment. If on certain occasions people in South-west Asia had not been willing to "oscillate from asymptote to asymptote" Judaism, Christianity, and Islam could hardly have developed as and where they did.

Economic Changes since 1939

By far the most significant feature of the last sixteen years has been an increase in wealth which, although varying considerably from region to region, has nevertheless affected South-west Asia as a whole. The change may amount to a very modest amelioration, as in Persia; or to a veritable transformation, as in Kuwait, where the average income of total population accruing to the State has risen from much less than £1 per head (1938) to over £200 per head in 1953.

The factors responsible for the changes since 1939 may be viewed as falling into two distinct but inter-related groups: development of resources within the Middle East itself—chiefly petroleum and cotton; and financial subventions of various kinds made directly by foreign countries and groups to Middle Eastern governments. The exploitation of oil, more than any other item, has enriched many Middle Eastern countries (Table 1), and since 1950 the Middle East has displaced the Caribbean area as the greatest oil-exporting region of the world—even allowing for the setback due to the loss of Persian production after 1951. Besides royalties actually paid to individuals and governments in the oil-producing countries, there are further payments to countries which lack oil but are crossed by pipelines, or include loading and refining terminals—e.g., Syria, Jordan, Israel, and the Lebanon. In addition, there are openings for employment as labourers and technicians at sites of production, in maintenance and supply along pipeline routes, and as dock workers and administrative staffs at the terminals. Beyond this still is the general stimulus to production and trade deriving from a higher native purchasing power, and from the presence of a group of highly paid foreign workers.

TABLE 1

Oil Royalties: Direct Payments by Oil Companies to Governments, in Million U.S. Dollars

YEAR	BAHRAIN	IRAN	IRAQ	KUWAIT	QATAR	SAUDI ARABIA
1940	1·0	16·0	8·1	—	—	1·5
1950	3·3	44·7	14·8	12·4	1·0	112·0
1951	3·8	23·3	38·5	30·0	3·8	158·0
1952	6·3	nil	110·0	139·0	9·0	160·0

Source: Petroleum Information Bureau, London.

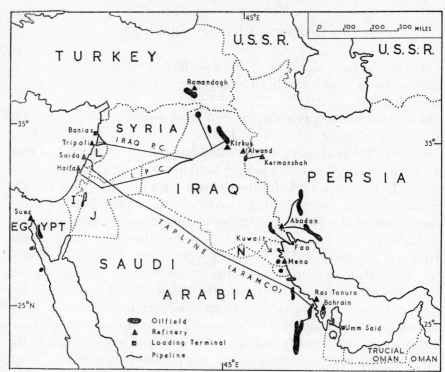

FIG. 4. THE OILFIELDS OF THE MIDDLE EAST

I = Israel, J = Jordan, L = Lebanon, N = Neutral territories, Q = Qatar. Concessions held as follows: Turkey, Turkish State; Persia, National Iranian Oil Co. (Persian); Iraq, Iraq Petroleum Co. (British, American, French, Dutch); Saudi Arabia, Arabian-American Oil Co. (U.S.A.); Kuwait (American and British); Bahrain (American); Qatar (I.P.C.); Egypt (American and British); Neutral territories (American).

The effects of oil exploitation (Fig. 4) may be followed as a case-sample in detail for one particular country—Saudi Arabia. In 1933 this

State could be described as a *tabula rasa*: a remote, isolated region, thought to lack any important oil deposits, almost without foreign trade, and governed by a vigorous, despotic, and patriarchal monarch, who held all power in his own hands. No State budget was thought necessary, as the king's privy purse, private income, and State revenue were one. His total income, upon which all government depended, came mainly from dues levied upon pilgrims to Mecca, and barely amounted to £150,000 per annum.

In 1952, after only thirteen years of operation, the Arabian-American Oil Company (Aramco) became the largest single oil-producing company in the world, with a production of 300 million barrels of crude oil; and the Saudi Arabian exchequer received in this one year £53 millions as royalties. Nearly 25,000 persons were employed by Aramco, of whom 15,000 were Saudi Arabian nationals, and 5000 nationals of near-by countries (India, Pakistan, Jordan, Arab Palestine, and Syria). The Company also contracted with 149 Saudi Arabian supply firms, who employed a further 11,000 people, and received in the one year payments of £4 millions.

The Saudi Arabian Government found itself able to embark on various public works: irrigation developments round Riadh, a railway from Dhahran to Riadh, costing 52 million dollars (£16·5 million), with a planned extension to Jidda; and the introduction of modern utilities (roads, drainage, the mechanization of local industry) on a small scale in many towns. The pilgrim traffic is now catered for by a fleet of 250 buses, nearly 4000 other vehicles, and twenty-five airfields. Taxes levied on pilgrimage were until recently very high, and thus tended to reduce the number of participants; but now that this revenue is no longer the mainstay of the State, dues have been virtually abolished, and the pilgrim traffic is now greater, with pilgrims arriving from as far afield as Morocco, Zanzibar, and Java—an interesting example of the inter-relationships of economic geography and religious life. A further index of the changes in Arabia is afforded by statistics of petrol consumption within the country. Since 1948 demand has quadrupled, from 260,000 barrels to $1\frac{1}{4}$ million in 1953, and there are now over fifty distributing depots within Saudi Arabia.

Another less spectacular but none the less valuable commodity is cotton, which has proved a major source of wealth to many landlords. The average price of Egyptian raw cotton in tallaris per cantar was 13·5 in 1938, 87 in 1950, and (following the outbreak of the Korean War, which led to stockpiling) attained 145 in 1951—*i.e.*, a rise of more than ten times the 1938 price, while the average price of goods imported by Egypt from abroad rose to only three or four times the 1938 average. Thus the terms of trade have moved enormously in Egypt's favour (bearing in mind that cotton accounts for over 70 per cent. of Egyptian exports); and in other Middle Eastern countries a similar, though smaller, benefit has been felt. The events in Korea produced a 'cotton fever' in Turkey, Syria, Iraq, and the Lebanon—mortgages were raised

TABLE 2

Value of Imports and Exports, in Million U.S. Dollars

YEAR	CYPRUS		EGYPT		IRAQ		ISRAEL/ PALESTINE	
	Im- port	Ex- port	Im- port	Ex- port	Im- port	Ex- port	Im- port	Ex- port
1938	11	12	184	147	41	18	56	28
1948	63	23	663	591	141	33	96	5
1950	38	31	564	504	105	60	287	35

YEAR	JORDAN		PERSIA		SYRIA AND LEBANON		TURKEY	
	Im- port	Ex- port	Im- port	Ex- port	Im- port	Ex- port	Im- port	Ex- port
1938	6	3	55	52	37	22	119	115
1948	47	11	131	56	213	36	275	197
1950	36	13	192	108	171	136	286	263

Source: U.N. World Economic Report 1950–51.

to acquire capital to purchase cotton seed, and in 1951 raw cotton displaced tobacco as the most valuable single item in the Turkish export trade.[10] This enhanced wealth, though by no means as extensive and spectacular as that gained from oil, has nevertheless brought about considerable changes, and it has reached a class of people who have not on the whole benefited greatly from oil royalties—smaller landowners, merchants, and business-men. Similarly, there has been a perceptible though again smaller increase in wealth from the high world prices of tobacco and wool, both of which are produced in quantity in Southwestern Asia.

A further important item in the economy of many Middle Eastern countries has been payments of various kinds originating from foreign

[10] Statistics from the *Monthly Bulletin of Statistics* (United Nations, 1951–52); and from the Petroleum Information Bureau, London.

governments and individuals, and in the main reflecting the enhanced strategic situation of South-western Asia. First, there have been the effects of two world wars and the Korean campaign of 1950–53. At least 50,000 foreign troops spent some time in the Middle East during 1914–19, and approximately one million in 1939–45. The combatant nations endeavoured to supply their troops as far as possible from local resources, and thus large numbers of Arabs and others found employment as servants, labourers, and technicians (e.g., 100,000 Egyptians were employed in Cairo and Alexandria alone), and in 1945 a debt of £500 million sterling was recognized by Britain as still outstanding to Egypt. Moreover, the presence of troops on leave, with a purchasing power much above that of the native population, stimulated a demand for accommodation and entertainment (the largest group of Egyptian hotels paid no dividend to stockholders in 1939, and 100 per cent. in 1944). A third minor 'boom' occurred in 1951. A prevailing downward trend in prices of raw materials was abruptly reversed, especially as regards cotton and wool (see above); stockpiling took place on a large scale, and for a time harbours and warehouses were unable to cope with the flow of merchandise.

Besides these purchases by foreign governments, direct payments as loans and subsidies have also been made. The principal source of these has been the United States (e.g., in 1948–50 governmental 'aid' amounting to 225 million dollars was given to Turkey and 25 million dollars to Persia, followed by 43 million dollars in 1952; and a non-governmental loan of 500 million dollars was floated in New York on behalf of the State of Israel). Other sums have also been made available either as direct military aid, or as subsidies to foreign cultural institutions in the Middle East—American, British, and French colleges and universities. The net effect of this has been to lighten considerably national budgets in the countries concerned. Some of the most influential educational establishments of South-west Asia are subsidised from abroad; consequently, for instance, the majority of Lebanese children who are at school attend non-State institutions.

Contemporary Economic Problems

The changes outlined above are now giving rise to certain acute problems. Because of the violent fluctuations in agricultural prices, with industrial raw materials (cotton, wool, tobacco) tending to fetch very high prices, the production of foodstuffs has tended to advance at a distinctly slower rate. Hence, bearing in mind that the populations of the Middle East are in rapid growth (in some regions this increase amounts to 2 per cent. per annum), it is thought that food supplies per head are below those of the years 1920–39.

This problem of over-population is by no means a feature of all parts of South-west Asia (Fig. 3). In Turkey, Iraq, and possibly Persia the size of existing populations is still inadequate to ensure full development of existing resources: over-population is a matter of concern only in Egypt, the Lebanon, Jordan, and Israel. In Egypt, however, conditions are critical, and one can go so far as to relate most of the principal political difficulties of the country to the single fact of high population density as compared with resources. With only 5 per cent. of the total land area regarded as cultivable,[11] population has grown from an estimated figure of 2½ millions in 1800 to 22¾ millions (1955). Only 4 per cent. of Egyptians do not live within the Nile valley, where in one or two localities densities have reached 6000 persons per square mile.

At present the annual increase in population amounts to 2 per cent. per annum (400,000 people), but in agricultural production an annual improvement of the order of 2 per cent. is extremely difficult to maintain over a long period. In fact, the yield of crops in Egypt per unit of cultivated land has tended to fall over the last fifteen years rather than rise, and, as maize and cotton yields are already the highest in the world, further improvement is in any case hard to achieve.

Until the modern system of perennial irrigation was developed, the average deposition of fertilizing silt by the river Nile amounted to 1·2 inches per century in Lower Egypt, and 4·1 inches in Upper Egypt. This was sufficient so long as one or two crops were taken annually; but now with perennial irrigation natural fertilizing by silt is greatly reduced[12] and at the same time two to four crops are taken. Already, in consequence, Egypt uses more artificial fertilizer per unit of cultivated land than do most other countries, and the dependence on imported fertilizers will tend to increase rather than decline. This was shown by

[11] This comprises the Delta area, and a strip some one to three miles wide on each side of the Nile south of the Delta.

[12] Under perennial irrigation the deposition of silt is only one-sixth of that under the older system of basin irrigation, giving a rate of deposition of 0·2 inches and 0·7 inches per century for Lower and Upper Egypt respectively.

the marked fall in yields during the second world war, when only 60 per cent. of requirements in fertilizers could be imported.

To this general demographic situation in Egypt can be related a number of political problems. Because of the slower development of resources, Egypt is most probably one of the Middle Eastern countries where the ratio of inhabitants to available foodstuffs has deteriorated— *i.e.*, the share of the individual is definitely less, as compared with 1930.[13] Hence, with such conditions of precarious or falling standards of life, it is not difficult to find one reason for the widespread xenophobia and civil unrest characteristic of contemporary Egypt.[14] The presence of foreign workers, who without exception enjoy inflated levels of living compared with the Egyptians, makes it easy for demagogues to represent that the hardships of peasants and artisans are due solely to foreign exploitation; and desperate underfed masses can be persuaded to turn eagerly to new political systems, however untried and violent.[15]

The present-day change-over from agricultural self-sufficiency to specialization in cash crops for sale abroad (cotton, rice, and vegetables) has political implications. Egypt is now increasingly affected by world trends in prices, yet her own production is relatively small and thus insufficient to exert any control on general price-levels. In consequence the country is subject to trade cycles over which she has little influence, and as a reaction to this position is developing a spirit of economic nationalism. Aware of her new standing as a minor but useful contributor to world trade, Egypt sets a higher value, possibly at times much exaggerated, upon her political importance. One might therefore suggest that we are now witnessing a change somewhat similar to that which occurred when England, for long a supplier of raw materials to Flanders and Italy, during Plantagenet times developed the beginnings of an independent economy and a parallel nationalism of outlook that later characterized the Tudor age.

Cotton by its nature is useless to the peasant grower until handled by merchants and middlemen; thus its wider cultivation within Egypt tends to enhance the financial position of the landlord, trader, and

[13] C. Issawi, *Egypt, an Economic and Social Analysis* (Oxford University Press, 1947). Issawi goes so far as to state that over the last twenty years, despite a population increase of one-third, the *absolute* volume of major foodstuffs available in Egypt is less, owing in part to increased cotton-growing, and in part to lower yields.

[14] It will be recalled that during riots in Cairo during 1951 some £40 million of damage was done, and ten foreigners killed.

[15] Almost all foreigners whom the Egyptian peasant sees appear to him extremely wealthy—even British private soldiers—and he could not therefore feel that their presence in his country was entirely disinterested.

merchant rather than that of the peasant grower. At worst, the peasant can eat any food he grows; but for a crop of cotton he must either find a buyer, or starve. Also, being marketable and unperishable, cotton can serve as a basis for credit manipulation and stock-exchange operations; and thus the relative emphasis to be placed on food production and on cotton-growing is now a most important political issue within Egypt. The peasant would prefer to grow more food, but landlords and dealers can far more easily make fortunes in cotton. It is not too much to say that widespread dissatisfaction over the manipulation of cotton prices in favour of individuals was one element in the downfall of the Egyptian monarchy in 1952.

As conditions now exist, most of the Nile water reaching Egypt is entirely utilized: there is no flow whatever to the Mediterranean in the few weeks before the flood season. But approximately 70 per cent. of river water is lost by evaporation in the Sudan, and, in addition, it is believed that a small fraction of artesian water occurring below the Western Desert may seep into the Nile between latitudes $23\frac{1}{2}°$ and $24\frac{1}{2}°$ N. Egyptian statesmen therefore feel a most compelling interest in political control of the Sudan (the so-called "Unity of the Nile Valley"), since all major schemes of improvement of irrigation in Egypt now rest on river control in the Sudanese reaches. They also recall an ultimatum presented by the British in 1924, to the effect that unless Egypt complied with certain demands the amount of water released to Egypt would be reduced. Hence to many Egyptians control of the Sudan represents both a vital strategic need and the key to improvement and control of Nile water—in other words, the obvious solution to the problem of over-population.

The general issue concerning Nile water has (1956) crystallized over specific proposals concerning the raising (for the third time) of the Aswan Dam, by an amount sufficient to give it a total storage capacity of 130,000 million cubic metres. Of this total, 70,000 million cubic metres would be available for extra irrigation purposes, the balance being either 'dead' water that must be retained in the bed of the reservoir to even out supply, or else provision for an exceptionally high flood.

Implementation of this scheme will cause the inundation of a large tract of land within the Sudan, containing the whole of the town of Wadi Halfa, and a total human population of 50,000, for whom entirely new settlements will have to be made. Further, the Sudan is at present unwilling to accept the High Aswan plan as drawn up by Egypt, because in the Sudanese view the existing division of Nile water is already unfairly weighted in favour of Egypt; and had the Sudanese been able to negotiate in the past as a free and independent State, present 'rights' and allocations now held by Egypt as long established and unalterable would not in fact have been agreed on. Also, the Sudan reserves the right to undertake further irrigation works higher up the Nile, thus, in the opinion of Egypt, prejudicing the success of the High Aswan scheme.

The Egyptian State cannot itself undertake the whole of the financial commitment involved in the High Dam project, and has hence applied for an international loan. This was not at first regarded favourably in London and New York, owing to the somewhat strained political relations with Egypt. But on becoming aware that overtures had been made to Russia, and that the Soviet Government was willing not only to provide the finance, but also constructional engineers as well, the nightmare of a large Russian colony (even temporary) in the heart of the Nile Valley induced the Western Powers to change their mind, and financial support has now been offered. The question of Egyptian-Sudanese differences still remains an issue, but will clearly turn on the general relations of the two countries. The international aspect is a remarkable demonstration of the opportunities now available to Middle Eastern countries to 'balance' between East and West.

Social Problems

Recent developments in South-west Asia have also tended to emphasize an issue that is in part related to the economic problems discussed above—the establishment of a stable and reasonably just social order. This is at present far from being realized. A prominent feature has long been the relatively sharp social division into rich and poor, with little of a 'middle' class. At present this discrepancy, though somewhat mitigated by the spread of education, which is producing a slightly larger group of professional and skilled workers, has in many cases been enhanced by the unequal way in which the benefits of the changes outlined above have reached different social groups. It is reasonable to state that, while the rich have definitely become much richer over the last few years, the standard of living of the poor has at best only slightly improved, or even (as in Egypt) may actually have fallen.

One reason for this unbalance is the nature of the developments themselves. Both oil and cotton, the two most valuable commodities, are exported, and relatively little used within the Middle East itself. Royalties and dues are paid over to a small group of politicians, notables, landowners, or even to a ruler personally; and there is no attempt to raise the question of the right of one or a few persons to enjoy total and untrammelled use of the new wealth. Provided that the local ruler guarantees security of exploitation to the concessionnaires, the latter are content to accept social conditions as they are; any attempt to influence the spending of royalties could be construed as interference in the internal affairs of the country concerned.[16]

TABLE 3

Proportion of National Taxation, 1951

TAXATION	SAUDI ARABIA	CYPRUS	EGYPT	IRAQ	ISRAEL
Direct (per cent.)	0	42	15	9	45
Indirect (per cent.)	100	56	48	68	40

TAXATION	LEBANON	PERSIA	SYRIA	TURKEY[1]
Direct (per cent.)	17	15	14	33
Indirect (per cent.)	70	56	85	67

Sources: Statistical Handbooks, Governments of Cyprus, Egypt, Israel, Lebanon, Syria, Turkey.
[1] Estimation.

Moreover, since the end of Ottoman rule, the wealthier Arabs who were once without political power are now the ruling classes of the new nationalist States. Under the Turks, a rich Arab lived circumspectly and avoided showing too much wealth in order to avoid heavy tax exactions; but now, able himself to control the fiscal policy of his country to his own advantage, he can more safely show his riches.

[16] Hence there arises a considerable dilemma for the oil companies. If they attempt to supervise and direct the spending of the royalties that they pay to local rulers they are in effect committed to some form of interference; if they do not, and allow social injustice to continue, they risk later the outbreak of revolution against a ruler with whom they have come to terms, and the consequent revocation of their concession. This is one of the fundamental issues in Persia.

Taxation is hence often maintained on a basis which places the greater burden on the poor—by imposts on necessities such as food. This kind of tax can be justified as the easiest to collect in a semi-literate community lacking a highly organized bureaucracy, but reliance on indirect taxation to produce the major part of State revenue can be socially unjust.

Ostentation has recently been greatly encouraged by the importation of Western luxuries, ranging from furs and refrigerators to radios and automobiles. There has been a profound change over the last fifty years —the rich are not only in fact very much better off relatively, but now *appear* far richer than formerly; and the psychological (hence also political) effects of this are increasingly apparent, leading to more persistent questioning of the social order. Bearing in mind the proximity of the U.S.S.R., which has a longer land frontier with the Middle East than any other State, and also developments in China and South-east Asia, where Communism has been accepted by many, it is not difficult to discern in this situation disquieting future possibilities.

Reference was made earlier to the disparity in wealth between town and country. One marked social effect of this is an extensive drift to the towns, which would appear to be rapidly growing in volume at the present time. Cairo, with a population of over two millions, is not merely the largest town in Egypt, but the greatest city in Africa and the entire Mediterranean basin. Beirut, a half-ruined site in 1921 with a population of 60,0000, now houses 300,000 people—one-quarter of the total population of the Lebanon. Ankara has grown from a "dusty village on a branch railway line" to a city of 250,000; and Tel Aviv in thirty years has changed from a hamlet to a capital of similar numbers. As a result, there is a corresponding rural exodus in certain districts leading to a decline of cultivation.[17]

At the same time a constant influx into the towns of needy, but somewhat more active and ambitious, former peasants has important political results. There is steadily growing a rootless, under-privileged, and increasingly restive proletariat, aware of the enhanced wealth now accruing in parts of South-west Asia, but debarred from sharing in this prosperity. The change-over to modern methods of industry, together with competition of foreign-made goods, is destroying a considerable native home industry that supplemented low returns from farming; yet

[17] In one district of the Lebanon the writer noted a decline of about 20 per cent. in the area under cultivation in the period 1942–51.

the towns cannot always provide employment for the stream of arrivals, and the prevailing stagnant political system (dominated by privilege and authoritarianism) breeds desperation and allows change only through sedition, armed revolt, and assassination.[18]

Moreover, the spread of education is creating an intellectual élite that can note the existence of radically different political systems in other parts of the world; and the fact that many of the best paid situations in Middle Eastern commerce, administration, and industry are still held by foreigners suggests imperialist exploitation either open or disguised, and produces a widely developed frustration and xenophobia on the part of the college-educated Middle Easterner.

The two groups, proletariat and students, often together form a very dangerous combination—the Middle Eastern city mob. The former element is concerned partly with looting and violence, partly with bringing about a change of rulers on a basis of desperation—almost any change will be for the better. The students are often more preoccupied with theories and ideas, but at the same time respond eagerly to slogans backed by solid offers of political appointment and jobbery. Unscrupulous demagogues can hence foment an outbreak of violence on a scale that is unknown in the West. Most years see an outbreak of rioting on a small scale—and no reports of these incidents reach Western newspapers. But from time to time, and, it would seem, with increasing frequency, events take a more serious turn, with widespread damage, some loss of life, and the overturning of a Cabinet or dynasty.[19]

[18] Within the last few years there have been several unsuccessful attempts on the lives of statesmen in Iraq, the Lebanon, and Libya; and successful attempts in Egypt, Jordan, Palestine, Persia, Syria, and the Yemen. Of the last four rulers of Syria, two have died on the scaffold, and two are in exile.

[19] E.g., the Cairo riots of 1951 and the Turkish outbreaks of 1955. In the latter instance damage exceeding £80 million sterling was done.

CHAPTER XXIX

South-west Asia: External Relations

W. B. FISHER

IN the previous chapter reference was made to geographical position as an influence in the internal political development of South-west Asia. Even greater importance can be attached to this same factor as an influencing element in external political relations, since the last half-century has witnessed an outstanding alteration of world conditions. During the last few decades of the Ottoman regime South-west Asia could be said to be remote from the main currents of world politics and trade; and future prospects appeared to indicate eventual absorption to a greater or less degree by outside Powers. Persia was in effect partitioned in 1906;[1] the Arabian Peninsula and Nile Valley had fallen largely within the British orbit; and the reduced Ottoman territories—for long preserved to the Turks because of rivalries among European Powers—were in 1916–18 definitively allocated as future zones of influence between France, Great Britain, Greece, Italy, and Russia.[2]

Since the first world war, however, considerable changes have supervened. On the one hand, there has been an eclipse or decline among most Western nations (Russia temporarily after 1917; Germany, Italy, and to some extent France and Great Britain after 1945), while in contrast certain nations of southern and eastern Asia have risen to positions of relatively enhanced economic and political influence.[3] Instead of a concentration of power in North-western Europe, there is now a wider dispersion over most major areas of the globe; and in consequence the

[1] The Curzon Agreement between Great Britain and Russia, which established within Persia a Russian sphere, a British sphere, and a central neutral zone.

[2] Sykes-Picot Treaty of 1916, with later emendations as the result of the collapse of Tsarist Russia.

[3] Cf. the change in political importance since 1945 of India and China. It would scarcely have seemed credible in the 1920's and 1930's that the latter could counter American and European military intervention with some success, as has happened in Korea, or that the former could act as mediator between the two warring sides.

Middle East, forming a principal way of access between three continents, has now become central rather than peripheral to world affairs.[4]

The Suez Canal

This situation is clearly shown by developments in the Suez Canal (Fig. 1). Since 1900 the annual number of transits has risen from 3400 to over 12,000; the number of passengers has approximately doubled,

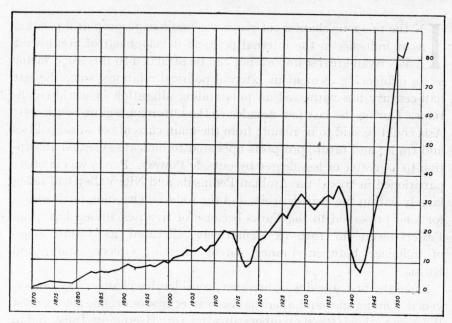

FIG. 1. TRAFFIC PASSING THROUGH THE SUEZ CANAL ANNUALLY (IN MILLIONS OF TONS)

and the tonnage of goods carried has risen more than ninefold, with spectacular increases since 1945.[5] Even the number of warships using

[4] One small indication of this is the fact that the British Overseas Airways Corporation operates more routine flights to and through the Middle East than to any other part of the world, excluding Western Europe. (In late 1954: Middle East, 35 flights weekly; N. America, 23; Africa (E., W., and S.), 25; India and Pakistan, 28; Australia and Far East, 19.)

[5] Figures in this section are from official publications of the Suez Canal Company. The writer wishes to record his appreciation of the facilities made available by this Company.

Port Said, with over 110 million tons of shipping passing through annually, now ranks as a principal port of the world, and in terms of movement of ships is ahead of London, New York, Antwerp, and Rotterdam.

TABLE 1

Suez Canal Traffic, 1900–1952

Year	Number of Passengers	Receipts (in million French francs)	Total Traffic (million tons)		Tanker Traffic (million tons)				Warships (million tons)
			N. to S.	S. to N.	N. to S.		S. to N.		
					loaded	empty	loaded	empty	
1900	283,000	90[1]	4·9	4·7	nil	nil	nil	nil	0·6
1913	282,000	129[1]	9·4	10·6	nil	nil	nil	nil	0·3
1930	305,000	192[2]	14·8	16·8	0·2	2·3	2·5	0·1	1·1
1938	480,000	1,649[3]	16·7	17·8	0·2	2·8	2·9	0·1	0·6
1952	571,000	26,849[4]	42·9	43·2	3·8	22·3	25·0	0·7	2·1

[1] 24 francs = £1 sterling.   [2] 55 francs = £1 sterling.   [3] 180 francs = £1 sterling.   [4] 980 francs = £1 sterling.

TABLE 2

Geographical Distribution of Suez Canal Traffic as Percentages of Total Traffic (Destination and Origin East of Suez only)

	Red Sea	East Africa	Persian Gulf	Indian Sub-continent	French Indo-China and Siam	Malaya and E. Indies	Australia	China and Japan
1913	<1	5	2	50	3	9	10	21
1952	5	4	57	12	3	5	7	6
Relative Increase in Volume (1913 = 100)								
1952	1,090	3,400	16,160	106	360	226	350	142

the Canal has increased—a commentary on world affairs, but also an indication of the enhanced strategic importance of the waterway. The increase is for the most part due to the development of oil-tanker traffic since 1913, but it should be noted that while crude and refined petroleum now form the principal item of northbound traffic, petroleum also ranks among the principal items of traffic southbound through the Canal— indicative of the growing markets for Middle Eastern oil in Asia, East Africa, and Australia.

Before the first world war the Suez Canal was important mainly because of the traffic to and from India, and China and Japan, which accounted for some 50 per cent. and 20 per cent. respectively of the total tonnage using the Canal. Since that time the total volume of this traffic has in fact increased; but Indian and Far Eastern traffic together now makes up only 20 per cent. of the total movement through the Canal, of which more than 60 per cent. now originates from ports within the Middle East.

Further, the nature of merchandise passing through the Canal has tended to alter. Before 1920 machinery and coal were the most important commodities (in terms of tonnage) that moved southward, and cereals and oil-seeds the most important items carried northward. As we have noted, petroleum is now overwhelmingly the most important single commodity moving northward (75 per cent. of all traffic), and in some years (e.g., 1952) also the chief commodity carried southward. The northbound cereal traffic has declined (four million tons in 1913, two million tons annually 1949–52), but the southbound traffic has increased, from negligible proportions before 1925 to two million tons in 1950–52, as has also the movement of chemical fertilizers, which totalled 1·5 million tons in 1952. Here is one indication of the serious problem con-

TABLE 3

Nationality of Ships passing through the

	American	British	Dutch	French	German
1880 .	0·1	76	4	8	1
1900 .	0·2	70	4	6	10
1913 .	—	60	6	5	17
1930 .	2	56	11	6	11
1938 .	1	50	9	5	9
1952 .	7	33	5	9	1

Source: Suez Canal

fronting southern Asia generally—the growing pressure of numbers and dependence at certain times on grain imported from Europe and America.

Two further points emerge from examination of the nationality of ships using the Canal. One is the predominant interest of Great Britain, which is still by far the largest user even at the present day; the other is the shift of commercial influence which has greatly reduced Britain's relative share of Canal trade in favour of the United States, Norway, and Sweden.

The figures given below provide one explanation of British interest in Middle Eastern affairs, and her tenacious attempts to retain military bases at or near the Canal. Though events of 1939–45 demonstrated that the Canal could be very vulnerable to air attack,[6] its strategic value remains great, both in peace and war, as shown by the great efforts made to keep it open, and by the campaigns undertaken to conquer the isthmus of Suez both in 1916 and in 1940–42.

The financial aspects of the Suez Canal concession may next be mentioned. The 1952 gross receipts amounted to approximately £30 million, and expenditure to £14 million. Allowing for certain fixed charges, there was thus available a net profit of some £14 to £15 million. The original terms of the concession as agreed in 1868 laid down that profits were to be distributed as follows: to the shareholders, 71 per cent.; to the Egyptian Government, 15 per cent.; to foundation members, 10 per cent.; and the balance of 4 per cent. to officials and employees. In 1936, however, the Egyptian Government found itself compelled to part with

---

[6] Traffic was reduced to roughly 20 per cent. of 1938 levels. As an instance of vulnerability it may be noted that, following the dropping of eleven mines on one night in February 1941, four ships were sunk in the Canal, and the fairway temporarily reduced to a depth of 20 feet, and a width of 85 feet.

Suez Canal as Percentages of Total Traffic

Greek	Italian	Japanese	Norwegian	Panamanian	Swedish
—	3	—	0·4	—	0·1
—	2	1	1	—	—
0·3	2	2	1	—	1
0·3	5	3	3	—	1
2	13	2	4	0·1	1
1	5	0·3	16	8	3

Company official returns.

its share in profits, and for some years received only an outright annual payment of £300,000. In 1949 payment was resumed at the rate of 7 per cent. of profits, which produced over £1 million annually. In addition, the Egyptian Government levies taxes on the Canal Company of the order of £3 million annually. These revenues (including profits) account for about 2 per cent. of the total Egyptian budgetary income.

With such financial arrangements, it is hardly surprising that differences of viewpoint have arisen. The Suez Canal Company can justifiably represent that considerable financial risk was initially taken by the concessionnaires, and can point to the undeniable further benefits that construction of the Canal has brought to Egypt: employment for over 4000 Egyptian workers, contracts placed within Egypt to the extent of £1 million annually, the acquiring of 'hard' currency in transit dues (£4·5 million in 1951), and the considerable developments arising from the growth of ports at Port Said, Suez, and Port Tewfik—ship-chandling and repairing, salt and oil refining, and the reclamation for agriculture of 70,000 acres of marsh and desert. In terms of shipping movements Port Said has displaced Alexandria as the chief port of Egypt, and the general rise in prosperity is indicated by the fact that, while in 1900 the average price per square metre of building land in Port Said was £2, it was £15 in 1949. Further, in justification of the terms of the Canal concession, it should be recognized that the Egyptian Government originally held a large number of shares in the company, and, also, that it was agreed from the start that the duration of the concession should be limited, with ownership passing to Egypt in 1968.

For many Egyptians, the operation of the concession at a high rate of profit, with 70 per cent. of the better-paid appointments held by foreigners, and the direct participation of both the British and French Governments as shareholders, suggest continued imperialist interference and exploitation on the unhappy pattern of 1880–1936. In the Egyptian mind the argument that British occupation was necessary for the protection of Egypt itself was merely a hypocritical excuse to conceal direct financial self-interest on the part of Britain; and the Canal hence served as a focal point for growing Egyptian nationalist emotion.

One other matter remains. From the geographical location of the major oilfields of the Middle East in relation to markets it will be clear that petroleum may not continue indefinitely to produce the greater proportion of Canal revenue. The larger number of tankers returning empty southward through the Canal (22 million tons in 1952), and the possibility of reducing the journey to the Mediterranean from Persia, Arabia, and Iraq by over two-thirds (with direct overland connexion) [7] has made the construction of pipelines a distinctly attractive economic proposition. It had, for instance, been calculated that with the Aramco 'Tapline' a saving is achieved of 4·90 dollars per ton of oil transported. As the capacity of the pipe is 15·5 million tons per annum, there is in prospect a saving of some 70 million dollars per annum when full operation is achieved; and the I.P.C. pipelines from Kirkuk to Tripoli and Banias are only 550 miles long, with a potential capacity of 22 million tons. It is also true that the Suez Canal Company has shown great sensitivity to the problem of oil transportation. Dues on empty tankers returning to the Middle East have been progressively reduced to a figure now less than half of the loaded rate, and in 1950 dues on individual passengers aboard ship were abolished, in order to counter the competition of air transport.

A Changed Outlook in South-western Asia

The more advantageous political situation and increased wealth of South-western Asia are bringing about a radical change of attitude among the leaders of Middle Eastern society. There is first a new self-confidence founded on realization of their own advance at a time of regression and decline in Europe. Contemplating their increased private fortunes based on oil, cotton, or wool, or derived from general trading during periods of war scarcity, at a time when Marshall Aid has been found necessary by formerly imperialist nations in Europe and when Great Britain negotiated a 1000 million dollars loan to maintain national solvency, Arab, Persian, and Turkish statesmen and politicians have become increasingly disinclined to accept political tutelage, economic domination, or even advice of any kind from the West.

Instead, following the lead given by India, the nations of South-western Asia have felt emboldened to adopt a policy of critical appraisal towards the West, with selective absorption of whatever might be offered in finance, ideology, and technology. This, coinciding with the division of the present-day world into Communist and non-Communist areas, has allowed more than ever an increasingly eclectic viewpoint,

[7] *E.g.*, the Aramco pipeline from Dhahran to Saida is 1200 miles long, as compared with a sea journey via the Suez Canal of 4000 miles (Chapter XXVIII, Fig. 4).

and the broad-scale effects of being able to choose between competing systems are now clearly apparent within South-western Asia.

Egypt pursues an increasingly nationalistic policy, with an internal economy based firmly upon *laissez-faire* capitalism. Turkey in contrast at first experimented deeply with State-control of industry and public utilities (étatism), sustained by political autarky—but since 1950 has undertaken a reversal of previous trends, with some sectors of production now returned to private ownership.[8] In the political field there is a distinct drift from the extreme secular nationalism that prevailed under Kemal Atatürk, and a much greater readiness to accept outside financial assistance, with concomitant treaty obligations involving extensive military alliances. Persia has experimented with a certain degree of State ownership—mainly as affecting oil exploitation, but also in distributing royal lands to peasant exploitation; Syria has tended to follow the Egyptian pattern of nationalism and private enterprise, while the Lebanon, Jordan, and Israel value at least a tenuous link with France, Great Britain, and the U.S.A. respectively.[9] Saudi Arabia has increased her economic ties with the United States, and Israel operates a mixture of étatism and private enterprise, owing to the overriding necessity of rapid development of resources to support an immigrant population at standards higher than those prevailing in most neighbouring regions of South-west Asia.

The marked division since 1945 between Communist and non-Communist States has made it possible for Middle Eastern politicians to 'play off' one foreign rival against another. Zionist leaders invoked both American and Soviet support in order to coerce Britain into granting independence to the Jews; Persia has been able to return to her traditional nineteenth-century policy of balance, with three major contestants for favours (Great Britain, Russia, and the U.S.A.) instead of the former two; and Syria and the Lebanon made use of British interest to enforce the ending of the French Mandate in 1944.

Moreover, by reason of their contacts—social, religious, and commercial—with the rest of the world, the inhabitants of South-west Asia can appeal to outside interest and assistance in a way that is denied to

[8] *E.g.*, a number of industries such as textiles and light engineering has been 'denationalized.' Turkey is an active member of U.N.O. (the Turkish contingent in Korea was, in proportion to the size of the country, second after that of the U.S.A.) and also of N.A.T.O., and she has recently concluded defensive military alliances with Greece, Yugoslavia, Iraq, and Pakistan (N.A.T.O. and Baghdad treaties).

[9] The Lebanese currency, despite strongly expressed Syrian disapproval, remains tied to the French franc; and Britain pays an annual subsidy to the State of Jordan.

many groups in other parts of the earth. The various religious sects, Hebrew, Christian, and Moslem, have often close connexion with larger bodies of co-religionists elsewhere, and the Jews are to an especial degree the object of interest and sympathy to devout Christians. Reinforcing these ties of religion are a number of social and commercial contacts. Syrian and Lebanese emigrants now settled in the Americas and West Africa still send back to relatives at home a substantial volume of remittances, often retain dual nationality, and even return to spend their last years; while a somewhat similar position holds in Southern Arabia, with much of the life and economy depending upon commercial ties and remittances from India and the East Indies. It is finally hardly necessary to recall the world-wide importance and connexions of the Jewish and Armenian communities.

As a consequence, the point of view and needs of many peoples in South-west Asia are frequently canvassed over the world, with an effectiveness that has little parallel elsewhere. The stock markets of New York, London, and Paris do not react with the same sensitivity to events among the Eskimo, Filipinos, or Peruvians as they do to events in Arabia or Persia; Tibetans, Koreans, or Australians are not represented in a majority of Cabinets and universities in the world, as are Jews and Roman Catholics; Kikuyu insurgents do not campaign in what is regarded as a holy land by millions living elsewhere; and Hottentot, Maori, or Malayan chieftains cannot negotiate fabulously wealthy mineral concessions as do the sheikhs of the Persian Gulf. In short, the world-wide associations of the natives of South-west Asia, both cultural and financial, have contributed under the changed circumstances of the last few decades to a notable growth of the influence in world affairs possessed by the States of that area.

Political Organization

There have been many sustained attempts to overcome the tendencies to political division and separation which arise in part at least from geographical environment in South-west Asia. The most successful single movement so far has been Islam, which by its simple theology and ritual, and its attempts at synthesis and pragmatism, came near to creating a single polity within South-west Asia. But the major separation into Sunni and Shi'a provided a fundamental weakness, and in the present century a growth of materialist nationalism has led many to reject Islam, which in many regions of the Middle East is now in real decline. Another attempt at unity was the Ottoman Empire, about which views have altered radically during the last few years. It was for long popular to regard the Ottoman system as inefficient, tyrannical, and wholly regrettable—as exemplified in the phrases "sick man of Europe" and "the unspeakable Turk." But contemporary research into Turkish history, together with certain other factors, have contributed to a distinct change of attitude regarding the merits of the Ottomans, who are now accorded appreciably more sympathy and respect. After experiences with Arab governments, the United States particularly has come to the view that Turkey, as currently the most progressive and stable political unit in the Middle East, must form the major local element in schemes of Western defence and anti-Communist containment.

At present two other movements envisage a closer linking of at least various parts of South-west Asia: the Greater Syria plan and the Arab League. The idea of a Greater Syria arises from the undoubted broad environmental unity of much of the Arabian peninsula, which the early Arab geographers classified summarily into Esh Sham (the left hand, or north) and El Yemen (the right hand, or south). This view was sustained by Sir George Adam Smith, who emphasized the undeniable elements of unity within an area stretching from the Mediterranean to the Tigris-Euphrates, and from the Taurus to the Sinai. At present, however, the region is partitioned among five sovereign States; and frontiers, far from being co-terminous with valid geographical boundaries, either represent an attempt to achieve maximum convenience in mere delimitation, or else reflect the balance of power between various nations which prevailed in 1918–26 and in 1948. For example, the head-waters of the river Jordan were deliberately allotted to Palestine (now Israel), to the disadvantage of Syria; Lebanese boundaries were liberally drawn so as to increase the viability of the new State *vis-à-vis* Syria; the present boundary between Jordan and Israel is a fortuitous stabilization of a military line as it existed on a particular day; and international bargains, rather than local feeling, determined the nationality of communities in the Hatay of Turkey and in the former Vilayet of Mosul.

One result of thus ignoring human and economic factors is that a considerable unbalance now exists between the various States. The

Lebanon must rely on imported food, and clings uneasily to her assets of a few good port sites, which, however, are likely to be gravely menaced by developments in near-by rival countries: *e.g.*, at Haifa, Banias, and Latakia. The country has a high proportion of reasonably skilled, adaptable, and industrious artisans, many of whom, owing to lack of local resources and restricted markets, cannot find full employment. Syria, on the contrary, exports food grains, and has areas in the northeast along the Euphrates and tributary rivers which are relatively empty and capable of further development. Unwillingness to rely on the non-Syrian ports of Beirut and Tripoli has led to the construction of a new harbour at Latakia on a not outstandingly good site.

Jordan, with her limited agricultural resources, could precariously maintain her pre-1948 population, but since the entry of nearly 800,000 destitute Arab refugees from Palestine must be considered definitely over-populated. Also, debarred from making use of natural port outlets at Haifa and Jaffa-Tel Aviv, Jordan is forced either to trade through the Lebanon—which both adds considerably to transport costs, and necessitates Syrian goodwill, since there is no common frontier—or, in default, to develop a port at Akaba. This in turn is expensive, because Suez Canal dues are then involved. In contrast, Iraq possesses considerable resources in irrigable land which are so far under-developed because of lack of people; and the country also depends for the marketing of its principal natural wealth, petroleum, upon the collaboration of Syria, the Lebanon, and Jordan, and even to some extent of Israel. The establishment of the State of Israel a generation after the setting up of the Jewish National Home in Palestine intruded into the Middle East a new, progressive, and (to Moslems) highly disturbing political force. Israel represents a novel 'State idea': a nation in the making, it is made up of immigrants, chiefly from Europe, and finds unity in its attachment to the historic land of its Jewish forefathers. With external financial help and with pioneering zeal, Israelis are energetically exploiting the small natural resources of their narrow territory, despite the hostility of, and barriers raised by, the Arab world around them.

There is in consequence no likelihood of this State forming a part of any purely Arab unit. But the fact that certain of the headwaters and tributaries of Israeli rivers, which are imperatively needed for irrigation, lie outside Jewish control, together with her urgent need to find markets for her expanding industry, suggests that inevitably, too, Israel will be drawn to interest herself in the question of a Greater Syria.

A current Arab fear is that Israel might be impelled from economic and political motives to create a Greater Syria under Jewish rule; and for the struggling Israeli State, where in 1953 exports covered only one-fifth of the cost of imports, a unified and hence stronger Greater Syria could under Arab control represent a deadly danger, but also, under Jewish hegemony, an aspiration and a guarantee of survival. One can thus see in the idea of a Greater Syria an acute problem of geopolitics, of the kind that fascinated German thinkers in the first half of the present century. Environmental conditions, with indeterminate physical and human boundaries, offer an invitation to movement and expansion, with consequent temptation for local statesmen.[10] The existing multiplicity of national units and tiers of government can inhibit full development of resources, and consequently perpetuate an unnecessarily low standard of life, with social distress and unrest. As the Danubian succession States discovered after 1918, the erection of several petty national States in place of one single large unit may exact an economic price. Creation of new frontiers and more national capitals does not necessarily produce a millennium of peace and prosperity.

Whether or not factors of economic geography can provide convincing evidence in support of a 'Greater Syria,' political conditions make its realization a remote possibility. The obvious candidate for rulership of a federation of the Lebanon, Syria, Jordan, and Iraq was for long the Hashemite Dynasty of Jordan in the person of the late King Abdullah.[11] But now that two young monarchs of almost identical age rule respectively in Amman and Baghdad, a designation of a single head of the Hashemites is no longer easy. Moreover, this family is suspect to many Arabs as too closely connected with Britain. Also, even if the monarchical principle could be accepted within Syria and the Lebanon, politicians and senior civil servants now have a personal vested interest in perpetuating republicanism and the *status quo*. Whatever was felt by the ordinary people, governmental personnel of the two regimes would not easily bring themselves to vote their own demise.

Other difficulties arise from the hostility of Egypt to the possible creation of a larger and probably more powerful State on its northern borders, ruled by a dynasty distinctly favourable to Britain. Finally,

[10] It is of interest to recall that on the day following the news of unrest and a *coup d'état* in Egypt (February 1954), one Israeli newspaper (*Maariv*) advocated an immediate annexation of Egyptian territory adjoining Israel, as far as the Suez Canal.

[11] Abdullah took part in the Arab Revolt of 1916–18, and a younger brother Feisul became the first king of Iraq. Grandsons of the two brothers now rule in Jordan and Iraq.

there has been the attitude of the late King Ibn Saud of Arabia, who was at personal enmity with the Hashemites, whom he ousted from Mecca in 1925. H. St J. Philby, a professed admirer of the Arabian king, states frankly that "determined opposition to the Hashemite rulers has for the last twenty-five years been the basis of Saudi Arabian policy,"[12] a matter which explains the inaction of Saudi Arabian contingents in the Arab-Israeli war of 1948.

The Arab League

This came into existence in 1945, following a conference in Cairo of representatives of the Arab States. Its aims are twofold: "to protect and safeguard the independence and integrity of member-states"[13] and to develop economic and cultural co-operation between the participating countries, which are Egypt, Iraq, Jordan, the Lebanon, Saudi Arabia, Syria, and the Yemen. Results achieved so far have, however, been few and disappointing. Joint action culminating in a declaration of war against Israel occurred in 1948, but the actual course of the fighting made clear that there was no overall strategic plan, and that each participating Arab State was determined to follow a separate policy closely reflecting its own particular interests. The failure of this joint military action, and the slight, almost negligible degree of economic and cultural co-operation which have so far been achieved, indicate that the Arab League lacks real political force. Though there are many references to potential strength, the practical importance of the Arab League itself in world affairs is at present minimal.

For this, the unequal size and wealth and the diverging situation and interests of the member States are chiefly responsible. Table 4, which represents an agreed estimate of relative economic strength, brings out clearly the great disparity in wealth that exists.

Egypt now feels fully capable of managing her own affairs, and is determined to avoid any policy that might involve dependence upon or even association with other nations, particularly Britain or America. Thanks to the high price of raw cotton, Syria began existence as a

---

[12] H. St J. Philby, *Arabian Jubilee* (Hale, London, 1952).

[13] Translation by the Arab Office, London. Delegates also represented Arab Palestine. Libya applied for admission to the Arab League in 1952, and Oman became a member in 1955.

2A*

TABLE 4

Suggested Capital Participation in Arab Development Bank
(sponsored by the Arab League, 1954)

Total Capital (£ E)

	AMOUNT	PERCENTAGE OF TOTAL ISSUE
Egypt	80,000,000	40
Iraq	34,000,000	17
Saudi Arabia	32,000,000	16
Kuwait	24,000,000	12
Syria	8,000,000	4
Qatar	6,000,000	3
Lebanon	4,800,000	2·4
The Sudan	4,000,000	2·0
Jordan	4,000,000	2·0
The Yemen	2,400,000	1·2
Bahrain	800,000	0·4

Source: *Bull. du Centre de Documentation et de Synthèse*, IV, i (Paris, 1954).

financially independent State[14] with a balanced budget that permitted
a modest programme of economic development—the drainage of marshes
along the Orontes and the construction of a railway and port at Latakia.
Like Egypt, Syria thus envisages reasonable prospects of following a
separate and nationalistic policy in both economic and political matters.

In the Lebanon a markedly different attitude prevails. Geographical
position makes the country pre-eminently a region of intercourse and
contact, where the Orient and the West meet and mingle. This is shown
by the varied racial and social composition of the population (there are
twenty-three active religious sects); and restricted natural resources tend
also to foster cosmopolitanism and openness to new ideas, with a real
dependence on outside connexions.[15] Tourism and the reception of
students from abroad are important to the national economy, while
international trade and exchange are relatively highly developed.[16] At
the same time, recognizing the somewhat unusual nature of certain

[14] *I.e.*, following the dissolution in 1950 of the joint customs union with the Lebanon.
[15] Lebanese daily papers carry current quotations of gold, both bar and coin, with
names that are rarely seen elsewhere: English guineas and sovereigns, French louis and
napoleons, and American 'eagles.' It was frequent even ten years ago to carry out day-
to-day transactions in Turkish gold pounds. Also significant of Lebanese business
acumen was the construction of a new airport for jet airliners—before any such machines
were actually in service in any part of the world.
[16] In addition to tourism and educational services, we may cite the receipt of remittances from the Americas, and, in bad years, the illegal sale of hashish, which in 1951
is thought to have totalled £11 millions—the largest single item in Lebanese exports.

sources of income, Lebanese statesmen are at pains to cultivate friendly relations with as many countries as possible, particularly the wealthier nations of the West. Moreover, as the one predominantly Christian state of South-west Asia, with only a slender basis for separate existence, the Lebanon must act circumspectly.[17] In consequence, Lebanese policy aims to demonstrate beyond dispute an ostensible solidarity with the Arab nationalist aims of her neighbours and of the Arab League, but at the same time to maintain reassuring contacts with non-Moslem countries—France and the United States especially.

Relations with the Great Powers

It will be clear that the main feature of the last decade has been a radical alteration in the relations of South-western Asia with the outside world, and in particular with the United States, Britain, France, and Russia. The Middle East is now a participant on a significant scale in world trade,[18] contributing certain highly strategic materials; and is in fact increasingly dependent on selling abroad a part of its production of these—chiefly petroleum, but also cereals, tobacco, and fruit. At the same time the higher volume of profits from these commodities encourages a more independent foreign policy, which finds its chief expression in a vehement nationalism, and engenders a changed outlook compounded in part of xenophobia, in part of a genuine respect for the material achievements of the West, and in part a vague desire, as yet unfulfilled, for some kind of revival of a Moslem 'Third Force' in the Old World between East and West. This latter aim takes root from the undoubted influence and superior culture once existing in South-west Asia; conscious of his once brilliant past, and now returning prosperity, the present-day Middle Easterner is quick to resent any suggestion of inferiority.

South-west Asia and the United States

We may examine in more detail the relations of South-western Asia and other Powers, beginning with the United States. Until 1940 it could

---

[17] It is probable that the Lebanon now has a Moslem majority, but this is concealed or minimized by a number of expedients: irregularities in Census returns and the counting of emigrants living abroad.

[18] E.g., in 1953–54 Turkey was the fourth largest world exporter of wheat.

be said that contacts were slight, being limited to a few cultural and missionary links (such as the American University of Beirut, which dates from 1866) and to a very small volume of trade. From the nature of her own production, the United States could hardly absorb much of the principal Middle Eastern exports—oil, cotton, and tobacco; and the relatively high price of American goods, together with the economic ties with Mandatory Powers, precluded a large import trade. During the

TABLE 5

U.S. Trade with Selected Countries of the Middle East
(in $000's)

COUNTRY	TRADE	1938	1950	1951	1953	1954
Egypt	Exports to U.S.A.	700	15,000	20,000	26,300	20,000
	Imports from U.S.A.	2,500	13,000	28,000	60,200	40,000
	Total trade	3,200	28,000	48,000	86,500	60,000
Iraq	Exports	2,900	—	2,700	2,000	16,000
	Imports	2,800	—	19,800	28,300	27,000
	Total	5,700	—	22,500	30,300	43,000
Israel	Exports	—	8,100	10,100	13,700	14,000
	Imports	—	106,000	109,200	92,000	74,000
	Total	—	114,100	119,300	105,700	88,000
Jordan	Exports	7	neg.	neg.	neg.	neg.
	Imports	7	1,200	4,900	2,100	3,500
	Total	14	1,200	4,900	2,100	3,500
Persia	Exports	1,400	23,600	32,000	22,700	19,300
	Imports	2,600	33,100	34,500	21,400	45,000
	Total	4,000	56,700	66,500	44,100	64,300
Turkey	Exports	320	—	67,000	74,000	64,600
	Imports	363	—	60,000	64,000	80,000
	Total	683	—	127,000	138,000	144,600

Sources: Official publications of countries concerned; Overseas Economic Surveys (H.B.M. Govt., 1947–55).

second world war, however, when South-west Asia was entirely cut off from many of its supplies of manufactured goods—from Germany, Italy, Japan, and France—and was forced to accept greatly reduced imports from the United Kingdom, a market was opened to American supplies.

Then the de Golyer report of 1944, which foreshadowed ultimate

American dependence on imports of petroleum,[19] focused attention in the United States not only on the importance of the Middle East as a future source of petroleum supplies, but also as a strategic region that might easily fall under Soviet domination.

Tension between Russia and the West has forced the United States to give attention to general strategic matters in South-west Asia. With the development of a 'zone of containment' extending along the borders of Russia and her satellites, South-west Asia and South-east Asia have come to be regarded as two major weak spots into which Communism might penetrate. In India there is the physical barrier of the Himalaya; in South-east Asia, China, and Korea, the issue has undergone decision by force; but in South-west Asia prospects are so far quite uncertain. Here, then, is one region where America can make strenuous efforts short of actual warfare to combat Russian influence; and this necessity was recognized in the attempt during 1953–54 to form a containing 'Islamic bloc' of Turkey, Iraq, and Pakistan. It will be noted that none of the three countries is wholly Arab. Two do not belong to the Arab League, and Iraq is in some respects different from its fellow members of the League by the predominance of Shi'a adherents and by the importance of non-Arab minorities: Kurds and Christians.

South-west Asia and the United Kingdom

If the interests of the U.S.A. in South-west Asia could be said to be mainly concerned with strategy and oil, those of Britain are both strategic and economic. In one sense, American expansion overseas is a matter of choice: her chief economic concern is production for an internal market, and the country itself provides sufficient basic foodstuffs and raw materials. But Britain is in the opposite position. Her geographical resources and conditions of life make essential the development of widest possible contacts, not merely as an adjunct to her economy, but as a vital necessity to survival. This in turn involves two matters—sensitivity to economic conditions and prevailing standards of life in other parts of the earth, and the maintenance of political strength in order to prevent interference with or discrimination against the normal flow of trade.

[19] Since 1950 the U.S.A. has begun to import petroleum chiefly from the Caribbean, but now to some extent from the Middle East.

In an imperfect world it would seem that these conditions may be best achieved by the possession of military bases, commercial concessions, and territorial advantages. Having once experimented with 'Free Trade,' Britain now finds that it is essential to retain some advantages as bargaining weapons and as an assurance of survival in time of war. Applied to South-west Asia, these aspects of British policy result in:

(1) A desire to possess actual military bases, or in default to have at least the right of occupation of strategic sites in time of war. This underlies the maintenance of British colonial rule in Aden and Cyprus, the 'protection' of sheikhdoms in southern and eastern Arabia; the payment of annual subsidies to Libya and Jordan in return for the right to keep troops there; and the special relationships with Iraq.

(2) Following the loss of preferential markets in other parts of the world, Britain is more interested in South-west Asia as a potential trading area. The increased purchasing power of some Arabs and the scope for capital development make the Middle East more attractive as a possible market. In 1950 British trade with Egypt alone amounted to £60 million sterling, and under favourable conditions a figure of at least £150 million might be reached for the Middle East as a whole.

(3) The direct participation of the British Government as a shareholder in the Suez Canal, the former Anglo-Iranian Oil Company (now the British Petroleum Company), and Iraq Petroleum Company inevitably means closer connexion with Middle Eastern affairs.[20] This, in the view of some, cannot always be disinterested.

Achievement of the aims indicated above demands a supple and imaginative British policy based on close understanding of the physical and human environment of South-west Asia, and sensitive to local developments. Unfortunately, this has of recent years rarely been attained. Anglo-French relations were gravely strained in 1944 over Syria and the Lebanon, without much corresponding gain in Arab friendship; in Palestine Britain managed to obtain the worst of both worlds— enmity from the dispossessed Arabs, and contempt from the Zionists; while as regards the Anglo-Iranian Oil episode it was perhaps a case of

[20] Note that whereas American interests in Middle Eastern oil are from individuals only, the British Government is itself a shareholder.

"too little and too late."[21] Though it is by no means true that present-day difficulties between the Middle East and the West (and Britain in particular) stem mainly from past British policy, at least it might be said that there has hardly been a full realization of the amplitude and nature of the changes now occurring in South-west Asia.[22]

South-west Asia and France

The position of France is no less complex. Besides direct economic links (e.g., France is currently the largest single importer of Middle East oil, and Lebanese currency remains linked to the French franc), France has strong cultural connexions with certain countries of South-west Asia, and now (following the end of British rule in India) rules the largest number of Moslem subjects. Many Egyptians, Persians, Turks, Syrians, and Lebanese speak French by choice, and send their children to French schools within the Middle East, and even, in some instances, to French universities. Also, now that France has withdrawn from Syria and the Lebanon her cultural influence and esteem are higher in those countries than at any time in the last fifteen years.

It is most unlikely that France would regain, or even wish to regain, direct political power in South-west Asia, but the relative success of her cultural approach to certain nations of the Middle East raises the interesting question of whether the contact of South-west Asia and Europe through French culture is more effective than through Anglo-Saxon exchanges.

[21] In the matter of oil royalties 16 per cent. of net profits were paid by the A.I.O.C. to the Persian Government up to 1951. In 1950–51 the Arabian American Oil Co. offered to the Saudi Arabian Government 50 per cent. of the net profits of the company in respect of its concession; and this 'fifty-fifty basis' quickly became standard for the remaining oil concessions in the Middle East, being in fact also offered by the A.I.O.C. during negotiations in 1951 with the Persians. In 1953 a German company (Karl Deilman A.G., of Bentheim) signed an agreement covering oil exploitation in the Yemen, which is reported to assign 75 per cent. of profits to the Yemenite authorities (*Bull. du Centre de Doc. et de Synth.* (Middle East), No. 2 (Paris, November 1953), IV, i.

[22] The most recent phase of British policy is an attempt to organize a 'northern tier' of States, under specific British impulsion—though with some American interest. The resulting alliance (the Baghdad Pact of 1955 involving Turkey, Iraq, and later Persia) could in some respects be regarded as recognizing a significant difference between those parts of South-west Asia that are purely Arab and orthodox Moslem and those that are non-Arab and follow heterodox forms of Islam.

South-west Asia and the U.S.S.R.

Direct economic contacts between the U.S.S.R. and the countries of South-west Asia are, except in Persia, generally small. Considerable tension exists with Turkey, and therefore exchange of all kinds is at a minimum. But a pact signed in 1953 with Persia envisaged the export of Russian textiles, consumer goods (chiefly electrical), sugar, and heavy machinery in return for Persian cereals, minerals, fruit, and carpets. The U.S.S.R. has also shown recent interest in trade with Egypt (as a buyer of cotton and oil) and with Israel (citrus fruit). Much more important was the decision in 1955 to supply military equipment and arms on a relatively large scale to certain Arab countries, thus increasing the likelihood of an Arab-Jewish conflict.

Parallel with this, however, is the ideological campaign carried on against certain Middle Eastern States, as, under their present forms of government, "satellites of America." This campaign covers several aspects:

1. The importance of the U.S.S.R. as a Moslem State. Apart from the countries of South-west Asia, the U.S.S.R., with twenty-one million Moslem subjects, ranks third in the world after Pakistan and South-east Asia. Two well-publicized pilgrimages to Mecca, led by a Moslem from Tashkent, have recently taken place, indicating, according to Russian views, the vigour and liberty of action accorded to religion in the U.S.S.R.[23]

2. The necessity and inevitability of social change within South-west Asia, and the lowered standard of living due to "colonial exploitation" by the West.

3. The Armenian question—an important matter when the intellectual ability, relative wealth, and wide distribution of Armenians within South-west Asia are borne in mind. Soviet propaganda emphasizes two themes:

   (a) The friendship and advantages offered by the U.S.S.R. to Armenians, underlined by the fate since 1900 of Armenians living in non-Russian territory—most of whom were exterminated. In contrast there is the functioning state of the

[23] Radio-Moscow, November 15 to 18, 1953.

Armenian S.S.R., with a population of nearly two millions, which is now a national home for all Armenians, even those living in Europe and the Americas.

(b) Armenian intellectual life finds widest expression in Soviet Armenia. When living as minorities in Turkey, Persia, or the Arab countries, Armenians can achieve no real intellectual or material progress.[24]

In a more general sense, the Soviet system can also make a powerful appeal to Arab psychology on the grounds of being itself a vigorous and successful State, and one that is likely to be even more powerful in the future. This point is well taken by Arabs, who tend to be much impressed by visible success. Secondly, Communism offers a way to material prosperity which rests on a mystical basis not entirely unlike that of early Islam—a brotherhood without class distinction dedicated to the overthrow of decadent empires by mass endeavour, and propagating direct, simply understood ideas. This appeal is the more dangerous from its many-sidedness and its skilful use of the varied elements, social and human, that characterize the environment of South-west Asia.

FURTHER READING

ANTONIUS, G., *The Arab Awakening* (Hamish Hamilton, London, 1938).

ARNOLD, T., and GUILLAUME, A., *The Legacy of Islam* (Oxford University Press, 1931).

ARBERRY, A. J., *The Legacy of Persia* (Oxford University Press, 1953).

BLANCHARD, R., *Asie Occidentale* (*Géographie Universelle*, vol. viii) (Colin, Paris, 1929).

BOARD OF TRADE, Overseas Economic Surveys (by individual country) (London, 1947 and after).

COON, C. S., *Caravan: The Story of the Middle East* (Holt, New York, 1951; Cape, London, 1952).

COOKE, H. V., *Challenge and Response in the Middle East* (Harper, New York, 1952; Hamish Hamilton, London, 1953).

DICKSON, H. R. P., *The Arab of the Desert* (Allen and Unwin, London and New York, 1949).

ETTINGHAUSEN, R. (editor), *Books and Periodicals dealing with the Middle East* (Middle East Institute, Washington, 1954).

FISHER, W. B., *The Middle East, a Physical, Social, and Regional Geography* (third edition; Methuen, London and New York, 1955).

GLANVILLE, S. R. K., *The Legacy of Egypt* (Oxford University Press, 1942).

HITTI, P. K., *A History of the Arabs* (Macmillan, London, 1952).

HOLLINGWORTH, C., *The Arabs and the West* (Methuen, London, 1952).

[24] Radio Erivan, November 20, 1953.

JACKH, E., *Background of the Middle East* (Cornell University Press, New York, 1952).

KEEN, B. A., *The Agricultural Development of the Middle East* (H.M.S.O., London, 1947).

KIRK, G., *A Short History of the Middle East* (Methuen, London, 1948); *The Middle East in the War* (R.I.I.A., 1951).

LAMBTON, A. K. S., *Landlord and Peasant in Persia* (R.I.I.A., 1953).

LONGRIGG, S. H., *Oil in the Middle East* (Oxford University Press, 1954).

ROYAL INSTITUTE OF INTERNATIONAL AFFAIRS, *The Middle East: a Political and Economic Survey* (London, 1951).

THORNBURG, M., SPRY, G., SOULE, G., *Turkey: An Economic Appraisal* (Twentieth-century Fund, New York, 1949).

WARRINER, D., *Land and Poverty in the Middle East* (R.I.I.A., 1947).

WORTHINGTON, E. B., *Middle East Science* (H.M.S.O., London, 1946).

CHAPTER XXX

The Impact of the Outer World on Africa

R. J. HARRISON CHURCH

PROBABLY no other continent still shows so vividly as Africa the influence of physical factors upon political, social, and economic development. Nor is there elsewhere such remarkable evidence of the imprint of external peoples and their policies. Varying political aims and methods have had immense effects upon Africa. In West Africa contrasting methods and results of French, British, Portuguese, Spanish, and Liberian policies are juxtaposed in rather similar natural regions.

Much of the interest and many of the problems of modern Africa arise from its being the least developed and most intractable of all continents, yet adjacent to Asia and Europe, both long developed, more intensively settled and politically organized than Africa.

As a result, Africa has been for centuries a challenge and a magnet to Asiatic and European peoples. Physical and other difficulties long retarded European entry to the inter-tropical areas, although the Arabs penetrated across the Sahara and settled on its northern and eastern fringes.

In the twentieth century Africa has acquired a new importance. Dependent territories have mostly become independent in Asia. Europe, and indeed the world, struggling to redress economic impoverishment from the second world war, are looking to the more intensive development of Africa. The United States, very concerned with its security, has a new strategic and economic interest in Africa. As *The Times*[1] put it:

Africa is the new continent; she is a focus of twentieth-century development, the centre of special problems of race, and the link between Europe and the Americas, on one side; and between Europe and Australia, New

[1] *The Times*, December 1, 1949.

Zealand and the Far East on the other. The importance of Africa is seen in Moscow as well as in London and Washington.

Even more certainly than elsewhere, the present in Africa can only be seen as the latest act of history, and to this we must turn.

The Ancient World and Africa

To explain the origin of Egyptian civilization, like those of the Tigris and Euphrates, Toynbee invoked[2] an inverted determinism, with his doctrine of the Challenge-and-Response. The challenge was an increasingly difficult environment and the response a civilization. The challenge was desiccation of the African grasslands after the close of the Great Ice Age, and one response was the emergence in Nilotic Egypt of Neolithic civilization following occupation and settlement by immigrant hunting people from the drying grasslands.

Attractive though this and other explanations be, they seem almost too simple. Did desiccation occur, and, if so, are we sure it had these effects on every one? Did those in unaffected areas remain Mesolithic hunters and food gatherers? Was agriculture invented here or elsewhere? Sauer[3] places the beginnings of agriculture, with plant selection by vegetative reproduction, and of animal domestication in South-east Asia; although one of his three centres of seed domestication was the Ethiopian Highlands. From them were probably obtained millets and, perhaps, other cereals, pulses, and possibly cotton.

The rise of ancient Egypt is probably more accurately but less elegantly explained by the transfer of techniques to an area of remarkable and renewable fertility, with an assured water supply in a desert so forbidding as to deter attack. Moreover, the Mediterranean fringes and especially the Nile delta were never pure desert. They lay astride one of the world's routeways and the meeting-place of the Mediterranean, Nile, and Red Sea.

The Phœnicians, Greeks, and Romans all remained within the Mediterreanean climatic zone in North Africa, or in areas adjacent to it, and were very dependent upon sea communications. The desert was

[2] Arnold J Toynbee, *A Study of History* (Oxford University Press, 1934), vol. i, pp. 304–306.
[3] Carl O. Sauer, *Agricultural Origins and Dispersals* (American Geographical Society, New York, 1952).

equally abhorrent to them, and cataracts and the Sudd region prevented southward movement up the Nile.

To the Ancients, as to the later Spanish, French, and Italians, North Africa appealed as an outlet for emigrants and as a source of food, because it enjoys a somewhat similar climate to that of their homelands. The vast interior of Africa remained beyond their range.

The Early Kingdoms of the Western Sudan

Environmental factors, linguistic, agricultural, social, and political differences have long contributed to contrasting traditions between savannah and forest peoples. Linguistic groupings and distributions in the savannah lands indicate large-scale prolonged movements of peoples over vast areas. These were possible because of ease of movement, grain cultivation, and cattle-keeping in country originally covered by open dry forest. Such activities were impossible in the desert to the north and in the dense rain forest to the south.

> The Western Sudan covered too vast an area and was too open to distinct external influences on too long a front for it to retain or to have imposed on it by migration or conquest any complete linguistic or cultural homogeneity. At the same time, the more open character of this country made it possible for expanding ruling groups to maintain partial unity, linguistic, cultural and political, over very extensive areas.[4]

Daryll Forde and others conclude that the various States of the Western Sudan traced their foundation to Hamitic-speaking, non-negroid invaders coming from north-east Africa by way of the Saharan routes and oases. Their introduction of the camel and the use of horses and donkeys enabled large-scale military and political organization, widespread transport and exchange of goods.

Early development of States in the Western Sudan had something of the same explanation as that of ancient Egypt. But in the Western Sudan Toynbee would find the invaders making the challenge. Compared, however, with Egypt, there is along the Niger far less alluvium, only incomplete seclusion by desert, but greater possibilities of cattle-keeping.

The Ghana Kingdom seems to have been founded in the fourth century A.D., and until the ninth century had 'white' rulers. Its zenith was

---

[4] Daryll Forde, "The Cultural Map of West Africa: Successive Adaptions to Tropical Forests and Grasslands," in *Transactions of the New York Academy of Sciences*, Series II, vol. xv (1953), pp. 206–219, at p. 210

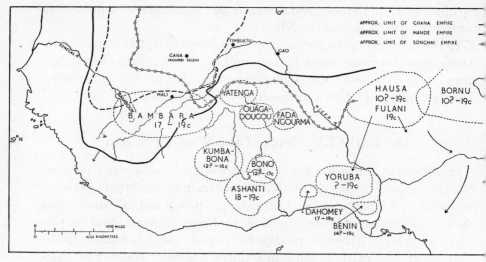

FIG. 1. THE KINGDOMS OF THE WESTERN SUDAN AND OF THE WEST AFRICAN
FORESTS
Mainly after Daryll Forde.

about A.D. 1000, when it extended roughly from Bakel on the Senegal
to Lake Faguibine in the east. The State is mentioned by an Arab
writer of A.D. 800, and in the following century by Ibn Hawqal. In the
eleventh century El Bekir devoted three pages to describing the capital
and countryside at a time when this State was not yet Islamized. Cotton
and millet were grown.

But in 1076 the capital was sacked by Moslem Berbers. Freedom was
regained from 1087 to 1240, but the State never knew its old prosperity
and decayed completely by the fourteenth century. Excavation has
located the capital at Koumbi Saleh, 205 miles north-north-east of
Bamako (French Sudan). Unfortunately, we so far have evidence only
of its later Islamized period.

Ghana was progressively supplanted by the Mande (or Mali or Man-
dingo) kingdom. Descendants of its rulers, who embraced Islam, are
still chiefs at Bamako. This kingdom was at its zenith in the early fourteenth century and included Gao and Timbuktu. Its capital of Mali was
described by the Arab Ibn Battuta,[5] who visited it in 1352. Decline
then set in, leading to final collapse and Bambara conquest in 1660.

Pressed on the west and east, many of its peoples moved up the Niger.

[5] Ibn Battuta, *Travels in Asia and Africa*, 1325–1354, translated and selected by
H. A. R. Gibb (Routledge, London, 1929).

In that direction lay forests less dense than those to the south, but in the north lay desert. Mande languages now predominate over the upper basins of the Senegal and Niger rivers, and Mende is spoken in Sierra Leone and western Liberia. Rice and cotton may first have reached the south-western coast of West Africa in this way. Cadamosto saw both on the Gambia river in 1455.

The eleventh century saw the rise of the Songoi Kingdom at Gao, on a trans-Saharan Arab trade route from Tripoli. Inhabitants of Gao were known as Songoi, and this name was applied to the whole empire. In 1468 Timbuktu was conquered, and in the west the Senegal river was reached in 1512. Katsina to the east was taken in 1515. This empire was conquered in 1591 by a Moorish and European mercenary army of four thousand men which had crossed the Sahara.

To the south were the entirely Negro and anti-Moslem Moshi Empires of Ouagadougou, Yatenga, and Fada N'Gourma, all of which survived to modern times. The Morho-Naba and his ministers still have ceremonial functions at Ouagadougou (Upper Volta).

In the east there is, until later, less documentation, though the indirect evidence of widespread oral tradition points to early pre-Islamic kingdoms likewise founded by 'whites' from the north.

All the above-mentioned kingdoms traded salt and cattle southward for slaves, ivory, gold, and kola-nuts from the forest. Some of the oldest African settlements were halting-places on these trade routes— e.g., Beyla in southern French Guinea, founded in 1230 and still a market for forest and savannah products. Slaves came from the politically weaker kin-organized tribes on the periphery of the kingdoms or empires. Gold was obtained from what is now the Gold Coast and also from Bambouk, on the borders of modern Senegal and the French Sudan. Kola-nuts came from what is now the Ivory Coast.

These goods and leather were also exchanged with Arab traders for European goods. The leather was later known erroneously as 'Morocco' leather. Early gold coins of Spain, Portugal, Genoa, and Venice may have been made of gold obtained overland, and some people maintain that Guinea is but a corruption of Ghana.

After the Moroccan conquest there were three centuries of anarchy, correlated, perhaps, with the Ottoman conquest of North Africa and the reduction of trans-Saharan trade and influence.

Arab Expansion in Africa

To Arabs the desert was natural, and so their realm of penetration in Africa was very different from that of the Ancients. Within a century of bursting out of Arabia in A.D. 632 they penetrated through North Africa and South-western Europe, inspired with the fervour of Mahomet's vision. North Africa became 'the western lands'—the 'Maghreb' of the Moslem Arab world.

The first great consequence of Arab conquest of Egypt in A.D. 639–41 was the isolation of Ethiopian Christendom for twelve centuries from the rest of the Christian world. The very individualized Ethiopian Coptic Church survived, although wedged between Islam and Paganism. In Ethiopia there also survived a Semitic language sandwiched between Hamitic and Nilotic linguistic areas, an individual if rather stagnant culture, and, until the air age, almost uninterrupted political freedom. The fastnesses and steep seaward edges of the Ethiopian Highlands are major explanations for these survivals.

The second effect of the advent of the Arabs was that, with the newly introduced camel, they were enabled to cross the Sahara, certainly from the tenth century onward. Beyond the desert the Arabs found the well-organized States described above. It is only through Arab chroniclers that we know anything (apart from quite recent archæological research at Koumbi Saleh and elsewhere) of these States. The writings have survived of Ibn Hawqal in the tenth century, El Bekir in the eleventh century, Ibn Battuta and Ibn Khaldum in the fourteenth century, and of the Berber Moor Leo Africanus. The last, a captive in Rome and a transient Christian convert, wrote a book on Africa in 1550. By a possible slip in asserting that the Niger flowed westward at Timbuktu he misled every one until Mungo Park proved otherwise in 1795–97.

From the eleventh century the Arabs converted some rulers of the Western Sudan to Islam, but the Negro peoples more slowly and the Moshi and their rulers not at all. Nevertheless, Arab influence on political organization was considerable. Moreover, Islam has since spread among most of the savannah peoples, and to-day is probably gaining more converts than Christianity in the forest lands. In East Africa Islam has spread far down the coast, where early Arab penetration reached as far as Sofala.

The Arabs engaged in trade with the successive empires of the middle

Niger. As intermediaries, they introduced European goods to them, although unknown to the European merchants. But the trade of greatest consequence was in slaves. For a thousand years the Arabs took Negro slaves across the Sahara and by sea along the east coast of Africa. Negro blood was introduced to Asia, North Africa, and Iberia. In the last, the idea of slavery was implanted and was soon to grow into massive proportions in the four centuries of European overseas slave trade to the New World.

Across and around the Sahara the Arabs also introduced such things as separate Moslem quarters to towns and greatly influenced architectural styles by bringing in their continuous and geometric patterns, massive walls, and the knowledge of vaulted and arched roofs.

To the Arabs the Sahara was "a hurdle and filter that restricted and selected the kinds of human movement and cultural forces that could penetrate and the sort of influence they could exert on the established populations."[6]

But the Arab world was severely weakened politically, reduced geographically, and shattered economically by reconquests, although at first these hardly affected North Africa. The Arab Empire was, however, ultimately destroyed there too, as the result of the mighty schism elsewhere between Sunnis and Shi'is and the Ottoman conquests provoked by that schism.

The Ottoman Influence in Africa

Until the early sixteenth century the Ottoman Turkish Empire had expanded north-westward into Europe. Further expansion seemed likely either there or, more probably, south-eastward into Azerbaijan and adjacent lands of the Osmanlis' birthplace. But the Shi'is revolution prevented this line of advance. Furthermore, the desperate need to forestall Shi'i influence in Arab lands caused rapid Ottoman conquests of Arabia and of North Africa as far west as Algeria between A.D. 1512 and A.D. 1574. There followed a period of decay in North Africa and in other lands previously penetrated by the Arabs. Ottoman influence was eliminated only in the nineteenth and twentieth centuries by French intervention in North Africa, British in Egypt, and Italian in Libya.

[6] Daryll Forde, *op. cit.*, p. 207.

Africa and the Route to India

The expulsion of the Arabs from Spain at the end of the fifteenth century led to great national upsurges there and in Portugal, and to a desire to undertake new crusades to spread the Christian faith and acquire the riches of the East. Religious and political hatred of the Moslem Arabs and Turks was intense. As the former had just been expelled from Iberia and the latter were obstructing the overland route to the East, there was a powerful amalgam of religious fervour, political hatred, and economic justification. There was also some jealousy, in Portugal at any rate, of Genoese trade with the Orient. For all these reasons a new maritime route to the East was in every way desirable and attractive. Nor may we dismiss the urge of sheer discovery, the hope of making contact with other Christian princes (through tales of Ethiopian Christianity), and of seeking gold south of the Sahara.

In the fifteenth century, especially between 1434 and 1498, many Portuguese expeditions explored the West African coasts, which in 1441 were reserved exclusively to the Portuguese by a Papal Bull. In 1494 the Treaty of Tordesillas gave them exclusive rights in all Africa and the Asiatic mainland, while to Spain was reserved most of the New World. Then in 1498 da Gama, by rounding the Cape, sailing up the east coast to Malindi and thence to India at Calicut, showed the practicability of the maritime Indian trade. He was also hopeful of supplementing it with gold and ivory from the East African coasts, after breaking the Arab monopoly. But he concluded that the other African coasts lacked possibilities of 'easy profit.' In this estimation he was wrong, for the West Coast provided most of the African trade of the next four centuries.

If the Ottoman Empire had conquered Morocco, and had based fleets on its Atlantic coast, it could have prevented Portuguese maritime trade with Africa and the East. Moreover, Ottoman conquests of Egypt in A.D. 1517 and of Iraq in A.D. 1534 were too late to prevent Portuguese footholds on the Indian Ocean.

European Coastal Footholds

For over three centuries the interests of maritime Powers were confined to two types of stations on the coast. The first type were calling-points or *points d'appui* on the route to India. These were sheltered coves where a fleet might rest and undertake repairs and where, above all, good supplies of water and possibly other goods such as vegetables were obtainable. Such were Portuguese Algoa Bay (east of modern Port Elizabeth, Union of South Africa) on their outward journeys to India (especially Goa) and Delagoa Bay (Lourenço Marques) on the return.

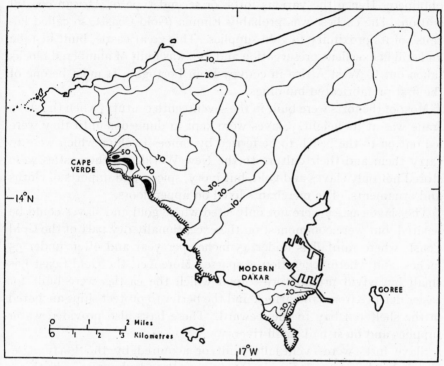

FIG. 2. CAPE VERDE AND THE ISLET OF GORÉE

The Portuguese were soon followed by the Dutch, who used Table Bay as a watering point and later made a settlement in 1652. The British first used St Helena (taken 1659) and then Cape Town after 1806. The French used Gorée (near modern Dakar), taken 1658, and Réunion, in the Indian Ocean, taken 1649.

The whole emphasis was on trade with Asia, because of its more advanced civilization and the greater opportunities which it offered compared with Africa. The latter also had formidable physical obstacles such as the surf-bound Senegal and Gulf of Guinea coasts, the paucity of deep sheltered and easily entered harbours, obstructed rivers, dense vegetation or desert, disease, and much more. Trade with North Africa would have been welcome, but the Turks made this impossible; South Africa seemed arid, useless, and difficult of entry; and the Arabs occupied the East Africa coast as far as 20° S. (Sofala).

Consequently, in Africa itself, opportunities were restricted and were confined to points where compact and valuable commodities could be obtained. Hence the various forts, or second type of African coastal station. The earliest was probably Elmina (Gold Coast), so called because of its proximity to gold supplies. This great castle, built in 1482 and still in excellent preservation and use, was built of numbered blocks taken out to West Africa in convoy from Portugal. It must be one of the first prefabricated buildings.

Most of the forts were built in the seventeenth century, when the slave trade was at its height. Slaves were kept in dungeons until they were led out on to the beach to be ferried by canoes to ships which were to carry them and their culture to the New World. In the castles were stored not only slaves and gold, but ivory, spices, and imports of cloths and ornaments. The merchants lived on upper floors.

The slave castles were not only sited where gold and slaves could be secured, but were commonest on the exceptionally dry part of the Gold Coast, where rainfall is under 45 inches per year and often under 35 inches, and where vegetation is sparse. Moreover, the Gold Coast has small but vivid promontories upon which the castles were built for easier defence from land attack and the better to protect ships anchored in the sheltered bay to the leeward. These bays also provided water supplies and most had small rivers. [7]

Slave forts were eventually built or acquired by the Portuguese, Dutch, English, French, Swedes, Danes, and Brandenburgers. The three-centuries-old Danish castle of Christiansborg, three miles east of Accra, is now the Governor's residence, and many other castles are now used for peaceful purposes.

The slave trade persisted longest to the east of the Gold Coast. On older maps the 'Slave Coast' is still indicated for the Dahomey and Western Nigerian coasts. There slaves were sold by the African States of Dahomey and Yorubaland (see Fig. 1) from among their political and military prisoners. Descendants of the Yoruba are numerous in Brazil.

Descendants of freed slaves often returned to West Africa as inter-

---

[7] For maps of rainfall and of slave castles in the Gold Coast, see *Atlas of the Gold Coast* (Gold Coast Survey Department, Accra).

mediaries in the slave trade. Hence the occurrence of so-called Brazilian or Portuguese quarters in towns such as Ouidah (Dahomey) and Lagos (Nigeria), where some houses have a Portuguese-Brazilian style of architecture.

The slave trade had three outstanding consequences in Africa. It made entry into Africa more difficult, because of the jealousy of the slave trade African intermediaries, and of the states which sold slaves such as Ashanti, Allada, Dahomey, Porto-Novo, Yorubaland, and Benin. There was also the hostility of the raided Africans.

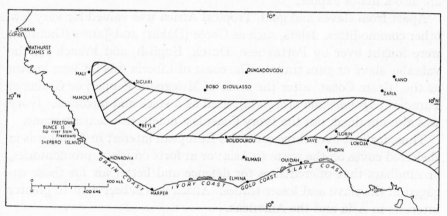

FIG. 3. THE POOR INTERMEDIATE OR MIDDLE BELT OF WEST AFRICA

Secondly, it is estimated that several million, perhaps twelve million, Africans were taken out of Africa in the course of a thousand years of Arab slave-dealing and of four hundred years by Europeans and Americans. Vast areas were depopulated, by actual removal of people, by peoples fleeing from slave raiders, and as the result of slave raiding which left the populations too small to reduce the vegetation harbouring tsetse flies and mosquitoes.

For this and other reasons, vast areas of low population density are among the outstanding features of modern Africa. The interior of West Africa suffered from both the Arab and European slave trades. One of its major modern problems is the Intermediate or Middle Belt between the rain forests and the savannah. On a population map it is startlingly clear. Not only are people few, but the soils are poor and the vegetation degraded. The belt has all the liabilities of the rain forests and savannah (e.g., their diseases), but none of their assets. From the Ivory Coast to

Nigeria, this is a vast negative zone which, for example, the railways cross without finding any significant traffic.

The last great consequence of the slave trade was that the Portuguese —the first in the trade—were faced with provisioning the captives in the forts and especially on the long voyage to the New World. Most local foodstuffs were too perishable, so that such crops as cassava (manioc), maize, new varieties of yams, sweet potatoes, groundnuts, and pulses which keep well were introduced. These have spread over Africa, all are now vital foodstuffs, manioc being a basic food, and groundnuts are also a major export.

Apart from slaves and gold, Tropical Africa was valued for very few other commodities. Islets, such as Gorée (Dakar) and James (Gambia), were fought over by Portuguese, Dutch, English, and French for the valuable slave or gum trades. The coast of Liberia was for long known as the 'Grain Coast' after the seeds of Melegueta Pepper, or Grains of Paradise (*Aframomum melequeta*), used as a spice and medicine. Ivory was also obtained, but the Ivory Coast is a nineteenth-century name.

Thus, for just over three centuries European interest in Africa was in sheltered coves on the route to Asia; or in forts on islets, promontories, or sandbars that offered sites for defence and better air for those engaged in the slave and lesser trades. Africa was subservient to greater interests in Asia and the Americas.

Ex-slave Settlement in Africa

Domestic slaves had been freed in the United Kingdom as the result of Lord Mansfield's judgment in 1772, but their condition was pitiable. Then in 1783 Britain was faced with another and far greater problem of ex-slaves who had fought with her against their American masters and were discharged and wretched in Nova Scotia or England.

The Sierra Leone Peninsula, one of the very few points where mountains meet the Atlantic in West Africa, was well known in Britain through the Royal African Company's fort on Bunce Island, up river. On the peninsula some thirty European traders had houses where they entertained with rum and dancing girls.[8] This well-known place was selected as the site of the first experiment in the resettlement of ex-slaves in Africa, and the pioneer party from England reached the peninsula in 1787. Another 1131 followed from the New World in 1792,

[8] Roy Lewis, *Sierra Leone* (Her Majesty's Stationery Office, 1954), p. 16.

when Freetown received its name. About 800 Maroons, or ex-slaves and their descendants, arrived from Jamaica in 1800, and many others were landed from captured slave ships between 1808 and 1854. In that same inaugural year of 1787, also one of the last of the unrestricted slave trade, we know that about 100,000 slaves were shipped from West Africa. The English carried away 38,000, the French 31,000, the Portuguese 25,000, the Dutch 4000, and the Danes 2000. Denmark was the first country to abolish the slave trade, but it will be realized that her noble gesture, which cost her dearly, made little impression upon the total trade.

It was quite otherwise with Britain's abolition of the trade in 1807, which was far more self-sacrificial. Convinced of the rightness of her cause and anxious to stop others reaping her abandoned profits, she set about stopping all other slave traders. A naval base was established for anti-slavery naval patrols at Freetown, a site for Bathurst was acquired in 1816 and used thereafter instead of Gorée (see Fig. 2), which was returned to France in 1817. Two bases were also leased between 1827 and 1833 on the Spanish island of Fernando Po, and Lagos was taken partly for the same purpose as late as 1861. At all of them, and especially at Freetown, the British Navy landed captives from slave ships who could not be repatriated.

The conscience over the slave trade gradually spread beyond Denmark and Britain. Americans with a real desire to help ex-slaves and those with less worthy motives worked together through the American Colonization Society. After an abortive attempt to settle ex-slaves on Sherbro Island, Sierra Leone, in 1820, their first successful establishment was on Providence Island, now part of Monrovia, Liberia, in 1822. Other societies established settlements along the coast, and by 1867, 13,136 settlers had gone to Liberia. In addition, there were 5722 exslaves sent by the U.S. Government or put ashore by the U.S. Navy. After 1867 the flow of settlers from America to Liberia practically ceased. Liberia had established its independence from the American Colonization Society in 1847 and chose the appropriate motto "The Love of Liberty brought us here." In 1857 Maryland in Liberia, around Harper, was fully incorporated.

Wherever freed slaves have been settled in Africa a Creole [9] community has developed, feeling itself apart from indigenous Africans. In Sierra

[9] In Africa the word 'creole' has a wider meaning than in America. It may mean a person of mixed blood, but is used primarily for people who are descended from exslaves, who have long abandoned tribal organization and have adopted (or have attempted to adopt) Western outlooks and ways.

Leone there is antipathy between "The Colony" (see Chapter XXXI, Fig. 3), where the Creoles live (although now outnumbered by pure Africans), and the Protectorate—the home of indigenous Africans. In Liberia it is seen in the similar social and legal contrast between the six

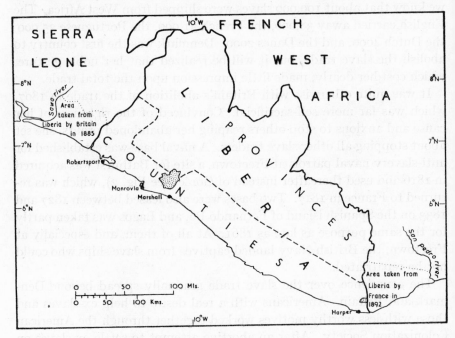

FIG. 4. MAIN ADMINISTRATIVE DIVISIONS OF LIBERIA
Rubber plantations are stippled.

Counties (including one called a Territory), which lie along the coast to a depth of about forty miles, and the three inland Provinces. In both Sierra Leone and Liberia, the real Africans have only very recently been represented in the central government.

If Negroes from West Africa have provided one of the major features of settlement in the New World, it is also clear that settlement of relatively small numbers of ex-slaves in Sierra Leone and Liberia led to immense contrasts in the social attitudes, political development, and settlement pattern between them and the indigenous peoples. Freetown, Bonthe, and the Creole villages around Freetown with such names as Wilberforce, Regent, and Waterloo and the America-Liberian towns of Robertsport, Monrovia, Marshall, and Harper have a style of architecture and layout taken direct from the southern states of America.

Their inhabitants, being neither true Africans nor Whites, form a separate nation. In Liberia it has attained statehood, with its colonial territory in the interior. If the Creoles attained political dominance in an autonomous Sierra Leone they might try to dominate the peoples of the interior.

Dahomey incorporates, near its southern coast, the territory of the erstwhile Dahomey kingdom (see Fig. 1), which had its capital at Abomey. When the slave trade was dying the Dahomey king was advised to use his prisoners to establish oil-palm plantations, as an alternative income. Here was the first appreciation of the new trade. The oil-palm plantations around Abomey and Porto-Novo are almost the only (and are certainly the oldest) extensive African-owned oil-palm plantations in West Africa. They still provide Dahomey's chief export.

The Scramble for Africa

For the first three-quarters of the nineteenth century Tropical Africa seemed to offer no trade prospects. But towards the end of the century increasing industrialization had ever greater need of tropical vegetable oils and other produce, such as timber and rubber. New markets for cheap cottons were also desired. Yet there were many other factors inducing a new interest in Africa.

France had occupied Algeria between 1830 and 1847, and Britain the Cape in 1806. The Afrikaners, and the Huguenots who had joined them later, had made a new nation in the south and could not tolerate the British and the abolition of slavery. The Great Trek took the Boers north to found new States. If, for a time, it eased their situation, the Great Trek brought Afrikaners more intimately in contact with the despised and less powerful Bantu. As sailing ships increased in size and gave way to more powerful steamships, so South Africa became more attractive for settlers. North Africa, so near France and Italy, exerted a similar attraction, though here competition for land with the Arabs, Berbers, and Moors soon became acute.

The opening of the Suez Canal in 1869 brought a struggle for control of points along the new all-sea route. France had ultimately to cede place to Britain in Egypt and the Sudan. Italy, France, and Britain all secured footholds flanking the Red Sea.

It was in East Africa that slavery persisted longest, because of Arab

2B

control. The stories that Livingstone, Stanley, and others had brought back encouraged a desire to intervene and stop slavery in Central and East Africa. Barbarity elsewhere—*e.g.*, in Benin—also caused European intervention to stop wholesale human sacrifices.

Lastly, power and prestige in Europe seemed to demand—in fact, be measured by—overseas possessions and settlement. The Brussels Conference of 1876 led to the establishment of the Congo Free State and the trade agreements of the Conventional Congo Basin. The Berlin Conference of 1884–85 led to the doctrine of effective occupancy for title to territory. There followed the "Scramble for Africa," and the present political map often indicates the relative speed or success of penetration by each Power from its coastal footholds and the way each offset the others.

Some flags had, however, already disappeared from Africa during the trade doldrums of the mid-century. Such was the cause of Denmark's departure from the Gold Coast in 1850, and this, and the cost of defence, had caused the Dutch exodus in 1872. These were offset by the newcomers to Africa, Italy and Germany. The present map will be examined in Chapter XXXI.

The Impact of Africa on the Outer World

Egypt apart, why have Africa and African cultures made so little impact upon the rest of the world? Why has Africa been retarded? The explanations are certainly partly, but not wholly, geographical. Tropical and southern Africa is shielded from Europe by the Sahara, and the occupation of North Africa by Arabs and Turks made this formidable natural obstacle a complete barrier. When the great navigators penetrated to the wet lands they found them forbidding. Because of surf, swell, and few deep indentations not impeded by bar or mangrove, landfalls were few. Moreover, the forest, the impeded rivers, the peoples, and diseases were antagonistic. The Arabs prevented access to the eastern coast north of about 20° S., and certainly north of 10° S.

Consequently Africans were isolated for centuries behind natural obstacles reinforced by the Arab barrier. African societies were self-evolving and self-sufficient. They gained few ideas or techniques from others. Their own cultures, often understandably poor in such harsh environments, often stagnated for lack of outside contact. The more vigorous ones such as Ashanti, Dahomey, and Benin debased their culture by appalling annual human sacrifices. What contacts Africa did have were almost exclusively to the continent's great disadvantage, notably the depopulation, degradation, and disruption of the slave trade.

During the last seventy-five years or so Africa has been rapidly occupied and opened up. It was the development of transport that made such opening up possible, the steamships and railways, then roads, and finally the 'plane. It is as easy to fly around Nigeria as within the United States. Nineteenth-century military technique soon overwhelmed most African peoples, but eighteenth-century or earlier military equipment might not have been so telling. Moreover, the lines of swiftest penetration were up the lower and middle Nile, up the Senegal and down the Niger, and through the South African Veld, precisely where the vegetation presents no obstacle and the conditions were more tolerable.

In the long historical view Africa was entered overnight. Her peoples have hardly had time to understand Western culture, from which most of them (certainly those in the interior) were isolated for so long. The greatest problem in tropical Africa to-day is not the appalling difficulty of the environment. Grim though they are, such things as leached soils, soil erosion, bad farming, ill-advised nutrition, and much more might soon be combated or overcome if they were in a Western society. The even greater problem is the fear of the supernatural which runs through African life and society. The uneducated African is often held back by fear and primitive customs which prevent him from making a proper impact on the outer world.

FURTHER READING

In addition to works cited in the footnotes, see:

E. W. Bovill, *Caravans of the Old Sahara* (International African Institute, London, 1933).

J. Greenberg, "Negro Kingdoms of the Sudan," in *Transactions of the New York Academy of Sciences*, series ii, vol. 4, pp. 126–135.

H. J. Wood, *Exploration and Discovery* (Hutchinson, London, 1951).

R. J. Harrison Church, *Modern Colonization* (Hutchinson, London, 1951), Chapters 2 and 4.

R. Earle Anderson, *Liberia—America's African Friend* (North Carolina University Press and Oxford University Press, 1952).

CHAPTER XXXI

African Boundaries

R. J. HARRISON CHURCH

BEFORE discussing typical boundary problems in Africa, it is valuable to examine briefly the outstanding effects of the main treaties, which defined the more important territories. In Chapter XXX it was shown that after the Berlin Conference of 1884–85 there was a scramble inland from coastal footholds. Between 1885 and 1904 most of the present political map of Africa was drawn, a process practically complete by 1919.

Although it had previously abstained from colonial adventure, Germany set about acquiring African territory with great vigour in and after 1884. British recognition of German rights in East Africa (Tanganyika) in 1890 prevented realization, while the Germans remained, of the then dearly held British aim of a Cape–Cairo railway. In German South West Africa, although Britain held a fifteen-mile-deep enclave at Walvis Bay, Germany won recognition of her claims to the rest of the coast and to the interior. This included the Caprivi Strip (see Figs. 1 and 2), one of the many territorial oddities of Africa. This twenty-five to fifty mile wide finger-like projection extends some 250 miles eastward, to reach the Zambezi river about thirty-one miles above Victoria Falls. At that time it drove a wedge between Portuguese territory and the British in Bechuanaland, which had itself been occupied by Britain in 1885 to prevent the Afrikaners from joining with the Germans. The Caprivi corridor gave the Germans a well-watered though remote link from the extreme north-east corner of their territory to the terminus, on the Zambezi, of one of the main lines of communication through Rhodesia. The Germans hoped that they would thus have a trade outlet eastward into Rhodesia, as well as westward by sea. As the Caprivi finger lay on the northern fringe of the Kalahari, it outflanked and neutralized the natural frontier.[1]

[1] Sir Thomas H. Holdich, *Political Frontiers and Boundary Making* (Macmillan, London, 1916), p. 241.

The original strategic value of the Caprivi Strip was largely lost by British victory in the South African War, 1899–1902, and the Germans had not built a railway or road (both of which would have been costly across the Okavango and Kwando rivers) by the time they lost South West Africa.

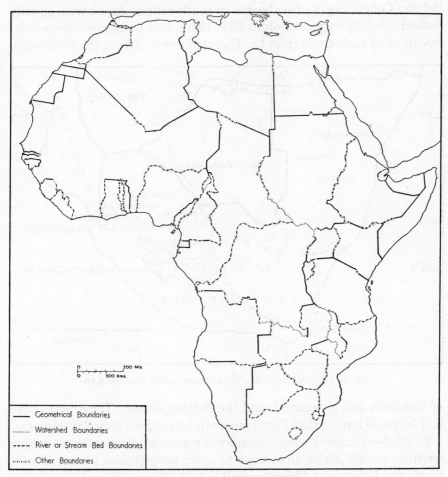

FIG. I. TYPES OF AFRICAN BOUNDARIES

To-day 'Africa's Polish Corridor' has potential economic and political importance from an opposite direction. If the Federation of Rhodesia and Nyasaland should decide on a new railway to South West Africa it might pass through the Caprivi Strip. Secondly, by possession of this finger, through its Mandate over South West Africa, the Union of South

Africa surrounds on three sides the British Protectorate of Bechuanaland (see Chapter XXXIII).

In 1890 Britain also recognized Portuguese interests in Africa.
While a Portuguese dream of continuous territory across southern Africa thereby faded, British and Congo Free State (after 1908 the
Belgian Congo) hopes of seaboards in south-central Africa were equally
dashed. But Portuguese Lobito Bay, Beira, and Lourenço Marques derive most of their trade from the Union of South Africa, the Federation

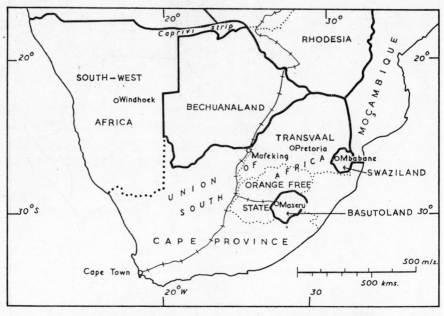

FIG. 2. BECHUANALAND, SWAZILAND, AND BASUTOLAND

of Rhodesia and Nyasaland, and the Belgian Congo. These ports have
had far more foreign than Portuguese capital put into their development.

In 1898–99 Anglo-French agreements prevented France from securing
territory across Africa from west to east; nevertheless French North,
West, and Equatorial Africa were all linked. Thus, although the British
had to drop their Cape–Cairo railway project, the French have never
finally given up their trans-Saharan one. Indeed, they pushed on with
it for a few months in 1941–42.

After Spain lost her American continental possessions she still retained, rather precariously, her Caribbean and Pacific islands. Even
more precarious was her hold on Spanish Guinea, which she had secured

from Portugal in 1778. Spanish Guinea had been obtained to enable Spain to have her own source of slaves. But her occupation of these African possessions was intermittent because of her defeat in America, political troubles at home, and Britain's watch on the Slave Coast after 1807.

In 1898 Spain suffered defeat by the United States and the loss of its Caribbean and Pacific islands, but Spanish Guinea survived. While Spain was still stunned, France managed in 1900 to confine Continental Spanish Guinea (often erroneously called Rio Muni) to its present small size. With the islands of Fernando Po and Annobon, this constitutes Spanish Guinea, over which France also secured the right of pre-emption. Spanish Guinea is Spain's only tropical possession, and high-land Fernando Po has a planter society and economy, dependent upon temporary immigrant labour, which comprises three-fifths of the population.

In 1904 France and Britain settled all outstanding boundary disputes. The Los Islands, off Conakry, French Guinea, were exchanged for territory around Kambia, now in Sierra Leone. Many boundaries were agreed elsewhere in West Africa. But most significant was French agreement to withdraw her claims in Egypt and to support Britain there, Britain doing the same for France in Morocco.

After the Agadir crisis of 1911 Germany withdrew her claims in Morocco in exchange for extension of the German Cameroons to the Congo and Ubangi rivers and the right of pre-emption over Spanish Guinea.[2] These gains were lost by the Treaty of Versailles, 1919. In 1912 France established a protectorate over the Sherifian Empire (Morocco).

In 1919–22 the former German colonies were assigned as Mandates to various Powers. Three were divided, not without protest from African peoples. The major parts of Togoland and the Cameroons were assigned to France. Ruanda-Urundi was separated from Tanganyika and assigned to Belgium. Adjacent to the Belgian Congo, Ruanda-Urundi is sharply contrasted with the Congo, the former being high and heavily populated. The rest of large Tanganyika became a British Mandate, except for a small piece given outright to Portuguese East Africa, to bring its northern boundary along the Ruvuma river. South West Africa was assigned to the Union of South Africa, which had become

---

[2] For a map of the various boundaries of the Cameroons, see R. J. Harrison Church, *Modern Colonization* (Hutchinson, London, 1951), p. 122.

independent in 1910, only nine years after the defeat of the Afrikaners. Although all other Mandates became Trusteeships in 1946, the Union of South Africa refuses to yield South West Africa to United Nations supervision and has effectively incorporated this territory in the Union.[3]

Under the Treaty of London of 1915, by which she joined the Allies in the first world war, Italy was promised a share of former German colonies in Africa if France and Britain secured additional territory. It was later argued that as France and Britain were accorded Mandates, rather than outright territorial cessions, this provision did not apply. Nevertheless, Libya was expanded by territory ceded by France, Egypt, and Britain between 1919 and 1934; and Italian Somaliland was much enhanced by the British cession of Jubaland, formerly part of Kenya, in 1924. None of these cessions was taken back after Italy's defeat in the second world war.[4]

After the unedifying wrangles of post-war years, it was decided that former Italian Somaliland should become an Italian Trusteeship, with the proviso that it shall be independent by 1960. Libya became independent, and Eritrea was federated with Ethiopia, so giving the latter a seaboard.[5]

The Character of African Boundaries

The key to understanding African boundaries is the speed with which they were defined. Most of them were decided between 1884 and 1919, and great lengths were agreed upon in each treaty.

Once a European Power had secured as much territory as was then thought possible and desirable, boundary definition was necessary, both for the development of the African possession and for the sake of peace in Europe. Many boundaries represent approximate limits of either military or political penetration in the past—e.g., the northern Gold Coast boundary. Some are the results of compromise, such as the north-

[3] The main difference between a League of Nations Mandate and a United Nations Trusteeship lies in the fact that the Mandates Commission had no right to visit or send observers to mandated territories, nor to hear witnesses from them. The Trusteeship Council, on the other hand, appoints visiting missions, and representatives of the local peoples may be heard by it. The Union of South Africa objects to such provisions.

[4] For changes in Libyan boundaries and the Jubaland boundary, see S. Whittemore Boggs, *International Boundaries* (Columbia University Press, New York, 1940), pp. 159–163.

[5] See R. J. Harrison Church, *op. cit.*, pp. 133–140; "The Problems of the Italian Colonies," in *World Affairs*, vol. iii, No. 1 (1949); Y. A. Haggag and R. J. Harrison Church, "Ethiopia, Eritrea, and Somalia," in *Geographical Review*, 1953, pp. 418–419 (with references).

western boundary of Nigeria. Others follow an exchange, such as the north-western Sierra Leone boundary.

Boundaries drawn on maps by European politicians bore little relation to the physical and even less to the social, economic, or political fabric of indigenous societies. Yet, of course, the rapid and intensive partition of Africa took place when little or no detailed knowledge was available of the terrain, peoples, and economy of the interior. Nevertheless, even if that knowledge had been available, the mood of the statesmen who partitioned Africa was not such as to suggest that they would have been willing to use it in their boundary deliberations.

As speedy decisions were called for in a little-known continent, it was natural that boundaries which could be easily conceived and quickly agreed upon were often chosen. Thus lines of latitude or longitude, arcs of circles, watersheds, rivers, and lakes were frequently adopted. Over one-third by length of Africa's international boundaries are geometrical. And if boundaries within federated territories (French West Africa, Nigeria, French Equatorial Africa, and Rhodesia and Nyasaland) and internal administrative boundaries be included, then the proportion must be quite one-half.

Boggs states[6] that with an area of nearly 11,400,000 square miles, Africa had some 28,670 miles of international boundaries in 1939, or about 2·5 miles of boundary for every 1000 square miles of area. On this count, Africa takes third place, after Europe and Asia, in degree of division by international boundaries. Yet the African measurements were made by Boggs on very small-scale maps, so that the real total is probably higher. Secondly, since 1939 Europe's boundaries have been shortened. Lastly, Boggs was naturally concerned only with international boundaries, but it is one of the characteristics of Africa that internal boundaries also much affect its political, social, and economic evolution. Boundaries of several kinds thus loom large in any discussion of Africa. Upon the pre-existing African political societies, with their always sensitive feelings to matters of boundaries and land, there came new divisions, imposed by outside Powers. Each boundary represented the knife-edged divide between contrasting and often conflicting colonial policies (see Chapter XXXIII).

---

[6] Boggs, *op. cit.*, p. 155.

2B*

The Physical Difficulties of Paper Partition

Paper partition by European politicians soon caused grave difficulties for boundary demarcators. Thus the 1894 agreement on the Belgian Congo–Northern Rhodesia boundary defined it as "the thalweg of the Luapula up to its issue from Lake Bangweolo. Thence it shall run Southwards along the Meridian of Longitude of the point where the river leaves the Lake." It was found, however, that the river did not flow from that lake but rises near Abercorn as the Chambezi, and flows through swamps to the south of Lake Bangweolo, after which it has the name Luapula. The longitude of Boundary Pillar 1 on the Congo-Zambezi watershed, erected by the Belgians in 1914, has been accepted instead of the longitude of the non-existent point of the exit of the Luapula from Lake Bangweolo. Furthermore, the newly adopted meridian has been extended in the reverse direction (south to north), until it intersects the Luapala river, the thalweg of which is then followed by the boundary to Lake Mweru.[7] As this boundary lies near a highly mineralized zone, its importance is obvious.

A more amusing example is also quoted by Boggs on the same page. For the Belgian Congo–Sudan boundary the Congo–Nile watershed was agreed. Before it was demarcated, and because the watershed is so flat, a missionary did not know in which territory his property was situated. So he engaged porters for several days to empty water on the land. The rill so created showed him to be in the Belgian Congo.

Again, the Congo-Tanganyika-Uganda boundaries were clearly defined in the treaties in geometrical terms. But, in the field, Mt Ruwenzori was found to be so much farther west than had been supposed that a meridian cut across its eastern gorges. An agreed strip for a proposed railway from Tanganyika to Lake Edward would have gone across Lake Kivu and through volcanoes. Definition by watershed was no alternative, since the Nile-Congo parting west of Lake Albert proved to be almost vertically above the lake shore. The British would then have had a sheer cliff beyond the lake to administer.[8] New locally surveyed boundaries were agreed in 1910.

The Moçambique-Nyasaland boundary was originally defined as following the eastern shore of Lake Shirwa. But the shore was found to be

---

[7] Boggs, *op. cit.*, pp. 166–167.

[8] A. R. Hinks, "Notes on the Technique of Boundary Delimitation," in *Geographical Journal*, vol. lviii (1921), pp. 417–443 (includes map).

marshy, vague, and variable. Demarcators might have marked out an agreed eastern shore or taken the eastern edge of the marsh, but they made a third choice—a straight line. Later this was found to bisect the lands of a chief who had long acknowledged allegiance to Portugal, and so the straight line was also modified.[9] Similarly, the Kagera river between Ruanda-Urundi and Tanganyika was found to be unsatisfactory as a boundary, because of its intricate meandering in a marsh. Straight lines were used instead, connecting inter-visible monuments.[10]

Sometimes politicians have misunderstood certain terms, and their errors have recoiled on their country. Thus the Liberian delegate, when he agreed in 1892 to France having the Ivory Coast boundary along the right bank of the southward flowing Cavally river, thought that the boundary would be the east bank and that Liberia would secure control of navigation. In fact, the boundary is the west bank, and France has control of navigation.[11]

In the least known parts of Africa geometric boundaries were frequently defined in treaties. When these boundaries came to be demarcated the surveyors were presented with a hazardous task. Thus the eastern boundary of former German South West Africa was defined as the meridian of 20° E. from the Orange River north to 22° S., thence east on that parallel to 21° E. and north on that meridian to 18° S. Some 450 miles long, this line ran through the Kalahari. The difficulties of demarcation were prodigious and the cost in money and lives so high that after five years the rest of the task was abandoned. It would have been much less expensive and more rational to have agreed upon a boundary in the same general location as the three lines but adapted to local topography. Such a line could have been quickly demarcated and would have been more visible to nomadic tribes. As there were so few of these, it was doubtful if a demarcated boundary of any kind was really necessary.[12]

The boundaries of the three Somalilands were demarcated with appalling difficulty. Moreover, because they are mostly straight, they are, in the main, unrelated to water resources and pastures. Although trans-

[9] Moçambique-Nyasaland Agreement, May 6, 1920, in *British and Foreign State Papers*, vol. cxiii (1920), pp. 409–423, annex 4.
[10] J. B. Laws, "A Minor Adjustment in the Boundary between Tanganyika Territory and Ruanda-Urundi," in *Geographical Journal*, vol. lxxx (1932), pp. 244–247.
[11] R. Earle Anderson, *Liberia—America's African Friend* (North Carolina University Press, 1952), p. 90. This boundary has importance since the small Firestone rubber plantation (see Chapter XXX, Fig. 4) is on the Liberian side of the river and the Company uses river transport. This has been challenged by French posts.
[12] T. H. Holdich, *op. cit.*, pp. 185–186.

boundary grazing rights have often been permitted, the boundaries would have been far more satisfactory if they had taken account of local physical and human geography.

It is frequently supposed that few African boundaries are demarcated, or that, if they are, demarcation is summary. Yet many are marked out on the ground in considerable detail and also well documented—e.g., the Belgian Congo–Uganda, Ruanda-Urundi–Tanganyika, Belgian Congo–Northern Rhodesia (for which there are maps on the 1:10,000 scale), British Somaliland–Ethiopia, Italian Somaliland–Kenya, and British and French Togoland boundaries.[13]

African Boundaries as Human Divides

As little account was taken of the distribution of African peoples when international boundaries were drawn, and as most tribal areas are relatively small, it is safe to assume that almost every boundary divides some African group.

Fig. 3 shows, by way of example, the international and internal boundaries of Sierra Leone and the distribution of its peoples, many of whom live astride these boundaries. Sierra Leone, as mentioned in the previous chapter, also suffers from the great historical, political, and cultural division between Colony and Protectorate. Sierra Leone further presents a mosaic of some 160 chiefdoms—all in a country smaller than Scotland and little larger than West Virginia.[14]

Fitzgerald has instanced [15] the division of the Angoni and Achowa peoples by the Rhodesia-Nyasaland boundary, and the Masai by the Kenya-Tanganyika line. Yet these divides are now less serious than formerly, the first because of the creation of the Federation of Rhodesia and Nyasaland, and the second because of closer association in the East African High Commission. Boggs[16] cites the Anuak, divided by the Sudan-Ethiopia line. The present author has described[17] partition of the

---

[13] For references to particular boundaries see bibliographies in S. B. Jones, *Boundary-making* (Columbia University Press, New York, 1945), and S. W. Boggs, *op. cit.*

[14] See 1:500,000 *Map of Chiefdom Boundaries* (Sierra Leone Survey). For maps of the present distribution of African peoples see 1:3,000,000 map of *Populations de l'Afrique Occidentale* (Direction Générale de la Santé Publique de l'A.O.F., Dakar, 1949); *Atlas of Sierra Leone*, 1953; *Atlas of the Gold Coast*, 1949; *Atlas Générale du Congo*; *Atlas of the Tanganyika Territory*, 1953; and publications of the Ethnographic Survey, International African Institute, London, E.C.4.

[15] W. Fitzgerald, *Africa* (seventh edition), p. 218.   [16] S. W. Boggs, *op. cit.*, p. 173.
[17] R. J. Harrison Church, *op. cit.*, pp. 116–121 and 138–140.

Ewe and Somali and the former division of the Dagomba peoples. These examples were chosen, not because they are unusual, but because they have received international notice.

FIG. 3. INTERNATIONAL AND INTERNAL BOUNDARIES OF SIERRA LEONE AS
HUMAN DIVIDES

In contrast to the many boundaries which partition African peoples because of the ignorance or indifference of the treaty-makers, the partition of the Kru was deliberate. These people, who live along the Liberian and Ivory Coast seaboards, are a relatively rare African example of a sea-loving people. They have for long been accustomed to service on ships engaged in the West African trades. Normally, ships pick them up on outward runs at Freetown (where there is an emigrant Kru colony), Monrovia, or Tabou, and disembark them again on the return voyage. During this period they are engaged aboard on cleaning and maintenance duties. Some are also more or less permanently employed on the ships —*e.g.*, as laundrymen or in the engine-room—as well as on naval vessels of several Powers. Until 1885 Liberia had always been recognized as extending eastward to the San Pedro river (see Chapter XXX, Fig. 4), so including all the territory inhabited by the Kru. But in that year the French claimed territory far to the west, and in 1892 the Cavally became the boundary. "France snapped up the sixty mile stretch of coast between the San Pedro and the Cavalla so as to have under her own flag a supply of Kru labour."[18]

As African peoples become more educated and nationalistic, richer and better versed in public relations, we may expect to hear more of their divisions, as we have already of the Ewe. Morocco, for example, although it remained unconquered for a thousand years, is now much divided. After the long period of Arab and Moorish rule the Spanish carried a revengeful sword into their enemy's country. Spain secured footholds at Melilla in 1497, the islet of Peñon de Velez de la Gomera in 1508, Ceuta in 1580 from Portugal, who had taken it in 1415, and the islet of Peñon de Alhucemas in 1673. These are governed as parts of Spain.

Spain also founded in 1456, on the Atlantic coast, Santa Cruz de Mar Pequeña, for the use of Canary Island fishermen. It was lost in 1524, but in 1860 the Sultan granted in perpetuity to Spain sufficient territory to refound it. Thus came into existence the territory of Ifni, sixty miles long by fifteen miles deep, on the coast of southern Morocco, recognized and confirmed by France in 1904 and 1912. It has been administered as part of Spanish West Africa since 1952. Apart from these early coastal footholds, Morocco resisted further intrusion and, as we have seen, was not conquered by the Ottoman Turks.

Then in 1912, although the unity of the Sherifian Empire was proclaimed, it came under the protection of France, who sub-leased to Spain the Spanish Protectorate, within limits proposed in 1904. The northern part of the Spanish Protectorate lay on the Atlantic and Mediterranean coasts. Because of political separation, the Sultan ap-

---

[18] Sir Harry Johnston, *Liberia* (Hutchinson, London, 1906), vol. i, pp. 280–296. He also gives a detailed account of the expansion of Sierra Leone by British aggression at the expense of Liberia. See also R. Earle Anderson, *op. cit.*, pp. 83–95, with a map of the areas seized (see also Chapter XXX, Fig. 4).

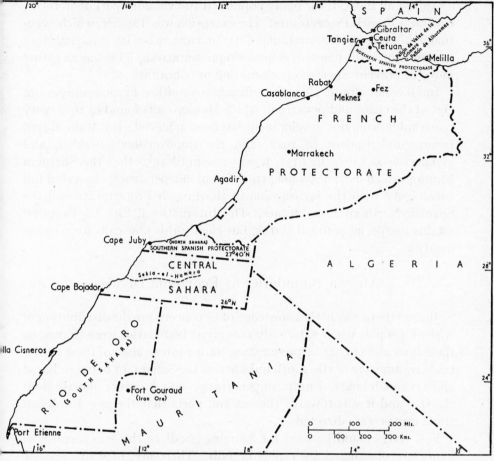

FIG. 4. NORTH-WEST AFRICA: POLITICAL DIVISIONS IN 1955

pointed the Khalifah of Tetuan as his local representative. On occasion
he was the Sultan's brother.

The southern part of the Spanish Protectorate lies between the Wadi
Draa and 27° 40' N. and is administered from Cape Juby, which is also
a fishing station. To the south lies the Sekia-el-Hamara, the extreme
limit of the old Sherifian Empire. Around this, between 27° 40' N. and
26° N., is a no-man's-land, which Spain may occupy at will. To the
south lies the Spanish colony of Rio de Oro. These three divisions have,
since 1952, been known respectively as the North, Central, and South
sub-divisions of the Sahara. Sahara and Ifni together comprise Spanish
West Africa.

Almost all the rest, the really populated and valuable part of Morocco, became a French Protectorate. The exception was Tangier, which eventually became an International City in 1923, with its unsatisfactory government in the hands of consular representatives. This was an astute move to prevent Spanish check-mating of Gibraltar.

In all zones almost all senior officials were either French or Spanish. Out of the chaos and poverty in which Morocco was found in 1912, very remarkable economic development has been achieved. But while Egypt became independent in 1922, and the impoverished, divided, and inexperienced Libya in 1952, it was not until 1956 that the Sherifian Empire, which had such a long tradition of independence, recovered full sovereignty with the retrocession of the French Protectorate and the Spanish Northern Protectorate. The International City of, Tangier[19] retains its special political status, but clearly this now calls for reconsideration.

African Boundaries as Economic Divides

Just as there was little knowledge of or concern for the distribution of African peoples when externally conceived boundaries were drawn, so these lines also cut across pre-existing trade routes. Most of these earlier trade routes were north–south links across the Sahara, or between forest and savannah lands. European penetration was, however, mostly from the sea, and it was towards the sea and ports that the new European trade routes were directed.

Few rivers could be used for bringing goods to the sea, because so many are obstructed by rapids or falls. There are, of course, a few exceptions—notably the lower Zambezi, the lower Niger, and the Senegal. But the last was gravely impeded by a difficult estuary and is now little used. Ironically enough, the really ideal Gambia is used only for local trade, because the very odd boundary, consisting of arcs of circles drawn closely around the navigable river, has cut it off from its natural hinterland. The French have completed the process by building a nearly parallel railway to Dakar, thereby also killing local traffic on the Senegal river.[20]

[19] See I. Bowman, *The New World* (fourth edition, New York, 1928), pp. 186–193; J. Ancel, *Géographie des Frontières* (Paris, 1938), pp. 20, 24–27, and 190–192; J. Célérier, *Maroc* (Paris, 1948); Jean Despois, *L'Afrique Blanche Française* (Paris, 1949); F. Joly and others, *Géographie du Maroc* (Delagrave, Paris, 1949); E. Guernier, *Encyclopédie Coloniale et Maritime-Maroc* (Paris, 1948).

[20] For a full analysis see R. J. Harrison Church, *op. cit.*, pp. 112–115.

Each Power sought to canalize trade to its own port by building a railway. This motive is constantly referred to in, for example, the early history of the French Guinea and Sierra Leone railways.

To control the upper Niger and drain its trade to a French port, the Conakry-Kankan railway was built across the incredibly difficult Fouta Dialon mountains. Had it not been for the existence of an international boundary, the railway might not have been built, since its economic value was for years very slight. If the railway had been required, however, a far better route could have been found over the low shoulder at about 9° N., between the Fouta Dialon and the Guinea Highlands. In conditions of economic nationalism this far better route was not considered, because the railway would have crossed a boundary. Furthermore, to make quite sure that the Sierra Leone and French Guinea railways could never be linked, different gauges were deliberately chosen.

Railways were, above all, political instruments and territorial trade canalizers or attractors. They cross international boundaries only in central Africa, where land-locked territories had to seek outlets in foreign territory. To get such outlets, the land-locked territories or their protectors often supplied most of the capital for construction of railways and ports—e.g., to and from Lobito Bay, Beira, and Lourenço Marques.

A similar problem is, however, being increasingly posed elsewhere, as economic development of more remote areas is desired. A rich iron-ore deposit near Fort Gouraud in west-central Mauritania (see Fig. 4) can be worked only if a railway is built. If it is constructed entirely in French territory, to Port Etienne, it will be 425 miles long and very costly. Alternatively, it could be 340 miles long and terminate at the same French port, but only by cutting across Spanish Rio de Oro. This solution is favoured at present, even though it would be more expensive than a 238-mile railway through Rio de Oro to the Spanish capital and port of Villa Cisneros. Franco-Spanish discussions may, of course, alter the decision in favour of the latter route.

Since the second world war there has been increased willingness to let trade flow across international boundaries in Africa. The Belgians and British were always willing, but the French are recent converts. Much Niger Territory produce is exported through Nigeria. Indeed, when the price of groundnuts is higher in the Niger Territory, Nigerian groundnuts have been known to go north across the boundary, only to come south again as Niger Territory produce for export.

Again, an international boundary bisects the excellent navigable

lagoon between Lagos, capital of Nigeria, and Porto-Novo, capital of
Dahomey. Were there no boundary, external trade would obviously
have passed through the deep-water harbour of Lagos and along the
lagoon. The French, however, were anxious to canalize trade at their
wharf at Cotonou and built a difficult connecting railway from Porto-
Novo to Cotonou in 1932. Nevertheless, cars and fuel oil are now often
brought in via Lagos and the lagoon, because of the congestion at
Cotonou wharf and its unsuitability for the handling of such goods.

The long isolation and economic stagnation of south-eastern French
Guinea have been ended by a through road to the free port of Monrovia,
Liberia. Again, most external trade of the northern Cameroons under
French Trusteeship passes through Garua and via the Benue river to
and from Nigerian ports. The Federation of Rhodesia and Nyasaland
is also increasing and improving its rail outlets through Portuguese East
Africa.

It seems that trade is flowing increasingly across African international boundaries, probably because European Powers, with American
encouragement, are impressed with the needs of and opportunities for
more rapid and rational economic development. Common defence requirements likewise point to increased contact across boundaries.

Frontier regulations and control along the British-French Togoland
boundary, so frustrating to Ewe people living on either side of the line,
have also been eased. There have been more signs of international collaboration over the development and use of the Nile waters. Administrators on both sides of almost all boundaries meet regularly and are on
cordial terms.

Revision of Boundaries

A number of African boundaries have been peacefully revised. The
most notable one was the cession in 1927 of three square kilometres of
Angolan territory near Matadi on the Congo river, against 3500 square
kilometres of territory then in the extreme south-west of the Belgian
Congo. The exchange was occasioned by Belgian need for more land to
extend the port facilities of Matadi and to realign the Matadi-Leopold-
ville railway, which circumvents rapids on the Congo river. The Belgians
also agreed to link up with the Lobito Bay Railway, and the through
route from Katanga to Lobito Bay was opened in 1931.

In 1925 and 1934 Egypt ceded to Libya the oases of Jaghbub and

Oweinat. Again, the boundary between Egypt and the Sudan (see Fig. 1), as defined by the treaty of 1899, was the 22° N. parallel to the Red Sea. But as that parallel cut across tribal territories a new "administrative boundary" was afterwards adopted. Although this rather zigzag boundary is the one generally shown, it has not the sanction of international treaty.[21]

There were also the earlier exchanges made during the primary partition of Africa, such as that already mentioned of the Los Islands ceded to France (French Guinea) in 1904, against the Kambia district to Britain (Sierra Leone). Lastly, some boundary rectifications have been made in the process of demarcation.

Reflection on the examples already quoted of the conflict of boundaries with the physical and human environment, as well as the study of large-scale maps, suggests that many more boundaries need revision.

The Gambia is a self-impoverishing enclave which denies the use of a magnificent river to the welfare of a larger hinterland. Furthermore, the geometrical boundary cuts across the Wolof and Mande peoples who live on either side, and it almost isolates Casamance from the rest of French Senegal. The more rational solution would be to put the international boundary along the river and to the north of MacCarthy Island, on which the old settlement of Georgetown lies. That town and Bathurst, the Gambian capital, would then remain British, and territorial compensation might be arranged to the south of the existing Gambian territory.

The divided Ewe wish for reunion. If the two Togoland Trusteeships were united, so reconstituting the territory as held by the Germans before 1914, some four-fifths of the Ewe would be included, but at the cost of redividing the now united Dagomba. On the other hand, the one-fifth or more of the Ewe now in the Gold Coast will, in any case, enjoy the forthcoming full self-government of that territory. Another two-fifths in Togoland under British Trusteeship could also enjoy it, if its peoples so desire and if the Trusteeship Council permit them. A third and possibly ideal solution would seem to be to put all the Ewe and Dagomba in a federal or unitary relationship with a self-governing Gold Coast. The rest of Togoland under French Trusteeship might then be administered with Dahomey.

By contrast, the Southern Cameroons under British Trusteeship has not been happy in association with the Eastern Region of Nigeria and

[21] S. W. Boggs, *op. cit.*, p. 199.

now has its own small-scale legislature. Communications are better with, and the economy more akin to, the French Cameroons than to Nigeria, though quite the contrary is true of the Northern Cameroons under British Trusteeship. Thus there might be a case for joining Southern British Cameroons with the French Cameroons, and Northern British Cameroons with Northern Nigeria.

Africa does not contain miniature States such as Monaco and the Vatican City. Nevertheless, Africa retains the Caprivi Strip of South West Africa and the Transvaal Panhandle between Swaziland and Natal, although Europe has lost its comparable Polish Corridor. Furthermore, Africa has its picturesque enclaves, appropriately associated with those most traditionalist of nations—Britain, Spain, and Portugal. The British High Commission Protectorate of Basutoland is entirely surrounded by territory of the Union of South Africa. The Spanish enclaves are in Morocco and Continental Spanish Guinea. The Portuguese are at Cabinda, north of the Congo mouth, and the 'Fort' of St John the Baptist at Ouidah, Dahomey. The latter may fairly claim to be the world's greatest territorial oddity. Comprising only eleven and a half acres, it is, nevertheless, substantially demarcated by eight boundary stones and contains a two-storeyed house and garden, with two governors but no population to govern. It is said that the two governors (one Military and one Civil) are stationed there in case one should die. Whatever boundary revisions may usefully be made in Africa, one hopes that the Fort of St John the Baptist may survive until the tourist trade reaches it.

CHAPTER XXXII

The Union of South Africa

KEITH M. BUCHANAN

THE most striking feature of the social geography of the Union of South Africa is the poverty of the great mass of its population. Estimates of the national income per head in terms of International Units[1] showed that in the period 1925–34 the national income per head in the Union was one-quarter that of Great Britain and below the figure for the U.S.S.R. Later estimates suggest that, while the gap between levels of income in the Union and in other Commonwealth countries has narrowed somewhat, national income per head is still only a fraction of that in other areas of relatively recent European settlement such as Australia or New Zealand.

In part, this poverty reflects the limitations of the geographical environment. Africa has been described as "the marginal continent," and even by African standards much of the Union is marginal or submarginal, with a difficult relief, shallow and impoverished soils, an erratic climate, and inadequate water resources. These environmental conditions pose very real problems, which would be by no means insuperable in a coherent State showing a strong consciousness of common purpose. In the Union, however, no such consciousness exists; instead, bitter racial antagonisms absorb much of the effort that might be devoted to a constructive policy of social and economic advancement, while the narrow sectionalism of the European community is an insuperable barrier to the progress of three-quarters of the Union's population. V. Gordon Childe has observed: "In practice, ideas form as effective an element in the environment of any human society as do mountains, trees, animals, the weather, and the rest of external nature."[2] The South

---

[1] Defined as "the quantity of commodities exchangeable for 1 dollar in the U.S.A. over the average of the period 1925–34."—C. Clark, *The Conditions of Economic Progress* (Macmillan, London, 1951), p. 19.

[2] V. Gordon Childe, *What Happened in History* (Penguin, London, 1942), p. 14.

African "pigmentocracy" provides a striking confirmation of the essential validity of the statement.

The Environmental Setting

The greater part of the Union consists of a vast elevated plateau, usually about 3000 ft. and rising to between 6000 ft. and 10,000 ft. along the great eastern scarp of the Drakensberg; its western edge is less imposing, rarely below 3000 ft. Over considerable areas it is relatively flat, broken only by occasional isolated hills developed on the horizontal sandstones and associated igneous rocks of the Karroo beds. Marginal coast plains are limited in extent. On the east a series of broad terraces or platforms at about 4500, 2500, and 600 feet provides a stepped descent to the coast. On the south the plateau is fringed by a well-developed belt of fold mountains, differing in detail in degree of dissection, in elevation, and orientation, but generally aligned subparallel to the plateau edge and sufficiently high and broken to constitute major barriers. Included within this southern fringing belt are important areas of slight relief, outstanding among which are the Little Karroo, between the Langeberg-Outeniqua Mountains and the Groote Zwartebergen, and the Great Karroo, overshadowed by the Nieuwveld scarp. The dissected character of these plateau margins has always tended to hinder communications with the coast, with obvious economic effects; it has also limited agricultural mechanization and the possibilities of irrigation. On the plateau itself the absence of pronounced breaks in relief, combined with conditions of semi-aridity and the tradition of large land-holding, have resulted in an unfavourable dispersion of population.

Partly as a result of the interception of rain-bearing easterly winds by the wall-like face of the Drakensberg, the greater part of the interior of the Union has a subhumid to arid climate. Two-thirds of the Union have less than twenty inches of rainfall; only the eastern terraced foreland and very limited parts of the Cape can be considered reasonably well-watered, but such areas, enjoying some thirty or more inches of rain, amount to barely one-tenth of the total. Rainfall, then, is limited in amount; it is also highly seasonal in character, 86 per cent. of the Union showing a marked summer concentration of rainfall (Cw type of Köppen), 10 per cent. in the south-west Cape, a marked winter maximum (Cs), and only a narrow coastal strip between Mossel Bay and East

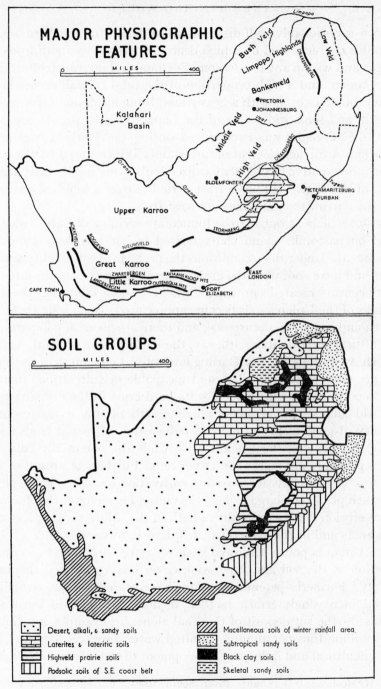

MAJOR PHYSIOGRAPHIC FEATURES

MILES 0 — 400

Limpopo
Bush Veld
Limpopo Highlands
Low Veld
DRAKENSBERG
Bankenveld
●PRETORIA
●JOHANNESBURG

Kalahari Basin

Middle Veld
Vaal

High Veld
BLOEMFONTEIN
DRAKENSBERG
Orange
PIETERMARITZBURG●
Tugela
DURBAN●

Upper Karroo
STORMBERG

BOKKEVELD
ROGGEVELD
NIEUWVELD
Great Karroo
EAST LONDON
ZWARTBERGEN
BAVIAANSKLOOF MTS
Little Karroo OUTENIQUA MTS
LANGEBERGEN
CAPE TOWN
PORT ELIZABETH

SOIL GROUPS

MILES 0 — 400

Desert, alkali, & sandy soils
Laterites & lateritic soils
Highveld prairie soils
Podsolic soils of S.E. coast belt

Miscellaneous soils of winter rainfall area.
Subtropical sandy soils
Black clay soils
Skeletal sandy soils

FIG. 1. UNION OF SOUTH AFRICA: MAJOR PHYSIO-
GRAPHIC FEATURES AND SOIL GROUPS

London a reasonably well-distributed rainfall (Cf). Furthermore, the rainfall is characterized by a high degree of variability, both from year to year and within any one season. Seasonal and intermittent droughts are common, and a high proportion of the total rainfall occurs in torrential thunderstorms with a heavy loss through run-off. Over most of the arid and semi-arid sector of the Cape an aggregate of some sixty months of drought was experienced during the fourteen-year period 1926–39.[3] A further element of uncertainty is introduced by the occurrence of destructive but highly localized hailstorms and by frost hazard; much of the High Veld has a frost period of over a hundred days, and only the narrow coastal plains are frost free.

Early settlement outside the immediate vicinity of Cape Town was based on pastoralism and characterized by an extremely loose land attachment. Under these conditions the problem of soil fertility scarcely arose, and it was not until the great mineral discoveries of the late nineteenth century created a growing market for arable crops that the shortcomings of the Union's soils became appreciated. Good soils are limited in area and patchy in occurrence, and there are no areas comparable in agricultural potentialities with, say, the Parana basin of South America or even Australia's Murray-Darling lowlands. Large areas in the humid east are stony, shallow-soiled, and incapable of cultivation; many of the deeper, heavier soils tend to set a hard crust in the dry season. In the arid and semi-arid sector alkaline soils occupy extensive areas. Scarcity of good soils and climate reduce the cultivated lands to less than 7 per cent. of the Union's area, while the potentially cultivable area is probably not more than 15 per cent. Further, as a result of some fifty to seventy-five years of robber cultivation (roofbou), soil depletion has taken place on a large scale in the cultivable sector of the Union and active erosion is a major problem both in the thinly peopled European farm areas and in the overcrowded Native Reserves.

The Union is poorly endowed with water resources, and a century's depletion of the soil and vegetation cover has aggravated this initial poverty. Formerly perennial streams have ceased to flow, rivers have become increasingly erratic in their regime, and their silt burden has increased—the silt deposit of the Vaal alone, for example, is estimated at $2\frac{1}{2}$ million tons per annum. Limited water resources handicap both the agricultural and industrial development of the interior. Because of

---

[3] J. H. Moolman, "The Orange River, South Africa," in *Geographical Review*, vol. xxxvi, No. 4 (1946), p. 655.

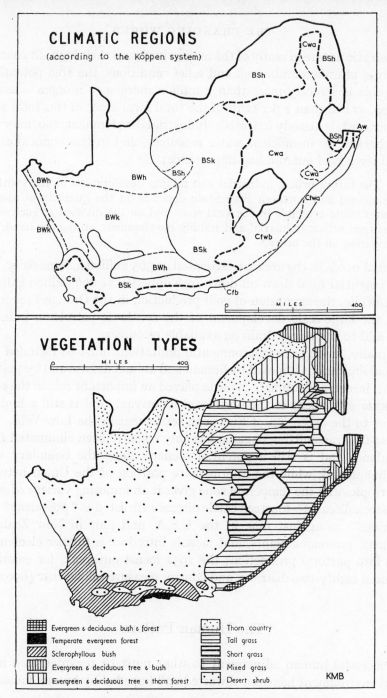

CLIMATIC REGIONS

(according to the Köppen system)

Cwa

BSh

BSh

Cwa

Aw

BSh

BSk

BWh

BSh

Cwa

Cwa

BWh

BWk

Cfwa

BWk

Cfwb

BSk

BWh

Cs

BSk

Cfb

MILES   400

VEGETATION TYPES

MILES

0   400

KMB

▦ Evergreen & deciduous bush & forest		⋮ Thorn country
■ Temperate evergreen forest		≡ Tall grass
▨ Sclerophyllous bush		≣ Short grass
⦀ Evergreen & deciduous tree & bush		≣ Mixed grass
⦀ Evergreen & deciduous tree & thorn forest		⋯ Desert shrub

FIG. 2. UNION OF SOUTH AFRICA: CLIMATIC REGIONS
AND VEGETATION TYPES

Köppen's system of climatic types is explained in W. Köppen, *Grundriss der Klima-kunde* (De Gruyter, Berlin, 1931).

the erratic nature of many of the major rivers and their high silt content, because of unfavourable soil and relief conditions, the area potentially irrigable is scracely more than 1 million morgen (1 morgen = 2·1165 acres), or less than 1 per cent. of the total farm area; of this total some 60 per cent. is already irrigated. Industrial development, too, may well be checked by insufficient water resources, and in this connexion the Vaal river is of outstanding importance:

> The future urban, industrial and mining development of the southern Transvaal and northern Free State depends on the quantity of assured water made available in the Vaal river and on the division of such water between urban, industrial and mining development, on the one hand, and irrigation on the other.[4]

Present needs in the area are estimated at 565 million gallons daily, and the potential total draw-off down to Kimberley at 800 million gallons; meanwhile, the expansion of gold production in the Orange Free State and the large-scale development of the synthetic petroleum industry will add to the heavy drain on available resources.

Finally, among the environmental limitations must be included biological limitations imposed by human and animal disease and by pests— plant, insect, and animal. Malaria played an important role in the early Trekker settlement of the north-east Transvaal, and is still a limiting factor to the extension of European settlement in the Low Veld. The tsetse-fly, transmitting nagana, has only recently been eliminated from Zululand, and is still a potential menace along the boundary with Bechuanaland, while the intermediate position of the Union between the tropics and the temperate zone gives it an imposing variety of other livestock diseases—fourteen cattle diseases are listed as "prevalent" and "serious" as against nine in the U.S.A. and four in New Zealand. Locusts, poisonous plants, and jackals introduce a further element of risk into pastoral production; the 1951 locust outbreak, for example, affected eighty-two districts, and control measures alone cost £600,000.

The Human Pattern

Successful human adjustment to what must be regarded as a marginal environment has been thwarted and impeded by human factors—

[4] J. P. Leslie, "Water—the Key to South African Industrial Progress," in *Optima*, vol. i, No. 3 (1950), pp. 7–11.

by the complex ethnic situation in the Union and by the racialism to which this situation has given rise.

The Union had a total population of 12·6 million (1951) and ranks, therefore, as one of the major population aggregates in Africa. This population is extremely unevenly distributed—geographically, ethnically, and economically. Since both the early European settlers and the Bantu were agriculturists and pastoralists there is a general concentration of population in the humid east; within this eastern sector, however,

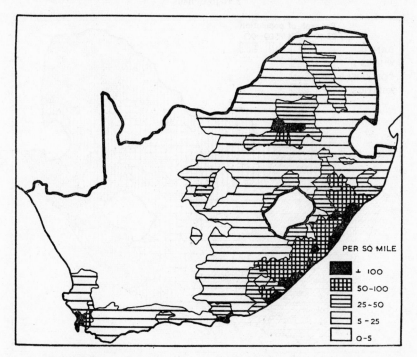

PER SQ MILE

+ 100
50–100
25–50
5 – 25
0–5

FIG. 3 UNION OF SOUTH AFRICA: DENSITY OF POPULATION

mining and industrial development has brought about a great aggregation of population in the Witwatersrand (1,632,000), while the great massing of population in the Transkei and the Natal coastal fringe (one-fifth of the Union's population on one-twentieth the Union's area) is due to the deliberate policy of concentrating the Bantu in restricted areas of Native Reserve territory rather than to any marked superiority of these areas in agricultural potentialities; the close settlement of the northern Transvaal may be explained in similar terms. Of the total population 42 per cent. is urban-dwelling, a proportion that has increased

steadily in the last half-century. The distribution of the population between the major ethnic groups is as follows (1951):

European	. .	2,643,000
Afrikaans-speaking	. .	57·31 per cent.*
English-speaking	. .	39·36 per cent.
Native (Bantu)	. .	8,535,000
Coloured	. .	1,102,000
Asiatic	. .	365,000

* 1946 Census

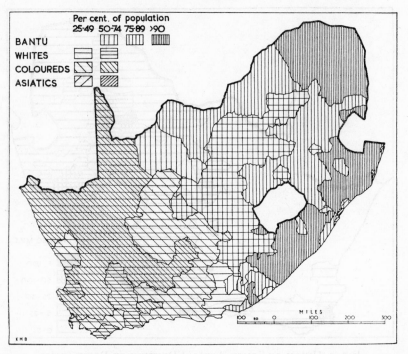

Fig. 4. Union of South Africa: Population and Distribution of
'Racial' Groups

As shown in Fig. 4, there are significant contrasts in the distribution
of these groups, contrasts resulting partly from historical accident,
partly from deliberate legislative pressure. The European population
shows a markedly peripheral pattern of distribution, half of the total
being found in the Cape coastlands and the southern Transvaal, a pattern which has become more and more marked with the decline of the
European rural population, and, above all, of the rural population in the
subhumid interior districts. Two major elements contribute to the

European group—the Afrikaner element, derived from the original Dutch settlers at the Cape, together with later infusions of Huguenot stock, and the English-speaking element, introduced first during the British occupation of the Cape during the Napoleonic wars, and strengthened by small-scale immigration in 1820 and 1849, and above all by massive immigration following the great mineral discoveries of the late

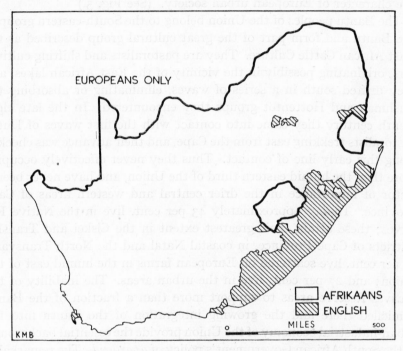

FIG. 5. UNION OF SOUTH AFRICA: HOME LANGUAGE

nineteenth century. The linguistic cleavage between these two groups is reinforced by religion—in 1936 out of an Afrikaans-speaking group of 1·12 millions, 1·02 millions belonged to the Dutch Reformed churches, which claimed only 33,000 adherents from the English-speaking group —and by contrasting historical experiences and political and economic attitudes. The two groups show contrasting patterns of distribution. The Afrikaans-speaking element dominates the rural areas, making up 82 per cent. of the rural population, and is the majority language group in the smaller towns (75 per cent.) and in some of the bigger centres such as Pretoria and Bloemfontein. The English-speaking group makes up two-fifths of the population, but is highly localized—firstly, in the larger urban areas which contain 77 per cent. of the English-speaking population; secondly, in two relatively compact 'pockets' in the east of Cape Province and central and coastal Natal. These two 'pockets' date from the early nineteenth century, but, as a result of Afrikaner infiltration, appear to be losing their exclusively English character; similarly, the entry of the Afrikaner into trade and industry is slowly transforming the character of European urban society. (See Fig. 5.)

The Bantu peoples of the Union belong to the South-eastern group of the Bantu and form part of the great cultural group described as the East African Cattle Culture. They are pastoralists and shifting cultivators, originating possibly in the vicinity of the East African lakes, and they drifted south in a series of waves, eliminating or absorbing the Bushman and Hottentot groups they encountered. In the late eighteenth century they came into contact with the first waves of Dutch pastoralists trekking east from the Cape, and their advance was checked along this early line of contact. Thus they never effectively occupied more than the humid eastern third of the Union, and have never been a factor of importance in the drier central and western areas of Cape Province. To-day approximately 43 per cent. live in the Native Reserves; these attain their greatest extent in the Ciskei and Transkei districts of Cape Province, in coastal Natal and the North Transvaal; 30 per cent. live scattered on European farms in the humid east of the Union; and 27 per cent. live in the urban areas. The inability of the Natives Reserve areas to support more than a fraction of the Bantu domiciled there and the growing integration of the Bantu into the urban-industrial economy of the Union provide the essential background to the South African Government's policy of *apartheid*. The remarkable regional distribution of Bantu males to females is shown in Fig. 6.

The Bantu never occupied central and western Cape Province, where their place is taken in the social and economic fields by the Coloured people.[5] This Census group comprises three main elements: the so-called aboriginal Coloured groups, such as the Khoisan peoples and the Korannas; the compact Cape Malay community of Cape Town; and the Cape Coloured group, derived from hybridization between aboriginal Khoisan and Bantu peoples, immigrant Europeans, and European-introduced slaves of Malay and Negro stock; this hybrid group makes up three-quarters of the Coloured population. The group as a whole is con-

[5] Keith Buchanan and N. Hurwitz, "The Coloured Community in the Union of South Africa," in *Geographical Review*, vol. xl (1950), pp. 397–414.

centrated in the western sector of Cape Province, and here it is the largest single ethnic group; one half of the total lives within 200 miles of Cape Town. Culturally it has taken over many of the forms of European society, including the Afrikaans language; economically and politically it enjoyed a relatively favoured position, at least in the Cape, though this has recently (1954) been lost as a result of the racialist policy of the Government.

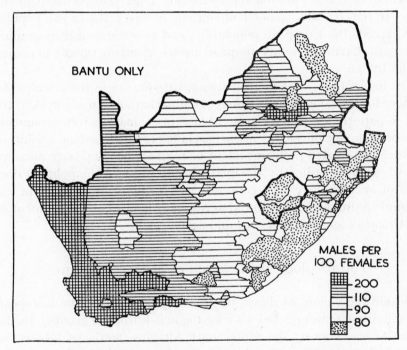

FIG. 6. UNION OF SOUTH AFRICA: POPULATION—SEX RATIO
The map shows the areas into which migrant male labour has been drawn.

The introduction of Malay and African slaves into the Cape to overcome labour shortages was paralleled at a later stage by the introduction of indentured Indian labour into the canefields of the subtropical coast belt of Natal.[6] During the present century the group has tended increasingly to move out of agriculture (only 28 per cent. were engaged in agriculture in 1936) and into secondary industry and trade, and the hardening of the South African attitude towards the Indian community

[6] Keith Buchanan and N. Hurwitz, "The Asiatic Immigrant Community in the Union of South Africa," in *Geographical Review*, vol. xxxix, No. 3 (1949), pp. 440–449.

has been explained largely in terms of the growing and successful competition of the Indian in these branches of economic activity. A further cause for concern has been the rapid growth of the Indian community, which demographically is a young community with high growth potential. The so-called "Indian problem" is, it must be stressed, highly localized: Indians make up less than 3 per cent. of the total population of the Union, and the districts where Indians constitute more than one-twentieth of the population represent only 1 per cent. of the Union's area. In the coastal area north of Durban, however, the Indian population exceeds the European population, and as a result of demographic factors the balance in many marginal areas is changing rapidly in favour of the Indian.

The uniqueness of the South African situation lies in the attempts to achieve for these four widely different cultural groups an adjustment to, and a pattern for peaceful coexistence in, a marginal environment. Recent economic development suggests the lines along which a solution to these two related problems might be reached, but any large measure of success is imperilled by the increasing strength of the political doctrine of *apartheid*. A brief comment on this powerful element in the cultural environment is essential as a background to any assessment of the Union's economic problems and achievements.

The Ideological Background of Development

Within the Union, as shown by figures quoted above, the European community is outnumbered 4 : 1 by the non-European groups. In the wider African context the white South Africans see themselves as the only single and distinct European nation in a continent of 210 million coloured people, a nation placed in South Africa "by God's hand and destined to remain as a nation with its own character and its own mission," a nation threatened by the rising tide of African nationalism over much of the remainder of the continent. At the same time it is recognized that the Bantu must be afforded the right of national self-expression and that "it is impossible indefinitely to follow a policy by which the Bantu—or at least the educated and civilized section of it—would be denied political rights and economic opportunities."[7] These two ends—the survival of the White South African group and the fuller

[7] N. J. J. Olivier, "Apartheid—a Slogan or a Solution?" in *Journal of Racial Affairs*, vol. vi, No. 2 (1954), p. 28.

development of Bantu life—are to be achieved through the policy of separate development or *apartheid*.

Apartheid is not a new policy, nor is it exclusively Afrikaner in inspiration. Some degree of racial separation has been implicit in the policies of the major political parties ever since Union, and, indeed, recently a United Party supporter accused his party of trying "to beat the Nationalists at their own game." What is unique in the present Government's policy is its coherence and forthrightness. There have been many expositions of the policy in recent years, but the clearest and fullest comes not from the Nationalist intellectuals but from Sir Godfrey Huggins, Prime Minister of the Federation of Rhodesia and Nyasaland:

> While there is yet time and space the country should be divided into separate areas for black and white. In the native areas the black man should be allowed to rise to any position to which he is capable of climbing. Every step in the industrial and social pyramid must be open to him, excepting only—and always—the very top . . . he must be protected from white competition in his own area. In the European area the black man will be welcomed . . . as a labourer, but it will be on the understanding that he shall merely assist and not compete with the white man. [8]

This, in essence, is the present South African policy; it is a policy which may achieve some measure of success in a recently settled country such as Rhodesia, but which presents insuperable difficulties in a country where a long process of economic development has brought about a complex interpenetration of the two societies, where the problem is aggravated by a large Asiatic community, and where a more catholic attitude to colour in the past has left as a legacy a half-caste group of one million. The aim of the policy is "the gradual and systematic disentanglement of the two groups," a policy to be pursued both territorially and economically and begun by legislation such as the Group Areas Act. Carried to its logical conclusion, it would involve the "Balkanization" of the Union, its fragmentation into separate European, Bantu, and Asian areas, each with its own pattern of self-government and economic life and possibly united on a federal basis. The lines of such a solution have been sketched by the South African historian A. Keppel-Jones in his work *Friends or Foes*. A solution along these lines might have something to commend it, were adequate land made available to the non-European groups; unfortunately, however, the dependence of European South Africa on coloured labour in all fields of

[8] Quoted by I. S. Lloyd, "Apartheid—South Africa's New Native Policy," in *Political Quarterly*, vol. xx (1949), No. 2, p. 128.

economic activity is so great, and the sacrifice which such a solution would demand of the European group so heavy, that complete separation must be regarded as impracticable; rather the trend of economic development is moving towards greater interdependence of the European and non-European communities.

As now applied (1956) the policy of *apartheid* has two aspects—a negative one and a positive one. Negatively, it involves growing discrimination against the non-European in such fields as skilled employment, land tenure, and freedom of movement. Positively, it involves an attempt to rebuild the fabric of Bantu tribal society and to develop the Native Reserves, both agriculturally and industrially, so that they can support a growing proportion of the Bantu population. Unfortunately, the negative aspects of the policy are the easier to put into force, and the initial results of the Nationalist Government's policy have been to increase discrimination against the non-European groups in almost all spheres of life. Whether the positive elements in the policy can ever be put into effect is questionable in the extreme. The process of detribalization is so far advanced that reconstruction of the old tribal system is impossible, even if it were desirable. The Reserves are already congested and are food-deficient areas, and to increase effectively their carrying power by industrialization or agricultural improvement would involve pouring in money and capital equipment on an immense scale; further, such a rehabilitation of the Native Areas would result in the drying-up of the flow of cheap migrant labour on which the whole economy of the Union rests. A dispassionate analysis of the situation suggests, in fact, that total *apartheid* is unrealizable and the most that can be achieved will be a degree of partial separation relegating the non-European groups to the category of second-grade citizens. Such a policy may temporarily ensure the predominance of the European minority, but it offers no permanent solution to the racial problem while the wastage and frustration of human abilities consequent upon the social and economic depression of three-quarters of the population contribute greatly to South African poverty.

Labour Problems

The industrial colour bar is designed to protect the level of living of the European worker by giving him a virtual monopoly of the more skilled and highly paid occupations. It is rooted in the erroneous belief that there exists a vast pool of potentially competitive non-European artisans and finds completest expression in the older-established industries such as mining; in these, trade union pressure, reinforced by law, effectively hinders the industrial advance of the non-European groups. The "white labour policy" is pushed with extraordinary vigour by Government departments, and especially South African Railways; in consequence, while only 29 per cent. of those employed in manufacturing industry are white, the proportion in the case of the Railways is 47 per cent. This policy of pushing Europeans into a reserved occupation at all costs may have been justified as a solution to the 'poor white' problem in the 1920's and 1930's, but has been rendered obsolete by the great expansion of the Union's economy in recent years. The resulting shortage of skilled European labour has been aggravated by a net outward movement of such labour to territories such as the Rhodesias. The problem is less severe in the newer industries, where the white labour tradition is less strongly developed and where the rate of expansion has made the employment of semi-skilled non-European labour essential; it is also less strong in the Cape, where the Coloured population has long participated in the industrial economy.

For non-European workers such restrictive practices mean that prospects of advancement are limited, there is little incentive to increase efficiency, earnings are low, and the rate of labour turnover high. Analysis of the records of 251 firms showed that half of the jobs taken by Africans lasted less than six months and three-quarters less than a year. [9] The situation is aggravated by the tendency of mining and much of secondary industry to depend on migrant labour, and by the refusal to follow the example of the Katanga and the Rhodesian copper belt in building up a stabilized urban-industrial African population. The migrant worker, with one foot in the Reserves and one foot in either the mine compound or the shanty town, has neither the opportunity nor the incentive to become an efficient worker; at the same time he is not an efficient agriculturist, and the rural economy and social life of the Reserves is shattered by the absence of a large proportion of its able-bodied male population for much of the year. [10] As a result of this general low level of efficiency, farming, mining, and manufacturing

[9] Sheila T. van der Horst, "The Native in South Africa's Industrial Revolution," in *Optima*, vol. iii, No. 2, p. 6.
[10] "The picture of the reserves is of an economy without men."—Leo Kuper, "Some Demographic Aspects of White Supremacy in South Africa," in *British Journal of Sociology*, vol. i, No. 2 (1950), p. 147. (See Fig. 6, p. 767, above.)

industry suffer from a chronic shortage of labour, and heavy labour immigration from surrounding territories has become an established feature; to-day almost two-thirds of the native labour used in the gold- and coal-mining industries are drawn from outside the Union. Meanwhile, growing population pressure in the Reserves ensures a continuous flow of would-be workers towards the shanty towns that fester on the edges of all the great mining and industrial centres.

The Economy of the Union

As a result of the territorial segregation of population the Union's economic life presents a twofold aspect—on the one hand there is the Western market-oriented economy typical of the cities and the European farm area; on the other the theoretically self-sufficient economy of the Native Reserves. The relationship between the two is complex; they compete for land, for Government assistance, and to some degree for markets; at the same time the two economies are becoming increasingly interdependent, since the Reserve economy is coming more and more to depend on imported foodstuffs, paid for by wages earned by migrant workers in the Western sector of the economy, while the European economy is dependent on the overpopulated Reserve economy for much of its labour. In spite of this interdependence it is advantageous to discuss the general features of the two economies separately; first, therefore, discussion is turned to the Western cash economy; the role and problem of the Reserves is then considered.

In spite of the continuing poverty of the great mass of the population the real national income of the Union has shown a marked increase in recent years, rising from an index of 100 in 1937–38 to 157 in 1950–1951. There have also been significant changes in the character of the economy during the last forty years, as shown by the following table giving the proportion of the net national production derived from various sectors of the economy:[11]

	1911–12	1948–49	1953–54
Farming . .	21 per cent.	14·9 per cent.	17·0 per cent.
Mining . .	36 per cent.	11·2 per cent.	11·0 per cent.
Manufacturing .	9 per cent.	23·0 per cent.	23·0 per cent.

[11] J. Goudriaan and D. A. Franzen, "Economic Factors," in *The South African Way of Life*, edited by G. H. Calpin (Heinemann, London, and Columbia University Press, 1953–54), p. 156, and *Report of South African Reserve Bank*, 1955, p. 11.

These changes have been accompanied by marked changes in the human pattern. The decline in farming with resultant outward migration from the poorer farming districts of the interior has emphasized the concentration of population in the coastlands of the Cape and Natal and the towns of the South Transvaal. Migration towards the expanding industrial centres is transforming their ethnic character: Africans resident in urban areas increased from 587,000 in 1921 to 1,689,000 in 1946, and by 1946 42·1 per cent. of the urban population was African, while the drift of the Union's Bantu away from mining and into secondary industry has led to an increased inflow of Tropical Africans to take their place in the mines. The proportion of Europeans living in the urban areas has increased from 65·2 per cent. in 1936 to 74·6 per cent. in 1951, a large proportion of the increase consisting of Afrikaners, so that the European population of the towns is becoming increasingly Afrikaner in character. Economic development, in short, is throwing together the various ethnic groups on a scale previously unparalleled, with the result that "to-day, whatever may be the theory, the towns in reality are mixed areas with members of the different racial groups inextricably interwoven in economic life."[12] The immensity of the task which the advocates of *apartheid* have set themselves is obvious enough; however, to the tiny minority of whites who realize that the interests of Europeans and non-Europeans are convergent rather than conflicting this growing economic integration is perhaps the most promising trend in the present-day development of the Union.

The Agricultural Economy. One-quarter of the Europeans, one-third of the Coloureds, and three-quarters of the African population are supported directly by farming, yet in recent years agriculture has accounted for scarcely one-seventh of the net national production. Yields per unit area are low (maize yields one-quarter those of Argentine, wheat yields one-half those of the U.S.A.); productivity per worker is only a fraction of that in other areas of newer settlement. In 1938 the value of the agricultural output was £53 million, produced by a labour force of 160,000 Europeans and 550,000 non-Europeans; Australian agricultural output, for comparison, was £112 million, produced by 175,000 male workers. Environmental disadvantages account in part for this low productivity, but their influence is aggravated by social factors, by the long-established tradition of large holdings, by the backwardness of

[12] Sheila T. van der Horst, *op. cit.*, p. 3.

the European farming community, and by the inefficient use of native labour; the overriding importance of the human factor is shown by the great range in maize yields within environmentally homogeneous areas of the Orange Free State.[13] Successive Governments have made little attempt to tackle the problem of low productivity, but have contented themselves with bolstering up the farming community by preferential treatment in the matter of railway rates and import dues, by guaranteeing prices and subsidizing exports. As H. J. Simons wrote:

> Farmers look to a paternal government to shield them from the consequences, not only of nature's harshness, but also of their own ignorance and inefficiency, and to ensure an abundant supply of non-European workers, who, illiterate, badly housed, fed, and paid, have neither the incentive nor the opportunity to acquire and apply the skill that agriculture so badly needs.[14]

Such a policy of support not only perpetuates inefficient husbandry, based largely on monoculture of cereals; it also encourages crop production on land submarginal for arable farming, with disastrous results to the soil. South African experts estimated in the early 1940's that the Union had lost one-quarter of its original reserves of soil fertility, and Jacks and Whyte, in their world survey of soil erosion, concluded that a national calamity due to erosion was more imminent in the Union than in any other country. While, therefore, it is not surprising that malnutrition and deficiency diseases should be so widespread, it is of the utmost gravity that, with a rapidly expanding population, the country should be changing from a food exporter to a food importer.

The general features of the farming pattern are summarized in Fig. 7. The relatively limited areas of even moderately intensive agriculture are evident; the highly localized character of the economy is evident from the fact that the 6 per cent. of cultivated land lying within these areas contributes to the national larder a larger quota of human food than the remaining 94 per cent. of the Union.

Mineral and Power Resources. The Union's mineral output in 1952 had an aggregate value of £214 million. Of this total, gold accounted for £146 million, coal for £41·6 million, diamonds for £14·8 million, and copper for £11·6 million. The value of gold production first exceeded

[13] *Agro-economic Survey of the Union* (Department of Agriculture, Economic Series, No. 34) (Pretoria, 1948), p. 100.
[14] H. J. Simons, "Race Relations and Policies in Southern and Eastern Africa," in *Most of the World*, edited by R. Linton (Columbia University Press, New York, 1949), p. 285.

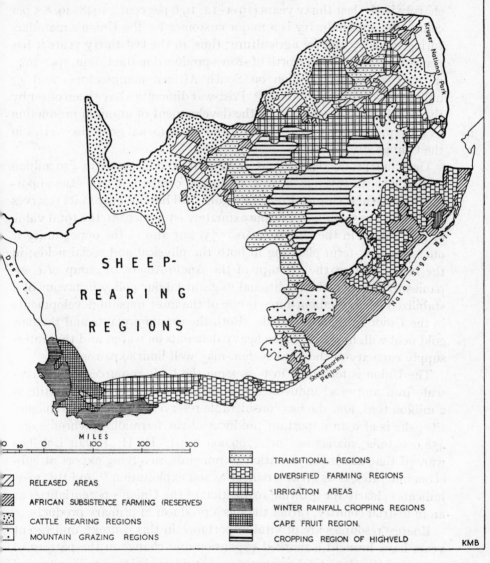

FIG. 7. UNION OF SOUTH AFRICA: FARMING TYPES

RELEASED AREAS

AFRICAN SUBSISTENCE FARMING (RESERVES)

CATTLE REARING REGIONS

MOUNTAIN GRAZING REGIONS

TRANSITIONAL REGIONS

DIVERSIFIED FARMING REGIONS

IRRIGATION AREAS

WINTER RAINFALL CROPPING REGIONS

CAPE FRUIT REGION

CROPPING REGION OF HIGHVELD

that of diamonds in 1892, and forty years later coal displaced diamonds as the second most valuable mineral produced.

Gold-mining is still of paramount importance; indeed, the gold industry has been termed "the flywheel of the Union's economy." While the percentage of national income earned in gold-mining has dropped sharply in the last thirty years (1911–12, 19·6 per cent.; 1948–49, 8·5 per cent.), the gold industry is a major customer for the Union's manufacturing industry and for agriculture; thus, in the last thirty years it has consumed £600 million worth of stores produced in the Union, spending, in 1951 alone, £44 million on South African manufactures and £7 million on local farm produce.[15] Post-war difficulties have been offset by the devaluation of sterling, by the development of uranium production as a by-product of mining, and by the phenomenal gold discoveries in the Orange Free State.

Uranium production will, it is estimated, add an extra £30 million annually to the revenue of the gold-mining companies, while the importance of the new Orange Free State gold field lies not only in its reserves (valued at £3350 million, or approximately equivalent to the total value of gold mined in the Union up to 1953) but also in the opportunity it offers for long-term planning in both the physical and social fields; in the latter context the attempt of the Anglo-American group of companies to abandon the traditional migrant labour policy in favour of a stabilized African labour force is one of the most hopeful developments in the Union in the last decade. Both the uranium plants and the new gold field will, however, make heavy demands on water, and the water-supply capacity of the Vaal system may well limit expansion.

The Union is fortunate in possessing the basic resources for a large-scale iron and steel industry. Her output of high-grade hæmatite is 2 million tons, and she has considerable reserves of titaniferous magnetite; she is also an important producer of the ferro-alloys (chrome ore, 458,000 tons; manganese ore, 709,000 tons). Dr H. J. van Eck has warned that unwise exploitation of minerals, involving export at sub-economic rates, is as great a danger as soil exploitation,[16] and this view indicates clearly the growing realization of the Union's potentialities as an industrial country, rather than as a producer of primary products.

Energy resources are of vital importance in this context, and recent years have brought a marked expansion and change in the pattern of energy production. Coal resources are considerable (2500 million tons of extractable high-grade coal, of which four-fifths are accounted for by the Transvaal fields), and exploitation is facilitated by the shallowness, thickness, and horizontal character of the seams; these features, coupled

[15] The Mining Survey, vol. iv, No. 5 (Transvaal Chamber of Mines, 1953), p. 1.
[16] H. J. van Eck, "Science and Our Natural Resources," in South African Journal of Science, vol. xlviii, No. 5 (1951), p. 156.

with very low non-European wage levels, have made it possible to produce at a pit-head price of 7–8s. per ton, as compared with overseas pit-head prices of 40–50s. Production in 1952 was 30 million tons, and expansion in demand has been at the rate of 900,000 to 1·2 million tons annually. ESCOM (Electricity Supply Commission) absorbs 4·25 million tons, and when the projected thermal power plants and the new coal-oil plant of SASOL (South African Coal, Oil, and Gas Corporation) are in operation ESCOM and SASOL together will absorb up to 11·75 million tons per annum. The concentration of generating stations on the coalfields makes it possible to utilize low-grade coals, while, in the future, gasification of these coals and the piping of the gas to the Witwatersrand may offer possibilities. Meanwhile, large-scale production of oil from coal (projected output 60 million gallons from 2 million tons of coal) will radically affect the transport situation by encouraging the greater use of Diesel-electric locomotives; such a development is of major importance in a country where water supply is a major problem on long stretches of railroad, and in the Western Cape will be more economical than electrification based on plants powered with Transvaal coal, which must be hauled 1000 miles and then converted into electricity with a thermal efficiency of only 20 per cent.[17]

Four-fifths of the Union's electric power are generated by ESCOM, and the total installed capacity of the Commission's undertakings is 1·758 million kW. New installations designed to cope with the steeply mounting demand for power have an aggregate capacity of 1·12 million kW; of this, almost three-quarters is accounted for by installations designed to serve the new Free State gold fields, including new stations at Taaibos (360,000 kW) and Vierfontein (210,000 kW) and extensions to the Vaal station. The significance of the mining industry as a consumer at present is indicated by the facts that half of the Union's capacity is accounted for by the Rand network and that the gold industry alone absorbs three-quarters of the output of the Rand stations.

The struggle for the gold and diamond resources of the interior fostered the early political development of the Union; to-day the Union's gold and uranium assets are of great importance in her relations with the United Kingdom and the United States, if only because their heavy capital investments in mining give these countries a vested interest in maintaining the existing social and economic pattern. The influence of the industry on the social pattern is more complex. The

[17] H. J. van Eck, *op. cit.*, p. 152.

2C*

system of low-paid migrant labour on which mining has been based has led to marked abnormalities in the age and sex structure of African populations in town and country (Fig. 6); these, together with the new set of values acquired by the semi-urbanized African, have been responsible for widespread moral and social disintegration. Its rigid industrial colour bar and discriminatory wage levels contribute greatly to the poverty and low purchasing power of the mass of the population; thus, in 1948, 38,359 European employees received wages totalling £24·24 million; 264,808 Africans received £12·8 million, and total working profits totalled £23·8 million. Finally, it is important to stress that the Afrikaner has played little part in the rise of the mining industry; its development has been due largely to English and Jewish interests, with the result that, while political power has passed in recent years decisively into the hands of the Afrikaner group, commercial and industrial power is concentrated equally decisively in non-Afrikaner hands. The impulse to rectify this anomaly goes far towards explaining the association of the Afrikaner with the "Revolt against Mining,"[18] the policy of industrial development designed to lessen the dependence of the country on the mining industry.

The Industrial Revolution. During the nineteenth and early twentieth centuries the high profits and wages offered by an expanding mining industry tended to divert attention from the development of secondary industry. To-day, however, the contribution of manufacturing to the net national production of the country is almost as great as the combined contribution of mining and farming. The recent rapid expansion of secondary industry reflects the growing economic maturity of the country; it reflects also an awareness of the dangers of excessive dependence on a precarious agricultural system and an unpredictable demand for the rarer minerals. Further, to many Afrikaners expansion of secondary industry represents a means of reducing the power wielded by the great mining groups, which, as has been indicated, are generally non-Afrikaner in character[19] and 'English' in their politics. The rate of expansion of industry in recent years is suggested by the table on p. 779.

[18] Basil Davidson, *Report on Southern Africa* (Cape, London, 1952), Part 2, Chapter 1.
[19] It is estimated that only some 10 per cent. of the capital invested in the Union is controlled by Afrikaner business-houses.—Leo Marquard, *The Peoples and Policies of South Africa* (Oxford University Press, 1952), p. 72.

Year	Number of Establishments	Number of Employees	Gross Value of Output
1932–33	7,669	192,483	90,948,000
1938–39	10,256	352,500	199,617,000
1943–44	10,684	457,176	330,557,000
1949–50	14,809	713,151	774,718,000

Source: *Official Yearbooks of the Union of South Africa.*

Since 1938–39 employment in industry has doubled (though European employment has increased only 50 per cent.), while gross value of output has quadrupled. For comparative purposes it may be noted that gross value of production is twice that of New Zealand but only slightly over half that of Australia; production per employee, however, is only half that in New Zealand.

Perhaps the most striking feature of the Union's industrial pattern is the high degree of concentration in four comparatively restricted areas: the Cape Western area, Port Elizabeth, Durban and Pinetown, and the Southern Transvaal, which together account for almost three-quarters of the industrial output of the Union. This concentration is most marked in the metal industries, in clothing, and textiles, furniture, and chemicals, and has shown a steady increase during the last thirty years; it reflects the dominating role of the market as a locational factor in the Union, due to the limited overseas market and the difficulties of communication which lead to high distribution costs within the Union. A second striking feature is the diversified character of the economy, with employment spread over a wide range of industries; food and drink, metals and engineering, clothing and textiles, building and chemicals are the major groups in terms of gross output, accounting together for two-thirds of the Union's production. Finally, and perhaps most significant of all, is the heavy and increasing dependence of industry on non-European labour; to-day two-thirds of the labour employed in manufacturing industry is non-European, and the proportion is likely to increase as the tempo of industrialization quickens.[20] The absorption of the non-Europeans has been slow in the more specialized industries and in the older industries with an established pattern of employment, but has been relatively rapid in groups such as metals and engineering. In such industries the African supplies not only the bulk of the unskilled labour force but also a growing proportion of the semi-skilled workers;

[20] Sheila van der Horst, *op. cit.*; J. D. Rheinallt Jones, "Industrial Relations in South Africa," in *International Affairs*, vol. xxix, No. 1 (1953).

he has, in short, set his foot firmly on the first rung of the industrial ladder.

A wide range of raw materials, an abundant (though at present wastefully used) labour force, and large potential markets in southern Africa provide the Union with a unique opportunity to relieve its burden of poverty through a far-sighted policy of industrialization. For its success, however, such a policy demands a drastic reorientation, so as to make the maximum use of the skills of all sections of the population, and a social policy directed to expanding the purchasing power of the depressed non-European masses. Except among a minority of liberal thinkers and industrialists there is little appreciation of these possibilities; rather is the growing economically motivated integration of black, white, and brown within the expanding framework of an urbanindustrial economy increasingly challenged by a racialist ideology valid only in a rural-patriarchal society long since dead.

The Problem of the Reserves

The Native Land Act of 1913 laid the basis for a uniform policy by demarcating native reserves; the policy was carried further by the 1936 Native Trust and Land Act, which made provision for the purchase of additional areas to alleviate overcrowding on existing reserves, established a Trust Fund for the financing of capital improvements, and set up a Native Representative Council to enable native opinion to be consulted. The basic concept behind this legislation was that the reserves should be maintained as a permanent home for the majority of the native population and that within the reserves guidance by European trustees would enable the African to "develop along his own lines."

The extent of Native Trust Land scheduled under the 1913 Act and later emendations was 10·59 million morgen; the 1936 Act provided for extensions to this not exceeding 7·26 million morgen in area and confined to certain areas delimited in the Act and termed "Released Areas." By December 1950 some 2·2 million morgen had been acquired. The general distribution of the reserves is shown in Fig. 7; the greater proportion lies in the humid or subhumid east, the largest blocks of reserve territory being the Transkei (25 per cent. of the total reserve area), Zululand (14 per cent.), and the North-east Transvaal (14 per cent.).[21]

[21] "The Native Reserves and their Place in the Economy of the Union of South Africa," in *Social and Economic Planning Council: Report No. 9* (Pretoria, 1946).

In theory, the reserves were to be the home for the majority of the Natives. To-day only two-fifths of the African population are domiciled in the reserves, yet the pressure of population is extreme. Taking the reserves as a whole, the density in 1936 was 57 per square mile; in the Natal Midlands it was 118, and in the reserves of the Natal coast belt it was 196.[22] Such densities, in areas often marginal because of soil poverty, erratic rainfall, or unfavourable relief, go far towards explaining the poverty, overcultivation, and declining fertility of the reserves. Agricultural productivity is very low; cereal output per head is estimated at 1·25 bags per annum compared with the 2·75 bags essential to provide a minimum diet. Cattle numbers appear to have reached a saturation level, yet in the Transkei two-fifths of the population have no cattle and the whole area is desperately short of dairy products. With total income in cash and kind estimated at £20 per family per annum and with the reserves producing less than one-half of the cereal needs of their population it was inevitable that the African should be forced out by economic pressure to become a wage-earner in the European economy. In 1936 54 per cent. of the male working population of the reserves were absent as migratory labourers, the proportion reaching 63 per cent. in the Ciskei and 69 per cent. in the Central Transvaal; the reserves, in short, far from becoming the home of a stabilized and self-sufficient peasantry, have become little more than economic appendages of the white economy, providing a vast pool of low-paid, unskilled migrant labour for the mines and factories of the Union.[23]

The avowed policy of the present Nationalist Government is directed towards developing the reserves as the home of a stable native population. Improved agricultural methods and the development of a wide range of secondary industries within, or within easy reach of, the reserves will, it is believed, help to solve the problem of over-population and stem the flow of the Bantu towards the cities. For the administration of the reserves the old tribal authorities, long since outmoded and little fitted to cope with the problems of a society in a state of rapid transition, are to be resuscitated; the Bantu Authorities Act "provides successively for tribal authorities, regional authorities, and territorial authorities in Native areas. . . . [It accepts] the tribal system as the springboard from which the Bantu may rise in their own areas to higher levels of culture and self-government."[24]

[22] *Ibid.*, p. 8.   [23] *Ibid.*, p. 45.
[24] H. F. Verwoerd, "Native Policy of the Union of South Africa" (Statement in the Senate of the Parliament of the Union of South Africa, May 1952). See also

It is doubtful how far such a policy can be, or is intended to be, implemented. The expenditure involved in agricultural rehabilitation of the reserves would be immense ; as an indication, it has been pointed out that assistance to European farmers in the last forty years has totalled £130 million and that the reserves would call for many times this sum for agricultural development alone. It takes little account of the demographic expansion of the Bantu, which, on a conservative basis, may well double or triple the population of the already congested reserves by the end of the century.[25] It attempts to stem or reverse the accelerating flow of Africans towards the urban areas, a migration becoming increasingly balanced in character and as essential to the industrial development of the Union as were the great rural-urban migrations of the nineteenth century to the industrialization of Great Britain. In its revival of the old tribal pattern of society and its refusal to attempt to integrate the African into the fabric of a democratic society it is diametrically opposed to political trends in the remainder of British Africa. While it would be folly to underestimate the strength of the ideological drive behind the present Nationalist policy it is difficult to resist the conclusion that their policy towards the reserves is little more than the last despairing move in what Sheila T. van der Horst has described as "a losing battle between an official policy aimed at keeping the different racial groups apart and the powerful forces making for economic integration."[26]

FURTHER READING

General Works

BROOKES, E. H., *South Africa in a Changing World* (Oxford University Press, 1953).
HELLMAN, E. (editor), *Handbook on Race Relations in South Africa* (Oxford University Press, 1949).
MARQUARD, L., *The Peoples and Policies of South Africa* (Oxford University Press, 1952).
PALMER, M., "Natal's Indian Problem," in South African Affairs Pamphlets, No. 99.

E. G. Jansen, *Native Policy of the Union of South Africa* (State Information Office, Pretoria, 1950).

[25] For population estimates see H. F. Verwoerd, quoted in "Report of U.N. Commission on the Racial Situation in the Union of South Africa" (New York, 1953), p. 154; also L. T. Badenhorst, "The Future Growth of the Population of South Africa," in *Population Studies*, vol. iv (1951), pp. 3-46.
[26] Sheila van der Horst, *op. cit.*

PATTERSON, S., *Colour and Culture in South Africa* (Grove, New York, and Routledge, London, 1953).

SAUVY, A., "Le problème démographique et racial en Afrique du Sud," in *Population*, vol. viii, No. 4 (1953), pp. 685–710.

SCHAPERA, I. (editor), *The Bantu-speaking Tribes of South Africa* (Routledge, London, 1937).

TINGSTEN, H., *The Problem of South Africa* (Gollancz, London, 1955).

WALKER, E. A., *The Great Trek* (Macmillan, New York, and Black, London, 1934).

WOODS, C. A., "The Indian Community in Natal," in *Natal Regional Survey* (Oxford University Press, 1953).

On the Ideological Background of Present Development and its Consequences

"Integration or Separate Development?" (South African Bureau of Racial Affairs, Stellenbosch, 1952).

Report of the Native Laws Commission, 1946–48 (Pretoria, U.G., 1948).

On Economic Life

BENNETT, H. H., *Soil Erosion and Land Use in South Africa* (Department of Agriculture and Forestry, Pretoria, 1945).

"Investigations into Manufacturing Industries in the Union of South Africa," in *Board of Trade and Industries Report*, No. 282 (1945.)

PENTZ, J. A., *An Agro-ecological Survey of Natal* (Pretoria, 1945). (Contains a generalized agro-ecological map of the Union.)

WELLINGTON, J. H., "Land Utilisation in South Africa," in *Geographical Review*, vol. xxii (1932), pp. 205–224.

CHAPTER XXXIII

Policies and Problems in Africa

R. J. HARRISON CHURCH

I N Africa there are six European Powers, which have different and
often diametrically opposed policies. Each is largely the reflection
of contrasted political, economic, social, and religious history, attitudes, and customs in the metropolitan country. Policy has also been
affected in some areas by the African environment: whether or not, for
example, it offers land and climate suitable for white settlers, or makes
possible plantation agriculture. The African social fabric has likewise
been a significant factor, but only where the metropolitan Power's pre-
disposition was to respect it. Thus, the political organization of the
Emirates of Northern Nigeria was retained under British policy, but
similar States in Mauritania, French Guinea, and the Upper Volta were
not retained by the French.

There are also at least five independent States in Africa, whose existence and widely different policies have repercussions throughout Africa,
largely through African newspapers, political parties, and by verbal
report from migrant labourers.

Nor should the influence of the outer world be forgotten. American
opinion makes itself known through African scholars in its universities,
through increasing interest in rapidly developing Liberia, and by muni-
ficent economic assistance to many territories. The direct influence of
the U.S.S.R. has been wildly exaggerated, and is more Marxian than
Russian. It appeals to those who desire political and land-owning
systems radically different from both traditional African and Western
ones. Far more important is the influence of India and Pakistan. Their
particular interest in Hindu and Moslem communities in Africa is
obvious, but the political interest of British Africans in India is more
widespread. African Moslems are also affected by the Arab League,
whose concern for events in Morocco, Algeria, and Tunisia is especially
evident.

British Policy in Africa

The basic aim is self-government, as already achieved by the Union of South Africa and, except for foreign affairs, by the Federation of Rhodesia and Nyasaland. The Sudan has now achieved full independence; Gold Coast, Western Nigeria, and Eastern Nigeria may attain it in 1956 or soon after. All three will then possess the right freely to leave the Commonwealth, should they so choose, as did Burma, the Irish Republic, and Sudan. Another choice before them will be to remain within the Commonwealth as self-governing republics, as India and Pakistan have done, and as Ceylon may also do.

Although the aim of self-government is clear enough for the Gold Coast, it is less so for the much smaller Sierra Leone and far from clear for such small units as the Gambia, whose area is only four times the size of Derbyshire or less than the area of Connecticut. It is problematical for such territories as British Somaliland or the islands of Mauritius, St Helena, or Ascension. In these, self-government by their own parliament or council might possibly be in association with the United Kingdom—as are Northern Ireland, the Isle of Man, Guernsey, Jersey, Alderney, and Sark, each of which has its own parliament, laws, and taxes. Such an association has been offered to Malta.

British colonial administration is also very decentralized. The Governor is the Monarch's personal representative and may, in his colony, override the Secretary of State for the Colonies. Two Governors at least have in fact done so in recent years. There is no Colonial Inspectorate, for the idea of the Colonial Office in London sending inspectors to examine the work of colonial administrators would be anathema to the very inner spirit of decentralized colonial administration. Decentralization was a lesson taught by the American War of Independence, and it was taken thoroughly to heart.

Decentralization likewise means that each territory has its own constitution, adapted to its own circumstances, drawn up sometimes by the peoples themselves, as in Nigeria and the Gold Coast; and sometimes partly in consultation with them, as in Kenya, Uganda, Tanganyika, Sierra Leone, and the Gambia. All have Executive and Legislative Councils. In some Executive Councils Africans have all the portfolios, as in Western and Eastern Nigeria, but more commonly they have a share with *ex-officio* members and representatives of other races.

Likewise, the Legislative Councils vary as to their degree of elected representation, African or otherwise. These Legislative and Executive Councils are, as their name indicates, law making and executing bodies. Laws, taxes, and the budget are all enacted in and by each territory.

Another fundamental aim has been to develop African cultures, customs, and institutions, rather than to supersede them with British ways and life. Indigenous political institutions were kept where possible, and, when practicable, Indirect Rule was established through the existing rulers.

Indirect Rule was especially well developed by Lugard through the Emirs of Northern Nigeria and by Cameron in Tanganyika. The Emirates of Northern Nigeria greatly expanded their revenues and government departments, their methods being improved to accord with Western ideas and practice. Some Emirate revenues were greater than those of poor sovereign States. And the power of the Emirs is illustrated by the fact that no Christian missions may be established in their territories without their permission.

Indirect Rule prevented over-hasty rupture with African tradition, conserved what was best or practicable in African society, and economized white officials. Yet, as time passed, the system has been much criticized, by Africans and by non-Africans alike. The existing chiefs were not necessarily liked or respected by their peoples, and even if they were they had to serve two masters, a problem found impossible in 1953 by the Kabaka of Buganda in central Uganda. The system often proved unduly conservative. Thus the Emirs excluded most Christian educational missions. But the scarcity of Christian educational missions in Northern Nigeria, compared with their widespread and long activity in Western and Eastern Nigeria, has resulted in there being few trained African leaders in Northern Nigeria. So that country now wishes to defer self-government until after 1956, which is the date proposed for Western and Eastern Nigeria. Moreover, under Indirect Rule, the educated élite often returned from their studies in Europe or America to scoff at the traditional and often illiterate chiefs. Lastly, in some areas, Indirect Rule was either a failure or was never applied because it was impracticable. Thus, the Ibo of Eastern Nigeria and the Kikuyu of Kenya never had chiefs in the ordinary sense of the word. Elsewhere, as in Sierra Leone, the small size and minute revenues of chiefdoms have presented great difficulty.

The present tendency in British territories is, therefore, rather to sidetrack the traditional chiefs. Especially is this seen in the Gold Coast and Nigeria, where the central legislative and executive power is in the hands of educated Africans not usually connected with and often hostile to traditional chiefs. African political leaders and European officials now favour and are developing elected local authorities, which again undermine the traditional African chiefs, previously encouraged and supported. The chiefs are understandably suspicious of the new constitutions and the recently emerged African politicians, and feel that their authority has been undermined by the British.

In the restricted areas known as "The Colony" (*e.g.*, around Bathurst and Georgetown in the Gambia, in and behind Freetown and the town of Bonthe in Sierra Leone, along the coast and near-by inland in the Gold Coast and Kenya, and around Lagos in Nigeria), English Common Law applies and the people are Citizens of the United Kingdom and Colonies. Elsewhere, African Customary Law and land tenure apply whenever possible, and the people are British Protected Persons.

British educational policy has been to educate in African languages at the primary and sometimes even at the secondary stage, on the argument that a child learns best in his own tongue. University education is encouraged: about 3000 British Africans attend universities in the British Isles. Many others attend university colleges in Sierra Leone, Gold Coast, Nigeria, Southern Rhodesia, and Uganda. Other Powers have hesitated to develop university education—there is no university in Portuguese Africa and few opportunities exist for Africans to attend Belgian or Portuguese universities. Yet it may be that the British have overemphasized general education and, until recently, underprovided technical education, in which the Belgians have especially believed.

The last outstanding characteristic of British policy is the lack of conscription of colonial peoples. An indigenous inhabitant of a British colony, whether living in his own country or in the United Kingdom, cannot be conscripted, even in wartime. This is in striking contrast with French practice. The French instituted conscription because of their low and practically static metropolitan population, by comparison with the larger and growing population of nineteenth-century Germany. Conscripted Africans were to help restore some sort of balance. They have always been used mainly in French overseas garrisons and campaigns. Apart from military considerations, the French consider that army service broadens the vision and improves the health and efficiency of conscripts. But while the conscripts are absent from home productivity (notably in agriculture) falls.

The fundamental British aim of self-government is relatively straightforward where there are no white settlers or other racial groups. But where these exist, the superior education, technical and business experience of whites, their possession of land often buttressed (as in Kenya) by special or concealed subsidies, give them great power. In Kenya, though by far the smallest racial group, the Europeans insist upon representation in inverse proportion in the Legislative and Executive Councils, so that they equal all other racial representatives put together. It is obvious that, as great power is accorded locally in British colonies, white settlers will tend to secure control, as in Kenya and in the Federation of Rhodesia and Nyasaland. In non-British territories, where administration is more centralized in Europe, white settlers are locally less powerful, although not less vociferous.

The Problem of the High Commission Protectorates

In vivid contrast to British policy stands that of *apartheid* in the Union of South Africa, which has been discussed above (see especially pp. 769–770).

But the British Government is still responsible for the Bechuanaland Protectorate, Basutoland, and Swaziland, which are semi- or complete enclaves within Union territory. They are under the immediate authority of the British High Commissioner (= Ambassador) accredited to the Union of South Africa. As he reports to the Commonwealth Relations Office, it is this office, and not the Colonial Office, which also administers these territories. Nevertheless, government is in accord with general British colonial policy, and Indirect Rule is the established method. These protectorates enjoy Colonial Development and Welfare grants, just as if they were ordinary colonies. Yet it is obvious that as semi- or actual enclaves they can hardly, in their present boundaries at any rate, look forward to eventual independence, as may other British territories.

Bechuanaland was taken under British protection in 1885 to prevent the Afrikaners linking with the Germans in South West Africa. But British Bechuanaland (the southern part) was later made a Crown Colony and then part of Cape Colony, which was later included in the Union of South Africa. Thus so-called British Bechuanaland is Union territory, where *apartheid* prevails. The Bechuanaland Protectorate is, however, British. Its administrative headquarters, Mafeking, actually lies over the border in the Union of South Africa—another of Africa's territorial oddities. If Seretse Khama had been permitted to become Chief of the Bamangwato tribe his white wife could hardly have accompanied him to the Bechuanaland Protectorate capital in Union territory, where mixed marriages are illegal. Moreover, Union of South Africa territory surrounds the Bechuanaland Protectorate on all but the north-east side, and the trunk railway running through the territory is operated by the Union, though owned by Rhodesia Railways. In 1946 the population of Bechuanaland was 292,755 Africans and 3555 non-Africans, in an area of 275,000 square miles.

Basutoland was British territory from 1868–71, again from 1884, and was always strongly anti-Boer. It alone of the three protectorates has no European settlers or landowners. Its capital, Maseru, lies only a mile from the western boundary, and Basutoland is entirely surrounded by Union territory. In an area of 11,716 square miles, its African population (1946) was 561,289, non-Africans being 2565.

Swaziland was originally under Afrikaner protection, later under joint Anglo-Boer control, and then, largely by an accident of administration, remained British. Because of concessions made by a chief in the eighteen-seventies, it has many white settlers, much of its land belonging to South African nationals. It also has mines, in which South Africa is interested. The Transvaal surrounds it on three sides and separates it from Natal by the "Piet Retief corridor," which is in places only a few miles wide. In 1946 the population of Swaziland was 181,269 Africans and 3946 non-Africans in an area of 6704 square miles, approximately the size of Wales, or less than Massachusetts. Though smaller than the other protectorates, it is richer and more varied in its resources, since much of Bechuanaland is semi-desert and Basutoland is partly composed of high mountains. Swaziland alone has important mineral workings, of tin and especially of asbestos. It also produces surplus rice, cotton, and tobacco.

All three are, however, basically cattle-rearing and -exporting lands, whose poor soils and lack of economic opportunity cause their young men to work as migrant labourers in the Union of South Africa, mainly in its mines. About 17,000 Bechuanas are absent annually out of a total African population of 293,000, some 9000 Swazis out of 181,000, and 64,000 Basutos out of 561,000.

The Union of South Africa's case for incorporation of the three High Commission protectorates is that it was foreseen and provided for in the South Africa Act of 1909. The Union's pride is obviously hurt by the existence of British areas within or on its borders in which a different social policy is pursued. The Union naturally resents Britain's distrust of its racial policy. Any country with such semi- or complete enclaves would desire to eliminate them, so making its own administration wider, easier, and tidier. The Union is also the natural market for the Protectorates' exports, including migrant labour, and a Customs Union hinders exports to other countries.

Bechuanaland has a Union-operated railway as its vital lifeline, but Basutoland and Swaziland lack railways, although there is one mile of track to Maseru, the Basuto capital. Many railways run near the borders, but the Union has deliberately left these two latter protectorates without railways, promising to provide them after incorporation. Lack of railways has been a grave handicap, particularly when roads were few. The main Johannesburg–Lourenço Marques road, however, runs through Swaziland.

It is certain that the Union could stifle these territories economically or occupy them overnight. If Britain had more fully educated their inhabitants, tried to make them independent of working in the South African mines, or permitted Seretse Khama to rule with his white consort, then the Union might very likely have demanded transfer.

The only argument against this has been the long-standing hatred of Union racial policy among protectorate peoples. They know the policy well, because so many have suffered from it as migrant labourers. Most of them prefer poverty and the more liberal British policy, to greater wealth, *apartheid*, and restrictions on their movements. If transfer were attempted there might be civil disorder.

Meanwhile, British Governments have frequently reiterated that Parliament would first have to agree upon transfer or change, that the Native populations would have full opportunity of expressing their views, and that safeguards would be required. But this latter pledge could not be enforced, and no British Government has yet said that the consent of the native populations is essential, only that they would be consulted.

Until 1940, at least, the protectorates were among the most neglected parts of the British Empire, but they have since received substantial grants, and Bechuanaland and Swaziland are the scenes of major experiments in ranching and irrigation respectively. The British Government is, however, anxious not to antagonize South Africa, because an unfriendly Egypt could close the Suez Canal. A friendly South Africa would then be even more vital along an alternative seaway.[1]

French Policy in Africa

The French territories in Africa, like the British, are in varied constitutional relationships with the home country. Algeria (especially Northern Algeria) is administered as a part of France, except for the application in certain circumstances of Moslem law and usage. There are three *départements* (Oran, Algiers, and Constantine), electing fourteen councillors of the Republic and thirty deputies. Réunion is also a *département* of France. Algeria and Réunion therefore come under the Ministry of the Interior, although the Southern Territories of Algeria are military territory, and so come also under the Ministry of War.

The third group was made up of the protectorates of Morocco and Tunisia, but these acquired political independence early in 1956. It is envisaged, however, as the formula 'independence with inter-dependence' suggests, that they should remain in some degree associated with France. This appears desirable if only because of the presence in Morocco and Tunisia of European minorities—predominantly French and Spanish in the former, and Italian, French, and Spanish in the latter. All other French territories in Africa come under the Ministry of Overseas France, formerly the Ministry of Colonies.

Despite the apparent diversity of the French overseas territories, the fundamental policy is that all shall eventually become *départements* or counties of a greater France. Before the second world war the policy was Assimilation to French civilization, but now it is the more liberal one of Association.

Modern French administrative aims and methods are based on the declarations of the Brazzaville Conference of 1944. The following one is basic:[2]

---

[1] On the problems of the High Commission Protectorates see Hailey, *Native Administration in the British African Territories*, Part 5 (H.M.S.O., 1953); M. Perham and Lionel Curtis, *The Protectorates of South Africa—The Question of their Transfer to the Union* (Oxford University Press, 1935); *The Official Year Book of the Union of South Africa* (Pretoria). The *Annual Report* for each territory, published by H.M.S.O., includes bibliographies.

[2] Quoted in French by W. R. Crocker, *On Governing Colonies* (Allen and Unwin, London, 1947), p. 92.

The aims of the task of civilization accomplished by France in the colonies put aside any idea of autonomy, all possibility of evolution outside the framework of the French Empire; even the eventual establishment in the colonies of self-governing constitutions is to be put aside. The aim is to affirm and guarantee the indestructible political unity of the French world. It is Paris which will preside over the planning of the whole Empire. Its economy shall be under the direction and control of the Mother-country.

Such denial of self-government within or outside the French Union and the concept of planning, direction, and control from Paris contrast strongly with British aims of self-government, decentralization, and local planning.

Thus the French Union is a tightly organized unity, not a loose Commonwealth. The French have also adopted the term 'territory,' instead of the more comely 'colony,' and speak of "territoires de la France d'Outre-Mer."

Administration is highly centralized in Paris or in the African capitals. Constitutions, all very similar, unlike the diverse British ones, are made in Paris, but in the presence of elected representatives from each overseas territory. Because of such representation in Paris, the local non-legislative Representative Assemblies and Councils of Government are largely confined in their powers to control of finance and to discussion of other matters.

Representation in Paris is, as for France, in the Chamber of Deputies and in the Council of the Republic, but in both cases with proportionately far fewer representatives than for France itself. Indeed, there are only thirty-seven deputies from all French 'Black' or Tropical African territories.

There is also an Assembly of the French Union at Versailles, the Assemblée de l'Union Française, but this has no legislative powers and meets infrequently for discussion only. African deputies in the Chamber of Deputies or councillors in the Council of the Republic (former Senate) reside in Paris for most of their elected term and necessarily become more French- or Paris-minded than African. They may lose touch with their African constituents, their lives and their problems. Thus it has been said:[3]

As a result the leaders of colonial opinion direct their attention to Parliament, and neglect both the local assemblies, where the immediate interests

[3] H. Laurentie, "Recent Developments in French Colonial Policy," in *Colonial Administration by European Powers* (Royal Institute of International Affairs, London, 1946), p. 15.

of the Colonies are discussed, and the Assembly of the Union, where the wider interests are debated. Furthermore, the balance between the representation of the interests of Frenchmen in the Colonies and those of the natives was sought in Parliament, under most unsatisfactory conditions, instead of in the Assembly of the Union, where such a balance could easily have been achieved. Lastly, opinion in the metropolitan country has taken exception on several occasions to the fact that the answer to purely domestic problems had depended on the vote of colonial deputies, some of them autonomists. This shortcoming is aggravated by the presence of colonial representatives in both houses.

The general aim is to make Africans as French as possible, while the British seem almost to resent Africans trying to be like themselves. Teaching is as much as possible in French and in French culture and traditions.

The French have instinctively allotted native culture and language no place in their educational system. This is true everywhere, or practically everywhere, of elementary education as well as of secondary and higher education. Consequently, French culture and language have become predominant everywhere. Moreover, the success obtained by our French education among the young natives encouraged us to continue along the same lines.[4]

African languages, culture, and tradition are given scant attention, except in museums and research institutions.

All rule in the past, outside protectorates, has been Direct, and chiefs have had purely ceremonial functions. Oddly enough, at the very moment when Britain seems to be abandoning Indirect Rule for elected local government, France is turning towards giving chiefs more power.

The French aim has always been to create an élite, which should exhibit and esteem French culture, so encouraging others in the same path. The British seem to dislike their African élite, and their aim is to develop African culture. In British colonies the bar has been colour (though it is diminishing), but in French territories it is culture—those évolués who have French culture, compared with those who have not.

Interdigitation of French and British territories in West Africa means that opposing policies are being worked out on either side of the boundaries. Particularly is this distressing where a people are divided, as are the Ewe.

In Togoland under French Trusteeship they are instructed in French, encouraged to become as French as possible, the men are conscripted

---

[4] H. Laurentie, *op. cit.*, p. 5.

(for local defence only, as it is a Trusteeship), and government is very centralized. But across a highly artificial boundary, in Togoland under United Kingdom Trusteeship,[5] they are taught in the Ewe language, encouraged to be good Ewe, are not conscripted, have representatives on local government District Councils and in the nearly self-governing Gold Coast's Legislative and Executive Councils.

Likewise, in adjacent French and British West Africa many striking contrasts arise from differing policies and social attitudes. An invariable feature of French administration seems to be an excessive number of white officials. Even minor ones, such as stationmasters, are often white in French West Africa, but are generally African in British West Africa. As land alienation is permitted in French West Africa, it also has Lebanese and French planter communities, as well as the usual traders. The latter too are more varied than their British counterparts, for in all French African territories there are the small café and hotel keepers, garage proprietors, and a semi-poor white class not seen in British territories, where trade is overwhelmingly in the hands of large companies with salaried staffs.

For these and other reasons, especially the fact that overseas territories are considered as Overseas France, Frenchmen (and women too) are willing to go out to work their way up from small beginnings. This may also be because France has fewer possibilities of emigration to temperate lands, such as Britain finds in the Commonwealth. Whatever the reason, the one-white-man business is common in French territories and almost unknown in British West Africa, though not in the healthier East and Central African territories.

The non-African population figures are, in consequence, very different. There are more non-Africans in Dakar alone than in all British West Africa. The contrast between Dakar, in parts a thoroughly European city and with very specialized quarters, and, say, Freetown, Accra, or Lagos is immense. Spanish Santa Isabel on Fernando Po is a small-scale model of Dakar, and both of them resemble Nairobi rather than any British West African town.

Portuguese Policy

Portuguese policy is similar to French in its high degree of centralization and the conception of Portuguese Africa as part of Overseas Portu-

[5] This may be terminated in 1956.

gal. There is no major colour bar, but rather, as in French territories, a cultural or economic one. On the other hand, although overseas territories are represented in the Portuguese Parliament, their deputies are generally recruited in Portugal and sometimes know nothing of the lands they represent. Nor is there conscription of unassimilated Africans; those who have become assimilated and have adopted Portuguese ways and become Citizens, though liable to be conscripted, are rarely compelled to serve.

Belgian Policy

Midway between the British and French conceptions stands the Belgian. M. Wigny, a former Minister of Colonies, envisages the possibility of a black democratic State, but, while considering political separation possible, would regard it as proof of failure.[6]

Like the French system, there is no local legislative council, but only a purely consultative one. Laws are made by the Belgian Parliament (but in which there are no Congo representatives), and there is a colonial inspectorate, although it is less powerful than the French one.

Akin to British practice is the degree of responsibility accorded to the Governor-General, provincial Governors, and other Congo officials. There is, likewise, great respect for the best in African life and institutions, no desire to Belgianize, and native languages are used and encouraged. The aim is not merely to have an élite; indeed, there seems to have been a fear of providing much secondary or university education. On the other hand, technical education is more advanced than in most other territories. Foreign trade regulations are also remarkably free, but internally the large semi-State companies are very powerful.

Some Specific Economic Aspects of Colonial Policies

In British West Africa the policy has been not to grant land concessions to non-Africans, although this restriction has never applied to mining leases. There are some six exceptions to the former rule, all of a scientific character. Almost all agricultural production therefore comes from African farms, most of them small.

[6] P. Wigny, "Methods of Government in the Belgian Congo," in *African Affairs* (1951), pp. 310–317, at p. 314.

The first Lord Leverhulme made prodigious efforts to persuade British officials in Nigeria to change this policy, but failed. He tried elsewhere, and in 1911 secured in the Belgian Congo a concession of 1,800,000 acres (reduced to 300,000 acres freehold in 1945), now operated by one of the Unilever group—Les Huileries du Congo Belge. Here oil-palm plantations were scientifically developed. Compared with most peasant production in Nigeria, Congo plantation yields are far higher, the oil content is greater and more is extracted, while the quality of the oil is generally superior and so commands a higher price.

In 1900 Nigeria produced almost all the world's supply of palm oil, which then represented 88 per cent. of her exports, but in 1938 it represented only 10 per cent. and her plantation rivals produced over three times as much. During and after the second world war the danger to Nigerian economy was eased, because exports from South-east Asia fell.

The problem so created for Nigeria was foretold by Lord Leverhulme. On the other hand, Nigerians retain their land, and small pioneer mills have been built to improve the rate of oil extraction and raise its quality. But poor cultivation methods are far more difficult to improve under existing African land tenure and social attitudes.

When Lord Leverhulme was refused Nigerian land concessions, early in the twentieth century, only the heavily populated areas of southern Nigeria were well known. To have granted concessions there would have caused grave land hunger. Since then, however, it has become clear that in the Cross river, and possibly in other areas, a few African plantations might be developed.

In almost all other African territories land alienation has been permitted and has enabled, for example, French Guinea and the Ivory Coast to develop large-scale banana and other fruit exports. This has also been possible from former German plantations in the Cameroons, but not, so far, from British African peasant farmers. Scientific large-scale rubber production in Liberia has only been possible because of the Firestone concession, on which some 100,000 acres have so far been planted, with ten to eleven million trees of clonal or budded rubber.

At the time of the British occupation of Kenya, the highlands appeared largely unoccupied, though this was misleading. The Kenya and Uganda Railway, which had been opened in 1901 to help suppress slavery, had proved exceedingly expensive. So in 1903 it was decided to encourage white settlement in the apparently empty and geographically favourable highlands, thereby developing the country and supporting the railway. Arabs had for centuries lived and traded in slaves in the country. Indians who had been brought in to build the railway often remained in petty commerce, and many others followed later. Europeans now complete the quadruple racial society.

Modern Kenyan problems stem from the strains and stresses of this multi-racial society, aggravated by the exclusion of Africans from land ownership in the 'white' highlands, where European settlers have large farms which they do not fully use. By contrast, African reserves, heavily overpopulated and overstocked with cattle, are badly farmed and becoming more eroded and infertile. "Poor soil makes poor people and poor people make poor soil worse."[7]

Solution of this grave problem calls for a revolution in African agricultural methods, full use of European lands, more equitable land holdings, the development of manufactures, and equal opportunities for all races. In the past, if not still, the Europeans have been heavily favoured. Thus for long they alone were permitted to grow coffee, and they have enjoyed special branch railways, favoured freight rates, and concealed subsidies.

In multi-racial industrial areas, especially where the colour bar has been most entrenched, as in British Central African territories, white trade unions have tended to reserve certain crafts and trades to themselves. More extreme is the situation in the Union of South Africa, where racial considerations very often determine who shall be employed. The greatest African problems centre around land and race; and it is in those territories with white settlers who, perhaps, also own industries and mines that these problems are most acute.

Some General Economic Aspects of Colonial Policies

A notable feature of all dependent territories has been the encouragement of external rather than internal trade. Every possible effort has been given to developing export crops and minerals. Research funds were, until 1939, almost exclusively applied to their problems. Only in

[7] See *East Africa Royal Commission 1953–1955 Report*, Cmd. 9475 (H.M.S.O., 1955); R. J. Harrison Church, *op. cit.*, pp. 56–57 and 86–87; G. W. Broomfield, *Colour Conflict* (*A Report to the United Council for Missionary Education*) (Edinburgh House Press, London, 1943); Norman Leys, *The Colour Bar in East Africa* (Hogarth Press, London, 1941); W. McGregor Ross, *Kenya from Within* (Allen and Unwin, London, 1927); M. Salvadori, *La Colonisation européenne au Kenya* (Larose, Paris, 1938) and *Land and Population in East Africa* (Colonial No. 290, H.M.S.O., 1952). This sentence is quoted in this at p. 5.

French West Africa was there a notable departure from this policy. There considerable research into food crops was undertaken because of the small population and the expressed aim, by means of better nutrition, to alleviate the labour shortage. But it is now usual to find some investigation into the problems of food crops, though the general emphasis is still overwhelmingly on cash crops. Until the standard of living is raised and taxable capacity increased this must continue, since revenues are largely dependent upon cash crops, minerals, and imports.

Exports often depend very considerably upon preferences accorded in metropolitan markets. Thus, coffee has become the main cash crop and export in the Ivory Coast because of a protected market in France. In the adjacent Gold Coast, in an area of similar climate and soils, where no comparable protected market exists, cocoa is much more profitable and is the main crop and export. Such instances are common.

Relative development has also been affected by availability of capital, so that most British territories have, in the past, been more developed than French or Portuguese lands. For a long time it was particularly difficult to attract French capital to mining in French territories, and Portugal has suffered from a general shortage of capital.

Since 1945, however, changes have been striking. Most territories have had increased metropolitan and often much United States aid, but there has been hesitancy of private capital towards certain British territories, because of the fear of nationalization in the event of self-government. As this is not envisaged in other colonial territories, no such deterrent exists. France has especially devoted much American aid to overseas development, and considerable 'refugee' capital is invested in Africa, being thought safer there than in France.

Africa has an excess of the general difficulties of the tropics and semitropics. It knows all the problems of poor soils, low yields, few natural fertilizers, seasonal and variable rainfall, water scarcity, primitive methods, and different attitudes from ours to economic incentives. For these and other reasons, Africa shows an economic development which is still patchy, and is the graveyard of economic stunts. Development has proceeded along the few lines of communication. Thus many more areas than Senegal, the Gambia, and Northern Nigeria are suitable for the cash cropping of groundnuts in West Africa, but have inadequate transport. Those products have been developed which are wanted outside Africa; such crops as cassava, yams, kola- and shea-nuts provide few exports, although much internal trade. Exports are insufficiently varied, and many territories are overwhelmingly dependent upon one commodity—the Gambia and Senegal on groundnuts, Northern Rhodesia on copper, and the Sudan on cotton. Eighteen territories have three or less commodities comprising 70 per cent. at least by value of their exports. Only Morocco has three major exports together accounting for under 50 per cent.

Diversification is not easy. New cash crops may generally only be introduced at the expense of food crops. Markets are often unwilling to accept Africa's green but sweet oranges, or its small bananas. New mineral workings require costly transport developments, and secondary industries have frequently proved uneconomic. Apart from physical difficulties, land and social systems are often highly resistant to quick economic development and change of any kind.

Production has depended, therefore, not only on physical factors and resources, but also largely upon governmental policies toward land alienation, white settlement, the power of such white settlers (great in British territories, moderate in French, and low in the Belgian Congo), occupational colour bars, encouragement of cash crops and external commerce, protected or unprotected markets, availability of capital, and investment policies.

Inter-territorial Co-operation

Outstanding dangers such as locusts have been the subject of international action in Africa for many years, but it is only recently that international collaboration has been extended from matters affecting sheer survival to those of defence, development, and welfare. This has happened as the result of common efforts in the second world war, the need for closer collaboration in the succeeding 'cold war,' the manifest advantages of freer movement of scarce commodities, and the need for pooling resources in the face of costly research and development.

Conferences on military, social, and economic matters seem now to be almost daily occurrences in Africa. Permanent international bodies have also become numerous, such as the Commission for Technical Co-operation in Africa South of the Sahara (C.C.T.A.) and its associated Scientific Council for Africa South of the Sahara (C.S.A.). There is also, for example, an Inter-African Soils Bureau, with headquarters in Paris;

and the World Health Organization has an African Regional Office at Brazzaville.

The various British territories, often so different in their government, are attempting to pool such matters as Transport and Communications, Customs and Excise, and Research. Thus there is the East African High Commission, in which are associated the Protectorate of Uganda, the Colony of Kenya, and the Trusteeship of Tanganyika. In West Africa the West African Inter-Territorial Secretariat associates the four British West African territories. There are also institutes supported by the several territories, such as the West African Cocoa Research Institute and similar institutes for rice, oil-palm research, fisheries, and other matters. The need exists, however, for further international pooling of research in all-Africa research institutes—e.g., into such matters as soil erosion and food crops.

Co-operation is easiest on technical and non-political problems. Contrasting types of government and political aims make closer political association difficult. Thus Uganda Africans fear domination by white settlers, if Uganda entered a British East African Federation of Uganda, Kenya, and Tanganyika. The same fear was expressed when the Federation of Rhodesia and Nyasaland was being discussed. Yet the logic of the modern world demands larger units, which alone can pool resources to command the capital for adequate development and social welfare.[8]

Proposals have come too from the Council of Europe for improving economic relations between member states of the Council and the Overseas Countries with which they have constitutional links.[9] The aim is to raise the living standards of the peoples of both groups, and to ease the balance of payment problems of the European countries concerned. On the continent of Europe much is heard of "Eurafrique," but Africans will be anxious to know whether the benefits will be mainly for Africa or for Europe.

While the whole European trend is towards larger units, there seems to be African distrust of them. Thus, as Nigeria reaches the threshold of self-government it is also becoming less unified. The unity achieved under British rule, by the creation of Nigeria in 1914, is now replaced by a loose federation, the individual regions of Western, Northern, Eastern

---

[8] The background to this for the Federation of Rhodesia and Nyasaland is set out succinctly in *Central African Territories: Geographical, Historical and Economic Survey*, Cmd. 8234 (H.M.S.O., 1951).

[9] *The Strasbourg Plan*, Council of Europe, 1952.

Nigeria, and the Southern Cameroons each having its own parliament and ministers. Further subdivision may occur, for in December 1953 Mr Awolowo, leader of the Action Group, the dominant Yoruba Western Region party, declared that "Nigeria should be divided into nine states, with the Northern Region partitioned into four parts, the Western Region into two, and the Eastern Region into three, with an Upper House at the Centre, in legal recognition of the equality of status of each state."[10] Nine states would reflect even more accurately the pre-European political mosaic.

One of the demands of the Kabaka of Uganda, before his deposition in December 1953, was for the independence of Buganda from the rest of the Protectorate. This would have made it an enclave, and as it has most of the resources and communications of Uganda, political separation would have ruined the rest of Uganda. The Kabaka may also have feared the association of Buganda with more backward tribes in the working of a more liberal constitution. Similar fears were noted above: that of the Creoles of the Colony of Sierra Leone and the Americo-Liberians of the indigenous Africans of the interior.

Upon the pre-European social mosaic of Africa a new European political structure was quickly superimposed after 1884. It in turn is now giving way to another. In East and Central Africa settler-dominated States may emerge. In Nigeria, the Gold Coast, and in the Sudan self-governing States of a truly African character are almost established. Tunisia and Morocco have yet to pass along either path. Other dependent territories may evolve to a closer association with European countries. Some of them may become autonomous units, such as the Isle of Man is within the United Kingdom. Others may become departments of Overseas France, Overseas Portugal, and Overseas Spain. The future political status of the Belgian Congo cannot yet be guessed.

History, looking back in retrospect on the part played by Imperial Powers in Africa, will be more concerned with the nature of the contribution which the European occupant will have made to the future of the African peoples, than with the profit or loss which the African connexion may have brought to Europe.[11]

[10] *The Times*, December 18, 1953.
[11] Lord Hailey, *An African Survey* (Oxford University Press, 1945), p. xxiii.

2D

FURTHER READING

In addition to works cited in the footnotes see:

HARDY, G., *Nos grands problèmes coloniaux* (Paris, 1942).

HARRISON CHURCH, R. J., *Modern Colonization* (Hutchinson, London, 1951).

HARROY, J. P., *Afrique, Terre qui meurt* (Brussels, 1942).

MACMILLAN, W. M., *Africa Emergent* (Penguin, London, 1949).

UNITED NATIONS, *Review of Economic Activity in Africa, 1950–54* (New York, 1955).

CHAPTER XXXIV

Australia and its Dependencies

O. H. K. SPATE

Location and its Significance

THE isolation of Australia is fundamental: its nearest continental neighbour—and by far the nearest to the developed core in the south-east—is Antarctica (Fig. 1). The continent is separated by 1200 miles of ocean from its nearest "white" neighbour, New Zealand; by 4500 miles from South Africa. By far the most usual approach is by Suez: it is 3120 miles, eight days' steaming, from Colombo to Fremantle. Only to the north-west is there any proximity of alien land: the farthest outpost of Asia, Timor, lies 500 miles from Darwin. North and north-east, indeed, New Guinea is only 100 miles from Cape York, New Caledonia within 700 miles of Queensland; but these islands are neither populous in themselves nor backed, as Timor is, by the millions of Indonesia. Beyond them lie 3300 miles of sea to Hawaii, and then a further 2400 before the Pacific coast of the United States is reached. Yet that is the nearest really powerful base of the "Western" world; and the nearness of "Asia's teeming millions" to her own empty North is ever present—perhaps to the point of obsession—to Australian political consciousness.

Obviously, then, mere distance from the European bases, whence Occidental power spread over the world, would by itself have retarded discovery and settlement. But a locational factor even more important than distance is the doubly isolating effect of latitude: Australia lies for the most part in Trade Wind latitudes, and is bypassed by the old sailing-tracks of Vasco da Gama and Magellan, which used the Indian Ocean monsoons and the south-east Trades respectively. It was left to the Dutch, making too much easting on their new route from the Cape to the Indies, to make the first known landfall on the Australian west coast. By the 1640's they knew the shores from Carpentaria to South

Australia, as well as the isolated fragment of Van Diemen's Land, the Tasmania of to-day.

But since the only continuous high relief lies close along the east coast

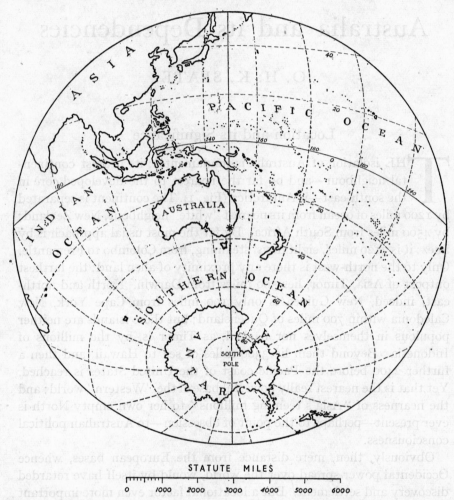

STATUTE MILES

0 1000 2000 3000 4000 5000 6000

Scale to read off distance from Canberra *

FIG. 1. THE HEMISPHERE AROUND AUSTRALIA

Zenithal equidistant projection centred on Canberra. (*Cf.* Fig. 3, p. 851.)

in Trade Wind latitudes, most of Australia lies as it were in a gigantic rain-shadow. The discovery of New Holland was the last fling of the Renaissance expansion of horizons; but these newest horizons were uninspiring. The Dutch stopped just short of the better country east of the Great Australian Bight; most of the coasts they knew were mangrove or semi-desert, with no sign whatever of spices or gold, inhabited by a few miserable savages not worth exploiting; nor were the Dutch interested in saving their problematical souls. Latitudinal position is thus responsible not only for the manner of the belated landfall, but also for the gap of nearly two hundred years between first sighting and first settlement. The well-watered east coast was hardly to be found except by deliberate search; and this was the aim and achievement of Cook in 1770. New Holland was valueless; New South Wales lay open to the first comer.

Even so, it was not until 1788, after the American War of Independence had sealed off the old dumping-ground of England's transported criminals, that the First Fleet passed through Sydney Heads to the best harbour but perhaps the worst site for settlement of all the temperate or sub-tropical east-coast lowlands. For any settlement other than a gaol, that is.

Thus the position of Australia in relation to the great wind-systems goes far to explain three fundamental features of Australian political geography: the unique fact of an entire continent forming one Commonwealth;[1] the paucity of the population; its overwhelming concentration in the south-east.

Limitations of the Physical Setting

The build of Australia is in outline simple; as in Africa, the dominance of peneplain forms and the paucity of large well-watered coastal lowlands are striking features. The western two-thirds of the continent are occupied by a great shield, mainly of ancient crystalline rocks; the only really high relief is in the plateaux of the Eastern Highlands, close along the Pacific coast and rarely exceeding 4000 feet except in the south-east. Between these two lie immense monotonous plains of Mesozoic and Tertiary sediments, from the Gulf of Carpentaria to the isolated horsts of South Australia and the mouth of the Murray.

Once more latitude is fundamental. Australia is rather less compact than South America or Africa, but although the extreme north-south

---

[1] In this chapter 'Commonwealth' without the adjective 'British' means the Commonwealth of Australia.

distance is slightly greater than the east-west, the bulk of the continent lies symmetrically on either side of 25° South. The only parts with less than the world mean of rainfall variability are the "Mediterranean" corners in the south; in the north a monsoon, and in interior New South Wales winter depressions, offset the rain-shadow. But the resultant of latitude, compactness, and relief is that Australia is dominated by aridity: 37·6 per cent. of its area receives less than ten inches of rain a year, while only 8·6 per cent. has over forty inches, a less proportion than in any other continent.[2] Probably no other country in the world, not even India, is so widely and deeply rainfall-conscious as Australia. The rainfall map is indeed a basic document of Australian history; it must of course be supplemented by considerations of effectiveness (Fig. 2).

Thus the heart of the continent has large areas of virtual desert, and around this core are wrapped concentric zones of rainfall, soils, vegetation; but terrain approaching semi-desert breaks the continuity of these girdles on the west coast north of Shark Bay, on the south at the head of the Bight. This, as it were, islands the "Mediterranean" corner in the south-west from the rest of developed Australia, a fact of considerable, if local, importance in history and politics.[3] Practically speaking, the only great system of normally perennial rivers, comparable with the major systems of other countries, is that of the Murray-Darling-Murrumbidgee.

While in perhaps one-quarter of the continent soils are moderately fertile and suited to extensive agriculture, a high proportion of this area lies within the really arid zone, and much of the rest is liable to severe erosion consequent upon excessive clearing or grazing and upon rainfall scanty but often coming in intensive downpours. By and large, the areas of really good and reliable rainfall are also areas of high or broken terrain and of relatively poor podsols, often lateritic. Soils of high fertility with good rain are restricted to very limited areas. Opportunities for irrigation—at least for arable as distinct from stock farming—are not great, even in the Murray-Murrumbidgee basin.

The magnificence of karri and mountain ash, the wide extent of fine woodland along the tourist-frequented roads of the Eastern Highlands

---

[2] *Official Year Book of the Commonwealth of Australia* (Bureau of Census and Statistics, Canberra; No. 40, 1954), p. 27 (cited as *Year Book* and source of all statistics, unless otherwise stated).

[3] At Albany, W.A., may be seen the first pole of the telegraph connexion (1875) "with the Australian and European Systems." Isolation could hardly be better expressed.

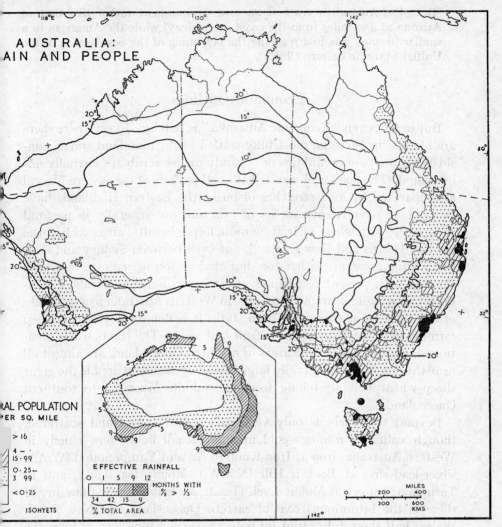

FIG. 2. AUSTRALIA: RAIN AND PEOPLE

and littoral, mask the extreme poverty of Australia's timber reserves: only about 120,000 square miles are under forest, of which less than two-thirds are even potentially exploitable, and only 5 per cent. softwoods. Perhaps the neatest summary is Griffith Taylor's:

> Indeed, the most striking fact in the geography of Australia is its division into . . . *Economic Australia* and *Empty Australia*. The former contains large areas of valuable lands which still await occupation. Probably they are the best second-class lands still open to white occupation anywhere . . .

[But] the Australian reached an arid environment rather like that of Arizona at 450 miles from the coast [at Sydney] while the American in a similar journey was just reaching the beginning of the best section of the United States in eastern Ohio.[4]

Economic Outlines

But in fact even "Economic Australia" is patchy. Everywhere there are blanks: in Victoria, most fully-settled of the mainland states, considerable tracts of mountains or of sandy mallee scrub are virtually uninhabited. The good well-watered alluvial pockets of the eastern littoral are separated by long stretches of bush; the Eastern Highlands have everywhere over twenty inches of rain and are generally in pastoral occupance, with wheat or fruit on more fertile basaltic areas such as the Darling Downs and New England, but even between Sydney and Canberra large areas are either too dissected or too infertile to be worth clearing with present techniques. Farming in South Australia is confined to the regions around the Gulfs, in Western Australia to a part only of the south-west corner; in both states it is dominantly wheat–sheep farming with small areas under fruit and vines. The tracts so far mentioned, and the sugar-cane areas of northern Queensland, are almost all near the coast; the only really large inland agricultural area is the great sheep–wheat belt stretching from the middle Murray into southern Queensland.

Beyond this there is only very sparse pastoralism and scattered, though valuable, mining: gold in many small fields, now chiefly in Western Australia; iron at Iron Knob (S.A.) and Yampi Sound (W.A.); silver-lead-zinc at Broken Hill (N.S.W.), Mount Isa (Qld.), and in Tasmania; copper at Mount Lyell (Tas.). More important than any of these is the bituminous coal of eastern Queensland and New South Wales; half the total output (of only 15,000,000 tons) comes from the lower Hunter valley behind Newcastle, the only extra-metropolitan industrial area (as distinct from isolated small towns), and at that a very thin development by European standards. In Victoria there are very considerable deposits of lignite, exploited mainly for electricity generation. New horizons are perhaps being opened by the discovery of important uranium ores at Rum Jungle (N.T.), Mount Kathleen (Qld.), and Radium Hill (S.A.), and by the oil strike near Exmouth Gulf (W.A.).

[4] *Australia: A Study in Warm Environments* (Methuen, London, fourth edition, 1947), pp. 4–5; *cf.* also pp. 52–53.

In this land of scanty unreliable rainfall and modest relief, major hydro-electric possibilities are severely limited. Some development is possible in Queensland, but the bulk of the potential (at most seven to ten million kW) is in Tasmania and the mountainous area on the New South Wales–Victoria border. Schemes constructed or planned in Tasmania will take up nearly a third of the estimated 1,865,000 kW potential; the Snowy scheme around Mount Kosciusko, if fully completed, could develop 3,000,000 kW, but it will probably be many years before any really considerable fraction of this is generated.

Nevertheless, a considerable manufacturing industry has been built up on these resources; it is mainly, though not entirely, concentrated around the state capitals. Indeed, the 1947 Census returned the following percentages for the occupied male population: manufacturing, 28·7; primary production, 19·4; commerce, 12·0; building, etc., 10·7; transport, 10·3; administration and professions, 8·8. It should be noted, however, that most factories, while modern enough, are small affairs: in 1950–51 no fewer than 28,644 of the total 43,147 employed under ten hands each; in fact, 13,393 had under four workers, and only sixty-eight over 1000. One clue to this structure is given by the fact that 5730 "factories" were concerned with automotive engineering and maintenance, and many of these are one-man-and-a-boy garages.

On a value of production (= "net added value") basis manufacturing output in 1950–51 amounted to £A843·6 million, the leading lines being metallurgy and engineering with 327 million, textiles with 126, and food, drink, and tobacco with 118.[5]

Against these figures for secondary production may be placed the values (with percentages) derived from fields and mines:

	1949–50		1950–51		1951–52	
Agriculture	199	(15)	196	(10)	247	(13)
Pastoral	343	(25)	709	(36)	400	(21)
Dairying	81	(6)	89	(5)	104	(5)
Mining*	68	(5)	89	(5)	119	(6)
All primary	691	(51)	1,083	(56)	870	(45)
Factory	661	(49)	844	(44)	1,024	(55)
Total	1,352	(100)	1,927	(100)	1,894	(100)

* Calendar years 1949, 1950, 1951.

[5] *Year Book*, pp. 975, 991. Of the metallurgy figure, machinery and machine tools, and motor engineering, accounted for over £A55·9 and 60·6 million respectively.

2D*

It should of course be borne in mind that 1950–51 was the year of the great wool boom, strikingly reflected in the exports of that year, when, of a total value of £A976 million, wool alone provided 633 (65 per cent.), wheat and flour 107, dairy products, hides, and meat 77·5; altogether (including minor items) agriculture and pastoralism accounted for over 90 per cent. of exports. Exceptional as was this year, in the preceding four years the percentages of export values from wool alone were 42, 37, 43, 51·5; in the succeeding year (1951–52) 48·4. Clearly manufacturing rests on the small, if highly consumptive, home market.

There is here a striking anomaly. The picture of the average Australian as a sunburnt bushworker is clearly far from the reality; nor could it be otherwise, when over two-thirds of the people are urban, and, indeed, half of them live in five cities. Of a total labour force (1947) of 3,196,000, only 506,000 were on the land; and this proportion is decreasing. Yet this half-million people, spread over twice as many square miles, contributed all but a small fraction of returns from exports; more striking still, in the last resort from one-third to two-thirds of these values were produced by the labour of the 96,000 workers in the grazing industry. These facts lie at the root of the internal problems of Australia, problems which may be summed up in one word: centralization.

Centralization

Although the state governments as governments are jealous of "encroachments from Canberra," in Australia centralization has reference to each individual state rather than to the Commonwealth; it means the dominance in each state of the state capital.

The reasons for this are inherent in Australian history and geography. The Australian frontier, unlike the American, was essentially a "big man's frontier": the costs imposed by distance to markets, the constant risk of drought, bushfire, and flood, made—and still make—Australia a land by and large inhospitable to the small farmer.[6] The small man has always looked to the state for assistance, but this meant organization and bureaucracy; in this land of vast distances and few men, the countryside had neither the money nor the men to run the machinery needed; these had to come, for the most part, from the existing com-

---

[6] *Cf.* B. Fitzpatrick, *The British Empire in Australia . . . 1834–1939* (Melbourne University Press, 1941), Chapters v and vii *passim*; F. Alexander, *Moving Frontiers* (Melbourne University Press, 1947), pp. 35–36.

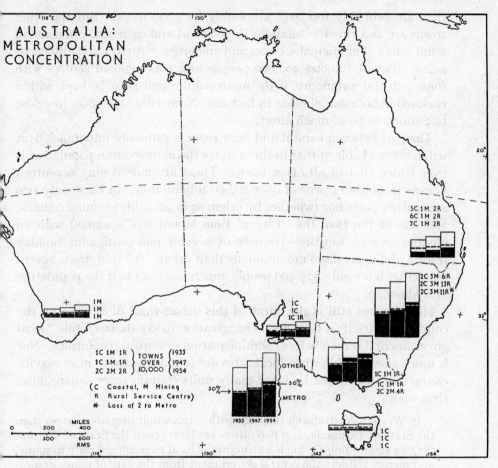

AUSTRALIA:
METROPOLITAN
CONCENTRATION

5C 1M 2R
6C 1M 2R
7C 1M 2R

2C 3M 6R
2C 3M 13R
2C 3M 11R *

1M
1M
1M

1C
1C
1C 1R

1C 1M 1R
1C 1M 1R
2C 2M 4R

1C 1M 1R) TOWNS (1933
1C 1M 1R } OVER (1947
2C 2M 2R) 10,000 (1954

(C Coastal, M Mining
R Rural Service Centre)
* Loss of 2 to Metro

OTHER

50% →   ← 50%

METRO

1933 1947 1954

1C
1C
1C

MILES
0   200   400
    300   600
         KMS

FIG. 3. AUSTRALIA: METROPOLITAN CONCENTRATION

mercial and administrative centres, the state capitals. The confusion
which arose over railway gauges in the 1860's accentuated the hegemony of the capital within each state, for only two adjacent states
(Victoria and South Australia) adopted the same gauge. Notoriously,
once centralization has been established it is self-reinforcing, even without such devices as deliberate fixing of railway routes and rates in
metropolitan interests.

The resulting concentration of well over half the population into five
state capitals (Fig. 3) has consequences for political life both wide and
deep. It is generally agreed, except by their more *exalté* business-men,
that the mainland capitals are too large relatively, and except for Perth

they are probably too large absolutely for good living. But the other towns are as a rule too small for the efficient and economic provision of a full range of municipal services and amenities.[7] Australia badly needs a few cities of 100,000–200,000 people to act as regional centres with some cultural autonomy, if the metropolitan pull is to be kept within reasonable bounds. She has in fact one, Newcastle (178,086), too close to Sydney to be of much effect.

The gap between capital and next town is probably unparalleled: it will be seen (Table 3) that in three states the metropolitan population is over thrice that of all other towns. There are indeed only seventeen non-metropolitan towns of over 20,000 inhabitants;[8] of these only two are neither ports nor (whether by origin or in actuality) mining centres; and one of the two, the "City of Blue Mountains"—named with an obvious eye to tourism—consists of several non-contiguous holiday resorts and is far more mountainous than urban. All told, these seventeen cities have only 825,000 people, much less than half the population of Sydney.

More serious still is the effect of this urban–rural disbalance on the countryside itself; it is no great exaggeration to say that as a rule "local government" is merely local administration of central regulations. Nor is much else possible when local rates are so inadequate to meet service charges, as they must be when many units contain more square miles than men:

> In Western Australia eleven local authorities administer areas larger than the State of Tasmania, and two others are larger than the State of Victoria [87,884 square miles]. Such a structure is local government only in name, and merely relieves the central government from the care of minor domestic matters.[9]

Though their functions are nominally many, the major concern of most local government organs (and the sole concern of some) is the upkeep of the local roads, and the condition of these bears incisive witness to the poverty of resources.

[7] Cf. A. J. and J. J. McIntyre, Country Towns of Victoria (Melbourne University Press, 1944), passim.

[8] Excluding Fremantle as being virtually metropolitan, but including Canberra. Some others included are not really single towns: the lignite group in Victoria, for instance, is returned as one unit of 37,341 people, but in fact consists of six entirely separate towns, only one of which reaches 9000. All these figures 1954 Census. See Tables 3 and 4.

[9] F. A. Bland, in C. Hartley Grattan (editor), Australia (United Nations Series; University of California Press, Berkeley and Los Angeles, 1947), pp. 126–127. It may be added that a perusal of annual reports of the Local Government Department of N.S.W. suggests that the central government does not care to be relieved of the most trivial domestic matters.

All this amounts to "apoplexy at the centre and anæmia at the extremities." Suggested cures, or rather palliatives, are three: decentralization, regionalism, "New States."

Decentralization is attractive enough in theory, and all parties pay lip-service to it. The obvious security risks of piling up the bulk of Australia's major secondary industry in half a dozen seaports led to some planning of industry away from the capitals during the second world war; but really effective decentralization would involve much more far-reaching and long-continued planning, probably under Commonwealth rather than state direction. For this there is no effective support, as is shown by the almost uniformly negative results of constitutional referenda. State sentiment still has a strong hold in this sphere, and in the states themselves half or more of voting power lies in the centres.

Regionalism has a certain following, and in the period of enthusiasm for reconstruction which possessed Australia, like other countries, around the end of the war several states established regional planning commissions. These, and Commonwealth agencies, have done much work, useful in its way, towards defining reasonable economic regions and publishing maps and statistical data on them. So far the chief beneficiaries have been geographers, since there has been very little sign of implementing the essential feature of regionalism—that is, some degree of local autonomy and initiative in development policies.

The "*New States*" movement appears more radical and has certainly, in some areas, more drive behind it. A better-balanced Commonwealth might have resulted if various nineteenth-century proposals had given it more foundation members. The constitution of the Commonwealth allows for the formation of new states, but only by consent of the legislatures of any old states involved. This in itself serves to prevent suggestions for new states from tampering with existing boundaries, since hopes of getting agreement from two adjacent states are Utopian. Yet in some cases—notably, for example, as between Victoria and South Australia—it is the state boundary which prevents a more rational organization of area.

New States movements are of some significance in two regions: northern Queensland, and New England in north-eastern New South Wales.

Separatism in northern Queensland has an obvious root in mere distance (Townsville, central on the coast, is 700 air miles from Brisbane), but it was strongest when the tropical north depended on coloured indentured labour—"kanakas" from the Pacific islands—for its sugar plantations; in 1891, indeed, the legislature adopted a resolution to split the state into three, but this was a snap vote. With federation and the acceptance of "White Australia" coloured labour was repatriated by 1912, the industry surviving with the help of considerable state aid and Italian labour. The development, still conceivable in the 1890's, of a region with an economic basis (indentured plantation labour) utterly different from that of the rest of Australia was thus ruled out, and with it went the most solid reason for separatism. Nevertheless the excessive eccentricity of Brisbane lends point to the distance-plus-neglect argument, and separatism survives, if not very vigorously.

The New England movement is more active and more serious, to the extent of holding embryonic constitutional conventions; in the 1954 local elections a large number of shires and municipalities disregarded the state government's disapproval and held local polls, in which some 70 to 80 per cent. of those voting (perhaps two-thirds of electors in the areas polling) opted for a new state. The core of its propaganda is neglect of the north by Sydney, and in this stronghold of the Country Party antipathy to "socialistic domination" by the metropolis is also a good cry. New England could indeed be a very workable unit by Australian standards: the boundaries claimed would give it an area of 64,000 square miles, a population of 690,000 (1954), and the coal and industry of the lower Hunter. It may be suspected, however, that one result of the creation of New England would be domination by Newcastle, which has already 26 per cent. of the people of the projected state. In the meantime the pronounced anti-labour bias of much New England propaganda ensures an almost complete absence of support from the centre itself, and without some such support New England could be attained only by revolutionary means, which in turn are not likely to command acceptance in New England itself.

The absence of sectionalism, in the American sense, is probably connected with the small number and large size of the states and the concentration of so much of their effective political power in the capitals; the great wool-wheat belt, for example, which in American conditions might well form a "section," is split between three (if not four) states, but is not dominant even in one of them. In some New State arguments it seems to be implied that an increased number of states might enable a stronger stand to be made against the growing range and weight of

Commonwealth as against state governmental activity; presumably by giving a wider spread of senatorial and Loan Council[10] votes and so allowing for sectional manœuvre and bargaining. At this point it is appropriate to consider Commonwealth-state relations.

The Commonwealth and the States

The Australian constitution was framed by men with the wealth of American and Canadian precedent at their finger-tips, but conscious that, except in Victoria and tiny Tasmania, their mass support was scarcely overwhelming. This was particularly true in the key state of New South Wales, where devotion to Free Trade reinforced a traditional aversion to agreeing with Victoria, which was Protectionist.[11] The lesser eastern states were anxious to guard against domination by a Victorian-New South Wales *bloc*; hence the adoption of the American principle of equal state representation in the Senate. Western Australia was distinctly lukewarm, except on the goldfields, where local discontents and the presence of many "t'othersiders" from the east forced the reluctant hand of Perth, in part by a separatist threat; as with British Columbia in Canada, the state made the building of a trans-continental railway a condition of entry. Isolated as it is, Western Australia has had less to gain by a high tariff policy than the eastern states, and it has often shown itself restive: as late as 1933 a referendum produced a two-thirds majority for secession, though the government presenting the referendum was defeated.[12]

The resultant constitution was a compromise, in which the positive powers of the centre were restricted to a defined list, residuary powers remaining with the states; and in fact not all powers allotted to the Commonwealth have been exercised—there is, for example, no uniform

[10] The Loan Council was set up in 1926–27 to co-ordinate Commonwealth and state borrowing; it consists of the Commonwealth Prime Minister and Treasurer, and the Premiers and Treasurers of the states. The Commonwealth has a double vote, plus a casting vote if need be.

[11] Percentage against federation of votes cast in the final referendum: N.S.W., 43.7; Qld., 39; W.A., 31; S.A., 20.5; Vic., 6; Tas., 6; total "No" vote 161,077 against 422,488 "Yes" (27.2 against 72.8 per cent.). A truer picture is perhaps given by the percentage of "Yes" votes to qualified electors: N.S.W., 34.9; Qld., 35.9; Tas., 38.9; S.A., 43.25; W.A. 46.6; Vic., 53.1; total only 42.9.

[12] K. A. MacKirdy, "Geography and Federalism in Australia and Canada," in *The Australian Geographer* (Sydney, 1953), vol. xi, No. 2, pp. 38–47, is an admirable analysis; see also R. S. Parker, "Australian Federation: The Influence of Economic Interests and Political Pressures," in *Historical Studies* (Melbourne, 1949), vol. iv, No. 13, pp. 1–2 t.

divorce law, though this is on the central list. The state powers on the whole come home more nearly to daily life; they include education, health, hospitals, roads, railways, agriculture, water supply, and liquor licensing. In theory the Commonwealth is concerned mainly with Australia as an international entity: with defence, external affairs, customs, overseas trade, civil aviation, migration, and territories. Over most of the continent its chief outward and visible sign is the Post Office and Savings Bank. As a result, though Australians have an intense loyalty to their way of life—to their continent and their culture—and to the Crown, loyalty to Australia *as a State* seems singularly weak compared with individual state loyalties: no one has died, and few have lived, for the ideal of the Commonwealth as such. Perhaps this is in part a reflection of geographical isolation: there are no land frontiers, no neighbour powers to give the internal cohesion which comes from long traditions of external differences or conflict. The nearest is the "Near North."

Nevertheless the over-all trend of Australian policy has undoubtedly been away from strict federalism, and the powers of the Commonwealth have grown at the expense of those of the states.

The need for rapid and decisive action on a continental basis in two world wars is, of course, largely responsible for extending the scope of central activity. But beyond this (which is, after all, a commonplace of the history of this century throughout the world) from the beginning of federation economic, social, and especially fiscal factors have worked together to weaken the position of the states.

It was foreseen that the obviously essential grant of customs and excise to the Commonwealth would give it greater financial resources, and constitutional provision was made for the distribution of surplus revenue to the states.[13] But these standard reimbursements were scarcely adequate for state developmental needs, especially after the depression of the thirties, when profits from railways, a major state resource, entered on a decline. The final blow was the taking over by the Commonwealth of income tax in 1942, a measure necessary to war financing but adopted over the resistance of state premiers. Despite the niceties of consultation, the Commonwealth is also dominant in the allocation of Loan Council moneys.

The Commonwealth has thus had to come to the assistance of the

---

[13] Changes in the method of making these basic Commonwealth contributions are irrelevant here. An excellent general picture is given in H. P. Brown's chapter on "Federal-State Financial Relations," in G. Sawer (ed.), *Federalism: An Australian Jubilee Study* (Cheshire (for Australian National University), Melbourne, 1952), pp. 49–70.

states: at first by general grants to enable poorer units (Western Australia, Tasmania, South Australia) to maintain administrative standards comparable with those of the east; by compensating the states for the losses incurred through the uniform income tax; and—increasingly—by special grants for defined purposes. As a result the states are becoming, in many respects, the creatures of the Commonwealth they themselves created. The trouble is that they are not very docile creatures.

They are the constitutional agents, within their boundaries, of most of the wide range of developmental activities and of many social services; but for these things they are increasingly dependent on Commonwealth funds. There is consequently, of course, much friction and delay; working agreements may take a long time to mature (and may even be constitutionally questionable); and increasingly the Commonwealth tends to duplicate state agencies, if only to ensure co-ordination, and to take a direct hand in development, as in the establishment (jointly with New South Wales and Victoria) of the Snowy Mountains Authority for hydro-electricity and irrigation. But since the states are more obviously and directly apparent in the day-to-day life of the citizens, there is very little support for the formal recognition of the Commonwealth's dominant role, as is shown by the persistent "No" vote in referenda on extensions of Commonwealth powers. The system, if anything so empirical can be called such, also tends to promote political irresponsibility, since the failings of state governments can easily be fathered on a niggardly Commonwealth. For this reason state governments are probably anything but anxious to be repossessed of the power of laying income tax, although, of course, they do not give wide publicity to this diffidence.

All this, clearly enough, springs in great part from the simple geographical facts of large area and small population. Inherent in the Australian federal system is a recognition of the difficulty—still largely valid in the air age—of adequately administering so huge and empty a land-mass from one single centre. Yet the whole trend has been towards the aggrandizement of that centre, ludicrous as this seems when one beholds its exceeding modesty: Canberra, "seven suburbs in search of a city," is the smallest national capital in the world, with a population of 30,000.

No clear trend of opinion on the subject is discernible. Few Australians are unificationists, even in Canberra; the Australian Labour Party once flirted with a scheme for a unitary government with a good deal of devolution to provinces or regions smaller than the existing states, but the vested interests of its state machines are strong enough to stifle any such imaginings. On the other wing are the strict federalists, generally more conservative members of the Liberal (= Conservative) and Country Parties, who wish to put the clock back to 1901. New State supporters apparently believe that more states would "restore the balance of the constitution" in some not clearly defined manner. But the Australian way of life is not adventurous in these matters, and probably nothing short of a really shattering economic-political crisis could work any radical change in a system which, after all, works in its fashion.

The Problem of the North: Immigration

Among the most serious of Australian problems is that of developing the empty tropical north, much of which—the Northern Territory—is a direct Commonwealth responsibility. Between 1900 and 1930 the white population of the Territory increased by 107 souls. In the next quarter-century the increase was over 150 per cent.; an achievement less striking when it is considered that the actual numbers in 1954 were 16,452, of whom half were in Darwin: this on an area of well over half a million square miles. Yet settlement was initiated as early as 1824, and for the last ninety years there have been persistent efforts, private and public, to exploit its undeniable resources. The charge that Australia has done nothing to develop its vast tropics cannot be sustained; there has been much labour, but trifling reward.

In essence this is due to the hard fact that the environment is by no means as favourable as the rainfall map suggests. A third of the Territory has over twenty inches, and the proportion with over forty is greater than that of any mainland state. But on the standard Australian formula for effective rainfall,[14] only the extreme north of Arnhem Land has a growing season of over five months (Fig. 2, inset). This, of course, is not a complete measure of possibilities: some areas are irrigable, others have a high water-table for much of the year. Yet, taken in conjunction with the fact that the area of reasonably good soils is very limited, it does mean that in the foreseeable future the economic development of

---

[14] All rain in excess of one-third of the evaporation from free water is regarded as effective ($P/E > 1/3$).

most of the north (except for mining) will remain pastoral. The Queensland coast must indeed be excepted; yet even there, where sugar supports the world's only considerable white population carrying out all manual operations in a humid tropical lowland, the physical climate has to be supplemented by a subsidy policy which keeps up the internal price of sugar to a point much resented by the consumers of the south. Research indicates that rice, tobacco, ground-nuts, and millets could be grown; but, except for millets, not on any very extensive continuous areas. For rice, irrigation would of course be necessary, and the costs of installation in these areas remote from labour and from the factories manufacturing basic equipment would be very high indeed. And, for any form of agricultural production, the fact must be faced that to almost prohibitive capital costs must be added a complete absence of local markets. Nevertheless rice production has been taken in hand.

Of the 600,000 square miles embraced between Cape York and the Kimberleys in the north of Western Australia, about one-third is good and one-third fair cattle land, though the good land is much split up. This area contains around 3,000,000 head of cattle, and undoubtedly this number could be greatly increased: the Barkly region, south of the Gulf of Carpentaria, for example, now carries rather under 300,000 head, but could maintain nearly 700,000. But for any considerable increase it is essential that transport should be greatly improved; and, indeed, inaccessibility is probably the major factor in the slowness of development in the north.

In part development has been hampered by historical factors. From 1863 to 1911 the Northern Territory was under South Australia, and all efforts at development were north from Alice Springs or south from Darwin. But this line lies across great stretches of utterly useless country, while the natural links of the Barkly region are south-east into Queensland, and the hinterland of Darwin would be a much more useful unit if combined with the Kimberleys, which have considerable potentialities but are cut off from the rest of Western Australia—itself a poor state—by the greatest deserts of the continent. One result of this approach has been that a few wharf workers in Darwin could virtually hold the Territory to ransom.

The projected south–north trans-continental railway is never likely to be constructed between Alice Springs and Birdum, the railhead south of Darwin; during the war the gap was spanned by a metalled road, the Stuart Highway (more generally known simply as "the bitumen"), and fair roads also lead south-east from the Barkly region into Queensland. There seems general agreement that the first essential is a railway from Birdum to Dajarra, the extreme railhead in western Queensland, and thence to Bourke on the Darling; though the advocates of "air-beef" believe that air transport by itself can open up the country. Meanwhile it is fair to say that there has been no lack of investigation and projecting, but very few projects (if any) have been pressed to a conclusion.

It is, of course, possible that mineral development may give the north a blood transfusion. Much of tropical Australia is highly mineralized: gold, tin, tungsten, have been historically important, but the only really solid developments at present are the silver-lead-zinc of Mount Isa (Qld.) and the iron of Yampi Sound (W.A.), though the uranium of Rum Jungle and Mount Kathleen, perhaps oil around Exmouth Gulf hold much promise. There is no doubt that a few reasonably stable mining towns could aid general development greatly, by providing both local markets and—probably more important—local bases and service centres for closer settlement.

"Closer settlement" must, of course, be understood in Australian terms; instead of vast holdings such as Victoria River Downs, larger than Belgium but with a permanent white population of about eight, plus ten times as many aboriginal stockmen, "small holdings" of 1000 square miles; perhaps in time less than that. Some at least of the inhibiting factors are yielding to new technical developments: aircraft and wireless greatly mitigate the rigours of pioneering for women, as, for example, through the Flying Doctor service, and this is an indispensable prerequisite of closer settlement. A more liberal land policy and special relief from taxation are loudly demanded by both pastoral and mining interests, and, since urban labour (both manual and clerical) in the Territory receives special rates, it does not seem that there could be much ethical objection to this. If Australia as a whole desires to people its north—so far as it can be peopled on white standards—it must be prepared to pay for it.

The desire is there, motivated largely by that unease before the hungry masses of Asia which we noted at the beginning of this chapter. It is, of course, arguable that since the Malays most certainly and the Chinese almost certainly knew of the north for centuries, if it had been any use for their type of culture they would have made at least some settlements beyond ephemeral fishermen's camps. Given several centuries of slow penetration, or several decades of modern technology with unlimited capital and shipping, it is possible that tropical Australia might be able to support several million people on Asian peasant standards. This could give no noticeable relief to Asian population pressure: one cannot empty an ocean into a pint-pot, and all that could result would be an extension of the world's poverty area, another virulent minority problem, and in all probability the subversion of a perhaps modest but at least democratic culture. For these reasons Australia's restrictive immigration policy seems justifiable, though many Australians to-day, recalling the blatancy with which it was at first propounded,[15] hardly like to mention it except in the guarded euphemisms of a Victorian evading discussion of the topic of sex.

But if Australians are entitled to hold their continent for their own way of life, this carries a correlative duty: to develop their resources so that they may make the fullest possible contribution to the rehabilitation of the economies of their hard-pressed neighbours. This certainly demands more intensive exploitation of "Economic Australia," and this in turn greater man-power. Since the war an unusually bi-partisan policy has resulted in an intake of migrants which has certainly been as great as the economy can reasonably absorb (Table 6). While the largest single contingent of immigrants continues to be British, and while on the whole the Dutch are the most popular of the new Continental arrivals, the long-established Italian and Greek communities have also been greatly increased, and a large proportion of "New Australians" have come from every country of east and south-east Europe. Although some assisted migrants are bound to work on the land or in specified industries (e.g., steel or the Snowy scheme), and others have brought European traditions of intensive agriculture to bear on orcharding and market-gardening, they have on the whole tended to accentuate the trend to metropolitan concentration. There are obvious risks: clannishness, sectionalism, the importation of ancient and modern feuds into politics; but the migrants have brought a touch of colour into a culture which needed it, and anyone seeing with what keenness their children assimilate in the schools will not worry unduly about the future in this respect.

---

[15] While Deakin, probably the greatest statesman Australia has produced, supported it on the grounds that the Chinese were a superior (i.e., more hard-working and thrifty) race, a Senator spoke of the Chinese as "a nation of yesterday." The Commonwealth was then seven years old.

Australia in the Pacific

Finally we may return to the overwhelming problem of Australia's external relations: the quest for security, seen always in a context of crowded Asia lying over against the empty three-quarters of the continent north of a line from Perth to Brisbane. It is almost comic to recall that one of the strongest factors in bringing the six colonies to a sense of common nationhood was also a threat to security, and from the north: it was in response to Australian sentiment, mightily afraid of French convicts, French morals, and French naval bases (and overlooking that all three were 600 miles nearer, in New Caledonia) that Great Britain insisted on a half-hearted share in the New Hebrides; and, more important, the light-hearted annexation of eastern New Guinea by Queensland in 1883, following reported German projects there, which led to the definitive British protectorate in its southern half, Papua, in 1884. The German hold on the north-east crumbled in a week of 1914, and Australia is now responsible for the western half of the island.[16]

Like the continental north itself, this holding is somewhat of a problem child. Although both Papua and the Trust Territory of New Guinea are now administered as a unit, the twenty-five years of German rule (which otherwise contributed little but reckoning in hectares and a few words of Pidgin) saw a considerable development of copra plantations. In Papua the tradition of government, British till 1906, has been rather more paternalistic, and plantation agriculture is far less developed. The Trust Territory again has the Wau goldfields, scene of the first large-scale mineral development carried out by air transport, and in the open grasslands of the central plateau an area which may well be climatically suited to white settlement.

Nevertheless the island as a whole is a difficult and/or unhealthy country of swampy lowlands or wildly dissected jungly hills. It suffers from an all but complete lack of land communications, and the costs of providing them would seem excessive in relation to the likely economic gains. Officials are isolated from the wealth of British colonial experience, and both men and money are spread too thinly for really effective administration. Large sums of money are still spent on the search for

---

[16] Papua: 90,540 square miles; estimated native population (1952), 369,975; "European" (1954 Census), 5,295. New Guinea: c. 93,000 square miles; native population (1952), enumerated 864,372, plus estimated 225,960; "European" (1954 Census), 8,020. Totals: 183,540 square miles; native population, 1,460,307; "European," 13,315.

oil, and, indeed, the geological structure makes the absence of any strikes surprising. There is a very large hydro-electric potential and some schemes for developing it, but it is difficult to see much real opportunity for its effective use in a country so retarded technologically. Indeed, it seems that private capital intake is stationary or actually declining, if allowance is made for depreciation and speculative losses.

There is perhaps more sentiment than sense in the persistent belief in the future of New Guinea as a field for white settlement on any large scale; this is understandable when we recall that precisely here the most deadly threat which has ever menaced Australia was parried, when the Japanese were turned back along the Kokoda Track in 1942. So far the Commonwealth Government has held fairly firm to its avowed policy of the paramountcy not only of current native claims, but of their future needs, although on different levels both the Liberal and Labour Parties are liable to pressure from those who wish for a White Melanesia before they have really got a White Australia.

There seems a general agreement among such observers as are both informed and detached that the best way of advance, however slow, is by developing native agriculture: the supplementing of shifting by sedentary cultivation, of roots (perishable, and wasteful to transport) by grain. Some of the inland tribes are barely out of the Stone Age, and indeed their rapid adoption of the steel axe is not an unmixed blessing: the jungle can be more quickly and thoroughly cleared, and hence erosion is now more than an incipient problem. Along the coasts, however, most of the natives have been exposed for half a century to various civilizing agents—missions, plantations, schools—and here there are at least signs of the emergence of a small class of petty entrepreneurs, notable around Rabaul in New Britain, a more solid town than the capital Port Moresby and in the best and best-developed plantation area.[17] That may also, of course, mean the emergence of a plural society.

The remaining dependencies of Australia call for little notice. Two of them, Lord Howe and Macquarie Islands, are in fact state territory, under New South Wales and Tasmania respectively; the latter, like Heard and Macdonald Islands, is used as a sub-Antarctic meteorological

[17] See O. H. K. Spate, "Changing Native Agriculture in New Guinea," in *Geogr. Review*, vol. xliii (1953), pp. 324–337, and South Pacific Commission, *The Purari Kompani* (Social Development Notes, No. 7, Noumea, 1951).

station.[18] The Australian Antarctic Territory is the sector between longitudes 160° and 45° E., less the six-degree sliver of French Adélie Land.

In the Pacific itself Australia possesses Norfolk Island, settled as an offshoot of New South Wales as early as 1788 and of some slight importance as a tourist centre. The Commonwealth also controls, as a Trust Territory, Nauru, only 5263 acres, but acres almost completely formed of rock phosphate. In the Indian Ocean, between Timor and Western Australia, lie the Ashmole and Cartier Islands, uninhabited except by occasional Indonesian fishermen; and in 1955 Cocos was transferred from Singapore to Australia in view of the importance of its airfield to Australian trans-oceanic communications.

These, however, are the small change of Australia's Pacific interests. We may end where we began. Before the war the rhetorical question was asked: from the point of view of defence, is there any real difference between six and nine millions?[19] In the modern world, not much; and hence, however strong the emotional ties with the homeland, Australia must look more and more to the nearest really powerful base of the Western world: to America, which it so much resembles in many features of the cultural landscape whether of bush or city. The links with the British Commonwealth are certainly not weakened in any absolute sense: it is sufficient to recall Australia's initiatory role in the Colombo Plan and its special significance to India, Pakistan, and Ceylon. But relatively at least Australia now feels increasingly another gravitational pull than that of Britain; of this the ANZUS Pact and the non-recognition of Communist China are tangible evidence. There are, of course, cross-currents: if there is some tendency to follow the American rather than the British line on China and Formosa, as regards Japan Australians have not taken to *Realpolitik* with the whole-hearted abandon of the Americans. But in the last resort it is probable that most Australians would agree with the predicate of the 1942 New Year's message of John Curtin, Prime Minister of Australia in the grim opening days of the Pacific War: "Without any inhibitions of any kind, I make it quite clear that Australia looks to America, free of any pangs as to our traditional links or kinship with the United Kingdom." The predicate,

---

[18] Transferred from the U.K. in 1947, Heard and Macdonald are under the laws of the Australian Capital Territory—an administrative detail almost as bizarre as the Condominium of the New Hebrides.

[19] A. G. B. Fisher, in J. C. G. Kevin (editor), *Some Australians Take Stock* (Longmans, London, 1939), p. 234.

not necessarily the emphatic adverbial clauses: not without inhibitions, not without pangs.

FURTHER READING

There is little geographical literature on Australia written by geographers; an idiosyncratic and thereby stimulating exception is:

GRIFFITH TAYLOR, *Australia: A Study in Warm Environments* (fourth edition; Methuen, London, 1947).

An elaborate Atlas of Australian Resources is being issued by the Department of National Development, Canberra. Two extremely valuable surveys are:

The Australian Environment (second edition; Commonwealth Scientific and Industrial Research Organization, Melbourne, 1950).

WADHAM, S. M., and WOOD, G. L., *Land Utilization in Australia* (second edition; Melbourne University Press, 1950).

An excellent introduction to the life of the continent is given in:

JOSE, A., *Australia, Human and Economic* (Harrap, London, 1932),

although it is in many respects superseded by perhaps the best single volume on Australia:

GRATTAN, C. HARTLEY (editor), *Australia* (United Nations Series, University of California, 1947).

Two brilliantly written outlines primarily historical, and both titled simply *Australia*, are those by HANCOCK, W. K. (Benn, London, 1930) and CRAWFORD, R. M. (Hutchinson, London, 1952), but perhaps the fullest modern treatment is in GREENWOOD, G. (ed.), *Australia: A Social and Political History* (Angus and Robertson, Sydney and London, 1955). A short and well-written presentation of the economic history is given in

SHAW, A. G. L., *The Economic Development of Australia* (revised edition; Longmans, London and Melbourne, 1946).

A stimulating survey, despite its old-fashioned liberal heresies, is

SHANN, E., *An Economic History of Australia* (Cambridge University Press, 1930).

Newer heresies in:

FITZPATRICK, B., *The Australian People, 1788–1945* (Melbourne University Press, 1946).

Current economic and political problems are discussed in HORSFALL, J. C., *Australia* (Benn, London, 1955).

On the problem of the North:

PRICE, A. G., *The History and Problems of the Northern Territory* (Macrossan Lectures, University of Queensland, 1930).

Report of Committee . . . into Land and Land Industries of the Northern Territory ("Payne Report"), Australian Parliamentary Papers Session 1937, vol. iii, pp. 817 sqq.

ABBOTT, C. L. A., *Australia's Frontier Province* (Angus and Robertson, Sydney and London, 1950).

Australian Institute of Political Science, *Northern Australia* (Angus and Robertson, Sydney and London, 1954).

For Papua and New Guinea:

REED, S. W., *The Making of Modern New Guinea* (Institute of Pacific Relations, N.Y., 1943).

MAIR, L. C., *Australia in New Guinea* (Christophers, London, 1948).

Resources of Papua and New Guinea (Department of National Development, Canberra, 1951).

Of the voluminous and often repetitive literature on Federalism and kindred problems in Australia, the following may be noted:

CANAWAY, A. P., *The Failure of Federalism in Australia* (Oxford University Press, 1930).

GREENWOOD, G., *The Future of Australian Federalism* (Melbourne University Press, 1946). (Unificationist, like the preceding.)

SAWER, G. (editor), *Federalism: An Australian Jubilee Study* (Cheshire/Aust. National University, Melbourne, 1952).

EGGLESTON, F. W., *Reflections of an Australian Liberal* (Cheshire/Aust. National University, Melbourne, 1953). (Almost the only thoughtful book by an Australian politician.)

ELLIS, U. R., *New Australian States* (Endeavour Press, Sydney, 1933). (Full historical account, strongly New States.)

TABLE 1

Australia: Area and Population[1]

STATE OR TERRITORY	AREA (*square miles*)	PERCENTAGE	POPULATION (1954)	PERCENTAGE	DENSITY TO SQUARE MILE
New South Wales .	309,433	10·40	3,423,718	38·10	11·06
Victoria .	87,884	2·96	2,452,337	27·29	27·90
Queensland . .	670,500	22·54	1,318,393	14·67	1·97
South Australia .	380,070	12·78	797,159	8·87	2·10
Western Australia	975,920	32·81	639,716	7·12	0·66
Tasmania .	26,215	0·88	308,783	3·43	11·78
Northern Territory	523,620	17·60	16,452	0·18	0·03
Australian Capital Territory . .	939	0·03	30,315	0·34	32·28
AUSTRALIA .	2,974,581	100·00	8,986,873	100·00	3·02

[1] Population in all tables excludes full-blood aborigines, who number about 47,000 (20,000 in W.A., 14,000 in N.T.), plus a few thousands still nomadic. About 27,000 of mixed blood are included in the Census. Tables 1–5 from Census, 6 from *Yearbook* (all adapted).

TABLE 2

Australia: Population at Four Censuses

State or Territory	1921	1933	1947	1954	Percentage Increase						
					1921–33 (12½ years)			1933–47 (14 years)			1947–54 (7 years)
					U.	R.	T.	U.	R.	T.	T.
New South Wales	2,100,371	2,600,847	2,984,838	3,423,718	45·3	19·6	23·8	37·2	4·6[1]	14·8	14·7
Victoria .	1,531,280	1,820,261	2,054,701	2,452,337	35·1	10·0	18·9	40·4	–5·7[2]	12·9	19·35
Queensland .	755,972	947,534	1,106,415	1,318,393	51·2	23·8	25·3	64·1	–0·2	16·8	19·2
South Australia .	495,160	580,949	646,073	797,159	46·0	10·1	17·3	50·4	–8·7	11·2	23·4
Western Australia .	332,732	438,852	502,480	639,716	39·2	41·0	31·9	47·0	–6·8	14·5	27·3
Tasmania .	213,780	227,599	257,078	308,783	17·3	4·4	6·5	58·5	–4·3	12·95	20·1
Northern Territory	3,867	4,850	10,868	16,452	11·9	33·5	25·4	62·1	155·2	124·0	51·4
Australian Capital Territory .	2,572	8,947	16,905	30,315	—	—	247·9	106·9	7·8	88·95	79·3
AUSTRALIA .	5,435,734	6,629,839	7,579,358	8,986,873	41·1	17·3	22·0	44·85	–1·1	11·4	18·6

U = Urban, R = Rural, T = Total.

[1] Increase largely due to abolition of small municipalities. [2] Decrease largely due to extension of metropolitan area.

TABLE 3

Australia: Urban and Rural Population, 1954

STATE	METROPOLITAN		OTHER URBAN		RURAL		TOTAL IN THOUSANDS
	Population in thousands	*Percentage*	*Population in thousands*	*Percentage*	*Population in thousands*	*Percentage*	
New South Wales .	1,862	54·4	962	28·1	591	17·3	3,424
Victoria .	1,523	62·1	470	19·2	450	18·3	2,452
Queensland .	502[1]	38·1	460	34·9	353	26·8	1,318
South Australia .	484	60·6	110	13·8	201	25·2	797
Western Australia .	348	54·4	105	16·5	183	28·7	640
Tasmania .	95	30·7	108	35·0	105	33·9	309
TOTAL .	4,814	53·8	2,215	24·8	1,883	21·1	8,940

[1] Includes *c.* 40,000 population really rural.

Minor discrepancies in totals and percentages due to rounding off and a few thousands migratory population.

TABLE 4

Metropolis and Next Largest City

STATE AND CITY	POPULATION (*in thousands*)			RATIO TO METROPOLIS— 1 TO:		
	1933	1947	1954	1933	1947	1954
N.S.W.: Newcastle .	104·5	127·1	178·2	11·8	10·9[1]	10·45
Vic.: Geelong , .	39·2	44·6	72·3	25·3	27·5[1]	21·1
Q'ld: Rockhampton .	29·4	35·0	43·2	10·2	11·5	11·6
(1954: Toowoomba)						
S.A.: Port Pirie . .	11·7	12·0	14·2	26·7	31·9	34·0
W.A.: Kalgoorlie . .	17·3	22·4	22·8	12·0	12·1	15·3
Tas.: Launceston . .	32·8	40·4	49·3	1·8	1·9	1·9

[1] Taking 1947 population of 1954 metropolitan area: N.S.W., 1:13·0; Vic. 1:29·0.

TABLE 5

Immigration and Natural Increase, 1947–53

YEAR	TOTAL INCREASE	NATURAL INCREASE	PERCENTAGE	NET IMMIGRATION	PERCENTAGE
1947	119,388	108,777	91·1	10,611	8·9
1948	156,252	101,137	64·7	55,115	35·3
1949	256,002	106,001	41·4	150,001	58·6
1950	264,909	112,404	42·4	152,505	57·6
1951	222,943	111,510	50·0	111,433	50·0
1952	214,085	120,053	56·1	94,032	43·9
1953	164,944	122,047	74·0	42,897	26·0
TOTAL	1,398,523	781,929	55·9	616,594	44·1

TABLE 6

Nationality of Migrants, 1950–52

(Figures in brackets are percentages of total)

Year	Total Net Migration	British (including Irish)	Dutch	German	Italian	Poles	Balts	Other E. and S.E. Europeans[1]	Stateless and Others
1950	152,505	48,748 (31·9)	11,092 (7·3)	1,446 (0·9)	12,798 (8·4)	31,873 (20·9)	8,133 (5·3)	29,563 (19·5)	8,852 (5·8)
1951	111,433	54,626 (49·0)	12,761 (11·5)	4,271 (3·9)	16,210 (14·5)	3,833 (3·4)	1,093 (1·0)	10,071 (9·1)	8,568 (7·6)
1952	94,032	35,679 (38·0)	14,819 (15·7)	6,778 (7·2)	26,652 (28·4)	856 (0·9)	220 (0·2)	4,514 (4·8)	4,514 (4·8)
Total	357,970	139,053 (39·0)	38,672 (10·8)	12,495 (3·5)	55,660 (15·6)	36,562 (10·2)	9,446 (2·6)	44,148 (12·3)	21,934 (6·0)

[1] Czechs, Slovaks, Greeks, Magyars, Russians, Ukrainians, Yugoslavs.

CHAPTER XXXV

New Zealand and its Dependencies

EILA M. J. CAMPBELL

NEW ZEALAND is a young country. Organized settlement by Europeans began only in 1840. In that year the Maori chiefs conferred upon the British Crown "the exclusive right of pre-emption" over their lands and received "all the rights and privileges of British subjects." Thereafter the immigrants were drawn mainly from the British Isles and from Australia, and in 1956 the population is overwhelmingly British by descent and in outlook. The pattern of life combines the traditional features of British origin, predominantly English and Scottish, with other elements drawn from the needs of a pioneer environment. Geographical position and world politics have played not insignificant parts in the development of New Zealand from an isolated British colony in the South Pacific to a leading Pacific State.[1] Since the end of the second world war its statesmen have taken in regional and international councils an increasingly important part—a part out of all proportion to their country's small total population of 2,164,734 (1955 estimate).

[1] New Zealand early received powers of self-government; in 1852, when the European population numbered only 27,000, the British Parliament passed a Constitution Act conferring representative institutions, and three years later the British Colonial Office agreed to the demand that the ministers should be responsible to the elected representatives; the first responsible ministry took office in 1856, and thereafter the colonists were entrusted with almost complete charge of their own political destinies. New Zealand has never paid taxes to the Government of Great Britain. Since the Imperial Conferences of 1917 and 1926 defined the status of the self-governing members of the British Empire and Commonwealth, New Zealand has in effect been a sovereign State, although the New Zealand Parliament chose to leave certain powers relating to constitutional change in the hands of the United Kingdom Parliament; in 1947 New Zealand adopted the Statute of Westminster and became in strict law what she had been in fact for thirty years—a fully sovereign State. However, a majority of New Zealanders, even in the second and third generations, continue to refer to Britain as "home," and many are still psychologically dependent upon the mother country. For a discussion of some of the factors that have contributed to the exceptionally close attachment of New Zealand to the United Kingdom see L. Lipson, *The Politics of Equality* (University of Chicago Press, 1948), pp. 496 *et seq.*

Demographic Considerations

Small Numbers and Immigration Policy. New Zealand's small numbers are to a large extent the result of a deliberate policy to remain small. During the first four decades of European settlement, numbers grew steadily by immigration; indeed, there was a rapid increase during the early 1870's in response to a deliberate attempt to expand. However, in the late eighties and the early nineties the young country had its first experience of an economic depression, and thereafter it has shown itself to be chary of expansion. For the last seventy years organized labour in New Zealand has feared that a too ready flow of immigrant workers will weaken its bargaining with employers by introducing into the country a pool of surplus labour. This fear persists, although for many years now there has been full employment. The fear that the newcomer will be a competitor in the labour market is not confined to Trade Unionists; the professions have not shown themselves any more ready to welcome newcomers whose ability might threaten the position of their members. All sections of the community set great store on a high degree of material comfort, and see in expanding numbers only a threat to their own standard of living. To New Zealanders generally, "The current recurring disadvantages of a large population increase, and therefore of a large volume of immigration, seem to be more clearly demonstrable than the advantages of the settled population which would result from them."[2] Successive Governments responsive to the sentiments of their electorates have framed their immigration policies accordingly. For many years now these have favoured selective immigration.

The Immigration Act of 1920 left every application for entry into the country to be decided on its individual merits. In theory New Zealand welcomes anyone from any nation provided he can appreciate the country and its way of life, but in practice it favours the immigration of selected North-west European, preferably British, settlers who will become assimilated in the shortest possible time. Integration is not sufficient. Furthermore, even carefully selected and assimilable immigrants must not be too numerous, for the country is not convinced that it either needs or can absorb them. The fear that an expanding population must, of necessity, threaten their own economic position haunts

[2] H. Belshaw, *Immigration Problems and Policies* (reprinted from *The New Zealand Financial Times*, Wellington, 1952), p. 31.

citizens and Ministers alike.[3] On this issue the two major political parties are somewhat divided. The Labour Party has tended to fear that immigrants will take work from New Zealanders; the National Party has argued that New Zealand workers themselves will benefit from the expanding economy which the immigrants will help to develop. Since 1949, when the National Government took office, the number of immigrants has increased substantially. A majority of the immigrants have continued to be of British descent, although a number of Dutch nationals—emigrants from the Netherlands and refugees from Indonesia—has also been admitted. The Dutch are very acceptable to New Zealand, but their number has fallen away since 1953; they have lost interest in an emigration scheme which offers them no great expectation of acquiring freehold land and of forming small 'colonies' as in Canada. Austrians, Danes, Germans, and Swiss have been invited to enter. A small number of displaced persons from Europe has also been allowed to enter New Zealand under an arrangement with the International Refugee Organization. From an occupational analysis of post-war 'contract migrants' it seems that for men with trade skills New Zealand must still rely upon Great Britain. To a country as machine-minded as New Zealand skilled hands are more important than cheap labour.

Expanding Numbers. In 1952, when New Zealand's total population passed the two million mark, it was growing at the rate of more than 2 per cent. per annum. It has been shown that if this rate is maintained the total population will reach 3,000,000 by 1975. The accelerated rate of growth since 1945 alarms many New Zealanders. They recall that it took nearly seventy years from the first organized European settlement for the population to reach the first million, and a further forty-five years for it to achieve the second million. Now they are faced with the possibility that their total numbers may exceed three million in only another twenty-five years. Even if immigration ceased immediately the total population might well exceed 2,800,000 by 1975, as the natural increase is high; indeed, it exceeds the current rates of both India and

[3] P. Fraser, in his last year of office as Prime Minister, stated the position thus: "We shall welcome people from any nation who can appreciate this country, its democracy, and its standard of living"; reported in *N.Z. Parliamentary Debates*, vol. 283 (Wellington, 1948), p. 2598. See also *Immigration into New Zealand: Report of a Study Group* (New Zealand Institute of International Affairs, Dunedin, 1950), pp. 17–21. In his *Economic Survey, 1953*, the Prime Minister considered how the country's economy could be expanded sufficiently to maintain at least the present standard of living for an increasing population; see *New Zealand Economic Survey, 1953* (Government Printer, Wellington, 1953).

2E

Japan. Hitherto only the European element has grown substantially by immigration, but in the coming decades the Polynesian element may well add to their numbers by migrants from the Cook Islands.

At present the Maoris constitute only some 6 per cent. of the total population, but they are increasing at a faster rate than the Europeans. Their natural increase is now over 33 per thousand compared with the European figure of only 15 per thousand. If they maintain their present rate of growth of some 34·7 per thousand[4] the Maoris will double their numbers in the next twenty-five years. It is highly probable that their rate of growth may increase, for they are a young population—nearly one half of their number is under fifteen years of age—and their mortality rate may well fall to that of the Europeans.

It is unfortunate that so many New Zealanders see only one aspect of their country's expanding population—its threat to their existing standard of living. For this reason the policy of selective immigration is applied in the face of pressure from underprivileged peoples wishing to enter the country. The equalitarianism which typifies New Zealand democracy at home is not projected into the realm of its international relations. At home New Zealanders have always subscribed rigidly to the Socialist doctrine that "none should eat cake until all have bread." Devoutly believing that all men are created equal, most New Zealanders assert unequivocally that all must be treated equally. But they have never allowed these ideals to influence their thinking on the subject of immigration into their country. The desire for economic security for themselves has prevented them from sharing their bread with others, especially with those seemingly most in need of it. However, in considering the New Zealand attitude to immigration it must be remembered that small numbers of like-minded people have assured the country of a high measure of economic security and of internal peace. The whole economy of the country is based upon the use of machinery giving a high output per man-hour. The country is prosperous because the racial and cultural character of the population has made it so. It cannot be expected that the grounds on which New Zealand's immigration policy rests are acceptable in overcrowded countries like Japan, which supports about twenty-five times as many people per square mile, but at a very much lower standard of living. However, it is for New Zealanders to decide who shall enter their country.

[4] This is more than double the current European rate, even allowing for a net annual increase from immigration of some 10,000 persons and the continuance of the present birth rate, which is substantially higher than that of the inter-war period.

European-Maori Relations. In the formative years of the nation New Zealand's island character and its remoteness from the main European and Asian centres of population allowed a single national, racial, and cultural tradition to develop, in spite of the fact that the country was already occupied when the British Government assumed responsibility for it. Thus, from this time, New Zealand was a plural community, but it was saved from many of the economic and social problems of some other multi-racial societies because equality for the Maori people was a cardinal principle of British thinking in New Zealand and was early formalized into constitutional law. Save for the brief interlude of the Maori King Movement in the North Island shortly after the Colony was granted self-government, New Zealand has always been free of inter-racial strife; yet, in spite of good relations, the two peoples have never become fully integrated, although there is no legal impediment to their so doing. A majority of the Maoris are still fundamentally Polynesian in their basic attitudes to life and in their allegiance to their tribe. The pull of the tribe, the meeting house, and the *marae*[5] may prevent the peoples from ever becoming a single society. They have been likened to "two rivers flowing side by side into a common sea. Occasionally a channel unites the two rivers and a little water flows from one to the other. For the most part, these cross channels are few and far between."[6] However, there is *de facto* as well as *de jure* equality for the Maori. At no time in New Zealand's history have the Europeans regarded the Maoris as a reserve of low-paid labour, endangering their own employment and wages. For many years now wage rates have been standardized throughout the country.

The two peoples have, however, always enjoyed a measure of geographical separation—the Maoris have been most numerous where the Europeans have been least numerous. Before the second world war an overwhelming majority of the Maoris lived in the rural areas of the North Island, notably in the North Auckland Peninsula and in the Poverty Bay area. A majority of the Maori people still live in these two regions, but, with the development of light industries during and since the war, there has been a steady increase in the number of Maoris seeking work in the cities of the North Island, especially Auckland, Wellington,

---

[5] Literally the open space in front of the meeting house, it has become the symbol of the Maori way of life.

[6] E. and P. Beaglehole, *Some Modern Maoris* (Whitcombe and Tombs, Christchurch, N.Z., 1946), p. 328. See also Metge, Joan, "The Maori Population of Northern New Zealand," in *The New Zealand Geographer*, vol. viii (1952), pp. 104–124.

and their satellites. European reaction to the increasing number of Maori youth seeking work in the cities is not wholly favourable, a fact recognized by many New Zealanders themselves. However, the total number of Maoris dwelling in urban areas is still small—only 16,010 at the 1951 Census; some 81 per cent. of those ranking as Maori for statistical purposes live in the rural areas. The ratio of Maoris per 1000 of other races in the urban areas naturally varies; Gisbourne and Auckland show the highest figures—60 and 24 respectively.

The Position of the Maoris in the State. The position of the Maoris in the State is an ambiguous one. They retain much of their tribal organization, although many Maoris living in the towns have become partly or wholly detribalized. The law recognizes and safeguards their ways and customs in certain matters—such as marriage, inheritance, and land-ownership. There is a special department of Maori Affairs to provide for the Maoris certain of the services provided for the Europeans by other departments; but many services are departmentally administered for both races. There is separate representation for Maoris in the House of Representatives, and most governments have included a Maori minister to represent the Maori race, although the portfolio of Maori Affairs has usually been held by a European. The existence of distinctive laws, separate representation, and a special department has from time to time been criticized as a hindrance to the development of a single New Zealand community. It has been defended on the ground that in some respects the Maoris still need special treatment and safeguards. A radical alteration of the present system is unlikely to be made in the near future, as it might well rouse racial feelings and thus endanger the prospects of any political party which proposed it.

The National Economy

New Zealand's major achievement during the last century has been the transformation of two isolated islands, almost completely covered by untouched primitive vegetation and without grazing animals, into a country of highly productive pastures.[7] In spite of expanding manufacturing industries, New Zealand is still basically an agricultural

[7] For an admirable account of the country's pastures, see P. D. Sears, "The Regional Variety of Pasture Growth in New Zealand," in *The New Zealand Geographer*, vol. i (1945), pp. 57-82.

country; indeed, its economy is dominated by its pastoral industries.[8] Together their products amount to nearly 90 per cent. of the value of all exports and earn the bulk of the overseas exchange (Table 1). But,

TABLE 1

Overseas Exchange Transactions, in Millions of £N.Z.

RECEIPTS

	1952	1953	1954	1955
(i) Exports:				
Butter . . .	50·7	48·4	50·4	30·6
Cheese . . .	17·0	17·4	20·5	9·6
Meat . . .	30·7	48·3	48·9	49·9
Wool . . .	115·9	73·9	87·2	91·5
Others . . .	37·4	39·1	32·9	34·7
(ii) Other receipts . .	25·9	26·1	31·6	58·2
Total receipts .	277·5	253·2	271·5	274·4

PAYMENTS

	1952	1953	1954	1955
(i) Government payments:				
Debt interest . .	2·5	2·5	2·7	2·9
Imports . .	21·7	29·1	25·1	20·8
Other . . .	9·2	8·9	11·7	11·4
(ii) Imports (excluding				
Government) . .	230·9	171·9	175·3	232·1
(iii) All other payments .	29·6	29·7	27·9	42·1
Total payments .	293·9	242·1	242·7	309·3
Balance . . .	− 16·4	+ 11·1	+ 28·8	− 34·9

Source: *Economic Survey of New Zealand* (1953, 1954, 1955). Figures given are for the year ending March 31 in all cases.

although the pastoral industries still form the mainstay of the country's economy, they employ only one-sixth of the labour force. Since 1939 the total labour force has increased by over 15 per cent., but the proportion of persons engaged in farming has fallen by nearly the same

[8] For a discussion of the geographical and historical factors influencing the development of these industries, see (i) R. O. Buchanan, *The Pastoral Industries of New Zealand*, Transactions of the Institute of British Geographers, vol. ii (1935); (ii) W. M. Hamilton, *The Dairying Industry in New Zealand* (Wellington, 1948).

percentage (Table 2). The farmers have met the shortage of hands by increased mechanization, and the country is probably second to none in the use of farm machinery. The drift of hired labour away from the land has been evident since the economic depression of the 1930's. It was encouraged by the Labour Government which came into office in 1935 through its programme of manufacturing industry, in the hope of reducing unemployment and cutting imports, at a time when a flight

TABLE 2

Estimated Distribution of Total Labour Force, 1939 and 1955

INDUSTRIAL GROUP	1939		1955	
	1000's	*Percentage*	1000's	*Percentage*
Primary Industries				
Farming	157 ⎫	26·6	135 ⎫	18·7
Fishing, Forestry, and Mining	22 ⎭		15 ⎭	
Secondary Industries				
Manufacturing . . .	131[1] ⎫		199 ⎫	
Building and Construction .	56 ⎬	27·8	69 ⎬	35·0
Power, water, and sanitary	⎮		⎮	
services	— ⎭		12 ⎭	
Tertiary Industries				
Transport and Communication	57 ⎫		77 ⎫	
Distribution and Finance .	100 ⎮		131 ⎮	
Administration and Professional	⎬	42·8	⎬	45·0
Services	76 ⎮		107 ⎮	
Domestic and Personal Services	51 ⎭		46 ⎭	
Armed Forces	3		10	1·3
Unemployed	19	2·8	—	—
TOTAL LABOUR FORCE . .	672	100·0	801	100·0

[1] Includes number of persons employed in power, water, and sanitary services.

Source: Based on Table 9 in (1) S. G. Holland, *Economic Survey of New Zealand*, 1954 (Government Printer, Wellington, 1954), p. 59, and (2) J. T. Watts, *New Zealand Economic Survey*, 1955 (Government Printer, Wellington, 1955), p. 54.

of capital was causing a balance of payments crisis. Since the war the trend away from direct employment in the primary industries has been accelerated, and to-day secondary and tertiary industries contribute the greater part of the national income. However, Table 2 obscures the fact that the most important group of manufacturing industries are those processing pastoral products; moreover, many of the workers employed in the secondary and tertiary industries are concerned with the marketing of pastoral products or of goods based on them. Nevertheless, since the second world war the output of the factory industries has expanded much more rapidly than that of the agricultural industries (Table 3).

TABLE 3
Index of Volume of Production

	YEAR	
	1938–39	1949–50
(i) All Farm Products .	100	123
(ii) Factory Production .	100	174
Total Production . .	100	136

Source: Table 4, "Value and Volume of Production," in S. G. Holland, *The New Zealand Economy, 1939 to 1951* (Government Printer, Wellington, 1952), p. 56.

Tariff barriers, customs duties, and, periodically, restrictions on the importation of certain manufactured articles continue to protect certain industries which, on account of high labour costs and the small internal market, appear to be uneconomic and wasteful of man-power.

The present concern of the Government is how to expand the country's economy sufficiently to maintain at least the present standard of living for a much larger population. Any marked changes in the pattern of the country's economy seem unlikely, and the nation will remain dependent on the production, mainly for export, of wool, butter, meat, and cheese. The only other commodities available in bulk for export are timber and wood pulp, but these are unlikely ever to surpass in importance the products of the pastoral industries. The country's poverty in raw materials suitable for processing makes it improbable that the manufacturing industries will ever contribute significantly to the earning of overseas exchange. High labour costs reinforce this conclusion. Thus it seems—and, indeed, this view is accepted by the New Zealand Government itself—that the national economy can be expanded only by an increase in livestock production; in this way the country will be able both to feed its increasing numbers and to buy the greater volume of imports they will require.

It has recently been estimated that to support a population of 3,000,000 at the present standard of living there must be a 60 to 70 per cent. increase in the production of butter fat, meat, and wool; such an increase entails a 50 to 60 per cent. increase in all types of livestock kept. [9]

[9] E. J. Fawcett, "Production for 3 Million 25 Years Hence," in *New Zealand Journal of Agriculture*, 87 (Wellington, 1953), pp. 194–196. In arriving at these figures the Director-General of Agriculture has, of course, had to make certain assumptions and has allowed a 20 per cent. upward adjustment in quantities to meet any fall in overseas trade. Technical developments may disprove his forecast.

Increases of this order are considered impracticable by 1975—the year when the country's total population will, if present trends continue, reach three million—and an increase in production of 30 per cent. is thought to be a more realistic figure; but to achieve even this increase it will be necessary both to intensify the use of land already in production and to develop marginal land.

The intensification of the use of the existing farm land is not a simple matter. Visitors from Asia or Europe may comment on the extensiveness of lowland agriculture, and on the amount of weed-infested farmland, but before suggesting subdivision as a stimulus to increased production they must take into account the fact that the New Zealand farmer thinks of high returns per unit of man-power. Moreover, he is already producing enough to ensure himself and his family a high standard of living and lacks the incentive to produce more. His prosperity depends upon external factors over which he has little control—for example, the terms of foreign trade and competition between butter and margarine or wool and synthetic fibres.

The greater volume of production necessitates increased capital expenditure in the form of new dairy factories and freezing works, improved transport, and larger port facilities. In the post-war period the proportion of gross national expenditure devoted to capital investment has been unusually high—it reached 23 per cent. in 1954—but the Government regards it as necessary in view of the high rate of population increase. The main fields of expenditure have been hydro-electric development, housing, and railways—in this order; land development, roads, and education have competed for fourth place; housing and education have not been neglected owing to their value as election planks. The continued demand for electricity gives priority to the harnessing of all available hydro-electric power.

It is, of course, impossible to predict with certainty the course of future events from current statistics or trends or from records of the past. But the degree of dependence of its national economy upon the overseas market makes New Zealand very vulnerable to events in the world at large, over which it can, on account of its smallness, exercise very little control. Any fall in demand for its pastoral products would present a very serious balance of payments problem. New Zealand's best customer has always been Great Britain, which still absorbs some 65 per cent. of its exports and supplies upward of 55 per cent. of its imports.

New Zealand has not the industrial resources to be able to maintain full employment and the existing standard of living without relying on overseas trade. Its development cannot therefore follow the same lines as that of the United States of America in the early days of industrial expansion; that country had sufficiently varied resources to support its rapidly expanding population from within itself. Domestic full employment in New Zealand can never replace world trade as the basis of the country's prosperity. Thus it must not only retain its existing markets but also seek new ones.

The Political and Administrative Organization

When its first Parliament met in 1854 New Zealand was a loose union of almost autonomous provinces. To-day it is a highly unitary State, in which local authorities perform a limited range of functions under the control of the central government. At first the provincial system dealt fairly well with the problems of government in a State composed of widely scattered, mutually averse settlements, but within twenty years it had become a serious obstacle to the development of the country. The Maori wars caused the central government to raid the provincial treasuries. In the early eighteen-seventies an extensive programme of public works was adopted to open up the territory to the scores of thousands of new settlers whom the national government was attracting into the country. The provinces, then nine in number, opposed some of the government's proposals, and in 1875 they were abolished, their powers being transferred to the national government.

This change made necessary a reorganization of the local authorities, which each provincial government had regulated in its own way. Sixty-three counties and thirty-six boroughs independent of the county authorities were organized to administer local services and affairs. Since 1876 the number of counties has doubled and the number of boroughs and towns independent of the counties has trebled (Fig. 1). In addition, over a thousand special authorities, of more than twenty different types, have been created to deal with many new services. The administrative structure of New Zealand now combines a plethora of small bodies, overlapping in functions, in area, or in both. This is the result of several factors. The increase in the number of boroughs and towns is an inevitable result of the growth of existing settlements and the establishment

2E*

of new ones. The increase in the number of counties is the result primarily of the localism which is a strong and persistent feature of New Zealand life. Each local community wants to improve its status and increase its degree of self-government. A small settlement seeks to become a township, and a township seeks to become either an independent borough or the county town of a new county. This local pride and ambition is not equalled by the interest in the working of local bodies. Thus participation in local elections is generally low, although participation in parliamentary elections is very high—New Zealand's record being better than that of any other country where voting is not made compulsory by law or by official pressure. Another important cause of the increase in the number of counties has been the legislation regulating local government finance, which has been more generous to small counties than to large ones, and has thus encouraged counties to divide. The proliferation of the basic local units has made them unsuitable for many new services which require larger areas for their efficient administration. Some new services have therefore been given into the charge of authorities specially created. The national government itself performs some functions which could be performed equally well by large local authorities, and it exercises over the basic units and the special bodies more control than it would have to exercise over larger authorities which could afford to employ more officials of higher quality.

Throughout the present century successive governments have recognized the desirability of reducing the number of local authorities. Yet although facilities for the amalgamation of neighbouring local bodies have been created, they have been used far less than the facilities for division, and it has always proved easier to create special-purpose bodies to administer new services than to reform the existing structure so that it could deal adequately with new needs.[10]

The national government itself is organized on the principle of centralism. Many of its departments have local offices throughout the country, but the power of decision is centralized in Wellington. To give a large measure of discretion to local officials, or even to regional officials, each supervising a number of local offices, would require more good-quality administrators than New Zealand can spare. More important, the tradition of New Zealand government has been that the

[10] For the problems of local and regional administration in New Zealand, see F. B. Stephens (ed.), *Local Government in New Zealand* (Wellington, 1949). For details of local authorities and their functions see *The New Zealand Official Year Book* (compiled by the Census and Statistics Department, Wellington, published annually since 1892).

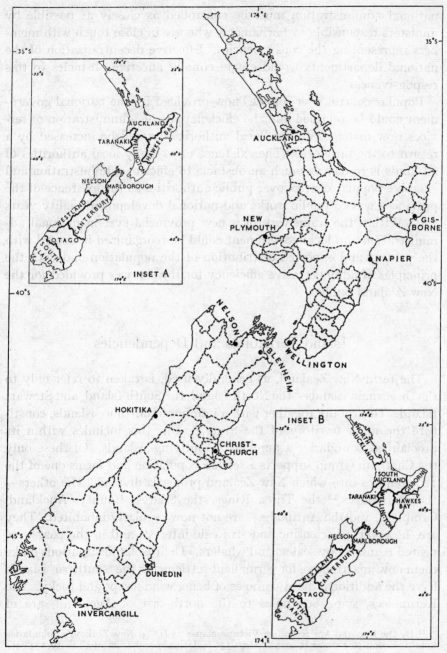

FIG. 1. THE COUNTIES OF NEW ZEALAND
Inset A: Provincial Districts; Inset B: Land Districts
The Chatham Islands (not shown) have county status

national administration must be controlled as closely as possible by ministers responsible to Parliament, who are in close touch with members representing the constituencies. Effective decentralization of the national departments would create equally effective obstacles to this responsiveness.

Popular control over services now provided by the national government could be retained and the efficiency of the administration of services now managed by the local authorities would be increased by a return to the provinces. The existence of so many local authorities of all kinds is to-day as much an obstacle to efficient administration and effective popular control over public authorities as the existence of the provinces was to public works and national development eighty years ago. Within the framework of a new provincial system national administration and local government could be reorganized in accord with the present and expected distribution of the population and with the principles of administrative efficiency for the services provided for the New Zealand public.

Island Territories and Dependencies

The term New Zealand, as generally used, is taken to refer only to the three main islands—the North Island, the South Island, and Stewart Island. This group, together with a number of off-shore islands, constitute the main territory of the State.[11] But this includes within its proclaimed boundaries a number of 'outlying' islands. Of these only the Chatham Group supports a settled population and forms one of the 129 counties into which New Zealand proper is divided. The others— the Kermadecs,[12] the Three Kings, the Snares, Bounty, Auckland, Campbell, and the Antipodes—are not now regularly inhabited. They are, however, of scientific and strategic interest, and in the past were visited regularly by sealers and whalers. Their isolated situations make them now unattractive for permanent settlement; the 'southern' islands have the additional disadvantages of being wind-swept and rocky. The Kermadecs, some 600 miles to the north-east of Auckland, are of

[11] By the Imperial Act 26 and 27 Victoria clause 23 (1863) New Zealand's boundaries were amended to extend from 33° S. to 53° S. latitude and from 162° E. to 173° W. longitude.
[12] By proclamation of July 21, 1887, declared annexed by the then Colony of New Zealand.

strategic importance, and there is an emergency air landing strip on Raoul, the largest. All these constitute New Zealand proper.

New Zealand's jurisdiction, however, extends over a very much greater area of the South Pacific Ocean than that included within the proclaimed limits of the State. Its annexed territories extend from some nine degrees south of the equator southward to the pole; they include the Cook Islands,[13] Niue,[14] the Tokelaus,[15] and the Ross Dependency.[16] In addition to these three territories over which New Zealand claims complete jurisdiction it also continues to assume responsibility for the United Nations trusteeships of Western Samoa, and, jointly with Great Britain and Australia, for that of Nauru.[17]

The total population of New Zealand's island territories numbers only about 104,000.[18] The islands are of strategic rather than of economic interest to the metropolitan government, for their resources are limited; indeed, they would not appear to be sufficient to allow the several island groups to become separate political entities in the modern world. At present independence is envisaged only for the Trust Territory of Western Samoa, but even its ability to stand alone is doubtful. Since the end of the second world war the public revenue of Western Samoa has been enough to meet the costs involved by New Zealand in administering the Territory, but any further development in self-government would require an expansion of services necessitating a considerable increase in the national income.

[13] The Cook Islands were proclaimed a part of New Zealand in 1901.

[14] Since 1903 Niue, the largest island in the Cook Group, has been separately administered.

[15] Formerly administered with the Gilbert and Ellice Islands by Great Britain, the Tokelaus were placed under the administration of New Zealand on October 1, 1925. By the Tokelau Act, 1948, the Group was included within the territorial boundaries of New Zealand.

[16] New Zealand claims that part of Antarctica and the off-shore islands lying between longitude 150° W. and 160° E. and extending south of latitude 60° S. to the pole. This claim, like the claims of other States to parts of Antarctica, is not recognized by the United States and some other countries. New Zealand does not participate in the whaling carried on in the waters of the dependency. See F. A. Simpson, "New Zealand Antarctica," in The New Zealand Geographer, vol. x (1954), pp. 1–24. For a discussion of the geopolitics of Antarctica, see below, Chapter XLII.

[17] See Trusteeship Agreement for the Territory of Western Samoa (Department of External Affairs Publication No. 32, Wellington, 1947). Nauru is administered by Australia on behalf of itself and the two other trustees.

[18] (i) Western Samoa, 83,565 (official estimate December 31, 1951).
(ii) Cook Islands (excluding Niue), 15,079 (September 25, 1951).
(iii) Niue, 4507 (September 25, 1951).
(iv) Tokelaus, 1600 (March 31, 1952).

For a full discussion of these islands see: (1) W. S. Lowe and W. T. G. Airey, "New Zealand's Dependencies and the Development of Autonomy," in Pacific Affairs, vol. xviii (1945), pp. 252–272; (2) E. Beaglehole, "Trusteeship and New Zealand's Pacific Dependencies," in Journal of the Polynesian Society, vol. 56 (1947), pp. 128–157.

The resources of Western Samoa, although greater than those of the Cook and Tokelau groups, are also small. A majority of the inhabitants still live at a subsistence level. In certain areas there is already a pressure of population upon the land. The amount of unoccupied land available for additional cultivation is limited, and would seem inadequate for the needs of the Territory's expanding numbers. Western Samoa's export surplus, which determines its income to an overwhelming extent, is highly vulnerable not only to price fluctuations on the world market but also to natural hazards, such as devastation by hurricanes. However, in due season, Western Samoa will doubtless become autonomous, although integration with New Zealand would probably ensure to the inhabitants a greater measure of economic security. At present the chiefs and village leaders desire independence, and will probably continue so to do. However, before New Zealand relinquishes the trusteeship and the Samoans assume entire responsibility it will be necessary for the United Nations Trusteeship Council to assure itself that the people, as well as their leaders, understand and practise democratic self-government, otherwise there is a danger of a reversion to autocratic rule, which in the past gave rise to intrigue and internal strife.

The Cook Islands, Niue, and the Tokelaus have all been proclaimed a part of New Zealand, and it may well be that the metropolitan government will gradually integrate them into the State and treat them as under-developed areas. Present population trends suggest that all three territories have inadequate resources to maintain even the existing standards of living. During the past ten years the Cook Islands and Niue have depended on subsidies from New Zealand amounting to more than half their total expenditure. The Tokelaus are also subsidized, but to a much smaller degree. Their inhabitants are more backward than those of the other islands and the Maoris of the Cook Islands, and the cost of their administration is very low; no European officials are stationed in the Group.

The prospects of the Cook Islands and Niue are substantially improved if they are regarded as economic outliers of New Zealand; government subsidies could make possible a programme of public works and social services far more expensive than that which can be maintained out of the local revenue. At present the living standard of the Cook Islanders is considerably below that of the Maori people of New Zealand proper, with whom they have close affinities. A small number of Cook Island Maoris regularly seek work in the North Island. At present the agricultural basis of the islands is not adequate for the maintenance of the growing population, and if, as one New Zealander has asserted, "the Cook Islands constitute an integral part of the Dominion of New Zealand both politically and economically,"[19] two questions, as yet unanswered, must then be posed—to what extent is the metropolitan government prepared to subsidize their economy and in what numbers may their inhabitants, should they so desire, migrate to New Zealand proper? The Cook Islands have been called "the tropical, insular, tenth 'province' of the dominion,"[20] but they have not yet been fully integrated into the State.[21]

New Zealand's interests in the island peoples of the South Pacific is not restricted to its own dependent territories. It is interested also in the Crown Colony of Fiji and the Kingdom of Tonga, both of which lie within its sphere of influence and which are in certain respects dependent on New Zealand. The State's experience in administering Western Samoa between the two world wars convinced it of the need for establishing a regional advisory council for the South Pacific area on the lines of the Anglo-American Caribbean Conference. Perhaps one of the most interesting outcomes of the agreement which it signed with Australia in 1944 has been the establishment of the South Pacific Commission. In January 1947 the two countries jointly convened the South Seas Commission Conference at Canberra to which they invited the governments of Great Britain, the United States, France, and the Netherlands. At this conference it was agreed to establish the South Seas Commission.[22] The participation of Great Britain and the United States enabled the Commission to establish research facilities which would have been beyond the capacity of Australia and New Zealand. From the beginning the initiators were determined that political matters were to be excluded from the scope of the Commission, and that it should be a purely advisory body promoting the health, education, and economic well-being of

[19] W. B. Johnson, "The Citrus Industry of the Cook Islands," in *The New Zealand Geographer*, vol. vii (1951), p. 138.

[20] *Ibid.*, p. 121.

[21] At present they are not represented in the New Zealand Parliament, and New Zealand laws apply to the Islands only if specifically extended to them.

[22] The original territorial scope of the Commission was defined as "all those non-selfgoverning territories in the Pacific Ocean which are administered by the participating governments and which lie wholly or in part south of the Equator and east from and including Netherlands New Guinea"; but on November 7, 1951, at the request of the U.S.A., an additional agreement was signed at Noumea on behalf of the six participating Governments, extending the scope of the Commission's activities to Guam and the American Trust Territories of the Pacific. See *Agreement extending the Territorial Scope of the South Pacific Commission, Noumea, November 7, 1951* (Department of External Affairs, Publication No. 116; Wellington, 1952).

the islanders. The Commission has two auxiliary bodies—the South Pacific Conference and the Research Council. The former is of special value in that it gives the indigenous peoples, through their representatives, the opportunity of discussing their problems and of bringing them to the attention of the Commissioners.

Since the Commission is only an advisory body, it is difficult to assess its value. Certainly it has the opportunity of making a contribution to the peace of the world if it succeeds in giving economic security to the islands included within its territorial scope. Some New Zealanders and Australians see the possibility of Great Britain, France, and the Netherlands suggesting that their South Pacific dependencies shall become the responsibility of the 'Canberra' Powers. But these are dreams of the future, for at present neither New Zealand nor Australia could afford to add to its financial commitments by assuming responsibility for additional dependencies, even were it given the opportunity to do so. Both countries need their surplus capital for developing to the full their own domestic resources.

External Relations

Historically New Zealand's foreign policy falls into three phases, and, in each, primary determinants have been the country's small size, its isolated position in the south-west Pacific Ocean, and its economic dependence on overseas markets. New Zealanders have always been acutely conscious of their country's smallness and of the necessity of being part of an organization bigger and more powerful than they alone can ever hope to form. Throughout the formative years of their development as a nation the 'protector' was found in the mother-country. By identifying themselves closely with Great Britain, upon whom they were psychologically as well as economically dependent, they acquired a sense of sharing in her greatness, thereby compensating themselves for the smallness of their own country and the feelings of inferiority that attend upon weakness. The greatness of the mother-country was reinforced by the additional sense of security that membership of the British Empire afforded.

The first phase in New Zealand's foreign policy lasted throughout the nineteenth century, and, in fact, there was no fundamental change in attitude until the first Labour Government came to power in the Dominion in 1935. For nearly a century successive governments ac-

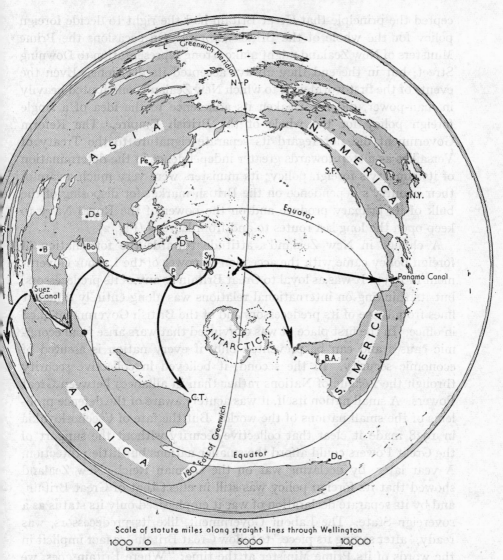

Scale of statute miles along straight-lines through Wellington

1000   0   5000   10,000

Zenithal equidistant projection centred on Wellington.

Fig. 2. New Zealand: Ocean Gateways to Great Britain

After map by J. W. Fox in "New Zealand and the Pacific: Some Strategic Implications," in *The New Zealand Geographer*, vol. IV (1948), p. 17.

A, Aden; B, Baghdad; Bo, Bombay; B.A., Buenos Aires; C, Colombo; C.T., Cape Town; D, Darwin; Da, Dakar; De, Delhi; L, London; M, Melbourne; N.Y., New York; P, Perth; Pe, Peking; R, Rome; S, Singapore; Sy, Sydney; S.F., San Francisco; T, Tokyo.

cepted the principle that Great Britain had the right to decide foreign policy for the whole of the British Empire. On occasions the Prime Ministers of New Zealand might make strong representation to Downing Street, but in the end they always accepted its decisions. Even the events of the first world war, to which New Zealand contributed heavily in man-power, did not weaken its adherence to the idea of a single foreign policy for the whole of the British Empire. The Reform Government did not regard its separate signature to the Treaty of Versailles as a step towards greater independence in the determination of its country's foreign policy; its ministers were very much aware of their country's dependence on the British market for disposing of the bulk of its primary produce and on the power of the Royal Navy to keep open the long sea routes to and from Europe (Fig. 2).

A change in New Zealand's attitude towards the formulation of foreign policy came with the accession to power of the Labour Government in 1935. It was as loyal to Great Britain as any of its predecessors, but its thinking on international relations was along entirely different lines from those of its predecessors and of the British Government then in office. In the first place, it was convinced that wars arise from economic causes and can be prevented only if every nation is assured of economic security. In the second, it believed in collective security through the League of Nations rather than in alliances between Great Powers. A small nation itself, it was acutely aware of the defence problems of the small nations of the world. But the fate of Czechoslovakia in 1938 made it clear that collective security without the support of the Great Powers could afford the smaller nations but little protection. A year later, by declaring war on the German Reich, New Zealand showed that its foreign policy was still in effect that of Great Britain, and by its separate declaration of war it emphasized only its status as a sovereign State. The Labour Government, like its predecessors, was ready, 'after saying its piece,' to follow Great Britain—a fact implicit in the words of its Prime Minister at the time: "Where Britain goes, we go; where she stands, we stand."[23]

In 1939, on the outbreak of the second world war, the average New Zealander, although over twelve thousand miles away, had a greater appreciation of the significance of events in Europe and North Africa than he had of those in Eastern Asia and the Western Pacific. His eyes

[23] Reported in the New Zealand Press generally for September 4, 1939. For an interpretation of the attitude of successive New Zealand governments see L. K. Munro, "New Zealand and the New Pacific," in *Foreign Affairs*, vol. 31 (1953), p. 641.

were focused on the Suez and Panama Canal routes to Great Britain
rather than on the islands lying to his immediate north (Fig. 3). The
front lines of defence of these routes were North Africa and the North

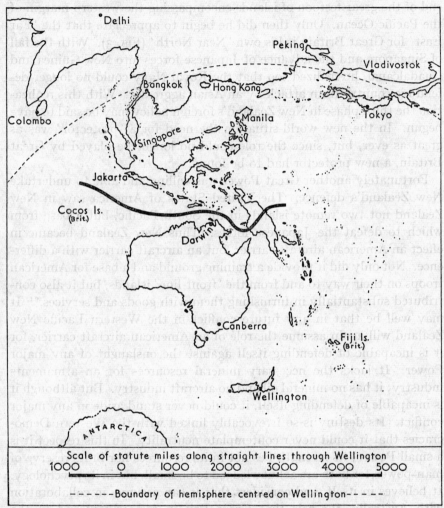

FIG. 3. NEW ZEALAND AND THE NEAR NORTH
The heavy black line marks the frontier of the British Commonwealth
over against Asia.

Atlantic Ocean. New Zealanders had long realized the importance of
the Mediterranean Sea and the Middle East in their country's destiny,
and had been vitally interested in any political moves that might result
in its closure to British ships.

It was only the rapid southward movement of Japanese troops, following upon the attack on Pearl Harbour in 1941, that made the New Zealander conscious of his country's vulnerable position at the southern end of the great festoon of islands encompassing the western margin of the Pacific Ocean. Only then did he begin to appreciate that the 'Far East' for Great Britain is his own 'Near North' (Fig. 3). With the fall of Singapore and the advance of Japanese forces into New Guinea and Guadalcanal, he realized too that the Royal Navy could no longer defend his country from attack by an Asian aggressor. With this realization the third phase in New Zealand's foreign policy may be said to have begun. In the new world-situation the need for a 'protector' was as great as ever, but, since the role could no longer be played by Great Britain, a new protector had to be found.

Fortunately another Great Power was willing and able to undertake New Zealand's defence. The United States of America saw in New Zealand not two remote islands in the South Pacific, but a base from which to defeat the Japanese forces. Thus New Zealand became in effect an American aircraft carrier, but an aircraft carrier with a difference. Not only did it provide a training ground and a base for American troops on their way to and from the 'front-line' islands, but it also contributed substantially in furnishing them with goods and services.[24] It may well be that in any future conflict in the Western Pacific New Zealand will again assume the role of an American aircraft carrier, for it is incapable of defending itself against the onslaught of any major Power. It lacks the necessary mineral resources for an armaments industry; it has no mineral oil and no aircraft industry. But although it is incapable of defending itself, it could never stand aside in any major conflict. Its destiny is so irrevocably linked with the Western Democracies that it could never contemplate neutrality. In this respect it is a small Power; its strength lies not in its resources nor in its reserve of man-power, for both are acknowledged to be small, but in its psychology. It believes in itself, and considers that it can assume, in collaboration with Australia, the role that Great Britain formerly played in the defence of South-east Asia and the South-west Pacific. Accordingly the two countries associated themselves in the Canberra Pact of 1944.[25]

[24] To the value of more than 280,000,000 U.S. dollars; see L. K. Munro, "New Zealand and the New Pacific," in *Foreign Affairs*, vol. xxxi (1953), p. 644.

[25] For the text, see *Australian-New Zealand Agreement*, New Zealand Department of External Affairs Treaty Series, No. 1 (Wellington, 1944). See also L. K. Munro, "The Canberra Pact and the Political Geography of the Pacific," in *The New Zealand Geographer*, vol. i (1945), pp. 48–56.

Thereby they asserted their determination to be consulted in any post-war settlement in the Pacific, especially in the treatment of Japan after its defeat. They also asserted their right to assume responsibility for the defence of the island arc "north and north-east of Australia to Western Samoa and the Cook Islands."[26] But a pact between Australia and New Zealand is not sufficient security for either country against any major aggressor. Australia, it is true, is capable of manufacturing major armaments and of being an indispensable base for an allied effort, but it could not offer adequate help to New Zealand were its own integrity threatened simultaneously.

New Zealand had hoped in 1944—and, indeed, for some years after Japan's capitulation—that the terms of the Japanese Peace Treaty would be severe. But in the post-war years it received little support in this aspiration from America, whose stature could enable it, in effect, to impose its will on its allies. So New Zealand found with its new protector, as it found with its old, that although it might express its opinions quite definitely, it was powerless to insist on their being accepted. However, New Zealand could and did insist on a security pact with the United States as the price of its acquiescence in the Japanese Peace Settlement.[27] Thus a treaty of mutual assistance between America, Australia, and New Zealand against any would-be aggressor in the Pacific area was signed.[28] The ANZUS Pact was unprecedented in the history of British Commonwealth relations, because for the first time New Zealand and Australia entered on their own, without Great Britain as a signatory, into a pact with a foreign Power. But New Zealand has been most anxious that none should think that the ANZUS Pact was intended to weaken its bonds with the Commonwealth, least of all with Great Britain. The terms of the treaty allowed for full consultation with Powers in the Pacific area interested in furthering the purposes of the Treaty—thus Great Britain, on account of its responsibility for the defence of Hong Kong, Malaya, Singapore, the Solomon Islands, and Fiji, has been kept informed of all developments under the

---

[26] Clauses 13, 26, 27.

[27] For the text, diplomatic background, and official attitude see: *Treaty of Peace with Japan and Related Documents* (Department of External Affairs, Wellington, 1951). See also *Must We Trust Japan?* (New Zealand Institute of International Affairs, Wellington, 1952).

[28] For the text, diplomatic background, and official attitude see: *Treaty between the Governments of New Zealand, Australia and the United States of America concerning Security* (Department of External Affairs, Wellington, 1952). See also (i) L. K. Munro, "New Zealand and the New Pacific," in *Foreign Affairs*, vol. xxxi (1953), pp. 634–635; (ii) W. F. Monk, "New Zealand Faces North," in *Pacific Affairs*, vol. xxvi (1953), pp. 220–229.

ANZUS Pact. The New Zealand Government looked upon the treaty as but "one of a series of Pacific defence arrangements, in conformity with the principles of the United Nations Charter."[29] New Zealand's desire not to be associated with any defence agreement of which Great Britain was not also a signatory was shown in its enthusiasm for S.E.A.T.O.

New Zealand has given full support to the United Nations and its specialized agencies, although it is a strenuous opponent of the power of veto vested in the Great Powers. For twenty years now it has been, first in the councils of the League of Nations and now in those of the United Nations, the champion of the rights of small States. Since 1945 its foreign policy has been a dual one of collective security through the United Nations and of common defence through regional organizations. In application of this policy it sent troops to Korea in 1950 and to Malaya in 1955. It also took an active part in the Geneva Conference on Indo-China in 1954.

As conference follows conference, and new treaties of mutual aid are signed in the hope of arresting the spread of Communism, it is clear that the New Zealand representatives have considered one of their principal tasks to be to help to strengthen agreement between Great Britain and the United States. On some issues, as in its attitude to the Chinese People's Republic, it has carefully adopted a position intermediate between its two great associates.

In the post-war years New Zealand has not lost sight of its belief that wars arise from economic causes and can be prevented by creating economic security for all nations, and its citizens are very conscious that political unrest in South-east Asia is encouraged by social inequality. In the underprivileged peoples of the Asian mainland it sees a threat to its own privileged condition. Thus New Zealand welcomed the Colombo Plan, and has been exceptionally generous in the financial and other aid that it has given to the Asian participators in the Plan. It has probably been over-generous in its contributions; conscious of its small size and its inherent weakness, it contributes a larger proportion of its income than it can afford, just as during the two world wars it sent abroad a larger proportion of its man-power than it could spare. But the New Zealander is prepared to give generously, for he is convinced that the continuance of his own high standard of living depends on the raising of that of his neighbours in the 'Near North.' He looks out from his position at the southern extremity of the island arcs fringing the Asian

[29] T. C. Webb, *New Zealand Parliamentary Debates*, February 27, 1953.

mainland, and sees a well-marked dividing line between his country and Australia on the one hand—both privileged nations—and the great numbers of underprivileged persons lying beyond them (Fig. 3). Yet, his country's financial contributions, and indeed those of the English-speaking peoples generally, will prove only Danegeld expedients against Communism unless they help to build up sound economies for the young Asian States.

This fact has been recognized, in part at least, by New Zealand in its desire to trade with Asia. In this respect it is reviving the traditional hopes of New Zealand farmers to find in Asia outlets for their meat, butter, and cheese which would reduce their dependence on the British market. But the food habits of the Asians, in conjunction with their low purchasing power, make such hopes unrealistic. Japan alone has the purchasing power, largely through American dollar aid, to buy on the New Zealand market, and its principal requirement is wool. But in trading with Japan New Zealand finds itself in a quandary. One of New Zealand's reasons for contributing so generously to the Colombo Plan was that it hoped thereby to create in South-east Asia a prosperous market for the Commonwealth, not least for British manufactured goods, so that Britain's own purchasing capacity for New Zealand's pastoral products might be sustained and even increased. Yet it is precisely in South-east Asia that Japan seeks a market for its manufactured goods. The two political parties and the country in general are divided on the policy that the country should adopt towards Japan. The farmers, who form the backbone of the National Party, welcome the economic advantage that the Japanese market would afford them; organized Labour, the nucleus of the Labour Party, is afraid of Japanese competition in manufacturing. The situation is complicated further by the attitudes of all sections of the community towards the inhuman behaviour of the Japanese during the war.

New Zealand is not happy about Japan's economic recovery and its participation in the General Agreement on Tariffs and Trade, but it has had to accept the facts, unpalatable though they are. It must trade with Japan, if only as a means of preventing that country from associating itself with the Communist camp. But as they look northward to Japan New Zealanders are all too conscious of the inherent threat to their own existence in a remilitarized Japan. Japan's expanding population alone constitutes a threat to the territorial integrity of New Zealand. The possibility that Japanese forces may again use the numerous small islands between Tokyo and the Kermadecs is not forgotten. But, in view of changes in military strategy in the atomic age and the uncertainty of the new Asia, it is not possible to forecast the future power pattern in the Western Pacific.

Conclusion

Certain facts, however, are clear. The development of New Zealand in less than a century into a comfortable, homogeneous, democratic nation was made possible by a power pattern that has passed beyond recall, and to-day New Zealand finds itself pulled in two directions; its military security depends on the goodwill of the United States of America, its economic prosperity rests on that of Great Britain. Fortunately for New Zealand its two 'protectors' are closely bound together by defence agreements, but any serious divergence on a major issue of foreign policy between them is a matter that New Zealand does "not care to contemplate."[30] It would like to be less dependent on the British market, but, sentimental considerations apart, it knows only too well that its expanding economy depends as much on keeping its traditional customer as on finding new ones. Were New Zealand to be prevented from marketing its pastoral produce overseas its high standard of living would inevitably fall.

New Zealand, like Australia, is acutely aware of the problem posed by the vulnerability of South-east Asia to the advance of Communism. The nation is a willing partner of S.E.A.T.O., but it is doubtful if its statesmen realize the complexity of South-east Asian politics. Between Western interests in the South-west Pacific and on the Asian mainland lies Indonesia, as yet politically uncommitted. Indonesian nationalists regard anyone of European extraction as a potential oppressor. The majority of New Zealanders are of European descent, and the Asian peoples generally identify them with the European Powers from whom many of them have only recently been liberated. They do not clasp the hand of friendship held out to them as quickly or as tightly as New Zealanders would wish. New Zealanders are puzzled by this reticence, forgetting that their country's policy of selective immigration —necessary as it is—suggests a colour bar to the underprivileged peoples

[30] N. Mansergh, *The Name and Nature of the British Commonwealth* (Cambridge University Press, 1954), pp. 27–28.

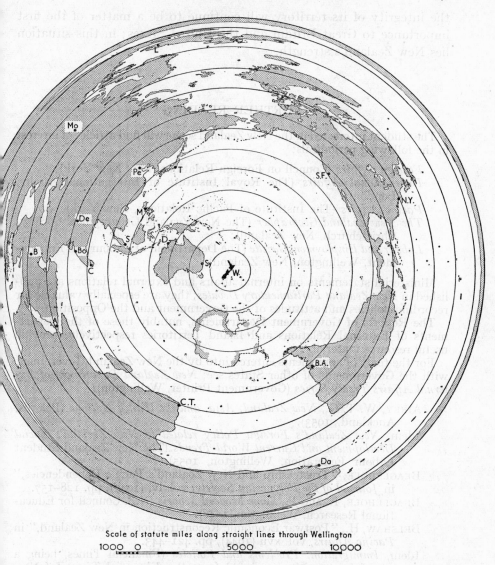

Scale of statute miles along straight lines through Wellington

1000 0 5000 10000

FIG. 4. THE WORLD: DISTANCES FROM WELLINGTON

Identifications as in Fig. 2, p. 849. Concentric circles have been drawn to show distances in multiples of 1000 statute miles from Wellington, the centre of the map projection (zenithal equidistant).

of their 'Near North.' Thus New Zealand remains in 1956 what it has always been—a small, isolated white community in the South-west Pacific Ocean (Fig. 4). But although the State is both small and weak, the integrity of its territory will continue to be a matter of the first importance to Great Britain and the United States; in this situation lies New Zealand's strength.

FURTHER READING

The student interested in the New Zealand scene will find articles of interest in the following periodicals:

Foreign Affairs (Council on Foreign Relations, Inc., New York);
International Affairs (The Royal Institute of International Affairs, London);
Pacific Affairs (The Institute of Pacific Relations, New York);
The New Zealand Geographer (The New Zealand Geographical Society, Christchurch, New Zealand);
Labour and Employment Gazette (The Department of Labour and Employment, Wellington, New Zealand).

Ministerial statements on internal affairs and external relations are published in *New Zealand Parliamentary Debates*; they are especially valuable for recording policies and attitudes of the Government and the Opposition.

The Reports of Government Departments, notably those of the Departments of External Relations and Island Territories respectively, provide useful resource material.

For the texts of agreements entered into by the New Zealand Government with the Governments of other States see: *New Zealand Department of External Affairs Treaty Series* (Government Printer, Wellington).

AIREY, W. T. G., *New Zealand, Asia, and the United Nations* (Pelorus, Auckland, 1953).

Idem, *New Zealand's Foreign Policy related to New Zealand's Social Development and Current World Trends* (The New Zealand Student Labour Federation, Wellington, 1955).

BEAGLEHOLE, "Trusteeship and New Zealand's Pacific Dependencies," in *Journal of the Polynesian Society*, vol. lvi (1947), pp. 128–157.

BEAGLEHOLE, E. and P., *Some Modern Maoris* (N.Z. Council for Educational Research, Wellington, 1946).

BELSHAW, H., "Postwar Economic Reconstruction in New Zealand," in *Pacific Affairs*, vol. xvii (1944), pp. 421–443.

Idem, *Immigration: Problems and Policies* (Financial Times, being a set of four articles reprinted from the *Financial Times* [of New Zealand], Wellington, 1952).

BILLING, G. C., *New Zealand Trade Policy* (The New Zealand Institute of International Relations, Wellington, 1946).

CAMPBELL, PETER, "Politicians, Public Servants, and the People in New Zealand," in *Political Studies*, vol. iii (1955), pp. 193–210, and vol. iv (1956), pp. 18–29.

CUMBERLAND, K. B., *Southwest Pacific* (Whitcombe and Tombs, Christchurch, N.Z., 1954).

CURRIE, A. E., *Crown and Subject: a Treatise on the Right and Legal Relationship of the Crown and the People of New Zealand as set out in the Crown Proceedings Act, 1950* (Wellington, 1950).

Economic Survey of New Zealand (Government Printer, Wellington, for years 1952, 1953, 1954, 1955).

FOX, J. W. L., "New Zealand and the Pacific: Some Strategic Implications," in *The New Zealand Geographer*, vol. iv (1948), pp. 15–28.

LEATHEM, S., *New Zealand's Interests and Policies in the Far East*, a data paper presented by the New Zealand Institute of International Affairs in connexion with the Lucknow Conference of the Institute of Pacific Relations in 1950.

LIPSON, L., *The Politics of Equality: New Zealand's Adventures in Democracy* (The University of Chicago Press, 1948).

MILNER, I. F. G., *New Zealand's Interests and Policies in the Far East* (Institute of Pacific Relations, New York, 1940).

NASH, W., *New Zealand, A Working Democracy* (Duall, Sloan and Pearce, New York, 1943; Dent, London, 1944).

The New Zealand Economy, 1939 to 1951 (Government Printer, Wellington, 1952—a government report presented by S. G. Holland).

PARKER, R. S. (editor), *Economic Stability in New Zealand* (New Zealand Institute of Public Administration, Wellington, 1953).

SIEGFRIED, A., *Democracy in New Zealand* (translated from the German edition of 1909 by E. V. Burns and with an introduction by W. D. Stewart (Bell, London, 1914)); this volume is still of value and should be read in conjunction with AIREY, WILLIS, "André Siegfried's *Democracy in New Zealand*—Fifty Years After," in *Political Science*, vol. vi, No. 2 (September 1954), pp. 33–51.

SIMKIN, C. G. F., *The Instability of a Dependent Economy—Economic Fluctuations in New Zealand, 1840–1910* (Oxford University Press, 1951).

SIMPSON, F. A., "New Zealand Antarctica," in *The New Zealand Geographer*, vol. x (1954), pp. 1–24.

SUTCH, W. B., *The Quest for Security* (Penguin edition, Harmondsworth, England, 1942).

The New Zealand Institute of International Relations:
    Contemporary New Zealand, a Survey of Domestic and Foreign Policy (Auckland, 1938);
    Immigration into New Zealand; Report of a Study Group (Dunedin 1950);
    Must we trust Japan? (Wellington, 1952).

WILLIAMS, J. W., *The New Zealand Economy in War and Reconstruction* (Institute of Pacific Relations, New York, 1948).

WOOD, F. L., *This New Zealand* (second edition; Paul's Book Arcade, Hamilton, N.Z., 1952); also published under the title *Understanding New Zealand* (Coward–McCann, New York, 1944). "New Zealand and Southeast Asia," in *Far Eastern Survey*, vol. xxv (1956), pp. 17–27.

CHAPTER XXXVI

The Caribbean and the Panama Canal

HENRY J. BRUMAN

LATIN AMERICA is slowly losing its traditional status as one of the world's great underpopulated areas. At a time when mankind is multiplying faster than ever before population growth in Latin America is fully twice the world average and exceeds that of any other major culture realm. Although most parts of the mainland are not yet overcrowded, many of the Caribbean islands have high population densities, and continuing rapid population increase is aggravating their economic and political problems.

The total population of the islands from the Bahamas south to Trinidad and west to Cuba and Jamaica increased from six million in 1900 to an estimated eighteen million in 1955. Population has run far ahead of food production, and there are few signs as yet that birth rates are declining. On some of the islands increasing industrialization is enhancing earning potential and the ability to pay for imported food, but the passage of time does not seem to be easing overall population pressure on available supplies of food. The disruptive influences of world Communism have seen in this situation a fertile ground for agitation and trouble-making, and the political prospect of the region as a whole cannot be viewed with complacency.

The Historical Background

The political geography of the Western Hemisphere is drawn mostly in rather broad strokes. Much of the land is occupied by independent States of fairly large size. But in the Caribbean the political units are small, and many of them have a status inferior to full sovereignty. In the islands of this New World Mediterranean there are three sovereign nations, one semi-independent Commonwealth associated with the United States, one United States Territory, and about a dozen European colonies divided among three European nations. Two of these island colonies are by law integral parts of a State whose main body politic lies thousands of miles away over open sea, whereas another is a component part of a kingdom in which it theoretically shares some aspects of equality with its European motherland. The reasons for this extraordinary political patchwork are to be found less in the intricate pattern of land and sea and of mountain and plain than in the historical development of the area by competing European Powers.

The very complexity of the Caribbean in the political sense gives it a kind of unity when contrasted with the rest of the Western Hemisphere. But an assertion of geopolitical unity can be justified on several grounds. In the sixteenth century the Caribbean was largely a Spanish lake. Spain was paramount by virtue of her control of the mainland rim and of the larger islands. After a while, it is true, pirates and freebooters of many flags harassed the Spaniards, and a convoy system had to be devised to protect the silver fleet, but only on occasion were these attacks more than a nuisance. Spain could not, of course, defend all the Caribbean islands—there were too many—and she was preoccupied with her sources of treasure in Mexico and Peru. In the course of time other nations established bases, especially in the Lesser Antilles, and these footholds could be used both for sniping at the plate fleets and for growing sugar. Eventually Spain was forced to recognize the interests of England, Holland, and France, and by the end of the eighteenth century the British Navy, even *in absentia*, was the main power in the Caribbean.

Many changes in sovereignty took place as a result of the French Revolution, the Napoleonic epoch, and the liberation of the mainland Spanish colonies. Of her vast New World empire Spain managed to retain only Cuba and Puerto Rico. The young United States began gradually to take an interest in the Caribbean area, acquiring frontage on the Gulf of Mexico through the purchase of Louisiana in 1803 and of Florida in 1819. The annexation of Texas and the Mexican War gave rise to a vital interest in Latin American matters, and the California Gold Rush brought thousands of Americans into the Gulf and the Caribbean on their way to the Pacific. American financiers surveyed the investment possibilities of the inter-oceanic portages at Tehuántepec,

Nicaragua, and Panama, and various schemes for development were proposed. One of the first railroads to be built in the tropics was completed in 1855 across the Isthmus of Panama.

This first period of American interest came to a close with the Civil War (1861–65), during which the Monroe Doctrine[1] could not be asserted. Not until the 1890's did real interest in the Caribbean on the part of the American public revive. Investments in Cuban and Puerto Rican sugar plantations helped to promote a sympathetic attitude by the American public toward revolutionary movements in Cuba which brought about the Spanish-American War (1898). The resultant responsibility of the United States for mapping the future of the former Spanish colonies introduced a new dimension into the political geography of the Caribbean. The Monroe Doctrine, as interpreted and amplified by Theodore Roosevelt, once again became highly significant in American political thought. There was concern that the Danish West Indies might be acquired by Germany; concern about a British-German-Italian blockade of Venezuela; concern about increasing European investments, especially in Central America. When Colombia seemed on the verge of refusing permission to the United States to build a canal through the Isthmus of Panama, and a revolt of the Panamanians occurred, the United States prevented Colombian militia from quelling the uprising, recognized the independence of Panama with a haste that in retrospect seems more wilful than diplomatic, and immediately concluded a treaty with Panama for the perpetual lease of a strip of land within which to build the canal. The United States had emerged as one of the great Powers, and the building of the Panama Canal was no longer to be denied.

The first three decades of the twentieth century were the period in American history to which the epithet 'imperialism' most nearly applies. There were several episodes of armed intervention in Haiti, the Dominican Republic, and Nicaragua, as well as supervision of financial matters, including customs collections, in Haiti and the Dominican Republic. Such interferences were rationalized in part by the fear that European Powers might otherwise intervene to protect the investments of their

---

[1] The Monroe Doctrine grew out of a message sent to Congress by President Monroe in 1823. In this he underlined the separateness of the New World by warning European States that any political interference in the affairs of the American republics would be regarded by the United States as an unfriendly act and as dangerous to its peace and safety. The ideas contained in this message became basic principles of the foreign policy of the United States, and were used in support of its interventions in the affairs of the Central American republics.—EDITORS' NOTE.

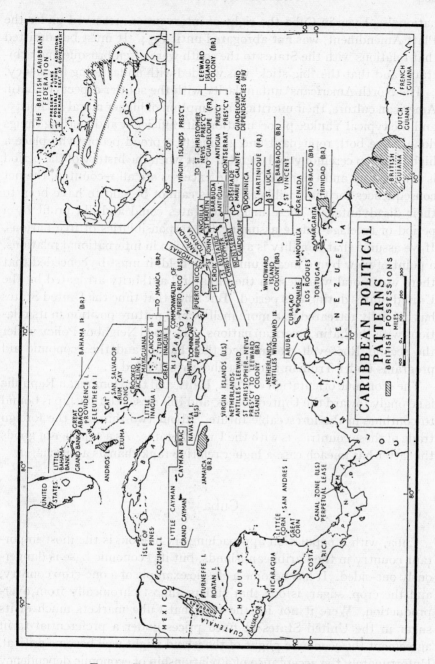

FIG. 1. THE CARIBBEAN: POLITICAL PATTERNS

nationals. Even in Cuba the right of intervention, reserved under the Platt Amendment, was not abrogated until 1934. It must be admitted that relations with the States to the south were often brusque and arbitrary, and that the 'big stick' was wielded with unflattering frequency.

The North Americans' unfamilarity with the subtler aspects of Latin American culture, their uncritical assumption of higher moral authority, and the typical Yankee preoccupation with efficiency and 'getting things done' were both repugnant and galling to a proud people who place a high value on ceremony and dignity. But when the history of the period is summed up and the mistakes and excesses are all recounted, the net consequences for the Caribbean States cannot be said to have been to their disadvantage. These incipient States could and did profit by a period of tutelage before assuming the responsibilities of free nations. If we assume that morality is a consideration in international relations, a point of view by no means universally held, it must be conceded that there was moral weakness in the unilateral authority arrogated by the United States during this period. But since that time the United States has officially retreated to a more mellow and mature position in its relations with the Latin American nations. The Good Neighbor Policy under the second Roosevelt exemplified the change, and the economic aid programs under Truman and Eisenhower extended it.

The economic orientation of Cuba, Haiti, and the Dominican Republic is strongly toward the United States, and this close relationship is bound to continue in the foreseeable future. About two-thirds of the foreign trade of these countries is with the United States. As a supplier of goods the latter has in each case a higher relative rank than as a purchaser.

Cuba

Cuba, with a population approaching six million, is the most important country in the Caribbean islands, but its economic base is dangerously one-sided. It has become a classic example of a one-crop country, and the crop, sugar, is one that suffers almost chronically from overproduction. Were it not for the fact that Cuba markets much of its sugar in the United States at fixed prices under a preferential tariff agreement the economic plight of the island might well become critical. Unfortunately the acceptance of a relationship of economic dependency diminishes both economic freedom and the incentive to find new markets. It is becoming increasingly evident that new markets must be found, and that agricultural diversification must be vigorously pursued. The seasonal rhythm of sugar growing and processing gives rise to widespread unemployment every year from May to November. The 173 sugar *centrales*, with their enormous investment, are closed more than half the time. Enforced idleness and reduced income lead to social unrest, and it is perhaps no accident that Cuba has had for years a large and active Communist movement.

Cuba's sunny winters and proximity to Florida have afforded a fine opportunity for the development of tourism. Unfortunately the facilities thus far developed and the treatment accorded visitors have not been universally acclaimed. Many tourists have come away dissatisfied, and long visits and return visits are not too common. Cuba at present appears to be far behind Mexico in the constructive attention it has paid to this great potential source of income.

Further developments are possible both in mining and in light manufacturing. Local supplies of the mineral fuels are scarce, which would seem to preclude the extensive development of heavy industry. A voluminous *Report on Cuba* published in 1951 by the International Bank for Reconstruction and Development gives a detailed analysis of the prevailing situation about 1950, and presents constructive recommendations for future development.

Haiti

The situation in Haiti is very different from that in Cuba. Haiti has a greater diversity of export crops than any other part of the West Indies, coffee and sisal being most important. It has also a well-developed subsistence agriculture, and is almost self-sufficient in food production. However, the problems of high birth rate, illiteracy, and poverty are extremely serious. Population densities are almost three times as great as in Cuba or the neighboring Dominican Republic, and the per capita income ranks near the bottom for all Caribbean areas. Soil erosion has been bad in this prevalently hilly country, and crop yields have not been maintained. Agricultural missions from the United States have made extensive studies of the needs of Haitian agriculture and various types of aid have been given, especially in the potentially highly productive Artibonite Lowland. The greatest problem is that of steadily

2F

increasing population pressure. Birth control has been of little help in this illiterate country. Migration has been proposed as a possible solution, but Haitian Negroes are not welcome elsewhere. Attempts to settle in the Dominican Republic have met with stern repression. In 1937 some 60,000 Haitians were living just east of their common border with the Dominican Republic. A campaign to drive them back to their own land, instigated by the Dominican Government, resulted in the death of many thousands of them. Sporadic attempts to find room in Cuba on an individual basis have also met with rebuffs. The Haitians are culturally and linguistically distinct from the other Caribbean peoples, and their salvation will probably have to be found in their own homeland. Industrialization promises little, as the prerequisites are largely absent. Commercial agriculture can be encouraged with the use of American capital, and the further development of coffee-growing would seem to have fair prospects. The dissemination of better agricultural techniques, including the use of fertilizer, will give higher yields of subsistence crops. But it will require great wisdom and extraordinary efforts to develop Haiti into anything more than a permanently poor backwater.

The Dominican Republic

The Dominican Republic has better prospects than Haiti. The country is almost twice as large and contains much greater areas of fertile agricultural land. Population pressures are not at all serious at present, and the Dominican Republic is the one country in the Caribbean which in the last three decades has actively promoted immigration. Various groups of European refugees have been encouraged to settle on unused lands in an attempt to exert a back-pressure against Haiti, to enhance further the Caucasian component in the prevalently mulatto population, and to introduce new skills which the nation can utilize. The Dominican Republic's greatest export is sugar, most of which is sent to the United Kingdom, for Dominican sugar is not accorded preferential treatment by the United States. The emergence to power of Rafael Leonidas Trujillo Molina in 1930 and his subsequent control of the Government brought a period of stability to the Dominican Republic which is unique in its history. It is the rule of a man on horseback, following a classical Latin tradition. While all opposition has been ruthlessly suppressed, education, production, and trade have been encouraged. The prevailing opinion among educated foreigners in the Dominican Republic is that the "era of Trujillo" has been of real benefit to the country, which is not ready for democratic government anyway. It is, of course, not easy to see how democratic government can ever be prepared for under these circumstances.

Cuba, Haiti, and the Dominican Republic all have republican constitutions, but they are not democracies. Periods of constitutional government based on legal elections have alternated with recurring dictatorships following on *coups d'état* and armed revolts. Respect by the parties in power for the rights of minorities is seldom found, and the related concept of "loyal opposition" by groups defeated at the polls is conspicuously absent. The concentration of economic and political control in the hands of a few families has brought about a self-perpetuating oligarchical domination of government. The development of a tradition of stable democratic government may depend as much on a wider distribution of property as on increasing literacy.

The Commonwealth of Puerto Rico

The last Spanish-speaking colony in the New World was Puerto Rico, an island too small and undeveloped to be set up as a separate country on the Cuban pattern after the Spanish-American War. It became a Territory of the United States, and in 1917 was given a Constitution which conferred United States citizenship on its people. With the passage of the years Puerto Rico was transformed into what amounted to a Latin American nation under the United States flag.

United States influence manifested itself in practical ways, such as the building of roads, the improvement of water supplies and sanitation, the construction of hydro-electric projects, and the introduction of higher standards of medical care and education. Commercial sugar plantations flourished under the influence of American capital, not always with due regard for the rights and basic needs of the Puerto Rican people. But the fundamental cultural attributes of Puerto Rican life were less profoundly affected. Five decades of instruction in English have not undermined the status of Spanish as the mother tongue. Less than a fourth of the population is truly bilingual to-day.

Mortality rates have constantly declined, while birth rates have remained very high. The average expectation of life at birth increased

from thirty-eight years in 1919 to fifty-eight years in 1954. The consequence has been a veritable explosion in population, one of the highest
rates of natural increase in the world. But for the safety valve of
emigration, the population of Puerto Rico would double in twenty-five
years, on an island that already has a population density of almost 700
per square mile. Although agriculture is the basic economy, there is less
than half an acre of arable land per person.

Paradoxically, Puerto Rico's political ties with the United States
have kept the population from increasing even more rapidly. As citizens
of the United States, Puerto Ricans have been free to come to the
mainland, and in the decade 1942–51 a net total of some 250,000 did so.
This number is equivalent to almost one-half the net increase in population for those years. Those who migrated were mostly young adults with
higher than average reproductive and lower than average mortality
rates. Had they remained on the island, the total population by 1952
would have been at least 320,000 greater than it actually was, allowing
for natural increase, or more than 2,600,000. Most of the migrants went
to New York City, which now contains as many people of Puerto Rican
extraction as San Juan. Their remittances to the homeland have helped
to support the island economy.

Since the establishment in 1952 of the Commonwealth of Puerto Rico
the people of the island have been completely self-governing in domestic
matters, but have retained their citizenship in the United States. They
elect their own governor and make their own laws, but defense and
foreign relations continue to be handled by the United States, and
federal agencies continue to serve Puerto Rico as though it were a state
in the Union. The Commonwealth differs from a state principally in
not having the right to send senators or voting representatives to Congress, and in not participating in presidential elections. Congressional
legislation applicable to the entire United States applies equally to
Puerto Rico—compulsory military service, for example. This surviving
aspect of legislation without representation troubles many Puerto Rican
leaders, for it is a vestige of colonial status. Puerto Rico sends to Washington only a Resident Commissioner, who since 1904 has been a member without vote of the House of Representatives. His status was not
changed in the Constitutions of 1917 or 1952. On the other hand,
'taxation without representation' is not at issue, since all taxes collected
under federal internal revenue laws and all customs duties collected in
the island are returned to the Insular Treasury, a practice which has

been in effect since 1901. Nor are the Puerto Rican people taxed to support federal agencies—*e.g.*, the post office. Such costs are borne wholly by the Federal Treasury.

In adopting the Constitution of 1952 the Puerto Rican people have voted to retain and reaffirm their connexion with the United States. The occasional terroristic acts of a small group of extreme nationalists moved President Eisenhower to declare in 1954 that if Puerto Rico ever chose to sever its ties with the United States he would ask Congress to pass the needed legislation. But the present insular Government and Puerto Rican intellectual leaders agree that it would be a fatal mistake to cast the small country adrift outside the United States tariff and immigration walls. Since 1948 Puerto Rico has been attracting an increasing number of small industries from the mainland by giving generous tax benefits for a period of years. The program, called "Operation Bootstrap," has created new employment and new sources of income for the island economy. Tourism has likewise been increasingly promoted, and the number of visitors from the mainland is now about 100,000 a year. Partly because of these new developments Puerto Rico's net national income increased from 228 million dollars in 1940 to 890 million dollars in 1952.

Even with continuing industrialization, improvement of agricultural production, and a gradually declining birth rate, the first signs of which have already appeared, large-scale emigration will be a continuing necessity for decades. Various schemes have been proposed to establish agricultural colonies of Puerto Ricans in South America, notably in Brazil and Surinam, but they have not materialized. So long as Puerto Rico retains her political ties with the United States her people are free to move to this country, and their chances of success here will not easily be surpassed elsewhere. Puerto Ricans have a distinguished record of service in the Armed Forces of the United States, and this training has broadened their vision and strengthened their feeling of identification with the United States.

The Netherlands Antilles

The Netherlands Antilles are not a colony in the eyes of the Netherlands Government. They are a part of the Kingdom of the Netherlands, and enjoy internal autonomy. There are two groups of islands. The

first, in the northern part of the Lesser Antilles, is not of great importance. The second group lies just north of the coast of Venezuela, and
includes Curaçao, Aruba, and Bonaire.

Curaçao and Aruba have had great economic and strategic significance since the first world war, when oil was discovered in the Maracaibo
Basin. A sandbar near the outlet of Lake Maracaibo prevented ocean-
going vessels from entering the lake, and facilities were established on
Curaçao and Aruba for tankers to load petroleum brought in by lighters.
Refineries have been located on Curaçao since 1916, and on Aruba since
1925. About 40 per cent. of the wage-earners of Curaçao are said to be
in the employ of the refineries and their shipping establishments; on
Aruba the figure rises to 70 per cent. These workers receive relatively
high wages, and Curaçao and Aruba enjoy the highest standard of living
in the entire Caribbean.

The culture of the islands is not emphatically Dutch. The most widely
used language, called *Papiamento*, is a local, regional development based
on Spanish.

The French West Indies

Since 1946 Martinique and Guadeloupe have had the status of departments of metropolitan France, and, like all other departments, have sent
deputies to the French National Assembly. They might thus be regarded as technically of higher political status than all other units in the
Caribbean except for the Commonwealth of Puerto Rico and the independent States (Cuba, Haiti, and the Dominican Republic). Their full
participation as part of the body politic of France would appear to be
somewhat comparable to the future status of Hawaii if and when that
territory is elevated to statehood. In actual fact, however, the French
Caribbean islands are still completely colonial in character, the bulk of
their population being composed of poor Negro and mulatto laborers
working on unprogressive and poorly managed plantations and on small
subsistence farms.

The first settlements on Martinique and Guadeloupe were made by
the French in 1635. Several of the islands now held by Britain in the
Lesser Antilles were formerly French, and even Martinique and Guadeloupe were repeatedly occupied by British forces in the seventeenth and
eighteenth centuries. Sugar plantations operated by Negro slaves became the dominant pattern in these islands, as well as in Saint Domingue,

now Haiti, which in the eighteenth century was France's greatest Caribbean sugar colony.

Slavery was abolished in the islands in 1848 and brought with it a crisis in the sugar industry. However, the crisis was not as severe as in the British islands, where the slaves had been freed a decade earlier, perhaps because the French had less feeling of race consciousness and had kept from unnecessarily alienating their slaves. At any rate, they did not find it necessary to bring in large groups of labor from other areas, the liberated slaves continuing to work the plantations. Thus the racial pattern in the French islands has remained relatively simple.

During the second world war the French Caribbean possessions became a serious problem for the Allies after the fall of France. Admiral Georges Robert, representing the Vichy regime, became governor in 1940, and an Allied blockade was imposed in order to deny the use of these islands to the German war effort. Until the ousting of Admiral Robert in 1943 Martinique and Guadeloupe underwent great privation, for necessary imports of food had been cut off by the blockade. Relief shipments of food were begun in 1943 by the United States, and the economic situation became once more stabilized with the end of World War II.

Sugar plantations are still dominant on Martinique and on Grande Terre. The French system of colonial preference has protected the planters from competition and has perpetuated inefficient techniques and poor management. The colored labor force lives in poverty; and housing, diet, and sanitation are all substandard. There is much rum-drinking and considerable alcoholism.

Since the war Communist influence has been very strong in both islands. Many of the local officials are Communists, as were four of the six deputies representing the islands in the French National Assembly at the beginning of 1954. So strong a Communist influence at the eastern approach of the Caribbean is a source of concern to all other Caribbean Powers, and in particular to the United States.

The British West Indies

Britain's interests in the Caribbean area are fully as ancient as her interests in North America. Her territorial claims date from the early 1620's, when a settlement was made in the Leeward Islands, followed almost immediately by a colony on Barbados. Jamaica was wrested from Spain in 1655, but Trinidad did not become British until 1797. Many of the British islands in the Caribbean have changed ownership repeatedly, having been claimed not only by Spain, but on occasion by France and Holland. During much of their colonial history these islands were modest pawns in contests of power whose main arena was Europe. Since the early nineteenth century, however, the British pattern of sovereignty in the West Indies has been relatively stable, and no changes in territory have occurred since 1815, when the Napoleonic Wars ended.

The use of a collective term like "British West Indies" gives an impression of cohesiveness and unity that is quite illusory when viewed in historical perspective. Only in recent decades have serious attempts been made to integrate these possessions with one other, and these efforts have not yet been crowned with success. Politically these islands have ignored each other through most of their history, and economically they have been more nearly competitive than supplementary. Their diverse histories have brought about a varied articulation in their administrative relationships to the Crown.

On the usual world map the Caribbean looks like a small region, and it is a convenient mental short-cut to lump it together as a unit. It comes as something of a shock to realize that Jamaica lies more than 1000 sea-miles from Trinidad, and that British Honduras is over 2000 miles from British Guiana. The British lands in the Caribbean are small bits of territory divided by much water and by the insular possessions of several other sovereign States. A tradition of tropical plantation agriculture is common to all of them, and sugar-growing has been the main source of income throughout their history. The native tribes, Arawaks and Caribs, disappeared early from most of the islands, and Negro slaves were brought from the Guinea coast to become the labor force. Plantation owners enjoyed widespread prosperity until the beginning of the nineteenth century, but since that time the people on the British sugar islands have lived mostly under a cloud of uncertainty, accentuated by periodic depressions. These recurring crises have had a multiple origin, and they can be explained only in part by the abolition of slavery (1834–38), by Britain's enactment of a free-trade policy, and by the rise in importance of beet sugar.

Until the middle of the nineteenth century the population of the islands had been mostly British, Negro, and mulatto, with the colored groups predominating numerically. But after the emancipation of the slaves large groups of indentured labor, mostly East Indian and Chinese, were brought in. The complex transfers of sovereignty on some of the islands assembled under British rule various groups of Dutch-, French-, and Spanish-speaking people, mostly colored. The sum-total of racial, cultural, and linguistic complexities in the British West Indies is as diverse as anywhere on the globe, and has been a powerful deterrent to cultural integration and to the growth of regional political maturity.

In one sense the problem of colonialism in the British West Indies differs from that in most other tropical colonies: there is no truly native population. With negligible exceptions the British are the oldest group in the area. But that does not mean that there is not a native problem; in fact, the problem, if anything, is multiplied. There is first the matter of geographic separatism. The Jamaican, no matter of what social stratum, considers himself a breed apart from the Barbadian, and *vice versa*. The same applies to inhabitants of Trinidad and the other islands. Superimposed is the complex problem of social and economic stratification, in which the East Indian groups, the Chinese groups, and the mulatto and Negro groups strive for political power at the expense of each other and of the politically and financially dominant but vastly outnumbered white groups. The undeniable fact that the non-whites have on the average a very low income; that their health, diet, sanitation and housing, though improving, leave much to be desired; that their large average family size and increasing population densities cause serious overcrowding in many areas; that they have a very low educational level and few effective opportunities to improve their education; and that they have not a few just grievances against their lot as they find it, has caused increasing numbers of them to feel not only dissatisfied but utterly frustrated, and has made them the easy prey of opportunist demagogues and Communist agitators.

Sugar at a few cents a pound is no longer the source of wealth that it was in the seventeenth and eighteenth centuries. For the last hundred years the British Caribbean colonies have been a net drain on the British Treasury, and this despite the fact that commercial agriculture has been diversified to include bananas, cacao, coconuts, oil palms, and many other crops; that Trinidad has become an important source of petroleum products; and that Jamaica has recently become an important source of bauxite. In spite of these developments the Caribbean islands have become an increasing financial burden to the United Kingdom. The

2F*

prestige that once went with the possession of colonies is now face to face with unpleasant economic realities. The modern trend, in the non-Communist world at least, is for colonies to be trained to assume a progressively greater share of self-government, leading eventually to a high degree of autonomy and perhaps eventual complete sovereignty. This has been the course of evolution in many parts of the British Empire, as it has also been the policy of the United States with respect to the Philippines and Puerto Rico. The conferences of the Organization of American States have repeatedly passed resolutions, the most recent in Caracas in 1954, to the effect that European colonies in the New World are anachronisms that must be eliminated. This brings up the question of a possible British Caribbean Federation, which might eventually become a self-governing dominion.

The British Caribbean Federation

For years there has been discussion among the inhabitants of the British West Indies and the various levels of government about the benefits that might result if the Caribbean colonies were more closely united. It has long been obvious that the colonies have problems in common, and it appears to many that co-operative effort might lead more directly and advantageously to common solutions. In other parts of the world administrative centralization, especially in technical matters, has frequently shown itself to be favorable to economic and social development.

It is not to be supposed that the West Indian colonies were completely unco-operative with each other even in the absence of specific plans for federation. Not only had there been various attempts at partial federation, but there had been co-operation in such matters as the Imperial College of Tropical Agriculture (founded in 1921 and located in Trinidad), the Barbados Sugar Cane Breeding Station, a Development and Welfare Organization (founded 1940), and the Anglo-American Caribbean Commission, which was set up in 1942. The latter was renamed the Caribbean Commission after France and the Netherlands joined in 1945. It has sponsored a number of important conferences, which have functioned as a forum for the exchange of ideas, and has created a Caribbean Research Council, whose technical committees have studied the basic problems of the Caribbean realm. The British colonies have contributed in many ways to the functioning of both the Commission and the Research Council.

In 1945 the British Secretary of State for the Colonies reopened the basic question of West Indian federation. He pointed out to the West Indian colonial governments that the initiative for political unity must come from within the area itself, and reaffirmed the British policy of promoting West Indian unity with the eventual aim of self-government. From this time on discussion of plans for federation has been vigorous.

Delegates from all the British West Indian colonies, with observers from British Guiana and British Honduras, held a conference in London in April 1953. They agreed to the establishment of a British Caribbean Federation, with headquarters in Grenada, to include all except the two mainland colonies.[2] By early 1955 full approval had not been obtained from the local colonial legislatures, and the future of the plan was very doubtful. The issues had been hotly debated, but not by the great mass of British West Indian subjects who, lacking political schooling, seemed to be largely apathetic. Federation is likely to come only if, in final balance, the problems of non-federation turn out to be even harder to bear than the problems of federation. It is obvious that federation *per se* will not solve the economic and social troubles of the islands, but it might create a more effective political framework within which solutions to common problems could be sought by co-operative effort.

The Panama Canal

The Canal Zone was established by the Treaty of 1903 between Panama and the United States. Within the Zone the latter was to have, in perpetuity, "all the rights, power and authority . . . which the United States would possess and exercise if it were the sovereign of the territory . . . to the entire exclusion of the exercise by the Republic of Panama of any such sovereign rights, power or authority." This extraordinary statement, an unprecedented compromise between North American necessity and Latin American dignity, is unfortunately subject to two interpretations. The United States has taken the position

---

[2] The original plan was to include British Honduras and British Guiana in the proposed Federation. But the two mainland colonies decided against the proposal for fear of being inundated by immigrants from the densely populated islands. In British Guiana the politically powerful East Indian group was afraid of being relegated to the status of a politically impotent minority.

that the Zone is completely under American control, and that Panama has little or no voice in how to run it. Panama, on the other hand, considers it Panamanian soil over which it has granted an easement and a few other concessions, but over which it has by no means relinquished all rights. The United States has at various times acceded to some of Panama's claims, but the two points of view have never been completely reconciled, and they have been a repeated source of irritation between the two countries. It is to be hoped that a new treaty concluded in 1955 will put an end to the misunderstandings of the past.

During the second world war the United States acquired 134 defense sites within the Republic of Panama, with a total area of fifty-eight square miles. The agreement provided that the United States might control these sites for the duration of the war and for one year after the signing of the definitive treaty of peace. By 1947 all but thirty-six had been returned. The United States wished to retain fourteen of the sites for a further period, especially the large Rio Hato Air Base, but the Panamanian National Assembly declined to extend the agreement, and the bases were returned forthwith. They were not reactivated even when the Republic of Panama invited the United Nations to make use of some of them after the outbreak of the Korean war in 1950. But the comprehensive treaty of 1955 between the United States and Panama included a clause by which the United States regained the use of the 30 sq. mile Rio Hato base for a further period of fifteen years.

The administration of the Canal Zone was modified in 1951 with the formation of the Panama Canal Company, a United States Government corporation. Formerly the Zone had been administered by the U.S. Army, and the Canal was considered of sufficient strategic importance to justify annual operating deficits. The new Company is required by its charter to be self-sustaining, and is expected to operate the Canal without expense to the U.S. Government. This change implies a reassessment of the role of the Canal in the strategy of the United States. It is evident that the strategic importance of the Canal declined during and after the second world war, partly because of the development of a two-ocean navy by the United States, but more particularly because of the emergence of effective intercontinental air power. Work begun before Pearl Harbor on a projected third set of locks has not been resumed, and the proposal to convert to a sea-level canal has received little real support. But the Canal's commercial importance, as measured by volume of maritime traffic, has constantly increased.

The pressure of the Panama Canal Company to avoid operational losses has resulted in the withdrawal of many of the perquisites which American civilian workers in the Zone had come to expect as their due, and resignations have been numerous since 1952. It was widely felt that toll rates should have been raised to make up operational deficits, instead of reducing the benefits that have compensated American labor for living in an alien, tropical environment. But toll rates have never been raised; they were, in fact, lowered slightly in 1936. Shipping interests in the States are not in favor of raising tolls, nor does the Administration of the Canal Company wish it, allegedly for fear that South Pacific traffic might be diverted elsewhere.

In August 1955 two years of negotiations were concluded between the Government of the Republic of Panama and the United States which resulted in a revision of the treaty arrangements regarding the use of the Canal Zone. The Panamanian Government asked for and received an increase in the annual payments made by the United States. The schedule of 250,000 dollars a year agreed on in the 1903 Convention was raised to 430,000 dollars in 1936, after Panama successfully argued that the dollar had been devalued by a corresponding amount. There has been further devaluation in the last two decades, while toll receipts have increased greatly. The new annuity is 1,930,000 dollars. Various other grievances have been resolved, among them competition in the Zone with Panamanian business interests, discrimination against Panamanian labor, and the relative inability of Panama to sell goods in the Zone because of restrictive American regulations.

The Panama Canal is becoming less a strategic focus vital to American security and more exclusively a commercial cross roads operated at cost by the United States for the benefit of itself and the world. The greatest beneficiary of the Canal is the Republic of Panama itself.

Conclusion

The Caribbean realm is a New World shatter belt in which political and economic colonialism survives to a greater degree than elsewhere in the Hemisphere. But the remnants of political colonialism are not necessarily an evil under present conditions. If democratic self-government is the aim, then the way must be prepared. Democracy cannot be imposed from above. Nor is economic colonialism all bad, provided that it involves a measure of self-determination and a goodly amount of local participation in the development of policy. For many Caribbean islands the sale of the fruits of tropical agriculture in non-tropical markets is the best way to create the wealth they need for their own advancement.

The course of history has made the United States the predominant Power in the Caribbean. Within this American hegemony, in friendly partnership with the other American States and the European colonial Powers, the future destiny of the West Indies must be unfolded. It is fortunate that public opinion in the United States and the rest of the western world has now advanced to the point where the development of the area will be watched with friendly eyes, to the end that the Caribbean peoples themselves may develop their lands in their own best interests.

FURTHER READING

BIESANZ, JOHN, "The Economy of Panama," in *Inter-American Economic Affairs*, vol. vi (1), 3–28 (1952).

BLANSHARD, PAUL, *Democracy and Empire in the Caribbean* (Macmillan, New York, 1947).

BURN W. L., *The British West Indies* (Hutchinson, London, 1951).

The Economic Development of Jamaica, Report by a Mission of the International Bank for Reconstruction and Development (Johns Hopkins University Press, Baltimore, Md., 1952).

FOX, ANNETTE BAKER, *Freedom and Welfare in the Caribbean, a Colonial Dilemma* (Harcourt, Brace, New York, 1949).

HANSEN, MILLARD, and WELLS, HENRY (editors), "Puerto Rico; a Study in Democratic Development," in *The Annals of the American Academy of Political and Social Science*, vol. cclxxxv (January 1953).

LEWIS, W. ARTHUR, "The Industrialization of the British West Indies," in *Caribbean Economic Review*, vol. ii (1), 1–61 (1950).

LISTOWEL, THE EARL OF, HINDEN, RITA, FARLEY, RAWLE, and HUGHES, COLIN, *Challenge to the British Caribbean* (Fabian Publications, Ltd, Research Series No. 150, London, 1952).

PATTERSON, BRUCE, "Britain's Caribbean Colonies: Tragic, Doomed Lands?" in *International Journal*, vol. 9 (1): 34–40 (winter 1954).

PERKINS, DEXTER, *The United States and the Caribbean* (Harvard University Press, Cambridge, Mass., and Oxford University Press, 1947).

PERLOFF, HARVEY S., *Puerto Rico's Economic Future: a Study in Planned Development* (University of Chicago Press, Chicago, Ill., and Cambridge University Press, 1950).

PROUDFOOT (MRS), MARY, *Britain and the United States in the Caribbean: a Comparative Study in Methods of Development* (Faber, London, 1954).

Report on Cuba: Findings and Recommendations of an Economic and Technical Mission organized by the International Bank for Reconstruction and Development in Collaboration with the Government of Cuba in 1950 (Johns Hopkins University Press, Baltimore, Md., 1951).

REVERT, E., "Géographie Politique du Monde Caraïbe," in *Annales de Géographie*, vol. lx (318), 34–47 (1951).

UNITED NATIONS: Report of the United Nations Mission of Technical Assistance to the Republic of Haiti (Lake Success, New York, 1949).

WHITSON, AGNES M., and HORSFALL, LUCY F., *Britain and the West Indies* (Longmans, London, 1948).

WILGUS, A. CURTIS (editor), *The Caribbean: Peoples, Problems and Prospects* (University of Florida Press, Gainesville, Fla., 1952).

TABLE 1
Caribbean Statistical Table

Name	Political Status	Area (square miles)	Population (thousands)[1]	Population Density	Capital	Population of Capital (thousands)
Cuba	Republic	44,206	5,871 (1953)	133	Habana	1,157
Haiti	Republic	10,714	3,200	308	Port-au-Prince	424
Dominican Republic	Republic	19,129	2,236	117	Ciudad Trujillo	182
Puerto Rico	Commonwealth (U.S.)	3,435	2,240	652	San Juan	360
Virgin Islands	U.S. Territory	133	24	180	Charlotte Amalie	11
Jamaica	British Crown Colony	4,411	1,472	334	Kingston	308
Trinidad (and Tobago)	British Colony	1,864	670	359	Port of Spain	111
Windward Islands	Four British Colonies under one Governor	821	293	357	St George's	6
Dominica	British Colony	305	57	187	Roseau	12
St Lucia	British Colony	233	83	356	Castries	24
St Vincent	British Colony	150	71	473	Kingstown	5
Grenada	British Colony	133	82	616	St George's	6
Leeward Islands	British Federal Colony	423	120	284	St John's	11
Antigua	Presidency	171	46 (1950)	269	St John's	11
St Kitts-Nevis	Presidency	147	47 (1951)	320	Basseterre	30
Montserrat	Presidency	38	16 (1951)	421	Plymouth	2
Br. Virgin Islands	Presidency	67	7 (1951)	104	Road Town	0.8
Barbados	British Colony	166	219	1,320	Bridgetown	15
British Honduras	British Crown Colony	8,867	73	8	Belize	17
British Guiana	British Colony	83,000	444	5	Georgetown	87
Guadeloupe	French Overseas Department	687	279 (1951)	406	Basse-Terre	13
Martinique	French Overseas Department	385	283	735	Fort-de-France	66
French Guiana	French Overseas Department	34,740	30	1	Cayenne	15
Surinam	Constituent part of the Kingdom of the Netherlands	54,291	227	4	Paramaribo	83
Netherlands Antilles	Constituent part of the Kingdom of the Netherlands	383	176	460	Willemstad	44
Curaçao		173	111	642	Willemstad	44
Aruba		70	56	800		
Bonaire		112	5	45		
St Maarten		13	2	154		
St Eustatius		12	1	83		
Saba		3.5	1	286		
Panama	Republic	29,224	864 (1953)	30	Panama	248

[1] Data for 1952 unless otherwise noted.

CHAPTER XXXVII

Latin America : State Patterns and Boundary Problems

PRESTON E. JAMES

THE outlines and internal patterns of the twenty independent countries of Latin America raise a number of problems of political geography. How did it happen that the several Portuguese colonies all joined together in one State of vast proportions? How did it happen that the Spanish colonies divided themselves into eighteen States, some of very small territorial spread? Were the States of Latin America formed by a process in any way similar to that common in Europe? Were they formed by a process common to all of Latin America? Are there similarities within the Latin American area with regard to the internal structure of the States? These and other questions call for investigation if we are to understand the meaning of the present political geography of Latin America.

All these twenty Latin American States came into being as independent political units over a period of a century. The first State to emerge was the Negro Republic of Haiti in 1804; the most recent one was Panama in 1903. In many, however, the boundaries have been shifted since independence was first established, in some by negotiation and arbitration, in others by war. Brazil is notable for the peaceful settlement of all its boundary problems; Argentina and Chile, after some show of hostility, submitted part of their common boundary problem to the King of England as arbiter. Notable boundary changes involving Chile and Peru–Bolivia, Paraguay and Bolivia, Peru and Ecuador, Haiti and the Dominican Republic resulted from hostilities. Mexico lost a vast northern area to the United States; and the United States was involved in the loss of Panama to Colombia. A few unsettled boundary problems remain, especially in Central America, and colonies of Great Britain are disputed in British Honduras by Guatemala, and in the Falkland Islands by Argentina. Boundary problems in Antarctica are mostly fought on paper. The geographic interpretation of these changes and of the contemporary situation is the subject of this chapter.

How Independent States appeared in Latin America

A modern, independent nation-State is a politically organized area established and maintained for the purpose of preserving, defending, and fostering the development of a distinctive body of traditions and institutions. The traditions and institutions that characterize a particular State constitute what is called the "state-idea," the *raison d'être* that commands the loyalty of the people of a State. Unless a great majority of the people in a politically organized area actually accept and support a state-idea the State is a relatively weak one and, under pressure, could easily break apart. If a state-idea is supported by a minority of the people, only a strong central authority can hold the State together. Fundamentally, States must be evaluated in terms of this intangible but none the less real concept.[1]

In the half-century that followed the Revolutionary War in Anglo-America, during which most of the Latin American countries established their independence, the idea on which all this revolutionary activity was based was the desire for freedom. But freedom from what and for whom? In the first place it should be clear that at no time was the desire for freedom felt to be an individual matter in Latin America. There was no question of the right of the individual to civil or religious liberty, or to any form of legal protection from a powerful and dictatorial government. This aspect of the desire for freedom, which found its way into the basic documents of Anglo-American independence, was not strong among the Latin Americans.

In Latin America the desire for freedom was an idea developed almost exclusively by relatively small circles of politically conscious people: American-born landowners, officers of the army, and the creole bureaucracy. These people resented their dependent status. The freedom they desired was from the control of emissaries of Spain; the purpose of revolt was to gain the right to do their own governing. But the great majority of the people who lived in Latin America were not directly concerned,

---

[1] Preston E. James and Clarence F. Jones (editors), *American Geography, Inventory and Prospect* (Syracuse, N.Y., 1954), pp. 168–225.

and when independence was established many of the new countries were essentially without a positive state-idea.

Political control from outside, then, was not tolerable for the politically conscious minorities of America. But outside of what areas? What determined the spread of the new national territories? In some cases several geographically distinct communities were grouped together in one country; in others similarly distinct communities established and maintained their political separation from each other.

It is a fundamental fact of Latin American geography that the pattern of population and settlement has remained one of isolated clusters.[2] There are distinct areas of concentrated settlement, each focused on a single urban nucleus. In few places is there an overlap between the supporting areas of two neighboring cities. Even in Brazil, where two cities of almost equal size are located within a few hundred miles of each other, the supporting territory of each city remains generally quite distinct, and an inter-fingering of urban services is found in only one small sector. In most places the areas of concentrated rural settlement are separated from each other by thinly peopled areas, through which the lines of communication are poorly developed.

Furthermore, the areas of concentrated settlement generally bear a simple relationship to the political territories. That is, each cluster of population forms the core of a politically organized area, and the boundaries usually run through the relatively empty country between the areas of concentrated settlement. There are a few notable exceptions to this general picture, where international boundaries actually cut through the middle of densely settled areas; yet the exceptions are not sufficiently numerous to destroy the validity of the generalization. In some cases the territory of an independent State encompasses just one core of concentrated settlement; more often the national territories include several such clusters. What factors determined whether a modern independent State embraces one area of concentrated settlement or several?

The two most important factors appear to have been: (1) position relative to the centers and boundaries of the Spanish colonial administrative areas, and (2) the relative strength of the local economy.

The Spanish authorities experimented during the colonial period with a variety of patterns of territorial organization.[3] The two outstanding

[2] Preston E. James, *Latin America* (Odyssey, New York, revised edition, 1950).

[3] C. H. Haring, *The Spanish Empire in America* (Oxford University Press, New York, 1947).

centers of Spanish colonization were Mexico City and Lima, each reflecting in its location the presence of one of the two major concentrations of Indians in America. Each of these cities became the administrative center of a viceroyalty, the Viceroyalty of New Spain and the Viceroyalty of Peru respectively. But as Spanish settlement spread the impossibility of maintaining effective administrative control from just two centers became obvious. Two other viceroyalties were set up, each reflecting the presence of secondary, but still important, concentrations of Indians: the Viceroyalty of New Granada administered from Bogotá, and the Viceroyalty of La Plata administered from Buenos Aires (rather than from Asunción, because of the difficulty of reaching it). But the territories of these four viceroyalties were further subdivided into captaincies-general and presidencies, in which there was a considerable measure of administrative independence. The Central American area, as far to the south-east as Costa Rica, was included in the Captaincy-General of Guatemala and administered from Guatemala. Similarly, Chile became a captaincy-general in the Viceroyalty of Peru; and the whole of Upper Peru from Lake Titicaca eastward was administered as the Presidency of Charcas, a part of the Viceroyalty of La Plata.

In the process of establishing independence the areas of concentrated settlement that were located close to the centers of colonial administration and had been effectively governed from these centers were included in the territory of the new independent States. These were Mexico, Peru, Colombia, and Argentina.

As distance from these centers of colonial power increased, the tendency for the separate clusters or groups of clusters to break off in additional independent States increased. Chile, compact around its single core of settlement, remote from Peru and isolated at the end of the hemisphere, became a sovereign State. Bolivia, remote both from Lima and from Buenos Aires, became independent. The single cluster of people in Paraguay, isolated both from the Andean centers and from Buenos Aires, became independent not because the political leaders of Asunción took positive steps to achieve this status but rather because the Argentines were too busy with Chile and Peru to bother with such an economically unimportant place.

The Central American areas of settlement were small and not very prosperous during the colonial period. Except for the Mayan area of Guatemala there were few concentrations of Indians; there were no great discoveries of gold or silver to attract the Spanish colonists. At first the whole area as far as Costa Rica was included in the territory of independent Mexico. After only three years, however, the politically ambitious ruling group of Guatemala was able to break away from Mexico City and to take under its control all the small communities that were even more remote from Mexico and had been included in the Captaincy-General of Guatemala. But the difficulties of communication, the weakness of the administrative machinery, and the general poverty of the area resulted, in 1839, in a further breaking down. Guatemala maintained its hold only on the areas of Mayan culture (except for Copán, which became a part of Honduras). Along the main highway south-eastward from Guatemala City, El Salvador, including a single area of concentrated settlement, established its independence. Farther along the highway the area of concentrated settlement in the Nicaraguan Lowland declared its independence as Nicaragua. Isolated in the highlands and off the main highway of communication, the politically conscious silver miners of Tegucigalpa established control over four small separate farming communities. Only in peripheral Copán were they able to penetrate Maya country. Finally, the settlements around San José in the highlands of Costa Rica, like Paraguay, became independent by default.

Bolívar's United States of Colombia also fell to pieces. The diverse and strongly contrasted communities scattered through mountainous Colombia were only held together with difficulty by the genius and enthusiasm of Bolívar. But even he was unable to hold the remoter communities of Ecuador and Venezuela. Peripheral Panama broke away when the negotiations for the building of a canal focused world attention on this isolated spot.

In the West Indies the Negroes of Haiti gained their independence from the French sugar planters in 1804, extending their control over the whole island of Hispaniola. In 1844, however, the small white group that survived on the eastern side of the island gained independence for the Dominican Republic from the mulatto rulers of Haiti. The independence of Cuba in 1898, as well as the establishment of Puerto Rico as a possession of the United States, were closely tied to internal politics in the United States and to the production of sugar-cane.

The eastern side of South America had been occupied by the Portuguese. Disregarding the original line of demarcation between Spanish and Portuguese spheres of interest (approximately the 50th meridian W. as established by the Treaty of Tordesillas), the semi-military expeditions which went out from São Paulo pushed the Portuguese-occupied territory westward as far as the beginning of dense forest (Chapter XXXVIII, Fig. 1). A belt of dense forest effectively separated the Spanish and the Portuguese settlements; where this forest belt reached the east coast between the Orinoco and the Amazon the Guiana colonies of England, the Netherlands, and France were established. The one place where Portuguese and Spanish colonists came into close contact was in grass-covered Uruguay. When Brazil declared its independence in 1822 the territory claimed as part of Brazil extended southward to the shores of La Plata. But the Argentines also had been active in the Banda Oriental, as the Uruguayan shore was called, and Argentina did not want to find the Portuguese firmly established on the main channel of the Plata. In 1828, through the intervention of Great Britain, Uruguay was recognized as an independent State—a typical buffer state.

The independence of Brazil was based on the same desire for freedom from outside political control that motivated the Spanish colonists. But there was a difference. From 1808 until 1822 the Portuguese emperor had used Rio de Janeiro as the administrative center of the Portuguese empire, during a period when the homeland had been under the control of Napoleon. When the emperor returned to Portugal, his son, remaining in Brazil, declared independence and the right to freedom from outside control. The Portuguese, who are not given to violent solutions, made the transition to independence by compromise and without dislocation of established administrative institutions.

The Significance of Physical Barriers

As we review all these new national territories, with boundaries generally drawn through the empty country between the areas of concentrated settlement, in how many cases is it possible to identify specific physical barriers that, by increasing the difficulties of communication, can be said to have been a causal factor in separating one new nation from its neighbors?[4] Certainly in the case of Brazil the belt of dense forest separating the Spanish and Portuguese spheres of interest in South America was a physical barrier which can be shown to have been a factor in the general location of the national boundaries. Only in the

[4] Robert S. Platt, *Latin America, Countrysides and United Regions* (McGraw-Hill, New York, 1942).

south where Brazil borders Uruguay and Argentina was there no physical barrier to use in the demarcation of the boundary. Between Argentina and Chile the great wall of the Andes interposed a physical barrier except in the far south; and in the north Chile was separated from its neighbors by the Atacama desert. Between Peru and Ecuador, too, there is a zone of very rugged terrain where the main Amazon tributaries have cut deeply into the Andes. Here even the Inca road descended to the coast on the way from Cuzco to Quito.

But where else can such physical barriers be found? The Titicaca Basin is no barrier; in fact, it has always been more difficult to travel from Cochabamba to Santa Cruz, both within Bolivia, than to travel from La Paz to Mollendo in Peru. There are no physical barriers separating Ecuador from Colombia, or Colombia from Venezuela, which are so difficult to cross as those to be found within the territories of these countries. Similarly, the physical difficulties of travel are much greater within Mexico than across the border of Mexico and Guatemala. No barrier separates Guatemala from either Honduras or El Salvador, or El Salvador from Nicaragua. Perhaps the climb from the Gulf of Fonseca or the Lempa Valley of El Salvador to the highland communities of Honduras offered some difficulties; yet these difficulties were no greater than must be encountered on a trip from Tegucigalpa to the other small clusters of people included within Honduras. No serious difficulties of terrain separate Nicaragua from Costa Rica, or Costa Rica from Panama. The difficulty of building a road from Medellín to Cartagena in Colombia is no greater than would have to be faced in building a road across the border into Panama. Even on rugged Hispaniola, where the mountainous terrain interposes great difficulties of communication, the ranges run at right angles to the international boundary between Haiti and the Dominican Republic.

Clearly it is false to insist that the separation of the Spanish colonial area into so many independent countries was a result of difficulties of communication imposed by physical conditions of the land.

Internal Patterns of Independent States

The new Latin American States did include internal barriers that made the establishment of efficient administration difficult. The internal barriers were, in some cases, the result of steepness of slope or of density of jungle growth. But in others it was a result of differences of language and tradition, even ethnic differences. And always there are the problems of connecting one area of settlement with another through intervening empty space. It takes a strongly ordered society to overcome such difficulties.

Each of these Latin American States began its independent existence with little in the way of a positive state-idea. The negative idea of throwing off the shackles of outside control had been achieved. There followed a period of conflict within each State during which the separate areas of concentrated settlement jockeyed for political power. In this jockeying each country has had a different history, and the results in the contemporary picture are different. Some have never formulated a clear state-idea that can claim the support of a majority of the people, and these countries have had to depend for their internal order on a strong central authority. But some have gained popular support for a distinctive national program. Brazil started with the great advantage of a language of its own, Portuguese, which served to distinguish it clearly from other American States. Haiti had the similar advantage of a language of its own, plus the relative purity of its ethnic make-up. The other countries lacked these advantages.

In the process of establishing a workable political order, whether based on a popular state-idea or on central authority, each State has had to adjust itself to a somewhat different internal pattern. In this connexion we are using the word 'pattern' to refer to geographic arrangement —that is, to the areal differentiation of the national territory. Other social-science disciplines make use of the same word to refer to functionally related institutions, which is another matter. We are discussing here the internal pattern of areally differentiated parts. In any analysis of a State with regard to the elements of its success or failure as a functioning political organization there are four fundamental parts to be distinguished.

First, it is necessary to distinguish between the total national territory and the effective national territory. The total territory is the whole of the area included within the national boundaries; the effective national territory is that part of the whole area from which the citizens of the country derive a living. Obviously any statistics of population density must be related to the effective national territory and not the total national territory.

Second, it is necessary to observe the areal relations of the areas of

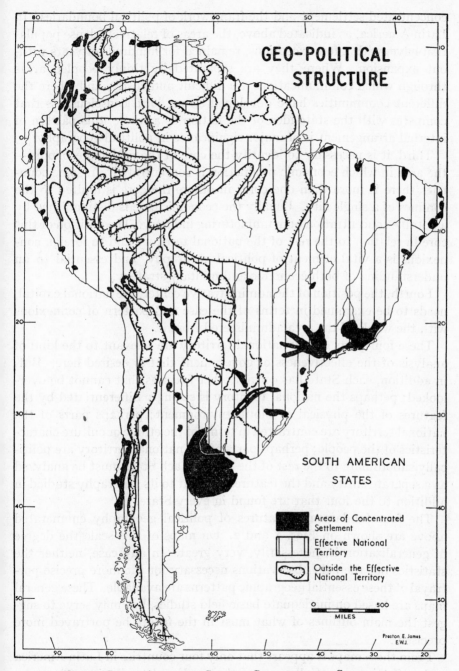

FIG. 1. SOUTH AMERICAN STATES: GEO-POLITICAL STRUCTURE

Inside the map:

GEO-POLITICAL
STRUCTURE

SOUTH AMERICAN
STATES

Areas of Concentrated Settlement

Effective National Territory

Outside the Effective National Territory

0   500
MILES

Preston E. James
E.W.J.

concentrated settlement and the framework of political boundaries. In Latin America, as indicated above, the areas of relatively dense population have, with a few exceptions, remained for hundreds of years without expansion. Where they are separated by thinly peopled areas through which communications are difficult and costly, and where the different communities have developed strong local consciousness that competes with the state-idea of the nation as a whole, this pattern of internal arrangement is of major significance in political geography.

Third, it is necessary to identify the core of the national economy— the area in which economic production is concentrated. In some countries there is more than one core; in others the core is limited to the confines of a single city. Usually the economic core is distinguished by a notable concentration of manufacturing industry. The position of this core in relation to the rest of the national territory and to foreign connexions is a vital element of political geography, and essential to an understanding of both economic and military strategy.

Fourth, the position of the administrative center, the national capital, needs to be examined in terms of the ease and pattern of connexions with the whole of the area administered from it.

These four parts of any national territory are relevant to the kind of analysis of the effectiveness of government that is desired here. But, in addition, each State has certain other features that cannot be overlooked; perhaps the national territory is strongly differentiated by the features of the physical or biotic environment; perhaps parts of the national territory are contrasted in terms of the ethnic or culture characteristics of the people; perhaps parts of the national territory are politically subordinate to the rest of the State. Each State must be analyzed as a separate entity and the features peculiar to its geography studied in addition to the four that are found in every State.

The four fundamental features of political geography enumerated above are shown on Figs. 1 and 2. On maps of this scale the degree of generalization is, necessarily, very great. In any case, neither the statistics nor the field observations necessary for the more precise portrayal of these essential geographic patterns are available. These general maps are based on inadequate basic field studies, but may serve to suggest the main outlines of what must in the future be portrayed more precisely.

From these maps it appears that only four countries in Latin America make effective use of all parts of their national territories. These are

Uruguay, El Salvador, Cuba, and Haiti. In all the other countries there are areas large enough to appear on Figs. 1 and 2 that are essentially unproductive.

On these same maps the areal relations between the areas of concentrated settlement and the national boundaries can be observed. These maps, being based on preliminary population maps published elsewhere,[5] are somewhat more precise than the maps of effective national territory,

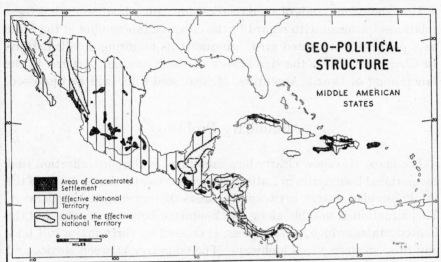

FIG. 2. MIDDLE AMERICAN STATES: GEO-POLITICAL STRUCTURE

although the progress of careful field studies will refine the outlines of these areas in detail. The countries of Latin America can be placed in four major categories, as follows:

(1) Countries in which there is a single major area of concentrated settlement containing the primate city of the country—Cuba, Guatemala, El Salvador, Nicaragua, Costa Rica, Chile, Paraguay, Uruguay.

(2) Countries in which there are several areas of concentrated settlement, each with its urban nucleus, but in which the urban nucleus of one of these areas is a primate city more than twice the size of the second city—Mexico, Honduras, Haiti, Dominican Republic, Venezuela, Colombia, Peru, Argentina.

(3) Countries in which there are several areas of concentrated settlement each with its urban nucleus, but in which the primate

[5] Preston E. James, *op. cit.*

city (which is more than twice the size of the second city) is situated outside the areas of concentrated settlement— Panama, Bolivia.

(4) Countries in which there are several areas of concentrated settlement, each with its urban nucleus, but in which there is no primate city (there are, instead, two cities of almost equal size)—Ecuador, Brazil.

How these four kinds of areal relationship came about, and what these relationships mean with regard to the effective functioning of the State as a politically organized area, are questions requiring detailed study. In Chapter XXXIX the significance of these internal patterns in the functioning of Brazil, Argentina, Mexico, and Chile will be discussed.

Boundary Problems

The maps also show clearly how important is the generalization that the national boundaries in Latin America are mostly drawn through the thinly peopled spaces between the areas of concentrated settlement. This situation is notable along the boundary between Mexico and the United States, which, nevertheless, is crossed by three major rail lines and three modern paved highways. The boundary between Mexico and Guatemala is not only drawn through empty country, but the sectors of the Pan American Highway in the two countries reach the common boundary at points which are separated by some fifty miles, and there is no all-weather connexion between the two ends. Although it is possible to drive on this highway from Guatemala to Costa Rica, it is not possible to cross either of the national boundaries of Panama.

The national boundaries in South America are similarly drawn for the most part through empty country. To be sure, there is a motor highway that is passable in all weather from Caracas in Venezuela to Puerto Montt in Chile; and there are trans-Andean highways and railroads between Argentina and both Bolivia and Chile. A railroad connects Argentina with Paraguay, and there are rail and highway connexions between Uruguay and Brazil, Argentina and Brazil, and between Brazil and eastern Bolivia. But these connexions have been built and maintained through many miles of empty country.

There are a few notable exceptions to this generalization. The boundary which partitions Hispaniola between Haiti and the Dominican

Republic marks the eastern edge of concentrated settlement in Haiti; but the Dominican side of the border is very thinly peopled. In South America there are four places where national boundaries pass through the midst of areas of concentrated settlement: (1) the Venezuela-Colombia border between Cúcuta and San Cristobal; (2) the Colombia-Ecuador border in the Basin of Tulcán; (3) the Peru-Bolivia border in the Basin of Lake Titicaca; and (4) the Argentine-Brazil border along the Uruguay river.

The first three of these exceptional situations are similar in origin. During the Spanish colonial period, and in the first decades of independence when the various separate communities were establishing their political positions, communities of Indians did not participate in the political affairs of the Spaniards. There was no movement for freedom on the part of the Indian community leaders. When boundary lines were drawn defining the area to be governed from a capital city the Indian communities were treated as part of the land. Here two contrasted cultures were superimposed: the political boundary is a concept which has meaning to the Europeans, but no meaning to the Indians. Specifically, in the case of the Colombia-Ecuador boundary, the position of the line through the midst of the Indian community of Tulcán was determined by conditions in Bogotá and Quito at the time of the break-up of Bolívar's United States of Colombia. The southern part of what has become Colombia might well have been included in Ecuador, for it had been occupied by Spaniards coming from Quito and had been administered from that place. But when the armed forces from Bogotá and Quito were in conflict a revolt in the Ecuadorean capital at that critical moment gave the armies from Bogotá the advantage. The boundary was established along the Tulcán river, which had been drawn on a map. But the map did not outline the area of concentrated settlement occupied by Indians, nor did it show the empty Páramo de Boliche just south of Tulcán that might have been used most effectively for the location of a boundary. The boundary between Peru and Bolivia crosses the Titicaca Basin along a line established in colonial times between the Viceroyalty of Peru and the Viceroyalty of La Plata which similarly bisects an area of dense Indian settlement.

The boundary between Argentina and Brazil, when originally drawn, did pass through empty country, just as did the boundary between Brazil and Uruguay. But during the present century both Argentina and Brazil have moved colonists into this boundary area for the purpose of creating dense settlement as a barrier to penetration from the other side. The intense rivalry between Portuguese and Spaniards of the colonial period has been carried on into the period of independence as rivalry between Argentina and Brazil. The critical and sensitive area where these two major powers face each other is along the Uruguay river.

During the century that followed independence there were numerous boundary disputes that had to be worked out, especially where the colonial lines of delimitation had been left vague.[6] One of the great accomplishments of Brazilian diplomacy has been the peaceful settlement of all its extensive boundaries, none of which was clearly marked at the time of independence. Only in Uruguay was a disputed zone actually fought over. Elsewhere peaceful negotiation was followed by joint boundary surveys. Argentina and Chile also settled their common boundary by arbitration. The one in the south attracted much attention because of the surveys carried out by a British expedition which established on maps the fact that " the highest crest of the Andes " did not, in fact, "separate the waters of the Atlantic and the Pacific."[7] The famous Christ of the Andes erected on the crest of the Uspallata Pass between Mendoza and Los Andes commemorates the fact that these two countries settled their dispute by peaceful means.

But not all the boundary disputes were settled in this way. Two major conflicts involved the boundaries of Bolivia. One of these wars resulted in pushing the national territory of Bolivia back from the Pacific Coast. In the early days of independence the political sovereignty in the Atacama Desert was defined in terms of the different oases, but clearly demarcated lines through the empty and then unproductive desert between the oases were not drawn. Peru's territory included Tacna and its port Arica. Bolivia's territory included Calama and its port Antofagasta. Chile's territory extended as far north as the oasis of Copiapó and its port Caldera. But, with the discovery and exploitation of sodium nitrate and copper, exactly defined boundaries became critical. Chile, which had been most active in developing the nitrate works, irritated by the insistent attempts of the Bolivians and Peruvians to extend their effective national territory over this previously empty area, finally resorted to war. The Chilean armies were successful, and in 1884 the Chileans drew new boundaries, leaving only the ownership of

[6] Gordon Ireland, *Boundaries, Possessions, and Conflicts in South America* (Cambridge, Mass., Oxford University Press, 1938).
[7] T. H. Holdich, *The Countries of the King's Award* (Hurst and Blackett, London, 1904).

the oasis of Tacna and its port Arica to be settled later. For many years this unsettled boundary problem remained to trouble the peaceful relations of the hemisphere, for not until 1929 did the two countries agree to the suggestion that Tacna should be given back to Peru, and Arica be given to Chile to administer as a free port for Bolivia.

One of the most dangerous areas of vague boundaries had been inherited from the colonial period in the Gran Chaco, a vast forested plain which lies between Bolivia, Paraguay, Brazil, and Argentina. In the colonial period the Spanish settlers at Asunción, in an area populated by the Guarani Indians, were isolated from the Andean mining communities by the difficulty of crossing the Chaco. To be sure, colonists from Asunción did push around the northern end of the Chaco to establish Santa Cruz near the eastern Andean piedmont in what is now Bolivia. But the chief direction of spread from Asunción was down the Paraguay and Parana rivers to Sante Fé, Rosario, and Buenos Aires (all of which were settled from Asunción). To cross the Chaco from the Parana river was not easy. The Chaco is a vast, featureless plain, sloping gently from the base of the mountains eastward. The rivers emerging from the Andes sprawl in winding and shifting channels: in the rainy season the flood waters spread over vast areas; in the dry season the river channels often become only strings of stagnant pools. Only the Salado and the Dulce, two rivers that run from the vicinity of Tucumán toward Santa Fé, provided a dependable supply of fresh water. Farther north the Chaco constituted a broad barrier between the Paraguayan settlers and those of the Andean piedmont. This great forested country remained essentially empty; and although the northern boundary of Argentina had been established along the Pilcomayo (when the channel of this river could be found), and the boundary of Brazil had been established along the Paraguay (except for the fortress of Corumbá on a range of hills west of the river), the limits between Paraguay and Bolivia remained vague. The boundary usually shown on maps was that of the Presidency of Charcas and had never been demarcated.

A variety of causes led to the war of 1932–35 between Bolivia and Paraguay. In a country like Bolivia, where the areas of concentrated settlement are small isolated mountain basins or long narrow ribbons along the valley bottoms, the establishment of an ordered society is most difficult. One way to gather the support of politically unstable communities is to claim attack from outside. Many Bolivians were told that the country was being encircled, shut off from the sea and so strangled, and that the war was an effort to establish an outlet through the Paraguay river (as if that river, which is not navigable for ocean vessels, could offer such an outlet). The problem also involved the possession of oilfields that were known to exist near the base of the Andes and were coveted by both Argentina and Brazil. The result of all this foreign intrigue, focused on an essentially empty area of vague boundaries and involving two countries in which the great majority of the people were quite ignorant of the geographic facts and the political realities, was a hard-fought war. The Paraguayans, brilliantly led, defeated the Bolivians, pushed them back almost, but not quite, to the mountain piedmont. The new boundary was established along the battle line when the two countries, exhausted and impoverished, and urged by the other American nations to stop fighting, agreed to accept and to demarcate a new boundary. [8]

Another area of vague boundaries in South America was in the upper Amazon. Here, in the midst of the trackless rain forest that so effectively separated the centers of Spanish colonization from those of the Portuguese, the only spots of settlement were along the river banks. The Brazilians had established their western boundary in this country by purchase from Bolivia of Acre Territory in 1903 and by negotiation with the other countries involved. But to the west of Brazil and east of the base of the Andes was a vast and mostly empty area claimed by Peru, Ecuador, and Colombia. Colombia, negotiating with Peru for territory claimed by Ecuador, succeeded in establishing a corridor along the Brazilian border southward to the Marañon, the main stream of the Amazon. [9] This narrow land connexion included within the total national territory of Colombia looks impressive on a political map, but it becomes geographic nonsense on a map of effective national territory. During the 1940's Peru used its army to press for a solution of its overlapping claims with Ecuador. The two countries agreed to set up a boundary commission to demarcate a boundary to be drawn some fifty miles upstream from the heads of launch navigation on the tributaries to the Marañon. Iquitos, the one center of Peruvian settlement on the upper Amazon, was no longer claimed by Ecuador. At last a line had been agreed upon through this empty country which is the last remaining

[8] P. M. Ynsfran (editor), *The Epic of the Chaco: Marshal Estigarribia's Memoirs of the Chaco War, 1932–1935* (Austin, Texas, 1950).
[9] Robert S. Platt, "Conflicting Territorial Claims in the Upper Amazon," in C. C. Colby (editor), *Geographic Aspects of International Relations* (Chicago, Lectures of the Harris Foundation, 1938).

location of the mythical El Dorado, the search for which makes such fascinating reading.

There are more unsettled boundary disputes in Middle America than in South America. Five such disputes among the Central American countries include two in which a considerable extent of territory is involved.[10] These two are on the border between Panama and Costa Rica, and on the border between Nicaragua and Honduras. Minor points of disagreement exist on the borders between Costa Rica and Nicaragua, and Honduras and El Salvador. On the Island of Hispaniola there is still not complete agreement on the boundary between Haiti and the Dominican Republic.

In two parts of Latin America there are colonies of Great Britain that are still disputed. In British Honduras there is a remnant of the much more extensive British holdings along the once empty forests of the Caribbean coast in Central America. The British colony in eastern Nicaragua has been absorbed in the national territory of Nicaragua. The Guatemalans from time to time press a claim to British Honduras based on the alleged failure of the British to co-operate in providing a means of transportation from the area of concentrated settlement in the Guatemala Highlands to the Caribbean near Belize, as agreed in the treaty of 1859. Another unsettled conflict is that between Argentina and Great Britain regarding the possession of the Falkland Islands, known in Argentina as the Islas Malvinas. From 1592, when the islands were first discovered by the British, until 1832, when a British expedition returned to reoccupy the islands and to claim them as a British possession, there was a long history of temporary settlement by British, French, and Argentine colonists. The United States was involved in connexion with a dispute concerning the rights of certain whaling and fishing vessels to make use of the islands. Since 1832 the British have held the Falklands, admitting no possibility of other claims; but the Argentines have nevertheless continued to press their claim. The islands might become important as a bargaining point if the two nations should be involved in negotiations regarding other quite different matters; but of themselves their value is small.

---

[10] Gordon Ireland, *Boundaries, Possessions and Conflicts in Central and North America and the Caribbean* (Cambridge, Mass., and Oxford University Press, 1940).

CHAPTER XXXVIII

Latin America : Economic and Demographic Problems

PRESTON E. JAMES

THE foregoing discussion of the origins of the politico-geographic patterns of Latin America points to the need for examining the associated economic and social patterns. The fact is that Latin America is strongly differentiated in terms of population and economy: there are great ethnic differences between predominantly Indian countries, predominantly white countries, and predominantly Negro Haiti; there are great differences in the density of population; and the way people make a living in Latin America ranges from isolated, self-sufficient economies to the most modern urban-industrial economy. Furthermore, the economic and social attitudes that have been inherited from Spain are quite different from those inherited from Portugal. The degree to which the people of any one country are attached to the system of international trade is suggested by such data as income per capita (Table 1). These data show that the Argentines produce more per person than do the people of any other Latin American country. This reflects a relatively large capital investment, a relatively large dependence on imports and exports, and a relatively high level of living. Some economists think of Argentina as the one Latin American country that is not 'under-developed.'[1] However, over-all figures averaged for large countries in which there are diverse economic conditions from region to region are usually misleading, and conclusions drawn from such data may be geographically unacceptable. Even in Argentina there are areas within which a large proportion of the inhabitants consume little that they do not themselves produce. In Latin America as

[1] The effect of the Perón regime has been disastrous. The attempt to make Argentina self-sufficient, to reduce imports, and to exact the highest possible price for exports has reduced the Argentine income per capita far below the level estimated in 1949. It may take years for the Argentine economy again to reach pre-Perón levels.

FIG. 1. SOUTH AMERICA: FORESTED AREA

a whole the proportion of people who do not participate to a significant degree in the exchange of products is enormously high; for these the level of living is low, and the countries may be classed as 'under-developed.'

TABLE 1

Latin American Countries: Economic Data (Pan-American Union)

COUNTRY	INDEX OF VOLUME OF AGRICULTURAL PRODUCTION, 1949–50[1]		INCOME PER CAPITA, 1949 (in dollars)[2]
	Total	*Per Capita*	
Argentina	68	50	346
Bolivia	174	154	55
Brazil	127	104	112
Chile	107	84	188
Colombia	163	130	132
Costa Rica	161	122	125
Cuba	191	150	296
Dominican Republic	120	89	75
Ecuador	140	130	40
El Salvador	127	137	92
Guatemala	122	119	77
Haiti	131	144	40
Honduras	146	148	83
Mexico	179	214	121
Nicaragua	166	190	89
Panama	149	98	183
Paraguay	117	80	84
Peru	128	106	100
Uruguay	119	106	331
Venezuela	112	74	322

[1] 1935–39: 100   [2] U.N. estimate

The attack on the associated problems of poverty, illiteracy, hunger, disease, and hopelessness takes different forms in different parts of the world. An easily popular program, for which political support is not difficult to find, calls for the redistribution of wealth which, in its extreme Communist form, results in the liquidation of the wealthy class. In an agrarian society, where the economy is based on the land resource, this calls for a redistribution of the land. Such a program runs into the fact that when the large estates are redistributed there is not enough land for every one. A program more difficult to explain to people who are economically illiterate involves the creation of new wealth through capital investment. Such a program results in the movement of people into cities, in the establishment of new manufacturing industries, and in an increase in the number and variety of jobs. This program also runs into a fact: that in densely populated countries the increase of job opportunities through new capital investment from private sources alone is insufficient to keep pace with the increase of population. In Latin America to-day we witness a race between those who would raise the level of living by redistributing the wealth, those who would solve the problem by creating new economic opportunities, and those who believe that only by doing both can satisfactory results be achieved fast enough.

TABLE 2

Latin American Countries: Population and Area
(Pan-American Union)

COUNTRY	AREA (in square miles)	POPULATION		
		1937	1951	1955[1]
Argentina	1,072,745	13,490,000	17,644,000	19,113,000
Bolivia	416,040	2,599,000	3,054,000	3,187,000
Brazil	3,286,169	38,685,000	53,377,000	58,404,000
Chile	286,396	4,754,000	5,912,000	6,250,000
Colombia	439,825	8,531,000	11,266,000	12,569,000
Costa Rica	19,238	576,000	825,000	937,300
Cuba	44,217	4,359,000	5,469,000	5,823,000[2]
Dominican Republic	19,129	1,556,000	2,167,000	2,315,000[3]
Ecuador	104,510	2,782,000	3,203,000	3,564,000
El Salvador	13,176	1,571,000	1,920,000	2,118,900
Guatemala	42,044	2,088,000	2,887,000	3,145,900
Haiti	10,700	3,000,000	3,112,000	3,400,000[4]
Honduras	59,160	1,020,000	1,505,000	1,607,200
Mexico	758,550	18,737,000	26,332,000	29,224,000
Nicaragua	57,144	926,000	1,088,000	1,229,200
Panama	28,575	575,000	817,000	861,200
Paraguay	150,516	934,000	1,425,000	1,518,000
Peru	482,257	6,695,000	8,558,000	9,359,000
Uruguay	72,172	2,080,000	2,353,000	2,543,000
Venezuela	352,141	3,415,000	5,071,000	5,676,000

[1] U.N. estimate. [2] Census 1953, revised 1954. [3] Estimate 1954. [4] Estimate 1954.

The figures for Latin America as a whole indicate that this part of the world is not so densely populated as some other parts (Table 2). Latin America includes 19 per cent. of the world's inhabited land area, but is occupied by only 7 per cent. of the world's population. Such figures, however, are dangerously misleading until they are examined more closely and in relation to the skills of the people and the nature of the land they occupy. There are some parts of Latin America, such as the Amazon Basin, in which the fundamental problem of economic development is a lack of people; but there are other parts of Latin America where the population is crowded and where the economy fails to provide adequately for the support of so many people. Population pressure, of course, is not solely a function of density. It may be that in an area of few resources inhabited by a people of limited skills even a thin population is too much—the Fuegian Indians, for example. On the other hand, the demand for a program to attack poverty increases as the density of population increases. In some places this demand is kept in check by central authority; in others it is given political expression through the action of leaders. In Latin America as a whole the demand for such action is increasing, and the need for it is becoming ever more critical. The geographical view of Latin America to-day sees that area as highly diversified in terms of the degree of pressure for economic development and in terms of the direction being taken by the programs to relieve the pressure.[2]

The Spanish Agrarian System

The countries of Latin America that have descended from Spain inherit, to a greater or lesser degree, the traditional Spanish agrarian system. Although this system does not exist in unchanged form anywhere in Latin America, it is necessary to understand its chief characteristics in order to interpret the contemporary conditions. There are four characteristics of this system that are relevant to the economic and social problems of the present time.

The first is the prestige value inherent in the ownership of land. The landlord, by virtue of his ownership of such property, was included in the aristocracy. He was the gentleman, the *caballero*, the man on horseback; he lived apart from other people in a different social and intellectual world; he alone patronized the arts and set the tone of life in the community. All those persons in a country who shared the traditional Spanish attitude toward land looked up to the owner of land and respected his position. The *peón*, the man on foot, stood hat in hand as

[2] Preston E. James, *Latin America* (Odyssey, New York, revised edition, 1950).

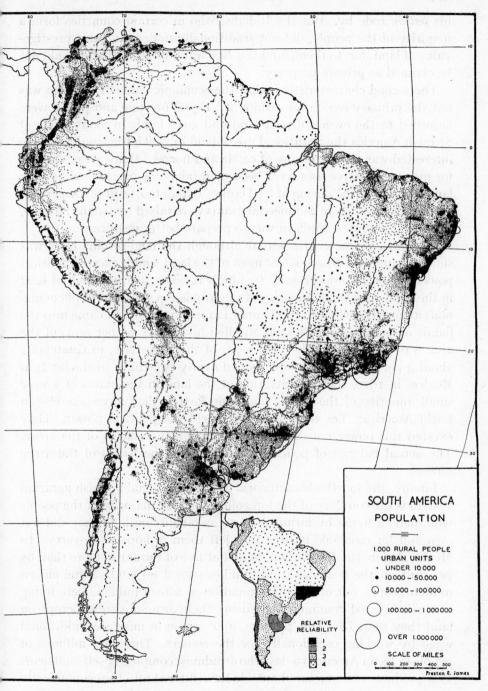

Fig. 2. South America: Population

his *patrón* rode by. But the Indians, who in certain countries form a majority of the people, did not traditionally understand this prestige-value of land, for, to them, land was like water or air in that it could not be claimed as private property.

The second characteristic is that the economic value of the land was not the primary reason for owning it. Equal prestige and power were accorded to the owner of poor land and good land. In many parts of Spanish America the traditional use of land in which the landlords were interested was for the raising of cattle and horses. Many areas suitable for more productive uses have been maintained as pasture, or as farm land devoted to the raising of feed crops. Often, too, as in the Argentine Humid Pampa, where commercial grains were raised by tenant farmers, the objective of the landlord was to prepare better pastures.

The third characteristic is that although the land-owning class was small it came into possession of most of the land, and it exerted political power out of all proportion to its numbers. The concentration of land in the hands of a small minority of the people is a well-known phenomenon: almost the whole of the Humid Pampa of Argentina came into the hands of some 300 families; in Middle Chile nearly 90 per cent. of the area was included in only 7 per cent. of the properties; in Guatemala about 3 per cent. of the people owned nearly two-thirds of the land; in Mexico, in 1910, the concentration of the land in the hands of a very small minority of the people had gone farther than anywhere else in Latin America. Yet these minorities held the political power. They exerted this power not directly, but through the officers of the army. The actual balance of political power was in the hands of the army officers.

Finally, the fourth characteristic of the traditional Spanish agrarian system is the corollary of the foregoing: the vast majority of the people who made a living by farming did so as tenants on land they did not own and for economic returns that left them in hopeless poverty. In Mexico, before the Revolution, in all but five of the states more than 95 per cent. of the heads of rural families owned no land. Some eleven million people, out of a total population of fifteen million, were living in small isolated communities, raising their own subsistence crops on land they rented for this purpose, and gaining a miserable additional wage by working occasionally for the owners. There are millions of people in Latin America to-day who are almost completely self-sufficient. Few products manufactured outside have filtered into the economically isolated communities: such products as the machete, the hoe, the ax, kerosene oil, and the five-gallon oil-can, which has been put to such a variety of uses in the economically under-developed parts of the world; the only piece of machinery widely used is the sewing-machine.

Not enough people shared in the benefits of the Spanish agrarian system to insure its survival unless it was protected by a powerful central government and by a loyal army. Agrarian unrest, often led by liberal-minded sons of the landlords, occasionally took the form of open revolt. Yet so strongly was the system entrenched that usually when political overturn had been accomplished the new leaders did no more than place themselves in a position to benefit, leaving the plight of the people unsolved.

Portuguese Economic Attitudes

There are poverty, illiteracy, hunger, disease, and hopelessness in Brazil too. But the attitudes of the politically powerful people differ in important ways from those of the similar groups in countries descended from Spain. In the north-east of Brazil, to be sure, a certain prestige was to be gained in the colonial period from land ownership; but also a hard and very practical business sense was involved. The unprofitable ownership of land has had little appeal to people of Portuguese economic traditions.

The economy of Portuguese Brazil is a speculative one. An economic venture that yields so little that the original investment is not returned within two or three years is not attractive. Furthermore, when the returns on money invested begin to drop, instead of seeking means of reducing costs through additional investment the tendency is to withdraw from the enterprise and to enter a new field with greater prospect of speculative returns.

So it is that Brazilian economic history has been marked by a series of cycles, in each of which a particular product rose rapidly, yielding fantastic profits to the entrepreneurs, and subsequently entered into decline. The first was the sugar cycle (1500–1700). For the first time in history sugar was produced from large cane plantations on a commercial scale and supplied to a constantly expanding market. This cycle was centered in North-east Brazil, on land that came into the possession of the planters without cost, and was based on the work of Negro slaves imported

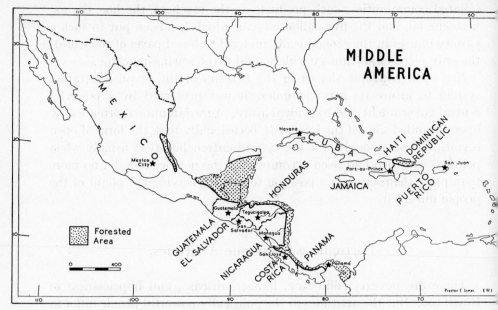

FIG. 3. MIDDLE AMERICA: FORESTED AREA

for the first time into the New World. But after the Dutch had occupied
a part of the North-east, and after them the French and the English
had started to plant sugar-cane in the West Indies and so had cut into
the. Portuguese market, the wealthy people in Brazil looked elsewhere
for a new source of speculative profits. Many moved into south-east
Brazil, into the newly discovered gold and diamond fields of Minas
Gerais (1700–1800). The gold-mining was restricted to the richer placer
deposits: the development of vein mining required too large a capital
investment, and there was no lack of gold-bearing gravels to work.
When the richer gold-bearing gravels had been combed over, however,
mining lost its attraction for the wealthy people. Coffee has had a
similar history to that of sugar-cane: Brazil was the first country to
reach an expanding market with low-cost coffee, based, this time, on the
work of Italian immigrants. The speculative cycle of coffee–planting,
which started during the nineteenth century, came to an end in 1930.
In 1934 there were 2,978,400,000 coffee-trees in Brazil, most of them in
São Paulo state. By 1950 the number had dropped to about 2000 million
and it is estimated that by 1960 another thousand million trees will have
gone out of production. New plantings since 1930 have been mostly on
poor soils or in areas of recurring frosts. A large proportion of these

speculative plantings in northern Paraná was wiped out by frosts in 1953. To-day a Brazilian with money to invest finds the most rapid returns in the construction of office and apartments buildings in São Paulo and Rio de Janeiro, or in the establishment of manufacturing plants. During the past century, too, there have been lesser cycles in rubber, cacao, cotton, oranges, and other products.

As in the Spanish agrarian system, the chief use of the land in Brazil is for the pasture of cattle. Stock-raising in Brazil is not so closely associated with status in the aristocracy as in the traditional Spanish system—except possibly among the 'gauchos' of Rio Grande do Sul, the southernmost of the Brazilian states. But there is a steady and even rising market for cattle, and when more profitable forms of economy fail the quickest returns on money invested can be had from the pasture of animals. There are vast areas of interior Brazil where no other form of land use has ever been successful; but even in the better agricultural lands the largest acreage is used for pasture.

In large parts of Brazil, where speculative agricultural cycles are not temporarily developed, the tenant farmers are included as an integral part of the pastoral system. They clear the forest and plant pasture grass; in the process they use the land for three or four years for the production of basic foods, such as maize, beans, and rice, or for cotton. The tenant farmers of Brazil, however, have no attachment to a particular landowner; they are far more mobile than the tenant farmers of most of the Spanish countries. The news of new economic opportunity, of free land to be had in a colony, of the beginning of a new agricultural cycle (such as sisal in the state of Paraíba) leads to a rapid migration, for the poor man is, at heart, as much of a speculator as his more wealthy neighbor.

During the four centuries of Portuguese settlement in Brazil, this form of land exploitation, this shift of people from place to place, has led to a serious amount of destruction of the resource base—to soil erosion, to the impoverishment of the land to the point where even pastoral productivity is seriously reduced. The parts of Brazil that have been most completely devastated and are to-day only thinly peopled are those close to the large cities, the very outskirts of Rio de Janeiro and São Paulo.

Small-farmer Settlement

But not all of Latin America is to-day dominated by the large land-owners, and some places have never been. In a number of places small landowners cultivate their own commercial crops, and there are a few countries in which political power is widespread among the people. In Haiti, for example, the land is mostly cultivated by small farmers, but political power is concentrated in a few hands. The countries in which liberal, democratic institutions are farthest developed and which, therefore, approach most closely to the ideal of democracy as developed in the English-speaking world are Costa Rica and Uruguay. These countries are exceptional in that they have to such a degree departed from the Spanish agrarian tradition with which they both started.

In the preceding chapter it was shown that the characteristic pattern of settlement in Latin America was that of isolated clusters of people, and that the areas of concentrated settlement had, generally, remained the same for centuries. There are four parts of mainland Latin America where the areas of concentrated settlement developed in the colonial period are now expanding, and this expansion takes the form of pioneer small-farmer movement toward a frontier. The population of the original nucleus, which is not supported by any important immigration, nevertheless remains dense. These places are the highlands of Costa Rica, Antioquia in Colombia, Southern Middle Chile, and South Brazil.

Costa Rica is strikingly different from any of its Central American neighbors. The 150 square miles that are included in the intermont basin in the highlands are occupied by nearly 1000 rural people per square mile; and, with a high birth rate but a low death rate, the net rate of increase is higher than for any other comparable area in Latin America. The people of this central area are of nearly unmixed European descent; they are predominantly small landowners who do their own farm work. They raise coffee, but also send food crops and dairy products to the city markets. Although few people are very wealthy, there are also few who are very poor; the economy is thoroughly commercial, the proportion of illiterates is low, and political power is widely spread among the voters. There is no army at all. How did such a situation appear in Costa Rica? This would be an interesting question

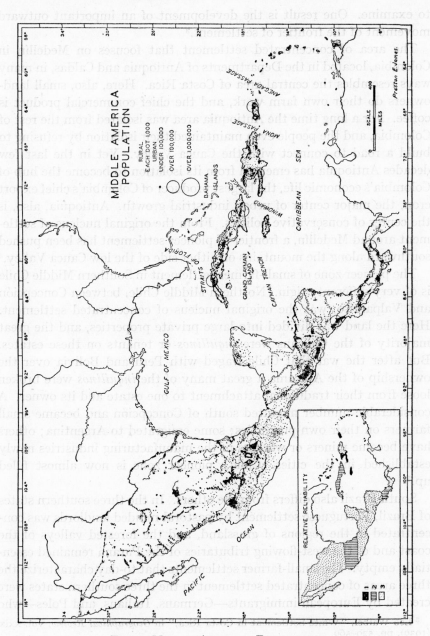

FIG. 4. MIDDLE AMERICA: POPULATION

to examine. One result is the development of an important outward movement of the frontier of settlement.[3]

The area of concentrated settlement that focuses on Medellín in Colombia, located in the Departments of Antioquia and Caldas, in many ways resembles the central area of Costa Rica. Here, also, small land-owners do their own farm work, and the chief commercial product is coffee. For a long time the Antioquia area was isolated from the rest of Colombia, and the people even maintained their isolation by refusing to build a road to connect with the Cauca Valley. Yet in the last few decades Antioquia has emerged from its isolation to become the hub of Colombia's economic life, the largest producer of Colombia's chief export crop, the major center of urban industrial growth. Antioquia, also, is the center of conservative politics. From the original nucleus of settlement around Medellín, a frontier of pioneer settlement has been pushed southward along the mountains on either side of the low Cauca Valley.[4]

The pioneer zone of small-farmer settlement in Southern Middle Chile is of very different origin. Northern Middle Chile, between Concepción and Valparaiso, was the original nucleus of concentrated settlement. Here the land was divided into large private properties, and the great majority of the Chileans were *inquilinos* or tenants on these estates. But after the war that Chile waged with Peru and Bolivia over the ownership of the Atacama a great many of the *inquilinos* were broken loose from their traditional attachment to one estate and its owner. A considerable number migrated south of Concepción and became small farmers on their own properties; some emigrated to Argentina; others have become miners or workers in the manufacturing industries newly established in the cities. Chile's pioneer zone is now almost filled up.[5]

South Brazil also differs from the others. In the three southern states of Brazil, Portuguese settlement by pastoral-minded landlords was con-centrated in the regions of grassland, and the forested valleys of the coast and of the west-flowing tributaries of the Paraná remained essen-tially empty. The small-farmer settlements that to-day characterize the three areas of concentrated settlement in the three southern states were created by European immigrants—Germans, Italians, and Poles—who

[3] Leo Waibel, "White Settlement in Costa Rica," in *Geographical Review*, vol. xxix (1939), pp. 529–560.

[4] James J. Parsons, "Antioqueño Colonization in Western Colombia," in *Ibero-Americana*, vol. xxxii (1949), pp. 1–225.

[5] George M. McBride, *Chile, Land and Society* (American Geographical Society, Research Series No. 19, New York, 1936).

came to Brazil mostly between 1870 and 1930.[6] While their use of the land has copied the destructive system of the Luzo-Brazilians,[7] they have nevertheless expanded the original areas of settlement by the outward movement of pioneer small farmers.

Changes in the Traditional Agrarian System

Clearly each country and in some cases each area of concentrated settlement must be examined separately in order to distinguish the unique character of its economic and demographic problems. The traditional agrarian system characterized by large landowners and tenant farmers has been subjected to an increasingly rapid modification in the countries of Latin America. To a certain extent the system has been challenged by business enterprises involving the investment of capital from foreign sources; in a major way the rise of an urban-industrial economy spells the end of the traditional system. The agrarian system is challenged most vigorously where there is a considerable pressure of population; it is challenged least where population pressure is low. The most spectacular attack was made in Mexico, where the Revolution of 1910–15 and the subsequent program of land redistribution has essentially eliminated the traditional landlord class. A profound change of the system is being carried out in Chile, so far without revolution. The next chapter discusses the particular cases of Mexico and Chile; it also examines two countries that are essentially unique—Argentina and Brazil.

But the traditional agrarian system has been challenged in other places too. Uruguay, which never had a large group of tenant farmers, but which was long torn by strife between rural and urban political parties, has been able to set up a number of liberal institutions providing for democratic political processes, for social security, and for other means of attacking the problem of poverty without resorting to revolution and dictatorship. Colombia is still struggling with apparently irreconcilable differences of political opinion. In Paraguay, Bolivia, Peru, and Ecuador the economic and demographic problems are aggravated by the presence of a large number of people of unmixed Indian descent

[6] Preston E. James, "The Expanding Settlements of Southern Brazil," in *Geographical Review*, vol. xxx (1940), pp. 601–626.
[7] Leo Waibel, "European Colonization in Southern Brazil," in *Geographical Review*, vol. xl (1950), pp. 529–547.

whose integration with the Spanish culture is still incomplete.[8] The problem of Bolivia is especially difficult, because the population of this country is divided into so many small clusters, some mere ribbons of settlement along the bottoms of mountain valleys, that no one area of concentrated settlement has been able to dominate the others, and no one of them has been able to develop enough productivity to pay the high costs of transportation development. The country is geographically weak; yet it possesses important resources of metal and oil coveted by others. Each of the great Latin American Powers—Argentina and Brazil—would like to bring Bolivia into its economic and political orbit. Competition of this sort could produce dangerous international friction.

There are some countries where the traditional agrarian system, although modified by a considerable small-farmer settlement, remains strongly supported in its essential outlines by a powerful central government and a strong army. The country often cited as among the most stable in all Latin America is Venezuela. Here the rich revenues from the oil companies, and now the potential revenues from the development of the iron mines, keep the government solvent and the army well paid. Stability results from the strict control of those processes of change which have gone forward more rapidly in other countries where the central government is not so strong financially. Stable, also, are the governments of the Dominican Republic and Nicaragua. Stable, also, was the government of Guatemala.

Foreign Economic Enterprise

Before turning to a discussion of the situation in Guatemala it is necessary to consider the role of foreign economic enterprise in building up the challenge to the traditional agrarian system. To get proper perspective it should be realized that foreign economic enterprise in Latin America began with the arrival of the Spanish and Portuguese colonists. The use of native Indian and imported Negro laborers for the low-cost production of commercial crops or of precious metals and gems had been fully established by the time other Europeans began to appreciate the possibility of utilizing the resources of the New World to bolster the failing economies of the Old. The Dutch, the French, and the British

---

[8] Ciro Alegría, *Broad and Alien is the World* (Farrar, New York, 1941; Nicholson and Watson, London, 1942).

invested money in the development of sugar-cane plantations, using Negro slave labor, chiefly in the West Indies.[9] By the time that the United States had grown large enough to turn its attention southward only the remnant island colonies of Spain remained, again with sugar cane as the chief economic interest. The story of Panama is unique in that it is tied to the construction of the Canal and to the interest of the United States in defending the Canal.

Foreign investment in sugar-cane production has been highly profitable but socially disastrous. The work of producing sugar has for centuries depended on a large amount of hand labor. Not only must the land be prepared for planting, and cultivated during the period when the cane is growing, but also a great army of workers must be mobilized for the harvest. In a few places, such as Trinidad, where the climate permits the harvesting of cane throughout the year, this work can be more or less evenly spread. But where there is a strongly marked dry season and rainy reason the harvest must be carried out within the period of a few months. During the remainder of the year, unless some other kind of occupation is available, many people must be unemployed. Usually, in sugar-cane areas, no other forms of employment are offered, and where the population is dense there may not even be room to permit these workers to raise their own food crops. This was the situation which developed in Puerto Rico, where almost all of the best land and much land of inferior quality were planted to cane, necessitating the importation of foodstuffs.

Another enterprise in tropical planting that is highly profitable is the production of bananas, chiefly in the Central American countries and Jamaica. In Central America the fruit companies moved on to land not previously utilized effectively, bringing in Negro workers from Jamaica, or recruiting Indian workers from the highlands. In the early decades of this century these foreign companies undoubtedly exerted considerable influence on the governments of the Central American countries, and sometimes this influence was applied with scant concern for the interests of the local ruling groups. That hospitals, schools, and homes have been provided for the workers and that wages have been higher than those paid elsewhere in the country are irrelevant, for the economic power of a large foreign corporation, even when administered with the utmost understanding and tact, necessarily restricts or seems to restrict the freedom of the local ruling groups. Freedom to do their own governing was,

[9] Derwent Whittlesey, *The Earth and the State* (Holt, New York, 1939), pp. 41-49.

after all, the basic motivation that led to the demand for independence from Spain. Only the fact that revenues to the treasury became a major part of the government's income has restrained the local authorities from taking steps to break the precarious but profitable hold of the companies on the banana lands.

The foreign mining companies face a similar situation. In many countries—notably Mexico, Venezuela, Peru, Bolivia, and Chile—foreign mining enterprises have opened up important new mining regions and dominate the economy of these regions. Maracaibo, a sleepy, dirty tropical town in 1920, is to-day more like a city in the United States than one in Venezuela. The mining interests in the mountains back of Lima in Peru, those in the highlands of Bolivia, and those in the deserts and mountains of Chile have provided important revenues for the governments in question. Yet the results are serious when a country becomes too completely dependent on such revenues. Before 1930 almost the whole revenue of Chile was derived from export duties on copper and nitrate. When the depression hit these products the revenue of the Chilean treasury dropped suddenly. Such dependence on foreign enterprise means that many decisions of policy vitally affecting the country are made somewhere else, often with little consideration for the impact of these policies in Latin America. The Brazilians, to avoid such a situation, have refused to give foreign enterprise a free rein in developing the iron-ore deposits or in carrying out exploration for oil.

Venezuela, on the other hand, has welcomed foreign enterprise, at the same time drawing up contracts which secure a large share of the profits to itself. No other Latin American country has gained more from foreign enterprise. The revenue of the Government was increased many times as the oil exports mounted, and, since 1934, oil exports have made up more than 90 per cent. of total exports. There is still a lot of oil in Venezuela; and now the discovery and development of the iron ores of the Guiana Highlands for the use of the ore-hungry steel industry of the United States promise another long-term and highly profitable economic relationship. Venezuela, as a result, has no foreign debt, can afford to pay its army well and provide it with modern weapons that ensure control of any popular uprising. For a few years Venezuelan liberals came into power, instituting a number of democratic political procedures; but at the first sign of a movement to impose additional regulations on the policies of the oil companies the army took back the control of the government. The traditional agrarian system throughout most of the country remains unchallenged.[10]

A large volume of foreign investment in the modern period is devoted to utilities and manufacturing industries. The development of hydro-electric power in Brazil provides the still not quite adequate basis for the industrial growth of São Paulo and Rio de Janeiro. Chile's development of electric power for industrial use is similarly supported by foreign capital. A phenomenon of increasing importance is the establishment around such places as São Paulo and Mexico City of branch plants of industrial concerns in Anglo-America and Europe.[11]

The Case of Guatemala

Starting, then, with the traditional Spanish agrarian system, each of the Spanish American countries has in one way or another modified this system, partly in response to purely domestic pressures, partly as a result of the impact of foreign economic enterprise. The world-wide transformation of the pre-industrial agrarian societies into industrial societies brings certain results wherever it takes place: prestige is inherent in the ownership of capital rather than of land; the number and variety of job opportunities and the share of the workers in the rewards of the economic life are all greatly increased; the concentration of people in cities makes possible programs of education and health, and results in enlargement of the share of the common man in the political life. These changes have gone on in other parts of the world: they are going on to-day in Latin America. In various ways the widespread agrarian poverty is under attack.

But the Communists also have a plan for an attack on agrarian poverty. The preliminary step is the expropriation of large land properties and the redistribution of the land to the former tenant farmers. It is clear, however, to all students of the agrarian problem that land redistribution by itself does not solve the problem of poverty for two chief reasons: (1) there is not enough good land in most areas to go around; and (2) the low-cost commercial production of agricultural products requires a large-scale enterprise. Almost everywhere the aftermath of land redistribution is a decline in per capita production. The

[10] Germán Arciniegas, *The State of Latin America* (Knopf, New York, 1952; Cassell, London, 1953).

[11] Lloyd J. Hughlett, *Industrialization of Latin America* (McGraw-Hill, New York, 1946).

Communists, after gaining wide popular support for land redistribution and after gaining control of the government, proceed to the second phase of their program. The land is removed from the private possession of the farmers and is consolidated in large collective farms owned by the State.

Guatemala has long provided an example of a relatively little-changed agrarian economy. The Mayan Indians of the highlands, who make up a majority of the people of Guatemala, have for centuries been concentrated on their ancestral lands. These lands, unlike many Indian lands in Latin America, were never divided into large private properties owned by people of Spanish descent. The Indian area is now divided into small properties around the different villages. But the pressure of population on these holdings has been gradually increasing, and the Indians have been forced to seek additional employment on the coffee plantations of the highlands or the banana plantations of the lowlands. The most successful coffee plantations were German-owned, and the banana plantations were developed by the United Fruit Company. The small group of Spanish-descended landowners and the army officers who held the political power have long eyed these successful plantation ventures covetously. During the second world war many of the German plantation owners were evicted and their lands taken over by Guatemalans. More than 60 per cent. of the area of Guatemala has come into the possession of only about 3 per cent. of the people. Most of the agricultural workers were landless, and the need of the Indians for additional land was steadily increasing. The whole situation was kept thoroughly under control by a strict military dictatorship.

But the dictatorship ceased to remain alert. Liberal-minded persons genuinely concerned about the plight of the peasants were able to come into office with the help of a group of dissatisfied junior officers of the army. The local Communist group, hitherto under cover as in most parts of Latin America, came gradually into the open, espousing the popular cause of finding and providing more land for the Indians. Step by step the United Fruit Company was pressed to cease planting bananas in Guatemala—not all at once, for the revenues to the treasury, as well as the employment of some 12,000 workers, could not be suddenly upset. It seemed to be only a question of time before the Communist-controlled government would expropriate the land not only of the United Fruit Company but also of the wealthy Guatemalans. With the Indians' traditional communal attitude toward land, it would not have been difficult to move directly to the establishment of collective farms. When the danger of this situation became apparent, however, the army again took control. An invading force met little real opposition and the Communists were thrown out of power. Whether this means that there will be a return to a strict military dictatorship or not remains to be seen.

Here is a case where the Communists took deft political advantage of an economic and demographic problem for which no other effective program of attack had been formulated. The danger to neighboring States was obvious. But a major lesson to be learned is that problems of economic distress and population pressure developed in a purely agrarian society can be neglected only at extreme peril.

The Case of Puerto Rico

Another case is offered by the island commonwealth of Puerto Rico. Here was a neglected Spanish colony, where the Spanish agrarian system was essentially unchallenged, that came into the possession of the United States in 1898. Large absentee sugar corporations developed the planting of sugar-cane, using for this purpose the best third of the agricultural land of the island. Meanwhile the application of health measures and the organization of medical services lowered the death rate, and the net rate of increase took a sharp upward turn. As late as 1932 the death rate was 22·3 per thousand; but in 1952 it was down to 9·0 per thousand. The density of population to-day is about 660 people per square mile. Before 1940 Puerto Rico was described as having the largest group of destitute people anywhere under the flag of the United States. More than 500,000 Puerto Ricans have emigrated to the United States, where most of them are concentrated in New York City.

Here is a quite familiar example of the ill-effects of colonialism. Yet since 1940 Puerto Rico has been transformed into a striking demonstration of how an agrarian system in an area of great population pressure can be effectively changed without resorting to Communist extremes. In 1940 the per capita income of the Puerto Ricans was 122 dollars; in 1952 the per capita income, adjusted to 1940 price levels, was 212 dollars.

The transformation of Puerto Rico was carried out under the direction of Puerto Rican political leaders, especially Governor Muñoz Marín. The first step was the enforcement of a law restricting the amount of land that could be owned by a corporation to 500 acres. At present the sugar companies operate the sugar refineries; the cane is bought from many small planters now working the former company lands. The whole island was surveyed in detail by geographers who plotted the land quality and the land use on large-scale maps. From these maps plans were made for a more effective use of the land. But none of these measures would have provided employment for all the people of crowded Puerto Rico. In addition, the island government adopted several measures calculated to attract manufacturing industries. Some 200 new manufacturing establishments have come to Puerto Rico, giving direct employment to between 12,000 to 15,000 workers.[12] It is recognized that for every worker employed in a basic industry, two workers are supported in commerce or in service activities. If each of these workers, one in the basic industry, two in the others, supports two dependents, it follows that when one new job is created in industry provision is made for the support of a total of nine persons.[13]

Industrialization

Latin America is in the throes of change from the traditional agrarian system to something else. Will it be a change carried out in the Communist pattern? Or will it be carried out along capitalist lines, leading to the establishment of a Latin American branch of the Industrial Society?

Industrialization is proceeding rapidly in some parts of Latin America. The largest industrial investment, and the largest concentration of workers employed in industry, is in São Paulo and Rio de Janeiro in Brazil. There is also a large industrial development in Buenos Aires and Mexico City; and only somewhat lesser development in the cities of Chile, in Medellín, and other places.

The basic idea of large-scale industry as developed by the Industrial Society is that by increased investment of capital in more efficient machinery and in the economy of large-scale operations it is possible to reduce the cost per unit of things produced. The reduction of cost is passed on to the consumer in the form of reduction of price. Profits

[12] Millard Hansen and Henry Wells (editors), *Puerto Rico, A Study in Democratic Development* (Annals of the American Academy of Political and Social Science, vol. cclxxxv, 1953).

[13] Harvey S. Perloff, *Puerto Rico's Economic Future, A Study in Planned Development* (Chicago University Press and Cambridge University Press, 1950).

result from the increase of consumers with each decrease of price; the rewards of the system are widely shared among the people.

The full and rapid development of this basic concept of the Industrial Society in most parts of Latin America is handicapped by several conditions. In the first place, as a result of the long dominance of the agrarian system, there is a great gap between the small minority of very wealthy people and the vast majority of very poor people. When a manufacturer invests in machinery that reduces the cost of his operations he cannot easily reduce the price, for such a reduction fails to bring him any commensurate increase of customers. Rather, he raises the price, which the wealthy can still afford to pay. By this form of inflation the poor are made even poorer than before.

He is handicapped also by the prevailing illiteracy of the people, which makes it not only difficult to find sufficiently skilled workers, but also makes it difficult to build up the market by the usual advertising methods. Both of these difficulties are being overcome by imaginative executives, but they retard the process of industrialization.

Industrialization can provide for an increase in the number of employment opportunities. The redistribution of land alone cannot possibly change the ratio of man to the land. It is necessary to promote the movement of people away from the rural areas and into the cities where not only are new economic opportunities offered, but where a real attack on illiteracy, ill-health, inadequate diet, and the spirit of hopelessness can be made.

TABLE 3

Principal Exports of Latin American Countries
(in percentages of total exports of each country)

ARGENTINA	1937	1952
	100	100
Corn	26	8
Wheat	21	1
Meat	10	15
Wool	7	16
Hides and skins	6	9
Quebracho	2	7
Others	28	44

BOLIVIA	1937	1952
	100	100
Tin	63	59
Lead	6	8
Tungsten	4	10
Zinc	4	9
Others	23	14

BRAZIL	1937	1952
	100	100
Coffee	42	74
Cacao	5	3
Cotton	19	2
Others	34	21

CHILE	1937	1952
	100	100
Copper	56	63
Nitrate	19	13
Others	25	24

COLOMBIA	1937	1952
	100	100
Coffee	65	82
Petroleum	23	16
Others	12	2

PARAGUAY	1937	1952
	100	100
Hides and skins	9	10
Cotton	37	34
Quebracho	19	18
Others	35	38

COSTA RICA	1937	1952
	100	100
Bananas	54	59
Coffee	36	34
Others	10	7

CUBA	1937	1952
	100	100
Sugar	78	85
Others	22	15

DOMINICAN REPUBLIC	1937	1952
	100	100
Sugar	60	45
Cacao	14	13
Coffee	10	23
Others	16	19

ECUADOR	1937	1952
	100	100
Bananas	4	27
Cacao	34	22
Coffee	17	26
Others	45	25

HAITI		1937	1952
		100	100
Sugar	. .	9	6
Coffee	. .	52	66
Others	. .	39	28

EL SALVADOR		1937	1952
		100	100
Coffee	. .	95	88
Others	. .	5	12

HONDURAS		1937	1952
		100	100
Bananas	. .	77	66
Coffee	. .	3	26
Others	. .	20	8

GUATEMALA		1937	1952
		100	100
Bananas	. .	25	5
Coffee	. .	68	82
Others	. .	7	13

MEXICO		1937	1952
		100	100
Coffee	. .	4	8
Cotton	. .	1	23
Copper	. .	7	6
Lead	. .	15	13
Zinc	. .	11	8
Others	. .	62	42

PERU		1937	1952
		100	100
Sugar	. .	9	14*
Cotton	. .	25	34*
Petroleum	. .	34	8*
Copper	. .	15	6*
Lead	. .	4	11*
Zinc	. .	1	6*
Others	. .	12	21*

* 1951.

NICARAGUA		1937	1952
		100	100
Bananas	. .	16	1
Coffee	. .	50	51
Cotton	. .	9	18
Others	. .	25	30

URUGUAY		1937	1952
		100	100
Meat	. .	16	14
Hides and skins		14	11
Wool	. .	46	33
Others	. .	24	42

PANAMA		1937	1952
		100	100
Bananas	. .	68	38
Cacao	. .	20	13
Others	. .	12	49

VENEZUELA		1937	1952
		100	100
Petroleum	. .	89	95
Others	. .	11	5

Source : Pan-American Union.

CHAPTER XXXIX

Latin American States : Four Case Studies

PRESTON E. JAMES

EVERY one of the twenty Latin American States is unique in the quality of its traditions, the direction and stage of the processes of change it is undergoing, and the character of its politico-geographic structure. This is true, of course, about every politically organized area, on whatever part of the earth. But it is a generalization that is especially important in connexion with Latin America because of the tendency of many writers to characterize this part of the world and its problems with broad, sweeping statements. Can it be said, for example, that all the under-developed countries of the American Hemisphere are in various stages of one process of economic development, all at various points of progress toward a single goal? This is frequently assumed by economists, and may well be an important source of error in the analysis of contemporary problems. For it seems that while stages of development can be identified, not all the countries are developing in the same direction, nor did they all start from the same beginnings.[1]

An analysis of the present problems and conditions in Latin America requires an understanding of three fundamental factors. The first is historical: the source of the cultural traditions, the direction of development, and the stage in the process of development. The second is geographic: the patterns of land and people, of physical and biotic resources, and of the uses to which people are able to put the resource endowment. The third is political: the manner in which historical process working in a specific environment has produced a particular political design, the state-idea that explains the degree of homogeneity achieved, and the effectiveness with which the social and economic problems can be attacked through political channels.

[1] Germán Arciniegas, *The State of Latin America* (Knopf, New York, 1952; Cassell, London, 1953).

Although it is not possible in this book to treat each of the twenty Latin American countries individually,[2] some idea of the diversity of conditions can be gained by a consideration of four case studies: Mexico, Chile, Argentina, and Brazil.

Mexico

Mexico has gone farther in attacking the problem of poverty by revolutionary change than has any other Latin American country. Here the Spanish agrarian tradition appeared in the most complete form, applied to a land already densely populated by well-developed Indian societies. By 1910 a small minority of landed aristocrats held private title to a larger proportion of the total area than anywhere else in Latin America, and the proportion of illiterate, sick, and hopeless rural people exceeded that of any other large area. Foreign investment had developed the metal and oil resources, and foreign markets offered inducements for the organization of certain agricultural enterprises, such as the production of henequen. The well-to-do were very well off indeed, and could afford to live in a genial and cosmopolitan atmosphere, leaving politics to the Army and worry about social unrest to the liberal teachers and their students. That was before 1910. Since then the idea of a landed aristocracy has disappeared, Mexico has struggled to achieve economic as well as political independence, democratic institutions have been planted and cultivated with difficulty, and a state-idea has been formulated that to-day commands the support of a majority of the people.

The Process of Change. The spirit of revolt against the Spanish agrarian system is not new in Mexico. Even the movement for political independence in the early nineteenth century was inspired by agrarian discontent. Unlike the independence movement in most parts of Spanish America, where American-born politically powerful people resented the continued rule by emissaries from Spain and set out to do their own ruling, in Mexico Father Hidalgo and Father Morelos led uprisings of peasants against the established order: against the system of large land properties, against the Roman Catholic Church as an institution supporting the economic *status quo*. But the movement was quickly turned

[2] Preston E. James, *Latin America* (revised edition, Odyssey, New York, 1950).

to political ends, and after independence from Spain had been achieved the Spanish agrarian system was changed. Benito Juarez, too, led an agrarian revolt, but it also was diverted from economic and social channels into the familiar channels of political change, the traditional dead-end street of Latin American politics. From 1884 to 1910 the rule of Diaz was not effectively challenged and the pressures of hopeless discontent were built up. The Mexican Revolution (identified by capital letters to distinguish it from lesser revolts) began under the leadership of Madero in 1910 and ended with Carranza in 1915. The platform of the Revolution, uncontrolled elections and land redistribution, was incorporated in the Constitution of 1917, the document that provides the legal basis for the fundamental changes made since that date.

Article 27 of this Constitution goes to the heart of the agrarian problem. It formulates the functional theory of land property: that the right to own property is dependent on socially harmonious use. This meant that no longer could a landowner use large areas of potential crop land for the pasture of cattle, no longer could a corporation hold land property idle awaiting the expansion of a commercial plantation crop. The constitution for the first time permitted the Government to expropriate idle land or land not used to capacity and to reassign this land to the rural communities, known as *ejidos*.[3] In the great majority of Mexico's more than 15,000 *ejidos* the land is parceled out among the individual families as essentially private property, although it cannot be sold. On the average the farm family in an *ejido* has received forty-four acres of land, but of this only about ten acres is considered suitable for crops. Some small private properties, not *ejido* lands, remain in Mexico, some being the remnants of the former *haciendas*; while some are large properties useful only for the pasture of cattle. But the way of life based on a small land-owning group and a large, landless peasantry is gone.

Has the Mexican Revolution been a success? This question has been argued from all points of view and with great heat. For many people, not only the dispossessed aristocracy, the Revolution has not been successful. As usual, when the property of the well-to-do is confiscated and redistributed, there is not enough to go around. The fact remains that less than 8 per cent. of the area of Mexico can be called crop land: land redistribution does not change the ratio of population to arable land;

[3] Eyler N. Simpson, *The Ejido, Mexico's Way Out* (Chapel Hill, North Carolina, and Oxford University Press, 1937).

unless land redistribution is accompanied by other programs the problem of poverty is not solved.

But declining agricultural production is not the whole story. Whetten[4] summarizes a study of the results of the land redistribution program in eight points:

1. The total production of basic food crops has declined.
2. There has been an increase in previously unimportant food crops that more than off-sets the decline in basic foods.
3. Clearly the *ejido* is a less efficient producing unit than was the *hacienda*.
4. Lack of technical knowledge among the farmers has greatly aggravated the problem of soil and water conservation.
5. But the percentage of illiteracy has dropped enormously.
6. There has been a notable increase in retail business.
7. The gain in personal freedom and the wide participation in political decisions, especially at the community level, have changed the former hopelessness of a majority of the people into a feeling of satisfaction.
8. Yet the fact must be faced that Mexico is a poor land for farming, even with the most advanced technology.

The rapid growth of manufacturing industries is the other factor in contemporary Mexico that promises an effective attack on the problem of poverty. New capital investment, much of it from foreign sources but strictly under Mexican control, has created a phenomenal industrial expansion, especially in and around Mexico City. Many new kinds of jobs are available to-day that did not exist a decade ago, and, as in Puerto Rico, each job in a basic industry gives indirect economic support to many people, including those employed in retail trade, in transportation, and in the service occupations.

Basic Patterns. All of these changes have been carried on in a national territory that is strongly differentiated in terms of its natural endowment. Only about 12 per cent. of the area of Mexico is adequately supplied with water throughout the year; and most of this area is mountainous. The fact is that Mexico is poor for farming; and the people are poor, in part because they are farmers, but also because they are concentrated in one of the poorer farming areas of the country. In the central area of Mexico is a concentration of maize acreage, visible on any world map of this crop. But this concentration is not economically similar to those also visible in the Corn Belt of the United States or the

[4] Nathan L. Whetten, *Rural Mexico* (Chicago University Press and Cambridge University Press, 1948).

Maize District of the Argentine Humid Pampa. In these other places maize occupies a large proportion of the farming area because it enjoys special advantages over competing crops—it brings higher returns to the farmer than wheat. But in the central area of Mexico there is an actual economic disadvantage in growing maize. The traditional diet of the Mexican people, however, is based on this grain, and where the Mexicans are concentrated they plant their basic food. If the central area were used for wheat and dairy cattle rather than maize its economic productivity would be increased; but the problem of educating the Mexicans

FIG. 1. MEXICO: RAILWAYS

to like milk and to eat white bread is not easy to solve. The best maize areas of Mexico are along the Gulf Coastal Plain, where population is thin and much of the land remains in woods. Irrigation works in the dry North can somewhat increase the area suitable for crops, but the possibilities of bringing additional water to the high meseta area are not great, owing to the pattern of drainage and the design of the surface features; and much of the North and most of the Pacific North-west are too cold.

There are many other elements of geographic arrangement in Mexico that should be considered in an appraisal of that country. Its position with reference to the United States; the fact that Mexico's international boundaries pass through empty country; the pattern of transportation that gives high strategic importance to the town of Celaya; the notable concentration of the Mexican people in the central area: these are all essential parts of the Mexican picture relevant to any interpretation of its social, economic, or political problems.

The Mexican State-idea. Mexico is making rapid strides in securing wide adherence to its distinctive state-idea. The concepts that to-day claim such wide support are those of the Party of the Mexican Revolution, many stemming from the formulations of the Constitution of 1917 as amended. Since the days of Carranza no opposition party worthy of the name has appeared. Even the Sinarquistas of the second world war days never actually gained the support of any considerable number of people. This was a counter-revolutionary movement with fascist trimmings that at the time caused more concern than it merited. But while the Revolution overthrew the Spanish agrarian system it has, so far, failed to create democracy. When even the tradition of public responsibility is lacking the creation of democratic ideals requires decades of patient work, most of it within the framework of the locality. To be sure, the spectacular expropriation of the foreign-owned oil-wells in 1938 gave rise to such a wave of public support as no Mexican government had ever received. Yet Mexico still has an essentially one-party system, and the normal differences of opinion regarding policy have no channels of political expression. Mexico still has a long way to go in its attack on poverty; but it has made a notable start.

Chile

In many ways the conditions in Chile parallel those of Mexico. In Chile, also, a small number of people came into possession of most of the land. Something like 60 per cent. of the arable land of Chile was owned by as few as 600 families. Even in the densely populated Central Valley of Chile the chief kind of land use in terms of acreage is for pasture and feed crops.[5] As in Mexico, also, foreign capital has been active in the development of mining.

But there are some very important contrasts between Mexico and

[5] George M. McBride, *Chile, Land and Society* (New York, American Geographical Society, 1936).

Chile. The Indians of Chile, the Araucanians, were not at all like the Indians of Mexico: possessing a culture that was not so elaborate as that of the Aztecs, the Chilean natives were, nevertheless, endowed to a much greater degree than were the Mexican natives with the spirit of independence. Furthermore, the Spaniards who established themselves in Chile differed from those who settled Mexico or Peru, for a large proportion of them were Basques and relatively few came from the south of Spain. Chileans are known for their progressive attitude toward economic and social questions, for their energy and resourcefulness, and for their practical and business-like approach toward the problems of readjustment in the modern period.

The Process of Change. Chile, like Mexico, has made an attack on the inherited agrarian system. But in Chile the attack has proceeded along quite different lines from those of Mexico. No class has been liquidated, no land expropriated; yet the redistribution of land is going on, and no other Latin American country has achieved so large a development of manufacturing production per capita. There have been two distinct phases to the process of change.

The first phase began at the conclusion of the War of the Pacific, during which the Chileans wrested control of the Atacama desert with its nitrate and copper resources from the Peruvians and Bolivians (1879–83). Before this war the Spanish agrarian system had remained unchallenged. The concentration of the people of Chile in the Central Valley (between Valparaiso and the Vale of Chile on the north and Concepción and the Valley of the Río Bío Bío on the south) was notable. In this central area the land was held in large properties, and the majority of the people were tenants (*inquilinos*) who were closely attached to the estates on which they were born. The War of the Pacific, however, tore many of the tenants loose: the Chilean army was recruited largely from the *inquilino* class.

At the end of the war the Chilean Government undertook to settle a considerable number of the returning veterans in the southern part of Middle Chile, south of the Bío Bío. The central part of Chile enjoys a Mediterranean climate with winter rains and summer droughts; but south of the Bío Bío the year-round rainfall supports a thick forest—the kind of country in which the Spaniards of the colonial period were at a disadvantage. Here the Araucanians had withstood the pressure of white settlement for three centuries. Not until German colonists settled

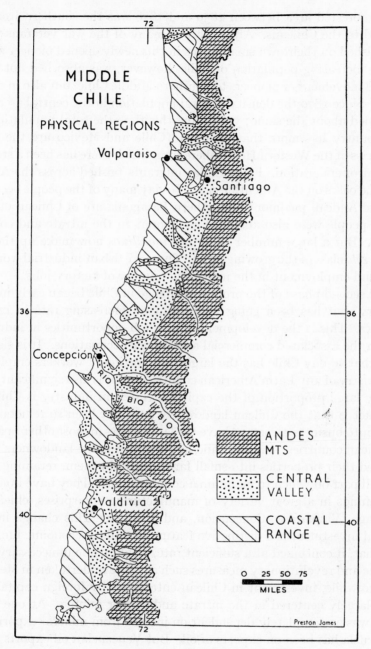

FIG. 2. MIDDLE CHILE: PHYSICAL REGIONS

in the forested area between 1850 and 1870 was the southern frontier opened to the Chileans. After the war many of the war veterans were established on their own small farms in this newly opened pioneer zone.

The increasing population of Chile, however, was absorbed not only by this movement of pioneers to Southern Middle Chile, but also in other ways. Since 1870 the density of rural population in the central area has remained about the same; yet during this time the total population of the country has more than doubled. Chile and Mexico are the only countries of the Western Hemisphere from which there has been a steady current of emigration. From Chile emigrants pushed across the Andes into the oases on the Argentine side. To-day many of the people occupying the Andean piedmont in northern Patagonia are of Chilean origin. Many people were also absorbed as laborers in the nitrate and copper mines. But a large number of former *inquilinos* now make up the so-called *roto* class of the growing cities. These are urban-industrial workers who find employment in the increasing number of factory jobs.

The second phase of the process of change in Chile began early in this century, but has been going forward at an increasing rate in recent decades. This is the development of new job opportunities in industry and in the associated commercial and service occupations. It is significant that to-day Chile has the largest proportion of workers employed in industry of any Latin American country; and it is also significant that a very large proportion of the capital invested in industry is Chilean. The fact is that the Chilean landowners have not been so reluctant to enter into business careers as have the landowners in most other Spanish American countries. In larger and larger numbers the landowners have divided their properties into small farms and sold them, retaining only a small part on which to maintain a country home. They have invested their funds in a great variety of manufacturing enterprises, chiefly in Santiago, Valparaiso, Concepción, and Valdivia. This change in the capital investment is a distinctive feature of Chilean economic life, and one that, if continued at a sufficient rate, would make unnecessary any drastic and revolutionary measures such as those undertaken in Mexico.

Meanwhile, investment in Chilean enterprises by foreign capital has been largely centered in the nitrate and copper mining. At one time Chile was as completely dependent on income from mineral exports, as Venezuela has been on exports of oil. But Venezuelan oil exports have never been subject to the violent fluctuations that have embarrassed the mining activities of Chile. The output of subsidized atmospheric nitrate plants in Europe and North America has seriously reduced the world demand for natural nitrate. And copper is subject to enormous fluctuations in the world markets. There was a time after the second world war when the revenue to the Chilean treasury dropped to only 15 per cent. of what it had been the previous year. Many of Chile's copper mines are owned and operated by subsidiaries of the Anaconda Copper Company. In 1950 Anaconda derived 36 per cent. of its profits from the Chilean mines. Where such close mutual ties exist between a foreign corporation and a Latin American government it is inevitable that decisions are often made deeply affecting affairs in Chile, and in the formulation of which the Chileans have no part. Much of the strong Communist activity in Chile is located in the mining camps, where workers are often out of work, where wages are very low, where real wages are getting lower, and where working conditions are generally dangerous and unhealthful.

A new steel plant has been built and put into operation near Concepción, utilizing Chilean raw materials. It is expected that numerous new steel fabricating plants will be established in the vicinity, thus further extending the job opportunities in basic industry. Little by little industrial employment is growing, and industrial wages are rising. Still the poverty of the *rotos* who inhabit the slum districts of Santiago and other industrial cities has not been solved, and the tide of discontent, started by the miners, is spreading to the urban workers.

Basic Patterns. Chile is remarkable as a country organized around a single central area of concentrated settlement. So strong is the focus on a single central city that the political subdivisions of Chile, the provinces, have no significance except as enumeration areas of the Census. There are no provincial police, no provincial governors or legislatures. This centralization of the political structure of Chile is matched with a similar centralization of the economic and social life. Some 90 per cent. of the people of Chile live in the central area.

The Chilean State-idea. Chile is one Latin American country in which a positive state-idea is well developed. From a purely negative desire for local self-government Chile went on to develop a strong sense of nationality among its citizens. Rich and poor alike are proud of being Chilean. The War of the Pacific added to the distinctive traditions of this country. Furthermore, although the national territory forms a long, narrow ribbon of land along the Pacific coast, the area of concentrated settlement, which is Chile to most Chileans, is a compact unit in which the development of a unified state-idea is facilitated.

The process of changing the inherited Spanish agrarian tradition to the modern urban-industrial society has resulted in a diversity of political groups. There are many diverse interests in Chile. The Chilean political system gives free channels of political expression to these groups: to-day Chile, like France, is burdened with a multiplicity of political parties, and governments represent special groupings or coalitions of parties. Yet the fact remains that Chile is making rapid strides in the direction of a liberal democracy.

Argentina

The case of Argentina involves totally different factors and processes. During the colonial period Argentina was remote from the Spanish centers, and a large part of its territory was unoccupied by white men. The settlements along the Paraná-Plata, which had been established by colonists moving downstream from Asunción, were not very prosperous. The major economic activity of the period was the production of mules for sale to the mining people of Bolivia and Peru. The focus of this mule trade on Tucumán and Salta gave these towns, especially the former, a head start in economic development. Here the agrarian tradition had its strongest hold in colonial times. Here independence from Spain was proclaimed.

Most of the traditions of modern Argentina were developed in the period after the fall of Rosas (1852). At that time Buenos Aires had become the political focus of the country and was in the process of becoming the economic focus. The Humid Pampa, however, was still occupied only along its northern edge. Not until after the Indian wars that ended in 1883 was the whole of the Humid Pampa opened to settlement. Then, in the Spanish tradition, most of this remarkable region was divided among some 300 families. To-day more than 80 per cent. of the productive capacity of Argentina is located in the Humid Pampa.

Development of the Humid Pampa. The development of the Humid Pampa, then, has taken place during the last hundred years. It was made possible, as in other great grassland regions of the middle latitudes around the world, by a series of technical innovations such as barbed wire, well-drilling machinery, agricultural machinery, and railroads. The development of the world's grasslands for the surplus production of grain and meat was associated in time with the rapid rise of modern great

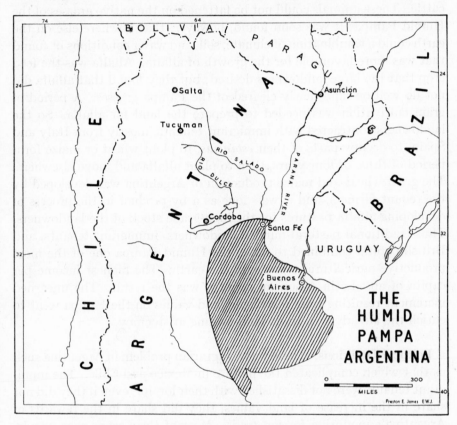

FIG. 3. ARGENTINA: THE HUMID PAMPA

cities and the industrial society. In no other grassland could grain and meat be produced for international trade at such a low cost per unit as in the Argentine Humid Pampa.

But commercial development in Argentina was based on two conditions. First was the Spanish agrarian tradition of large land holdings, tenant workers, a pastoral economy, and political power in the hands of army officers. The second was the investment of foreign capital, chiefly British, in the development of railroads, docks, and other facilities. The small group of people into whose hands came the possession of most of the Humid Pampa, and whose *estancias* included hundreds of thousands of acres, were almost exclusively interested in the raising of high-grade stock—cattle, horses, and sheep. But the British market demanded fat beef; and from English sources the landowners imported English beef cattle. These animals could not be fattened on the native grasses of the Humid Pampa; it was soon found, however, that nowhere else on the earth could a combination of climate, soil, and water conditions be found that was more favorable for the growth of alfalfa. Alfalfa was the feed crop that the large landowners desired; but they found that alfalfa did not do well on land newly cleared of the Pampa grasses. A period of grain cultivation was needed to prepare the land for alfalfa. So the landowners contracted with immigrant tenants, mostly from Italy and Spain, to occupy parts of their *estancias*, to plant wheat or maize for a period of three or four years, then to plant alfalfa and move elsewhere. The great wheat and maize production of Argentina was developed by the tenant farmers, and it was done as a by-product in the process of developing alfalfa pastures for the high-grade stock of the landowners. Thus traditional pastoral-minded landowners, immigrant tenants, and British capital combined to make the Humid Pampa one of the most productive agricultural regions on the earth. The highest income per capita of any Latin American country was the result. The unearned increment resulting from increasing land values on the Pampa went to enrich the already well-to-do land-owning aristocracy.

Political Traditions. There was no agrarian problem in Argentina such as that which complicated the picture in Mexico and Chile. The immigrant tenants were not dissatisfied with their lot, for, even if they did not share in the increase of land values, they did share in the rewards of Argentina's mounting foreign trade. Most of them were poor people, seeking economic opportunities in the New World that were denied them in the agricultural systems of Italy and Spain. Many did very well indeed in Argentina, and all were better off than they had been at home.[6]

Politically the tenants had little opportunity to express themselves. On the *estancias* at election times the tenants voted under the eye of the landowner or his representative. No government could survive, it was said, that did not have the approval of the landowners. But the landowners, as a class, did not take active part in politics, leaving that to others, and not meddling so long as the system was undisturbed. After

[6] Carl C. Taylor, *Rural Life in Argentina* (Baton Rouge, Louisiana, 1948).

the harsh dictatorship of Rosas, Argentina was led by several distinguished liberals and seemed to be well on the way to the establishment of democratic institutions. In Buenos Aires two of the world's leading free newspapers, *La Prensa* and *La Nación*, were published. At several great universities liberal traditions were nurtured. Yet the great majority of the people did not enjoy political freedom.

The Effects of the Second World War. World wars have a serious impact on any country involved in international trade. The great prosperity of Argentina was based on access to foreign markets, and when those markets were shut off by war the results on Argentine economic and political life were profound. During the first world war, for example, Argentina was suddenly faced with a shortage of the manufactured items it had been accustomed to import, chiefly from Great Britain. Even wheat had been shipped to Britain and British flour had been shipped back. Many new manufacturing industries were established during and after the second world war, chiefly the result of foreign investment, for the Argentine wealthy class was not interested in this kind of opportunity. Furthermore, the Government was not especially concerned to protect the new industries. In fact, tariffs were so arranged that it was cheaper to import manufactured articles from abroad than to manufacture them in Argentina. For a variety of reasons, some of them obvious, Argentina adopted a policy of neutrality in the world's conflicts, and became strongly anti-United States and anti-British.

The second world war, however, had the most profound effect on Argentina.[7] Soon it became apparent that Britain could no longer spare the ships to carry on the accustomed trade with so distant a country. The British decided to try to produce more wheat in Great Britain and to limit Argentine shipments, so far as possible, to meat. Argentina easily reacted to this change in trade. The large landowners dismissed their tenant grain farmers. Wheat and maize acreage declined enormously as the tenant farmers moved into Buenos Aires. Fortunately, during this period, there was no shortage of jobs in the metropolis: there was a vast program of slum clearance, new construction, and new industrial expansion that offered employment to all who wanted jobs. A huge new port was being built for Buenos Aires. But the most important effect was the removal of the former tenants from the political supervision of the landowners.

[7] Felix J. Weil, *Argentine Riddle* (John Day, New York, 1944).

Perón rose to power on the votes of the workers, the ones he described as *descamisados*, or shirtless. His social program, his promises, and the personal appeal of himself and his wife, Eva Perón, commanded the enthusiastic support of voters who never before had been free to express themselves politically. The program he announced was immensely pleasing to people who combined a burning national pride with a lack of education in the basic economic facts and principles. These people, moreover, had never enjoyed civil liberty. They supported enthusiastically a strong central dictatorship that stamped out all liberal movements, closed the liberal newspapers, dismissed the liberal professors, and which at the same time proclaimed Argentina's independence from outside forces and her own national self-sufficiency. That such a program could lead only to economic ruin in a land endowed with none of the basic resources, even of fuel or potential hydro-electric power, could not be understood.

How could Perón defy the political power of the army and of the landowners? By the time that he had received the support of a vast majority of the people, the army could no longer control the political situation, and its officers were unwilling to face the possibility of having to shoot down the citizens of their own country. Perón's program incorporated the old ideas of national self-sufficiency together with numerous economic and social benefits promised to the workers. He decreed higher minimum wages, social security, health insurance, vacations with pay, and other popular measures which were pleasing indeed to the laboring classes. With the aid of a secret police, secret arrest, trial by torture, and the elimination of all sources of public news, he was able to keep strictly in line people opposed to his program. The atmosphere of emotional patriotism, of high-sounding attacks on the world's great Powers, of military might, and of complete national unity was intoxicating.

But eventually the facts caught up with Perón. His economic program brought Argentina to ruin. The income per capita dropped well below that of Venezuela and even of Puerto Rico. Supplies of meat were inadequate even for the domestic market, and this for a people accustomed to eating steak three times a day was a really serious matter. Furthermore, the many Argentines who were bitterly opposed to their loss of civil liberties and who were working underground began to find supporters from among the workers. When Perón launched a bitter attack on the Catholic Church, arresting priests and demanding the exile of the leaders of the Church in Argentina, it was clear that he had become desperate. The revolt which forced him into exile in 1955 started with the officers of the armed services. Because Perón had removed officers of doubtful loyalty to the provinces, the revolt began in Córdoba. It spread rapidly, however, and soon the army was back in control. Strikes called by the former Perónista labor leaders failed because the workers, disillusioned by Perón's failure to deliver what he had promised, were now ready to support another government.

The Argentine State-idea. Argentina is a country with divergent state-ideas. The majority would certainly subscribe to an extreme form of nationalism which aims at complete self-sufficiency. The Argentines achieved their advanced stage of economic development because of British investment in the period after 1853. But seldom indeed are there examples in the world of the people of a country being grateful for economic development resulting from foreign investments. Usually the people are bitterly resentful. The basic idea of freedom—that is the right to political and economic independence—has long been frustrated in Argentina precisely because of Argentina's relative prosperity. The idea of economic interdependence, so necessary for a country with such unbalanced natural resources, has few adherents. Perón's program of national self-sufficiency had great popular support. In fact, one of the underlying causes of his downfall was an agreement he had made with certain large North American oil companies to undertake oil exploration and development. This was too much for the army.

On the other hand, Argentina has a long tradition of liberalism. Its great newspapers, especially *La Prensa*, have long carried the banner of civil liberty, of freedom of access to knowledge. Argentine professors and their students were, before Perón took rigid control, strongly liberal. Can liberalism, and freedom of access to knowledge be reconciled with violent nationalism and with programs of economic self-sufficiency? This is Argentina's great problem.

Brazil

Totally different, again, is Portuguese Brazil. The Brazilians are a commercial-minded people, always alert for the chance of quick profit, always ready to compromise to avoid a conflict. Brazil's national terri-

2H*

tory is larger than that of the United States, and within its borders are a variety of different kinds of people and contrasts of economic development.

The Process of Settlement. Brazilian landowners have never been content with the prestige of holding landed properties. Always they have sought speculative gain. Brazil's economic history is divided into cycles in each of which a kind of economy has been built up speculatively to the vast profit of the entrepreneurs. And when competition with other producing areas, or increasing costs of production due to soil impoverishment, result in a decrease of profits the tendency is to sell the land or other property and enter a new and more promising venture. From 1500 to 1700 sugar cane in the North-east was bringing great wealth to the small number of landowners, whose plantations were worked by Negro slaves. From 1700 to 1800 the chief speculative profits were made in the mining of gold and diamonds, most of it in the South-east, the region inland from Rio de Janeiro. From 1850 to 1930 great profits were made from coffee planting, chiefly in São Paulo state. The present high coffee prices are the result of the decline of new coffee planting after 1930, when the Government withdrew its support of coffee prices and speculative profits were no longer insured. Since that time the best way to derive quick returns on money invested would seem to be in the construction of apartment and office buildings in the big cities.

There have been other economic cycles in Brazil during all this time. Rubber production was stepped up in the Amazon region until, after 1910, competition with the plantations of South-east Asia reduced the possibility of quick profits. There have been speculative cycles in cacao, oranges, and, after the second world war, in sisal.

Underlying all these cycles is the basic pastoral economy. The large landowners of Brazil would not hesitate to make the most profitable use of their lands; but when all else fails there is always a steady demand for beef, and this requires relatively little investment to produce. The great majority of the Brazilian farmers work as tenants; they are welcomed by the pastoral-minded landlords because they clear the forest and, after a few years during which they grow maize, rice, beans, and perhaps cotton, they plant pasture grass and move away.[8]

The Brazilian agricultural system has been applied, during the course of four centuries, to one kind of land—to the area originally covered by

[8] T. Lynn Smith, *Brazil: People and Institutions* (Baton Rouge, Louisiana, 1946).

tropical forest.[9] This forest is not so luxuriant as the rain forest of the Amazon, where soil conditions outside of the alluvial flood-plains are very poor; but the tropical forest is denser than the mixture of low scrubby trees and savanna described as *Cerrado* (Fig. 4). Brazilians

FIG. 4. BRAZIL: NATURAL VEGETATION

sometimes look at simple political maps showing the vast area of the country and the relatively small part of the coastal fringe within which the several areas of concentrated settlement have been built up, and they fail to appreciate the relationship between the farming areas and the area of tropical forest. By 1954, also, the tropical forest had been almost entirely cleared. Except for small areas in western Paraná and Santa Catarina, or in northern Minas Gerais and southern Bahia, no virgin

[9] Preston E. James, "Trends in Brazilian Agricultural Development," in *Geographical Review*, vol. xliii (1953), pp. 301–328.

tropical forest remains. Near the cities the forest has been cleared again and again until the land has been so impoverished that it has little productivity left.

What happens next? Is there to be a westward movement into the *Cerrado* of the interior? Is the capital to be moved into this still empty area? Not enough is known about the character of the soil, surface, and drainage conditions or the climates of this interior to provide a proper guide to any process of new settlement. There is great need for a survey of resources, somewhat like the great Land Utilisation Survey of Great Britain or the Puerto Rico survey, but on maps of smaller scale.

The Brazilian State-idea. The development of a distinctive state-idea in Brazil is facilitated by the use of a distinctive language. No other American State speaks Portuguese, and this fact alone serves to create a feeling of unity in the minds of the varied people who make up the Brazilian population. People who speak and read Portuguese are influenced by a distinctive set of books and ideas.

There are, to be sure, certain conditions in Brazil that work against the establishment of an ordered political life.[10] Chief among these is the very uneven economic development of the country. Nearly 40 per cent. of the productive capacity of Brazil is in the state of São Paulo and more than 70 per cent. is concentrated around the two metropolitan cities of Rio de Janeiro and São Paulo. The tempo of the economic life in São Paulo reminds one of that in Detroit or Chicago. The rest of the country is much poorer.

These forces, however, are countered by others that point toward closer unity. The fact that São Paulo is near the center of the country rather than on its border is important, for separatist tendencies can develop most easily on the periphery of a national territory, as in Catalonia in Spain. No centrally located state has ever been known to secede from the outlying sections of a federation such as that of Brazil. Modern techniques of transportation and communication are rapidly overcoming the isolation of one area of concentrated settlement from another; whereas the governor of Goiás once needed twelve days to get from his state capital to the national capital, it now takes him a few hours, and he can talk by radio or telephone at any time.

Brazil still has serious economic problems to solve. Centuries of

---

[10] *Idem*, "Forces for Union and Disunion in Brazil," in *Journal of Geography*, vol. xxviii (1939), pp. 260–266.

exploitive land use have seriously damaged the resource base for a pre-dominantly agricultural economy. Yet the Brazilian farmer is not so fixed in position, either socially or geographically, as his counterpart in most of the Spanish countries. The poor people of Brazil are highly mobile, and quickly travel across the vast interior of the country in search of better economic opportunities. There is no agrarian problem at all comparable with that of Mexico or Chile. But there is still a great gap between the very wealthy and the very poor, and until this gap is narrowed the development of modern large-scale manufacturing in-dustry is handicapped. As explained in a previous chapter, industriali-zation under these conditions results in a rise of prices and the progres-sive impoverishment of the people.

Nevertheless, industrialization, as elsewhere, provides the jobs that must eventually close the gap. São Paulo city and its environs is the location of the largest concentration of industrial investment in all Latin America. The new steel plant, located midway between Rio de Janeiro and São Paulo is the largest steel plant in all Latin America. Few countries enjoy such a large domestic market area, unimpeded by tariffs; and in no other country are the possibilities of increasing the domestic market so enormous.

CHAPTER XL

Maritime Boundaries

A. E. MOODIE

W HEN Columbus discovered America he could not have foreseen the difficulties to which the developments of the "Columban Age" were to lead. His great contribution to geographical knowledge was his demonstration that the barrier function of the oceans could be overcome, and the efforts of later explorers and traders were to illustrate what has now become a commonplace—that the seas are links between the coastal communities of the world. For four centuries world maritime trade steadily increased, overseas empires were established, and for much of that time the Royal Navy maintained at least a semblance of order on the High Seas. While advancing knowledge of surveying and cartography enabled the nineteenth-century States to define and demarcate their land boundaries, little or no attention was paid to the delimitation of maritime limits. The well-known "cannon-shot rule," as enunciated by the Dutch jurist Bynkershoek in 1737, whereby the sovereignty of a maritime State extended over the territorial sea to a limit of three nautical miles, was generally accepted. For obvious reasons such limits could not be demarcated and "For centuries, because of the vastness of the sea and the limited relations between States, the use of the sea was subject to no rules; every State could use it as it pleased."[1]

The Need for Maritime Boundaries in the Twentieth Century

Bynkershoek's rule was designed with an eye to defence and became obsolete with the development of modern artillery. Throughout the nineteenth century increasing attention was paid to the use of the seas.

[1] Señor Alvarez, "Fisheries Case (United Kingdom v. Norway)," *Reports of Judgments, Advisory Opinions and Orders* 1951 (International Court of Justice, Leyden, 1951), p. 146. Señor Alvarez was the Chilean member of the Court.

Coastal States rapidly expanded their overseas trade, and even interior Powers sought a share in the new maritime activities. Imperial Russia acquired "a window on the Baltic," and Austria-Hungary built the ports of Trieste and Fiume (Rijeka) at the head of the Adriatic. The opening of the Suez Canal reinvigorated the trade of the Mediterranean, and Japan joined the rivals for sea power. These activities were reflected in the building of warships as well as merchant fleets, so that by the opening of the twentieth century Britain no longer held the sole responsibility of maintaining the *Pax Britannicum* on the High Seas. The world had awakened to the possibilities which Columbus had inadvertently indicated.

Three sets of geographical conditions affecting the use of the seas have emerged during the first half of the present century. First, sea-borne trade has increased enormously. Accompanied by a ceaseless search for markets and sources of raw materials, and assisted by the growth of navigational aids and new means of communication, maritime traffic has reached an unprecedented peak and has brought about such a close network of international relationships that a high degree of economic integration has been achieved in this field. "The ocean was one ocean all the time, but the practical meaning of that great reality was not wholly understood until a few years ago—perhaps it is only now being grasped in its entirety."[2] Such a realization finds its expression not only in the increased appreciation of the use of the seas to the benefit of mankind, but also in the foreign policies of the governments concerned.

Secondly, the great increase of world population has been accompanied by a lower rate of increase in the production of food, but, simultaneously, by a vast expansion in the consumption of the raw materials of industry. Nothing is further from the truth than the assumption that the Industrial Revolution has been completed. Technological developments, new sources of industrial energy, and new materials are coming forward at a greater tempo than ever before. In a recent and stimulating study Fairfield Osborn wrote, "We Americans have used as much of the earth's riches in forty years as all people, the world over, have used in four thousand."[3] Doubts may be cast on the statistical validity of this statement, yet there can be no denial of the dangers of the rapid consumption of irreplaceable raw materials. For our present purpose the important factor is its essential corollary in the search for new sources.

[2] Sir H. J. Mackinder, *Democratic Ideals and Reality* (Constable, London, 1919), p. 39.
[3] F. Osborn, *The Limits of the Earth* (Faber, London, 1954), p. 60.

For many centuries the sea has been a provider of food, but it may now have to play a greater role in meeting the world deficit. Furthermore, the sea-bed in all probability contains rich mineral deposits to which men are already looking to counterbalance the impending exhaustion of land sources. For these cogent reasons littoral States are concerned with their authority over adjacent sea areas.

Thirdly, and partly as a result of two world wars, the number of independent or quasi-independent States in the world has increased considerably during the twentieth century. "States, national and multinational, are the stars of the international scene."[4] The activities of each are dominated by the desire to maintain sovereign independent status within a clearly defined sphere, the delimitation of which may give rise to conflict with both contiguous States and those more remotely situated but with common interests in neighbouring areas. On land territorial claims have been met by treaty arrangements, bilateral or multilateral, and the habitable surface of the earth is now more or less clearly marked out by international boundaries, although it would be a mistake to consider all these arrangements as permanent settlements of boundary disputes. Because of the economic and strategic interests outlined above, maritime independent States have become increasingly conscious of the need to define their spheres of sovereignty seaward. When it is remembered that the majority of States possess marine frontages, and even those that are landlocked have interests in seaborne trade the significance of this new phase of boundary definition will be appreciated. In international law all States are theoretically equal and politically independent, however unequal and economically interdependent they may be in practice. When they proceed to stake claims over adjacent seas and their beds by unilateral action, conflicts inevitably develop, especially when there are wide divergences of interest between individual States or groups of States. This is precisely what has happened during the last thirty years. Strategic, economic, and political interests have combined to bring about a state approaching that of chaos in the seaward extension of sovereignty. The increasing number of international disputes falls into two groups, those concerned with the continental shelf and with the territorial sea respectively.

[4] G. Schwarzenberger, *Power Politics* (second edition; Stevens, London, 1951), p. 126.

Maritime Boundaries and the Continental Shelf

Like all natural phenomena, the continental shelves are irregularly distributed. Nowhere do these gently sloping submarine surfaces extend to very great distances from the continental shores, yet they have been important to the inhabitants of the adjacent littorals. Outstanding are their value as fishing grounds: witness the contributions of the shelves of middle latitudes—those of Western Europe, eastern North America, and the Far East—to the food supply of the temperate countries. At the same time it may be recalled that the unsubmerged parts of continental shelves are islands whose peoples have frequently played a major role in the activities of the inhabitants of the near-by mainlands, the British and Japanese archipelagos providing excellent examples. In spite of their obvious importance, the shelves have never been claimed as State territory[5] until recent years. Beyond the territorial seas they have been regarded either as *res nullius* (no-man's-land) or as *res communis*—i.e., incapable of acquisition by any State; and the doctrine of the Freedom of the High Seas has generally been accepted in peacetime as granting unrestricted use of the sea to all comers. Under this regime of the High Seas no difference was made between the waters covering the continental shelves and those of the ocean deeps, and no question of a legal definition of the extent of the shelves arose. Hydrographers discovered that there is normally a pronounced break of slope between the continental shelf and the continental slope at a depth of about 100 fathoms, but this break does not occur regularly and exactly at such a depth. Nevertheless, the 100-fathom isobath has been widely accepted as the outer limit of the continental shelf by geographers, hydrographers, and geologists. The aggregate area of all such areas between the 100-fathom line and the mean low-water mark of the adjacent land masses has been estimated to reach as high a figure as ten million square miles.

Another characteristic feature of the world's continental shelves is their variation in width. Their existence results from tectonic movements in the earth's crust which in themselves are notable for their range of amplitude. Thus the western coasts of the Americas and the whole of Africa show very little development of shelves, whereas Eastern United States and Canada, North-western Europe, and parts of Eastern and South-east Asia have extensive platforms inside the 100-fathom

[5] With the possible and unique exception implied in the Treaty of Tordesillas of 1494.

isobath. In each of these latter instances considerable areas of the shelves are unsubmerged, the most important islands being Newfoundland, the British Isles, the Japanese archipelago, and the East Indies. Any territorial claims to the continental shelves made by adjacent States are affected by these geographical conditions. Furthermore, and owing to the peculiar irregularity of the distribution of States on the earth's surface, there is wide variation in the numbers of claims which can legitimately be made to parts of any one shelf. The Western European Shelf, for example, is bordered by eleven independent States (excluding those bordering on the Baltic only), each of which may claim rights over parts of the adjacent submarine platform. By contrast, the shelf off the eastern coasts of North America, with a greater extent from north to south, is subject to claims by two States only—the United States and Canada. In view of these and other differences it is not difficult to envisage some at least of the complex problems which arise as soon as claims to total or partial sovereignty over the shelf itself or over its superjacent waters or both are made. Such claims are very recent. All of them have been put forward as unilateral declarations, each State clearly aiming at obtaining what it considers to be the maximum possible.[6]

A preliminary phase to extending sovereignty seaward may be detected in the Declaration of Panama, which was issued after a meeting of the Foreign Ministers of the American Republics in October 1939. Under this declaration a security zone with a minimum width of 300 nautical miles was established off the coasts of the Americas. At that time the second world war had begun, and the American Republics hoped to preserve their neutrality behind this extensive belt of water, a hope which was destroyed by the disaster of Pearl Harbour. Nevertheless, the strategic importance of adjacent waters was not forgotten, as is shown by the Treaty of Petropolis of September 1947, which defined a region of reciprocal assistance by the signatories of the Panama Declaration and extending from the North Pole to the South Pole. Such international agreements can be successfully implemented only with the help of powerful naval and air forces, and it appears that the United States Navy is now undertaking a function comparable with that for long performed by the Royal Navy.

When the second world war ended the Declaration of Panama automatically became invalid, because it infringed the rights exercised by

[6] Most of these claims are given in M. W. Mouton, *The Continental Shelf* (The Hague, 1952).

nations under the doctrine of the Freedom of the High Seas. The multi-lateral agreement of October 1939 was followed by a series of unilateral declarations which was initiated by the Proclamation (No. 2667) of the President of the United States of September 28, 1945. This so-called Truman Declaration, it is important to notice, was very carefully worded and claimed sovereignty only over the sea-bed and subsoil of the adjacent continental shelf—not over its superjacent waters. Even so, the American Government appeared to have considerable hopes of economic advantage from their claim, for, as Mr Harold L. Ickes, the Secretary of the Interior, wrote in his Annual Report for 1945, "Alaska cost us $7,200,000, the Dutch West Indies $25,000,000, the Louisiana Purchase $27,000,000. The Continental Shelf cost us only the forethought that was required to assert our sovereignty over it."

The Truman Declaration was soon followed by twelve other American Republics, but most of these made greater claims than that of the United States in so far as they claimed sovereignty over the epicontinental sea—*i.e.*, the waters lying on the shelf, as well as the sea-bed and subsoil of the shelf. In particular, Chile issued a Presidential decree in June 1947 which "Confirms and proclaims the national sovereignty over the seas adjacent to its coasts . . . for 200 marine miles from the whole circumference." This was followed in August 1947 by a Decree of the President of Peru, which differed from that of Chile only by making special reference to the extension of sovereignty over the guano deposits of the offshore islands. In 1952 the Governments of Chile, Ecuador, and Peru issued at Santiago a joint declaration in which they ". . . proclaim as a standard of their international maritime policy exclusive sovereignty and jurisdiction . . . up to a distance of 200 nautical miles." This was tantamount to an extension of the territorial seas of the three countries and, as such, had no precedent. It evoked strong protests from the United Kingdom and other maritime Powers, yet late in 1954 part of the Onassis whaling fleet was arrested within the 200-mile limit and taken in custody to a Peruvian port. The subsequent payment of a fine of $3 million by Lloyds' agents as insurers of Mr Onassis may be taken as implying recognition of the Peruvian claim; at the least, it establishes a very undesirable precedent.

By 1948 the legal position regarding the continental shelf had become so involved that the United Nations Organization recommended to the International Law Commission that it should give priority in its discussions to the regime of the High Seas. After prolonged argument the

Commission submitted to the General Assembly of the United Nations its proposals concerning the continental shelf. These Draft Articles[7] defined the shelf as ". . . the sea-bed and subsoil of the submarine areas contiguous to the coast, but outside the area of the territorial sea, to a depth of two hundred metres," and state that "The coastal State exercises over the continental shelf sovereign rights for the purpose of exploring and exploiting its natural resources," but "The rights of the

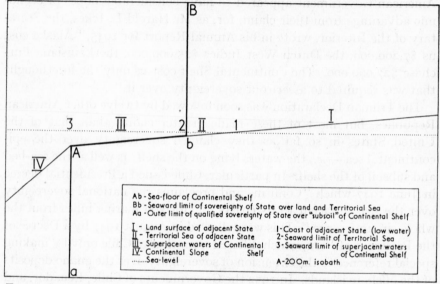

FIG. 1. SCHEMATIC CROSS-SECTION OF THE SEAWARD BOUNDARY OF A LITTORAL STATE

coastal State over the continental shelf do not affect the legal status of the superjacent waters as high seas," nor do these rights ". . . affect the legal status of the airspace above the superjacent waters." The Ninth Session of the General Assembly agreed to defer consideration of the Draft Articles to the Tenth Session in 1955, in order to give member countries further opportunities of studying them, but some of their possible effects may be considered here.

The point is often overlooked that all international boundaries are, in law, not lines but planes. On land the demarcated boundary is a line and appears as such on maps, but in legal theory the boundary extends upward and downward so that the State controls the air-space above its

[7] "Draft Articles on the Continental Shelf," Report of the International Law Commission, in *General Assembly of the United Nations Official Records*, Eighth Session, Supplement No. 9, A/CN/4/76 (New York, 1953), pp. 12–19.

territory, both land and sea, as well as the resources beneath it. Furthermore, States are very unwilling to allow any infringement of their rights within these vertical planes. The development of the so-called Continental Shelf Theory introduces a new concept into the field of boundary-making. If the littoral State possessed full sovereignty over the adjacent part of the shelf and its superjacent waters, then its seaward boundary would be a vertical plane passing through the 200-metre

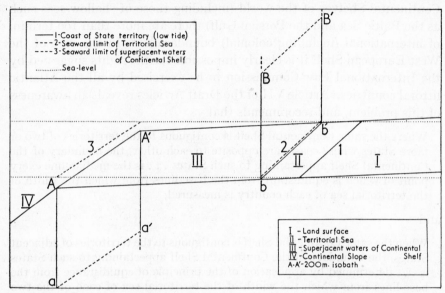

FIG. 2. THREE-DIMENSIONAL REPRESENTATION OF THE SEAWARD BOUNDARY OF A LITTORAL STATE

Plane AA′ aa′ represents the outer limit of qualified sovereignty over the subsoil of the Continental Shelf. Plane AA′ bb′ represents the floor of the adjacent Continental Shelf below which the littoral State will exercise qualified sovereignty. Plane BB′ bb′ represents the seaward limit of full national sovereignty over the air-space and the waters of the Territorial Sea. Continued vertically downward, it would indicate the outer limit of full sovereignty over submarine resources.

isobath. This would mean a very great extension of the authority of some coastal States and might well prove to be a hindrance to navigation and fishing.

Should the International Law Commission's recommendations be adopted the seaward boundary of the littoral State will have three parts as indicated diagrammatically in Figs. 1 and 2.[8] It is difficult to

[8] These two diagrams are reproduced from the writer's paper, "Some Territorial Problems associated with the Continental Shelf," in *The Advancement of Science*, vol. xi, No. 41 (1954), by permission of the British Association for the Advancement of Science.

envisage any suitable methods of demarcating these new limits. Presumably the hydrographic charts of the future will be contoured in metres. The 200-metre isobath at least should be plotted, but the old problem of navigators, especially of fishermen, of knowing, or, worse still, of proving, when they are just inside or outside the territorial sea will remain. Further problems will arise where two or more States lie adjacent to the same continental shelf. "On the sea coasts of the Continental Shelves of the world (including those of shallow seas such as the Baltic Sea and the Persian Gulf) there are more than 100 termini of international (including colonial) boundaries."[9] In the case of the West European Shelf it is clearly impossible for the rights suggested by the International Law Commission to be exercised by all the Atlantic littoral countries. Article VII of the Draft Articles reveals an awareness of this problem, and recommends that

> Where the same Continental Shelf is contiguous to the territories of two or more States whose coasts are opposite to each other, the boundary of the Continental Shelf appertaining to such States . . . is the median line every point of which is equidistant from the base-lines from which the width of the territorial sea of each country is measured,

and

> When the same Continental Shelf is contiguous to the territories of adjacent States, the boundary of the Continental Shelf appertaining to such States is . . . determined by application of the principle of equidistance from the base-lines from which the width of the territorial sea of each of the two countries is measured.

Fig. 3 shows a possible interpretation of these recommendations, but, unfortunately, the Draft Articles do not prescribe methods for dealing with problems arising from the existence of islands such as the Channel Isles and Bornholm. The members of the Commission probably had such cases in mind when they added the provision ". . . in the absence of agreement between those States or unless another boundary line is justified by special circumstances" to the two parts of their Article VII.

The present position concerning the legal status of the continental shelf and its superjacent waters is hardly more than one of claim-staking. A twentieth-century Alexander could say with justice that there are no more worlds to conquer, at least not on *terra firma*. The land surface of the earth has already been shared out; now man's atten-

[9] S. W. Boggs, "National Claims in Adjacent Seas," in *Geographical Review*, vol. xli, No. 2 (New York, 1951).

tion has been turned to the sea-bed and its subsoil and to the possibilities of exploiting their resources. Petroleum has been extracted from the sea-bed of the Gulf of Mexico at a distance of twenty-five miles from the shore of the state of Texas, and improved techniques combined with

FIG. 3. SHARING OUT THE CONTINENTAL SHELF OF NORTH-WESTERN EUROPE

A possible arrangement of international maritime boundaries, here drawn at equal distances from opposite coasts. The occurrence of off-shore islands causes difficulties which are illustrated in this map by the cases of the Channel Islands, and Danish Bornholm and Swedish Gotland in the Baltic.

ever-increasing demand may push the seaward limit of mineral exploitation of the sea-bed even farther out. Sir Rupert Hay reports that the oil companies operating in the Persian Gulf States are interested in prospecting for oil under the sea and that

. . . in 1949 the Rulers of all the States in the Persian Gulf proper issued

declarations that the sea-bed and subsoil lying beneath the high seas of the
Persian Gulf, contiguous to their territorial waters and extending seawards
to boundaries to be subsequently defined, belonged to them and were subject
to their absolute jurisdiction.[10]

These and other developments indicate increasing interest in previously
inaccessible areas which will inevitably lead to more territorial problems. Finally, it may be recalled that the Draft Articles expressly
exclude the superjacent waters of the continental shelf from State
sovereignty. If they are accepted and implemented through the United
Nations they will invalidate the claims of the South American Republics, and fishing rights outside the territorial sea will remain free to all
except where international arrangements such as those of the International Whaling Commission and the International Convention for the
High Seas Fisheries of the North Pacific Ocean may be applicable.
Nevertheless, there remain the problems associated with the territorial
seas, which, although they are part of the superjacent waters of the
continental shelf, fall into a different legal category.

The Territorial Sea and Maritime Boundaries[11]

For nearly three centuries there has been general acceptance of the
three-mile limit as the seaward boundary of the territorial sea. In effect
this water body, together with its associated air and submarine spaces,
is considered as an extension of the territory of the adjacent State which
exercises full sovereign rights over the whole complex with the single
exception of the right of "innocent passage" in peacetime. In recent
years two factors have been primarily responsible for numerous demands for extensions of the limits of the territorial seas. First, the old
cannon-shot rule is no longer applicable as a defensive measure—
Bynkershoek's dictum "The dominion of the land ends where the power
of arms ends" is patently absurd in these days of aircraft and guided
missiles. Indeed, it is debatable whether any width of such adjacent
zones would be effective in wartime, but obsession with security measures has given rise to some extravagant demands. Secondly, the economic resources of the territorial sea and its floor have assumed greater

[10] Sir Rupert Hay, "The Persian Gulf States and their Boundary Problems," in
Geographical Journal, vol. cxx, Part 4 (1954).
[11] "Territorial sea" is preferred in legal circles to the older form "Territorial waters,"
as it avoids confusion over "inland waters," etc.

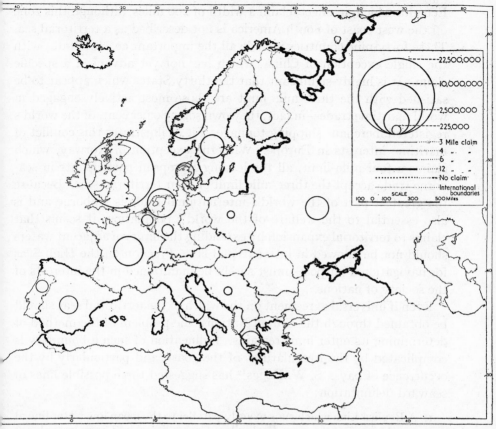

FIG. 4. THE CLAIMS OF EUROPEAN MARITIME STATES TO TERRITORIAL SEAS AND
THEIR SEABORNE TRADE

Circles are proportional to overseas trade in tons (1954); thicknesses of
coastlines in proportion to territorial seas in marine miles.

importance than ever before. In particular, as States possess absolute
rights over the fisheries of their territorial seas, it is to their economic
advantage to extend their areas of control. Any such extensions immediately reduce the freedom of action of other States and may lead to
conflicts.

At the present time, therefore, there is no universal agreement on the
width of territorial seas. Thirty States (including the United Kingdom
and the French Union) claim a three-mile limit, four States claim a four-
mile limit, one State (Honduras) claims a five-mile limit, Mexico claims
a nine-mile limit, and the U.S.S.R. stands alone in its claim to a twelve-
mile limit. The most extreme cases are those of Chile, Peru, and

Ecuador which, in effect, claim a width of 200 miles, although this zone off the west coast of South America is not described as a territorial sea. These forty-nine countries include all the important coastal States with the single exception of China, which has not yet advanced a specific claim. It is highly significant that the thirty States which appear to be satisfied with the three-mile limit are those most actively engaged in world maritime trade—in fact, they own some 80 per cent. of the world's registered merchant-shipping tonnage. Fig. 4 illustrates this conflict of maritime interests in Europe. With the exception of Norway, which claims a four-mile limit, all the leading European participants in sea-borne trade accept the three-mile limit of their territorial seas. Because the greatest part of the world's international trade is seaborne and is also essential to the welfare of the world's population, it seems that claims to territorial expansion by extending the limits of adjacent waters should not be allowed in international law. Freedom of the High Seas for navigational purposes must surely be maintained in the interests of the society of nations.

Even if universal agreement on the width of the territorial seas should be obtained through the United Nations, the problem of the method of determining its outer limit remains. Delineation of such a boundary is complicated by the irregularities of the coast, and particularly by the occurrence of bays. S. W. Boggs[12] has suggested three possible lines of seaward delimitation:

1. A Replica Line which runs exactly parallel to the mean low water line at a distance of three nautical miles. Such a line would be as irregular as the coast itself and would be difficult to delineate cartographically.
2. A Conventional Line which is drawn parallel to a series of base-lines joining selected points on the coast.
3. An Envelope Line. Like 1 and 2 this is a geometrical boundary and is defined as the envelope of the arcs of circles of three-mile radius drawn from all points on the mean low water line. It is a much simpler and less irregular line than the replica line, and yet, unlike the conventional line, it adheres literally to the three-mile requirements.

All three of these methods are further complicated by the occurrence of offshore islands as well as by the morphology of the coast itself. Nowhere has the envelope method been applied, although it was proposed, unsuccessfully, by the American delegation to the Hague Conference for the Codification of International Law in 1930. The replica

[12] S. W. Boggs, "Delimitation of the Territorial Sea," in *American Journal of International Law*, vol. xxiv (New York, 1930).

method or variants of it is most commonly used, but cases of the application of the conventional method have recently been the cause of international disputes (see pp. 956–959 below). Both the replica and envelope lines are measured from mean low water lines, but, as Shalowitz[13] points out, tidal conditions vary along different coasts, so that, for example, nautical charts of the United States show mean low water for the Atlantic coast and mean lower low water for that of the Pacific. But the greatest difficulty in fixing datum lines from which the width of the territorial sea is measured arises from the occurrence of coastal indentations such as bays and estuaries.

Bays and the Semicircular Rule. As long ago as 1910 the North Atlantic Fisheries Tribunal investigated a dispute between the United Kingdom and the United States over the rights of American nationals to fish within three miles of the Newfoundland coasts. It decided that "In the case of bays, the three marine miles are to be measured from a straight line drawn across the body of water where it ceases to have the configuration and characteristics of a bay,"[14] but, did not define the "configuration and characteristics of a bay." It did, however, decide that the three-mile limit in open bays should be measured "from a straight line across the bay in the part nearest the entrance at the first point where the width does not exceed ten miles." This ruling does not consider the penetration of the indentation and does not help in the differentiation between 'open' and 'closed' bays. Hence it was desirable to evolve a geometrical formula which could be used in all cases of bays and estuaries to determine where an indentation of the coast is sufficient to be regarded as a closed bay—i.e., as a part of the inland waters of the State concerned. Such a formula was worked out in the United States as follows. If the area of a bay in nature, measured between the shoreline and a line joining the headlands, exceeds the area of the semicircle whose diameter is the line joining the headlands, the bay is a closed bay and the seaward boundary of inland waters is the headland-to-headland line. If its area is less than the area of the semicircle, the bay is an open bay and the boundary line of inland waters would be the mean low water mark following the sinuosities of the bay. This is known as the semicircular rule.

[13] A. L. Shalowitz, "Cartography in the Submerged Lands Oil Cases," in *The Journal*, No. 4, Coast and Geodetic Survey (New York, 1951), pp. 68–78.
[14] A. L. Shalowitz, *op. cit.* The author gives a series of useful cartographic representations of the methods of drawing envelope lines.

S. W. Boggs introduced a refinement of this rule. He proposed that the radius of the semicircle should be equal to one quarter of the length of the line between headlands, and that the landward limit of the territorial sea—*i.e.*, the seaward limit of inland waters—in bays should be the envelope line of arcs drawn at a distance equal to the radius of the semicircle from all points on the mean low water line. This proposal was incorporated in the American delegation's suggestions to the Hague Conference in 1930, but was not accepted, although it provides a sound working method of solving problems associated with coastal indentations. The delegation also proposed that in the case of bays wider than ten miles at the outer headlands a line should be drawn across the bay where it first narrows to ten miles, and that this line should be used to determine the radius of the arcs under the semicircular rule. That all these proposals and the seemingly endless legal arguments concerning the methods of determining the extent of the territorial sea are of more than academic interest is suggested by the number of disputes which have arisen since the end of the second world war. In the United States there have been several disputes between the Federal Government and state governments, the upshot of which has been a ruling by the Supreme Court that the territorial sea is subject to the sovereignty of the United States and not of any one of its component parts. More important in the international field are two disputes in which the United Kingdom has been involved, one with Norway and the other with Iceland. In a strictly legal sense, each of these two cases is concerned with the delimitation of fishing zones with a view to conservation measures and exclusion of foreign fishermen except by special arrangement, but in the former at least, it was assumed that the area in dispute was the territorial sea. For a number of reasons, of interest to geographers and lawyers alike, the two cases are worthy of brief analyses.

The Fisheries Case (United Kingdom *v.* Norway).[15] In 1951 the United Kingdom asked the International Court of Justice

> to declare the principles of international law to be accepted in defining baselines, by reference to which the Norwegian Government is entitled to delimit a fisheries zone, extending to seaward four sea miles from these lines and exclusively reserved for its own nationals, and to define the said baselines in so far as it appears necessary in the light of the arguments of the Parties in order to avoid further legal difficulties between them.

[15] *Reports of Judgments, Advisory Opinions and Orders, 1951* (International Court of Justice, Leyden, 1951).

Sixteen years earlier, on July 12, 1935, a Norwegian Royal Decree had determined a fisheries zone northward of 66° 28' N. latitude to Traena in the County of Nordland. Norway claimed that this decree was based on well-established national titles of right, the geographical conditions prevailing on its northern coasts, the safeguarding of the vital interests of the northernmost parts of the country, and the Royal Decrees of 1812, 1869, 1881, and 1889. The Decree of 1935 prescribed the outer limit of the fishing zone as running parallel with straight base-lines drawn between fixed points on the mainland, on islands or on rocks. The Court upheld the Norwegian action, thus supporting the use of a conventional line as the outer limit of a territorial sea. The case is important as being the only one of its kind which has been referred to the International Court. The judgment was accepted by both parties.

The Iceland Fisheries Case.[16] In 1950 the Icelandic Government issued "Regulations concerning the Conservation of Fishing Rights off the North Coast of Iceland," which prohibited all trawling and Danish seine-netting in the area between Horn and Langanes inside four nautical miles from a base-line between the outermost points of the coast, islands, and rocks; in bays the basic line was drawn across the openings irrespective of their width. In the area defined, only Icelandic citizens may fish for herring, and for such fisheries Icelandic vessels must be used. This was followed in 1952 by "Regulations concerning Conservation of Fisheries off the Icelandic Coasts," which defined base-lines connecting forty-eight points on the mainland and four islands. All foreign fishing was prohibited within a four-mile zone measured from these base-lines. As Fig. 5 shows, the prohibited area includes Faxa Floi, which had been "a sort of fisherman's Eldorado for British trawlers since the 1890's." This unilateral action by Iceland seriously affected the deep-sea fishing industry of other countries, in particular that of Great Britain. Unfortunately Iceland is unwilling to submit her claims to international arbitration, so that the legal issues have led to an inconclusive exchange of notes between the British and Icelandic Governments. On the economic side the dispute has resulted in the refusal of British port authorities to allow landings of Icelandic-caught fish to the detriment of British consumers and Icelandic fishermen.

Some measure of the importance of rival claims to national rights over adjacent waters is provided by these two cases in which otherwise

[16] *Report of the International Law Commission* (New York, 1953), pp. 53 *et seq.*

friendly States have been involved. In each case the United Kingdom has suffered serious economic losses, but at the same time it is difficult not to sympathize with the Icelandic claim, for, as its Government reported to the International Law Commission, "It can truly be said that the coastal fishing grounds are the *conditio sine qua non* of the Icelandic people, for they make the country habitable."

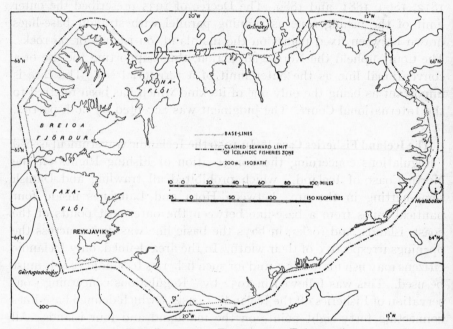

FIG. 5. THE ICELANDIC RESTRICTED FISHING AREA

Based on "The Law concerning the Scientific Conservation of the Continental Shelf Fisheries, dated April 1948." This is not strictly a territorial sea, as only fishing rights are claimed. *N.B.* The outer limit of the fishing area passes seaward of the 200-metre isobath in places, and, to that extent, infringes the recommendations of the International Law Commission.

Conclusion

The first half of the twentieth century has produced many and varied claims concerning the continental shelf and the territorial sea. Contemporary with the increasing 'touchiness' of modern maritime States over their rights to adjacent waters has grown a series of conflicts of interests, strategic and economic. It is obvious that the reasonable settlements of disputes cannot be achieved by unilateral declarations, yet many years may pass before universal agreement on the definition of maritime boundaries is achieved. It is equally obvious that the International Law Commission is striving strenuously to formulate rules for the political adaptation of human activities to the maritime parts of the physical environment. Given the accepted pattern of States, these rules must be primarily directed to the definition of maritime boundaries.

CHAPTER XLI

The Political Geography of the Arctic

TREVOR LLOYD

DEFINITION of "The Arctic" presents perennial problems which have no easy solution. A climatic definition which has become generally accepted includes the area north of the 50° F. (10° C.) isotherm for July. This agrees fairly closely with the 'tree-line' which separates the northern coniferous forest from the tundra. To exclude certain areas with cool maritime climates the annual mean temperature should be below 32° F. (0° C.).[1] It is even more difficult to select a boundary for the area discussed here, since this must include not only the true Arctic and considerable areas of the subarctic, but contiguous areas of less extreme climates. As the present purpose is to discuss geographical factors from a political standpoint, a political delimitation of the area is desirable. Hence the inclusion of the whole Territory of Alaska, the Yukon, Northwest Territories and Quebec Province north of 52° N. Lat. and Labrador in Canada, Greenland, Iceland, Scandinavia north of 68° N. Lat., and the U.S.S.R. north of 62° N. Lat.[2]

The main topics selected for discussion here are: (1) contemporary importance of the far north; (2) the basis and extent of territorial sovereignty, with comments on some boundary questions; (3) resources and their exploitation; (4) transportation routes; (5) strategy and defense. In conclusion there will be a brief comment on possible future developments in the light of the area's political geography.

[1] For a non-technical discussion of polar climates, see V. C. Finch and G. T. Trewartha, *Physical Elements of Geography* (McGraw-Hill, New York, 1949), pp. 205–209. See also M. J. Dunbar, "Note on Delimitation of the Arctic and Subarctic Zones," in *Can. Field Naturalist*, vol. lxi, No. 1 (1947), for a definition from a marine biological viewpoint. *Arctic Bibliography* (Washington, 1953) has arrived at a useful delimitation for bibliographical purposes, but excludes Iceland for non-geographical reasons. For the poleward limits of various trees, see I. Hustich, "The Boreal Limits of some Conifers," in *Arctic*, vol. vi, No. 2, pp. 149–162.

[2] The southern limits mentioned are selected for convenience and have no precise justification.

Contemporary Importance of the Far North

The widespread present-day interest in the far north is a reminder that until a century or so ago it was regarded as a potential world travel route. The disastrous failure of the Franklin expedition in search of a north-west passage and the discouraging geographical knowledge acquired during the subsequent search, the lack of success in finding a practicable north-easterly route and the opening of the Suez Canal, led to a decline in the significance of the north as a possible short-cut from Europe to the Far East. The remarkable present-day surge of northern development is in striking contrast to the century of neglect that pre-ceded it. What factors have brought about this changed attitude? The chief cause is the area's location on the earth in relation to the main centres of population and to modern means of travel.

Geographers long ago deduced, as any schoolboy with a globe and a piece of string can discover for himself, that the shortest routes from Western Europe to Eastern Asia lie to the North. The choice was merely between a north-east and a north-west passage. There was no lack of purpose, skill, and courage among the navigators who for so long failed to find such a passage. But they lacked technical equipment, such as mechanical power for ships, and vehicles able to use the only world-wide thoroughfare—that is, the atmosphere. To-day the use of aircraft makes the open sea, ice-filled waters, or rugged land almost equally unimportant. It is man's ability to use the short-cuts across the world that now brings the higher latitudes into strategic focus. Reinforcing the importance of northerly routes is the uneven distribution of world population centres on the globe. The most important urban areas—which in general are the sources from which spring the world's greatest travel routes—are within the northern hemisphere. Since the Great Circle routes linking the main population centres run northward, we are witnessing a northward shift of the highways of commerce. It is, in part, this north-ward trend of the world's routes, long ago foreseen,[3] that explains the present growth in significance of Alaska, northern Canada, and Green-land, and of corresponding areas on the other side of the North Pole. For example, in justifying the expansion in civil and military activities in the north some years ago the Prime Minister of Canada stated:[4]

[3] V. Stefansson, "The Arctic as an Air Route of the Future," in *National Geographical Magazine* (August 1922), pp. 205–218, map.
[4] Canada: *House of Commons Debates* (February 12, 1947), pp. 359–361.

"New geographical factors have been brought into play. The polar regions assume new importance as the shortest routes between North America and the principal centres of population of the world."

The far north is of growing importance for a related reason. There are, militarily speaking, two outstandingly powerful States in the modern world—the United States and the U.S.S.R. The area we are discussing lies between them. In a warring world it would be on, or close to, the main routes of attack. In an age of long-range missiles no imagination is needed to recognize the danger zone should the catastrophe of a world conflict come about.

The geographical factors which make the far north important militarily are also, and more happily, significant in determining the course of inter-continental civil aviation. We are as yet only beginning to use the 'straight-line' routes northward, long known to exist but out of reach for lack of technological skill. There is little room for doubt that they will in time become extremely important.[5]

Increased flying in the Arctic and middle latitudes has led to other developments, particularly to intensive study of the characteristics and behaviour of the atmosphere. Weather is the common property of all mankind, and nations with territory in the far north are called on to provide detailed and continuous information concerning the atmosphere above it. This has led to the establishment of an elaborate network of far northern weather stations, which is still being expanded.

While it is easy to overestimate the wealth of natural resources which may exist north of the densely settled areas, enough is known to suggest that should the need arise there is room for increased population based on agriculture; that livestock breeding can be expanded, and that there are commercial occurrences of metallic minerals and oil. Should the climatic amelioration of the past thirty years be more than a short-cycle phenomenon, and the limits of certain crops be pushed northward, the crowding of the settled zones to the south may be relieved by a considerable northward expansion of settlement. One does not need to be an uncritical advocate of a "Friendly Arctic" to recognize that valuable resources and large areas of useful land are at present lying untouched beyond the "railway belt."

[5] Commercial air routes have been established for a decade from Canada and the United States to the Far East by way of Alaska. Corresponding routes in the Atlantic frequently cross southern Greenland and use Iceland as a way-station. In November 1954 service was started from Los Angeles to Copenhagen by way of central Greenland and would have used the Thule air-base still farther north but for military objections. A route from Vancouver to Amsterdam via Greenland began in 1955.

The intensified activity in the Arctic, both by military authorities and by commercial or scientific agencies, makes the exact delimitation of territory of great importance. Mining claims, fishing rights, allocation of air routes, and authority to carry out scientific exploration are being eagerly sought. The following discussion indicates that there are still some uncertainties concerning the limits of territorial sovereignty.

Territorial Sovereignty in the Far North

In the classic work on the subject, Miller points out that "discovery," and "settlement," and "notification of the fact" have been traditionally accepted as contributing to a claim to sovereignty, but that "settlement in the Arctic regions can hardly be regarded as precisely synonymous with settlement elsewhere."[6] Subsequent writers have emphasized that settlement is not a necessary element in effective occupation—thus, in the East Greenland case discussed later, the Court of International Justice held that Denmark possessed sovereignty over the area during long periods when no settlement existed at all.[7] Certainly, discovery alone does not provide title to an area.

Stated briefly, the bases of sovereignty in the Arctic are as follows:

Alaska. The territory of Alaska was acquired by the United States by purchase from Russia in 1867. The boundaries described in a convention of March 30, 1867, have been retained to the present. There is no uncertainty about definition of the line separating Alaska and Russia as laid down in 1867, but an official military air chart reveals that the International Date Line is sometimes erroneously marked as the boundary. Misunderstandings of this kind in such an area may have serious consequences.

In the case of the eastern boundary—*i.e.*, the 141st meridian—the convention was supplemented by an official statement by the Minister of the Interior of Canada in 1925. There have been no international disagreements about this boundary, which has been demarcated since

[6] David Hunter Miller, "Political Rights in the Polar Regions," in *Problems of Polar Research* (American Geographical Society, New York, 1928).

[7] Examples cited from the polar regions may be found in: Elmer Plischke, "Trans-Arctic Aviation," in *Economic Geography*, vol. xix, No. 3 (1943), pp. 283–291, and C. H. M. Waldock, "Disputed Sovereignty in the Falkland Islands Dependencies," in *British Yearbook of International Law* (1948).

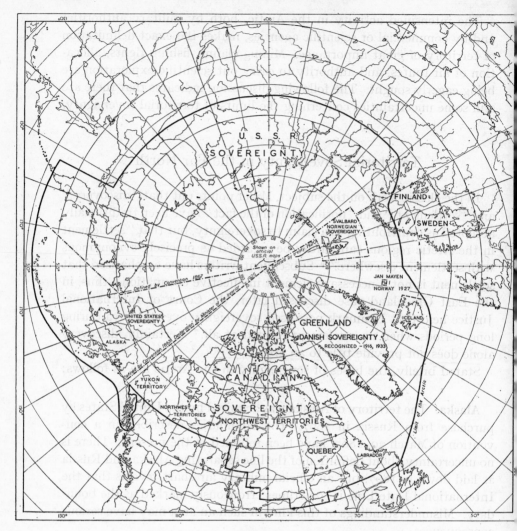

FIG. 1. POLITICAL SOVEREIGNTY IN THE ARCTIC

1913.[8] The extent to which sovereignty may extend beyond the Alaska mainland is discussed later.

Canada. Canada's title to the mainland and known islands between

[8] Hon. Charles R. Stewart, *House of Commons Debates*, vol. lx, No. 84 (June 10, 1925).

Stuart R. Tomkins, "Drawing the Alaskan Boundary," in *The Canadian Historical Review*, vol. xxxvi, No. 1, 1–24 (1945).

Thomas Riggs, "Running the Alaska Boundary," in *The Beaver*, Outfit 276, pp. 40–43 (September 1945).

Greenland and 141° W. Long. has not been challenged in recent years and is not likely to be questioned, since lands customarily shown as Canadian on official maps are everywhere recognized as being Canadian. The basis of Canada's title is effective occupation, including the administering of the law throughout the area, and undisputed official announcements over a long period, as, for example, in 1897, when the District of Franklin was defined as including "all those lands and islands comprised between the 141st meridian of longitude west of Greenwich on the west and Davis Strait, Baffin Bay, Smith Sound and Kennedy Channel and Robeson Channel on the east." The naming of the Arctic archipelago after Queen Elizabeth is a recent example of the exercise of State activity in the area.[9]

Greenland. Greenland is part of the Kingdom of Denmark. There have been some uncertainties about the rights of other nations there, although no question has been raised for more than two centuries about Danish title to the more densely populated south-west coast. Danish title to north-west Greenland has not been in doubt since the United States surrendered any possible claim to parts of the area in 1916 at the time of cession to the United States of the Danish West Indies.[10]

Danish title to East Greenland was challenged by Norway in 1921 on the basis of long-established hunting rights there. A treaty between them, signed in 1924, settled certain points about hunting and the operation of weather stations, but when Norway occupied parts of East Greenland in 1931 the question was referred to the Hague Court, whose decision in 1932 recognized Danish sovereignty.[11] The treaty of 1924 remained in force, and, because of most favoured nation treaties, the rights granted to Norway automatically extend also to Britain and France.

[9] *Canadian Weekly Bulletin*, vol. ix, No. 15 (February 12, 1954), p. 2. For discussions of territorial claims in northern Canada see: W. R. King, *Report upon the Title of Canada to the Islands North of the Mainland of Canada* (Ottawa, 1905); Miller, *op. cit.*; V. K. Johnston, "Canada's Title to the Arctic Islands," in *Canadian Historical Review*, vol. xvi, No. 1 (1933), pp. 24–41; Y. Beriault, *Les Problèmes Politiques du Nord Canadien* (University of Ottawa, 1941); and N. L. Nicholson, *The Boundaries of Canada, its Provinces and Territories* (Queen's Printer, Ottawa, 1954).

[10] The standard work, now somewhat outdated by the passage of events is: Gustav Rasmussen, "The Status of Greenland in International Law," in *Greenland*, vol. iii (Copenhagen, 1929). See also Convention for the Cession to the United States of the Danish West Indies, signed in New York, August 4, 1916: *Senate Documents*, Washington, 1910–23, vol. iii, pp. 2558–2566. Britain was careful, when recognizing Danish sovereignty over Greenland in 1920, to reserve certain rights.

[11] Legal Status of East Greenland, 1933. *Publications de la Cour permanente de justice internationale*, Série, A/B, No. 53. For a useful summary see: *Geographical Journal*, vol. lxxxii (August 1933), pp. 151–166.

The presence of United States forces in Greenland during the 1939–45 war in no way modified Danish sovereignty. They were there on the basis of a temporary agreement for the period of the war.[12] Administration of the colony remained in Danish hands. Some military forces remained after the end of the war, as Denmark had not given the required notice to terminate the treaty. The situation was clarified in 1951 by a new agreement between Denmark and the United States under which certain rights were granted by Denmark for the use of small enclaves as N.A.T.O. bases.

The international status of Greenland has changed in recent years. It is no longer closed to non-residents as it was for 200 years; yet because of its remoteness and the physical difficulties of travelling in it, the change is unlikely to bring an influx of Danes or foreigners.

An important change in internal status took place in 1953, when Greenland was, by a change in the Danish Constitution, incorporated into Denmark as an 'Amt' or county, with the right to elect two members to the Danish Parliament.[13] This act has important consequences for Greenlanders, but there are unlikely to be any immediate effects internationally, except that Denmark no longer reports annually on the status of Greenland under Article 73 of the U.N. Charter.

Iceland. Iceland was declared a republic in 1944, when sovereignty of the Danish king over the island ceased following a plebiscite which favoured republican status.

Norwegian Arctic Possessions. The archipelago of Svalbard, which includes Bear Island, has a unique status in international law. With a very long history of exploration by many nations, it passed under Norwegian sovereignty as recently as 1925. As an offshoot of the Versailles Treaty negotiations, a treaty was signed by nine nations allocating sovereignty to Norway but retaining equal economic right in the island for all signatories and forbidding use of the islands for military purposes.

[12] "In agreement between Denmark and the United States on the defence of Greenland, in 1941 . . . the United States expressly reaffirmed their recognition of Danish sovereignty over the whole of Greenland, including areas used by the Americans for defensive purposes under the agreements." Brun, Eske, in *Greenland* (Copenhagen, 1952), p. 30.

[13] Effective June 5, 1953. See *Report on Greenland* (Copenhagen, 1953), p. 5, and *Grønlandsposten*, Nr. 13 (1953), p. 210. The United Nations formally recognized the change in November 1954.

The Soviet Union adhered to the treaty in 1924 and a few years later many other States followed suit.[14]

Jan Mayen is not a part of Svalbard. It was occupied by the Norwegian weather service in 1921 and annexed by Norway in 1927.

Soviet Union. Territories of the U.S.S.R. have already been referred to incidentally. The boundary with Alaska was laid down in 1867, and the present territorial limits on the west date from the end of the second world war, when the boundary with Norway was re-established.[15] There has been one important adjustment of this since, when by a special agreement in 1947 Finland agreed to sell to the U.S.S.R. an area in the Pasvik river valley to provide water power-sites needed for developing nickel mines in the Petsamo area.[16] Soviet maps usually show a westward 'sector' limit at about 31° 20′ E. Long. with a 'jog' in the Svalbard area to 35° E. Long.

The only territorial disagreement in the Soviet Arctic concerned claims to Wrangel Island in 1920, but as they were private and never supported by Canada or Britain, they had no formal status.[17]

Territorial Waters. Increased military and civilian activity in far northern lands, coupled with expansion of coastal fisheries in some areas due in part to moderating sea temperatures, have increased the significance of territorial boundaries at sea.

In Norway and more recently Iceland special limits have been laid down to exclude some fishing vessels.[18] So far these have not been adopted elsewhere, although their use in Greenland is a possibility, where Disko Bay has long been acknowledged as Danish waters. Hudson Bay has similarly been recognized as Canadian since early in this century. The twelve-mile limit appears to be claimed as the outer limit of Soviet jurisdiction, although under a special agreement dating from 1930 British trawlers were permitted to operate to the three-mile limit.

[14] Anders Orvin, "Twenty-five Years of Norwegian Sovereignty in Svalbard, 1925–1950," in *The Polar Record*, vol. vi, No. 42 (July 1951), pp. 179–185. The boundaries of Svalbard are longitude 10° and 35° E. and latitude 74° and 80° N.

[15] Before this the boundary had been at the eastern limit of the Finnish Petsamo 'corridor.' The first general claim to Arctic territories by Russia was announced in a diplomatic Note of December 1916.

[16] See Trevor Lloyd, "The Norwegian-Soviet Boundary, a Study in Political Geography," 39 pp., maps, illus., in *Technical Report ONR* 438–03–01 (Hanover, New Hampshire, 1954).

[17] See V. Stefansson, *The Adventure of Wrangel Island* (Macmillan, New York, 1925).

[18] See Chapter XL.

On the other hand, the White Sea has been closed to Norwegian sealers since the second world war.

The Sector Principle. Independent of offshore territorial boundaries is the so-called "Sector Principle." Many political maps of the north polar regions show a series of meridional national boundaries converging on the north pole. A typical example is the 141° W. meridian forming the Canada-Alaska boundary, which is on Canadian maps extended to the Pole from Demarcation Point on the shore of the Arctic Sea.[19]

It is not easy to discover a precise meaning for such lines. The nations have not laid formal claim to the sea itself, nor have they excluded from the sector subjects of other nations engaged in fishing or other peaceful pursuits. The generally accepted meaning is that any land which may eventually be discovered within the particular sector is pre-empted by the nation having territory to the south. The "Canadian Sector" was shown on an official Canadian map as long ago as 1904, and had been defined by an Order in Council issued at Ottawa seven years earlier. The first official, unqualified promulgation of the sector theory was in 1925, when the Minister of the Interior confirmed that Canadian claims extended ". . . right up to the Pole." The principle did not have the force of law in the U.S.S.R. until 1926.[20]

The United States apparently makes no formal claims to an Arctic Sector if maps can be taken as a criterion.

Air-space above a sector of the sea cannot be claimed. Soviet aircraft are known to fly within the Canadian sector, but, when flights such as those by the S.A.S. from Oslo to Tokyo might have followed a more direct route on the 'Soviet side' of the Pole, they have apparently kept to the longer route on the North American side. Aeronautical charts of Alaska indicate that both the U.S.A. and U.S.S.R. exercise a degree of control over waters extending a long way off-shore toward the north.

A new complication was introduced into interpretation of the sector principle when the U.S. Air Force occupied a floating ice-mass, usually referred to as "Ice-island T-3," within the polar basin. This island drifts with the wind about the polar sea and enters the various sectors

[19] This line on land was originally accepted as a boundary between Russian territory in Alaska and British North America, in the Treaty of 1825, and incorporated in the U.S.-Russian Treaty of 1867 governing purchase of Alaska. The English text describes the line as extending "as far as the Frozen Ocean."

[20] It was incorporated in Soviet Municipal law by decree of April 15, 1926, and is invariably shown on official Soviet maps. The longitude lines used were 32° 04′ 35″ E. and 160° 49′ 30″ E. A boundary change bringing Soviet territory in contact with Norway has complicated the western limit of the sector.

from time to time. It was manned by U.S. military personnel for about two years, but was evacuated in 1954. The Soviet Union has manned similar ice stations in the polar basin. It would take an intrepid international lawyer to offer an opinion on national jurisdiction over a floating ice-island drifting from sector to sector in the Polar Sea, although events could conspire to make the matter far from academic.

In summary, although the Sector Theory has never been advanced as a sole basis for territorial claims in the far north, its tacit use by Canada and the U.S.S.R. has not been formally challenged and seems to be accepted doctrine as far as title to any land masses within the specified meridians may be concerned. Hesitation of the United States to accept the theory in the Arctic is apparently due mainly to a distaste for having it applied in the Antarctic, where large areas of land are involved, and where the United States neither claims territory nor recognizes the claims of others.

Official Canadian maps show the international boundary between Canada and Greenland as lying near the middle of Davis Strait, Baffin Bay, and the other waters separating the two land masses northward to the Arctic Sea.[21] This line dates from 1925, when the Canadian Minister of the Interior defined it as the eastern limit of territorial claims. It does not appear on Danish maps of Greenland. There is apparently no convention defining the boundary between Canada and Greenland.

Two factors which may lead to sovereignty problems in the far north, or elsewhere, are the tremendous increase in long-distance aviation, both commercial and military, and the tendency for States to extend their territorial claims seaward in pursuit of food supplies from the sea, or mineral resources from the continental shelf. When, combined with these, there is an urge to exclude an unfriendly Power from an area for strategical reasons friction is probable. The Arctic area where Soviet and United States interests overlap is clearly in this class.

Resources and Economic Development

Just as definitions of territorial ownership in the far north in some cases remain uncertain because of the lack of development in the area, so all too little advance has taken place in use of the natural resources.

[21] An extension of this line carries it to the northern tip of Labrador on maps in N. L. Nicholson, *op. cit.* No official government support for the change can be found.

21*

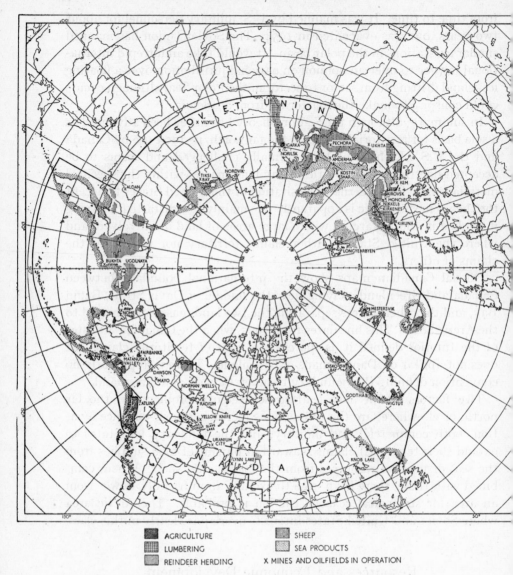

FIG. 2. ECONOMIC RESOURCES OF THE ARCTIC

Even mining, which has often been a spearhead of settlement in remote corners of the globe, is here still in embryo, except in particularly favoured areas such as Ivigtut, Greenland, Yellowknife, Canada, Kirkenes, Norway, Longyearbyen, Svalbard, and the Kola region of the U.S.S.R.

To say this is not to discount the eventual development of northern resources, but rather to stress the very long period that may elapse between discovery and dividends. On the other hand, modern technology is doing much to speed up this process, by the use of aeroplanes, helicopters, powerful ice-breakers, and, of course, the modern aids to rapid mapping of unknown lands. The map of mineral resources in the far north is now a guide to development, rather than the rough record of discoveries it once was. The ways in which exploitation of northern resources is likely to advance most in the next few years are as follows:

Mining. In Europe, coal production in Svalbard from both the Norwegian and Soviet concessions seems to be stabilized at about 700,000 tons per annum. Improved equipment and methods may increase the total somewhat, but the available market can probably be expanded little. In northern Scandinavia iron ore is mined profitably at Kirkenes, mainly because the mines are almost at the ice-free sea-coast.[22] Inland there may eventually be some exploitation of base metals, including copper. Near by in the Soviet Union are the successful nickel mines at Nikel, and another farther south-east at Monchegorsk. The world's largest apatite mines are at Kirovsk, also in the Kola peninsula of European U.S.S.R. Pechora coal, now of great importance both to the Leningrad area and the northern shipping route, is accompanied by oil production and refining near Ukhta. The mainland south of Novaya Zemlya produces fluorspar, lead, and zinc. Still farther east, beyond the lower Yenisei valley, the Noril'sk area has a variety of mines and refineries producing nickel, copper, gold, and platinum. Salt from Nordvik (on the coast of the Laptiev Sea) plays an important part in the fish industry of the U.S.S.R.'s Far East, and brown coal has been mined at Tiksi Bay. The north-eastern area of Siberia appears to be undergoing important development based particularly on minerals (tin and gold) in the Kolyma valley.

The name of Alaska has long been synonymous with Arctic gold, from the 'rushes' of more than sixty years ago. Since then the more profitable alluvial workings have been mechanized, and there is now a steady output. There probably remain considerable unknown reserves. The leading possibilities for future expansion in mining appear to be gold, copper, silver, coal, and perhaps oil, the latter particularly on the northern Arctic slope, where the United States Navy recently terminated intensive studies which had been carried on for a decade.

[22] See Trevor Lloyd, "Iron Ore Production at Kirkenes, Norway," in *Economic Geography*, vol. 31, No. 3 (July 1955), pp. 211–233.

Mineral development of northern Canada is likely to expand rapidly. Numerous mineral 'finds' have been mapped in the past fifty years, but because of remoteness, technical difficulties, inability to find an assured market or to raise the necessary capital, few have reached the stage of producing metals, let alone dividends. Yet the sum total of experience gained has been enormous, and there is now little doubt that mining settlements will grow up in many formerly remote regions. The first commercial mineral operation, apart from gold mining in the Yukon at the turn of the century, was oil at Norman Wells on the Mackenzie River, near the Arctic Circle, shortly after the first world war. A decade later came the discovery of radium and uranium at Great Bear Lake, where the mining town Radium grew up. Shortly before the last war gold mining on the north side of Great Slave Lake led to the building of Yellowknife, which has continued to flourish. The post-war years have seen widespread surveying, prospecting, and some actual mining in other areas. There have been notable uranium strikes on the northern edge of the Prairie provinces, and older established metal mines, including those in the Yukon, have expanded. In the subarctic of eastern Canada, at Knob Lake[23] on the Quebec-Labrador boundary, a large iron-mining centre was built in a few years and is now linked to the north shore of the St Lawrence. This development was based almost entirely on the use of aeroplanes, for surveying, carrying equipment, and moving personnel. A new mining community is rising at nickel mines on Rankin Inlet on the west shore of Hudson Bay.

There is good prospect that new mining centres will be built at Leaf Lake on Ungava Bay (iron), at some point on the eastern side of Hudson Bay (nickel, copper, and gold), and on the zone running north-west from Lake Athabaska to Great Bear Lake and beyond to the Arctic coast (many metals). Throughout this zone there is potentially a plentiful supply of hydro-electric power. Still farther north is the longer range possibly of coal and oil production on the Queen Elizabeth Islands.

Greenland's mineral resources have so far been more limited. One mine alone has been very productive. This is the world's only cryolite mine at Ivigtut in the south-west, almost ideally located for exploitation near the ice-free coast, and midway between the European and American markets.[24] A second mineral, coal, has long been mined in the Disko

---

[23] It is now officially named 'Schefferville.'
[24] See Trevor Lloyd, "Ivigtut Cryolite and Modern Greenland," in *The Canadian Geographer*, No. 3 (1953), pp. 39-52.

Bay area for local use, but it is of indifferent quality. Some marble was formerly mined farther north for the Danish market. Since the last war an apparently rich discovery of lead and zinc has been made at Mesters Vig, north of Scoresbysund on the east coast, and is now being developed energetically by a joint Danish, Swedish, and Canadian concern. Any mineral occurrence, however rich, on this coast faces the serious handicap of severe ice conditions, even in summer.

Furs, Forests, Farms. Other northern resources are more traditional and less likely to produce startling developments. Fur trading has long been the leader among them, but it is increasingly apparent that it does not provide a satisfactory foundation for permanent development because of the double hazard of low prices due to fashion changes and low quantities due to biological causes. So governments are increasingly anxious to supplement it by ensuring more dependable sources of living for the natives, particularly the Eskimos. The earliest of these was the introduction of reindeer herds into some areas, and still later, especially in Greenland, the stimulation of commercial sea-fishing. The latter has been made possible by a slight warming of the ocean water, the arrival of Atlantic cod, and the migration northward of seals. Consequently Greenland's population of a little more than 20,000 now depends mainly on salting, drying, and freezing fish for export. West Greenland waters have in recent years become very attractive to European fleets, notably those of Norway, the Faeroes, and Portugal, but not excluding Britain, France, and Denmark. In fact, Norwegian interests have a large shore-based station at Faeringehavn, and there are other 'international' fishing stations at several points along the coast. Alaska has long had a commercial fish-canning industry, concentrated for the most part on the southern part of the coast. It is really a northward extension of the American industry, employing native labour when this is more profitable. Large-scale fisheries in the Soviet White Sea area, Barents Sea, and the Far East are also long-established.

The fishing industry of Northern Norway is outstanding. It is based in part on near-by waters, but, as already mentioned, the fleet also goes as far afield as Greenland, and also fishes in the Svalbard area, off Iceland, and as far east as the Murman coast. Sealing, based on some north Norway ports, is equally widespread—from Newfoundland to Svalbard and east to Novaya Zemlya and the White Sea. There is an increasing tendency everywhere to exclude foreign vessels from rich coastal waters; thus British trawlers have suffered serious losses by being excluded from Norwegian and Icelandic waters, while Norwegian sealers complain about the closing of the White Sea, formerly one of their most profitable areas.

Resources of the soil in the north are less spectacular than those of the sea, but they are not unimportant. Apart from areas which have long been cultivated, or which have traditionally supplied forest products, there are marginal areas whose development is likely to be worth while only as a supplement to some other industry, such as mining, or in order to provide fresh produce for scientific or military stations. No attempt will be made here to summarize northern agriculture and forestry, but a few examples are cited to indicate the possibilities.

Old-established lumbering industries exist in southern Alaska, and in many parts of the Soviet north. Less well-known areas are the northern part of Finnish Lapland, which once shipped out lumber by way of Petsamo, and which is at present searching for profitable outlets by way of the north Norway fjords. Norway itself once had a very productive forest industry based on the Pasvik valley and export of the products from Kirkenes, but the Pasvik river is now shared with the U.S.S.R. and is no longer available for floating.

The widespread coniferous forests of northern Canada have long provided timbers for building and mining, but are not well situated for export. However, they reduce very considerably the costs and difficulties of exploiting other resources in the area. There are no lumber towns, such as Archangel and Igarka in the Soviet Union, and none likely to develop, because of the lack of natural transportation routes.

Great efforts have been made, particularly where there are urban populations, to produce fresh foods in the far north. The Matanuska experiment in Alaska is an outstanding example. Yet, despite the presence of a guaranteed market in the large military camps near by, the ultimate success of the project is still doubtful. In northern Canada the Mackenzie valley is promising, and small-scale cultivation for local needs has gone on for over a century. As the need arises this can be expanded to provide more potatoes, fresh vegetables, and dairy produce.

South-west Greenland is noteworthy for a considerable growth of sheep-raising and small-scale cultivation during the past few decades. In the Julianehaab District and near Godthaab the former has been shown to be not only practicable but to offer Greenlanders an alternative to fishing. In the far south considerable quantities of hay and potatoes are grown, while good vegetable gardens are common along the coast as far as Disko Bay. North Norway has large areas of potential agricultural land, and the long distance from other sources of supply must eventually lead to expansion of the present relatively small areas. There are particularly promising districts in the Pasvik valley and around Alta fjord, but small-scale dairying and horticulture are fairly widespread.

There is considerable evidence that high-latitude cultivation has gone farthest in the U.S.S.R., where strenuous efforts have been made to provide mining centres and scientific or military stations with fresh produce. While small herds of dairy cattle are found in most subarctic areas in all countries, reindeer are the most widespread of the 'domesticated' herds. They are now found in all the larger polar areas—having been introduced into Alaska about sixty years ago, into Canada a generation later, and most recently into Greenland, where a herd appears to be thriving at Godthaab fjord. The largest herds are in northern Scandinavia and the U.S.S.R.

Taken as a whole, far northern resources from the soil are clearly limited—apart from the specially favoured areas already mentioned— to those places where poor transportation or other handicaps place a premium on local supplies. Expansion will probably be greatest where mining creates large urban centres and fresh foods and lumber can be provided more economically than they can be shipped from outside.

In all these matters the situation of Iceland is unique. There a comparatively small population (about 150,000) has long been adjusted to the available resources—resulting in sheep-raising and dairying on land and deep-sea fishing to provide not only the local population but export products to pay for large imports of food and other essentials. There is probably little room for expansion of this type of economy within the island, although more efficient use of resources (as, for example, in the artificial drying of hay) can do something to improve the output.

Logistics and Strategy

It is difficult to separate commercial and military operations in the far north, and, as transportation plays such a large part in both, they will be discussed together. As has already been stressed, the air provides a universal means of transit, and is the only one that can take full

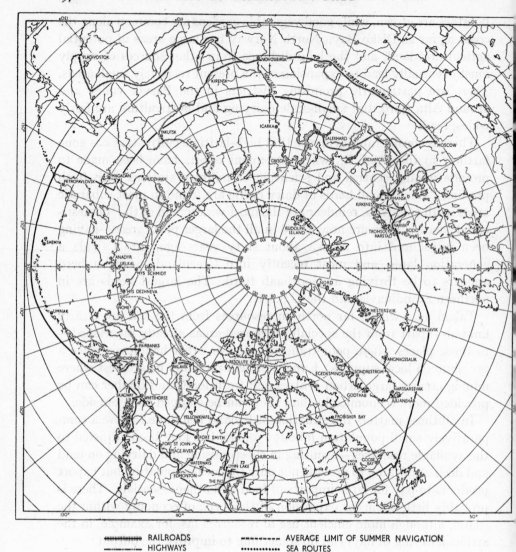

RAILROADS	AVERAGE LIMIT OF SUMMER NAVIGATION
HIGHWAYS	SEA ROUTES
RIVER ROUTES	LIMIT OF THE ARCTIC
⊗ MAIN AIRPORTS	

FIG. 3. ARCTIC TRANSPORTATION

advantage of Great Circle paths across the Arctic. Moreover, flying conditions are on the whole better in the Arctic proper than farther south. The present political barriers between countries of the 'Soviet bloc' and others reduce considerably the value of high-latitude travel, since the northern lands are, in effect, divided into two approximately equal compartments, neither of which can be used by the other. While the commercial air route from Los Angeles to Copenhagen by way of Greenland is about 500 miles shorter than that by New York, real economies begin to appear when still longer routes farther north are followed, as, for example, between Los Angeles and Calcutta, Vladivostok and New York, London and Tokyo.

All northern air routes are dependent upon elaborate servicing and repair bases, and these in turn are supplied by sea, for only by sea can the vast quantities of fuel be provided economically. Hence aviation in the far north is to a degree tied to the traditional sea routes, and these in turn depend on the distribution of open water and the availability of good harbours.

Arctic Sea Routes. The pattern of northern shipping lanes depends on the seasons. Despite the remarkable efficiency of modern ice-breakers and the relatively large number now available, freight tonnages are still greatest where ice is least. The oldest established route is that which follows the "gulf of warmth" extending north-eastward from the Atlantic Ocean to Murmansk in winter and still farther east in summer, when the mouth of the Yenisei is accessible to ordinary ocean-going vessels. Corresponding to this on the west side of Greenland is a stretch of open water extending north of Godthaab in winter and beyond Thule in summer. This is complicated in the south in summer by polar pack-ice which rounds Cape Farewell from East Greenland. The west coast of Alaska is even more open in winter south of the Aleutians, and in summer vessels are able to penetrate Bering Strait and reach the Canadian western Arctic.

On east coasts in these latitudes conditions are more severe, since the currents flow southward carrying cold water and heavy ice toward middle latitudes, and the prevailing air masses are formed over the colder land masses to the west. Thus East Greenland is reached with difficulty even in summer and is closed in winter. The same is true of parts of the Canadian eastern Arctic and the north-east coast of Siberia.

Powerful ice-breakers aided by helicopters and long-range aircraft have done much to extend the sea lanes into regions where ice is heavy even in summer. Thus the Soviet Northern Sea Route from Barents Sea to Bering Strait can be used throughout its length for about two months each year.[25] For the first time, in 1954, a deep draught naval ice-breaker went through the Northwest Passage from Davis Strait to Bering Strait (and eventually circumnavigated North America), a journey made previously only by small specially constructed schooners. The regular supply of mining and other operations in East Greenland also depends on specially built vessels.

Even very powerful ice-breakers have their limitations. In a recent summer no less than three at work in the Canadian eastern Arctic were so seriously damaged that they needed to return to bases far to the south for extensive repairs, and one was almost compelled to winter in the ice near Ellesmere Island. Some weather stations in Arctic Canada and Greenland, and doubtless also in the U.S.S.R., have not yet been reached by sea. The present slight amelioration of climate in the high latitudes may ease this situation somewhat, as it has already brought about more favorable ice-conditions than those typical of the past century.

Land Routes. A few land routes link centres of dense population and advanced technology in the south with outposts in the north. In time the supply and maintenance bases needed for servicing even more remote northern settlements will be pressed still farther north. Some examples follow.

First to be used as overland routes were the rivers, which carried explorers and fur traders to the shores of the Arctic seas; such were the Yukon and Mackenzie rivers in North America and the Ob, Yenisei, Lena, and other northward-flowing streams in Siberia. They are still important, and will doubtless always remain so for the movement of heavy and bulky cargoes during the open season. The first land routes were developed to make contact with these and similar rivers, by trail, road, and railway. The first railroad in the Yukon was built to link the river of that name with the Pacific Ocean at Skagway; a railroad northward from Edmonton, Alberta, tapped the Mackenzie waterway at Waterways, and later a road reached it even farther north at Hay river. In the U.S.S.R. the Trans-Siberian Railway crossed many northward-flowing rivers near their navigable heads, and as recently as 1954 a branch line built east of Krasnoyarsk provided the first direct contact with the Lena river at Ust' Kut.

[25] See T. E. Armstrong, "The Soviet Northern Sea Route," in *The Geographical Journal*, vol. cxxi, Part 2 (June 1955), pp. 136–148.

In some areas land transport has reached the shores of the Arctic Sea, either by road or rail, and this tendency will probably continue if only to provide the year-round transportation essential to modern industry. In Canada a railroad reached Hudson Bay at Churchill a generation ago, and the route is now important both economically and as a link in northern military supply routes. Farther east a railway reaches the shores of James Bay, and in Quebec the new railway (carrying iron ore) points a 350-mile-long finger northward from the St Lawrence toward Ungava Bay. Plans have been revived to build a railway to reach the Mackenzie valley at Hay river.

In Scandinavia the former through road from southern Finland and Sweden to the Barents Sea is now blocked at the Soviet frontier, but an alternative route gives access to the sea at Porsanger Fjord in Norway, and also at Kirkenes farther east. Railroads both in Norway and Finland extend at present barely beyond the Arctic Circle, although Narvik in northern Norway is linked to the Swedish rail net through Kiruna. The Soviets have three railroads giving direct access to the northern seas; on the west are those to Archangel and Murmansk, and farther east the Pechora valley railway has been extended to the shores of the Ob estuary. A road of some value reaches as far as Igarka on the Yenisei.

In addition to recognized highways in the north are others which serve as supplementary routes in winter. They are sometimes used by trucks, and more usually by tractor trains, often taking advantage of lakes and other water-courses. In this way the old tradition that Arctic travel was far better in winter than in summer is continued in our mechanized age.

From the growing network of northern transportation routes, certain 'nodes' or focal points are emerging. Some are important for sea, land, and air transport, while others are more limited. Fairbanks, Alaska, is one such focus, and Churchill another. Farther north a possible focus exists in the Aklavik area, and another at Thule. In Eurasia, Tromsø has long been recognized as an important base for Arctic transport, and Kirkenes or Alta somewhat to the east may develop as rivals. Murmansk, Igarka, and Yakutsk are Soviet examples. Looking to the day when inter-continental commercial aviation may become commonplace, the possible termini on the margins of the far north may be London or Copenhagen, Montreal, Winnipeg, or Edmonton, Leningrad, Omsk, Krasnoyarsk, or Irkutsk, with more northerly foci at Nome, Fairbanks,

Aklavik, Resolute Bay, Thule or Søndrestrøm Fjord, Reykjavik, Kirkenes, Dikson Island, Tiksi, and Ambarchik near the Kolyma delta.

Of greater immediate importance is the fact that most high-latitude flying, and probably most other forms of transport, are keyed to military planning. No less than three complete radar screens now extend from Alaska across Canada to Greenland, the northernmost of them beyond the Arctic Circle. To supply and man these alone is a major problem in military "logistics" calling for greater tonnages than any civilian operations in the past. Between them and the north pole there are even more remote weather stations and air bases which require regular servicing, if need be at all seasons of the year. To maintain perhaps 5000 men at Thule in Greenland is a staggeringly expensive undertaking. Doubtless there are comparable stations in the higher latitudes of the U.S.S.R., although sea transportation there may be less of a problem, if only because of the longer experience in operating the route.

From a strictly military standpoint there is still no agreement as to the part the Arctic regions may play. At one extreme are those who believe that intercontinental bombers and guided missiles will flow in steady streams across the pole, between the United States and the Soviet Union. At the other extreme are those who remain convinced that any future war will conform to the traditional "east–west" strategy of the 1939–45 war, and that any activity in the far north will be only diversionary. Between the two views is the more generally accepted one that the far north will be an active theatre of war, but that ground operations will be very limited. Local attacks may be expected, particularly on weather and radar stations, air bases or supply dumps, but most of the activity will be in the air. Long-distance raids will be made on industrial targets on both continents, but, unless interrupted, such aircraft will travel at a great height and usually leave the Arctic proper unaffected. If this is a sound forecast, then military planners are unlikely to attempt any large-scale garrisoning of the far north, but will use the area for defence in depth, man it with radar networks, and choose selected key sites as 'strong points' to be defended.

At the moment there is apparently little divergence in interest between military and civilian planners in the north. Both need more detailed maps, greatly improved transportation, better weather stations, more suitable mechanical and other equipment, better local food supplies, and so on. There may be minor disagreements due to military security in areas where civilian activities need greater freedom, and there may, of course, be the traditional competition for public funds. Of importance also is the danger that military activities may permanently disorganize the traditional way of life of the native population. Since, however, the military activities are directly controlled by governments, this danger may well be less than that from the activities of commercially minded civilians. Whatever may be the details of future developments in the far north, it is now apparent that the area has been 'opened up' and can never again return to its former isolation. The intercontinental routes of the future cross it, and this alone will require a large measure of development both for its people and the resources at their command.

FURTHER READING

AHLMANN, H. WISON, *Glacier Variations and Climatic Fluctuations* (American Geographical Society, New York, 1953).

ARMSTRONG, TERENCE, *The Northern Sea Route* (Cambridge University Press, 1952).

GEOGRAPHICAL BRANCH, *The Canadian Arctic* (Department of Mines and Technical Surveys, Ottawa, 1951).

GREENLAND DEPARTMENT, *Report on Greenland, 1954* (Copenhagen, 1954).

JOERG, W. L. G. (editor), *Problems of Polar Research* (American Geographical Society, New York, 1928).

JONES, STEPHEN B., *The Arctic: Problems and Possibilities* (Yale Institute of International Studies, New Haven, 1948).

LUIHN, HAAS, *Finnmark, en okonomisk analyse* (Oslo, 1952).

Mid-century Alaska (Department of the Interior, Washington, 1951).

NORDENSKJØLD, O., and MECKING, L., *The Geography of the Polar Regions* (American Geographical Society, New York, 1928).

STEFANSSON, V., *The Arctic in Fact and Fable*, Headline Series No. 51 (Foreign Policy Association, New York, 1945).

WEBSTER, C. J., "The Growth of the Soviet Arctic and Subarctic," in *Arctic*, vol. iv, No. 1 (1951), pp. 27–45.

WEIGERT, HANS, and STEFANSSON, V., *Compass of the World* (Macmillan, New York, and Harrap, London, 1944).

CHAPTER XLII

The Partition of Antarctica

L. P. KIRWAN

THE political map of Antarctica is of comparatively recent development. Though its beginnings may be traced back to the first quarter of the nineteenth century, it is only within the last fifty years that it has taken coherent shape; and one sector, the "Pacific" Sector, with a perimeter of over one thousand miles, is still unallotted to any nation.

Geographically, the Antarctic may be defined as the area lying southward of the Antarctic Convergence, the line along which the cold northward-moving Antarctic surface water sinks beneath the warmer sub-Antarctic water. This line probably forms the extreme northerly limit of the pack-ice and is for the most part precisely identifiable by the sudden change in surface temperature. Within this hydrological zone lies the compact land mass of the Antarctic Continent, some six million square miles in area, roughly equal to the combined areas of Europe and the United States of America.

The Political Map of Antarctica

The partition of this "last continent," the central feature of the political geography and geopolitics of Antarctica, has resulted in five geographical "sectors"—three British, one Norwegian, one French—with a sixth, "Pacific," sector unallotted, though partially claimed by the Government of Chile. This sector principle was first proposed, with reference to the Arctic, by Senator Poirier in the Canadian Parliament in 1907.[1] The three British sectors of Antarctica are administered respectively by the Government of the Falkland Islands, by New Zealand, and by Australia. The Falkland Islands Sector consists of the

---

[1] *Debates of the Senate, 1906–7*, pp. 266 ff.

Falkland Islands Dependencies as defined by Letters Patent of July 21, 1908, and of March 28, 1917; the latter constituting the first declaration of a Polar sector, specifically applied. The New Zealand sector, known

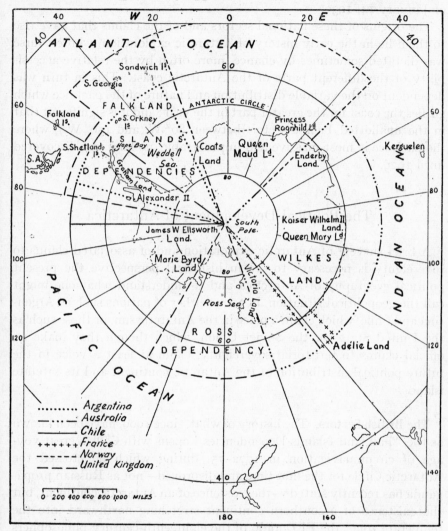

FIG. 1. THE ANTARCTIC CONTINENT

as the Ross Dependency, was defined by an Order in Council of July 30, 1923; and the Australian sector, known as Australian Antarctic Territory, by an Order in Council of February 7, 1933. The French sector, Adélie Land, is no more than an enclave within Australian Antarctic

Territory. It was annexed to France by a decree of April 1, 1924. Finally, the Norwegian sector, Queen Maud Land or Dronning Maud Land, was brought under Norwegian sovereignty by a Norwegian decree of January 14, 1939.

The origins of these national sectors and of the claims that gave rise to them lie in the early history of Antarctic exploration, whose course was dictated sometimes by chance, more often by the relative accessibility of the different parts of the Antarctic coast. This in turn was dependent on the variable distribution and nature of the pack-ice which girdles the coast for the greater part of the year; and it is significant that in the unallotted Pacific sector (between 80° W. and 150° W.), where the pack-ice is most massive and impenetrable, no land was discovered until 1929.

The Political Development of Antarctica

A brief survey[2] of Antarctic exploration and of associated claims to sovereignty is necessary to see in historical perspective the present political geography of Antarctica and to understand what one might call the geopolitical situation, in terms either of nations such as Argentina and Chile, which claim a place in the Antarctic sun, or those such as the United States or the Soviet Union, which though they make no official claims to territorial sovereignty, claim at least a voice in the future political distribution of the Antarctic continent and its satellite islands.

The British Sectors. The history of what, since 1909, have been known as the "Falkland Islands Dependencies" opens with Cook's great voyage of circumnavigation in 1772–75, during which he crossed the Antarctic Circle for the first time and disproved—not as Russian propaganda has recently stated[3]—the existence of an Antarctic continent, but the existence of a southern continent stretching northward into the temperate zone; the El Dorado of the eighteenth-century philosophers and geographers. It was during this voyage that Cook landed in South

[2] *The Antarctic Pilot* (1948), pp. 6–25. "Chronological List of Antarctic Expeditions, with brief notes on each, 1802–1948," compiled by Dr B. B. Roberts (Hydrographic Dept., Admiralty, 1948). The survey here is with reference to nationalities and sectors.
[3] "The Soviet Memorandum on the Antarctic, 1950." For text, see *Polar Record*, vol. vi (41), pp. 120–121.

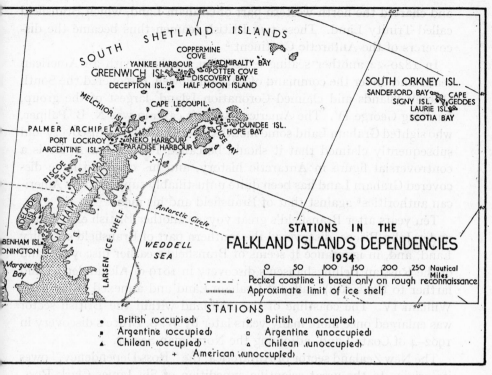

SHETLAND ISLANDS

SOUTH

GREENWICH ISL.

COPPERMINE
COVE
YANKEE HARBOUR ADMIRALTY BAY
POTTER COVE
DISCOVERY BAY
DECEPTION ISL. HALF MOON ISLAND

MELCHIOR ISL.

CAPE LEGOUPIL

PALMER ARCHIPELAGO

PORT LOCKROY NEKO HARBOUR
ARGENTINE ISL. PARADISE HARBOUR

DUNDEE ISL.
HOPE BAY

DUSE BAY

BISCOE ISL.

GRAHAM LAND

Antarctic Circle

SOUTH ORKNEY ISL.

SANDEFJORD BAY CAPE
SIGNY ISL. GEDDES
LAURIE ISL.
SCOTIA BAY

BENHAM ISL.
ONINGTON ISL.

ADELAIDE ISL.

LARSEN ICE SHELF

WEDDELL
SEA

Marguerite
Bay

STATIONS IN THE
FALKLAND ISLANDS DEPENDENCIES
1954

0   50   100 150   200   250 Nautical
                                  Miles
- - - - - Pecked coastline is based only on rough reconnaissance
Approximate limit of ice shelf

STATIONS

• British (occupied)   o British (unoccupied)
■ Argentine (occupied)   □ Argentine (unoccupied)
▲ Chilean (occupied)   △ Chilean (unoccupied)
+ American (unoccupied)

FIG. 2. STATIONS IN THE FALKLAND ISLANDS DEPENDENCIES, 1954
From " The Polar Record" (Scott Polar Research Institute, Cambridge)

Georgia and took possession of it for King George III. He also discovered the South Sandwich Islands. And it was Cook's reports of the rich fauna of the Antarctic seas, the abundant whales and seals, that gave the first great impetus to Antarctic exploration. British sealers which started to work in South Georgia in 1778 were soon followed by others from the United States. By 1791 no fewer than one hundred sealers were at work in this part of the Southern Ocean.[4]

The next event in the growth of this British Sector was the landing by a sealing captain, William Smith, on King George Islands, South Shetlands, in 1819, and its annexation in the name of King George III. Later in the same year Smith sailed again, this time with Midshipman Edward Bransfield, R.N., who was placed in command of the Brig *Williams* by the Admiralty. Their voyage was an historic one. For, in addition to carrying out a survey of the South Shetlands, they discovered

[4] *Antarctic Pilot* (1948), p. 7, footnote.

and charted the north-western part of Graham Land, which Bransfield called Trinity Land. These two British seamen thus became the discoverers of the Antarctic Continent.[5]

In 1820–22 another sealing expedition, working with an American sealer and under the command of Captain Powell, discovered the South Orkney Islands and claimed Coronation Island, largest of the group, for King George IV. The American sealer's captain was N. B. Palmer, who sighted Graham Land some months after Bransfield's discovery and subsequently claimed that it should be called Palmer Land. He is a controversial figure in Antarctic history, and his claim to have discovered Graham Land has been quite unjustifiably supported by American authorities[6] against that of Bransfield and his men.

Ten years after Bransfield's great voyage another British expedition, under John Biscoe, discovered the southern part of Bransfield's Trinity Land, and, in ignorance it seems of Bransfield's earlier discovery (and of the Russian Bellingshausen's discovery in 1819 of Alexander I Land farther to the south), called it Graham Land and annexed it for King William IV. The coastline of the mainland within the British sector was enlarged once more many years later by W. S. Bruce's discovery in 1902–4 of Coats Land, adjoining the Norwegian Sector.

The New Zealand sector of Antarctica, the "Ross Dependency," owes its origins to the great scientific expedition of Sir James Clark Ross, who, in *Erebus* and *Terror*, discovered the Ross Sea and Barrier and roughly charted some 500 miles of coastline in Victoria Land. This, with a number of islands in this area, he claimed for the British Crown. These British discoveries were further extended by the Antarctic expedition of 1898–1900, under Borchgrevink.

British discoveries and claims in the New Zealand sector were still further enlarged by the British National Antarctic Expedition under R. F. Scott in 1901–4, and by Shackleton's British Antarctic Expedition of 1907–9. Scott discovered King Edward VII land, adjoining the Pacific sector; a discovery renewed a few years later by Roald Amundsen, who claimed the territory for King Haakon VII. Shackleton, after discovering nearly 500 miles of new mountain ranges in Victoria Land, renewed the British claim to this area, and claimed the Polar plateau

---

[5] A. R. Hinks, "On Some Misrepresentations of Antarctic History," in *Geographical Journal*, vol. xciv, No. 4 (1939), pp. 309–330. R. T. Gould, "The Charting of the South Shetlands, 1819–28," in *Mariners' Mirror*, vol. xxvii (1941), pp. 206–242. For the contemporary accounts of Bransfield's voyages, see *Polar Record*, vol. iv (32), 385–393.

[6] Hinks, *op. cit.* It is called Palmer Land on U.S. maps.

for King Edward VII. Still further explorations in Victoria Land and on the Ross Barrier were carried out by Scott in 1910–13, and Oates Land, lying across the present boundary between New Zealand and Australian Antarctic territory, was also discovered by him.

The third British sector, known since 1933 as "Australian Antarctic Territory," owes its origin to John Biscoe's discovery of Enderby Land during his voyage of circumnavigation of 1830–32. A British Expedition, under John Balleny in 1838–39, then discovered Sabrina Land, so called after one of Balleny's two ships. This discovery was later confirmed by the United States Exploring Expedition, under Charles Wilkes, who also discovered Knox Coast; Wilkes's name was subsequently given to the whole of this area of Australian Antarctic Territory. In 1833 the territory was further increased by the addition of Kemp Land, discovered by Peter Kemp in the British brig *Magnet* in December of that year. Kaiser Wilhelm II Land, also included in this territory, was first discovered by the German South Polar Expedition of 1902, under Dr E. von Drygalski. It was seen at that time only from several miles away; its eastern portion was subsequently seen, and sketched, by the Australian Antarctic Expedition in 1912.

This Expedition, under the famous Australian polar explorer Sir Douglas Mawson, made during the years 1911–14 some of the most important additions to Australian Antarctic Territory, both King George V Land and Queen Mary Land being discovered and claimed for the British Crown. Then, in 1929–31, the joint British-Australian-New Zealand Antarctic Expedition, also led by Mawson, discovered Mac-Robertson Land, made a number of landings elsewhere in this region, proved the connexion between Kemp Land and Enderby Land, and finally annexed the whole of what is now Australian Antarctic Territory in the name of King George V. One remaining section of the coast, King Leopold and Queen Astrid Land, was discovered from the air in 1934 by Lieutenant Gunnstad of the Norwegian whaling factory *Thorshavn*.

The French and Norwegian Sectors. Included in Australian Antarctic Territory is the French enclave known as Adélie Land, so called after the wife of its discoverer, the French explorer J. S. C. Dumont D'Urville, who sighted it on January 20, 1840. A week later the same coast was sighted by Lieutenant Charles Wilkes of the United States Exploring Expedition. But the charting of the coast was left to the Australian

Antarctic Expedition of 1911–14 and to British expeditions in 1931 and 1938. It was claimed for France by a French decree of April 1, 1924.

The first land in what is now the Norwegian sector of the Antarctic was seen by the great Russian explorer Admiral Bellingshausen during his remarkable voyage of circumnavigation in 1819–21, to which reference has already been made. He sighted and described, but did not recognize as land, part of the mainland now known as Princesse Ragnhild Land.[7]

The subsequent history of the exploration of this region is almost exclusively Norwegian, carried out by expeditions whose primary object was the defence of Norwegian whaling interests. In 1930 General Riiser-Larsen, in a series of reconnaissance flights from the *Norvegia*, discovered and roughly charted Princesse Ragnhild Land, sighted by Bellingshausen a hundred years before. He claimed this territory for Norway, and also flew over Kronprins Olaf Land. In 1936–37 further flights from the factory ship *Thorshavn* discovered Prins Harald Land, which was photographed from the air and claimed for Norway. During the next two years a German Antarctic Expedition, personally sponsored by General Goering and including German Air Force and Naval personnel, spent three weeks in the Princesse Astrid and Kronprincesse Martha area. The two aircraft carried by this expedition photographed about 350,000 square kilometres of territory between 14° W. and 20° E. This they named Neu-Schwabenland, and, throwing down iron stanchions stamped with swastikas, they implicitly claimed it for Nazi Germany.[8] It was perhaps to counter a possible formal German claim that Norway, in January 1939, approved the decree, not disputed by the other Antarctic Powers, annexing the whole of Norwegian Antarctic Territory under the general name of Dronning Maud Land. The Norwegian title was reinforced after the second world war by the Norwegian Expedition of 1949–52,[9] which, with British and Swedish participation, maintained a base for two winters in this area. Widespread exploration and mapping by land and by air were carried out and the many inaccuracies in the German maps rectified.

The Pacific Sector. Finally there is the Pacific sector, within which only one island, Peter I Øy, has so far been annexed; in this case by

[7] Terence Armstrong, "Recent Soviet Interest in Bellingshausen's Antarctic Voyage of 1819–21," in *Polar Record*, vol. xxix (1950), pp. 475–478.

[8] Ritscher, *Deutsche Antarktische Expedition* (Leipzig, 1942).

[9] G. de Robin, "An International Expedition to Antarctica," in *Geographical Journal*, vol. cxix (June 1953), p. 155.

Norway in 1929. The island had first been discovered by the Russian Bellingshausen,[10] but he was unable to land. The first, and indeed the only, landing made was from the Norwegian research vessel *Norvegia*, in February 1929.

Credit for the discovery of the hinterland of this inaccessible coast must go to the numerous United States Expeditions under Admiral Byrd, of 1928–30, 1933–35, and 1939–41; discovery in each case being from the air. A more thorough examination of the coastline, still only roughly located, was made again from the air by Admiral Byrd's United States Navy Expedition, Operation "High Jump," in 1946— the largest expedition yet to visit the Antarctic. This sector of the Antarctic has still to be annexed. Despite the multitude of American personal names that appear upon the map, and despite the personal claims made in 1928–30 by Admiral Byrd to Marie Byrd Land, by the aviator Lincoln Ellsworth in 1935–36 to Ellsworth Land, and by Ellsworth again in 1938–39 to adjacent areas, none of these claims has ever been officially recognized by the United States Government. Only the Government of Chile lays claim to any part of this area, to the strip adjacent to the British Falkland Islands Dependencies.

It is clear from this brief survey of discovery in the Antarctic sectors that, with few exceptions, the nation whose citizens have contributed most to that discovery is the one which, unchallenged when its claims were made, now holds the sovereign title. The exceptions, however, may be important, since they may in future be used to substantiate claims or to contest the claims of others. Thus the Russians have recently given much prominence to the first sighting of land by Bellingshausen in what is now the Norwegian sector; and to his discoveries in the Falkland Islands Dependencies.

The political divisions that have developed from these explorations and annexations, though acceptable among those nations possessing Antarctic territories, are by no means accepted by the world at large.[11] Both Argentina and Chile have put forward claims, overlapping with each other, to the Falkland Islands Dependencies, those of Chile extending into the adjacent Pacific Sector. The United States, which neither makes any territorial claims nor recognizes those of others,

---

[10] Armstrong, *op. cit.*, p. 476.

[11] Norway promised in 1929 not to contest the claims of the British Commonwealth. See *American Journal of International Law*, vol. xxxix (1940), Suppl., p. 84. France in 1938, in agreeing to reciprocal rights of air passage, also implicitly recognized British claims (Treaty Series, No. 73 (1938), Cmd. 5900).

nevertheless reserves the rights of discovery for itself and for its own citizens,[12] while paradoxically denying at the same time that discovery by itself gives any right to title. Finally, the Soviet Union, recalling the part played by the Imperial Russian Navy in Antarctic discovery, and Soviet interest in Antarctic whaling, claims on these grounds the right to be consulted on the future political organization of the Antarctic. The Soviet Union has not yet, however, made any specific claims to territory. She has been content so far to contest the claims of others.

The most pressing problem in the Antarctic to-day and one in which stalemate has virtually been reached is that of the claims of Argentina and Chile to the British Falkland Islands Dependencies. Some consideration of the activities of all three countries is necessary if we are to see the different aspects of this dispute in terms of contemporary opinion and international law.

Argentine and Chilean Activities in the Antarctic. There is no evidence of any discoveries by either Argentina or Chile in Antarctica during the nineteenth century. Argentina entered the Antarctic only in 1903, when she took over from W. S. Bruce, leader of the Scottish National Antarctic Expedition, a meteorological station on Laurie Island in the South Orkneys, for the upkeep of which Bruce could not obtain the necessary funds from Great Britain. Four Argentine Government scientists, conveyed to the island in Bruce's own ship, the *Scotia*, hoisted the Argentine flag, and the *Scotia* sailed for Cape Town with letters bearing special Argentine stamps and post-marks.[13] Argentina, which later claimed possession of the islands, has maintained the station at Laurie Island ever since. Argentine claims to the South Orkneys in 1906 were followed in 1927 by claims to sovereignty over South Georgia.

This was the limit of Argentine activity in the Antarctic up to the second world war. Apart from a certain amount of privately organized sealing and whaling, the latter under licence from the British Government, Chilean activity for the same period is similarly limited, in this case to the rescue in 1916 of the crew of Shackleton's *Endurance* from the South Shetland Islands. In the political field, however, Chile in 1907 made a proposal to Argentina which is important because it fore-

[12] The position was thus stated by Acting Secretary of State Dean Acheson on December 27, 1946.
[13] R. N. Rudmose Brown, *A Naturalist at the Poles* (Seeley, Service, London, 1923), pp. 172–173.

shadowed the present claims of both countries to the Falkland Islands Dependencies. That was for a treaty between Chile and Argentina defining their respective zones as regards the "islands and the American Antarctic Continents." Argentina declined to take part.[14] No official comment was made by either country during this period on the British Letters Patent of 1908 and 1917, which proclaimed British sovereignty over the Dependencies (including, it is worth noting, Laurie Island).[15]

At the start of the second world war both Argentina and Chile, encouraged presumably by the United Kingdom's preoccupation with more vital issues, began to formulate their claims to the whole of the Dependencies. In Argentina a convenient starting-point for the launching of a national campaign was provided by the proposed International Polar Exhibition and Congress of Polar Explorers which was to have been held in Bergen from May to September 1940.[16] Great prominence was given in the Argentine Press to Argentina's intention to participate, much play being made with statements of Argentina's geographical proximity and contiguity to the Antarctic Continent by way of the so-called "Scotia arc" (comprising South Georgia, the South Sandwich Islands, the South Orkneys, and the northward-jutting peninsula of Graham Land). Much emphasis was laid on Argentina's yearly expeditions to the meteorological station on Laurie Island.

When the Bergen Congress was postponed because of the war the Argentine Government set up a National Antarctic Committee, a permanent organization responsible for the "defence and development of Argentine interests in the Antarctic or in the Antarctic Continent."[17] Meanwhile, throughout the years 1940–42 the Argentine Press published numerous articles, illustrated by maps, which extended earlier Argentina claims (to the South Orkneys) to the whole of the Falkland Islands Dependencies between longitude 25° W. and 68° 34' W. (subsequently amended to 74° W.) and south of latitude 60° S.

In 1943 Argentine sent an expedition to the South Shetlands and to West Graham Land which deposited on Deception Island an "Act of Possession." This was the first official Argentine claim to the whole sector, within the limits described above.[18] Two years earlier, in 1940,

[14] C. H. M. Waldock, "Disputed Sovereignty in the Falkland Islands Dependencies." *Year Book of International Law* (1948), p. 311. An excellent survey of the legal issues involved, by the Professor of Public International Law at Oxford.

[15] Waldock, *loc. cit.*

[16] For the texts of the Argentine and Chilean decrees, see *Polar Record*, vol. iv, 32 (July 1946), pp. 412–417.

[17] *Polar Record*, No. 32 (July 1946), pp. 412–417.   [18] See *Antarctic Pilot* (1948), p. 24.

Chile, stimulated by Argentine interest in the Antarctic, had formulated her own claims in a Presidential Decree which declared that:

All lands, islands, islets, reefs of rocks, glaciers, already known, or to be discovered, and their respective territorial waters, in the sector between longitudes 53° and 90° W. constitute the Chilean Antarctic or Chilean Antarctic territory.[19]

This Chilean claim, to which Japan somewhat unexpectedly entered a reservation, overlaps the Argentine claim and extends into the otherwise unclaimed Pacific sector.

It is unnecessary for the purpose of this survey of the geopolitical position in Antarctica to relate in any detail the story of the successive expeditions and of the setting up of bases, Argentine, Chilean, and British, that followed the formulation of Argentine and Chilean claims to the Falkland Islands Dependencies. The Argentine challenge of 1942 and 1943 was answered, despite British involvement in the second world war, by a visit of H.M.S. *Carnarvon Castle* to the South Shetlands and South Orkneys in 1943. Argentine emblems were removed and the British flag was hoisted. Diplomatic courtesies at the same time were carefully observed by a British call on the Argentine meteorological station at Laurie Island. In 1944 the United Kingdom established the Falkland Islands Dependencies Survey, first under the Admiralty and later under the Colonial Office, whose function it was (and is) to conduct from bases within the sector a long-term programme of exploratory research and development, with special emphasis on meteorology. Each base is in charge of a resident "Magistrate," and all bases of the Survey, to which each year a relief expedition is sent from Great Britain, are annually inspected by the Governor of the Falkland Islands.[20] At the present time (June 1956), there are ten British as against eight Argentine and four Chilean bases within the Falkland Islands Dependencies sector; an unusual position in territory administered as a British Crown Colony.

It is remarkable that the continuous dispatch of expeditions by all three countries and the setting up of bases simultaneously by both sides in this Antarctic desert has not resulted in serious incidents. An Argentine armed party, admittedly, opened fire with a machine-gun (apparently without authority) on the British landing at Hope Bay in 1952. And in the following year the British arrested two Argentine citizens at

[19] *Polar Record*, vol. iv (32), p. 416; Waldock, *op. cit.*, p. 333.
[20] *Polar Record*, vol. v (January–July 1948), p. 228.

Deception Island under the Falkland Islands Aliens Ordinance of 1949.[21] But for the most part the various moves and counter-moves of the rival Powers have been followed by nothing more violent than the painting out of national emblems and the exchange of protests or declarations of sovereignty either between the rival explorers of each nation in some remote and glaciated wasteland or through diplomatic channels in Buenos Aires, Santiago, or London. That serious incidents have generally been avoided is largely due to the Tripartite Antarctic Naval Declarations, which have been renewed annually since 1948, whereby the United Kingdom, Argentina, and Chile have by agreement refrained from sending warships south of latitude 60° S.[22]

The powerful nationalist sentiment for which these Antarctic activities have provided an outlet has been stimulated in Chile through emulation of Argentine ambitions in the Antarctic. In Argentina they were stimulated by the deliberate policy of Juan D. Perón, elected in February 1946 President of the Republic. Under his five-year plan Argentina was to become a great industrial State, no longer dependent on foreign finance or on foreign manufactured goods. Foreign balances accumulated during the War were to be expended in buying out foreign-owned utility companies. Argentina was to be recognized, not as a mere subsidiary to the British economic system or as a pawn in the diplomatic game played by the United States in Latin America, but as a Great Power in her own right. The decision to stimulate Argentine claims in the Antarctic was but another aspect of this general revival of Argentine nationalism.

The appeal, shrewdly timed and carefully calculated, was based on the British assertion that the Antarctic Dependencies were dependencies of the Falkland Islands. From childhood every Argentine had known of the Falkland Islands, the "Islas Malvinas." They had always been presented as part of the Motherland through inheritance from Spain, and as territory which had been brutally seized by Great Britain at a time when Argentine was struggling to create herself out of the ashes of the old Spanish Empire.[23] This appeal to recover the "Malvinas Dependencies" found an immediate response among all classes and all parties in Argentina.

[21] The diplomatic correspondence arising from these incidents is published in *Polar Record*, vol. vii (48), 212–226.

[22] *Polar Record*, vol. vii (48), 226.

[23] F. A. Kirkpatrick, *The Argentine Republic* (Cambridge University Press, 1931), p. 245 ff. See Argentine Note of 1948 in *Polar Record*, vol. v, pp. 233–234.

2K

The Legal Case for Sovereignty in the Falkland Islands Dependencies

South American Claims and International Law. The evident British reluctance to use force to remove the Argentine and Chilean parties thus established in the Falkland Islands Dependencies has its origin in a desire first to obtain an authoritative decision as to British legal rights.[24] In this they have so far failed. It is of interest, therefore, to examine the Antarctic claims of the three countries in the light of international law.

The possibility of acquiring sovereignty over the polar regions has for nearly half a century been debated by international lawyers. At the beginning of the century the view was expressed (in the United States) that the polar regions, being incapable or extremely difficult of permanent settlement by man, could not be brought under sovereignty by effective occupation.[25] This view was based on the now exploded theory that actual settlement or use of territory was essential to its effective occupation. But the decisive test of effective occupation, it is now held, is not exploitation or settlement, but the display of State functions; in other words, evidence of the effective activity of the State within the territory, or externally in relation to other States.[26]

The meaning of the term 'effective occupation' is important, because on it hinges the whole question of sovereignty in Antarctica and the evaluation of the rival claims. There are, of course, other possible foundations for the title of sovereignty, such as geographical proximity or contiguity, and discovery. But neither has any appreciable legal value unless supported by effective occupation, in the sense of the actual, peaceful, and continuous display of the functions of a State.[27]

Argentine and Chilean claims are fundamentally based on historical and geographical considerations; indeed, with the exception of the Argentine meteorological station on Laurie Island and a certain amount of Chilean whaling activity, conducted under British licence, there is no evidence of any State activity by either country before 1925. On historical grounds both countries base their claims on inheritance from Spain. But there is no acceptable evidence of Spanish discoveries or

[24] *Hansard*, vol. cdxlviii, col. 1685.
[25] *American Journal of International Law* (1909), p. 928; (1910), p. 265. Waldock, *op. cit.*, p. 314.
[26] A change in concept that followed the Berlin Conference of 1885 on the Partition of Africa.
[27] Waldock, *op. cit.*, p. 334.

claims within the area covered by the Falkland Islands Dependencies.[28] Nor is Spain ever believed to have specifically claimed any of the territories now claimed by either Argentina or Chile. And if there were no Spanish annexations or discoveries before 1810, when the Buenos Aires Government broke away from Spain, then there can be no question of succession by Argentina or Chile.

The second basis for South American claims is the outmoded one of geographical contiguity; the argument of the "Scotia Arc" based on the family resemblance between the volcanic and intrusive rocks of Graham Land and the South Shetlands and those of the Andes and Patagonia.[29] In fact, however, the sectors claimed by the South American countries do not form a geographical unit with Chile, still less with Argentina, even if such geological similarities are accepted. The Antarctic Continent is itself a natural geographical unit. And its satellite island groups are separated by many miles of ocean from South America.

The British case by contrast is allegedly based not on discovery, but on effective occupation,[30] which appears indeed to be the most acceptable basis in law for a title to sovereignty; it is, moreover, a case reinforced by discoveries to which neither Argentina nor Chile can lay claim. Until 1940, when Chile first formulated her claim to Antarctic territory, and until 1942, when Argentina deposited her "Act of Possession" on Deception Island, neither country had displayed any substantial signs of State activity. By this date the British title 'by occupation' appears to have been well established.

British State activity, apart from discovery and proclamation of annexation more often than not without official endorsement, came into being with the introduction of modern whaling into the Antarctic in 1904. In the following year the United Kingdom demanded payment of royalties by Norwegian whalers on all whales caught from the Falkland Islands and from South Georgia. The Norwegians, thereupon, inquired as to the sovereignty of the territories in the whaling areas, and in 1904 were told that the South Shetlands, South Georgia, South Orkneys, and Graham Land were British possessions. Applications for whaling licences, they were also told, should be addressed to the Governor of the Falkland Islands.[31] It was these regulations that led to the formulation

[28] Such as it is, it is reviewed by Waldock, *op. cit.*, p. 319.
[29] *Antarctic Pilot*, p. 66, "Geology," communicated by J. M. Wordie.
[30] British Note of December 23, 1947. *Polar Record*, vol. v, p. 232.
[31] Falkland Islands Ordinance, No. 3 of 1906.

of the Letters Patent of 1908, amended to avoid any misunderstanding as to their extent, in 1917. To these reference has already been made.[32]

The Letters Patent of 1908, declaring the above territories to be dependencies of and subject to the Executive Council of the Falkland Islands, defined the Dependencies as follows:

> The groups of islands known as South Georgia, the South Orkneys, the South Shetlands, and the Sandwich Islands, and the territory known as Graham's Land, situated in the South Atlantic Ocean to the south of the 50th parallel of south latitude and lying between the 20th and 80th degrees of west longitude.

Since the territories claimed are specifically named there is no substance in the accusation, first voiced by the South American countries, that some hundred thousand square miles of Patagonia and Tierra del Fuego were also included in the claim.[33]

There was, however, in the first geographical definition some doubt about the extent of the British claim to Graham Land. In 1917, therefore, a new version was issued. In these amended Letters Patent the present definition of the Falkland Islands Dependencies was given as follows:

> All islands and territories whatsoever between the 20th degree of west longitude which are situated south of the 50th parallel of south latitude; and all islands and territories whatsoever between the 50th degree west longitude and the 80th degree of west longitude which are situated south of the 58th parallel of south latitude.

The definition of 1908 based on the naming of specific territories was thus replaced by a claim to a geographical sector. Neither of these Letters Patent evoked any protest or counter-claim from any other country; either from Argentina or Chile, or from countries such as Russia or the United States whose nationals had (like Bellingshausen, who discovered Alexander I Land) first discovered parts of the territories in question.

The Letters Patent, important State acts but by themselves paper claims, are supported by much evidence of State activity which amounts to effective occupation of most, if not all, of the territory claimed. Whaling ordinances, in force since 1906, have been applied ever since, though licences decreased with the advent after 1930 of pelagic whaling,

---

[32] For texts, see *Polar Record*, vol. v, p. 241.
[33] For Argentine and Chilean Notes, see *Polar Record*, vol. v, pp. 235 and 240. See also David Winston Heron, "Antarctic Claims," in *Foreign Affairs* (July 1954), p. 663.

involving sea-going factory ships instead of land bases. Magistrates, customs, and police officers were appointed in the whaling areas. In South Georgia leases for mining and grazing rights were granted to a number of countries, and since 1909 a stipendiary magistrate has been continuously resident, supported since 1912 by police and customs and post-office services. Similar examples of State activity may be cited for other parts of the Dependencies. From 1912 to 1930, for instance, a customs officer with a magistrate's commission functioned in Deception Island in the South Shetlands, and in 1912 the Hektor whaling company, a Norwegian concern, took a twenty-year lease of land on the island from the British Government.[34] In 1923 the Discovery Committee was instituted under the Colonial Office to carry out Antarctic research, with special reference to the Dependencies, and numerous and extensive explorations were made between 1926 and 1938. Similarly, between 1934 and 1937, the British Graham Land Expedition, sponsored by the Royal Geographical Society, made far-reaching surveys of the Graham Land Peninsula.

On the basis of these activities the United Kingdom can put forward a strong claim to sovereignty on grounds of effective occupation; a claim which in so far as it antedates would render illegal and invalid the activities of Argentina and Chile. If the Argentine claim to Laurie Island be excepted, Argentine activities in the Dependencies were, as has been seen, relatively insignificant until in 1942 her "Act of Possession" was deposited on Deception Island. Chilean claims, too, are as recent as 1940, the date of her Presidential decree, followed in 1943 by evidence of State activity in the form of the dispatch of a Chilean observer with an Argentine expedition.

It is on this basis, on the basis of effective occupation and not as is sometimes stated of discovery, that the United Kingdom in December 1947 informed both Argentina and Chile that she was willing to submit her title to the Dependencies to the jurisdiction of the International Court at The Hague.[35] The offer was not then, nor has it since, been accepted. Both Argentina and Chile have argued that such a move would be presented as a request for something which already belonged to them, but over which they did not exercise effective possession. Argentina referred also to the impossibility of independent reference to the Court because of the Declaration of July 12, 1947, whereby both

---

[34] Waldock, op. cit., pp. 327–331.
[35] British Note of December 23, 1947; Polar Record, vol. v, p. 232.

countries agreed that "it is their desire to arrive as soon as possible at the conclusion of a Treaty between Argentina and Chile regarding the demarcation of boundaries in the South American Antarctic."[36] Not even a unilateral, and fully documented, application by the United Kingdom to the International Court in 1955 could induce any change in the Argentine or Chilean attitude.

Meanwhile this cold war in the Antarctic continues; the United Kingdom, pledged to a peaceful solution of the problem, but unable to obtain an authoritative decision on her title, maintains her Antarctic bases through the yearly expeditions of the Falkland Islands Dependencies Survey. Argentina and Chile, unmoved by protests, conscious maybe of the weakness of their case if put to legal test, prefer to continue unimpeded their campaign of "saturation," to which Perón was dedicated,[37] and to which his successors appear equally attached.

Antarctic Interests of the United States and the Soviet Union

Two powerful countries with political interests in the Antarctic, though neither has yet made specific or official claims to sovereignty, are the United States and the Soviet Union.

The history of United States' activity in the Antarctic dates back to the early nineteenth century, when sealers from New England ports were active in the Falkland Islands sector. One of them, Captain Palmer, has been championed, unjustifiably on the evidence, as the first discoverer of the Antarctic Continent in preference to Bransfield.[38] Another, Christopher Burdick, a Nantucket whaling captain, has more recently been preferred in the United States even to Palmer as the first man to recognize the Antarctic Mainland.[39] Neither, however, put forward any territorial claims at the time (whatever may be claimed for

[36] *Polar Record*, vol. v, pp. 236–240. Argentina in her note of January 28, 1948, offered Buenos Aires as a seat for an international conference, in place of The Hague. The United Kingdom's case was put to the Court on May 4, 1955. On March 17, 1956, the Court refused to consider the case on the grounds that Argentina and Chile continued to refuse to accept the jurisdiction of the Court. The case was then removed from the Court's list.

[37] Speech by President Perón.

[38] *Geographical Journal*, vol. xciv, No. 4 (1939), pp. 309–330.

[39] Edouard A. Stackpole, "A First Recognition of Antarctica," in *Boston Public Library Quarterly*, vol. iv, No. 1 (1951), pp. 5–19. See also Stackpole, *Voyage of the Huron and Huntress* (Mystic, Conn., 1955), p. 51, where a good case is made out for a first landing on the Antarctic Continent by the American sealer Captain Davis on February 7, 1821.

them to-day), and there is no evidence of such claims or annexations on the part of any North American Antarctic explorers until the twentieth century.

In his expeditions of 1928–30 Admiral Byrd claimed to have discovered extensive territories in Marie Byrd Land on behalf of the United States. And further claims, reported to have been made by him in southern Graham Land on his expedition of 1940–41, if supported by the United States Government, might conceivably compete with British claims to sovereignty in an area of Graham Land where British activity has been less than in the northern half of the peninsula.[40] No official claims, however, have yet been made by the United States to this or any other part of Antarctica, nor do they recognize the claims of other countries. The United States reserves, on the other hand, any rights arising out of claims made by its explorers; an attitude which has given rise to doubts as to the legality of excluding, as it may be at some future date, other States from areas over which the United States herself does not profess to display sovereignty.[41]

The reluctance of the United States to make formal claims may be traced, it appears, to the opinion held by Secretary of State Hughes in 1924.[42] This was in line with earlier American legal opinion, which maintained that effective occupation requires permanent settlement. In so far as this implies that discovery by itself gives no claim to title the specific reservation by the United States of rights of discovery by its nationals is not easy to follow.

A more recent development in the geopolitics of Antarctica was the attempt made by the United States in 1948 to gain agreement to the placing of Antarctica under United Nations Trusteeship.[43] All the countries with Antarctic territories were approached, as well as Argentina and Chile. It was a courageous proposal, given the inevitable necessity sooner or later of a United States vote in the embarrassing dispute between the United Kingdom and her South American rivals. Whether a majority of those with Antarctic possessions would have supported the proposal is doubtful.[44] However that may be, the United States proposal seems to have been dropped; partly, it may be, because it provoked an immediate intervention in Antarctic affairs by the Soviet Union.

[40] Waldock, *op. cit.*, p. 350.   [41] *Idem*, p. 352.
[42] U.S. Dept. of State, *Foreign Relations of the United States* (1924), vol. ii, pp. 519–520.
[43] *Hansard*, vol. cdlvi, Written Answers, cols. 10–11.
[44] Waldock, *op. cit.*, p. 312. It was favoured by the United Kingdom and New Zealand, but not apparently by the other five countries. *The Times*, January 20, 1949.

No sooner had the news of the United States approach reached Russia than a Memorandum was dispatched in 1950 to all the interested parties[45] making it clear that the Soviet Union intended to have a full say in any discussions on a future regime for the Antarctic. The Russian Memorandum was given world publicity through the Tass Agency.[46] It was ostensibly inspired by a Resolution of the All-Union Geographical Society at Leningrad, drawing the attention of the Russian public to the important part played by Russian explorers in Antarctic discovery in the nineteenth century. The Russian navigators, Bellingshausen and Lazarev, it contended, were the first discoverers of the Antarctic Continent. It stressed also Russia's concern with Antarctic whaling and with the scientific research important to it. And finally it recalled the protest the Soviet Union had already made at an allegedly unilateral decision regarding Antarctic sovereignty, a reference to the Soviet Note of January 27, 1939, contesting the right of the Norwegian Government to annex Peter I Øy, an island first sighted by Bellingshausen and situated in the Pacific sector.[47]

As far as the discovery of the Antarctic Continent is concerned, the Russian claims are unsubstantiated. Neither Bellingshausen nor those who sailed with him in 1819–21 (their accounts have recently been discovered and published) claimed that in the "ice field strewn with hummocks" seen off Princesse Ragnhild Land in 1820 they recognized the legendary Southern Continent.[48]

Nor in the hundred years and more that have elapsed since the voyage have any such claims been voiced by the Russian Government. Of more immediate importance is the evident Russian intention to have a voice in any future distribution of Antarctic territory. If, for example, at some future date the United States were to endorse the claims of Byrd and Ellsworth to territories in the Pacific Sector, it seems not unlikely that the Soviet Union, as in the case of Peter I Øy, might find it opportune to intervene.

The abortive American proposal of 1948 has not discouraged a recent revival of the Trusteeship idea, in the first instance by Mr Walter Nash, leader of the Opposition in New Zealand. According to reports (February 1956), India is shortly to raise with the United Nations

[45] Polar Record, vol. vi (41), pp. 120–121, for full tenor.
[46] The text was broadcast in full from the Soviet Union in all languages.
[47] Polar Record, vol. vi (41), p. 121.
[48] See Armstrong, op. cit., and "From Eye-witness Accounts of Bellinghausen's Antarctic Voyage of 1819–21," in Polar Record, vol. vi, No. 41, pp. 85–87.

proposals for a Trusteeship over Antarctica. But even if a majority of the nations now holding Antarctic territories favour the idea (which they did not in 1948), it is difficult to see what the practical result will be. Agreement on the allocation of trusteeships would seem to imply a prior settlement of the Falkland Islands dispute. This, with two of the three parties refusing to attend, can hardly now come out of the International Court. It can, surely, only be reached by a political settlement between the United Kingdom, Argentina, and Chile. The chief importance of the Antarctic, putting national rivalries aside, is as a scientific laboratory for international use. Trusteeship under the United Nations for such a territory seems the most appropriate, if not the most easily attainable, form of government for this vast and uninhabited territory.

Motives for International Rivalry in Antarctica

In concluding this sketch of political geography and geopolitics in Antarctica it is worth considering the possible motives that inspired all this international rivalry. National prestige and ambition have always been inseparable from Antarctic exploration except in the days, perhaps, of the early sealers, who worked in terms of secret commercial competition rather than of proclamations of territorial annexation. This is true even of the period since 1895, when the Sixth International Geographical Congress inaugurated the era of scientific exploration in which the true importance of Antarctica lies. Recently, this rivalry has been intensified by increasing reference to the economic and strategic importance of the Antarctic.

Since 1945 whaling has certainly gained in importance, owing to postwar national food shortages, and both the Netherlands and the Soviet Union have entered the Antarctic whaling field. Whaling, fortunately, is an unlikely source of international dispute, since it is well regulated by the International Whaling Convention. Another factor in stimulating national interest in the Antarctic has been the growing realization that the economic development of parts of Antarctica may technically be within sight. Coal (low grade but with large reserves), tin ore, lead ore, copper ore, iron sulphide, iron pyrites, even gold and silver in small quantities, have been found in the British Sectors of Antarctica.[49] Who

[49] *Antarctic Pilot* (1948), pp. 21–22.

2K*

can say that, in such a vast and relatively unexplored region, oil or minerals for the production of nuclear energy may not also be found? Difficult as economic exploitation may now appear to be, it is not impossible that future world shortages, coinciding with the development of new techniques, will make a national stake in Antarctic territory a worthwhile long-term investment.

In the air, flights across Antarctica by Great Circle courses have yet to be developed. These might involve permanent meteorological stations and, possibly, emergency landing grounds on the Antarctic Mainland. Strategically, Antarctica seems of little importance in terms of the contemporary struggle for power, except perhaps as a military training ground in Polar techniques, as in the case with the United States naval and air exercise "Operation High Jump."[50] Bases in the Antarctic were used by German raiders during the second world war for their forays against shipping in the South Indian and South Atlantic Oceans. And Drake Strait, south of Cape Horn, ice-free throughout the year, might well offer a welcome alternative to the ice-bound Northwest Passage if enemy action were to close the Panama Canal.

But neither economic nor strategic prospects yet seem predominant factors in the present international rivalry for territory in Antarctica.

FURTHER READING

HAYES, J. GORDON, *Antarctica* (Richards Press, London, 1928).
HAYES J., GORDON, *Conquest of the South Pole* (Thornton Butterworth, London, 1932).
CHRISTIE, E. W. HUNTER, *The Antarctic Problem* (Allen and Unwin, London, 1951).
HINKS, A. R., "Some Misrepresentations of Antarctic History," in *Geographical Journal*, vol. 94 (1939), No. 4, pp. 308–330.
RUDMOSE-BROWN, R. N., *The Polar Regions* (Methuen, London, 1927).
The Antarctic Pilot (Admiralty Hydrographic Department; second edition, 1948).
MILL, HUGH ROBERT, *The Siege of the South Pole* (Alston Rivers, London, 1905).
The Polar Record (published by the Scott Polar Research Institute, Cambridge).
The Geographical Journal (published by the Royal Geographical Society, London).
Accounts of the various expeditions under the names of the leaders, Scott, Amundsen, Shackleton, etc.

---

[50] It has been suggested that the Antarctic Continent would be the ideal dropping-grounds for the various forms of 'atom' bomb.

CHAPTER XLIII

Some Aspects of Applied Geography

L. DUDLEY STAMP

IN the thirty-five years since Isaiah Bowman was writing *The New World* no problem has forced itself on world attention more insistently than that of the growing pressure of population on resources. The days of exploration in the old sense are past, the extent of the earth's surface of land and sea are known, and every year sees closer estimates of actual and potential resources. These material resources of land and water, including the extent of cultivable lands and the sources of energy, however large, are certainly finite and measurable. On the other hand, the ability of the human species to multiply, if not infinite, is not yet measurable. Given present trends it is not difficult to calculate that the population of the world, estimated at about 2,528,000,000 in 1954 and known to be increasing at not less than 1 per cent. per annum (probably 1·3 per cent.), will have exceeded 3,000,000,000 by 1975 and 4,000,000,000 by A.D. 2000—within the lifetime of many who will read these words. The day when, at the same rate, there would be 'standing room only' is not far ahead in terms of the vast æons of the earth's past history—in about a couple of thousand years.

The dynamic relationship between population and resources has been behind most of the political upheavals of the past quarter century. The realization that the erstwhile land of infinite resources, the United States, could narrowly estimate its remaining stores in many directions was obviously behind the policy of restricting immigration. Population pressure in Germany and the difference between the 'haves' and the 'have nots' was a powerful force behind the rise of the Hitler regime. The movements in so many countries towards resource conservation is an obvious result, so too is the interest of the United Nations evidenced by the calling of the great conference on Land and Water Resources at Lake Success in 1949 and the World Population Congress at Rome in 1954. The latter conference showed the attention now being given almost universally to the accurate enumeration of population and the study of population trends. In general the spread of 'death control' has overtaken that of birth control. Causes of human disease are known and can now be countered on a huge and increasing scale as health services and medical skill become more widely available, with resulting increases in expectation of life. In contrast, birth control is still scarcely known or not used among half mankind.

The Rome conference brought out yet another sharp contrast between the Soviet bloc and the Western world. The delegates from countries behind the Iron Curtain sought to identify restriction of population to meet diminishing resources with capitalist countries and to stigmatize it as 'neo-Malthusianism,' contrasting the viewpoint of Communist ideology which was to develop natural resources to meet any increases of population which were in fact to be encouraged. That these Russian ideas have been absorbed by the leaders of the People's Republic of China is evidenced by the objective declared in 1954 of aiming at a net population increase of 12,000,000 per annum over a total of Chinese in the world published as 601,000,000 in that same year.

These sharp national contrasts emphasize the need to study the relationships between population, land, and resources at four different levels.

First there is the overall global position—the ability of the world as a whole to support the increasing population. Although this is the favourite approach of the many recent writers on the subject, it is in reality of mainly academic interest so long as nations continue to exist whose leaders can set up restrictive barriers and so long as the countries of the world enjoy different standards of living.

The second level is the essentially realistic one of the country or nation. Conscious efforts at international co-operation have been, and are constantly being, countered by the growth of political and economic nationalism. Universal free trade which would encourage each region of the earth to produce those commodities, be they primary produce or manufactured goods, for which it is most suited by natural endowments is further from realization than ever before. Instead, industrialization has come to be regarded as an index of 'development' and national maturity. As a result, every nation is compelled to approach the population-resources problem as a national one and each is having to work out its own salvation. In particular the older established industrial countries of Europe are being compelled to reassess their positions in the world. The exchange of their manufactures for the foodstuffs and raw materials of the primary producers, which had become traditional since the Industrial Revolution, is being profoundly modified. The new national isolationism thinks in terms of over-population when the land of the country is unable to feed the people. In many respects contrasts between one country and another are becoming more rather than less marked.

At the third level every country of any size is a heterogeneous unit with marked contrasts between one region and another. This is familiar ground to the geographer, but attempts to measure scientifically the 'carrying capacity' of different types of land or their ability to support varying densities of population are still in their infancy. Some countries, especially those of vast extent and still unproved resources such as Brazil, exhibit extreme contrasts between regions.

And fourthly there are the vital though essentially local relationships between people and land which is the sphere of town and country planning. There may be a pinpoint relationship between the physical conditions of a particular site and its ability to produce a given crop—the peaches on a south-facing wall in southern England. Similarly, the popular concept that the sunny side of the street has advantages over the other can sometimes be substantiated from health statistics. In this sphere much work remains to be done.

World Population

The problem of feeding the world's population from the world's food resources seems likely to become more rather than less of an academic exercise. Something like a third of the world's resources and rather more than a third of the world's people—in the U.S.S.R., China, and satellites—lie behind what is widely called the Iron Curtain, within which is a self-contained world. The Dollar Curtain, which enshrouds the United States, is of a very different character, but is none the less a very real barrier. Nearly every country has its tariff wall, its currency restrictions, or its immigration regulations, all joining to prevent the free flow of men, materials, and services. Within the broad picture of world population growth there are many contrasts between the continents, between races, and between nations.

The contrasts between the continents are clear from the following table:

TABLE 1

CONTINENT	POPULATION, IN MILLIONS			ANNUAL RATE OF INCREASE (1900–50)
	1800	1900	1950	
Europe . .	187	401	539	0·7
North America .	5·7	81	165	2·1
Central and South America .	19	63	163	3·2
Oceania . .	2	6	13	2·3
Africa . .	90	120	198	1·3
Asia . .	602	937	1,322[1]	0·8
World .	906	1,608	2,400	1·0

[1] Including a rough estimate of fifty millions for Soviet Asia.

This table suggests that in the last half century the already crowded countries of Europe have shown population increases well below world average. The same is true of Asia as a whole, despite what is known of phenomenal increases in Japan, the East Indies, and Siberia. On the other hand the new lands of the Americas and Oceania are showing a remarkable growth in population: Africa is beginning to pick up after centuries of stagnation, disease, and the slave trade. These figures have a special interest when translated into a percentage distribution of population over the world.

TABLE 2

Percentages of World Population

CONTINENT	1800	1900	1950
Europe	20·6	24·9	22·4
North America . . .	0·6	5·1	6·9
Central and South America .	2·1	3·9	6·8
Oceania	0·2	0·4	0·5
Africa	10·0	7·4	8·3
Asia	66·5	58·3	55·1
	100·0	100·0	100·0

The figures given in the preceding tables should serve at least to remove the popular concept that the white races are being overwhelmed by the black and yellow. Given that English is the language of the United States, Australia, and much of Canada, English-speaking whites are increasing four times as rapidly as the population of the world as a whole, and now number (1950) about 206,000,000 or over 8 per cent. of the total. Nevertheless, because of the huge numbers of Chinese and Indians, even with a smaller rate of increase, the annual addition is enormous. If the net annual increase in the world is between twenty-five and thirty millions, about one-third is of Chinese, a quarter Indian. The latest United Nations estimate is 36,000,000.

But other changes of fundamental importance are taking place. What is now frequently referred to as death control is spreading much more rapidly than birth control. Within the past few decades so remarkable has been the growth of medical knowledge and skill, so efficient the development of health services, that many killing diseases have lost their terrors. Malaria, the very cause of which was unknown within living memory, has been eliminated over huge areas; yellow fever, cholera, typhoid, smallpox, are firmly under control by inoculation; leprosy, syphilis, and many other dreaded diseases are curable. The surgeon too has played his part—appendicectomy is a simple operation, Cæsareans are usual in difficult cases of childbirth. Penicillin, the sulphonamides, and numerous new drugs are to hand in treatment of disease. Wherever modern medicine has penetrated, and yearly that means more and more of the world, there has been a phenomenal fall in the death rate.

On the other hand in many of the most populous countries there has been little fall in the birth rate. Asia's birth rate is forty to forty-five per 1000 per annum, but the death rate is still twenty-five to thirty-two per thousand, so the net increase is only moderate and the expectation of life at birth is still only about twenty-seven years. In Catholic Latin America the birth rate is about forty per thousand, but the death rate has dropped to seventeen, giving a net increase of twenty-three.

The essential lesson of such figures (though little more than intelligent guesswork still in many cases) is that the world's population position is very fluid and great changes may be expected in the near future. Not least is the likelihood that Africa, now within reach of medical skills, will show a phenomenal rise. But the changes are affecting the age structure of the population of every country. In England and Wales a child born in 1880 could have expected to live to forty-three or forty-four; in 1945 the expectation of life was over sixty-five. There are two important aspects of population age structure. One is the number of 'under-age' dependants to be supported. As education becomes more widespread and the school-leaving age is raised in one country after another, and when an ever higher proportion of adolescents go on to college, this proportion may increase even if the actual proportion of children is less. But perhaps even more serious is the proportion of 'over-age' dependants—the retired or old age pensioners. Already more than 11 per cent. of the total population of Britain are over sixty-five, yet in many professions retiring age is sixty. No wonder Oxford and Cambridge have seen the red light and in 1954 raised the retiring age of professors from sixty-five to sixty-seven.

The implications of demographic changes have been neglected in geographical writings. Even detailed cartographical representations of population changes have only recently been undertaken in many countries, yet they are vital in any work of physical planning.[1]

The World's Lands

The surface of the earth is roughly 196,836,000 square miles or 509,805,000 km². Of this total rather less than two-fifths is land, so that the total land surface is approximately 55,786,000 square miles. This is divided between the continents as follows: Europe, 4,093,000 square miles; Asia, 16,677,000; Africa, 11,699,000; North and Central America, 8,658,000; South America, 7,047,000; Oceania, 3,201,000; Antarctica, 4,411,000.

It need hardly be emphasized that the vast icy wastes of Antarctica, though they may one day yield a quota of minerals to world supplies, are unlikely ever to be occupied by a resident population living off the land. Just as Antarctica may thus be ignored when considering the habitable land surface, so there are other huge areas incapable for one reason or another of supporting permanent settlement. Considerable interest, of obvious practical importance, attaches to efforts to measure the œcumene, or habitable surface of the earth. Some years ago the late Professor C. B. Fawcett made a number of calculations and latterly estimates have been published by the United Nations Food and Agriculture Organization (F.A.O.). In broad general terms a fifth of the land surface is too cold to support permanent settlement—including both the areas permanently covered by snow and ice and those extensive regions

[1] G. T. Trewartha, *Annals of the Association of American Geographers*, 43 (1953), pp. 71–97; 44 (1954), pp. 135–193; E. C. Willatts, *Geographical Journal*, 119 (1953), pp. 431–454; S. W. E. Vince, *Transactions of the Institute of British Geographers*, 18 (1952), pp. 53–76.

of permafrost where the soil remains frozen at depth below a superficial layer of summer thawing. Another fifth is too dry and is without
water resources to support irrigation. Another fifth is too elevated or
mountainous. Of the 40 per cent. left perhaps a quarter can be eliminated through absence of soil—where bare rock outcrops may support
a growth of trees but scarcely of the crops chosen by man or his grazing
animals. We are accordingly left with something of the order of 30 per
cent.[2] of the land surface as potentially capable of supporting a permanent settled population, or about 16–17,000,000 square miles for
2,500,000,000 people.

This area of the *œcumene* is equivalent to 10,500,000,000 acres or
4 acres per head of the existing population. F.A.O. has endeavoured to
collect figures of actual cultivated area throughout the world. Sir John
Russell has warned that even in the best documented countries agricultural statistics are liable to an error of $\pm$ 5 to 10 per cent. and in peasant
countries $\pm$ 25 per cent.[3] With this in mind we may note that total
cultivated area is given by F.A.O. at 3,006,000,000 acres or 1·2 acre
per head of population. Estimates of other categories are:

TABLE 3

	MILLION ACRES	MILLIONS OF SQUARE MILES	PERCENTAGE
Arable or cropped . .	3,006	4·7	9·1
Meadow and pasture .	5,269	8·2	15·9
Forest and woodland .	8,702	13·6	26·3
Unused but potentially pro- ductive . . .	936	1·5	2·8
Waste land, built over, etc.	15,200	23·7	45·9
	33,113	51·7	100·0

These figures exclude Antarctica, but show a slightly greater total for
the remaining land area than that given above.[4]

From these figures and other calculations quoted we may draw the
following conclusions:

(1) At the varied levels of nutrition and equally varied levels of

[2] This was the figure reached by C. B. Fawcett, "The Extent of the Cultivable Land,"
in *Geographical Journal*, 76 (1930), pp. 504–509. He considered a further 30 per cent
might be classed as productive (forest and grazing) but not cultivable.
[3] E. John Russell, *World Population and World Food Supplies* (Allen and Unwin,
London, 1954), p. 8.
[4] F.A.O. *Yearbook of Food and Agriculture Statistics*, 1949.

farming efficiency it requires an average of 1·2 acres of arable or cropped land and 2·1 acres of pasture (generally rough grazing or rangeland) to support each human being at present.

(2) Taking F.A.O. figures of arable, plus a proportion of the 'pasture' and 'forest' and the potentially productive land, Fawcett's estimate of the *œcumene* at 30 per cent. of the land surface is of the right order of magnitude.

(3) Only 9 per cent. of the surface is actually cropped against 30 per cent. which might be. Allowing for known low levels of production, it is difficult to avoid the conclusion that the world could, with full application of present knowledge, support at least three or four times the present population.

This brings us to the problem of the under-developed lands.

The Under-developed Lands. The words undeveloped and under-developed have come to be used very loosely and interchangeably as an acceptable substitute for 'backward,' which is held to imply a stigma by those countries to which it might be applied. The problems associated with under-development have long been a special concern to the European colonial Powers who, despite the oft repeated charges of 'exploitation,' have in general recognized the mutual advantages for themselves, the territories concerned, and the world as a whole in fostering material progress in the less developed areas. These countries of recent years have been brought into the forefront of world affairs by a rapid growth in political consciousness both from within and without and by the provision of a forum in the United Nations for the full international discussion of their affairs. Further, perhaps even more important, has been the focusing of the American spotlight on the problems of under-developed lands. The interests of the United States as a colonial Power had been limited in the past to Alaska, the Philippines, Hawaii, Puerto Rico, the Virgin Islands, and, to a less extent, Liberia. That they now intervene widely in world affairs is important because of the wealth and power which they command. This intervention stems especially from the now famous declaration of President Truman in his Address to Congress of January 20, 1949:

> Fourth, we must embark on a bold new program for making the benefits of our scientific advances and industrial progress available for the improvements and growth of under-developed areas. More than half the people of the world are living in conditions approaching misery. Their food is inade-

quate. They are victims of disease. Their economic life is primitive and stagnant. Their poverty is a handicap and a threat both to them and to more prosperous areas. For the first time in history humanity possesses the knowledge and the skill to relieve the suffering of these people.

It was not long after this declaration that an active "Point IV program" was initiated and has played a large part in hastening change in many countries.

The definition of 'under-development' presents many difficulties. In determining what countries shall be eligible for assistance under Point IV, under-development has been officially equated with poverty. If per capita income falls below a certain level the country is under-developed, despite the fact that every inch of its land may be intensively cultivated and all known natural resources used. On the other hand, Australia or the United States might not farm a single acre of their vast lands, but would not be classed as under-developed. Without attempting to argue the case between an economic and geographic definition of under-development, it may be an advantage to look at the more obvious meaning of the word. Any survey of the world's natural resources reveals that there are vast areas of land not yet yielding the quota of food and raw materials for the support of mankind which, by their physical advantages of soil and climate, they could be made to do. Similarly, vast stretches of forest are not yet managed so as to produce the range of products in sustained yield of which they are capable. Immense mineral wealth lies untouched. Countries where, for one reason or another, such potential wealth lies untouched would seem to qualify for the designation under-developed. In another sense all countries are under-developed in that known technological advances have not yet been applied in full to the stimulation of output. Most countries show crop yields a half or less of those known to be possible. Most countries employ systems of production—such as the shifting cultivation of tropical lands, or the monocultural cereal cultivation of the great mid-latitude plains—which afford yields per unit area far below the maximum possible. These matters are closely bound up with the concept of 'efficiency' in production, especially of food production. The most efficient systems of production measured in output per unit area may be reached only by an excessive use of labour—as in China; the most efficient system in terms of man-hours may give very low yields per acre. As Sir John Russell puts it, however, even within the limits imposed by the Law of Diminishing Returns enormous improvement is possible.

The Measurement of Agricultural Efficiency. If it is true that half the world is hungry and getting hungrier—the amount of food per head produced is less than it was even a few years ago—what matters is output per unit area. Half the world's population is in south-east Asia, where a labour supply presents no problem and where, indeed, any reduction in demand for labour creates dangerous and far-reaching problems. The need is maximum output of food per unit area. The much extolled virtues of agricultural mechanization are applicable only to certain parts of the world.

If one takes output per acre as a measure, it is still far from simple to secure an accurate assessment of efficiency. Crop yields can be converted into calories per acre, and this eliminates to some extent differences in crops. Cereals can be converted into 'wheat equivalent' or directly into calories. It is found that the 2,500,000,000 people in the world probably consume rather over 900,000,000,000 lb. of cereals a year—about 1 lb. per day, which is 1650 calories. This is almost exactly half the caloric intake in the United States, and if we accept 2500 calories a day as a proper standard for health we see how this figure, in view of the reliance on cereals as the staples of diet throughout so many parts of the world, reflects the low standard in the world as a whole. F.A.O. has calculated too that whereas in 1934–38, 38 per cent. of the people in the world had less than 2200 calories a day this proportion had increased to 60 per cent. in 1949–50.

Clearly the great need is for increased yields. Actually yields show staggering differences. In 1951 the world average for yield of wheat was 17·2 bushels per acre, but it ranged from 10·3 in India to 54·0 in the Netherlands. Rice, with a world average of 18·1 bushels, showed a range of 12·9 in India (12·7 that year in Thailand and the Philippines) to 65·2 in Spain. Combining nine or ten crops commonly grown in all of the following twenty countries one can get a ranking coefficient (Kendall) of efficiency in output. The order in 1934–38 was: Belgium, Denmark, Netherlands, Germany, Britain, Ireland, New Zealand, Egypt, Austria, France, Japan, Italy, United States, Canada, Spain, Chile, China, Argentina, Australia, India. In the post-war years the order remained broadly correct: increased yields in corn (maize) due to the use of hybrid corn had pushed up the United States to ninth place; the ravages of war had dropped Japan to seventeenth place.

The order is interesting geographically. The countries at the head of the list enjoy both a reliable climate and an advanced technology. The low positions occupied by Australia and Spain reflect vagaries of climate, but that of India is the result of technological inefficiency rather than climate. The relatively low position occupied by the United States indicates that efficiency in output per man-hour is not to be equated with efficiency in output per unit area and justifies the use of the term 'under-developed.'

If these and other criteria are applied where are the world's under-developed areas? They may be grouped as follows:

(1) The Equatorial Lands, with certain exceptions such as Java and parts of Malaya, where heat and moisture are adequate but where many difficulties remain to be overcome.

(2) The Tropical Lands, notably large parts of Africa, where there are still many unsolved problems in land, and especially soil-management, the control of water, and the vagaries of the climate, as well as a whole range of problems linked with the people, their distribution and social organization.

(3) The Mid-latitude Lands, where output is still low. Herein lies the dilemma. If a larger output of food and raw materials is needed, authorities are agreed that it is easier to get this by an increased output in such countries as the United States, Canada, and Argentina than in the Tropics, where conditions are still imperfectly understood. On the other hand, this is no answer to the problem of developing the under-developed lands, which lie so largely in the Tropics.

So far our emphasis in considering under-development has been on food and renewable resources. When we take resources of industrial power into consideration, the evidence is that resources of coal and oil are not only of limited extent but within sight of exhaustion in many countries. Water power does not provide a full answer, and other sources of power must be sought. However, with both renewable resources of power (*i.e.*, water) and capital resources of minerals many of the under-developed countries are destined to play an increasing part in world economy. The oil of the Middle East—Arabia, Kuwait, Bahrain, Iraq, Persia—of Indonesia, and of South America; the tin of Bolivia, Nigeria, and Malaya; the copper of the African Copper Belt; the bauxite of the Guianas and West Africa; and many other examples could be quoted to show how the natural resources of the under-developed lands are those in urgent demand by the rest of the world.

What emerges as soon as one attempts seriously to consider the problems of the under-developed lands is nearly always the lack of accurate factual knowledge. Nowhere is this more apparent than in the field of land use. A hazy guess as to the existing use of land, 'statistics' with a margin of error of ± 25 per cent. or more, no detailed maps, all combine to make it quite impossible to know why people in the under-developed lands live where they do, what they do, and why their patches of cultivation are found where they are.

Survey and Analysis. It has been said with considerable justification that any country has but two ultimate assets—its land and its people. The starting point in the factual objective study of the *people* is a full census, followed by both a demographic and a geographic analysis. Into the geographic analysis must enter the many and varied systems of the mapping of population distribution and movements. The starting-point in the factual objective study of the *land* should be a survey of its use and non-use, followed by an analysis which seeks to trace the influence of the several physical, economic, historical, and social factors which have led to the present position. Too often a statistical statement of land use—the acreage in forest and farm, in crops, grass, and various forms of development—is regarded as adequate for the purpose, ignoring the obvious necessity of relating the determinant factors to specific areas, even to pinpoint them.

Land-use surveys inspired by these simple principles have now been carried out in a number of countries, but the work of the Land Utilisation Survey of Britain may be quoted as an example fully worked out. The survey was carried out mainly in the years 1931–34, and the initial object was to record the then existing use of every acre of England, Wales, and Scotland. The work was of course greatly facilitated by the existence of a complete series of maps on the scale of six inches to one mile (1:10,560). The work involved some 15,000 map sheets and an army of volunteers to do the primary survey and later checking. The results were reduced to the scale of one inch to one mile, and the series of sheets on that scale were in due course published for the whole of England and Wales and the more populous parts of Scotland. The maps reveal the very complex land-use pattern, which is the result of at least 2000 years of settlement and development with the post-industrial revolution spread of an urban-industrial pattern over the older mature rural-agricultural. An attempt was made in a series of ninety-two county reports to trace the varied influence of the numerous factors in determining the pattern. Looked at as a snapshot picture in a long-continued process of scenic evolution, such a survey reveals not only correlations but trends. It also reveals the complex position from which any planning for the future must start. Physical planning can be seen as a conscious effort either to reverse a trend regarded as undesirable or to encourage a trend regarded as desirable. Such is the relationship between policy and the factual objective survey.

Britain by contrast with most parts of the world was already well known and well mapped. Although the revelations of such a land-use survey are remarkable, this is very far from being the only basis for planning. Accurate knowledge and mapping of solid and surface geology, mineral resources, climatic factors and soils, among the physical factors, are obvious desiderata. Interpretations such as types of farming and classification or types of land involve something at least of subjective judgment and come after; whole series of population studies of density, distribution, movement, and development are vital.

It is sometimes urged that a survey of the use or non-use of land is neither necessary nor desirable. What one requires to know is land potential, which, say some critics, is essentially a function of soil. A soil survey and an interpretation in the form of potential land-use classification is, they say, what is required, especially for the underdeveloped lands. When the International Geographical Union at its Lisbon Congress in 1949 set up a Commission to report on a project for a World Land Use Survey or Inventory under the chairmanship of Professor Samuel Van Valkenburg all these points of view came under review. The Commission reported in favour of a survey of the actual position in every country, drew up a 'master key,' the classification proposed being adaptable according to local needs but permitting of worldwide correlation of results. Pilot surveys carried out in widely separated parts of the world have shown that in most areas, even the seemingly monotonous parts of tropical Africa, the pattern of land use is so complex that no scale smaller than one inch to one mile (1:63,360) can normally show it, though much basic information can be conveyed on 1:250,000 or even 1:1,000,000. It has been found that such a survey can be made from air photos with a small amount of ground checking. The Commission took the view that, since any planning must start from the present position, the reasons for the existing land-use pattern must be determined. A soil map is a vital adjunct, not a substitute.

Land Classification. Both land-use surveys, properly interpreted, and soil surveys read in conjunction with other relevant factors can lead to schemes of land classification while land classes give the lead to planning. Empirical schemes, provided each class is defined in precise terms of site and soil, seem to provide satisfactory results. As an example may be quoted the eight land-potential classes used in the Survey of the Pacific North West, or the ten-fold scheme drawn up by the Land Utilisation Survey of Britain and used in a number of official investigations. This latter scheme may be briefly outlined:

I. Good Quality Land
    1. First-class land capable of intensive cultivation, especially of fruit and vegetables for direct human consumption.
    2. Good general-purpose farmland.
    3. First-class land with water conditions especially favouring grass.
    4. Good but heavy land with consequent restriction on period of working and range of crops.

II. Medium Quality Land
    5. Medium quality light land.
    6. Medium quality general-purpose farmland.

III. Poor Quality Land
    7. Poor quality heavy land.
    8. Poor quality mountain land.
    9. Poor quality light land.
    10. Poorest land.

These types of land are defined in physical terms. The concept of marginal land is an economic one, but broadly speaking marginal lands as at present understood would fall into Major Category III. It should be noted that such a classification has nothing to do with land-use policy, but policy can be and is related to it. For example, it is a policy decision that housing and other development should as far as possible be avoided on the good lands—types 1 to 4 inclusive, other things being equal.

The Carrying Capacity of Land and the Concept of the Potential Production Unit

There is much yet to be learnt in land classification, and any really scientific basis for determination of types of land or their optimal use is in its initial stages. We have already seen that, taking the world as a whole, there is about 1·2 acre of cropped land for each individual. In very broad general terms it may be stated that an acre or rather more at the standard of farming in north-western Europe, including England, is required to support each individual at the standard of living there current.[5] In India 0·8 acre has to suffice—at low yields and low standards. The yardstick of an acre a head gives at least a rough measure of the carrying capacity of a country in terms of population and farm acreage.

If we accept for the moment that one acre of average improved farm land in a given country can support one person we can make a number of simple deductions:

(1) The carrying capacity of the land is 640 persons per square mile of improved farm land—*i.e.*, crops or, in countries such as Britain, crops and improved grass.

(2) A density below this leaves room for population expansion: a density above this gives a measure of 'over-population.'

(3) The actual figure will vary widely from country to country, according to the basic foodstuffs, type of farming, and so on.

(4) In a given country the 'average acre' of average farm land can be used as a unit. This I have called a P.P.U., or Potential Production Unit. An overall improvement in yield would, of course, raise the value of the unit.

(5) But land is of varying quality. The better lands may have an output equivalent to 2 P.P.U. It has been the practice of the Ministry of Agriculture in England and Wales to consider 10 acres of rough grazing as equivalent to 1 acre of improved farm land—*i.e.*, to rate it at 0·1 P.P.U.

(6) If each *type* of land in a country can be given a P.P.U. rating it is possible to express its total productive capacity.

(7) It is well known that a meat diet makes a more extravagant use of land than a cereal diet. Preliminary results suggest that 1 P.P.U. can be equated with 0·4 stock units. In other words, a cow or a bullock requires 2½ acres of average improved land.

There is frequently a confusion of thought between the carrying capacity of land, as expressed in the number of people its produce is able to support, and the actual farming population required to produce food. The two concepts are entirely different. The 1940–41 Farm Survey

[5] A very careful and detailed analysis by James Wyllie has shown a considerable variation from year to year. At the height of the war effort in 1943–44 it required the produce of 1·15 acre. In 1948–49 and 1949–50 it was 1·27 acre. Both these figures are much lower than in the careless pre-war days—1·85 acre in 1936–37.

in England and Wales showed that the average full-time holding was just under 100 acres of improved land (crops and grass). Such a holding is commonly run by the farmer, his wife, and one other adult worker. With dependants this can be equated to 7 persons, or a total of 45 per square mile. This is the "Primary Rural Population." S. W. E. Vince, working out in detail my preliminary results, finds that the "Secondary Rural Population" is almost exactly half the Primary. This gives a total rural population of 68 per square mile under the individual farm organization of England and Wales to produce the food of 640 per square mile: let us say 11 per cent. of the population engaged in actual agricultural production. This interesting line of research needs to be followed up, but it illustrates how little is yet known of the scientific background of planning.

For here geographical analysis fades into physical town and country planning. Here it should be clear that geographical survey and analysis should be part of the prelude to planning, the geographer one of the investigational team. If 5000 acres of land are needed for a new town it can either absorb 10,000 P.P.U.'s of the country's productive capacity or only 500, according to the type of land taken. An optimum rural population to produce food may not be large enough to maintain the social structure of the countryside, and it may be necessary to encourage an adventitious rural population—living in the country, but drawing its livelihood elsewhere.

Such is a small part of the fertile new field of Applied Geography.

FURTHER READING

FREEMAN, OTIS W., and MARTIN, HOWARD H. (editors), *The Pacific North-West: An Overall Appreciation;* (second edition; Wiley, New York, and Chapman and Hall, London, 1954) (first edition 1942).

RUSSELL, E. JOHN, *World Population and World Food Supplies* (Allen and Unwin, London, 1954).

WYLLIE, JAMES, *Land Requirements for the Production of Human Food* (Wye College, University of London, 1954).

Report of the Commission on World Land Use for the period 1949–1952 (International Geographical Union).

STAMP, L. DUDLEY, *Our Underdeveloped World* (Faber and Faber, London, 1953) (American title: *Land for Tomorrow* (American Geographical Society and Indiana University Press)); *The Land of Britain: Its Use and Misuse* (Longmans, London, 1950); *The Underdeveloped Lands of Britain* (Soil Association, London, 1954).

UNITED NATIONS, *Demographic Yearbook.*

United Nations Food and Agriculture Organization, *Yearbook*, and other publications.

Putnam, P. C., *Energy in the Future* (D. Van Nostrand, New York, and Macmillan, London, 1953).

P.E.P. (Political and Economic Planning), *World Population and Resources* (Allen and Unwin, London, 1955).

Postscript

W. GORDON EAST
and
A. E. MOODIE

THE mid-century world has witnessed four remarkable geopolitical changes, of which the advent of the U.S.S.R. as the dominant military power in Eurasia is the most outstanding. This is a more important fact than the ideology with which she is associated, for the U.S.S.R. now stands with the United States as one of the two greatest of Powers. Continental in her location and scale, and rapidly increasing her industrial strength at a higher rate than that of the western democracies, she commands a numerous and growing population and so-called 'interior lines' of communication beyond the periphery of her territory to Western Europe, the Middle East, and the Far East. The second outstanding event of recent years is the success of Communist forces in China. This country, now in alliance with the U.S.S.R., affords her substantial support on her Asian flank. The principal effect on Europe of this rise in Soviet power has been the division of the continent into two *blocs*. The simplicity of the pattern is marred by the special political positions of five European States: Sweden, Switzerland, and Austria stand neutral between the Soviet and Western *blocs*, while Spain and Yugoslavia occupy anomalous positions.

The third outstanding fact in the present geopolitical situation is the emergence of the United States as the protagonist of the western world. No longer withdrawn within her own continent, and now aware of her grown stature and of the external dangers to her security, she has taken the active leadership of those many democratically organized peoples who are prepared to defend themselves against the encroachment of the Russian and Chinese Communist Powers. Distrustful of imperialism, yet in need of outlying bases if she is to keep war as far as possible from American soil, the United States has sought by diplomatic means to rally friends and neutrals, to restore and strengthen their economies, to acquire air and naval bases overseas, and to organize effective systems

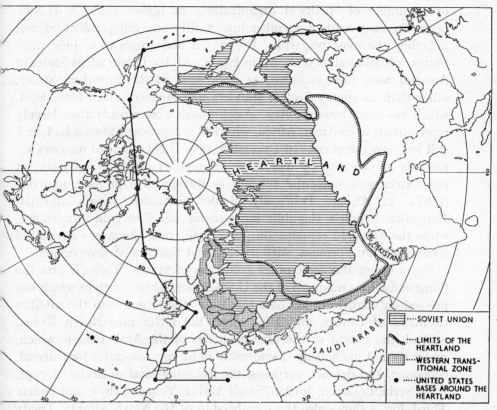

FIG. 1. UNITED STATES BASES AND THE 'HEARTLAND'

of defence. Fig. 1 illustrates with what success she has pursued a policy of 'containing' the Soviet Union and the Chinese Republic. It shows the incomplete ring of bases which has been drawn from the Aleutian Islands to both the Philippines and Libya in countries friendly to the United States. And it emphasizes how the American policy of defence against possible dangers originating in the Heartland area[1] of Eurasia—an area controlled by the U.S.S.R. and China—necessarily rests on the control of the sea lanes and the use of air and naval forces.

Fourthly, the breakdown of European imperialism in southern Asia and the emergence there of nationalist States constitute another significant factor in geopolitics to-day.

Already before the second world war had ended the attempt was made by the successful belligerents to organize the world for peaceful living by the creation in 1945 of the United Nations Organization, one

of a number of 'political organizations at higher ranks.'[2] U.N.O.
began in 1945 with a membership of fifty-one independent States,
including the most powerful. By 1954 it had grown to include sixty
States, distributed as is shown in Fig. 2. All the independent States of
America were then included, as were most of the European States,
other than ex-enemy States, statelets like Monaco, and Switzerland,
which has never sought entry. Asian States were already then largely
represented; in contrast, Africa, with few independent States, had, and
still has, few members. In December 1955 U.N.O. moved measurably
towards universality by increasing its membership to seventy-six: of
the sixteen new entrants[3] ten are in Europe, five in Asia, and one
(Libya) in Africa. Politically divided Germany, Japan, and the
Mongolian People's Republic have so far failed to gain admittance,
while the anomaly remains (in June 1956) that China is represented
territorially by Formosa, with its so-called Nationalist Government.

Fig. 2 shows also some other groupings of States. There is first the
Communist *bloc*, made up of the U.S.S.R. and China, each of which has
pressed outward from her own territory—the former into the satellite
countries of Europe and High Asia, the latter into North Korea.
Second, the extent of the nine countries of the Arab League which,
under the not unchallenged leadership of Egypt, associates for cultural,
economic, and defence purposes, the following Moslem States: Egypt,
Iraq, Syria, Lebanon, Jordan, Saudi Arabia, Yemen, Libya, and Sudan.
Third, Fig. 2 shows also the membership of the North Atlantic Treaty
Organization, on which the defence of Western and Southern Europe
principally depends. Fourth, the eight States which, it was proposed,
should form the European Defence Community—but this project failed,
to be replaced by the West European Union, organized under the Treaty
of London of 1954. Lastly, the grouping of the three Pacific States,
effected by the ANZUS treaty of mutual defence, is depicted in Fig. 2.

Thus in their struggle for security the States of the world have
created many large-scale groups, and no single comprehensive organization of all the nations is in sight. Rather, it appears that a threefold
political division exists in the world, as in Europe and Asia, its two most

---

[1] See Chapter XVIII.
[2] See R. Hartshorne's discussion in *American Geography: Inventory and Prospect*,
edited by Preston E. James and Clarence F. Jones (Syracuse University Press, 1954),
pp. 211–213.
[3] The ten new European members are: Albania, Austria, Bulgaria, Finland, Hungary,
Ireland, Italy, Portugal, Romania, and Spain. The five new Asian members are Cambodia, Ceylon, Laos, Nepal, and Jordan.

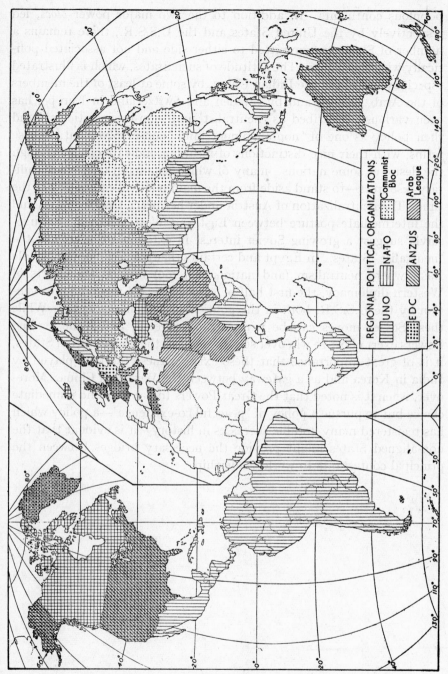

FIG. 2. REGIONAL POLITICAL ORGANIZATIONS IN 1954

Outline by courtesy of the Cartographical Department of the Clarendon Press

populous continents. In addition to the two major power *blocs*, led respectively by the United States and the U.S.S.R., there remains a number of States uncommitted to either side and not associated politically with each other. The attitude of such States, which is illustrated especially by that of the Indian Union, by some at least of the members of the Arab League, and by Sweden and Switzerland in Europe, has been variously described as 'neutralist' and 'non-interventionist' and their policy as one of 'non-alignment' and 'non-involvement.' These terms, with their nice distinctions of meaning, indicate clearly enough the desire of some nations—many of which command only small military resources—to stand aside from the main political contention of the time. The neutralization of Austria under her peace treaty of 1955 and the intermediate posture between East and West assumed by Yugoslavia suggest a growing Soviet interest in extending the area of the 'neutralist' States. In Egypt and certain other countries of the Middle East, where neutralism (and nationalism too) impede the efforts of Western diplomacy, the first half of 1956 witnessed vigorous intervention by the U.S.S.R. both in the political and economic fields. While these Soviet moves can be variously interpreted, and while leading Powers exert effort to win over some at least of the uncommitted States, it is of great importance that these exist, witness the part played by India in Korea and as a gateway between the West and China. Moreover, when it is noted that the Great Powers to-day have no immediate choice but to pursue a policy of 'peaceful co-existence'—a policy which has registered many notable successes in history—it is evident that the non-aligned States might provide the necessary bridges between the principal contestants to world leadership.

Index